Lore of Running

Fourth Edition

TIMOTHY D. NOAKES, MD, DSc

Discovery Health Professor of Exercise and Sports Science
University of Cape Town
Cape Town, South Africa

Human Kinetics

Library of Congress Cataloging-in-Publication Data

Noakes, Timothy, 1949-
  Lore of running / Tim D. Noakes.--4th ed.
    p. cm.
  Includes bibliographical references (p.) and index.
    ISBN: 0-87322-959-2
    1. Running. 2. Running--Training. 3. Running--Physiological aspects. I. Title.
  GV1061 .N6 2002
  796.42--dc21

ISBN-10: 0-87322-959-2
ISBN-13: 978-0-87322-959-3

First published in 1985 by Oxford University Press Southern Africa

Fourth edition published in 2001 by Oxford University Press Southern Africa
Reprinted by arrangement with Oxford University Press

Acquisitions Editor: Martin Barnard; **Developmental Editor:** Julie Rhoda; **Managing Editor:** Carla Zych; **Assistant Editor:** John Wentworth; **Copyeditor:** KLM Words; **Indexer:** Craig Brown; **Graphic Designer:** Fred Starbird; **Graphic Artist:** Kimberly McFarland; **Cover Designer:** Jack W. Davis; **Photographer (cover):** ©Tony Demin/ImageState; **Photo and Art Manager:** Carl D. Johnson; **Printer:** United Graphics, Inc.

Human Kinetics books are available at special discounts for bulk purchase. Special editions or book excerpts can also be created to specification. For details, contact the Special Sales Manager at Human Kinetics.

Printed in the United States of America   15   14

Human Kinetics
Web site: www.HumanKinetics.com

United States: Human Kinetics, P.O. Box 5076, Champaign, IL 61825-5076
800-747-4457
e-mail: humank@hkusa.com

Canada: Human Kinetics, 475 Devonshire Road, Unit 100, Windsor, ON N8Y 2L5
800-465-7301 (in Canada only)
e-mail: info@hkcanada.com

Europe: Human Kinetics, 107 Bradford Road, Stanningley
Leeds LS28 6AT, United Kingdom
+44 (0) 113 255 5665
e-mail: hk@hkeurope.com

Australia: Human Kinetics, 57A Price Avenue, Lower Mitcham, South Australia 5062
08 8372 0999
e-mail: info@hkaustralia.com

New Zealand: Human Kinetics, Division of Sports Distributors NZ Ltd.
P.O. Box 300 226 Albany, North Shore City, Auckland
0064 9 448 1207
e-mail: info@humankinetics.co.nz

For Marilyn, forever my best friend,

and for our most treasured gifts,

Candice Amelia and Travis Miles

Contents

Foreword

One useful classification of human personality divides us into four categories: analytical, expressive, driving, and amiable. Most of us have one primary characteristic. Many have two. A few have three. Timothy Noakes is one of the few people I have met who possesses all four in almost equal degrees. He is completely disarming in debate because he is so amiable. He is rarely without a smile on his face. He is a scientist devoted to exact proofs, an investigator who never allows emotion to get in the way of his judgment. At the same time, Timothy is an expressive who sees beyond all this logic and achievement to the nonrational areas of life. He allows himself to express the deepest and most fundamental human emotions. He is a rare combination, and that makes this a rare book.

Noakes has a training, an intelligence, a sensitivity, and experience that few writers on the athletic life can equal. On every page we can see the work of a scientist. He has studied the physiology and pathology of athletic training in depth. No problem in running, whether it be an intractable orthopedic injury or sudden death on the road, is foreign to him. He is not only familiar with the medical literature; in many instances he is the medical literature. His published material covers running in virtually every aspect. And he has explored the areas of living beyond the physical. He has integrated the science and art of living.

Noakes is also a physiologist and an expert in human performance. He tells us how to become and remain athletes. Noakes is a runner who has gone through the varied experiences of running: the contemplation, the conversation, the competition. He is familiar with both the joy and the boredom of running, its peaks and valleys.

The result is a book that appears deceptively simple. It puts into words our own thoughts as yet unexpressed and leads us to insights not yet discovered. We all have within us the drive toward excellence. Timothy Noakes writes of how he sought this excellence . . . and in so doing blazes a path for us all.

George Sheehan, MD
Ocean Grove, New Jersey

Preface to the Fourth Edition

The affection with which the running public both in South Africa and internationally have accepted *Lore of Running* is a constant source of pleasure to me. To be told that your book has influenced even one life is reward beyond measure. It seems that *Lore* has achieved some of the goals that inspired its creation: in particular, that of producing a comprehensive, interesting, and practical book, which would be scientifically accurate yet be understood by those who lack formal training in the biological sciences.

So what, you may wonder, enticed me to return pen to paper, to produce this fourth edition? Partly, it was the subtle pressure of the publishers, Mary Reynolds and Rainer Martens, to whom, now that the task is complete, I am most thankful.

But mostly it resulted from the fact that, as they age, scientific publications can no longer reflect the cutting edge of inquiry. And in one vitally important matter, the need to replace what now seems to me obsolete wisdom in previous books on running (including previous editions of *Lore*) has become compelling.

It was while writing the first edition that I researched some historically important studies in the exercise sciences. Then I uncovered a crucially significant scientific blunder that had lain unexposed for 75 years and that has formed part of the foundation of a great deal of teaching and research in the exercise sciences. I alluded to the error in the third edition, but I did not then comprehend its full implications. In the 10 years since, it has been possible to examine it rigorously, to develop a novel theory of how the body really does function during exercise and training—and to discard much of the baggage of past wisdom.

The product is this, the fourth edition. It is the first book written by an exercise physiologist to acknowledge the dominant role played by the brain in determining performance in any form of physical activity. I have tried throughout the book to explain the practical implications of this new theory for both training and racing.

I have also updated all the other material and have included significant new information; this includes training histories of world-class athletes who have sprung to eminence in the recent past as well as a new and expanded reference list. We offer this reference list in an online format at www.humankinetics.com/references/noakes.pdf. Providing this extensive list online allows the book to remain as affordable as possible and also allows us to add the newest significant studies and research to the list as they are published. (For a printed copy of the list, within the United States, please send a self-addressed, postage paid, 8-1/2 x 11 envelope to *Lore of Running* Editor, Human Kinetics, P.O. Box 5076, Champaign, IL 61825-5076.)

May this new edition add joy to your running, and to your life.

Tim Noakes

Acknowledgments

We acknowledge too infrequently the women who shape our lives.

I learned the English alphabet at my mother's knee on the sands of Glencairn beach, some 50 years ago. My mother's devotion to my education and her faith in me have sustained and inspired me ever since then.

Marilyn Anne has been the single greatest influence on my life. Her purity and generosity of spirit, coupled with a necessarily astute understanding of the person behind the image, forms the foundation for all that we have collectively achieved, including all the elements of our shared lives that made this book possible.

Pam Peters has now typed and retyped every letter in three editions of this book. Her fastidiousness, support, unfailing good humor, and willingness to do "whatever was necessary" for more than 15 years, without ever even the slightest suggestion of complaint, is appreciated beyond measure. She is indeed the underrecognized coauthor of this book.

Human Kinetics cast their professional eyes over the American edition of *Lore,* ruthlessly identified what could be improved, and thus produced a book with an enhanced flow for easier comprehension. Jenni Middleton Horn at Oxford University Press then skillfully edited the resulting revisions and meticulously managed the crucial, and unexpectedly complicated, final two trimesters of the book's gestation, during which the infant threatened to reach a size beyond the ability of modern technology to deliver. Karen Sharwood kindly assisted in the production of numerous line graphs while Bronwen Lusted and the late Jeannette Venter contributed illustrations of very high quality.

Of the inspiring men in my life, none has been more important than my late father, who taught me that honesty is the first requirement in life. His great sense of humor, his love of a good story skillfully told, and his global view, allied to a disdain for authority and pretense, made him the perfect mentor for a career in science and education. He also had the brilliant foresight to leave me, as a young child, in the care of Thomas Taravinga, my first friend, whose Zimbabwean warmth and brilliant smile I have tried all my life to emulate.

The genius of the late Professor Christiaan Barnard inspired me to study medicine at the University of Cape Town, where I learned to run under the expert tutelage of Drs. Edward (Tiffy) King and Manfred Teichler, all of us inspired by the exploits of Dave Levick. There too, I came under the influence of Professors Lionel Opie and Wieland Gevers. It was Wieland Gevers's offhand remark that we should not assume that muscles become anaerobic during exercise, with his insistence on the term "oxygen-independent" (not anaerobic) metabolism, that ultimately led to the research that produced the maverick theories presented for the first time in this book. That research has been funded by the University of Cape Town and the Medical Research Council for an unbroken period of 26 years.

Adrian Gore, Neville Koopowitz, and Johan van Rooyen of Discovery Health were instrumental in establishing the Chair in Exercise and Sports Science with substantial additional research funding. Without the unwavering support of all these great institutions, the pivotal ideas in this book would never have evolved.

I first met the late Dr. George Sheehan, the running writer without equal, at the Conference on the Marathon in New York City in 1976. His writings, which continue to set the standard against which all else is measured, and the friendship we shared for 15 too-short years, are forever.

For the enthusiasm, passion, and faith of those colleagues who were there in the basement at the beginning—Mike, Vicki, Steve, Andrew, Wayne, and Martin—and whose work forms a cardinal part of this book, my sincerest thanks. History will yet judge with great favor the contributions you have already made and those yet to come.

In 1992, South African rugby icon Morné du Plessis helped us found the Sports Science Institute of South Africa. The achievement of our collective vision would not have been possible without the substantial patronage of Mr. Johann Rupert.

I wrote this book to provide a bridge with the past I did not know and a future I will not live to experience. Yet, teachers live on through their students. To all those students who have enriched my life for the past 20 years, my joy is to know that the future is yours.

And your best is yet to come.

Tim Noakes

Introduction
Some Reflections on Running

Like many, I discovered running quite by accident. It was in 1969, while training for rowing, that I started running regularly. But during those years, I seldom ran more than twice a week and never for more than 25 minutes. Until one day in 1971 when, for no logical reason, I decided to run for an hour. That run was absolutely decisive. For during that run I finally discovered the sport for which I had been searching. At school I had been taught that sport was cricket and rugby; the pressure to conform to these sporting norms was extreme, and I was not then secure enough to question what was good for me. But my doubts about the real attraction these games held for me first started, I suppose, at age 15, when I discovered surfing. For the first time I discovered a sport in which it was possible to be completely alone. I loved it. No rules, no guidelines, no teams, no coaches, no spectators, and in those distant days, few other participants. Just me, my surfboard, my thoughts, and an almost empty ocean. In short, what I discovered in surfing was a sport in which the external human factor was almost totally removed and nothing could detract from my enjoyment.

Surfing also brought me for the first time into direct physical contact with nature and her naked, frequently stark and always awesome beauty. And sometimes, when the water was cold and the offshore wind was strong, so that each passing wave left an icy, stinging spray that bit my wetsuit and scratched my eyes, this starkness was intensified. And I knew that it was good to be alive, and independent and vigorous, and so close to nature's embrace that, in each wave, I could hear her heart beat. I found the attraction to surfing alarmingly powerful.

Later, at university, I learned to row. What I found in rowing was a team sport that demanded total dedication, physical perfection, and an acceptance of pain and discomfort. Rowing first introduced me to my need for self-inflicted pain—the special nauseating deep-seated pain that accompanies repetitive interval training and racing.

At first, I merely followed this need intuitively. Only later would I begin to suspect that it is the continual exposure to, and mastery of, that discomfort that is an essential ingredient for personal growth. And in training for rowing, I was led to running. Now, 30-odd years down the road, this book provides the opportunity to reflect on what running has meant to me.

The first way in which running has influenced my life is that it has taught me who I am and, equally important, who I am not. I learned through running that I love privacy and solitude.

I have come to accept that, in common with a good number of other runners, I share the emotional and personality traits that William Sheldon (1945) ascribed to those whom he called ectomorphs and whose body builds resemble those of champion distance runners. Do not, for a moment, think that I am suggesting that you might mistake my generously endowed frame for that of a champion runner. Not so! Rather, I share some of the personality characteristics that Sheldon attributed to that physical group: a love of privacy, an overwhelming desire for solitude, and an inability to relax or talk in company; an overconcern with physical health; typical patterns of mental behavior that include daydreaming, absentmindedness, procrastination, and an inability to make decisions. According to Sheldon, the ectomorph's eternal quest is to understand the riddles of life.

> *Even if the day ever dawns in which it will not be needed for fighting the old heavy battles against nature, muscular vigor will still always be needed to furnish the background of sanity, serenity, and cheerfulness to life, to give moral elasticity to our disposition, to round off the wiry edge of our fretfulness and make us good humored and easy of approach.* William James (1892)

Given these characteristics, the attractions of running are obvious. For a start, it provides complete solitude. Even in the most crowded races, the point is reached when fatigue drives us back into ourselves, into those secluded parts of our souls that we discover only under times of such duress and from which we emerge with a clearer perspective of the people we truly are. Running can also allay our overconcern with health by giving us evidence that we are still well. The emotional release and physical fatigue induced by running improve our sleep. And running can provide a context for looking at the world, for seeking explanations to the riddles of life.

Second, running made me newly aware of my body and of my responsibility to look after it. Having a physically improved body showed that I cared—that I had self-pride and, more important, self-discipline. Running has also given me pride in what I can get that body to do if I prepare it properly. Like most runners, I am not really designed for running. I am too ungainly and far too tall, with too much fat, muscle, and bone. But these very disadvantages have heightened the rewards. Because, like any skill that one has acquired, the more effort that goes into its acquisition and the more difficulties overcome, the more rewarding the result.

Next I discovered that the successful completion of severe running challenges, such as finishing an ultramarathon as fast as I could, gave me the confidence to believe that, within my own limits, I could achieve whatever physical or academic target I set myself, as long as I was prepared to make the necessary effort. I learned that rewards in running, as in life, come only in direct proportion to the amount of effort I am prepared to exert, and the extent to which I can summon the required discipline and application.

Yet running also taught me a heightened degree of self-criticism and self-expectation. I realized that it is never possible to do one's absolute best, to reach the pinnacle of absolute perfection. Beyond each academic or sporting peak there will always, indeed, must always, be another peak waiting to be tackled. Mavis Hutchison realized this the very moment she had completed her life's ambition—to run across North America. As she finished, she saw that she still had a lifetime ahead of her with other goals and other ambitions to achieve.

Fourth, running in competitions taught me the humility to realize my limitations and to accept them with pride, without envy of those who might have physical or intellectual gifts that I lack. While I will never run like the elite athletes described in this book, I can still devote the same effort to my more mundane talents as they do to theirs, and so attempt to derive as much pleasure and reward from running as they do.

Humility starts, I think, with modesty and self-criticism. Percy Cerruty, who knew many great athletes, wrote that the really top athletes he had coached were never superior, insolent, or rude. Rather they were circumspect, modest, thoughtful, and anxious to acquire new knowledge, and they hated flattery—attributes that I have found in virtually all the top distance runners I have had the privilege to know. Indeed, I suspect that these characteristics are essential in sport, in which success and failure are so dreadfully visible, and in which the duration of success is so ephemeral—lasting, at most, a handful of summers.

I suggest that to achieve real success in running, as in any worthwhile activity, there must always be the fear of failure: a very real fear that the day will come when we will fail, regardless of how hard we have prepared. It is that very insecurity that keeps our carefully nurtured self-confidence from becoming arrogance. And it is also in our inevitable failures that the seeds of real personal growth are sown and eventually blossom.

Fifth, running has taught me about honesty. There is, you see, no luck in running. Results cannot be faked, and there is no one but yourself to blame when things go wrong.

So running has shown me that life must be lived as a competition with oneself. It has made me appreciate what I now believe to be a very real weakness in many team and skill sports: in those sports you do not have to admit to your imperfections; there is always someone or something else to blame, if you so choose.

The real competitions are those in which we test ourselves in company with others. Peter Pollock, who achieved immortality in cricket, had to run the Comrades Marathon before he could write: "You have not lived in the world of competitive sport until you have fought a battle that is not against an opponent, but against yourself."

Sixth, in recent years, I have learned to use running for relaxation and creativity, as my form of play. I have found that running is one way of living with everyday mental hassles. And it provides the time for the creativity that is important in my work. So I have written articles, prepared speeches, designed research experiments, and, indeed, refined this book during the hours that I have spent running. And I have found that my thinking during those hours is more creative and insightful than at any other time of my day.

Running has taught me that creativity is not the result solely of hard work. To me, it seems that regular play, like running, provides the childlike activity necessary for the creative act to occur, for novel thoughts to appear apparently from nowhere, and for old-established ideas suddenly to take on a new meaning.

It may be as the mathematician Morris Kline wrote: "The creative act owes little to logic or reason. Indeed, it seems to occur most readily when the mind is relaxed and the imagination roaming freely."

Finally, running can teach us about our spiritual component—the aspect that makes us uniquely human. This, I suspect, is the need to discover and to perfect, the need to keep moving forward. Running epitomizes that struggle by teaching us that we must not stop. Paavo Nurmi wrote: "You must move, otherwise you are bound for the grave" (chapter 7). Arthur Newton felt similarly: "You never stay put at any stage; either you advance or slip back" (1949). So we inherit this desire to push to the limits to find out what makes us what we are, and what is behind it all.

The rewards of doing it right are those that the runner experiences in the predawn excitement at the start of any marathon: "God made a home in the sky for the sun, it comes out in the morning . . . like an athlete eager to run a race."

PHYSIOLOGY AND BIOCHEMISTRY OF RUNNING

Part I of this book deals with the physiology and biochemistry of running. Chapter 1, therefore, starts by focusing on the structure and function of muscles. Chapter 2 expands on this by explaining how oxygen and fuel are delivered to the muscles. Chapter 3 describes how the muscles and other bodily organs alternately store and then use the energy contained in the body's stored chemicals—the process of metabolism. Chapter 4, in turn, focuses on how the body maintains a safe body temperature by removing from the muscles the excess heat produced by metabolism and by dissipating that excess heat into the environment.

All humans, including scientists, interpret the meaning of information based on their own preconceived ideas of how the world works. These preconceptions are called paradigms, or axioms, or, in the physiological sciences, models. We may never know whether the axioms or models we use are true or correct, only that they have yet to be disproved. And if they have been disproved, we may still not yet know that information, or we may simply choose to ignore it. That our models may ultimately be incorrect (although as yet unproven) does not matter. As Stephen Hawking, author of the most popular scientific publication of all time, *A Brief History of Time* (1988), says: "One cannot say that one model is more correct than the other, only more useful."

At one time, the most popular model of the earth was that it was flat. Christopher Columbus disproved this model in 1492, however, when he successfully sailed west from Spain to North America—without falling off the edge. Today, membership of the Flat Earth Society is reserved for those who choose to ignore the unequivocal results of Columbus' liberating discovery.

Since the early 1920s, our understanding of exercise physiology has been dominated by a model that holds that the most important, perhaps the only, determinant of exercise ability is the capacity to transport oxygen to active muscles during exercise. Supporters of this model argue that muscle fatigue, particularly during high-intensity exercise of short duration, occurs when the exercising muscles' need for oxygen outstrips the ability of the heart to satisfy that demand. As a result, in the absence of an adequate oxygen supply, the muscles are forced to contract anaerobically. I have called this the Cardiovascular/Anaerobic Model (Noakes 1998a; 1999a). In terms of this model, which I evaluate in chapter 2, the world's best athletes are those with the greatest capacity to transport oxygen to their muscles during very hard exercise. As suggested in previous editions of *Lore of Running*, I have never been a devotee to that cause; now I am an active opponent (Noakes 1998a; 1999a). For, as described in chapter 2, I believe that this traditional model leads to heart damage during exercise. I therefore conclude that the more important organ—the heart—and not the exercising muscles, must be protected from oxygen deficiency during exercise. If this theory takes some of the gloss off the Cardiovascular/Anaerobic Model, it also provides us with the liberating opportunity to explore a broader range of models that attempt to explain the physiology of human athletic performance. Additional models that are presented in this book, perhaps for the first time, are the following:

- The Central Governor or Integrated Neuromuscular Recruitment Model (chapter 2)
- The Biomechanical Model (chapter 2)
- The Muscle Power Model (chapter 2)
- The Energy Supply/Energy Depletion Model (chapter 3)

Before we enter these uncharted waters, let us begin our own voyage into this New World of exercise physiology by considering the structure of muscles and how they work.

Muscle Structure and Function

Muscle contraction is the essential physiological event that enables us to run. Thus, a description of how muscles are constructed and how they contract will help build an understanding of the physiology and biochemistry of running.

There are three types of muscle in the body: heart, or cardiac, muscle; skeletal muscles, which are attached to the skeleton and which contract to produce locomotion; and smooth muscles, which form the muscular lining of many organs, in particular, those of the digestive organs of the intestine.

Of these three, only skeletal muscle and, to a lesser extent, cardiac muscle are of any real relevance to running. In this chapter, we focus exclusively on the structure and function of skeletal muscle.

Each skeletal muscle is composed of a vast number of individual muscle cells, or fibers. These cells lie parallel to one another and are separated by connective tissue containing blood vessels and nerves (figure 1.1). In humans there are two types of muscle cells—Type I and Type II fibers. There is a random mix of Type I and Type II fibers in all the skeletal muscles in the body.

STRUCTURAL COMPONENTS OF SKELETAL MUSCLE

The connective tissue surrounding the muscle cells contains nerves and tiny blood vessels, or capillaries. As a result, each muscle cell (whether Type I or Type II) has its own nerve and blood supply. In general, each muscle cell is surrounded by about five capillaries, and this number increases with training (Saltin and Gollnick 1983).

Myofibrils, Sarcomeres, and Myofilaments

Every muscle cell is made up of a multitude of tiny rods called myofibrils, which lie parallel to one another. Each myofibril, in turn, contains many shorter components, called sarcomeres, which lie end to end. Each sarcomere contains a large number of even tinier rods, the myofilaments. These myofilaments also lie parallel to one another.

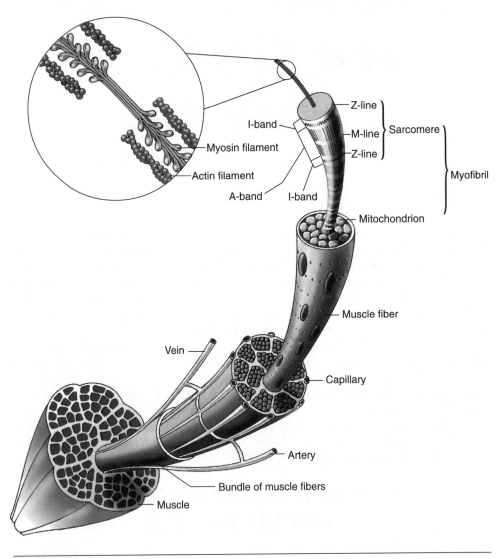

Figure 1.1   The structure of muscle showing the organization of muscle fibers, myofibrils, and sarcomeres, including the actin and myosin filaments.

A myofilament consists of two parts: a thick filament made up of myosin molecules, and a thin filament made up mostly of actin molecules. These thin filaments also contain two other proteins, troponin and tropomyosin molecules. When we run, these thick and thin filaments interact in a complex way to produce muscle shortening (concentric contraction) or lengthening (eccentric contraction) of the whole muscle. This interaction within the muscles enables us to run.

An important feature of the sarcomeres is that they are striped, or striated (see figures 1.1 and 1.2), which is why skeletal muscle is sometimes also called striated muscle. The sarcomeres look striped because the thin filaments are situated at the outer ends of the sarcomeres, while the thick filaments lie between them and extend across the center of the sarcomeres. The striations are due to the overlap of both filament types at the inner sections of the sarcomere, the A-bands (figures 1.1 and 1.2). But the immediate function of these structural proteins is to transmit the force generated by the sarcomeres to the tendon some distance away.

Until recently, interest in skeletal muscle function focused on the interaction of these contractile proteins of the sarcomeres. Surprisingly, less attention was paid to other proteins found in muscle, which are among the largest proteins in the human body. What is important is that these structural proteins bind the

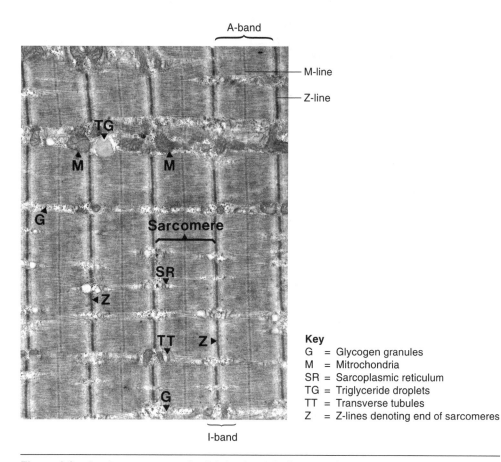

Key
G = Glycogen granules
M = Mitrochondria
SR = Sarcoplasmic reticulum
TG = Triglyceride droplets
TT = Transverse tubules
Z = Z-lines denoting end of sarcomeres

Figure 1.2 An electronmicrograph of skeletal muscle. Sample is from Lindsay Weight, winner of the 1983 and 1984 Comrades Marathons.

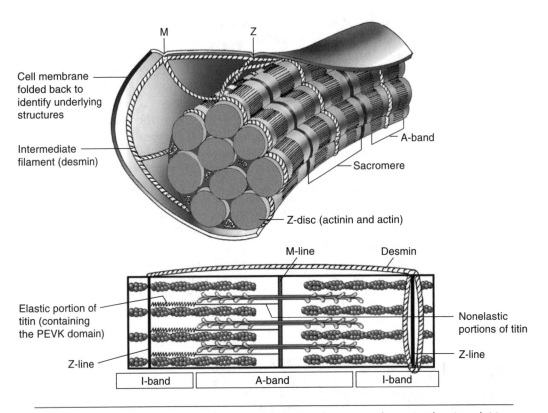

Figure 1.3   The detailed structure of sarcomeres, showing the structural proteins desmin and titin within the muscle fiber. The other proteins (nebulin, talin, vinculin, and dystrophin) are not shown.

sarcomeres together and prevent their disruption when they produce force during contraction (figure 1.3).

The Biomechanical Model of Exercise Physiology (see chapter 2) proposes, in part, that because these proteins influence the elastic recoil of the muscles and, probably, their resistance to damage during repeated eccentric contractions, they may contribute to athletic ability, especially when running events longer than 30 km. Perhaps exhaustion of this elastic function could explain why runners suddenly "hit the wall" during marathons and longer races and why weight-bearing sports such as running are so much more difficult to master than non-weight-bearing activities like cycling. In fact, the elastic properties of the muscle tendon complex are altered in runners, being less elastic or stretchable than that of nonrunners (Kubo, Akima, et al. 2000). Furthermore, the less compliant this structure, the less able it is to use the elastic energy stored in each running stride (Kubo, Kawakami, et al. 1999). These findings lead the authors to postulate that the elastic properties of the musculotendinous complex of athletes may well contribute to their running ability. Also, these elastic properties can alter substantially and rapidly—with as little as 20 days' bed rest (Kubo, Kanehisa, et al. 2000).

The first such protein is titin, which extends from the Z-disc to the M-line, effectively binding myosin to the Z-disc (figure 1.3). Titin maintains the structural integrity of the myofibril and provides resistance to the stretch of the sarcomere (and hence, the muscle). Titin is also designed to act as a spring, as this section of the protein, which extends into the I-band (the PEVK portion), can unfold. The more elastic Type II fibers have more titin than the less elastic Type I fibers. Damage to titin causes the A-bands to lose their normal regular arrangement. This is an important component of the damage that occurs with repetitive eccentric exercise, such as marathon running (see chapters 7 and 14).

Nebulin is the structural portion of the thin filament and probably regulates the number of actin, tropomyosin, and troponin molecules that are allowed in each thin filament. Sarcomeres are kept in register by the protein desmin, which binds adjacent sarcomeres at the Z-discs. Finally, sarcomeres are attached to the cell membrane by another group of proteins, the talin, vinculin, and dystrophin proteins. A genetic defect in the production of these proteins causes a form of muscular disease (dystrophy) in children.

Mitochondria

Another important feature of the skeletal muscle cell is clearly shown in figure 1.2. The semicircular structures, marked M, are called mitochondria. These structures lie next to the muscle filaments, and their main function is to produce the energy needed to power muscular contraction. As a result, mitochondria have been termed the powerhouses of the cell. In terms of the Energy Supply/Energy Depletion Model (see chapter 3), running ability and fitness are partly related to the total ability of the mitochondria to produce energy in the runner's body.

The fact that the mitochondria are strategically placed next to the muscle filaments is important—it means that the energy produced in the mitochondria can be transported easily to the site where it will be used in the muscle filaments.

We do not fully understand the complex way in which mitochondria produce energy. For our purposes, it is sufficient to know that each mitochondrion consists of a bag of enzymes, which are biological catalysts. (Catalysts are substances that speed up chemical reactions without undergoing a change themselves.) These enzymes change the energy contained in the foods we eat into a molecule known as adenosine triphosphate (ATP). ATP is the form in which energy is used in the body—it is the body's energy currency.

The enzymes in the sarcoplasm provide a metabolic pathway, or route for energy transfer that does not require oxygen. (More accurately, a metabolic pathway is a series of chemical reactions, each of which is catalyzed by enzymes, in which energy is released to do work within the body—muscle contractions, cell maintenance, nerve conduction, and so on.) This particular pathway is known as the oxygen-independent glycolytic pathway—it means that stored muscle glycogen and blood glucose can be used to produce energy independent of an oxygen supply. (Unfortunately, the incorrect term, *anaerobic* glycolysis, has persisted in the literature. We discuss the reason for this in chapter 2.)

Fat Droplets

The circular fat droplets constitute a third important feature of muscle cells. These fat droplets consist of triglyceride molecules—marked TG in figure 1.2—and are the form in which fat is stored in the body. These molecules are among the main sources of energy for muscular contraction.

The triglyceride molecule, in turn, is made up of three fatty acid molecules linked to a single glycerol molecule. (*Cellulite* is a euphemistic term used to describe excessive accumulation of these triglyceride molecules in the subcutaneous layer.)

For the triglyceride molecule to provide energy for muscular contraction, it must first be broken into its free fatty acid and glycerol components. This is done by the action of a specific biological catalyst, the enzyme triglyceride lipase. The free fatty acid molecules then enter the bloodstream and travel to the muscle mitochondria where they are used as an important energy fuel. However, free fatty acids released from the triglyceride broken down inside the muscle cell are transported directly to the mitochondria—they do not need to enter the bloodstream. The glycerol molecules are used by the liver to produce new glucose units in a metabolic process known as gluconeogenesis. Both these processes are important in providing energy during prolonged exercise, in particular during marathon and ultramarathon racing.

Glycogen

Figure 1.2 shows clumps of fine granular material scattered throughout the cell. These granules, marked G, constitute the second important source of energy inside the cells. They consist of many individual glucose molecules bound together into long branching chains called glycogen. Glycogen is the only form in which both the muscles and the liver store the ingested carbohydrates. As we shall see further on, according to the Energy Supply/Energy Depletion Model, these glycogen stores may play a critical role in determining performance in both marathon and ultramarathon races.

In vegetables and fruits, on the other hand, energy is stored as a different large molecule, starch. We will discuss the importance of ingested starch and its derivatives, the glucose polymers, as a fuel for muscles during exercise in greater detail in chapters 3 and 4.

With this background, we can now discuss the more detailed structure of the thick and thin filaments and how they interact to produce muscular contraction.

BIOCHEMICAL EVENTS OF MUSCLE CONTRACTION

In the early 1900s, it was realized that, during the contraction of a muscle, the sarcomere shortens in such a way that the A-band (see figures 1.1 and 1.2) remains the same width and the I-band becomes thinner. The British scientist A.F. Huxley proposed that the thin filaments of the I-band had slid or been pulled into the A-band by the action of the A-band (thick filament) proteins. Huxley was deservedly awarded the Nobel Prize for Biology for his sliding filament theory of muscle contraction. Today, this hypothesis is still considered to be correct (Poldosky et al. 1983), although, as discussed later on in this chapter, one iconoclastic and maverick Japanese scientist, Toshio Yanagida, has proposed a different idea.

The thick filaments that constitute the A-band are made up of myosin molecules, each of which has a body and a head. The individual myosin heads point toward the actin proteins of the thin filaments. There is a strong attraction between the myosin and a region of the actin molecule called the actin-binding site. In a resting muscle, this mutual attraction is physically blocked by the tropomyosin molecules of the thin filaments (see figure 1.1). Therefore, before muscle contraction can occur, some mechanism must operate to move the tropomyosin molecule out of the way.

The trigger that activates this move is the element calcium. When we decide to move a particular muscle, the brain sends a message in the form of an electrical impulse, down the spinal cord, and from there to the peripheral nerve that supplies the muscle. There is a special site, called the motor nerve end-plate, at the point where the peripheral nerve joins the muscle cell that it serves. When the electrical current passes through the motor nerve end-plate, a special chemical messenger, acetylcholine, is released into the gap between the motor nerve end-plate and the outer covering of the muscle cell (figure 1.4).

Once it crosses this tiny gap, the acetylcholine molecule binds to special receptors on the muscle cell. This binding causes an electrical current to travel along the outer envelope of the cell and down its extensions, called the transverse tubules (marked TT in figure 1.2; also shown in figure 1.4), which penetrate the inside of the cells. In a way that is yet to be explained, this causes calcium stored deep inside the cell to be released very rapidly. The calcium is stored in a structure called the sarcoplasmic reticulum (SR in figure 1.2; also shown in figure 1.4).

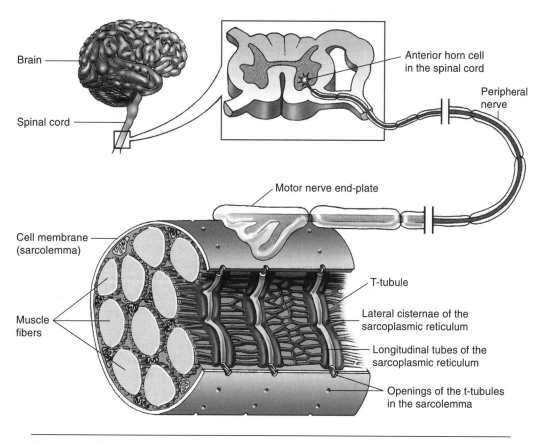

Figure 1.4 Pathways by which a nerve impulse travels from the brain to the muscles.

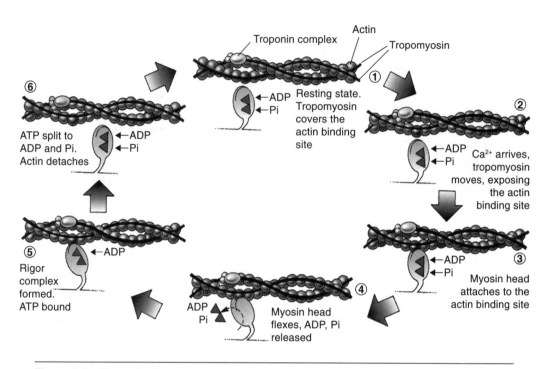

Figure 1.5   The molecular mechanism involved in muscular contraction.

The calcium now floods into the cell sarcoplasm surrounding the muscle filaments and binds to specific calcium-binding sites. These are found on a special calcium-binding protein, troponin-C, attached to both the tropomyosin and the actin (position 1 in figure 1.5).

This binding of calcium causes the troponin-C molecule to undergo a complex twisting movement. The result is that the tropomyosin molecule is moved from its blocking position between actin and myosin (position 2 in figure 1.5). This allows the myosin head to attach itself to actin, the essential first step in muscular contraction.

The next ingredient required for muscular contraction is a source of energy—supplied by ATP molecules produced in the mitochondria. These travel to specific ATP-binding sites on the myosin heads. The ATP is stored here as two ATP breakdown products, adenosine diphosphate (ADP) and phosphate (Pi) (position 2 in figure 1.5). The breakdown of ATP to ADP and Pi is prompted by the enzyme myosin ATPase. The importance of this particular enzyme is that the speed at which any specific muscle can contract is largely determined by the activity of the predominant form of myosin ATPase that it contains.

When the energy-loaded myosin head attaches itself to actin (position 3 in figure 1.5), the Pi and ADP are released, almost immediately, one after the other by the myosin-binding site. This action causes the myosin head to undergo a complex sequence of events in which its flexible neck bends 45 degrees from its normal vertical angle (position 4 in figure 1.5). This bending action, known as the power stroke, causes the thin filaments to be pulled toward the center of each sarcomere as the myosin molecule acts as the lever arm. This movement, repeated

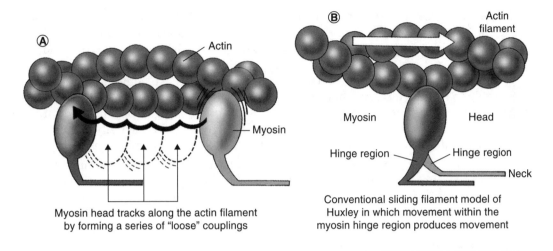

Myosin head tracks along the actin filament by forming a series of "loose" couplings

Conventional sliding filament model of Huxley in which movement within the myosin hinge region produces movement

Figure 1.6 Toshio Yanagida's model of muscle contraction *(A)* compared with the accepted sliding filament model of Huxley *(B)*.

in many millions of thick and thin filaments in millions of sarcomeres in a single muscle, produces the visible muscle shortening that we recognize as movement.

The fully contracted position, in which the myosin head is bent to the 45-degree position and is bound to actin, is known as the rigor complex (position 5 in figure 1.5). To break the rigor complex to relax the muscle, first the mitochondria must supply fresh ATP to the ATP-binding site on the myosin head, and second, the calcium bound to the troponin-C must be removed so that tropomyosin can again move into its blocking position between the actin and myosin (position 6 in figure 1.5).

The somewhat modified theory of muscle contraction proposed by Japanese scientist Toshio Yanagida (Cyranoski 2000) suggests that instead of binding firmly to a single actin-binding site, as shown in figure 1.5, the myosin head tracks along the actin filament, forming a series of loose couplings (figure 1.6A), quite unlike the original single tight-coupling model of Huxley (figure 1.6B). As scientists find it difficult to disprove Yanagida's model, the debate is likely to remain unresolved for some time to come. One of the possible advantages of Yanagida's model is that it is better able to explain eccentric muscle contractions, which are difficult to imagine according to the tight-coupling model.

The Cross-Bridge Cycle

The complete sequence shown in figure 1.5 is known as a single cross-bridge cycle. The following three important practical points should be noted:

1. The rate at which the cross-bridge cycle takes place determines the speed at which an athlete runs.

2. The total number of cross-bridges formed (in the active muscles) determines how powerfully the muscle contracts—for example, when lifting a heavy

(continued)

weight. The speed is determined by the rate at which ATP is bound and split on the myosin head by the enzyme myosin ATPase (positions 5 and 6 in figure 1.5). The power, in turn, is determined by the amount of calcium bound to troponin-C. We can therefore predict that athletes with muscle fibers that can bind and split ATP most rapidly, because of a high myosin ATPase content, should be able to run the fastest, whereas those whose muscles are best able to deliver and bind calcium and have the most available cross-bridges, because they are large muscles, will be the most powerful. The myosin ATPase activity of muscle fibers differs and is used in their classification.

Furthermore, sprinters (in both human and other species, including grey-hounds, cheetahs, and thoroughbred racehorses) do indeed have muscles with greater myosin ATPase activities than do nonsprinters. For instance, the greater sprinting ability of thoroughbred racehorses compared with draft horses, such as the Percheron, is believed to be related to the remarkable differences in the contractile capacities of the muscles of these two horse breeds (Potard et al. 1998). Thus, thoroughbreds have muscles that not only contract more rapidly (because of greater myosin ATPase activity), but they are also surprisingly much more powerful than the muscles of the outwardly more powerfully built draft horses. This suggests that the skeletal muscles of thoroughbreds also have a greater capacity to bind calcium. The greater capacity of the thorough-breds to transport blood and oxygen to their muscles, associated with their larger and more powerful hearts, is the result, not the cause, of their superior capacity for muscular work (Potard et al. 1998).

I speculate throughout this book that the same may also apply in human athletes: that the ability to supply a great deal of oxygen to a very powerful heart, associated with superior contractile function of both the heart and the skeletal muscles, causes superior athletic performance. The high rate of oxygen delivery to those skeletal muscles, which is needed to sustain their function during maximum exercise, is the result, not the cause, of an athlete's superior exercise capacity (chapter 2).

Interestingly, there have been relatively few studies of the contractility of muscle fibers taken from biopsy samples of athletes and studied in isolated systems in the test tube outside the body (that is, in vitro; literally *in glass*). These studies show that the contractility of Type I muscle fibers from trained runners are altered so that they contract more rapidly (Widrick et al. 1996a), but with Type IIa fibers, they produce less force as a result of the smaller size of both those fiber types in trained athletes than in untrained people (Widrick et al. 1996a; 1996b).

3. We can speculate that a muscle cramp results from the development of a rigor complex (position 5 in figure 1.5). This might occur either because there is no fresh ATP available to the myosin head to allow relaxation, or because there was a breakdown in the mechanism whereby calcium is released from troponin-C and pumped back into the sarcoplasmic reticulum. Alternatively, the neural stimulation of the muscle may be excessive, causing persistent electrical activity in the cell envelope and the transverse tubules. This will cause a continual release of calcium into the cell sap. As discussed in chapter 15, this is the most likely explanation for exercise-related muscle cramps.

TYPES OF MUSCLE FIBERS

The two main types of muscle cells, or fibers, are randomly mixed in all human muscles. These fibers are differentiated on the basis of their color, the quantity of mitochondria they contain, and the speed with which they contract, the latter being determined by the myosin ATPase content.

Type I muscle fibers are red and have a high concentration of mitochondria. Their redness is due to a high content of myoglobin, the protein whose function it is to transfer the oxygen carried in blood to the mitochondria and to act as an oxygen store in the muscles. The Type II fibers are white, owing to a low myoglobin content. They also have a low mitochondrial content. Surprisingly, despite the belief that myoglobin is an integral component in oxygen use by the muscles, especially during exercise, mice that have been genetically engineered so that their heart and muscles contain no myoglobin do not have any physical impairments and have a normal exercise capacity (Garry et al. 1998). Their muscles are paler, however, because of the lack of myoglobin. This study adds further fuel to the debate surrounding the contentious role of oxygen transport and athletic ability (chapter 2).

As early as 1873, the German physiologist Ranvier observed that muscles made up primarily of red fibers contract and relax more slowly than muscles made up primarily of white fibers. More recent work has confirmed this. In line with the most modern classification of muscle fiber type, these fibers are either defined as red, Type I, slow-twitch (ST) fibers or white, Type II, fast-twitch (FT) fibers. The understanding is that the Type II muscle fibers contract rapidly because they have a high myosin ATPase activity, whereas Type I fibers have a lower myosin ATPase activity.

It now seems, however, that the situation is not quite this simple; the myosin ATPase activity is not simply either fast or slow, and there may be varying grades of fastness or slowness among the Type I and Type II fibers. Thus, the Type I (ST) fibers of some athletes may have contraction speeds that approach those normally found in Type II (FT) fibers.

In addition, the Type II fibers can be divided into at least five subtypes: IIa, IIb, IIc, IIab, and IIac (Staron 1997). The Type IIa fiber is similar to the Type I fiber as it has a high concentration of mitochondria, and therefore an increased capacity to produce ATP by oxygen-dependent metabolism in the mitochondria. This fiber type is mainly found in long-distance runners and other endurance athletes such as cross-country skiers (Saltin, Henriksson, et al. 1977). Thus, the Type IIa fiber is believed to be a Type II fiber that is adapted for endurance exercise. The Type IIb fiber conforms to the classical description of the Type II fiber in that it has low mitochondrial content, whereas the Type IIc fiber is of uncertain origin and may be an uncommitted, primitive fiber capable of developing into either a Type IIa or a Type I fiber. Interestingly, the percentage of Type IIc fibers is highest in long-distance runners (Staron et al. 1984) and in those who do orienteering (Jansson and Kaijser 1977). Differentiation of fiber types is determined by the nature of the myosin molecule present in the fiber—in particular, the type of myosin heavy chain that is present, which is specific for the different fiber types (I, IIa, IIb, IIc). More recently, the Type IIc fiber has also been named a Type IIx fiber (Widrick et al. 1996a; J.L. Andersen et al. 2000). In vitro studies show that Type IIx fibers produce about twice as much power (force at speed) as Type IIa fibers, which are about five times as powerful as Type I fibers (Widrick et al. 1996b).

Fiber Type Composition:
Sprinters Versus Endurance Athletes

A number of studies have shown that the muscles of elite athletes exhibit specific and predictable patterns of muscle fiber content according to the sports in which the athletes excel. Thus, the muscles of sprinters, jumpers, and weightlifters contain a high percentage of Type II fibers. Middle-distance (400 m to 1500 m) runners, cyclists, and swimmers tend to have equal proportions of both Type II and Type I fibers. In long-distance (10 km to 42 km) runners and cross-country skiers, the percentage of Type I fibers is higher (table 1.1).

These differences between sprinters and distance runners are probably genetically determined (Komi, Viitasalo, et al. 1977; Komi and Karlsson 1979). If that is so and if these different fiber patterns are essential for success in the various sports, then it strongly suggests that a person's ultimate potential for success in endurance sports may be determined, in part, by being born with a high percentage of Type I fibers. Similarly, raw speed and weightlifting strength may also be determined by the number of Type II fibers with which the athlete is born.

One of the most interesting sporting phenomena is the domination by athletes of African origin. A more careful analysis shows that different athletic events are dominated by athletes from opposite sides of the continent. Sprinting and long-jump events are dominated by African-American and Caribbean athletes originating from Central West Africa, including Senegal, Liberia, Nigeria, and the Ivory Coast. Events longer than 400 m are dominated athletes from East and North Africa, predominantly by those from Kenya, Morocco, and Ethiopia, and, to a lesser extent, Algeria, Tanzania, and South Africa.

Table 1.1 Muscle fiber composition in athletes	
Types of athlete	**Type I muscle fibers (%)**
Sprinters	26
Sprinters and jumpers	37–39
Weight lifters	44–49
Cyclists and swimmers	50
Middle-distance runners	45–52
Elite half-marathon runners	54
Canoeists	60
Elite rowers	60–90
Elite distance runners	79–88
Cross-country skiers	72–79

Table 1.2 Different physiological and physical requirements of sprinters and distance runners		
Attribute	**Sprinter**	**Distance runner**
Size	Large (> 80 kg)	Small (< 50 kg)
Explosive power	Very high	High
Aerobic capacity	Unimportant	Important
Fatigue resistance	Unimportant	Crucial
Muscularity	Essential	Disadvantage
Body type	Mesomorphic	Ectomorphic
Muscle fiber composition	80% Type II (FT)	60% Type I (ST)

What is striking about this phenomenon is that there are different physiological and biochemical requirements for success in sprinting and in distance running (table 1.2). Sprinters are designed to be big, muscular, and explosive, but they are unable to sustain their effort for longer than 20 to 40 seconds. In contrast, distance runners must be small but exceptionally powerful for their size. A large capacity to transport and use oxygen (aerobic capacity) is important, but the crucial capacity is fatigue resistance, which can be described as the ability to sustain a high percentage of the maximum exercise capacity for minutes to hours. These differences are explained, at least in part, by the different fiber compositions of the muscles of sprinters and distance runners shown in table 1.1.

Sprinters have a greater proportion of fast-contracting Type II fibers, whereas endurance athletes have a majority of fatigue-resistant, slower-contracting Type I fibers. As a result, the lower limbs of sprinters are able to contract more powerfully and more rapidly than those of endurance athletes. Sprinters also have larger muscles with longer muscle fascicle lengths, which are a measure of the number of sarcomeres stacked end to end (in series) in their muscles (Abe, Kumagai, et al. 2000). Sprinters, especially African-Americans, also have a different muscle shape with greater muscle thickness in the upper parts of the muscles near where they originate from the skeleton (Abe, Brown, et al. 1999; Abe, Kumagai, et al. 2000). The pennation angle, which is a measure of the angle at which the muscle fibers insert into the tendons, is also less in sprinters than in distance runners (Abe, Kumagai, et al. 2000).

These real differences between sprinters and distance runners in terms of body size and muscularity are likely genetically determined. The extension of the argument is that the different performance capabilities of West African sprinters and East African distance runners may also be linked to their genetic backgrounds.

So, exercise scientists might ask: How were the different genes for ability in sprinting or distance running distributed to the west and east of Africa during African prehistory? What local factors contributed to the clustering of the "sprinting genes" in the west and the "distance running genes" in the east, north, and south? And what of the countries in between? Which athletic genes did their peoples inherit? Are there common genetic links between the peoples of Kenya, Tanzania, Ethiopia, Morocco, Algeria, and South Africa, who produce the great distance runners? If not, are there environmental factors common to these different peoples that can explain their uncommon sporting prowess? The significance of such research is that it will be the most direct way of unraveling the nature of the different genes determining success in sprinting and in distance running—if such genes exist. The identification of any such genes may also establish the exact physiological and biochemical attributes needed for success in sprinting and in distance running.

Only the Fast and Strong Die Young

A number of studies have shown that athletes proficient in endurance sports outlive those who are blessed with speed and strength. While the usual explanation is that this results from the greater health benefits achieved by participating in aerobic (endurance) sports compared with the explosive sports such as sprinting or weightlifting, there is some evidence that these differences could be due to inborn, hereditary factors, perhaps related to the type of muscle fibers with which athletes in either group are born. Thus, people with a high proportion of Type II muscle fibers may be more prone to developing hypertension, diabetes, and obesity (Bassett 1994).

Indeed, Heikki Tikkanen, a Finnish sports physician from Helsinki, has shown that the percentage of Type I fibers in a person's thigh muscles influences that person's level of fitness, chosen levels of habitual physical activity, and serum cholesterol concentrations, especially the concentrations of serum HDL-cholesterol (Tikkanen, Härkönen, et al. 1991; Tikkanen, Näveri, et al. 1996; Tikkanen, Hämäläinen, et al. 1998; 1998b). It was found that people with a high percentage of Type I fibers were more likely to be physically active, to have higher blood HDL-cholesterol concentrations, and to be fitter. In contrast, those with low percentages of Type I fibers were more likely to be physically inactive, physically unfit, and to have coronary heart disease. These authors have concluded that skeletal muscle, in particular the percentage of Type I fibers, contributes to the long-term health of the heart. Thus, among former athletes, the least healthy are those who are physically inactive and physically unfit, perhaps, in part, because they have a low proportion (less than 44%) of Type I fibers. Members of this group are more likely to have been sprinters or weightlifters in their youth. In contrast, the most healthy group were those who were the most physically active and had the highest fitness levels, and who also had a high proportion (greater than 66%) of Type I fibers (Tikkanen 2001).

Another study found that the percentage of Type I fibers in the thigh muscles was inversely related to percentage of body fat so that those with the most Type I fibers were the leanest (Wade et al. 1990). Furthermore, during exercise, those with more Type I fibers burned more fat as a fuel. According to the Energy Supply Model and Energy Depletion Model (chapter 3), burning more fat during exercise should enhance performance during prolonged exercise.

These researchers concluded that people endowed with a high percentage of Type I fibers have a natural aptitude for physical activity and are therefore more likely to participate in physical activity throughout their lives. In addition, the high percentage of Type I fibers may also endow these endurance athletes with higher blood HDL-cholesterol concentrations and perhaps a greater capacity to adapt both to training and to other favorable health benefits of exercise. In this way, physical activity further enhances the health of those born to be healthy. Thus, genetic skeletal muscle fiber composition may determine the likely lifetime physical activity patterns and, in part, the risk of developing heart disease. This might support Lean and Han's view that men with a natural ability in "power sports" are at increased risk of developing cardiovascular disorders, compared with men with a natural ability in endurance sports. It might also explain why "a predominance of Type II, glycolytic muscle fibers, presumably of genetic origin, may predispose to cardiovascular disorders" (Lean and Han 1998). This finding, however, does not negate the evidence that both the genetically fit and the genetically unfit benefit from regular, vigorous exercise and that the magnitude of these benefits may indeed be greatest for those who are the least fit.

I am not convinced that a high percentage of Type I fibers is essential for success in prolonged endurance activities such as marathon running, as suggested by the findings reported in table 1.2. I suggest that the different muscle fiber composition found in middle- and long-distance runners is somewhat artificial and that within the next 20 to 50 years, the muscle fiber composition of the elite marathon runners will be found to approach that currently found in elite middle-distance runners (that is, approximately 50% Type II fibers). Those athletes who excelled at the marathon distance when these initial studies were performed probably did so because they were not quite fast enough for success in middle-distance running, possibly because their muscles have too few Type II fibers. A good example is the former marathon world record holder, Derek Clayton, who chose to specialize in the marathon when he realized he could not be Australia's next Herb Elliott (chapter 6).

Perhaps the selection pressures at play in the 1970s and 1980s forced slower milers with a low percentage of Type II fibers to compete at longer distances at which faster milers, who have faster muscles and a higher percentage of Type II fiber content, did not choose to compete and for which they were not ideally suited.

As the longer distance races, especially the standard marathon, become more lucrative and therefore as attractive as track running, however, these elite middle-distance runners with higher percentages of Type II fibers will begin to dominate these races. A repeat today of the study done by Fink et al. (1977) on elite American marathon runners of the 1970s may show different results and could indicate that athletes with an even mix of Type I and Type II fibers are probably better able to succeed in marathon and ultramarathon races than are those with a high percentage of Type I fibers. Our data on world-class black distance runners shows this to be the case; these runners have between 40% and 60% Type II fibers (Coetzer et al. 1993). Certainly, I predict that the sub-2-hour marathon, the probable ultimate goal of Ethiopian Haile Gebrselassie, will not be achieved by a runner with a low proportion of Type II fibers.

Training to Develop Specific Muscle Fiber Types

Gaining an understanding of the different muscle fiber types helps us appreciate why, during exercise, the fibers in the active muscles are activated in a specific pattern. Both the type of exercise and its intensity and duration determine this activation pattern. During low-intensity running, Type I fibers are initially active, but as the exercise intensity increases, a greater number of Type II fibers become active in the sequence of Type IIa > Type IIb (Saltin 1981). There is also a recruitment sequence during prolonged exercise, with the Type I fibers being activated first. One theory is that as the Type I fibers become progressively energy-depleted, the Type IIa fibers become active, followed finally by the Type IIb fibers. Thus, the noncompetitive jogger who exercises at a low intensity for a short duration will train predominantly Type I fibers, while the middle-distance runner who includes high-intensity training will train both Type I and Type II fibers.

Logically, optimal training should be at all running intensities so that all muscle fiber types are trained equally. Indeed, the success of the peaking training technique developed by Forbes Carlile (1963) and Arthur Lydiard (Lydiard and Gilmour 1978) and described by Daws (1977), Osler (1978), and others (see chapter 6) may be that it achieves optimum training of the Type II fibers.

Muscles are recruited by messages coming from a special part of the brain—the motor cortex. Thus, recruitment patterns are, at least initially, determined centrally in the brain. The Integrated Neuromuscular Recruitment Model holds that this central recruitment influences and perhaps determines athletic performance in ways that are not yet fully appreciated. This model predicts that these changes in muscle recruitment patterns during exercise are not so much related to metabolic and other changes in the exercising muscles—for example, depletion of their energy reserves (the Energy Supply/Energy Depletion Model; see chapter 3)—as they are to motor patterns programmed into the motor cortex, or perhaps to information coming from a variety of receptors in the body. Controllers whose functions have already been identified include the following:

- The cardiostat—controllers that limit exercise of maximal intensity or at high altitudes when the oxygen supply to the heart or brain is at risk (see chapter 2; Noakes, Peltonen, et al. 2001)

- The glycostat—receptors monitoring blood glucose and perhaps muscle glycogen concentrations and the rates of their use during exercise (see chapter 3)

- The thermostat—those measuring the extent and rate of body heat accumulation during prolonged exercise (see chapter 4)

In all these situations, the action of these controllers is to protect the body from harming itself during exercise. For example, preventing maximum skeletal muscle recruitment during exercise at altitude reduces the work of the heart. This ensures that the heart does not develop an imbalance between its oxygen demand and its oxygen supply, the latter being substantially reduced by the very low blood oxygen content at altitude. Similarly, reducing skeletal muscle work when the blood glucose concentration is low prevents the brain from being damaged. Glucose is the brain's preferred fuel, and an inadequate supply of glucose to the brain will cause brain damage.

An alternative explanation to this integrated model is that muscle recruitment is reduced at fatigue because the brain itself becomes tired—so-called central (nervous system) fatigue (J.M. Davis and Bailey 1997). This model holds that changes in the brain's concentration of the chemical serotonin, and perhaps other neurotransmitters, including dopamine and acetylcholine, reduce the rate of firing of the motor centers in the brain. This reduces the recruitment of muscle fibers in the active muscles, hence producing (central) fatigue. Inasmuch as this model has no logical reason to exist, other than to explain some experimental findings, I expect it plays a less important role than does the purposeful reduction in muscle recruitment that occurs when the body is either hot, exercising at altitude, or exercising with a low or falling blood glucose concentration, or when the energy stores in the active muscles are depleted by prolonged exercise.

Another possibility currently under investigation (St. Clair Gibson, Lambert, et al. 2001; 2001a; 2001b) is that the brain is preprogrammed by prior experiences to progressively reduce muscle recruitment during very prolonged exercise. This model, which also provides the basis of the expanded Central Governor Model, holds that the increasing feeling of fatigue and the progressive reduction in the capacity of the exercising muscles to maintain a constant work output during prolonged exercise results from currently unrecognized processes in the brain, which presumably act to prevent bodily harm during such exercise. This model theorizes that performance during exercise is determined by two separate phenomena:

1. A pacing strategy that is preprogrammed into the athlete's subconscious brain as a result of previous training and racing experiences.

2. Acute alterations to that preprogrammed strategy resulting from sensory input from a variety of organs—heart, muscle, brain, blood, and lungs, among others—to the exercise controller or governor in the brain. Output from the controller to the motor cortex then determines the mass of skeletal muscle that can be activated and for how long, thereby determining the pacing strategy that the subconscious brain adopts during exercise (chapter 2).

At the same time, information is sent from the controller to the emotional and other centers in the brain. These influence the level of discomfort that is felt, the emotional response, and the self-talk and self-doubt that are additional but poorly understood features of the fatigue that develops during exercise (see chapter 8).

CONCENTRIC AND ECCENTRIC MUSCLE CONTRACTIONS

Figure 1.5 predicts that when an unloaded muscle (that is, a muscle that is not bearing a weight) contracts, it always shortens. This is called a concentric muscular contraction. An example of this would be picking up a very light weight. In contrast, during an eccentric contraction, the muscle length increases when it contracts. An example would be putting something down. This occurs when a force applied to the muscle exceeds the force that the muscle can produce during contraction. In this type of contraction, the myosin heads are pulled out to angles of 90 degrees or beyond during contraction, rather than flexing to 45 degrees (figure 1.5). It should be noted, however, that the actual mechanics of an eccentric contraction are not understood and that there are many theoretical objections to this simple model. The loose binding theory of Toshio Yanagida (see figure 1.6) is far more convincing since it would allow the myosin head to slip over the actin-binding sites during the lengthening phase of the contraction without requiring the myosin head to be flexed forcibly, as this action could produce damage. Nevertheless, eccentric muscle contractions use less oxygen and ATP, and they recruit fewer muscle fibers than do equivalent concentric contractions (Friden 1984). Eccentric contractions produce nearly twice as much force in each muscle fiber that is active, which is why such contractions increase the risk of both muscle and tendon injuries (see chapter 14). This force enhancement is believed to be influenced in some way by the action of the structural proteins, including titin (Komi and Nicol, 2000).

In running, eccentric muscle contractions occur in both the quadriceps and the calf muscles with each running stride. This is exaggerated, especially in the upper thigh (quadriceps) muscles, during downhill running because the forces that pass through these muscles can equal three times the body weight, particularly as the foot lands on the ground. The initial contraction of the quadriceps is not quite strong enough to overcome this force; thus, this muscle is stretched in an eccentric contraction for a brief instant, every time either foot hits the ground. Muscles were not designed for repetitive eccentric contractions and are susceptible to damage when forced to contract in this way (Friden 1984). This explains why downhill running can be especially painful and why it takes so much longer for postrace muscle stiffness to abate after downhill races than it does after uphill races; during eccentric contractions (downhill running) the muscles act as brakes and heat up just as brakes do when continually used. Exercise-induced muscle damage is discussed in greater detail in chapter 14.

Weight training uses concentric and eccentric contractions. For example, the standard leg press exercise activates a concentric contraction of the quadriceps muscle as the knee is extended and the weight pushed away from the body, and an eccentric contraction of the same muscle as the knee is flexed and the weight returns to its initial position (see figure 14.11, exercise D).

Training with weights causes the trained muscles to enlarge (hypertrophy) from an increase in the number of myofilaments, without an increase in the total number of muscle cells (fibers). The important benefits of static exercise such as weight training are that, when performed regularly, such exercise prevents the gradual loss of strength and bone mineral content that occurs naturally with age. Thus, runners who train only their lower limbs when running will benefit if they also use light weight training for their upper bodies. Furthermore, it seems likely that eccentric muscle contractions strengthen the elastic elements of the muscle. According to the Biomechanical Model (chapter 2), it is also likely that eccentric muscle contractions reduce the risk of injury, as well as enhancing performance. Training the quadriceps muscles with eccentric contractions probably aids performance in marathon and ultramarathon racing by reducing muscle damage.

Many great runners, including Herb Elliott and Bruce Fordyce , believe that weight training improves running performance. The scientific evidence is somewhat less clear. For example, both Hickson (1980) and G.A. Dudley and Djamil (1985) found that the training-induced increase in maximum oxygen consumption ($\dot{V}O_2$max) is not enhanced by combining weight training and running training any more than it is by changes produced only by running training (chapter 2). As we shall see, however, $\dot{V}O_2$max is not a reliable predictor of changes in running performance. Indeed, Hickson, Rosenkoetter, et al. (1980) have shown that a program of weightlifting did indeed improve actual running performance in short-duration, high-intensity exercise lasting up to 6 minutes. Furthermore, their subsequent study (Hickson,

Overland, et al. 1984) showed that heavy resistance training of the quadriceps muscle increased endurance time during maximal cycling or running exercise by 47% and 12% respectively. In that and other studies (Hickson, Dvoroak, et al. 1988; Marcinik et al. 1991) showing a beneficial effect, weight training was added to endurance training and not substituted for an equal time of endurance training. When strength training was substituted for a portion of the endurance training undertaken by cyclists, there was no benefit in comparison with spending the same time cycling (Bastiaans et al. 2001). Similarly, in another study of female cyclists, a 12-week weight training program added to a standard cycling program did not improve cycling performance to any great extent (D. Bishop et al. 1999).

In contrast, Finnish researchers Leena Paavolainen and her colleagues have shown that explosive strength training involving sprinting and a variety of jumping exercises (some of which were performed with additional weights), as well as conventional leg-press and knee flexion-extension exercises, significantly improved the 5-km running performance of trained runners (Paavolainen, Häkkinen, et al. 1999). The effect was due to neuromuscular adaptations, which most likely reduced neuromuscular exhaustion.

These researchers have also shown that the ability to produce force rapidly when the foot is on the ground, thereby maintaining a short ground contact time, is a factor predicting 5-km running time (Paavolainen, A.T. Nummela, et al. 1999). Furthermore, exhaustion during a 10-km running trial was associated with a significant impairment in all these variables—ground contact time increased and muscle activation decreased. Hence, explosive-type strength training may improve running performance as a result of neuromuscular adaptations that ensure that muscle activation remains high during the full duration of a race. This will ensure rapid force production when the foot is on the ground, reducing the ground contact time, thereby ensuring that a high running speed is maintained.

In contrast to these positive effects, the gains in strength that result from weight training appear to be impaired by concurrent endurance training (Hickson 1980; G.A. Dudley and Djamil 1985; Kraemer et al. 1995; G.J. Bell et al. 2000).

It would seem that although strength training may indeed enhance some aspects of running performance, running training impairs the muscles' ability to adapt to strength training. Thus, those who wish to develop strength only would be unwise to run as well. In contrast, there seems to be proven benefit in adding strength training if a runner wishes to improve running performance over distances from 5 to 90 km. There is no evidence, however, that cycling performance at any distance is improved by weight training. In chapter 6 we discuss the experiences of Yiannis Kouros, whose ultradistance running performances are unmatched. It appears that the stronger he became, the better he performed in races lasting from 24 hours to six days. This anecdotal experience should alert us to the possibility that strength training may become progressively more beneficial as the racing distance increases.

FINAL WORD

This chapter introduced the notion that all physiological findings are interpreted according to popular models of how the human body works. Currently, in terms of the most popular model, exercise performance is determined by each athlete's ability to transport oxygen to the exercising muscles. In the absence of an adequate oxygen supply, the exercising muscles are forced to contract anaerobically, a state that cannot be maintained indefinitely. In fact, the predictions of this model were described in detail more than 50 years ago:

> *First, the sprinter very quickly creates what is termed an "oxygen debt"; second, the valuable glycogen inside the muscle fibers is turned into poisonous lactic acid, the muscles become tired and stiff, dwindle in power, and finally refuse to function until the lactic acid has been turned back to glycogen during the recuperative processes of rest. (F.A.M. Webster 1948, p. 75)*

While Webster referred specifically to the theoretically poisonous role of lactic acid in sprinting, this description has been used loosely to explain how exhaustion develops in many sporting activities, not just sprinting. Here I have attempted to broaden this understanding by introducing some additional models of how the body functions during exercise. I have even suggested that all fatigue may be purely the sensory component of a subconscious pacing strategy that originates in the brain as part of a regulated process. It is this process that prevents bodily harm during exercise. I expand on these ideas in subsequent chapters.

The bulk of this chapter was devoted to describing how muscles are made up, how they contract to produce movement, the different muscle fiber types that exist, and how this influences athletic ability and perhaps longevity and susceptibility to various diseases. I have also speculated that the inborn characteristics of certain skeletal muscles may explain why most of the great sprinters in the world originate from central West Africa and why the presence of other muscle characteristics may explain why East, North, and South Africans, especially Kenyans, dominate international middle- and long-distance races.

Oxygen Transport and Running Economy

Why are some athletes able to run faster than others? How does training improve our fitness and racing times? What factors can predict running performance? In this chapter, I attempt to answer some of these questions by focusing on the relationship between oxygen transport through the body and exercise performance. I discuss the much-used, but frequently misunderstood, concepts of maximum work rate, maximum oxygen consumption ($\dot{V}O_2max$), and running economy. I also describe why most runners, and many exercise physiologists, have come to accept the notion, perhaps incorrect, that most forms of exercise are limited by a failure of oxygen delivery to the active muscles and that when forced to contract without an adequate oxygen supply (anaerobically) these muscles fatigue, thus terminating the exercise. I outline some of the new ideas that challenge this model, which I have termed the Cardiovascular/Anaerobic Model of Exercise Physiology and Athletic Performance.

HOW OXYGEN REACHES THE MUSCLES

Figure 2.1 shows the pathway by which atmospheric oxygen, which constitutes 21% of the air we breathe at sea level, is transported from the air to the mitochondria in the muscle cells.

Exhale CO_2

Inhale oxygen-rich air

Oxygen-poor air
to lungs

Oxygen-rich blood
from lungs to body

CO_2 enriched,
O_2 depleted
blood returns
to the heart

Exercising muscle
uses oxygen

CO_2 ← ← O_2

ATP

Figure 2.1   The pathways by which oxygen is transported from atmospheric air to the active muscles.

When we inhale, air containing oxygen is transported deep into the lungs, where it is brought into contact with blood carried in fine blood vessels. Therefore, the lungs are the meeting place of the oxygen in the air and the red blood cells contained in the blood. The red blood cells approaching the lungs have no oxygen left, but are loaded with carbon dioxide. (Carbon dioxide is the major waste product of energy production in the mitochondria.)

As blood passes through the capillaries in the lung, the red blood cells release their carbon dioxide, which is then passed out of the body via the lungs. At the same time, some of the oxygen that has come into the lungs dissolves into the fluid portion of the blood. A larger fraction of this oxygen is taken up by the red blood cell protein, hemoglobin, which has a high attraction to oxygen. The oxygen is transported in the bloodstream with the hemoglobin to all the cells of the body. During exercise, the oxygen requirements of the active muscles can be increased instantaneously by as much as 20 times. However, the requirements of the inactive muscles remain unchanged. The heightened metabolic activity of the muscles facilitates the release of biochemical signals that cause the blood vessels in the active muscles to dilate, increasing their flow. At the same time, the rate at which fuels enter the mitochondria rises. The result is that the energy and oxygen supplied to the active muscles are increased selectively.

Another mechanism for increasing blood supply to the active muscles has been termed the *splanchnic shunt*. Here blood is shunted away from the less active tissues—in particular, those supplied by splanchnic (gut) circulation (the intestine, kidneys, liver, etc.)—and redirected to the active tissues. All these tissues normally have an overabundant blood flow at rest and are able to survive on a reduced blood supply for fairly prolonged periods, certainly for a few hours of exercise. They do this by increasing the amount of oxygen they extract from the reduced blood flow. This enhanced oxygen extraction ensures an adequate oxygen use.

THE CONCEPT OF $\dot{V}O_2MAX$

As can be expected, there is an increase in oxygen consumption as the body goes from rest to exercise. This occurs as follows—as exercise increases in intensity, the motor regions in the brain recruit more muscle fibers and hence more myofibrils to produce ever more powerful muscular contractions. This demands increased rates of energy requirement, and this, in turn, a greater oxygen supply.

Early Studies

British physiologists, Nobel Laureate A.V. Hill and Hartley Lupton, were among the first to measure oxygen consumption during exercise and to speculate on the role of oxygen as a determinant of athletic ability (1923). On the basis of certain assumptions now shown to be incorrect (Noakes 1988b; 1997; 1998b; 2000c; Noakes, Peltonen et al. 2001), Hill and Lupton postulated that during exercise of increasing intensity humans use two energy sources.

At low exercise intensities, all the energy comes from aerobic (oxygen-requiring) sources (figure 2.2), corresponding to adenosine triphosphate (ATP) production in the mitochondria. Hill and Lupton believed, however, that these aerobic sources could only provide energy to a maximum rate of 4 liters per minute in humans, corresponding to the energy required to run at 13 km per hour. This precipitated Hill and Lupton's first conclusion that there was a maximum rate of oxygen consumption of 4 liters per minute in all humans (Noakes 1998b; 2000b).

Thus, when humans wished to run faster than 13 km per hour, they had to access a second energy source and this, Hill and Lupton proposed, was provided by anaerobic (meaning in the absence of oxygen) metabolism. As shown in figure 2.2, they also calculated that anaerobic metabolism could provide substantially more energy than could aerobic metabolism. Thus, at running speeds faster than 20 km per hour, approximately 75% of the energy came from anaerobic metabolism, with the remainder coming from aerobic metabolism in the mitochondria. As often happens in science, what Hill and Lupton actually believed and what subsequent generations of exercise physiologists interpreted as their beliefs were two quite different ideas (Noakes 1998b; 2000c; Noakes, Peltonen et al. 2001).

In 1955, the American physiologist Henry Longstreet Taylor and his colleagues (1955) reported that Hill and Lupton's work proved that during exercise of increasing intensity the oxygen cost ($\dot{V}O_2$max) rises as a linear function of the exercise intensity, or running speed. Then, shortly before athletes reached their maximum work rate, or maximum running speed, the rate of oxygen consumption reached a plateau (the so-called plateau phenomenon) and did not increase further. Although able to exercise a little harder, the athletes took up no more oxygen. At this point, the athletes were said to have reached their maximum rate of oxygen consumption, or $\dot{V}O_2$max (figure 2.3). Central to this belief is the idea that each person has a unique $\dot{V}O_2$max value that can be determined only by individual measurement in a laboratory. The annotation V is simply scientific shorthand for a rate of (volume of) flow. Thus, $\dot{V}O_2$max is the maximum rate of oxygen flow, and it is usually expressed relative to body weight (that is, in milliliters of oxygen per kilogram of body weight per minute (ml O_2/kg/min).

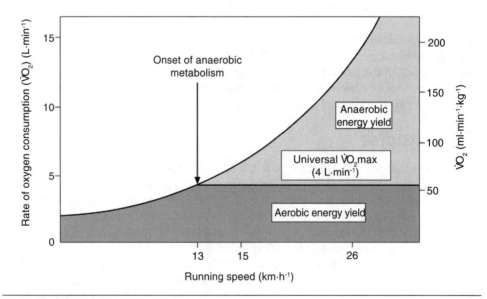

Figure 2.2 Hill and Lupton's concept of aerobic and anaerobic energy production and the "universal $\dot{V}O_2$ max" during progressive exercise to exhaustion.

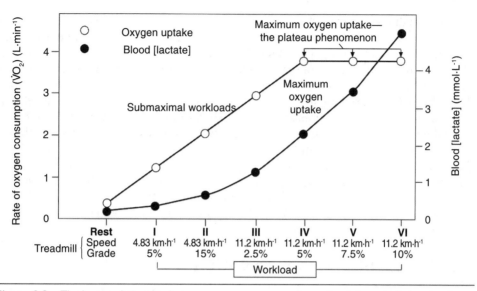

Figure 2.3   The linear relationship between oxygen consumption and running speed, showing the point at which maximum oxygen consumption ($\dot{V}O_2$max) is reached and the plateau phenomenon is believed to occur.

From J.H. Mitchell and Blomqvist (1971), pp 1018-22. © 1971. Adapted by permission, 2001. Massachusetts Medical Society. All rights reserved.

In fact, Hill and his colleagues neither described nor supported any of this. First, they believed that oxygen consumption rose as an exponential (nonlinear) function of running speed (see figure 2.2). Second, their model made no provision for the concept of the individual $\dot{V}O_2$max. Rather, they believed that there was a universal human $\dot{V}O_2$max of 4 liters per minute (Noakes 1998b; 2000c). Third, they made no mention of any plateau phenomenon, although their model predicted that $\dot{V}O_2$ would always reach a limiting maximum value in all humans at running speeds greater than 13 km per hour. The notion that a plateau phenomenon can be identified in individual athletes who may have $\dot{V}O_2$max values either less or more than 4 liters per minute was not their idea. This was the interpretation credited to Hill's mythical findings by Longstreet Taylor and his colleagues (1955), among others (Noakes 1998b). Fourth, they believed that "anaerobic metabolism" began only after the athlete had achieved the universal $\dot{V}O_2$max of 4 liters per minute at a running speed of 13 km per hour.

Although there is now good reason to believe that the plateau phenomenon is an artifact of dubious physiological significance (J.N. Myers 1996; J.N. Myers et al. 1989; 1990; Noakes 1988; 1997; 1998b; M. Doherty et al. 2002), it remains one of the most enduring, influential, and hotly defended concepts in the exercise sciences (Bassett and Howley 1997; Bergh et al. 2000; Wagner 2000; Ekblom 2000). In subsequent sections, I explain what I believe to be its true meaning and why Hill was much closer to the truth than this introduction might suggest.

Measuring $\dot{V}O_2$max

$\dot{V}O_2$max (however it may be defined) is measured during exercise on a treadmill or stationary bicycle. The athlete starts exercising at a low work rate. The work rate is then gradually and progressively increased at regular intervals—usually every minute—over a period of 8 to 15 minutes. Eventually, the athlete reaches exhaustion and stops exercising. The absolute maximum work rate that an athlete can achieve is reached in a 100-m sprint. But such a short event would not allow sufficient time for oxygen consumption to reach its maximum, hence the proviso that the test must last a reasonable time if the athlete's $\dot{V}O_2$max is to be measured. The $\dot{V}O_2$max measured in a progressive test to exhaustion is probably no different from that which would be measured when the athlete exercised as hard as possible to exhaustion within 5 to 8 minutes. The questions that remain to be answered are: What does the $\dot{V}O_2$max test really measure? What is its value to athletes? And why do humans stop exercising at $\dot{V}O_2$max if not because their exercising muscles have become "anaerobic" according to the popular interpretation of Hill's original idea? To assist our understanding of these ideas, we need to analyze the Cardiovascular/Anaerobic Model in greater detail.

Cardiovascular/Anaerobic Model

A number of conclusions followed naturally from Taylor et al.'s interpretation of the $\dot{V}O_2$max and the plateau phenomenon (figure 2.3).

1. If the oxygen consumption did indeed reach a maximum some time before the athlete became exhausted (that is, if it showed a plateau phenomenon), then it was clearly the development of a progressive oxygen deficiency in the exercising muscles that explained this exhaustion. Continued exercise beyond the plateau could only occur if the additional energy requirement was provided by oxygen-independent or anaerobic sources.

2. If that was indeed so, then the fastest runners would be those who had the greatest capacity to take up and utilize oxygen. Thus, the $\dot{V}O_2$max of elite athletes would always be the highest, and this measurement alone would be able to classify all athletes according to how well they would run in competition.

3. The limitations to exercise performance could be explained in terms of oxygen delivery to the muscles, oxygen utilization by the muscles, or both. Thus, the high $\dot{V}O_2$max values of the fastest runners would result either from their superior hearts being able to pump very large volumes of blood (and oxygen) to the muscles, or from their superior muscles, which could take up large volumes of oxygen. Note that the emphasis here is on the muscles' ability to use oxygen, as opposed to other properties that might determine their capacity to exercise at high intensity. These properties include the contractile capacity of the muscles, believed to be related to their myosin ATPase activity, their shape or their fascicle lengths (D. Abe et al. 2000), or their elasticity, influenced perhaps by their titin content or the collagen content of the elastic tendons in the lower limbs. This model also completely ignores any role of the brain in recruiting those muscles—by recruiting either more or less muscle (Kay, Marino, et al. 2001; St. Clair Gibson, Schabort, et al. 2001) or the more powerfully contracting muscle fibers (Paavolainen, Häkkinen, et al. 1999; Paavolainen, A.Nummela, et al. 1999; Paavolainen, A.T. Nummela, et al. 1999).

4. Anything that increased oxygen delivery to, or oxygen uptake by, the muscles and that therefore acted to delay or prevent the development of this oxygen deficiency in the muscles would improve the athlete's performance.

5. It is well known that the muscles of athletes, whether sprinting or running very long distances, always tire without developing contracture or rigor, shown as the rigor complex in figure 1.5. Yet, the rigor complex must be the final outcome of any model that holds that the muscles tire because they are unable to generate ATP with sufficient rapidity. (Recall from figure 1.5 that ATP is required to allow the rigor complex to be broken and the myosin head to be released from its binding to actin.)

For reasons that remain unclear since he could not have foreseen these arguments, Hill believed that the rising concentration of lactic acid, a chemical he considered to be a by-product of anaerobic metabolism, interfered with the processes of muscular contraction, inducing exhaustion before the development of skeletal muscle rigor. An inability to supply oxygen to the muscles produced a peripherally located, metabolite-induced exhaustion of the exercising muscles.

Together, these five points define what I have termed the Cardiovascular/Anaerobic Model of Exercise Physiology and Athletic Performance (Noakes 2000c). Restated, this model holds that high-intensity exercise is ultimately limited by the development of anaerobic conditions in the active muscles. This absence of oxygen results from the heart's inability to increase its output above some limiting maximum value. As a result, oxygen delivery to the active muscles plateaus, forcing the muscles to rely on anaerobic metabolism for their energy supply. The by-products of this anaerobic metabolism eventually accumulate in the muscle, causing exhaustion (figure 2.4). The unambiguous characteristic of this model is that the heart is the slave of the exercising muscles.

The fact that Hill and Lupton did not establish any of the theories subsequently accredited to them does not mean that those ideas and the model they created are definitely wrong. There is much, however, that reduces the plausibility of the Cardiovascular/Anaerobic Model.

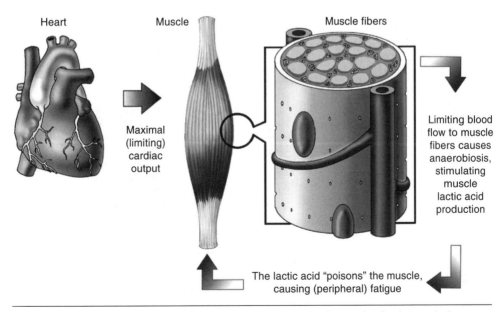

Heart   Muscle   Muscle fibers

Maximal (limiting) cardiac output

Limiting blood flow to muscle fibers causes anaerobiosis, stimulating muscle lactic acid production

The lactic acid "poisons" the muscle, causing (peripheral) fatigue

Figure 2.4   The sequence of events leading to exhaustion, according to the Cardiovascular/Anaerobic Model.

Modern studies suggest that this plateau phenomenon can be identified in approximately only 30% of tested subjects (Noakes 1998b; M. Doherty et al. 2002), and in children the plateau phenomenon is seldom identified (Rowland 1993; Rowland and Cunningham 1992). Note that the absence of a plateau does not imply that these athletes could go on using more and more oxygen indefinitely. They clearly become exhausted and stop exercising, but the absence of the plateau indicates that sufficient oxygen is reaching the muscles at the time they stopped exercising. This is analogous to the rate at which gasoline is supplied to an engine. While we might be able to supply more and more fuel, there will still be a limit to the amount of additional work that engine can do. This would be due to limitations, not in the rate of fuel (oxygen) supply to the engine, but in other factors inherent in the engine (muscle) itself. By analogy, supplying fuel at the same maximum rate to the engines of a Formula 1 racer and a family sedan would not eliminate the performance difference between the two.

The presence of a plateau phenomenon does not necessarily mean that a true oxygen deficiency has developed in the muscles (J.N. Myers et al. 1989; J. Myers et al. 1990; J.N. Myers 1996). Indeed, this relationship has always been assumed, never proven. In the most recent attempt by experts to determine whether muscles become anaerobic during maximum exercise, the opposite conclusion was drawn: "these data demonstrate that, during incremental exercise, skeletal muscle cells do not become anaerobic . . . since intracellular PO_2 [the oxygen pressure in the muscles] is well preserved even at maximal exercise" (R.S. Richardson et al. 1998).

A more careful review of the work by Hill and his colleagues (Noakes 1998b; 2000c; Noakes, Peltonen, et al. 2001) has revealed that Hill foresaw a critical flaw in his own theory that muscles became exhausted when the heart was no longer able to increase blood supply to the muscles (figure 2.4). He reportedly realized that for this to happen, the heart had to fatigue first, before the skeletal muscles. But

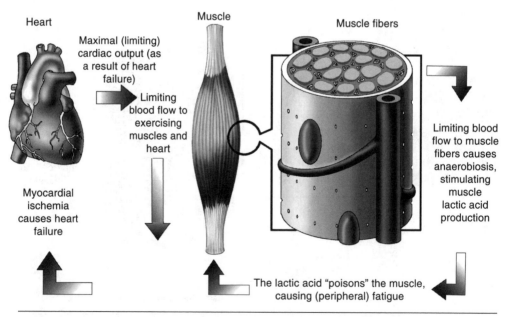

Heart

Muscle

Muscle fibers

Maximal (limiting) cardiac output (as a result of heart failure)

Limiting blood flow to exercising muscles and heart

Limiting blood flow to muscle fibers causes anaerobiosis, stimulating muscle lactic acid production

Myocardial ischemia causes heart failure

The lactic acid "poisons" the muscle, causing (peripheral) fatigue

Figure 2.5 The development of an inadequate blood flow to the heart muscle (myocardial ischemia) as predicted by the Hill model.

what was the nature of that heart exhaustion, preceding, as it must, exhaustion in the exercising muscles? The heart is itself a muscle dependent on an adequate oxygen supply. But, unlike skeletal muscle, the pumping capacity of the heart is not only dependent on, but also the determinant of, its own blood supply. (This is because the pumping action of the heart generates the pressure in the arteries that drives oxygenated, arterial blood through the coronary arteries that feed the heart.) Thus, if the pumping capacity of the heart limits the supply of oxygen to the active muscles, as is presumed by the plateau phenomenon and the Cardio-vascular/Anaerobic Model, then this must result from a failure of blood flow and oxygen delivery to the heart itself (figure 2.5).

Hence, if the Cardiovascular/Anaerobic Model is correct, then for the muscles to become exhausted during vigorous exercise, the heart must become exhausted first, presumably as the result of an inadequate blood supply. This leads to the conclusion that the organ at greatest risk of developing anaerobiosis during exercise is the heart, not skeletal muscle. In the original words of Hill and his colleagues,

> *Certain it is that the capacity of the body for muscular exercise depends largely, if not mainly, on the capacity and output of the heart, it would obviously be very dangerous for that organ to be able, as the skeletal muscles are able, to exhaust itself very completely and rapidly, to take exercise far in excess of its capacity for recovery. . . . The enormous output of the heart of an able-bodied man, maintained for considerable periods during vigorous exercise, requires a large contemporary supply of oxygen to meet the demand for energy. . . . When the oxygen supply becomes inadequate, it is probable that the heart rapidly begins to diminish its output, so avoiding exhaustion; the evidence for this, however, is indirect, and an important field of research lies open in the study of the recovery process in heart muscle, on the lines of which it has been developed in skeletal muscle. (1924b, p. 443)*

As a result, "It would seem possible that a deciding factor in the capacity of a man for severe prolonged exercise may often be the efficiency of his coronary circulation" (A.V. Hill 1925, p. 108). Thus, Hill and his colleagues were quite content with the idea that the heart could tire during exercise and that such exhaustion would not only precede, but also cause, exhaustion in the exercising muscles. What they did not know then is that the heart has no capacity to contract anaerobically and to develop an oxygen debt. Rather, when exposed to an inadequate oxygen supply, the heart's contractile activity is immediately impaired—causing the reduction in output foreseen by Hill and his colleagues—with the development of the characteristic chest pain (angina pectoris) that signals the onset of an inadequate blood supply to the heart.

An early protégé of A.V. Hill was the American David B. Dill, who, with A.V. Bock, developed the Harvard Fatigue Laboratory, one of the most important laboratories in the historical development of the modern exercise sciences (Horvath and Horvath 1973). Dill, too, believed that the heart became exhausted during maximum exercise because of an inadequate oxygen supply:

> *The blood supply to the heart, in many men, may be the weak link in the chain of circulatory adjustments during maximum exercise, and as the intensity of muscle exertion increases, a point is probably reached in most people at which*

the supply of oxygen to the heart falls short of its demands, and the continued performance of work becomes difficult or impossible. (Bainbridge 1931, p. 75)

Hence, Dill and Bock proposed that "another factor, which may contribute to the production of this type of fatigue, is fatigue of the heart itself." They believed that although the occurrence of exhaustion of the heart in health is not very clearly established, a temporary lowering of the functional capacity of the heart, induced by exhaustion of its muscular fibers, might result in too little blood being supplied to the skeletal muscles and brain. As they state, "the lassitude and disinclination for exercise often experienced on the day after a strenuous bout of exercise, has been ascribed to fatigue of the heart as its primary cause."

Like Hill, Bock and Dill overlooked the problems for the heart's own blood supply if the functional capacity of the heart was allowed to be impaired. Yet they understood that a greater and more immediate problem than any insufficient blood supply to the skeletal muscle and brain was an inadequate blood supply to the heart itself.

The major weakness of the Cardiovascular/Anaerobic Model is that it predicts something that does not occur: the heart does not fatigue as a result of anaerobiosis during maximal exercise, nor do healthy subjects terminate exercise because they develop chest pain (angina pectoris) resulting from an inadequate oxygen supply to the heart. Thus, proponents of this model face the challenge of explaining how blood supply to the exercising skeletal muscles can be inadequate while that to the heart is adequate (judged by the absence of chest pain at peak exercise in healthy athletes and the absence of evidence that the heart fatigues or fails during maximum exercise even at extreme altitude; Noakes 1988; 1998b; 2000c; Noakes, Peltonen, et al. 2001).

Hence, for there to be a plateau in oxygen delivery to the exercising muscles, the first organ to be affected by any postulated oxygen deficiency will be the heart itself. Furthermore, the immediate result of a deficient oxygen supply to the heart will be a drastically impaired pumping capacity. This would further reduce the heart's cardiac output and, as a result, its own (coronary) blood flow, leading to a vicious cycle of progressively increasing ischemia (inadequate blood supply). Were this to be the real model, all vigorous exercise in humans would be terminated by the development of chest pain (angina pectoris) that indicates the heart is being forced to continue contracting despite an inadequate oxygen supply. This finding, not uncommon in people with disease of the coronary arteries, has never been described in healthy athletes.

Anticipating this dilemma, Hill and his colleagues (A.V. Hill, Long, et al. 1924b) proposed that it would clearly be useless for the heart to make an excessive effort if, by doing so, it merely produced a far lower degree of saturation of the arterial blood (supplying the heart). They suggested that there was a mechanism in the body (either in the heart muscle or in the nervous system) that caused a slowing of the circulation as soon as a serious degree of unsaturation occurred, and vice versa. This mechanism, they said, acted as a governor.

Hill and his colleagues had correctly realized that, even if the ultimate limits of maximal exercise are set by the cardiovascular system, some mechanism other than skeletal muscle anaerobiosis must be present to terminate exercise before the heart itself is damaged by the very plateau in cardiac output that is (theoretically) necessary to explain the plateau phenomenon and the development of skeletal muscle anaerobiosis. Hence, they proposed that a governor, in either the heart or the nervous system, specifically terminated exercise before myocardial damage developed.

On the basis of this logic, I now believe that the heart's pumping capacity, determined, in part, by the maximum coronary blood flow, may indeed limit maximal aerobic exercise performance in events lasting a few minutes. This capacity is determined by the heart's maximal pumping capacity at the point at which the maximal blood flow to the heart is about to be reached. This must be a regulated process, however, as the actual maximal blood flow to the heart must never be achieved (or else chest pain and heart damage would result). Rather, as Hill and his colleagues proposed, there must be a governor that terminates exercise before the heart and exercising skeletal muscles are forced to contract anaerobically.

It seems probable that the heart's maximum ability to pump blood does determine the $\dot{V}O_2$max, but not by the mechanisms popularly presumed. Exercise must terminate before the heart itself becomes anaerobic, or ischemic, as it is the heart, not the skeletal muscles, that is at greatest risk of developing anaerobiosis during maximal exercise (see figure 2.5). This concept was well recognized by the early researchers, including A.V. Hill and David Dill (Noakes 2000c) .

To prevent the heart from becoming anaerobic during exercise, there would indeed be a need for a governor that anticipated when the blood and oxygen supply to the heart was about to become inadequate. Physiologists do not like the idea of subconscious physiological processes that function by anticipation (that is, by predicting the future). Prediction of the future is, they believe, reserved exclusively for the conscious processes in the higher brain centers. Yet, the evidence that this governor has anticipatory capacity is shown by human responses to a reduced oxygen supply in the inspired air, as occurs at altitude. This governor, presumably located in the brain, would, in response to information from the heart, and perhaps even the coronary blood vessels, reduce the recruitment of the muscles already active (figure 2.6). Alternatively, the governor might prevent the recruitment of additional muscle fibers necessary to further increase the work output and oxygen consumption. Were this to occur, additional demands would be placed on the heart, increasing its oxygen demands and thereby precipitating myocardial ischemia, or anaerobiosis.

Hence, the postulated governor would cause exercise to terminate before there was a plateau in whole body oxygen consumption or, more important, in the heart's blood supply and oxygen consumption. In this way, neither the heart nor the skeletal muscles would develop anaerobiosis during maximal exercise, and exercise would terminate as a result of a plateau in the recruitment of any additional fibers in the exercising muscles by the brain.

Accordingly, this model should, perhaps, be more correctly termed the Integrated Neuromuscular Recruitment Model of Exercise Physiology and Athletic Performance or, in short, the Central Governor Model.

Central Governor Model

This (new) Hill and Noakes model of maximum exercise performance holds that the heart is the organ at greatest risk of developing an oxygen deficiency during stressful conditions—especially vigorous exercise at extreme altitude. Thus, a mechanism must exist to restrain the overvigorous use of the exercising skeletal muscles,

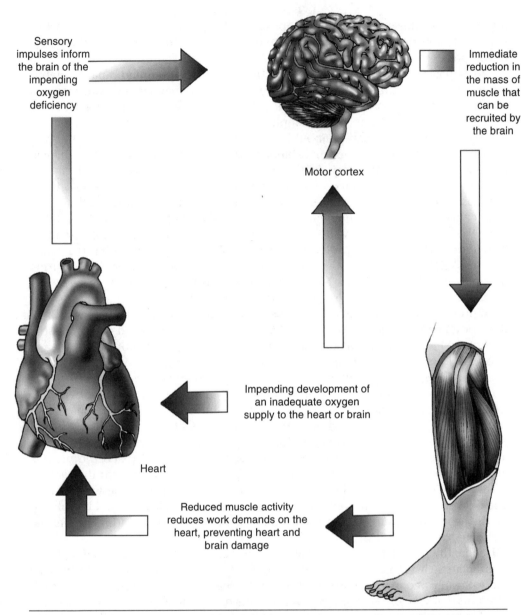

Sensory impulses inform the brain of the impending oxygen deficiency

Immediate reduction in the mass of muscle that can be recruited by the brain

Motor cortex

Impending development of an inadequate oxygen supply to the heart or brain

Heart

Reduced muscle activity reduces work demands on the heart, preventing heart and brain damage

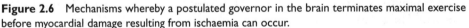

Figure 2.6 Mechanisms whereby a postulated governor in the brain terminates maximal exercise before myocardial damage resulting from ischaemia can occur.

which would imperil the heart. This model proposes the existence of a governor that monitors the state of oxygenation of the heart and perhaps other organs (such as the brain and diaphragm) as well. When the oxygenation approaches the limits of what is safe, the brain's motor cortex, which recruits the exercising muscles, is informed, and it stops recruiting additional muscle. As a result, the following occurs:

- The body experiences fatigue. Note that, like pain, fatigue is always sensed exclusively by the brain, even though it appears to be coming from elsewhere; for example, in the muscles (exhaustion and discomfort) or on the skin (pain).

■ The work output of the muscles and the heart falls, which leads to a reduction in the oxygen demands of the heart, thereby protecting the more delicate heart from damage caused by oxygen starvation.

Thus, this model predicts that maximum exercise capacity is a process, coordinated subconsciously by the brain, limited by the maximum capacity of the coronary blood flow to supply oxygen to the heart, and regulated to prevent heart damage during maximal exercise. The maximum work output (exercise capacity) achieved at that limiting coronary blood supply, however, will be determined by the mechanical efficiency, contractility, and elasticity of both the heart and the skeletal muscles of any person (figure 2.7). Thus, individual differences in human exercise capacity may result from different capacities in maximum coronary blood flow and in heart and skeletal muscle efficiency, contractility, and elasticity, or any combination of these. In addition, the governor may be activated at different levels of impending oxygen lack in different people.

The prediction is that the very best athletes will be those with the highest maximum rates of coronary blood flow, perhaps because they have larger coronary blood vessels with a greater capacity to dilate during exercise (Haskell et al. 1993), and the most economical hearts and muscles with the greatest contractility and elasticity. The governors in their brains may also allow their hearts to continue contracting to lower oxygen concentrations in their hearts.

You may be asking what the practical value of the new Central Governor/Integrated Neuromuscular Recruitment Model is to athletes and their coaches? My personal bias (Noakes 1988b; 1997; 1998b; 2000c) is to believe that the maximum rate of oxygen transport to and use by the muscles ($\dot{V}O_2$max) is not the critical factor determining exercise performance. I suggest that the $\dot{V}O_2$max is the result of two distinct physiological processes.

1. The maximum pumping capacity of the heart. This determines the peak rates at which blood and oxygen can be transported to the exercising muscles at the point at which the heart is itself about to become ischemic, or anaerobic,

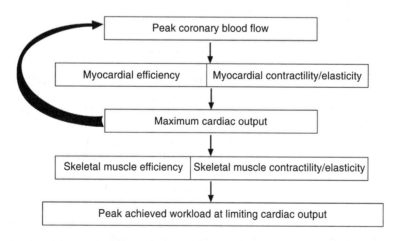

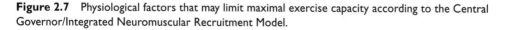

Figure 2.7 Physiological factors that may limit maximal exercise capacity according to the Central Governor/Integrated Neuromuscular Recruitment Model.

and at which the governor is activated, causing skeletal muscle recruitment to plateau and exercise either to terminate or to decline in intensity. This, in turn, is determined by the peak rate of (coronary) blood flow to the heart; the contractile ability of the heart, which very likely varies between people; and the efficiency of the heart.

Thus, hearts with greater contractility and greater efficiency produce a greater blood flow (cardiac output) to the muscles at that limiting coronary flow. Interestingly, trained athletes have more efficient hearts than do untrained athletes (Heiss et al. 1976) and require less blood flow and oxygen to produce more work.

This process, however, is tightly regulated in the Central Governor Model to prevent the absolute maximum coronary blood flow from ever being reached, at least in health. Were this to happen, the athlete's life would be endangered.

2. The athlete's exercising muscles. The best athletes would be those whose muscles have superior contractility, either on the basis of superior myosin ATPase activity or enhanced capacity to bind calcium (see chapter 1), superior efficiency, superior elasticity, and superior fatigue resistance (see figure 2.7). This enables them to achieve higher work rates that they can sustain for longer, before the maximum (safe) pumping capacity of their hearts is reached. The result is that their $\dot{V}O_2max$ values tend to be high, leading to the erroneous conclusions that $\dot{V}O_2max$ is the sole and exclusive predictor of athletic potential and that oxygen availability to the exercising skeletal muscles (rather than the heart, as I argue) must therefore be the most important factor limiting exercise performance.

Rather, superior and more efficient heart function and superior skeletal muscle contractility and efficiency all combine to produce high $\dot{V}O_2max$ values. Thus, the $\dot{V}O_2max$ is the rather simple laboratory measure of a number of complex processes, only one of which (oxygen supply to the heart) is exclusively an oxygen-dependent function.

To make this point more clear, it could be said that athletes' heart and muscle strength and fatigue resistance enable them to run at high speeds; once the high speeds are reached, athletes need a high rate of oxygen consumption (that is, a high $\dot{V}O_2max$). But the high rate of oxygen consumption does not create the ability to run fast—rather, the high $\dot{V}O_2max$ is the complex result of heart and muscle factors that determine the ability to run fast (and therefore the capacity to use oxygen at high rates). Ultimately, the oxygen supply to the heart may indeed set the (safe) limit for the $\dot{V}O_2max$. But the actual $\dot{V}O_2max$ that the athlete achieves does not simply reflect the ability of the heart to pump oxygen to the muscles, or the muscles' capacity to consume oxygen and thus prevent the development of anaerobiosis. Nor does it mean that the higher the value, the better the athlete. High values could be achieved, for example, by athletes with inefficient hearts and muscles that consume large volumes of oxygen but have poor contractile function and inferior fatigue resistance.

Conversely, relatively low $\dot{V}O_2max$ values might be achieved by elite athletes who have hearts and muscles that have superior contractility, efficiency, and fatigue resistance and that are able to produce high rates of work at low oxygen cost for prolonged periods without becoming exhausted. The value of this adaptation is that these more efficient athletes produce less heat when they run fast; hence, they accumulate less heat when running fast during prolonged exercise. This has relevance to the Biomechanical Model discussed later in this chapter.

In support of this interpretation, we (Noakes, Myburgh, et al. 1990a; Scrimgeour et al. 1986) and others (L.N. Cunningham 1990; Krahenbuhl and Pangrazi 1983; D.W. Morgan, Baldini, et al. 1989; B.K. Scott and Houmard 1994; Berthon, Fellmann, et al. 1997; S. Grant et al. 1997; Yoshida et al. 1993; Lacour et al. 1990; 1991; Padilla et al. 1992; A.M. Jones and Doust 1998) have found that it is the maximum achieved work rate rather than the $\dot{V}O_2$max that is the best predictor of running potential. This confirms that it is indeed a combination of heart and skeletal muscle factors, other than those regulating oxygen use by the active muscles alone, that determine athletic potential (Noakes 1988b; 1997; 1998b).

Thus, even if the pumping capacity of the heart limits exercise of high intensity lasting a few minutes, the best athletes must still be those whose exercising skeletal muscles are able to produce the greatest amount of work and have the greatest fatigue resistance when their hearts are approaching that maximum capacity. This helps explain the finding that the fastest athletes in endurance events of 5 km or longer tend also to be faster over the short distances from 100 m to 1500 m. Indeed, Lydiard and Gilmour (1978) and Gordon Pirie (1961) observed that the distance runners who are fastest over the shortest distances are also the fastest at all longer distances, including the ultramarathons. This issue is discussed further in chapter 6. Finally, and most interestingly, this model predicts that the best way to train is not at altitude, breathing oxygen-depleted air (hypoxia), but rather below sea level, breathing oxygen-enriched air (hyperoxia). The logic for this blasphemy is described in chapter 13.

Muscle Power Model

The original Cardiovascular/Anaerobic Model ignored the possibility that muscles may differ in their ability to produce force (that is, in their contractility) and that this might contribute to differences in athletic ability. Yet, it is well known that Type II (FT) fibers, more common in sprinters than in distance runners, have greater contractility than do Type I fibers, which are more common in distance runners. Thus, it seems a reasonable assumption that muscle contractility differs between sprinters and distance runners and that this difference could explain their different running abilities. Furthermore, it seems probable that muscle contractility may differ within humans and between athletes and that this could contribute to differences in performance, both at short and long running distances.

Accordingly, the Muscle Power Model holds that muscle contractile capacity (that is, that ability of individual muscle cross-bridges to generate force) is not the same in the muscles of all humans. Those with superior athletic ability have muscles with a superior capacity to generate force (superior contractility) by the individual cross-bridges of the different muscle fibers. This model is readily accepted by cardiac physiologists who believe that the contractile state of the heart is determined, in health, by the sum of the inherent contractilities of each individual cardiac muscle cross-bridge, which is essentially independent of the oxygen or fuel supply to each cross-bridge.

I could only find one recent statement in which this model is used to explain superior athletic performance, specifically in swimming:

The strength of the muscles used in swimming is a major determinant of success in events from 50 to 1500 m. Though this may not seem surprising, it must be remembered that strength per se does not indicate fast swimming. The forces generated by the muscle must be effectively applied to the water if they are to propel the body. Thus, strength specifically is the key to swimming success. (Costill, Maglischo, et al. 1992)

There are rather few studies of the contractility of single muscle fibers taken from the skeletal muscles of athletes and studied in vitro in the laboratory. These studies generally show that endurance training reduces skeletal muscle contractility (Fitts, Costill, et al. 1989; Widrick et al. 1996a; 1996b). This establishes that skeletal muscle contractility is not an immutable characteristic of the different muscle fiber types (Fitts and Widrick 1996). By extension, we might speculate that the contractility of the specific muscle fiber types might differ between athletes of different abilities in different sporting disciplines. This theory forms the basis of the Muscle Power Model.

In summary, the Muscle Power Model predicts that changes in exercise performance may result from increased muscle contractile function caused by biochemical adaptations in muscle that increase force production or the rate of sarcomere shortening, or both, independent of changes in neural recruitment by the brain. But, according to the Central Governor Model, the increase in performance resulting from these adaptations would only occur if the cardiovascular limits for exercise performance were not exceeded.

Athletic Mammals

Cheetahs, thoroughbred racehorses, and the pronghorn antelope are the mammals best known for their athletic abilities. Cheetahs are essentially lightweight sprinters (approximately 50 kg) that are able to run at up to 100 km per hour for short bursts of a few hundred meters. If a cheetah does not capture its prey within 20 to 30 seconds, it will terminate the hunt, probably from a rapid rise in its body temperature to values of 42°C or higher (C.R. Taylor and Rowntree 1973). Indeed, this physiological characteristic is used as a harmless way to catch cheetahs in the wild. A car follows the cheetah, which becomes overheated after running for about 2 km. When in this state, the cheetah is as tame as a domestic cat and can be easily restrained.

The physiological basis for the cheetahs' speed is unknown but is probably related to their muscle fiber composition, as yet unstudied, and the efficiency of movement resulting from their long elastic limbs and flexible spine.

The 30-kg pronghorn antelope, which inhabits the North American prairie, has a top running speed only marginally slower than that of the cheetah. Yet, unlike the cheetah, the pronghorn is an endurance sprinter able to run 10 km in less than 10 minutes, averaging 65 km per hour (Lindstedt et al. 1991). When measured in the laboratory, the $\dot{V}O_2max$ of two pronghorn antelopes was an astonishing 300 ml O_2 per kg per min, or about three times higher than the normal $\dot{V}O_2max$ value (90 ml O_2 per kg per min) of a 30-kg dog. To achieve their $\dot{V}O_2max$, the antelopes "jogged" at 36 km per hour on a treadmill set at an 11% incline for 5 minutes. This equals the peak speed achieved by top human sprinters such as Carl Lewis or Michael Johnson during a 100- to 200-m race that lasts

10 to 20 seconds and is run on the flat. The superior endurance and speed of the pronghorn antelope is particularly remarkable given that there is no predator in North America capable of matching this athletic ability. Why then did the pronghorn antelope develop such athleticism?

The exercise capacity of thoroughbred racehorses has been studied extensively. Like the pronghorn antelope, thoroughbreds have very high $\dot{V}O_2$max values (150 to 200 ml O_2 per kg per min; Potard et al. 1998), which is especially remarkable given the very large size (approximately 550 kg) of the thoroughbred. There is an inverse relationship between $\dot{V}O_2$max and body mass so that such high $\dot{V}O_2$max values are usually measured only in mammals weighing 100 g to 1 kg.

The Cardiovascular/Anaerobic Model ascribes this superior athletic ability of the thoroughbred to a large heart, which is able to pump ample volumes of blood and oxygen to the exercising muscles. But a novel study (Potard et al. 1998) compared exercise capacity and muscle power in thoroughbred and Percheron horses (draft horses, which are powerful but slow). This study found that when pulling the same weights, thoroughbred horses ran about twice as fast as the draft horses. As a result, the thoroughbreds achieved $\dot{V}O_2$max values and peak running speeds that were twice those of the draft horses. More important, and contrary to the usual assumption, thoroughbreds were twice as powerful as the draft horses. Furthermore, peak power was achieved at much lower speeds in the draft horses.

Potard et al. (1998) therefore concluded unequivocally that the difference between thoroughbreds and Percherons lay primarily in their muscles, which have quite different contractile characteristics. This means that thoroughbred skeletal muscle has been selectively bred for high-intensity exercise in high-speed tasks with low external forces whereas Percheron muscle has been bred for low-intensity exercise in low-speed tasks with high external forces.

The insight gleaned from this study of horses showed that the Muscle Power Model best explains the greater exercise capacity and cardiorespiratory function of the horse, the domesticated mammal with the highest $\dot{V}O_2$max value, higher than those of elite athletes (see table 2.1). This thinking is in line with that predicted by the Central Governor Model. Elite endurance athletes must also have muscles with superior contractility that allow them to run very fast at the limiting output of the heart.

Using $\dot{V}O_2$max Correctly

Although the $\dot{V}O_2$max concept is misleading because it erroneously suggests that oxygen uptake by the active muscles is the sole factor determining maximum work rate achieved during exercise testing in the laboratory, it nevertheless remains a popular talking point among runners. As one of my students recently challenged me, "The $\dot{V}O_2$max concept is so simple, appealing, and easy to understand. Why do you have to complicate it?"

In light of the preceding discussion, it is important to use the term only when it is understood as being an indirect equivalent of the maximum achieved work rate during physiological testing and as being determined by the complex interaction of heart, brain, and skeletal muscle factors. $\dot{V}O_2$max provides an indirect measure

Table 2.1 Maximum oxygen consumption ($\dot{V}O_2$ max) values in elite endurance athletes

Athlete	$\dot{V}O_2$ max value (ml·kg⁻¹·min⁻¹)	Major performance	Reference
John Ngugi	85.0	5 times World X-C Champ	Saltin, Larsen, et al. (1995)
Dave Bedford	85.0	10 km WR 1973	Bergh (1982)
Steven Prefontaine	84.4	1 mile 03:54.6	Pollock (1977)
Henry Rono	84.3	10 km WR 1978	Saltin, Larsen, et al. (1995)
Said Aouita	83.0	5 km WR 1987	Zur & Hymans (1991)
Gary Tuttle	82.7	02:17:00 marathon	Pollock (1977)
Kip Keino	82.0	2 km WR 1965	Saltin & Astrand (1967)
Don Lash	81.5	2 mile WR 1937	Robinson et al. (1937)
Craig Virgin	81.1	02:10:26 marathon	Cureton et al. (1975)
Jim Ryun	81.0	1 mile WR 1967	Daniels (1974)
Steve Scott	80.1	1 mile 03:47.69	Conley et al. (1984)
Joan Benoit	78.6	02:24:52 marathon	Daniels & Daniels (1992)
Bill Rodgers	78.5	02:09:27 marathon	Rodgers & Concannon (1982)
Matthews Temane	78.0	21 km WR 1987	Coetzer et al. (1993)
Don Kardong	77.4	02:11:15 marathon	Pollock (1977)
Tom O'Reilly	77.0	927 km in 6-day race	Davies & Thompson (1979)
Sebastian Coe	77.0	1 mile WR 1981	Zur & Hymans (1991)
John Landy	76.6	1 mile WR 1954	Astrand (1955)
Alberto Salazar	76.0	02:08:13 marathon WR 1981†	Costill (1982)
Johnny Halberstadt	74.4*	02:11:44 marathon	Wyndham et al. (1969)
Amby Burfoot	74.3	02:14:28 marathon	Costill & Winrow (1970b)
Cavin Woodward	74.2	48 to 160 km WR 1975	Davies & Thompson (1979)
Kenny Moore	74.2	02:11:36 marathon	Pollock (1977)
Bruce Fordyce	73.3*	80 km WR 1983	Jooste et al. (1980)
Grete Waitz	73.0	02:25:42 marathon WR 1980	Costill & Higdon (1981)
Buddy Edelen	73.0	02:14:28 marathon WR 1963	Dill et al. (1967)
Peter Snell	72.3	1 mile WR 1964	Carter et al. (1967)
Zithulele Sinqe	72.0	02:08:05 marathon	Coetzer et al. (1993)
Frank Shorter	71.3	02:10:30 marathon	Pollock (1977)
Willie Mtolo	70.3	02:08:15 marathon	Coetzer et al. (1993)
Derek Clayton	69.7	02:08:34 marathon WR 1969	Costill et al. (1971)

NOTE: WR = world record; X-C = cross country
* Predicted sea level values from measurements recorded at medium altitude by adding 11 percent.
† Subsequently not ratified (short course).

of that work rate and allows us to compare athletes in different sports in which the maximum work rate may be difficult to measure or to compare. (It is, of course, not always easy to determine the $\dot{V}O_2max$ for athletes in all sports since the activity needs to be recreated in a laboratory to measure it accurately. For example, though it may be relatively simple to measure the rate of work performed on a bicycle, it is far more difficult to do this in activities such as rowing or swimming.)

Use the term $\dot{V}O_2max$ when it is understood that the value is the athlete's maximum rate of work, rather than his or her maximum oxygen consumption, that predicts athletic performance. This maximum work rate is the result of a complex interaction of heart and skeletal muscle factors that combine to establish the measured maximum rate of oxygen use by the muscles at that peak work rate ($\dot{V}O_2max$). But the measured peak rate of oxygen consumption is the result, not the cause, of the peak work rate that is achieved. Unfortunately, exercise physiologists have only recently begun to appreciate this complexity. Originally, in line with the Cardiovascular/Anaerobic Model, they assumed that the skeletal muscles stopped working when they became anaerobic at the $\dot{V}O_2max$. Thus, they naturally assumed that the best athletes would simply be those with the highest $\dot{V}O_2max$ values, who were able to deliver more oxygen to their exercising muscles, thereby delaying the onset of the anaerobic metabolism that would ultimately cause exhaustion.

Thus, the emphasis in research of human performance has focused on the measurement of $\dot{V}O_2max$ in elite athletes and the effects of various interventions, including training, on the $\dot{V}O_2max$. Inasmuch as higher $\dot{V}O_2max$ values generally reflect the capacity to reach higher maximum work rates, the work adds to our understanding of human exercise physiology.

FACTORS THAT AFFECT $\dot{V}O_2MAX$

Keep in mind the intellectual constraints imposed by the simplistic view that oxygen deficiency in the skeletal muscles limits exercise performance and that it is exclusively the capacity to offset that limitation that is measured by the $\dot{V}O_2max$. Rather, the $\dot{V}O_2max$ encompasses the complex interaction of heart and skeletal muscle factors and is not itself synonymous with athletic potential. With this proviso, it is safe to read the following review of the factors that influence athletic potential (by altering one or more of the complex factors of heart and muscle that determine exercise performance and hence, indirectly, the measured $\dot{V}O_2max$).

Age

It is acknowledged that in healthy but inactive people, there is a gradual decline in $\dot{V}O_2max$, equivalent to about a 9% decrease per decade, after the age of 25 years. There is some evidence, not supported by all studies (M.J. Rosen et al. 1998), that vigorous exercise maintained for life may reduce the age-related rate of fall in $\dot{V}O_2max$, which has been estimated to be only 5% per decade in lifelong athletes (G.W. Heath, Hagberg, et al. 1981; Pollock, Foster, et al. 1987).

Alternatively, according to the theory that heart and skeletal muscle contractility and efficiency also contribute to the $\dot{V}O_2max$ and the maximum achieved work rate, the decrease in $\dot{V}O_2max$ and maximum work rate with age may reflect a progressive decrease in contractility, efficiency, and fatigue resistance of the heart and skeletal muscles with age. It may also reflect a loss of muscle mass with age

(Fleg and Lakatha 1988; M.J. Rosen et al. 1998) or perhaps even a progressive fall in the capacity to deliver oxygen to the myocardium, resulting from changes in or even disease of the coronary blood vessels.

Gender

Women have lower $\dot{V}O_2$max values than men. This is due in part to their higher body fat content, their smaller muscle mass, and, probably most important, to their "less powerful" muscles (see chapter 12). It seems likely that peak coronary flow rates and peak cardiac outputs would be lower in women than in men, but not all of these possibilities have been studied.

Fitness and Training

Healthy people who embark on running programs similar to those outlined in chapter 9 can expect an increase in $\dot{V}O_2$max of only about 5% to 15% (J.T. Daniels, Yarbough, et al. 1978). This indicates that $\dot{V}O_2$max is, per se, a poor measure of fitness. (This is because, with training, an athlete's running speed or endurance, especially, increases by a much greater percentage [see chapter 13]. Furthermore, the differences in running ability between groups of either trained or untrained people are greater than 15%.) This suggests that if there are major differences (that is, greater than 15%) in $\dot{V}O_2$max between people, then that is probably a result of hereditary factors rather than of training. Age does not influence the degree to which $\dot{V}O_2$max increases with training; this increase is the same in the young and the old (Hagberg, Graves, et al. 1989; Meredith, Frontera, et al. 1989).

It is also apparent, however, that the 5% to 15% increase in $\dot{V}O_2$max with training is the average result and that the extent to which any person adapts his or her $\dot{V}O_2$max with training may differ from as little as 0% to as much as 60%, the latter being more likely in elite athletes.

Interestingly, it has been found that there is a likely genetic basis for these high and low responders to both endurance and weight training (Thomis et al. 1998). Moreover, the low responders (Prud'homme et al. 1984; Lortie et al. 1984) may show none of the adaptations to training that have been described. They simply do not and cannot improve with training, regardless of their efforts.

Attempts to identify genetic markers for superior athletic performance (Rivera et al. 1997a; 1997b; Rivera, Wolfarth, et al. 1998; Rivera, Pérusse, et al. 1999; Bilé et al. 1998; Manning and Pickup 1998; A.G. Williams et al. 2000; R.R. Taylor et al. 1999; Alvarez et al. 2000; Hagberg, Ferrell, et al. 1998; Wolfarth et al. 2000; Bouchard, Wolfarth, et al. 2000) and for high and low adapters to training (Bouchard, Chagnon, et al. 1989; Bouchard, An, et al. 1999; Bouchard, Rankinen et al. 2000; Dionne et al. 1991) are currently in progress.

Changes in Altitude

Changes in altitude have the most marked effect on $\dot{V}O_2$max. With an increase in altitude, the barometric pressure and the oxygen content of the air decreases. This fall in the oxygen content of the air causes a predictable fall in $\dot{V}O_2$max equivalent to about 10% for every 1000 m above 1200 m (Squires and Buskirk 1982). On the summit of Mount Everest (8848 m), the $\dot{V}O_2$max of the average mountaineer is only 15 ml

O_2 per kg per min, or about 27% of the sea level value, and barely greater than the lowest oxygen consumption required to sustain life, 7 ml O_2 per kg (West, Boyer, et al. 1983). This explains why, even when breathing supplemental oxygen, mountaineers struggle to climb near the summit of Everest and progress at a rate of approximately 50 m per hour near the summit. But the reasons why climbers complain of weakness in their muscles and an inability to climb rapidly at extreme altitude are not, as discussed subsequently, those that might seem the most obvious.

The $\dot{V}O_2$max of Reinhold Messner, arguably the most remarkable high-altitude climber of all time, is only 48.8 ml O_2 per kg per min (Oelz et al. 1986), essentially the same as that of Sir Edmund Hilary, who in 1953 became the first person to reach the summit of Mount Everest (Pugh 1958). These values are little better than those found in untrained but healthy young men. Thus, $\dot{V}O_2$max is certainly not a very good predictor of high-altitude mountain-climbing ability.

In fact, the key to successful climbing at altitude is an ability to sustain a higher than expected oxygen tension in the arterial blood supplying both the heart and the brain (and it has nothing to do with the capacity of the exercising muscles to use oxygen). The ability to sustain higher arterial oxygen tension is most likely due to a superior capacity to transport oxygen across the lung membranes into the blood, as well as a greater drive to increase the rate and depth of breathing at that altitude.

Indeed, exercise at altitude provides the single best test of the Central Governor Model (Noakes 1998b; 2000c; Noakes, Peltonen, et al. 2001). The three crucial findings are the following:

1. Blood lactate concentrations fall progressively at peak exercise with increasing altitude (E.H. Christensen and Forbes 1937; Green, Sutton, et al. 1989a; 1989b).

2. Heart rate and heart (cardiac) output—the amount of blood pumped by the heart, most of which goes to the muscles during exercise—decreases at increasing altitude (Noakes 1998b).

3. Most crucial of all, recruitment of skeletal muscle also falls during exercise at altitude (Kayser, Narici, et al. 1994). Hence, neither the heart nor the skeletal muscles become anaerobic during exercise at extreme altitude, when the oxygen content of the inspired air is so low that it is barely able to sustain human life. But according to the Cardiovascular/Anaerobic Model, the skeletal muscle and heart must surely become anaerobic under these conditions, and the heart must increase its output to maximize oxygen delivery to the muscles since, in this model, the heart is merely the slave to the exercising muscles, acting always to maximize their oxygen delivery.

What is more likely is that in response to the reduced oxygen supply to the heart (or perhaps the brain) during exercise at altitude, the protective reflex proposed in figure 2.6 prevents the brain from recruiting the leg muscles to the extent that is possible at sea level (Kayser, Narici, et al. 1994). As Kayser and colleagues have concluded, "during chronic hypobaric hypoxia (reduced oxygen content in the air), the central nervous system may play a primary role in limiting exhaustive exercise and maximum accumulation of lactate in the blood" (p. 634). If the muscles were able to work normally, as at sea level, the oxygen content of the blood supplying the heart (and brain) would drop so low that the normal functioning of the heart and brain would be impossible, inducing unconsciousness. Without this control, mountaineers would risk death from heart and brain hypoxia whenever they ascended above 5000 m. Indeed, we can safely predict that if the human body had been designed by exercise physiologists according to the Cardiovascular/Anaerobic Model, no human would have survived a climb above base camp on Mount Everest, much less have reached the summit.

Fortunately, modern exercise physiologists were not consulted when the human was designed. This begs answers to two important questions. First, why was the human built with just enough capacity to enable only a handful of people with the very best design to reach the summit of Mount Everest without breathing supplemental oxygen? Indeed, it has been argued that if the summit of Mount Everest were 20 to 50 m higher, no human would have reached it without supplemental oxygen and returned to tell the tale. Does the Creator have a sense of the dramatic?

Second, why was this method of control (reduced muscle recruitment by the brain when the oxygen content of certain organs falls) built into the human in the first place? Did the Creator foresee that humans would one day wish to summit Mount Everest, a geographical feature that only developed during the evolution of the Earth? Or is it simply that this mechanism of control is not uniquely active only at extreme altitude but also terminates exercise performed at sea level? It is a question that proponents of the Cardiovascular/Anaerobic Model would do well to ponder.

Ventilatory Muscle Action

During maximum exercise, the rate of ventilation increases substantially and may reach values as high as 150 liters per minute. But during maximum exercise at extreme altitude, even values as high as 180 liters per minute have been measured (J.R. Sutton, Reeves, et al. 1988). This possibly indicates that humans have ventilatory reserves when exercising maximally at sea level.

Other evidence that ventilatory failure does not directly limit the $\dot{V}O_2max$ is the finding that the arterial oxygen partial pressure (PaO_2) does not usually fall during maximum exercise. This indicates that the lungs are functioning appropriately since their main function, besides excreting carbon dioxide, is the maintenance of the PaO_2.

Nevertheless, some elite athletes allow their PaO_2 to fall during both submaximal and maximal exercise (Dempsey et al. 1984), probably because they choose to breathe less rapidly during exercise than is necessary to maintain the arterial PaO_2.

Underbreathing during exercise will have two effects:

1. It saves energy since there is a substantial oxygen cost associated with very high rates of ventilation, so much so that as much as 10% of the oxygen consumption at $\dot{V}O_2max$ may be used to support the respiratory muscles.

2. The fall in PaO_2 could theoretically be sensed by the central governor and may be one of the signals leading to the termination of exercise before damage to the heart can occur.

These two responses are in opposition, and whichever is greater will determine the effect of underbreathing on performance during maximum exercise.

There is also strong evidence that the diaphragm and other respiratory muscles may become exhausted during both short-duration, high-intensity exercise (Bye et al. 1984) and more prolonged exercise such as standard marathon running (Loke et al. 1982). While the implications of the finding are not yet clear, it may indicate that training of the ventilatory muscles by methods other than running may be necessary. Such training has been achieved experimentally by having athletes repeatedly exhale against resistance. Also, a commercial product that purportedly improves athletic performance by improving the strength and endurance of the respiratory muscle has been widely marketed in Great Britain. The scientific evidence to support these alleged claims is less than convincing, however, and more studies are required. For example, Israeli scientists (Inbar et al. 2000) found that the strength and endurance of the ventilatory muscles can indeed be increased by a dedicated 10-week training program; however, this training did not either alter the $\dot{V}O_2$max or prevent any fall in arterial oxygenation during maximal exercise.

$\dot{V}O_2$MAX VALUES OF ELITE ATHLETES

Given the linear relationship between oxygen consumption and running speed (see figure 2.3), it is logical to conclude that elite athletes who have the ability to maintain the fastest running speeds for prolonged periods of time must have a much greater capacity for maximum oxygen consumption than do ordinary mortals. This is indeed so, and table 2.1 shows the range of $\dot{V}O_2$max values recorded in some elite athletes.

The highest reported $\dot{V}O_2$max value in male runners is that of Dave Bedford and John Ngugi (85 ml O_2 per kg per min) and in a female runner, that of Joan Benoit (79 ml O_2 per kg per min), winner of the inaugural 1984 Women's Olympic Marathon in Los Angeles (J. Daniels and Daniels 1992). The highest value ever recorded in any athlete is a value of 93 ml O_2 per kg per min, that of a Scandinavian cross-country skier (Bergh 1982). In contrast, $\dot{V}O_2$max values measured in otherwise healthy young men are much lower, usually between 45 and 55 ml O_2 per kg per min (Kruss et al. 1989; Wyndham et al. 1966), about 60% lower than in elite athletes. As we have already concluded that $\dot{V}O_2$max can be improved, on average, by only 5% to 15%, even with intensive training, it is clear that the average healthy person can train as much as he or she likes yet will never achieve a $\dot{V}O_2$max value anywhere near that of the elite athletes. Therefore, inasmuch as $\dot{V}O_2$max is a (indirect) measure of potential for success in endurance activities, it is clear that hereditary factors (Fagard et al. 1991) must play an important role in determining champions.

$\dot{V}O_2$max values may vary quite dramatically, even among elite athletes with similar performances. For example, consider the cases of Steve Prefontaine and Frank Shorter, two athletes whose $\dot{V}O_2$max values differed by 16%, yet whose best 1-mile (1.6-km) times differed by less than 8 seconds (3.4%) and whose best 3-mile (4.8-km) times differed by even less (0.2 seconds). If differences in running performance can be ascribed solely to $\dot{V}O_2$max, then Prefontaine should have been better by at least 16% at all distances. Similarly, why was Mark Plaatjes's marathon time not considerably faster than that of Zithulele Sinqe or Derek Clayton, who held the world marathon record despite a relatively poor $\dot{V}O_2$max value of 69.7 ml O_2 per kg per min?

Looking at it another way, why do some athletes with quite similar $\dot{V}O_2$max values have quite different running performances? For this we need to look no further than the examples provided by the Americans Alberto Salazar and Joan Benoit, the Norwegian Grete Waitz, and the Briton Cavin Woodward, whose best marathon times differed greatly, despite similar $\dot{V}O_2$max values (table 2.2).

Table 2.2 An example of four athletes with similar $\dot{V}O_2$max values but with substaintially different standard marathon times		
Athlete (country)	$\dot{V}O_2$max value (ml·kg^{-1}·min^{-1})	42-km marathon time (h:min:s)
Joan Benoit (USA)	78.6	02:24:52
Alberto Salazar (USA)	76.0	02:08:13
Cavin Woodward (UK)	74.2	02:19:50
Grete Waitz (Norway)	73.0	02:25:29

$\dot{V}O_2$MAX AND RUNNING ECONOMY

The idea that the $\dot{V}O_2$max test can predict how well any runner will ever perform on the road has been propagated in many scientific and lay publications (for example, Bassett and Howley 1997; 2000; Costill 1967; Martsui et al. 1972; Costill, Thomason, et al. 1973; C. Foster, Costill, et al. 1978; Miyashita et al. 1978; C.T.M. Davies and Thompson 1979; Wyndham et al. 1969; C. Foster 1983). One of the most striking features of all these studies is the fact that they have looked at groups of athletes of quite different abilities, including the very good and the very bad. Not surprisingly, such an approach delivers predictable results—slow athletes have low $\dot{V}O_2$max values and fast runners much higher $\dot{V}O_2$max values.

However, when groups of athletes with similar running performances are studied (see table 2.1), then the $\dot{V}O_2$max becomes a far less sensitive predictor of performance (Costill and Winrow 1970a; 1970b; Pollock 1977; Conley and Krahenbuhl 1980; Noakes, Myburgh, et al. 1990a; Coetzer et al. 1993; B.K. Scott and Houmard 1994; D. Abe et al. 1998).

How, then, are we to explain these anomalies? David Dill and his colleagues (Dill, Edwards, et al. 1930), David Costill (Costill and Winrow 1970a; Costill 1979), and Jack Daniels (1974) were probably the first scientists to suggest that there may be differences in the amount of oxygen athletes actually require when running at the same speeds and that these differences in running economy could be a major factor explaining differences in running performance in athletes with similar $\dot{V}O_2$max values (Noakes 1988b). In more simple terms, we could compare this to two different cars, one of which uses less fuel than the other when traveling at the same speed and is therefore said to be more economical.

To avoid confusing the concept of running economy with that of the $\dot{V}O_2$max, it is important to point out that running economy relates to the amount of oxygen used by the athlete when running at a constant (submaximal) running speed, whereas $\dot{V}O_2$max refers to the rate of oxygen use by the athlete when running at the maximum speed that that particular athlete can sustain for between 5 and 8 minutes. Therefore, to determine the relative running economies of different athletes, they should be tested at the same speed. Analogously, it would be pointless to test the economy of one car at 80 km per hour and that of another at 100 km per hour. For example, Costill and Winrow (1970a) reported that the oxygen consumption of

McDonagh and Corbitt, two veteran ultramarathoners with similar $\dot{V}O_2$max values but with different running performances, differed substantially when tested at four submaximal running speeds (below 100% $\dot{V}O_2$max) between 10.8 and 16 km per hour. McDonagh required less oxygen to run at each running speed and was therefore labeled more economical than Corbitt. Interestingly, the relative difference in their economies was about 11%, which is about twice the difference (5%) in their best marathon times at the time they were studied. Others (Dill, Edwards, et al. 1930; Sjodin and Shele 1982; Daniels et al. 1985; Sjodin and Svedenhag 1985) have also reported that, even in trained athletes, running economy can differ by as much as 30%.

The best athletes are usually the most economical (Noakes 1988b). This finding has been clearly shown by Conley and Krahenbuhl (1980), who studied a group of 12 runners whose best 10-km times were closely bunched between 30:31 and 33:33. They found that the runners' $\dot{V}O_2$max values, which ranged from 67 to 78 ml O_2 per kg per min, could not be used to predict their 10-km times. For example, the second-fastest runner had the second-lowest $\dot{V}O_2$max value. There was a correlation between the amount of oxygen that each runner used at each of three submaximal running speeds (14.5, 16.1, and 17.7 km per hour) and that runner's best time for the 10-km race. Thus, the runners who used the least oxygen at each of these running speeds, and were therefore the most economical, had the fastest 10-km times.

The authors concluded that a high $\dot{V}O_2$max (anything above 67 ml O_2 per kg) helped each athlete gain membership of this elite performance group. Within this select group, however, running economy, and not $\dot{V}O_2$max, was the factor controlling success in the 10-km race.

I interpret these data differently. To join the elite group of runners, the athlete needs a superior and efficient heart, which is able to achieve a high cardiac output at the maximum coronary blood flow, and also muscles with superior efficiency, contractility, elasticity, and fatigue resistance. A combination of superior heart and skeletal muscle function then allows the athlete to achieve a high work rate during the maximum test to exhaustion. The high work rate demands a high rate of oxygen consumption that is interpreted as a high $\dot{V}O_2$max. But the exact $\dot{V}O_2$max value that each athlete achieves (whether in the laboratory or during racing) will be determined by his or her running economy (Noakes 1988b), and it is independent of the exact peak work rate that is achieved. At the same maximal work rate, uneconomical runners will have higher $\dot{V}O_2$max values, and economical runners will have much lower values. But the real predictor of performance is the maximal work rate (running speed) that is achieved, not the $\dot{V}O_2$max measured at that work rate. Just as the authors failed to relate 10-km performance to the peak achieved work rate, they may also have failed to identify the real explanation for the different performances of the athletes in their study.

So, runners whose performances do not seem to match their very high $\dot{V}O_2$max values (Tuttle and Virgin in table 2.1) are probably less economical runners who require more oxygen than average to run at any speed. Similarly, the relatively low $\dot{V}O_2$max values of outstanding long-distance runners such as Salazar, Clayton, Shorter, Sinqe, and Ngugi indicate that they are extremely economical runners.

Some evidence for this hypothesis is provided by the data in figure 2.8, which compares the running efficiencies of Derek Clayton (Costill, Branam, et al. 1971), Jim Ryun (J.T. Daniels 1974), Frank Shorter (Pollock 1977), Zithulele Sinqe (Coetzer et al. 1993), Craig Virgin (Cureton, Boileau, et al. 1975), John Ngugi, and Julius Korir (Saltin et al. 1995) with those of a group of children studied by C.T.M. Davies (1980c).

It is clear that Clayton, Shorter, Ngugi, and Korir are the most economical of the runners studied; that Jim Ryun's economy is slightly better than that of the Scandinavian runners; and that Craig Virgin is the least economical of these runners. The difference in economy between Clayton and Virgin ranges between 15% and 20%, despite the fact that both these athletes were equally trained. This suggests that although training may improve running economy, there are inherent differences in running economy between athletes and that these differences cannot be completely removed by training (J.T. Daniels et al. 1985). The nature of these differences is at present unclear but may relate to differences in energy return from elastic recoil of muscle. It is particularly interesting to note that the two of the most efficient runners yet studied are Kenyans.

Figure 2.8 also shows that children are even less economical than Virgin, and that at a running speed of 16 km per hour, the difference in economy between Clayton and the children is 33%. Changes in body mass or in muscular elasticity or muscle recruitment with age may explain why children become more economical with age.

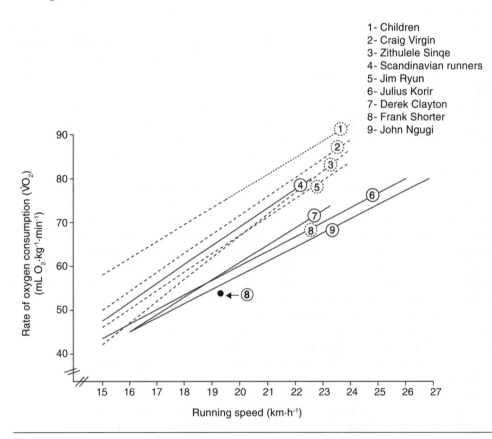

Figure 2.8 Running efficiencies of Derek Clayton, Jim Ryun, Frank Shorter, Zithulele Sinqe, Craig Virgin, John Ngugi, and Julius Korir, and Scandinavian runners compared with those of a group of children.

Why $\dot{V}O_2$max Doesn't Necessarily Predict Performance

The first reason $\dot{V}O_2$max is a relatively poor predictor of performance is because athletes differ in their rate of oxygen consumption at any submaximal running speed (running economy) and in the peak running speed they reach during the maximal treadmill test. Figure 2.9 uses this information to explain possible differences in running performance in athletes with similar $\dot{V}O_2$max values or, conversely, similar running performances in athletes with dissimilar $\dot{V}O_2$max values. The figure compares the $\dot{V}O_2$ at submaximal running speeds (running economy) and the maximal running velocity and $\dot{V}O_2$max in three idealized runners, A, B, and C. The first difference between the three runners is their $\dot{V}O_2$ values at any submaximal running speed. Hence, runner C is shown to be the most economical as his $\dot{V}O_2$ value at 18 km per hour is about 55 whereas the less economical runners B and A have corresponding $\dot{V}O_2$ values of 60 and 65 respectively at that running speed.

When runners A and B reach their peak treadmill running speed at about 20 km per hour, the least economical runner (A) has a higher $\dot{V}O_2$max value (approximately 71) than runner B (approximately 68). Yet, the most economical runner, runner C, reaches a higher peak treadmill speed (approximately 22.5 km per hour) than both runners A and B. However, C's $\dot{V}O_2$max (approximately 68) is only equal to that of B and is lower than that of A.

So, which of these runners is likely to be the fastest in races of 3 to 21 km? The answer is that the peak treadmill running velocity achieved during the $\dot{V}O_2$max test is, as described, a very good predictor of running performance. Hence, according to that prediction, runner C would be the fastest runner at any distance, despite having a lower $\dot{V}O_2$max value than runner A. C's low $\dot{V}O_2$max value is due to his superior running economy; his superior performance is due to his ability to achieve the highest peak treadmill running speed. The runner

(continued)

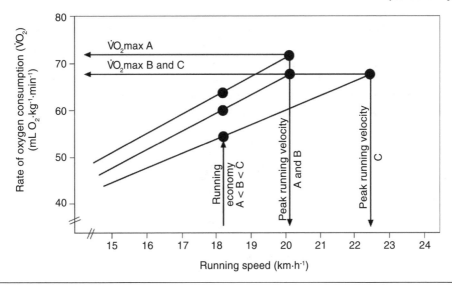

Figure 2.9 Comparison of running economy, peak treadmill running speed, and $\dot{V}O_2$max in three theoretical runners (A, B, and C) during a progressive exercise test to measure $\dot{V}O_2$max.

in table 2.1 who most closely fits this description would be Derek Clayton, who is known to have been one of the most economical runners yet studied (see figure 2.8). He held the world record for the marathon despite having a relatively low $\dot{V}O_2$max value of 69.7.

Runner A performs less well than her high $\dot{V}O_2$max would predict because she is the least economical of the three runners and only reaches the same peak treadmill speed as does runner B, despite a higher $\dot{V}O_2$max. Hence, her performance would only ever equal that of runner B and would be inferior to that of runner C, whose $\dot{V}O_2$max is lower. The runners in table 2.1 who best fit these characteristics are American Craig Virgin and Norwegian Greta Waitz, both of whose performances do not appear to be as good as their high $\dot{V}O_2$max values would predict.

The second reason that $\dot{V}O_2$max alone is a relatively poor predictor of performance is because it cannot account for the proportion of the $\dot{V}O_2$max that different athletes can sustain during prolonged exercise. We have termed this ability *fatigue resistance*. In short, it is found that regardless of their actual $\dot{V}O_2$max values, the most successful athletes are those who can sustain a high percentage of $\dot{V}O_2$max during racing at any distance, because they have superior fatigue resistance. Therefore, another reason why the $\dot{V}O_2$max is a poor predictor of running ability is because it neither measures nor predicts fatigue resistance during prolonged submaximal exercise. This is largely because the $\dot{V}O_2$max measures a single physiological variable during a single bout of progressive, maximal exercise to exhaustion in a test that lasts a few minutes. But each athlete's fatigue resistance can only be measured during prolonged exercise in the laboratory, on the basis of his or her performances in a series of races of different distances.

The reason that running economy is considered such an important factor is because athletes with good running economy burn less fuel at any running speed than do less economical runners. If depletion of body fuel stores explains exhaustion during marathon and ultramarathon racing (see the Energy Supply/ Energy Depletion Model in chapter 3), then it is obvious that the more economical the runner, the farther that athlete will be able to run on the same amount of fuel. More important, according to the Integrated Neuromuscular Recruitment Model , which holds that the rate of heat accumulation also influences endurance performance, the more economical runners will accumulate heat less rapidly and hence may have superior endurance.

FACTORS THAT AFFECT RUNNING ECONOMY

In the same way that the $\dot{V}O_2$max is influenced by factors either internal or external to the runner, running economy is also influenced by a range of variables.

Up-and-Down Movement

There is evidence to suggest that uneconomical runners expend more energy bobbing up and down when they run than do more economical runners (C.T.M. Davies

1980b; Miyashita et al. 1978), who tend to glide over the ground with very little vertical oscillation (Higdon 1981).

Clayton has described how he thinks he became an economical runner:

When I started training for marathon distances, my style changed naturally. Running 20 miles a day cut down on my stride length. It also eliminated the tendency to lift my knees. Gradually, my power stride evolved into one of economy. Despite the energy-draining action of my upper body, I developed a very natural leg action I call "The Clayton Shuffle." Through miles and miles of training, I honed my leg action to such a degree that I barely lifted my leg off the ground. "The Clayton Shuffle" is probably the best thing that ever happened to my running. It was economical and easy on my body. (Clayton 1980, p. 62)

Arthur Newton, discussed in more detail in chapter 5, had similar advice:

Learn to run in an easy and serene manner without an atom of wasted energy. Use short strides. The longer your stride, the more you bob up and down. You ought to almost slither your feet over the ground, going as near to touching it without actually doing it. (Newton 1935, pp. 21-22, 36; 1949, p. 87)

Muscle Capacity to Store Energy

With each running stride, the muscles of the landing leg store impact energy as they contract eccentrically to absorb the shock of landing (K.R. Williams 1985; 1990). Most of the stored energy is then used during the concentric muscle contraction that propels the body forward during the next stride; that is, we use the impetus of landing to assist the muscular effort of takeoff.

Indeed, there is growing evidence to suggest that the elastic recoil provided by the tendons contributes a significant proportion (about 30%) of the energy for propulsion, at least when running on flat terrain. It is possible that the muscles of the more economical runners have a greater ability either to store or to utilize this form of impact energy (Bosco, Montanari, et al. 1986).

In this regard, cyclists with a higher proportion of Type I fibers were found to be more economical (Coyle, Sidossis, et al. 1992). Coyle and colleagues speculate that this results from a metabolic difference between the muscle fibers, with Type I fibers producing energy more economically than Type II fibers. As cycling is a non-weight-bearing activity, the contribution of elastic recoil to cycling economy is likely to be less than in running. It is generally believed that Type II fibers have superior energy return (elasticity) than Type I fibers.

A popular idea, implicit in the description of how muscles work (see figure 1.5) is that it is the shortening of contracting muscles that propels the body forward when we run. But running is really a series of bounces in which muscles, tendons, and ligaments alternately store and release the energy absorbed as the feet hit the ground. Indeed, it is similar to the action of a pogo stick or a bouncing ball (R.McN. Alexander and Bennet-Clark 1977; R.M. Alexander 1987; Wingerson 1983). The realization that the legs alternately store and release elastic energy during running, that this elasticity probably contributes to running ability and possibly also explains some forms of exercise exhaustion, is the basis of the Biomechanical Model.

The notion that running is really a bouncing action is not new; it received renewed impetus with a recent study of muscle and tendon function in turkeys (Pennisi

1997). By placing sensors in the muscles and the tendons of turkeys, T.J. Roberts et al. (1997) were able to show that when running on flat surfaces, the turkeys' leg muscles contracted shortly before the foot landed on the ground. The muscle contraction was just enough to keep the tendon stretched when the foot was on the ground, thereby storing energy for the next stride. As a result, the muscle shortened relatively little and used only a small amount of energy when the turkeys ran on flat surfaces. Most of the work of running was done passively in the elasticity of the muscle and tendon. When the turkeys ran uphill, however, their muscles shortened more, and substantially more muscle was recruited to produce the same force as on the level. Roberts et al. concluded that, "running economy is improved by muscles that act as active struts rather than working muscles" (1987, p. 1113).

It is likely that all animals use elastic recoil to improve their efficiency of locomotion (Prilutsky et al. 1996), but the kangaroo is the animal in which this phenomenon is best exemplified. When moving at less than 8 km per hour, the kangaroo has an ungainly gait in which the tail acts as a fifth leg. But at any higher speed, the animal begins to hop, and it is then that its extraordinary adaptation becomes apparent, for the energy cost of hopping at speeds from 8 to 25 km per hour does not increase (T.J. Dawson and Taylor 1973). In contrast, humans must expend three times as much energy when increasing their running speeds from 8 to 25 km per hour (see figures 2.3 and 2.8).

Kangaroos achieve this energy saving by having unusually long and large Achilles tendons, very long heel bones that act as the lever to which the Achilles tendons insert, and a large ligament in the tail. All these structures act as the springs that allow the efficient use of the stored energy of landing. In this way, greater speed increases the amount of energy stored without requiring any additional muscle contraction and hence energy use. The muscles of the kangaroo's leg, like those of the turkey's, take up the slack in the elastic elements so that, on landing, the elastic springs stretch, not the muscles.

Muscle elasticity in humans comes from the titin within the muscles and the collagen fibers that, arranged as long, parallel fibers, make up tendons and ligaments. Aging is associated with a loss of elasticity in the collagen. Long-term training in both rats and humans reduces muscle elasticity (Kovanen and Suominen 1988; Kubo, Kanehisa, et al. 2000), an effect that may also occur in older distance runners with many years of heavy racing and training. In contrast, short bouts of training improve muscle elasticity, at least in rats (Gosselin et al. 1998).

Thus, the most current biomechanical model of leg action during running is that all the elastic elements in the lower leg muscles act as a single linear spring. The stiffness of that spring can be varied, however, particularly in response to the softness of the surface over which the athlete runs (D.P. Ferris and Farley 1997). This is important because the stiffness of the spring determines how the body reacts with the ground during the contact phase of the running cycle (chapter 14).

A fundamental finding is that the stiffness of the leg spring is independent of running speed but alters with changes in stride frequency. Thus, at the same running speed, the leg spring becomes stiffer the higher the stride frequency (and the shorter the stride length). The stiffer the spring, the less energy that will be absorbed. These findings suggest that the naturally chosen stride frequency when running at the same speed by different runners (of similar mass), must reflect individual differences in the elasticity of their legs.

Studies in humans (D.P. Ferris and Farley 1997) show that runners can alter their leg stiffness by more than threefold. In particular, they do this when running on surfaces that differ in hardness. The result is that the combined stiffness of the leg and the contact surface remain the same. As a result, the length of the time that the foot is on the ground (ground contact time) and the duration of the airborne phase remain the same. Consequently, the stride frequency and the vertical oscillation of the body do not change, irrespective of the softness of the surface on which the subject runs. A failure of this adaptation would mean that the duration of the ground contact phase would increase by about 70% when running on very soft surfaces.

As a result of increases in leg stiffness, there is reduced flexion of the knee during ground contact. Running with increased flexion of the knee is wasteful of energy. This "Groucho Marx" style of running increases oxygen consumption by up to 50% (McMahon et al. 1987). In contrast, there is a general finding that less flexible runners—measured as flexibility of the hip or calf muscles, either at rest (Craib et al. 1996; Gliem et al. 1990) or during exercise (Heise and Martin 1998)—are more economical. Acute changes in leg stiffness occur predominantly as a result of changes in ankle stiffness. Thus, as the surface becomes softer, ankle stiffness increases, and knee bend is reduced on landing. How changes in leg stiffness are brought about is not known, but it is not simply the result of increased muscle activation (recruitment) since this is reduced when running on harder surfaces (Farley et al. 1998).

Biomechanical Factors

Biomechanical factors, such as differences in limb lengths and body weight distributions, may also contribute to differences in running economy (K.R. Williams 1985; 1990), but the precise relationships between these factors are unclear.

Interestingly, athletes appear to choose the stride length at which they are most economical—that is, at which their oxygen uptake is the least for that particular running speed (Cavanagh and Williams 1982). When forced to take either shorter or longer strides but to maintain the same running pace, they become less economical and require an increased oxygen uptake. As Arthur Newton said, "Don't draw the line too fine about the length of your stride . . . just make a habit of acquiring a reasonable length and Nature will attend to the rest." With training, distance runners increase the length of their strides and reduce their stride frequency (R.C. Nelson and Gregor 1976). This is believed to optimize running economy since increasing stride frequency is a less economical method for increasing running speed than is an increase in stride length, at least in distance runners. The effect cannot be evaluated in sprinters.

Technique and Type of Activity

Running economy may change for the same athlete during different types of exercise, such as during uphill or downhill running (Gregor 1970), or during different activities such as cycling or step-climbing (J.T. Daniels et al. 1985). Thus, it is possible that runners who are economical on flat terrain may be uneconomical while running either up- or downhill. Alternatively, some economical runners may be less economical at cycling than other runners who are less economical runners.

Fitness and Training

It seems that people beginning exercise become more economical with training (S. Robinson and Harmon 1941). The same applies to people who are already trained but who continue heavy training (Conley et al. 1981a; 1984) or who introduce interval training (Franch et al. 1998). For example, Svedenhag and Sjodin (1985) found that the running economy of a group of elite Swedish distance runners improved between 1% and 4% during the course of one year. Changes of similar magnitude (up to 4%) were also measured in a group of adolescent runners (J. Daniels and Oldridge 1971). The authors speculated that the continual improvement in the running performance of these Swedish athletes was due to a slowly progressive improvement in their running economies, rather than an increase in $\dot{V}O_2$max. The latter was relatively fixed, increasing only during that phase of the season when the athletes were performing high-intensity interval-type training. This training effect has also been shown in a group of elite Czech runners (Bunc et al. 1989). Others have also found that changes in running economy are better predictors of changes in running performance than are changes in $\dot{V}O_2$max (Ramsbottom et al. 1989).

The effects of training have been summarized by D.W. Morgan, Bransford, et al. (1995), who conclude that trained runners are more economical than untrained runners and that, as a group, elite runners are usually more economical than less talented athletes, but that economical and uneconomical runners can be found in all categories of athletes.

Age

Children are less economical runners than adults (see figure 2.8; Krahenbuhl and Pangrazi 1983; Krahenbuhl and Williams 1992) but become more economical with age (J. Daniels and Oldridge 1971; Krahenbuhl and Williams 1992; Ariëns et al. 1997). This is due partly to training (J. Daniels, Fitts, et al. 1978) but also to their weight gain (MacDougall, Roche, et al. 1983) and, perhaps, also to increases in stride length and in elastic energy return. For example, children may be less able to store and use elastic energy during running (Thorstensson 1986), something that possibly improves with maturation. Improvements in running performance in adolescents appear to be a result of changes in running economy, not in $\dot{V}O_2$max (Krahenbuhl, Morgan, et al. 1989). Instruction in running technique did not improve the running economy of 10-year-old boys (Petray and Krahenbuhl 1985).

Fatigue

The energy cost of running at a specific speed increases during exercise and is substantially increased at the end of long-distance running (Helgerud 1994; Xu and Montgomery 1995) and triathlon events (Hausswirth et al. 1996). This response can be detected after runs of 60 minutes and is not reduced by fluid or fuel ingestion during exercise (Sproule 1998). It is possible that this effect results from the muscle exhaustion and damage that occurs during repetitive eccentric muscle contractions.

Paavo Komi and colleagues at the University of Jyväskyla in Finland have contributed innovative work that—perhaps better than any other—may explain why runners hit the wall during marathon racing. This model may also explain why fatigue causes a reduction in running economy.

Komi was one of the first to appreciate that most human muscles do not contract in vivo (in the live situation) in exactly the same way as they do when tested either as isolated muscle samples in the laboratory (in vitro), or even when measured with expensive laboratory equipment that measures their concentric, eccentric, or isometric strength.

During weight-bearing exercise such as running, muscles, particularly of the lower limb, are first stretched before they contract. Komi coined the term the stretch-shortening cycle (SSC) to describe this more realistic description of how muscles really work during weight-bearing exercise. The important characteristics of the SSC are the following:

- The prestretch of the muscle increases the performance of the muscle during the subsequent contraction.
- The prestretch activates nervous reflexes that alter the stiffness of the muscle.
- Repetitive stretching, which causes eccentric muscle contractions, can lead to muscle damage of varying degrees (see chapter 14). What this information predicts is that while the SSC increases the power output of the muscle, the cost of this benefit is muscle damage caused by overstressing the elastic elements of the muscle. Komi's insightful contribution was to ask whether repeated SSC contractions, as occur in the calf and quadriceps muscles, could induce a special type of exhaustion (for example, during marathon and ultramarathon running).

Komi's laboratory experiments showed that repeated SSC contractions induce a specific form of muscle exhaustion in which the muscle is unable to compensate for a progressive reduction in the power output of the muscle fibers by increasing muscle recruitment. Thus, characteristics of this exhaustion are a failure of the contractile capacity of the exercised muscles, accompanied by a reduced tolerance to muscle stretch and a delayed transfer from muscle stretch to muscle shortening in the SSC cycle. As a result, the duration of both the braking and push-off phases in the running stride are increased, leading to mechanical changes in the stride with landing occurring on a more extended leg but with greater subsequent knee flexion.

As these abnormalities persist for many days after the race, they cannot be explained by acute, reversible metabolic changes produced by exercise. Thus, they cannot be explained by acute changes in oxygen or substrate delivery to the muscles, or by the elevated body temperature during exercise, as required by the other models of exercise physiology.

A series of studies from Komi's laboratories (C. Nicol et al. 1991b; Pullinen et al. 1997) has found that peak muscle function is reduced for at least seven days after a marathon race. This is associated with a reduced ability to activate (recruit) the damaged muscles whose endurance is also reduced (C. Nicol et al. 1991c). Hence, these studies show evidence of impaired central (brain) recruitment of the muscles—so-called central fatigue—that persists for some days after the marathon. This is consistent with the belief that central (brain) fatigue limits performance during prolonged exercise, such as marathon running.

During the experimental marathon, a progressive fall in the maximum sprinting speed was measured repeatedly throughout the race. Gait changes also developed as exhaustion progressed during the race. Firstly, the foot contact phase of the landing cycle increased. Secondly, the forces generated during the push-off phase were reduced. As a result, the knee went into a greater degree of flexion on landing. Together, these changes prolonged the push-off phase of the running cycle and reduced the bounciness of the running stride (Avela and Komi 1998a; 1998b), reducing running economy (C. Nicol et al. 1991a). Similar changes have been reported by Heikki Rusko's group, also in Jyväskyla, Finland, during a simulated 10-km race (Paavolainen, A. Nummela, et al. 1999). This study showed that this effect is not only specific to marathon running but may also occur during competition over any running distance, becoming increasingly more obvious at racing distances greater than 5 km.

In summary, these studies have found that repeated eccentric muscle contractions produce progressive muscle damage that reduces the power output of the damaged muscles. As a result, during repeated SSC contractions, there is reduced elastic energy recoil and impaired running economy. Runners show this form of fatigue when they hit the wall in marathon and ultramarathon races. This condition can be diagnosed by changes in gait, in particular a deeper knee bend during the stance phase of the running cycle and a prolonged contact phase. The finding that these changes are still present for at least seven days after the marathon confirms that they are not due to metabolic changes in the muscle. Instead, they appear to result from fatigue of the processes that regulate the stiffness of the leg with a resulting inhibition of nerve impulses coming to the muscles from the controlling cells—the alpha motor neurons—in the spinal cord. As a result, the use of elastic energy is impaired (Avela and Komi 1998b). These studies confirm that exhaustion during exercise can result from many different processes not accounted for in the original Cardiovascular/Anaerobic Model.

Gender

Although $\dot{V}O_2$max values differ between the sexes, gender appears to have no effect on running economy: trained men and women are generally considered to be equally economical (J. Daniels, Krahenbuhl, et al. 1977; C.T.M. Davies and Thompson 1979; P. Hopkins and Powers 1982; Maughan and Leiper 1983; J. Daniels and Daniels 1992).

Padilla et al. (1992) have argued, however, that women are in fact more economical than men, probably because they are better able to use stored elastic energy than men, as they are more elastic (Komi and Bosco 1978; Winter and Brookes 1991). Padilla et al. argue that body mass is an important determinant of running economy—heavier adults, for example, are more economical than lighter adults or children. Most women are lighter than men; thus, if they are as economical as the heavier men, they would actually be more economical than men of the same weight. Using this logic, Padilla et al. (1992) calculated that, at the same body mass, women are about 10% more economical than men. They proposed that "studying the mechanics of the female (running) stride could open a way to improve male performance" (p. 565).

Race

Running economy may also be influenced by race. Asians and Africans have been found to use 17% less energy than Europeans when lying down, sitting, or standing, but no studies were performed during exercise (Geissler and Aldouri 1985). A more recent study (Ferretti et al. 1991) found that African pygmies were about 10% more economical than Caucasians when running but not when walking. The authors speculate that this difference could be the result of ethnic differences in the recoil of elastic energy stored in the stretched tendons.

In our study of elite runners of different racial groups, we found no race-related differences in running economy (Coetzer et al. 1993). But as shown in figure 2.8, the two best Kenyan runners yet studied, John Ngugi and Julius Korir, are among the most economical runners studied to date. The same is true of the average economy of the best Scandinavian runners (figure 2.8). In addition, we found that subelite African runners were more economical than subelite Caucasian runners (Weston, Mbambo, et al. 2000). This difference increased when differences in body weight between the heavier Caucasians and lighter Africans were normalized by expressing the oxygen consumption to body weight$^{0.66}$.

Added Weight of Clothing and Shoes

Athletes' economy can also be influenced by what they wear. E.D. Stevens (1983) has calculated that changing from nylon clothing weighing about 150 g to cotton clothing weighing about 240 g would increase the time taken by a world-class runner to complete the marathon by about 13 seconds (and that of the average 03:40 marathoner by about 23 seconds). Running in a full cotton tracksuit weighing 985 g would increase the average runner's marathon time by about 4 minutes.

Laboratory experiments, however, do not necessarily substantiate these calculations. Thus, Cureton, Sparling, et al. (1978) found that the addition of up to 4 kg to the torso increased the oxygen cost of running by only about 2.5%, or about 0.5% for 1 kg of extra weight.

Extra weight added to the legs or feet appears to have a greater effect on running economy. The addition of 0.5 kg to each thigh or to each foot increased the oxygen cost of running by 3.5% and 7.2% respectively (P.E. Martin 1985). Other studies (Catlin and Dressendorfer 1979; Stripe 1982a; E.C. Frederick, Clarke, et al. 1983; B.H. Jones, Toner, et al. 1984; D.A. Jones, Newham, et al. 1986) have shown that the addition of 1 kg to the feet increases the oxygen cost of running by between 6% and 10%, or about 1% per 100 g increase in the weight of footwear. The increase is the same in men and women (D.A. Jones, Newham, et al. 1986).

Clearly, a 1% saving in energy expenditure during a standard 42-km marathon race, for example, is not inconsiderable. If translated directly into a 1% improvement in performance, it would mean a saving of 77 seconds at world record marathon pace, equivalent to a sub-02:05 standard marathon. But it has yet to be proven that we can assume that this energy saving will cause an equivalent improvement in running performance.

In-shoe orthotics used in the treatment of a number of running injuries (see chapter 14) increase shoe weight and have an adverse affect on running economy. In the study by Burkett et al. (1985), the addition of orthotics, each weighing 80 g, to each running shoe increased the oxygen cost of running by about 1.4%; smaller increases (0.4% to 1.1%) were reported by Berg and Sady (1985). It would seem that the added weight of the orthotic decreases running economy in direct proportion to its weight.

The air sole introduced by Nike in the early 1980s reduced the oxygen cost of running by an average of 2.8% (Stripe 1982b) and 1.6% (E.C. Frederick, Clarke, et al. 1983) respectively at a running speed of 16 km per hour. Once again, if these savings are directly translatable into equivalent improvements in racing performance, then they are sufficiently real, at least for the top athletes, to be taken seriously. Further research is needed to study this possibility.

Chester Kyle and his colleagues (Kyle 1986; Kyle and Caiozzo 1986) have studied the effects of athletic clothing on aerodynamic drag and therefore on the runner's economy. They showed that the aerodynamic drag experienced by the runner was increased by the following factors:

- Shoes with exposed laces (0.5%)
- Hair on limbs (0.6%)
- Long socks (0.9%)
- Short hair (4%)
- Loosely fitting clothing (4.2%)
- Long hair (6.3%)

They also calculated that by reducing aerodynamic drag by as little as 2%, equivalent to cutting the hair short, runners would reduce their running times over 100 m by 0.01 seconds, and in a standard marathon by 5.7 seconds. Even better results could be achieved by running in a custom-fitted speed suit with a tight-fitting hood to cover the hair and ears. Such a suit made of polyurethane-coated, stretchable nylon reduces aerodynamic drag by smoothing the air flow around the streamlined areas of the chin, ears, and hair, and by eliminating the flapping of loose clothing. Calculations suggest that wearing such clothing would reduce running time in the 100 m race by 0.284 seconds (3%) and by 1:34.50 (1%) in a standard marathon (Brownlie et al. 1987a). Unfortunately, this clothing is impractical for runners because its streamlining prevents heat loss (Brownlie et al. 1987a). The first attempt to use the streamlined hood in Olympic relay competition had disastrous results—the 1988 U.S. Olympic 100-m relay team was disqualified in the preliminary rounds when one runner received the baton outside the legal zone because he was unable to hear the approach of the other runner. These runners also broke one of the cardinal rules of racing—never try something new for the first time in competition.

Environmental Conditions

Environmental conditions, including the running surface, wind speed and direction, and up- and downhill running, have the biggest effects on a runner's economy. T.A. McMahon and Greene (1979) have suggested that optimizing the spring constant of a running track so that it is "tuned" to the human leg will probably improve running performance and running economy (and thereby reduce the risk of injury).

The influence of the running surface on the oxygen cost of running was first noted by Passmore and Durnin (1955), who showed that the oxygen cost of walking across a ploughed field was 35% greater than the cost of walking at the same speed on a smooth, firm surface. Running on sand has a similar effect (Wyngard et al. 1985). Running over ground in dense forest, the chosen activity of orienteers, is associated with a reduction of about 50% in running economy (K. Jensen et al. 1999), which explains why orienteering is such a physically demanding sport. However, orienteers are more economical when running in forests than are track-trained runners (K. Jensen et al. 1999). This could be a result of their training or perhaps because orienteers are born with that unique ability and hence are attracted to that sport.

One of the first scientists to study the influence of wind speed on running performance was the British physiologist Griffiths Pugh, whose work on the effects of altitude on athletic performance is one of the most significant contributions to that topic (Pugh 1958; 1967b). Pugh's studies (1970a; 1970b) showed that the extra cost of running into a facing wind increased as the square of the wind speed, whereas the extra cost of running uphill increased as a linear function of the gradient.

Pugh also showed that at the speeds at which middle-distance track events were run in the 1970s (6 m per s; about 67 s per 400 m), about 8% of the runner's energy is used in overcoming air resistance. But by running directly behind a leading runner at a distance of about 1 m, the athlete can save 80% of that wasted energy. In a middle-distance race this would be equivalent to a saving of about 4 s per lap. Pugh considered it unlikely, however, that, in reality, the following athletes would ever be able to run close enough to the lead runner to gain any substantial benefit. By running slightly to the side of the lead runner, the following runner would probably benefit by about 1 s per lap (Pugh 1970a, 1970b).

Chester Kyle (1979) has also evaluated the benefits of drafting. His calculations suggest that at world record mile pace, running 2 m behind the lead runner would effect an energy saving of about 1.66 s per lap, thus confirming the general accuracy of Pugh's estimations. Interestingly, in cycling, the benefits of drafting increase with the size of the group and the distance from the front of the pack. It is entirely possible, although as yet untested, that the same could apply in running. The studies of Brownlie et al. (1987b) indicate that the optimum drafting position is indeed 1 m directly behind the lead runner. At a running speed of 28 km per hour, this would be equivalent to a saving of 4.32 s per 400-m lap if the lead athlete wore traditional nonaerodynamic running shorts and a singlet and while the following athlete wore an aerodynamic Lycra bodysuit (Brownlie et al. 1987b). In contrast, aerodynamic drag is increased when runners are positioned abreast, because the larger frontal area results in a larger shared drag (Brownlie et al. 1987b). Thus, running next to another runner increases the effort of both runners. This could become a tactic to slow an opponent if members of a running team regularly rotated their position next to the opposing lead runner.

These findings clearly explain why track athletes find pacers such an essential ingredient in their attempts at world track records. In addition, they explain why world records in the sprints are set at altitude (see chapter 12). This is because during sprinting the energy cost of overcoming air resistance rises to between 13% and 16% of the total cost of running. Thus, the sprinter benefits greatly by running at altitude, where air resistance is considerably reduced. It is interesting that when racing on a circular track, an athlete's optimum strategy is to accelerate into the wind and to decelerate when the wind is from behind, the opposite to what one would expect (Hatsell 1974). The reason for this is that the retarding effect of a headwind is greater than the assisting effect of a tailwind; hence, you will be using your energy in the most economical way. Obviously, when running into the wind, it is particularly valuable to draft.

The Welshman C.T. Mervyn Davies (1980b; 1981) extended Pugh's findings. He used essentially the same techniques as Pugh but included observations on the effects of downhill running and of following winds of different speeds. When measured on the treadmill, facing winds of up to 18 km per hour had no effect on the oxygen cost of running. This does not mean that on the road, running into a wind of 18 km per hour will have no effect. On the contrary, it will have a very marked effect. On the treadmill, the athletes do not move forward. Thus, they do not expend energy overcoming air resistance. When you are running on the road into a wind of 18 km per hour, however, you face an actual wind speed equal to that of your running speed, plus that of the prevailing wind.

The practical relevance is that, on a calm day, anyone running slower than 18 km per hour (about a 2:21 marathon pace) will not benefit by drafting in the wake of other runners. Runners stand to gain considerably by drafting when running at faster speeds, however, or when running into winds that, when added to their running speeds, would make the actual wind speed greater than 18 km per hour.

Of course, both the men's and the women's world marathon record is run at a pace faster than 18 km per hour. This means that athletes intent on setting world marathon records would be well advised to draft for as much of the race as possible. Front-running in the marathon is almost as wasteful of energy as is front-

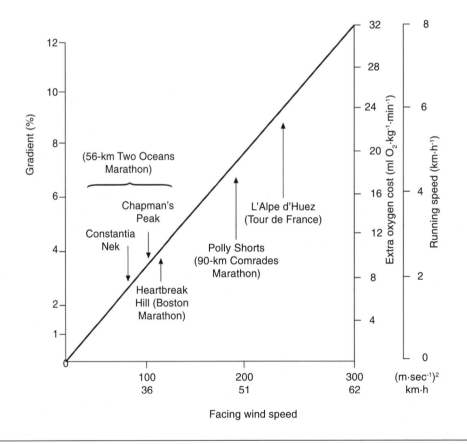

Figure 2.10   The additional oxygen cost of running up differing gradients or running into headwind speeds (facing wind speeds) of different velocities.

Based on the data of C.T.M. Davies (1980b; 1981).

running on the track. The appearance of pacers in marathon races in the past decade indicates that this fact is now more widely appreciated.

Besides drafting, the only other way to reduce wind resistance is to run with a tailwind of which the speed is at least equal to that of the runner. Under these circumstances, Davies calculated that the removal of the energy required to overcome wind resistance at the then men's world marathon pace (19.91 km per hour) would increase the runner's speed by about 0.82 km per hour, equivalent to a reduction in racing time of about 5 minutes. Drafting in a tightly knit bunch for the entire race would be expected to reduce air resistance by about 80%, allowing the runner to run about 4 minutes faster.

Davies found that the effect of a tailwind was about half that of a headwind (although obviously this effect was to the athlete's advantage). Thus, as discussed, a tailwind of 19.8 km per hour is of little assistance to runners running slower than 18 km per hour, but a tailwind of 19.8 km per hour would assist a marathon world record attempt by increasing the runner's speed by 0.5 km per hour. Higher tailwind speeds of 35 to 66 km per hour would improve running speeds by 1.5 to 4 km per hour.

At higher headwind speeds, the oxygen cost of running increases enormously. Wind speeds of 35 km per hour would reduce running speeds by about 2.5 km per hour, and with speeds of 60 km per hour by about 8 km per hour (figure 2.10).

Finally, Davies calculated the additional oxygen cost of running uphill or, conversely, the energy saving of running downhill. He found that the energy saving when running downhill was only half of the energy that would be lost when running on an equivalent uphill gradient. Thus, uphill running increased the energy cost by about 2.6 ml O_2 per kg per min for each 1% increase in gradient. This is equivalent to a reduction in running speed of about 0.65 km per hour. Downhill running was associated with a reduction in the oxygen cost of running by about 1.5 ml O_2 per kg per min for each 1% gradient, equivalent to an increase in speed of about 0.35 km per hour.

The practical value of this information is threefold:

1. It indicates that time lost going up a hill can never be fully regained by running an identical downhill gradient.

2. The data can be used to estimate how much time a runner can expect to lose or gain on a particular section of a race as long as the gradient of that section is known.

3. It provides the information necessary to predict three of the crucial factors required for a running world record—pacemakers and a flat course with windstill conditions. (The fourth factor, cool conditions, is discussed in chapter 4.)

By reducing wind resistance, altitude aids performance in short-distance events. This advantage is offset, however, by the reduced oxygen content of the arterial blood. This reduces the oxygen delivery to the heart and therefore reduces the athlete's peak power output (according to the Central Governor Model). These opposing effects cancel each other out in events lasting about 90 seconds. Running events completed in less than 90 seconds are enhanced at altitude; those lasting longer are impaired (see chapter 9).

TRAINING TO
IMPROVE RUNNING ECONOMY

Early physiological research into the effects of running training focused almost exclusively on the effects of training on the athlete's $\dot{V}O_2$max. Yet, it is now clear that the $\dot{V}O_2$max value of a healthy person is stable and changes relatively little, even with intensive training (J.T. Daniels 1974; J.T. Daniels, Yarbough, et al. 1978; Svedenhag and Sjodin 1985; Bunc et al. 1989). Thus, the question may be asked: Why does running performance continue to improve with training if the $\dot{V}O_2$max does not show a corresponding increase?

One proven explanation is that training increases the running speed at the lactate turnpoint (see chapter 3) and that this change correlates closely with actual changes in running performance (K. Tanaka et al. 1984). Another important possibility is that athletes who train heavily show a gradual and progressive increase in running economy, which even continues to improve for some years after their $\dot{V}O_2$max has reached its highest possible value. Svedenhag and Sjodin's (1985) findings provide evidence of this.

Our own findings are in accord with this interpretation. Scrimgeour et al. (1986) found that the group of runners who trained the least ran at a significantly higher percentage of their $\dot{V}O_2$max during a 10-km race than did the runners who trained the most. But they also ran more slowly because they were less economical and required more oxygen to run at any (slower) speed. Others have noted that weekly training distance does not predict the percentage $\dot{V}O_2$max that an athlete can sustain during competition, so elite runners do not necessarily run at a higher percentage $\dot{V}O_2$max during competition than do slower runners (C.T.M. Davies and Thompson 1979; C.L. Wells, Hecht, et al. 1981; C. Williams and Nute 1983; Maughan and Leiper 1983; Sjodin and Svedenhag 1985). This is a particularly remarkable finding as it conflicts with the logical assumption that training increases the effort we can sustain during competition. In contrast, this finding suggests that training improves performance during competition by reducing the effort expended. An important and perhaps overlooked benefit will be to reduce the rate of heat accumulation during competition and to delay fatigue by keeping the athlete cooler. This is the second prediction of the Integrated Neuromuscular Recruitment Model, which is discussed in more detail in chapter 4.

In summary, Scrimgeour et al. (1986) found that training more than 60 to 100 km per week did not increase the intensity of effort, measured as the percentage $\dot{V}O_2$max, that athletes could sustain during marathon and ultramarathon races. The more heavily trained runners, however, were more economical. Thus, it seems that their extra training increased their running economy so that for the equivalent effort during competition, the more trained runners ran faster. In their study, Sjodin and Svedenhag (1985) essentially reported the same finding, except that they concluded that the cutoff training distance was 120 km per week. Together, these studies suggest the possibility that one substantial benefit of very high weekly training distances may be a progressive increase in running economy. In view of the risks associated with heavy weekly training distances, are there not better and less risky ways of improving running economy?

Alternatively, the reason why few studies have managed to identify the major physiological adaptations that explain why training improves running performance may simply be that they have failed to identify the organ system on which training-induced changes in running performance are dependent. If it is changes in brain function and muscle recruitment that explain these adaptations, and if such function has not been studied, then it is understandable why scientists have overlooked these.

At present our understanding of all the factors that determine running economy is incomplete. In addition, we do not yet know how these factors might be altered for greater effect. The evidence presented so far does suggest that to optimize running economy, greater attention needs to be paid to minimizing the weight of shoes and clothing worn during competition; to developing a longer stride length with a lower stride frequency; and to minimizing the weight of the moving limbs, in particular the legs, in much the same way that cyclists strive to keep the weight of their revolving wheels to a minimum. In addition, runners need to be more aware of their aerodynamic profile. Thus, Chester Kyle (1986) has suggested that a reduction of between 2% and 6% in aerodynamic drag can be achieved by runners who run with tightly fitting clothing, with short hair, and without socks. This change would be the equivalent of running 12 cm less in the 100 m and 30 m less in a standard marathon. Shoelaces should also be covered as exposed laces also increase aerodynamic drag and slow the runner down.

Armed with new knowledge, it is likely that in the future running shoe manufacturers will concentrate on producing products that improve running economy, bioengineers will aim to increase their understanding of the factors that influence running economy, and coaches will develop new training techniques to improve the running economy of their athletes. Even the psychologists may have a role to play, given the finding that hypnosis can influence running economy (Benson et al. 1978). An obvious area for development is the "tuning" of running shoes to enable a maximum amount of energy to return to the foot with each stride (Kyle 1986)—in much the same way that running tracks have been tuned to allow faster running times. The development of the Nike Shox running shoe range (figure 2.11) represents the first innovation based on this concept.

Figure 2.11   A Nike Shox running shoe, which incorporates springs in the heels to increase elastic recoil during running.

PREDICTING RUNNING PERFORMANCE

A fascination with the belief that the $\dot{V}O_2$max is the alpha and omega of exercise physiology has blinded us to the possibility that factors other than those relating only to oxygen delivery to and use by the athlete's muscles are better predictors of running performance (Noakes 1988b; 1997; 1998c; 2000b).

The first of these untested factors is the peak running speed reached at exhaustion during the maximal exercise test (that is, the maximum work rate). In all the quoted studies, the maximum work rate and the running speed at the lactate turnpoint (discussed in chapter 3) were the best physiological predictors of running performance; $\dot{V}O_2$max was a less reliable predictor. But the best predictor of performance at any longer distance, even up to 90 km, was the 10-km running time (Noakes, Myburgh, et al. 1990a). I interpret these findings to indicate that muscle and neural (brain) factors contribute to running performance at any distance. This muscle factor has two components, neither of which appears to be related to factors determining oxygen transport to or oxygen use by the exercising muscles (Noakes 1988b). The first factor is superior heart and skeletal muscle function, which allows the fastest athletes to maximize their muscle power output (peak achieved work rates or running speeds) at the maximum coronary flow and cardiac output that limits maximal (short duration) exercise performance, according to the Central Governor Model.

The second factor, more likely a combination of neural and muscle factors, is the ability to resist fatigue during more prolonged exercise. I speculate that during high-intensity exercise of short duration (up to 4 to 6 minutes), the capacity to produce a high maximum power output is the more important determinant of success and is controlled by the protective action of the central governor, the goal of which is to prevent heart damage by controlling the mass of skeletal muscle that can be recruited, and determined by the contractile characteristics of the muscle fibers that the governor allows to be recruited. As the duration of exercise increases, however, the ability to resist the development of fatigue becomes the increasingly more dominant determinant of exercise performance (Coetzer et al. 1993). The extent to which this is also regulated by the central governor—responding in this case to the different signals, including perhaps the body temperature, the state of the muscle glycogen stores, and the blood glucose concentration as well as the extent of any eccentrically induced skeletal muscle damage—is currently unknown, but it is likely to be important.

The finding that the best sprinters are not the best long-distance runners suggests that these two physiological determinants of success do not coexist to maximum capacity in any one type of human muscle. The brains and muscles of sprinters, who are able to achieve very high rates of energy production for short duration, fatigue more rapidly than do the brains and muscles of middle- and long-distance runners, whose muscles are not quite as powerful. Thus, at distances greater than 400 m, the less talented sprinters with the less powerful but more fatigue-resistant brains and muscles will begin to outperform the elite sprinters, whose brains and more powerful muscles fatigue too rapidly.

Thus, in groups of equally trained distance runners, I suspect that the best runners at any longer distance are those who are fastest over distances from 100 to 800 m and whose brains and muscles are also highly fatigue resistant. There is no better example of this than Daniel Komen, the Kenyan phenomenon. Komen's best

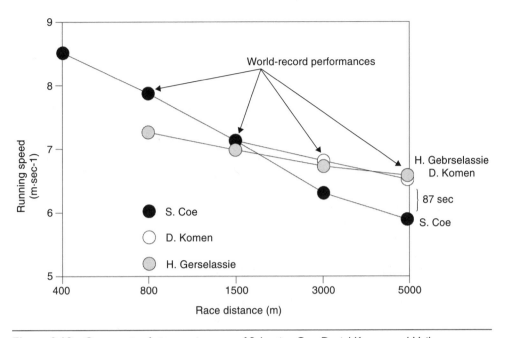

Figure 2.12 Comparative fatigue resistances of Sebastian Coe, Daniel Komen, and Haile Gebrselassie.

time over 1 mile is about 1 s faster than that of the former 800-m world record holder, Sebastian Coe. But at 5000 m, Komen's best performance is 83 seconds, or 10%, faster than Coe's, indicating that Komen's success is due to an unusual combination of world-class speed over 800 to 1500 m allied to a degree of fatigue resistance previously unmatched by any runner in the history of this sport and equaled only by that of the Ethiopian runner, Haile Gebrselassie (figure 2.12). But the more important determinant of Komen's and Gebrselassie's success in the distance events is their superior fatigue resistance.

This concept of fatigue resistance, including the way in which it can be predicted from performance at different running distances, is described in greater detail in the section of this chapter dealing with the Mercier-Leger-Desjardins nomogram, and its role in the prediction of world running records by Péronnet and Thibault is discussed in chapter 12.

All these findings suggest the following:

1. $\dot{V}O_2$max is an indirect measure of athletic potential because in effect what is measured is the oxygen consumption at the peak achieved work rate or running velocity. In groups of runners who have equal running economy, the runners who reach the highest work rates (the highest running speeds during the $\dot{V}O_2$max test) will also have the highest $\dot{V}O_2$max values and will also be the best runners. But the true predictor of their potential is the peak running velocity or work rate they achieve during the maximal test, not the actual $\dot{V}O_2$max value (Noakes 1988b; Noakes, Myburgh, et al. 1990a; figure 2.9). This, as I have argued, is determined by the maximum coronary blood flow; the efficiency and contractility of the heart, which maximizes the cardiac output at that maximum coronary blood flow; and the efficiency, contractility, and

elasticity of the skeletal muscle that maximizes the workload that can be achieved at that maximum cardiac output.

2. The best predictor of running performance at any longer distance is a running test (time for 10 km or shorter). This is a most important finding as it proves what the best athletes have always known—that a person's state of preparedness for any race longer than 10 km, including marathons and ultramarathons, can be predicted from his or her recent 10-km times. Thus, it is not necessary to test your preparedness for a marathon by running the full distance. This prevents the eccentrically induced muscle damage and prolonged recovery that results from racing distances longer than 25 km.

3. Laboratory testing on the treadmill is not yet as effective in predicting performance as is an actual running test. Although running potential can be predicted to some extent from maximal exercise testing, most especially from the peak achieved workload, the prediction is not particularly accurate as it fails to account for fatigue resistance, which can really only be measured during tests lasting from tens of minutes to hours. For example, such testing might be able to identify a group of runners able to run 42 km in less than 2:14, but it would probably be unable to select either the fastest runner in that group or those runners able to run under 2:07.

In the absence of laboratory tests of fatigue resistance or the identification of the specific brain and muscle factors that determine this characteristic, the best predictors of running performance at any longer distances are athletes' running performances at shorter distances. This is because athletes' individual degrees of fatigue resistance are predictable from the rate at which their performance falls off with increasing distance. Runners whose running speeds at increasingly longer distances fall little, like those of Komen and Gebrselassie, have high fatigue resistance; those whose speeds drop off more steeply have lesser fatigue resistance.

Finally, these findings also indicate that the tables predicting running performance on the basis of a hypothetical $\dot{V}O_2$max (see the following section) are accurate, not because they are based on some unique physiological characteristic but because they predict performance at all distances on the basis of performance at shorter distances. They therefore incorporate the two physiological determinants of running performance—the peak achieved workload and the rate at which the athlete fatigues.

Prediction Tables

Few athletes in the world have ready access to laboratories that are equipped to measure $\dot{V}O_2$max, running economy, maximum work rate (that is, peak treadmill running speed), or the brain and muscle factors that determine fatigue resistance. Thus, the information that we have covered in some detail in the previous pages may be very interesting but, at first glance, may seem to be of little practical value to the average runner. As the best predictor of running performance at any distance, however, is running performance at other shorter distances, it is possible to predict with reasonable accuracy your potential running performances at all distances, without ever entering an exercise laboratory. Five groups of researchers—Davies-Thompson, Daniels-Gilbert, Osler, Gardner-Purdy, and Mercier-Leger-Desjardins—have provided tables that allow prediction of performances at different distances. These tables are discussed in the sections that follow.

Davies-Thompson

It is not possible to run at 100% $\dot{V}O_2$max for more than a few minutes. Thus, it has been found that trained athletes can maintain an average of 94% (range 89% to 100%) of their $\dot{V}O_2$max for a 5-km race, 82% (range 76% to 87%) for the standard 42-km marathon, 67% (range 53% to 76%) for the 85-km London-to-Brighton race, and about 45% for a 24-hour race (C.T.M. Davies and Thompson 1979; see figure 2.13).

It follows, then, that if you know athletes' $\dot{V}O_2$max and their oxygen cost of running (running economy), it is simple to calculate the running speed that those athletes should be able to sustain for a certain period of time and therefore their expected race time at any distance.

If an athlete has a $\dot{V}O_2$max value of 60 ml and can sustain 50% of his or her $\dot{V}O_2$max for 17 hours, then the athlete's average oxygen consumption during that period will be 30 ml O_2 per kg per min. To determine how fast the athlete will be running during that time, we need to know the running speed to which that rate of oxygen uptake corresponds. This can either be measured directly in the laboratory or predicted from the following equation devised by C.T.M. Davies and Thompson (1979):

$$\text{running speed (km/h)} = (\text{oxygen uptake } [\text{ml } O_2 \cdot \text{kg} \cdot \text{min}^{-1}] + 7.736) \div 3.966$$

By substituting an oxygen uptake of 30 ml O_2 per kg per min in the above equation, we can predict that our athlete should be able to sustain a running speed of 9.5 km per hour for 17 hours. To know how far this athlete would run in 17 hours is a simple matter of multiplying the calculated running speed in km per hour (9.5 km per hour) by the running time. The answer is a final distance of 161.8 km.

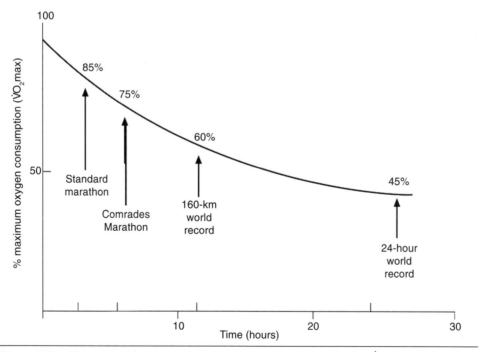

Figure 2.13   The sustainable exercise intensity (expressed as a percentage of $\dot{V}O_2$max) falls progressively with increasing exercise duration.

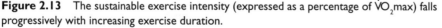

Table 2.3   Predicted equivalent running times (h:min:sec) for different racing distances related to predicted $\dot{V}O_2$ max

Predicted $\dot{V}O_2$max (ml·kg·min)	Distance							
	1500 m	I mile	5 km	8 km	10 km	16 km	21 km	30 km
93.6	(3:50)	(4:07)	10:00	(20:43)	(25:59)	42:16	55:52	01:20:41
89.9	(3:59)	(4:16)	11:00	(21:29)	(26:57)	43:51	57:59	01:23:48
82.7	(4:18)	(4:36)	13:00	(23:12)	29:07	47:26	01:02:46	01:30:49
79.1	(4:28)	(4:48)	14:00	24:11	30:21	49:27	01:05:27	01:34:46
75.5	(4:40)	(5:00)	15:00	25:14	31:43	51:38	01:08:23	01:39:05
71.9	(4:43)	(5:14)	16:00	26:23	33:08	54:02	01:11:55	01:43:49
68.2	(5:06)	(5:29)	17:00	27:39	34:43	64:40	01:15:06	01:49:01
64.6	(5:22)	(5:45)	18:00	29:03	36:28	59:33	01:18:59	01:51:45
61.0	(5:38)	(6:03)	19:00	30:55	38:25	01:02:46	01:23:17	02:01:08
57.4	(5:57)	(6:23)	20:00	32:17	40:34	01:06:20	01:28:04	02:08:15
53.7	(6:18)	(6:46)	21:00	34:12	42:59	01:10:20	01:33:27	02:16:15
50.2	(6:41)	(7:11)	22:00	36:21	45:37	01:14:50	01:39:30	02:25:18
46.5	(7:08)	(7:39)	23:00	38:47	48:44	01:19:57	01:46:24	02:35:37
42.9	(7:38)	(8:12)	24:00	41:34	52:17	01:25:49	01:54:18	02:47:28
39.3	(8:13)	(8:44)	25:00	44:47	56:21	01:32:35	02:03:28	03:01:15
35.7	(8:54)	(9:33)	26:00	(48:32)	1:01:05	01:40:31	02:14:11	03:17:26
32.1	(9:41)	(10:24)	27:00	(52:57)	1:06:41	01:48:54	02:26:55	03:36:42
28.5	(10:39)	(11:25)	28:00	(58:16)	1:13:25	02:01:11	02:42:14	03:58:58
24.8	(11:48)	(12:40)	29:00	(1:04:44)	1:21:37	02:14:59	03:01:00	04:28:33
21.2	(13:15)	(14:13)	30:00	(1:12:48)	(1:31:51)	02:32:14	03:24:29	05:04:22

NOTE: Running times that appear in parentheses seem to be unrealistic. From C.T.M. Davies and Thompson, 1979. © 1979 by Springer-Verlag Heidelberg. Adapted by permission. Calculations provided by J. Affleck-Graves.

Most athletes, however, do not wish to know how far they will run in a certain time. Rather, they wish to know how fast they can run various distances. As the mathematics of this was quite beyond me, I approached mathematician John Affleck-Graves, a marathoner and former professor of business administration at the University of Cape Town. He provided table 2.3, which gives all possible performances over virtually all distances up to 24 hours that any runner would wish to race. As running speeds will not be different for distances close to 90 km, reworking of the data will allow fairly accurate predictions of likely times for both the London-to-

			Distance				24-hour distance
32 km	42 km	50 km	56 km	90 km	100 km	160 km	(km)
01:26:23	01:56:02	02:19:33	02:38:07	04:32:43	05:09:55	09:37:48	309.2
01:29:43	02:00:37	02:25:08	02:44:31	04:44:36	05:23:44	10:07:39	299.1
01:33:20	02:05:34	02:30:45	02:51:28	04:57:33	05:38:51	10:40:28	288.9
01:37:15	02:10:57	02:38:46	02:59:01	05:11:44	05:55:25	11:16:43	278.8
01:41:31	02:16:48	02:44:56	03:07:15	05:27:19	06:13:38	11:56:44	268.6
01:46:09	02:23:12	02:52:46	03:16:17	05:44:30	06:33:48	12:40:58	258.5
01:51:14	02:30:13	03:01:23	03:26:13	06:03:32	06:56:12	13:29:51	248.3
02:03:01	02:46:30	03:21:27	03:49:23	06:48:34	07:49:18	15:22:48	228.0
02:09:53	02:56:02	03:33:13	04:03:01	07:15:22	08:21:01	16:27:09	217.9
02:17:33	03:06:43	03:46:26	04:18:19	07:45:46	08:57:03	17:36:37	207.8
02:25:11	03:18:44	04:01:21	04:35:38	08:20:28	09:38:13	18:50:49	197.6
02:35:36	03:32:24	04:18:19	04:55:23	09:00:22	10:25:31	20:09:14	187.5
02:47:04	03:48:01	04:37:47	05:18:05	09:46:31	11:20:06	21:31:24	177.3
02:59:53	04:06:04	05:00:29	05:44:24	10:40:16	12:23:15	22:56:59	167.2
03:14:47	04:27:07	05:26:41	06:15:15	11:43:07	13:36:17	24:25:56	157.0
03:32:17	04:51:56	05:57:52	06:51:48	12:56:43	15:00:20	25:58:36	146.9
03:53:08	05:21:37	06:35:15	07:35:37	14:22:41	16:36:03	27:35:99	136.7
04:18:20	05:57:35	07:20:33	08:29:49	16:02:12	18:23:32	29:18:55	126.6
04:49:18	06:41:53	08:16:22	09:34:09	17:55:49	20:22:23	31:10:00	116.5
05:04:22	07:37:22	09:26:00	10:55:10	20:03:29	22:32:29	33:12:20	106.3

Brighton race (85 km) and the 100-km race. Distances below 5 km and beyond 24 hours cannot be calculated accurately because the equation used by C.T.M. Davies and Thompson (1979) develops certain mathematical problems at very short and very long time periods.

The practical relevance of this information lies in demonstrating how inborn factors determine what the runner can hope to achieve. Furthermore, the tables provide accurate information on predicting the time in which particular athletes can expect to cover a certain distance on the basis of times they have run for other, shorter distances. The information also helps athletes determine whether their performances at all distances are equivalent or whether they are underperforming at certain distances.

As we have already established, $\dot{V}O_2$max is ultimately limited by hereditary factors, and even with the most intensive training it can be increased by only 5% to 15% in the average runner. (Elite athletes are different and are likely to be "high adapters"; that is, they may increase their $\dot{V}O_2$max by 25% or more in response to intensive training.) This means that the average athlete can only ever hope to achieve the racing performances that fall within a small range of times; perhaps the performances covered by only two or three consecutive rows in table 2.3. Thus, if we take the typical healthy but untrained male who has a $\dot{V}O_2$max value of about 50 (Wyndham et al. 1966), and we train him as we would a world champion, his $\dot{V}O_2$max value might, with luck, increase to about 57 (an upward shift of two columns in table 2.3), giving him a best 5-km time of about 20 minutes. If allowed to race the standard marathon, this highly trained runner would, according to the data in table 2.3, run the race in a solid 3:06:43.

If we were now to have this same runner compete in a 90-km ultramarathon after training every bit as hard as the world's best ultramarathon runners, and if we were to ensure that he ran the race with the same degree of courage and intelligence as those great runners, his predicted race time would be 7:45:46. Even if he did everything right, the average runner could only ever hope to finish some 2:15:00 behind the winner.

And now to add the final insult. According to table 2.3, if the winner of that ultramarathon runs the distance in 5:27:19, he should have a predicted $\dot{V}O_2$max value of 79, a value not very different from that recorded by Bruce Fordyce (see table 2.1). If someone with this $\dot{V}O_2$max value were to run the race without any training whatsoever, so that he would be able to maintain about 50% $\dot{V}O_2$max for the race (equivalent to an oxygen cost of 39.5 ml O_2 per kg per min), he would still complete the distance in 7:49:48, or just 4 minutes behind our highly trained, intensely motivated average runner.

Examples that confirm the general accuracy of this calculation do in fact exist. Fordyce's time in his first ultramarathon, for which he trained only moderately, was 6:45:00, equivalent to an effort of about 57% $\dot{V}O_2$max.

As the famous Swedish physiologist Per-Olaf Åstrand said, "If you want to be a world beater then you must choose your parents carefully" (cited in Wyndham et al. 1969). Of course, what tends to happen is that most runners do not accept this. They assume that the rapid improvements they make when they start training will continue forever; that with training they too will become world champions. But what happens is that, after a year or so of running, they enter the area of diminishing returns. At first, performance and fitness improve dramatically, so that for a small input of, say, 60 km of training a week, our trained average runner with a $\dot{V}O_2$max value of 57 might be able to run the standard 42-km marathon at 50% to 60% of his $\dot{V}O_2$max. This would give him a finishing time of 3:58:48. But to improve his fitness by another 26% so that he could run his personal record of 3:06:43, he might have to treble his training mileage up to 160 to 180 km per week. While this training load might be acceptable for the potential champion looking to cut seconds off his time, for the average runner it is likely only to result in injury, illness, overtraining, family disharmony, and poor racing form. It will, of course, never allow him to run faster than his 3:06:43 threshold. Table 2.3 enables runners to predict whether they will ever be able to complete longer-distance races before the cutoff times. Thus, to finish a standard marathon in under 4:30:00, you must be able to run 5 km in about 25 minutes; to complete a 90-km ultramarathon in under 11 hours, you will need a slightly faster best 5-km time of about 24 minutes.

Daniels-Gilbert

Using the same principles—namely, that the percentage $\dot{V}O_2$max that can be sustained falls predictably with running time (see figure 2.13)—J. Daniels and Gilbert (1979) calculated predicted running times for virtually every possible racing distance on the track in metric or imperial measures and for distances on the road from the half-marathon to 50 km. Each performance time on each list was related to a reference $\dot{V}O_2$max value, as we did for the Davies-Thompson data in table 2.3. Table 2.4 gives all the distances also listed by Davies and Thompson up to 56 km. Distances for which Daniels and Gilbert have not provided data have been calculated from the equations they provided.

Comparing the Daniels-Gilbert data with those of Davies and Thompson shows a relatively good correspondence between their respective predicted marathon times for 5-km times in the range 14 to 22 minutes. Outside these values, however, the results are quite different, with the data of Thompson and Davies predicting marathon times that are considerably slower than are those of Daniels and Gilbert.

The reason for this is that the equations that these two groups of researchers derived for the percentage $\dot{V}O_2$max that can be sustained for running times shorter than one hour and for those longer than four hours are quite different. This would happen if the populations of runners studied by the two groups were different.

The Daniels-Gilbert data can also be used to give reference $\dot{V}O_2$max values for all world records, for both men and women. Table 2.5 compares the relative quality of each world record, and it also compares the performances of men and women. The data in table 2.5 show that the reference $\dot{V}O_2$max value for both men's and women's records falls with distance, which could indicate that athletes do not run as hard in the longer road races as they do in the shorter track races. Alternatively, it seems likely that environmental factors such as running gradients, wind, and heat could also be important factors explaining the relatively poorer performance over longer distances. Similarly, internal physiological factors in the heart or muscles may explain this difference.

It is of interest that the $\dot{V}O_2$max reference values for the women's records are at least nine points lower than those of the men at all distances. This suggests that until women can improve their performances over the shorter distances, they will not match men over the longer distances. This disproves a popular myth that women's and men's running performances at all distances will one day be equal (Whipp and Ward 1992; see chapter 12). Some women, it seems, may indeed have an athletic advantage, but if that exists, it occurs only at the very longest running distances and perhaps only in subelite women compared with subelite men.

Osler

Tom Osler, the veteran runner/mathematician/writer of whom we will hear much in chapters 6 and 7, supplied a graph in *The Serious Runner's Handbook* (1978) showing equivalent effort performances in races of distances from 1 mile to the marathon. Osler does not mention how he arrived at these data. Nevertheless, it is interesting to compare his data with those of the other researchers cited. Table 2.6 shows that Osler's data compare quite accurately with those of Davies and Thompson and Daniels and Gilbert, at least in the range of 5-km times between 12 and 22 minutes. Thereafter, the data are remarkably close to those of Daniels and Gilbert.

Table 2.4   Predicted equivalent running times (h:min:sec) for different racing distances related to a reference VO₂max

Reference VO₂max (ml·kg·min)	Distance					
	1500 m	1 mile	5 km	8 km	10 km	16 km
112.1	2:40	2:53	10:00	16:29	20:52	34:25
100.2	2:56	3:10	11:00	18:07	22:55	37:47
90.5	3:12	3:27	12:00	19:44	24:57	41:10
82.4	3:28	3:45	13:00	21:22	27:01	44:35
75.5	3:44	4:02	14:00	23:00	29:04	48:01
69.7	4:01	4:20	15:00	24:38	31:08	51:28
64.6	4:17	4:38	16:00	26:16	33:12	54:56
60.2	4:34	4:56	17:00	27:54	35:17	58:25
56.3	4:51	5:14	18:00	29:33	37:21	01:01:54
52.8	5:08	5:33	19:00	31:11	39:26	01:05:23
49.7	5:25	5:51	20:00	32:49	41:31	01:08:53
47.0	5:42	6:09	21:00	34:28	43:36	01:12:22
44.5	5:59	6:28	22:00	36:06	45:41	01:15:52
42.2	6:16	6:46	23:00	37:44	47:46	01:19:21
40.1	6:33	7:05	24:00	39:22	49:51	01:23:50
38.3	6:51	7:24	25:00	41:00	51:56	01:26:18
36.5	7:08	7:42	26:00	42:38	54:00	01:29:46
35.0	7:25	8:01	27:00	44:16	56:04	01:33:12
33.5	7:42	8:19	28:00	45:53	58:08	01:36:38
32.2	7:59	8:37	29:00	47:30	01:00:12	01:40:14
30.9	8:16	8:56	30:00	49:07	01:02:15	01:43:28

NOTE: Based on equations derived from data in J. Daniels and Gilbert, (1979), © 1979 by J. Daniels and J.R. Gilbert. The exact data can be derived from *Oxygen Power*. The book can be purchased by writing to Jack Daniels, SUNY Cortland, Box 2000 Park Center, Cortland, NY 13045.

Gardner-Purdy

James Gardner and Gerry Purdy produced a table for the common racing distances from 100 m to 80 km (1970; table 2.7). What is particularly interesting about this table is that it relates performance times at the sprint distances to those at the ultradistances. Again, my hunch is that performance in distance races in trained

| Distance | | | | | |
21 km	30 km	32 km	42 km	50 km	56 km
45:46	01:06:31	01:11:15	01:35:44	01:54:44	02:09:24
50:17	01:13:08	01:18:21	01:45:17	02:06:08	02:22:14
54:50	01:19:49	01:25:31	01:54:53	02:17:35	02:35:05
59:25	01:26:32	01:32:42	02:04:31	02:29:02	02:47:55
01:04:02	01:33:16	01:39:56	02:14:09	02:40:29	03:00:44
01:08:40	01:40:02	01:47:10	02:23:47	02:51:55	03:13:31
01:13:19	01:46:48	01:54:25	02:33:25	03:03:19	03:26:16
01:17:58	01:53:35	02:01:39	02:43:01	03:14:40	03:38:57
01:22:38	02:00:21	02:08:54	02:52:34	03:25:58	03:51:34
01:27:19	02:07:06	02:16:07	03:02:06	03:37:13	04:04:08
01:31:59	02:13:51	02:23:19	03:11:35	03:48:24	04:16:37
01:36:36	02:20:34	02:30:29	03:21:00	03:59:32	04:29:01
01:41:18	02:27:15	02:37:37	03:30:23	04:10:35	04:41:21
01:45:57	02:33:54	02:44:43	03:39:42	04:21:34	04:53:36
01:50:34	02:40:32	02:51:47	03:48:57	04:32:28	05:05:47
01:55:11	02:47:07	02:58:48	03:58:08	04:43:18	05:17:21
01:59:46	02:53:39	03:05:46	04:07:16	04:54:03	05:29:52
02:04:20	03:00:09	03:12:42	04:16:19	05:04:44	05:41:47
02:08:53	03:06:37	03:19:34	04:25:19	05:15:09	05:53:37
02:13:24	03:13:01	03:26:24	04:34:14	05:25:51	06:05:22
02:17:53	03:19:23	03:33:10	04:43:06	05:36:17	06:17:01

distance runners is related to their sprint times, which echoes Arthur Lydiard's and Gordon Pirie's opinions.

Trained sprinters cannot use this table to predict how well they would do in the distance races, however, because their hearts, brains, and muscles will not have the same resistance to fatigue as those of the trained distance runners on whose performances these tables are based. Although this could be due to training-induced differences, it is far more likely to be due to the fact that sprinters are born with a predominance of those Type II (FT) muscle fibers that lack the capacity to become greatly fatigue resistant, even with appropriate endurance training, or that their central governors cannot be trained for endurance exercise, perhaps because their hearts have lower peak coronary blood flows.

Table 2.5 Relative performance ratings of men's and women's world records at distances from 0.8 to 42 km				
Distance (km)	Time		Reference $\dot{V}O_2$max (ml·kg⁻¹·min⁻¹)	
	Male	Female	Male	Female
0.8	01:41.11 Kipketer, 1997	01:53.28 Kratochivilova, 1983	82.4	72.8
1.5	03:25.00 El Guerrouj, 1998	03:50.46 Qu Yunxia, 1993	83.8	73.1
1.6 (mile)	03:43.13 El Guerrouj, 1999	04:12.56 Masterkova, 1996	83.4	72.2
2	04:44.79 El Guerrouj, 1999	05:25.36 O'Sullivan, 1994	82.7	70.9
3	07:20.67 Komen, 1996	08:06.11 Wang Junxia, 1993	83.5	74.5
5	12:39.36 Gebrselassie, 1998	14:28.09 Jian Bo, 1997	84.7	72.5
10	26:22.75 Gebrselassie, 1998	29:31.78 Wang Junxia, 1993	84.8	74.2
15	00:42:13 Tergat, 1994	46:47 Meyer, 1991	80.4	71.0
21.1	00:59:17 Tergat 1988	66:44 Meyer, 1999	82.6	71.9
25	01:13:55.8 Seko, 1981	01:29:29.2 Szabo, 1988	78.8	63.3
30	01:29:18.8 Seko, 1981	01:47:05.6 Szabo, 1988	79.4	64.4
42.2	02:05:42 Khannouchi, 1999	02:18:47 Ndereba, 2001	81.5	72.6

NOTE: Data current to March 2001.

Mercier-Leger-Desjardins

In 1986, Mercier et al. of the University of Montreal, Canada, developed a nomogram (see figure 2.14) to predict equivalent running performances at different distances. The nomogram is based on equations relating percentage $\dot{V}O_2$max to duration of running (Leger, Mercier, et al. 1984). Their predictions did not differ much from those of Gardner and Purdy in table 2.7, but the beauty of the nomogram is that it is able to predict performances from any best time for the common running distances. Tables 2.3, 2.4, 2.6, and 2.7 are only able to predict performances for a limited range of times at the different running distances.

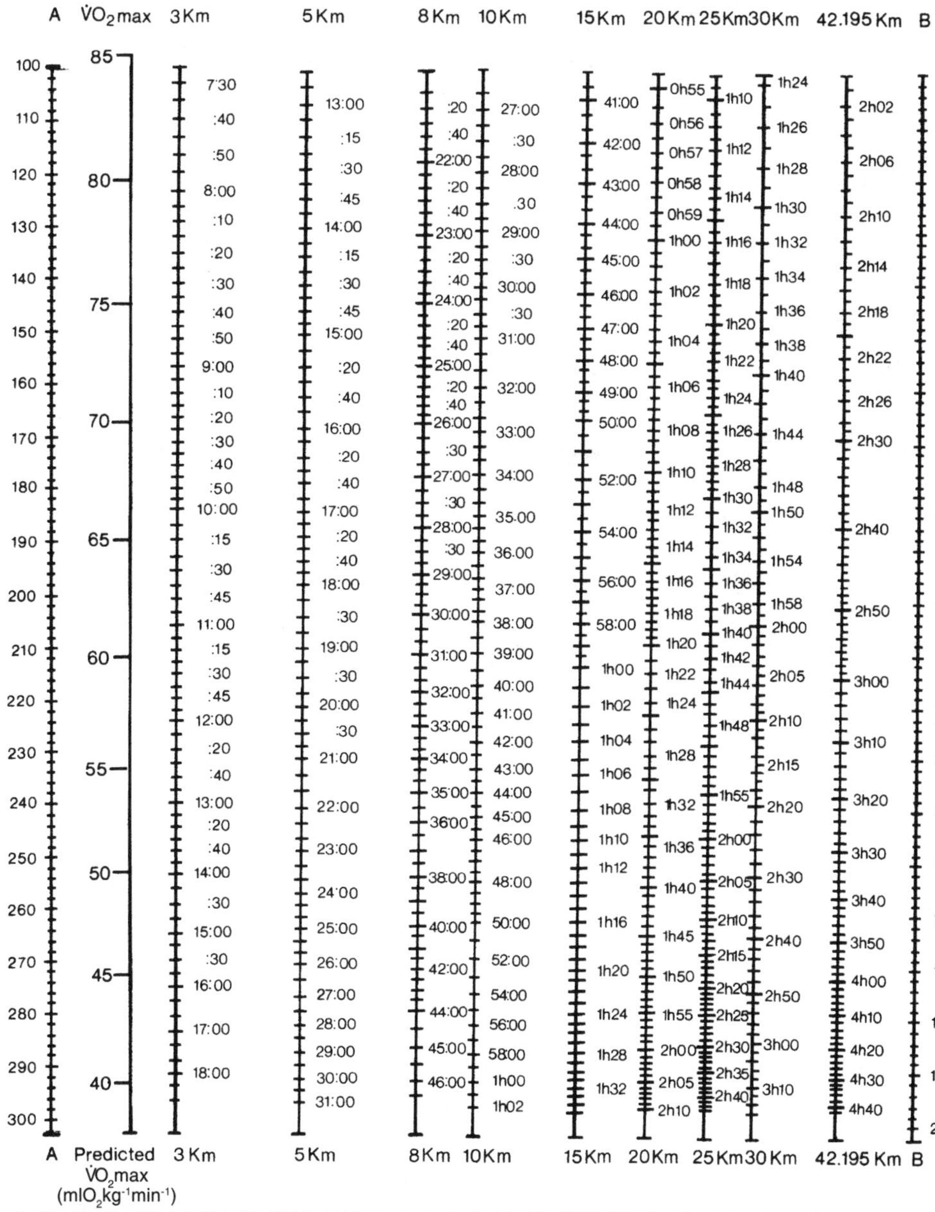

Figure 2.14 The Mercier-Leger-Desjardins (1986) nomogram predicting running performance at distances from 3 to 42 km. For details on how to use the nomogram, refer to pages 76 and 77.

From Mercier et al. 1986.

Reprinted with permission.

Table 2.6   Predicted equivalent running times (h:min:sec) for different racing distances related to a performance rating

Performance Rating*	Distance		
	1 mile	5 km	8 km
2000	3:34	12:00	20:53
1960	3:54	13:00	22:22
1910	4:18	14:00	24:02
1870	4:36	15:00	25:46
1830	4:54	16:00	27:26
1780	5:17	17:00	29:10
1740	5:34	18:00	30:44
1690	5:57	19:00	32:19
1650	6:15	20:00	34:08
1600	6:38	21:00	35:48
1560	6:55	22:00	37:27
1510	7:19	23:00	39:06
1470	7:37	24:00	40:46
1420	7:50	25:00	42:25
1380	8:07	26:00	44:05
1330	8:31	27:00	45;44
1290	8:49	28:00	47:24
1240	9:12	29:00	49:03
1200	9:29	30:00	50:42

NOTE: From Osler (1978, p. 169). © 1978 by T. Osler. Adapted by permission.

To predict $\dot{V}O_2max$, performance at other distances, and level of fitness on the basis of best running times at two other distances, use the following simple technique:

1. Place a ruler connecting the two measured racing performances and read off the times for equivalent performances at other racing distances along the edge of the ruler.

2. Read estimated $\dot{V}O_2max$ values off the scale relating $\dot{V}O_2max$ to 3-km running time (the second column on the left).

Distance				
10 km	16 km	21.1 km	32 km	42 km
26:43	44:25	59:53	01:33:28	02:05:52
28:35	47:24	01:03:49	01:39:24	02:13:44
30:39	50:42	01:08:11	01:46:03	02:22:29
32:50	54:11	01:12:46	01:53:01	02:31:39
34:54	57:30	01:17:08	01:59:38	02:40:24
37:05	01:00:59	01:21:44	02:06:36	02:49:35
39:03	01:04:08	01:25:53	02:12:54	02:57:53
41:01	01:07:17	01:30:02	02:19:12	03:06:11
43:18	01:10:55	01:34:50	02:26:29	03:15:48
45:22	01:14:14	01:39:13	02:33:07	03:24:32
47:26	01:17:33	01:43:35	02:39:45	03:33:17
49:30	01:20:52	01:47;57	02:46:22	03:42:01
51:35	01:24:11	01:52:19	02:53:00	03:50:46
53:39	01:27:30	01:56:42	02:59:38	03:59:30
55:43	01:30:48	02:01:04	03:06:15	04:08:15
57:47	01:34:07	02:05:26	03:12:53	04:17:00
59:52	01:37:26	02:09:48	03:19:31	04:25:44
01:01:56	01:40:45	02:14:19	03:26:08	04:34:28
01:04:00	01:44:04	02:18:33	03:32:46	04:43:13

*The performance rating is calculated as the year in which world records for the listed distance will equal the times given.

3. Read the values in column A (extreme left-hand side of the nomogram) and column B (extreme right-hand side of the nomogram) corresponding to the points at which the columns are crossed by the line describing the athlete's performances at the different distances. Subtract the value in column B from that in column A to determine a fitness level on a scale of −100 to +100. A value of 100 corresponds to a horizontal line joining performances at 3 and 42 km and is equivalent to the performances of the world's best athletes.

Table 2.7 Predicted equivalent running times (h:min:sec) for different racing distances related to a performance rating						
Performance rating*	Distance (m)				Distance (km)	
	100	200	400	800	1.6	5
1080	10.42	21.0	44.1	1:41.3	3:45.1	13:00
950	10.42	21.0	47.0	1:48.5	4:01.7	14:00
840	10.95	22.1	49.8	1:55.3	4:17.8	15:00
740	11.47	23.2	52.6	2:02.4	4:34.3	16:00
650	11.99	24.4	55.4	2:09.5	4:51.2	17:00
570	12.50	25.4	58.1	2:16.6	5:08.0	18:00
500	12.97	26.5	1:00.8	2:23.5	5:24.3	19:00
440	13.41	27.4	1:03.3	2:29.9	5:39.8	20:00
380	13.88	28.4	1:05.9	2:37.0	5:56.9	21:00
330	14.30	29.3	1:08.3	2:43.4	6:12.4	22:00
280	14.75	30.3	1:10.9	2:50.3	6:29.4	23:00
240	15.13	31.1	1:13.2	2:56.3	6:44.2	24:00
200	15.52	32.0	1:15.5	3:02.8	7:00.1	25:00
170	15.83	32.7	1:17.4	3:07.9	7:12.8	26:00
130	16.26	33.7	1:20.1	3:15.3	7:31.1	27:00
100	16.60	34.4	1:22.2	3:21.2	7:45.9	28:00
70	16.96	35.2	1:24.2	3:27.4	8:01.7	29:00
40	17.34	36.0	1:26.7	3:34.1	8:18.5	30:00

NOTE: From J.B. Gardner and J.G. Purdy. © 1970 by Tafnews Press. Selected data adapted by permission.
*Performance rating is an arbitrary scale indicating the relative quality of different performances; the higher the rating, the better the performance.

Using the Tables to Predict Performance

Despite having tarnished the credibility of the $\dot{V}O_2$max as a predictor of athletic performance, I have used the data from Davies and Thompson; Daniels and Gilbert; and Mercier, Leger, and Desjardins to make the strongest possible case that $\dot{V}O_2$max can predict performance accurately. How can this anomaly be explained? What these tables actually show is that performance at one distance can predict performance at another distance. Indeed, the nomogram of Mercier et al. (1986) is based entirely on tests of running performances at different distances (Leger, Mercier, et al. 1984). In addition, these tables provide a physiological explanation for this, namely, that there is a predictable relationship—a measure of each individual athlete's fatigue resistance—describing the percentage $\dot{V}O_2$max or, more accurately, the percentage of peak running speed that can be sustained for a given running time. Note that figure 2.13 is based on an average fatigue resistance for the popula-

			Distance (km)			
8	**10**	**16**	**32**	**42.2**	**50**	**80**
21:31.7	27:14	45:07	01:34:24	02:06:18	02:33:04	04:16:47
23:11.4	29:21	48:39	01:41:53	02:16:22	02:45:04	04:37:34
24:48.6	31:25	52:06	01:49:12	02:26:13	02:57:19	04:57:59
26:29.6	33:34	55:41	01:56:50	02:36:30	03:09:50	05:19:19
28:13.0	35:45	59:22	02:04:41	02:47:06	03:22:45	05:41:20
29:56.8	37:57	01:03:04	02:12:36	02:57:46	03:35:46	06:03:36
31:38.7	40:06	01:06:43	02:20:24	03:08:17	03:48:38	06:26:38
33:15.7	42:10	01:10:11	02:27:51	03:18:21	04:00:56	06:46:44
35:22.2	44:28	01:14:03	02:36:08	03:29:34	04:14:38	07:10:18
36:42.0	46:34	01:17:36	02:43:47	03:39:55	04:27:10	07:32:07
38:30.6	48:53	01:21:31	02:52:13	03:51:24	04:41:19	07:56:17
40:05.5	50:53	01:24:56	02:59:37	04:01:23	04:53:36	08:17:32
41:48.4	53:04	01:28:40	03:07:41	04:12:20	05:07:02	08:40:48
43:11.7	54:50	01:31:41	03:14:14	04:21:13	05:17:56	08:59:43
45:11.6	57:25	01:36:03	03:23:42	04:34:05	05:33:44	09:27;11
46:49.2	59:29	01:39:36	03:31:25	04:44:36	05:46:40	09:49:42
48:33.9	61:43	01:43:25	03:39:46	04:55:57	06:00:37	10:14:04
50:26.9	64:08	01:47:33	03:48:47	05:08:15	06:15:45	10:40:32

*Performance rating is an arbitrary scale indicating the relative quality of different performances; the higher the rating, the better the performance.

tions of runners evaluated in that study. The advantage of the nomogram in figure 2.14 is that it enables athletes to calculate their own individual degrees of fatigue resistance and to determine how that improves with training and, conversely, deteriorates with detraining or illness. Athletes who know their own fatigue resistance are better able to predict their performance in long-distance races.

The actual $\dot{V}O_2$max values in tables 2.3 and 2.4 and in figure 2.14 are completely arbitrary, however, and relate only to runners whose economy falls within the normal range of runners tested in those particular studies. Problems arise when the economy of the runner differs from what was predicted. Thus, if we take the examples of Derek Clayton and Craig Virgin from table 2.1, we would predict using table 2.4 that, based on Clayton's $\dot{V}O_2$max value of 69.7, his best marathon time would be 2:23:47, whereas Virgin, with a $\dot{V}O_2$max value of 81.1, would be expected to run the marathon in about 2:04:31. Both these predictions are wrong because the two runners have different running economies that differ greatly from the average (see figure 2.8). Clayton's marathon time (2:08:34) is under the predicted time because he is more economical than the average runner, whereas Virgin's (2:10:26) time is over the predicted time because he is less economical than the average runner.

Thus, there is no point in attempting to predict marathon performance on the basis of a $\dot{V}O_2$max value that does not take the runner's economy into account. Performance in shorter-distance races, particularly at 10 or 21 km, remains the best predictor. In our studies (Noakes, Myburgh, et al. 1990b), we found that a 42-km marathon time could be predicted from either 10-km or 21-km time, using the following equations:

$$\text{time for 42 km (min)} = 5.48 \times \text{10-km time (min)} - 28.00 \text{ (min)}$$

$$\text{time for 42 km (min)} = 2.11 \times \text{21-km time (min)}$$

The equation using the 21-km time was found to be the more accurate predictor.

It is important to remember that the $\dot{V}O_2$max measures the total oxygen-using capacity of all the skeletal muscle mitochondria that are active during maximum exercise. Yet there are additional sources of energy production for which oxygen is not needed, which are not measured by $\dot{V}O_2$max testing. These sources comprise "oxygen-independent" ATP production by glycolysis. These biochemical pathways, which are important during all short-term exercise lasting up to about 45 s, will be discussed in chapter 3. At present, the capacity of these oxygen-independent pathways for energy production is best measured in the field rather than in the laboratory. It makes little sense to devise a laboratory-based measure of sprinting ability, when a time-trial on a 100-m track will give the answers.

CHANGES WITH AGING

A sad reality is that we all age. Yet the good news is that people who do a moderate amount of running age better than people who do not exercise. We need to understand how the body ages, however, so that we can optimize our training at all ages. Logically, we cannot maintain either the intensity or the volume of training that we are capable of doing at age 20 when we reach age 60 or even 70.

Much of the research into bodily changes that occur with aging has focused on age-related changes in $\dot{V}O_2$max, which, according to the Cardiovascular/Anaerobic Model, predicts that it is changes in cardiac function and oxygen-transport capacity that determine how aging affects running performance. Other factors such as changes in the mechanical function of muscle (the Biomechanical Model) or in the ability to recruit as much muscle during exercise as we age (the Integrated Neuromuscular Recruitment Model) are equally important.

Reduction in $\dot{V}O_2$max

Earlier in this chapter we reviewed the evidence that the $\dot{V}O_2$max falls with age, but we did not quantify either the extent of that reduction or the extent to which that reduction may be prevented by continued training for life. We also did not allude to any of the factors that might explain why this reduction occurs.

Figure 2.15 shows the average changes in $\dot{V}O_2$max that occur with age in athletes and sedentary subjects (Marti and Howald 1990). The annual rate of decline in the $\dot{V}O_2$max is actually greater (0.5 versus 0.4 ml per kg per min per year) in the active

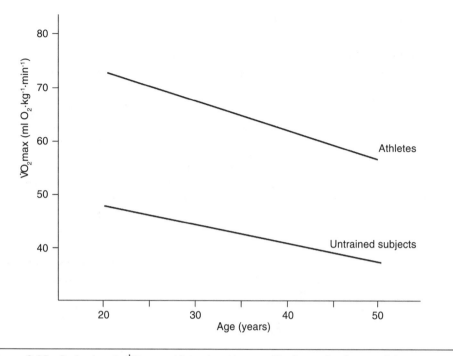

Figure 2.15 Reductions in V̇O₂max with age in athletes and in those who do no training.

group than in the sedentary group simply because the active group starts with a much higher V̇O₂max value at age 20 (72 versus 48). But, when expressed as a percentage change per decade, the fall is about half as great in the group that continues to train than in the sedentary group (approximately 5% versus 10% per decade, respectively [Marti and Howald 1990; M.A. Rogers, Hagberg, et al. 1990; Trappe et al. 1996]). Not all studies, however, conclude that training reduces the age-related decline in V̇O₂max (T.M. Wilson and Tanaka 2000).

Proponents of the Cardiovascular/Anaerobic Model assert that this age-related fall in V̇O₂max is explained by age-related changes in the heart. They ascribe the fall to an inability of the heart to reach the same high maximum heart rates of which it was previously capable. If this model is correct, then peak blood lactate levels at exhaustion must be the same regardless of age, since it is the elevated muscle and blood lactate concentrations that act to constrain the muscles' function, causing exhaustion during maximal exercise. Evidence of a "lactate paradox" with aging— that is, lower peak blood lactate concentrations at exhaustion in older compared to younger runners, analogous to the lactate paradox at altitude—would surely indicate that something other than lactate constrains the maximum exercise of aging athletes.

Those who, like myself, believe that a central governor and not an elevated muscle lactate concentration determines exhaustion during maximum exercise would propose that the age-related fall in V̇O₂max could have at least four components, according to the concept developed in figure 2.7:

1. A reduced maximum blood flow to the heart, perhaps related to a reduced capacity of the coronary blood vessels to dilate or else to an inevitable coronary atherosclerosis that develops in most runners as they age.

2. A reduced myocardial contractility; as a result of these two changes (1 and 2), the maximum allowable cardiac output that can be achieved without the development of myocardial ischemia will fall with age.

3. A decrease in the permissible mass of skeletal muscle that the central governor will allow to be recruited during maximum exercise, as the maximum blood and oxygen supply to the heart fall with age.

4. A possible reduction in the skeletal muscle contractility or muscle quality (strength per unit of muscle), similar to that of the heart (Lindle et al. 1997).

As a result of these two additional changes noted in number 4 above, less muscle of a poorer quality will be recruited during exercise so that the peak work rate will also fall. Since older athletes are unable to achieve the same peak work rate as when they were younger, the $\dot{V}O_2$max will fall in proportion to the smaller muscle mass that can be recruited during maximum exercise and the age-related fall in the contractile capacity of that muscle.

Regardless of whether the heart's function itself is altered by aging and whether this explains the age-related fall in $\dot{V}O_2$max, there is good evidence to suggest that regulation of circulation alters with age. Thus, leg blood flow at any absolute workload is reduced with aging (Proctor et al. 1998), as is blood flow to the skin during heating (Minson et al. 1998).

Muscular Components

Fleg and Lakatta (1988) ascribe the fall in $\dot{V}O_2$max with age to the progressive decline in muscle mass and the contractile ability of aging muscles. In fact, one of the best correlates of the fall in $\dot{V}O_2$max with age is the age-related reduction in muscle mass (Fleg and Lakatta 1988). Muscle undergoes specific and, in some cases, profound changes with aging (Jakobsson et al. 1990; M.A. Rodgers and Evans 1993; F.W. Booth et al. 1994; S.V. Brooks and Faulkner 1994).

In humans, the deterioration of skeletal muscle with age begins between the ages of 50 and 60 and is characterized by the following (F.W. Booth et al. 1994):

- Muscle strength is relatively well maintained until age 50, whereafter there is a 15% loss of muscle strength per decade up until age 70. Between 70 and 80, a further 30% of muscle strength is lost.

- Total muscle mass peaks at about 24 years of age and falls by about 10% by age 50. Thereafter, the loss of muscle accelerates so that another 30% of muscle mass is lost by the age of 80.

- This muscle loss is due to an equivalent loss of both Type I and Type II muscle fibers, but whereas the surviving Type I fibers retain their normal size, the remaining Type II fibers are smaller than their peak adult size.

- The number of motor nerve cells in the spinal cord—the anterior or ventral horn cells—falls after age 60, again by about 10% per decade. Loss of those cells causes a loss of all the muscle fibers that each anterior horn cell innervates unless these muscle fibers are reinnervated by nerves supplying adjacent muscle fibers.

Whereas the different muscle fibers are randomly distributed in healthy skeletal muscle, fiber grouping occurs with aging and disease (figure 2.16). In fiber group-

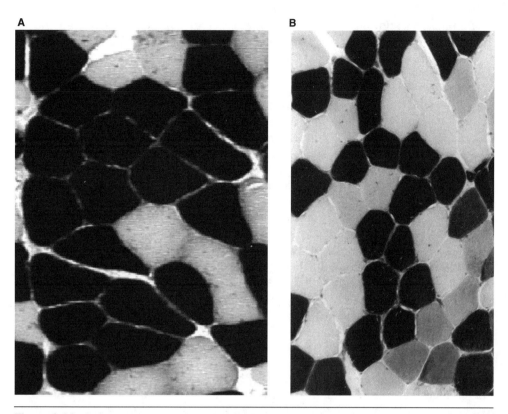

Figure 2.16   Light microscopic picture showing fiber grouping in diseased skeletal muscle (A) compared to skeletal muscle fibers from a healthy athlete (B).

Histological slides prepared by Ms. Liesl Grobler, MRC/UCT Research Unit for Exercise Science and Sports Medicine.

ing, fibers of the same type are found in clumps throughout the muscle. This indicates that reinnervation from adjacent muscle fibers has occurred. This, in turn, implies that there has been a loss of anterior horn cells with reinnervation coming from nerves supplied by anterior horn cells that continue to survive.

The oxidative capacity of skeletal muscle falls with age (Houmard, Weidner, et al. 1998) but is reversible with training (Berthon, Freyssenet, et al. 1995; Coggan, Spina, et al. 1992). The extent of all these changes is not inevitable, however, and can be reduced by training after age 50 (Fiatarone et al. 1990; Klitgaard et al. 1990; M.A. Rodgers and Evans 1993).

Body Composition

Another factor causing a reduction in $\dot{V}O_2$max with age is a change in body fat content. Regular training, however, can reduce the increase in body fat content with age (Marti and Howald 1990; Horber et al. 1996). In one study, Marti and Howald (1990) followed a group of champion Swiss runners over a 15-year period—from age 27 to 42. The runners followed one of three patterns. A total of 19% remained highly active and actually increased their volume of training from 104 to 112 km per week between ages 25 and 40. The majority (48%) reduced their training volume to about 50 km per week. The third group (33%) stopped running.

The important finding was that only the active groups remained within 1 kg of the weight they carried when they were competitive. The sedentary group gained about 9 kg in weight (mainly fat), representing an 11% increase in body weight. When changes in $\dot{V}O_2$max were related to changes in body composition, it was found that about 50% of the variance in the $\dot{V}O_2$max of the still-active runners, and 40% of the variance in those who had stopped running, could be explained by changes in body fat content. What these authors discovered was the (possibly obvious) point that changes in body fat content with age have an important effect on the $\dot{V}O_2$max. $\dot{V}O_2$max can still fall in those athletes whose body weight and body fat content do not change with age, however (M.A. Rogers, Hagberg, et al. 1990). Hence, even the avoidance of weight gain with age will not prevent an outright age-related fall in $\dot{V}O_2$max.

One additional benefit of preventing any age-related rise in body fat content is that this increase is associated with, and possibly causes unfavorable changes in, blood fat concentrations, in particular increases in serum LDL-cholesterol concentrations and a reduction in HDL-cholesterol concentrations (Marti, Knobloch, et al. 1991) with development of a less favorable HDL-cholesterol to total cholesterol ratio. This would indicate an increased propensity to develop heart disease.

Training Changes

A fourth factor explaining the fall in $\dot{V}O_2$max with age is the reduction in the volume and the intensity of training that occurs with age. Marti and Howald (1990) showed that changes in training volume and training intensity accounted for 28% and 35% respectively of the variance in $\dot{V}O_2$max with age in their runners. This is not an independent variable as the fall in training intensity would be an expected result of changes in cardiac and skeletal muscle function. The change in the training volume would result from the inability to recover as rapidly after each training session.

Hence, the fall in $\dot{V}O_2$max with age is the result of age-related changes in skeletal muscle, the heart, and body composition (especially a reduction in lean body mass and an increase in body fat content) and a reduction in training volume and intensity. Thus, the rate at which $\dot{V}O_2$max falls can be reduced by maintaining training volume and trying to prevent or limit any change in body composition, especially the increase in body fat content. Sounding a cautionary note, P.T. Williams (1997) asserts that achieving those goals alone is detrimental as some deterioration in function is inevitable, even in athletes who are able to train the most. I also suspect that the rate of deterioration in these variables and the ability to maintain higher volumes of training with age are probably genetically linked. Athletes whose skeletal muscles are able to sustain higher training volumes may also be genetically programmed to age less rapidly in their other organs. Training at an older age thus selects out those who are already advantaged; their training may then further delay the age-related fall in their performance capacity.

Is there any benefit in reducing the rate of fall of $\dot{V}O_2$max with age? F.W. Booth (1989) has suggested that the rate of fall of $\dot{V}O_2$max with age can be used to predict longevity. He proposes that life must terminate when the declining $\dot{V}O_2$max finally reaches the basal metabolic rate (3 ml per kg per min). Figure 2.17 shows that three different studies indicate that athletes with $\dot{V}O_2$max values of 50 to 60 ml per kg per min at the age of 20 would, on the basis of this hypothesis, be predicted to

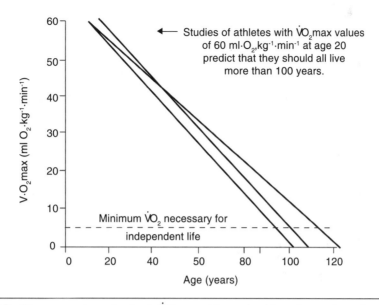

Figure 2.17 The progressive reduction in $\dot{V}O_2$max with age should predict maximum longevity, according to Booth's Theory.

live for 100 to 125 years, provided they maintained their physical activity so that their rate of decline in $\dot{V}O_2$max remained constant. Of course, the reason few athletes ever achieve such longevity is that disease intervenes and their longevity is somewhat less than predicted in Booth's optimistic hypothesis.

Capacity to Absorb Landing Forces

In chapter 12, I review the studies that show that running performance falls with age. For now, suffice it to say that the affect of age on running performance is greater in the marathons and ultramarathons than in distances of 10 km or less. This reality became very clear to me once I had passed my midthirties: whereas I could still run 10 km between 10% and 15% slower than the times I ran at my peak, even with a modicum of training, my best marathon times, even with substantial training effort, fell by about 30%.

Bill Rodgers, my American marathon idol of the 1970s and 1980s, discovered the same in 1999 when he attempted to set the world marathon record for 50-year-olds in that year's Boston Marathon. He had run 16 km in less than 53:00 in training, so that a marathon time faster than the (then) world age-group record of 2:31:00 seemed entirely possible.

Rodgers retired from that race after the 30-km mark, not because he was undertrained or not sufficiently motivated, but because, in my view, his aging muscles were no longer able to absorb the additional pounding after 30 km. The stiffness and soreness he experienced prevented any realistic attempt at breaking the record.

It is unrealistic to expect the marathon champion from a previous decade to be the champion two to three decades later, the reason being that the damage caused by intensive training and frequent racing in earlier years is not reversible. Indeed, the study by M.I. Lambert and Keytel (2000) showed that the total number of years

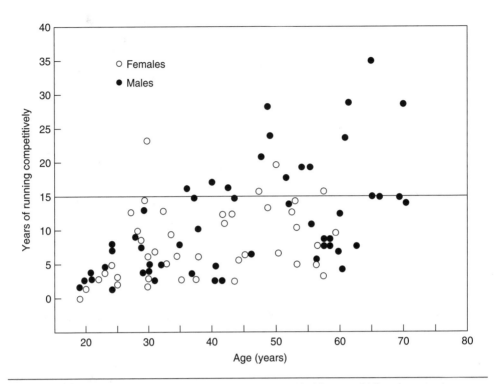

Figure 2.18 Number of years running for age-group record holders in a 56-km ultramarathon. Note that, with the exception of some runners older than 45 years, the majority of records are held by runners who have trained and raced for fewer than 15 years (horizontal line).

From M.I. Lambert and Keytel (2000, p. 30).

that the age-group record holders in the 56-km Two Oceans Marathon had been racing is seldom more than 15 years, even for those who set the records at ages above 60 years (figure 2.18). This implies that peak racing performance, at least in ultramarathons, can only be sustained for up to 15 years. After this, it becomes impossible to maintain the training volume and intensity necessary to be a champion. Thereafter, it is the opportunity for athletes in that same age group but who have raced for fewer years to become the champions.

These suppositions were strengthened by the correspondence I have had over the years with Basil Davis, a unique South African who has run 122 42-km marathons (88 in less than 3 hours), 34 Comrades Marathons (23 in less than 7.5 hours), and 56 other ultramarathons ranging from 50 to 58 km. During this time, he kept meticulous records of his training and his racing performances—possibly a unique record and certainly one that merits analysis (Lambert, Bryer, et al. 2002). In 37 years of running, he trained a total of about 153,944 km and raced 16,604 km.

During this time, his training volume rose progressively from about 1000 km per year at age 26 to peak at approximately 5900 km per year at age 42, whereafter it returned as a mirror image of its rise to a volume of 1000 km per year at age 63 (figure 2.19). The highest training volume undertaken by Davis in any one year was 7600 km at age 33.

What has Davis learned about the human body from this lifetime of ultramarathon racing? He has made three principal observations.

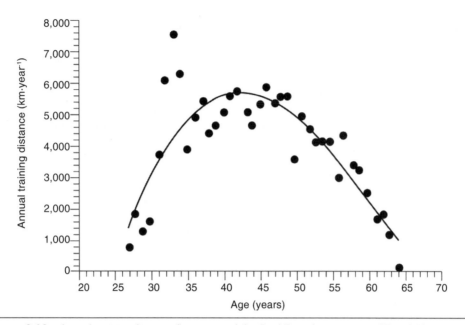

Figure 2.19   Annual training distance (km per year) for Basil Davis between ages 27 and 64.
From M.I. Lambert, Bryer, et al. (2002).

1. After age 50, his body could no longer absorb the high training mileage per-formed in his youth. He became increasingly stiff and tight in his legs and buttocks, especially in the mornings. He writes that he always "seems to be stiff." In training, it takes at least 4 km for him to fall into his normal training pace of about 5:30 per km; his first kilometer may take as much as 7:00. Rodgers also documented his observation that now low-grade muscle stiff-ness "is almost always there" (B. Rodgers 1998).

2. His 42-km marathon performances fell with age as would be expected from the predictions provided in chapter 12. After the age of 45, however, by which time he had been racing marathon and ultramarathon races for more than 20 years, he felt that his performances deteriorated more rapidly than he would have expected. In addition, he noticed that other veteran runners of the same chronological age, who had run for far fewer years than he, were easily able to beat him in races. His impression was that they would not have beaten him had they competed against one another during his younger years when he was training and performing at his peak.

3. In earlier years he could predict his 42-km marathon time to within a minute on the basis of his 10-km time. In his later years, however, this was no longer possible.

Davis's major conclusion was that he had trained and raced too much in his earlier years. "I have definitely noticed that runners who start running later in life (older than 45 years) run better than those who, like me, have been running for 30 years or more." Davis also provides examples to show that the best-aged South African ultramarathon runners are those who started running relatively late in life. The same would seem to apply to international marathon running: The best marathon runners over the age of 40 were also not the best 20-year-old runners since they were not yet competitive.

For example, the fastest 40-year-old marathon runners of all time, New Zealanders John Campbell and Jack Foster, did little running in their twenties and thirties; Foster only started running competitively at the age of 32 (Lenton 1981). Similarly, South African Titus Mamabola, the marathon world record holder for 50-year-olds, was a champion track athlete in his twenties who did no distance running in his thirties and forties.

Subsequent to Davis's own interpretations, Lambert et al. (2002) performed a statistical analysis of Davis's performances at 10, 21, and 42 km, as well as in the up-and-down Comrades Marathons at different ages. They compared the rate of decline in his performance at those distances with the decline with age of the world records at those distances (figure 2.20).

The analysis shows that the rate of decline in Davis's racing speeds over the different distances matched the rate of decline of the world's best until age 40 for 10 and 42 km, until age 47 for 21 km, and until age 48 for 90 km. After those ages, however, Davis's racing speeds declined more steeply than those of the same-aged runners who had established the world's best performances at those distances, exactly as Davis had concluded.

Interestingly, the rate of decline was worse at the shorter distances than at the longer ones. This is somewhat surprising, given that the reason for the rapid decline in running performance in runners who have trained and raced too hard for too long seems to be due to the inability of the muscles to bear weight for many hours.

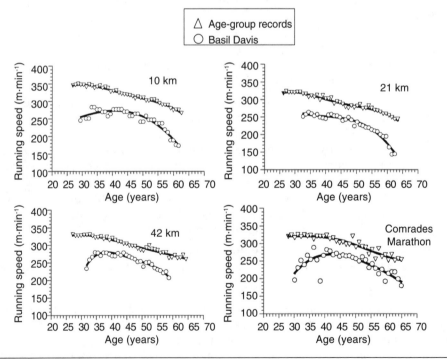

Figure 2.20 The average running speeds at 10, 21, and 42 km and at the Comrades Marathon (90 km) at different ages for Basil Davis (lower curves) compared to United States national age-group records for the shorter distances and the Comrades Marathon age-group records (upper curves).

A possible answer might be that muscles may lose the resilience needed to absorb the landing shock produced by weight-bearing activities such as running, and that this capacity is even more important in short-distance races, since the landing forces are greater the faster you run.

For example, the human Achilles tendon can conserve 35% of the total energy required during each stride (Farley et al. 1991). Yet, there are many additional springs in the lower limb that could return more of this mechanical energy stored during the stance phase of the running cycle (Farley et al. 1991). If the efficiency of energy return produced in this manner was 100%, then the running human would be like a person hopping on a pogo stick. For the pogo stick stores the energy of landing in a powerful spring, which then uses that energy to propel the next jump.

The Biomechanical Model proposes that an important function of the muscles, and of the brain and nerves that control their function, is to maintain the tension in the tendons when stretched at foot strike, as well as during the first part of the stance phase of the running cycle. This then allows the spring (Achilles tendons and other structures) to be stretched actively. Return of the spring to its unstretched position at toe-off then provides a good proportion of the energy needed for the next stride (Bosco, Tihanyi, et al. 1982). If this model is correct, it predicts that any age-related change in the function of these springs could have unexpectedly large influences on running performance. But why do these changes have a greater effect on performance in shorter-distance races than in 10-km races in those who, like Basil Davis, have probably raced and trained as much as any other human?

The Biomechanical Model predicts that an important component of running ability is the nature of our connective tissue and its capacity to act as a spring to store and return the energy of landing. Furthermore, a component of the exhaustion that develops during racing occurs in these connective tissue springs, either because they themselves become less able to absorb energy or because they alter the patterns of muscle activation that determine muscle function and stride characteristics when fatigued.

When exhaustion develops during racing, the elastic tissues and the muscle reflexes may become less able to store elastic energy and to absorb the shock of landing. This will cause the runner to slow down and to alter the running stride to lower the total mechanical loading on the body, particularly on the joints. Accordingly, this theory predicts that the reduction in running speed, which occurs during 10 to 21 km races in aging runners like Davis and at the marathon "wall" in all of us, is a result of a subconscious reflex that cannot be overridden by the conscious efforts of the runner. The aim of this subconscious reflex is to protect the body, especially the joints, from excessive loading when the muscles and tendons are less able to absorb the shock of landing. As cycling, swimming, and cross-country skiing do not involve weight bearing, the exhaustion that develops in those sports cannot be due to failure of these springs and must reflect true exhaustion of the mechanical properties of the muscles. Alternatively, this fatigue may result from the actions of a central governor that is responding to other sensory information.

Therefore, I suggest that the greater detrimental effect that many years of heavy racing and training has on performance in those who have run many marathon races can probably be best explained by age- and racing-dependent changes in tendon and muscle elasticity and the function of the reflexes that reduce the impact shock of landing.

The body can only accept a certain maximal loading with each stride. Therefore, once these shock-absorbing mechanisms are damaged (perhaps by years of intensive training and racing) or become fatigued during races (perhaps prematurely in competitive veteran runners), the central governor in the brain will force the body to run at a slower pace to protect the muscles and joints from damage.

A large cross-sectional study of 654 men and women aged 20 to 93 years lends support to these theories. The study found that the capacity to utilize elastic stored energy falls with age in men but may actually improve in women (Lindle et al. 1997).

There is also good evidence that the quality of our connective tissue deteriorates with age (Ippolito et al. 1980; Gosselin et al. 1998), with the result that our connective tissue is less extensible (Larsson 1978), causing us to become stiffer and less able to absorb the shock of landing (Akiya et al. 1998). Thus, we would expect that performance in those weight-bearing activities that most stress the connective tissue, especially weight-bearing activities such as running, would be the most severely affected.

In chapter 6, I review convincing anecdotal evidence that the running performance of the most elite athletes can fall precipitously after a few exceptional races. No reason has yet been advanced to explain this phenomenon. Could it be that irreversible damage (rapid aging) occurs to the connective tissue, which is never again able to absorb the stresses of another 2:08 marathon, or is this effect due to alterations in the responses of the central governor? These are questions that, I suspect, will be answered within the next decade.

In a first attempt to study this possibility, Sharwood et al. (2000) evaluated muscle function in a group of 20 veteran marathon and ultramarathon runners after they had run downhill on a laboratory treadmill for 40 min. The study found that runners who had accumulated more than 5000 km in racing used a different neural recruitment strategy to maintain muscle function than did those who had raced less. In other words, there was evidence for an alteration in the action of the central governor. The authors ascribed their findings to one of the following causes: longstanding skeletal muscle damage; increased muscle stiffness; an inability to recruit Type II muscle fibers; or a more economical use of the available muscle mass, so-called muscle wisdom. Any or all of these could alter the responses of the central governor. This study is a start, but much remains to be learned about this intriguing and clearly important phenomenon.

Recovery

A frequent complaint of aging athletes is that they are simply not able to train as hard and as frequently as before. A study (Manfredi et al. 1991) has found that when exposed to the same training load, the muscles of older subjects showed more severe damage than did those of subjects under 30 years of age. What this shows is that aging muscle must be treated with respect. Recall the marked reduction in training volumes that Basil Davis was able to sustain toward the end of this racing his career.

Chronic Orthopedic Disabilities

Running does not cause osteoarthritis in those who start running with healthy joints and who do not train as hard as elite athletes (see chapter 14). Yet, many runners start running on abnormal joints. They need to be aware that if symptoms begin to develop during running as a result of joint degeneration, then non-weight-bearing activities, such as swimming and cycling, will protect the joint more effectively than running and will delay the rate at which progressive joint degeneration occurs.

The point to remember is that all joints previously damaged by surgery or other trauma deteriorate with age, and this deterioration will probably be more rapid in those who stress the joints the most, particularly in weight-bearing activities. The presence of any joint abnormality would be an important reason to modify your training mode and intensity as you age, most especially to consider the introduction of more non-weight-bearing activities.

Ability to Adapt to Training

Aging does not seem to affect your ability to adapt to training, at least when measured during activities of relatively short duration (Makrides et al. 1990). Thus, neither the rate of adaptation nor the extent to which the body will adapt to training is altered with aging. It follows that it is never too late to begin at least a moderate exercise training program.

The volume and intensity of your training, however, must be reduced as you age, for the reasons described in this section.

FINAL WORD

This chapter began by introducing the traditional concept that the sole determinant of athletic ability is the athlete's capacity to transport oxygen to the exercising muscles. The limitations, both theoretical and practical, of the concept that the heart exists only as the slave of the exercising muscles have been reviewed in detail. Other models were also introduced, and in particular those that emphasize the action of the muscles and the functioning of the central governor (the brain). The governor is responsible for protecting the athlete's body from damage by safely controlling the intensity that the athlete can sustain during any type or duration of exercise. These ideas represent a substantial break from exercise physiology as it has historically been taught since the early 1920s.

3

Energy Systems and Running Performance

In this chapter I focus on the effects of the foods we eat on exercise performance by answering the following questions:

- How do these foods fuel the body?
- Is carbohydrate the ultimate fuel, as most runners believe?
- Why is the role of fat, or indeed protein, in the athletic diet attracting newfound interest among researchers?
- How does training affect the storage and use of body fuels?
- To what extent will the body adapt to training?

HOW THE BODY USES FOOD

Most of the foods we eat are ingested in the form of complex molecules. These molecules must be broken down into smaller molecules before they can be absorbed through the linings of the intestine to enter the bloodstream. Once in the bloodstream, they are transported to the appropriate tissues, particularly the liver, muscle, and fat (adipose) tissue, where they are stored until required to provide energy (for example, during exercise).

This breaking down process begins when food travels via the esophagus into the stomach, where it stimulates the secretion of various digestive enzymes. These enzymes begin to break down the complex carbohydrate and protein molecules

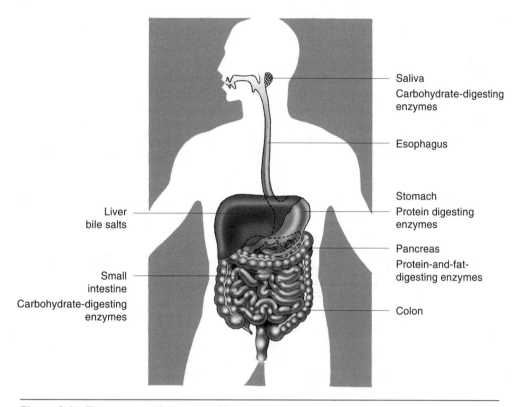

Saliva
Carbohydrate-digesting
enzymes

Esophagus

Stomach
Protein digesting
enzymes

Pancreas
Protein-and-fat-
digesting enzymes

Colon

Liver
bile salts

Small
intestine
Carbohydrate-digesting
enzymes

Figure 3.1   The passage and digestion of food in the intestine.

into simpler constituents, in particular, glucose, galactose, maltose, and fructose from carbohydrates, and amino acids from proteins (figure 3.1).

Once sufficiently digested in the stomach, the food is released into the upper reaches of the small intestine. Here secretions from the liver (bile salts) and the pancreas break food down further. The bile secretions have a detergent effect, breaking the fats into an emulsion (a dispersion of fine fat droplets); the pancreatic and intestinal secretions contain most of the enzymes that digest carbohydrates, fats, and proteins. The result is that when the food enters the lower parts of the small intestine, it has already been broken down into its basic components and is ready to be absorbed. The carbohydrates, fats, and proteins are absorbed in the upper and middle parts of the small bowel; minerals, certain vitamins, and iron are absorbed at the end of the small bowel. The main function of the large bowel is to absorb water that escaped absorption in the small bowel and to allow fermentation of those (resistant) carbohydrates that have escaped digestion in the small bowel.

Once exercise begins, the fuels that have been stored during the resting period must be mobilized to provide the adenosine triphosphate (ATP) necessary for muscular contraction. We learned in chapter 1 that ATP is the energy currency of the body.

Carbohydrate

The absorbed carbohydrates now in fully digested forms—glucose, fructose, and maltose—all travel to the liver, where fructose is converted to glucose. Glucose may then be stored as glycogen in the liver or may be exported to the skeletal muscles and heart to be stored as muscle glycogen, depending on the state of the glycogen stores in those muscles. Glycogen is the only form in which both the liver and the muscles store carbohydrates. Glycogen consists of branching chains of glucose molecules.

Alternatively, some of the glucose may be burned by certain tissues, such as the brain, the kidney, and the red blood cells, all of which depend on blood glucose for their normal functioning. We will see later that without an adequate glucose supply, the brain is unable to function normally. Hence, a reduced blood glucose concentration (hypoglycemia) is an important cause of central nervous system (brain) fatigue that can develop in those who do not ingest adequate amounts of carbohydrate, either before or during prolonged exercise.

Glycogen stored in the liver is broken down to glucose, which then enters the bloodstream, from where it is extracted by the muscles, brain, kidneys, and red blood cells. This occurs at a rate of about 10 g per hour at rest (Felig and Wahren 1975). During exercise, most of the blood glucose is taken up and used by the active skeletal muscles. The rate at which glucose is both released from the liver and used by the muscles is greatly increased during exercise to about 60 g per hour. This has relevance to the development of low blood glucose concentrations (hypoglycemia) during exercise and the optimum amounts of carbohydrate that need to be ingested during prolonged exercise (see chapter 4).

Blood glucose levels represent a balance between the rate at which the liver produces glucose and the rate at which muscles and other tissues use glucose. When tissues are taking up and using blood glucose faster than the liver is producing it, blood glucose levels fall. This results in impaired body functioning. The brain in particular is affected as it is dependent on glucose for its energy.

Symptoms of hypoglycemia include a reduced ability to concentrate, a sudden feeling of weakness, and the intense desire to stop running. Typically, the athlete senses the impossibility of completing the race.

Hypoglycemia

The first report of hypoglycemia in marathon runners reportedly came from doctors at the Peter Bent Brigham Hospital in Boston (S.A. Levine et al. 1924). These doctors studied runners who took part in the 1924 Boston Marathon and found that postrace blood glucose concentrations were decreased in all runners. They noted a strong correlation between the condition of the athletes at the end of the race and their blood glucose levels. Athletes with low blood glucose levels presented with "asthenia, pallor and prostration." In fact, one of the athletes was arrested by the Boston Constabulary, who mistook his symptoms for alcohol intoxication.

During the 1925 Boston race, those runners who had developed hypoglycemia the preceding year were encouraged to eat a high-carbohydrate diet for the 24 hours before the race and to start eating sweets after they had run about 24 km (Gordon, Kohn, et al. 1925). These techniques were very effective. The runners on the carbohydrate trial completed the race in excellent physical condition; their postrace blood glucose levels were elevated and their performances had improved greatly.

At about the same time, a series of classic studies at the Harvard Fatigue
(continued)

Laboratory (Dill, Edwards, et al. 1932) established that their most famous research mammals, the dogs Joe and Sally, were able to run indefinitely for up to 24 hours, without apparent exhaustion, if fed sweets during exercise. Without carbohydrate ingestion, both became exhausted, manifesting low blood glucose concentrations within less than 6 hours. (Paradoxically, dogs bred for endurance, like the Alaskan huskies, perform best when adapted to a high-fat diet and become increasingly less able to exercise when eating a high-carbohydrate diet. The results of the studies on Joe and Sally need to be interpreted with caution, at least with respect to dog physiology.) Similarly, in Stockholm, Christensen and Hansen (1939) showed that cyclists, exhausted after exercising for approximately 90 minutes, were able to continue after ingesting a high-carbohydrate drink containing about 200 g of carbohydrate. Carbohydrate ingestion reversed low blood glucose concentrations present at exhaustion.

As a result, David Dill (1936) concluded: "The ingestion of a heavy carbohydrate meal a few hours before the marathon race and a supply of glucose before and during the race are logical." Or, as Grace Eggleton (1936) wrote in her textbook, *Muscular Exercise,*

> *When [long-distance runners] have run to exhaustion, the level of blood sugar is found to be abnormally low. . . . If the eating of sugar candy during a race was encouraged. . . it seems possible that new records might be achieved in long-distance running. (p. 153)*

For reasons that still escape my understanding, the convincing results of these studies from both sides of the Atlantic were largely ignored by both exercise physiologists and athletes. As a result, for the next 56 years, most researchers dismissed the possibility that hypoglycemia could be a factor causing fatigue during marathon running. For example, a highly influential paper by Felig et al. (1982) evaluated the effects of carbohydrate ingestion during laboratory exercise in a group of recreational but noncompetitive bicyclists. The study found that the group ingesting carbohydrate during exercise did not perform better than the group that ingested placebo and who consequently developed hypoglycemia, in some cases profound. The authors concluded,

> *These findings do not support a role for glucose ingestion during prolonged exercise, and they may have relevance to endurance sports such as marathon running. In addition, the ability to continue prolonged exercise despite frank hypoglycemia suggests that the so-called phenomenon of "hitting the wall" during marathon running is probably due to factors other than a low blood glucose concentration. (p. 899)*

Unlike the liver, muscle is unable to produce glucose as an end-product of its glycogen breakdown. Instead, glycogen is broken down in the muscles to give an end-product called pyruvate (figure 3.2). According to the most recent theory, lactate is the dominant end-product of glycolysis (G.A. Brooks 1998; G.A. Brooks, Dubouchard, et al. 1999) and can either enter the bloodstream and be shuttled around the body, or enter the mitochondria to fuel the Krebs cycle.

An important feature of this glycogen/lactate pathway is that it can proceed without an adequate oxygen supply; hence, we speak of oxygen-independent glycolysis.

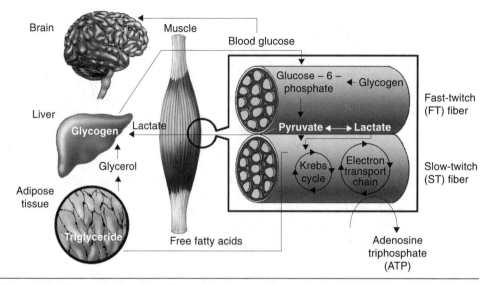

Figure 3.2 The metabolic pathways for carbohydrate and fat metabolism by the liver, muscles, and brain.

Glycolysis simply means the breakdown of glucose precursors to pyruvate in a series of sequential metabolic reactions—a metabolic pathway. The term *oxygen-independent glycolysis* is preferable to the old term, *anaerobic glycolysis,* which suggests that glycolysis only occurs when there is anaerobiosis (that is, an inadequate oxygen supply). We now know, however, that glycolysis becomes very active during high-intensity exercise such as sprinting, even though there is an adequate oxygen supply to the muscles. The idea that muscles produce lactate only when they contract anaerobically is an incorrect legacy of the work of A.V. Hill and his colleagues (see figure 2.5).

Most of the lactate produced in this way will cross the mitochondrial membrane either as pyruvate or, according to a new theory, as lactate itself (G.A. Brooks, Dubouchard, et al. 1999). It then enters the final metabolic pathway common to both fat and carbohydrate, the so-called *citric acid cycle* or *Krebs cycle,* after the Oxford biochemist who first described it. At various points in the Krebs cycle, hydrogen is released and transferred to a third metabolic pathway, the electron transport chain, for the production of mitochondrial ATP. The ATP produced in the mitochondria is then transferred to the head of the myosin molecule, where it is used to fuel the cross-bridge cycle (see figure 1.5).

Fat

Fats present in the diet are digested in the intestine by the pancreatic enzymes (see figure 3.1). The constituent glycerol and free fatty acid components are absorbed into the bloodstream, reconstituted, and transported to the liver, where they are repackaged and transported to the major fat storage sites in fat (adipose) tissue and in muscle. They are stored at both sites in the form of triglyceride molecules. Adipose tissue is widely distributed throughout the body, forming the subcutaneous (below skin) fat layer that serves to conserve heat, as well as surrounding major organs such as the heart, kidneys, and intestines. Women have a different fat distribution from men, with more fat being concentrated in the breasts, upper thighs, and buttocks (they are said to be pear-shaped). In men, the distribution tends to be around the abdomen (producing an apple shape). These differences have important health implications. It appears that the female (gynoid) type of fat accumulation is not associated with greater health risks, in particular the elevated blood pressures, blood cholesterol concentrations, and increased risk of diabetes and heart attack that are present in men whose fat accumulation is in the android distribution around the belly.

We learned in chapter 1 that the triglyceride molecule consists of three fatty acid molecules attached to one glycerol molecule. For fat to be used as an energy source, the fatty acid components of the triglyceride molecule must first be freed from the glycerol molecule. This is achieved by an enzyme, hormone-sensitive lipase, which exists in the adipose (fatty) cell membrane.

The term *hormone-sensitive* indicates that the action of the enzyme is regulated by hormones in the blood. The two most important hormones are insulin, which reduces the activity of this enzyme, thereby preventing fat from being used, and adrenaline, which activates the enzyme, thereby accelerating the use of fat. During exercise, insulin levels fall and adrenaline levels rise so that the breakdown of fat and the mobilization of the released free fatty acids and glycerol is stimulated. In contrast, a high-carbohydrate meal can cause insulin levels to rise and impair fat mobilization.

After they have been released from triglyceride molecules in adipose tissue, free fatty acids and glycerol pass out across the adipose cell membrane and enter the bloodstream, where the free fatty acid molecules bind to a carrier protein, albumin. When the circulating free fatty acid molecules reach the capillaries supplying the muscle cell, they can be taken up into the cell and either metabolized in the Krebs cycle to produce ATP or reformed and stored as muscle triglyceride. There is evidence to suggest that these muscle triglyceride stores are also an important fuel during both high-intensity and prolonged exercise. Some believe that an important effect of training is to increase the amount of muscle triglyceride used for energy, with a sparing of muscle glycogen (Hurley et al. 1986), but others argue that this effect, if present, is not as great as originally believed (G.A. Brooks and Mercier 1994; Friedlander, Casazza, et al. 1998a; 1998b).

Protein

When proteins are digested, they are broken down into their constituent building blocks, the amino acids. The amino acids are then transported to the liver, where they may contribute to glucose and glycogen production. More importantly, amino acids are used by all body tissues, in particular muscle, to replace proteins that are continually being broken down. The major function of the protein stores is to produce movement through the interaction of the two principal proteins—actin and myosin. Protein is used as an energy source during exercise, and only under extreme conditions, such as complete starvation or prolonged exercise lasting three or more hours (especially under conditions of carbohydrate depletion), does its contribution reach even 10% of the total energy production (P.W.R. Lemon and Mullin 1980). Under such conditions, the major role for protein is to provide the liver with fuels from which it can produce glucose when the liver glycogen stores are low.

Energy Supply Model

The central premise of the Cardiovascular/Anaerobic Model is that it is the provision of a substrate (oxygen) to muscle that limits exercise performance so that fatigue during high-intensity exercise is a direct consequence of a failure of oxygen delivery to the exercising muscles. A subtle extension of this idea produces a second model, which proposes that fatigue during high-intensity exercise may, alternatively, result from the inability to supply another substrate (ATP) sufficiently fast to sustain exercise. A.V. Hill (1927), whose research in the 1920s was directly responsible for the development of the Cardiovascular/Anaerobic Model, wrote: "The fact remains, however, that the chief factor in many forms of athletic achievement is the supply of energy and its proper and economic utilization" (p. 237).

This model predicts that performance in events of different durations is determined by the capacity of the different metabolic pathways—including the phosphagens, oxygen-independent glycolysis, aerobic glycolysis, and aerobic lipolysis—to produce energy (ATP). Superior performance is then explained by a greater capacity to generate ATP in the specific metabolic pathway(s) that predominate(s) during that activity. Thus, the sprinter is assumed to have a greater capacity to generate ATP from the intramuscular phosphagen stores and from oxygen-independent glycolysis, whereas the ultramarathoner has a superior capacity to oxidize fat (aerobic lipolysis; figure 3.2). Whether this hypothesis is true is uncertain, as it has yet to be evaluated systematically. To prove this model would require that:

1. The metabolic capacities of these different pathways be shown to be causally related to performance in events lasting the different durations.

2. The specific metabolic pathways be shown to adapt predictably with specific training.

3. These adaptations alone explain the changes in performance that result from training with exercises lasting the different durations.

Until these studies are completed, this model remains hypothetical, but interesting. The weakness of the model is that it predicts that exercise must terminate when muscle ATP depletion occurs—that is, when the muscle develops rigor, the irreversible contracture that normally develops after death (rigor mortis). Yet, all the evidence clearly shows that the ATP concentrations, even in muscles forced to contract under ischemic conditions, do not drop below about 60% of resting values. This indicates that muscle ATP concentrations are "defended" to prevent the development of skeletal muscle rigor (Fitts 1994).

The nature of the "governor" preventing total muscle ATP depletion during exercise is uncertain but could reside either in the brain, as postulated in the Central Governor/Integrated Neuromuscular Recruitment Model (see chapter 2), or in the muscle cells themselves. This hypothesis holds that when the rate of ATP production by oxidative sources becomes inadequate, high rates of anaerobic glycolytic ATP production produce metabolites, particularly H+, which interfere with energy production and cross-bridge cycling, causing exhaustion and a failure of muscle contraction. This is the basis of the traditional belief, described in chapter 1, that lactic acid "poisons" the exercising muscles.

In this way, muscle contraction fails, not because of a failure of central recruitment (as predicted by the Central Governor Model), but because of a peripherally located inhibition of muscular contraction. Proponents of this model can cite substantial evidence showing that a number of metabolites can interfere with muscle cross-bridge cycling measured in vitro (in the test-tube, outside the body) in isolated muscle fibers (Fitts 1994). The necessary assumption is that skeletal muscle contracting in vitro, in the absence of an intact nervous system, behaves exactly as it would in vivo (in the intact body) when operating under the influences of the central nervous system. But there is a body of evidence that is not compatible with these assumptions and conclusions. For example, a large range of muscle pH concentrations is measured at exhaustion in humans (Mannion et al. 1995). Furthermore, this model is unable to explain the increasing sense of fatigue that develops during races lasting between 10 and 50 minutes. In those races, fatigue is increasing while blood lactate concentrations are falling. In addition, the progressive sense of fatigue that develops in marathon and ultramarathon races cannot be explained on the basis of muscle or blood lactate concentrations, which are typically low during such races.

In summary, a metabolic basis limiting high-intensity exercise of short duration is widely assumed but incompletely documented. There is a need to establish whether those metabolic factors that appear to limit muscle function in vitro also play a role in vivo, when the muscle is also under the influence of the central nervous system. The possible contribution of neural factors to this form of exhaustion needs to be excluded before results from in vivo studies are extrapolated, without qualification, to the in vitro condition. There is mounting evidence to suggest that the central nervous system plays the predominant role, limiting performance during bouts of high-intensity exercise. For example, Kay, Marino, et al. (2001) had athletes cycle for 1 hour at their own best pace in a laboratory-based time trial. Every 10 minutes, subjects were asked to cycle all out for 60 seconds. The electrical activity in their exercising muscles was measured by means of electromyography (EMG).

The study showed that both the EMG activity and the all-out power produced by the cyclists fell from sprints 2 to 5, recovering somewhat in sprint 6 (see figure 3.3). That athletes are suddenly able to sprint near the end of races of any distance is a common observation. Yet, it cannot be explained by a model based on the theory that exhaustion during high-intensity exercise of short duration of the type studied develops because of the progressive accumulation of poisonous metabolites including lactate and H+. If this were the case, it would be impossible to sprint near the end of a race when accumulation of poisonous metabolites would have to be greatest (or else why would the athlete show a progressive fatigue?).

Similarly, neither the Energy Supply Model nor the Energy Depletion Model (discussed later in this chapter) is able to explain why exhausted marathon and ultramarathon runners are nevertheless able to increase their speeds for short distances near the end of those races. If depletion, specifically of muscle glycogen, was the sole cause of their exhaustion, then such a finishing sprint would not be possible.

But the study of Kay, Marino, et al. (2001) clearly establishes that the major cause of the reduced power output in sprints 1 to 5, with a sudden increase in

(continued)

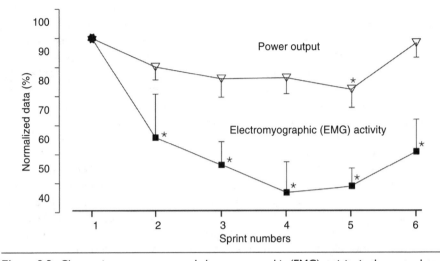

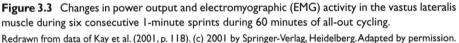

Figure 3.3   Changes in power output and electromyographic (EMG) activity in the vastus lateralis muscle during six consecutive 1-minute sprints during 60 minutes of all-out cycling.

Redrawn from data of Kay et al. (2001, p. 118). (c) 2001 by Springer-Verlag, Heidelberg. Adapted by permission.

the final sprint 6, is the reduced EMG activity, indicating a reduced drive from the brain to the muscles, so-called central fatigue. The increased power output in the final sprint (figure 3.3) is associated with an increased EMG activity, indicating that the inhibitory influence of the central governor had been reduced, allowing a greater mass of muscle to be recruited and hence a higher power output to be achieved.

In a related study on which the research of Kay, Marino, et al. (2001) was based, St. Clair Gibson, Schabort, et al. (2001) showed identical responses during a 100-km cycling time trial that also included all-out sprints of 1 and 4 km. Again, power output and EMG activity fell with successive sprints, indicating the development of a progressive central fatigue. Unlike the finding in the 60-minute cycle, however, cyclists were unable to increase either power output or EMG activity in the final sprint of the 100-km time trial. In summary, both these studies show that central (brain) fatigue, regulated by a central governor, determines exhaustion during prolonged exercise.

HOW THE BODY STORES FUEL

Figure 3.4A shows the percentage contribution of the different body organs to the mass of a 70-kg man. The largest organ is muscle, which comprises about 26 kg, or 37%, of total body weight, followed by fat tissue (10.5 kg; 15%), and bone (10 kg; 15%). The fat and carbohydrate stores of the body are also depicted. Women are generally lighter than men, with slightly less muscle and more fat, but the differences between athletic men and women are less. The proportional distribution of muscle, fat, and bone tissue listed here would be appropriate for athletic women weighing less than 70 kg.

Water is the major constituent of the human body, accounting for up to 64% of total body weight, or 83% of the weight of the body's water, fat, and carbohydrate

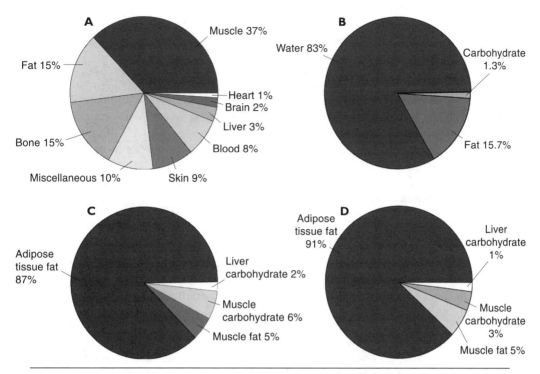

Figure 3.4   Percentage by weight of the different organs of the body (A) and of the body water, fat, and carbohydrate stores (B); percentage of total body energy store (g) that is present as carbohydrate or fat in either adipose tissue or muscle (C); percentage of total body energy store (kJ) found in adipose tissue fat, muscle fat, and muscle and liver carbohydrate (D).

stores (figure 3.4B). The more important practical point is that fat is the largest energy store in the body and can total as much as 9 kg even in a relatively lean (70-kg) male athlete or 7.5 kg in a lean (50-kg) female athlete. By comparison, the carbohydrate stores are quite trivial, at most 600 to 700 g. Figure 3.4C shows the percentage of the total body energy store in grams that is found as fat in either adipose tissue or muscle, or as carbohydrate in either liver or muscle. Note the high percentage (87%) of energy stored as adipose tissue fat. Because fat is more energy-dense than carbohydrate, when these stores are expressed as a percentage of the total body energy store in kilojoules (KJ), adipose tissue fat comprises 91% of all the body's energy stores (figure 3.4D). To emphasize the importance of this difference in the size of the body fat and carbohydrate stores, let us consider for how long it is possible to run at men's world-class marathon pace if burning exclusively carbohydrates or exclusively fats.

The oxygen cost of running at world record marathon pace (for men, 19.8 km per hour) for an athlete of average economy is about 67 ml O_2 per kg per min. The total oxygen consumption each minute by a 70-kg athlete running at 20 km per hour would therefore be (70 × 67 ml per min), that is, 4.69 liters per minute. We know that each liter of oxygen used produces approximately 20 kJ; thus our athlete will be burning 93.8 kJ per minute. As 1 g of carbohydrate provides 16.65 kJ (Newsholme and Leech 1983), it follows that the athlete will be burning carbohydrate at the rate of 5.65 g per minute so that the total body carbohydrate stores in this particular athlete would last only 125 minutes (2:05:00). In contrast, the body fat stores, which provide 37.5 kJ per gram, could fuel exercise for 59 hours and 1 minute (59:01:00).

But our empirical observation is that no world-class marathon runner could ever hope to run at 20.1 km per hour for close to 60 hours. Clearly, fats are never called on to provide all the energy required at world-class marathon pace. Rather, as we shall see, when the exercise intensity exceeds about 80% of $\dot{V}O_2$max in most but not all athletes, virtually all the energy comes from carbohydrate metabolism (G.A. Brooks 1998; G.A. Brooks and Mercier 1994). This helps explain why competitors in more prolonged exercise sustain an exercise intensity closer to 67% $\dot{V}O_2$max for the duration of the race. This allows the competitors in those events to use both fats and carbohydrate for energy. Even then, the most successful triathletes are likely to be those who are able to extract most of their energy from fat, especially during the final 42-km marathon section of that race.

Carbohydrate Storage

Although figure 3.4 might suggest that the body can only store a fixed amount of carbohydrate, in fact this amount can vary significantly from person to person and may vary markedly at different times in the same person. Let us consider the factors that explain this observation.

One factor is the level of training (Greiwe et al. 1999). Untrained subjects eating a normal diet store about 280 g of carbohydrate in their muscles (Hultman 1967; Blom, Costill, et al. 1987), whereas values of up to 720 g are usually found in trained athletes who have not exercised for 24 to 48 hours and who have allowed their muscles sufficient time to fill all their carbohydrate stores completely (Costill, Sherman, et al. 1981; Noakes, Lambert, et al. 1988b; W.M. Sherman, Costill, et al. 1983; see table 3.1). On days when they are training, their average muscle glycogen stores will be lower, about 420 g.

A small part of this difference in muscle glycogen storage capacity between trained and untrained subjects will be a result not of training but of a dietary change, because as people become fitter, they tend to eat a higher carbohydrate diet, which will increase muscle glycogen stores. However, untrained subjects encouraged to eat a high-carbohydrate diet increase their muscle glycogen stores to about 360 g (Hultman 1967; Jardine et al. 1988), or about half the values measured in trained athletes. Similarly, muscle glycogen levels in trained subjects eating a low-carbohydrate diet are about twice values measured in untrained subjects eating the same diet. This indicates that the muscles of trained athletes are better able to store carbohydrates than are the muscles of the untrained subjects eating the same diet (Greiwe et al. 1999).

Additional evidence that training increases the muscle capacity to store glycogen is shown by the finding that the muscle glycogen content of the legs is greater than that of the arms, almost certainly because the legs are used more and are therefore "fitter" (Hultman 1967). (This study was performed on runners. Triathletes, swimmers, rowers, and canoeists who train their upper bodies are likely to have increased muscle glycogen stores in their arms, but this has not been studied, in part because of the difficulty of sampling tissue from the smaller arm muscles without damaging other structures such as nerves and arteries.)

Liver glycogen stores in untrained subjects are about 100 g (Hultman and Nilsson 1971; Nilsson and Hultman 1973) and are increased to about 130 g on a high-carbohydrate diet.

Another factor influencing the size of body carbohydrate stores is the effect of different diets, including fasting. Table 3.1 shows that a high-carbohydrate diet (greater than 70%) causes a small increase in muscle glycogen stores in untrained subjects from 280 g to about 360 g, and in trained subjects from 280 g to about 420 g. A 24-hour fast causes a rapid depletion of liver glycogen stores but has little effect on muscle glycogen stores.

As already described, maintenance of the normal blood glucose concentration is dependent on the rate at which the liver manufactures glucose. If prolonged exercise were to begin after a long period of fasting, the liver would be unable to produce glucose fast enough to satisfy the increased demands of the exercising muscles for glucose. As a result, the blood glucose concentration would fall, leading ultimately to exhaustion caused by hypoglycemia (low blood glucose concentration). This can be prevented by ingesting carbohydrate-containing drinks during exercise (chapter 4). However, the ideal is to ensure that the body carbohydrate stores are replete *before* exercise. This can be achieved by eating a carbohydrate-containing meal 3 or more hours before competition.

A crucial failing of the original studies of carbohydrate loading and carbohydrate depletion on exercise performance was that hypoglycemia developed rapidly in those on the low-carbohydrate diets. Hence, it is not possible to determine whether exhaustion really resulted from muscle glycogen depletion or from liver glycogen depletion, causing hypoglycemia.

Since we have been able to increase the exercise capacity of athletes with muscle glycogen depletion by more than 25%, simply by infusing glucose into the bloodstream at rates sufficient to prevent hypoglycemia (Claassens et al. 2001), my bias is to believe that hypoglycemia, secondary to liver glycogen depletion, may be the more important contributor to the fatigue that develops during prolonged exercise when muscle glycogen depletion is also present.

The rapid decline in liver glycogen levels during exercise or fasting results from liver glycogen being used to maintain the blood glucose level. At rest, liver glycogen provides the blood glucose that is used principally by the brain, which, at least in the short term, uses only glucose for its energy. The reason is that the energy-producing pathways in the brain are designed to use carbohydrate, especially glucose. Only with a more prolonged period of fasting does the brain's metabolism switch to using fats, especially ketone bodies in the bloodstream. The brain's daily glucose requirement is about 125 g, or about 100% of the total liver carbohydrate stores in people eating a high-carbohydrate diet (table 3.1). Thus, the brain's daily glucose requirement alone is almost sufficient to deplete the liver glycogen stores within 24 hours. Note that liver glycogen stores fall by about 9 g per hour so that liver glycogen depletion can occur after a fast of only 18 hours.

In contrast, either eating a low-carbohydrate, high protein-fat diet, or fasting for up to five days, causes muscle glycogen levels to fall by only about 30% to 40%, if only normal daily activities are performed (Hultman 1971). This indicates that muscle glycogen levels fall markedly only if vigorous exercise is performed for which carbohydrate is the main fuel source. Furthermore, glycogen levels fall more in the exercised muscles (Hultman 1971). This finding has practical relevance. By studying the relative rates of muscle glycogen use during exercise, it is possible to determine which muscles are most active during different exercises.

Subjects	Type and time of diet	In muscle	In liver	Total carbohydrate stores (g)**
Untrained	Average (45%) CHO diet	14	54	380
	High (75%) CHO diet	18	70	490
Trained	When training daily (low-CHO diet)	14	30	330
	When training daily (high-CHO diet)	21	70	550
	24-hour fast	21	10	440
	Glycogen stripping (3 days low-CHO diet with exercise)	7	10	158
	Immediate premarathon (3 days CHO-loading)	36	90	880
	Immediate postmarathon	4-5	23*	130
	24 hours postrace (high-CHO diet)	15	90	460
	48 hours postrace (high-CHO diet)	27	90	700
	1 week postrace (high-CHO diet)	30	90	620

Table 3.1   Effects of different interventions on muscle and liver glycogen stores (g·kg wet tissue⁻¹)

NOTE: To convert from g per kg⁻¹ to mmol per kg wet muscle⁻¹, multiply by 5.56. Notice that although liver glycogen stores are intact after a 42-km race, muscle glycogen concentrations are very low. CHO = carbohydrate.
* Calculated at a liver glycogen utilization rate of 40 g per h⁻¹ during exercise at 75 to 85% $\dot{V}O_2$max (Ahlborg & Fll 1982) for an athlete running 42 km in 2.5 hours and not ingesting carbohydrate.
** Calculated assuming 20 kg of muscle and 1.8 kg of liver.

Fat Storage

In figure 3.4, page 101, we have assumed that fat constitutes 15% of the body weight of an average male. In reality, there is a wide variation in percentage body fat among people. This is shown in figure 3.5, which gives the distribution of body fat in a group of male and female medical students at the University of Cape Town (Koeslag 1980). Notice that the distribution of people with increasing levels of body fat is described by a symmetrical, convex curve. In this curve, there are small numbers of people at the extremes of very low and very high percentage body fat (the left and right ends of the curve), but the average or middle reading in the curve is about 15% for males and 25% for females. These figures are probably similar to those for other comparable groups of young Caucasian adults around the world. Note that aging flattens the curve and shifts it to the right, quite markedly to higher percentages of body fat.

Elite marathon runners are at the extreme left-hand corner of this curve. Studies by Costill, Bowers, et al. (1970), Pollock, Gettman, et al. (1977), and Coetzer et al. (1993) have shown that male marathon runners have 4% to 7% body fat, or about half that found in average healthy people. The lowest percentage body fat measured was 3.5% in "Mosquito" Madibeng (Coetzer et al. 1993), then the ninth-fastest half-marathon runner of all time. A study of the top American female distance runners of the early 1970s recorded an average body fat reading of 15%, with the lowest value being 6% (Wilmore, Brown, et al. 1977). A more recent study reported

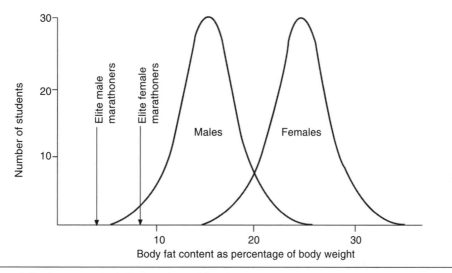

Figure 3.5   Percentage body fat in males and females.

identical findings (Graves et al. 1987). Former world marathon record holder, Grete Waitz, recorded an 8% body fat reading in 1981 (Costill and Higdon 1981).

It therefore seems fair to conclude that female distance runners have greater fat stores than do male distance runners, but that both have about 10% less of their body weight as fat than do average healthy untrained people.

Protein Storage

The size of the body protein stores is more tightly regulated than the sizes of either the body carbohydrate or fat stores. Starvation produces a progressive and ultimately fatal reduction in body protein stores. These stores are slowly broken down by metabolic conversion from protein to provide the glucose necessary to sustain the function of certain obligatory carbohydrate-using organs, including the kidney, the red blood cells, and the brain.

Body protein stores increase acutely (that is, for a short time, whenever the body is in positive energy balance—when energy intake exceeds energy expenditure). However, a new equilibrium is soon achieved. Weightlifting exercise, especially when combined with the use of anabolic steroids (see chapter 13), can produce spectacular changes in total body protein stores in those people whose muscles have the genetic capacity to increase in this way.

Most elite male runners are genetically programmed to have a small muscle bulk, which increases little, if at all, in response to weight training programs. This most likely reflects a reduced capacity of their muscles to respond to the muscle-building (anabolic) properties of the male hormone, testosterone. Women only have a small amount of circulating testosterone and therefore tend to show smaller increases in muscle bulk in response to weight training. But because women have naturally low blood levels of testosterone, they tend to show quite large increases in athletic performance and muscle bulk when they use any of the illegal anabolic steroids. In fact, the regression in women's performance in track and field since the fall of the Berlin Wall in 1989 has been ascribed to the more effective elimination of anabolic steroid use from women's athletics since the 1990s.

FACTORS AFFECTING FOOD STORAGE AND RATE OF USAGE

Here we discuss those other factors, open to modification by the athlete, that determine the rate at which the different body fuel stores are used during exercise.

Exercise Intensity and Duration

During exercise, muscle glycogen levels fall progressively with time (Hultman 1971), as shown in figure 3.6. The rate of glycogen breakdown is initially rapid and constant until muscle glycogen levels reach about one-third of their starting values; thereafter the rate of use slows (Bosch et al. 1993). The initial rate of glycogen breakdown is critically dependent on the intensity of exercise so that the higher the exercise intensity (expressed as percentage $\dot{V}O_2$max), the more rapid the rate of glycogen use (Saltin and Karlsson 1971).

Figure 3.6 also shows that severe muscle glycogen depletion does not occur during continuous exercise at high intensities (greater than 90% $\dot{V}O_2$max). This is because at such high exercise intensities, fatigue develops rapidly. The Energy Supply Model discussed earlier in this chapter predicts that this exhaustion is caused by the rapid accumulation of hydrogen (protons) within the muscle cell, which increases the acidity of the muscles. Hence, that model predicts that an increasing acidity ultimately interferes with muscle contraction, causing the exhaustion typical of this kind of exercise. Alternatively, according to the Central Governor Model, this fatigue may also be limited by a reduced central nervous system (brain) recruitment of the exercising muscles, as established in the form of exhaustion (see figure 3.3).

However, if exercise of high intensity is performed intermittently (the dotted lines in figure 3.6), allowing for the metabolism of the excess protons during recovery (and perhaps also allowing the brain a chance to recover), then a marked degree of muscle glycogen depletion can occur within a short period of time. As a result, high-intensity interval training will produce low muscle glycogen concentrations that, through an action of the central governor, could perhaps contribute to the reduction in interval running speed at the end of such a session.

Continuous exercise at 70% to 85% $\dot{V}O_2$max, sustained for periods of more than 2 hours, causes the greatest degree of muscle glycogen depletion. Therefore, if muscle glycogen depletion causes exhaustion during prolonged exercise (according to the Energy Depletion Model), then to improve performance, it would be advisable to employ strategies that increase the muscle glycogen stores before competition. The strategies used will also slow the rate of glycogen use during exercise, especially in events that last more than 2 hours (such as long-distance running, cycling, swimming, cross-country skiing, etc.).

During prolonged exercise at 70% to 90% of an athlete's maximum capacity ($\dot{V}O_2$max), intensities that are typically sustained at running distances from 21 to 90 km, glycogen depletion occurs to the greatest extent in the endurance-type Type I (ST) muscle fibers (Thomson, Green, et al. 1979). It occurs somewhat less in the Type IIa (FT) fibers and least in the Type IIb (FT) fibers (P. Andersen and Sjogaard 1976; Gollnick, Armstrong, et al. 1973; Gollnick, Piehl, et al. 1974; Vollestad and Blom 1985; H.J. Green, Smith, et al. 1990). After a standard-marathon race, Type I

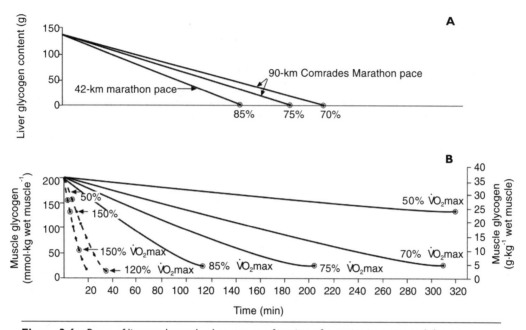

Figure 3.6 Rates of liver and muscle glycogen as a function of exercise intensity and duration.

and Type IIa fibers are completely glycogen-depleted, with only the Type IIb fibers retaining some glycogen (W.M. Sherman, Costill, et al. 1983). During supramaximal (greater than 100% $\dot{V}O_2$max) exercise, all three fiber types become glycogen-depleted, although depletion is greatest in the Type IIb fibers, least in the Type I fibers, and intermediate in the Type IIa fibers (Essen 1978; J.A. Thomson et al. 1979). At lower exercise intensities (40% to 60% $\dot{V}O_2$max), the greatest glycogen breakdown occurs in the Type I fibers (Vollestad and Blom 1985). (The concept of exercising at greater than 100% $\dot{V}O_2$max is discussed later in this chapter.)

It was recently discovered that glycogen is stored in muscle in two different pools—an acid-soluble macroglycogen (MG) and an acid-insoluble proglycogen (PG)—that are used to different extents during exercise. Thus, a greater fraction of the MG pool than of the PG pool is used during marathon running (Asp, Daugaard, et al. 1999). Whereas the PG pool is replenished rapidly after exercise, the MG fraction is replenished more slowly. The practical importance of this finding has yet to be established.

In summary, Type I fibers are active during exercise at all training and racing intensities. As either the exercise intensity increases or the exercise duration is prolonged, more Type IIa and then finally the Type IIb fibers are also activated. As most athletes train at a variety of exercise intensities, they train all their Type I, Type IIa, and Type IIb fibers. As a result, all the fiber types become endurance-adapted, so that the original Type IIb fibers convert to Type IIa fibers.

We know less about changes in liver glycogen levels during exercise than we do about muscle glycogen levels. However, indirect evidence suggests that the rate of liver glycogen use increases in a linear fashion with increasing intensity and averages about 1 g per min at exercise intensities of 70% to 85% $\dot{V}O_2$max (Bosch et al. 1993). Figure 3.6 shows that if the total liver glycogen stores are 135 g before a marathon race, these stores will be completely depleted within about 2 hours 20 minutes of exercise at 70% to 85% $\dot{V}O_2$max if no carbohydrate is taken by mouth during that period. As muscle glycogen stores could last up to 4 hours during prolonged exercise at that intensity, this means that liver glycogen depletion is likely to occur before muscle glycogen depletion in the athlete who takes no carbohydrate by mouth during prolonged exercise at 70% to 75% $\dot{V}O_2$max—the typical intensity at which 50- to 100-km ultramarathons are run. Athletes complete shorter-distance races of 5 to 21 km at between 90% and 95% $\dot{V}O_2$max and thus burn glycogen at very high rates. However, the duration of exercise is short, which means that these athletes complete the exercise with muscle glycogen stores that are still adequate (W.M. Sherman, Costill, et al. 1981).

The extent of muscle and liver glycogen depletion during exercise depends on the intensity and duration of the exercise and will be greatest after prolonged exercise at 42-km standard marathon (85% $\dot{V}O_2$max) or ultramarathon (70% to 75% $\dot{V}O_2$max) pace. However, at exercise intensities of 70% to 75% $\dot{V}O_2$max, depletion of liver glycogen stores likely occurs before depletion of muscle glycogen stores. Shorter distance races of 5 to 21 km do not produce either liver or muscle glycogen depletion. So dietary intervention either before or during races of these distances are, in theory, less important determinants of performance, although there is some evidence suggesting that ingesting carbohydrate can improve performance in exercise events lasting as little as 1 hour (15 to 20 km; Below et al. 1995; Jeukendrup, Brouns, et al. 1997). The practical importance of this concept is discussed in the following section.

Eating a High-Carbohydrate Diet

Immediately after exercising, glucose produced by the liver is used first to return blood glucose levels to normal and then used to restock the glycogen stores—first of the heart and then of skeletal muscles (Gaesser and Brooks 1980).

This resynthesis of glycogen is aided by a high-carbohydrate diet. Trained athletes eating a high-carbohydrate diet (more than 70% of energy from carbohydrate) can probably restock their entire carbohydrate stores within 24 hours (Costill and Miller 1980; Brouns 1988). The rate of muscle glycogen resynthesis after a standard marathon race is somewhat slower (W.M. Sherman, Costill, et al. 1983), probably because racing-induced muscle damage caused by repetitive cycles of stretch/shortening muscle contractions, as described by Paavo Komi and his colleagues slows the normally high rate of glycogen resynthesis in trained subjects.

The classic studies of the effects of exercise and dietary manipulation on muscle glycogen levels were performed in 1967 by Scandinavian groups led by Jonas Bergström (Bergström, Hermansen, et al. 1967; Bergström and Hultman 1967a; 1967b) and Bjorn Ahlborg (B. Ahlborg, Bergström, et al. 1967a; 1967b). These studies led directly to the widespread use by marathon runners in the 1970s of the prerace carbohydrate depletion/carbohydrate loading diet. Figure 3.7 is a synthesis of the findings in the study by B. Ahlborg, Bergström, et al. (1967a). For that study, Ahlborg and his colleagues took three groups of Scandinavian army conscripts (Groups A, B, and C) and exposed them to the following experimental regime:

Group A performed exercise to exhaustion on day –3 then ate a high-fat-protein, low-carbohydrate (less than 10% of total energy) diet for the next three days. On day 0, they again exercised to exhaustion, and for the next seven days (days 1 to 7) they ate a high (90%) carbohydrate diet.

Group B exercised to exhaustion on day –1. Then, after 24 hours on a high-fat-protein diet, they again exercised to exhaustion (day 0) before eating a high-carbohydrate diet for the next seven days.

Group C only performed one exercise bout on day 0 then ate a high-carbohydrate diet for the next seven days.

The results of this experiment were the following:

- Exercising to exhaustion made muscle glycogen levels to fall to very low levels.
- There was minimal glycogen resynthesis when a high-fat-protein diet (carbohydrate depletion) was eaten by Group A between day –3 and day 0 and by Group B between day –1 and day 0.
- A high (90%) carbohydrate diet (carbohydrate loading) caused muscle glycogen levels to be resynthesized rapidly so that preexercise muscle glycogen levels were exceeded within 24 hours (see lines for all groups between day 0 and day 1).
- The muscle glycogen levels in Groups B and C peaked after four days of carbohydrate loading and rose no further. The final values in Group B were about twice the normal resting values.
- Muscle glycogen levels in Group A continued to increase for the entire duration of the experiment, reaching final values close to three times the normal resting values.
- The subjects tested were relatively unfit. This is shown by their low starting muscle glycogen levels of about 14.4 g per kg wet muscle, values that correspond to those found in untrained subjects.

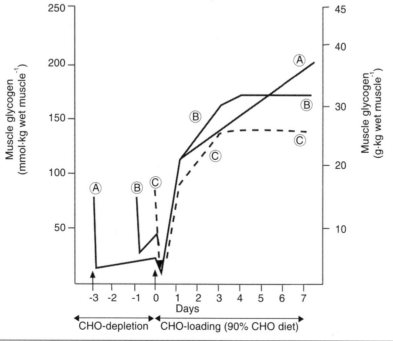

Figure 3.7   The effects of the popular carbohydrate-depletion/carbohydrate-loading exercise diet regime on muscle glycogen levels. Three groups of exercisers are represented by A, B, and C.
Ahlborg, Bergström, et al. (1967a, p. 91).

On the basis of these studies, the carbohydrate depletion/carbohydrate loading or so-called carbo-loading diet was established, in which athletes followed the same exercise/diet regime undertaken by Group A in figure 3.7 and ate a high-carbohydrate diet for the last three days before the race. Yet, it is clear from the figure that optimum carbohydrate loading would only have been expected to occur if the carbohydrate loading phase had lasted for seven days. Despite this obvious criticism and the fact that only untrained subjects were used, the practical result of this study was that from the time of its publication until at least the mid-1980s, most endurance athletes, including some of the world's very best, rigorously followed this strict dietary regime before major competition.

However, it was the study of W.M. Sherman, Costill, et al. (1981) that suggested that we might have been wasting our time. These workers studied the extent of muscle glycogen storage at various stages during the different diets:

- After the traditional seven-day carbohydrate depletion/carbohydrate loading diet exercise regime used by B. Ahlborg, Bergström, et al. (1967a; figure 3.7)
- After eating a 50% carbohydrate diet for the entire seven days of the study
- After eating a 50% carbohydrate diet for the first three days of the study, followed by a high (75%) carbohydrate diet for the last three days

As illustrated in figure 3.8, the results showed that the traditional carbohydrate depletion/carbohydrate loading diet (group A) did not cause muscle glycogen levels to be any higher than did the high-carbohydrate diet eaten for only the last three days before competition (group C). Thus, the conclusion is that the traditional carbohydrate depletion/carbohydrate loading diet carries no advantages, at least for those who are well trained. Provided the subject eats a high-carbohydrate diet for the last three days before competition, carbohydrate storage will be optimized. As expected, muscle glycogen levels were lowest in subjects who ate the 50% carbohydrate diet for the entire duration of the experiment (group B). Interestingly, the extent of muscle glycogen depletion during a 21-km time trial on day 7 was the same in all groups, irrespective of the initial prerace muscle glycogen levels. If the Energy Depletion Model is correct, this might suggest that carbohydrate loading is of no value before exercise of such short duration (30 to 90 minutes). Indeed, the study of Hawley, Palmer, et al. 1997 failed to show any benefit of carbohydrate loading in a 20-km cycling time trial lasting about 30 minutes.

Blom, Costill, et al. (1987) have shown that the amount of running done on the last three days before the start of the carbohydrate-loading phase does not influence the extent to which muscle glycogen levels rise when carbohydrate loading. In fact, they were unable to detect the so-called supercompensation effect shown in figures 3.6 and 3.7. This failure could not be ascribed to an inadequate carbohydrate intake as the subjects took in 600 g carbohydrate daily when carbohydrate loading. Others (G.M. Fogelholm, Tikkanen, et al. 1991) have also failed to show that the muscles of all athletes will definitely show a carbohydrate-loading effect. The study of K.M. Roberts et al. (1988) also showed that optimum glycogen storage can be achieved without a carbohydrate depletion phase.

These studies confirm that the athlete's level of training and the amount of carbohydrate eaten daily are the main determinants of muscle glycogen levels during carbohydrate loading. Muscles restock their muscle glycogen stores at rates of about 5 mmol per kg of muscle per hour, so it takes at least 20 hours for depleted

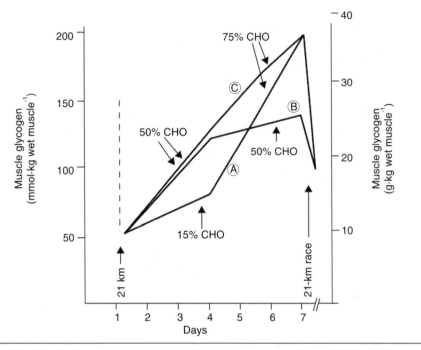

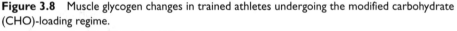

Figure 3.8 Muscle glycogen changes in trained athletes undergoing the modified carbohydrate (CHO)-loading regime.

From Sherman, Costill, et al. (1981, p. 116)

stores to be repleted, provided sufficient carbohydrate of the correct type is eaten during that period (Coyle 1991). Only if glucose is infused intravenously can muscle glycogen stores be replenished more rapidly, perhaps within 8 hours.

The Energy Depletion Model

A characteristic of the exercise sciences is that each new technological advance produces a rash of research based on that novel technology. Then, the results of that research are interpreted as the final solution for all the unresolved issues in our particular field of science. When the Scandinavian researchers reintroduced the muscle biopsy technique (B. Ahlborg, Bergström, et al. 1967a; 1967b; Bergström, Hermansen, et al. 1967; Bergström and Hultman 1967a) with which they measured muscle concentrations of glycogen (and later triglyceride, the phosphagens, and a host of other biochemicals), it was perhaps natural that muscle glycogen should follow oxygen and lactic acid as the newest hypothetical chemical determinant of exercise performance and exhaustion, only this time in more prolonged exercise.

Three crucial findings ignited the theory that the size of the preexercise muscle glycogen stores is the single most important determinant of performance during prolonged exercise at approximately 60% to 80% $\dot{V}O_2$max. I term this theory the Energy Depletion Model of Exercise Physiology and Athletic Performance.

1. Muscle glycogen concentrations were extremely low in athletes who became exhausted during prolonged exercise at 60% to 80% $\dot{V}O_2$max. It was natural to assume that such low concentrations must contribute to fatigue.

2. If athletes were placed on a high-fat (90% of total energy), low-carbohydrate diet, their exercise performance was markedly impaired compared to their performance when they had eaten a high-carbohydrate diet before exercise (Bergström, Hermansen, et al. 1967). Starting muscle glycogen concentrations were also much lower as a result of the low-carbohydrate diet.

3. Athletes who carbohydrate loaded before competition were able either to exercise for longer or to maintain a higher work rate over a fixed distance than those who did not carbohydrate load before exercise (B. Ahlborg, Bergström, et al. 1967a; Bergström, Hermansen, et al. 1967; Karlsson and Saltin 1971). Thus, there appeared to be a linear relationship between the preexercise muscle glycogen concentrations and the duration for which athletes could exercise at about 70% $\dot{V}O_2$max (see figure 3.9).

The conclusion was that the superior performance of athletes ingesting a high-carbohydrate diet before exercise resulted from their larger preexercise muscle glycogen stores, which delayed the onset of exhaustion by allowing more exercise to be performed before the onset of muscle glycogen depletion. It became the accepted dogma that it is the depletion of a specific energy substrate, muscle glycogen, that uniquely causes exhaustion during more prolonged exercise.

The logical corollary was that all athletes, but especially those involved in endurance events, must be advised to eat high-carbohydrate diets both in training and especially before competition. Indeed, it could be argued that this interpretation forms the central pillar onto which the profession of sports nutrition is cemented, as high-carbohydrate diets are now considered ideal for both health and sport.

While this interpretation appears to be entirely logical and is accepted by the vast majority of exercise physiologists, it conceals two crucial weaknesses. First, all the relationships described are associational; that is, each different phenomenon is linked only by its temporal association to the others. There is no direct evidence that any one phenomenon, for example, muscle glycogen depletion, actually causes another (in this case, exhaustion during prolonged exercise). It could be argued that progressive muscle glycogen depletion occurs at the same time as some other physiological change (or changes) that actually causes the exhaustion in athletes who happen, at the same time, to have muscles depleted of glycogen. Possibilities include a reduced blood glucose concentration (Johannessen et al. 1981; Claassens et al. 2002), which is entirely probable given that liver and muscle glycogen depletion occur at the same time during prolonged exercise (see figure 3.6); a rising body temperature; the stretch-shortening cycle fatigue that develops in weight-bearing activities such as running; or even central (brain) fatigue, perhaps related to changes in brain neurotransmitters. Alternatively, the low muscle glycogen concentrations might activate the glycostat (discussed further in chapter 13), which causes exhaustion indirectly by activating the central governor, which then in turn reduces skeletal muscle recruitment, specifically to prevent the development of ATP depletion and skeletal muscle rigor.

Thus, carbohydrate loading could conceivably produce another physiological effect that enhances performance, quite separate from its effect of increasing muscle glycogen concentrations and thus delaying the onset of muscle glycogen depletion and the resulting sensory feedback to the central governor.

One such effect might be on the belief system of the athletes. If athletes subconsciously believe that the intervention will be successful, then they are likely to

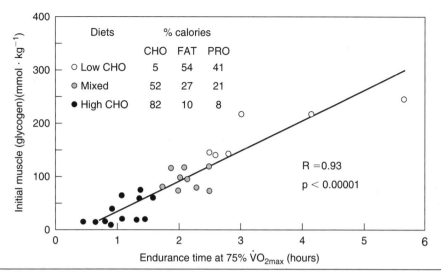

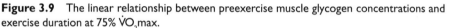

Figure 3.9   The linear relationship between preexercise muscle glycogen concentrations and exercise duration at 75% $\dot{V}O_2$max.

Adapted from data in Hermansen, Hultman, et al. (1967).

perform better. This is called the placebo effect. The effect is considered so powerful that all studies of any intervention or therapy must control for it by including a placebo group of subjects who do not receive the active intervention (such as carbohydrate loading). It is essential that the placebo group should believe that they have received the actual active intervention. To date, only two carbohydrate-loading studies have included adequate placebo controls (Hawley, Palmer, et al. 1997; Burke et al. 2000), and both failed to show any added benefit, over placebo, of the active intervention, in this case carbohydrate loading. In scientific terms, this proves that a placebo effect may indeed be present. Hence, the classical studies (B. Ahlborg, Bergström, et al. 1967a; Bergström, Hermansen, et al. 1967; Karlsson and Saltin 1971) are, in scientific parlance, scientifically worthless because, in addition to other limitations, they lacked adequate placebo groups.

Another possibility is that the magic of the carbohydrate-loading diet may actually rest in the three days of carbohydrate depletion, during which it is likely that the blood glucose concentration is lower than normal, especially in those who continue to run longer distances during this phase of the diet. This exposure to hypoglycemia could preprogram the central governor to accept lower blood glucose concentrations during subsequent exercise. We are beginning to learn that the central governor can be retrained very rapidly, perhaps with as little as one exposure to hypoglycemia.

The fact that few acknowledge this heretical analysis of the validity of the classical studies is understandable since the credibility of the carbohydrate industry relies, at least in part, on the continued acceptance of those studies by the scientific community and, through them, the general public, including runners. Surprisingly, it is often these same scientists who, quite correctly, emphasize the scientific limitations of studies evaluating the effects of high-fat diets on athletic performance, who are not equally critical of glaring failings of the classical carbohydrate-loading studies. The reality is that were carbohydrate loading to be marketed according to the laws governing the pharmaceutical industry, it would not pass scrutiny since, as yet, carbohydrate loading has not been shown to be more effective than placebo, at least during prolonged exercise (L.M. Burke et al. 2000).

This does not mean that carbohydrate loading does not improve performance; only that the mechanism whereby it might be effective, including a possible placebo effect, has yet to be determined.

Part of the problem is that the only direct way to prove that muscle glycogen depletion alone determines exhaustion during prolonged exercisewould be to show that exhaustion is immediately reversed by rapid muscle glycogen repletion during exercise. But this cannot ever be achieved—full muscle glycogen repletion takes at least 12 to 24 hours. This means that the exact causal effect of muscle glycogen depletion on fatigue cannot be measured directly. In the absence of such evidence, we have two choices: either to accept this model and its practical implications, in particular, that all endurance athletes should always eat high-carbohydrate diets, or to evaluate all the evidence dispassionately, including any that might conflict with the predictions of this model.

Indeed, there is some important evidence that suggests that the supposed causal relationships between muscle glycogen depletion and exhaustion (or between elevated preexercise muscle glycogen concentrations and enhanced endurance performance) may be spurious.

The original study showing that muscle glycogen depletion occurred at the same time as exhaustion ignored any causal or contributory role of a reduced blood glu-

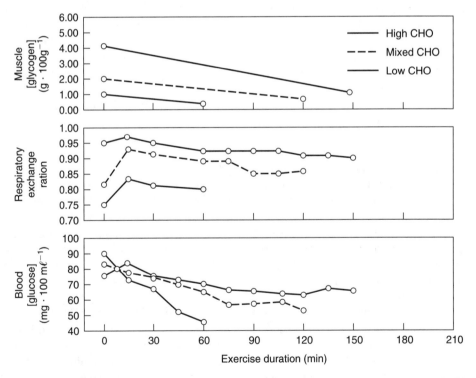

Figure 3.10 Hypoglycemia occurs rapidly in subjects eating a low-carbohydrate diet before exercise.

Data from Bergström, Hermansen, et al. (1967).

cose concentration (hypoglycemia) in that fatigue. Yet, it is well known that a low-carbohydrate diet will cause liver glycogen depletion within as little as 12 to 24 hours so that any exercise undertaken after this will most likely result in the rapid onset of hypoglycemia. In those classical studies in which the data were reported, profound hypoglycemia was also present at exhaustion in subjects who started exercise with low muscle glycogen concentrations following a low-carbohydrate diet (Bergström, Hermansen, et al. 1967; figure 3.10). Hence, it is not possible, on the basis of the original studies, to exclude the possibility that exhaustion was caused by the development of liver glycogen depletion and hypoglycemia, coincidental with the onset of muscle glycogen depletion.

Modern studies of the effects of carbohydrate loading on exercise performance (Madsen et al. 1990; Brewer et al. 1988; Widrick, Costill, et al. 1993; Kang et al. 1995) are all characterized by the following experimental procedures:

- Subjects knew when they had eaten the high-carbohydrate diet. As a result, a placebo effect could not be excluded.
- Subjects fasted for at least 12 hours before exercise.
- In studies showing a positive effect of carbohydrate loading, subjects did not ingest carbohydrate during exercise (Brewer et al. 1988).
- Blood glucose concentrations fell to a greater extent during the exercise that followed the normal or low-carbohydrate diets than after the high-carbohydrate diet. When carbohydrate is ingested during subsequent exercise, the differences in exercise performance between subjects who do carbohydrate load before prolonged exercise and those who do not are either small (Widrick, Costill, et al. 1993; Kang et al. 1995) or absent (L.M. Burke et al. 2000). Or, stated differently, if blood glucose concentrations are the same during the performance trial, then preexercise carbohydrate loading does not improve performance during that trial (Widrick, Costill, et al. 1993; L.M. Burke et al. 2000; Madsen et al. 1990). But if exercise after carbohydrate loading does cause blood glucose concentrations to fall, then carbohydrate ingestion during subsequent exercise further enhances performances even after carbohydrate loading (Kang et al. 1995).

This therefore confirms that optimum performance during prolonged exercise requires both preexercise carbohydrate loading and carbohydrate ingestion during subsequent exercise (Bosch et al. 1996a; 1996b).

All these findings are compatible with the conclusion that carbohydrate loading improves endurance performance principally by delaying the onset of liver glycogen depletion, which causes hypoglycemia, so that when carbohydrate is ingested during exercise, any added benefit of carbohydrate loading is absent or masked.

Thus, the prevention of hypoglycemia by glucose infusion increases exercise time to exhaustion by about 25% in those who begin exercise with very low muscle glycogen concentrations (Claassens et al. 2002). However, exercise performance is not normalized, suggesting that either a low-carbohydrate diet impairs performance by factors other than changes in liver or muscle glycogen concentrations or that terminal fatigue does indeed occur when muscle glycogen concentrations are nearly exhausted. According to the governor theory, sensory feedback from the low muscle glycogen concentrations would stimulate the governor to terminate exercise before complete muscle energy depletion and rigor developed.

The original studies showing the close relationship between preexercise muscle glycogen concentrations and subsequent exercise performance (see figure 3.7) applied specifically to an acute effect—that is, one lasting a few (less than seven) days. But it has been known for more than 50 years that humans perform very poorly when placed acutely on a carbohydrate-free, high-fat diet (Kark et al. 1945; Consolazio and Forbes 1946). In contrast, dogs, especially Alaskan sled dogs, thrive on the high-protein (about 35%), high-fat (greater than 60%), low-carbohydrate (about 5%) diet (R.C. Hill 1998; Hinchcliff et al. 1997) that is quite unacceptable to humans (Kark et al. 1945).

But there is now a large body of evidence showing that athletes can adapt to a high-fat diet without sacrificing their endurance performance (Goedecke, Christie, et al. 1999). Some have even suggested that exercise performance, especially during prolonged exercise, might actually be enhanced following adaptation to a high-fat diet (E.V. Lambert, Speechly, et al. 1994; Muoio et al. 1994; Hoppeler et al. 1999) without adverse health effects such as increased body weight or body fat content (R.C. Brown et al. 2000; Leddy et al. 1997) or alterations in blood lipid concentrations (Leddy et al. 1997; R.C. Brown and C.M. Cox 1998).

In fact, blood concentrations of the protective HDL-cholesterol fraction increased on the high-fat diet (Leddy et al. 1997), whereas unfavorable changes in total cholesterol and triglyceride concentrations were measured in the group ingesting the high (about 70%) carbohydrate diet (R.C. Brown and C.M. Cox 1998). This is in line with the possibility that a high-carbohydrate diet comprising foods with a high glycemic index may be detrimental to health. However, detailed studies of Helge, Richter, et al. (1996) show that untrained subjects who ate a high-fat diet while undergoing an eight-week exercise training program improved as much as those eating a high-carbohydrate diet for only the first four weeks of training. Thereafter, those who ate a high-carbohydrate diet performed better. These findings suggest that trained and untrained subjects may differ in their responses to a high-fat diet.

The idea that exercise terminates only when a specific (critically low) muscle glycogen concentration is reached does not apply in subjects who have adapted to a high-fat diet (Helge et al. 1996) or in those who fatigue while exercising in the heat (González-Alonso, Calbet, et al. 1999; Febbraio, Snow, et al. 1994; Parkin et al. 1999; Pitsiladis and Maughan 1999b).

Hence, Helge, Richter, et al. (1996) concluded that "Factors other than carbohydrate availability are responsible for the differences in endurance time between groups (eating high- and low-carbohydrate diets)," and that "These observations also indicate that fatigue during prolonged moderately intense exercise does not always seem to be closely related to glycogen depletion, as is usually stated."

Similarly, Fitts (1994) wrote that "It seems unlikely that muscle glycogen depletion, low blood glucose, and the resultant decline in carbohydrate oxidation is an exclusive fatigue factor during prolonged exercise." Fitts also acknowledges that "a possibility exists that muscle glycogen depletion is causative in fatigue via a mechanism independent of its role in energy production." Such a role could, of course, be via the central governor, with one of its goals being to terminate exercise before muscle glycogen and ATP depletion leading to rigor could occur.

The Energy Depletion Model cannot explain how elite competitors in the Hawaiian Ironman Triathlon are able to swim, cycle, and run at more than 65% $\dot{V}O_2$max for about 8 hours without slowing down. Yet, they must develop profound muscle glycogen depletion in their active leg muscles at the end of the cycle leg and are still able to complete the marathon leg in midday heat in less than 2:40:00. If muscle depleted of glycogen is unable to sustain a high work rate (about 65% $\dot{V}O_2$max), then these performances are physiologically impossible.

Athletes do not always eat high-carbohydrate diets in training, nor does the addition of extra carbohydrate to the diet of athletes in training necessarily improve their performance (Lamb, Rinehardt, et al. 1990; Simonsen et al. 1991). Indeed, two of the greatest ultraendurance athletes of all time—Mark Allen, perhaps the greatest male triathlete of the past century, and his female counterpart, Paula Newby-Fraser, overall Triathlete of the Century—have suggested that their training diets were not particularly high in carbohydrate. Allen (1998a) stated, "For me, 40% carbohydrate: 30% fat: 30% protein, that's my ideal diet." Similarly, Paula Newby-Fraser claims never to have carbohydrate loaded for any race in her life.

The Energy Depletion Model fails to explain why exhaustion develops when the muscle is glycogen depleted. The assumption is that exhaustion results because "what is clear is that, in glycogen-depleted muscle, ATP is being used up faster than it can be manufactured, and so force output is diminished" (Conlee 1987). However, that which is apparently most clear is often somewhat more complex. For if ATP is being consumed more rapidly than it is being produced, then ATP depletion must occur, leading to rigor. But skeletal muscle ATP stores are not depleted at fatigue (Febbraio and Dancey 1999) even in muscle fibers that are glycogen depleted (Ball-Burnett et al. 1991). Hence, something else is regulating performance. As Howard Green (1991) has concluded: "Most studies report no or only minimal changes in ATP concentrations at fatigue and no further changes in the by-products of ATP hydrolysis. These findings suggest that fatigue might be caused by other non-metabolic factors."

One such factor would be the associated hypoglycemia, which would act via a governor to cause a reduction in skeletal muscle recruitment, specifically to prevent damage to the brain, which relies on a normal blood glucose concentration for its healthy functioning.

The other factor would be central fatigue, the progressive reduction in central brain drive to the muscles (St. Clair Gibson, Schabort, et al. 2001). This central drive might fall as a direct result of feedback to the governor from the declining muscle glycogen concentrations via the glycostat. Hence, declining or low muscle glycogen concentrations would indeed "cause" the exhaustion, but the effect would be indirect, acting not peripherally in the muscles themselves, but centrally via the neural (brain) governor. Alternatively, other inputs to the governor would cause the development of a central, regulated fatigue that coincided with, but was not caused by, muscle glycogen depletion.

There is also little convincing evidence that carbohydrate loading increases the capacity to generate energy via oxygen-independent glycolysis during short bursts of high-intensity exercise (Bangsbo, Graham, et al. 1992). As a result, performance during single bouts of high-intensity exercise of short duration may be independent of the starting muscle glycogen concentrations (Grisdale et al. 1990; Hargreaves, Finn, et al. 1997; Pitsiladis and Maughan 1999a). Only when the exercise includes many repeated bouts of exercise does the preexercise muscle glycogen concentration influence the number of repetitions that can be performed and the amount of work in each repetition (Balsom et al. 1999).

This finding is also compatible with the central governor theory, in which, to prevent the development of rigor, less work would have to be performed as the muscle becomes progressively glycogen depleted.

In summary, the jury has not yet returned to deliver its final verdict on the second most popular dogma in the exercise sciences. Until such time as the issue is resolved, it is good to continue experimenting and to keep an open mind. The proven value of a high-carbohydrate diet is that it prevents excessive weight gain in athletes who must maintain low body weights. By maintaining higher blood glucose concentrations during exercise, preexercise carbohydrate loading reduces the probability that hypoglycemia will develop during exercise. In addition, according to the governor theory, complete muscle glycogen depletion should not be allowed to occur during exercise since this would lead to muscle rigor. Hence, it is probable that, during prolonged exercise, the governor must be continually updated by the glycostat about the state of the muscle glycogen stores so that it can reduce skeletal muscle recruitment before complete glycogen depletion occurs. The governor theory therefore predicts that preexercise carbohydrate loading will delay exhaustion and enhance performance by increasing the duration of exercise before muscle glycogen depletion occurs. This activates the central governor to reduce skeletal muscle recruitment. But, in this model, muscle glycogen is the indirect cause, indeed the signal, for that fatigue and acts via a neural (brain) mechanism—the glycostat—not by a direct chemical action in the exhausted muscles.

The current consensus is that the fastest initial rates of muscle glycogen resynthesis are achieved when 1.2 g carbohydrate per kg per hour are eaten every 30 minutes over 5 hours (about 400 g) (Van Loon, Saris, et al. 2000).

It is improbable that such a high rate of carbohydrate ingestion could be sustained for much longer than 5 hours without producing diarrhea and gastrointestinal distress. It is usually presumed that optimum carbohydrate loading can be achieved if about 600 g carbohydrate is ingested daily for two to three days. It is probably not important whether the carbohydrate is a simple (glucose) or complex (starch) carbohydrate. Our findings suggest most of the most commonly eaten carbohydrates are rapidly digested and absorbed in the intestine so that their released glucose enters the bloodstream at much the same rate as if glucose had been ingested, at least during exercise (J.A. Hawley, Dennis, et al. 1992a). The carbohydrate can also be eaten either as frequent small meals or in two large meals (Costill, Sherman, et al. 1981), or it can be taken in liquid form. However, muscle glycogen repletion occurs more rapidly if glucose is infused directly into the bloodstream, in which the absolute peak muscle glycogen concentrations of 40 g per kg wet muscle can be achieved within about 8 hours (Hansen et al. 1999).

Finally, in the absence of exercise, muscles with a high glycogen content retain those elevated levels for at least three days and probably for much longer.

Repleting Muscle Glycogen Without Food

One of the classic experiments that influenced A.V. Hill in developing his Cardiovascular/Anaerobic Model was performed by Walter Morley Fletcher and F.G. Hopkins at Cambridge University in 1907. Like Hill, Fletcher represented his university in track and field against the universities of both Oxford and Yale.

In their historic study, Fletcher and Hopkins showed that when frog muscle, isolated from the animal, was electrically stimulated to contract in vitro in the absence of an oxygen supply, its production of lactate increased. But when oxygen was reintroduced, the lactate slowly disappeared (W.M. Fletcher and Hopkins 1907).

The authors concluded that anaerobic conditions caused the contracting muscle to produce lactate from an unknown "lactic acid precursor" (now known to be glycogen), whereas the reintroduction of aerobic conditions ensured the resynthesis of that lactic acid precursor.

Hill used this experiment to explain the sequence of physiological events that occur during high-intensity exercise of short duration. He postulated that during such exercise, an inadequate oxygen supply to the muscles caused them to contract anaerobically, producing lactic acid from an undetermined precursor. During recovery, as the oxygen supply to the muscle again became adequate, that precursor, subsequently identified as glycogen, was resynthesized from the lactate that disappeared from the muscle. Hill estimated that 80% of the lactate removed in this way was resynthesized to glycogen, whereas the remaining 20% was oxidized in what later became known as the Krebs cycle (see figure 3.2). In this way, it provided the energy for the resynthesis of the muscle glycogen stores.

However, modern studies have shown that in both rats (Brooks et al. 1983; Nikolovski et al. 1996) and humans (Åstrand, Hultman, et al. 1986; Bangsbo, Gollnick, et al. 1991; Peters-Futre et al. 1987), this pathway cannot be significant as there is little resynthesis of glycogen directly from the lactate produced during high-intensity exercise. Rather, the resynthesis must occur from the glucose derived from dietary carbohydrates. This explains why significant muscle glycogen resynthesis does not occur in humans and rats unless carbohydrate is ingested and why the more carbohydrate that is ingested, the more rapid the glycogen resynthesis.

Researchers in Western Australia (Bräu et al. 1999) wondered whether this inability to resynthesize glycogen directly from lactate would apply to all mammals, especially those living in desert conditions in which access to carbohydrate-containing foods was restricted for prolonged periods of the year. They wondered how, for example, the desert-dwelling Western Chestnut mouse would survive predation if it were unable to resynthesize its muscle glycogen stores rapidly after being chased by a predator, and before a second attack was made.

Accordingly, they studied a group of Western Chestnut mice. They found that 50 minutes after they had been chased for 3 minutes around a circular running track in the laboratory, the mice experienced near total muscle glycogen depletion and a steep rise in muscle lactate concentrations. But 50 minutes later (after recovery), muscle glycogen concentrations were back to preexercise values, even though the mice had not eaten for 40 hours.

It appears that some mammalian muscle can be adapted to resynthesize glycogen rapidly after exercise from sources other than glucose derived from ingested carbohydrate. Clearly, either humans have never developed that capacity or they have lost it during their more recent past.

We now have an idea of how the body's energy stores are mobilized; let's look at factors that determine in what proportions these fuels are used during exercise.

FACTORS THAT AFFECT THE TYPE OF FUEL USED

There are a number of factors that determine whether the body will choose to burn fats, carbohydrates, or protein during exercise.

Exercise Intensity

When the intensity of exercise increases, carbohydrates become more important for energy production (Coyle, Jeukendrop, et al. 1993). This is because as exercise intensifies, more muscle glycogen and blood glucose are used with reduced rates of oxidation of plasma-free fatty acids at all exercise intensities greater than 60% $\dot{V}O_2$max and of muscle triglycerides at exercise intensities above 80% $\dot{V}O_2$max (Romijn et al. 1993; Van Loon, Greenhaff, et al. 2001). The rate of muscle glycogen use speeds up significantly at exercise intensities above 75% $\dot{V}O_2$max. At exercise intensities greater than 95% $\dot{V}O_2$max, only carbohydrate is burned (Saltin 1973; G.A. Brooks and Mercier 1994; G.A. Brooks 1998).

This finding led George Brooks and his colleagues from the University of Berkeley (G.A. Brooks and Mercier 1994; G.A. Brooks 1998) to postulate the crossover concept of energy metabolism during exercise (figure 3.11).

But our own data suggest that fat, especially intramuscular triglyceride, does contribute to energy metabolism, even at exercise intensities of up to 100% $\dot{V}O_2$max (Lambert et al. 1992). The practical point is that at high exercise intensities, carbohydrate, especially muscle glycogen, is used at very high rates and is probably the principal energy fuel.

Figure 3.11 shows that as exercise intensity increases (increasing percentage $\dot{V}O_2$max), there is a curvilinear increase in the proportion of energy derived from carbohydrate use with a reciprocal decline in the proportion of energy coming from fat. The greater use of carbohydrates at higher exercise intensities to the fact that there are more glycolytic enzymes than lipolytic enzymes in human muscle fibers. The crossover point occurs at about 35% $\dot{V}O_2$max in figure 3.11.

G.A. Brooks and Mercier (1994) speculate that the exact exercise intensity at which metabolism crosses over is determined by the athlete's degree of training (which

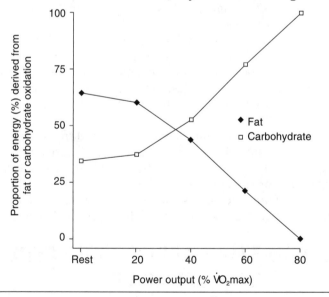

Figure 3.11   The crossover concept of George Brooks features a relative increase in energy derived from carbohydrate (CHO) oxidation and a proportional reduction in energy from the oxidation of fat with increasing power output.

Reprinted by permission of G.A. Brooks.

favors increased fat metabolism at low exercise intensities) and the degree of sympathetic nervous stimulation (which favors increased carbohydrate metabolism at higher exercise intensities).

The value of this concept comes from the knowledge that many athletes train at greater than 70% $\dot{V}O_2$max (that is, at exercise intensities at which carbohydrate is the main fuel for exercise). Furthermore, the most effective training for rapid improvements in performance is done at even higher exercise intensities (greater than 90% $\dot{V}O_2$max), at which carbohydrate is used exclusively.

This might suggest that enhancing the body's capacity for carbohydrate metabolism could improve performance during high-intensity exercise of relatively short duration (5 to 21 km). In contrast, and in keeping with the Energy Depletion Model, training at lower exercise intensities might enhance the body's capacity to burn fat and therefore spare the body's limited carbohydrate stores.

Nevertheless, the practical point is that at high exercise intensities, carbohydrate, especially muscle glycogen, is used at very high rates and is the principal energy fuel in most, but not all, athletes.

There is individual variability in all human responses, including dietary changes. For example, in the famous pemmican trials, in which humans were exposed to high-fat diets for short periods (Kark et al. 1945; Consolazio and Forbes 1946), most became so ill that they would rather starve than have to eat such intolerable food. Yet, one subject was quite the opposite. He ate 200 g of pemmican per day for the first three days, then ate between 400 and 674 g daily for the remaining six days (Consolazio and Forbes 1946). If people's habitual dietary preference can differ so much, and if such preferences cause long-term metabolic adaptations (Goedecke, Christie, et al. 1999), then that perhaps suggests that people differ in their metabolic responses during exercise. Any genetic influences on metabolism might further increase these differences.

In an earlier study from our laboratory at the Sports Science Institute of South Africa in Cape Town, Andrew Bosch and colleagues (1993) found that not all subjects were able to complete a 3-hour exercise bout after carbohydrate loading if they did not also ingest carbohydrate during exercise. They also noted that subjects who burned more carbohydrate during exercise, so-called carbohydrate burners, were more likely to fatigue prematurely than were subjects who burned more fat, the so-called fat burners. The concept that different people might be either fat or carbohydrate burners and that this might influence the dietary advice the different groups should be given, was first proposed in our laboratory by Professor Vicki Lambert. Intrigued by this possibility and under the direction of Lambert, doctoral student Julia Goedecke set out to determine whether there was any evidence for this individual variability in metabolism during exercise.

By studying a large number (61) of equally performing recreational cyclists, Goedecke was able to show that following an overnight fast, there is a great variability in the metabolism of these people, both at rest and during exercise (Goedecke, St. Clair Gibson, et al. 2000). Thus, at rest, the percentage fat oxidized as an energy fuel by the different subjects was normally distributed and varied from 100% to about 25% (figure 3.12A).

Furthermore, during exercise at 25%, 50%, and 70% of peak work rate, this normal distribution was maintained but shifted to the right (figure 3.12B), indicating that although all participants had increased the amount of carbohydrate they burned with increasing exercise intensity, there were still people in whom about 40% of

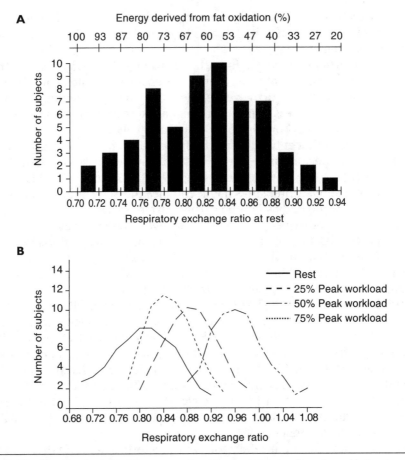

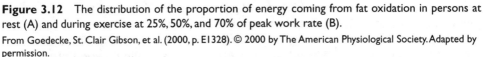

Figure 3.12   The distribution of the proportion of energy coming from fat oxidation in persons at rest (A) and during exercise at 25%, 50%, and 70% of peak work rate (B).

From Goedecke, St. Clair Gibson, et al. (2000, p. E1328). © 2000 by The American Physiological Society. Adapted by permission.

their energy came from fat oxidation at 70% of peak work rate, whereas in others, 100% came from carbohydrate and 0% from fat oxidation at that work rate.

Hence, that study establishes—perhaps in a significant way, and for the first time—that metabolic individuality exists such that, in the fasted state, some will continue to derive a meaningful proportion of their energy from the oxidation of fat, even during intensive exercise, whereas others will derive more than 90% of their energy from carbohydrate oxidation, even when exercising at a very low intensity (25% maximum work rate; figure 3.12B).

The study also showed that the key determinants for these metabolic differences at rest were muscle glycogen content, training volume, the proportion of Type I skeletal muscle fibers, resting blood free fatty acid and lactate concentrations, and the percentage dietary fat intake. At 25% maximum work rate, the key determinant of metabolic fuel use was the concentration of blood-borne fuels; at 50% maximum work rate, it was muscle substrate and glycolytic enzyme concentrations; and at 70% maximum work rate, the blood lactate concentrations.

This study shows that not all athletes are metabolically the same so that, at least when tested in the fasted state, some burn substantially more carbohydrate than others. Regardless of the physiological exercise model to which you adhere, carbohydrate burners are likely to be at a substantial disadvantage during prolonged exercise since they are more likely to develop hypoglycemia and muscle glycogen depletion prematurely, causing the early termination of exercise. These subjects would benefit substantially from preexercise carbohydrate loading and carbohydrate ingestion during exercise. In contrast, fat burners would be less likely to benefit from either of these interventions, and they could perhaps benefit more from interventions that would further enhance their capacity to burn fat during prolonged exercise. Indeed, the differences in fatigue resistance during very prolonged exercise might result from differences in the capacity to burn fat.

Exercise Duration

As the duration of exercise increases, at any exercise intensity, fat becomes an increasingly important energy source. For example, in our studies (Bosch et al. 1993) in which athletes exercised at 70% $\dot{V}O_2$max for 3 hours, the breakdown of fat accounted for only 6% of the energy production at the start of exercise but increased to 43% after 3 hours of exercise in subjects who did not carbohydrate load before exercise (figure 3.13). Rates of fat use were also reduced in those who had carbohydrate loaded before exercise. Our subsequent studies (Weltan, Bosch, et al. 1998a; 1998b) have shown that it is the muscle glycogen concentration that determines this response since high muscle glycogen concentrations inhibit (and low muscle glycogen concentrations enhance) fat metabolism, independent of the effects of either of these interventions on blood glucose concentrations.

Costill (1970) found similar changes during 120 minutes of treadmill exercise at 65% $\dot{V}O_2$max in non-carbohydrate-loaded subjects. At the start of exercise, 39% of energy came from fat, whereas at the finish, 67% of energy came fat.

The change from predominantly carbohydrate to predominantly fat as a fuel as the exercise duration increases is due to a slowing of the rate of muscle glycogen breakdown as muscle glycogen concentrations fall, and not to a reduced rate of blood glucose uptake by the muscles. In fact, the rate of glucose uptake by muscle rises substantially when the duration of exercise is increased (see figure 3.13).

The practical point is that as exercise is prolonged, there is a progressively greater reliance on blood glucose as the fuel for muscle metabolism. But this glucose comes mainly from the liver, which will become progressively more glycogen-depleted as the exercise continues. Ultimately, liver glycogen depletion will be so advanced that the rate of glucose production by the liver will be less than the rate of glucose uptake by the exercising muscles. Under those circumstances, blood glucose concentrations will fall, leading to the symptoms of hypoglycemia. This is one form of exhaustion that can be avoided by drinking suitable carbohydrate-containing drinks during prolonged exercise.

Degree of Fitness

The physiological and biochemical adaptations that occur with training are reviewed in detail later in this chapter. According to the earlier interpretations, the major effect of these adaptations is that during any exercise, regardless of its intensity or duration, more energy comes from fat than from carbohydrate (Henriksson 1977;

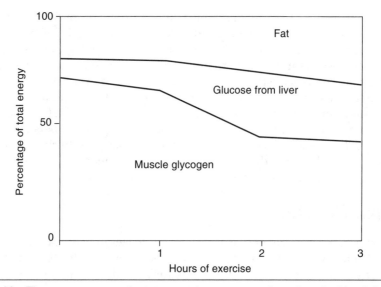

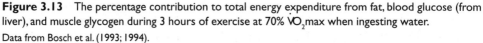

Figure 3.13   The percentage contribution to total energy expenditure from fat, blood glucose (from liver), and muscle glycogen during 3 hours of exercise at 70% $\dot{V}O_2$max when ingesting water.
Data from Bosch et al. (1993; 1994).

Hurley et al. 1986). The result is that increased fitness reduces the amount of carbohydrate burned during exercise. Proponents of the Energy Depletion Model argue that this adaptation allows trained athletes to exercise longer before they become exhausted, owing to depletion of carbohydrate, specifically muscle glycogen.

However, G.A. Brooks and Mercier (1994) have suggested that this interpretation is simplistic. They contend that the evidence showing that trained athletes burn more fat, specifically in their muscles, at all exercise intensities is not supported by much of the scientific literature (Helge, Richter, et al. 1996; Kanaley et al. 1995). Instead, they argue that other evidence shows that training may increase rates of fat oxidation at low exercise intensities, probably as a result of the increased use of intramuscular triglyceride stores (W.H. Martin et al. 1993; W.H. Martin 1997; Hurley et al. 1986) and enhanced oxidation of free fatty acid taken up from the bloodstream (Klein, Coyle, et al. 1994). At moderate to high-exercise intensities (above 75% $\dot{V}O_2$max), training increases the capacity to use blood glucose, thereby reducing the reliance on fat oxidation. This is associated with increased activation of the sympathetic nervous system.

Carbohydrate Stores

It was known as early as the 1920s that the preexercise diet influenced the type of fuel used during subsequent exercise (E.H. Christensen and Hansen 1939; Krogh and Lindhard 1920). Thus, athletes who followed a carbohydrate-free diet for a number of days used an increased amount of fat. A number of studies have shown that this effect is enhanced when athletes adapt to a high-fat diet, so-called fat loading (E.V. Lambert, Speechley, et al. 1994; Helge, Richter, et al. 1996; Goedecke, Christie, et al. 1999).

E.H. Christensen and Hansen (1939) also noted that the length of time that exercise could be sustained was influenced by the diet followed in the last few days before exercise and was greatest after a high-carbohydrate diet and least after a high-fat-protein diet. As discussed earlier in this chapter in the section on the Energy Depletion Model, it has since been assumed that this difference is explained by the higher preexercise muscle glycogen levels after the high-carbohydrate diet (Bergström, Hermansen, et al. 1967a). But, as I have argued, the effect could be due to higher pre-exercise liver glycogen levels that delay the onset of hypoglycemia during exercise.

When a high-fat diet is followed for sufficiently long (5 to 15 days) so that specific adaptations occur, this relationship is not found. The endurance of trained subjects adapted to a high-fat diet is not impaired (Phinney et al. 1983; Jansson and Kaiser 1982; E.V. Lambert, Speechley, et al. 1994; Goedecke, Christie, et al. 1999; Van Zyl et al. 1999 and is reportedly enhanced in some studies (E.V. Lambert, Speechley, et al. 1994; Van Zyl et al. 1999); Muoio et al. 1994; Hoppeler et al. 1999). Previously untrained subjects who were trained on a high-fat diet showed lesser gains in endurance after seven weeks than did those who trained on a high-carbohydrate diet; these performance differences were not present in the first four weeks of training (Helge, Richter, et al. 1996).

These studies emphasize the complexity of this topic. Perhaps the most important conclusion is that athletes can increase the fat content of their diets without affecting their endurance performance, either in training (Lamb, et al. 1990; Simonsen et al. 1991) or in competition. Even though few studies have shown that adaptation to a high-fat diet enhances endurance performance, this may be because the type of exercise in which this adaptation is likely to prove beneficial (prolonged exercise lasting more than 4 to 5 hours at 65% $\dot{V}O_2$max—typical of the Ironman Triathlon or 100-km or longer road races) has not been studied. The probable reason why the body chooses to burn more fat when a high-fat diet is followed is because this diet reduces muscle glycogen content in those who are regularly active. Work from our laboratory at the Sports Science Institute in Cape Town has established that muscle glycogen depletion increases fat oxidation directly (S.M. Weltan et al. 1998a; 1998b). This effect is not prevented by the infusion of glucose at high rates, indicating that it is muscle, and not liver, glycogen depletion that influences the rate of fat oxidation during exercise.

What Was Last Eaten and When

It is generally believed that whether a person is resting or exercising, the amount of energy that the muscles can extract from fat metabolism during exercise is determined by the rate at which free fatty acids are supplied to the muscles by the bloodstream (Newsholme and Leech 1983). This, in turn, depends on free fatty acid levels in the blood and the rate of blood flow to the active muscles. Thus, given a constant muscle blood flow, more of the total energy bill can be paid from fats when free fatty acids levels in the blood are high, at least when a person is resting. Conversely, when free fatty acid levels are low, the muscles must burn fuels other than fats, in particular muscle glycogen and blood glucose. As described in the previous section, we found that the muscle glycogen content determines the rate of fat oxidation during exercise by changing the free fatty acid concentrations in the blood, which are low when muscle glycogen concentrations are high and vice versa (S.M. Weltan et al. 1998a; 1998b).

This finding conflicts with a popular theory proposed by a group of Oxford biochemists in the 1960s. This group hypothesized that carbohydrate metabolism by the muscles is regulated directly by the concentration of free fatty acids in the bloodstream. Thus, high levels of circulating free fatty acids stimulated fat and inhibited carbohydrate metabolism, whereas low levels allowed unrestrained carbohydrate use. They termed this the Glucose-Fatty Acid Cycle (Randle et al. 1963).

When the Energy Depletion Model came in vogue in the late 1960s, exercise scientists theorized that an important technique to enhance endurance performance would be to stimulate fat metabolism and inhibit carbohydrate metabolism by invoking this Glucose-Fatty Acid Cycle. In this way, the rate of muscle glycogen use would be slowed during exercise, and the time taken to reach critically low muscle glycogen concentrations would be prolonged, thereby delaying fatigue. But if it is the muscle glycogen concentration that regulates fat metabolism—the Reverse Glucose-Fatty Acid Cycle—then manipulating the circulating free fatty acid concentrations will have little, if any, effect on the rates of muscle glycogen use and the duration of exercise that can be sustained before fatigue.

To test this hypothesis, a variety of techniques have been used to elevate free fatty acid concentrations in the blood artificially before or during exercise (Sidossis 1998). These techniques include caffeine ingestion (Bellet et al. 1968; B. Berglund and Hemmingson 1982; Costill, Dalsky, et al. 1978; Essig et al. 1980; Weir et al. 1987); injections of heparin (Costill, Coyle, et al. 1977) or fat emulsions, the latter into the bloodstream (Auclair et al. 1988; Hargreaves, Keins, et al. 1991; Vukovich, Costill, et al. 1993; Bracy et al. 1995; Dyck et al. 1993; Odland et al. 1998); or a high-fat meal immediately before or during exercise (Ravussin et al. 1986; Whitley et al. 1998). These studies have produced variable results that indicate that the Glucose-Fatty Acid Cycle does not exist, at least at physiological free fatty acid concentrations in the blood of humans. However, evidence for this effect can be found at the higher free fatty concentrations (0.8 mmol per liter) (Odland et al. 1998) that are present during prolonged exercise when muscle glycogen concentrations are low.

There is overwhelming evidence in support of the Reverse Cycle, in which the rate of carbohydrate metabolism, in particular, the muscle glycogen content and the availability of glucose in the cell, regulates fat metabolism in exercising humans (Coyle, Jeukendrup, et al. 1997; S.M. Weltan et al. 1998a; 1998b; Sidossis, Stuart, et al. 1996; Sidossis and Wolfe 1996).

We can perhaps conclude from these studies that it is not possible to increase the amount of fat the body will burn during subsequent exercise simply by altering the fat content of the last meal eaten before exercise. As Whitley et al. (1998) have concluded, "the pattern of substrate oxidation during endurance exercise is remarkably resistant to alteration." Perhaps this is because the amount of fat oxidized during exercise is determined principally by individual characteristics, including the muscle glycogen stores, which are not influenced by the amount of fat ingested immediately before exercise, but which can be increased by carbohydrate ingested 2 to 4 hours before exercise. Thus, it is the amount of carbohydrate burned during exercise that is the more easily modifiable.

The practical point is that any carbohydrate ingested before exercise increases the amount of carbohydrate used during subsequent exercise (Coyle, Coggan, et al. 1985; Montain, Hopper, et al. 1991), in part because such carbohydrate increases the starting muscle glycogen content (Coyle, Coggan, et al. 1985). The effect is measurable for about 6 hours after a high-carbohydrate meal (Montain, Hopper, et al. 1991). Thereafter, people's metabolism during exercise would be the same as if they had fasted for 12 to 14 hours.

Irrespective of the physiological exercise model you support, muscle glycogen concentrations should influence performance by acting either directly in the muscle or indirectly as a result of activation of the central governor. Thus, delaying, by whatever means, the time at which muscle glycogen depletion occurs should theoretically enhance performance.

Ingesting Caffeine and Fat

Caffeine ingestion appears to have no metabolic value, especially during exercise (Casal and Leon 1985; Erickson et al. 1987), possibly because caffeine loses its ability to mobilize fat in people who have carbohydrate loaded (Weir et al. 1987). However, the fact that caffeine does not appear to increase fat metabolism during exercise does not mean it cannot increase a person's ability to perform work. In fact, the evidence is quite the opposite; caffeine is remarkably effective in enhancing time to exhaustion when exercising for prolonged periods at a predetermined, constant workload. That this may be independent of any effect on metabolism but could result from a stimulatory effect, acting either centrally in the brain or on skeletal muscle contractility, might suggest that the Integrated Neuromuscular Recruitment Model is much more likely to explain exhaustion during prolonged exercise than the metabolically based Energy Depletion Model.

Much of the most convincing work in this field has been undertaken by Terry Graham of the University of Guelph in Ontario, Canada. Paradoxically, this work was initiated by the Ben Johnson doping scandal, which profoundly affected the Canadian sporting community. Graham wished to prove that caffeine, which was widely used by Canadian athletes of all ages and in many sports, was without any beneficial effect. Unfortunately, this work, which was initially funded by Sport Canada, whose mission, among others, is to reduce drug use in Canadian sport, proved the exact opposite.

One of their early studies (T.E. Graham and Spriet 1991) found that caffeine ingestion within the legal limits imposed by the International Olympic Committee (IOC) increased endurance performance during cycling and running at 85% $\dot{V}O_2$max by between 20% and 50%. The mechanism for this action was not determined. There are three possibilities for this.

1. The caffeine may have acted directly on skeletal muscle (Lopes et al. 1983; Mohr et al. 1998), possibly to increase its resistance to fatigue (the Muscle Power Model).

2. The caffeine may have acted on the brain to reduce the perception of fatigue, thereby enhancing endurance (the Central [Nervous System] Fatigue Hypothesis).

3. The caffeine may indeed have increased fat use by the muscles and spared muscle glycogen use. But this effect seems unlikely because caffeine enhances performance during high-intensity exercise at $\dot{V}O_2$max without affecting the rate of muscle glycogen use (Jackman et al. 1996). A number of studies show that endurance performance is increased after caffeine ingestion without evidence of increased whole body fat metabolism with carbohydrate sparing (Mohr et al. 1998; Van Soeren and Graham 1998).

As a result of these studies, T.E. Graham, Hibbert, et al. (1998) concluded that "The mechanism through which caffeine acts as an ergogenic aid is unlikely to be through changes in available metabolic substrates or catecholamines, but rather through some direct action of caffeine on tissues as yet to be described" (p. 1500).

Although caffeine also improved performance during maximum exercise lasting 4 to 5 minutes, no such effect was found during short-duration (30 seconds) exercise of very high intensity (Greer et al. 1998) nor, surprisingly, did the caffeine in coffee produce any effect (Graham, Hibbert, et al. 1998). Thus, some substance is present in coffee that prevents the usual ergogenic effect of caffeine. But despite the remarkable effects of caffeine on exercise performance in open-ended trials in which subjects were asked to continue exercising as hard as possible for as long as possible, no such effect was found in one study in which athletes were asked to complete a 100-km cycling time trial as quickly as possible (Hunter et al. 2002).

The practical implications of these divergent findings are discussed in more detail in chapter 13.

Ingesting a High-Carbohydrate Meal

Whereas the ingestion of fat has minimal effects on carbohydrate metabolism during exercise, a high-carbohydrate meal eaten shortly before exercise, like carbohydrate loading before exercise (Bosch et al. 1993; Bosch et al. 1996a), will increase the amount of carbohydrate oxidized during subsequent exercise (Coyle, Coggan, et al. 1985; G. Ahlborg and Bjorkman 1987; Montain, Hopper, et al. 1991).

For many years, runners have been encouraged not to eat a high-carbohydrate meal within 15 to 90 minutes before the start of exercise. The perceived logic for this is that blood concentrations of the hormone insulin increase after a high-carbohydrate meal and could have detrimental effects during exercise.

When carbohydrates are ingested, they cause a variable increase in the blood glucose concentration 30 to 60 minutes later. This is most likely determined by the rate at which the carbohydrates are emptied from the stomach, digested, and absorbed. Rapidly digested and absorbed carbohydrates formerly called refined or simple carbohydrates but now known as carbohydrates with a high glycemic index (GI), cause a rapid rise in the blood glucose concentration. This stimulates an increase in blood insulin concentrations. The function of insulin is to lower the blood glucose concentration by increasing both the removal of glucose from the blood and its storage as liver or muscle glycogen. It is considered unwise to begin exercise with elevated blood insulin concentrations as these will prevent the accelerated rate of liver glycogen breakdown necessary to supply the glucose to the bloodstream at increasing rates during exercise.

As the exercise intensity increases, the rate at which the active muscles extract glucose from the bloodstream rises. Any imbalance between the rates of liver glucose release and muscle glucose uptake will cause the blood glucose concentrations to fall, resulting in the premature termination of exercise.

In contrast, carbohydrates that are emptied from the stomach, digested, and absorbed more slowly, formerly described as complex or unrefined carbohydrates, but now known as carbohydrates with a low GI, cause a smaller, more delayed rise in blood glucose and hence in blood insulin concentrations. It is postulated that the ingestion of carbohydrates with a low GI before exercise would be less likely to induce hypoglycemia during subsequent exercise.

The differential effect of carbohydrates with either a low or a high GI are outlined in figure 3.14, which shows the blood glucose (A) and insulin (B) responses to the ingestion of either a carbohydrate-free placebo, or equal amounts (of energy) of potatoes with a high GI or pasta with a low GI. The glucose and insulin response to potatoes, originally regarded as a complex carbohydrate, is substantially greater than to pasta, showing that potatoes have a high GI.

The new GI terminology was introduced to accommodate the uncertainty as to whether some seemingly complex carbohydrates are able to produce changes in blood glucose concentrations similar to those measured when refined carbohydrates such as glucose or sugar (sucrose) are ingested. Currently, carbohydrates like potatoes, bread, sucrose (sugar), and confectionery, which produce a large glucose and insulin response, are said to have a high GI, whereas those like pasta, lentils, rice, and beans are said to have a moderate or low GI (Horowitz and Coyle 1993; L.M. Burke, Claassen, et al. 1998; see table 3.2).

Low GI carbohydrates are thought to be beneficial for health. As discussed subsequently, when carbohydrate is ingested during exercise, any metabolic differences caused by the ingestion of either high or low glycemic carbohydrates before exer-

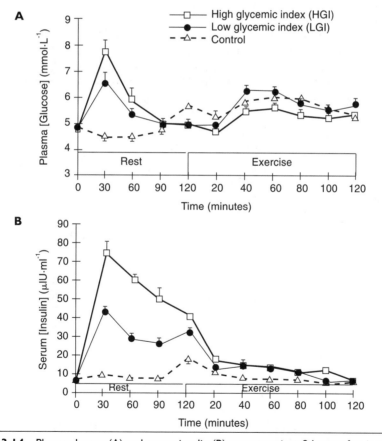

Figure 3.14 Plasma glucose (A) and serum insulin (B) concentrations 2 hours after ingestion of high and low glycemic index (HGI and LGI) carbohydrates at time 0, followed by 2 hours of exercise during which subjects ingested carbohydrate at regular intervals. In the control trial, subjects did not ingest carbohydrate before exercise.

From L.M. Burke, Claassen, et al. (1998, p. 2222). © 1998 by The American Physiological Society. Reprinted by permission.

cise is minimized, as also shown in figure 3.14. Irrespective of the GI of the carbo-hydrate in the preexercise meal, blood glucose and insulin concentrations during exercise were not found to be substantially different.

However, if no carbohydrate is ingested during exercise, preexercise meals com-prising low GI carbohydrate foods may enhance performance more than do high GI carbohydrates (Thomas et al. 1994; Kirwan, O'Gorman, et al. 1998). The reason for this is perhaps because blood glucose concentrations are higher, and insulin concentrations lower, during exercise that follows ingestion of a low GI food (Tho-mas et al. 1994). Thus, the optimum type of carbohydrate ingested before exercise depends on if carbohydrate is ingested during exercise. Furthermore, the addition of fat (butter or margarine) to the carbohydrate reduces the glycemic response to ingestion of the carbohydrate (Horowitz and Coyle 1993).

Insulin is the "anti-exercise" hormone that inhibits fatty acid mobilization from the fat cells and stimulates glucose uptake and storage (as glycogen) in the muscles and liver. Thus, in theory at least, if exercise starts when blood insulin levels are high, the rate of removal of glucose into the liver for glycogen storage may be accelerated, increasing the risk that blood glucose levels will fall precipitously, causing hypoglycemia (Short et al. 1997). Under these circumstances, muscle gly-cogen use is increased. However, for whatever reasons, hypoglycemia does not occur to any significant extent in the majority of athletes (Devlin et al. 1986; Seifert et al. 1994; Chryssanthopoulos, Williams, et al. 1994; Tokmakidis and Volaklis 2000),

Table 3.2 Food classification according to the glycemic index

Foods with a high glycemic index

Sugars	Glucose and sucrose
Syrups/jams	Honey, corn syrup, molasses, cane, and maple sugar
Beverages	All athletic drinks containing glucose and glucose polymers (maltodextrins)
Cereal products	Bread and cornflakes
Fruit	Raisins
Vegetables	Sweetcorn and baked, boiled, or mashed potatoes

Foods with a moderate glycemic index

Cereal products	Spaghetti (pasta), macaroni, noodles, rice, and whole grain rye bread
Fruit	Grapes and oranges
Vegetables	Yams and corn
Legumes	Baked beans

Foods with a low glycemic index

Fruits	Apples, cherries, dates, figs, grapefruit, peaches, pears, and plums
Legumes	Butter beans, kidney beans, chick peas (Garbanzo beans,) green beans, navy beans, red lentels
Dairy products	Milk and yogurt

so the risks of eating a high-carbohydrate meal shortly (15 to 45 minutes) before exercise may have been overemphasized. Nevertheless, some people are extremely sensitive to this phenomenon (Kuipers, Fransen, et al. 1999).

In contrast, strong evidence suggests that ingesting food 45 minutes to 4 hours before exercise may enhance performance (Coyle, Coggan, et al. 1985; Neufer, Costill, et al. 1987b; Anantaraman et al. 1995; El-Sayed et al. 1997; MacLaren et al. 1994; W.M. Sherman, Brodowicz, et al. 1989; Wright and Sherman 1989; Wright et al. 1991; Thomas et al. 1991; Kirwan, O'Gorman, et al. 1998; W.M. Sherman, Peden, et al. 1991; Schabort, Bosch, et al. 1999) by providing an additional store of carbohydrate in the intestine that is used at a constant rate during subsequent exercise. The effect is enhanced when carbohydrate is ingested during subsequent exercise (Chryssanthopoulos and Williams 1997). Ingesting the carbohydrate even 1 hour or less before exercise enhances performance (W.M. Sherman, Peden, et al. 1991; Goodpaster, Costill, et al. 1996a), provided the exercise bout is not too short (Palmer et al. 1998) or too intense (A.C. Snyder, Moorhead, et al. 1993). Performance was enhanced despite an increased rate of carbohydrate use during exercise after preexercise carbohydrate ingestion. This conflicts with the Energy Depletion Model, which predicts that performance is enhanced only when carbohydrate use is reduced by increasing the amount of fat burned.

In addition, we (L.M. Burke, Claassen, et al. 1998) found that the ingestion of carbohydrate during exercise minimizes any metabolic effect of carbohydrate ingested before exercise. Blood glucose and insulin concentrations and fuel choices during exercise were essentially the same in subjects who ingested approximately 60 g of carbohydrate per hour during 2.5 hours of exercise that followed ingestion of either a high or low GI carbohydrate meal.

However, some runners are extremely sensitive to the effect of a preexercise carbohydrate meal, and they develop profound hypoglycemia with severe incoordination and clouding of consciousness if they exercise within 90 minutes of ingesting a high-carbohydrate meal, without also ingesting carbohydrate during exercise. The lesson to be learned is that these athletes should avoid eating carbohydrates shortly before exercise or that they should only eat low GI carbohydrates that induce a small rise in blood insulin concentrations (Thomas et al. 1991). They should avoid carbohydrates for the 4 hours before exercise. Alternatively, they may eat before exercise, provided they ingest carbohydrate at about 60 g per hour during exercise.

For the rest of us, a high-carbohydrate meal eaten before exercise is essential because this practice clearly enhances performance during subsequent prolonged exercise, especially if combined with carbohydrate ingestion during exercise.

Exercise-Related Hypoglycemia

When South African marathoner Josiah Thugwane won the gold medal in the 1996 Olympic Marathon in Atlanta, his victory came as a surprise to many South Africans, who had perhaps hoped that a South African would win but had installed Gert Thys (figure 3.15) as their favorite.

At the 35-km mark, Thys, who was running close to the leaders, experienced a sudden onset of leg weakness. In two subsequent races he experienced identical symptoms. On both occasions, Thys was forced to drop off the pace, which

(continued)

Touchline Media

Figure 3.15 Gert Thys, the most consistently fast marathoner of all time, in the 2000 London Marathon.

cost him both a good position and a fast finishing time. As a result, he consulted a sports physician and was referred to Andrew Bosch at the Sports Science Institute of South Africa. On careful questioning, Bosch ascertained that Thys's symptoms strongly suggested hypoglycemia resulting from carbohydrate ingestion. But this was an unusual response, particularly since Thys's usual practice was to ingest his first carbohydrate-containing drink late in the race, when liver glucose output would already have been low as a consequence of lowered liver glycogen stores. This form of hypoglycemia contrasts with the more common forms of exercise-induced hypoglycemia, which develop in those who either ingest high GI carbohydrate foods 30 to 90 minutes before exercise or become liver glycogen depleted during exercise because they fail to carbohydrate load before exercise or to ingest adequate amounts of carbohydrate during prolonged exercise.

Tests were done in the laboratories of the Sports Science Institute to investigate how Thys responded to carbohydrate ingestion during exercise. His blood glucose concentration at the start of running was 4.8 mmol per liter. After running at race pace (20 km per hour) for some time, he ingested the sucrose-containing drink that he would normally use in a marathon. This caused symptoms identical to those he experienced during his races. His blood glucose concentration was then measured and found to be 3.5 mmol per liter. His insulin concentrations were high, confirming that he had developed hypoglycemia in response to carbohydrate ingestion late in exercise. In the next experiment, he was given a different carbohydrate drink containing glucose polymers soon after he started running. In contrast to the previous experiment, he did not develop any symptoms, and his blood glucose concentration remained normal at 5.4 mmol per liter with normal blood insulin concentrations. It was concluded that Thys was ingesting carbohydrate too late in a race, in insufficient quantities, and not of the most suitable type. He was advised to experiment with different types of carbohydrate, particularly different glucose polymer solutions, and to ingest these drinks as a 10% solution earlier in the race. He was to continue using this solution throughout the race.

The results have been particularly gratifying. In 1998 Thys became the only athlete ever to run two 2:07:00 marathons in the same calendar year. Then, in the Tokyo Marathon in Japan in February 1999, he became the world's second-fastest marathoner at that time, winning the race in a time of 2:06:30. When the times for his fastest five marathons are summed, he was the most consistently fast marathoner of the 20th century.

Nicotinic Acid Concentrations

Nicotinic acid is one of the B-group vitamins which, when present in the blood in high concentration, has an insulin-like effect and inhibits fat mobilization (Carlson et al. 1963; Bergström, Hultman, et al. 1969). It should therefore not be ingested within hours of starting exercise. Nicotinic acid is also used in the treatment of high blood cholesterol. As a result, some runners use this drug to lower their blood cholesterol concentrations.

Fortunately, the effects of nicotinic acid on running performance are mild. Thus, time in a 10-km race was not impaired when nicotinic acid was ingested before the race (B. Norris et al. 1978). Another study found a minimal detrimental effect of nicotinic acid on the performance of subjects who first cycled for 120 minutes at a fixed exercise intensity before cycling 5.6 km as rapidly as possible (Murray, Bartoli, et al. 1995).

Other cholesterol lowering agents, such as the HMG-Coenzyme A reductase inhibitors, simvastatin and gemfibrozoil, have little effect on fat metabolism during exercise, whereas acipimox, a nicotinic acid derivative, consistently inhibits fat metabolism during exercise (Head et al. 1993).

Fasting Before Exercise

Fasting increases free fatty acid levels in the blood, which induces fat metabolism during exercise (Montain, Hopper, et al. 1991). The increased use of fat is proportional to the length of the fast. However, performance in both submaximal (Loy et al. 1986; Zinker et al. 1990) and maximal (Gleeson, Greenhaff, et al. 1987) exercise is impaired by fasting: the former happens because of the premature onset of hypoglycemia; the latter, according to the Energy Supply Model, as a result of the reduced ability of muscle and blood to neutralize acid after fasting. Fasting also has effects in the brain that influence exercise performance.

Taking in Fuel During Exercise

Glucose either taken by mouth or infused into the bloodstream during exercise does not reduce the overall rate of muscle glycogen use during exercise (B. Ahlborg, Bergström, et al. 1967b; Bergström and Hultman 1967b; Coyle, Coggan, et al. 1986; Noakes, Lambert, et al. 1988; Bosch et al. 1994; Jeukendrup, Raben, et al. 1999; Jeukendrup, Wagenmakers, et al. 1999; MacLaren et al. 1999) but may reduce the rate of glycogen use in Type I muscle fibers (Tsintzas et al. 1995a; 1996a). However, during intermittent high-intensity exercise typical of team sports such as soccer and hockey, carbohydrate ingestion during exercise has a marked glycogen-sparing effect (Nicholas et al. 1999). The main fate of the ingested glucose is oxidation by the muscles in place of blood glucose derived from the liver (Bosch et al. 1994; Jeukendrup, Raben, et al. 1999; Jeukendrup, Wagenmakers, et al. 1999; figure 3.16). Thus, glucose or other carbohydrate ingested during exercise reduces the rate at which glycogen depletion of the liver occurs without affecting the rate of muscle glycogen depletion. However, it may alter the metabolic fate of the end-products of glycogen metabolism, especially lactate (Bosch et al. 1994).

A fascinating finding is that there is a maximum rate of glucose output by the liver during exercise (J.A. Hawley et al. 1992a; 1994a; 1994b; Jeukendrup, Raben, et al. 1999; Jeukendrup, Wagenmakers, et al. 1999). Ingesting carbohydrate does not increase this maximum amount; the carbohydrate ingested simply substitutes for all or part of the glucose released by the liver and any excess is stored as liver glycogen. Hence, there is a maximum rate at which carbohydrate should be eaten during exercise. This information forms the scientific basis for determining the optimum solutions for carbohydrate ingestion during exercise (see chapter 4).

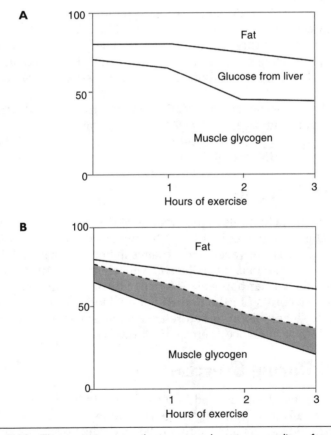

Figure 3.16   The percentage contribution to total energy expenditure from fat, blood glucose (from liver), and muscle glycogen during 3 hours of exercise at 70% V̇O₂max when ingesting water (A) or carbohydrate (B). Ingested carbohydrate is used in preference to liver glucose. Hence, glucose ingestion during exercise spares liver but not muscle glycogen stores.

Data from Bosch et al. (1994).

The Athlete's Regular Diet

While many exercise scientists around the world have become convinced that the ingestion of a high-carbohydrate diet is the secret to optimum performance during prolonged exercise, Phinney et al. (1983) found that the exercise performance of athletes who had adapted to a high (greater than 50%) fat diet was not impaired. Subsequently, as discussed earlier in this chapter, a number of studies have shown that athletes who adapt to a high-fat diet perform as well both in daily training and during prolonged exhaustive exercise as do those on a high-carbohydrate diet. But there is still no conclusive evidence that adaptation to this type of diet enhances performance more than does a high-carbohydrate diet, although isolated studies do report this effect (E.V. Lambert, Speechley, et al. 1994; Muoio et al. 1994; Hoppeler et al. 1999; E.V. Lambert, Goedecke, et al. 2001). However, the possibility remains that this diet may only enhance the performance of people involved in prolonged exercise lasting at least 4 to 6 hours and typified by ultradistance triathlon and running events (Brown et al. 2001). Interestingly, the endurance performance of rats is greater in those eating the less healthy n6 polyunsaturated fatty acids (PUFA) than in those eating n3 PUFAs (Ayre and Hulbert 1997). The authors conclude:

> Owing to publicity surrounding the findings that n3 fatty acids are beneficial for the cardiovascular system and neural development, there has been an increase in human consumption of foods such as canola-based products and fish. Clearly, however, the side-effects of such increased consumption on physical performance in humans need to be investigated.

Until studies evaluating this possibility have been completed, the simplest conclusion is that humans appear to have the capacity to adapt equally well to a variety of diets, without impairing their endurance performance. Perhaps this is to be expected.

There are also examples in the animal kingdom of superior endurance athletes that eat either a mixed grain diet (thoroughbred and Arabian race horses), a predominantly protein-fat diet (the African hunting dog), or a high-fat/moderate protein/absent carbohydrate diet (the Alaskan huskies that compete in the Iditarod Trail Race; Hinchcliff et al. 1997). It is of some interest that the athletic performances of Alaskan huskies fall immediately when they are placed on a high-carbohydrate diet, whereas thoroughbred race horses placed on a high-carbohydrate diet risk developing the muscle breakdown syndrome, myoglobinuria, or "tying up."

A point made at the 1976 New York City conference on the marathon has perhaps escaped critical assessment. In discussions at the conference, D.S. Kronfeld (1977) from the University of Pennsylvania made the following statement about the prevailing dogma that human athletes must eat exclusively high-carbohydrate diets:

> When the chimp came out of the trees 3 to 5 million years ago and started to chase, he was running on a diet of raw meat, and that was for 5 million years; and about 10 thousand years ago we learned how to cook and started to eat those cereal grains that started to sweep across the Middle East after the Ice Age. It is hard for me to see how an animal, and man is still an animal, that adapted to a very low carbohydrate, high meat, and high-fat burner for 5 million years suddenly in 10,000 years becomes a great glucose burner. I still am in the direction of thinking that we should be using nutritional strategies that favor fatty acid oxidation during long exhaustive work, and my thinking in that direction comes from studies of comparative nutrition. (p. 956)

The studies of comparative animal nutrition to which he refers show that most animals with high endurance perform more poorly on high-carbohydrate than on moderate- to high-fat diets (Kronfeld 1973; Kronfeld et al. 1977). Perhaps it is time again to emphasize the metabolic individuality of humans.

Gender

In the early 1970s, before running became popular and indeed before women were allowed to run in the Olympic Marathon, Joan Ulyott, a cardiac surgeon and ultramarathon runner from California, postulated that women had greater endurance than men. She theorized that this resulted from their greater capacity to burn their larger fat stores during exercise. However, it took two decades for the theory to be evaluated.

Although an original study found no difference in the capacity of men and women to burn fat during exercise, more recent, carefully conducted studies have all shown that women use more fat than do men during exercise at exercise intensities of 65% to 75% $\dot{V}O_2$max. In rats, equivalent exercise produces a lesser depletion of muscle glycogen in females than in males. Female rats also outperform males. These differences seem to be due to the female hormone estrogen, as treatment of male rats with estrogen both increases their exercise endurance and reduces their rate of muscle glycogen use in a dose-dependent manner (Tate and Holtz 1998). Other evidence for gender-determined differences in fat metabolism is the finding that women, but not men, increase the amount of fat they use at the same relative (percentage $\dot{V}O_2$max) exercise intensity after training (Friedlander, Casazza, et al. 1998a; 1998b).

There is at present suggestive evidence that women may burn more fat and less carbohydrate than do men when exercising at the same moderate (65% to 75% $\dot{V}O_2$max) relative workload. Whether or not this might favor women during prolonged exercise has not been established but seems unlikely, at least in terms of the model that holds that muscle glycogen depletion is not the exclusive cause of fatigue during prolonged exercise and the finding that, at least at the elite level, women do not have superior fatigue resistance compared to men.

Environmental Temperature

The rate of muscle glycogen use appears to increase during exercise in the heat (Fink, Costill, et al. 1975). Originally, this was considered to be a possible factor explaining impaired running performance in the heat. More recently, as discussed in chapter 4, it was established that exercise performance in the heat is impaired by a rising body temperature that induces a protective response that, in turn, reduces muscle recruitment, thereby decreasing heat production and decreasing the risk of heatstroke.

Warming Up

Warming up before exercise does not slow the rate of muscle glycogen use during exercise (Robergs, Pascoe, et al. 1991), but increases the blood flow to, and the temperature of, the active muscles.

Increasing Carbohydrate Stores Before Exercise

The Energy Depletion Model predicts that when the body's carbohydrate stores are depleted, the exercise intensity falls, possibly because some limiting concentration of muscle glycogen is reached.

Hence, according to that model, exercise performance during prolonged exercise of 1 hour or more can potentially be enhanced by increasing the amount of carbohydrate stored before exercise, by reducing the rate at which those stores are burned during subsequent exercise, and by ingesting carbohydrates in the appropriate amounts during exercise to maintain high rates of carbohydrate use, particularly when fatigued. While there may be significant reservations about the correctness of this model, the balance of evidence shows that eating a high-carbohydrate diet before and ingesting carbohydrate during prolonged exercise is the most effective way of improving performance during prolonged exercise at 70% to 90% $\dot{V}O_2$max. Time may yet prove that eating a diet with a higher fat content is a better option for very prolonged exercise (of 4 to 10 or more hours) at 65% $\dot{V}O_2$max or less, typical of the Ironman Triathlon and running races of 90 to 160 km or longer. However, this possibility remains speculative at present.

Figures 3.7 and 3.8 show that a high carbohydrate diet (75% to 90%) eaten for the last three days before exercise causes maximum filling of muscle (and liver) glycogen stores. To achieve this, the carbohydrate content of the diet for a 70-kg athlete needs to be of the order of 600 g per day. Lighter women would need to ingest 400 to 500 g a day.

For those who habitually eat a high-carbohydrate diet, the length of time for which prolonged submaximal exercise can be sustained has traditionally been linked to the size of the preexercise muscle glycogen stores. Karlsson and Saltin (1971) found that time in a 30-km cross-country race was best when the prerace muscle glycogen levels were of the order of 440 g (high-carbohydrate diet) but was 12 minutes slower when prerace muscle glycogen levels were only 230 g (fat-protein diet). When extrapolated to the marathon distance, these data suggest that athletes eating a low-carbohydrate diet would run about 30 to 45 minutes slower than if they had eaten a high-carbohydrate diet. Of course, no one would suggest that athletes should eat a low-carbohydrate diet before exercise, so that the actual magnitude of any effect may have been exaggerated in that study. Furthermore, in that study, there was no relationship between the extent to which the muscle glycogen stores were increased before exercise, the extra amount of muscle glycogen used during the race, and the individual improvements in racing performance. Hence, in that study, some factor other than an increased muscle glycogen storage and use explained the superior performance after carbohydrate loading. Since the study was not placebo-controlled, a placebo effect cannot be excluded.

In a more recent laboratory study, Bebb et al. (1984) showed that subjects who carbohydrate loaded before exercise were able to run 12% longer at 70% $\dot{V}O_2$max than those who only followed their normal diets for the three days before the exercise. Brewer, Williams, et al. (1988) found even larger increases (23% to 26%) in performance in those subjects participating in a similar experimental design who carbohydrate loaded by eating a 70% simple or complex carbohydrate diet for the final three days before exercise. In both studies, increased endurance was again associated with increased carbohydrate use during exercise in the carbohydrate-loaded group. Similar findings were reported by Tsintzas et al. (1996b). But these latter two studies are not especially relevant as athletes are more interested in completing a given distance in as short a time as possible, rather than maintaining a constant pace for longer (although this would probably also result in a faster finishing time for a set distance). Surprisingly, there are few modern studies that address this issue.

Brewer et al. (1988) showed that trained runners who supplemented their normal diets with carbohydrate confectioneries for the seven days before exercise ran 2:36:00 (1.9%) faster for 30 km than did a group who supplemented their diets with an equivalent amount of fat- and protein-containing foods. Both groups fasted for the 12 hours before exercise. This would have reduced liver glycogen stores in both groups. However, the effect would have been more important in the group ingesting the fat-protein diet as they would start exercise with lower liver (and muscle) glycogen concentrations and hence be at greater risk of developing hypoglycemia during subsequent prolonged exercise. Most of the benefit of carbohydrate loading was achieved in the last 5 km, in which the carbohydrate-loaded group ran significantly faster. An important effect of carbohydrate loading was to maintain higher blood glucose concentrations during the last 10 km of the race, again raising the possibility that it was the maintenance of higher preexercise liver glycogen and hence high glucose (rather than muscle glycogen) concentrations during exercise that really explained how carbohydrate loading works. For example, another study from the same group found that eating a high-carbohydrate meal (about 135 g) 4 hours before and ingesting water during exercise had the same effect on performance as did ingesting a total of about 85 g of carbohydrate at regular intervals during exercise that followed the same 12-hour fast (Chryssanthopoulos, Williams, et al. 1994). Both interventions maintained blood glucose concentrations during exercise.

The only other metabolic difference between groups was that the carbohydrate-loaded group burned about 30 g more carbohydrate during the trial despite eating 1270 g (1.27 kg) more carbohydrate for seven days on a high-carbohydrate diet. This is about the same additional amount burned in their earlier trial in which 30-km running performance was enhanced by the ingestion of carbohydrate during exercise (C. Williams et al. 1990). In that study, as in another of carbohydrate ingestion during exercise (Tsintzas et al. 1993), performance was enhanced to a similar degree to that achieved with preexercise carbohydrate loading.

These studies beg the obvious question: Why must so much carbohydrate be ingested before exercise to achieve the same benefit achieved when only a fraction of the same amount is ingested either some hours before or during exercise? As carbohydrate ingested during exercise really only substitutes for stored (endogenous) glucose derived from the liver (Bosch et al. 1994) (see figure 3.16), the beneficial effect of carbohydrate ingestion on exercise performance in these studies must have resulted from an effect on liver glycogen metabolism and possibly the prevention of hypoglycemia. Hence, these studies suggest the following:

- Substantially more carbohydrate must be ingested before (in the form of carbohydrate loading) than during (in the form of carbohydrate-rich drinks) exercise to prevent hypoglycemia during exercise.
- Discrepancy between the large amount of carbohydrate (about 1 kg) needed to be ingested before exercise to enhance performance and the small additional amount of carbohydrate actually burned during that improved perfor-

mance (about 30 g; Brewer et al. 1988 can best be explained if that additional carbohydrate contributes to the maintenance of higher blood glucose concentrations during exercise. As the liver usually contains about 100 g of carbohydrate, a 30-g increase would represent a substantial (30%) change in liver glycogen content and use during subsequent exercise, whereas it represents a negligible change (1.5%) in the estimated 500 g of glycogen stored in the muscles.

Thus, one way of interpreting this series of studies from the same research group (C. Williams et al. 1990; Brewer et al. 1988; Chryssanthopoulos, Williams, et al. 1994; Tsintzas et al. 1993; Tsintzas et al. 1995b) is that they have developed an excellent laboratory model to evaluate the effects of carbohydrate loading for the last days before exercise, eating a high-carbohydrate meal hours before exercise, and ingesting carbohydrate during exercise. These studies show that all three interventions are equally effective, provided hypoglycemia develops in the group not ingesting the carbohydrate. Hypoglycemia is made more likely by fasting the subjects for the 12 hours before exercise, the same technique used by Coyle, Coggan, et al. (1986) to establish the value of carbohydrate ingestion during exercise. As carbohydrate ingestion mainly affects liver glycogen depletion (Bosch et al. 1994), the likely conclusion is that all these interventions enhance performance, principally by preventing the development of hypoglycemia.

A theoretical weakness of the study of Brewer et al. (1988), as of most similar studies, was that the subjects and perhaps the experimenters knew when the athletes had carbohydrate loaded. In other words, they were not blind to the intervention that was being evaluated. It is well established that this knowledge can affect the outcome of the results as it tends to magnify any effect that is being studied. This would occur, for example, if the runners had ever read any literature on the topic and believed that carbohydrate loading improves performance.

To obviate this possibility, L.M. Burke et al. (2000) compared the effects of carbohydrate loading with real carbohydrate (in the form of potato starch) to that of a placebo (in the form of a low-energy jelly). Subjects were informed untruthfully, but in an ethically acceptable way, that both supplements contained the same amount of carbohydrate.

Despite an increased muscle glycogen use in the carbohydrate-loaded group, there were no differences in performance between the groups during a subsequent 100-km cycling time trial in the laboratory in which carbohydrate was ingested. This study raised at least two possibilities—either carbohydrate loading acts, at least in part, through a placebo effect, or, alternatively, the ingestion of carbohydrate during exercise minimizes any beneficial effect of carbohydrate loading, perhaps by maintaining blood glucose concentrations during subsequent exercise. The other possibility is that another factor, perhaps heat accumulation according to the Integrated Neuromuscular Recruitment Model, causes exhaustion during prolonged exercise. Provided the body has sufficient carbohydrate stores to prevent the early development of fatigue due to a falling blood glucose concentration (hypoglycemia), then heat accumulation or some other factor may become the mechanism limiting endurance performance.

Although a number of studies suggest that a high-carbohydrate preexercise diet may also enhance performance during exercise at 100% or more of $\dot{V}O_2$max (Maughan and Poole 1981; Greenhaff, Gleeson, et al. 1987a; 1987b; 1988a; 1988b; I. Jacobs 1987; Jenkins et al. 1993), other important studies have failed to show this effect. The failure to find any effect, even in subjects who are not blind to the intervention, suggests that a sufficiently high muscle glycogen content does not limit the rate of energy supply during high-intensity exercise (Energy Supply Model) as essentially proven by Bangsbo, Graham, et al. (1992). Alternatively, psychological factors, influenced by the placebo effect, may play little role in high-intensity exercise of very short duration. Indeed, the actual biochemical factors limiting such exercise remain uncertain (Fitts 1994). My bias is to believe that the central governor is especially important in this type of exercise.

Finally, the two findings that habituation to a high-fat diet for five or more days reverses the impaired performance of the first few days of a low-carbohydrate diet even though muscle glycogen concentrations remain low and that exhaustion occurs at different muscle glycogen concentrations after the different diets indicate that performance during prolonged exercise is not determined exclusively by the size of the preexercise muscle glycogen stores (Helge, Richter, et al. 1996).

CARBOHYDRATE LOADING AND DEPLETION

The metabolic effects of carbohydrate loading and carbohydrate depletion have been studied intensively. Bosch et al. (1993) found that carbohydrate loading increased muscle glycogen content before exercise and delayed the time at which very low muscle glycogen concentrations were reached. Interestingly, the main metabolic effect of carbohydrate loading was to decrease the amount of fat used during exercise. Thus, carbohydrate loading has a fat sparing effect during exercise. So, any beneficial effect of carbohydrate loading must result from its effect in increasing carbohydrate, and reducing fat, oxidation during prolonged exercise. This conflicts with the Energy Depletion Model, which predicts that superior endurance performance, following an intervention, must result from an increased capacity to use fat and hence to spare carbohydrate, most especially muscle glycogen, during prolonged exercise bouts.

The work of Weltan et al. (1998a; 1998b) has helped explain this finding. These studies established that the amount of fat used during exercise is determined by the muscle glycogen concentration. High muscle glycogen concentrations inhibit fat oxidation, and low muscle glycogen concentrations accelerate it. This explains the controversy surrounding the Glucose-Fatty Acid Cycle (Randle et al. 1963) and the Reverse Glucose-Fatty Acid Cycle (Sidossis, Stuart, et al. 1996; Sidossis 1998). In both cases, it appears that it is the muscle glucose concentration (in the form of glycogen) that has the predominant role in regulating fat metabolism by the muscle. It may therefore be very difficult, perhaps impossible, to increase fat oxidation and limit muscle glycogen use when muscle glycogen stores are elevated as they are after carbohydrate loading.

Reducing the Rate of Muscle Glycogen Use

Getting used to a high-fat diet seems to be the only technique that definitely slows the rate of muscle glycogen use during exercise (E.V. Lambert, Speechley, et al. 1994; Helge, Richter, et al. 1996; Goedecke, Christie, et al. 1999; E.V. Lambert, Goedeke, et al. 2001). Indeed, this effect probably explains how habituation to a high-fat diet returns endurance performance to normal after a few days on this diet and allows equivalent performance to that achieved on a higher carbohydrate diet (Goedecke, Christie, et al. 1999; Helge, Richter, et al. 1996). By increasing the body's capacity to mobilize fat and the muscles' capacity to use fat, this diet reduces the dependence on carbohydrate metabolism during exercise. As a result, the rate of muscle glycogen used is decreased. Most importantly, the increased ability to derive energy from fats may allow the fat-adapted athlete to continue exercising for longer at exercise intensities of 70% $\dot{V}O_2$max or less when muscle glycogen stores are at levels that would terminate exercise in the carbohydrate-adapted athlete.

Why the Hawaiian Ironman Triathlon Is a Metabolic Impossibility

One of the great challenges for exercise scientists who believe in the Energy Depletion Model is to explain how anyone is able to complete the Hawaiian Ironman Triathlon in as fast a time as the best triathletes—perhaps most notably, Mark Allen and Dave Scott in the 1989 Ironman Triathlon. After swimming 3.8 km in 51:17 minutes and cycling 180 km together in 4:37:52, they completed the final 42-km marathon in 2:40:04 and 2:41:03 respectively. The physiological anomaly is that if the Energy Depletion Model is correct, it would have been impossible for these two athletes to have run as fast as they did in the marathon, as no human has sufficient carbohydrate to sustain 8 or more hours of such high-intensity effort.

For example, our laboratory studies (Bosch et al. 1993, 1994; Rauch, Hawley, et al. 1998) predict that after 4.5 hours of cycling, an elite male Ironman triathlete would be expected to have oxidized about 700 g of carbohydrate and 175 g of fat. This compares to predicted whole body carbohydrate and fat stores of 520 g and 5000 g respectively. Hence, this model predicts that at the end of the cycle leg, an elite athlete would have depleted his body carbohydrate stores, yet must still run 42 km at close to 16 km per hour if he wishes to be successful.

Our other laboratory data suggest that after 4.5 hours of cycling at about 40 km per hour, the carbohydrate contribution to whole body energy metabolism would comprise a blood glucose oxidation rate of 1.2 g per minute (21 kJ per minute) and a lactate oxidation rate of 0.6 g per minute (10.5 kJ per minute). Together with the average maximum rate of fat oxidation that we have measured after 3 hours of laboratory cycling (0.76 g per minute; 28 kJ per minute), this provides a total rate of energy production of 59.5 kJ per minute. This would provide energy at a rate sufficient to sustain a running speed of approximately 12 km per hour, only enough to complete the 42-km marathon leg of the Ironman Triathlon in 3:30:00 (figure 3.17). To run the marathon in under 2:40:00, Allen was, according to these calculations, required to oxidize fat at a rate of 1.15 g per minute (figure 3.18). This rate is about 50% higher than the rates we have measured in national-class athletes in our laboratory.

If this metabolic model of fatigue in the Ironman Triathlon is correct, then the difference between running the final marathon in 2:40:00 versus 3:30:00 may simply be a 51% (0.4 g per minute) greater capacity to oxidize fat when body carbohydrate and, especially, muscle glycogen stores are depleted. Of course, this model does not negate the requirement that such high rates of fat oxidation can only be achieved if the central nervous system continues to recruit an appropriately large mass of muscle able to produce an appropriate force (St.

(continued)

Clair Gibson, Schabort, et al. 2001) This requires that the athlete's body temperature should also be sufficiently low.

It is this calculation that suggests that adaptations of fat metabolism rather than carbohydrate may be more important for ultraendurance athletes than for those involved in running events of up to 42 km, which are usually completed within 3 hours at a higher percentage $\dot{V}O_2$max(75% $\dot{V}O_2$max or higher). It also suggests that Allen may have exceptional physiological capacity for fat oxidation that is uniquely beneficial for the Ironman Triathlon. Allen's other achievement as one of the most successful Olympic distance triathletes of all time would not be explained by this capacity, as such events are too short to produce whole body carbohydrate depletion.

The theoretical and as yet untested predictions of these studies suggest that optimum preparation for endurance events lasting more than 4 to 6 hours—events involving exercise at approximately 70% $\dot{V}O_2$max and typified by ultramarathons of 56 km or longer, or more especially the Ironman Triathlon—should include a period of 7 to 10 days during which the athlete adapts to a high-fat diet (Goedecke, Christie, et al. 1999). Before competition, the athlete should switch to a high-carbohydrate diet. This ensures three benefits for the athlete:

Ironman simulation

To run 42 km in:	$\dot{V}O_2$ (ml $\cdot$ kg^{-1} $\cdot$ min^{-1})	% $\dot{V}O_{2max}$	Energy required (kj $\cdot$ min^{-1})
02:40:00	53	66	74
03:00:00	48	60	65
03:30:00	42	52	58

Energy comes from oxidation (g $\cdot$ min^{-1}) of:

	Blood glucose	Lactate	Fat
g $\cdot$ min^{-1}	1.2	0.6	0.76
kj $\cdot$ min^{-1}	21	10.5	28

42 km in 03:30:00	59.5 kj $\cdot$ min^{-1}

Figure 3.17 Ironman simulation: the table at the top of this figure shows the oxygen requirement ($\dot{V}O_2$), the exercise intensity (percentage $\dot{V}O_2$max), and the rates of energy expenditure that would be sustained by a world-class athlete completing the final 42-km marathon running leg of the Ironman Triathlon in times of 2:40:00, 3:00:00, and 3:30:00. Laboratory studies suggest that after a 3.8-km swim and a 180-km cycle, the athlete's body carbohydrate stores would be depleted so that energy for the running leg would come from oxidation of (mainly ingested) blood glucose and blood lactate and from circulating free fatty acids derived from muscle and adipose tissue triglyceride. To complete the marathon running leg in 3:30:00, the athlete would have to sustain a $\dot{V}O_2$ of 42 ml per kg per min (52% $\dot{V}O_2$max), equivalent to an energy expenditure of 59.5 kJ per min. Laboratory simulations (table at bottom of figure) suggest that under these conditions of near total carbohydrate depletion, peak glucose oxidation rates are 1.2 g per min and peak lactate (from glycogen) oxidation rates are 0.6 g per min. If these data for the maximum capacity to oxidize glucose and lactate in the carbohydrate-depleted state are correct, then to sustain the rate of energy expenditure necessary to run the marathon in 3:30:00, the carbohydrate-depleted triathletes must oxidize fat at a rate of 0.76 g per min.

Calculations courtesy of Andrew Bosch.

1. The athlete's muscle glycogen concentrations would be maximized before exercise.
2. The athlete might use that glycogen more slowly during exercise due to a greater capacity to burn fat.
3. The increased capacity for fat metabolism would allow the athlete to continue exercising at a moderately high intensity (about 70% $\dot{V}O_2max$), even when the muscle glycogen stores are very low. However, this advice still needs to be verified in a laboratory.

Ironman simulation

To run 42 km in:	$\dot{V}O_2$ (ml $\cdot$ kg^{-1} $\cdot$ min^{-1})	% $\dot{V}O_{2max}$	Energy required (kj $\cdot$ min^{-1})
02:40:00	53	66	74
03:00:00	48	60	65
03:30:00	42	52	58

Energy comes from oxidation (g $\cdot$ min^{-1}) of:

	Blood glucose	Lactate	Fat
g $\cdot$ min^{-1}	1.2	0.6	1.15
kj $\cdot$ min^{-1}	21	10.5	42.50

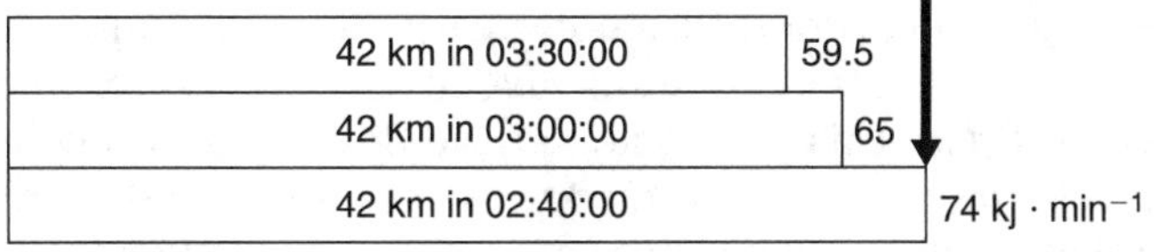

42 km in 03:30:00	59.5
42 km in 03:00:00	65
42 km in 02:40:00	74 kj $\cdot$ min^{-1}

Figure 3.18   Ironman simulation: To complete the marathon running leg of the Ironman Triathlon in 2:40:00, currently the fastest running time yet recorded in the Hawaiian Ironman Triathlon, the athlete would have to sustain a $\dot{V}O_2$ of 53ml per kg per min (66% $\dot{V}O_2max$), equivalent to an energy expenditure of 74 kJ per min. If the maximum capacity to oxidize glucose and lactate in the carbohydrate-depleted state is unchanged from values given in figure 3.17, then to sustain such a high rate of energy expenditure, the athlete must oxidize fat at a rate of 1.15 g per min. This model predicts that the superior ability of the elite Ironman triathlete may result from a greater (about 50%) capacity to oxidize fat than has been measured in our laboratory experiments of very prolonged laboratory exercise involving subelite athletes (Rauch, Hawley, et al. 1998).

Calculations courtesy of Andrew Bosch.

Maintaining Liver Glycogen Stores

The importance of maintaining liver glycogen levels and hence the rate of liver glucose production during exercise is that failure to do so will cause blood glucose levels to fall for the reasons already described. As the brain is dependent on an adequate glucose supply, declining blood glucose levels (hypoglycemia) ultimately lead to exhaustion, owing to impaired brain functioning. The typical symptoms of hypoglycemia are incoordination, an inability to concentrate or to think clearly, and extreme physical weakness, leading to collapse.

As might be expected, training increases the liver's ability to produce glucose, particularly from circulating blood lactate (Bergman, Horning, et al. 2000). This would be another mechanism explaining why training increases the rate at which lactate is removed from the blood in trained subjects.

Central Governor's Role During Prolonged Exercise

In chapter 4 we focus on a lost period between 1930 and 1986, during which scientists seemingly ignored evidence suggesting that carbohydrate ingestion during exercise might aid performance. However, in 1986, a study by Coyle, Coggan, et al. finally restored a historic truth.

Professor Eddie Coyle studied a group of elite cyclists who exercised for as long as they could at a fixed exercise intensity when ingesting either placebo or approximately 100 g carbohydrate per hour. As shown in figure 3.19, carbohydrate ingestion increased exercise time to exhaustion by about 1 hour, probably by preventing hypoglycemia (figure 3.19A). This study became a classic because it confirmed what had been known in the 1920s and 1930s and subsequently forgotten.

One important finding had been overlooked. Athletes ingesting carbohydrate terminated exercise after 4 hours, even though their blood glucose concentrations (figure 3.19A) were elevated. Also, their rates of carbohydrate oxidation (figure 3.19B) and their muscle glycogen concentrations (figure 3.19C) had remained unchanged. Why should these trained cyclists have fatigued at 4 hours if their metabolic profile was not greatly different from what it had been at 3 hours, after which they were still able to continue exercising for a further hour?

To investigate this phenomenon, we developed a new method of tracking the development of exhaustion during very prolonged exercise. Instead of having athletes either exercise for as long as possible at a fixed work rate or completing a time trial as fast as possible, we introduced repeated 1- and 4-km sprint intervals during a 100-km cycling time trial in the laboratory. Subjects were encouraged to complete each individual sprint trial, as well as the total distance, as fast as possible (L.M. Burke et al. 2000; St. Clair Gibson, Schabort, et al. 2001). We wanted to determine exactly when sprinting performance would begin to decline, as this would indicate when the subjects were starting to tire. We believed that the model used by Coyle, Coggan, et al. (1986)—open-ended trials in subject exercise at a fixed intensity for as long as possible—could not identify when fatigue first develops, since the point of fatigue is defined as the point at which exhaustion develops and exercise terminates, for example at 3 and 4 hours in the placebo and carbohydrate trials respectively (figure 3.19).

It was noted that peak sprinting speed fell progressively from the very first sprint for both the 1- and 4-km sprints (figure 3.20). Fatigue had already developed during the first 25 km of the 100-km time trial, analogous to the progressive slowing in marathon and ultramarathon runners, described further in chapter 10.

But perhaps the most important finding in that study was provided by Alan St. Clair Gibson, an expert in neuromuscular function during exercise. By measuring the electromyographic (EMG) activity in the *vastus lateralis* muscle of the cyclists, he was able to show that EMG activity fell progressively during the 1- and 4-km sprints. This was a crucial finding because it clearly differentiates

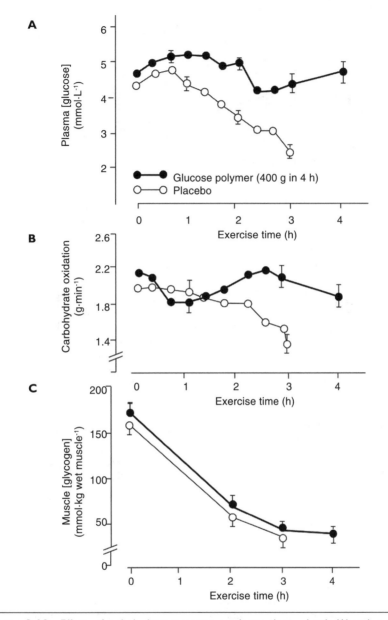

Figure 3.19 Effects of carbohydrate ingestion on plasma glucose levels (A) and on the rates of carbohydrate oxidation (B) and muscle glycogen concentrations (C) during prolonged exercise at 70% V̇O₂max. Carbohydrate ingestion during exercise maintains blood glucose levels and rates of carbohydrate oxidation without affecting the rate of muscle glycogen use.

From Coyle, Coggan, et al. (1986, p. 167). © 1986 by the American Physiological Society. Adapted by permission.

between peripheral fatigue best described as exhaustion in the exercising muscles and a centrally regulated fatigue that originates in the brain. For if the muscles become fatigued, the brain should recruit more muscle fibers to assist the fatiguing fibers, thereby maintaining a constant force output. This would be measured as increased EMG activity in the muscles. But the opposite occurred,

(continued)

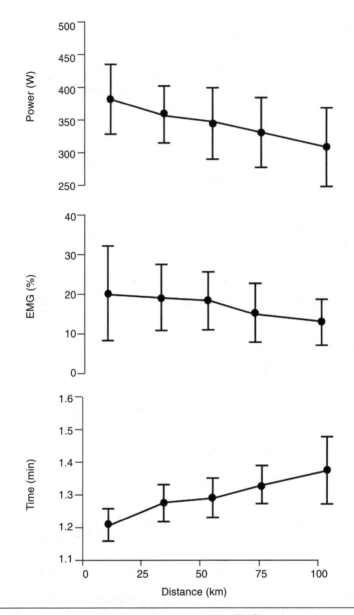

Figure 3.20   Power outputs, electromyographic activity (EMG), and time during consecutive 1-km sprints during a 100-km cycling time-trial in a laboratory.

Redrawn from St. Clair Gibson, Schabort, et al. (2001, R190). © 2001 by the American Physiological Society. Adapted by permission.

indicating that the brain had chosen to reduce the overall number of skeletal muscle fibers that were activated.

The conclusion that could be drawn from that study (St. Clair Gibson et al. 2001) was that the progressive fatigue shown as a progressive reduction in 1- and 4-km sprinting speed during the 100-km time trial was due to a progressive reduction in central neural recruitment. This suggests the action of a central governor, the goal of which is to reduce the mass of muscle that can be recruited during prolonged exercise gradually, thereby preventing the development of muscle glycogen depletion and muscle rigor or of hyperthermia leading to heatstroke.

The action of a central governor, which progressively reduced the mass of muscle that could be recruited, is the probable reason why the subjects in the study by Coyle, Coggan, et al. (1986) stopped exercising after 4 hours when they continued to ingest carbohydrate and were not hypoglycemic. After 4 hours, the brain was no longer able to recruit a sufficiently large muscle mass to maintain the original power output. As a result, exercise at that work rate would have to terminate. However, exercise could continue at a lower power output as this required a smaller muscle mass to be active.

If correct, this suggests that the central governor will allow exercise of approximately 70% $\dot{V}O_2$max to continue for up to 4 hours before it demands a reduction in the exercise intensity. However, if hypoglycemia develops before that time, it will cause a dramatic, but reversible, reduction in skeletal muscle recruitment. As shown in figure 3.19, this hypoglycemia will lead to the termination of exercise after 3 hours. But beyond 4 hours, provision of carbohydrate at high rates will not enhance performance at 70% $\dot{V}O_2$max any further. The governor, responding to other sensory information not yet identified but perhaps related to low muscle glycogen concentrations and coming from the glycostat, will decide that that particular exercise intensity is no longer sustainable and will signal that it must be reduced. The governor theory is the only model able to explain why exercise can continue during very prolonged exercise at a lower exercise intensity after exhaustion develops at a higher exercise intensity.

As a result of these ideas, Lambert, St. Clair Gibson, and I devised a new definition of fatigue, which we presented for the first time at the 2001 Annual Congress of the American College of Sports Medicine (ACSM). The traditional definition of fatigue is the inability to sustain the desired or required force (Edwards 1981). To this, St. Clair Gibson has added that fatigue is actually a central (brain) perception, in fact a sensation or emotion and not a direct physical event. This stems directly from our interpretation that exhaustion results from changes in central (brain) commands to the muscles (figure 3.20), rather than as a result of changes in the muscles themselves. My contribution has been to suggest that fatigue is merely the physical manifestation of a change in pacing strategy. Recognizing that the real reason why most of the models of exercise physiology fail is because they all try to explain fatigue exclusively, we exercise scientists have become conditioned to studying fatigue as if it and exhaustion are the most important phenomena in our discipline.

Yet, the reality is that pacing is the really interesting athletic phenomenon, since pacing and the absence of fatigue or exhaustion is the hallmark of success. And, since exercise fatigue is never absolute (at least this side of the grave)—we can always continue, but at a slower pace—it follows that all that happens at fatigue, when we are no longer able to sustain "the required force," or running speed, is that we have simply adopted a new, albeit slower, pacing strategy. To this, Lambert has added that the cause of this altered pacing must be to ensure that internal body homeostasis is maintained so that the muscles do not develop ATP depletion and rigor during either high-intensity or prolonged

(continued)

exercise when muscle glycogen stores are depleted; that the heart does not develop myocardial ischemia during high-intensity exercise; that the body temperature does not rise too high; and that the brain is not damaged by continued exercise when the blood glucose concentrations are low. Thus, our definition holds that fatigue is a (central brain) perception, which is based on the sum of the sensory feedback from a variety of organs to the central governor, and which is expressed physically as an alteration in pacing strategy (running speed) caused by a reduction in the muscle mass activated by the motor cortex in the brain.

This new understanding of fatigue brings together all the different models of exercise physiology. In fact, the findings of the separate models can all be explained by the action of a central governor that regulates exercise to ensure that internal body homeostasis is maintained and bodily damage avoided. Fatigue is merely the emotional expression of the subjective symptoms that develop as these subconscious controls wage a fierce battle with the conscious mind to ensure that the conscious ultimately submits to the superior will of the subconscious.

Preventing Hypoglycemia

My personal interest in the problem of hypoglycemia originated during the 1980 Comrades Marathon, for which I had not prepared properly. During this race, I experienced difficulty in concentrating. My mind would clear for 5 to 10 minutes every time I drank 100 ml of Coca-Cola. By 65 km, my pace began to fall, and by 80 km, I was forced to sit on the side of the road to keep from falling over. After about 5 minutes, I recovered enough to walk the remaining 10 km to the finish. On the road, I met two other runners who had suffered the same fate. They both concurred that, like me, they had started to feel faint and giddy and could simply not continue running. All three of us were intensely hungry and craved something sweet.

As a result of my experiences during this race, I have often wondered why, once you start walking, having run as fast as you can in an ultramarathon, it is virtually impossible to run again. Perhaps this is another effect of the central governor, which decides that once you have started walking, then walking is perhaps the safest way for you to progress toward the finish line.

Since then, two incidents of almost certain hypoglycemia in elite Comrades Marathon runners came to my attention. In the 1979 race, in his first attempt at a race longer than 56 km, Johnny Halberstadt led the race convincingly from the start and established a record time at the halfway mark. During the race, he drank an electrolyte drink with a low-carbohydrate content. He continued in this way, but 14 km from the finish he became disorientated, was unable to concentrate, and had to lie down to avoid falling over. He also had an intense craving for something sweet. What is of particular interest is that shortly after drinking a liter of Coca-Cola, which contains some 100 g of carbohydrate, Halberstadt took off with renewed vigor, just failing to win the race. Later Halberstadt told the press that he had diluted his body salts. In fact, he had simply not drunk enough carbohydrate during the race. Nor, as he later admitted, had he eaten breakfast. Both promote the development of hypoglycemia during prolonged exercise.

This remarkable recovery is identical to those reported by the pioneering Scandinavian exercise physiologists, who showed that exhausted, hypoglycemic subjects were again able to exercise without distress after they had been given drinks containing high concentrations (about 200 g) of sugar (Boje 1936; E.H. Christensen and Hansen 1939).

In the same 1979 Comrades Marathon, Bruce Fordyce, then young and unknown, also went through a bad patch 20 km from the finish. He recalls that he was suddenly unable to maintain his running pace. Fordyce's father forced him to drink a high-carbohydrate solution (Coca-Cola with added sugar). The results were quite dramatic; he finished strongly in third place and kick started his ultradistance running career.

Subsequent field studies show that whereas only 2% of runners develop hypoglycemia in a 42-km standard marathon, this figure increases to 6% after a 56-km ultramarathon and to 11% after the 90-km Comrades Marathon (P.S. McArthur et al. 1983). This suggests that carbohydrate ingestion, especially during ultramarathon races, likely enhances performance by preventing hypoglycemia.

I personally fieldtested this possibility in two ultramarathon races in 1982. In a 60-km race, I induced hypoglycemia after 50 km by neither carbohydrate loading nor resting beforehand, nor ingesting sufficient carbohydrate during the race. When reduced to a walk, I ingested about 25 ml of corn syrup (glucose polymer or maltodextrins). Within 5 minutes, the symptoms had resolved completely and I ran the last 8 km of the race as fast as I have ever run in any ultramarathon race.

Two months later, in the 1982 Comrades Marathon, I ran the last 40 km of the race with a tube filled with corn syrup from which I sucked the contents every 5 to 10 minutes. The 100 or so additional grams of carbohydrate had a clear effect—my mind remained clear for the entire duration of the race, and I experienced none of the emotional trauma typical of such events. More significantly, the fastest kilometers of my race were the final three.

This experience, aided by the insights of Fordyce, led to the development of a range of commercial carbohydrate products, the so-called Leppin FRN Squeezies. These products, which derived their name from the three developers [F(ordyce) R(ose) N(oakes)], were the first packaged carbohydrates for ingestion during marathon and longer races.

The question remains as to why hypoglycemia occurs in elite ultramarathon runners but is apparently uncommon in standard marathon runners (Noakes, Lambert, et al. 1988). The answer can be found in figure 3.6, which suggests that at standard-marathon pace (85% $\dot{V}O_2max$), muscle glycogen stores (B) will be depleted after about 115 minutes, whereas liver glycogen stores should last more than 140 minutes. However, at ultramarathon pace (70% to 75% $\dot{V}O_2max$), muscle glycogen is used at a much slower rate and should last for at least 310 minutes. Interestingly, the study of C.T.M. Davies and Thompson (1986) supports this finding because it found that complete muscle glycogen depletion had not occurred in a group of ultramarathon runners who ran for 4 hours at 67% to 73% $\dot{V}O_2max$. Their data therefore fit the prediction of figure 3.6 quite accurately.

However, the rate at which liver glycogen is used is not decreased by very much at 75% $\dot{V}O_2max$ compared to 85% $\dot{V}O_2max$, with the result that liver glycogen depletion would occur after only 220 minutes of exercise, in a shorter time in those who fast for 12 or more hours before exercise (see figure 3.19A). Thus, the prediction is that in athletes who do not ingest carbohydrate during an ultramarathon, liver glycogen stores will be depleted long before muscle glycogen stores. In contrast to marathon running (Noakes, Lambert, et al. 1988), ultramarathon running is more likely to be limited by the premature onset of hypoglycemia. Nevertheless, hypoglycemia can occur in marathoners who fail to ingest sufficient carbohydrate during competition (Cade et al. 1992).

But if a hypothetical athlete drinks 400 ml of a sports drink, with a carbohydrate content of 60 to 70 g per liter, every hour that he runs, he will extend the time he takes to become hypoglycemic. The onset of hypoglycemia would occur at about 5:10:00, at much the same time that it took both Halberstadt and Fordyce to become hypoglycemic during the 1979 Comrades Marathon.

Carbohydrate Ingestion During Exercise

Only recently have studies established that the ingestion of carbohydrate during prolonged exercise not only reduces the perception of fatigue (Lonnett et al. 1991; Wilber and Moffatt 1992; Utter et al. 1997) but also delays fatigue and enhances performance (Brooke et al. 1975; Macaraeg 1983; Coggan and Coyle 1987; 1988; 1989; Coyle, Hagberg, et al. 1983; Coyle, Coggan, et al. 1986; Ivy, Miller, et al. 1983; W.M. Sherman, Brodowicz, et al. 1989; J.B. Mitchell, Costill, et al. 1989b; Murray, Eddy, et al. 1987; Murray, Paul, et al. 1989; Murray, Siefert, et al. 1989; Williams et al. 1990; M.L. Millard-Stafford, Sparling, et al. 1992; M. Millard-Stafford et al. 1997; Tsintzas et al. 1993; Tsintzas et al. 1995; 1996a; 1996b; McConell, Kloot, et al. 1996; Jeukendrup, Brouns, et al. 1997; Kang et al. 1995b; Below et al. 1995; Maughan, Bethell, et al. 1996). Carbohydrate should be ingested throughout exercise. When ingested late in exercise, performance is not enhanced (McConell, Kloot, et al. 1996).

The beneficial effect of carbohydrate ingestion during exercise has been shown in the studies of Coyle, Coggan, et al. (1986) and Coggan and Coyle (1987; 1988; 1989); as discussed on pages 144 and 148, these researchers established that glucose polymer ingestion improved endurance performance by preventing hypoglycemia and maintaining a high rate of carbohydrate use (see figure 3.19). Interestingly, carbohydrate ingestion did not reduce the rate of muscle glycogen use (Bosch et al. 1994; Mitchell, Costill, et al. 1988), as was found in runners during marathon and short ultramarathon races (Noakes, Lambert, et al. 1988) or even in cyclists receiving large intravenous infusions of glucose (Coyle, Hamilton, et al. 1991). However, there may be sparing of muscle glycogen use in Type I muscle fibers when carbohydrate is ingested during prolonged exercise (Tsintzas et al. 1995a; 1996a).

Coggan and Coyle (1988) then showed that glucose infused at a rate in excess of 1 g per minute, beginning at the point of exhaustion, can prolong performance. (This finding has little practical value to runners as it would constitute doping in competition.) Carbohydrate ingestion at the point of exhaustion was less effective, probably because the rate of delivery from the intestine was unable to match the high rate at which it was being used (Coggan and Coyle 1987). Exercise performance was enhanced even if the carbohydrate was ingested late in exercise but before the onset of exhaustion (Coggan and Coyle 1989). The authors therefore suggested that there was no benefit in ingesting carbohydrate throughout prolonged exercise. They proposed that the ingestion of a very concentrated drink (20% to 50%) 30 or more minutes before the time at which exhaustion was expected to occur might have the same effect. The evidence published since that study shows that carbohydrate should be ingested throughout exercise, not least because it reduces the sensation of fatigue. However, it is still too early to accept this possibility unconditionally. If fatigue during prolonged exercise lasting up to 4 hours is caused by hypoglycemia rather than muscle glycogen depletion, then this proposal of Coggan and Coyle (1989) is correct. Ingestion of adequate amounts of carbohydrate late in exercise would be as effective in preventing hypoglycemia and in enhancing performance as would carbohydrate ingestion throughout exercise.

Interestingly, it seems that the beneficial effect of carbohydrate ingestion during exercise occurs sooner in running than in cycling (Wilber and Moffatt 1991). In one trial, carbohydrate ingestion enhanced running performance over the last 15 km of a 30-km time trial (C. Williams et al. 1990). In another study, runners who ingested carbohydrate during the first 35 km of a 40-km time trial ran 11% faster over the last 5 km than did those who ingested only water (M.L. Millard-Stafford, Sparling, et al. 1992). More recently, Below et al. (1995) showed that carbohydrate or water ingestion during high-intensity exercise of short duration (70% $\dot{V}O_2$max for 50 minutes) enhanced performance during a subsequent bout of all-out effort lasting 10 minutes. The magnitude of the independent effects of water and carbohydrate ingestion were about the same (6%): replacing both water and carbohydrate during exercise improved performance by about 12%. M. Millard-Stafford et al. (1997) showed that performance during the last 1.5 km of a 15-km race was far better when carbohydrate was ingested before and during the run than when only water was ingested.

Other studies have shown that carbohydrate ingestion improves performance during high-intensity exercise of short (1-hour) duration (Jeukendrup, Brouns, et al. 1997), although no effect was found in exercise lasting only 30 minutes (Palmer et al. 1998). The physiological explanation for this is unclear and cannot be due to the prevention of hypoglycemia, which did not occur in those studies.

Preexercise Carbo Loading

A final insight into this topic is provided by studies comparing the effects on performance of preexercise carbohydrate loading, with or without carbohydrate ingestion during subsequent exercise. The most illuminating study is that of Kang et al. (1995), who showed that carbohydrate ingestion (approximately 45 g per hour) increased the duration that carbohydrate-loaded subjects could exercise at 70% $\dot{V}O_2$max by about 35 minutes (about 23%). Carbohydrate ingestion (approximately 143 g during 190 minutes of exercise) increased total carbohydrate oxidation by about 100 g and prevented a progressive decline in the blood glucose concentration after 20 minutes of exercise in carbohydrate-loaded subjects who did not ingest carbohydrate during exercise but who had fasted for 12 hours before exercise (and who therefore began exercise with substantially reduced liver, but not muscle, glycogen concentrations). The authors observed that carbohydrate loading seemed to slow the rate of blood glucose decline in subjects who did not ingest carbohydrate during exercise so that preexercise carbohydrate loading "could reduce the minimal dosage of carbohydrate that should be ingested during exercise" to prevent the development of hypoglycemia and impaired performance.

The converse study of Widrick, Costill, et al. (1993) showed that the endurance performance of subjects who did not carbohydrate load before exercise but who ingested carbohydrate during exercise was almost as good as that of subjects who carbohydrate loaded before exercise, fasted for 12 hours before exercise, and did not ingest carbohydrate during exercise. Blood glucose concentrations were essentially the same with either carbohydrate loading before exercise (and no carbohydrate ingestion during) or with only carbohydrate ingestion during exercise. In contrast, blood glucose concentrations fell precipitously and performance was impaired in those who did not carbohydrate load, fasted, and failed to ingest any carbohydrate during exercise.

My interpretation of all published studies in which body carbohydrate stores are manipulated either before or during exercise is as follows:

- The most important carbohydrate stores influencing exhaustion are in the liver, because the stores are quite small (approximately 100 g); they are used up at an obligatory rate of between 10 and 60 g per hour during rest and exercise respectively; and, when depleted, they cause hypoglycemia, which rapidly terminates exercise via a central governor mechanism.

- Perhaps the most important effect of carbohydrate loading is to increase the liver glycogen stores at the start of exercise. This increases either the duration or the intensity of exercise that can be sustained before the development of hypoglycemia induces fatigue and terminates exercise.

- Ingesting carbohydrate during exercise is the most effective way of preventing hypoglycemia. Carbohydrate ingestion during exercise is at least as effective in improving endurance performance as carbohydrate loading alone. To achieve this benefit, much less carbohydrate must be ingested during exercise than before exercise. This is because all the carbohydrate ingested during exercise is used to prevent hypoglycemia (Bosch et al. 1994) whereas only a portion of the carbohydrate ingested before exercise is ultimately used by the liver to maintain the blood glucose concentration. A far greater proportion is used by the muscles. Indeed, the rate of muscle glycogen use is increased after carbohydrate loading (Bosch et al. 1993).

Of course, exhaustion will still develop during prolonged exercise, even if the blood glucose concentration remains normal (Coyle, Coggan, et al. 1986; A.P. Burke et al. 1999). This is assumed to be caused by muscle glycogen depletion acting directly in the active muscles themselves. However, I suspect that the central governor, responding to low muscle glycogen concentrations, is the more likely explanation.

Type and Amount of Carbohydrate

Most forms of carbohydrate, except for some starches, are able to supply glucose to the bloodstream sufficiently fast, if ingested at rates of about 60 to 90 g per hour during exercise (Hawley et al. 1994a; 1994b; Jeukendrup and Jentjens 2000).

The current proviso is that virtually any palatable carbohydrate can be ingested during exercise, in either solid or liquid form, at rates of 40 to 80 g per hour. The more prolonged the event, the more important such ingestion becomes. It is possible that optimum performance in events of less than 90 minutes can still be achieved without carbohydrate ingestion. However, in events lasting more than 2 hours, this becomes increasingly improbable.

Restocking Glycogen

The prevailing belief is that athletes whose training involves prolonged high-intensity exercise must eat a high-carbohydrate diet if they wish to maintain their liver and muscle glycogen levels. In general, the greater the carbohydrate content of the diet, the more rapid the rate of glycogen resynthesis. Surprisingly then, studies comparing the performance, during training, of athletes following either high- or more moderate carbohydrate diets have not shown any substantial performance benefits in favor of the high-carbohydrate diets (W.M. Sherman, Doyle, et al. 1993; Lamb, Rinehardts, et al. 1990). Furthermore, studies of the real dietary habits of athletes, as opposed to the theoretical ideas they have been taught about what they should eat, show that few, if any, eat high-carbohydrate diets (J.A. Hawley, Dennis, et al. 1995). This raises the question of whether such diets are really necessary during training (Sherman and Wimer 1991; Noakes 1997) or whether adaptation in fat metabolism allows athletes to perform optimally, at least during training, even when eating diets containing a suboptimum carbohydrate content.

It is possible that low muscle glycogen stores may not affect muscle performance as adversely as is generally believed (Grisdale et al. 1990). Any diet that prevents the development of hypoglycemia during exercise may be all that is required.

However, Simonsen et al. (1991) found that whereas rowers who underwent four weeks of intensive training maintained muscle glycogen content and power output during a short-duration test of high intensity while eating a diet containing 5 g carbohydrate per kg body weight per day, their performance and muscle glycogen content was enhanced by a diet containing 10 g carbohydrate per kg body weight per day. Although this finding might be specific to an activity such as rowing, in which performance was tested during high-intensity exercise of relatively short duration (6 minutes), the value or necessity of ensuring that body carbohydrate stores are replaced daily by eating a high-carbohydrate diet remains unproven, at least in runners.

Despite this still unresolved controversy, athletes who wish to restock their liver and muscle glycogen stores as rapidly as possible should eat the same high-carbohydrate diet that they would eat before competition. Athletes competing on consecutive days for more than 4 hours daily can ensure optimum muscle glycogen resynthesis each day if they also ingest high-carbohydrate solutions during competition (Brouns 1988).

Only recently have studies determined the amount of carbohydrate needed to restock carbohydrate stores in athletes training heavily each day, as well as the effects of daily carbohydrate repletion on performance. These studies have shown that a minimum of 8 g carbohydrate per kg body weight must be eaten daily but that muscle glycogen concentrations may still fall despite such a high carbohydrate intake (Kirwan, Costill, et al. 1988).

Other factors influencing the rate of muscle glycogen resynthesis have been identified more recently. Although one study suggested that women have a reduced capacity for glycogen resynthesis (M.A. Tarnopolsky, Atkinson, et al. 1995), this finding was not apparent in another study by the same group (M.A. Tarnopolsky, Bosman, et al. 1997). Resynthesis is more rapid when carbohydrates with a low GI are eaten (L.M. Burke, Collier, et al. 1993; Jozsi et al. 1996) or when protein is ingested with the carbohydrate (Zawadzki et al. 1992; Van Loon, Saris, et al. 2000). However, the most important determinant is simply the amount of carbohydrate ingested (Van Loon, Saris, et al. 2000). Not surprising, trained humans resynthesize muscle glycogen about twice as fast as do the untrained (Hickner et al. 1997). The same is found in rats (Akira et al. 1997).

The rate of muscle glycogen resynthesis is unaffected by the physical nature of the carbohydrate, whether liquid or solid (Lamb, Snyder, et al. 1991; Coleman 1994) and whether the same amount of carbohydrate is eaten as small, frequent snacks or as large meals (L.M. Burke, Collier, et al. 1996). However, resynthesis is most rapid if the carbohydrate ingestion begins immediately after the termination of exercise (Ivy 1991). The amount ingested should be about 50 to 80 g repeated twice hourly, starting immediately after exercise and continuing for the first 6 hours after exercise (Ivy 1991; W.M. Sherman 1992). But even higher rates can be achieved if the same amount is ingested every 30 minutes for 5 hours (Van Loon, Saris, et al. 2000).

Muscle glycogen resynthesis is impaired for the first few days after marathon racing (W.M. Sherman, Costill, et al. 1983; Asp, Rohde, et al. 1997), probably as a result of muscle damage (described in chapter 7). Adequate carbohydrate ingestion during the early phase of recovery improves performance during a second exercise bout undertaken either 4 hours later (Fallowfield et al. 1995; Bilzon et al. 2000) or 24 hours later (Fallowfield and Williams 1993; Nevill et al. 1993).

ENERGY PRODUCTION DURING SUPRAMAXIMAL EXERCISE

Up to this point, we have confined our discussion to metabolism during prolonged exercise at intensities less than 100% $\dot{V}O_2$max, for which virtually all the energy comes from oxygen-dependent mitochondrial metabolism. Yet some distances, such as the 100- and 200-m sprints, are run at speeds that require a rate of energy production that exceeds those that can be sustained by purely oxygen-dependent (or oxidative) metabolism. Thus, a 100-m sprint in 10 seconds, a speed of 36 km per hour, requires an oxygen consumption of 140 ml O_2 per kg, far greater than the highest value ever measured in a human. This indicates that the body is able to produce energy from other oxygen-independent pathways in each muscle cell.

ATP and PCr Stores

Within the muscle there are stores of adenosine triphosphate (ATP) and phosphocreatine (PCr), which provide the immediate energy for muscle contraction. The stores can only provide energy for about 7 seconds of maximum exercise.

Oxygen-Independent Glycolysis

Once intensive activity, such as sprinting, begins, glycolysis is instantly activated to supplement energy production from the ATP and Pcr stores. In this pathway, glycogen is broken down to lactate (Brooks et al. 1998) and ATP is produced to replenish the ATP stores of the muscle (refer to figure 3.2). Lactate is then transported across the mitochondrial membrane to serve as a substrate in the Krebs cycle.

In theory, the muscles contain sufficient glycogen to maintain a maximum sprint of 80 seconds (Newsholme and Leech 1983). Yet, from watching the world's leading sprinters, we all know that it is impossible to maintain peak sprinting speed for more than about 5 to 20 seconds. Why should this be?

One possibility is that such high-intensity exercise may threaten the safe functioning of the heart, activating the governor described in chapter 2 to regulate muscle recruitment and running speed. Clearly, this model must become active within the first 1 to 3 minutes of exercise, whereafter the maximum cardiac output and maximum coronary blood flow is achieved. If the central governor is not activated within 2 to 3 minutes of the onset of exercise of high intensity, then myocardial ischemia will develop (figure 2.5).

Alternatively, the Energy Supply Model predicts that important by-products of glycolysis and of ATP and PCr breakdown, in particular hydrogen ions (H+), accumulate within the muscle fibers and reduce the muscle's ability to continue contracting at high intensity (Fitts 1994). This control mechanism functions in the same way as the governor in the heart that was originally postulated by Hill, who believed that this governor reduced the contractile capacity of the heart when ischemia developed. The action of this "peripheral governor" during intensive exercise of short duration prevents normal human muscle from depleting its energy content to such low levels that irreversible muscle damage and muscle cell death results. As a result of this safety mechanism, runners are forced to slow down, thereby preventing death.

Given this background knowledge, it is possible to describe the exercise duration for which each of these intracellular fuels is especially important during high-intensity exercise, such as sprinting.

A single maximal muscle contraction (for example, lifting a heavy weight) uses only ATP. Thereafter, glycolysis and PCr breakdown are activated to the greatest possible extent, peaking within about 3 to 6 seconds (Boobis 1987; Spriet 1987; Hultman, Spriet, et al. 1987). The rates of glycolysis and PCr splitting then become progressively inhibited, and oxygen-requiring (oxidative) metabolism in the skeletal muscle mitochondria becomes increasingly important. After about 90 to 120 seconds, oxidative metabolism becomes the predominant energy source. The rate of energy production from the breakdown of ATP and PCr and from glycolysis exceeds, by far, that from purely oxidative pathways. This is why we can only do intense exercise for brief periods.

This information also helps explain the different metabolic pathways activated by high-intensity interval training of different durations, as well as the nature of the fatigue experienced during high-intensity exercise.

Exercise to exhaustion in less than 6 to 10 seconds stresses PCr and glycolytic metabolism to their limits and is probably limited by the rapid accumulation of metabolic end-products, the rising concentrations of which are probably sensed by muscle receptors, which then inform the central governor to reduce the mass of muscle that it is prepared to activate. This explanation contrasts with the more popular theory—based on the ideas of A.V. Hill—that the accumulation of those metabolites acts as a peripheral governor that "poisons" the exercising muscles.

This historical explanation is easily refuted by means of a simple observation. Sprinters in 200-m races maintain the same speed from about 50 to 180 m. If their top speeds are limited by the accumulation of "poisonous" metabolites, they should continue to speed up progressively until poisonous metabolite levels are reached, whereafter they should slow progressively and inexorably. But this simply does not happen, since peak and constant speeds are achieved and maintained for the greater duration of those races, just as they are in races of most distances up to 10 km. In fact, sprinters reach their peak velocities within 3 seconds and then sustain the same velocity for another 17 or so seconds. Changes in muscle lactate and pH cannot occur so quickly that they set the optimum pace within the first 3 seconds of exercise.

Only a neural regulator that determines the mass of skeletal muscle that is active (and hence the rate at which the supposedly poisonous metabolites can accumulate) can produce a constant peak running speed, achieved within 2 to 3 seconds of starting exercise and, at least initially, independent of the rate of accumulation or the absolute intramuscular concentrations of the poisonous metabolites. As the exercise continues, this central governor in the brain sets the pace on the basis of prior experience and in response to sensory feedback from a number of organs.

Since the heart is not at risk during high-intensity exercise of up to 60 seconds, the actions of the central governor are aimed not at sparing the heart but rather at preventing the development of rigor in the exercising muscles. But the central governor might apply the logic that if this same exercise intensity were to be maintained for 2 to 3 minutes, then heart damage would occur when a limiting cardiac output and coronary flow is reached sometime after that. If the central governor has the capacity for such logic, then the lower power output during high-intensity exercise lasting 2 to 5 minutes might indeed be due to the action of the central governor choosing to recruit a smaller mass of muscle from the outset of the exercise, rather than by any direct action of poisonous metabolites in the muscles, causing a peripherally based, metabolite-induced fatigue. Because glycolysis is active for only a very short time during high-intensity exercise of 6 to 10 seconds, the blood concentrations of its by-product, lactate, remain relatively low.

During exercise lasting between 6 and 30 seconds, glycolysis is the predominant energy source, and blood lactate concentrations are increased somewhat. If exercise of between 6 and 30 seconds is repeated in an interval training session, it is probable that much of the lactate produced during the exercise period would be removed during recovery. Steady-state blood lactate levels are reached after two or three intervals (Åstrand and Rodahl 1977; figure 3.21). The benefit of this form of training would probably be to speed up the rate of lactate removal from muscle during the recovery period.

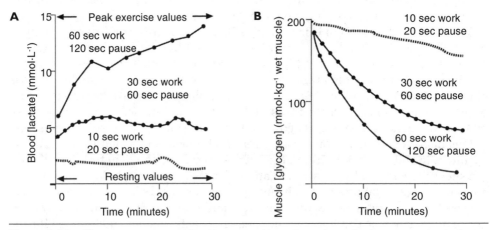

Figure 3.21 Changes in measured blood lactate and in estimated muscle glycogen concentrations during repeated intervals lasting 10, 30, or 90 seconds separated by an equal period of rest in the ratio of 2:1 (duration of rest period: duration of exercise period).
Used with permission of Åstrand and Rodahl (1977 p.300).

If the exercise duration is longer than 30 seconds, glycolysis makes a maximum contribution to energy production, resulting in large increases in muscle and blood lactate concentrations (figure 3.21). In addition, the acidity of the muscle increases sharply. If interval sessions are performed with the exercise repeats lasting more than 30 seconds, it is probable that there is a progressive accumulation of lactate in muscle and blood as metabolism of lactate during the rest intervals is not swift enough to prevent its accumulation (Åstrand and Rodahl 1977). Muscle acidity also increases. Thus, this type of interval training probably stresses the ability of the muscles to continue contracting even when their acidity is greatly increased. Exercise lasting 60 minutes or more stresses carbohydrate and fat metabolism, as already described.

Lactate Metabolism

There are so many misconceptions surrounding the glycolytic product known as lactate that it is important that these be adequately addressed.

Lactate is one of the products of glycolysis (refer to figure 3.2). In fact, according to one new hypothesis it may be the key end-product (Brooks et al. 1998; Brooks 1998; Dubouchaud et al. 2000). It is both produced and used by the muscles; its rate of production increases as the exercise intensity increases and as more carbohydrate is used to fuel exercise. In the body, lactate usually exists in combination with sodium (as sodium lactate), not in the acidic form of lactic acid.

Lactate was one of the first chemicals that the early exercise scientists were able to measure. An unfortunate result was that every possible problem associated with exercise—including fatigue, muscle cramps, the stitch, postexercise muscle soreness, and oxygen debt—were laid at the door of this molecule. We now know that lactate is innocent on all these counts (Brooks 1998). In fact, lactate may be one of the most important energy fuels in the body. Let us banish once and for all the bad publicity that lactic acid has attracted for so long and elevate it to its rightful place as one of the most important of the body's fuels.

The original thinking was that muscles only began to produce lactate when their oxygen supply was inadequate to meet their oxygen demands. The muscles therefore became anaerobic and, as a result, the end-products of glycogen breakdown could not be metabolized in the mitochondria, as oxygen is required for them to function. As a result, it was believed that the muscles released lactate in increasing amounts.

The origin of this belief can probably be traced to the early studies of W.M. Fletcher and Hopkins (1907) and the subsequent influence of A.V. Hill, who proposed that lactate was the signal that initiated muscle contraction and that the function of oxygen was to remove the lactic acid once it had been formed (Hill 1927a). It is now clear that lactate is a product of, not the cause of, muscle contraction. More important, there is little evidence that lactate is released only by muscles that are anaerobic or indeed that muscles ever become anaerobic during exercise.

First, muscles are able to release lactate even when their oxygen supply is more than adequate (Connett et al. 1984; 1986; MacRae et al. 1992; R.S. Richardson et al. 1998; Graham and Saltin 1989). Thus, muscle lactate production is not contingent on anaerobic conditions in the muscles.

Second, there is no conclusive evidence to suggest that muscles become anaerobic during exercise at intensities approximating the lactate threshold (Connett et al. 1985; Gayeski et al. 1985) or even during maximal exercise (Graham and Saltin

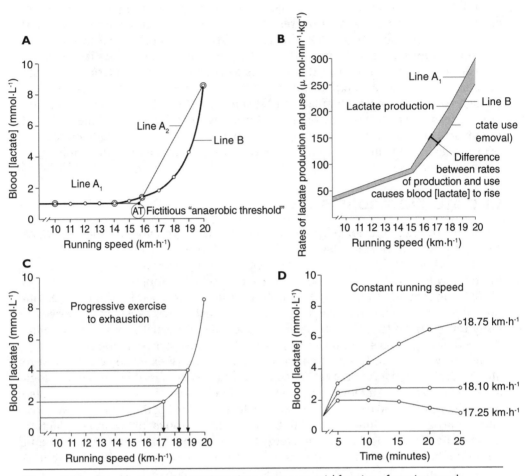

Figure 3.22 Blood lactate concentrations rise as an exponential function of running speed.

1989; R.S. Richardson et al. 1998).

At one time, the prevailing belief was that blood lactate concentrations suddenly increased at a threshold exercise intensity, variously called the anaerobic threshold, the lactate turnpoint, or the ventilation threshold.

Figure 3.22 shows that blood lactate concentrations measured during the same progressive treadmill test used to determine the $\dot{V}O_2max$ remain low at low running speeds. Ultimately, a running speed is reached above which blood lactate levels appear to rise more precipitously. This point has conventionally been called the anaerobic threshold because it was proposed that at that exercise intensity the muscles became "anaerobic" for the first time. The belief was that as the exercise intensity increased further, the muscles became progressively more anaerobic so that the trickle of lactate into the bloodstream became a flood, and blood lactate concentrations rose precipitously.

This mistaken conclusion resulted from at least two errors. First, too few blood samples were measured. For example, if only four blood samples had been drawn at running speeds of 10, 14, 16, and 20 km per hour (figure 3.22A, lines A1 and A2), then a fictitious anaerobic threshold (AT) would have been identified at 15.5 km per hour. But measuring blood lactate concentrations repeatedly—for example, every km per hour (figure 3.22A, line B)—shows that blood lactate concentrations rise exponentially without any evidence of a threshold phenomenon. Second, it was not understood that lactate is both produced (figure 3.22B, line A) and used (figure 3.22B, line B) by the exercising muscles (and also used by the heart and liver), so that the exponential rise in blood lactate concentrations results from the progressively greater rise in the rate of lactate production than in the rate of its removal, and hence its progressive accumulation in blood. Note that the rates of lactate use are greatest at the highest running speeds. This could not happen if the muscles were "anaerobic."

It is now clear that the blood lactate concentrations do not show a clearly defined, abrupt threshold response during exercise of progressively increasing intensity. Rather, blood lactate concentrations begin to rise as soon as progressive exercise commences. However, at low exercise intensities, the rate of the increase is so slow that it is barely noticeable. Only when the exercise becomes more intense does the rise become apparent, which perhaps explains the erroneous impression that blood lactate concentrations increase abruptly when the lactate threshold is reached.

Figure 3.22 also shows another technique for determining an athlete's level of fitness by measurement of blood lactate concentrations during progressive exercise to exhaustion (C) and during sustained exercise at the same running speed (D). Figure 3.22C shows that blood lactate concentrations of 2, 3, and 4 mmol per liter are achieved at running speeds of 17.25, 18.10, and 18.75 km per hour during the progressive exercise test. When running at those speeds for 25 minutes (figure 3.22D), blood lactate concentrations fall after an initial rise at 17.25 km per hour, stay constant at 18.10 km per hour, or rise progressively at 18.75 km per hour. According to this test, the athlete's maximum lactate steady state—the maximum running speed at which lactate use matches lactate production—occurs at 3 mmol per liter in the progressive test to exhaustion (Borch et al. 1993). Accordingly, the running speed during the progressive exercise test that elicits a blood lactate concentration of 3 mmol per liter may be the most meaningful measure of each athlete's "lactate threshold."

When mathematical techniques are used to quantify the changes in blood lactate concentrations, they show that the concentrations rise as a continuous function of the exercise intensity without showing an abrupt threshold effect (M.E. Campbell et al. 1989; Dennis et al. 1992; Hughson, Weisiger, et al. 1987; Bosch et al. 1993). In other words, lactate is a natural product of carbohydrate metabolism during exercise. As the rate of energy production rises, so more carbohydrate is used, and, as a result, more lactate appears in the bloodstream. Hence, a rising blood lactate level only indicates that more carbohydrate is being burned. It does not mean that the muscle's work is becoming more anaerobic.

For these reasons, the terms anaerobic threshold, lactate threshold, and lactate turnpoint are no longer justifiable. With the lack of a suitable alternative, we have continued to use the term lactate turnpoint in this text. This term refers to the exercise intensity at which blood lactate concentrations begin to rise visibly. It is limiting in that it identifies a point that is determined visually, not mathematically, and that it suggests some sort of abrupt threshold, when no such threshold exists.

More accurate techniques to define this same point mathematically rather than visually are available (M.E. Campbell et al. 1989; Dennis et al. 1992; Hughson, Weisiger, et al. 1987). These techniques measure the gradient of the slope of increasing blood lactate concentrations. Thus, the lactate turnpoint can be identified as a point on the curve at which the gradient for increasing blood lactate concentration is, for example, 108. Alternatively, as shown in figure 3.22, the lactate turnpoint might be best defined as the exercise intensity or running speed that produces a blood lactate concentration of 3 mmol per liter during a progressive maximal exercise test to exhaustion.

This is because when exercise is continued at running speeds below that critical speed, blood lactate concentrations do not rise further but tend to fall (figure 3.22D). This suggests that the exercise intensity can be sustained for some reasonable time.

Biochemical Explanations for Increased Lactate

As the exercise intensity increases, so does the rate of carbohydrate use. When high exercise intensities (greater than 85% to 95% $\dot{V}O_2$max) are achieved, virtually all the energy comes from carbohydrate oxidation (G.A. Brooks and Mercier 1994; Brooks 1998). This means that the rate of energy flow through the glycolytic pathway increases steeply with increasing exercise intensity. The result is that the rate of lactate production increases inside the muscles. The high rate of glycolytic ATP turnover also produces acidic (hydrogen) ions, or protons, which acidify the inside of the muscle cell and which, according to Hill's peripheral governor theory, interfere with muscle contraction. To counteract this, the protons are exported from inside the cells into the bloodstream. But this process requires that lactate be cotransported with the protons (Dennis et al. 1992). In this way, lactate appears in the bloodstream whenever the rate of carbohydrate use is high. The presence of lactate in the bloodstream is the by-product of a process that aims to prevent the muscles from becoming acidic too rapidly.

An important aspect of endurance training is that it shifts the lactate turnpoint to a higher running speed or a higher percentage of $\dot{V}O_2$max (see figure 3.23). These changes in the lactate turnpoint appear as an early response to training. In one 36-week study, as a group of subjects increased their weekly training distances from 20 km per week to 73 km per week in preparation for a marathon race, their lactate turnpoints increased from 63% to 71% $\dot{V}O_2$max within the first 12 weeks of training and did not change after that. Their $\dot{V}O_2$max values continued to increase for 24 weeks before stabilizing (D.A. Smith and O'Donnell 1984). Gaesser and Poole (1986) showed that the rate of change in the lactate turnpoint was fastest in the first two to three weeks of training. Subsequently, Gaesser and Poole (1988) showed that the half-time for this adaptation is 10.5

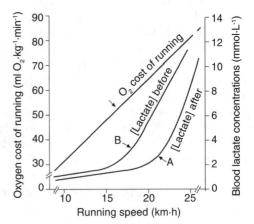

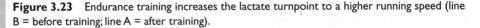

Figure 3.23   Endurance training increases the lactate turnpoint to a higher running speed (line B = before training; line A = after training).

days; that is, half of the total adaptation (to the constant training load) will be achieved within 10.5 days of training. This study also showed that adaptations in the $\dot{V}O_2$max and the lactate turnpoint occur at different times.

Interestingly, the capacity of the muscle cell membranes to transport lactate is high in trained athletes and is proportional to the percentage of Type I (ST) muscle fibers (Pilegaard et al. 1994).

Lactate Turnpoint

A number of studies suggest that the visually determined lactate turnpoint may indeed be a good predictor of marathon running performance. This was first shown by P.A. Farrell et al. (1979), who found that the velocities runners were able to maintain for the standard marathon were 0.45 km per hour faster than the treadmill speeds at which their lactate turnpoints occurred.

Other studies confirmed these findings in race walkers (Hagberg and Coyle 1983), in road racers competing at distances from 3 to 21 km (LaFontaine et al. 1981; Kumagai et al. 1982; S.R. Powers et al. 1983; Tanaka, Matsuura, et al. 1983; C. Williams and M.L.G. Nute 1983; Yoshida et al. 1993; Roecker et al. 1998; A.M. Jones and Doust 1998), and in marathoners (Lehman et al. 1983; Noakes, Myburgh, et al. 1990a; Sjodin and Jacobs 1981; Sjodin and Svedenhag 1985; Tanaka and Matsuura 1984; Roecker et al. 1998). In addition, Sjodin and colleagues (1981) showed that a runner's lactate turnpoint was related to training volume and to the percentage of Type I muscle fibers and the capillary density in the runner's leg muscles. Thus, the greater the percentage of Type I fibers, the greater the training volume. Also, the more muscle capillaries athletes had, the greater the speed at which their lactate turnpoints occurred and therefore the faster their marathon paces. Training-induced changes in road racing performance at distances from 5 to 10 km also correlate best with changes in the lactate turnpoint (Tanaka, Matsuura, et al. 1984).

The practical relevance of this information is twofold. First, it suggests that the exercise intensity that can be sustained for 42 km is very close to the intensity at which blood lactate concentrations first begin to rise above values present during mild exercise. Hence, at least theoretically, this test might be useful in helping athletes predict their likely marathon times.

Second, this test could be used to monitor an athlete's fitness level if repeated frequently during training.

However, in reality, it is relatively time-consuming to identify the lactate turnpoint in the laboratory. Also, it is probably a less accurate predictor of marathon performance than either the peak treadmill running velocity measured during the $\dot{V}O_2$max test; the prediction based on racing performance at shorter distances (see tables 2.3, 2.4, 2.6, and 2.7 and figure 2.13); or even the athletes' own predictions, provided they are experienced marathoners. Indeed, in equally well-trained cyclists, measurement of blood lactate parameters during exercise was found to be of negligible value in predicting their performances (Hoogeveen and Schep 1997).

Despite the hype that surrounds the value of lactate testing in predicting performance in runners, the expectations have unfortunately not been met. Changes in blood lactate concentrations during exercise can give some indication of whether the athlete's fitness has improved or regressed, but there is little added value in using blood lactate measurements for the prediction of performance.

Conconi Test

Much attention has been given to the possibility that the lactate turnpoint can be predicted on the basis of the so-called Conconi test, which measures heart rate changes that occur during exercise (Conconi et al. 1982; Bodner and Rhodes 2000).

Conconi, after whom the test was named, suggests that at work rates below the lactate turnpoint, the heart rate increases linearly with increasing work rate or running speed, as in the protocol used for $\dot{V}O_2$max testing. However, at and above the running speed or work rate that corresponds with the lactate turnpoint, the heart rate no longer rises in a linear fashion but reaches a plateau, the so-called heart rate inflection point. Thus, the authors have suggested that determining the running speed at which the heart rate inflection point occurs is a noninvasive technique of predicting the lactate turnpoint. If this were true, this simple test could also be used to predict running performance and to measure improvement in fitness, as well as to predict overtraining (see chapter 7) and imminent or established illness.

However, we (Dennis et al. 1992) and many others (Ribeiro et al. 1985; Kuipers, Keizer, et al. 1988; Coen et al. 1988a; 1988b; Leger and Tokmakidis 1988; Tiberi et al. 1988; Francis et al. 1989; Hofmann et al. 1994; 1997) have only been able to identify this phenomenon in a few subjects. Others have found that the test fails to produce reproducible results (A.M. Jones and Doust 1995). Furthermore, when a heart rate inflection point is achieved, it occurs at work rates well above the traditionally defined lactate turnpoint (Ribeiro et al. 1985; Tokmakidis and Leger 1992; A.M. Jones and Doust 1997; Hofmann et al. 1997; Bourgois and Vrikens 1998; Vachon et al. 1999). The test results are also believed to be influenced by nutritional status (Thorland et al. 1994).

As a result, runners who use the Conconi method to determine the intensity at which they need to exercise to train at or above their lactate turnpoints are exercising at too high an intensity and thereby run the risk of overtraining.

My conclusion is that this heart rate inflection point is not a true and reproducible physiological phenomenon. It is of little practical value and can be damaging if used to assess training intensity. I would not advise athletes to use this technique as a training or fitness assessment method, even though the test has even been incorporated into the software programs of some systems that measure heart rate during exercise and that use the heart rate inflection point to prescribe different exercise intensities for training.

Lactate Shuttle

George Brooks (1986a; 1986b) of the University of California at Berkeley has pioneered the concept of the lactate shuttle. He suggests that lactate is not a useless byproduct of glycolysis but is possibly the most important metabolic fuel used by muscle, especially during exercise.

Brooks proposes that the skeletal muscles actively produce and consume lactate both at rest and during exercise (figure 3.22b). He suggests that the lactate produced as the end-product of glycolysis is transported directly into the mitochondria for further metabolism in the Krebs cycle or is released into the bloodstream, where it can be used by the heart or other skeletal muscle fibers (for energy production) or by the liver (for the production of blood glucose). As the exercise intensity increases, the rate of carbohydrate use by the body increases (G.A. Brooks and Mercier 1994). As a result, glycolysis is activated; lactate production in both Type I and Type II muscle fibers rises (Ivy, Chi, et al. 1987) so that at the lactate turnpoint, lactate production exceeds the rate of lactate consumption in the exercising skeletal muscles. Lactate then appears in increasing amounts in the arterial and venous blood. In this way, lactate is shuttled to other tissues, in particular the liver, the heart, and the inactive skeletal muscle. The liver may use lactate for producing new glucose and glycogen; in the heart, the lactate becomes the preferred fuel for oxidative (mitochondrial) metabolism. The inactive muscles store the lactate, thereby lowering the lactate concentrations in the blood and active muscles.

An important feature of the lactate shuttle is that it allows carbohydrate to be transferred from one muscle group to another while the muscles are at rest or during exercise. Unlike the liver, muscles lack the enzyme necessary to convert stored glycogen to glucose, and are therefore unable to export glucose derived from glycogen into the bloodstream for use by other glycogen-depleted muscles. The lactate shuttle provides a convenient method by which body carbohydrate stores can be redistributed from glycogen-replete areas to glycogen-depleted areas during and especially after exercise (G. Ahlborg et al. 1986). During and after leg exercise, for example, glycogen reserves in the inactive arms are metabolized to lactate, which is then transported via the blood to serve as an additional carbohydrate energy source for the active leg muscles and to assist in replenishing the leg muscle glycogen stores after exercise.

The practical importance of this shuttle was shown in our study of athletes who exercised at 60% $\dot{V}O_2$max for 6 hours in the laboratory (Rauch, Hawley, et al. 1998). Lactate oxidation was an important contributor to overall metabolism and, most especially, during the last few hours when levels of muscle glycogen in the active muscles were low. As the calculations presented in figure 3.17 show, when the body is carbohydrate depleted, lactate oxidation totals about one-half of the energy derived from blood glucose oxidation. Without this additional energy source, it would be more difficult than ever to complete the Hawaiian Ironman Triathlon in a reasonable time.

Lactate and Exhaustion

Lactate is a totally innocuous substance that, if infused into the bloodstream, has no noticeable effects. Rather, it is the excess acidic ions released during rapid carbohydrate turnover that may be related to fatigue during high-intensity exercise. In addition, the low lactate levels found after prolonged exercise cannot explain exhaustion in marathon and longer-distance races.

Lactate Removal After Exercise

A frequent question is whether the stiffness that athletes feel after a hard training session or, in particular, after a marathon race is caused by the presence of lactate in those stiff muscles. One old theory even proposed that the lactate caused needlelike crystals to form in the muscles and that it was these needles that caused the pain we feel.

Within an hour of an intensive interval training session during which blood lactate levels reach the highest achievable values (15 mmol per liter), muscle lactate levels will return to normal (Peters-Futre et al. 1987). Furthermore, the worst muscle soreness is always evident after long races that are run at speeds below the lactate turnpoint and that do not, therefore, elevate either blood or muscle lactate levels. For both these reasons, lactate cannot be a cause of the muscle soreness or stiffness felt after exercise (Schwane, Johnson, et al. 1983). In chapter 7, I argue that this stiffness is almost certainly due to racing-induced muscle cell damage, especially to the elastic elements in the skeletal muscles.

High-Intensity Training and Lactate Metabolism

As I discuss in chapter 6, one of the most important techniques that can be used to improve running performance is to include high-intensity training (so-called peaking training) for a short period of time. Although the effects of peaking training are usually dramatic, the physiological explanation for these effects has only recently been determined.

Edmund Acevedo and Allan Goldfarb (1989) have shown that high-intensity training improves running performance and lowers blood lactate concentrations at the high exercise intensities used in training, without altering the $\dot{V}O_2$max. This indicates that the addition of peaking training will further improve the changes in lactate metabolism produced by more gentle endurance (base) training. These changes in lactate metabolism are then markers of the enhanced performance following peaking training.

Our studies also showed that 12 sessions of high-intensity training, which improved 40-km time trial performance by about 3% (Lindsay et al. 1996; Stepto et al. 1999; Westgarth-Taylor et al. 1997), reduced blood lactate concentrations and shifted the lactate turnpoint to a higher workload (Westgarth-Taylor et al. 1997). This training also improved muscle buffering capacity (Weston, Wilson, et al. 1996).

Interestingly, these metabolic changes could not explain why performance improved by approximately 3.0% in the 40-km cycling time trials, since cyclists achieved higher rates of carbohydrate oxidation and higher predicted blood lactate concentrations during the time trial after training, the opposite of the expected result (Westgarth-Taylor et al. 1997). However, these findings are entirely compatible with a resetting of the central governor with high-intensity training, which ensures that a higher constant workload can be sustained during subsequent time trials as a consequence of the higher muscle mass that can be recruited by the (trained) central governor.

METABOLIC ADAPTATIONS TO TRAINING

In previous sections, we have highlighted four metabolic adaptations that occur with training:

1. An increased $\dot{V}O_2$max, indicating an increased capacity to recruit a larger muscle mass during maximal exercise. This enables a higher workload to be achieved and, in turn, increases the oxygen consumption by the mitochondria in the active muscles. According to the Hill/Noakes Central Governor Model, any beneficial training effect that increases oxygen consumption by the muscles is dependent on there first being an increased oxygenation of the heart. The better-oxygenated heart is then able to increase oxygen delivery to the muscles without endangering its own supply.

2. An increased capacity to store muscle and liver glycogen.

3. An increased rate of fat usage with decreased glycogen usage during exercise at all work rates. Whether this adaptation also occurs during high-intensity exercise is currently a source of debate. Evidence suggests that at the same relative (percentage $\dot{V}O_2$max) work rate after training, there is little if any change in the percentage of fat that is used, at least in men. Women may indeed increase the proportion of fat that they burn at the same relative work rate (percentage $\dot{V}O_2$max) after training (G.A. Brooks and Mercier 1994; G.A. Brooks 1998).

4. A shift in the lactate turnpoint to a higher running speed or percentage $\dot{V}O_2$max as the result of a reduced rate of lactate production by the muscles and an increased capacity of the body to clear the lactate produced in the active muscles and elsewhere (MacRae et al. 1992; Bergman, Wolfel, et al. 1999).

The metabolic adaptations occur in the glycolytic pathway with sprint training and in the mitochondria with endurance training.

In the following sections, I discuss some of the anatomical and biochemical adaptations in the skeletal muscles that explain these changes. It is likely that related changes also occur in the heart, especially in the capacity to increase blood flow via an increased capillary network or a greater capacity of the coronary blood vessels to dilate, perhaps resulting from a greater capacity to generate nitric oxide, the endothelial-derived vasodilator.

Increased Capillarization

The number of blood capillaries surrounding muscle fibers increases with training (P. Andersen and Henriksson 1977), facilitating transport of oxygen and fuel to the muscle mitochondria. Blood flow to muscles is increased after training. These adaptations may be especially important for facilitating free fatty acid uptake by the muscle mitochondria. A faster rate of fat delivery to the muscles would increase their capacity to produce energy from fat metabolism (Newsholme and Leech 1983).

Glycolytic Pathway Adaptations

Sprint training increases the activity of certain glycolytic enzymes (A.D. Roberts et al. 1982; MacDougall, Hicks, et al. 1989) and also the ability of the muscle fibers to continue exercising despite high levels of acidity, probably because the neutralizing (buffering) capacity of the trained muscle is increased (R.L. Sharp et al. 1986; Weston, Wilson, et al. 1996). Mitochondrial enzyme activities remain unchanged if the exercise duration is short (K.J.A. Davies, Packer, et al. 1982; Gillespie et al. 1982; A.D. Roberts et al. 1982; B. Dawson et al. 1998) but increase when the exercise duration is 30 seconds (MacDougall, Hicks, et al. 1998).

These longer exercise bouts produce an increase in $\dot{V}O_2$max, an unexpected response to high-intensity training of short duration but compatible with a resetting of the central governor allowing a greater muscle mass to be recruited during maximal exercise.

The practical relevance of these studies is to show that the duration of the high-intensity exercise bout influences the nature of the training adaptation and may therefore produce different effects on racing performance.

Changes in the Mitochondria

The traditional Energy Depletion Model proposes that the most important adaptation to submaximal (dynamic) exercise training occurs in the mitochondria, which increase in number and size (Kirkwood et al. 1987) and alter in composition. The mitochondrial enzyme content, particularly the content of those enzymes in the Krebs cycle and the respiratory chain (figure 3.2), increases. An increase is also found in the concentration of enzymes associated with fatty acid metabolism—including the (fatty acid binding) proteins that transport free fatty acids across the cell membranes (Turcotte et al. 1999)—and the shuttle systems that transfer the acidic ions generated during high-intensity exercise into the mitochondria for use in the respiratory chain (K.J.A. Davies, Packer, et al. 1981; Holloszy and Coyle 1984). An additional adaptation is the increase of resting muscle glycogen, triglyceride, and myoglobin stores. The increase in the capacity for muscle glycogen storage can be identified as early as day four of training (H.J. Green, Jones, et al. 1989).

Gollnick and Saltin (1982; Saltin and Gollnick 1983) explain how the increased mitochondrial enzyme content increases the rate of fat breakdown and the shift in the lactate turnpoint after training. An important signal that controls cellular metabolism is the ratio of ATP to its breakdown products, ADP and Pi, represented scientifically as the (ATP):(ADP)(Pi) ratio. During exercise, the ratio falls progressively as the exercise intensity increases. A fall in this ratio increases the rate of carbohydrate metabolism by first activating the breakdown of glycogen and increasing glucose uptake by the cell, thereby stimulating glycolysis. In this way, carbohydrate becomes the preferred energy fuel during high-intensity exercise when the intracellular (ATP):(ADP)(Pi) ratio falls.

The pretraining line A in figure 3.24 shows that the rate at which ATP can be produced by oxidative metabolism in the mitochondria from untrained muscle rises with increasing concentrations of free fatty acids in the bloodstream. However, the rate of ATP production approaches its maximum value at relatively low free fatty acid concentrations in the blood and can be increased relatively little even with further large increases in fuel supply, represented as increased free fatty acid concentrations in the blood. The practical implication is that the capacity of untrained

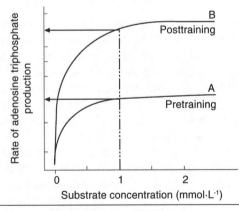

Figure 3.24   Training increases the rate of energy (ATP) production from the oxidation of substrates, especially free fatty acids. After training, the same blood substrate concentration can support a substantially higher rate of ATP production by the exercising muscles.

From Gollnick and Saltin (1982, p. 4). © 1982 Blackwell Science Limited. Adapted by permission.

mitochondria to produce ATP rapidly from blood-borne free fatty acids is relatively limited. Thus, even at quite low work rates, mitochondria would be unable to use mainly fats since this would cause a decline in the (ATP):(ADP)(Pi) ratio, which would be the signal to increase energy provision from the major alternative source, carbohydrates.

However, when the number and volume of mitochondria increase as a result of training (posttraining, line B in figure 3.24), the immediate effect is that the capacity of each mitochondrion to produce ATP at any free fatty acid concentration in the blood is greatly enhanced. Thus, at any rate of energy production (exercise intensity), each mitochondrion will be able to work at a higher (ATP):(ADP)(Pi) ratio and will therefore be less dependent on carbohydrate metabolism for energy.

This means that after training, fat can provide more energy at higher exercise intensities than it could before training, with less need to activate carbohydrate metabolism. Thus, the rate of production of acidic ions in the muscles is reduced and, as a result, less lactate needs to be cotransported out of the cells with these ions. This reduction in the rate of lactate production after training explains, in part, the shift in the lactate turnpoint with training. G.A. Dudley, Tullson, et al. (1987) and Kent-Braun et al. (1990) have shown that the muscle (ATP):(ADP)(Pi) ratio is indeed higher during exercise in trained than in untrained muscle. Muscle acidity is also lower at any work rate after training (Kent-Braun et al. 1990).

In addition, evidence now indicates that the abilities of tissues (such as the heart, kidney, liver, and inactive and active skeletal muscles) to extract and metabolize any lactate produced by the active muscles during exercise are also increased with endurance training (Donovan and Brooks 1983; MacRae et al. 1992; Bergman, Wolfel, et al. 1999). These adaptations are significant in explaining the reduced rate of lactate accumulation in the blood during exercise.

However, newer evidence suggests that this theory does not explain all the findings. In particular, it fails to explain why, at higher exercise intensities (greater than 80% $\dot{V}O_2$max), training does not increase fat metabolism but alters carbohydrate metabolism. Thus, in contrast to earlier findings suggesting that exercise training dramatically increases the capacity for fat metabolism (Hurley et al. 1986; W.H. Martin et al. 1993; S. Klein, Coyle, et al. 1994; S. Klein, Webber, et al. 1996) and reduces carbohydrate turnover (Mendenhall et al. 1994), more recent studies suggest that some of the measured difference may have been artifactual; that is, introduced by errors in the experimental methods used to study a complex phenomenon. In addition, the original theory may apply to women but not to men.

These studies suggest that endurance training may have a relatively small effect on metabolism in men tested at the same relative workload(percentage $\dot{V}O_2$max), before and after a training program that increases the maximum workload and $\dot{V}O_2$max (Bergman, Butterfield, et al. 1999; Friedlander et al. 1997). At the same absolute workload (running or cycling speed), fat metabolism is enhanced. But this may simply occur because the brain perceives this exercise to be less intense; that is, after training it requires a smaller percentage of the greater $\dot{V}O_2$max. As a result, the hormonal response to that exercise is reduced, favoring fat metabolism.

At present, the evidence suggests that if training alters fat metabolism in men, this effect only occurs at lower exercise intensities of less than 50% $\dot{V}O_2$max (G.A. Brooks and Mercier 1994; G.A. Brooks 1998; Bergman and Brooks 1999). At higher exercise intensities, the body crosses over to carbohydrate metabolism (see figure 3.11). As most athletes train at more than 50% $\dot{V}O_2$max most of the time, it is unlikely that the major effect of training would be to alter fat metabolism. Thus, the finding that athletes burn more fat than nonathletes at the same relative (percentage $\dot{V}O_2$max) workload (Jeukendrup et al. 1997; S. Klein et al. 1994; 1996; Van Loon, Jeukendrup, Mensink, et al. 1999) could be the result of genetic differences that preselect for the endurance sports those with a greater capacity to oxidize fat, in accordance with the concept of metabolic individuality.

In contrast, women show a different response and increase in their fat oxidation, exclusively from increased oxidation of blood-borne free fatty acids, at both the same relative and absolute workloads after training (Friedlander et al. 1998a; 1998b). In part, this might be explained by a lesser reliance in women on muscle glycogen use during exercise (Friedlander et al. 1998b).

If fat metabolism measured at the same percentage $\dot{V}O_2$max before and after training is not altered by endurance training in men, what of carbohydrate metabolism? Logic suggests that two adaptations in carbohydrate metabolism would be beneficial. Firstly, the body would benefit if it could increase the amount of energy it derived from ingested (exogenous) carbohydrate. But this does not occur (Jeukendrup, Mensink, et al. 1997). Secondly, the body would benefit by increasing its capacity to generate glucose in the liver from other carbohydrate (lactate) and noncarbohydrate (amino acids and glycerol) sources. This could increase the rate of glucose use by muscle without the risk of hypoglycemia developing, especially as exercise becomes more prolonged.

Evidence suggests that this adaptation exists in rats (Donovan and Sumida 1997), which explains why trained rats are able to exercise for longer without developing hypoglycemia. The livers of trained rats are better able to convert lactate and the amino acids alanine and leucine to glucose. Thus, they produce more glucose, which continues to be taken up at the same rate by the exercising muscles (Sumida and Donovan 1994). As a result, after training, blood glucose concentrations can be maintained at higher levels during prolonged exercise.

This adaptation also occurs in humans (Bergman, Horning, et al. 2000). Given the important role of hypoglycemia in limiting prolonged exercise performance, the value of this adaptation is obvious.

Changes in Muscle Contractility

The fascination that modern exercise physiologists have with the Cardiovascular/ Anaerobic Model may have blinded us to the possibility that muscle power, or contractility, may also influence performance and that training may bring about important changes in muscle contractility (Noakes 1988b). These changes would probably result from increased skeletal muscle myosin ATPase activity and enhanced calcium handling by the sarcoplasmic reticulum. Alternatively, the ability to resist fatigue may also result from local changes in skeletal muscle contractile function according to the Muscle Power Model. In chapter 2, I reviewed the evidence showing that training does in fact alter skeletal muscle contractility. However, it remains unclear how this explains superior fatigue resistance with training.

Increased Capacity to Recruit Muscle Mass

According to the Integrated Neuromuscular Recruitment Model, any improvement in performance with training must result from an increased capacity of the brain to recruit a larger muscle mass for longer, thereby enhancing performance. Throughout this book, I have highlighted examples in which observed phenomena are more effectively explained by a central brain adaptation than by any other model of exercise physiology. Since so few scientists have looked for evidence of this central brain adaptation, we are unable, as yet, to show that it definitely exists. That proof will have to await a future edition of this book.

Effects of Short-Term Training

A surprising finding is that training can produce measurable effects in previously untrained athletes within as few as 5 to 10 training bouts, provided each exercise bout is prolonged (1 to 2 hours; H.J. Green, Jones, et al. 1991; H.J. Green, Helyar, et al. 1992; H.J. Green, Ball-Burnett, et al. 1995; H.J. Green, Cadefau, et al. 1995; S.M. Phillips, Green, et al. 1995; 1996b; Putman et al. 1998). These changes reportedly occur before any measurable changes in either the size or enzyme content of the mitochondria—a conclusion that has been challenged (Spina et al. 1996).

These changes include higher resting muscle glycogen concentrations and reduced rates of muscle glycogen use, lactate production, and blood glucose oxidation, compensated for by an increased rate of fat oxidation, principally from the intramuscular triglyceride stores. All these changes were reported at the same absolute cycling workload before and after training. Whether or not they are also present in the same relative (percentage $\dot{V}O_2$max) workload was not tested but seems unlikely, given that long-term training does not appear to alter metabolism at the same relative workload to any great extent.

The relevance of these studies is that all these changes occur *before* there are measurable changes in mitochondrial enzyme content or mitochondrial oxidative capacity. Hence, they challenge the theory that the whole-body metabolic changes measured in trained subjects result specifically from alterations in skeletal muscle oxidative capacity (Noakes 1997). Rather, they suggest adaptations in feed forward control from the brain.

EFFECTS OF TRAINING AND DETRAINING

The adaptations of $\dot{V}O_2$max to training occur so quickly that in humans it is possible to detect an increase in $\dot{V}O_2$max within a week of beginning an intensive training program (Hickson, Bomze, et al. 1977). As described in the previous section, metabolic adaptations also occur rapidly. But unless the intensity of the training program is increased progressively, no further increase in $\dot{V}O_2$max may occur after three weeks of training at the same intensity and duration (Hickson et al. 1981d).

Just as these adaptations to training occur rapidly, so too do they regress when all training ceases; that is, when detraining commences. With detraining there is a rapid fall in $\dot{V}O_2$max in the first two to three weeks, with a more gradual decrease thereafter (Coyle, Martin III, et al. 1984).

The time course of muscle enzyme changes with training has been less clearly defined. Whereas some argue that measurable changes in enzyme activities only occur after about 30 days of training (H.J. Green, Helyar, et al. 1992; 1995; S.M. Phillips,

Green, et al. 1995; 1996b), others argue that they occur far more rapidly (that is, within five to seven days of the start of the training program) (Spina et al. 1996). In studies lasting up to 12 weeks, enzyme concentrations appear to show a gradual and progressive increase. At present, it seems that the rate and magnitude of these changes is a function, within limits, of the total amount of muscle contractile activity. The rate can be increased either by performing more contractions in a given time period (increasing exercise intensity) or by maintaining the same frequency of contraction for a longer period (increasing exercise duration; Holloszy and Coyle 1984). As will be discussed, it seems that the former method of increasing the exercise intensity may produce more rapid and greater results than the latter but at a great risk of overtraining.

It also seems that these adaptations do not continue forever. Thus, in rats it was found (Dudley, Abraham, et al. 1982) that 60 minutes of training five days a week at any exercise intensity produces the maximum adaptation in mitochondrial enzyme content. Longer daily training periods or the addition of two exhaustive training sessions a week (Katsuta et al. 1988) produce no further increase in mitochondrial oxidative enzyme changes. A most interesting finding was that high-intensity interval training at approximately 116% $\dot{V}O_2$max for relatively short periods (15 min per day) produced as great an increase in mitochondrial enzyme content as did exercise of 90 min per day at 83% to 94% $\dot{V}O_2$max. Thus, there is a limit to the extent to which the mitochondrial enzymes can adapt, and this limit is reached more quickly with less total training time by performing high-intensity exercise of short duration (speed work) than by running at much lower intensities for very much longer.

A number of researchers have used the decrease in the mitochondrial enzyme content that occurs when training stops as a measure of the rate at which fitness is lost when a person stops training. In addition, they have studied the amount of exercise required to maintain those adaptations. An important and potentially erroneous assumption of these studies is that these changes occur in tandem with, and can therefore predict, changes in running performance. These conclusions are based on the Energy Supply/Energy Depletion Model, which predicts that it is changes in these muscle enzyme activities that alter metabolism sufficiently to delay the onset of muscle glycogen depletion during exercise.

But we found that this assumption certainly does not hold during the adaptations to increased training: the increase in mitochondrial enzyme content does not occur simultaneously with increases in exercise capacity (M. Lambert and Noakes 1988), as also argued by Green and colleagues (H.J. Green, Helyar, et al. 1992; H.J. Green, Cadefau, et al. 1995). We have also found that the performance of trained cyclists can be further improved with a short period of high-intensity training that does not alter mitochondrial enzyme content (Lindsay et al. 1996); this training actually increased, rather than decreased, the rate of carbohydrate oxidation during a subsequent time trial in which performance was enhanced (Westgarth-Taylor et al. 1997).

Accordingly, these studies must be interpreted with caution. The most relevant studies are those that monitor changes in actual exercise performance during detraining. To some extent, the latter studies suggest that performance can change quite dramatically with little, if any, change in mitochondrial function. Hence, the conclusion that can be drawn from these studies in which mitochondrial enzyme changes are interpreted as a surrogate for changes in exercise performance may be erroneous, perhaps because of the logical flaws in the Energy Supply/Energy Depletion Model already identified.

In general, it seems that the elevated mitochondrial enzyme contents that result from training are lost within about four to eight weeks (Holloszy and Coyle 1984; Coyle, Martin III, et al. 1984; R.L. Moore et al. 1987) in those who have trained for less than six months, with no further loss thereafter (Coyle, Martin III, et al. 1984). However, humans who have trained for much longer (6 to 20 years) show a much more gradual decline in mitochondrial enzyme content and, even after 12 weeks of inactivity, have mitochondrial enzyme contents at least 40% to 50% above those of subjects who have never trained (Chi et al. 1983; Coyle, Martin III, et al. 1984). This is compatible with either or both of two different explanations:

1. These athletes may have had higher mitochondrial enzyme contents before they started training—in line with the belief that athletes who continue to train for many years are genetically different.

2. Alternatively, prolonged training over years may provide changes that are not replicated by short-term studies. Certainly, it is a common observation that complete inactivity of even a month or two does not cause athletes who have trained for many years to revert to a completely unfit state. In addition, some elite athletes, including Mark Allen, report anecdotally that they observe continual improvement in certain measured physiological variables, such as running speed at a particular heart rate, over many years of training. Yet, exercise physiologists seldom perform such long-term studies in human athletes.

One of the first studies to measure the effects of detraining on performance was that of Hickson and his colleagues (Hickson et al. 1981; Hickson, Kanakis, et al. 1982). They exercised groups of subjects six days a week for 40 min per day for 10 weeks, whereafter they exercised either less frequently (two to four days a week) at the same intensity or for a shorter time (13 min per day or 26 min per day) but at the same intensity and frequency. They found that the fitness of the subjects was maintained even though the exercise program of some of the subjects had been reduced by almost two-thirds. However, similar one-third or two-third reductions in exercise intensity failed to maintain the elevated $\dot{V}O_2max$ values resulting from training (Hickson, Foster, et al. 1985).

It is interesting to note that, with detraining, performance time to exhaustion during short-duration (5 minutes) and prolonged (200 minutes) exercise did not decrease to the same extent as did the $\dot{V}O_2max$, again suggesting that other factors besides $\dot{V}O_2max$ are important in determining performance during short-duration and prolonged exercise.

Studies in swimmers (Costill, King, et al. 1985; Neufer et al. 1987a) and runners (Houmard, Costill, et al. 1990; Shepley et al. 1992) indicate that reducing training volume by up to 70% for up to 21 days does not influence performance negatively, provided the exercise intensity is retained (Neufer 1989; Houmard 1991). Indeed, the study of Shepley et al. (1992) found that a seven-day taper that included high-intensity training enhanced performance compared to either a taper in which training intensity was less or a taper during which the athletes did not train. Hence, tapering by reducing volume but maintaining intensity enhanced performance more than resting alone, at least in short-distance races (Shepley et al. 1992).

But what practical value can be derived from this knowledge? First, the mitochondrial adaptations to training only occur in the trained muscles and in the muscle fibers that are active during the specific exercise. This indicates that, when training for a particular event or sport, an athlete must concentrate on using the correct muscle groups and, more specifically, the appropriate muscle fibers and the appropriate metabolic pathways in those fibers. For example, the runner who trains exclusively on the flat is untrained for uphill running because different muscle groups are involved in those two activities (Costill, Jansson, et al. 1974). Similarly, the noncompetitive jogger will train a different fiber type than the middle-distance runner who exercises at a higher intensity and therefore activates both the Type I and the Type II muscle fibers. This wisdom underlies an important principle of training known as the *specificity of training*. Of course, this conclusion is based on the assumption that it is these changes that are important determinants of exercise performance.

Second, the studies of detraining show that it is not necessary to maintain the same high intensity of training all year round. Thus, a reduction in training by as much as two-thirds may maintain a decent level of fitness. This becomes important when we consider the concept of recovery and rest before a major competitive effort (see chapters 9, 10, and 11). Indeed, these studies raise a very important question: If performance, achieved by so much training, can be maintained by so little training, was that large volume of training necessary in the first place? My feeling is probably not; either a large proportion of the massive volume of training done by many athletes is wasted, or else training is producing additional adaptations, unrecognized and therefore unmeasured in these studies, that may be necessary for some but not all activities.

For example, to train adequately for marathon and ultramarathon races, I frequently ran long distances in training. These long runs, it seems to me, were necessary to adapt the muscles and tendons so that they were able to carry my weight for many hours during competition. This perhaps has something to do with the Biomechanical Model of Exercise Physiology. But it is not clear whether the specific adaptations induced by such overdistance training are necessary for athletes who never race at distances further than 21 km. It is absurd and even detrimental for athletes competing at shorter distances to train to the extent that marathon and ultramarathon runners do, as it reduces their speed over shorter distances. As indicated in chapter 2, it is speed over the shorter distances that also predicts performance in events at any longer distance.

But the only way we shall ever establish the ideal training program that produces maximum benefit in terms of enhancing performance while minimizing the risk of injury or overtraining, with minimum input, will be by studying, in carefully controlled experiments, the effects of different types and amounts of training on competitive performance. Sadly, though, there are too few of these studies. In 1991, in one of the first studies of its kind, David Costill and colleagues found that the performance of a group of collegiate swimmers did not improve when they increased their daily training volume from 90 to 180 minutes. In fact, the sprinting performance of the longer-training swimmers was marginally impaired by their heavier training. There is an almost total dearth of similar studies conducted among runners.

Third, the concept of different training intensities producing different training effects allows the tailoring of individual training goals. According to the Energy Supply/Energy Depletion Model, the aim for sprinters must be to increase muscle contractility and the rates of ATP resynthesis and glycolysis. Middle-distance runners, on the other hand, must adapt their hearts to an increased oxygen delivery so that the central governor becomes operative only at higher exercise intensities and cardiac outputs. In addition, their muscles must become progressively more resistant to the increasing acidity that develops during exercise of high intensity. Marathon runners, on the other hand, must shift their lactate turnpoints to a higher running speed; they must increase their capacity for fat use so that they can spare their carbohydrate stores during racing, thereby delaying the action of the governor, which seeks to protect the muscles from becoming totally energy depleted during prolonged exercise; they must maximize their ability to store liver and muscle glycogen before exercise; and they must increase their capacity to absorb carbohydrate during competition and to produce glucose in the liver from lactate and other substrates. They need also to adapt their muscles to the rigors of repeated eccentric muscle contractions and to improve their running economy.

If fatigue during prolonged exercise has a central (brain) component, then marathon runners need also to adapt their brain function accordingly. For example, the serotoninergic Theory of Central Fatigue holds that any increase in brain serotonin levels promotes fatigue (J.M. Davis and Bailey 1997). How training might influence this rise is not known.

In addition to adapting their brain function to develop the optimum pacing strategies, ultramarathon runners must adapt their muscles to ensure that they become shock absorbers that are resistant to racing-induced muscle damage, according to the Biomechanical Model of Fatigue.

HEREDITARY CAPACITY TO ADAPT TO ENDURANCE TRAINING

As described in chapter 2, $\dot{V}O_2$max is largely determined by hereditary factors and shows a familial resemblance (Bouchard, Daw, et al. 1998). It is now also known that endurance performance is determined, to an even larger degree, by genetic factors (Bouchard, Lesage, et al. 1986), as is the extent to which any person can adapt to an endurance training program (Bouchard and Lortie 1984; Prud'Homme et al. 1984; Hamel et al. 1986; Simoneau et al. 1986). Adaptation to endurance training also shows a familial aggregation (Bouchard, An, et al. 1999). Thus, as much as 70% to 80% of endurance performance and adaptability to training may be determined by genetic factors. In children, the variation in athletic ability is due more to genetic than to environmental factors (Maes et al. 1996). At present, there is a great deal of interest in determining the specific genes involved in these specific characteristics (Gagnon et al. 1997; Rivera, Dionne, et al. 1997a; 1997b; Bouchard 2000). It is also interesting that the extent to which other beneficial changes develop with training, including the reduction in serum cholesterol concentrations, may also be genetically determined (Després et al. 1988).

Currently, the race is on to identify the specific genes that confer superior athletic ability and superior capacity to adapt to athletic training. Genetic markers for superior athletic ability have been mapped to chromosomes 4q12; 8q24.12; 11p15.1, and 14q21.3, whereas genes relating to the responsiveness to training have been mapped to chromosomes 1p11.2; 2p16.2; 4q26; 6p21.33, and 11p14.1 (Bouchard, Wolfarth, et al. 2000).

There has been substantial interest in a report that a specific copy of a single specific gene, the 1 allele of the angiotensin-1-converting enzyme (ACE) was more prevalent in a sample of British mountaineers who had ascended to altitudes in excess of 7000 m and in British military recruits who showed superior adaptation to weight training (H.E. Montgomery et al. 1998; H. Montgomery et al. 1999). Similarly, Australian national rowers (Gayagay et al. 1998) and professional Spanish athletes (Alvarez et al. 2000) also show a higher than expected frequency of this allele. The $\dot{V}O_2$max of postmenopausal women with this allele was also higher than that of women without the allele (Hagberg, Ferrell, et al. 1998). In addition, British army recruits with this allele showed greater gains in mechanical efficiency with cycling training (A.G. Williams et al. 2000).

Conversely, a study of elite Australian athletes (R.R. Taylor et al. 1999), the Genathlete Study—a collaborative study of elite athletes in five different countries (Bouchard 2001)—as well as our own unpublished studies of Ironman triathletes and elite South African rugby players (M. Collins, unpublished data) have all failed to show a higher than normal prevalence of this specific allele in those athletic populations.

Other genes that may be linked to athletic performance include the alpha-2A-adrenoreceptor gene (Wolfarth et al. 2000) and the creatine kinase MM gene, the latter in relation to the adaptability to training (Rivera, Pérusse, et al. 1999) but not in relation to $\dot{V}O_2$max and hence elite athletic status (Rivera, Dionne, et al. 1997a; 1997b).

The elite athletes are not only superiorly endowed with those attributes necessary for success—such as high $\dot{V}O_2$max values, lactate turnpoints that occur at fast running speeds, fast peak treadmill running speeds (Noakes, Myburgh, et al. 1990b), and muscles with a higher capacity to generate ATP from oxidative metabolism even when untrained (J.H. Park et al. 1988)—they also have the genetic gift that all these variables will adapt to the greatest possible extent with training.

FINAL WORD

In this chapter I have reviewed the important aspects of exercise-related metabolism, focusing in particular on information that is of practical value to athletes. Perhaps the most important recent advances in our understanding are the realization that carbohydrates may not be the only important constituents of the athletic diet, that the human metabolic response during exercise is quite individual, and that the brain is by far the most important determinant of exercise performance, since it establishes the optimum pacing strategy for any race. I have also introduced the novel concept that fatigue is nothing more than a sensation that is associated with the reduction in running speed that we experience when "fatigued," particularly when we hit the marathon wall. When we are fatigued, the brain adopts an altered pacing strategy to guide us to the finish at minimum risk of irreversible damage to our bodies. The ultimate goal of the (selfish) brain is to protect itself from damage.

I advise the wise runner to experiment with the different ideas developed in this chapter rather than to continue accepting time-honored dogmas that may be significantly flawed.

CHAPTER

4

■ ■ ■ ■ ■

Temperature Regulation During Exercise

One of the physiological problems that runners face during exercise is how to lose the excess body heat produced by muscle contraction. The converse challenge—maintaining a normal body temperature when running in the cold when heat loss is increased—becomes a problem only when exercising under extreme environmental conditions without adequate clothing to provide protection against wet and wind (Noakes 2000a). The reason the body has great difficulty staying cool during exercise is that so much excess heat is produced when exercising.

To live, we humans must keep our body temperatures within a narrow range (35 to 42°C) despite wide variations in environmental temperatures and differences in levels of physical activity. During exercise, however, the conversion of chemical energy stored in adenosine triphosphate (ATP) into the mechanical energy that permits exercise is extremely inefficient; as much as 70% of the total chemical energy used during muscular contraction is released as heat rather than as athletic endeavor.

Thus, when Bruce Fordyce and Don Ritchie won ultramarathons at an average pace of 16.3 km per hour, they used about 56 kJ of energy every minute (figure 4.1), or about 18,480 kJ in the 5.5 hours that they ran. Of the total amount of kilojoules used, only 4000 kJ helped transport them from the start to the finish of their races. The remaining 14,480 kJ was nothing more than a hindrance, serving only to overheat the runners' bodies. To prevent their temperatures from rising to over 43°C, which would have resulted in heatstroke, these athletes had to lose more than 90% of this heat.

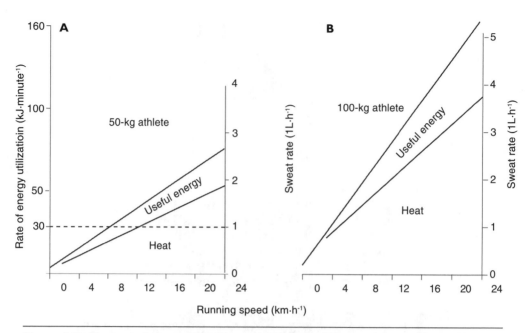

Figure 4.1   The rates of energy expenditure and sweating at different running speeds in a 50-kg athlete (*A*) and a 100-kg athlete (*B*). Energy production rises linearly with increasing running speed (see chapter 2), but only about 20% of the energy produced by the body is used to support the athletic endeavor (useful energy). The remaining 80% simply heats up the body. Sweating is one mechanism for losing that heat and preventing the body temperature from rising excessively. Also note that a sweat rate of I liter per hour (*A*) can remove about 30 kJ per minute (1800 kJ per hour) from the body.

From Costill (1977, p.162). © 1977 by the New York Academy of Sciences. Adapted by permission.

It is clear that to control the heat rise associated with exercise and in so doing prevent overheating and heatstroke, the body must be able to call upon a number of very effective heat-diffusing mechanisms. Although in cold, wet weather the dangers of overheating are less likely, it is nevertheless important to know how to keep the body dry and the temperature regulated.

TEMPERATURE REGULATION DURING EXERCISE

As exercise begins, the blood flow to the muscles is increased. Not only does the heart pump more blood, but blood is preferentially diverted from nonessential organs toward the working muscles and skin. As it passes through the muscles, the blood is heated and distributes the added heat throughout the body, particularly to the skin. As a result, heat is conducted to the skin surface. Heat conduction to the skin is also achieved by direct transfer from muscles lying close to the skin. Circulating air currents then carry this heat away by convection. (Convection is simply the transfer of heat energy into the surrounding air: the body heats up the air around it.) Any nearby object whose surface temperature is lower than the skin temperature—for example, trees or the road surface—will attract this heat, which travels by electromagnetic waves in a form of energy transfer known as radiation. In contrast, when surrounding objects are hotter than the body—for example, hot tar roads—heat is transferred by convection from those objects to the runner's body.

Surface heat is also lost when the sweat produced by the sweat glands in the skin evaporates. It is important to appreciate that sweating itself does not cause heat loss: it is the evaporation of the sweat into the atmosphere that causes heat to be lost.

FACTORS THAT AFFECT HEAT BALANCE

A number of factors affect heat balance, including the rate at which the athlete produces heat and the efficiency of the heat loss mechanisms, convection or sweating. As discussed below, some of these factors can be modified by the athlete.

Exercise Intensity

As the intensity of exercise increases, the body determines whether to pump more blood to the muscles, thus maintaining their increased energy requirements, or to increase its blood flow to the skin, thereby facilitating heat dissipation. When faced with these conflicting demands, the body always favors increased blood flow to the muscles. The result is that while the production of body heat increases, the ability to lose that heat decreases.

It appears that athletes running at world-record speeds, at least in races of up to 16 km, have markedly limited blood flow to the skin and therefore a limited ability to lose heat. They thus run in a microenvironment in which their ability to maintain heat equilibrium depends entirely on the environmental conditions being sufficiently cold (Pugh 1972). If these conditions are unfavorable, the athletes will continually accumulate heat until their body temperatures reach the critical level at which heatstroke occurs. Fortunately, the brain, responding to information from internal temperature sensors, will usually terminate exercise before the body temperature exceeds about 41°C, thereby preventing the risk of developing heatstroke during exercise. Indeed, one possibility is that it is the feedback from those sensors, in response to the rate at which the body temperature is rising, that sets the exercise intensity (running speed) that the brain will allow in different environmental conditions (Marino et al. 2000). Yet, sometimes this thermal governor can be overridden by an athlete's free will, leading to heatstroke. Heatstroke therefore serves as the body's shutoff mechanism. As discussed under the Integrated Neuromuscular Recruitment Model (see chapter 2), the brain stops athletes from exercising before heatstroke develops. What is unclear is why this mechanism sometimes fails.

There are three documented and somewhat legendary examples of athletes who ran at world-record pace and developed heatstroke when forced to race in unfavorable environmental conditions—Jim Peters in the 1954 Empire Games Marathon in Vancouver, Canada; Alberto Salazar in the 1980 Falmouth 12-km road race; and Gabrielle Andersen-Schress in the 1984 Los Angles Olympic Marathon. All these races were run in unusually warm conditions. As was then the practice, the 1954 Empire Games Marathon was held in the afternoon during an unseasonable heatwave in British Columbia. Similarly, the Falmouth race, which always takes place in August in Falmouth, Massachusetts, has since become an important testing ground for determining techniques to lower body temperature in athletes with very high body temperatures (Armstrong et al. 1996). Not surprisingly, the scheduling of the Olympic Marathon in Atlanta in 1996 unleashed a wave of predictions, not least of which was that performances would be impaired and that the event might even be dangerous (Nielsen 1996; Sparling 1995; 1996; 1997). It is not for nothing that Atlanta is nicknamed Hotlanta. In the end, although the race times were somewhat slower than might have been expected (Sparling 1997), relatively few cases of heat injury were reported. This shows that in most cases the body's natural defense mechanism against heatstroke acts to limit exercise and prevent injury, even in Olympic competition.

There is evidence to suggest that a high body temperature causes the central governor to reduce muscle recruitment during prolonged exercise. In the early 1990s, Bodil Nielsen and research colleagues in Copenhagen, Denmark (Nielsen et al. 1990) observed that during heat acclimatization studies, subjects stopped exercising when their body temperatures reached a value that was constant for each person. These researchers subsequently showed that when the subjects reached their exhaustion points when exercising in the heat, muscle blood flow was high, whereas the muscle metabolism was normal (Nielsen et al. 1993). They found that fatigue could not be explained by peripherally located changes in skeletal muscle metabolism, analogous to the so-called lactate paradox, the logical challenge posed to the Cardiovascular/Anaerobic Model by fatigue at extreme altitude (chapter 2).

Thereafter, those researchers (González-Alonso, Teller, et al. 1999) showed that the rise in body temperature was indeed the factor that caused the termination of exercise since precooling prolonged exercise time to fatigue whereas preheating had the opposite effect. Irrespective of the kind of intervention, however, subjects terminated exercise at the same body temperatures (Walters et al. 2000).

More recently, Nybo and Nielsen (2001) have shown that this fatigue is caused by a reduced capacity of the "hot" brain to recruit skeletal muscle during exercise, and it is not due to any heat-induced, direct impairment in skeletal muscle function. Hence, an elevated body temperature causes a central governor to reduce skeletal muscle recruitment during exercise, as predicted originally in 1997 and subsequently in 2000 (Noakes 1997; 2000c).

High running speeds constitute the greatest risk factor for heatstroke. Conversely, slow running speeds usually prevent heatstroke, irrespective of environmental conditions. Hence, heat injury is a major danger in short races in which athletes run at near maximal effort for 15 to 60 minutes (5 to 21 km for world-class performers). In recent years, this danger has become more marked because, unlike marathons, many short races are organized by nonrunning organizations, such as charities and other sports clubs, and not by licensed athletics organizations. Organizers are often unaware of the risk factors for heatstroke and may not even ensure the presence of medical personnel at such events, which can have potentially disastrous results. In addition, because sports medicine practitioners have fixated on dehydration as the most significant cause of heatstroke (discussed in the section on dehydration), they often incorrectly assume that heatstroke can only occur in marathon and longer races. However, the opposite is true: in my experience, heatstroke occurs much more frequently in short-distance races than in marathons (Noakes 1981b). For example, in a 12-year study (1982 to 1994) of the Twin Cities Marathon in Minneapolis-St. Paul, Minnesota—the largest documented study of its kind—only 17 of 81,277 entrants (0.02%) required medical care for a rectal temperature greater than 40°C (Roberts 2000). Nearly three times as many runners (46, or 0.06% of all race entrants) required treatment for hypothermia (a reduced body temperature). In this instance, cold posed more of a threat than heat. In recent years, the number of people who enter marathons has mushroomed. This increases the probability, particularly among runners who run at less than 10 km per hour, that cold will become a more serious problem during marathons, especially in races run in cold conditions.

Wind

High facing wind speeds cause a large volume of unwarmed air to cross the skin. Therefore these winds allow for greater heat loss by convection. Both running and cycling produce an effective wind speed, which aids convective heat loss but which may not be sufficient to increase heat loss adequately in severe environmental conditions. Obviously, a wind coming from behind at a speed equal to the speed at which you are moving forward will cause you to run in a totally windless environment, which will prevent convective heat loss. In contrast, the wind speed developed by cyclists appears to be sufficient to compensate even for severe conditions and explains why heat is not as great a problem for endurance cyclists as it is for runners (that is, until they hit the ascents on the long mountain stages). When climbing, elite cyclists work at very high metabolic rates, generating large amounts of heat. Yet, they travel slower than they do when racing on the flat and, as a result, convective heat loss is reduced. The situation is dramatically reversed on the descent and explains why professional cyclists wear additional clothing or insert sheets of paper in their cycling tops immediately before they begin fast descents in competition. This is because convective heat loss increases dramatically on the descent as the cyclists reach speeds of up to 80 km per hour. Yet, their rates of heat production are substantially reduced because they do less pedaling as they descend.

High Temperatures

At rest, the body skin temperature is about 33°C. If exercise is undertaken in environmental temperatures greater than 33°C, heat cannot be lost by convection because the air temperature is higher than that of the body surface. Therefore, the direction of heat transfer is reversed, and the tissues near the surface of the body gain heat from the environment. In these conditions, the only avenue for heat loss is sweating. Sweating removes between 1,092 and 2,520 kJ of heat per liter of sweat evaporated (figure 4.1), depending on whether all the sweat evaporates or, as usually happens, a substantial percentage drips from the body without evaporating. As the air humidity increases, the ability to lose heat by sweating decreases. This is because humidity is a measure of the water content of the air. If the humidity is high, the air cannot absorb additional water. Hence sweat does not vaporize from the skin but simply drips off the body, without producing a cooling effect.

Although exercise physiologists have emphasized the dangers of exercising in hot environments, they have tended to focus their attention on the air temperature and not on humidity. Yet, it is clear that sweating is the most important method of heat loss during exercise, at least when the wind speed is low and the athlete is traveling at less than 20 km per hour (as do most runners), thus reducing convective heat loss. As the effectiveness of heat loss by sweating is strongly related to the humidity of the air, humidity must be the more important determinant of the ease with which athletes will be able to cool themselves during exercise in the heat. This concept is especially relevant to larger, heavier athletes.

Why All Great Marathoners Are Small

It does not take a genius to notice that the great distance runners are often very small. South African Josiah Thugwane (figure 4.2), gold medal winner in the 1996 Olympic Marathon in Atlanta, tips the scales at 43 kg and is less than 1.52 m tall. Haile Gebrselassie of Ethiopia, world record holder at 10,000 m and the athlete most likely to take the world marathon record to 2:00:00 or below, is built equally slim. This is not a new phenomenon.

An analysis of the Boston Marathon winners shows that the average heights and masses of the winners have not changed in the past hundred years (figure 4.3, *A* through *C*) and average 171 ($\pm$5) cm, with a range of 155 to 191 cm, and 61.1 ($\pm$5.1) kg, respectively. In contrast, the average height of U.S. citizens (Norton et al. 1996) has increased by about 1 cm per decade in the same period. Hence, if height was not a factor predetermining marathon running ability, today's Boston Marathon winners should, on average, be 10 cm taller than the runners 100 years ago. Similarly, the mean mass of the winners has remained relatively constant for the same period, as has the body mass index (BMI), which measures the ratio of the body mass (in kilograms) to height (in meters; figure 4.3*B*).

Touchline Media

Figure 4.2   Josiah Thugwane, gold medalist in the 1996 Atlanta Olympic Marathon. Thugwane (43 kg) beat the silver medalist, South Korean Lee-Bong Ju (45 kg), by 8 seconds in the closest finish in Olympic history.

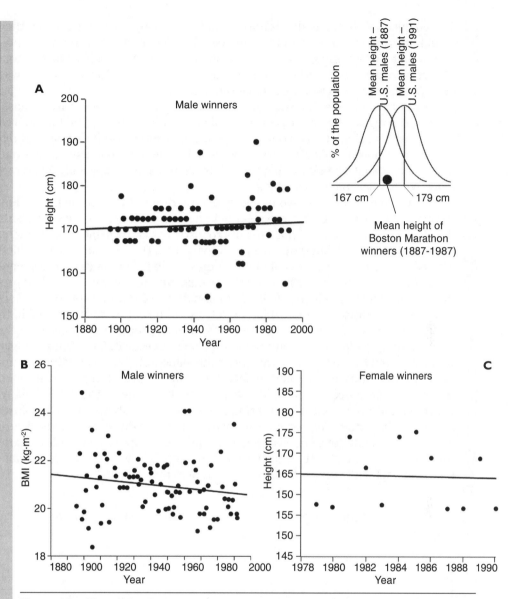

Figure 4.3 The relationship between the year of winning the Boston Marathon and the height (A) and body mass index (BMI) (B) of male winners, and the height of female winners (C).

Also, the height of the female winners did not change in the first decade that women competed in the Boston Marathon (figure 4.3C). Why should this be?

When I read a scientific report predicting the heat balance in the 1996 Olympic Marathon by Bodil Nielsen, the Danish expert and innovative researcher of the physiology of exercise in the heat, I was struck by one obvious inconsistency (Nielsen 1996). Her analysis predicted that the 65-kg winner of that race would have to lose 2.1 liters of sweat per hour when racing in 35°C at humidities above 60%. These predictions are similar to those shown in figure 4.1. Nielsen concluded that if the humidity was greater than 60%, any runners racing at

(continued)

2:10:00 pace would be unable to lose sufficient heat by sweating; instead they would store heat and succumb to heatstroke. Hence, Nielsen indirectly predicted that a 65-kg runner would be unable to win the Atlanta Marathon if conditions were severe and other runners were able to run at 2:10:00 pace. She was correct. The race was won by a 43-kg runner.

For her calculations, Nielsen chose a marathon runner of 65-kg body mass. But when Thugwane won the race, my colleague Steven Dennis and I wondered how Nielsen's calculations would change if they were made for runners of different body masses. This led to some very interesting conclusions and one possible explanation of why small size may be beneficial, especially when racing at world class pace in the heat.

For example, as also shown in figure 4.1, the rate of heat production at any running speed rises much more steeply in heavier runners (figure 4.4A). This does not pose a problem if the capacity to lose heat is the same in all runners, irrespective of their different masses. But when we (Dennis and Noakes 1999) plotted the ability of athletes of different mass to lose heat under more severe environmental conditions (figure 4.4B), we discovered, as Pugh (1972) had predicted, that there are clearly defined combinations of running speed and environmental conditions above which athletes of different masses are unable to match their rate of heat loss to their rate of heat production. Consequently, when running under those conditions, they must overheat. More interestingly, we discovered that when they ran under the same hot, humid conditions, runners of lower body mass could maintain adequate rates of heat loss at much higher running speeds than could heavier runners (figures 4.5 and 4.6). Finally, we compared the effects of increasing humidity on the ability of 45- and 65-kg runners to maintain heat equilibrium when racing at different speeds (figure 4.7). These calculations showed that at humidities of 50% to 90%, a 65-kg marathon runner racing at 2:10:00 pace (line A in figure 4.7) would be able to maintain heat balance at respective air temperatures of 36 and 18°C.

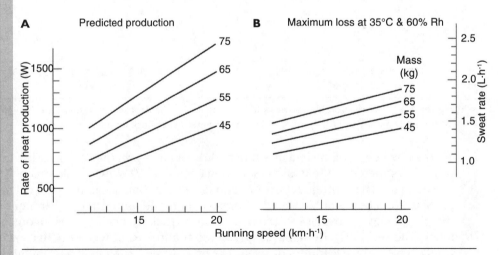

Figure 4.4   Predicted rates of heat production (A) and predicted maximum rates of heat loss (B) for athletes of 45, 55, 65, and 75 kg when running in hot environmental conditions (35°C; 60% relative humidity [Rh]).

From Dennis and Noakes (1999).

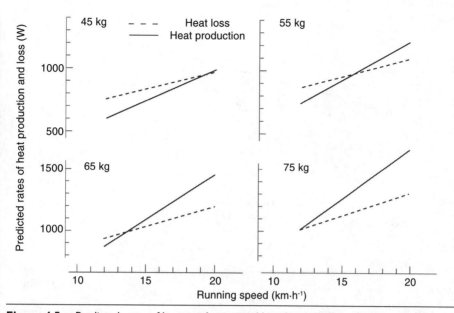

Figure 4.5   Predicted rates of heat production and heat loss at different running speeds in athletes of 45, 55, 65, and 75 kg when running in hot environmental conditions (35°C; 60% relative humidity [Rh]). Note that the running speed at which the predicted rate of heat production exceeds the predicted rate of heat loss represents the fastest speed the athlete could expect to run in these environmental conditions.

From Dennis and Noakes (1999).

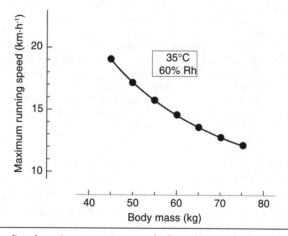

Figure 4.6   Predicted maximum running speeds that athletes of different masses can sustain in hot environmental conditions (35°C; 60% relative humidity [Rh]).

Based on the data presented in figure 4.5.

At the combination of 25°C and 70% relative humidity actually measured in the 1996 Atlanta Olympic Marathon (Sparling 1997), a 65-kg runner would just have been able to maintain heat balance when running at a pace of 2:10:00.

In contrast, a 45-kg runner racing at the same pace (line B in figure 4.7) would be able to maintain his body temperature at the same environmental temperatures (18 to 36°C) as well as at humidities in excess of 80%, easily surpassing the severity of the conditions prevailing during the 1996 Olympic Marathon.

(continued)

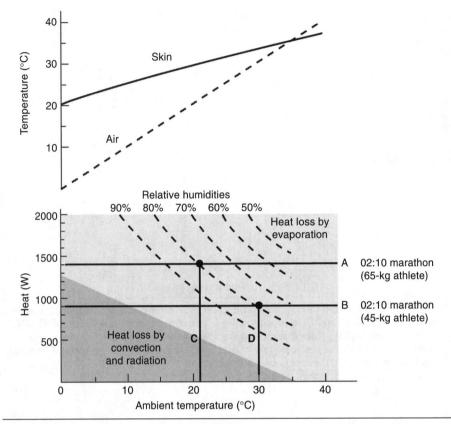

Figure 4.7 Comparison of predicted heat production and possible avenues of heat loss at different relative humidities and ambient temperatures in a 65-kg marathon runner (line A) and a 45-kg marathon runner (line B) when running at 2:10 marathon pace. The ambient temperature at which line A or B crosses the prevailing humidity (or vice versa) indicates the maximum environmental conditions under which the athlete can sustain a 2:10 marathon pace. Whereas the 65-kg runner in this example can maintain that pace at 80% relative humidity and 21°C (vertical line C), the 45-kg runner can run at that pace and at that humidity even at a temperature of 30°C (vertical line D).

In summary, smaller athletes produce less heat at any running speed than do heavier athletes. When the ability of the environment to cool the athlete becomes limiting—largely because of an increased humidity that prevents heat loss by sweating—heavier athletes are disproportionately disadvantaged and must reduce their running speeds to maintain heat balance (figure 4.6). In contrast, the lighter the athletes, the faster they can run in more severe environmental conditions since the environment can absorb their much lower rates of heat production more easily.

It seems clear from the sidebar that a greater capacity to run fast in severe heat would explain why smaller runners dominate those marathons that are run in hot environmental conditions.

But does this alone explain why the winners of the Boston Marathon are always so small? Unlike many marathons in Asia and the southern hemisphere, the Boston Marathon is sometimes run in quite cool conditions. Hence, small marathon runners must also enjoy other benefits. Perhaps smallness also delays the rate at which stretch shortening cycle (SSC) fatigue develops. According to the Biomechanical Model (see chapter 2), this would be another plausible explanation for the dominance of marathon races by smaller runners, independent of the prevailing environmental conditions.

Low Temperatures

Although the medical image of marathon running is usually one of hot conditions and the risk of heat injury (Wyndham 1977), in reality, many marathons, especially in Europe and parts of North America and Asia, are run in cold conditions. In addition, many runners around the world train in autumn and winter.

The essential problem encountered during hot-weather running is the body's inability to lose the heat it is producing and thus prevent a dangerous rise in body temperature. When in extreme cold, the critical danger is that the rate of heat loss from the body may exceed the rate of body heat production, causing the body temperature to fall. Once the body temperature falls below 35°C, mental functioning is impaired and the blood pressure falls. Below 33°C, mental confusion develops and the limb muscles become rigid and immobile. Unconsciousness develops shortly thereafter and can lead to death from hypothermia if the body is not rewarmed rapidly.

In reality, as noted by Roald Amundsen, leader of the first team to the South Pole (Huntford 1985), the exercising body is a furnace so that with sufficient clothing, the human can survive exercising in extremely cold conditions.

It is essential that sufficient clothing be worn to prevent hypothermia. Despite the body's ability to produce an enormous amount of heat during exercise, it has a relatively limited ability to reduce its rate of energy transfer to the environment. Staying dry and maintaining a high rate of heat production (by continuing to exercise and not resting) are also crucially important in reducing the risk of hypothermia in those who are caught in severe cold without adequate clothing (Noakes 2000a)

Cloud Cover

Finally, the body can absorb additional heat from the environment, particularly from the sun, but also from the hot road. This is because the body temperature is cooler than that of the sun. Thus, it absorbs the sun's radiant energy. Obviously, the amount of radiant energy to which the athlete is exposed is greatest when there is no cloud cover and least when cloud cover is absolute.

The WBGT Index

The four environmental factors that determine the athlete's ability to lose heat—wind speed, humidity, air temperature, and radiant energy load—are measured by means of the Wet Bulb Globe Temperature (WBGT) index. This index integrates the measurement of the dry bulb temperature with the wet bulb temperature. The dry bulb temperature measures the prevailing air temperature. The wet bulb temperature is measured by a thermometer covered by a wick permeated with water. The difference between the wet bulb temperature and the dry bulb temperature is a measure of the humidity of the air and therefore

(continued)

a measurement of the ease with which sweat will vaporize, transferring heat from the athlete to the air. Furthermore, wind blowing over the wet wick of the wet bulb thermometer will increase the rate of evaporative cooling and therefore lower the wet bulb temperature. In this way, the WBGT index is also influenced by the prevailing wind speed. Finally, the radiant energy coming from the sun and other bodies that are hotter than the skin temperature is measured as the temperature of a globe that is painted black and hence absorbs any radiant energy in the environment.

More recently, the Corrected Environmental Temperature (CET) has been proposed as an even better predictor of heat stress during running. The American College of Sports Medicine (ACSM) has adopted yet another method combining knowledge of the dry bulb temperature and the humidity.

Although the WBGT index is widely used, it tends to underestimate the "hotness" of conditions in which humidity is high with the environmental temperature somewhat lower. As shown in figure 4.7, conditions of high humidity but relatively low temperature (and hence lower WBGT index) can be dangerous, especially for heavier runners who are trying to run fast in humid but otherwise relatively mild conditions.

Clothing

Aesthetic reasons apart, the usual rationale for wearing clothing is to trap a thin layer of air next to the body. As air is a poor conductor of heat, this thin layer rapidly heats to body temperature and acts as an insulator, preventing heat loss. Clearly, during exercise in the heat, any clothing that is worn must be designed to achieve the opposite effect: promoting heat loss. Marathon runners have learned that light, porous garments, such as mesh singlets and shorts made of a breathable fabric, are best for achieving this.

We often observe runners training in the heat in full tracksuits or other heat-retaining outfits. It is probable that these athletes, including many novice runners, believe that the more they sweat, the harder they must be exercising, and therefore the more weight they will lose. The unfortunate truth is that in running, the energy cost for any individual runner is related only to the distance run. Thus, to lose weight, we need to run further.

Excessive sweating, by dehydrating the body, will effect a sudden drop in total body weight—the procedure used by boxers, jockeys, and wrestlers for "making weight." By exercising in the heat for as little as half an hour, it is possible to lose as much as 1 kg, but this is a fluid loss that will be rapidly replaced once the athlete rehydrates. In contrast, to lose a real kilogram of body weight, we need to expend about 37,500 kJ of energy, equivalent to running about 160 km.

The insulating capacity of clothing is expressed in clothing (CLO) units. One CLO unit is equivalent to the amount of insulation provided by ordinary business apparel, which provides comfort at temperatures of 21°C when both wind speed and humidity are low. The clothing of the Eskimo provides 10 to 12 CLO units and is essential for life in polar conditions. However, because of the considerable heat production during exercise, clothing that will provide 1 CLO unit of insulation may be all that is required when running in temperatures as low as –22°C, provided that there is little or no wind. As soon as there is any wind, convective cooling increases as an exponential (nonlinear) function of the wind speed. Hence, clothing must be increased whenever conditions are windy.

Whereas a resting human needs to wear 12 CLO units of clothing to maintain body temperature at –50°C (figure 4.8A), when running at 16 km per hour at the same temperature, the same person would be adequately protected by only 1.25 CLO units of clothing. Allowance must also be made for clothing that becomes wet because the insulating properties of clothes are then lost.

In practice, sweating alone will not cause clothing to lose its insulating properties completely, especially when running in cold, dry conditions. Problems will arise when the athlete runs in drenching rain with strong facing winds for periods exceeding 1 to 2 hours. The rain will saturate the clothing, destroying its insulating properties. Almost without exception, fatal cases of hypothermia occur in people who underestimate the cooling capacity of the environment; they become soaking wet because their jackets are not water resistant, and they stop exercising because of fatigue but cannot shelter from the wet and cold (Pugh 1966; 1967b; Noakes 1000a). Under these conditions, an impervious water-resistant jacket must be worn. In all other conditions, garments that breathe by allowing sweat to vaporize through pores in the material are more comfortable as they keep the garments closer to the skin drier for somewhat longer.

To calculate the coldness of the environment in which we are to exercise, it is necessary to know both the dry bulb temperature and the expected wind speed and direction. Wind dramatically increases the feeling of coldness of any given dry bulb temperature, in effect reducing the temperature to which the body is exposed

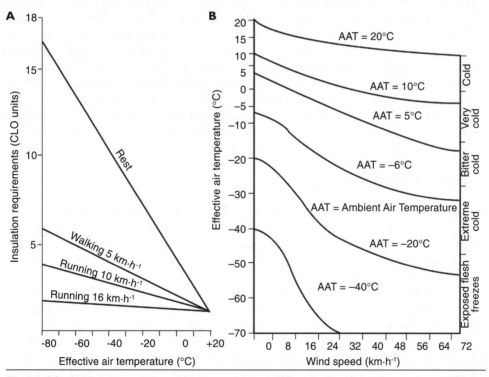

Figure 4.8 Insulation requirements during exercise at different effective air temperatures (A) and the effects of different wind speeds on the effective air temperatures at different ambient air temperatures (AAT) (B).

and thereby increasing the rate of energy loss from the body. This is known as the wind chill factor. Figure 4.8*B* is a plot of the effective temperature for different actual still-air dry bulb temperatures and wind speeds. To calculate the effective temperature, it is important to remember that a person's running speed into the wind increases the effective wind speed by a speed equal to their running speed, whereas running with the wind from behind reduces the effective wind speed by an equivalent amount. Notice also that it is not safe to run at effective temperatures below about –56°C. At lower temperatures, exposed flesh freezes within 30 seconds, leading to frostbite.

Figure 4.8 is designed to help runners decide how much clothing to wear, depending on the speeds at which they will be running and the effective air temperature. Note that even when running at quite slow speeds (10 km per hour) in effective air temperatures as low as –50°C, as little as 3 CLO units will provide adequate protection. Appropriate clothing under these most extreme conditions would include a cotton T-shirt, two nylon sweatshirts, underpants (one or two pairs), long johns (cotton, polypropylene, or Lycra), shorts, sweatpants, a hood, mittens, a ski mask or face protector (including a sweat band) to protect the tip of the nose, shoes, and socks. If it is also wet, a rainproof jacket with a hood must also be worn. At higher temperatures, the outer layers of clothing can be discarded easily.

Wear sufficient clothing to keep warm, but not so much that you start to sweat profusely, as sweat reduces the insulating properties of clothing. Always start running into the wind when you are fresh so that the wind comes from behind when you are tired. In this way, the cooling effect of the environment is greatest when you are freshest, running the fastest, and therefore generating the most body heat, and least when you are tired, running the slowest, and producing the least heat. Always plan to run in well-populated areas so that help is close at hand should hypothermia develop, and never run so far that you become tired and have to walk. As shown in figure 4.8, walking dramatically increases the amount of clothing that must be worn to keep warm at low effective air temperatures. Finally, wear clothing that is easily adaptable, such as a lightweight rain jacket with a zip-up front and a hood, which can be worn either zipped or unzipped and with or without the hood. (You should be able to carry it easily.) It is also sensible to choose running routes that provide as much shelter from the wind as possible.

Heat Acclimatization

It is well documented that the performance of athletes who train exclusively in cool weather is impaired when they are suddenly confronted with hot, humid conditions. With perseverance and continued training in the heat, however, the body becomes acclimatized and performance soon improves, returning within a short period to normal for those conditions.

Heat acclimatization begins after the first exposure to exercise in the heat and is fully developed after 7 to 14 days (Armstrong and Maresh 1991). The optimum method for achieving this adaptation is to train daily at exercise intensities greater than 50% $\dot{V}O_2$max. Training should clearly be done in the heat for gradually increasing periods of between 30 and 100 minutes for an initial period of 10 to 14 days (Shapiro et al. 1998). However, continued improvements in heat acclimatization may occur for up to 30 days (Kubica et al. 1996). I suspect that full heat acclimatization is always superior in those who have always lived in hot environments. Optimum heat acclimatization is achieved with a wide variety of combinations of exercise intensities (40% to 75% $\dot{V}O_2$max) and durations (30 to 90 minutes) performed in a wide range of environmental temperatures (30 to 40°C) and humidities (20% to 85% relative humidity; Nielsen 1998). Nielsen (1998) concludes that it is the daily exposure to rising body temperatures and prolonged exercise that induces these adaptations. Hence, any exercise in the heat that causes the body temperature to rise progressively will induce acclimatization to heat.

Once established, heat acclimatization can be fully retained for about a week after returning to the cooler climate. Thereafter, it is lost at rates that vary from person to person, but usually within 28 days. It is best retained by those who stay in good physical condition and who reexpose themselves to exercise in the same heat on a regular basis.

The important changes that occur with heat acclimatization are that the heart rate, body temperature, and sweat salt (sodium chloride) content during exercise decrease (Armstrong and Maresh 1991; Nielsen 1998). However, the sweating rate increases owing to the increased secretory capacity of the sweat glands (Buono and Sjoholm 1988; Nielsen 1998). In addition, the metabolic rate and the rate of muscle and blood lactate accumulation are decreased by heat acclimatization (A.J. Young et al. 1985), as is the rate of carbohydrate (Febbraio et al. 1994) and muscle glycogen utilization (King et al. 1985; Kirwan et al. 1987).

The importance of heat acclimatization is that it not only provides considerable protection from heat injury, but in competition in the heat, heat-acclimatized athletes will always have the edge over their equally fit but unacclimatized opponents. In a later chapter, I describe the way in which Ron Daws (1977) used heat acclimatization to qualify for the 1968 Olympic Games. It is noteworthy that recent important marathon races held in the heat—such as the 1992 and 1996 Olympic Marathons in Barcelona and Atlanta and the 1998 Commonwealth Games Marathon in Kuala Lumpur, Malaysia—have been dominated by athletes living and training in warm conditions in Africa and Asia.

Dehydration

With sweating, fluid is removed from the body, causing dehydration. This loss of fluid may be compounded by vomiting and diarrhea or excessive urinary fluid losses. It is popularly believed that dehydration is the single greatest threat to the health of the athlete. In fact, we seldom read popular (or indeed even scientific) articles on this topic that do not cite dehydration as the important cause of fatigue or exhaustion or indeed any form of ill health that develops during prolonged exercise, irrespective of whether or not it is undertaken in the heat. Thus, in popular use, dehydration has become a lay synonym for fatigue or almost any illness that develops during exercise, regardless of its nature or duration.

For example, athletes will say: "I dehydrated and slowed down" indicating that, in their minds, fatigue and dehydration are synonymous. Similarly, race commentators or the press will report that an athlete has been admitted to a medical facility for the treatment of "dehydration," as if dehydration were a clearly defined medical illness with its own specific and reproducible symptoms. It is interesting to record how these ideas have evolved and the unexpected consequences they have had.

The first comprehensive series of scientific studies that evaluated the effects of dehydration on exercise performance and human physiology were performed in the Nevada Desert during the World War II (Adolph 1947). These studies clearly established a range of findings that have withstood the scrutiny of the next 50+ years of scientific research.

Not all of these findings have received equal exposure, which means that evidence supporting the supposed dangers of dehydration has been perpetuated. Surprisingly, evidence that downplayed these dangers has been rigorously ignored, perhaps even suppressed, for reasons that I have yet to understand.

The Nevada Desert Study revealed the following (Noakes 1993):

- Even when given free access to adequate fluids, subjects drank less than they lost in sweat or urine. Hence, they developed voluntary dehydration that was corrected only after exercise was completed and food was eaten, as eating promoted fluid intake and corrected any residual dehydration.

- Unless corrected, the progressive dehydration that developed in the heat was associated with premature fatigue. As a result, in experiments in which groups of soldiers drank freely or not at all during day-long marches in the desert heat, a much greater percentage of those who drank during exercise were able to complete the exercise bout.

- Subjects in the groups who did not drink during exercise usually stopped when they were dehydrated by between 7% and 10% of body weight. In this dehydrated state, they tended to experience difficulty maintaining their blood pressures when attempting to stand upright. However, they recovered rapidly and were able to resume walking within minutes of lying down and ingesting fluid.

- Dehydration did not reduce either the sweat rate or the rate of urine production during exercise. However, the rectal temperature and heart rate rose as linear functions of the level of dehydration. This increase in temperature was between 0.2 and 0.3°C for each 1% level of dehydration.

- There were no immediate health risks associated with the levels of dehydration (7% to 10%) that were present at the termination of exercise. Only at very high levels of dehydration (15% to 20%) was there a risk of serious organ failure, in particular kidney failure.

Interestingly, these studies, which clearly established the value of fluid ingestion during exercise, had little impact on the athletic community as at that time runners were encouraged not to drink during exercise. It was only the studies of Pugh et al. (1967) and Wyndham and Strydom (1969) that finally drew attention to the need for fluid ingestion by athletes during prolonged exercise.

Pugh et al. (1967) showed that the top finishers in an English marathon only drank 400 ml (approximately 160 ml per hour) and developed a mean weight loss of 2.9 kg (6% of initial body weight). As fluid loss, sweat rate, and postrace rectal temperature were highest in the race winner, the authors concluded that "a high tolerance to fluid loss" seemed to be an important requirement for success in distance running. But they did not propose any role for fluid ingestion during exercise, nor were they particularly concerned about any possible dangers that these quite marked levels of dehydration posed for those race winners.

So, it was into this intellectual vacuum that one of the most influential studies in the modern exercise sciences exploded. The study (Wyndham et al. 1969) was completed as an adjunct, perhaps as an afterthought, to a larger study measuring the effects of a high carbohydrate, specifically a sucrose-supplemented, diet on running performance in 30-km footraces (McKechnie et al. 1970). The authors were unable to measure any ergogenic effect of the high sucrose diet. However, they had also measured the rates of fluid ingestion and the levels of dehydration that developed in the runners during those races. It was these findings that were to become so influential and important.

The principal findings were that the athletes drank less than they sweated; hence, all the athletes lost weight, developing voluntary dehydration as did the army recruits studied in the Nevada Desert Study. More specifically, as also found in the army recruits (Adolph 1947), there was a linear relationship between levels of dehydration greater than 3% and the athletes' postexercise rectal temperatures. Hence, the authors concluded that the level of dehydration that develops during exercise is the most important factor determining the rectal temperature during exercise. This, in turn, meant that the avoidance of weight loss (dehydration) was the critically important factor preventing heat injury during prolonged exercise (Wyndham 1977). Interestingly, the authors did not speculate that dehydration might influence running performance. Their finding, identical to that of Pugh et al. (1967), that the race winners had the highest rectal temperatures and were the most dehydrated (Wyndham and Strydom 1969), may have dissuaded them from doing so.

To reach their conclusion that dehydration determined the rectal temperature during exercise, the authors had to ignore their own published findings, which established that the rate of energy expenditure during exercise, the metabolic rate, is a major determinant of the rectal temperature during exercise (Wyndham et al. 1970).

The real influence of the study, however, came not so much from its findings as from its provocative title: "The danger of an inadequate water intake during marathon running." However, the research neither studied nor identified any dangers of an inadequate fluid intake during marathon running. What they did establish was that the most dehydrated runners won the races. Thus, a disinterested runner might well have concluded that dehydration had beneficially enhanced the performances of the race winners. Indeed, given this unexpected finding and the low rate of reported cases of heatstroke and other health disorders in marathon runners at that time, despite their hopelessly inadequate fluid intakes, a more appropriate title for that historic study might perhaps have been: "Remarkable resistance of marathon runners to any detrimental effects of dehydration."

The immediately beneficial effect of that study was that the International Amateur Athletics Federation (IAAF) reviewed the rules governing international distance races. As a direct result, rule changes were introduced in 1977 that allowed fluid ingestion every 2.5 km after the first 5 km of long-distance races. In 1990, the rule was again modified to allow the ingestion of water and carbohydrate every 3 km after the first 2.5 km of long-distance races. The origin of all these rule changes is unquestionably the stimulus provided by Wyndham and Strydom's historic study.

The less desirable effect of this study was that sports medicine practitioners began to extol the dangers of dehydration in endurance athletes, as well as the need to ingest vast amounts of fluid during exercise. Attempts to question this theory have usually been greeted with derision, not least because they may be perceived to threaten some lucrative dogmas. Thus, those who were influenced by the article's title seem to have adopted the following (incorrect) logic: Progressive dehydration during exercise causes heatstroke; hence, the most important method to prevent heatstroke during exercise is to ensure that athletes ingest as much fluid as possible.

But heatstroke is also the most important cause of collapse during exercise. Hence, all people who collapse after exercise have a heat disorder and must necessarily be dehydrated. Therefore, intravenous fluid therapy is the logical treatment of choice for all athletes who collapse during or after exercise. The illogic in this argument should be apparent, but it is not often appreciated, much less accepted, by those managing collapsed athletes.

In summary, the studies of Adolph (1947), Pugh et al. (1967), and Wyndham and Strydom (1969) established that subjects drink less than they sweat during exercise and that, in marathon runners, the difference can be very marked. As a result, during exercise, athletes develop dehydration of varying degrees. In addition, the body temperature is raised in proportion to the level of dehydration. The studies of Adolph (1947) showed that the proportion of subjects who completed a walking task in desert heat increased with fluid ingestion during exercise. In contrast, the winning runners in the distance races studied by Pugh (1967) and Wyndham and Strydom (1969) were both the most dehydrated and the hottest.

Subsequent generations of exercise physiologists have interpreted these findings according to their particular biases. All studies have been interpreted to indicate that dehydration alone can cause heat injury (that is, if athletes become dehydrated during exercise, they must develop heatstroke; the flaws in this logic are reviewed later in this chapter). Other researchers have interpreted the finding of Adolph (1947) as evidence that "exercise performance" is impaired by dehydration. In fact, these studies showed that subjects who were dehydrated by about 7% of body weight (because they did not drink at all during exercise) fatigued prematurely and were unable to sustain the same exercise intensity for as long as those who ingested fluid during exercise. That study provides no information on the much more relevant question: Does the maintenance of levels of dehydration less than 5% during exercise—the more usual values measured in competitive athletes (Noakes 1993)—lead to superior performance in competitive events, especially in sports such as running, in which the body's weight must be carried and in which the goal is to complete the race in the shortest possible time? This question has received remarkably little attention, even by those scientists who consider the effects of dehydration during exercise to be worthy of study.

Thus, the original studies of the effects of dehydration on exercise performance were all performed on army personnel (Adolph 1947; Bean and Eichna 1943; Eichna et al. 1945; Ladell 1955; Pitts et al. 1944; Strydom et al. 1966) during prolonged walking, usually in the heat. The general finding was that more subjects completed the set task when they ingested fluid during the activity.

Most researchers also reported that fluid ingestion had more obvious effects on the psyche than on the soma. The description of Bean and Eichna (1943) is typical of subjects who did not ingest fluid during exercise:

An important change which the chart does not show was the actual condition of the men, their low morale and lack of vigor, their glassy eyes, their apathetic, torpid appearance, their "don't-give-a-damn-for-anything" attitude, their uncoordinated stumbling, shuffling gait. Some were incapable of sustained purposeful action and were not fit for work. All they wanted to do was rest and drink. (p. 155)

Eichna et al. (1945) reported that dehydrated subjects were "reduced to apathetic, listless, plodding men straining to finish the same task" that they completed energetically and cheerfully when fully hydrated (page 50). Similarly, Strydom et al. (1966) reported that fluid restriction caused their subjects to become morose, aggressive, and disobedient toward their superiors.

Since 1966, relatively few studies have looked specifically at the effects of fluid ingestion alone. Instead, the evaluation of carbohydrate ingestion has been emphasized (Coggan and Coyle 1991; Montain and Coyle 1992b; Hawley et al. 1992a). These studies generally show that carbohydrate ingestion enhances performance (Coggan and Coyle 1991; Montain and Coyle 1992b), and the assumption is that this is only due to a metabolic effect, probably by forestalling the development of hypoglycemia (see chapter 3). However, the addition of glucose to the ingested solution increases fluid absorption (Gisolfi et al. 1990; 1991). Hence, the beneficial effect of carbohydrate ingestion during exercise could theoretically be due to an influence of the added carbohydrate on fluid balance.

Relatively few studies have compared the exercise performance of subjects when they ingested or did not ingest only water during exercise. Maughan et al. (1989) found that ingestion of either water or concentrated carbohydrate solutions did not increase endurance time at 70% $\dot{V}O_2$max, which exhausted subjects in 70 to 75 minutes. However, endurance was increased in subjects who ingested a dilute carbohydrate/electrolyte solution.

In contrast, Barr et al. (1991) showed that subjects who did not ingest fluid during very prolonged exercise (4 to 6 hours) at 55% $\dot{V}O_2$max terminated exercise approximately 90 minutes earlier than when they ingested fluid. Levels of dehydration at exhaustion were greater than 6%. Montain and Coyle (1992) also found that when they did not ingest fluid, subjects were less likely to complete exercise in the heat at 65% $\dot{V}O_2$max, whereas Fallowfield et al. (1996) found that subjects increased their running endurance at 70% $\dot{V}O_2$max by 33% when they ingested water during exercise.

Three studies have assessed the effects of water (or saline) ingestion or infusion at higher exercise intensities. Dechamps et al. (1989) reported that an intravenous saline infusion did not enhance performance at 84% $\dot{V}O_2$max, which exhausted subjects in approximately 21 minutes. However, Walsh et al. (1994) found that subjects were able to exercise significantly longer during a subsequent exercise bout at 90% $\dot{V}O_2$max when they ingested fluid during a preceding 1-hour exercise bout in the heat at 70% $\dot{V}O_2$max. This effect was not caused by differences in any measured physiological variable, including rectal temperature, and it occurred despite a difference in fluid balance of only 1.1 kg between dehydrated and fluid-replete subjects. Ratings of perceived exertion were significantly lower when fluid was ingested. The study of McConell et al. (1997) reported the same findings when the exercise bout preceding the performance trial lasted 90 minutes.

The study of Below et al. (1995) showed that the ingestion of either carbohydrate or water during exercise had equal effects but that ingesting both produced additive effects. Hence, the ingestion of either water or carbohydrate during exercise improved performance by about 2% during a high-intensity exercise bout requiring athletes to complete a fixed amount of work in the shortest possible time, which followed 50 minutes of exercise at 80% $\dot{V}O_2$max. The performance improvement doubled (4%) when the same amount of carbohydrate was ingested with water (that is, in the form of a carbohydrate drink).

A striking feature of most of those studies—with the exception of those by Walsh et al. (1994) and Below et al. (1995)—is that exercise performance was measured during open-ended trials in which athletes exercised at a fixed intensity for as long as they were able. These studies have a high coefficient of variation between trials (that is, they are not particularly reproducible). As a result, the performance of athletes undertaking these trials varies substantially from day to day. This suggests that external factors, such as boredom, may influence the results. For example, fluid ingestion might enhance performance simply by alleviating boredom.

In contrast, exercise tests in which the athlete freely chooses the exercise intensity and is asked to complete a fixed amount of work, for example, a 40-km cycling time trial in the shortest possible time, are highly reproducible on a day-to-day basis (Schabort, Hawley, et al. 1998) and are therefore likely to be the more accurate measures of the real effects of any intervention on athletic performance.

It is interesting that the few studies in which athletes were asked to complete a fixed amount of exercise in the shortest possible time do not show any beneficial effects of different rates of water ingestion on exercise performance (T.A. Robinson et al. 1995; McConell et al. 1999; Daries et al. 2000). Hence, McConell et al. (1999) conclude that the benefits of fluid ingestion alone on performance may only become apparent if the exercise lasts more than 2 hours or is undertaken in the heat. Even then, ingesting fluid at rates equal to rates of sweat loss does not appear to be more beneficial than simply drinking ad libitum (T.A. Robinson et al. 1995; McConell et al. 1999; Daries et al. 2000).

In summary, the balance of evidence indicates that the ingestion of water enhances the ability to sustain the same exercise intensity for longer during both very prolonged exercise of low intensity and during exercise of somewhat higher intensity but shorter duration. However, this effect is less than that achieved when the fluid contains carbohydrate either alone (C. Williams et al. 1990) or with electrolytes (Maughan et al. 1989; Coggan and Coyle 1991; Below et al. 1995; Tsintzas et al. 1993; 1995b). This is because carbohydrate ingestion consistently prevents the development of a hypoglycemia associated with a progressive reduction in the peak exercise intensity that can be sustained (C. Williams et al. 1990; Tsintzas et al. 1993). The most consistent finding is that fluid ingestion markedly reduces the perception of effort during exercise at both low (Adolph 1947) and high intensities (Walsh et al. 1994). It is also possible that exercise performance during high-intensity exercise is impaired at levels of dehydration that do not influence performance at lower exercise intensities (Adolph 1947).

An important finding of these studies is that the closer the rate of fluid ingestion approaches the sweat rate, the less the degree of physiological disturbance that develops during exercise (Montain and Coyle 1992a; 1992b). If the degree of physiological disturbance resulting from dehydration determines the degree to which exercise performance will be impaired, then, logically, athletes should drink at rates that equal their rates of fluid loss if they wish to optimize performance. Currently, four studies have evaluated the effects on performance of drinking fluid at rates that match the rates of fluid loss.

McConell et al. (1997) found that replacing 100% of the sweat lost during exercise did not improve exercise performance more than did replacing only 50% of that loss. Daries et al. (2000) reported essentially the same finding. Drinking fluid ad libitum (approximately 400 ml per hour) during 90 minutes of exercise that preceded a 30-minute all-out bout of exercise produced the same performance as did drinking at about twice that rate (approximately 900 ml per hour), a rate of ingestion that is in line with the guidelines of the American College of Sports Medicine

(ACSM). T.A. Robinson et al. (1995) found that ingesting fluid at very high rates (greater than 1 liter per hour) during a 1-hour cycling time trial caused abdominal fullness and impaired exercise performance compared to not drinking any fluid during the same period. Similarly, McConell et al. (1999) found that fluid ingested at 50% or 100% of the rate of fluid loss during 45 minutes of exercise did not improve performance during a subsequent 15-minute bout of all-out exercise, compared to trials in which no fluid was ingested. Cheuvront and Haymes (2001) have also reported that forced drinking did not enhance the performance of female runners more than did ad libitum drinking during 2 hours of running. Hence, there is at present no scientific support for the belief that performance will be optimized if fluid is drunk at the same rate that it is lost during exercise. This guideline, entrenched in the Position Stand of the ACSM (1996a), is not supported by any scientific evidence.

Although none of these studies have clearly identified the mechanism whereby dehydration impairs the ability to sustain the same exercise intensity for prolonged periods, it is well established that dehydration increases the heart rate and body (rectal) temperature during exercise (Montain and Coyle 1992b; González-Alonso et al. 2000) and reduces the heart's output and stroke volume (González-Alonso et al. 2000), as well as the blood flow to the skin (González-Alonso et al. 1995) and the exercising muscles (González-Alonso et al. 1998; González-Alonso, Calbet, et al. 1999), all in proportion to the degree of dehydration (Montain and Coyle 1992a; 1992b). Furthermore, dehydration increases muscle glycogen use (Hargreaves et al. 1996); increases the blood levels of the fluid-regulating hormones, including vasopressin (ADH), renin, aldosterone, and atrial natriuretic factor (McConell et al. 1997); and increases the discomfort experienced during exercise (Noakes 1993). The circulatory effects are mainly due to a reduction in the central blood volume, as they disappear when exercise is undertaken in the supine (lying) position (González-Alonso, Mora-Rodriguez et al. 1999). This latter finding predicts that simply lying flat should reverse all of the cardiovascular effects of dehydration, a point that we emphasize in the management of our collapsed, often dehydrated, runners.

The cardiovascular penalty (that is, the rise in heart rate and the reduction in cardiac output and skin and muscle blood flow) increases with increasing exercise intensity, whereas the thermal penalty (that is, the elevation in core temperature) is independent of the exercise intensity and is between +0.1 and +0.2°C for each 1% body weight loss resulting from dehydration (Montain, Sawka, et al. 1998). Dehydration has not been shown to alter gastrointestinal function during exercise (Ryan et al. 1998), metabolism during high-intensity exercise of short duration (Montain, Sawka, et al. 1998), or the sweat rate (Noakes 1993).

As exercise in the heat seems to be limited by a rising body temperature, the reduction in body temperature resulting from fluid ingestion during exercise would appear to be an important mechanism whereby fluid ingestion enhances endurance performance. The same applies to the heart rate, since an elevated heart rate may impair performance and may increase the perception of effort, thereby inducing premature fatigue. Hence, keeping levels of dehydration as low as possible may be necessary if optimum performance is to be achieved during high-intensity exercise in the heat. However, ingesting fluid to the point at which gastrointestinal symptoms or hyponatremia develops will impair performance. Similarly, there may be a tradeoff if high rates of fluid ingestion mean the athlete must carry more weight, especially in weight-bearing activities such as running.

Thus, my conclusion is that all the evidence indicates that ad libitum fluid ingestion during exercise appears to be as beneficial as higher rates of forced ingestion.
Such fluid ingestion will improve performance during very prolonged bouts of exercise in which the goal is to maintain the same exercise intensity or during exercise of more than 1 hour in which the goal is to complete a fixed amount of exercise
in the shortest possible time. However, ingesting carbohydrate with the water has
a much greater effect, not least of which is the potential for a placebo effect (V.R.
Clark et al. 2000).

PREVENTING HEAT-IMPAIRED PERFORMANCE

Anyone who has run a marathon or longer race in the heat knows that such races
are much more difficult than races of the same distance run in cold conditions. The
first hint of a likely explanation should have come from a series of studies showing
that precooling of the body or the active muscles before exercise prolongs endurance time to exhaustion in both dogs and humans (Schmidt and Bruck 1981;
Hessemer et al. 1984; Kruk et al. 1985; Kozlowski et al. 1985; Olschewski and Brück
1988; Lee and Haymes 1995; González-Alonso, Teller, et al. 1999; Kay et al. 1999;
Marsh and Sleivert 1999). Precooling keeps the body and muscle temperature lower
during subsequent exercise and alters the metabolic response by decreasing the
rates of muscle glycogen utilization, muscle lactate accumulation, and the decline
in muscle high energy phosphate content (Kozlowski et al. 1985). Thus, according
to the Energy Supply/Energy Depletion Model, it was originally assumed that these
metabolic changes explained the enhanced performance with precooling.

However, humans (B. Nielsen et al. 1990; 1993; 1997; Gonzalez-Alonso, Teller, et
al. 1999) and other mammals (C.R.Taylor and Rowntree 1973; Fuller et al. 1998) tend
to stop exercising at a characteristic body temperature (specific for each individual)
without any evidence of impaired blood or oxygen delivery to, or metabolism by,
the active muscle (B. Nielsen et al. 1990; 1993; Gonzalez-Alonso et al. 1998; González-
Alonso, Mora-Rodriguez et al. 1999). Moreover, the muscle glycogen stores are not
as depleted as they are during exercise in cooler conditions (Febbraio and Dancey
1999; Pitsiladis and Maughn 1996b; Parkin et al. 1999), in which the subjects can
exercise harder for longer (Dill et al. 1931; MacDougall et al. 1974; Kozlowski et al.
1985; S.D.R. Galloway and Maughan 1997). These findings indicate that it is the elevated body temperature that causes fatigue.

Thus, Nielsen (1994) has concluded:

> It was the rise in core temperature to about 40° C which coincided with exhaus-
> tion and an inability to sustain exercise, not only during acute heat exposure, but
> also after acclimatization to heat.... It is therefore suggested that a high core
> temperature is the ultimate cause of fatigue due to heat stress. This high tempera-
> ture may adversely affect the function of motor centres, reduce the ability to
> recruit motor units for the required work—or perhaps decrease the "motivation"
> for muscular activity. (p. 56)

According to this model, precooling or exercising in a cooler environment aids
performance by increasing the duration of exercise required to produce sufficient
additional heat storage. It achieves this by raising the body temperature to the

limiting value at which central (brain) recruitment of muscle is reduced to prevent the development of heatstroke. Of course, cooling does not only have to occur before exercise. Logically, continued cooling during exercise would also be of value. It was this possibility that led to the development of a cooling jacket by the Australian Institute of Sport. The jacket, made of neoprene, included pouches containing ice that maintained reduced skin temperatures before and during exercise. The system was used by Australian athletes at the 1996 Atlanta Olympic Games and was generally well accepted.

Logically, however, cooling of either the brain or of the blood flow to the brain is likely to be the most effective technique for enhancing performance since the temperature of the blood reaching the brain is more likely to be the variable sensed by the central governor. Indeed, one study found that cooling the face increased the exercise time to fatigue at 75% $\dot{V}O_2$max in moderate heat by 50% (Marvin et al. 1999). Cooling lowered the temperature of the inner ear membrane and presumably also that of the brain. This study suggests that cooling the blood in the large arteries in the neck, the carotid arteries, which carry blood to the brain, would be an even more effective cooling strategy.

Sponging the Body

It is vitally important to sponge the body during exercise, particularly in the heat. As the skin temperature rises, it causes blood to pool in the veins of the arms and legs because the veins become progressively more dilated as the skin temperature increases. The veins soon fill with a large volume of blood that is effectively lost from the circulation and only can be returned to the circulation if the skin temperature is again lowered. This can be achieved by sponging, provided it is able to lower the skin temperature effectively or, better, the temperature of the blood reaching the brain.

Lowering the skin temperature induces a reflex constriction of the veins and arteries in the cooled limb, thereby reducing the volume of blood previously stored in the dilated veins. Such sponging must reduce and maintain a (lower) skin temperature if it is to be effective.

A recent study confirmed that skin wetting did in fact lower the skin temperature during exercise but did not aid heat loss (Bassett et al. 1987). Thus, the benefits of skin wetting during exercise probably relate to its ability to increase return of blood from the limb veins to the central circulation. As a result, the volume of blood filling the heart increases, and this aids the heart in maintaining a high stroke volume and cardiac output at a lower heart rate.

Ingesting Fluids

Ingesting the correct amount of fluid during exercise aids performance. In the following section, I outline the volumes and frequency with which runners should drink before and during exercise. I also suggest what that drink should contain.

Before Exercise

The enthusiasm that many athletes have for drinking large volumes of fluid during exercise sometimes also extends to the preexercise period. Many runners believe that it is important to drink quite large volumes of fluid before exercise to ensure that they begin exercise in a state of optimum hydration. More recently, this enthusiasm has spread to increasing salt intake in the days before ultradistance events such as the Ironman Triathlon.

Humans, like mammals such as the desert-dwelling camel and Bedouin goat (Choshniak et al. 1987), are designed to operate in a moderately dehydrated state, which is then corrected by fluid ingestion. In humans, this is usually associated with meals; it occurs in camels when they finally locate an oasis. Thus humans, like camels, live in a state of perpetual dehydration except for a short period at night after the evening meal. Like the real camel and unlike the myth, humans cannot store either fluid or salt to any great extent to reduce the degree of dehydration that occurs before the next opportunity to drink. Rather, all mammals drink until they are no longer dehydrated; the uniqueness of the camel and the Bedouin goat is that both are able to sustain fluid losses of up to 30% of body weight without ill effect before they again need to drink. In contrast, humans are unable to exercise if they are dehydrated by more than 10%. Death in humans occurs at dehydration levels of 20% or greater. The other unique characteristic of camels is that they can correct their fluid loss within minutes of beginning to drink. Also, despite such large fluid deficits, they never overdrink, unlike some humans. In fact, camels have an almost mystical ability to know exactly how much they need to drink to correct a deficit accumulated over weeks or months, and to stop drinking the instant they have drunk enough to correct that deficit.

In humans, the aim of ingesting fluid before exercise is to ensure that we are appropriately hydrated at the start of exercise. This is quite easily achieved by ensuring adequate fluid intake with meals. We do not need to drink continually for the 12 to 24 hours before competition. Overdrinking will simply result in more frequent trips to the toilet, effecting an increased loss of sodium and potassium in the urine. Only if drinks with an unpalatably high sodium content are ingested is there a small (approximately 7%) expansion of the plasma volume (Greenleaf, Looft-Wilson, et al. 1998), equivalent to an increase in whole body water storage of perhaps 500 ml. Normally, body water comprises about 65% of an athlete's weight, or about 45 liters in a 70-kg male. Thus, even a 500-ml increase represents a very modest (1%) change.

Optimum hydration can be assessed easily by monitoring urine color. L.E. Armstrong et al. (1998) showed that a very lightly colored urine is the best measure of the optimum hydration state.

Accordingly, before competition, athletes should drink sufficiently to ensure that their urine is lightly colored. As it takes between 1 to 2 hours for ingested fluid to be fully absorbed and the obligatory urine response to have occurred, athletes should probably take their last drink about 2 hours before exercise. For reasons discussed subsequently, they should carry 400 to 500 ml of fluid to the start line of any race longer than 10 km and ingest that fluid in the last minute or two before the race begins.

But even if the body were able to store fluid before exercise, there is no evidence that this would necessarily be beneficial. Preexercise overhydration with glycerol ingestion did not alter either performance or cardiovascular function during exercise in moderate (Latzka et al. 1997) or severe (Latzka et al. 1998) heat. In contrast, preexercise blood volume expansion with the use of an intravenous dextran solution reportedly improved cycling performance by more than 10% (Leutkermeier and Thomas 1994). But this degree of improvement seems unrealistic, suggesting that some other factors also influenced the outcome of that study.

Sadly, some may attempt to use these techniques to disguise their use of the banned drug erythropoietin (chapter 13), which increases the mass of circulating red blood cells. Expanding the plasma volume can disguise the presence of a greater than allowed concentration of red blood cells.

During Exercise

The idea that we should drink during exercise, especially marathon running, is of recent origin. This is surprising, given that the early military studies (Adolph 1947) established that fluid ingestion aided performance and prolonged survival during exercise performed in the desert heat.

That early marathon runners were unaccustomed to drinking fluid regularly during races is shown by the trivial amounts drunk by Arthur Newton during his races (see chapter 6). This was probably a legacy of the beliefs of the original marathon runners. American Joseph Forshaw, who finished fourth in the 1908 Olympic Marathon and tenth in the 1912 Olympic Marathon, had written: "I know from actual experience that the full race can be covered in creditable time without so much as a single drop of water being taken or even sponging of the head" (Sullivan 1909, page 73; Martin and Gynn 1979, page 45).

The advice given to marathon runners of the early 1900s included the following caveats: "Don't take any nourishment before going 17 or 18 miles. If you do, you will never go the distance. Don't get into the habit of drinking and eating in a marathon race; some prominent runners do, but it is not beneficial" (Sullivan 1909, page 39).

Then, 50 years later, Jim Peters, whom I consider to be the greatest marathoner of all time, enunciated the conventional wisdom of his day:

> [In the marathon race] there is no need to take any solid food at all and every effort should also be made to do without liquid, as the moment food or drink is taken, the body has to start dealing with its digestion, and in so doing some discomfort will almost invariably be felt. (J.H. Peters et al. 1957, page 114)

Arthur Newton expressed similar sentiments: "You can't lay down a hard and fast rule [about fluid ingestion during exercise]. Even in the warmest English weather, a 26-mile run ought to be manageable with no more than a single drink or, at most, two" (Newton 1948, page 15).

To check whether these statements accurately reflected the actual behavior of these runners in races, I asked Jackie Mekler how he ate and drank during his competitive racing career, which began in 1945 and ended in 1969. He confirmed that these comments tallied with the practices of his day:

> In those days it was quite fashionable not to drink, until one absolutely had to. After a race, runners would recount with pride, "I only had a drink after 30 or 40 km." To run a complete marathon without any fluid replacement was regarded as the ultimate aim of most runners, and a test of their fitness. (Mekler 1991, personal communication)

Later Mekler told me that he held one world record that would never be challenged. In one 90-km Comrades Marathon he had his first drink at 60 km. Yet, he won the race. In another 160-km race, he took his first drink even later, after 100 km.

The landmark scientific study that reversed these beliefs was that of the Johannesburg-based physiologists, Cyril Wyndham and Nick Strydom (1969) who studied runners in a 32-km road race and showed that the body temperatures of athletes who became dehydrated by more than 3% of their body weight were elevated to levels that Wyndham and Strydom considered unacceptable. They concluded that the dehydration that develops during exercise is detrimental because it causes the body temperature to rise excessively and must predispose the athlete to heatstroke (figure 4.9). Yet, as already argued on pages 190 through 192 of this chapter, they discovered no such dangers, and their conclusion that dehydration alone explained the elevated rectal temperatures in that particular study may not be entirely correct (Noakes, Lambert, et al. 1988; Noakes 1995), because it is now known that the intensity of exercise, rather than the level of dehydration, is the most important factor determining the body temperature during exercise. Nevertheless, the 1969 study was of great practical significance, for it drew attention to the potential dangers of the International Amateur Athletic Federation's Rule No. 165.5, which stipulated that marathon runners could drink no fluids before the 11-km mark of a 42-km marathon and thereafter could only drink every 5 km. This ruling was an improvement of the 1953 rule that stated that "refreshments shall (only) be provided by the organizers after 15 km. No refreshments may be carried or taken by a competitor other than that provided by the organizers." These early rulings discouraged marathon runners from drinking during races and promoted the idea that drinking was unnecessary and a sign of weakness.

From the results of their original study, Wyndham and Strydom (1969) concluded that marathon runners should aim to drink 250 ml of fluid every 15 minutes during exercise to give a total of 1 liter per hour, a value that matched their sweat rates. It

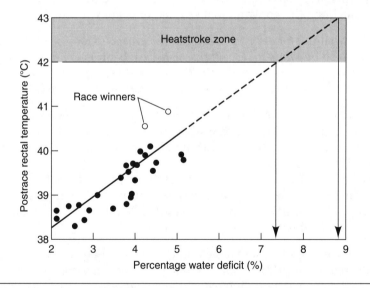

Figure 4.9 An apparent relationship between postrace rectal temperature and level of dehydration led to the (incorrect) theory that dehydration is the most important risk factor for heatstroke in marathon runners. Note that the highest rectal temperatures were found in the race winners, that heatstroke could only be expected in runners who were dehydrated by between 7% and 8.5%, that the highest levels of dehydration in these runners were 5%, and that their rectal temperatures ranged between 38.3 and 41.0°C.

Adapted from Wyndham and Strydom (1969, page 895).

is now clear that no competitive runner in the long history of the sport has ever achieved such high rates of fluid ingestion. Only in intermittent activities in the heat have such high rates of fluid ingestion been reported (Morris et al. 1998). The only runners who are capable of drinking so much are those who develop water intoxication—the hyponatremia of exercise. Most of those athletes are noncompetitive, finishing in the last quarter to half of the field. However, competitive Ironman triathletes can develop the hyponatremia of exercise if they drink excessively during the bicycle leg and continue that practice during the running leg. Wyndham and Strydom's own data found that the marathoners in their study only drank about 100 ml per hour. More recent studies confirm that the voluntary fluid intake by runners during races is closer to 500 than 1000 ml every hour (Shephard and Kavanagh 1978; Maughan 1985; Noakes, Lambert, et al. 1988; Noakes 1993), as also found in laboratory studies (McConell et al. 1999; Daries et al. 2000; Haymes et al. 2001). Despite this, current guidelines for runners suggest they should aim to drink between 600 and 2000 ml per hour during competition (ACSM 1985; 1987; 1996; Gisolfi and Duchman 1993). Yet the only proven effect of such high rates of fluid ingestion (greater than 1 liter per hour) is the development of water intoxication (hyponatremia) and impaired exercise performance.

Unfortunately, all these recommendations are based on inadequate data and the unshakeable belief in a dogma that holds that any weight loss that develops during exercise represents a fluid loss that must be prevented if a profound drop in performance (said by some to equal 40% for a 5% level of dehydration) is to be avoided and if heatstroke is to be prevented. Yet, I am plagued by the persistent question: If these fears are indeed valid, how was it possible for the marathoners and ultramarathoners of the first part of this century to survive, let alone run astonishing times, when they drank essentially nothing, neither water nor carbohydrate, during competition? My empirical observations of the television images of leading runners in modern marathon races do not suggest to me that they drink very much— certainly nowhere near the 1 to 2 liters per hour that scientists say they must. In my view, a figure closer to 200 to 400 ml per hour might be more likely.

ACSM's Fluid Replacement Guidelines: Not Evidence-Based

Perhaps the most compelling change in the conduct of medicine in the past decade has been its move to include only those medical practices that are evidence-based—those that have been shown, by independent clinical trials, to offer the patient more benefit than simply doing nothing. It would be interesting to establish the extent to which the drinking guidelines of the ACSM are evidence-based.

During the past 25 years, the ACSM has produced four different Position Statements pertaining to fluid ingestion and the prevention of heat injury during exercise (ACSM 1975; 1987; 1996a; 1996b). Each is somewhat different, particularly with regard to the nature of the claims made surrounding the benefits of such fluid replacement and the volumes of fluid that should be ingested during exercise.

In 1975, the simple advice was that athletes should "be encouraged to frequently ingest fluids during competition." (ACSM 1975) Frequently was considered to be every 3 to 4 km in races of 16 km or longer, suggesting that fluid

(continued)

ingestion was of lesser importance in races less than 16 km. This advice was entirely appropriate in 1975 since, for the previous 100 years, athletes had been advised to avoid fluid ingestion during exercise. The rationale behind fluid ingestion was to "reduce rectal temperature and prevent dehydration." No reference was made to the possibility that fluid ingestion alone would influence the risk of, much less prevent, heat illness during exercise.

The subsequent Position Stand of 1987 introduced two additional statements of relevance to this debate:

> *Fluid (water) consumption before and during the race will reduce the risk of heat injury,* particularly in longer runs such as the marathon *[my emphasis] (Costill et al. 1970 [sic]; Wyndham and Strydom 1969; Gisolfi and Copping 1974). . . . Such dehydration will subsequently reduce sweating and predispose the runner to hyperthermia, heatstroke, heat exhaustion, and muscle cramps. (ACSM 1987, p.530).*

The three quoted references do not support that conclusion, however, because all of these researchers only studied the effects of fluid ingestion on rectal temperature during exercise, and none—including the original historic paper of Wyndham and Strydom (1969; figure 4.9)—studied the incidence of heatstroke, heat exhaustion, or muscle cramps in marathon runners, nor the influence of different rates of fluid ingestion on that incidence. Rather, the sole finding of that study was a relationship between the postexercise rectal temperature and the extent of weight loss in competitors in 32-km running races, which I think may have been spurious (Noakes 1993; 1995). Of interest was the finding that the winners of those races were also the most dehydrated and hyperthermic, which is at variance with the theory that dehydration impairs athletic performance and increases the risk that heat illness will occur.

Of these studies, none could conclude that fluid ingestion reduces the risk of these medical complications in marathon runners. In addition, the study of Costill, Cote, et al. (1970) was incorrectly referenced. Hence, this Stand, which introduced a fundamentally novel concept not present in the 1975 Statement, was not based on any new evidence that had become available since 1975.

Nine years later, the 1996 Position Stand On Heat and Cold Illnesses During Distance Running proposed that dehydration will "predispose the runner to heat exhaustion or the more dangerous hyperthermia and exertional heatstroke (Pearlmutter 1986; Hubbard and Armstrong 1988; ACSM 1996b, p iii)." However, this statement is not evidence-based since the two referenced articles are literature reviews: they do not provide any new findings (since the 1987 Position Stand) that support the conclusion that dehydrated runners are at increased risk of "dangerous hyperthermia" or heatstroke.

Furthermore, the 1996 Position Stand appears to be contradictory since it later states that "excessive hyperthermia may occur in the absence of significant dehydration," (page iv) especially in short-distance races when the rate of heat production is high. That statement is evidence-based.

The 1996 Position Stand also includes the statement that "adequate fluid consumption before and during the race can reduce the risk of heat illness, including disorientation and irrational behavior, *particularly in longer events such as a marathon* [my emphasis] (Wyndham and Strydom 1969; Costill et al. 1970 (sic); Gisolfi and Copping 1974; ACSM 1996b)." Again, the same three references from the 1987 Position Stand are quoted, none of which had measured the effects of different rates of fluid ingestion on the incidence of heat illness, disorientation, or irrational behavior in any running races, including marathon races. The statement also proposes that athletes should be encouraged to "replace their sweat losses or consume 150 to 300 ml every 15 minutes (600 to 1200 ml per hour)" (ACSM 1996b, p. i). No scientific rationale for that proposal was provided.

The Position Stand also includes the statement that "intravenous (IV) fluid therapy facilitates rapid recovery (in runners with heat exhaustion) (Hubbard and Armstrong 1989; Nash 1985; ACSM 1996b)." But that statement also references two review articles, which do not contain evidence from controlled clinical trials proving that novel claim.

The related 1996 Position Stand on Exercise and Fluid Replacement (ACSM 1996a) extends these new claims by stating that the "most serious effect of dehydration resulting from the failure to replace fluids during exercise is impaired heat dissipation, which can elevate core temperature to dangerously high levels (i.e., greater than 40° C)" (p. ii). Later the statement is made that dehydration during exercise

> presents the potential for the development of heat-related disorders . . . including the potentially life-threatening heatstroke (Sutton 1990; Wyndham 1977). It is therefore reasonable to surmise that fluid replacement that offsets dehydration and excessive elevation in body heat during exercise may be instrumental in reducing the risk of thermal injury (Hubbard and Armstrong 1988). (ACSM 1996a, p. ii)

These conclusions are again not evidence-based; all the material cited to support these new ideas are review articles that represent the individual beliefs of the authors. None provide specific data showing either that athletes who are dehydrated are at greater risk of heatstroke during exercise or that fluid ingestion during exercise can reduce that risk, as repeatedly argued (Noakes 1993; 1995).

The Position Stand on Exercise and Fluid Replacement confirms the belief that the rate of fluid ingestion during exercise should equal the sweat rate and that "fluid and carbohydrate requirements can be met simultaneously by ingesting 600 to 1200 ml per hour of solutions containing 4% to 8% carbohydrate" (ACSM 1996a, p. iv). In addition, runners are encouraged to "consume the maximal amount that can be tolerated" (p. i). Although there is substantial evidence supporting the proposal that ingesting carbohydrate at rates of about 60 g per hour can enhance performance during prolonged exercise by preventing hypoglycemia, there is no published evidence to prove that fluid should be ingested at rates equal to sweat rates to prevent heat injury.

Thus, over the course of four revisions, the ACSM Position Stands have become progressively more forceful in promoting the belief that high rates of fluid ingestion during exercise are necessary to prevent heatstroke and other heat illnesses. None of them, however, refer to specific prospective studies from which such definite conclusions can be drawn. Furthermore, there are no published cross-sectional studies showing that runners with heat illnesses are more dehydrated than are those who do not develop heat injury during exercise. Rather the conclusions of the four ACSM Position Stands are based

(continued)

on a "reasonable to surmise" doctrine. Moreover, they promote high rates of fluid replacement during exercise, sufficient to replace sweat losses (without ever referring to urine losses), but without providing a scientific validation for that conclusion.

The Stands acknowledge that high-exercise intensities are more likely to produce heatstroke, regardless of the levels of dehydration that develop in runners. Yet, the evidence presented in this chapter indicates that ad libitum drinking is probably optimum during exercise. The extent to which the ACSM guidelines have contributed to overdrinking during exercise and the development of hyponatremia (water intoxication) must await the judgment of history. For example, although the 1996 Position Stand warns about the dangers of overconsumption of fluid during exercise, the advice is confused by the popular but unproven dogma that salt ingestion can lessen the risks caused by overdrinking:

> *Excessive consumption of pure water or dilute fluid (i.e. up to 10 liters per 4 hours) during prolonged endurance events may lead to the harmful dilutional hyponatremia (Noakes, Goodwin, et al. 1985) which may involve disorientation, confusion, and seizure or coma. The possibility of hyponatremia may be the best rationale for the inclusion of sodium chloride in fluid replacement beverages. . . . One reason for including sodium in rehydration drinks is to avoid hyponatremia. To prevent the development of this rare condition during prolonged exercise (longer than 4 hours), electrolytes should be present in the fluid or food during and after exercise. (ACSM 1996b).*

The scientists who develop these guidelines would be best advised to warn runners and cyclists that drinking too much can kill you and that there is seldom, if ever, the need to drink more than 400 to 800 ml per hour during exercise.

Ingestion Equal to Sweat Rate

The detailed studies of Montain and Coyle (1992a; 1992b) have established that when studied during exercise in the heat, the detrimental effects of dehydration on the various physiological functions occur as a linear function of the level of dehydration. Thus, for each liter of unreplaced fluid loss, the heart rate increases by 8 beats per minute, cardiac output falls by 1 liter per minute, and rectal temperature rises by 0.3°C. Logic suggests that if these detrimental effects were prevented, performance would be optimized. Hence, the assumption is that the rate of fluid ingestion should equal the sweat rate if performance (and not just physiological function) is to be optimized. But there are a number of caveats to this logic.

First, these studies were performed in the laboratory under environmental conditions in which, according to the ACSM guidelines, competitive sport should not be permitted (32°C, relative humidity 50%, with inadequate convective cooling). Their relevance to the real world of competitive sport is, at best, dubious. In field trials of athletes competing in real competition, there is no relationship between the level of dehydration and the postrace rectal temperature (Noakes, Adams, et al. 1988; Noakes, Myburgh, it al. 1990b; Noakes 2001a; figure 4.10).

Second, athletes who drank enough to replace their sweat rates (1.2 liters per

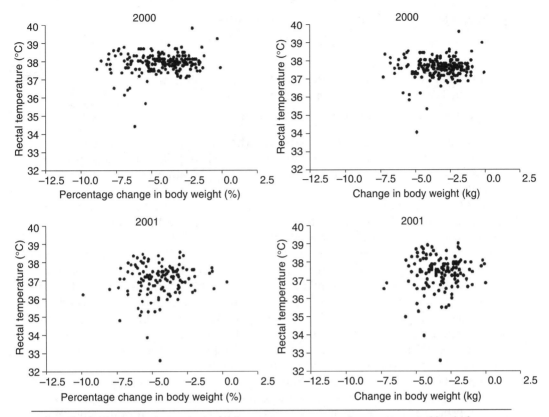

Figure 4.10 Absence of any relationship between postrace rectal temperature and level of dehydration in competitors in the 2000 and 2001 South African Ironman Triathlons. Note that the range of postrace rectal temperatures is similar to that reported by Wyndham and Strydom (1969; figure 4.9) even though some triathletes in this study were substantially more dehydrated.

Data from the 2000 and 2001 Ironman Triathlons, Cape Town, collected by K. Sharwood, T.D. Noakes, and colleagues, unpublished.

hour) finished the exercise 2.3 kg heavier than athletes who did not drink during exercise and 1.4 kg heavier than those who drank 300 ml per hour. As the study did not include a true performance trial, especially one in which the effect of this extra body weight was measured, we do not know whether the detrimental effects of this extra weight outweighed the physiological benefits of maintaining lower heart rates and body temperatures.

The third caveat is that no one has yet accurately established how best to determine the exact level of dehydration, particularly in athletes involved in prolonged exercise. A portion of the weight lost during more prolonged exercise does not constitute a fluid loss that contributes to dehydration. As yet, scientists have not decided whether this is a small amount totaling a few hundred grams or whether it is a large amount of 2 to 3 kg (Noakes, Adams, et al. 1988; Pastene et al. 1996; G. Rogers et al. 1997; Speedy et al. 1999). If it is the latter, advice on how much to drink during exercise should be altered substantially. For example, Pastene et al. (1996) calculated that 1.8 kg to 2.0 kg of weight loss incurred by athletes running 42 km on a treadmill at a mean speed of 12.6 km per hour, during which they drank an average of about 1.5 liters (approximately 450 ml per hour), could be apportioned as follows:

Metabolic fuels (carbohydrate and fats) oxidized	557 g
Water released from stored glycogen used during exercise	1280 g
Total	1837 g
Additional metabolic water produced by metabolism and contributing to sweat losses but not to weight loss	402 g
Total weight loss not requiring replacement	2239 g

According to those calculations, athletes who lost 2 kg during that experimental marathon would finish the race overhydrated by 239 g. Drinking to prevent any weight loss during that marathon would have caused the athletes to be overhydrated by 2.2 kg.

If these calculations are correct, they explain why ad libitum rates of fluid ingestion of approximately 500 ml per hour are so common in athletes during competition (Noakes, Adams, et al. 1988; Noakes 1993).

Similarly, during an event such as the Hawaiian Ironman Triathlon, about 800 g of carbohydrate and 200 g of fat must be burned to complete the event. This would produce about 1.2 kg of metabolic water that would contribute to sweat losses without requiring replacement. In addition, another 1 to 2 kg of water stored with liver and muscle glycogen must be released and lost from the body, either as urine or as sweat, as that glycogen is used. As a result, up to 3 kg of the weight lost during prolonged exercise may not represent a true fluid loss that needs to be replaced during prolonged exercise if dehydration is to be prevented.

Support for this theory comes with the finding that Ironman triathletes lose about 2.5 kg of weight over the 48-hour period from immediately before the race to one day after the race (Speedy et al. 1999; 2001b). Why should these triathletes remain 2.5 kg lighter 24 hours after finishing the race? Perhaps because their muscle glycogen stores (500 to 800 g) and the associated water content (1500 ml to 2000 ml) have not yet been restored. If this were correct, then an Ironman triathlete who lost 2.5 kg during the race would have finished the race in a state of optimum hydration and any lesser weight loss would indicate a state of overhydration.

The fourth caveat is that, at least during competitive running, it is simply not possible to replace fluid at rates equal to the sweat rate when the sweat rate exceeds about 600 ml per hour. This is due, in part, to the gastrointestinal distress caused by higher rates of fluid intake during competitive running (Costill, Cote, et al. 1970; Brouns et al. 1987; Mitchell and Voss 1991).

We are left then to ponder what evidence there is to show that maintaining a particular body weight and completely preventing any dehydration during exercise will measurably enhance performance.

The only studies that have compared the effects on performance of moderate (ad libitum) to high rates of fluid ingestion during running are those of McConell et al. (1999) and Daries et al. (2000). Daries et al. (2000) found that performance during a 2-hour running test was not different in athletes who drank either ad libitum or at two levels of replacement suggested by the ACSM (150 or 350 ml per 70 kg of body mass every 17.5 minutes, equivalent to intakes of about 0.4 and 0.9 liter per hour. Interestingly, the rate of ad libitum drinking was similar to both the lower ACSM recommendation and the ad libitum fluid ingestion rates measured in runners in competition (Noakes, Adams, et al. 1988; Noakes 1993) or in other laboratory studies (Cheuvront and Haymes 2001). There was no measurable physiological difference with the higher rates of fluid ingestion except that they produced greater levels of intestinal discomfort. Essentially, the same findings were reported by McConell et al. (1999).

Another unpublished study found that 75% of triathletes who ingested more than 700 ml per hour during a standard triathlon reported feeling bloated after exercise, compared to only 37% of athletes who ingested 400 to 700 ml per hour, or only 29% of athletes who ingested less than 400 ml per hour.

Hence, the fifth caveat is that—unlike the clear evidence that any weight loss during laboratory exercise in very hot conditions produces a predictable and presumably detrimental effect on physiological functioning (Montain and Coyle 1992a; 1992b) no direct effect on performance has yet been shown, at least in runners (McConell et al. 1999; Daries et al. 2000). Furthermore, the optimum fluid replacement rate for cyclists has yet to be determined, as too little (200 ml per hour; Below et al. 1995) or too much (1500 ml per hour; T.A. Robinson et al. 1995) impairs performance.

There is currently no evidence to suggest that drinking more than ad libitum holds any particular advantages during running in the usual conditions present during competition (McConell et al. 1999; Daries et al. 2000; Cheuvront and Haymes 2001). Perhaps the advice should simply be to drink ad libitum. Those who wish to drink more should bear in mind that there is little scientific evidence to support this practice.

Calculating the Sweat Rate

If you wish to drink more than ad libitum and to match sweat losses, then it is necessary to understand the factors that regulate sweat rate, as sweating is by far the most important cause of water loss during exercise.

The metabolic rate is the most important factor determining the sweat rate (Noakes et al. 1990a). It is affected by the speed of running and body weight (Costill 1977). Figure 2.9 shows that the rate of oxygen consumption and the rate of metabolic heat production increase linearly with increasing running speed. As sweating is the most important avenue of heat loss during running, it is likely that the sweat rate also increases linearly with the increasing rate of heat production. Recall that figure 4.1 shows that heavier body mass increases metabolic heat production at any given running speed in direct proportion to the greater body mass. Thus, a 100-kg runner will produce twice as much heat as a 50-kg runner when running at the same speed. The larger runner's sweat rate will also be twice as high.

In competition, smaller runners often run faster for a shorter time and the heavier runners run more slowly for a longer time. If their finishing times are in the same ratio as their body weights, their total sweat losses should be very similar.

Barr and Costill (1989) have provided a prediction of sweat rates at different weights and running speeds in marathon races. Their prediction is that a sweat rate of 1 liter per hour is likely in a 50-kg runner who completes the marathon race in about 2:50:00 or a 90-kg runner who takes more than 5 hours to complete the race. Still, the actual sweat rates of all runners in competitive races are not known. Most evidence suggests that sweat rates may be lower than these predictions and that they are only greater than 1 liter per hour under unusual conditions, at least in marathon races. Such high rates are likely only in the fastest runners under the very worst environmental conditions. Most marathons are now held in the early morning when temperatures are usually mildest. Higher sweat rates are possible in training because athletes usually run harder for shorter periods in training, or they run either in the afternoon heat of the day or in the morning when the humidity is high. To my knowledge, the highest sweat rates yet recorded for sustained periods were those in marathon runners in Atlanta, Georgia, who were participating in simulated marathons (Millard-Stafford et al. 1992; 1997). Sweat rates of 1.8 liters per hour were recorded during exercise at temperatures of between 25 and 32°C and relative humidities of 70% to 80%, conditions considered to be of high or hazardous heat stress. Hence, unusually high sweat rates can be expected when environmental conditions are more severe, especially when the humidity is high. Even under those conditions, runners could only ingest about 750 ml per hour.

One of the problems of extrapolating laboratory experiments to competitive racing is that laboratory experiments are often undertaken in hotter conditions than would be allowed in competitive races (Noakes 2001a). But, more important, convective cooling is usually only provided by a fan in the laboratory, whereas in competition the athlete generates a (cooling) wind speed equal to the rate of forward progression. This wind speed is higher if there is a facing wind speed and lower if the wind is from behind.

Superior convective cooling when running outside the laboratory would lower the sweat rate since more heat would be lost by convection, requiring less to be lost by evaporation (sweating).

To calculate your sweat rate, or to find out by how much your current drinking pattern during races falls short of replacing your sweat losses, try the following experiment: Weigh yourself naked on a scale calibrated in kilograms, immediately before (WB) and immediately after (WA) a marathon run in conditions and at a pace to which you are accustomed. During the race you need to measure carefully the total amount of fluid in liters that you ingest while running (F). Your sweat rate

$$\text{Sweat rate (liters per hour)} = \frac{(WB - WA)}{\text{running time (hours)}}$$

can be calculated fairly accurately:

Your fluid replacement will have been adequate if, after races longer than 30 km, you lost less than 2 to 3 kg and are not dehydrated by more than 3%, calculated by the following equation:

$$\text{Dehydration (percent)} = \frac{(WB - WA) \times 100}{WB}$$

The highest sweat rates measured during marathon races in more mild environmental temperatures (11 to 23°C) are up to 1.2 liters per hour in the fastest runners (Wyndham and Strydom 1969; Pugh et al. 1967; Maughan 1985; Noakes, Adams, et al. 1988). However, once the environmental temperature and humidity rise to uncomfortable levels, sweat rates are much higher and can reach 1.8 liters per hour (Millard-Stafford et al. 1992; 1997).

I believe that the amount of heat lost by convection and the extent to which convective heat loss is influenced by the environmental conditions are factors that have been seriously underestimated in our predictions of sweat rates in runners. For example, it has been shown that the sweat rates of cyclists riding outdoors are much lower than those measured in the laboratory (S.L. Brown and Banister 1985). This results from the higher facing wind speeds generated by cycling outdoors, when the cyclist moves forward through the air. When cycling in the laboratory, the cyclist does not move forward, so that convective heat losses become negligible.

Another study of cyclists performed in an environmental chamber (W.C. Adams et al. 1992) found that increasing the wind speed flowing past the cyclists from 0.7 to 11 km per hour dropped the sweat rate by about 200 ml per hour. This is a large effect despite a small change in wind speed; competitive cyclists seldom travel slower than 40 km per hour and elite runners seldom slower than 18 to 22 km per hour.

I suspect that the same may apply to runners. Most of the data predicting sweat rates in runners were collected in the laboratory, where the capacity to lose heat by convection is minimized because there is no wind movement—the runners do not move forward but remain in the same place on the treadmill. In contrast, when running outdoors, runners are exposed to the wind speed generated by their own pace, as well as by any prevailing headwinds. As all runners soon learn, the wind always comes from the front. Furthermore, the higher the wind velocity, the greater the heat loss by convection and consequently the lower the sweat rate.

Differences in the capacity to lose heat by convection may be another, perhaps less important, reason why heavier people have more difficulty maintaining body temperature during exercise in the heat (S. Robinson 1942). This is because the surface area available for convection in heavy people is smaller relative to their body weight. Thus, heavier people have a reduced capacity for losing heat by convection, yet they produce large amounts of heat even when running quite slowly. In contrast, when exposed to cold, heavier people are better able to maintain body temperature as they lose less heat by convection.

In summary, it would seem that running speed and body weight are the most important determinants of sweat rates when running in the relatively moderate environmental conditions enjoyed by many runners throughout the world. Maximum sweat rates are seldom greater than 1.2 liters per hour and may be considerably lower, especially in slower runners or when heat loss by convection is increased, as occurs when running into a strong headwind. Furthermore, it is important to remember that all the weight lost during exercise does not need to be replaced to prevent dehydration.

Rate of Fluid Ingestion and Absorption

A frequently made assumption is that any amount of fluid taken by mouth will be absorbed rapidly from the intestine into the bloodstream. But this assumption has never been tested during exercise, and the current evidence suggests that there may be a limit to the rate at which both fluid and carbohydrate are absorbed from the intestine during exercise and that absorption may occur at lower than expected rates (Noakes 1993). In addition, there may be a wide range of individual variability in this capacity.

The most obvious basis for this conclusion is the finding that during running, athletes have great difficulty ingesting more than about 700 ml per hour with the increasing probability that they will feel bloated should they try to ingest more. This bloating must indicate the presence of a volume of unabsorbed fluid in the intestine. Vomiting during or after exercise is another indication that there is a large volume of unabsorbed fluid present in the intestine, not just in the stomach as is usually concluded.

Serious dehydration will occur if rates of fluid ingestion by runners during exercise are far lower than their sweat rates. It is usually believed that severe dehydration is an inevitable consequence of racing in marathons or longer-distance races, yet this is not supported by published evidence; levels of dehydration are modest in the majority of marathon runners (Noakes, Adams, et al. 1988; Noakes 1993; 1995) and may become even lower in competitors in ultramarathons and ultratriathlons, some of whom actually gain weight during these races (Salvato et al. 1990; Speedy et al. 1997; 1998; Speedy, Rodgers, et al. 2000a; 2000b; 2000c; Speedy, Noakes et al. 2000 2001a; 2001b; Noakes, Myburgh, et al 1990b). Thus, rates of fluid ingestion of about 500 ml per hour (Noakes, Adams, et al. 1988; Noakes 1993) are probably acceptable in most runners, with the increasing probability that the fluid intakes of runners competing in very long races will be greater than required.

It would seem that the only runners whose fluid intakes may be inadequate are those who run the fastest in races of between 10 and 42 km. These runners compete at 85% or more of $\dot{V}O_2$max. At these high-exercise intensities, rates of gastric emptying (table 4.1) and possibly intestinal absorption are likely to be impaired. In addition, their high rates of ventilation make the actual process of drinking both difficult and uncomfortable. High pressures inside the abdomen induced by running faster compound this discomfort. Of course, the fast running speeds of these elite athletes ensure high metabolic rates and therefore also rapid sweat rates. Thus, it is precisely these runners, who require the highest rates of fluid intake during exercise, who also have the greatest difficulty replacing their fluid losses during exercise. For reasons that are not yet established, cyclists do not experience the same difficulties and can ingest much larger volumes of fluid (possibly up to 2 liters per hour) even during intense competition, such as in the Tour de France or the cycling leg of the Ironman Triathlon. Possible contributing factors include the relatively lower exercise intensity (approximately 65% in the Ironman Triathlon and somewhat lower during the longer stages of the Tour de France); the lower intra-abdominal pressures in cycling than in running; the freer access to fluid provided by seconding crews in those events; and, most probable, frequent exposure to high drinking rates producing a training effect that increases the rate at which fluid empties from the stomach and is absorbed by the intestine.

Slower runners, especially during ultramarathon races, have less difficulty in drinking adequately since they travel slowly and walk frequently, and some may even have too much of a good thing. For example, by drinking 1000 ml instead of

Table 4.1 Factors determining the gastric emptying rate		
Accelerating factors	**Decelerating factors**	**Factors that have no effect**
Large ingested volume	Small ingested volume	Training
Isotonic solutions	Hypertonic solutions	Rest
Fluids	Solids	Water and hypotonic solutions
Cold foods and beverages	Hot foods and beverages	
Low fat/protein content	High fat/protein content	
Carbohydrate content <0.30 kcal·ml^{-1}	Carbohydrate content <0.30 kcal·ml^{-1}	
Running at <75% $\dot{V}O_2$max	Any exercise at >75% $\dot{V}O_2$max	
Calm mental attitude	Anxiety	
	Dehydration	
	Severe environmental conditions	

500 ml each hour during an ultramarathon, some ultradistance runners and triathletes develop the potentially fatal condition known as overhydration, water intoxication, or hyponatremia (low blood sodium concentration). We (Noakes, Goodwin, et al. 1985) first reported this condition in four athletes competing in ultramarathons or ultratriathlons. Of 17 runners who were hospitalized after the 1985 Comrades Marathon, 9 had hyponatremia; after the 1987 race, 24 similar cases were reported (Noakes, Norman, et al. 1990). Among these were runners who were critically ill: three of them nearly died. At least two marathon runners in the United States have died from this avoidable condition (Manier and Deardorff 1998; Ayus et al. 2000), as have military personnel (Montain et al. 1999; Garigan and Ristedt 1999). Similar cases have also been described in American ultramarathons (Frizzell et al. 1986; J.M. Clark and Gennari 1993; Surgenor and Uphold 1994) and marathons (M.Young et al. 1987; D. Davis et al. 1999; 2001); in the Hawaiian (Hiller et al. 1985; Hiller 1989; O'Toole et al. 1995) and New Zealand Ironman Triathlons (Speedy et al. 1997; 1999; Speedy, Rogers, et al. 2000a; 2000b; 2000c; Speedy, Noakes, 2000; 2001a; 2001b); in recreational hikers, especially in the Grand Canyon National Park (Backer et al. 1993); and in military personnel (Galun et al. 1991; Montain et al. 1999; Garigan and Ristedt 1999; Flinn and Sherer 2000). The incidence in United States Army personnel increased substantially after the introduction of new drinking regulations that "emphasized the importance of adequate hydration and prevention of dehydration" (Montain et al. 1999) but failed to warn of the dangers of overhydration. As Garigan and Ristedt (1999) concluded,

> The occurrence of excessive fluid intake in soldiers, athletes, and hikers can be attributed to heightened emphasis on water for the prevention of heat injury and the widespread ignorance of the condition of water intoxication. The presence of a strict authority that emphasizes forced hydration, such as the chain of command for military trainees, may result in people drinking more than they should.

The condition has also been reported in a laboratory experiment of exercise in the heat (Armstrong et al. 1993) and in a football player who received a large volume of fluid intravenously as treatment for muscle cramps (Herfel et al. 1998). In excess of 70 case reports of this condition have been published in the medical literature in the last 15 years (Speedy, Rodgers, et al. 2001c), and most of these patients have been extremely ill. In contrast, I am unaware of a single case report in the medical literature that clearly establishes that an athlete became critically ill during exercise as a result of dehydration only (Noakes 1995; 2001a).

Initially, there were two conflicting theories on how this condition was caused. Researchers working at the Hawaiian Ironman Triathlon concluded that it resulted from the large water and sodium losses incurred during the race, which is held under extreme environmental conditions of high temperatures and humidity. When the sodium losses were not replaced and only water was drunk, hyponatremia resulted. They argued that hyponatremia was caused by large sodium losses during very prolonged exercise and was compounded by dehydration and the ingestion of sodium-free drinks during exercise (Hiller et al. 1985; Hiller 1989; O'Toole et al. 1995). However, there is no scientific evidence to support this theory. In particular, levels of dehydration were never measured in triathletes diagnosed with hyponatremia.

In contrast, in the first series we reported (Noakes, Goodwin, et al. 1985), we were concerned by the high rates of fluid intake reported by those who developed the condition. We suggested that athletes should be wary of overdrinking during prolonged exercise (Noakes, Goodwin, et al. 1985) and should perhaps restrict themselves to an intake of about 500 ml per hour during exercise (Noakes, Adams, et al. 1988), which now appears to be the ad libitum intake of most runners during competition.

But as this conflicted with the popular dogma of the day, which held that "you cannot drink enough during exercise" and that athletes who drank anything less than 1 to 2 liters per hour during exercise risked their lives, the idea was greeted with much derision and hostility.

To resolve this dispute, my doctoral student, Tony Irving, hospitalized eight ultramarathon runners who developed severe, symptomatic hyponatremia during the 1988 Comrades Marathon. Overnight, as they recovered, he collected all urine that they passed and monitored any fluid or salt that they ingested. By the time all had recovered, the answer was clear. All had been in positive fluid balance (overhydrated), as they lost between 2 and 6 liters of fluid during recovery. In addition, none seemed to be in serious sodium deficit, which implies that none of them could have lost excessively large amounts of sodium during the race. We concluded that excessive fluid retention, the opposite of dehydration, causes this condition and that sodium losses play, at best, an accessory role (Irving et al. 1991; Noakes 1992a; 1992b). This conclusion has since been confirmed by a growing number of studies (Armstrong et al. 1993; Speedy et al. 1997; Speedy, Noakes, et al. 1999; 2000; Speedy, Rodgers, et al. 2001a; 2001b).

If this condition is caused by excessive fluid retention, then it is easier to understand why the typical runners or triathletes who develop hyponatremia are not the elite, most competitive athletes but those who are completing these ultradistance events in between 9 and 13 hours (Noakes 1992b; Speedy et al. 1997; Speedy, Noakes, et al. 1999; 2000; 2001c; Speedy, Rodgers et al. 2000a; 2000c). Female athletes are at much greater risk than males (Speedy, Noakes, et al. 2001c)—perhaps because their smaller size increases the ease with which they become overhydrated, particularly if they drink fluid at rates more appropriate for heavier males, who run faster and thus sweat more. The slow running speeds of these athletes allow them ample time to drink fluid from the vast number of feeding stations available during these races; a significant change from the absolute lack of fluid refreshment stations in the races held before 1980s. In addition, these runners were encouraged to "drink as much as possible" to prevent the supposedly lethal effects of dehydration.

Equally important, because of their slow running speeds and resultant low metabolic rates, nonelite runners sweat at much slower rates than those calculated by previous workers, who studied only elite marathoners (Pugh et al. 1967; Wyndham and Strydom 1969). It is clear that sweat rate calculations based on elite runners are erroneous if applied to the average runner of the same body mass, who runs much more slowly, and especially if applied to smaller women.

For example, researchers originally believed that if a 50-kg runner loses 5.5 liters of sweat during a 5:30:00 ultramarathon, then that runner should obviously drink a liter of fluid every hour to maintain a water balance. This calculation ignores the weight of fat and carbohydrate that is burned irreversibly during exercise and that may amount to 800 g of carbohydrate and 200 g of fat in an Ironman Triathlon. The water lost from glycogen may constitute up to 2 kg. None of these weight losses contributes to dehydration. Thus, the ACSM devised the general (but incorrect) rule (ACSM 1996a; 1996b) that a 50-kg person should drink a liter of fluid for every hour of running and that those who are heavier should drink a little more.

We now know that this advice is only appropriate if the runner is able to finish the race in 5:30:00. A less competitive 50-kg runner who religiously followed that advice but took 10:00:00 to complete the race would finish the race with a fluid credit of 4 liters, enough to cause severe symptomatic hyponatremia if the runner were unable to excrete the excess fluid (Noakes 1992b). The finding that the incidence of hyponatremia is on the increase among slower ultramarathoners (Noakes, Norman, et al. 1990; Noakes, Berlinski, et al. 1991) in the Hawaiian Ironman Triathlon and in military personnel (Montain et al. 1999) suggests that this is happening more frequently.

Why should this extra fluid cause the runner to develop hypontremia? Originally, it was believed that it is not so much the absorbed fluid that is the problem, but rather the large volume of unabsorbed fluid in the intestine. This theory postulated that humans may have a limited capacity to absorb water from the small bowel during exercise. If this maximum capacity is only 500 ml per hour, then an athlete who ingested 1000 ml per hour would accumulate fluid in the small bowel at a rate of 500 ml per hour. Within a few hours, this unabsorbed fluid would be sufficient to cause hyponatremia (Noakes 1992b), as sodium moves from the cells lining the gut into the undigested fluid to equalize the sodium content in the two body compartments. (Whenever a fluid that does not contain sodium is ingested, sodium moves into the fluid before it is absorbed. In other words, sodium is needed for water to be absorbed into the intestine. Sodium moves out of the cells lining the gut into the ingested water.) The loss of this sodium then causes the osmotic pressure in the bloodstream to fall. As a result, water moves from the bloodstream into all the cells of the body, causing them to become soggy. This sogginess causes the brain to swell. But as the brain is contained in a rigid skull, any swelling of the brain will cause an increase in the pressure inside the skull. Death results as the rising pressure causes the brain centers controlling breathing to stop functioning.

In fact, it now seems more likely that the excessive fluid retention in this condition is not caused by a failure of fluid absorption by the intestine, causing the relocation of sodium into the unabsorbed fluid in the intestine, but by the fact that the fluid accumulates in the blood, in the (interstitial) fluid surrounding the cells, and inside the cells, diluting the sodium content (Speedy, Rodgers, et al. 2000a). Therefore, the abnormality in this condition must be principally a failure of the kidney to excrete all the ingested fluid.

The reason why athletes drink too much is almost certainly due to hysteria attached to the supposed dangers that dehydration poses to athletes and to the belief that fatigue is caused by dehydration so that replacing more fluid than is lost during exercise will ensure optimum performance. I find no scientific support for either belief (Noakes 2000a; 2001).

In the following section, I highlight the importance of replacing fluid during exercise, outlining in particular current thinking on the appropriate content of ingested fluid.

Electrolyte Content of Fluid

It is essential that the fluid consumed contain substances needed to restore the body's supplies. Obviously, one possible aim of fluid ingestion during exercise might be to match the electrolyte losses in sweat. Electrolytes are chemical substances that, when dissolved or melted, dissociate into electrically charged particles (or ions such as sodium and potassium). Electrolytes are vital for the normal functioning

Table 4.2   Electrolyte contents of sweat and blood and the effects of fitness and heat acclimatization

Electrolyte	Blood	Sweat of unacclimatized, unfit subject	Sweat of fit but unacclimatized subject	Sweat of fit, acclimatized subject
Sodium (Na$^+$)	140.0 (6.1)	80.0 (3.5)	60.0 (2.6)	40.0 (1.8)
Potassium (K$^+$)	4.0 (0.1)	8.0 (0.2)	6.0 (0.15)	4.0 (0.1)
Magnesium (Mg$^+$)	1.5 (0.1)	1.5 (0.1)	1.5 (0.1)	1.5 (0.1)
Chloride (Cl$^-$)	101.0 (2.9)	50.0 (1.4)	40.0 (1.1)	30.0 (0.9)

All values in mmol·L^{-1} (g·L^{-1}). Based on data from Verde, et al. (1982, pp. 1541, 1543) and Costill (1977, p. 162). ©1982 and 1977 by the American Physiological Society and the New York Academy of Sciences, respectively. Adapted by permission.

of all cells. Some electrolytes, such as magnesium, are necessary for the activities of certain enzymes, particularly myosin ATPase. Sodium and potassium are the crucial determinants of the water contents of the extracellular and intracellular fluid volumes. Thus, the amount of sodium in the body determines the extracellular fluid volume, whereas its potassium content determines the volume of the intracellular space. Table 4.2 compares the electrolyte content of sweat (Costill 1977; Verde et al. 1982) with that of blood.

It is clear from table 4.2 that both fitness and heat acclimatization reduce the sodium content of sweat in particular. The amount of sodium lost in the sweat of the heat-acclimatized, fit athlete is not very large, amounting to little more than 2 g per hour of running (assuming a sweat rate of about 1 liter per hour), or about 6 to 8 g in a 42-km marathon and 10 to 16 g in an ultramarathon.

The average daily salt intake of the average runner exceeds normal requirements by about 8 g and is therefore more than enough to cover the salt requirements of running even a marathon a day. Even after an ultramarathon, the normal daily salt intake would replace sodium losses within 24 hours. For this reason, we might argue that extra salt is not required when exercising. However, we now know that the issue is somewhat more complex.

Our calculations (Noakes, Norman, et al. 1990) suggest that during prolonged exercise, even in those who replace all the fluid lost in sweat, the body is forced to deplete its fluid stores as a consequence of the sodium chloride losses in sweat. (This is because the amount of sodium and potassium in the body determines the amount of water: the balance of these electrolytes determines the water balance, not the other way around.) If this did not occur and if the body fluid stores were allowed to remain normal in response to drinking during exercise, a dilutional hyponatremia with potentially catastrophic effects would develop in all runners competing in races lasting more than 4 hours. The term dilutional is used because if more water than sodium were retained by the body, the remaining sodium would be diluted.

It follows that the only way to prevent dehydration during exercise is to replace both the sodium and the water losses in sweat, as these losses develop (Carter and Gisolfi 1989; Ryan et al. 1989; Sanders et al. 1999; 2001), by drinking an appropriate fluid that contains the optimum amount of sodium. At present, most athletic drinks contain about 20 mmol per liter of sodium. There are historical reasons for this, and these tend to perpetuate this formulation.

1. Original sports drinks such as Gatorade contain this concentration of sodium. As other sports drinks have developed in different parts of the world, they have tended to copy the successful Gatorade formulation.

2. Much of the relevant research has evaluated sports drinks containing this amount of sodium, in part, because this research is frequently funded by the manufacturers of the most successful sports drinks. Hence, there has been little financial incentive to study sports drinks with different sodium concentrations.

3. Most of the experts in the field believe that there is no benefit in ingesting more concentrated sodium drinks during exercise (ACSM 1996a). As a result, it is unlikely that this state of affairs will change in the immediate future.

One of the important physiological problems is that an optimum fluid balance requires that all the water and sodium lost during exercise be replaced as the losses develop. Yet, we have already shown that, if the sweat rate exceeds about 750 ml per hour, it is impossible to replace all that fluid, probably because the fluid cannot be ingested and absorbed by the intestine at such high rates, at least during exercise. It is also not yet known if all of that fluid needs to be replaced since some of the weight lost during exercise does not contribute to dehydration, as already discussed.

However, if that rate of fluid replacement were possible, it would itself be excessive unless the sodium chloride losses were corrected at the same time. If not, the body would have to excrete the appropriate volume of fluid (in a ratio of 1 liter of fluid for every 140 mmol of sodium that had been lost) to ensure that the osmotic concentration of the body remained constant and that the blood sodium concentration did not decrease as a result of dilution. Thus, even if fluid is ingested at sufficiently high rates to replace all the water lost, that fluid must also contain sodium in the same concentrations found in sweat, which is between 40 and 80 mmol per liter (table 4.2), or from two to four times higher than the sodium concentrations currently found in athletic drinks. Why, then, are the exercise scientists so adamant that the ingested solution contain only 20 mmol per liter?

The original argument was that athletes must decide whether they wish to optimize carbohydrate or sodium replacement during exercise; they cannot do both. The rate at which carbohydrate and water are absorbed in the intestine is largely determined by the osmolality of the ingested solution, and the optimum osmolality for fluid absorption is reportedly about 270 mmol per liter (Rolston et al. 1990; Shi and Gisolfi 1998; Shi, Summers, et al. 1995). Table 4.3 shows how a solution with that osmolality could be constituted. It shows that the only solution that contains an adequate sodium chloride content would have a low carbohydrate content, which would be undesirable given that carbohydrate ingestion enhances performance by preventing hypoglycemia. More than one carbohydrate type should also be present, either a glucose/sucrose/fructose/glucose polymer or a soluble starch.

However, when a solution containing both a high carbohydrate (6-8%) and a high sodium (50 mmol per liter) content was evaluated so that the osmolality was also high (330 mosmol per liter), the rates of water and carbohydrate absorption were not lower. In addition, sodium absorption was slightly faster than from the solutions containing 25 mmol or less of sodium (Gisolfi, Summers, et al. 1995). Other studies confirm that the addition of sodium at concentrations of up to 50 mmol per liter neither increases nor retards the rate of carbohydrate absorption by the intestine (Hargreaves et al. 1994; Massicotte et al. 1996).

The most likely explanation for this surprising finding is that the composition of any fluid is rapidly altered in its passage through the upper reaches of the small intestine. Thus, glucose is absorbed, and sodium and potassium are added (Gisolfi et al. 1995; Shi et al. 1995; Duchman et al. 1997). The greatest effects are on sodium absorption and the rapid removal of carbohydrate. Consequently, within about 50 cm of entering the small bowel, the carbohydrate content of the solution drops between 50% and 66% (Shi, Summers, et al. 1995), and the sodium content increases to at least 80 mmol per liter (Gisolfi, Summers, et al. 1995). As a result, the osmolality of all solutions, regardless of their initial osmolality when constituted outside the body, converges to a value of between 270 and 300 mosmol (Shi, Summers, et al. 1995; Gisolfi, Summers, et al. 1995; 1998; Lambert et al. 1996; Duchman et al. 1997) within the first 50 cm of entering the small bowel. Only ingested water maintains its lower osmolality (Gisolfi, Summers, et al. 1998). Hence, changes in the osmolality of the ingested solution are brought about rapidly in the small bowel by glucose and water absorption from, and sodium secretion into, the intestinal contents.

As a result, the most recent study has shown that water, sodium, and carbohydrate fluxes are not different from solutions that differ in their original osmolality from 200 to 412 mosmol because of differences in carbohydrate content (Gisolfi et al. 1998). These studies show that increasing the sodium content of drinks is logical if the sodium and water balance is to be optimized during prolonged exercise. Whether this seemingly obvious conclusion will lead to changes in the composition of sports drinks seems unlikely at present because of concerns that a high sodium intake is unhealthy and may predispose to the development of hypertension (Greenland 2001) and because drinks with high sodium contents are unpalatable, certainly when ingested at rest. Hence, drinks with higher sodium contents would be appropriate only for those involved in more vigorous exercise.

Anticipating that drinks with an increased sodium content might be beneficial, we have evaluated the effects on fluid balance, but not on performance, of ingesting solutions containing either 50 or 100 mmol per liter of sodium (Sanders et al. 1999; 2001). An important effect of drinks with high sodium concentrations is to reduce urinary losses and to increase the blood volume. Overall fluid balance is enhanced by ingesting the high sodium drinks when fluid intake matches the sweat rate of about 900 ml per hour.

Indeed, the ingestion of current sports drinks with even quite low sodium concentrations is beneficial when the rates of ingestion are high, matching sweat rates.

Table 4.3 Equivalent drinks that would optimize absorption of carbohydrate and water in the intestine

	High energy drink to replace carbohydrate	Low energy drink to replace fluid
Na+ (mmol·L^{-1})	20	60
Cl– (mmol·L^{-1})	20	60
Carbohydrate (mmol·L^{-1})	230 (10% maltodextrin glucose polymer or solution)	120 (6% maltodextrin solution); 167 (3% sucrose)
Osmolality (mosmol·L^{-1})	270	240 (6% maltodextrin solution) or 287 (3% sucrose solution)

Thus, Vrijens and Rehrer (1999) showed that drinking water at high rates during exercise produces a progressive fall in serum sodium concentrations, which is reduced by ingesting a popular sports drink with a sodium concentration of only 18 mmol per liter. But drinks with a higher sodium concentration may have been even more beneficial. However, the important lesson from the study of Vrijens and Rehrer (1999), not reflected in the title of their paper, is that it is the ability to maintain urine production, thereby preventing fluid retention, rather than the small extra amount of sodium ingested, that reduces the fall in blood sodium concentrations in all athletes, regardless of how much sodium they ingest. As already argued, it is the ability to maintain urine production that prevents the development of hyponatremia in those who ingest fluid at excessive rates.

Thus, on the basis of these studies, I see no reason why the sodium content of drinks should not be increased to higher values of about 60 mmol per liter, provided they continue to be palatable. As runners are not at risk of developing deficiencies of either magnesium or potassium during exercise, neither needs to be replaced until after exercise.

Ann Trason's Salt Ingestion During Ultramarathons

Often when there is doubt, it helps to ask the experts. Here is the opinion of Ann Trason (1998), one of the greatest ultramarathon racers of all time.

Electrolyte replacement, in my opinion, becomes critical when running hundred milers. I have noticed that ultrarunners in the US are much more concerned about consuming enough sodium and potassium during the long races than are runners in South Africa. Replacement drinks, such as Cytomax, just do not contain enough electrolytes for ultras. Most ultrarunners (including myself) take some sort of electrolyte pill or consume table salt or sea salt. Many of my friends, from the US, that have run the Comrades Marathon were surprised that there was no salt or salty food on the racecourse, for example. I take electrolytes for two reasons. First, it seems to help combat problems I have with nausea. Second, it helps with cramping.

There are two types of electrolyte pills I like. One is Therma Tabs. Each pill contains 450 mg sodium chloride and 30 mg potassium chloride. The other pill that is popular in the US these days is Succeed buffer/electrolyte caps. They have 350 mg sodium and 21 mg potassium per capsule. Succeed electrolyte caps are made and distributed by Karl King, Professor of Biochemistry at the University of Wisconsin, who is also the race director for one of our larger 50-miler trail races (Ice Age 50). He is also an avid ultrarunner. I will take either pill (they seem to work equally well for me) every 2 to 4 hours, depending on the conditions. The hotter the ambient temperatures, the more salt I take. Many ultra-runners in this country get their salt by consuming pretzels, or potatoes that have been dipped in salt, or by drinking soup.

This information is interesting because it shows that runners develop a salt craving during longer distance races. Interestingly, the amounts ingested by Trason are quite small, about 200 mg per hour as against a predicted loss of sodium chloride in sweat and urine of 1 to 3 g per hour. Perhaps an intake of two tablets per hour (approximately 900 mg per hour) would be more appropriate.

Carbohydrate and Fat Content of Fluid

One consensus of all this research might be that the more important factor determining performance during exercise is the carbohydrate content of the ingested solution. Chapter 3 outlined the argument that carbohydrate must be ingested during prolonged exercise that is undertaken at up to 75% $\dot{V}O_2$max and lasts more than 4 hours. Carbohydrate ingestion prevents hypoglycemia, which profoundly affects performance. To choose the most appropriate type of carbohydrate, we need to look at factors that determine the rate at which fluid leaves the stomach (gastric emptying), as well as the rate at which it can be absorbed into blood from the intestine (gastrointestinal absorption).

Table 4.1 listed some factors that influence the rate of gastric emptying, particularly under resting conditions. These factors were first studied in detail by Costill and Saltin (1974). The results of their experiments are detailed in figure 4.11.

Costill and Saltin found that up to an exercise intensity of 60% $\dot{V}O_2$max (figure 4.11A), the rate of gastric emptying is about 750 ml per hour with a 2.5% glucose solution, but thereafter the rate falls steeply and is only about 320 ml per hour at an exercise intensity of 90% $\dot{V}O_2$max.

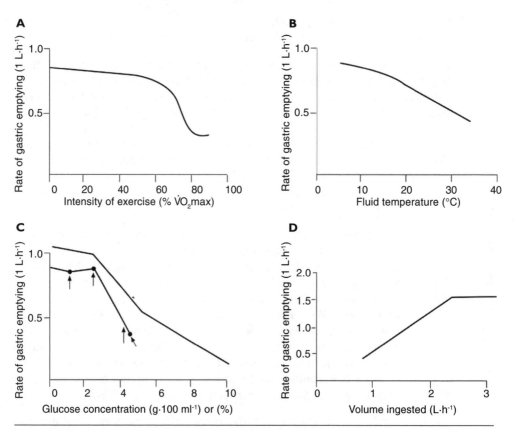

Figure 4.11   The effects of exercise intensity (A), fluid temperature (B), glucose concentration (C), and ingested volume (D) on the rate of gastric emptying. Also included are the data for four commercial drinks from the study of Coyle, Costill, et al. 1978.

From Costill and Saltin (1974, p. 681). © by the American Physiological Society. Adapted by permission.

The stomach empties more slowly as the temperature of the ingested fluid rises (figure 4.11*B)* and is only 350 ml per hour at a temperature of 40°C, whereas it is almost 900 ml per hour at 5°C. More recent studies dispute this finding and show that the temperature of the ingested solution has little effect on the rate at which it leaves the stomach (K.E. McArthur and Feldman 1989). Cold fluids are still preferable because they are more palatable and encourage fluid ingestion during exercise.

The rate of gastric emptying falls steeply as the glucose content of the ingested fluid increases (figure 4.11*C)* and is about 100 ml per hour at a glucose concentration of 10 g per 100 ml (10%). This graph also shows the gastric emptying rates of three American drinks, Brake Time, Body Punch, and Gatorade, which were studied by Coyle et al. (1978). The amount of liquid emptied by the stomach increases as the volume ingested increases (figure 4.11*D),* and the rate is highest at an ingestion rate of 2.4 liters per hour. This critical finding, which has been completely overlooked by exercise physiologists and athletes, is discussed in more detail below.

Costill and Saltin (1974) did not study the effects of increasing the osmolality of the ingested solution by adding electrolytes. (Osmolality is determined by the concentration of all the particles—electrolytes, proteins, etc.—dissolved in the solution. Osmolality is therefore proportional to the total number of all the molecules dissolved in the solution.) However, the addition of any electrolytes that would increase the osmolality of the solution might be expected to delay gastric emptying (table 4.1).

Drinking Patterns and Rates of Carbohydrate and Fluid Delivery

Adolph's desert studies (1947) showed that subjects almost always drink less than they sweat during exercise and hence develop voluntary dehydration, which is only corrected when they next ingest food, usually at night. This suggests that drinking patterns may be influenced by other physiological clues. Only recently has it been appreciated that factors in the drink itself may influence drinking behavior.

A series of studies have established that, at least in exercising boys, voluntary dehydration can be prevented if the boys are offered a grape-flavored drink that has a carbohydrate content of 6% and a sodium concentration of 18 mmol per liter (Wilk and Bar-Orr 1996; Wilk et al. 1998; Rivera-Brown et al. 1999). Excluding any of these constituents reduced voluntary fluid intake. One recent study in adults found that subjects drank more of a carbohydrate than a water solution during recovery but not during a 90-minute run at 60% of $\dot{V}O_2$max, during which they drank about 1 liter of fluid (Wilmore, Morton, et al. 1998). Another study (Lambert et al. 1993) showed that athletes drank more if the solutions were not carbonated and if they contained 6% compared with 10% carbohydrate. One study found that if subjects started the exercise bout dehydrated by walking in the heat, their fluid intake increased five-fold (Armstrong et al. 1997). This is the greatest effect on the rate of fluid intake during exercise yet measured. We must ask whether the same mechanism might not also exist during exercise and whether this increased drive to drink as dehydration develops may be inhibited only when running at moderately-high exercise intensities (greater than 65% of $\dot{V}O_2$max). The probable conclusion is that fluid ingestion during exercise is increased when carbohydrates, electrolytes, and flavorings are present (Passe 2001), as they are in modern sports drinks.

Figure 4.11C indicates that increasing the carbohydrate content of the ingested solution beyond about 6% begins to have a rather marked effect on the rate of gastric emptying. It was this finding more than any other that suggested to these original workers that carbohydrates either should not be included in the solutions ingested during exercise or should be present only at concentrations less than 2.5% (Costill 1979, p. 68). This formed the basis of the original ACSM guideline that warned against the consumption of carbohydrate solutions in concentrations greater than 2.5% (ACSM 1975). Thus, in the revised edition of his book, David Costill (1986) wrote:

> *Since dehydration is the primary concern during hot weather running, water seems to be the preferred fluid. Under less stressful conditions where overheating and large sweat losses are not as threatening, runners might use liquid feedings to supplement their carbohydrate supplies. A number of sports drinks containing carbohydrates are currently on the market, grossing more than $100 million each year. Unfortunately, many of the claims used to sell these drinks are based on misinterpreted and often inaccurate information. (pages 75-76)*

It is this finding that drinks containing carbohydrate empty quite slowly from the stomach (figure 4.11C), at least under the constraints of this experimental model, which explains why water was promoted as the preferred drink during exercise. It also explains why the early, classic experiments of the 1920s and 1930s that established the value of carbohydrate ingestion during exercise were ignored by exercise physiologists until the first conclusive study of Coyle, Coggan, et al. (1986)(see chapter 3).

In retrospect, the methodological error in Costill and Saltin's (1974) studies was that they were performed in subjects who ingested the solutions only once, and the rate of gastric emptying was really the average over the entire period, rather than the fastest or slowest rates measured. (We now appreciate that gastric emptying is not constant, being fastest when the stomach is fullest and slowing thereafter. The average rate of emptying is therefore much slower than the fastest initial rates when the stomach is fuller.) However, more recent studies show that this single ingestion method is inaccurate in determining the rates of gastric emptying of fluids ingested repeatedly as it fails to produce repeated changes in gastric volume (Noakes, Reher, et al. 1991). This is important because during competition athletes ingest fluid repeatedly, and the effect of repeated bouts of fluid ingestion needs to be considered.

These more recent studies (Owen et al. 1986; J.M. Davis et al. 1987; J.B. Mitchell et al. 1988; 1989b; 1994; Ryan et al. 1989; Mitchell and Voss 1991; Lambert et al. 1996) have found that if the solutions are ingested repeatedly during exercise so that the stomach is kept in a more distended state during exercise, then higher rates of gastric emptying can be achieved, as predicted by Costill and Saltin (1974; figure 4.11D). Thus, differences in the rates of gastric emptying between water and solutions with quite high carbohydrate and electrolyte content can be minimized if the more concentrated solutions are ingested repeatedly during prolonged exercise so that the amount in the stomach at any time remains high.

For practical purposes, when ingested repeatedly, the rates of gastric emptying for water and for carbohydrate and electrolyte solutions at concentrations of less than 10% are essentially the same at rest and even during exercise at up to 70% $\dot{V}O_2max$ (Mitchell et al. 1989b; Rehrer, Beckers, et al. 1989; Sole and Noakes 1989). In contrast, when ingested as a single amount (bolus), solutions with glucose concentrations as low as 4% empty more slowly than water (Vist and Maughan 1994; 1995), confirming the original study of Costill and Saltin (1974). However, higher carbohydrate concentrations (greater than 15%) empty significantly more slowly than does water both at rest (Rehrer, Beckers. et al. 1989; Sole and Noakes 1989) and during exercise (Davidson et al. 1988; Moodley et al. 1992), even when ingested repeatedly. But the rate of carbohydrate delivery to the intestine from these more concentrated drinks increases as the carbohydrate content increases, even up to 18% carbohydrate solutions (Davidson et al. 1988; Rehrer, Beckers. et al. 1989; Sole and Noakes 1989; Mitchell et al. 1989b; Moodley et al. 1992; Vist and Maughan 1994; 1995). Higher concentrations have not been studied, but there is no reason to believe that the rate of carbohydrate delivery would not continue to rise with further increases in the carbohydrate concentration of the ingested solution.

The reason why frequent drinking affects the rate of gastric emptying can be inferred from the detailed studies of Rehrer, Beckers, et al. (1989). The critical finding in these studies was that the rate of gastric emptying for any solution is a logarithmic function of the amount of fluid present in the stomach at that time; in essence, this means that during any equivalent time period, a constant percentage of the drink that was present in the stomach at the start of that period would have been emptied. Rehrer et al. found that approximately 65% of a water solution (that is, plain water), 50% of an isotonic solution (having the same osmolality as blood), 7% of a carbohydrate solution, and 25% of a 15% glucose or 18% glucose polymer solution would be emptied during successive 10-minute time periods when exercising at approximately 70% $\dot{V}O_2$max. (In other words, for the concentrated glucose solution, 25% of the original volume present in the stomach at the start of the 10-minute sampling period would be emptied every 10 minutes, and so on.)

This information has been used to construct figure 4.12, which shows the volume of fluid remaining in the stomach at successive 10-minute intervals after the initial ingestion (at time 0) of 400 ml of plain water and a 7% or 18% glucose polymer solution. Figure 4.12 shows that the most important factor determining the rate of gastric emptying is the volume of the solution in the stomach, not its carbohydrate content.

The rate of gastric emptying of the 18% carbohydrate solution between 0 and 10 minutes is 100 ml every 10 minutes, which exceeds the rate of emptying of water at all times after 10 minutes (approximately 80 ml every 10 min) and of the 7% glucose polymer solution at all times after 20 minutes (approximately 50 ml every 10 min).

Figure 4.13 uses this information to show the hypothetical effects of two different drinking patterns on carbohydrate and water delivery during exercise. Figure 4.13A shows a practical drinking pattern for an athlete who is able to run with a stomach containing 400 ml of fluid; figure 4.13B depicts the drinking pattern of an athlete who can tolerate a stomach volume of 800 ml. These drinking patterns are not the optimum, but they can be applied practically, at least while running races. The optimum method, which could be used by cyclists and canoeists who carry their fluids with them, would be to drink fluid continually at a rate exactly equaling the rate of gastric emptying, thereby maintaining a constant gastric volume and maximizing the rate of gastric emptying.

Using the more practical approach of drinking at regular intervals, both runners fill their stomachs to capacity immediately before exercise. Every 10 minutes thereafter, each runner again drinks sufficiently to replace the volume of the solution that had emptied during that 10-minute period, thereby refilling the stomach to the

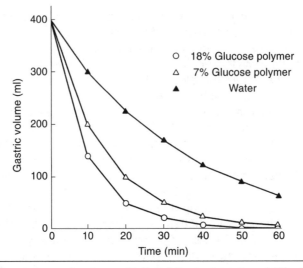

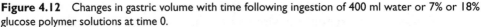

Figure 4.12   Changes in gastric volume with time following ingestion of 400 ml water or 7% or 18% glucose polymer solutions at time 0.

From Noakes, Rehrer, et al. (1991, p. 309). © 1991 by Lippincott, Williams, and Wilkins. Adapted by permission.

maximum volume each person can tolerate. The volumes of fluid that each can ingest every subsequent 10 minutes will depend on the carbohydrate content of the ingested solution and will be 65% of the initial volume of water ingested (520 or 260 ml); 50% of the 7% isotonic carbohydrate solution (400 or 200 ml); or 25% of the 18% glucose polymer solution (200 or 100 ml). On completion of exercise, total fluid delivery from the three solutions during 1 hour will be 3120, 2400, and 1200 ml respectively for the athlete able to maintain a gastric volume of 800 ml (figure 4.13*B)* and half that (1560, 1200, and 600 ml) for the athlete able to maintain a gastric volume of only 400 ml during exercise (figure 4.13*A).* The respective rates of carbohydrate delivery for these drinking patterns will be 168 and 216 g per hour (figure 4.13*B)* and 84 and 108 g per hour (figure 4.13*A).*

The accuracy of these predictions is confirmed by the results of some recent studies. Ryan et al. (1989) reported a rate of gastric emptying in excess of 1 liter per hour in subjects who drank 5% glucose, glucose polymer, or glucose polymer/fructose solutions at rates of 350 ml every 20 minutes, similar to the drinking pattern proposed in figure 4.13*B.* A gastric emptying rate of 1.2 liters per hour was measured by Lambert et al. (1996) in subjects who ingested 400 ml of a 6% carbohydrate solution with a sodium concentration of 16 mmol per liter at the start of exercise and 200 ml every 10 minutes thereafter. In contrast, a rate of gastric emptying of only 460 ml per hour for a similar (6%) carbohydrate solution was reported by Mitchell et al. (1989b) in subjects who only ingested 150 ml every 15 minutes.

These calculations demonstrate two very important points. First, that it is theoretically possible to ingest large volumes of fluid during exercise if you drink frequently and maintain a large gastric volume. This would explain why it is possible to develop water intoxication (hyponatremia) during exercise. Second, different drinking patterns can produce similar rates of carbohydrate delivery during exercise from solutions with different carbohydrate concentrations (compare in figures 4.13*A* and *B* the total carbohydrate delivery from the 18% carbohydrate solution when drunk at a rate of 600 ml per hour with the 7% carbohydrate solution when ingested at a rate of 2.5 liters per hour).

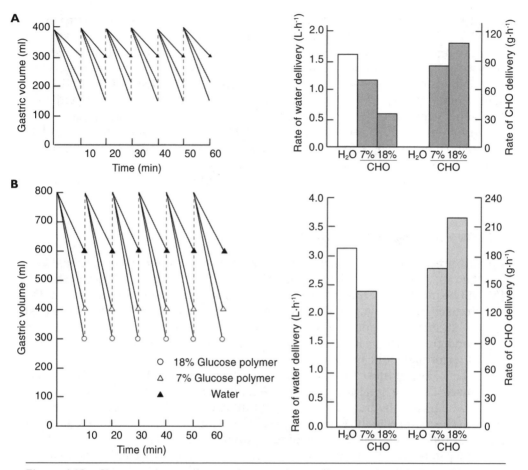

Figure 4.13   Changes in gastric volume with time and rates of water and carbohydrate delivery from two different drinking patterns for water and for 7% and 18% glucose polymer solutions. In the top graphs (A), the athlete maintains a gastric volume of 400 ml every 10 minutes; in the lower graphs (B), a volume of 800 ml every 10 minutes. The figure shows that it is possible to provide high rates of water and carbohydrate delivery even from solutions with high carbohydrate contents.

From Noakes, Rehrer, et al. (1991, p. 310). © 1991 by Lippincott, Williams, and Wilkins. Adapted by permission.

In summary, the practical relevance of this finding is that the maximum rate at which the carbohydrate and water content of an ingested solution can be delivered to the intestine is determined solely by the average volume of fluid athletes will allow in their stomachs during exercise. The greater the degree of gastric distension an athlete maintains during exercise, the more carbohydrate and water will be delivered to the intestine, irrespective of the carbohydrate content of the ingested solution (Noakes, Reher, et al. 1991). How, then, do you make sure that you aren't drinking too much? The answer is that vast majority of runners do not drink enough to match their sweat rates and hence are not at risk of developing hyponatremia. Only those drinking more than 1.0 to 1.5 liters per hour for many hours are ever likely to get into trouble—runners who drink less than this should be within safe limits, unless they are very light (less than 45 kg) and run very slowly.

There are other factors that influence the rate of gastric emptying of fluids. Dehydration (Neufer et al. 1989a; Rehrer, Beckers, et al. 1990) and severe environmental conditions (greater than 35°C dry bulb temperature; 20% relative humidity; Neufer et al. 1989a) impair gastric emptying. However, running at exercise intensities lower than 75% $\dot{V}O_2$max is associated with increased rates of gastric emptying as compared to rest (Neufer et al. 1986; 1989a). Training appears not to influence the rate of gastric emptying (Rehrer, Beckers, et al. 1989), which is the same during cycling and running at the same exercise intensities (Neufer et al. 1989b; Rehrer, Brouns, 1990; Houmard et al. 1991). The addition of sodium chloride to the ingested solution either accelerates (Hunt 1963) or has no effect on the rate of gastric emptying (Naveri et al. 1989; Rehrer, Brouns, et al. 1990). However, hypertonic electrolyte solutions (those having an osmolality greater than that of blood) empty more slowly than either isotonic solutions or water (Rehrer, Brouns, et al. 1990). The carbonation of an ingested solution (for example, Coca-Cola) also fails to influence its rate of gastric emptying (Ryan, Navarre, et al. 1991).

Muscle Uptake of Carbohydrate

The preceding discussion indicates that most researchers have assumed that the rate at which the energy in an ingested drink reaches the muscle where it will be used is determined by the rate at which the solution empties from the stomach. But this ignores the obvious anatomical consideration that, once past the stomach, the solution must still be absorbed from the intestine into the bloodstream, where its glucose content is taken up by the muscles and used as a fuel for metabolic oxidation.

Thus, any of these four processes—gastric emptying, intestinal absorption, muscle glucose uptake, or oxidation—could be the real factors limiting the rate at which carbohydrate provided by mouth can actually be used by the active muscles. Accordingly, solutions that empty rapidly from the stomach might not produce the highest rates of fuel provision to, and fuel utilization by, the active muscles if the factors controlling the rates of gastric emptying, intestinal absorption, muscle glucose uptake, and oxidation differ.

However, by comparing the maximum rates of glucose oxidation from carbohydrate ingested by mouth (Rehrer 1990; Hawley, Dennis, et al. 1992a; Moodley et al. 1992) to those achieved when the glucose is infused directly into the bloodstream, our research team (Hawley, Bosch, et al. 1994b) was able to show that the factor limiting the oxidation of ingested carbohydrate is the rate of glucose released by the liver. As this is set at about 1 g per minute, it follows that ingesting carbohydrate at rates much faster than 1 g per minute during exercise will not be beneficial, as the carbohydrate will be stored in the liver and not used during exercise.

The factors that influence the rate at which water, electrolytes, and energy fuels are absorbed in the intestine have been studied by intubating the small bowel and studying the absorption of carbohydrates, electrolytes, and water across that small segment of the bowel, usually 50 cm, that lies adjacent to the tube (Leiper and Maughan 1988; Gisolfi et al. 1990; 1991). These early studies showed that water absorption is fastest from an ingested solution that is hypotonic (Gisolfi et al. 1990), whereas electrolytes are absorbed most rapidly from ingested hypertonic solutions. Absorption is further enhanced if carbohydrate is included in the ingested solution at least at concentrations of up to 6% (Gisolfi et al. 1991). This led to the acceptance that the commercially available sports drinks, formulated even before this research had been completed, were optimum because they were hypotonic with glucose and sodium concentrations of 6% and 18 mmol per liter respectively.

In truth, however, it would be surprising if the original sports drinks, designed "to replace what is being lost in sweat" and formulated before we enjoyed this detailed knowledge of intestinal function, should serendipitously have arrived at this ideal solution. It is also unlikely that the intestine would be designed in such a way to ensure that only one specific solution is ideal for ingestion during exercise.

It is now apparent that intestinal design is too clever for this. By rapidly adding sodium and absorbing water and glucose, the intestine quickly prepares the ingested solution to one that is most rapidly absorbed in the main absorptive area in the small bowel. As a result, it appears that, within reason, absorption of water, electrolytes, and carbohydrates will be very similar to a range of different solutions that conform to the general characteristics of the popular sports drinks (Gisolfi et al. 1998). However, it is also clear that the range of different compositions of drinks that could be absorbed at equal rates in the intestine is much greater than is currently available commercially.

Many of these studies of fluid and carbohydrate absorption are now performed during exercise. Indeed, exercise itself may also influence the rate of intestinal absorption of carbohydrate. Three studies (J.H. Williams et al. 1976; Barclay and Turnberg 1988; Maughan et al. 1990) suggest that exercise impairs carbohydrate ingestion during exercise; another that exercise at 70% $\dot{V}O_2$max had no such effect (Gisolfi et al. 1991). However, the latter study did show that only 37% of a solution infused at a rate of 900 ml per hour was absorbed. This suggests that even if exercise does not alter rates of intestinal absorption of water, these rates are not as rapid as is usually assumed.

It is clearly important to know what the maximum rate of fluid absorption is and whether this is reduced during exercise. Various studies suggest that the maximum rate of fluid absorption by the intestine at rest may be as high as 1.3 liters per hour (Schedl et al. 1994). During exercise, maximum rates of fluid absorption measured in the first 50 cm of the small bowel have been as high as 20 ml per cm per hour (Lambert et al. 1996), suggesting a maximum rate of fluid absorption in excess of 1 liter per hour in the small bowel (assuming that the absorptive surface of the small bowel exceeds 50 cm).

But the conclusion is dependent on the assumption that the length of the small bowel involved in such rapid absorption exceeds 50 cm, that all sections of the small bowel have the same absorptive capacity, and, perhaps more critically, that intestinal absorptive capacity is identical in all humans. The latter certainly seems unlikely as the tolerance for high rates of fluid ingestion clearly differs from person to person, with some developing intestinal fullness, nausea, and vomiting when ingesting fluid at rates as low as 600 to 800 ml per hour for many hours of exercise. Clearly, there is a need for much more research of this topic. Indeed, it is now apparent that a specific water carrier exists in the body (the water-channel protein, aquaporin 1 [AQP1]; Marples 2000). Humans who lack AQP1 have been described and are apparently normal (Preston et al. 1994). But it is possible that people without AQP1 or with lesser amounts of AQP1 might have a reduced capacity to absorb fluid during exercise and might therefore be more likely to develop nausea when they ingest larger amounts of fluid.   *(continued)*

Finally, the influence of the type of carbohydrate and the timing of its absorption on the rate at which the active muscles take up and oxidize the ingested carbohydrate during exercise has only very recently been researched and defined. This is indeed one of the most intriguing paradoxes in the modern exercise sciences.

As discussed in chapter 3, from 1939 to 1986, exercise physiologists fastidiously ignored any potential role of carbohydrate ingestion during exercise. They disregarded the original data and were completely paralyzed by the fear that the addition of carbohydrate to the fluid ingested during exercise would promote the risk of heatstroke by delaying the rate of gastric emptying, as described earlier in this chapter.

In addition, an early study erroneously concluded that ingested carbohydrate was not used to any great extent during exercise (Van Handel et al. 1980). That study ignored the finding of another study, ironically from the laboratory of Wyndham (whose work had been so influential in shaping the dogma that only water should be ingested during exercise), which showed that ingested carbohydrate was rapidly oxidized by the active muscles during exercise (Benadé, Janson, et al 1973; Benadé, Wyndham, et al. 1973).

The result was that in the "state-of-the-art" proceedings of the 1976 New York Academy of Sciences Conference, "The Marathon: Physiological, Medical, Epidemiological, and Psychological Studies" (Milvy 1977), there was not a single reference to carbohydrate ingestion during exercise. Only when Coyle, Coggan, et al. (1986) finally established that carbohydrate ingestion during exercise prolonged the duration of exercise that could be sustained at a constant workload did this area of research become attractive and receive appropriate attention.

As a result of the research initiated by that classic study, we now know that the fate of the ingested carbohydrate is the same whether it is taken 3 hours before (Jandrain et al. 1984) or 15 or 120 minutes after the start of exercise (Krzentowski et al. 1984). The ingested carbohydrate is burned by the muscles in place of blood glucose derived from the liver (Bosch et al. 1994). The rate of combustion of the ingested carbohydrate increases with increasing exercise intensity (Pirnay et al. 1982) up to an exercise intensity of about 60% $\dot{V}O_2$max (Pirnay et al. 1995) and with the amount of carbohydrate ingested (Pallikarakis et al. 1986). Trained athletes may oxidize more of an ingested carbohydrate load than untrained subjects (Burelle et al. 1999), but there is uncertainty about whether a low-carbohydrate diet before exercise either increases (Péronnet et al. 1998) or reduces (Jeukendrup, Borghouts, et al. 1996) this rate of oxidation. When ingested as a 25% solution at a rate of 100 g per hour during 4.75 hours of exercise at 45% $\dot{V}O_2$max, ingested glucose was combusted at a rate of 70 g per hour, thereby providing between 85% and 90% of the total carbohydrate expenditure during the latter phase of exercise (Pallikarakis et al. 1986).

It is now believed that ingested carbohydrate is oxidized at a maximum rate of about 1 g per minute during exercise, provided the rate of ingestion is at least 70 to 100 g per hour (Hawley, Dennis, et al. 1992; Wagenmakers et al. 1993; Saris et al. 1993). The optimum fuels for ingestion are glucose, maltose (comprising two glucose molecules; Hawley and Burke 1998), and fructose polymers, or soluble, branched-chain starches with high glycemic indexes, as present in spaghetti, bread, and potatoes (Wagenmakers et al. 1993; Saris et al. 1993; Guezennec et al. 1993).

In contrast, fructose, the sugar present in fruits (Massicotte et al. 1986; 1989; Guezennec et al. 1989; Jandrain et al. 1993; Adopo et al. 1994; Burelle et al. 1997), galactose (Leijssen et al. 1995), lactate (Péronnet, et al. 1997) and alcohol (ethanol; Massicotte et al. 1993) are all oxidized to a lesser extent than is glucose ingested during exercise. Hence, glucose, glucose polymer, or branched-chain starches with high glycemic indexes are the preferred carbohydrate source for ingestion during exercise. The sole proviso is that the total oxidation from carbohydrate is increased when glucose and fructose are ingested in the same solution (Adopo et al. 1994). This is probably because fructose is absorbed across the intestinal wall by a carrier separate from that of glucose. Thus, at least in theory, fructose might be included with glucose, glucose polymer, or starch as a fuel for ingestion during exercise. In addition, fasting increases the rate of fructose oxidation during exercise (Massicotte et al. 1990).

However, the ingestion of even quite modest amounts (about 50 g) of fructose, like that of lactate (Peronnet et al. 1997), produces gastrointestinal discomfort (Murray, Paul, et al. 1989) because there is a limited capacity to absorb fructose from the intestine. Any unabsorbed fructose travels to the colon, where its metabolism by bacteria produces chemicals that induce colonic discomfort. Furthermore, the intestinal absorption of fructose is markedly reduced during exercise (Fujisawa et al. 1993). As a result, compared to glucose, too little fructose can ever be ingested during exercise to match the rates of oxidation achieved when glucose is ingested.

The effects on whole body metabolism are the same if the different carbohydrates are ingested as a solid or a liquid, or in combination (Mason et al. 1993; Lugo et al. 1993; Roberts et al. 1998).

In summary, there is a maximum rate at which carbohydrate ingested during exercise can be used by the muscles. The rate-limiting step appears to be the rate of release of glucose by the liver (Hawley, Bosch, et al. 1994). Only when a "second liver" is introduced—by infusing glucose directly into the bloodstream at much faster rates (up to 3 g per minute) than the normal liver chooses to release glucose (1 g per minute)—can muscle glucose oxidation rates be increased to what may be a maximal capacity of about 2.5 g per minute (Hawley, Bosch, et al. 1994b). However, this procedure produces very high blood glucose concentrations (approximately 10 mmol per liter), which are twice the normal values.

The conclusion must therefore be that the human was designed to maintain a blood glucose concentration of about 5 mmol per liter. This is achieved by a balance between the rate of glucose release by the liver and its use by the muscles. During prolonged exercise (longer than 90 minutes), this balance is reached at a rate of glucose release by the liver and its use by muscles, both equal to 1 g per minute. When carbohydrate is ingested at sufficiently rapid rates (approximately 80 g per hour), the ingested carbohydrate completely suppresses liver glucose production so that all the glucose oxidized by the muscles (1 g per minute) comes from the ingested carbohydrate.

One reason for the limiting rate of liver glucose release might be the relatively small amount of carbohydrate (approximately 120 g) stored in the liver. Were very high rates of glucose release possible, the liver's glycogen stores would be rapidly depleted, causing hypoglycemia, and exercise would be terminated.

(continued)

Perhaps this is another example of the Creator's wisdom and foresight in the design of the human physiology.

Inspired by the finding that there is a limited rate at which ingested carbohydrate can be oxidized during exercise, a number of researchers have attempted to find alternative, noncarbohydrate sources that might aid performance by substituting especially for the use of the limited muscle glycogen stores (according to the Energy Supply/Energy Depletion Model).

According to the original Glucose-Fatty Acid Cycle hypothesis, which holds that increasing the availability of fat (free fatty acids) in the bloodstream will slow muscle glycogen use, the focus has now shifted to finding ways in which the concentrations of free fatty acids in the blood might be increased, especially by fat ingestion during exercise.

Long chain length triglycerides (LCTs)—the predominant source of fat present in the diet—are digested in the intestine, and they travel by the lymphatic system to the liver, where they are bound with protein and transported in different fat/protein combinations as the main constituents of the blood cholesterols and triglycerides. As such, they have rather more to do with whole body metabolism and the risk of heart disease than with muscle energy metabolism. Hence, ingesting the usual triglyceride-rich (fatty) foods in the diet is not of great use for energy metabolism during exercise (Ivy et al. 1980). Glycerol ingestion is also not of any benefit (J.M. Miller et al. 1983; Gleeson et al. 1986; Murray et al. 1991).

In contrast, medium chain length triglycerides (MCTs) are semisynthetic oil products prepared from coconut oil. They are water-soluble and enter the bloodstream directly after ingestion. They then travel directly to muscle, where they enter the cells with relative ease and are available for oxidation. A number of studies have now evaluated the value of MCTs ingested during exercise.

Beckers et al. (1992) showed that replacing the carbohydrate in drinks ingested at rest with equicaloric amounts of MCT increased the rate of gastric emptying of the solution. Hence, MCT/carbohydrate solutions empty more rapidly from the stomach than do equicaloric carbohydrate solutions.

Other studies have shown that MCTs are readily oxidized during exercise (Satabin et al. 1987; Massicotte et al. 1992; Jeukendrup et al. 1995) and can reach rates of 0.15 g per minute after about 90 minutes of exercise. This rate appears to be limited by the quite small amounts of MCT (about 30 g) that can be safely ingested during exercise without the development of gastrointestinal symptoms. Although one study (Van Zyl et al. 1996) suggested that the ingestion of slightly larger amounts (about 50 g) of MCT might slow the rate of muscle glycogen use and enhance performance, subsequent studies have failed to prove that MCT ingestion affects either the rate of total carbohydrate or specifically muscle glycogen use (Massicotte et al. 1992; Jeukendrup, Saris, et al. 1996; Goedecke, Elmer-English, et al. 1999), even in subjects who start exercise in a carbohydrate-depleted state (Jeukendrup, Saris, et al. 1996b). These studies have also been unable to show that MCT ingestion enhances performance more than does carbohydrate ingestion alone (Jeukendrup, Saris, et al. 1998b; Goedecke, Elmer-English, et al. 1999). In fact, when ingested at high rates, MCT may produce such disabling gastrointestinal symptoms that exercise performance may be substantially impaired. Hence, a search that began with such promise (Van Zyl et al. 1996) has returned empty-handed. Perhaps the reason for this failure is simpler than we expected; we might have been looking for something that does not exist.

The logical basis for any theory that fat ingestion improves performance during exercise rests squarely on the veracity of the Glucose-Fatty Acid Cycle hypothesis. If that cycle does not exist, as now seems likely (see chapter 3), then there is no reason to believe that fat ingestion during exercise should have any special effect. Thus, it is perhaps not surprising that research has failed to show that the ingestion of fat-containing energy bars, including the "Access Fat Conversion Activity Bar" (Kolkhorst et al. 1998) and a bar containing high concentrations of fat and protein (Rauch et al. 1999), enhances performance during prolonged exercise.

Indeed, the study of Rauch et al. (1999) was particularly illuminating. It showed that, compared to the ingestion of carbohydrate, ingestion of the bar containing both fat and protein impaired exercise performance despite increased fat oxidation during exercise. Subjects who ingested high-fat/protein bars performed poorly because they became hypoglycemic as a result of inadequate carbohydrate replacement during exercise. This is compatible with the belief that the prevention of hypoglycemia is the crucial ergogenic effect of carbohydrate ingestion during exercise.

During Recovery

As also applies during exercise, increasing the sodium content of the fluid ingested during recovery reduces the urine losses and increases the rate of rehydration in proportion to the sodium concentration of the ingested fluid (Maughan and Leiper 1995; Shirreffs et al. 1996; Wemple, Morocco, et al. 1997; Shirreffs and Maughan 1998; Ray et al. 1998). Although solutions with a sodium concentration of 100 mmol per liter are most effective in restoring fluid balance, in practice, subjects will drink more of solutions with a more palatable sodium concentration of 25 mmol per liter (Wemple, Morocco, et al. 1997). As fluid ingestion will initiate some urine loss, the ingested volume needs to exceed the total fluid deficit by 25% to 50%.

The Ideal Sports Drink

Our argument has so far shown that the maximum rates of fluid loss for the faster runners competing in moderate environmental conditions is about 1000 ml per hour. However, no one has yet shown that, in competition, these runners can ever drink more than 700 ml per hour without developing symptoms of fullness and bloating. Nor is it yet certain that fluid ingestion must match the rate of fluid (or weight) loss during exercise if dehydration is to be prevented. This is because some of the fluid lost during exercise probably comes from water stores that are released while liver and muscle glycogen are oxidized. In addition, some of the weight lost during exercise results from irreversible oxidation of fat and carbohydrate stores. As calculated earlier, these sources could be as much as 2 kg. Perhaps it is not surprising that during more prolonged exercise athletes incur a remarkable constancy in the weight loss (2 to 3 kg). This appears to be relatively independent of either the type or duration of the activity (Noakes 1993).

There is also no definite evidence suggesting that drinking fluid at rates greater than ad libitum, which corresponds to between 400 and 600 ml per hour, is more beneficial than lower rates, but doing so is certainly more likely to cause abdominal bloating and fullness (McConell et al. 1997; 1999; Daries et al. 2000; Haymes et al. 2001).

The key to developing the optimum replacement fluid for ingestion during exercise would seem to be to develop a drinking pattern that provides optimum fluid, electrolyte, and carbohydrate replacement at an ingested rate of 500 to 800 ml per hour without causing gastric distress by forcing the athlete to maintain a large gastric volume or abdominal fullness as a result of a failure of fluid absorption.

The proposal outlined in figure 4.13 shows that even an 18% carbohydrate solution ingested at a rate of 100 ml every 10 minutes in an athlete prepared to maintain a gastric volume of 400 ml would provide a gastric emptying rate in excess of 600 ml per hour. The same athlete could achieve the same results from a 7% carbohydrate solution if he or she also ingested 100 ml every 10 minutes and maintained a gastric volume of only 200 ml. This is probably the more usual drinking pattern chosen by most athletes during competition.

It is clear that different carbohydrate concentrations ingested in different ways could provide the required fluid replacement of 500 to 800 ml per hour but would provide quite different rates of carbohydrate delivery. The rate of carbohydrate delivery, rather than the rate of water delivery, may really be the more important factor to consider, at least during more prolonged exercise lasting more than 3 hours (Noakes 1990a).

The ingested solution could vary in osmolality from 200 to 400 mmol per liter (Gisolfi et al. 1998), but to optimize intestinal absorption of carbohydrate and water and to replace the sodium lost in sweat, it should have a sodium chloride content of about 60 mmol per liter. The higher osmolality drinks would be those that also have a higher glucose content (greater than 10%).

When drunk frequently during exercise, the solution ensures high rates of gastric emptying (Rehrer, Beckers, et al. 1989). The carbohydrate can be of any source—glucose, maltose, glucose polymer, or starch—as all seem to be used by the body at equivalent rates. The intake must be sufficient to provide the muscles with 1 g per minute of glucose. This is probably achieved with an intake of 60 to 90 g per hour. Higher rates do not appear to aid performance further (Mitchell et al. 1989a).

At a practical level, what should the average runner do? We are currently working on developing an ideal solution (assuming a drinking rate of 500 to 800 ml per hour) that is also palatable, along the following lines:

Carbohydrate content: 7.5% to 12% (depending on the rate of drinking)

Carbohydrate type: Anything but fructose

Osmolality: 200 to 400 mosmol per liter (osmolality will depend on the type of carbohydrate used—glucose polymers will have lower osmolalities at any carbohydrate concentration)

Sodium content : 60 mmol per liter

At present, there is still no solution conforming to the above criteria. Here are some guidelines, however, on what to look for when buying currently available sports drinks.

Palatability. The most scientifically formulated drink is of no value if it is so unpalatable that it cannot be drunk.

Carbohydrate concentration of 5 to 10%. Higher carbohydrate concentrations only become important near the end of prolonged, competitive exercise when the desire to drink falls but the need for carbohydrate replacement is greatest.

Carbohydrates from a variety of sources. A mixture of carbohydrate sources (glucose, fructose, and maltodextrins) is necessary to maximize palatability and to maintain a low to moderate osmolality.

Sodium concentration of 20 to 60 mmol per liter. The higher sodium concentrations aid fluid balance when athletes are able to ingest fluid at high rates.

HEAT HAZARDS

The history of the marathon, more than any other sport, is etched with the tragedy of heat-related deaths. The hero of the 1908 Olympics in London, the diminutive Italian Dorando Pietri, lay in a semicoma desperately close to death for the two days following his collapse in the final meters of the marathon. In the 1912 Olympic Games in Stockholm, the Portuguese runner Francisco Lazaro collapsed from heatstroke after running 19 miles and died the next day. Jim Peters, the first marathon runner to break the 2:20:00 barrier, entered the Vancouver Stadium 15 minutes ahead of his nearest rival in the 1954 Empire Games Marathon, only to collapse before reaching the finishing line (figure 4.14). The words of the stunned broadcaster, "God! He's running backwards!" captured, better than anything, the horror of the moment. Jackie Mekler, who finished second in the same marathon, recalls that environmental conditions were so severe that he had chosen to run conservatively, finishing more than 14 minutes slower than his best time. Worse, in accordance with the rules of the day, there were few watering stations. Those that did exist were unattended, as the officials had chosen to return to the stadium to watch the Landy-Bannister "Mile of the Century" that was run 20 minutes before Peters arrived in the stadium. Thus, there was no one to tell Peters that he had a huge lead and could win comfortably even if he walked the last 3 km. Peters was not treated according to the modern principles of rapid cooling in an ice-cold bath. Instead, he reportedly languished for some hours before making a full recovery. He never again raced a marathon. He feared that if he were again to race in the heat, particularly in the 1956 Melbourne Olympic Marathon, he would be unable to restrain himself and would suffer the same fate. A better understanding of human physiology would have allowed Peters to have run that race, even in the heat. A slower running pace, appropriate to the environmental conditions, some fluid ingestion during the race, and rapid immersion in ice-cold water if he had overheated should have been sufficient to allow him to race.

Fortunately, since these disasters, there have been three major changes that have reduced the risk of runners developing heatstroke during races longer than 3 km.

1. Running races longer than 3 km are no longer held in the heat of the day, as was the case in the 1954 Empire Games Marathon. Rather, these races are usually scheduled (with the notable exception of the men's 1984 Olympic Marathon) in the early morning or late evening.

2. The facilities for providing the athletes with fluid replacement during races have greatly improved. When I ran my first marathon, drinking was allowed only after the first 10 km, and then every 5 km. In fact, as I recall, there were

only three watering stations over the entire course. Today, refreshment stations are provided every 2 to 3 km and often more frequently at the most popular races.

3. Athletes have become aware of the need to preacclimatize by training in the heat if they are to run races of 5 km or longer in the heat, as well as of the need to run conservatively, especially if the race is between 5 and 21 km.

One of the remarkable paradoxes of medicine is that we observe and describe the unusual and then assume that it is the commonplace. Thus, we remember Jim Peters' collapse because it was so unusual; yet, we then assume that heatstroke must be a common risk for all marathon runners when the exact opposite applies. The remarkable observation is how few reports there are of heatstroke in marathon runners during the past century, despite the hazardous environmental conditions in which many of those races were held. Perhaps a more apt conclusion would be that marathoners are relatively immune to heatstroke even when racing in conditions that are especially hazardous. I believe there are two primary reasons why this is so.

Figure 4.14 Jim Peters collapses near the finish of the 1954 Vancouver Empire Games Marathon. Chris Brasher (jacketless in a white shirt), organizer of the first London Marathon in 1981, is pictured behind Peters. Brasher won the gold medal in the 3000-m steeplechase at the 1956 Olympic Games in Melbourne. He was also the pace setter for the first 800 m of the first sub-4-minute mile.

First, there is evidence to suggest that the brain continually receives information about the body's skin, brain, and core body temperature. When the temperature exceeds 39 to 40°C in most runners, the brain reduces its recruitment of the exercising muscles and subconsciously informs the athlete that he or she is "tired." As a result, the athlete either slows down or stops completely. This reduces the rate at which the body produces heat and, provided the athlete seeks a cool, shady, preferably windy place, soon results in the body temperature returning to normal, thereby preventing heatstroke.

Second, the most important cause of heatstroke, as so clearly shown in the case of Jim Peters, is the metabolic rate that the athlete can sustain during the race. The metabolic rate can be estimated from the product of the running speed and the athlete's mass. Metabolic rate is therefore highest in those races, especially of 5 to 10 km, that are run at the highest speeds and are somewhat lower in the marathon. Hence, there is a greater likelihood that heatstroke will develop in the shorter-distance races than in the marathon. It is really in these races that more attention needs to be paid to preventing this condition.

Perhaps what Jim Peters and other athletes with heatstroke show is that the internal controls that should prevent heatstroke sometimes fail. When they do, it is important to recognize the condition to know how to prevent and treat it.

Heatstroke

If a previously healthy athlete shows evidence of marked changes in mental functioning—collapse with unconsciousness, a reduced level of consciousness (stupor, coma), or mental stimulation (irritability, aggression, convulsions)—in association with an internal body temperature (measured rectally) over 41°C (Peters' was reportedly 42°C), then the diagnosis is heatstroke. The diagnosis can be confirmed during the first 48 hours after collapse by a rise in blood levels of certain enzymes that leak from the muscles into the blood as a result of heat damage.

Diagnosing Heatstroke

The only conditions with which the heatstroke may initially be confused are heart attack (cardiac arrest), a severe fall in blood glucose levels (hypoglycemia; see chapter 3), or hyponatremia (water intoxication). In patients with cardiac arrest, the heart stops beating and the patient does not breathe; thus, a pulse will not be felt and the chest wall will not move. In contrast, in heatstroke, the pulse rate is rapid, usually more than 100 beats a minute, and breathing is more rapid and obvious. Thus, simply feeling the pulse will differentiate between heatstroke and cardiac arrest.

Identifying hypoglycemia or hyponatremia is not as simple. In the words of Sir Adolphe Abrahams (1951): "When exhausting exercise is undertaken in circumstances conducive to heatstroke, it is impossible to separate the symptoms caused by an accompanying hypoglycemia" (page 1188). Abrahams was the British Olympic team doctor for many years; brother of Harold Abrahams, the sprinter; and one of the fathers of modern sports medicine. His words were, of course, written before carbohydrate ingestion was advocated during exercise. We now know that such ingestion reduces the probability that hypoglycemia will develop.

The distinction between heatstroke and hypoglycemia can be made only on the basis of the rectal temperature, which is usually lower than 40°C in hypoglycemia and hyponatremia, and by measuring the blood glucose and sodium concentrations. Blood glucose concentrations below about 4 mmol per liter and blood sodium concentrations below 130 mmol per liter may cause the symptoms of hypoglycemia and hyponatremia, respectively.

Heat Injury in Children During Exercise

Four factors are believed to reduce the young athlete's ability to lose heat while exercising in a warm environment.

1. Children produce more metabolic heat per unit of mass than do adults during exercise at the same workload.
2. They have a lower sweating capacity than do adults.
3. They have a reduced ability to transfer heat from the body core to the body surface (skin).
4. They have a greater surface area to weight ratio, which facilitates heat gain from the environment during exercise in the heat or, conversely, heat loss to the environment during exercise in all other conditions, including mild heat (Delamarche et al. 1990) or cold. In addition, children acclimatize to heat more slowly than do adults (American Academy of Pediatrics 1983).

While these differences do not interfere with children's ability to exercise in a cool environment, they may limit their ability to exercise safely in a warm or hot environment although not all studies support this conclusion (Docherty et al. 1986; Delamarche et al. 1990). In particular, their greater surface area to weight ratio means that children lose more heat by convection than do adults. So, to maintain the same rectal temperature, they need to sweat less during exercise (Delamarche et al. 1990). In addition, their smaller size means that, when running at the same speed as a larger adult, the smaller child will produce less heat and should therefore be at a thermoregulatory advantage (Dennis and Noakes 1999). Nevertheless, the following recommendations have been made by the American Academy of Pediatrics (1983):

- In hot environmental conditions, children should either reduce the intensity of their activities or avoid exercising for longer than 30 minutes at a time.
- When moving to a hot climate, or at the start of the summer season, children should allow 10 to 15 days for heat acclimatization to occur. During this time, they should gradually increase the intensity and duration of their exercise sessions.
- Children should wear lightweight, porous clothing and drink fluids regularly during exercise—300 ml per hour for a child weighing 40 kg. Rubberized sweat suits must never be used in an attempt to produce a rapid weight loss.

Fortunately, the risk of heatstroke will always be negligible, even if children exercise in the heat. This is because the central governor usually terminates exercise before the body temperature reaches dangerous levels.

A simple, practical approach, advisable only when facilities to measure the blood glucose concentration are not readily available, is first to correct any hypoglycemia in a collapsed runner by giving adequate amounts (about 10 to 20 g) of glucose intravenously. The athlete with pure hypoglycemia will recover rapidly with this treatment; the condition of runners with heatstroke and hyponatremia will be unaffected. This treatment is also safe. In practice, the diagnosis of hyponatremia is usually made on the basis of exclusion: if an athlete is unconscious or severely confused or has a vacant stare and the rectal temperature is not elevated, the most likely diagnosis is hyponatremia, especially when the blood glucose concentration is also found to be normal. Furthermore, in healthy runners, hypoglycemia alone seldom causes the degree of mental confusion seen in hyponatremia or heatstroke. Also, hypoglycemia never causes unconsciousness in healthy, nondiabetic athletes. However, the incorrect (excessive) use of insulin by exercising diabetics or of insulin-like growth promoting factor (IGF-1) by athletes participating in (illegal) doping programs can cause profound hypoglycemia and coma that may be more difficult to reverse.

The personal and environmental factors that predispose to heatstroke are those that disturb the equilibrium between the rate of heat production and that of heat loss. The rate of heat loss is controlled by the air temperature, its humidity, the rate of wind movement across the athlete's body, and the athlete's sweating capacity. The rate of heat production is determined by the athlete's mass and running speed. Thus, the rate of heat production and the risk of heatstroke is greatest in short-distance races (Noakes, Adams, et al. 1988; Noakes 1981; 1990a; 1991; 1993; 1995), not in the marathon, as is commonly believed. Indeed, this is a critical point that is not appreciated by many athletes or race organizers: the major factors causing heatstroke during races are the environmental conditions, the speed at which the athletes run, and individual susceptibility, including whether or not the athlete has preacclimatized to running in the heat (Noakes, Adams, et al. 1988). If longer-distance races are held when either the WBGT index or the dry bulb temperature is greater than 28°C, heat injury will occur to a significant number of competitors, regardless of how much they drink and sponge during the race or how they are dressed. Adequate fluid replacement during racing is only one of many factors that reduce the risk of heat injury; it is certainly not the only factor and may not even be a very important factor (Noakes, Adams, et al. 1988; Noakes 1981; 1990a; 1991a; 1993; 1995; 2000; 2001).

In this context, it is of some historical interest that the highest incidence of heatstroke in an Olympic running event occurred not in a marathon race, but in the 10,000-m cross-country race at the 1924 Olympic Games in Paris. Competing at 3:30 p.m. on a day that was "unbelievably hot" (Lovesey 1968), only 15 of the 39 entrants completed the race; four runners collapsed on the track. Lovesey writes that the runners arrived looking like "victims from an action on the Front.... The state of the pathetic figures who tottered into the stadium in the wake of the leaders so shocked those present that cross-country running was banned from future Olympic track and field programs" (Lovesey 1968, page 112).

Other factors that determine the rate at which the athlete loses heat include

- clothing, because the more clothing people wear, the less heat they will lose by convection and sweating;
- the state of heat acclimatization, because heat acclimatization increases both

people's ability to lose heat by sweating and their resistance to an elevated body temperature; and

- the athletes' state of hydration, because dehydration impairs the ability to lose heat by sweating.

Finally, it is clear that only certain people are prone to heatstroke for reasons that are at present unknown. It seems likely that some may have an hereditary abnormality of muscle cell metabolism (Noakes 1987a).

For example, one feature of malignant hyperthermia, a hereditary condition, is the uncontrollable rise in body temperature under conditions of stress, most especially during surgical anesthesia with the drug halothane (Simon 1993) but possibly also during vigorous or prolonged exercise (Jardon 1982). Patients with this condition often die suddenly under unusual circumstances, perhaps from an unrecognized heatstroke. The genetic physiological abnormality in this condition is a "leaky" sarcoplasmic reticulum in the skeletal muscles (MacLennan et al. 1990). When exposed to halothane or other triggering stimuli, these abnormal sarcoplasmic reticulae leak calcium, which then stimulates rapid glycogen breakdown in the affected muscles. Body temperature rises rapidly, muscle and blood lactate concentrations increase, and pH falls, leading to death unless the condition is reversed by rapid cooling and the use of the drug dantrolene sodium, which reverses the abnormality in the sarcoplasmic reticulum.

The point is that this condition mimics the heatstroke seen in exercising athletes. Hence, at least some cases of heatstroke may actually be better described as exercise-induced malignant hyperthermia. This contrasts to environmentally induced heatstroke, in which an otherwise completely healthy athlete develops heatstroke as a result of running too fast in conditions that are either too humid or too hot, or both, as did Jim Peters.

Athletes may increase their individual susceptibility if they are not properly acclimatized to running in the heat; if they exercise when they are ill, especially if they are feverish; and if they take medications that interfere with their ability to lose heat, especially by sweating.

Treating Heatstroke

The first priority is to lower the body temperature to below 38°C as quickly as possible because the amount of tissue damage caused by the high body temperature is related to the time during which body temperature exceeds that value. Such cooling can best be done at the medical facility at the race finish.

The most effective cooling method is to place the athlete's torso in a bath of ice water, placing the arms and legs over the edge above the water. This is best achieved by using a small, child's size, plastic bath. The body temperature should drop to 38°C within 3 to 6 minutes of this exposure (Armstrong et al. 1996). It is dangerous to leave the athlete in the bath for too long, as the body temperature may drop too far, inducing hypothermia. Rates of cooling close to 1°C per minute can be achieved with this form of cooling (Armstrong et al. 1996).

When body temperatures are changing rapidly, the rectal temperature lags behind the core (esophageal) temperature. Thus, active cooling must be terminated before the rectal temperature reaches the normal body temperature. Shivering indicates that the core temperature has decreased to 37°C or below.

If a bath of iced water is not available—such baths should be mandatory at all races longer than 3 km, except those run in very mild environmental conditions—then ice packs should be placed over as large an area of the body surface as possible.

As soon as a cooling procedure is started, correction of dehydration and possible hypoglycemia with intravenous fluids and glucose can be instituted. However, no more than 1 to 2 liters of fluid should be given, as there is no evidence to support that such treatment is either necessary or beneficial (Noakes 1991b; 2000b; 2001a). By itself, administration of fluids is not an acceptable form of treatment for heatstroke (Noakes 2001a). Provided the patient is not suffering from fluid overload, this relatively small volume of fluid is safe. Once the temperature has been reduced to below 39°C, athletes usually regain consciousness, in which case they can continue to be managed at the facility at the race finish and can usually be discharged within 60 to 90 minutes. If an athlete fails to regain consciousness or develops other complications, it is best to transfer him or her to the nearest hospital for further cooling and observation in case any of the serious complications of heatstroke, in particular kidney failure and organ damage, should occur. It is important that the body temperature be monitored while the athlete is being transported to hospital, as well as after hospital admission, as the temperature tends to rise once the active cooling procedures cease.

How Best to Treat Heatstroke—Forgotten Lessons

A striking characteristic of "truth" is that it tends to be cyclical. That is, wisdom developed in one generation sometimes fails to make it through to the next, only to be rediscovered by some misguided, malcontent maverick in some following generation.

When I began running, we were taught that athletes with heatstroke should be cooled by placing towels saturated with cold water over their bodies and by increasing the flow of air over the body with the use of large fans. How this was to be implemented in the field was never explained to us. This approach was based on a study that showed that this method produced a more rapid rate of cooling than did either immersing athletes in cold water or leaving them to recover in still air conditions (Wyndham et al. 1959). This technique soon became the world standard. Proponents of this method argued that placing patients with heatstroke in an iced water bath would be detrimental, as doing so would cause immediate constriction of the blood vessels in the skin, thereby preventing heat loss from convection and evaporation. In line with this thinking, an athlete with heatstroke placed in an ice-cold bath would be expected to "heat up" (Strydom et al. 1982). Given that humans who swim in cold water for prolonged periods develop hypothermia (Noakes 1985; 2000c), not heatstroke, the ludicrousness of this advice should have been immediately apparent (Noakes 1986).

A number of studies have finally proven that the best technique for cooling the athlete with heatstroke is to apply ice or iced water directly to the skin, preferably by placing the athlete's torso in a small bath of iced water with the legs and arms hanging over the edge of the bath (Kielblock et al. 1986; Armstrong et al. 1996; Costrini 1990).

First, Kielblock et al. (1986) showed that cooling rates of 0.03°C per minute could be achieved by placing 24 to 28 ice packs over the entire skin surface.

(continued)

This rate of cooling was the same as that achieved with the conventional method, using either compressed air evaporation or cooling with a large fan (approximately 0.04°C per minute). Next, Costrini (1990) showed that ice-bath immersion produced a cooling rate of 0.15°C per minute in Marine Corp recruits who developed heatstroke during basic training; that was four times faster than the conventional method.

Armstrong et al. (1996) showed that athletes who developed heatstroke in the Falmouth Road Race could be cooled at a rate of about 0.4°C per minute when placed in a bath of ice-cold water. This technique of cooling is superior to any of the other techniques that had become the accepted standard over the years.

Remarkably, the first successful use of ice-water baths in the treatment of heatstroke was reported in 1917 (Gauss and Meyer) so that by 1940 this method was recommended as the treatment of choice (Ferris et al. 1938; Talbott 1940).

Indeed, in 1948, Daily and Harrison (1948) showed that ice-water baths produced the most rapid rates of cooling (approximately 2°C per minute in rats) and the highest number of survivors in experimental heatstroke in dogs, rats, and mice. Ice-water baths generally produced rates of cooling that were twice as rapid as those produced by fanning. The authors noted that

> there are two criticisms of the ice-bath in the literature: that it is less effective than evaporative cooling because of physical principles, and possibly vaso-constriction, and that it may be dangerous, producing "shock." Our experiments on the rate of temperature reduction in the rat and dog denies [sic] the first objection, and the greater survival of mice treated with ice-baths, as compared to those treated by evaporative cooling, denies the second. (p. 53)

Their conclusion was that "If a patient is comatose, or if the body temperature is above 41°C (106°F), the patient should be immersed in ice water" (p. 54). Half a century later, the study of Armstrong et al. (1996) verified their conclusion once and for all.

Daily and Harrison made one other interesting observation—that "massive" intravenous infusions produced heart failure in rats with heatstroke, whereas the same infusions were well tolerated by rats with normal body temperatures. They concluded that the heart had a reduced functional reserve at high body temperatures.

This cautionary note is especially important because of the tendency of some to believe that heatstroke is caused solely by dehydration that must be corrected immediately by rapid infusions of large volumes of intravenous fluids. This is a component of the "dehydration myth" that has been perpetuated over the years (Noakes 1997; 2000c). Clearly, because of the risk of inducing heart failure and flooding of the lungs (pulmonary edema), such fluids must be used cautiously in those with markedly elevated body temperatures.

In addition, a number of studies have failed to show that intravenous fluids increase the rate of recovery from exercise (Polak et al. 1993; Castellani et al. 1997; Riebe et al. 1997), even in those treated for exercise-associated collapse (EAC; Ellis et al. 1990). In fact, they may be dangerous if used indiscriminately, as they can produce hyponatremia (Noakes 1999a; 1999b; 2000; Noakes, Berlinski, et al. 1991). Indeed, one study (Casa et al. 2000) suggests that physiological function during a subsequent exercise bout is better if subjects drink fluid rather than receive it intravenously during recovery from a previous exercise bout.

Preventing Heatstroke

The following proposals for preventing heat injury during running are based on the proposals of ACSM (1975; 1985; 1996a; 1996b). Unfortunately, they are not entirely foolproof—some athletes will suffer heatstroke during exercise, regardless of the precautions they take.

Nevertheless, the overall risk to all athletes can be reduced by paying close attention to these proposals. The single most important point here is that the risk of heatstroke is inversely related to the distance of the race (that is, it is least in the longest races) and is directly related to the environmental temperature.

- ✔ Competitive races longer than 5 km should not be conducted when the Wet Bulb Globe Temperature (WBGT) index exceeds 28°C or the dry bulb temperature is greater than 27°C in summer, less in winter (figure 4.15).

- ✔ During periods of the year when the daylight dry bulb temperature often exceeds 25°C, distance races should be conducted before 9:00 a.m. or after 4:30 p.m.

- ✔ It is the responsibility of the race sponsor and organizer to provide drinking/sponging stations, at least every 3 to 4 km for all races longer than 4 km.

- ✔ Runners should be encouraged to drink approximately 100 to 125 ml of fluid every 10 to 15 minutes during competition and to consume approximately 400 to 500 ml of the same solution before competition. However, even regular and adequate drinking will not necessarily prevent heatstroke, at least in races of up to 10 km (England et al. 1982). As described earlier in this chapter, ad libitum fluid ingestion is all that is required.

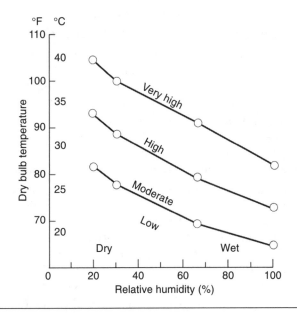

Figure 4.15   Guidelines from the American College of Sports Medicine for classifying the heat risk when exercising at different relative humidities and dry bulb temperatures.
From ACSM (1987, p. ii).

✔ Runners should sponge frequently. Water applied to the skin acts as artificial sweat and aids the body's cooling system. In one study, runners who suffered heat injury in a 10-km race had used sponging facilities much less frequently than those who had completed the race safely (England et al. 1982). Although it should be remembered that even elite, highly trained athletes can suffer heatstroke if forced to race in inappropriate environmental conditions (Noakes 1981a), the runners most likely to develop heatstroke are those who

- are overweight;

- are inadequately trained;

- are not acclimatized to running in the heat;

- overestimate their running ability and therefore attempt to run too fast during the race, especially near the end;

- have suffered heat injury before;

- are taller than 1.79 m (England et al. 1982);

- ignore warning symptoms of impending heatstroke, such as weakness, clumsiness, stumbling, headache, nausea, dizziness, apathy, aggression, and any gradual impairment of consciousness (Sutton and Bar-Or 1980; unfortunately, most runners who develop heatstroke have either none or only one of these warning symptoms; England et al. 1982);

- have recently recovered from a febrile illness or are harboring illnesses such as influenza, gastroenteritis, or upper respiratory tract infection;

- have a genetic predisposition (Jardon 1982), possibly on the basis of an inherited abnormality of skeletal muscle metabolism (Jardon 1982; Noakes 1987a);

- have previously suffered heatstroke; or

- take certain medications, including diuretics and antidepressants.

✔ All competitors must be educated to train properly and to acclimatize for hot weather running; to avoid competition if they have recently been ill or are running a temperature; to drink adequately during competition; and to stop running should they develop symptoms of impending heatstroke.

✔ Responsible and informed personnel should supervise drinking stations. They should have the right to remove from the race any runners who exhibit clear signs of heat exhaustion or impending heatstroke or, conversely, any of those who have drunk too much and have developed hyponatremia.

✔ Suitably qualified personnel should be present at all races in which there is a substantial risk that heatstroke or hyponatremia will occur. Such personnel must have free access to the facilities, equipment, and medications necessary to diagnose and treat those conditions—a basic medical kit for the immediate treatment of heat injury. The kit should contain at least the following: rectal thermometers, fluids for intravenous administration, instant ice packs, and one or two large electrically driven fans.

✔ Facilities for ice-bath treatment should always be available in the medical facility at the race finish.

✔ Suitable vehicles should be on standby to transport seriously ill athletes to the nearest hospital.

✔ All races should end in open, well-exposed areas so that those athletes who collapse near the finish of the race can be spotted easily. Deaths from heatstroke have occurred in two North American races because the athletes became disorientated and collapsed in dense vegetation close to the finish, only to be discovered hours or days later.

Other Heat-Related Disorders

Much of the confusion surrounding the amount of fluids athletes should ingest during exercise comes directly, in my view, from the lack of clarity about what constitutes a heat illness. For example, when I began running marathons in 1972, there were no medical tents at the end of races. What was more likely was that runners would have had to present a medical clearance indicating that they were fit to start the race. Once you started, you were essentially on your own. At that time, heatstroke was the only serious heat illness that was recognized.

In the 1970s, however, when marathons moved from the suburbs to the big cities and attracted more runners, it became necessary to provide medical care during and after races. It is possible that nowadays runners use the facilities simply because they are there. So, quite suddenly, a new industry developed—the care of the collapsed athlete after marathon and ultramarathon races. And what a growth industry it proved to be. Some 10%, and in the case of the Hawaiian Ironman Triathlon, 30%, of entrants in those races sought medical care at the postrace medical facilities. This presented race doctors with a new problem—the need to come up with appropriate diagnoses for this new hoard of medical casualties.

Unfortunately, the medical diagnostic categories were formulated unscientifically, without appropriate measurements to justify the new nomenclature. Thus, "dehydration" became one of the diagnostic categories. Since dehydration is a physiological term, not a medical term for a specific disease, this was clearly inappropriate. Furthermore, the diagnosis was always made without measuring the weight that the athlete had lost during the race and without an intellectual assessment of its real physiological relevance.

The second related category was heat illness, a term borrowed from military experience and based on research largely undertaken before and during World War II. The heat illnesses were said to include "heat cramps," "heat exhaustion," and "heat syncopy." These illnesses were all believed to be due to dehydration, which led to an elevated body temperature, which, in turn, then caused the collapse, a less serious form of heatstroke. The only problems with this logic are that there is no published evidence showing that dehydration causes any of these conditions; the body temperature is not abnormally elevated in any of these conditions; and unlike heatstroke, all these conditions are treated without any need for external cooling of the body, hence proving that they are not real heat illnesses.

But the inadvertent, illogical trap into which many fell was that if the number of runners needing treatment for heat illness after marathon races had suddenly increased, then it was because they were becoming dehydrated from not drinking enough. Hence, the preventative strategy was to force marathon runners to drink more and the treatment for such collapses was intravenous fluids. The result of this illogical thinking was a rising incidence of hyponatremia, with some fatal results.

Apart from our description of the first cases of the hyponatremia of exercise (Noakes, Goodwin, et al. 1985), there were two other findings that convinced me that these ideas were hopelessly incorrect. These included our finding that runners with so-called heat illness were no hotter than other runners who finished the race without heat illness and that 85% of marathon runners admitted to the medical tent collapsed after they finished the race. Clearly, it is the act of stopping, and not the act of running, that causes the majority of postrace collapses.

As a result, we (but perhaps not everyone else) now think that the vast majority of athletes treated in the medical facility at the end of marathon races are suffering from nothing more serious than a precipitant drop in blood pressure that results from suddenly stopping exercise, so-called Exercise Associated Collapse (EAC). But to explain how we arrived at that conclusion, we first need to discuss the historically described "heat illnesses."

Heat Cramps

Heat cramps were probably first described in 1923 among coal miners in the north of England. Eventually this condition became known as miner's, fireman's, stoker's, or cane cutter's cramps or, simply, heat cramps.

The popular belief still current is that heat cramps are caused by the severe dehydration and large sodium chloride losses that develop during exercise, especially in hot conditions (Eichner 1999). But the original descriptions of the condition postulated that the cramps resulted from an excessive fluid intake.

Thus, these early researchers believed that heat cramps were caused by the ingestion of large volumes of water without adequate replacement of sodium chloride; but they did not base their conclusions on solid scientific evidence. It was also believed, as is still advocated today (Eichner 1999), that heat cramps could be prevented by the addition of sodium chloride to water ingested during exercise or could be treated with sodium chloride infusion. However, no controlled clinical trials to evaluate these beliefs have ever been reported.

Two modern studies have extended our knowledge of this phenomenon. Maughan (1986) showed that there were no differences in the serum electrolyte concentrations and changes in plasma volume between runners who developed cramps during a 42-km marathon race and those who did not. He concluded that "exercise-induced muscle cramp may not be associated with gross disturbances of fluid and electrolyte balance (p. 31)" Another study compared fluid balance and serum electrolyte changes during a 56-km ultramarathon footrace in a group of runners with a history of frequent exercise-related cramps and a control group of competitors without such a history, who were competing in the same race. There were no differences in either fluid balance or serum electrolyte changes between members of the cramp-prone group, who developed cramps during the ultramarathon and the noncramping controls. Hence, the only modern studies of fluid and electrolyte balance have failed to show that either fluid or electrolyte imbalances play any significant role in exercise-related cramps.

In summary, there is no published evidence to support the popular belief that heat cramps are caused by dehydration or by excessive sodium chloride or other electrolyte losses invoked by exercise. After a lifetime studying sodium balance in people exercising in desert heat, Epstein and Sohar (1985) concluded that "salt deficiency heat exhaustion [and by extension, salt deficiency heat cramps] is an example of christening by conjecture. . . . Such a syndrome has never been proven to exist."

Furthermore, clinical observation confirms that cramps can occur at rest or during or after exercise undertaken under in mild environmental conditions. Hence, cramps are neither specific to exercise, nor to exercise in the heat. The more modern hypothesis proposes that cramps are probably the result of alterations in spinal neural reflex activity by fatigue in susceptible people (Bentley 1996; Schwellnus et al. 1997; Schwellnus 2000). Thus, persisting with the term *heat cramps* cannot be justified and continues to prevent a better understanding of the real, probably neurological, nature of this condition. Nor should we continue to believe (Eichner 1999) that salt has anything to do with either the cause or cure of this condition, since no such evidence exists.

Heat Exhaustion

In current understanding, heat exhaustion, or heat syncope, describes a condition in which an athlete collapses during or after exercising in the heat. The condition is believed to be due to dehydration-induced heat retention insufficiently severe to cause heatstroke, according to the original Wyndham/Strydom hypothesis. Hence, heat exhaustion is described as a mild form of heatstroke caused by dehydration—which, unless correctly treated, will progress to heatstroke. Some of the errors in logic leading to these incorrect conclusions have already been described in this chapter. In this section, I outline the evidence that suggests that heat exhaustion is not a true heat disorder caused by abnormalities in heat balance that in turn induce a progressive rise in core body temperature during exercise.

First, rectal temperatures are not abnormally elevated in people with heat exhaustion (Holtzhausen et al. 1994; Holtzhausen and Noakes 1997), those with the experimental condition termed *heat strain* (Sawka et al. 1992; 1996), or those with exercise-associated collapse (EAC; W.O. Roberts 2000). Second, there is no published evidence that people with heat exhaustion will develop heatstroke if left untreated or that they are more dehydrated than participants in the same events who do not develop the condition. The largest modern study of subjects who sought medical attention after marathon races has shown that only a tiny proportion have markedly elevated rectal temperatures, and few require hospitalization (W.O. Roberts 1996; 2000). These findings refute the popular belief that the majority of subjects who collapse after prolonged exercise suffer from a heat disorder that progresses inexorably to heatstroke.

Third is the critical finding that most athletes (85%) who collapse and who would therefore fulfill the diagnostic criteria for heat exhaustion do so after they have stopped exercising (Holtzhausen et al. 1994). This finding alone is incompatible with the belief that dehydration or hyperthermia are determinants of this condition. The simple reason for this is that either of these conditions should cause collapse to occur while the athlete is exercising vigorously, not after exercise when the exercising stress has been removed and the rate of heat production by the body is falling.

Indeed, both logic and the published evidence point to the fact that heat exhaustion will not lead to heatstroke. The simple act of stopping exercise will reduce the rate of heat production in subjects with heat exhaustion, causing them to begin cooling immediately on collapse. This contrasts to the situation in true heatstroke, in which physiological and biochemical abnormalities in skeletal muscle cause the rate of heat production to remain elevated even after the athlete stops exercising. Thus, the body temperature in heatstroke will remain in excess of 41°C unless lowered by active cooling to below 38°C.

The more likely explanation for heat exhaustion is that the sudden cessation of exercise induces a rapid drop in blood pressure (postural hypotension) by causing blood to pool in the dilated capacitance veins in the lower limb. Usually those veins are emptied by the second heart action of the lower limb musculature, which squeeze blood from the veins with each contraction. With the sudden cessation of exercise, this pumping action is lost. The blood then dams up in the veins instead of returning to the heart. As a result, blood pressure can fall precipitously. One explanation is that heat syncope or heat exhaustion is an incorrectly labeled condition, which is actually caused by the sudden onset of postural hypotension on the cessation of exercise, probably induced by the sudden pooling of blood in the dilated, capacitance veins in the lower limbs, which reduces blood return to the heart, and interferes with normal blood pressure regulation (Noakes 1988a; Holtzhausen et al. 1994; Holtzhausen and Noakes 1995).

Historical studies of collapse in people exposed to exercise in hot environmental conditions, so-called heat exhaustion, emphasized that all had postural hypotension but that their rectal temperatures were not abnormally elevated. The cardiovascular instability and associated symptoms disappeared as soon as the subjects lay prone, without the need for intravenous fluid therapy (Talbott et al. 1937; Adolph 1947; Eichna et al. 1945; 1947). Thus, these authors did not believe that dehydration contributed to the condition.

For example, Adolph (1947) noted that patients with heat exhaustion were "still producing sweat and keeping cool" but that they showed evidence of postural hypotension. Adolph and Fulton (1924) concluded that

> *The peripheral blood vessels are greatly dilated during exposure to high temperatures, and this dilation continues indefinitely. The lack of a high resistance in the peripheral blood vessels prevents blood from returning to the heart. The heart rate increases steadily and rapidly, and is even able to increase the systolic blood pressure. In spite of this compensating activity on the part of the heart, the blood flow back to the heart finally becomes inadequate. At this point, circulatory collapse or shock is complete, with faintness.*

Adolph (1947) also noted that patients with this condition needed "merely to lie down to feel better." The shock-like circulatory failure appeared to be the crucial element in this condition.

Thus, the conclusion from these early studies must be that, historically, the terms *heat exhaustion, heat prostration,* and *heat syncope* were used only to describe a condition of collapse due to postural hypotension that develops in people exercising in the heat. The terminology should not be misinterpreted to indicate that the collapse is caused by an elevated body temperature due to a failure of heat regulation and that it is therefore a mild form of heatstroke. Ever since these early studies, however, researchers have rigorously ignored the possibility that heat syncope or heat exhaustion could be due to nothing more evil than a sudden drop in blood pressure in people stopping exercise suddenly.

Rather, as an extension of the dehydration myth, we have been encouraged to believe that dehydration and an elevated body temperature are the exclusive causes of this condition. In my view, we have been conditioned to follow the wrong treatment options.

Exercise-Associated Collapse (EAC)

Exercise-associated collapse is the condition that is seen most frequently in athletes completing marathon and ultramarathon races, especially in the heat. Shortly after finishing the race, in which they experienced no or only minor discomforts, they suddenly begin to feel light-headed and nauseated, complaining that they wish to faint. Unaided, they fall to the ground. On examination in the lying position, they are usually pale with a low normal blood pressure (about 100 to 110 mm Hg systolic). Their heart rate is seldom more than 110 beats per minute in the lying position. Their symptoms usually abate rapidly when lying down and can be reversed almost instantly if they are nursed in the head-down (Trendellenburg) position. Standing, however, rapidly reproduces their symptoms of fainting. As a result, they remain unwilling to attempt standing for some time, usually for about 20 to 30 minutes; however, most athletes recover within about 30 minutes. Our clinical impression is that recovery is expedited in those patients who are nursed in the head-down position from the moment they collapse. Indeed, the "no intravenous fluids" rule (except under extremely exceptional conditions) is now the accepted standard at the South African 226-km Ironman Triathlon and the 56-km Two Oceans Marathon.

There is no evidence that athletes suffering from exercise-associated collapse are any more dehydrated than those who do not collapse after such races, nor are their rectal temperatures unusual (Holtzhausen et al. 1994; W.O. Roberts 2000). Hence, there is no need to give these athletes fluids intravenously. Instead, they should be encouraged to drink a carbohydrate-electrolyte solution ad libitum.

We have proposed that most athletes who collapse after exercise have postural hypotension and should be managed by lying supine with legs and pelvis elevated above the level of the heart (Holtzhausen and Noakes 1997). This treatment has proved particularly effective and, in our hands, has essentially removed the need for intravenous fluid therapy from the management of the vast majority of athletes who collapse after completing marathon and ultramarathon races. In fact, since using this strategy of recovery in the head-down position, we have not needed to use intravenous fluids for the management of postexercise collapse.

Confusion about the etiological role of dehydration in the incorrectly termed "heat illness" in athletes stems from the misinterpretation of the real findings of Wyndham and Strydom's (1969) study, as well as the results of laboratory studies of the experimental condition known as heat strain (Sawka et al. 1992; 1996). Heat strain is defined as the condition of exhaustion that develops when people exercise in severe environmental conditions, specifically chosen so that thermal balance cannot be achieved. The result is that all subjects collapse from heat strain, provided the exercise duration is sufficiently long. Under such extreme environmental conditions, in which athletic competition would neither be safe nor allowed, severe preexercise dehydration (hypohydration; 8%) is associated with premature termination of exercise with heat strain. Yet, and this is the point of logic that has been overlooked, the finding that all subjects developed heat strain even when they exercised in the fully hydrated state proves that dehydration is not an etiological factor for the development of heat strain. Rather, severe hypohydration influenced only the duration of exercise that could be sustained before the onset of heat strain.

Indeed, despite a decade of searching, I have failed quite dismally to unearth any published evidence showing that those who develop heatstroke or heat illness during athletic competition are any more dehydrated than are those who complete the same races with more normal body temperatures. The absence of such information is understandable, given the very low frequency with which heatstroke occurs in modern athletic competition, especially since the introduction of suggested limiting environmental conditions under which such competitions should not be held. It would be very unlikely that severe dehydration alone can explain why only one or two people develop heatstroke in races involving tens of thousands of competitors, the majority of whom will become dehydrated to varying degrees but without developing heatstroke. Rather, as already described, it is far more likely that, for reasons that are at present unknown, only certain people are prone to heatstroke during exercise.

In summary, whereas dehydration may affect exercise performance in the heat to varying degrees (Walsh et al. 1994; Below et al. 1995), there is no evidence to suggest that dehydration of the levels present in endurance athletes (1% to 8% of body weight; Noakes, Adams, et al. 1988; Noakes, Myburg, et al. 1990a) exercising under more moderate environmental conditions poses any major health risks or that it even predisposes to heatstroke. Given the historical evidence, it would seem unlikely.

The classic studies of exercise dehydration performed during World War II (Adolph 1947; Brown et al. 1947) found that military personnel forced to exercise without fluid replacement would continue to exercise in hot, desert conditions until levels of dehydration of greater than 7% to 10% were reached.

Dehydration exhaustion, characterized by circulatory instability with, in particular, an elevated heart rate (tachycardia), postural hypotension, and psychological alterations, including heightened aggression and a loss of discipline, terminated exercise. The crucial observation is that despite levels of dehydration almost never reached by endurance athletes in modern competitions, none of the subjects lost consciousness. Hence, loss of consciousness is not a characteristic of exercise-induced dehydration.

In addition, subjects were not markedly hyperthermic, nor did they show significant alterations in renal function. All recovered quickly when they lay down and ingested fluid. Recovery occurred even before any physiological effects could have resulted from the fluid ingestion. On the basis of those studies, Brown (1947) concluded that dehydration posed significant health risks only at levels of dehydration of 15% to 20%. These levels of dehydration are two to three times greater than those normally measured in endurance athletes (Noakes 1993; 2001a). Perhaps "dehydration exhaustion" or "heat strain" acts to prevent athletes from continuing to exercise to levels of dehydration that cause medical complications.

Based on this historic evidence, together with our own studies of exercise-associated collapse (Holtzhausen et al. 1994; Holtzhausen and Noakes 1995; 1997; Sandell et al. 1988; Noakes 1988a; 1995; 1998a; Noakes, Adams, et al. 1988; Noakes, Berlinski, et al. 1991; Noakes, Myburgh, et al. 1990a) and extensive clinical experience in the management of this condition in collapsed ultramarathon runners and Ironman triathletes (Noakes 2001), we have suggested that the principal pathophysiological change that explains this condition of postexercise collapse (exercise-associated collapse, heat exhaustion, or heat syncope) is a postural hypotension that develops as a result of three specific changes.

First is an increased blood flow in the blood vessels closest to the skin to regulate body temperature. This response is increased in hot conditions and leads to a redistribution of the blood to the peripheral veins. This reduces the pressure of blood filling the heart (González-Alonso, Mora-Rodriguez, et al. 1999). The higher the environmental temperature, the greater the skin blood flow and thus the greater this peripheral location of blood, particularly on the cessation of exercise. This theory would explain why the number of athletes who collapse during or after endurance events is linearly related to the ambient temperature (Richards and Richards 1984).

Second, the action of the calf muscle pump reduces the volume of blood stored in the capacitance veins of the lower limb and maintains an adequate return of blood to the heart. With the cessation of exercise, this action of the calf muscle ceases, and blood accumulates in the dilated capacitance veins of the lower limb, threatening the maintenance of an adequate arterial blood pressure.

Third, evidence shows that training-induced adaptations occur in the autonomic nervous system. These adaptations include an increased baseline parasympathetic (vagal) activity, associated with a resting bradycardia and a blunted sympathetic response to any stress that reduces the blood pressure. As a result, the normal response to a lowering of blood pressure, including an immediate increase in heart rate together with increased tone in the blood vessels, occurs to a lesser extent in endurance trained athletes.

If this theory is correct, then the most logical approach to the treatment of EAC would be to elevate and cool the athlete's legs and pelvis to reduce the skin blood flow and the volume of blood in the cutaneous and, perhaps more important, the splanchnic veins. When this is done, the cardiovascular instability supposedly from dehydration is removed (González-Alonso, Mora-Rodriguez, et al. 1999), indicating that such instability is due to the upright posture, not the dehydration (González-Alonso, Mora-Rodriguez, et al. 1999). Subjects considered to be dehydrated may ingest fluid orally. This is the treatment approach we have developed in the medical tents that we direct. Using this form of treatment, we have dramatically reduced the need for intravenous fluid therapy in collapsed ultramarathon runners, simultaneously improving the amount of care that can be lavished on those who are really ill and have serious medical conditions.

TREATING COLLAPSED ATHLETES

A number of novel ideas were introduced in the previous sections. The first is that the majority of exercise-related collapses are not due to heat disorders but probably result from the onset of postural hypotension immediately on cessation of exercise; second, that dehydration does not appear to be an important factor in any of these conditions; and third, that overhydration is a cause of a serious and potentially fatal form of exercise-related collapse. In addition, we now know that hypothermia can even occur in those events that are traditionally associated with heatstroke, such as marathon running. This information can now be used to good advantage and can be integrated into a guided approach to providing effective medical care at endurance sporting events.

The following list, compiled from various sources, includes the most common medical conditions that may be encountered in runners who collapse during or after endurance events:

- Exercise-associated collapse (heat syncope or heat exhaustion)
- Muscle cramps
- Heatstroke
- Hypoglycemia
- Hypothermia
- Hyponatremia
- Cardiac arrest
- Orthopedic conditions, including stress and traumatic fractures
- Other medical conditions

This list is not exhaustive but is practical. Certain conditions are more specific for particular sports and different prevailing environmental conditions. Contrary to the general expectation, heart attack (cardiac arrest) is rarely seen and is more common in those events that attract older participants. The most frequently encountered condition at these events is postexercise collapse, also termed exercise-associated collapse (EAC), the diagnostic characteristics of which have been described in detail.

Symptomatic hyponatremia, profound hypoglycemia, and exercise-induced hyperthermia (heatstroke) are the three serious emergencies likely to be encountered in long-distance footraces, especially in hot environmental conditions. In cold weather conditions, hypothermia should be anticipated.

Initial Management

In the past, one of the major downfalls in the management of collapsed athletes was that treatment was often initiated before a rational differential diagnosis was considered. This probably resulted from the (unrealistic) fear that any delay in the initiation of treatment would prejudice the patient's outcome. But the emergency treatment of life-threatening conditions, including heatstroke and hyponatremia, can safely be delayed for 1 or 2 minutes while the rectal temperature is measured and a reasonable working diagnosis is established. If the rectal temperature is greater than 41°C, then the diagnosis is heatstroke, and cooling should commence immediately. The obvious exception to the rule is cardiac arrest, which occurs uncommonly, and the diagnosis of which is unambiguous.

One reason treatment is often initiated expeditiously is that the rate of admission to the medical facility can be extremely high. For example, close to 50% of the 14,000 competitors in the Comrades Marathon complete the race in the last hour of the race. If 4% of those subjects collapse as might be expected, the average rate of admission during that period will exceed four patients per minute and is likely to be even faster in the last 10 minutes of the race when the rate of finishing accelerates further. Such high rates of admission rapidly swamp the available medical resources unless, of course, the problem has been anticipated and an appropriate action plan developed.

Another reason treatment is often initiated without a diagnosis is of the near-universal dogma that dehydration is the sole important etiological factor causing all forms of athletic collapse. Physicians who hold this belief must assume that all collapsed athletes are severely dehydrated and therefore require intravenous fluid therapy that must be initiated without delay.

Table 4.4 Guidelines for determining the severity of the collapsed athlete's condition	
Nonsevere	Severe
Immediate assessment	**Immediate assessment**
Conscious	Unconscious or altered mental state
Alert	Confused, disoriented, aggressive
Rectal temperature < 40°C	Rectal temperature > 40°C
Systolic blood pressure > 100 mm Hg	Systolic blood pressure < 100 mm Hg
Heart rate < 100 beats·min	Heart rate < 100 beats·min
Specialized assessment	**Specialized assessment**
Blood [glucose] 4 to 10 mmol·L^{-1}	Blood [glucose] < 4 to > 10 mmol·L^{-1}
Serum [sodium] 135 to 148 mmol·L^{-1}	Serum [sodium] < 135 to > 148 mmol·L^{-1}
Body weight loss 0 to 5%	Body weight loss > 10%
	Body weight loss > 2%

But race-day clinicians must be discouraged from assuming this unproven dogma (Noakes 1995; 2001a). Rather, like all patients, the collapsed athlete first deserves a rational diagnosis (Noakes 1988a; Holtzhausen and Noakes 1997) before the most appropriate therapy is initiated. There is no evidence to support the view that if the diagnosis is not readily apparent, there will be detrimental consequences if the correct therapy is withheld for a few minutes. A part of this more rational approach is an analysis of the athlete's fluid status, either under- or overhydration.

Furthermore, it is possible to manage high rates of admission to the medical facility only if those select patients who require urgent, sophisticated management receive such treatment. If all collapsed athletes are treated identically without differentiation on the basis of the nature and severity of their condition, it will never be possible to provide a medical staff sufficiently large to cope with the high rates of admission expected, especially in those distance races that are run in the heat and that include large numbers of relatively less well-trained participants (as do most of the popular large city marathons).

We have proposed the need for a triage system in which the severity and nature of each athlete's condition is rapidly assessed. The athlete can then be referred to the correct area of the medical facility for immediate and appropriate treatment. The criteria that we have developed for determining the severity of collapse are described in table 4.4. The initial assessment is made on the basis of the athlete's level of consciousness, assisted by knowledge of where in the race the athlete collapsed. It has been found that patients who are seriously ill will show alterations in their level of consciousness and will almost always collapse before completion of the race, as discussed subsequently.

Thus, the level of consciousness and site of collapse are the initial criteria used for the immediate classification and early management of EAC. Additional information can be obtained by measuring the rectal temperature, blood pressure, and heart rate, as this helps determine the severity of the condition. In longer races (longer than 25 km), when hypoglycemia is more likely, the facility to measure the blood glucose concentration with a glycometer should also be provided. In mass events of much longer duration (longer than 4 hours), including ultramarathons and ultratriathlons, it is essential that equipment for measuring the serum sodium concentration be available so that the potentially lethal condition of exercise-related hyponatremia can be diagnosed quickly. Our standard approach is that intravenous fluid therapy should only be considered after the serum sodium concentration has been measured and has been shown to be greater than 135 mmol per liter. If the value is below 130 mmol per liter, the increasing probability is that the athlete is suffering from mild to increasingly severe overhydration (Speedy, Noakes, et al. 2001e; Noakes 2002).

Diagnostic Steps for Collapsed, Unconscious Athletes

If the collapsed athlete is unconscious, then the initial differential diagnosis is between a medical condition not necessarily related to exercise—for example, cardiac arrest, grand mal epilepsy, subarachnoid hemorrhage, diabetic coma—and an exercise-related disorder—especially heatstroke, hyponatremia, or severe hypoglycemia. The latter is an uncommon cause of exercise-related coma in nondiabetic subjects.

The focus here is not on the diagnosis of medical conditions unrelated to exercise, as the differentiation of these conditions is usually obvious to experienced physicians. The critical issue in the vast majority of cases of collapse is the rapid differentiation of the serious from the benign and the expeditious initiation of the correct treatment for the serious conditions. If the patient is unconscious, the crucial initial measurement is the rectal temperature, followed by heart rate and blood pressure. If the rectal temperature is greater than 41°C, the diagnosis is heatstroke, and the patient must be cooled immediately according to the techniques already described.

If the rectal temperature is less than 40°C in an unconscious patient, if the blood pressure and pulse are not grossly abnormal, and if there is no other obvious medical condition to explain the unconsciousness, the probability is that the athlete has the hyponatremia of exercise or, rarely, another electrolyte abnormality, such as hypochloremia, also causing cerebral edema. As argued earlier, there is absolutely no evidence for the belief that dehydration, in the range measured in endurance athletes, causes unconsciousness.

The diagnosis of hyponatremia is confirmed only by measuring the serum sodium and chloride concentrations. If the diagnosis is suspected, there is little risk in delaying the diagnosis, provided that any intravenous fluids the patient receives are of a high sodium content (3% to 5% saline) and given at a very slow rate (less than 50 ml per hour), until a diagnosis is established. In most cases, the symptomatic hyponatremia resolves spontaneously as soon as the patient begins to pass copious volumes of very dilute urine. Final correction of the serum sodium concentration may take substantially longer, usually up to 24 to 48 hours.

The finding that symptomatic hyponatremia results from fluid overload (Noakes 1992b; 2000a; 2001b; 2001c; 2002; Speedy, Noakes, et al. 2001c) makes it essential that some assessment of the collapsed athlete's fluid status be performed. The recognized clinical indicators of dehydration include a loss of skin turgor, recessed eyeballs, drying of the mouth, and an inability to spit caused by inhibition of parotid secretions, which occurs at dehydration levels of greater than or equal to 5%. Fluid overload is likely if the athlete complains of feeling bloated and swollen and of vomiting clear fluid during the race. The latter indicates fluid accumulation in the stomach and small intestine and is not a feature of dehydration. Another helpful sign is that rings, race identification bracelets, and watchstraps may all feel noticeably tighter. The athlete may indeed indicate that the watchstrap had to be loosened during the race. The fit of the race bracelets worn in triathlon events is a helpful indicator, as these are fitted before the race and are usually loose-fitting. A bracelet or watch that cannot be moved easily is suggestive of fluid over-load. Visible edema over the back of the hands and in front of the tibia are also suggestive, as is the presence of water in the lungs (pulmonary edema). This may present as the coughing up of blood-stained sputum.

An athlete who is confused but has a normal rectal temperature and normal blood sodium concentrations may be hypoglycemic. Exercise-induced hypoglyce-mia occurs when liver glycogen causes liver glucose production to lag behind the rate of muscle glucose uptake by muscle from the blood. Hypoglycemia occurs more commonly in long-distance events lasting less than 4 hours, especially in athletes who fail to eat and drink sufficient carbohydrate before or during these events. During events of shorter duration, the higher exercise intensity increases the probability that factors other than hypoglycemia will initiate fatigue before the liver glycogen stores are depleted.

People who voluntarily restrict their intake of carbohydrates, usually young women with overt or covert eating disorders, are especially at risk. In our experi-ence, the development of hypoglycemia in unusual circumstances should raise the possibility of an eating disorder with long-term carbohydrate restriction. A characteristic of young female athletes with eating disorders appears to be to run long-distance races without carbohydrate replacement specifically so that they can develop a large energy deficit.

In most cases of severe hypoglycemia, the level of consciousness dictates that the glucose replacement be given intravenously as a 50% solution. Recovery is always rapid (within minutes) if hypoglycemia is the sole cause of collapse. Pa-tients who are conscious can ingest concentrated glucose solutions orally.

Diagnostic Steps for Collapsed, Conscious Athletes

By definition, these athletes are suffering from exercise-associated collapse (EAC). This condition is analogous to the classically described heat exhaustion, or heat syncope, and can be diagnosed with almost absolute certainty by asking athletes where they collapsed in the race (at or after the finish), simultaneously establish-ing that they are fully conscious and have a normal concentration span and the absence of the hyponatremic stare. In contrast, athletes with hyponatremia have difficulty concentrating and experience frequent lapses in concentration.

Nursing athletes with EAC in the head-down position is almost always dramati-cally effective, producing a more stable cardiovascular system within 30 to 90 sec-onds and, usually, the instant reversal of symptoms. This indicates that symptoms of dizziness, nausea, and vomiting frequently associated with this condition may result simply from a sudden reduction in blood pressure, including a dramatic fall in the elevated pressures maintained during exercise.

Subjects with EAC should be encouraged to ingest fluids orally during recovery. Sports drinks containing both glucose (5% to 10%) and electrolytes (Na, 10 to 20 mM) should be offered. Most athletes with EAC will be able to stand and walk un-aided within 10 to 30 minutes of appropriate treatment, in particular lying in the head-down position. They should be encouraged to leave the medical facility within that time.

Avoiding the Hazards of Sunburn

There is a growing realization that excessive exposure of the skin to the UVA and UVB bands of the ultraviolet light from the sun increases the rate at which the skin ages, as well as the likelihood of developing skin cancer. For this reason, I advise runners, especially those with skins that burn easily and tan poorly, to protect their skins from sun damage by following these precautions:

- Wear hats and sunglasses to shield the face and eyes from intense sun while running.

- Wear long-sleeved T-shirts so that the shoulders are covered. If you can see your hand through the fabric, it is too thin. This will be difficult if the day is very hot, but these are precisely the conditions likely to cause the greatest sun damage.

- Run before 10 a.m. and after 4 p.m. (that is, avoid the hours of sunshine that are the most dangerous).

- Use sunscreen lotions on all exposed skin surfaces when running in sunny conditions. The face, shoulders, arms, and legs especially need to be protected. Depending on your skin type, sunscreens with a sun protection factor (SPF) of 15 or higher may need to be used.

About 30 ml of sunscreen is needed to cover an adult's body; most people tend to use about half the optimum amount. Using a lotion with a higher SPF compensates in part for this. Sunscreens should also be used on cloudy days, as clouds do not protect from harmful UV radiation. It is especially important to cover the tops of the ears and the head if you are bald or have thinning hair. If you sweat heavily, use water-resistant sunscreen lotions and reapply them at hourly intervals to make up for the loss of protection through sweating and sponging.

COLD HAZARDS

So much attention has been paid to the dangers of heatstroke during marathon running that we have been slow to appreciate that athletes can also suffer from hazards of running in the cold.

Hypothermia

Hypothermia has long been recognized as a most serious condition, often with fatal consequences, for mountain hikers (Pugh 1966; 1967b), mountain runners, and channel swimmers (Pugh and Edholm 1955; Noakes 1985; 2000a). However, it has really only been the growth in popularity of mass-participation marathons in the northern hemisphere, especially in Britain, that has focused our attention on the risk of hypothermia developing during marathons and longer races.

The risk of hypothermia is not as great in short-distance races because they are run at a faster pace so that the metabolic rate, which determines the rate of heat production, is higher. In addition, exposure to cold is for a shorter duration, reducing the possibility of hypothermia developing.

Australian John Sutton was probably the first to consider hypothermia as the cause of death in two runners competing in a "Go-As-You-Please" race to the summit of Mount Wellington in Tasmania in 1903 (J.R. Sutton 1972). The race was held in a snowstorm with a strong wind blowing, and the runners were dressed only in "singlets and light knickers." Soon the competitors in the race were "lying over logs, on the ground, and under trees, too exhausted to continue." The deceased runners almost certainly froze to death before they could be rescued.

The first documented case of hypothermia in a modern marathon runner was described by Ledingham and his colleagues (1982), who reported a rectal temperature of 34.3°C in a runner who collapsed in the Glasgow Marathon, which was run under dry but cold conditions (dry bulb temperature 12°C) with a strong wind of 16 to 40 km per hour. Subsequently, Maughan (1985) measured the rectal temperature of 59 runners completing the 1982 Aberdeen Marathon, run under more favorable weather conditions (dry bulb temperature 12°C; dry with humidity of 75%; and a wind speed of about 26 km per hour). Despite the relatively mild conditions of the race, including the absence of rain, four runners finished the race with rectal temperatures below the normal 37°C, showing that body temperature can fall even when running in relatively mild conditions.

Our own studies have shown that even conditions in South Africa can on occasion be sufficiently unfavorable to cause hypothermia (Sandell et al. 1988). A study of all the runners admitted to the medical tent at the end of the 1985 Two Oceans Marathon, run under unusually cold conditions for the Southern Hemisphere (wet bulb globe temperature 19.8°C; rain; and a wind of 30 km per hour), showed that eight (28%) of the collapsed runners had rectal temperatures below 37°C. Despite maintaining a high running speed in excess of 17 km per hour, one very thin elite runner collapsed on the course and was brought to the medical tent, where his rectal temperature was found to be 35.0°C.

As detailed earlier in this chapter, the three factors that predispose athletes to the development of hypothermia during distance running are the environmental conditions, the athletes' clothing and body builds, and the speed at which they run.

Using the data in figure 4.8, we are able to calculate that the effective air temperatures prevailing in the three marathon races described above, in which runners became hypothermic, would have been between 1 and 3°C. Were those conditions to prevail for the duration of the race, runners running at 16 km per hour would need to wear clothing providing about 1.1 CLO units, whereas those who were reduced to a walk (5 km per hour) during the run would require approximately 2 CLO units of insulation. In reality, it is probable that most runners are unaware of the dangers of marathon running in the cold so that they fail to wear clothing that provides sufficient insulation, especially under conditions of wet, cold, and wind.

Experience with the English Channel swimmers (Pugh and Edholm 1955) has shown that body build, especially the body muscle (but also the body fat) content, is a critical factor determining the rate at which a swimmer will cool down during a long-distance swim (Noakes 2000a). I suspect that the same applies to runners: those who have little body fat and are not muscular will probably be the most affected by the cold and the most likely to become hypothermic. Frank Shorter is one such thin runner who found that he ran poorly in the cold (see chapter 6) and conversely rather well in the heat. Possibly this indicated that thin runners, like Shorter, have difficulty maintaining a normally elevated body temperature when running in the cold. In contrast, thin, light runners are at a significant advantage when running in the heat (Dennis and Noakes 1999; Kay et al. 2001).

The role of running speed in protecting against hypothermia has been discussed and is highlighted in figure 4.8. The important point to remember is that the change from running to walking has a marked effect on the clothing needed to maintain body temperature, even at relatively mild effective temperatures. Thus, clothing with at least four times as much insulation is required to maintain body temperature at rest at an effective air temperature of 0°C as when running at 16 km per hour. For this reason, it is most probable that hypothermia will occur in those marathon runners who are lean, lightly muscled, and lightly clothed and who become fatigued and are forced to walk for prolonged periods during marathon races run in effective air temperatures of less than 5°C. This condition can be prevented by ensuring that extra clothing is available should you be forced to walk when running races in cold conditions.

Frostbite

Tissues exposed to very cold temperatures, such as effective air temperatures of –35°C or lower, will freeze rapidly, and if rewarming does not occur within a short time, the frozen tissue dies, necessitating amputation. Frostbite is the classic complication of high-altitude mountain climbing so that few who climb the world's highest mountains retain all their toes and fingers. Toes and fingers are the classical sites of frostbite in mountaineers. In runners, the exposed parts of the face and the hands are most at risk if mittens are not worn. However, other more vital organs may also be in danger.

Melvin Hershkowitz, a New Jersey physician, reported in the *New England Journal of Medicine* (Hershkowitz 1977) that after 25 minutes of running at –8°C in shorts, two T-shirts, a sweater, and a rain jacket that extended just below the belt line, he developed severe pain at the tip of his penis. This forced him to curtail his run 5 minutes later, at which time the physical examination of the sensitive area indicated the presence of early frostbite. Manual rewarming rapidly returned the circulation to the affected area, thereby sparing Hershkowitz the trauma of amputation. To prevent this situation, an athletic supporter and cotton warm-up pants can be worn. Others have suggested that a spare pair of socks placed in the front of the underpants are highly effective.

FINAL WORD

For a long time runners have been advised to drink "as much as possible" to prevent fatigue and heat illness during exercise. In fact, this has been one of the most pervasive mantras of the past 15 years.

In this chapter, I have attempted to show that heat balance during exercise is regulated by a number of factors, of which fluid balance is perhaps only a minor contributor, especially when exercise is undertaken out of doors in mild to moderate environmental conditions.

Rather, the athlete's size and running speed and the environmental conditions, especially the humidity, determine the risk of heat illness. Even then, the presence of a central governor, in this case the thermostat, will usually force most athletes to stop exercising before their body temperatures reach the heatstroke range.

This overemphasis on drinking, especially during prolonged exercise, has produced an undesirable result, demonstrated by the sudden increase in the number of athletes treated for water intoxication in the past 15 years. In the past decade, many more cases of water intoxication than of heatstroke have been reported in distance runners.

The balance of modern evidence suggests that runners should avoid excessive drinking in extreme heat; drink as your thirst dictates (ad libitum) during exercise, irrespective of its duration or intensity or the environmental conditions.

Fortunately, good sense seems to have prevailed with the more widespread acceptance that the advice runners have received, especially in the United States in the past 10 years, is dangerously wrong. What we wrote in 1985 (Noakes, Goodwin, et al. 1985) seems now finally to have been accepted: ". . . advice (on fluid replacement during exercise) should be tempered with the proviso that the intake of hypotonic fluids in excess of that required to balance sweat and urine losses may be hazardous in some individuals" (p. 375).

PART II

TRAINING BASICS

aving explored the phenomena that occur within the body during running in part I, we can now put that knowledge to use in training the body to perform optimally. Part II opens with information about building a foundation for training. Newcomers to running often need a more detailed training plan than veteran runners to help them train appropriately and safely. Following the 14 steps and 15 Laws of Training outlined in chapter 5 will help any runner develop a smart, solid program. Chapter 6 proceeds from this foundation and relates how several world-class runners over the past 150 years have applied the key principles to their own training, highlighting the training ideas that seem to have brought success as well as those that seem to have failed these talented runners.

Most often, the failure of training stems from the phenomenon of overtraining—training too much for too long without allowing sufficient time to rest. Chapter 7 provides insights for recognizing the signs of overtraining and learning to avoid this common pitfall. Finally, perhaps the "final frontier" of running training is understanding the interaction of the mind and body in training and performance and discovering how to use that understanding to optimize performance. Chapter 8 explains the role of the mind in running success.

CHAPTER

5

■ ■ ■ ■ ■

Developing a Training Foundation

This chapter provides practical training advice and is particularly written for those who have just started running. More experienced runners—or those who want more specific training details for 10-km races, half-marathons, marathons, and ultramarathons—should skip to part III or, alternatively, refer to the books of Gardner and Purdy (1970), Henderson (1977), Daws (1977), Osler (1978), Lydiard and Gilmour (1978), Galloway (1984; 1996), Glover and Schuder (1983), Martin and Coe (1997), S. Edwards (1997), Daniels (1998), and Hawley and Burke (1998). I have steered clear of giving any detailed training program of my own, apart from the one for novice runners in table 5.8 later in this chapter, as my personal inclination has always been to train according to a general plan and to run each day as I feel. But I am equally aware that some runners benefit from a more regimented approach.

Many neophytes make the common error of training too much, too soon, and they thereby run a high risk of becoming injured early on. It is for this reason that they require a more detailed training program.

The tendency is for neophytes to want to run slightly more each day to prove that their fitness is improving. However, the ideal prescribed training program should ensure a low training load for the first three to six months of training to enable the body to adapt gradually to the added mechanical loading. An added advantage of following a strict program at the outset is that it helps induce the discipline necessary for long-term running success.

Here follows advice for the runner who is just beginning.

STEP I: ANALYZE
YOUR MOTIVATION AND DISCIPLINE

When starting out, beginners may not find running particularly easy or enjoyable. It takes great motivation and personal discipline to survive the first three months before running becomes a habit controlled by the subconscious. I suspect that this process is part of the subconscious programming that occurs in the central governor, discussed in chapter 2. It is in this learning process that the subconscious governor begins to discover the body's capabilities. Interestingly, once the novice has been through this process, it need never be repeated. Irrespective of the duration for which you do not run, be it months, years, or even decades, you will never again need to go through this learning process; starting to run will never again be as difficult, regardless of how unfit you may have become. This suggests that the neural processes of running become hardwired into the subconscious, much as does the ability to ride a bicycle. Since this process takes time, one consequence is that many beginners often fall by the wayside, as they are unable to look beyond the glamour of running and are totally unaware of this unexpected demand of the sport.

I suspect that those who find it easiest to stick to a running program have previously exhibited self-efficacy and perseverance, are mentally healthy, and tend to succeed in whatever they put their minds to (Sallis et al. 1992; Du Charme and Brawley 1995). Having been successful previously in sport or, alternatively, having a reasonable measure of running ability is probably a very important determinant of who will most likely stick with the running program (Dennison et al. 1988). Other factors predicting adaptation to and maintenance of an exercise program include years of education and support from family and friends (Sallis et al. 1992). In contrast, it has been found that those who drop out are more likely to have failed previously and may have low levels of self-esteem (Lobstein et al. 1983). Indeed, studies have shown that cardiac patients who dropped out of exercise programs to which they had been referred after suffering heart attacks were more depressed, hypochondriacal, anxious, and introverted and had lower ego strength than did those who remained in such programs (Blumenthal et al. 1982b). Another factor is each person's capacity to accept responsibility for determining his or her own fate.

At present, our knowledge of how best to help those likely to drop out of a regular running program is limited so that it essentially becomes an individual problem for each runner. What is important is that you realize your weaknesses and that you get others to help and support you. In particular, plan to run in a group of people who meet regularly and who will assist in motivating you. Unfortunately, many running clubs have not yet evolved a system whereby they guide novice runners through these first difficult steps. I hope that this will change in the future. John Martin and Patricia Dubbert from the University of Mississippi at Jackson (Martin and Dubbert 1984) suggest the following strategies to assist the beginner.

Goal setting. It is always important to set achievable, short-term goals in training (in respect to either distance or time run each day or week) and also to have long-term goals, like running in a fun-run, 10-km race, half-marathon, or marathon. New runners might find it useful to keep a logbook to help them set goals and to reinforce successful behaviors. (See Law 14 in the section describing Step 5, later in this chapter.)

Shaping. Shaping is a process in which a target behavior (that is, becoming fit enough to become a competitive runner) is broken down into a series of steps that eventually achieve the desired goal. Martin and Dubbert suggest starting with a simple, easily performed task. In running, the initial shaping goal during the first 8 to 12 weeks should therefore not be to become fit, but to develop the habit of regular exercise. Thus, some initial shaping strategies might include the following:

- Allocating a certain amount of time each day for your running. This should include time to prepare for the run and to shower and dress after exercise. Usually, a total of 45 to 60 minutes will be required for a reasonable session.
- Deciding what time of day is best for your running. Lunchtime is ideal but may be impractical. Afternoon is the next best but may result in you arriving home too late. Early morning may be the most practical as it interferes least with other aspects of your life, but it is also the most demanding: this is when the body, as a result of the circadian (24-hour) variation in exercise capacity, is the least well prepared for exercise.
- Running with a group. Try to find others with whom you can share the joys and tribulations of the new challenge.

Reinforcement control. Any encouragement that reinforces the exercise habit will be beneficial—such as running in a group, experiencing the benefits of the exercise, and, in particular, enjoying increased physical fitness. Running is a social activity, and the more benefit you draw from that social interaction, the easier it will become to keep running.

Stimulus control. This method uses stimuli or prompts to encourage exercise—perhaps laying out running clothing the night before, wearing exercise clothes around the house, or always having exercise attire in the car. Associating with regular exercisers and discussing personal training and performances, as well as reading about running, can also increase the desire to exercise.

Associative and dissociative strategies. This concept is discussed in greater detail in chapter 8. In short, when running, either think about everything but what you are doing (dissociation) or concentrate purely on the activity and how your body feels as you run (association). In general, it is believed that competitive runners do best if they associate during races. However, it also appears that novice runners do best if they dissociate. As soon as they start associating—thinking about their running and how their bodies are hurting—they are less likely to continue exercising. Running in pleasant and varied surroundings, rather than on monotonous roads and tracks, helps the dissociation process.

Dissociation is generally easiest when the athlete is running at relatively low exercise intensities. But as the exercise intensity increases or fatigue develops, the mind starts associating naturally, especially when the run is either so hard or so long that pain intrudes. By running either faster or slower, novice runners will soon learn how to switch naturally between associative and dissociative mental states.

Coping thoughts. As a novice runner, learn positive self-talk methods (discussed more in chapter 8) such as "I'm doing well to exercise at all today since I wasn't looking forward to it," "I'm nearly halfway," or "I'm nearly finished . . . let me notice what's going on around me—that sunset is beautiful." At first, it is better to be excessively self-congratulatory about your efforts. Stricter self-examination can be instituted once the exercise habit is ingrained.

If you are a highly dedicated person, then the problem is the reverse. Rather than doing too little, you are likely to aim too high, too soon. It is important to set realistic goals and to start gradually. Be aware that, in the beginning, the mind, heart, and lungs are infinitely stronger than are the bones, tendons, and ligaments of the lower limb, and a serious running injury is virtually guaranteed to befall anyone who starts training too intensively too soon.

STEP 2:
DECIDE IF YOU NEED MEDICAL CLEARANCE

A question that inevitably arises is whether people taking up exercise in middle age should have an exhaustive medical evaluation before they start. Ideally, the answer should be an unqualified yes, because it is obviously desirable that any medical problem that could be aggravated by running be identified early.

This form of logic led the American College of Sports Medicine (ACSM) to advise that anyone over 35 years of age who planned to start an exercise program should have a full medical examination, including an electrocardiogram, recorded before, during, and after maximal exercise (that is, a maximal exercise or stress test). In addition, the ACSM felt that people under 35 who had certain risk factors for heart disease (a family history of heart disease, a history of heavy smoking, high blood pressure, high blood fat levels—cholesterol or triglycerides or both) should also undergo this test. The purpose of the maximal exercise test was to identify all those who had heart disease and were therefore at high risk of dying suddenly and unexpectedly during exercise.

Subsequent research has shown this method to be inconclusive and prohibitively expensive. When formulating its guidelines in the 1970s, the ACSM was unaware that maximal exercise testing was a relatively insensitive method of identifying those people who have the type of heart disease likely to cause sudden death during exercise. Worse, maximal exercise testing also identifies a group of people who do not have heart disease even though their electrocardiographic response to exercise is identical to that of people with the disease; thus, the maximal exercise test cannot diagnose heart disease conclusively.

One of the best ways to determine without doubt whether or not a person has serious heart disease is to perform coronary angiography, a specialized procedure performed only in the cardiac unit of a major hospital. During this procedure, a small plastic tube (catheter) is introduced into a large leg or arm artery and carefully guided until it enters, in sequence, each of the arteries supplying the heart muscle, the coronary arteries. A radio-opaque dye is then injected down each coronary artery, and pictures are taken as the dye travels down the arteries. Any irregularities or atherosclerotic plaques in the arteries are shown as narrowings, which indicate the presence of coronary atherosclerosis (hardening of the arteries), the disease most likely to cause sudden death in older athletes (those over 40) during exercise.

However, coronary angiography does have some significant limitations. It is a specialized procedure requiring admission to the hospital, and it is not without risk. For every 1000 coronary angiograms performed, there is likely to be one death attributable to the procedure. In addition, coronary angiography only identifies those people who have coronary atherosclerosis. If we were to perform coronary angiography on all male runners, we would expect that between 20% and 30% (the national average for most western countries) would have coronary atherosclerosis of varying grades of severity. Yet, our data show that very few runners (possibly one in 6000 to 7000) develop cardiac problems during any single year (P.D. Thompson et al. 1982; Noakes et al. 1984b). At present, we are unable to identify specifically those few runners with severe coronary atherosclerosis who are at risk of sudden death during exercise, from that much larger group of other runners who have equally severe coronary atherosclerosis but for whom, for reasons unknown, exercise does not pose such an inordinate risk of sudden death (Ciampricotti et al. 1990; Siskovick et al. 1991).

Bearing in mind the risks involved in these medical tests and their present costs, the National Heart, Lung and Blood Institute in 1983 formulated a set of eight guidelines advising anyone who conforms to one or more of the eight criteria below to consult a doctor before beginning any exercise program. Therefore, it is advisable to consult a doctor if any of the following are true:

1. You are over the age of 60 and are not accustomed to vigorous exercise.
2. You have a family history of premature coronary artery disease (under the age of 55).
3. You frequently have pains or pressure in the left side of the neck or the left shoulder or arm (as distinct from a "stitch") during or immediately after exercise.
4. You often feel faint, have spells of severe dizziness, or experience extreme breathlessness after mild exertion.
5. You do not know whether your blood pressure is normal or have high blood pressure that your doctor confirms is not under control.
6. You have heart trouble or a heart murmur or have had a heart attack.
7. You have bone or joint problems such as arthritis (confirmed by your doctor).
8. You have a medical condition not mentioned here that might need special attention in an exercise program (for example, insulin-dependent diabetes).

I agree with this advice and would only advise exercise testing for older athletes and for those with any symptoms suggestive of heart disease. Indeed, if there is any suggestion that the athlete has symptoms that might be due to heart disease, it is essential that a full medical evaluation, including maximum exercise testing, be performed so that the unexplained symptoms are reproduced (chapter 14).

However, there are ways in which people can protect themselves without recourse to medicine. First, you must start the exercise program gradually and train gently. If heart disease is present, it will show itself when the heart is forced to work harder than it is able.

Second, you must be aware of those specific symptoms that might develop during exercise and that indicate heart disease. In the largest collection of cases of sudden deaths and heart attacks in marathon runners reported in a scientific paper (Noakes et al. 1984b; Noakes 1987b), it was found that the majority (81%) had warning symptoms that they chose to ignore. These symptoms included severe chest pain and shortness of breath sufficiently severe to prevent their normal running. Despite this, a number continued to train and even to race; three even completed the 90-km Comrades Marathon despite marked chest pain and shortness of breath.

In two of the runners studied, the symptoms of heart disease were unfortunately misinterpreted by their doctors, who may have concluded that because the runners were so "fit" they could not have had heart disease. This error could possibly also be traced to those medical zealots who popularized the incorrect theory that marathon running prevents heart disease (Bassler 1977).

The message is simple: before starting any exercise program, check the eight starting questions provided by the National Heart, Lung and Blood Institute. If your answers to these questions indicate that it is necessary, visit your general practitioner, who will decide what else needs to be done. But regardless of whether or not you initially consulted your doctor, you should do so immediately if you develop any of the symptoms described earlier, either during or after exercise. If your doctor considers it likely that the symptoms derive from the heart, you will be advised to be evaluated exhaustively in a hospital cardiac unit, and it is likely that you will undergo at least a maximal exercise test and possibly coronary angiography as well.

But even if everyone were to follow religiously the guidelines described here, there would unfortunately still be runners who die suddenly during or after exercise. There are two main reasons for this.

1. Coronary atherosclerosis, the form of heart disease most commonly associated with sudden death during exercise, can cause death within minutes when a previously stable atherosclerotic plaque in the coronary arteries (supplying the heart muscle) suddenly becomes unstable (Goldstein et al. 2000). This occurs, for example, when a plaque that is not sufficiently large to interfere with the blood flow in a coronary artery (and does not therefore cause symptoms resulting from inadequate blood flow through that artery to the heart muscle) suddenly ruptures, exposing the center of the plaque to the circulating blood. This rapidly initiates the formation of a blood clot at the site of the original plaque. If this clot fills the entire blood vessel, then blood flow in the affected coronary artery ceases. As a result, the blood flow to that part of the heart muscle normally nourished by that specific artery stops. This initiates a heart attack or, in some cases, a fatally abnormal heart rhythm. Thus, people without symptoms of heart disease but with unstable coronary atherosclerotic plaques are always at risk of a sudden plaque rupture inducing sudden death, even in a coronary artery only mildly affected by atherosclerosis.

   Interestingly, exercise training, drugs that lower the blood cholesterol concentration (in particular, the statins), and anti-inflammatory drugs (such as aspirin) all help stabilize atherosclerotic plaques, thereby reducing the risk of plaque rupture.

2. The next most common cause of sudden death during exercise is a form of heart disease known as hypertrophic cardiomyopathy, which is extremely difficult to detect medically. It frequently does not cause any symptoms until the fatal event. In addition, the enlarged heart of the athlete with hypertrophic cardiomyopathy may, using current methods of detection, be difficult to distinguish from the normally enlarged heart of the athlete.

STEP 3:
CHOOSE APPROPRIATE RUNNING SHOES

The next step is to choose an appropriate pair of running shoes. This is easier said than done. The choice of running shoes has become enormously complex, and there are probably in excess of a hundred different models on the market. This problem is further compounded by our inability to define those minor individual differences in body structure that determine which shoes are best for a particular person (Cavanagh 1980). Nor, surprisingly, are we yet certain of the exact characteristics of running shoes that prevent, cause, or cure different running injuries. In the face of such uncertainty, I feel that the choice of the appropriate running shoe is best determined by two principal factors: whether you are a novice and whether you are injured. If you are uninjured, the choice of shoe will be determined by whether you run enough to warrant expensive shoes and by the purpose for which you want to use the shoes. If you are injured, your choice will depend on the type of injury you have.

Shoes for Novices

It is always best to start running in a relatively modestly priced pair of shoes bought from a reputable running shoe dealer. If, after some months of running, an injury occurs, the nature of the injury will indicate which type of shoe is likely to help cure that injury and prevent similar injuries in the future. (This is discussed in detail in chapter 14.) Even if you are to enter the sports shop prepared to buy an inexpensive running shoe, it helps to know something about the different features of running shoes and about how these features affect the performance of any particular model.

Shoe Anatomy

Running shoes have five major anatomical features, as shown in figure 5.1: outersole, midsole, slip or board lasting, heel-counter, and other devices—either in the shoe (arch or shank supports) or in the midsole (variable density midsoles)—that help reduce the excessive muscular activity associated with abnormal ankle pronation

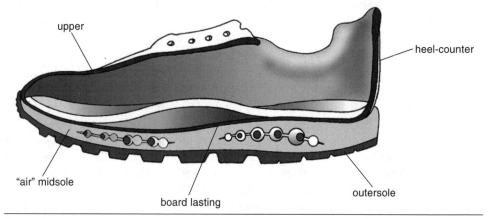

Figure 5.1   Anatomical features of the typical running shoe.

(the excessive inward rolling of the ankle and forefoot during the early part of the stance phase of running; see also chapter 14). Also important (and discussed later in this section) are the nature of the shoe last (whether it is straight or curve lasted) and the degree of medial and lateral midsole heel flaring.

Outersole

The outersole comes into direct contact with the ground. Today, outersoles are made from a variety of materials and are of different designs. The main design innovation in the past 25 years was the development of the waffle sole. The term originated after coach Bill Bowermann (at the University of Oregon at Eugene) filled a waffle iron with urethane, producing the first outersole with this characteristic pattern.

The most important features of the outersole are that it not wear down too quickly and that it provide traction. Its greatest durability is ideally in the areas of greatest wear, particularly at the outer heel edge. Durable material is not used uniformly throughout the outersole, because the more durable the material, the heavier it is. Thus, the nonuniform outersole saves weight. The only benefit of a soft and therefore nondurable outersole is that it provides additional cushioning, which may be useful to those runners for whom exceptional shock absorption is essential.

Waffle soles were originally designed for cross-country running, not road running, as they give better traction on uneven ground (Cavanagh 1980). They also increase shock absorption. Today, however, most modern outersoles are designed with patterns similar to the original waffle design.

The life expectancy of a shoe is determined more by the compression of the midsole than by the wear to the outersole. The midsoles of most shoes, with the exception of those using air or other noncompressible materials, wear out after about 500 to 700 km of use. Thus, the optimum life expectancy of most running shoes is probably between 500 and 1000 km.

If you start to notice wear at the heel of your outersole, it is not necessary to replace the shoes unless it threatens to go right through to the midsole; the heels wear to accommodate the natural heel strike of the athlete. The athlete whose foot lands with the heel in marked supination, so that the heel strikes the ground at an increased angle, tends to show heavier wear at the heel. To repatch such a heel constantly prevents proper adaptations of the shoe to the athlete's particular heel strike pattern. You are probably better off allowing the outersole to wear out completely, even exposing the midsole.

Midsole

The midsole—the heart of the shoe—is the feature that I always notice first. The most important feature of the midsole is the degree of softness or hardness. The midsole has three functions:

1. To absorb the shock of the landing of the heel (heel strike) and of the front of the foot (forefoot strike)
2. To resist excessive inward rotation of the ankle (pronation) as the foot progresses from heel strike to toe-off (the belief that excessive muscular activity produced by this exaggerated movement causes running injuries is detailed in chapter 14)
3. To flex at a point about two-thirds from the heel, as the heel starts to come off the ground leading to toe-off

Before the mid-1970s, midsole material was made only from rubber, which has the dual disadvantages of being heavy and absorbing shock relatively poorly. In 1974 Jerry Turner, then of the Brooks Shoe Company, contracted a chemical engineer, David Schwaber, to produce a lighter material with better shock-absorbing properties (Cavanagh 1980). The result was a compound called ethylene vinyl acetate (EVA). Tiny gas bubbles are trapped in the EVA when it is cooled at high pressure. These bubbles make the material light and provide good shock-absorbing properties. The major disadvantage is that, with wear, the tiny gas bubbles are expelled from the EVA, which flattens out, becomes harder, and absorbs shock less well. When the EVA compacts down unevenly, either in the heel or in the midsole, the shoe distorts badly, and this may be an important cause of injury. Another problem arising from the manufacturing process is that it is difficult to produce EVA of consistent hardness. As a result, the quality of the midsole can vary from shoe to shoe. For these reasons, it is essential that prospective buyers check the

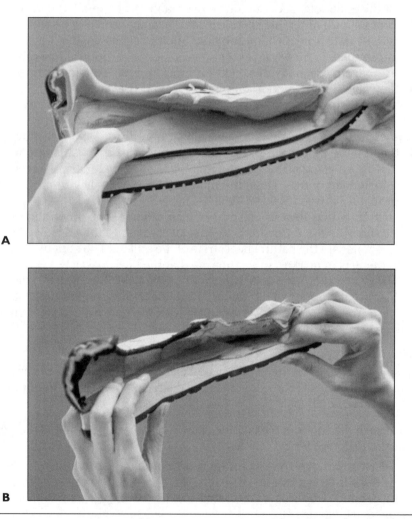

Figure 5.2   The thumb compression test. A hard or firm midsole compresses very little (A); a softer midsole compresses more, providing greater shock absorption (B).

midsole hardness of all the shoes they buy and learn to use the thumb compression test (figure 5.2) to test the midsole hardness that best suits them.

In this test, the midsole at both the heel and forefoot is squeezed between the fingers of both hands, and the relative hardness of the midsole is estimated. The greater the degree of midsole indentation produced by this method, the softer the shoe and, therefore, the more shock the shoe can absorb, but the more quickly it will tend to compact down. Conversely, the less indentation caused by the thumb compression test, the harder the shoe and the less shock it will absorb, but the less likely it will be to compact down rapidly.

I have already mentioned that the midsole must combine a capacity for shock absorption with an ability to resist the excessive muscular activity induced by exaggerated ankle pronation. It must also provide adequate flexibility. Yet, to some extent, two of these characteristics are mutually exclusive. On the one hand, a midsole with good shock absorption will be soft and therefore have good flexibility but very poor pronation control. On the other hand, a midsole that prevents excessive muscular activity caused by exaggerated pronation will be hard and inflexible and will have poor shock-absorbing characteristics.

In an attempt to compensate for these mutually exclusive characteristics, shoe manufacturers have used midsoles of differing hardness in different areas: a soft, shock-absorbing material is sometimes used along the outer heel border and under the ball of the foot to increase shock absorption and flexibility, and a firmer material along the inner border of the shoe, extending from heel to midfoot, to control pronation.

By and large, these techniques have been successful. The only problem that has not been effectively dealt with is that of the midsole underneath the ball of the foot. This area does not absorb the highest forces during landing—that is done by the heel—but it is exposed to moderately high pressure for a much longer time. Thus, it tends to compact down even more than the heel. Yet, it must be soft enough to allow flexibility and good shock absorption.

The Nike Company came up with one potential solution to this problem in the form of the revolutionary Nike Tailwind, first released in 1979 and rereleased in 1999. In this shoe, the midsole contained a series of five polyurethane tubes extending from heel to forefoot, into which Freon gas was injected at a pressure of about three atmospheres (Cavanagh 1980). While this shoe ultimately proved unsatisfactory because it had poor rear foot control, its progeny over the past 20 years have clearly shown that the air sole does not compact down as quickly as does conventional EVA or other midsole materials. However, the air sole does not extend to the forefoot in all these shoes. If the air sole is present only in the heel, the EVA under the forefoot is still prone to compaction in those runners who land heavily on the forefoot. In 1987, Asics running shoes introduced a gel-containing midsole that, like the air midsole, resists compaction, yet it has a shock-absorbing capacity that is equivalent, if not superior, to that of EVA. Other major shoe manufacturers, including Reebok, Converse, Hi-Tec, Saucony, and Turntec, responded by introducing so-called energy return systems to their midsoles (see chapter 14).

In summary, the features of the midsole that require consideration are its hardness and whether or not it is made of mixed material. As we shall see, runners who require shock absorption in their running shoes because they have a "rigid" lower limb structure must look for shoes with soft midsoles; those with mobile feet need firmer shoes (chapter 14).

Slip or Board Last

When running shoes are made, the nylon material that constitutes the shoe upper—the part that covers the foot—is stitched together, and its lower part is glued onto the top of the midsole. If this part of the upper is stuck directly to the midsole and no additional material overlies it, the shoe is said to be slip lasted. Alternatively, if a brown-colored board overlies and hides the tucked-under portion of the upper, the shoe is said to be board lasted (see figure 5.1).

Board lasting increases the ability of the shoe to resist pronation. The board may extend from heel to toe, in which case the board lasting is said to be conventional, or it may end just behind the ball of the foot, in which case we speak of partial or combination lasting. The benefit of partial board lasting is that it does not reduce flexibility in the forefoot, yet it retains some ability to resist ankle pronation. Figure

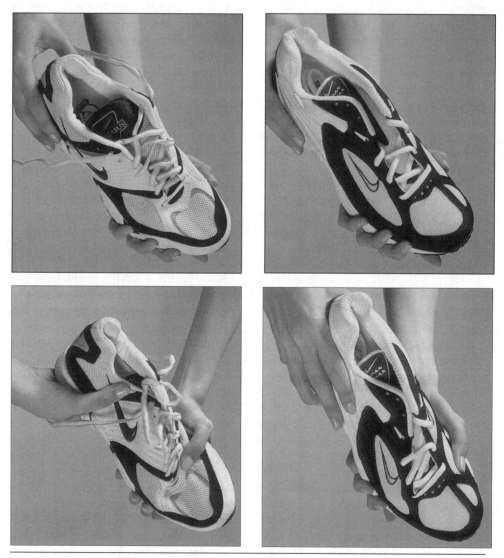

Figure 5.3 The Noakes Running Shoe Pronation Testing Technique. The shoe on the left is easily twisted in the vertical plane, whereas the shoe on the right is designed to resist rotation in the vertical plan, analogous to pronation in the ankle joint.

5.3 demonstrates a simple but useful technique for testing a shoe's pronation-resisting qualities. In general, board lasted shoes will benefit those runners who require shoes that control the excessive muscular activity associated with exaggerated ankle pronation, whereas slip lasted shoes are best for those with rigid feet that require as much movement as possible.

Heel-Counter

The heel-counter is made from a firm thermoplastic material that is molded into the correct shape during a special heating process (Cavanagh 1980). Some heel-counters extend further on the inner than on the outer side of the shoe, and today

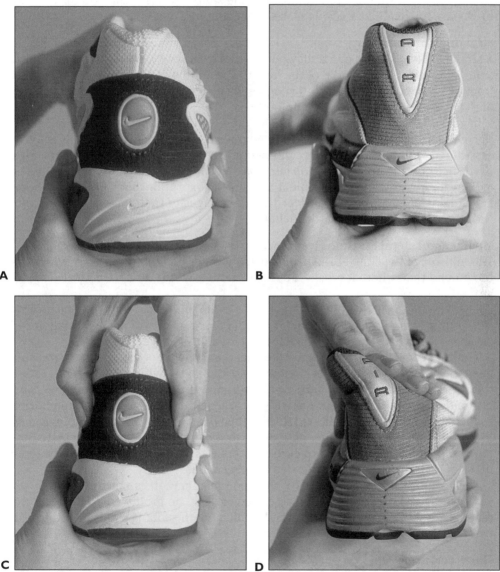

Figure 5.4   Testing the strength of the heel-counter of the running shoe. The heel-counter in *A* and *B* resists deformation better than the shoe in *C* and *D* and would probaby control the excessive muscular activity associated with ankle pronation more effectively.

most are associated with special stabilizing structures that tend to bind the heel-counter more firmly to the midsole. The aim of the heel-counter is to reduce ankle pronation. The athlete who requires a shoe that will limit this movement should obviously choose a shoe with a strong heel-counter.

There are two ways to test the strength of the heel-counter. First, pinch the middle of the heel-counter on its inner and outer edges between the thumb and the index and second fingers of your dominant hand (figure 5.4). Determine how much pressure is required to distort the heel-counter toward the center of the shoe. Then, holding the heel-counter as before, grasp the midsole of the shoe in the palm of the other hand and determine how much torque is required to distort the heel-counter to the inside or to the outside of the shoe. The less distortion produced by these maneuvers, the stronger the heel-counter.

Straight or Curved Last

A straight lasted shoe is one that, when viewed from below, is symmetrical around a line drawn from the middle of the heel to the middle of the toe. In contrast, the front of a curved (banana) lasted shoe bends inside a line drawn from the middle of the heel to the middle of the midfoot.

In general, because it contains considerable additional midsole material under the midfoot, a straight lasted shoe will help resist the excessive muscular activity associated with ankle pronation and should therefore be used by runners who need such control. In contrast, the curve lasted shoe is of benefit to those athletes looking for increased foot movement and shock absorption. Such athletes usually have high-arched feet, tend to wear the outer edges of their shoe soles, and run with their toes pointing inward (toeing in).

Medial and Lateral Midsole Heel Flares

The midsole of the shoe at the heel is usually wider on both sides where it meets the ground than where it meets the foot—in other words, it is flared from foot to ground.

The flare on the inside of the shoe resists ankle pronation; the flare on the outside probably increases the muscular activity associated with ankle pronation because it acts as a lever, forcing the foot inward at heel strike.

Thus, it seems likely that the medial heel flare may be of value to runners who need to limit the abnormal muscular activity associated with ankle pronation, but the lateral flare is probably more of a hindrance than a help. Indeed when Nike introduced the LDV 1000, a shoe with an exaggerated lateral flare, a number of runners using the shoe developed the iliotibial band friction syndrome (Cavanagh 1980). At the time, our running patients with this injury were most fascinated by our advice that if they wished to cure their injuries, they should cut off the lateral flares of their still new and expensive running shoes.

The result of this experiment by the shoe manufacturers ensured that shoes with excessive lateral heel flares would never again be produced. Rather, the extent of lateral heel flares has decreased on all modern running shoes over the past two decades.

Other Features

There are a number of other less important features that are worthy of note.

Uppers. Most modern shoe uppers are made of nylon or materials with similar properties. Leather tends to stretch once wet and needs to be dried slowly, so it's not ideal.

Additional arch support. Additional arch support systems are provided in some running shoes, as shown in figure 5.1. By and large, these systems offer too little to help runners who pronate excessively but may assist those with only minor degrees of excessive ankle pronation. In general, however, this is a cosmetic feature. Runners who pronate excessively usually require custom-made orthotics to control the excessive muscular activity associated with this exaggerated ankle movement.

Achilles tendon protector. The Achilles tendon protector is the extension of the material at the top of the heel-counter. Although some suggest that this protector may be the cause of inflammation in the Achilles tendon, there is no scientific support for this theory. However, should the protector cause discomfort, simply cut it off, as it does not affect the function of the shoe in any way.

Method of lacing. The way in which a shoe is laced may affect its comfort. The two most common lacing methods are variable-width lacing, in which there are two rows of nonaligned eyelet holes—this allows the athlete to choose either a narrow or a wide lacing system—and speed lacing, in which originally plastic but now cloth D-shaped or circular rings are substituted for the conventional leather eyelets. The friction between the plastic or cloth and the lace is considerably less than between lace and leather, making lacing quicker. Although pressure distribution is said to be more even with the D rings, plastic D rings are hard and can cause considerable pressure on the top of the foot, which explains why they have largely been replaced by cloth in modern running shoes.

Ensuring Proper Fit

Having decided which model of shoe you are going to buy, make sure that it fits properly.

✔ Always test the fit of new shoes in the afternoon and buy shoes slightly larger than your conventional shoe size; the foot swells about one half size during the day and during running. To test whether the shoe is the correct size, you should be able to fit the width of the index finger between the end of the longest toe (this is not always the big toe!) and the front end of the shoe upper.

✔ Make sure there is sufficient height in the toe-box to allow free up-and-down movement of the toes. Athletes with very wide or very narrow feet need to look to manufacturers whose normal width range tends to be either broader or narrower than the average running shoe. The most important width fitting is over the middle (bridge) of the foot.

✔ The shoe should feel comfortable as soon as you walk on it. A shoe that feels uncomfortable in the shop will simply become more so on the road. If possible, jog in the shop or outside to test the shoe.

✔ Make sure your heel does not slip out of the heel-counter of the shoe at toe-off.

Shoes for Experienced, Uninjured Runners

If you are a novice and have been running for some time without an injury, you eventually become an uninjured nonnovice runner, and the choice of the second pair of shoes requires several new considerations. If you suffer an injury that may be related to your previous choice of running shoe, then your choice of shoe may be determined by a different set of factors. These are detailed in chapter 14.

Uninjured runners fall into two categories: those who are at risk of injury but who are not yet running enough to become injured and those fortunate few who can do whatever they like without ever becoming injured. This latter group includes many experienced runners. If you happen to fit into this group, your choice of shoe can be made entirely without recourse to the information contained here. One way for uninjured novices to check whether they may be injury-prone is to try the pinch test. The pinch test is effective because damaged tissues become tender to the touch long before they actually cause pain to be felt during or after running. A feeling of tenderness or discomfort, either when the Achilles tendon is pinched between the thumb and forefinger or when firm pressure is applied along the borders of the shin-bone (the tibia) or the knee-cap, indicates trouble. If this is allowed to go unchecked, the result may be a debilitating injury.

Tenderness in any of these areas indicates, among other things, that you are training harder than your tissues, usually the bones and tendons, can tolerate. In addition, there is likely to be a biomechanical imbalance somewhere in the lower limb. The reason for this might be that the foot is pronating either too much or too little, in which case you should wear a shoe with features that either restrict or alternatively promote the muscular activity associated with different degrees of ankle pronation (chapter 14). Usually this finding also indicates that you need to modify your training, often by reducing the total training volume and by introducing more rest days.

It is important not to race in shoes that are either too light or too worn out. The muscles normally provide a good measure of overall shock absorption during running, but near the end of a long training run or race they become too exhausted to help so that the shoe is left to absorb the shock unaided. A shoe that feels adequate at the start of the run may not be optimum when left to cope without the help of the muscles.

All running shoes with EVA midsoles have a limited life expectancy—a probable maximum of six months of daily wear—before their ability to absorb shock or control ankle movement is lost. Therefore, it is advisable to change these shoes every six months or so.

Runners frequently ask whether they should train in shoes that are heavier than the ones in which they normally race. The weight of the training shoe probably does not make any difference to the overall training effect because the weight differences are so negligible. Distance and speed are the factors that count in training, and shoes should be chosen on the basis of the comfort and protection they provide. Shoes for cross-country training and racing can sacrifice some cushioning and should have a thin midsole, especially at the heel, to increase stability on uneven ground. Shoes for high mileage training or ultramarathon racing need more cushioning. Joggers who train fewer than three times per week or who run less than 20 km per week probably do not need the additional protection built into the very expensive running shoes, although they may if they become injured.

As far as different brands or models of shoes are concerned, if you are comfortable in a particular brand, you should stay with it. I am comfortable in only a small range of shoes. A number of other shoes that seem to have identical characteristics to these shoes are, for no apparent reason, simply not comfortable. Stay with the shoes that feel comfortable, and choose shoes that are appropriate for racing and training at different distances.

Many (uninjured) runners who are unable to justify the high price of modern running shoes ask how the great runners of the past were able to do so much running in the ordinary-looking walking shoes worn by Clarence de Mar and Emil Zatopek or the 7s.6d. plimsolls (canvas tackies) used by Jim Peters. My answer, right or wrong, is that in those days the top runners had undergone a vigorous process of self-selection. Only those with perfect biomechanical function were able to survive training; those with less than perfect function were soon injured and dropped the sport. Today, many runners who have very bad biomechanics are able to run prodigious distances only because of the very real improvement in the design of running shoes. In the past, they would simply have had to stop running because of recurring injuries.

Recently, I had the interesting opportunity of advising Wally Hayward (chapter 6) about what running shoes he should choose. In his first 50 years of running in canvas shoes, he had few injuries besides recurrent calf muscle tears that probably bore little relationship to shoe choice. Since he had been running in modern shoes, however, he had suffered a series of knee injuries. Following the reasoning outlined above, I advised him to go back to plimsolls, but with an elevated heel. He seemed perfectly happy with that advice. More important, his cheaper shoes allowed him to continue running without developing the same injury.

STEP 4: CHOOSE APPROPRIATE CLOTHING

As highlighted in chapter 4, the key is to dress as lightly as possible when running. When it is warm, a pair of shorts and a porous T-shirt are likely to be all that is required. Sleeveless shirts are ideal in that they are much cooler than T-shirts, though they do expose more skin to the dangers of sunburn. A track suit should only be worn when the temperature is near zero, when there is a strong, cold wind blowing, or when the athlete is trying to acclimatize to hot-weather running (chapter 4).

Most authorities advise active women to wear specially designed sports bras to minimize breast injury and soreness during strenuous activity. Yet, there are few scientific studies of which sports bras are best for use during exercise. Lorentzen and Lawson (1987) compared the ability of eight different sports bras in the United States to control breast motion during running. Not unexpectedly, they showed that large-breasted women required more rigidly constructed bras than did small-breasted women. They suggested that runners should wear bras with firm, non-slip, nonstretch straps connected directly or almost directly to a nonelastic cup; that the bra should be of firm, durable construction and should have no irritating seams or fasteners next to the skin; and that the silhouette should hold the breasts in a rounded shape close to the body.

Additional criteria proposed by C.L. Wells (1991) are that the material used should be absorptive, nonallergenic, and nonabrasive; that the straps should be wide, nonelastic, and designed in such a way that they do not slip off the shoulders during movement; and that the base of the bra should be made of a wide cloth band or similar material, to prevent riding up of the bra over the breasts during running. Sports bras are sometimes not available in small cup sizes; they may not be necessary in such cases.

STEP 5: LEARN THE 15 LAWS OF TRAINING

Before the development in the early 1970s of modern sports science as a legitimate academic discipline, we knew very little about the real factors that determine running ability or about how the body adapts to training. As you may have noticed while reading chapters 1 through 4, most of the definitive work in this area was done in the last two decades. As a result, virtually all the ideas about training that accumulated over the first 150 years of the sport (since the mid-1800s) are based on the intuition and personal observations of many individual athletes and their coaches. Few of these ideas have been subjected to independent scientific evaluation; they owe their truth only to the perceived credibility of the person making the claims or to untested observation that, when applied to many athletes on many different occasions, these training methods seem to produce the desired result of improved athletic performance.

In writing this section, I read a wide selection of the more readily accessible writings on training and racing by most of the outstanding coaches and athletes of the past 150 years. When combined with what is now known about the physiology of human performance and how the body adapts to training, this information led me to propose that there are 15 basic laws of athletic training that apply to all runners. These will now be introduced. Chapter 6 includes some additional refinements that are probably more relevant to elite athletes wishing to perform optimally for extended periods (years to decades). These ideas may also be of value to other competitive athletes seeking to make the most of their running careers.

Arthur Newton's Contributions to Training

As I researched the writings of the pioneering runners and coaches of the late nineteenth and early twentieth centuries, it became increasingly clear that one, the Englishman Arthur Newton (whose athletic career is described in chapter 6), was the first to describe in the English language a set of training ideas that modern experience has shown to be essentially correct. Newton's ideas evolved between 1922 and 1935, the 13 years he ran competitively. It is not difficult to understand why Newton was the first to write of his experiences in such detail. He began his international running career at the advanced age of 38, so that he retired from running and perhaps from other professional responsibilities when in his early fifties. As a result, he was able to concentrate on this writing, which, besides his remarkable athletic achievements, became his legacy. It is clear that there were nine aspects of training about which he frequently wrote. I have used his own words to describe how he understood these nine laws (marked by * below). I have added another six laws about which Newton did not write, but which I consider complimentary to the laws he described. Together these constitute what I consider the 15 Laws of Training (presented in full in italics at the beginning of each of the following 15 sections):

1. Train frequently, all year-round*
2. Start gradually and train gently*
3. Train first for distance, only later for speed*
4. Don't set your daily training schedule in stone*
5. Alternate hard and easy training
6. At first, try to achieve as much as possible on a minimum of training
7. Don't race when in training or run at race pace for distances above 16 km*
8. Specialize*
9. Incorporate base training and peaking (sharpening)
10. Don't overtrain*
11. Train with a coach
12. Train the mind*
13. Rest before a big race*
14. Keep a detailed logbook
15. Understand the holism of training

Law 1: Train Frequently, All Year-Round

First practice your event as often as possible, paying less attention to other activities. If you want to be a good athlete, you must train all the year round, no matter what. What is really required is a little exercise constantly; this will benefit you permanently to a far greater degree than single heavy doses at long intervals.

This advice of Newton's no longer sounds particularly remarkable, yet for the amateur runners of his era it certainly was. When Newton started running in 1922, the great amateur distance runners of the day or of the immediate past were Walter George, Alf Shrubb, Hannes Kolehmainen, Paavo Nurmi, and Clarence de Mar (see chapter 6). None of these runners trained as much as Newton did, and only De Mar trained consistently all year round. Kolehmainen trained only 64 km per week and George no more than 3 km per day (Lovesey 1968; Krise and Squires 1982). Even Nurmi trained for only five months of the year (between April and September), and before 1924 he seldom ran more than 10 km per day.

The books about marathon training that Newton might have read were those by Walter Thom (1813), Alfred Downer (1900), Walter George (1902; 1908), Alf Shrubb (1909; 1910) and his coach Harry Andrews (1903), James Sullivan (1909), J.H. Hardwick (1912), Sam Mussabini and C. Ransom (1913), and Alec Nelson (1924). None of these advised that training should be as frequent as Newton proposed or that it should be practiced all year round.

For example, Shrubb's advice was to train for marathons by walking:

Get out for a 16-mile walk three or four times a week, and walk at 4-miles-an-hour pace [6.4 km]. On the other days, go 8 miles [12.8 km] only at about 5 miles [8 km] an hour, saving one day for a 16-mile [26 km] steady road run. (Shrubb 1910, p. 64)

Shrubb suggested that this training program be followed for four to six weeks. For the last month before the race, he recommended that the long run be increased to 20 or even 25 miles [32 or 40 km] and that this should be done either twice per week or three times a fortnight. Andrew's advice was similar, although he emphasized the need to run more:

> To train for long distances a great amount of walking must be done. It is necessary to negotiate many miles both of walking and running at a stretch, the distance to be regulated according to the number of miles a man is training for. . . . At first long road-walks, 15, 20, or 30 miles 24, 32 or 48 km] a day, alternate with runs of a like distance on the track, but at the easiest of speeds. (Andrews 1903, pp. 72-73.)

In his book, *Marathon Running* (1909), James Sullivan wrote that "distance walking is one of the best forms of preparing for distance races; alternate daily running one day and walking the next." Athletes were advised to start walking about 4.8 km at first and to build this up as they felt comfortable. Similarly, it was recommended that athletes start running 8 or 9.6 km three times per week and build this up so that they could go 8 or 16 km without tiring. Sullivan advised athletes to compete in cross-country races and in the marathon only after this level of training had been achieved. However, running the full marathon distance was not recommended until runners had covered at least 40 km several times in training. They were also advised to use George's "100-up" exercises, in which athletes ran on the spot, lifting their knees up in sets of 100.

American John Hayes, who won the marathon in the 1908 Olympic Games in London, apparently only ran 4.8 km in the evenings. If he ran further than this, he would not do any training the next day but would walk on the second day after his run and would go back to running on the third day. However, before the 1908 Olympic Games in England, the American runners were stranded in England for a month, during which time they became bored and therefore trained harder—sometimes 19 to 48 km on their longer runs. In addition, during the last two weeks of their marathon training, the Americans ran the full marathon distance several times. Perhaps because of this sudden training spurt, Americans finished first, third, fourth, ninth, and fourteenth at the Olympics. (The second runner was C. Hefferson of South Africa.)

Before setting the American marathon record in 1908, Matt Maloney only ran three times per week—24 km on the first day, 6 km on the third day and 11 km on the fifth day. On two or three other days of the week, he would walk up to 16 km per day. He also advised runners to run up to 24 km on one of the three training days as they became fitter. On this training, Maloney set the then world record of 2:35:26.2. As there are few modern runners who could run so fast on so little training, his performances again indicate the value of genetic endowment for running ability.

The advice of Alec Nelson (1924), who set the professional half-mile record in 1905 and who was coach to Cambridge University and the British Olympic Team, was very similar: "First of all, then, to build up the body and stamina, it is necessary to specialize in long strong walks." He suggested that the athlete should train twice per week—one of these training sessions should be a long walk, the other a run of gradually increasing distance. He added that "if the athlete feels that he is quite capable of turning out more frequently, additional runs of from 6 to 8 miles

Week	Walking distance (km) (one session)	Running distance (km) (one session)	
1	24	8	
2	24	8	
3	24	8	
4	16	16	
5	16	24	
6	16	16	
7	24	24	Training speed $4{:}04$ km^{-1} to $4{:}23$ km^{-1}
8	16	41	
9	24	20	
10	16	48	
11	24	16	
12	16	16	
13	16	32*	
14	24	16	Training speed $3{:}45$ km^{-1}
15	16	24	
16	24	16	

Table 5.1 Alec Nelson's 16-week marathon training program

* Final trial
From Nelson (1924, pp. 75-76).

may be included." Nelson also provided a 16-week marathon training program that is reproduced in table 5.1.

Only in the books by Thom (1813) and Downer (1900) is reference made to the more exacting training methods of the pedestrians—the professional walkers/runners of the late nineteenth century, who are discussed in detail in chapter 6 and whose approaches were more similar to Newton's. It seems likely that Newton borrowed heavily from the ideas of those professionals.

Newton's contact with Walter George (chapter 6), who was a friend of the great pedestrian, Charles Rowell, as well as with pedestrians Len Hurst and John Fowler-Dixon, who set amateur world records at 40, 50, and 100 miles in the 1870s and 1880s, would have exposed him to the training methods of the pedestrians. For example, George informed Newton of experiments undertaken by Rowell and Harry Shaw, in which they perfected the running style that reduced knee bend to a minimum. This style involved running on the heels with hands and arms in front of the body, causing the rear leg to swing "from toe to heel without exertion" (Dillon and Milroy 1984, p. 48). It is likely that Newton ultimately revised his ideas on the basis of that additional information (Milroy 1987), particularly in respect of the very large volumes of training undertaken by the professional pedestrians competing in the six-day races. Milroy (1992b) makes the point that, during the Transcontinental race of 1928, Newton would also have met the Finns Willi Kolehmainen and Arne

Souminen. He apparently stayed with the three Kolehmainen brothers among the large Finnish community in New York. Thus, Newton was also exposed to the training methods of the first great Finnish runners. This would also explain why a book describing the Finnish training methods was found among Newton's possessions after his death.

Newton would have learned that the pedestrians would train for up to 8 hours per day by walking and running up to 80 km (Milroy 1983). As they were training for six-day races in which they usually averaged about 9 km per hour, it is probable that they trained considerably slower than did those who, like Newton, were preparing for shorter distance races run at a faster pace.

Newton was really breaking new ground for amateur, but not professional, runners by stating that training must be continued all year round, as frequently as possible; that most of the training should involve running; and that runs of 32 km should become a daily, not a weekly, occurrence.

This first law is also known as the consistency ethic (Liquori and Parker 1980). When starting to run, the key is to train regularly. For the jogger interested only in improving health, 30 minutes of exercise three or four times per week is probably all that is required (ACSM 1978). For the competitive runner, training needs to be done at least six days per week. Although most elite runners probably aim to train for at least 11 months of the year, I now believe this to be wrong. Athletes who wish to have successful careers that last for more than a few brief summers need, I think, to rest completely from all training for at least two months each year and to train slowly and consistently for another three months every year. I learned this approach from Mark Allen, perhaps one of the most consistently successful endurance athletes of all time.

Law 2: Start Gradually and Train Gently

Nearly all of us dash into it hoping for and expecting results which are quite unwarranted. Nature is unable to make a really first-class job of anything if she is hustled. To enhance our best, we need only, and should only, enhance our average. That is the basis we ought to work on, for it succeeds every time when the other fails. So, in running, it is essential to take to it kindly.

Newton proposed that the most effective training method for beginners is to run longer distances at a comfortable pace that is much slower than race pace and not to race in training. This type of training was rediscovered in the 1960s and termed long slow distance (LSD) by the American runner Joe Henderson (1969; 1974; 1976; 1977).

The wisdom in Newton's ideas is borne out by the training methods of the modern distance exponents, who do most of their running at slower than race pace and who are seldom able to reproduce their racing performances over distances longer than about 21 km in practice.

How the body is able to produce competitive performances greatly in excess of what is achieved in daily training is not known, but it must relate to either the accumulated effects of training or to specific programming of the brain, according to the Integrated Neuromuscular Recruitment Model. Nevertheless, it is clear that this very real phenomenon must be appreciated if the athlete is ever to achieve lasting success. The novice runner who repeatedly attempts to reproduce racing performances in training simply becomes overtrained (see chapter 7). It is also clear that runners who train only at low exercise intensities will not perform to their potential in competition (see Law 3), at least at running distances up to 100 km.

We now appreciate that another reason why training should initially be gentle is because the bones, tendons, and muscles, even of young healthy humans, are simply not able to adapt overnight to the cumulative stress of regular training. For this reason, it is best to begin training with a period of walking and to start jogging slowly at first and for short periods of time only.

The beginner's training program in shown in table 5.8 incorporates an initial walking period like this. As training volumes increase, it is invaluable to include some walking in the training program.

It is only necessary and possible for average runners to train at race pace for 5% to 10% of their total training distance. Most of the world's best marathon runners do most of their training at a speed of between 30 and 50 seconds per km slower than their race pace. Two excellent examples are Alberto Salazar and Rob de Castella (see chapter 6), both of whom did most of their training at 3:45 per km yet raced standard marathons at close to 3:00 per km. Wally Hayward seldom trained faster than 5:00 per km yet set world records in ultramarathon races by averaging 4:05 per km for up to 90 km. In simple terms, this means that the novice runner who ultimately plans to run a standard marathon in 4:30:00 will need to run the marathon at 6:00 per km. Therefore, an appropriate training speed would be between 6:00 and 7:00 per km. Similarly, this rule applies to races at other distances.

The best way for a novice to achieve the correct intensity of training is to monitor how the body responds to the effort. While running, you should feel that the effort is comfortable. You should also be able to carry on a conversation with your running companions. This ability to speak intelligently without becoming short of breath while running is known as the "talk test." Should the effort of the run become noticeable and result in you being unable to talk, you are straining, not training, and should slow down.

Another important point is that runners should never be ashamed to walk during training runs if they become overtired. At the start, at least, beginners should always finish each run feeling only pleasantly tired, knowing that, if they had to, they could comfortably run the same distance again.

The first scientist to observe that athletes could accurately predict how hard they were exercising on the basis of how they felt was Gunnar Borg. Borg (1973; 1978) noticed that there was a close relationship between the exercising heart rate, which, as we saw in chapter 2, is directly related to the intensity of the exercise, and how athletes actually perceived the effort they were making. He produced his Borg Scale, which provides a scoring system ranging 6 to 20, based on how the athlete feels when running (see table 5.2a). The figures he chose relate quite closely to the heart rate (divided by 10) that the athlete would achieve while exercising at those different ratings.

More recently, the original Borg Scale was modified to accommodate the observation that the perception of effort does not increase in a linear fashion with increasing exercise intensity. Rather, as the runner approaches the lactate turnpoint, the perception of effort increases very steeply. The new Borg Scale (Noble et al. 1983; Borg 1998), listed in table 5.2b, takes this into account by reducing the range of ratings that describe mild to moderate exercise (0–3) and increasing the range of ratings for heavy exercise (4–10). Using the scale, the athlete is able to describe

Table 5.2A The original Borg Scale Rating Perception of Effort (RPE)

Rating	Perception of effort
6	
7	Very, very light
8	
9	Very light
10	
11	Fairly light
12	
13	Somewhat hard
14	
15	Hard
16	
17	Very hard
18	
19	Very, very hard
20	

From Borg (1973, p. 92). © by Lippincott, Williams & Wilkins. Adapted by permission.

Table 5.2B The category-ratio scale of perceived exertion—the new Borg Scale

Rating	Perception of effort
0	Nothing at all
0.5	Very, very weak (just noticeable)
1	Very weak
2	Weak
3	Moderate
4	Somewhat strong
5	Strong (heavy)
6	
7	Very strong
8	
9	
10	Very, very strong (almost maximal)
>10 (any number)	

From B.J. Noble et al. (1983, p. 523). © by Lippincott, Williams & Wilkins. Adapted by permission.

with far greater precision the exact intensity of any exercise, but particularly that of more vigorous exercise. One of the best uses to which the runner can put the new Borg Scale is to record it in a logbook and use that information to calculate both the strain and monotony of the training program, as described in chapter 7.

Another method of determining effort during running is to monitor heart rate during exercise. It is traditionally taught that maximum heart rate falls with age, but this does not necessarily appear to be the case in those who remain vigorously active for life (S. Edwards 1997). A simple equation used to predict the maximum heart rate (in beats per minute) is 220 minus age in years. Therefore, the predicted maximum heart rate of a 40-year-old is (220–40) beats per minute, which equals 180 beats per minute. However, there appears to be little or no scientific basis for this calculation (S. Edwards 1997). Thus, it is recommended that should you wish to use your heart rate to determine your appropriate exercise intensity, you should first establish your maximum heart rate.

Two factors that influence the maximum heart rate are endurance training and heart disease. All younger, highly trained athletes and most patients with heart disease have maximum heart rates that are lower than expected for their ages. In contrast, highly trained athletes over 50 years of age have higher maximal heart rates than predicted by this equation. Unless you are young and untrained, in which case the 220 minus age equation may be reasonably accurate, it is more appropriate to establish your maximum heart rate more accurately.

This can be done in one of two ways. If necessary (see chapter 2), you can visit an exercise laboratory and have an exercise scientist perform a maximum exercise test, during which your maximum heart rate, $\dot{V}O_2$max, and lactate turnpoint are measured. Alternatively, you can use a heart rate monitor and perform your own maximal exercise test. Maximal heart rates are usually achieved at exhaustion during all-out exercise that terminates within 4 to 10 minutes. Thus, the highest heart rate you achieve when running as hard as you can for 4 to 10 minutes will be your maximum heart rate. However, this test should not be undertaken in an unsupervised setting by people whose heart conditions are not known.

The popular training dogma is that maximum benefit is achieved by training at between 60% and 90% of maximum heart rate. Ideally, heart rates should fall between these values for most of the training time. Values higher than these should only be achieved during short-duration speed training with lower values achieved only when you are jogging during the days of recovery from hard training or racing. Table 5.3 and figure 5.5 have been drawn up for those who wish to control their exercise intensities on the basis of their exercising heart rates. Note that these heart rate ranges are for people with normal hearts. Anyone with known heart disease should first seek specialist medical advice before embarking on a training program. Sally Edwards (1997) has compiled one of the most comprehensive books on the use of heart rate monitors during training. She contends that the 220 minus age calculation for predicting the maximum heart rate has no solid scientific basis and stresses therefore that individual runners must establish their own maximum heart rates if they wish to use this method for establishing the correct training intensity.

A recent study of Ironman triathletes indeed confirms the accuracy of Edwards's concern. That study (O'Toole et al. 1998) found that although the 220 minus age formula for calculating the maximum heart rate was more accurate than another popular formula of 210 – (0.5 × age), individual variation in maximum heart rate was great. Thus, individual triathletes had maximum measured heart rates during

	Table 5.3 Maximum heart rates and target range for different ages		
Age	Maximum heart rate (beats·min⁻¹)	Target heart rate (beats·min⁻¹)	Target heart rate range (beats 15·sec⁻¹)
20-29	200	120-180	20-30
30-39	190	114-168	19-28
40-49	180	108-162	18-27
50-59	170	102-150	17-25
60-69	160	96-144	16-24
70+	150	90-132	15-22

cycling that could be either 35 beats per minute below or 16 beats per minute above those predicted by that equation. During running, the range was from 25 beats per minute below to 19 beats per minute above the predicted values. The authors also found that maximal cycling heart rates were substantially lower than maximum heart rates measured when running. Edwards also argues that the training guidelines of 60% to 85% of maximum heart rate are too broad to be of real value. Instead, she proposes five training heart rate zones. Table 5.4 identifies those zones and the frequency and duration of training in those zones, as well as the type of activity that will take you into those different zones.

Sally Edwards has competed in ultradistance endurance events for the past 30 years, having completed, among others, the Hawaiian Ironman Triathlon on numerous occasions. In her book, *Smart Heart* (1997), she describes the following five training heart rate zones:

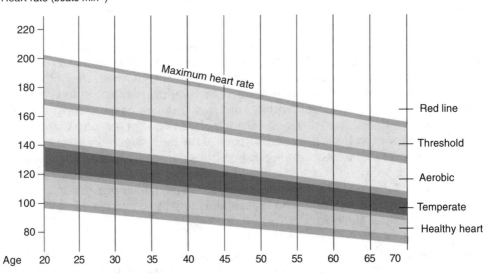

Figure 5.5   The five heart rate training zones of Edwards and Burke.

Table 5.4   Exercise prescription according to five training heart rate zones: The methods of Sally Edwards and Edmund Burke

Zone	Frequency times/ week	Intensity (% of maximum heart rate)	Intensity (% $\dot{V}O_2$max)	Time (min)	Activity	Rating of perceived exertion (Borg Scale)	Descriptive rating, perceived exertion
Red line	0-2	90-100%	>85	2-4	Racing, intervals speed work	18-20	Very hard to very fast. Quite heavy breathing
Threshold	1-3	80-90%	75-84	15-55	Run, spinning, cross-country skiing	16-17	Hard to very hard. Heavier breathing
Aerobic	4-6	70-80%	63-74	20-120	Jog, swim, cycle step	13-15	Somewhat hard but still able to talk
Temperate	3-4	60-70%	50-62	15-30	Jog/walk, swim cycle	11-12	Fairly light. Brisk but comfortable. Breathing becomes slightly noticeable
Healthy heart	2-3	50-60%	40-49	10-60	Walk, low-impact aerobics	9-10	Very comfortable and light. Able to converse with ease

Adapted, by permission, from Iknoian (1998, p. 47).

Zone 1: Healthy Heart—50% to 60% of the maximum heart rate. Training in this zone for sufficiently long (10 to 60 minutes, two to three times per week) produces the health benefits of exercise described in chapter 15.

Zone 2: Temperate—60% to 70% of the maximum heart rate. Exercising in this zone produces the same health benefits as those achieved in Zone 1 but, for the same time commitments, the benefits are greater. In addition, when the habitual training load is closer to 70% than to 60% of the maximum heart rate, the benefits begin to include adaptations that will improve running performance.

Zone 3: Aerobic—70% to 80% of the maximum heart rate. The bottom rung of this zone (70% of maximum heart rate) is still more gentle exercise but the upper range (80% of maximum heart rate) corresponds to exercise that is "somewhat hard" or "hard" according to the Borg Scale (tables 5.2*a* and 5.2*b*). According to Edwards, training in this zone for sufficient durations produces major physiological adaptations (in the heart, in the exercised skeletal muscles, and in metabolism) that enhance endurance running performance.

Zone 4: Threshold Zone—80% to 90% of the maximum heart rate. This zone is strictly for those interested in high performance. It reflects the transition from the Aerobic Zone, a training zone that can be sustained for hours, to one that can be sustained by elite athletes for prolonged periods of at least 60 minutes, but only with some difficulty. When added to a sustained period of training in the Aerobic Zone, training in this zone produces rapid gains in performance and is most effectively used in the period immediately before competition. However, training too often and for too long in this zone, without adequate rest, will precipitate the overtraining syndrome (see chapter 7).

Zone 5: Red Line—90% to 100% of the maximum heart rate. Interval training at running distances up to 400 m provides entry into this training zone. This training produces the same results as those achieved by Zone 4 training.

Edwards made an important additional contribution by demonstrating how her training zone concept allows a more accurate quantification of the amount of training achieved with each training session. She suggests the following formula to make this calculation:

$$\text{Workload (points)} = \text{duration} \times \text{zone}$$

Thus, exercising for 30 minutes in Zone 3 (with a heart rate of 70% to 80% of maximum) produces 90 points. When the training for each week is summed, a total weekly training load can be calculated. This information can then be used to calculate the exact amount of training that produces optimum racing results without the risk of overtraining.

Using Heart Rate Monitors in Training

The first heart rate monitors used by modern athletes can be traced to a meeting held in 1976 between Professor Seppo Säynäjäkangas of the Oulu University Electronics Laboratory in Oulu, Finland, and the coach of the university's cross-country skiing team. The coach sought the professor's help because of his conviction that he would be a better coach if he knew what the heart rates of his athletes were during training and competition.

Appropriately challenged, Säynäjäkangas formed the family-controlled company, Polar Electro, in Kempele, Finland, in 1982, subsequently leaving the university to devote his time exclusively to his new company. In 1998, in excess of 2 million Polar heart rates monitors were sold worldwide, establishing Polar as the leading manufacturer in the field and proving that athletes around the world endorse this technology.

Modern heart rate monitors vary considerably in their levels of sophistication. The simplest heart rate monitors display heart rates in real time and are therefore useful in controlling the appropriate exercise intensity by heart rate (figure 5.5). The added advantage of some, like the Polar Smart Edge, is that they also calculate the number of calories expended during each exercise session. This calculation is based on the measured relationship between heart rate and oxygen consumption, adjusted for the subject's gender, body mass, and maximum exercise capacity predicted from the $\dot{V}O_2$max.

These models are appropriate for novice athletes who do not wish to analyze their training in any great detail and do not foresee themselves becoming committed racers. Any runner who plans to become a serious racer with long-term performance goals, however modest, needs to consider the next advance in heart rate monitoring, which is the ability to store heart rate information from either a single exercise session (Polar Coach) or multiple exercise sessions (Polar Accurex Plus; Polar X Trainer Plus; Polar Vantage NV) and then to download that information via either a sound link or an interface unit. This allows all the heart rate information collected during each exercise session to be stored on a personal computer for analysis at a later stage. This information has additional value:

- As you become fitter, your heart rate at any running speed falls. Thus, improvements in fitness can be more easily gauged. For example, if you run a favorite route at a lower average heart rate but at the same or faster speed, then your body is adapting positively to your training.

- The rationale behind using frequent running tests to establish whether your body is adapting effectively to your specific training program is that, as you become fitter, your heart rate after exercise will return more quickly to its normal resting value.

- Once you are overreaching or overtraining (chapter 7), your heart rate will be increased at any running speed. When you observe this, you need to rest, not train.

- Should you notice that your heart rate is abnormally elevated during a training session, you should abort the session before greater damage is done.

- By quantifying the amount of time spent in each training zone, you are able to determine the exact training load you achieved in each session. When you subsequently evaluate your racing performances, you will be able to calculate the amount of training measured as the accumulated time you spent training in each heart rate zone. Conversely, if you perform poorly, then you will have an indication of where you went wrong—whether you did too much training at intensities that were too low or too high.

- By using a heart rate monitor, you will soon learn the heart rates you can sustain for different distances. This can help prevent you from starting out too fast in longer distance races.

The Polar Coach heart rate monitor enables you to download training information daily, by sound, into a computerized training logbook that stores the information for later analysis. You can then integrate this information into a series of different training programs developed by running experts, including Jeff Galloway, Arturo Barrios, and Ray Benson, among others. Novice runners who use this system can therefore follow more personalized training programs not covered to any great extent in this book.

The most recent advance on this technique comes from the novel idea of South African-schooled Crispian Hotson, who realized that the value of heart rate monitoring resides not in the technology but in the intelligent interpretation of the information stored in the heart rate monitor. The key then is to link the heart rate monitor to the exercise scientist who understands that information and who is able to interpret it most effectively for the exerciser. In this way, the exerciser can be coached at a distance using heart rate monitoring and access via the Internet to appropriately trained exercise scientists working in university research laboratories around the world.

Winning Wellness, the company that has developed Body iQ in collaboration with our research team at the University of Cape Town and the Sports Science Institute of South Africa, now provides training advice and distance coaching

(continued)

to those with access to the Internet who use either Polar Heart Rate monitors or the Body iQ Binky Heart Rate Monitoring system, the Body iQ Max product. The product includes a sophisticated logbook function and a unique electronic personal medical and training folder, accessible via the Internet.

Phillip Maffetone (1996) is another scientist/coach who has become well known for training ideas that incorporate heart rate monitoring. Coach to world class triathletes Mike Pigg and Mark Allen, Maffetone developed his "180 minus" formula for establishing the peak heart rate you should achieve during the first three months of training at the start of the new training year. The same formula is probably also appropriate for the beginner runner. To calculate your "180 minus" training heart rate, you subtract the following from the number 180:

your age (in years);

10, if you are recovering from a major illness or recent hospital visit, or if you are on any regular medication; and

5, if you have not exercised before, or if you have not recently been exercising normally because of injury, illness, or lack of interest; or

0, if you have recently been exercising regularly without interruption.

Finally, if you have been exercising for more than two years without interruption and your fitness has steadily improved, you should add 5 to your total. Thus, a 50-year-old runner with no known medical conditions who has never exercised before would exercise at a peak heart rate of 180 – 50 – 5 + 0, or 125, beats per minute. If the same runner had a known medical condition for which he was receiving treatment, his peak heart rate would be 10 beats per minute lower, or 115 beats per minute. If, on the other hand, he was completely healthy and had been training without incident for two years, his peak heart rate would be 135 beats per minute. While there is no firm scientific basis for these calculations, their great value is that they give a fixed and easily understandable guideline, they are extremely conservative, and they encourage you to train gently for a prolonged period (three months) with little risk of illness or injury.

Mark Allen has ascribed much of his success during an astonishing 14-year career to his adherence to the Maffetone principle for at least three months per year. Allen calls this period of training his "patience phase." Patience in training is indeed an excellent maxim for most runners.

Law 3: Train First for Distance, Only Later for Speed.

If you are going to contest a 26-mile event, you must at least be used to 100 miles a week. . . . As it is always the speed, never the distance, that kills, so is it the distance, not the speed, that has to be acquired. In the early days of training, you must endeavor only to manage as great a distance on each practice outing as you can cover without becoming abnormally tired. . . . Your aim throughout, should be to avoid all maximum effort while you work with one purpose only and that is to achieve a definite and sustained rise in the average speed at which you practice, for that is the secret of ultimate achievement. . . . You must never, except for short temporary bursts, practice at racing speed.

The notion that you should never, except for short, temporary bursts, practice at racing speed is essentially a corollary to Newton's second law, in which he warned against the dangers of excessive speed training. In this law, Newton elaborated on his principal belief that the goal of training is to gradually increase the speed that can be maintained for prolonged distances. And this, he believed, could be achieved only by training that emphasized distance, not speed. Interestingly, Alf Shrubb (1910, page 64) had drawn the same conclusions: "It is the distance and not the pace that is going to kill in the long-distance race."

Newton was the first, after the professional pedestrians, to describe two components that are central to the training beliefs of the New Zealand running coach, Arthur Lydiard: the 100-mile training week and the belief that the human body already has sufficient speed and lacks only endurance.

However, since Newton's era, training has evolved considerably, with more emphasis being placed on the need for regular weekly sessions of speed training or speed work. The first reference that I could find to an athlete who regularly performed speed training was Alf Shrubb (1910). At least twice per week, Shrubb ran at close to race pace for distances from 4 to 16 km. Hannes Kolehmainen probably also used speed training and has been credited as one of the first runners to practice speed play (fartlek), in which the athlete surges with bursts of speed over varying distances, usually on the road or across country (Doherty 1964). Kolehmainen probably also influenced the next great Finnish runner, Paavo Nurmi, to include speed work in his training. As described in chapter 6, Nurmi considered his early years of training to be less than optimal because he had not included sufficient speed training. He believed this to be the reason why he remained a "slow trudger" until 1924, when he first included regular speed training sessions, having already developed the training base that Newton advocated.

With this evidence, I have altered this third law from Newton's to read: Train first for distance, *only later* for speed.

Thus, Nurmi's principal method of speed training was interval repeats, first of 80 to 120 m and later of 400 to 600 m. This type of training was subsequently refined independently by the German team of physiologist, Hans Reindell, and coach, Woldemar Gerschler (Pirie 1961; Doherty 1964; Burfoot 1981a) and by Franz Stampfl, the British coach of Roger Bannister (Stampfl 1955; Lenton 1983a). Bannister used pure interval training to break the 4-minute mile barrier, whereas Zatopek was the first to use large numbers of intervals, run at varying paces, to accumulate both a volume and an intensity of training not previously matched. In the 1950s and 1960s, marathoners Jim Peters and Buddy Edelen then adapted these principles for marathon training, as did Alberto Salazar in the 1970s and Steve Jones in the 1980s (chapter 6). Also, it seems likely that the East, North, and South African distance runners, who began to dominate the marathon in the 1990s and into the new millennium will continue to do so.

The wide acceptance of speed work today suggests that it is both effective and essential for all runners who wish to improve and to be competitive. But this should not detract from Newton's observation that the greatest performance improvements occur, at least initially, after the athlete has developed a strong endurance base through long, slow, distance training. My own feeling is that speed work should be approached with extreme caution, preferably with the help of a knowledgeable coach, or after consulting the appropriate writings of the training experts listed earlier in this chapter.

Thus, Newton's advice that you should never undertake speed training clearly only applies to novice runners and to athletes who run for enjoyment and who are not concerned about improving their speed. There is no doubt that the standard of competitive running has progressed significantly since Newton's day, and it would be unthinkable for a modern elite distance athlete to try to succeed in competition without doing some speed training. As we shall see when we discuss the training methods of several athletes in chapter 6, it becomes clear that even ultradistance runners need speed training.

In summary, the key to successful training, at least for the first 12 months or so, is the amount of time you spend running each week, rather than the distance you cover or the speed at which you run. Therefore, you should initially aim to run for a certain time each session. You will run farther when you are fresh and rested than when you are tired. In this way, the effort will be controlled. Remember that the initial goal in distance training is to increase gradually the speed or effort that can be maintained for prolonged distances.

It has been found that after 12 or more months of training, athletes who only do distance training reach a definite plateau. To improve beyond this, the athlete must either further increase the distance run in training or else run the same distance but run some of that distance at a faster pace—that is, use speed training.

The evidence clearly indicates that increasing the distance run in training is frequently counterproductive, particularly when the weekly training distance goes beyond about 190 km per week. By judiciously using a limited amount of speed training at the correct time, it is possible to achieve quite dramatic improvements in performance (see Law 9 on pages 307-324).

If you wish to experiment with speed training, first read all you can about the different methods of speed training (Gardner and Purdy 1970; Henderson 1977; Daws 1977; Osler 1978; Lydiard and Gilmour 1978; Galloway 1984; Glover and Schuder 1983; S. Edwards 1997; Martin and Coe 1997; Daniels 1998). Then speak to the experts, the speed-trained athletes and their coaches, and find a group of experienced runners whose running performances are similar to yours but who do regular speed training as part of their peaking program. Or else consider using a computerized training program, such as the PC Coach Athletic Training software, which has programs for training purely by heart rate for distances of 800 m to 10 km (developed by Coach Ray Benson), 10 km (by Arturo Barrios), 21 to 42 km (by Jeff Galloway), and 42 km (by Uta Pippig). Or, if you have Internet access, consider the Body iQ option (**www.BodyiQ.com**).

The reasons for doing speed work relate to both physical and mental needs. Faster running trains the quadriceps muscles and the Type II muscle fibers in all the lower limb muscles. These are the muscle groups and the muscle fibers that are needed during longer distance races but remain untrained if you run slowly during training. Another benefit is learning to relax at speed. Furthermore, it is likely that the fast running adapts the ventilatory muscles for high work rates and may help prevent stitches.

Speed work also trains the central governor to allow for greater effort. A target is set, and a time is laid down. But the governor resists by testing the will, arguing that such effort is unnecessary. As a result, speed work becomes a test of that will. The choice is simply between doing and not doing the chosen task. There is no place for explanations, excuses, and rationalizations. Only when you have successfully faced that reality in the unforgiving solitude of the track are you ready for that best race.

Indeed, according to the Integrated Neuromuscular Recruitment Model, the real benefit of interval training may simply be to reset the central brain governor so that it allows a greater skeletal muscle recruitment during maximum exercise. This theory predicts that the very high-intensity training achieved during the intervals teaches the governor that such exercise can indeed be undertaken without risk of damage to the body. Thus, the governor learns to allow higher levels of skeletal muscle recruitment during subsequent bouts of high-intensity exercise.

But speed work is not without risk: the twin dangers are running the sessions too often and running them too fast, the natural trap for athletes who are overeager or for those who consider their inability to run faster a result of not training sufficiently hard (rather than a lack of genetic endowment—see chapter 2). My ideas about this type of training are described in greater detail at the end of this chapter. Those of some of the world's greatest runners are presented in chapter 6. All agree that high-intensity training is one of the two pillars on which successful racing is based.

Law 4: Don't Set Your Daily Training Schedule in Stone

Don't set yourself a daily schedule; it is far more sensible to run to a weekly one, because you can't tell what the temperature, the weather, or your own condition will be on any day.

Here Newton introduces the concept of listening to your body, an idea subsequently popularized by George Sheehan (1972; 1975). Using this technique, runners monitor how they feel before and during their runs and then adjust their training on any given day according to how they feel during each run.

Many runners choose to run each day according to a prearranged schedule. This approach is less than ideal because, as Newton pointed out, the weather may not always be appropriate. On that particular day, your body may not be up to undertaking the scheduled training. In particular, factors either within the body (minor illness or muscle soreness indicating lingering fatigue from the last workout) or external to it (work and family commitments, lack of sleep, and travel) may reduce the body's ability to perform on that day and, more important, its ability to benefit from that particular training session. Inappropriate training performed with sore and damaged muscles will not only be ineffectual, as the damaged muscles are unable to perform properly, but will also delay muscle recovery.

A daily schedule should act only as a guideline. You should be flexible about modifying the plan if conditions such as the weather or any other factor mitigate against adhering to it. The key to knowing how much to train on any given day comes from learning to listen to your body. This, of course, is much more difficult than religiously following a detailed training schedule because it demands insight and flexibility, attributes that not everyone possesses. Yet, in the end, the ability to know how much training to do on any particular day ultimately determines your running success. There is immense wisdom in Marti Liquori's statement: "What is pain or discomfort to a relatively inexperienced runner is merely information to the elite runner" (Liquori and Parker 1980, page 78).

Be attuned and monitor how your legs feel at the start of each run, as well as during the run. When you are training hard, it is usual for your legs to feel slightly tired and lethargic at the start of a run. However, this feeling should lift rapidly as the run progresses. Muscle stiffness and soreness that either persist or get worse during a training run indicate that your legs have not recovered. In this instance, you should abandon your run and rest for a period to allow muscle recovery before undertaking another hard or long training session. If your legs do not regain their feeling of strength after 24 to 48 hours of rest, then your body is telling you that you are well on the road to overtraining (see chapter 7).

Law 5: Alternate Hard and Easy Training

This is one of the laws that Newton did not practice. His training was relatively similar from day to day, a luxury he enjoyed first as a self-employed farmer in KwaZulu Natal and later as a professional runner. The danger of training monotonously in this way, by following a heavy but unvaried daily training schedule, is that it increases the probability of illness and overtraining.

Bill Bowermann and Bill Dellinger, the coaches behind the dynasty of great runners that has emerged from the University of Oregon at Eugene, were the first to teach that training should not always be of the same intensity and duration, day in and day out (Burfoot 1981b). They observed that their runners progressed best when they were allowed a suitable recovery period after each hard training session. For some, this period was only 24 hours; for others, it might have been as long as 48 hours. This is what is known as the hard day/easy day training program. Author and marathon Olympian Kenny Moore, who trained under Bowermann and Dellinger (K. Moore 1982) and who was one of the runners needing 48 hours' recovery, called his personal variation the "hard/easy/easier training method" (Galloway 1984).

Dellinger claims that the hard day/easy day description of the Oregon training approach is inaccurate: "Strictly speaking, it's misleading to say that we follow a hard-day/easy-day pattern. Our kids run two workouts that I consider fairly hard, on Tuesday and Saturday. On Thursday they might do a little quality work, but it's short and not very intense" (Burfoot 1981b, page 57).

Researchers have not established why the body is unable to train hard every day, but the phenomenon is probably due to muscle damage of the same type as that caused by marathon racing, although less severe. It is probable that this degree of muscle damage requires about 24 to 48 hours to recover fully, rather than the six to eight weeks needed after a 42-km marathon race.

Training is not simply a matter of stocking up with fuel and repeating what was done the previous day. To be a wise runner, you must learn that if the previous training session was hard, regardless of what your mind tells you or what you imagine your competitors might be doing in training, you must allow your body to recover so that it can restock its energy stores and repair the microdamage caused by the previous day's heavy training. Hard training when the body is not fully recovered simply compounds damage already done.

All athletes must establish for themselves how frequently they can train hard. Their success will, to a large extent, depend on whether or not they achieve this balance. Paula Newby-Fraser, eight-time winner of the women's division of the 226-km Hawaiian Ironman Triathlon, has also written that she built her training around three key workouts per week:

These sessions are the foundations of my training, and they rarely change in structure. They are my "bread-and-butter" work. During these workouts, I focus all my energy—mentally, physically, emotionally—in every possible way. Key workouts are the best measure of my peak fitness and are the acid tests for speed, endurance, and strength. After a key workout, I can accurately judge where I am on my performance scale. Key workouts are a much better measure of fitness than total mileage because, even though you're racking up the miles, weaknesses such as lack of speed, endurance, or strength may be camouflaged. (Newby-Fraser and Mora 1995, p. 161)

Law 6: Achieve As Much As Possible on a Minimum of Training

This law, which was not ever formulated by Newton, would seem to be the opposite of the first law, which emphasizes the importance of training frequently all year round. The point, perhaps, is that it was only after Newton's example in the 1920s that amateur runners around the world began to train as hard as their bodies would allow. Before that, only the professional pedestrians had pushed their bodies to their physical limits in both training and racing.

But since the first running boom of the 1970s, an increasing number of runners have begun to believe that the more they train, the more successful they will be. In fact, there is a limit to the amount of training the body can benefit from. Training beyond that limit produces progressively poorer performances, leading ultimately to overtraining.

Thus, for some reason, part of the macho image of running is built on the myth that the top runners and Ironman triathletes achieve greatness by enduring training programs quite beyond the level of the rest of us. The best runners, the world would have us believe, are those who train the hardest. Nowhere do you ever read about the many great athletic performances that have been achieved on very little training nor, as described in chapter 6, about how well these top runners perform even when they train very little. In part, this results from a prevailing international ethic that holds that the environment contributes far more to who we are and what we become than do factors that are beyond our control and that may have an hereditary (genetic) component.

But it is clear that genetic ability has more to do with why the great athletes beat us than their harder training, and there is no earthly way in which training can reverse the physiological realities and thus reduce the chasm that divides us from them. Unfortunately, too many runners believe that they must train hard to run well and end up doing too much to try to compensate for their genetic deficits. But, by starting with a modest training program and then gradually increasing and modifying the balance between increasing training distance and training speed (see Bruce Fordyce, chapter 6), the crossover point where increased training leads to compromised, not better, performance and increased injury risk can be clearly identified.

For example, who ever records that exceptional runners like Walter George and Alf Shrubb achieved quite remarkable performances on very low mileage? George ran a mile in 4:10.6 and a 16-km run in 49:29 on little more than 3 km of training per day. Even Paavo Nurmi, the most medalled Olympic runner of all times, trained pathetically little but performed exceptionally, even by today's standards. The outstanding performances of the black African runners, from Kip Keino to Matthews Temane, have also been achieved on relatively little training in which high quality but relatively low volume has been emphasized.

My own experience has backed this up. If I had my running career over again, I would seldom run more than 120 km per week, the maximum training distance suggested by the University of Oregon's Bowermann and Dellinger. I would see what I could achieve by maintaining that training load for a few years. If I still wished to improve, I would then increase my amount of speed training and perfect the peaking technique. Only when these methods failed to improve my running would I consider further increasing my training distances.

So I would suggest that, when starting a running career, you should decide on the amount of time you can commit to your training. Provided this is less than 6 to 8 hours per week, there is little possibility that, on this volume of training, you will be able to overtrain to the point that your running performances will be impaired by training too much. Thus, any amount of training that can be completed in less than 8 to 10 hours per week can be undertaken quite safely.

The danger starts when you wish to train for more than 10 hours per week, equivalent to a training volume of 120 to 160 km per week for average and elite runners respectively. This is the point beyond which the law of diminishing returns begins— that is, more training produces progressively less benefit with the increasing possibility that you will start to perform worse than if you had trained less (figure 5.6).

How, then, do you determine the individual training threshold at which your training volume produces maximum benefits (figure 5.6, zone of optimum training benefits)? I would suggest that your first priority is patience—you have many years to answer this question, so a measured approach is essential. Take the long-term view that running is something worth doing for at least 5 to 15 years and that, during that time, your goal should be a progressive but gradual improvement. This is to be achieved first by finding the training volume that produces the best results and then by gradually increasing the intensity of some (perhaps 15% to 30%) of that training to optimize training.

Thus, your weekly training volume during the more intensive training period of the year can be gradually increased until the point of optimum training is identified. This training threshold can really only be identified if you train both less and, finally, more than this optimum amount. Accordingly, your training volume needs to be increased gradually and progressively until the training volume at your individual failure threshold is identified. This corresponds to the training volume that produces a deteriorating, not an improved, racing performance. The identification of this training threshold is a crucial exercise in ultimately helping you determine how you achieve success. Runners such as Bruce Fordyce and triathlete Mark Allen, who consistently achieve levels of excellence, largely owe their success to their ability to identify their individual failure thresholds that they never again exceeded in their training. Interestingly, Mark Allen originally failed to win the 226-km Hawaiian Ironman Triathlon because he trained less than he needed to (see chapter 6)— an uncommon failing in runners but perhaps more likely in triathletes, who spend most of their training time in non-weight-bearing activities.

In contrast, athletes whose success is intermittent and who are never certain of how they will perform, such as Ron Hill, have never identified their individual training thresholds. Usually they train beyond their thresholds, perform poorly, and

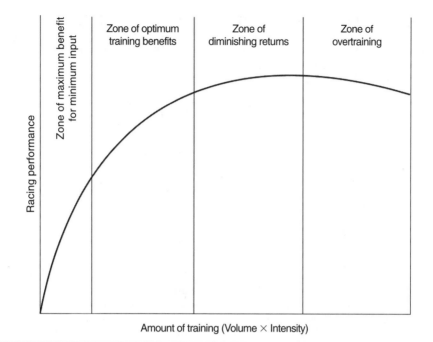

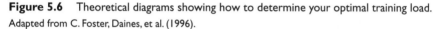

Figure 5.6   Theoretical diagrams showing how to determine your optimal training load.
Adapted from C. Foster, Daines, et al. (1996).

conclude that their failure proves exactly how lazy they are. Thus, they train even harder, and their performance deteriorates as they enter the zone of overtraining.

Only when these runners stop trying, lose interest, and train less do they again start performing to their potential. Only then, when it is too late, do they begin to understand the training threshold concept, and only then do they learn that too much training was more detrimental to their performance than too little training.

Quantifying Your Training Load

To identify your optimum training load, you must be able to quantify exactly how hard you are training. Most runners measure the number of kilometers they run each week and assume that mileage alone accurately measures their training loads. Yet, that measurement does not quantify the quality of that training. Furthermore, the quality of the training is probably a better predictor of both future performance and the risk of overtraining (chapter 7). Hence, a measure of both the quantity and quality of training is required. Carl Foster of the Milwaukee Heart Institute is one scientist who has pondered this challenge.

Foster and his colleagues (Foster et al. 1996) evaluated the performances of 56 competitive athletes as they increased their training. They calculated the training load as the duration of the session multiplied by the average rating of perceived exertion (RPE; tables 5.2*a* and 5.2*b*) during the session. However, to facilitate ease of use, they developed slightly different phrases to describe the different ratings on the Borg Scale (table 5.5). Then, to work out the mean weekly

(continued)

Table 5.5   The modified Borg Scale for RPE used to calculate training load according to the method of Foster et al. (1996).

Rating	Verbal description
0	Rest
1	Really easy
2	Easy
3	Moderate
4	Sort of hard
5	Hard
6	
7	Really hard
8	
9	Really, really hard
10	Just like my hardest race

Subjects were asked to describe the overall perception of effort during the session as if they were responding to their mothers' question: *How was your workout, honey?* Permission granted by C. Foster.

duration of high-intensity training, they calculated the minutes of training during the week that elicited an RPE greater than 5. Figure 5.7 illustrates some of their findings.

Figure 5.7*A* shows the improvement in 10-km times achieved by four different speed skaters as they increased their training loads. Observe that the rates of improvement with increasing training load (the slopes of the four curves) are quite different for the different skaters.

Whereas skater B shows the steepest improvement in performance with increasing training load, skater D improves very little with increased training. Skaters A and C show improvements that lie within these two extremes. Hence, the response to training is highly individualized, as frequently stated.

Figure 5.7*B* represents the average percentage improvement that an athlete in that study could expect with increases in training load. Point A represents the baseline performance that an athlete with a weekly training load of 500 units (100 minutes of exercise at an RPE of 5, table 5.5) could expect. If the athlete doubled her training to point B on that figure, she could expect her performance to improve by 3%. Further training increases of 1000 units per week (points C, D, E, and F) would produce progressively smaller improvements in performance of 2.5%, 1%, and 0.5% respectively. Thus, because of this logarithmic relationship between training load and performance, a 9% increase in performance requires a 10-fold increase in training load (figure 5.7*B*). Perhaps this too is expected as it confirms the law of diminishing returns. However, the importance is that the method of Foster et al. (1996) allows you to evaluate your training load (chapter 7). Plotting your training load against your own performance will enable you to determine your own optimum training load, as suggested in figure 5.6.

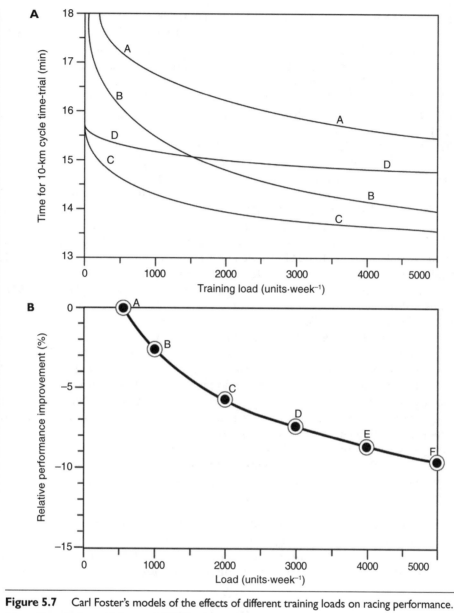

Figure 5.7   Carl Foster's models of the effects of different training loads on racing performance. Adapted from C. Foster, Daines, et al. (1996).

Law 7: Don't Race When in Training or Run at Race Pace for Distances Above 16 Kilometers

I decry such things as time-trials. . . . I am convinced that they are nothing more than a senseless waste of time and energy. They can't tell you any more than the race itself could. . . . Racing, then, should be the only time-trials, and should only be run every two, or preferably three, weeks apart. . . . six weeks between events would be more suitable for a marathon runner, but once every two months is probably better.

It is clear that Newton was strongly opposed to time trials and races other than the major event for which he was training. We have to presume he meant time trials over marathon distances, rather than over distances of 8 to 12 km, which would seem to be essential for elite 10-km, marathon, and ultramarathon runners and probably for any experienced athletes wanting to improve their performances (Law 3). However, I believe that all novice runners should avoid time trials initially and should rather follow Newton's ideas about building endurance and not speed.

The accuracy of Newton's observation that a period of six to eight weeks must be allowed between longer-distance races has only really been reinforced in recent years. We now know that races longer than about 25 km produce marked muscle damage that takes a considerable time to repair (Biomechanical Model of Exercise Physiology), probably longer than Newton estimated. The essential points to remember are that fast running exhausts not only the body but, equally important, the mind. Thus, the amount of fast training and racing that you do must be carefully controlled. As Bruce Fordyce (1996) has so frequently stated: "When I am preparing for a major effort in an ultradistance race, I have one rule about entering other long-distance races—don't. If I could have my way I would force my running friends not to race a single race of 42 km or longer in the six months preceding the [90 km] Comrades" (p. 32).

A rule of thumb is that the shorter the race, the more frequently it can be run, but approach runs beyond 25 km with caution as it appears that racing-induced muscle damage starts to occur in races longer than 25 km (Strachan et al. 1984). Generally, only race two to three races longer than 32 km each year. By racing, I mean running to total exhaustion. An athlete can certainly enter shorter races more frequently but again, exercise restraint (see chapter 9 for more information on racing distances shorter than the marathon).

On the issue of time trials, those who have studied Lydiard's training methods (Lydiard and Gilmour 1978) are aware that he advocates regular time-trials during the peaking phase. Yet, it is clear that he shares Newton's concerns about the dangers of racing in training, for he states,

> The word "time-trial" is often misleading. Basically, a time-trial is used to develop coordination in running races over certain distances, and to find weaknesses and use the appropriate training to strengthen them. Time-trials should not be run at full effort, but with strong, even efforts, leaving you with some reserves. (p. 76)

Lydiard also advised strongly against racing in training and placing too much reliance on the stopwatch. Too much concern with time can result in athletes' losing confidence, particularly as they may be tired from heavy training. In his own words: "Remember that when you are doing time-trials, you are still training hard, so good times cannot always be expected. You cannot train hard and perform well simultaneously."

An error that many runners make in running regular time-trials is to think that each trial must be faster than the last. This is neither desirable nor possible. The surest indication that you are improving is if you are able to run the same or better times in successive time-trials but at a lower heart rate, with less effort, and with a more rapid recovery.

Law 8: Specialize

Specialization nowadays is a necessity. Modern exponents have raised the stan-dards to such a height that nothing but intensive specialization can put a fellow anywhere near the top. Before the 1914 to 1918 war, the marathon was consid-ered an event for only the favored few who had unusual toughness and stamina.

It takes anything from 18 months to three years to turn a novice into a first class athlete. You will have to drop the bulk of your present recreations and spend the time in training; anything from 2 to 3 hours a day will have to be set aside. Athletics must be your major engagement for at least two years on end, your business or means of making a livelihood being at all times of secondary importance.

In this rule, then, Newton was suggesting nothing less than making running a profession, a choice he made when he entered the 1928 Transcontinental Race across North America. Until the early 1980s, Newton's ideas were quite contrary to prevailing thought, perhaps best epitomized by Sir Roger Bannister (1955), the world's first sub-4-minute miler (chapter 8). Bannister has always seen sport as a diversion, rather than a profession:

I believe . . . that running has proved to be a truly amateur activity after all, one on which it is neither necessary nor desirable to spend unlimited time and en-ergy. Fitting running into the rest of life until one's work becomes too demand-ing—this is the burden and joy of the true amateur. (p. 221)

In my view, Sir Roger's ideas are not wrong. But times have changed, and what Newton foresaw more than half a century ago has now materialized.

For those of us who will never break into the professional ranks, I like to think that this rule stresses the importance of specific training. For we now appreciate that training is absolutely specific and that we are fit only for the sport for which we train.

Most runners will already have experienced this. They will know that while they can run effortlessly for hours, they are quite unable to swim comfortably even for a few minutes. The reason for this is that running and swimming train different muscle groups. When a runner exercises the untrained upper body in swimming, for example, the body responds as if it were essentially untrained.

Whereas running principally exercises the legs, leaving the upper body muscu-lature relatively untrained, canoeing and swimming mainly train the upper body, leaving the legs untrained. Swimming and canoeing training do not improve run-ning ability, or vice versa. This distinction may be even more subtle. Novice run-ners frequently find hill running difficult. This is because uphill running stresses the quadriceps (the upper thigh muscle)—a muscle that is much less important during running on the flat and is therefore undertrained in people who run exclu-sively on flat terrain. Similarly, running is the only form of training that adapts the legs for prolonged periods of weight bearing. According to the Biomechanical Model, weight-bearing exercise causes a specific form of exhaustion not encountered in a non-weight-bearing activity, like cycling. Hence, running is the sole method of train-ing that will adapt the body to this type of exhaustion.

Training specifically also includes speed training, hot weather training, and alti-tude acclimatization. As discussed in chapter 1, the speed or intensity of training determines which muscle fibers will be active in the particular muscle groups being exercised. Thus, if you train slowly and then race at a faster pace, you may utilize muscle fibers that are relatively untrained. Similarly, to race effectively in the heat or at altitude, it follows that you need to train under these conditions as well to allow the body to adapt to them (chapters 4 and 9).

The result is that the more closely you tailor your training to the specific demands of the sport for which you are training and to the environment in which you will be expected to compete, the better you will perform.

Despite what I have written here, there is one observation that is at variance with the concept of the absolute training specificity. Some of the very best triathletes in the world have achieved prodigious endurance running performances, despite relatively modest running training. Some, like Mark Allen (chapter 6), have concluded that this is because of all the cycling training that they do. For example, in each of the four weeks of intensive training leading up to the Hawaiian Ironman Triathlon, Allen cycles up to 800 km per week while running about 128 km (Allen 1996b). This would equal about 20 hours of cycling and 8 hours of running per week. It seems possible that Allen's ability as a runner at the end of the Ironman may, in part, result from his cycling training.

Thus, one possibility is that cycling may provide the same metabolic stress as running without the same loading stresses on the muscles and the skeleton (see chapter 3). Cycling may produce training benefits for runners without the risk of muscle damage. Indeed, part of that training adaptation may be to preprogram the brain to accept that the brain was originally prepared to allow it. It is noteworthy that Allen observed that he became a winner of the Hawaiian Ironman Triathlon only after he included training sessions that lasted as long as his winning time in that race. This begs the question: does walking also have a similar programming effect on the brain?

Historically, it is interesting that walking was a central component in training all runners, including Paavo Nurmi. Newton also commented on the role of walking and cycling as additional training methods for long-distance running. Walking was very much in vogue in the 1920s, and there were many popular walking races, including the London-to-Brighton Stock Exchange race, the predecessor of the London-to-Brighton running race. As described in chapter 6, all runners of that era believed that walking should be the major component in long-distance training and that running should be performed only a few times per week. Even Newton's attitude was clear: "Walking is a waste of time. Long walks, even quick walks, do not help a man to run." (Newton 1949, p. 56)

Given this attitude, it is difficult to understand why Newton also walked more than 47,000 km during his running career. His explanation was that "There was a definite purpose in this walking, viz., to make me used to being on my feet nearly all the time. . . though at a much later date I decided it might have been better to run, for running was my job, not walking" (Newton 1947a, p. 64). Ultimately, he concluded that "the average young man would be better off if he left long walks until later on in life when strenuous exercise won't have so great an appeal" (Newton 1949, page 56). What is interesting is that walking is again earning respect as a training method, at least for older runners, especially those who have run many miles and countless marathons in their youth. The training circle continues to turn.

As one such runner, my observations are that very few runners are able to continue training hard and racing longer distances, especially marathons, indefinitely.

Sooner or later, reality strikes and we discover that an unexplained X factor, present when we were younger, has gone missing. Of course, the most popular explanation is that we simply lack the desire to train and race as hard as we had in our youth. While this is certainly a possibility, my belief is that the loss of desire to train and race hard comes after we first notice changes in our bodies, partly due to aging and partly due to the accumulated effects of many years of heavy training and racing. My bias is dependent on observation made on myself and from following the careers of some great runners who are approximately my age, as well as the experiences of other runners described at the end of chapter 2.

First, I ran my best Comrades 90-km ultramarathon on my first attempt. Despite training as well, and perhaps better, for later races, I noticed that I ran differently in those races and consequently, I suggest, slower. I seemed to have lost some bounce in my stride in later years.

Second, close observation of Bruce Fordyce's running over the years during which he won nine Comrades Marathons suggested to me that he was not as fast or as consistent in his later years, when his running stride clearly changed. Previously light and bouncy, he seemed to become progressively more earthbound. The changes that were observed were similar to those sudden changes detected when runners hit the wall in the marathon and their running mechanics change as a result of the stretch-shortening cycle fatigue.

Third, it has become clear that the best young marathon runners of any generation are only the best for about the first 20 years of their careers. Thereafter, another group of their chronological peers, who began competitive running perhaps 15 years later, begin to dominate.

This explains why the world-class runners described in chapter 6 dominated world running before the age of 40 but no later. Any analysis shows that beyond age 40 it is a different group of runners who dominate, especially marathons. Then again, another different group of runners will dominate marathon races for 60-year-olds when that same group of chronological peers reaches that age. This tends to suggest that the best 80-year-old marathon runners will be those who take to the sport only after they turn 70. This factor alone explains why it has never been possible for one runner to dominate the sport at each group from, say, 20 to 60. An interesting recent example is Bill Rodgers (figure 5.8), who, with Frank Shorter, was the dominant marathon runner of the 1970s.

In 1999, at age 51, Rodgers set out to better the world marathon record for athletes over 50 years. In training, he completed one 16-km race in 52:15, a remarkable achievement for a 51-year-old athlete. Yet, he dropped out of the Boston Marathon at 30 km. In my analysis, this occurred because he hit the wall at that distance because his aging legs, altered by decades of heavy training and many marathon races, were no longer capable of coping with the eccentric loading necessary to complete the marathon without hitting the wall. What this means is that Rodgers is able to race almost as well as ever over the shorter distances, at which his muscles are still able to absorb the eccentric loading without failing.

But there is a racing distance that becomes shorter with increasing age and miles of races run at which this failure occurs, inducing the so-called wall phenomenon at increasingly shorter distances with age. It may also be that the running speed you can sustain after hitting the wall slows progressively as the result of this continued muscle aging and eccentric muscle damage.

In his book (Rodgers 1998), Rodgers provides insight into what I think has happened:

There have been other changes as I've aged. Starting in my late 30s and early 40s, I noticed a pretty much perpetual soreness in my legs that wasn't there before. I would definitely get sore 20 years ago, but when I did, it was an acute soreness, limited to one spot on my legs, and I could usually figure out why I had it. For example, if I wore spikes on the track, I could usually count on my calves being sore the next day, and I could count on that soreness disappearing within a few days. What I experience now is different, it's more low grade but it is almost always there. (p. 156)

I interpret the increased stiffness described by Rodgers as evidence of a fixed alteration in his muscle structure and function, causing a progressively reduced capacity to absorb shock and return elastic energy. This results in the earlier onset of fatigue and hitting the wall, especially during marathon races.

Thus, for older athletes, the value of walking (or cycling) may be that a measure of fitness can be achieved without risking further damage to the shock-absorbing and energy return systems in the legs. There may be a brain preprogramming component, as well.

Photo courtesy of the Boston Athletic Association.

Figure 5.8 "Boston Billy" Rodgers—arguably America's favorite marathoner of the 1970s and 1980s.

Finally, in keeping with his ability to foresee trends in physical activity 50 years later, Newton also expressed some ideas about training for the triathlon or, at least, about the effects of cycling and swimming on running performance. He commented that walking, cycling, and swimming made no difference to his running abilities but did serve the purpose of keeping him "thoroughly fit."

Law 9: Incorporate Base Training and Sharpening

This rule implies that peak racing performance only occurs when a period of high-intensity, low-volume training (peaking or sharpening) follows a prolonged buildup period consisting of low-intensity, high-volume training (base training).

Franz Stampfl, the coach who had more to do with the first sub-4-minute mile than is generally acknowledged, was one of the first coaches to introduce the idea of background and peaking training (Stampfl 1955). But unquestionably, the coaches who refined this concept and first described it in detail were the Australian swimming coach, Forbes Carlile (1963), and the New Zealand running coach, Arthur Lydiard (Lydiard and Gilmour 1978).

In his book, Carlile (1963) provided the first detailed description of peaking that I could find. Figure 5.9 summarizes his ideas. Carlile divides the year into four quarters (periods I to IV) and into either a one-peak or two-peak year. For a one-peak year, period I comprises a complete rest from hard training, with emphasis on forms of exercise other than swimming. During period II, swimming training is increased, with the emphasis on technique, while period III is reserved for very heavy swimming training. This leads to period IV, the competitive period, during which the athlete tapers while competing regularly. In a two-peak year, all four periods are shortened, and less heavy training is done during period III.

Two runners of that era who achieved their greatest success using this Carlile/Lydiard method of peaking were New Zealander Peter Snell and the "Flying Finn," Lasse Viren. Their stories illustrate the value of peaking. More recently, the great Kenyan runners have developed their own unique method of peaking.

Snell, the 1960 800-m Olympic gold medalist, had been written off by the press four weeks before the 1964 Olympic Games because he was unable to run the mile in less than 4 minutes. However, at the finals, Snell was unbeatable. While his competitors had already peaked by the time they arrived at the Olympics, Snell used the heats as the speed work he needed to bring him to his peak.

In January 1962, Snell completed what J. Kenneth Doherty (1964) considers the greatest middle-distance running the world has ever seen. In early December, Snell completed a standard marathon as part of Lydiard's base training program and began sharpening training in mid-December. With only two and a half weeks of speed training, he ran a mile in 4:01.3. During the following five weeks, he ran 880 yards in 1:48.3 and 1:47.3 and ran 800 m in 1:46.2; three days after the latter event, he ran a mile in the world record time of 3:54.4, followed one week later by a world record 800 m in 1:44.3 and 880 yards in 1:45.1. Snell fulfilled Lydiard's belief that his system would bring runners (you) "to your peak slower than many runners [ensuring that] you will be running last when they are running first. But when it is really important to run first, you will be passing them" (Lydiard and Gilmour 1978, p. 33).

Similarly, Lasse Viren—a winner of very little besides four gold medals, two each at the 5000 m and 10,000 m in the 1972 and 1976 Olympic Games—appeared to be

Time	Southern hemisphere	Northern hemisphere	Relative amounts of training	
			One-peak year	Two-peak year
PERIOD I Recuperation	April to June	November to January		
PERIOD II Gentle training	July to September	February to April		
PERIOD III Hard training	October to December	May to July		
PERIOD IV Hard competition	January to March	August to October		

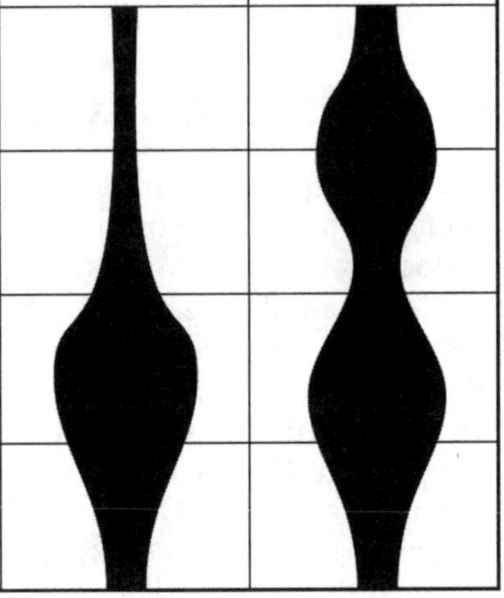

Figure 5.9 The Forbes Carlile yearly training plan.
Adapted from Carlile (1963, p.17). © 1963 by Forbes Carlile.

an "ordinary" athlete in non-Olympic years but beat the world by following Lydiard's ideas and choosing to peak only once every four years. I vividly recall watching a replay of the 1976 Olympic Games 10,000-m final. With Viren leading the British hopeful Brendan Foster by half a lap, English broadcaster Ron Pickering remarked in dismay, "But Brendan Foster has beaten Lasse Viren four times this year." Viren spent four years of background training preparing for a single peak at the Olympic Games. And when he peaked, no one was near him. Of this ability Viren commented: "Some do well in other races, some run fast times, but they cannot do well in the ultimate, the Olympics. . . . The question is not why I run this way, but why so many cannot" (Daws 1978).

One of the less well appreciated facts about the rise of the great dynasty of Kenyan runners since 1985 was that Kenyan running began to sink into the (relative) doldrums in the early 1980s, in part because Kenya boycotted both the 1976 and the 1980 Olympic Games. As a result, a generation of runners was denied the incentive for excellence offered by the Olympic Games. However, former Kenyan international runner Michael Kosgei, who was appointed as the new national Kenyan coach in 1984, came up with a radical solution. He proposed that, in the future, teams chosen to represent Kenya in major international events (in particular the World Cross Country Championships) would be selected only from the best runners present at a three-week training camp held at altitude immediately before those international competitions. The effect was that Kenya's best runners at those camps would know that, to represent their country, they would have to race each other daily in training for those 21 days. The result is that Kenyan teams competing in international meets now represent the survivors of the hardest peaking training program ever undertaken by human athletes. For those who survive this ultimate peaking program, international competition must feel like a day off. Since adopting this model, the Kenyans have absolutely dominated the World Cross Country Championships and have achieved unequalled success in the Olympic Games (see chapter 6).

Somewhat easier and more conventional peaking methods have been described by Carlile (1963), Osler (1967 and 1978), Daws (1977), Lydiard and Gilmour (1978), and Daniels (1998), where more detailed explanations of the ideas and programs followed by these runners can be found. I personally found the books of Daws and Osler the most readable and easiest to follow. Their ideas are outlined in the section that follows.

Base Training

Base training consists mainly of long, slow distance (LSD) running. The aim is to run as high a mileage as possible without overtraining and to increase gradually the average speed and distance of the training sessions.

Tom Osler (1978; figure 5.10) suggests that base training should continue for at least six months and preferably one year before beginning any sharpening training. He also writes that the guiding principle during base training is that, after any training session, the runner should feel able to turn around and complete the same workout again if demanded.

According to Osler (1967 and 1978), base training provides the following benefits:

- It develops robust health.
- It conditions the cardiovascular system.
- Its slow pace helps keep injuries to a minimum.
- It fosters a continual, slow improvement. (Osler calls this an improvement in the runner's "base performance level.")
- It has a desharpening effect and conserves what Osler calls "adaptation energy."

No one knows precisely what adaptation energy is. Osler also refers to this energy form as "competitive juices." He suggests that we all have limited reserves of these juices, which must be expended with care. This concept is similar to that proposed by Hans Selye in his General Adaptation Theory and is also alluded to by Lord Moran (1945) in his discussion of the battle-weary troops in the trenches at the battle of the Somme during World War I. Moran wrote,

In war, men wear out like clothes. All around me are the faces of men who do not seem to have slept for a week. Some who were tired before, look ill; the very gait of the men has lost its spring. The sap has gone out of them. They are dried up. (Moran 1945, p. 70)

Later, Moran described similar observations in the Royal Air Force Bomber Command in World War II:

When a pilot's behavior on the ground changes, when a lad that had been the life and soul of the mess becomes silent and morose, when he loses interest and zest, and becomes critical and bad-tempered, then it is too late to save him. Moods were the (silent) language in which they spoke to us of their distress. (Moran 1945, p. 43)

Osler contends that stressful conditions of training hard and racing, like fighting a war, use up these competitive juices and that, when they are exhausted, the athlete is no longer able to perform to potential. Osler's theories have since been confirmed by our studies (Barron et al. 1985) showing that overtrained runners are unable to respond normally to stress by releasing the appropriate stress hormones or juices.

Osler warns that although base training is a very safe training method, its main disadvantage is that it fails to prepare either body or mind for the stresses of racing. In particular, it fails to develop the coordination and the relaxation at speed that are necessary for peak performance. Also, it fails to produce those biochemical adaptations specific to speed training (see chapter 3).

Thus, the athlete who only does pure base training may be able to run forever at a slow pace and will recover very quickly from even the most demanding performance but will never run to full potential. All the authors cited here agree that to achieve this, each athlete must undergo a period of sharpening.

Sharpening

Sharpening consists of any of a number of different training methods, the common feature of which is that they are all performed at race pace or faster, for varying lengths of time. The most common sharpening techniques are interval running and speed play (fartlek), hill work, and short races or time-trials of up to 8 to 10 km (Doherty 1964; Daws 1977; Galloway 1984; Lydiard and Gilmour 1978; Osler 1967; 1978; Glover and Schuder 1983; Martin and Coe 1997; Daniels 1998; see also chapter 6). These sessions become the focal point of training and may be performed one to three times per week, depending on the experience and physical strength of the athlete.

The Science of Sharpening Training

Surprisingly few studies of the effects of different training regimes on athletic performance have been quantified in scientifically designed trials (Hawley, Myburgh, et al. 1997). In part, this is because few exercise scientists have considered this to be important, choosing rather to study how the body adapts to training at the cellular and molecular level (Mujika 1998). Perhaps they believe that neither the Nobel Prize in Physiology or Medicine nor its sporting equivalent, the International Olympic Committee Science Prize, will be won by the exercise scientist who first discovers the most ideal athletic training program.

Another reason is that many of these studies have used surrogate physiological measures, such as a change in $\dot{V}O_2max$ (chapter 2) or in the "anaerobic threshold" (chapter 3), as predictors of an expected change in athletic performance according to the Cardiovascular/Anaerobic Model. Yet, changes in athletic performance frequently occur without any change in these physiological variables and vice versa (Madsen et al. 1993; McConell et al. 1993). Hence, studies based on that premise are not likely to establish the real effectiveness of different training programs.

A series of studies in our unit at the University of Cape Town and the Sports Science Institute of South Africa have attempted to evaluate the effects of specific additional "sharpening" training on the performance of athletes who have generally chosen to train exclusively with endurance-type training with little exposure to a systematic program that includes regular sessions of high-intensity training.

Our first study (Lindsay et al. 1996) showed that replacing 15% (about 50 km) of a group of cyclists' usual 300-km-per-week training with six twice-weekly sessions of 6 to 8 five-minute rides at 80% of the athletes' $\dot{V}O_2$max or 90% of their maximum heart rates improved their times in a 40-km cycling time-trial in the laboratory by 2 minutes (3.6%). Doubling the total number of training sessions by lengthening the high-intensity training program from three to six weeks did not produce any additional benefit (Westgarth-Taylor et al. 1997).

In the next study (Stepto et al. 1999), different groups of subjects performed high-intensity training of different durations (0:30 to 8:00) at different intensities (80% to 175% $\dot{V}O_2$max). Interestingly, only race pace (4:00 at 85% $\dot{V}O_2$max) or very high-intensity (0:30 at 175% $\dot{V}O_2$max) training improved cycling performance during a 40-km time-trial.

Hence, the surprising finding from those studies was the rapidity with which quite large changes in cycling endurance can be achieved with relatively little training. This provides documentary proof needed to verify the anecdotal observations reported by Osler.

This conclusion that measurable changes in performance can be produced rapidly by sharpening training is extended by the study of T.P. Smith et al. (1999) from Tasmania. Smith and colleagues measured the effects of sharpening training with two interval sessions per week for four weeks. Subjects trained at the maximal treadmill speed achieved during the $\dot{V}O_2$max test ($v\dot{V}O_2$max or V max; chapter 2). The duration of each interval was set at between 60% and 75% of the duration that each person could sustain when running at the V max. This duration was called T max. Each training session involved the repetition of either five or six of these intervals.

The authors made two interesting practical observations. First, when the exercise duration was 60% to 75% of T max, subjects maintained heart rates of approximately 90% to 95% maximum during all the intervals. However, when the exercise duration was 70% to 75% of T max, the heart rate would rise to 100% of maximum after the second or third repetition, suggesting that the intervals were too long and too stressful. Second, if the heart rate did not drop below 125 beats per minute between intervals, the next interval would always elicit a maximum heart rate.

But their main finding, in agreement with ours, was that this period of high-intensity training significantly increased V max, T max, and 3000-m time-trial performance, the latter by 2.8% (0:17). They also suggested that using V max as the exercise intensity and 60% and 70% of the T max as the exercise duration might be particularly useful in exercise prescription for athletes, a suggestion I find appealing for a number of reasons.

The first is because the variables are easily measurable and do not require any sophisticated equipment, other than a treadmill to measure V max and T max. The second is because the method does not require the measurement of blood lactate concentrations and the prescription of exercise according to biological phenomena like the anaerobic threshold, the physiological basis of which is in doubt (see chapter 3). Third, the incorporation of heart rate monitoring

(continued)

provides another tool to determine when the interval duration has been too long or the number of intervals too many.

Hence, the conclusion from this group of studies is that large improvements in performance can be achieved quite dramatically by the addition of six to eight sessions of high-intensity interval training over a period of three to four weeks, confirming the accuracy of the ninth law.

An intriguing question is: What is the physiological basis for these changes? According to the Cardiovascular/Anaerobic Model, high-intensity training would be expected to improve oxygen delivery to the trained muscles, thereby rendering them less anaerobic. Alternatively, sharpening training might improve the ability of the exercising muscles to contract under anaerobic conditions, perhaps by increasing their capacity to contract when muscle pH is low.

My bias is to suggest that such physiological changes are unlikely to occur either as rapidly or to the same extent as do the large changes in performance produced by sharpening training. I tend to believe that these rapid changes occur in the nervous system, so that sharpening training increases the mass of skeletal muscle that can be recruited during exercise before the central governor is maximally activated, terminating exercise. According to this theory, sharpening training reprograms the subconscious brain to accept a higher exercise intensity as safe than the governor was prepared to allow before sharpening training took place.

According to Osler, an important advantage of sharpening is that it teaches you to run relaxed even at race pace. More important, it produces specific, physiological adaptations that yield quite dramatic improvements in racing performances, as shown by the experience of Peter Snell. Osler reports that after eight weeks of sharpening, he runs 10 to 20 sec per mile faster than previously and expects an 11-minute improvement in his marathon time.

But even more than base training, sharpening training has serious disadvantages. In particular, it is very taxing and uses up adaptation energy; it increases the risk of injury and reduces resistance to infection. When sharpening, the athlete is on the knife's edge that divides a peak performance from a disastrous race. For this reason, sharpening can only be maintained for relatively short periods of time, with a probable maximum of between 8 and 12 weeks. I believe that this rule crosses all human activities, mental or physical. How, then, to achieve a peak?

Figure 5.10, which owes nothing to science and everything to the anecdotal experiences of great runners such as Lasse Viren and Peter Snell and great runner-thinkers such as Tom Osler and Bruce Fordyce (chapter 6), was first formulated by Osler (1967; 1978). The diagram compares the performance improvements that would be experienced by a runner following two different training methods of 32 weeks each. A hypothetical runner who chooses to do only base training in the 32-week period can expect to improve her racing performance along the line A–G. Osler calls this the improvement in the runner's base performance level.

If, however, our hypothetical runner chooses to start sharpening at the twelve-week point on the graph (point B) and, instead of only doing long, slow distance running, she now includes speed training, her racing performance will improve quite dramatically along the portion B–C–D of the graph. Eight weeks after starting sharp-

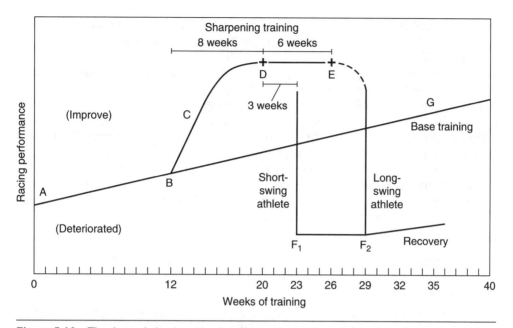

Figure 5.10   The theory behind peaking. Note that the performance of short-swing athletes begins to fall after about 11 weeks of sharpening training whereas that of long-swing athletes may continue to improve for up to 14 weeks of sharpening training.

ening training, her potential racing performance will probably start to plateau (point D). Please note that the time intervals shown on the graph are somewhat arbitrary and have been arrived at by empirical observation of rather small numbers of runners rather than by careful scientific study. Some runners will take either longer or shorter periods to arrive at the various points on the diagram.

To my knowledge, the first author to identify that people differ in the rapidity with which they adapt during peaking was Ludwig Prokop (1963-64), who noted that there are two types of athletes, the "short-swing" and the "long-swing" types. Short-swing athletes are able to improve their condition very quickly but can maintain their performances for only short periods of time before they must return to base training. These athletes are able to peak several times during the season. Long-swing types, on the other hand, need considerably more training to reach their peak, which they can also sustain for much longer.

Prokop reported that his athletes usually required seven to eight weeks' sharpening training to reach a peak that would last for between three and six weeks before their performances would start to fall. Two great athletes who observed this in themselves were Derek Clayton (1980) and Ron Hill (1981; 1982), who found that their running improved steadily for approximately 10 weeks. Beyond this period, they were easily tired, slept badly, were often injured, and raced poorly.

Once this hypothetical runner reaches her peaking plateau (line D–E in the diagram), she is ready for her best race, and all she need do is maintain her sharpening training. As coach Jumbo Elliott said: "After you start hard racing, hard training will get you nowhere" (Liquori and Parker 1980, page 150).

A frequent problem is that once a runner realizes he is on to a peak, he will seldom be happy with just one good race, unless that race happens to be in the

Olympics. Inevitably, the now-greedy runner tries to pack in too many races, the last of which he runs when his performance level is already on the precipitous downward slide of the performance curve. The result is that he ends up injured, ill, and thoroughly overtrained—depicted as points F1 and F2 on the diagram and described in detail in chapter 7. An important feature of the line E–F2 is its steepness. I suspect that it takes only three weeks to go from a best-ever performance to the point at which you are physically incapacitated.

Two final points shown on the graph are the slow rate of recovery from overtraining and the way in which a sharpening runner can perform either much better or much worse than a runner who has performed only base training.

It is possible to monitor the success of peaking. Just as runners who do too much develop specific warning symptoms (chapter 7), so runners' bodies tell them when they are sharpening correctly. Once again, Osler (1967; 1978) first recorded these symptoms:

- During the speed-training sessions, the body no longer needs to be forced through the session. Rather the body "surges forward at its own will" and "thirsts to accelerate."

- In the hour following training, the runner feels supreme vigor, quite unlike the normal postexercise feelings of mild fatigue.

- Everyday physical activities, such as climbing stairs, become easier.

- The runner becomes increasingly sensitive to everyday situations and is mildly irritable as the body is "prepared for action and is ready for the fight."

- As the body becomes flooded with previously latent energy, a heightened sexual awareness is often evident.

With regard to speed training during this peaking phase, I have observed that proper speed work training probably requires the presence of a coach (Law 12). Speed work requires more finesse and understanding than does long, slow, distance running (LSD), as it is more likely to cause injury or physical breakdown. For these reasons, it is essential to train with someone else who can analyze objectively whether the speed work is having the desired effect. Something coach Arthur Lydiard has written may at first seem to contradict this advice:

> There is no coach in the world who can say exactly what athletes should do as far as the number of repetitions, distances and intervals are concerned. Not even physiologists can tell an athlete that. The important point is that the athlete knows what he is trying to achieve and goes out and works at it until he does. (Lydiard and Gilmour 1978, p. 12)

The point I believe Lydiard is making is that interval coaching is as empirical as are all forms of coaching, and that is all the more reason to have two heads—an athlete's and a coach's—working on the problem rather than one.

Fast running is best done when the body and mind demand it. Fast running should be an enjoyable change from the occasional monotony of long training runs. When it is not, it indicates that the body is too tired and that the session must be postponed until the speed session again becomes pleasurable. (Refer to the different approaches of John Walker and Derek Clayton in chapter 6.) If Walker struggled in an interval training session, he packed up and went home; when Clayton struggled, he carried on until he had completed what his mind said that his body should do.

Such obsessiveness is inevitably destructive and probably explains why Clayton was injured so frequently.

But Walker's experience teaches another lesson. Attempting to become the first athlete aged over 40 to run a sub-4-minute mile, Walker was forced to retire from the sport as a result of crippling Achilles tendinosis. American miler Steve Scott experienced the same end to his career.

My impression had been that speed work becomes increasingly dangerous with age, especially in those who, like these two great milers, have trained heavily for decades. I predicted that the first person over 40 years old to break the 4-minute barrier would be a relatively unknown runner.

However, in 1994 Irishman Eamonn Coghlan—the indoor mile record holder of the 1970s—disproved this theory when he came out of retirement to become the first athlete over 40 years of age to break the sub-4-minute mile. It is surprising that though he had exposed his legs to decades of heavy training, especially speed work, he was still able to survive the quantity and quality of speed work necessary to run a sub-4-minute mile after 40. He did, however, retire a second time after this performance due to Achilles tendinopathy.

You cannot do speed training indefinitely within a season. Carlile and Lydiard have taught us that six to eight weeks' intensive training, when added to a solid period of base training, is all that is needed for a peak performance, and this is something on which everyone seems to agree (Osler 1967; 1978; Daws 1977; Galloway 1984; Glover and Schuder 1983; Dellinger and Freeman 1984). Derek Clayton (1980) wrote that he could sustain heavy training for only 10 weeks before his performances began to deteriorate.

Significantly, Ron Hill came to precisely the same conclusion (Hill 1982, page 160), for he wrote, "my ideal build-up to a peak occupies a period of ten weeks." When two of the world's best marathoners, as well as Mark Allen, arguably the greatest male triathlete of all time, come to the same conclusion independently, then there is likely to be some truth in it.

All too often I have seen not only runners but also other endurance athletes who, in attempting to maintain heavy training for longer than this period, have performed poorly in their target races. This is always a tragedy: they invest so much effort that, for the want of just a little knowledge and moderation, is wasted.

The most beneficial forms of speed training for marathon and ultramarathon runners seem to be hill running and fast, long intervals on the track. For those interested, the principles of hill training have been best described by Ron Daws (1977) and Bruce Fordyce (1996). Although Lydiard includes the use of short intervals (100 and 200 m) in his marathon training methods, I think that longer intervals (800 m to 1.6 km) are probably better for 10-km and marathon training.

One of the joys of speed training is the rapid improvement you feel. Very little effort produces remarkable rewards. I found that when I started my interval training sessions, I was able to run only two, or possibly three, 1-km repetitions, each of which was very tiring. But after four or five such sessions, I was able to do twice as many repetitions, much faster and without the distress I experienced in the first session.

As long as I was running as fast as or faster than before with the same or less effort, I knew that the speed training was beneficial. However, if the sessions became increasingly difficult and the interval times started to slow, then I knew that I was in trouble and that my body was telling me that it had done too much and required a period of rest with no training, not more and harder training.

Where many runners make a critical error is that they believe that the fall in performance during these sessions indicates they are not sufficiently motivated and are being lazy. Instead of resting, they try harder and compound the error and the risk of overtraining. There is a danger that by training under these conditions, athletes not only damage themselves physically but also use up the motivation they should be conserving for their one all-out racing effort.

Short races of 5 to 16 km are an excellent form of speed training. Run these as hard efforts controlled by perceived effort or by heart rate, rather than by the stopwatch (Law 7). These races should serve as the equivalent of a hard interval session. By starting the race at a comfortable pace that you increase gradually with each kilometer, you will end the race having run 4 to 8 km at a hard pace (equivalent to an interval session of three to five 1.6-km repetitions). But because you started slowly without concern for your total time and did not race the entire distance, the overall stress of the race is reduced and you will recover more quickly.

Another reason for running these short races this way is that short-distance races usually fall on weekends when a long training run is also required. Galloway (1984) and Glover and Schuder (1983) emphasize not combining speed work or a race and a long training run on the same weekend: "Never put two stress days together under any circumstances" (Galloway 1984, page 134). Indeed, Galloway suggests that even after a race of only 10 km you should take about one week's easy running before tackling speed work or another long run. He also stresses that two easy days should follow each hard session or long training run (Law 5).

By racing half or less of the total race distance in these races, you can run them more frequently. I ran only 7 to 10 speed sessions during the entire peaking phase. This conforms closely to Galloway's suggestion of running only one speed session per week when training for a 10-km race and one every second week before the marathon. Galloway (1984) also proposes that you should never complete an interval session feeling totally fatigued and that you should rest for as long as desired between each interval repeat.

The keys to high-intensity training are the following:

- The volume of high-intensity training completed each week must not exceed a certain proportion of the total weekly training volume.
- The intensity (running speed) of each high-intensity training session must be tailored appropriately for each athlete's individual running ability.
- The duration (weeks) of the high-intensity training program must be carefully controlled.
- There needs to be some variety in the types of high-intensity training that the athlete performs during the period of high-intensity (peaking) training.

The man who has best described his philosophy in concise, easily understandable terms is the running guru, coach, and exercise physiologist, Jack Daniels, former coach to the Nike Athletics West Club in Eugene, Oregon, who is considered by some North Americans to be "the world's best coach."

Jack Daniels' Training Philosophy

In *Daniels' Running Formula* (1998), Daniels describes the wisdom he has acquired in the course of 36 years of coaching many of North America's most successful athletes. His success has been aided by his training in exercise physiology, including his doctoral thesis, in which he evaluated the effects of altitude training on the sea-level performance of a group of elite distance runners, including Jim Ryun (Daniels and Oldridge 1970). He is also coauthor of the crucially relevant *Oxygen Power*, from which the data in table 2.4 were extracted.

As a result of his training in classical exercise physiology, Daniels uses specific physiological terms to describe both the nature of his different training sessions and the physiological adaptations that will result from those training sessions. The strength of this approach is that it fixes in athletes' minds the exact reason *why* they are doing a particular workout.

However, the terminology used by Daniels and by Pete Pfitzinger (who appears to have been a disciple of Daniels and whose ideals are described subsequently) indicates that they are dedicated proponents of the Cardiovascular/Anaerobic Model. Hence, they both define the exercise intensities for their different sessions in terms of the different (anaerobic) thresholds that are at the core of that model. Furthermore, they explain the adaptations that are likely to occur, purely in terms of altering capacities of oxygen delivery to and use by the muscles, with resulting changes in skeletal muscle lactate production.

While these objections may be valid, they do not detract from the clear evidence that Daniels has achieved great practical success with this training method. That he uses an unproven and perhaps dated model to explain the physiological reasons for his success is of no consequence. In time, science will catch up with Daniels and will provide a more correct physiological explanation as to why his methods, field-tested for more than three decades, produce the superior results his athletes have achieved.

Thus, Daniels proposes that there are six physiological processes, each of which needs to be adapted optimally if the athlete is to achieve optimum competitive performance:

1. Improving the body's ability to transport blood and oxygen
2. Increasing the ability of the running muscles to use the available oxygen effectively
3. Raising the lactate threshold to a faster running speed
4. Increasing aerobic capacity, $\dot{V}O_2max$
5. Improving running speed
6. Lowering the energy demand of running (improving running economy)

Daniels further concludes that there are unique exercise intensities that will specifically adapt each of those different physiological processes.

However, to my knowledge, there are no published studies that prove that training at a particular exercise intensity uniquely adapts only one of the six physiological processes listed by Daniels. Perhaps this lack of evidence is simply because scientists have not yet researched this possibility in sufficient depth. Alternatively, as seems more likely to me, it may be that the body adapts all these different physiological processes during all training, regardless of its intensity, but that certain adaptations are emphasized at specific running intensities. For example, long, slow distance training may well enhance the mitochondrial capacity to oxidize fats, but it is also likely to adapt the connective tissue in the lower limbs, enabling it to cope better with repeated eccentric loading. Similarly, any training at intensities greater than the incorrectly labeled "anaerobic threshold" is likely to alter whole body lactate mechanics (Macrae et al. 1992), whether that training is at 80% or 100% of $\dot{V}O_2$max.

Remember, then, that the physiological goals listed by Daniels are specific for the Cardiovascular/Anaerobic Model and do not take into account the other models of exercise that may equally determine running performance at different distances. Thus, this training ethos does not acknowledge that adapting the muscles to absorb the shock of running may be another important adaptation for marathon running specifically, as described in chapter 2. Furthermore, consideration is not given to the possibility that training adaptations may also occur in the brain and that these changes could possibly explain how training improves running performance.

With those points of scientific clarification, it is then appropriate to explain in detail how Daniels advises you to structure a high-intensity training program and what he believes are the specific physiological benefits of each of the different training methods that he advocates.

The first form of high-intensity training proposed by Daniels is the so-called VDOT training. This is training performed at the running speed at which the $\dot{V}O_2$max is achieved. We have already used the ideas of Daniels and others to explain the concept that a particular VDOT or $\dot{V}O_2$max value predicts the likely running performances at other distances. Thus, the athlete who wishes to determine a VDOT value on the basis of the best running performance according to the Daniels method should refer to table 2.4.

In table 5.6, Daniels (1998) lists the six training intensities (as a percentage of VDOT) that he considers most effective in enhancing running performance. The six different intensities are:

Easy/Long (E/L) Pace. This intensity refers to the pace the athlete should maintain for easy and long runs. These are run at about 70% of $\dot{V}O_2$max and, according to Daniels, enable the body to cope with fluid loss and glycogen depletion and to burn more fat during prolonged exercise. Such training probably also helps adapt the muscles, enabling them to cope with the loading requirements of prolonged exercise. Columns 2 and 3 in table 5.6 list the E/L pace that should be achieved by athletes with different VDOT values.

Marathon Pace (MP). This is the pace that the athlete may hope to maintain during a marathon race. The appropriate pace in minutes per mile is listed as column 4 in table 5.6.

Threshold (T) Pace. These runs are considered to occur at the anaerobic threshold, which is at about 88% of VDOT ($\dot{V}O_2$max) or at 90% of either the maximum heart rate or the running speed at the $\dot{V}O_2$max (v$\dot{V}O_2$max). Daniels describes such training as comfortably hard running at about 25 to 30 seconds per mile (16 to 19 seconds per km) slower than current 5-km race pace. Daniels stresses that it is important to run at this pace and not any faster, which is hard for many overenthusiastic runners to do. He argues that running at a higher intensity does not enhance the physiological adaptations to this type of training. Columns 5, 6, and 7 in table 5.6 list the T pace that should be achieved by athletes with different VDOT values. Daniels also defines tempo runs as 20-minute runs at the threshold pace. Similarly, cruise intervals are repeated runs of between 3 and 15 minutes at threshold pace, broken up by short recovery

Table 5.6 Training paces (min:sec) based on the current VDOT ($\dot{V}O_2$max) method of J. Daniels (1998)

1	2	3	4	5	6	7	8	9	10	11	12	13	14
VDOT	E/L Pace		MP	T Pace			I Pace				R Pace		
	km	mile	mile	400	1000	mile	400	1000	1200	mile	200	400	800
30	7:13	12:16	11:02	2:33	6:24	10:18	2:22	–	–	–	67	2:16	–
32	7:16	11:41	10:29	2:26	6:05	9:47	2:14	–	–	–	63	2:08	–
34	6:56	11:09	10:00	2:19	5:48	9:20	2:08	–	–	–	60	2:02	–
36	3:38	10:40	9:33	2:13	5:33	8:55	2:02	5:07	–	–	57	1:55	–
38	6:22	10:14	9:08	2:07	5:19	8:33	1:56	4:54	–	–	54	1:50	–
40	6:07	9:50	8:46	2:02	5:06	8:12	1:52	4:42	–	–	52	1:46	–
42	5:53	9:28	8:25	1:57	4:54	7:52	1:48	4:31	–	–	50	1:42	–
44	5:40	9:07	8:06	1:53	4:43	7:33	1:44	4:21	–	–	48	98	–
45	5:34	8:58	7:57	1:51	4:38	7:25	1:42	4:16	–	–	47	96	–
46	5:28	8:48	7:48	1:49	4:33	7:17	1:40	4:12	5:00	–	46	94	–
47	5:23	8:39	7:40	1:47	4:29	7:10	98	4:07	4:54	–	45	92	–
48	5:17	8:31	7:32	1:45	4:24	7:02	96	4:49	4:49	–	44	90	–
49	5:12	8:22	7:24	1:43	4:20	6:55	95	3:59	4:45	–	44	89	–
50	5:07	8:14	7:17	1:42	4:15	6:51	93	3:55	4:41	–	43	87	–
51	5:02	8:07	7:09	1:40	4:11	6:44	92	3:51	4:36	–	42	86	–
52	4:58	7:59	7:02	98	4:07	6:38	91	3:48	4:33	–	42	85	–
53	4:53	7:52	6:56	97	4:04	6:32	90	3:44	4:29	–	41	84	–
54	4:49	7:45	6:49	95	4:00	6:26	88	3:41	4:25	–	40	82	–
55	4:45	7:38	6:43	94	3:56	6:20	87	3:37	4:21	–	40	81	–
56	4:40	7:31	6:37	93	3:53	6:15	86	3:34	4:18	–	39	80	–
57	4:36	7:25	6:31	91	3:50	6:09	85	3:31	4:15	–	39	79	–
58	4:33	7:19	6:25	90	3:45	6:04	83	3:28	4:10	–	38	77	–
59	4:29	7:13	6:19	89	3:43	5:59	82	3:25	4:07	–	37	76	–
60	4:25	7:07	6:14	88	3:40	5:54	81	3:23	4:03	–	37	75	2:30
61	4:22	7:01	6:09	86	337	5:50	80	3:20	4:00	–	36	74	2:28
62	4:18	6:56	6:04	85	334	5:45	79	3:17	3:57	–	36	73	2:26
63	4:15	6:50	5:59	84	3:32	5:41	78	3:15	3:54	–	35	72	2:24
64	4:12	6:45	5:54	83	3:29	5:36	77	3:12	3:51	–	35	71	2:22
65	4:09	6:40	5:49	82	3:26	5:32	76	3:10	3:48	–	34	70	2:20
66	4:05	6:53	5:45	81	3:24	5:28	75	3:08	3:45	5:00	34	69	2:18
67	4:02	6:30	5:40	80	3:21	5:24	74	3:05	3:42	4:57	33	68	2:16
68	4:00	6:26	5:36	79	3:19	5:20	73	3:03	3:39	4:53	33	67	2:14
69	3:57	6:21	5:32	78	3:16	5:16	72	3:01	3:36	4:50	32	66	2:12
70	3:54	6:17	5:28	77	3:14	5:13	71	2:59	3:34	4:46	32	65	2:10
71	3:51	6:12	5:24	76	3:12	5:09	70	2:57	3:31	4:43	31	64	2:08
72	3:49	6:08	5:20	76	3:10	5:05	69	2:55	3:29	4:40	31	63	2:06
73	3:46	6:04	5:16	75	3:08	5:02	69	2:53	3:27	4:37	31	62	2:05
74	3:44	6:00	5:12	74	3:06	4:59	68	2:51	3:25	4:34	30	62	2:04
75	3:41	5:56	5:09	74	3:04	4:56	67	2:49	3:22	4:31	30	61	2:03
76	3:39	5:52	5:05	73	3:02	4:52	66	2:48	3:20	4:28	29	60	2:02
77	3:36	5:48	5:01	72	3:00	4:49	65	2:46	3:18	4:25	29	59	2:00
78	3:34	5:45	4:58	71	2:58	4:46	65	2:44	3:16	4:23	29	59	1:59
79	3:32	5:41	4:55	70	2:56	4:43	64	2:42	3:14	4:20	28	58	1:58
80	3:30	5:38	4:52	70	2:54	4:41	64	2:41	3:12	4:17	28	58	1:56
81	3:28	5:34	4:49	69	2:53	4:38	63	2:39	3:10	4:15	28	57	1:55
82	3:26	5:31	4:46	68	2:51	4:35	62	2:38	3:08	4:12	27	56	1:54
83	3:24	5:28	4:43	68	2:49	4:32	62	2:36	3:07	4:10	27	56	1:53
84	3:22	5:25	4:40	67	2:48	4:30	61	2:35	3:05	4:08	27	55	1:52
85	3:20	5:21	4:37	66	2:46	4:27	61	2:33	3:03	4:05	27	55	1:51

Reprinted, by permission, from J. Daniels (1998, pp. 250-53).

periods of usually 1 minute or less. The total amount of quality running for a cruise interval workout must never exceed 10% of the weekly mileage with a minimum of 6000 m or 13,000 m per week.

Interval (I) Pace. Daniels defines this running intensity as the speed that can be maintained for 10 to 15 minutes in a race situation that, for an elite athlete, is about the 5000-m race pace. The interval pace is described as demanding or hard running but does not involve all-out running. Daniels again warns that completing intervals at too fast a pace is of no value as the results will be no better than if you had run at the designated pace. In addition, the excessive pace will probably prevent full recovery before your next quality training session. Columns 8, 9, 10, and 11 give the interval pace for interval training according to the different VDOT values. Daniels also stipulates that interval training should never include more than 5 minutes of intense running. The total amount of quality running in an interval session should be less than 8% of the weekly mileage with a 10-km maximum. As these intervals are without doubt the most demanding training you can do, you must never do too many. Hence Daniels's six criteria for interval training are the following:

1. Run intervals of between 0:30 and 5:00 duration.

2. Stick to the I pace for all aspects of quality running.

3. Run easily during recoveries.

4. Keep recovery periods equal to or shorter than the work bouts they follow.

5. Let the quality portion of an interval session total up to 8% of your current weekly mileage with a nonnegotiable upper limit of 10 km.

6. Allow sufficient time to recover so that you feel you can perform the next interval as well as you did the previous one.

Repetition (R) Pace. Running at this pace, which is faster than $\dot{V}O_2$max pace, aims to develop your speed, economy, and relaxation when running at the fastest speeds of which you are capable. Daniels suggests that this training does not influence either the $\dot{V}O_2$max or the lactate threshold. The final three columns in table 5.6 list the repetition paces for athletes with different VDOT values.

Rest. The unsolved paradox of training is that while training allows you to run faster both in training and in racing, it also causes a progressive, accumulated fatigue without which you would run even faster. Frequent rest allows partial recovery from that accumulating fatigue, hence better training. Proper tapering before competition allows a more complete recovery, without which a peak performance is not possible.

Daniels advises runners to remain at the same training intensity for at least three or four weeks and at the same overall training volume for at least three weeks before increasing the mileage. Daniels's specific training programs, in which he combines all the different training sessions into comprehensive and coherent training programs for 10- to 21- and 42-km races, are presented in chapters 9 and 10. A final insight by Daniels is his classification of four different types of runners:

Type 1. Those with high ability and motivation. It is from this group that the champions come.

Type 2. Those with high ability but little motivation. These are the athletes who will forever frustrate the coach.

Type 3. Those with little ability, but high motivation. These are the athletes who frustrate themselves and are the potential overtrainers.

Type 4. Those with little ability and little motivation. These people should not do any sports that require discipline. They are in the wrong activity.

Pete Pfitzinger's Training Advice

Pete Pfitzinger is a two-time member of the U.S. men's Olympic Marathon Team. In 1984, he was voted America's best distance runner and was named Runner of the Year by the Road Runners' Club of America. He is also a two-time winner of the San Francisco Marathon and finished third in the 1987 New York City Marathon. He has coached for 18 years and holds an MSc degree in exercise science from the University of Massachusetts. His book, coauthored by runner/writer Scott Douglas (Pfitzinger and Douglas 1999), provides another approach to the training of serious distance runners.

Pfitzinger describes five components of training:

1. Short, fast speed work to improve "leg turnover and running form"
2. Longer repetitions of 2 to 6 minutes at 3- to 5-km race pace to improve the $\dot{V}O_2max$
3. Tempo runs of 20 to 40 minutes at 10-mile (16-km) race pace to increase the lactate threshold
4. Long runs to build endurance
5. Easy recovery runs to allow a maximum effort on the hard training days

Pfitzinger's ideas match those of Jack Daniels, as do his methods of achieving the different physiological adaptations. Note also that the Cardiovascular/Anaerobic Model is again used to explain the physiological adaptations that result from training.

Pfitzinger proposes that the optimum training to improve $\dot{V}O_2max$ is to run 4 to 8 km of intervals per workout. He proposes running one workout like this each week, and he suggests that the most appropriate form of training is to do repetitions of 2:00 to 6:00 duration (600 to 1600 m per interval). These intervals should be run at your 3- to 5-km race pace to ensure that you are running at between 95% to 100% of your $\dot{V}O_2max$. The duration of recovery should be sufficiently long so that your heart rate drops to 65% of maximum between intervals. Pfitzinger also believes that the classic workout to improve your lactate threshold is the tempo—a continuous run of 20 to 40 minutes at your lactate threshold pace, which is your 15- to 21-km race pace. He also proposes the use of Daniels's cruise intervals.

To improve pure endurance, Pfitzinger believes that your long runs should be completed at between 70% and 85% of your maximum heart rate. This, he suggests, is approximately 0:45 to 1:30 per mile (0:28 to 0:56 per km) slower than your marathon race pace or 1:00 to 2:00 per mile (0:38 to 1:16 per km) slower than your 15- to 21-km race pace. He also suggests that you should start these long runs at the slower end of the range and gradually increase your pace during the run. Recovery runs should be at less than 70% of your maximum heart rate, as also advocated by Daniels. Pfitzinger's specific training programs for 5- to 21- and 42-km races are presented in chapters 9 and 10.

Pfitzinger also expresses strong views on two additional aspects of training. He very expressively portrays the mental dilemma faced by many runners in the last few weeks and days before an important race:

To taper effectively for a marathon takes about three weeks. Unfortunately, our self-confidence is fragile. Our egos require the positive reinforcement of a hard workout every few days. If we take a few days easy—let alone three weeks—we go through withdrawal. Our distance runners' paranoia makes us fear that our muscles will turn to mush and that we will waste all those months of hard work. (Pfitzinger and Douglas 1999, p. 92)

The section on tapering in this chapter indicates that tapering for three weeks improves rather than hinders racing performance. In chapter 6, world champion triathlete Mark Allen describes how, once you start to train vigorously, your body becomes overstimulated and unable to recover properly. Pfitzinger describes a similar observation: constant sympathetic stimulation (induced by heavy training) leads to the feeling that your mind and body are always engaged; your fight or flight response is always activated (meaning that it's controlling you, rather than the other way around). As a result, you are simultaneously "on" and fatigued and therefore unable to relax fully or perform at your best.

Additional Advice on Training Intensities

Additional guidelines for the correct pace during interval training are provided by Galloway (1984). He suggests that you should run 400-m repetitions 5 to 7 seconds faster than your goal race pace, 800 m in 10 seconds faster than your goal pace, and the mile 15 to 20 seconds faster than your goal pace. The athlete who is unable to achieve these goals during interval training is almost certainly putting in too much mileage and will need to cut back to benefit optimally from this type of training.

Burfoot and Billing (1985) also believe that optimum training is achieved by including regular runs at three different intensities in your weekly training. They suggest that most of your training needs to be done at intensities between 65% to 75% $\dot{V}O_2$max, which correspond to the pace below that at which you run the 42-km marathon. The purpose of these runs, they suggest, is to improve running efficiency.

These authors also prescribe a once-a-week run of 5 to 10 km at 85% $\dot{V}O_2$max to shift the lactate turnpoint to a higher percentage $\dot{V}O_2$max. This exercise intensity corresponds to the speed you can maintain during races of 10 to 21 km. It is not necessary to run the 5 to 10 km of this session continuously. Rather, the authors suggest that this workout be run on the track or road as a series of repeat runs of 2 to 3 km.

Finally, run one session per week at a running pace eliciting $\dot{V}O_2$max. This intensity corresponds to the fastest speed at which you can run 3 km. Burfoot and Billing suggest 3 to 6 × 800 m or 8 to 12 × 400 m. However, these distances may be too short for less competitive marathon runners. If you find running these distances too demanding, you might try running 1-km to 1-mile intervals.

David Costill (1986) has also provided a list of what he considers appropriate times for different intervals, based on your best 10-km time (table 5.7). He divides the interval sessions into anaerobic, aerobic, and aerobic-anaerobic. He suggests that the anaerobic sessions should be 10 × 200 m with 2 minutes' rest between intervals; the aerobic intervals 20 × 400 m with 10 to 15 seconds' rest; and the aerobic-anaerobic intervals 10 × 400 m with 60 to 90 seconds' rest between intervals.

Table 5.7 Optimum running times for interval training based on best 10-km time

Best 10-km time (min:sec)	Intervals		
	200 m (anaerobic)*	400m (aerobic)*	400m (aerobic-anaerobic)
46:00	00:46	2:00	1:51
43:00	00:43	1:52	1:44
40:00	00:40	1:45	1:37
37:00	00:38	1:37	1:29
34:00	00:36	1:30	1:16

*These terms are not physiologically based (chapter 2) but refer to intervals that are either more (anaerobic) or less (aerobic) stressful because they are run either faster or slower after rest periods of different durations between intervals.

Adapted from Costill (1986, pp. 98, 101, 103). Permission granted by D.L. Costill.

Law 10: Prevent Overtraining

Perhaps one of the chief points is to regulate your training so as to be sure of always being on the safe side: the least sign of overdose will surely lead to trouble. Go so far every day that the last mile or two become almost a desperate effort. So long as you are fit for another dose the following day, you are not overdoing it. But you must never permit yourself to approach real exhaustion; you must never become badly tired. A good way to judge whether you are overdoing it is by your appetite. A really fearsome thirst is a definite sign that either the pace or the distance has been too much. Not only are you unbearably thirsty, but your appetite disappears entirely, even for many hours after the event.

Newton mentions some symptoms that the athlete who is doing too much will experience. The probable reason why he only lists a few is because he seldom, if ever, wore himself down by training too much and was unaware of the myriad other symptoms that appear when an athlete trains too hard. Of course, Newton lived in the era before runners had learned to train as hard as or harder than their bodies would allow. In addition, there were fewer races to run and few financial incentives to entice runners of that amateur era into racing too frequently.

Once again, Newton was 50 years ahead of scientists in his observation that an increased thirst at night is an indicator of overtraining. Richard Brown, exercise physiologist and former coach of Mary Slaney and of the Athletics West Club in Eugene, Oregon, has since shown that one of the earliest indicators of overtraining is an increased fluid intake in the evening (R.L. Brown 1983).

Chapter 7 contains a complete description of the overtraining syndrome and offers readers guidelines on how to avoid this major problem.

Remember also that if you follow the approach and guidelines proposed under Law 6 (achieve as much as possible on a minimum of training), you should only overreach or overtrain once in your career. Once you have identified your individual training threshold (figure 5.6), you need never again risk overtraining.

Law 11: Train With a Coach

When I began running, I was totally unaware of the potential value of a coach. Now that I have read more widely and have met and worked with some excellent coaches in different sports, including team sports, I liken the successful coach to a highly skilled artist whose work is infinitely more difficult than that of scientists like myself. Performing experiments in the laboratory, in which virtually all factors are rigorously controlled, is so much easier than trying to do the same with athletes who live in the real world and must therefore cope with the problems that life brings and that, inevitably, affect their running performances. I now also appreciate that, at least in international competition, the margin between success and failure is razor thin. It takes a special person, different from the more risk-averse scientists, to choose to live a professional career on that margin.

The more I have read, the more I have realized that a running coach is needed not necessarily for the physical preparation of the athlete but for inspiration and support, and to provide an objective analysis of when the athlete is doing too much. Franz Stampfl (1955, page 146) said as much himself: "The coach's job is 20% technical and 80% inspirational. He may know all there is to know about tactics, technique, and training, but if he cannot win the confidence and comradeship of his pupils, he will never be a good coach." In *Testament of a Runner*, W.R. Loader (1960) said much the same, and James Counsilman, the brilliant swimming coach of Indiana University, pinpointed another important role of the coach: "the most practical judgment of the point at which the swimmer has had exactly enough training is exercised by the coach. Perhaps the ability to do this effectively marks the difference between a good and a poor coach" (Counsilman 1968, page 234). He also wrote that the coach must contribute enthusiasm, create team unity, and provide guidance. "I prefer to visualize our experience as that of a well-informed coach talking to an intelligent group of athletes in a situation in which everyone has a common goal, that of achieving the full potential of each person and of involving each intellect in the process" (page 4).

Few athletes are made exclusively by training. Chapter 6 shows that there really are no training secrets known only to the most successful athletes. Many runners train just as hard, if not harder in some cases, yet they never achieve the same degree of success.

Marti Liquori, the American miler who trained under Jumbo Elliott, the coach generally considered to be the greatest ever produced in the United States (Elliott and Berry 1982), wrote, "Much of running is mental, and the guru coaches probably have been successful more because they knew how to harness a runner's heart and mind than because of any mysterious secret training formula" (Liquori and Parker 1980, page 35). Of Jumbo Elliott himself it was written: "His coaching method was a non-method. He insisted on their attention to studies. His method was in the application of his knowledge of the athletes, knowing which psychological approach would be most effective and when his man was ready" (Elliott and Berry 1982, pages 186-187).

This is the crux of good coaching—treating each athlete as a person and knowing which psychological approach will work best. For the athlete, the challenge remains to find the coach to whom you best relate. That coach should be sufficiently knowledgeable to prevent you from overtraining and should be able to extract the most from you. In Arthur Lydiard's words, "Two brains are better than one" (Lenton 1981, page 69).

Law 12: Train the Mind

When you begin training you will find that the longest and most strenuous mental and physical exertions all come at the start. . . . It seems to me that stamina is just as much a mental attribute as a physical one. Make your mind healthy and it will do the rest. If it is not normally healthy, you will never make a decent job of anything.

The idea that the mind is important in such an outwardly physical sport as running is also something that, even today, is not always appreciated. In fact, until very recently, there were very few contributions to running literature on the mental aspects of training, and even reviews on the evolution of training methods over the years pay scant attention to mental preparation for running (Burfoot 1981a).

It may be that success in running is ultimately determined not so much by training the body as by training the mind. This helps explain why consistently successful runners can always be relied on to perform well, why equally trained runners seldom perform equally, and why some runners who perform superbly in training never succeed in racing.

Percy Wells Cerutty was one of the first coaches to write openly about the importance of mental preparation for running. Certainly, Cerutty (1964, page 29) recognized that his greatest protégé, Herb Elliott, was mentally different: "Herb Elliott had the 'gift' of being able to exhaust himself. That is shared by very few. It is a type of personality, individuality, not of training. You have it—or you do not have it. Elliott had it 100%. His greatness as a runner rested in this."

Later, Elliott wrote, "If you emphasize the physical side of training you may become superbly conditioned but mentally not advanced at all. On the other hand, if you concentrate on the mental aspect, it is inevitable that the physical side will follow. My golden rule is to train for the mental toughness and [not to] train for the physical development" (Lenton 1981, page 32).

Another great miler, Marti Liquori, wrote: "The athletes who truly make it are mentally some of the toughest people in the world. No one is born with that kind of toughness, and it doesn't come overnight. You must develop it, cultivate it, cherish it!" (Liquori and Parker 1980, page 149)

In chapter 8, I focus on the mental aspects of training, as there is indeed a physiological basis to this concept of mental toughness required in running

Law 13: Rest Before a Big Race

Cut out all racing . . . during the last month of your training; you will need certainly three weeks to put the finishing touches to your stamina and reserve energy. When you consider what a vast amount of work you have already gone through, you will admit that a fortnight or so longer is a relatively trifling matter. Endeavor to keep all your spare time fully occupied with reading, writing: anything that will keep you still, anything to divert your mind from harping on the forthcoming event.

Before Newton, no other writers seem to have discussed the importance of resting up before a major race—a practice now referred to as tapering. Certainly, Alf Shrubb trained hard right up to the day of competition. Four days before he set his 16-km and 1-hour world records, he ran a 16-km time-trial in 50:55, just 15 seconds slower than his subsequent world record. The reason Shrubb was successful, even though he did not taper, was probably either because he was remarkably gifted or because he was not a heavy trainer. He also did not compete in races longer than 18 km. I believe that the harder athletes train and the longer the distances they race, the more vital the tapering process.

The Science of Tapering

Most of the information on tapering in this chapter is based on the advice given by the world's most successful athletes. Only recently have scientific studies evaluated the effects on performance of different tapering regimes.

Perhaps the first scientific study of this kind was reported as recently as 1992. Shepley et al. (1992) found that a high-intensity taper in which subjects ran 5 × 500 m on day 5 before the race, 4 × 500 m on day 4, 3 × 500 m on day 3, 2 × 500 m on day 2, and 1 × 500 m on the last day before the race produced significantly better performances during a maximal run lasting 6 minutes than did either complete rest or low-intensity training entailing a total of 30 km of running at 50% to 60% $\dot{V}O_2$max over the same five-day period. Certain metabolic changes were identified in the skeletal muscles of those who tapered with the high-intensity protocol. These changes included increased citrate synthase activity and higher muscle glycogen concentrations. However, it is difficult to understand how these minor changes could improve performance in a 6-minute run. It is possible that the main effect of this tapering program, which includes elements of sharpening training, may also be in the brain and its ability to recruit a larger muscle mass for longer during subsequent exercise.

A two-week taper in which cyclists reduced their high-intensity training by 88% and their total training by 66% improved their performance by 8% in a cycling test in which the work rate increased over 30 to 40 minutes (D.T. Martin et al. 1994). Interestingly, muscle power increased as a result of the taper, suggesting that recruitment of the muscles by the brain was altered with tapering.

Houmard and colleagues (1994) studied a group of subelite runners who reduced their daily training volume from about 10 km per day to about 1.5 km per day over seven days. Training during the taper took the form of 400-m intervals runs at 5-km race pace, with 100- to 200-m intervals added to complete the appropriate daily training volume. This taper resulted in a 2.8% improvement in 5-km running performance of between 9 to 30 seconds. Heart rate during the 5-km time-trial was higher after the taper, reflecting, in part, the faster running speed. Performance improved even though $\dot{V}O_2$max and blood lactate concentrations did not alter, indicating that the Cardiovascular/Anaerobic Model could not explain how this taper improved racing performance. These authors indeed concluded that "neural structural and biomechanical factors," consistent with the other performance models described in chapter 2, should be considered when explaining the beneficial effects of tapering. Further, they concluded that tapering seems to produce a 3% improvement in performance, regardless of the quality of the athlete or the volume or intensity of the preceding training.

The surprising point is that simply reducing the volume of training by up to 70% does not have the same effect (Houmard et al. 1990; 1992). Thus, the key would seem to be to do very little training during the taper, but to train only at race pace.

Banister et al. (1999) have evaluated whether it is better to reduce training during a two-week taper either by a small stepped reduction in daily training volume, or by a rapid, exponential reduction in volume. They found that the more rapidly training is reduced in the taper, the better the racing performance. Thus, the most effective taper was one in which training was reduced by 50% on the third day of the taper and by 75% on the sixth day with a continuing reduction for the next eight days.

In summary, the scientific evidence confirms that tapering produces a dramatic improvement in performance. The effect is greatest if there is a rapid reduction in training volume already in the first few days of the taper and if training during the taper is at high intensity, approximating 5-km race pace for runners. My advice is that once you decide to taper, do as little training as your mind will allow, but do that little training at a fast pace.

Other distance runners of the day were unaware of the importance of tapering. The day before the 1912 Stockholm Olympic Marathon, Christian Gitsham, the South African who finished second in that race, set out to run the complete marathon distance. Fortunately, his coach caught up with him after he had run 20 km and angrily returned him to his hotel. Some 11 days before the 1920 Antwerp Olympic Marathon, the team of four United States runners ran the course in 02:46:55, a time that they could barely repeat on race day (Temple 1981). On the race day, Joseph Organ ran 2:41:30, Carl Linder 2:44:21, and Charles Mellor 2:45:30 (Martin and Gynn 1979). The fourth United States runner did not finish.

One of the first authors to discuss the importance of resting before competition was Stampfl (1955), who insisted that his distance athletes rest for four full days before competition. But it was really Forbes Carlile (1963) who first emphasized the importance of resting up or tapering before competition. Incidentally, the term tapering was first coined by Carlile and Frank Cotton in 1947.

Carlile and Cotton found that after two or three months of hard training, their swimmers performed best if they eased their training for the last three weeks before major competition. At the end of the first week of tapering, the swimmers would complete a time-trial. "A poor time generally indicates that the swimmer needs more rest" (Carlile 1963, page 33). The 1962 European Swimming Championships proved the correctness of this approach. Before these championships, Carlile was appointed national coach to the Dutch swimming team, which had previously performed very poorly. Carlile's approach was to send each swimmer a document alerting them to the dangers of hard training during the last three weeks before competition. At the championships, all members of the team swam their best times of the year and all but two achieved personal bests as they "swept all before them."

Runners have only recently begun to realize that, as in the case of swimming, adequate taper also enhances running performance. Physiologist Ned Frederick (1983b) used the term "the Zatopek Phenomenon" to emphasize the importance of resting before competition. Frederick recounts that Emil Zatopek (chapter 6) was training very intensively for the 1950 European Games in Brussels when he became so ill that he had to be hospitalized for two weeks. He was released two days before the 10,000-m race, which, thanks to the enforced rest, he won by a full lap. A few days later, he won the 5000-m race by 23 seconds.

Other famous examples exist (see chapter 6). Dave Bedford set the 10,000-m world track record in 1973 after a minimum of training. Towards the end of 1973, Derek Clayton ran a 2:12:00 marathon after one of his "easiest preparations" (Clayton 1980). Four months later, he failed to complete the 1974 Commonwealth Games Marathon owing to injury. "I think," he later wrote, "there is a message here as I often thought I trained harder than necessary." (Clayton 1980, p. 130) British marathoner Ron Hill reported essentially the same experience. When 37-year-old Carlos Lopes won the 1984 Olympic Games Marathon in commanding style, he did so after an accident had prevented him from training for the last 10 days before the race. Similarly, Joan Benoit—who later became the first woman to win the Olympic Marathon gold medal—won the 1984 United States Olympic Marathon Trial only days after arthroscopic knee surgery for a condition that had interfered with her preparation. Later, she concluded that the surgery was probably the most important contributor to her victory since it forced her to train less.

I have also wondered whether the long and harsh Scandinavian winters, which forced former Norwegian world marathon record holder, Ingrid Christiansen, to train indoors on a treadmill for some months, in any way explained why she set the women's world record in the London Marathon in early spring 1985. Perhaps training indoors reduced the probability of overtraining as might have happened had she trained outdoors.

Thus, our understanding of the value of reduced training before competition has come a long way. It seems that no one knows how long the optimal tapering period before a big race should be. My own view is that it may take at least 10 to 14 days, and possibly even longer, for the body to recover fully from months of heavy training and racing and that this may be an individual response. Mark Allen would, for example, taper for four weeks before the Hawaiian Ironman Triathlon. The optimum volume of training needs to be determined by each person, so each runner needs to experiment with different tapering programs to determine which program produces the best results for the different distances. Guidelines for tapering are provided in chapter 10.

Law 14: Keep a Detailed Logbook

The runner's logbook serves the same function as the scientist's notebook, for it records the result of each day's experiment. When sufficient raw information has been collected, the data can be analyzed, theories developed, and new experiments planned.

The goal of each runner's training experiment is to be a better or, perhaps, healthier runner. The hypothesis under investigation is that this can be achieved effectively by a certain type of training. Thus, the key experiment that each runner must undertake is to determine the exact amount of training, appropriately quantified, that will achieve the desired result at the least possible cost in terms of time and the lowest risk of injury, illness, or overtraining (see figures 5.6 and 5.7).

As many athletes do not understand that they are involved in any such experiment, the outcome of which is not initially predictable, they fail to record those crucial daily measurements that will enable the necessary conclusions to be drawn and their optimum individual training programs to be developed by continual experimentation over a lifetime of running.

As a result, those ill-informed runners continue to wander, lost in the training wilderness, never quite knowing exactly how they should be training. If you do not wish to join those lost souls, you must learn early in your running career to record that daily information that will help you become an effective trainer, reaping maximum benefit from a minimum input.

Besides these advantages, a well-kept logbook is a runner's best friend, as it records the path that has been traveled in the search for fitness. It also provides a continuing source of motivation, as well as providing those important clues as to which training methods have been successful or, alternatively, not so successful.

Ultramarathoner Bruce Fordyce believes implicitly in the importance of keeping detailed logbooks, which he calls "textbooks" (Fordyce 1983). By comparing his performances in the same training sessions over the years, he was able to judge his fitness at any time of the year with pinpoint accuracy. The result was that he was always right on race day and thus established a degree of consistency never before seen in ultradistance running and equaled by very few other athletes.

The essential information to include in the logbook are the date, the training route, the details of the training session, the shoes worn, the running time and distance, running partners, and the weather conditions. These are the basic descriptive data to which you will return over the years to see, for example, how much and how fast you are now running in comparison with what you did in the past.

There are nine additional pieces of information that may be included in the logbook, not because they have any historical value initially, but because they will tell you whether or not you are overtraining. I have listed all possible indicators that you may wish to include; with experience you will learn which you find to be the most useful.

How the run felt. Pay particular attention to muscle soreness, the level of fatigue, and the intensity of the effort. In chapter 7, I describe how this information is used. The athlete who consistently trains on broken-down legs should rest until the legs recover.

Effort rating. Use the Borg Scale (tables 5.2A and 5.2B). This information tells you when you are reaching your peak, as you will run at a higher intensity but will feel less fatigued. In contrast, high perceived exertion ratings during exercise of low intensity indicate that you are tired and that you need to rest.

Enjoyment rating. On this scale, a score of 1 indicates a run that was not enjoyable at all; a score of 3, a neutral run; and a score of 5, a very enjoyable run (J.E. Martin and Dubbert 1984). If the runs score consistently low on the enjoyment rating scale, then you need to analyze the cause. You may be running too much and may be overtired, or you may be running at too high an intensity. If the runs continue to be unpleasant, the chances are that you will drop out and stop exercising. In such instances, my advice would be either to rest completely or to do gentle exercise until the desire to exercise returns and the exercise-related symptoms disappear.

Training load. A method for determining the training load was described on page 290. Figure 5.6 details how that information can be used to determine optimum training load.

Waking pulse rate. Measure and record your pulse rate within a few minutes of waking in the morning. If your waking pulse rate suddenly increases more than five beats a minute above the normal value, you have done too much the previous day and should either train very little that day or rest completely (chapter 7). You may refine the technique by remeasuring the heart rate exactly 20 seconds after first getting out of bed in the morning. Your heart rate increases when you stand up, and the degree of this increase can also indicate overtraining. Although there are as yet no publications to support this theory, we have collected some evidence to suggest that elevated sleeping heart rates may also be an early indicator of overtraining the previous day. Perhaps there is some value also in recording sleeping heart rates. If they too are consistently elevated, you may be training too hard.

Early morning body weight. As you become fitter, your body weight will fall progressively before stabilizing. But if it falls too much you may be overreaching or overtraining, or you may have an eating disorder. Indeed, a continuing loss of weight is a late indicator of overtraining (see chapter 7). The idea that you can never be too light to run is false. As originally observed by Arthur Newton, there is an optimum racing weight for each athlete; going below the weight will result in poorer performances, not better ones.

Postworkout body weight. This is a valuable indicator that can be used to quantify your sweat rate. It will help you calculate how much you need to drink while exercising (see chapter 4).

Bedtime and number of hours' sleep. Again, changes in sleeping pattern provide another easily measured indicator of overtraining. The changes that should arouse concern include going to bed progressively later at night, sleeping restlessly, waking earlier, and, as a result, sleeping less than normal (chapter 7). A restless night may also be shown by frequent, sudden spikes in the sleeping heart rate.

Record your heart rate and times during all training sessions (especially during speed work sessions and races). The value of any training information is greatly enhanced if there is additional information from the heart rate data measured during exercise. This can be achieved if a heart rate monitor is worn during every training session, especially if the monitor has the ability to download the information to a computer-based training logbook like the PC Coach or to interact with exercise scientists via the Body iQ system. This information allows you to calculate the weekly training load in terms of the strain of *your* body. This is roughly proportional to the number of heartbeats expended during training. In addition, this information enables you to compare your heart rates during similar training sessions, not just from month to month, but from year to year. Provided your heart rate is the same or lower during sessions in which you performed equally (presuming equivalent environmental conditions), then your fitness is either the same or improving.

An alternative testing method proposed by Philip Maffetone, and subsequently dubbed the Maximum Aerobic Function (MAF) test, is to determine your running speed at the "180 minus" training heart rate (the 2nd Law of Training). This can be done weekly or biweekly on any measured running track. If your running speed at that heart rate continues to improve, so too will your fitness level. Once your heart rate at that running speed is no longer falling, it may be time to include some training of a higher intensity in your overall training program.

Women should record their menstrual cycles so that they can determine whether their performance is influenced by their menstrual cycles or vice versa, and, if so, whether they wish to alter the timing of menstruation, particularly before competition. Women should also evaluate whether training or their diet influences their menstrual patterns.

Law 15: Understand the Holism of Training

The term *holistic running* was first coined by Kenneth Doherty (1964), who made the very simple but profound observation that most training methods "limit their attention to what happens during the few training hours each day and ignore the remaining 20 or more hours, which are often just as effective in determining success in running." (page 121)

Thus, you need to be aware that you are in training 24 hours per day and that everything you do can affect your running. But you should also be aware that there is a holism to training itself. In his analysis of the different methods of training, Doherty (1964) suggested that the success of Lydiard's training was due to the balance Lydiard achieved between training and competition; between races that were important and those that were merely training; between mileage and enjoyment; between different kinds of terrain; between endless year-round training and maintaining motivation through six different types of training; and between steady-state and uneven speed running. Clearly, it is important for runners to achieve this balance in their own training. Equally important, runners must balance a commitment to running to all the other components of life—family, work, recreation, and other relationships.

Everything affects how you run and train. Unfortunately, only the professional athletes are ever able to control their lives so completely that running becomes their central focus. For the rest of us, running must compete with various other activities. But to do our best, we must first recognize these enemies and try to keep them from interfering with running.

There are four major factors that must be taken into account when you are training hard—eating an appropriate diet, getting the right amount of sleep, avoiding physical effort during the day, and reducing work stress.

When training heavily, most athletes probably take in slightly fewer kilojoules than they burn and, as a result, lose some weight. Many will also reduce the amount of fat they eat, although few runners actually eat as little fat as the dieticians suggest they should (Hawley et al. 1995.) This paradox was addressed in chapter 3. Galloway (1984) has suggested that fatty foods seem to impair running performance and that this effect becomes more marked with age. However, in chapter 3, I discuss the possible value of fat in the ultraendurance athlete's diet.

Most runners generally sleep an additional hour per night on those days that they train hard or long. Even Plato observed that "the athlete in training is a sleepy animal." Another essential training trick is to avoid, where possible, excessive work stress, such as working overtime, endless traveling, and meetings. These aspects are discussed later in this chapter.

STEP 6: FOLLOW THESE PRACTICAL TIPS

Once you have progressed through steps 1 to 5, you are ready to put the following tips to use in your runs.

Learn Proper Breathing

Correct breathing is *yoga breathing,* or *belly breathing,* which involves breathing predominantly with the diaphragm, rather than with the chest muscles. With belly breathing, the chest hardly moves at all. Instead, the abdomen (stomach) appears to be doing all the work, for as you breathe in, the stomach goes up, and when you exhale, the stomach retracts. Note that the term *belly breathing* is incorrect, albeit descriptive. The diaphragm, not the belly, is doing the work.

Proper breathing can prevent side stitches from developing. Side stitches occur only during exercises that are undertaken in the erect posture and that involve running or jolting or both (Sinclair 1951; Abrahams 1961; Rost 1986). The pain of the stitch is usually felt on the right side of the abdomen, immediately below the rib margin. Frequently, the pain is also perceived in the right shoulder joint, where it feels as if an ice-pick were being driven into the joint. However, a recent study (Morton and Callister 2000) found that a clear majority of athletes report that pain occurs most commonly in the middle abdominal areas, suggesting that multiple mechanisms may be causing the problem. The pain is exacerbated by downhill running and by fast, sustained running, as in short road races or time-trials. Other factors that predispose runners to developing side stitches are eating and drinking before exercise; lack of training; weakness of the abdominal muscles; cool weather; nervousness; and starting a race too fast (Rost 1986). In addition, constitutional factors would seem to be involved, as only certain people are susceptible to stitches. Swimmers are often affected by the condition (Morton and Callister 2000). Since vertical jolting of the ligaments does not occur in swimming, another mechanism is involved. Morton and Callister propose that irritation of the abdominal lining, the parietal peritoneum, most adequately describes all the clinical features of this condition.

If you have a side stitch, lie down immediately with the hips elevated; this helps differentiate the stitch from other conditions, including chest pain due to heart disease, as the pain of the stitch disappears very quickly on lying down. Indeed, this characteristic explains why so little is known about it. It is extremely difficult to study a phenomenon that disappears mysteriously the moment exercise stops. About 20% of athletes have residual discomfort on deep inspiration for two to three days after getting a side stitch (Abrahams 1961).

For various complex anatomical reasons, the fact that side stitches cause discomfort in the shoulder joint suggests that the diaphragm is one cause of the pain, but it is likely that other factors may also contribute. The historical explanations for this condition (Sinclair 1951; Abrahams 1961; Rost 1986) are based on the anatomical finding that a group of ligaments that support the stomach, the liver, and the spleen are also attached to the diaphragm. Vertical jolting of those organs during running is believed to put strain on the diaphragm, which ultimately goes into spasm, causing the pain of the stitch. The tension is greatest at the insertion of the diaphragm into the rib margin, explaining why the discomfort is often felt under the rib margin. Rost (1986) suggests that the stitch can be prevented by avoiding food and water for 2 to 4 hours before exercise, by training the abdominal muscles with appropriate sit-ups (see chapter 14), and by learning how to breathe with the diaphragm. Forced exhalation is the most effective technique to break a stitch that is caused by a cramp of the diaphragm.

To learn how to belly breathe, lie on the floor and place one or more large books on your stomach. Concentrate on making the books rise when you breathe in and

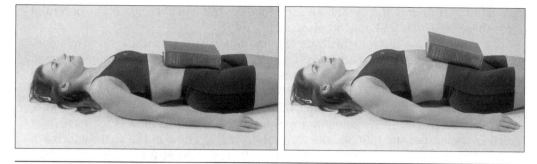

Figure 5.11   Learning how to belly breathe. As the athlete breathes in, the book should rise, indicating the contraction of the diaphragm.

fall when you exhale (figure 5.11). As it takes about two months to learn to do this while running fast, it is important to start practicing well before an important race.

A change in breathing pattern may help relieve the stitch. Within a short period of starting to run, breathing becomes synchronized with footfall. Thus, we automatically breathe in on one leg and out when landing either on the same leg or on the opposite leg. This phenomenon was first reported by Bramble and Carrier (1983). Of particular interest was their finding that most runners begin and end a respiratory cycle on the same foot, usually in a stride-to-breathing ratio of either 4:1 while jogging or 2:1 while running faster. Runners then become habituated to breathing out on the same leg, day after day. This produces asymmetrical stresses on the body and could be a factor in both the stitch and certain running injuries.

Train With Company

When starting to train, it is best to do so with others to help to maintain interest and motivation. Only train with experienced runners if they will run at your pace. Generally, experienced runners are more comfortable running faster than novice runners typically run. Do not attempt to impress experienced runners by trying to stay with them in training. The end result will be that you run too far, too fast, too soon and will develop a running injury, such as tibial bone strain (shinsplints) or a stress fracture.

Choose Safe and Appropriate Training Routes

Hill running stresses the anterior thigh (quadriceps) muscles, which are often untrained in people whose previous major activity has been walking on flat terrain, which stresses mainly the calf muscles. For this reason, it is better to walk or jog on flat terrain initially, using muscles that are not totally untrained. Attempt to run hills only if you are able to run comfortably on the flat for about 30 minutes.

Before I started running, I did not appreciate the scenic beauty that surrounded me. I believe that one of the attractions of running is that it brings us back into contact with our environment and enhances our awareness of nature.

Once your fitness improves, it becomes necessary, sooner or later, to run on the roads. When this happens, runners become exposed to their greatest enemy—the motor vehicle. I have lost four friends who were knocked down and killed while either running or cycling; others were lucky to escape when cars hit them. As the number of runners (and cyclists) on the roads continues to escalate, the potential for these tragedies will only increase all the more.

As shown in a study from the United States, many of the tragedies can be avoided. The study revealed that collisions between runners and cars typically occurred after dark, when the joggers were running on the road in the same direction as the traffic. Most often, the runner who was struck was running abreast of another runner and was closest to the road (A.F. Williams 1981). In only 27% of cases were the drivers primarily responsible for the collision, and in most such cases the driver was under the influence of alcohol or drugs. Thus, in the vast majority of cases, the jogger was either totally or partially responsible for the collision. Runners can greatly reduce the risk of such tragedies by adhering to the following simple rules (modified from Osler [1978] and A.F. Williams [1981]):

- Run facing the oncoming traffic.
- Adopt a defensive attitude when running on the road.
- Constantly watch every oncoming car and listen for cars coming from behind. Be ready to jump to safety at the first indication of trouble.
- Select roads with little traffic and very wide shoulders.
- Run on the verge, not on the road itself.
- Run in single file or not more than two abreast. Large running groups are particularly dangerous, especially when the groups divide so that runners are on both sides of the road. When this happens, drivers of oncoming cars are unable to drive onto the verge in the case of an emergency.
- Do not run at dusk or at night.
- Wear the brightest, most visible colors, with reflective material attached. Osler (1978) writes: "Yellow, orange and red might not be the colors you prefer from the standpoint of fashion, but you must make yourself as visible as possible to motorists. Never wear blue, brown or dark gray."
- Be especially careful when tired. Fatigue impairs the concentration, slows the reflexes, and unfortunately seems to make runners feel that they are indestructible—a combination of factors not unlike the effects of alcohol intoxication.

The most worrying situation involves, as Osler (1978) points out, the car that moves onto your side of the road and comes up behind you to overtake a car ahead of it on its side of the road. Although you are running facing the oncoming traffic, you will still have a car approaching from the rear in this situation. This is the nearest I have ever come to being hit by a car.

I was not always as careful as I now am when running on the road. I have learned many lessons, however, and remain gravely concerned by the needlessly cavalier attitudes of many runners toward road safety. These runners seem to act as if they own the roads and exhibit extreme arrogance toward other road users. This attitude is not only unnecessary but also extremely foolish. In an accident with a car, the only loser is the runner, irrespective of who is at fault.

Stretch and Strengthen Regularly

Running causes the muscles that are active to become strong and less flexible, whereas the opposing muscles, which are relatively underused, become weaker. To maintain flexibility and the correct muscle balance between opposing muscle groups, perform special exercises regularly (see chapter 14).

Eat What Your Body Dictates

The body by and large dictates its requirements. Thus, there is no need to follow a special diet. As a person becomes more active, the major alterations that occur in dietary preference are the desire to eat more carbohydrates (starches), in particular sweets and fruits, and the inclination to increase the fluid intake. These are natural responses. The carbohydrate content of the diet determines how rapidly the muscle and liver glycogen stores will be replenished after exercise, and a high-carbohydrate diet ensures that these stores will be most rapidly replaced (chapter 3). Fluid intake increases spontaneously to replace that lost from sweat and expiration. Drink fluid during exercise only if the exercise bout lasts more than an hour. Drink about 500 ml of cold fluid for every hour that you run (chapter 4).

Salt losses during short-duration exercises are negligible, so it is not necessary to increase salt intake when training. There is also no need to increase protein intake specifically, nor is there convincing evidence that taking vitamin and mineral supplements is necessary since you will automatically increase your intake of vitamins and minerals through increased consumption of fruits and vegetables.

Get Enough Sleep

Although the amount of time that people sleep can vary quite remarkably, with some sleeping as little as 4 hours per night, the average person sleeps between 7 and 8 hours per night. With harder training, the amount of time spent sleeping definitely increases. Arthur Newton (1935) described the changes that occur in sleeping patterns with increased physical activity:

> I used to find 5 hours [of] sleep quite sufficient to recover from heavy mental work; but no sooner did I shear off into vigorous training than I noticed a 7 to 8 hour stretch, or even more, was desirable. When it is a matter of superintensive training, you may require as much as 9 hours in bed each night.

Many runners get too little sleep because they fail to allow for the time that running takes out of their day. If you are running 2 hours per day and sleeping an extra hour every night, then you have "lost" 3 hours per day, and whatever you would normally do during that time must give way. In other words, you need to budget three hours per day for running.

Be Sensible About Weather Conditions

Take special precautions when exercising in severe environmental conditions (see chapter 4). Don't exercise vigorously very early in the morning if the temperature is very low (below freezing). The likelihood of developing upper respiratory tract infections is increased if you consistently train very hard in very cold air. Wear a rain suit if it is raining heavily and there is a strong wind blowing. Wind increases the wind-chill factor and could cause the runner whose clothes are wet to develop a critical reduction in body temperature (hypothermia) when running for too long under such conditions.

This advice is slightly different from that of Arthur Newton who, as a competitive runner, was less inclined to be put off by the weather. He observed correctly, despite incorrect reasoning, that running in the cold weather is altogether less taxing than is running in the heat.

Don't Let Running Become a Cause of Stress

I frequently see runners who do not understand why they are unable to work and run hard at the same time. They are unaware that running is an additional cause of stress that, when piled on top of their already highly stressful lifestyles, may prove too much.

Runners are usually involved in many demanding activities, each of which they try to do with the same perfection they desire of their running. But once the total stress from all your various activities exceeds your stress-coping capacities, you will in time break down, the most obvious indication of which is the overtraining syndrome. A prime example is the runner who wrote to tell me that he had tried to combine training for the standard marathon with a heavy workload. This meant he had to run early in the morning under very cold conditions and often had to work late. Added to this were the stresses of a high-powered business environment. All these pressures led to recurring bouts of flu. The result was that, aiming to run a 3:30:00 marathon, he was forced to walk from the 23-km mark to the finish, completing the distance in a shade under 5 hours. For the next three days, this athlete was bedridden with flu-like symptoms.

The most obvious diagnosis is that this runner thought he could add the stress of running to his already over-filled life without taking something else away to make room for it. By getting up early, he was cutting back on his sleep. Worse, he was running in very cold conditions, which increased the likelihood of a respiratory infection. A vicious cycle developed in which he was simply becoming progressively more fatigued and therefore less able to cope, not only with running, but also with all the other aspects of his life.

To avoid this predicament, this runner needed to temper his enthusiasm and understand the nature of his sudden preoccupation with running. What particularly sparked his conversion? He needed to ask why it was so necessary for him to complete the marathon in less than 3:30:00. Did the seeds of his failure perhaps lie in the totality of the forces compelling him towards that goal? And what was he prepared to forfeit to allow him to train hard enough to reach that ephemeral goal?

The answer is that the time to train for your best marathon is not when business and other personal pressures are on the increase, forcing you into irrational choices. The time to train for a best marathon is when your life is the least cluttered by all the other demands that interfere with optimum training and racing.

STEP 7: START WITH A PLANNED TRAINING PROGRAM

Although following a rigid daily training program violates the 4th Law of Training, I have found that most novice runners require some kind of training program to assist them in their initial year of running. In particular, the program enables them to run without constantly worrying about what they should be doing. Indeed, I ran my first (and most successful) 90-km Comrades Marathon after following a training program drawn up by two famous Comrades runners, Hardy Ballington and Bill Cochrane.

The program was successful because it provided daily, weekly, and monthly training goals in terms of total distance run; it emphasized a gradual progression of training and, importantly, did not prescribe at what intensity that training should be. The goal was simply to condition the body so that it could run a long way, the primary requirement for a 90-km ultramarathon. Only later did I learn that the addition of peaking, a period of more intensive training, together with more frequent racing over shorter distances, would have produced an even better result.

Over the years, there have been many different publications featuring different training programs for those wishing to start running (Henderson and Maxwell 1978; Temple 1980; Bloom 1981; Squires 1982; Galloway 1984; Glover and Schruder 1983; Galloway 1996; Daniels 1998; Pfitzinger and Douglas 1999). More recently, computerized training programs have become increasingly available. I am sure that all these programs are quite similar and equally effective. Therefore, your choice of program will depend on what information you can find, as well as on your inclination to use newer technologies. However, to my knowledge, few programs have been scientifically tested in a sufficiently large group of subjects to determine their real effectiveness in practice. They probably all work quite similarly because they have common origins, and they work on the simple physiological principle that the body adapts optimally to a gradually increasing physical load, applied gently. The beginner's training program that I have included in this chapter has undergone at least some field testing, as have the highly successful programs of Jeff Galloway (1996).

Selected training programs for both beginners and more advanced runners wishing to compete in races from 10 to 90 km, or longer, are described in chapters 9 to 11.

Basic Beginner's Marathon Program

Between August 1982 and March 1983, a research group at the University of Cape Town trained a group of subjects, some of whom had previously been totally sedentary, to run a 42-km standard marathon. In the end, 26 finished the standard marathon in times ranging from 2:59 to 6:05. The program these runners followed was originally modeled on the Henderson and Maxwell (1978) marathon training program, to which an initial eight-week walking program was added. The original program has been adjusted slightly in light of the results we achieved.

We found that even reasonably healthy, young, and otherwise athletic people will almost certainly develop injuries between the 8th and 12th week of training if they do not start with a solid base of walking. We also found that performances suddenly improved dramatically after 20 weeks of training. Our third finding was that our original program of seven months was too short for the average beginner who wished to train for a standard marathon. Very athletic people can do it in this time, but the average person requires eight to nine months.

In this chapter, we present the first part of that program. The beauty of this program is that it enables previously sedentary people to run in training without incurring a high risk of injury and to increase their fitness so that they can comfortably complete races of 10 to 21 km (chapter 9), 42 km (table 10.1) or longer (table 11.1).

The original aim of this program was to train a group of sedentary nonrunners to complete a 42-km marathon. Based on that program, we devised a 58-week training

Table 5.8 A scientifically evaluated 20-week training schedule for beginners

Day	Week 1	Week 2	Week 3	Week 4	Week 5	Week 6
1	W20	–	W20	W15, R5	–	W20
2	–	W20	W20	W20	W20	W20, R5
3	W20	–	–	–	–	–
4	–	W20	W20	W20	W20	W15, R5
5	W20	–	W10	–	–	–
6	–	W20	W20	W20	W15, R5	W15, R5
7	W20	–	–	W10	–	–

Day	Week 7	Week 8	Week 9	Week 10	Week 11	Week 12
1	W5, R5	W5, R5	W5, R5	R10	W15, R5	W10, R10
2	W15, R10	W20, R5	20, R5	W20, R10	W20, R10	W15, R15
3	–	–	W10, R10	–	–	–
4	W15, R5	W15, R5	–	W20, R10	W20, R10	W20, R10
5	–	–	W10, R10	–	–	–
6	W15, R5	W20, R5	–	W20, R10	W20, R10	W15, R15
7	–	–	W15, R10	–	–	–

Day	Week 13	Week 14	Week 15	Week 16	Week 17	Week 18
1	W10, R10	W10, R10	W5, R15	W5, R25	R30	R30
2	W10, R20	W10, R20	W5, R25	–	–	–
3	–	–	–	R30	R30	R30
4	W15, R15	W10, R20	W10, R20	W5, R15	R20	R20
5	–	R10, W10	W5, R25	R30	R30	–
6	W10, R20	W10, R20	–	–	–	R30
7	–	–	W10, R10	W5, R15	R20	R20

Day	Week 19	Week 20
1	R30	–
2	–	R30
3	R30	R20
4	R30	–
5	–	R30
6	R20	R30
7	R0	R15

All measurements are in minutes. W = walk; R = run.

program to train novices to go from being completely sedentary to being able to complete a 90-km ultramarathon in less than 11 hours. The initial 20-week section of the program is presented in table 5.8.

The 20-week training program was designed to allow a novice with no previous running experience to be able to run continuously for 30 minutes within 17 weeks. Of course, it is possible for a novice to train so that she can run 30 minutes continuously in a much shorter time. But there is a high risk that any further increases in training volume, should she wish to start running races of longer distances, will increase the risk of injury. In the program, substantial emphasis is placed on walking. Table 5.8 lists the time (in minutes) you should exercise each day. W refers to walking, and R refers to running. Thus, the code *W20* for day 1 of week 1 means that you should walk for 20 minutes on that day.

Although many people think that to become runners they must begin by running, it is essential that you refrain from running for the first three weeks of your training program, at the very least. During this time, you should only concentrate on walking. Only after this should you start running slowly. It is far better to walk for the first six weeks of the program than to be forced to stop running for six weeks due to an injury such as a stress fracture—the injury to which novices are most prone. Furthermore, the initial walking period allows the bones time to strengthen so that they can resist the more demanding stresses to which they will be exposed later (chapter 14). This period also allows new runners to ascertain whether they need a medical evaluation. The main aim is to acquire the exercise habit rather than to become fit, which conforms with the concept of shaping described in this chapter.

After completing this program you can progress to the 26-week marathon training program (table 10.1) and the 22-week ultramarathon training program (table 11.1).

To Run Faster, Walk More?

Runners, I have observed, usually have a very poor opinion of walkers and walking. The reverse, I am sure, is equally true. Much of my medical education was spent in vigorous debate with a medical professor who failed to share my enthusiasm for running. Most of his spare time was spent exploring, photographing, and describing the diverse flora of our shared mountain playground (Jackson 1977). There was no room on his mountain or in his comprehension for running, something he considered to be a brainless activity.

I never had any difficulty understanding the runner's aversion to walking. The runner trains precisely so that he need never again walk. For the runner to walk is to admit failure and defeat; a giving-in to the baser weakness; a failed reformation. Thus, perhaps subconsciously, we runners ascribe to walkers all those negative characteristics we wish to avoid. We distance ourselves from the walkers lest we be contaminated by their perceived failure. Perhaps it is time for a broader view.

All I know about walking and walkers I have learned from my wife, Marilyn Anne. It is when we walk together on the mountain trails I discovered through running that I learn how different the worlds of the runner and the walker are. Compatible as we are, when we walk, we frequent two quite different worlds.

When I run, my mind is elsewhere, full of everything but that which I am

(continued)

doing at the moment. Perhaps I am vainly trying to understand humanity, or writing this book or planning some new experiment that will finally explain all of exercise physiology. Only occasionally does my environment impinge on my activity—usually when I need a rest. When too tired to think clearly, I sometimes survey the beauty of the environment and notice, for the first time, the trees of the forest. But too soon, the details are forgotten, the trees recede, and I return to that endless stream of consciousness that plunges me back into the future.

When I walk with Marilyn Anne, I learn that the environment I overlook so easily is filled with the most exciting discoveries. She harvests the beauty that my absented mind fails to recognize. Each step brings a new discovery of exquisite colors, sights, sounds, and smells. Her senses, heightened by the moment, take in everything. At every opportunity, she directs my distracted mind to a delicate flower or one with a special scent or to the distant call of a secretive bird that, in my masculine impatience, I have hurried by.

What place, you may ask, does this section describing the hidden pleasures of walking have in a book of running? Simply that, to be a better long-distance runner, you may need to overcome your entrenched bias and consider the possible value of walking, especially during marathon and ultramarathon races.

In his classic, *The Serious Runners Handbook,* Tom Osler (1978), one of the first Americans to run ultramarathons, describes how he learned to complete an 80-km training run, irrespective of how fit he was. The secret, he discovered, was to walk frequently. He proposed that the ideal combination was to run for 25 minutes and then to walk for 5 minutes. But Osler confined his advice to ultramarathoners and did not extrapolate the advantages he discovered to other running distances.

More recently, another legendary American runner and writer, Jeff Galloway, author of another classic, *Galloway's Book on Running* (1984), refined this advice. His proposal is that, when racing marathons, you should only run for 2:30 before walking for 0:30. His observation is that the muscular exhaustion of long-distance running develops much less rapidly when we walk frequently. Perhaps it is because frequent walks delay the rate at which stretch-shortening fatigue develops. As a result, a much greater distance can be covered before severe exhaustion sets in.

The probable reason why frequent walking delays the onset of fatigue is because walking reduces the eccentric loading of the weight-bearing muscles, allowing them to recover their shock-absorbing capacity. Repeated often enough, these frequent rest periods must delay the onset of the terminal failure of the muscles' load-bearing function that causes the "wall," according to the Biomechanical Model.

Australian ultradistance runner Alan Peacock has described to me his own experiences of alternating walking and running during competition. By mixing running with walking right from the start, he was able to complete 207 km in a 24-hour race without developing leg stiffness after the race. When he applied the same principle to his long Sunday training runs, in which he runs for 15 minutes and walks for 2 minutes, he is able to recover more quickly, within 24 hours, even after long runs of 4 hours. By Tuesday, he is sufficiently recovered to do more intensive interval-type training. Peacock's point is that walking in training is still considered unacceptable by the fastest runners. Yet, he suggests that everybody could benefit by including regular walking in their long training runs since the same distance would be covered, yet recovery would be enhanced. As a result, there would be less need to recover during the rest of the week and more intensive speed training session could be undertaken.

Perhaps this is an idea whose time has come. Osler's innovation needs to be practiced more widely.

The first marathon boom began in 1976. One of the features of the second marathon revolution (chapter 10), which started in the 1990s, is that it has been led, in part, by the aging baby boomers who were also central to the first marathon running revolution in the 1970s. But now that they are older and wiser, with less competitive urges, their advice has changed somewhat. In particular, walking in either racing or training, anathema 30 years ago, is now being touted as a valuable training and racing aid. The leader of this latest revolution is Jeff Galloway, a former Olympic 10,000-m runner and American record holder at that distance.

Galloway explains, "The human body wasn't designed for running continuously for long distances" (Galloway 1996, page 48). Thus, "by alternating running and walking, from the beginning of a run, we can extend our endurance limits dramatically." His explanation is that walking allows the leg muscles to "regain resilience before they reach a significant level of fatigue. . . . I believe that this reduction in intensity, [actually a break from eccentric loading—my edit] allows the main running muscles to make adaptations inside so that they can continue to perform at the level you request for much longer than if used continuously." (page 48) According to the Biomechanical Model, frequent walking allows the muscles to recover from repetitive eccentric loading, delaying the onset of stretch-shortening cycle fatigue.

Galloway promises that those who convert to his heresy will be able to run further, faster, sooner; that they will improve their endurance; and that they will lower their marathon times by 10 to 45 minutes compared to the times they would need to run the full marathon distance. This advice is probably aimed at those who, because of age, a lesser running ability, or a lack of time have been unable to follow the training programs given in chapter 10 and are running the marathon in 4 hours or more. The advice is even more relevant for ultramarathoners (chapter 11). Much of the advantage of walking frequently is achieved near the end of the race, when you will be able to maintain your pace instead of slowing down. As a result, you will pass those runners who, in ignorance, chose to run the complete marathon distance. According to Galloway, additional benefits include recovering more quickly from races and being able to fit in long training runs. The risk of injury may also be reduced. To be effective, Galloway suggests that walk breaks must be taken early enough and often enough.

He suggests that beginners should take "jogging breaks in their walks" so that they walk for a minute for every 5 minutes that they run. As they become fitter, they should take a 2- to 3-minute walk for every 2 to 3 minutes that they run. Average runners should take walk breaks every 3 to 8 minutes in long runs. In races, Galloway suggests that you take 1-minute walk breaks for each mile (1.6 km) that you run.

Perhaps it is now time for a scientific study to determine the cut-off marathon time for which the introduction of walking improves performance by preventing a drop-off in performance at "the wall." Probably all runners who slow dramatically over the last 10 km of the marathon would benefit by walking early and frequently, as proposed by Galloway.

The program in table 5.8 advises that you walk for the first three weeks, and only on the first day of the fourth week may you begin running. The designation *W15, R5* for that day indicates that you should walk for 15 minutes and jog/run for 5 minutes. Over the next 14 weeks, the amount of time spent jogging will gradually increase until, after 17 weeks, each training session will include only running—this is shown as *R30*. By then you have completed your beginner's program. Should you continue to run for 30 minutes, three or more times per week for the rest of your life, you will be doing sufficient exercise to measurably enhance your health, increase your life expectancy, and reduce your life-time medical costs and your risk of developing certain chronic diseases. Should you continue training at that level for the rest of your life, you will be expending between 6000 and 7000 kJ of energy per week and can expect a reduction in heart attack risk of about 25% and an increase in life expectancy of between one and two years, depending on the age at which you first started running (Paffenbarger et al. 1986).

It seems probable that increasing the amount of running you do beyond 2 to 4 hours each week will not necessarily enhance your health to any great extent. Just as there is a point at which further training does not enhance performance—the Law of Diminishing Returns—so too is there a point at which running more does not improve health. Once you run more than 2 to 4 hours per week, you are no longer training principally for enhanced health benefits but, rather, to improve your competitive racing performances.

From week 4 to 17, you may experience certain symptoms for the first time. These include persistent calf-muscle soreness and discomfort along the border of the shin bone, the tibia. This condition is known as tibial bone strain (shinsplints). Both tend to disappear with time, without recourse to the more involved treatment regime described in chapter 14. Symptoms like these indicate that training, however light it might seem, has been too intensive and, at least for a few weeks until the symptoms abate, your body will need more rest days. You should also reduce the distance that you run. If these simple measures do not alleviate the symptoms, then consider changing running shoes and possibly seeking professional advice.

The main objective during this period is to run without becoming breathless or overly tired. The average training pace will probably be 5 to 10 minutes per kilometer, depending on your age and genetic athletic ability. Eventually, after some months, you will settle into a comfortable running pace, one that will be influenced by your genetic athletic ability.

Resist any desire to start running earlier than is indicated on your schedule, because increasing your intensity during this time increases your risk of injuring yourself after 10 to 12 weeks. It is not known why the risk of injury is so high during this stage, but the phenomenon has also been noted in army recruits, who become most prone to injury after about two months of training.

Current evidence shows that bones in the lower limb undergo some demineralization during the first three to five months of training, before becoming stronger after about 10 months (Kuusela et al. 1984). Unfortunately, the fitness of novice runners starts to improve quite rapidly after about 10 weeks of training so that they want to start training more intensively at the very time when their bones are weakest. For this reason, it is best to start slowly so that both the extent of bone demineralization and the rate of fitness enhancement are reduced.

Grete Waitz's Beginner's Program

Grete Waitz has developed a training program for beginners that will allow the armchair athlete to run 5 km continuously within 10 weeks.

During the first four weeks of Waitz's program, the break-in period, pay close attention to your body and learn to read its signals of fatigue or stress (chapter 7). Each session should be comfortable, and a warm-up and cool-down are strongly advised. Don't hesitate to walk during training. Exercise sessions are scheduled three days per week and take approximately 45 to 60 minutes, including 5 to 10 minutes of warming up and cooling down, followed by stretching and strengthening exercises. There should be one day's rest between training sessions. Waitz's program is presented in table 5.9.

The initial objective of Waitz's program is simply to go out and move. The emphasis should be on the joy of running. Waitz suggests that running should be a group experience and that the novice runner should find a group of running partners. Consistency is vital, but interest should be maintained by varying the course, the terrain, and the location.

Waitz also writes that it is natural to feel discouraged, bored, or apathetic at times. These mood swings in running are natural, but negative feelings should be

Table 5.9	Grete Waitz's training program for beginners	
Week 1	Alternatively jog and walk 100 m for a total of 1.6 km. Repeat three times during the week.	
Week 2	Alternatively jog and walk 200 m for a total of 2 km. Repeat twice during the week for a total of three exercise sessions.	
Week 3	Alternatively jog and walk between 200 and 400 m for a total of 2.5 km. Repeat twice during the week.	
Week 4	Alternatively jog and walk, but walk only half the distance of each jog. Vary the distances between 400 and 800 m for a total of 3 km.	
Week 5	Session 1	Alternate 800-m jog with 400-m walk for a total of 3.2 km.
	Session 2	Alternate 1.2-km jog with 800-m walk for a total of 3.2 km.
	Session 3	Jog 3.2 km without walking.
Week 6	Session 1	800-m jog followed by 400-m walk, followed by 1200-m jog, followed by 400-m walk, followed by 800-m jog for a total of 3.6 km.
	Session 2	1.6-km jog followed by 400-m walk, followed by 1.6-km jog for a total of 3.6 km.
	Session 3	3 to 3.6-km jog with no walking.
Week 7	3.8-km jog on three days of the week.	
Week 8	4.4-km jog on three days of the week.	
Week 9	4.8-km jog on three days of the week.	
Week 10	5-km jog on three days of the week.	

All distances are in kilometers or meters.

Excerpted from Galloway (1984, p. 109). Reprinted by permission.

translated into positive ones. Thus, the experience should be seen not as a struggle to get into shape but as a new way of feeling and a new and better way of life. Finally, Waitz suggests that the beginner should run for at least one to two years before training for a marathon or other long race.

Jeff Galloway's Beginner's Program

Jeff Galloway (figure 5.12) is undoubtedly one of the founding fathers of modern distance running in the United States. Galloway set the American record for 10 miles and represented his country in the 10,000 m at the 1972 Olympic Games. By 1978 he had established a nationwide chain of Phidippides running stores with headquarters in Atlanta, Georgia, where he now lives.

At the Galloway Vacation Fitness Camps held each summer and in his book, *Galloway's Book on Running* (1984), Galloway shares the knowledge he has acquired as a competitive runner and running guru. More recently, Galloway has been instrumental in training many thousands of middle-aged executives to run marathons. His experiences are described in his most recent books (Galloway 1995; 1996).

In his first book, Galloway provides a basic training program for running 10 km in less than 50 minutes after 28 weeks of training. The basis for each of Galloway's training programs is that he divides his training into three components: a base training program of 14 to 19 weeks; a period of hill training that lasts 3 to 8 weeks; and a final period of speed work training that lasts 5 to 9 weeks. Speed work comprises predominantly interval sessions on the track. Hill work involves running repetitions on a hill of moderate gradient (10% to 15%). These hill repetitions should be run at about 85% effort, equivalent to 10-km race pace, and should not exceed 200 m each. Table 5.10 lists Galloway's proposed 28-week training program for novice runners. More advanced programs for those who wish to race 10- and 42-km races according to the Galloway method are included in chapters 9 and 10.

Figure 5.12   The 1976 Peachtree Road Race in Atlanta, Georgia, featuring Don Kardong (771) and Jeff Galloway (513). Kardong won, Bill Rodgers was second, and Jeff Galloway fourth.

From Galloway (1984), p. 281. © 1984 by Jeff Galloway, Shelter Publications, Inc., P.O. Box 279 Bolinas, CA 94924, USA. Reprinted by permission.

Table 5.10   Jeff Galloway's training program for beginners wishing to run 10 km in 50 minutes

Week Number	Mon	Tue	Wed	Thu	Fri	Sat	Sun (Longer runs)
Base training							
1-10	0-3	5-7	0-3	5-6	0-3	0	Starting with longest run in last 2 weeks, increase 1.6 km per week up to 19 km
10-19	0-3	7-8	0-3	6-8	0-3	0	
Hill training							
20	0-3	6 (hills)	0-3	6-8	0-3	0	19
21	0-3	8 (hills)	0-3	3-5	0-3	0	9
22	0-3	9 (hills)	0-3	6-8	0-3	0	19
23	0-3	11-13 (hills)	0-3	6-8	0-3	0	9
Speed work							
24	0-3	6 × 400 in 01:52	0-3	3-5	0-3	0	9
25	0-3	8 × 400 in 01:52	0-3	6-8	0-3	0	19
26	0-3	10 × 400 in 01:50	0-3	6-8	0	10 (time-trial)	3-8
27	0-3	6 × 400 in 01:50	0-3	6-8	0	5 (race)	16
28	0-3	6 × 400 in 01:50	0-3	3-5	2-3	0	10 (race)

All distances are in kilometers or meters.

Excerpted from Galloway (1984, p. 109). Reprinted by permission.

STEP 8:
ENTER PROGRESSIVELY LONGER RACES

Running races is quite different from training because it produces its own peculiar stresses, including large numbers of experienced runners, the confusion of trying to get a drink, sponging, and learning to pace yourself. It is therefore best to run a number of short-distance races before tackling a longer race. By the time you run your first longer race, you can concentrate on what it takes to go the distance rather than the distractions that surround racing. A suggested progression is to run races of 2, 4, and 8 km before attempting the first 10-km race; 10-, 12-, and 16-km races before the first 21-km race; and then 24- and 32-km races before the 42-km marathon. (A 56- to 60-km race should be run before tackling an ultramarathon of 90 to 100 km). These races will also enable you to practice the racing advice in chapters 9 through 11 and establish what pace you will be likely to run in the longer races.

STEP 9:
LEARN FROM PERSONAL EXPERIENCE

Every athlete is a unique person, different from all others. As George Sheehan famously described: "We are each a unique experiment of one." While the training approach described here and in chapters 9 to 11 can generally be applied to all athletes, the specific details vary from person to person—in particular, in respect of the relative emphasis that different athletes place on different aspects of their training.

The only way for you, the individual runner, to determine what is most appropriate is to observe carefully how you personally respond to different training methods. Continue experimenting until you finally discover the training methods that produce the best results for you, regardless of how unusual they may be. Where possible, speak to experts who can help you analyze your own experiment. But be certain to choose creative advisers who are not themselves tied to a particular dogma.

One of the first factors that you need to ascertain is the rate at which you adapt to training. This will determine the optimum duration of the intensive training during the peaking period (the 9th Law of Training). Those who adapt rapidly must shorten the duration of their peaking programs (figure 5.11).

The best method to determine this individual rate of adaptation is to undergo a relatively short peaking period of, say, three to five weeks and to monitor the results. You can then increase the duration of the peak training by, say, a one-week period before your next major race. Ultimately, when the peaking period approaches or exceeds 10 weeks, your performance in the race for which you are training will not be as good as expected. This indicates that the optimum peak training duration has been exceeded. The optimum duration of the peaking period will range from 6 to 10 weeks.

STEP 10: SET REALISTIC
TRAINING AND RACING GOALS

No amount of training can compensate for poor genetic material. Difficult as it may be, we have to accept our limited abilities with dignity and humility. Unrealistic goals lead to unrealistic expectations and unrealistic training volumes—the deadly combination for the unfulfilled runner.

With regard to establishing career goals, frequent mention has been made of the inability of most runners to avoid either training or racing speed, or both. When they are training hard and racing well, the primary focus of their lives usually extends no further than the next race; they lack the ability to plan more than three months ahead, let alone 3 or 30 years. Yet, the need to plan ahead is crucial.

It is crucial because all athletes, regardless of their ability, have only so many good races in them during their careers. This point is emphasized by the experiences of exceptional runners such as Buddy Edelen, Alberto Salazar, Steve Jones, Dick Beardsley, and Frith van der Merwe, all of whom had meteoric careers that lasted only a few brief summers.

Similarly, I suspect that the body can only absorb so much heavy training over many years. Possibly 20 years of heavy training is the greatest duration that the average distance runner can expect. Therefore, it is essential to plan your running career within those guidelines. Thus, I advise you to plan to still be running in 20 years, at least. Seen from this perspective, it no longer becomes important that you race a marathon or other race every few months. Rather, you need to do whatever is necessary to ensure that you remain a motivated and enthusiastic runner for the rest of your life.

STEP 11: SET YEAR-LONG TRAINING GOALS

A problem with all the training programs described in this chapter, as well as those in chapter 6, is that they focus on a single event, such as a 10-km race or a marathon. While this is appropriate for the recreational athlete intent only on running one of two races per year, it is inappropriate for those who wish to develop a year-long training program.

One of the most readable training guides I have encountered was written by Robert Sleamaker, an exercise physiologist, cross-country skier, and duathlete from Vermont. In *Serious Training for Endurance Athletes* (Sleamaker and Browning 1996), Sleamaker offers advice on how to devise a year-long training program. His scientific training, during which he studied the effects of exercise training in women who are pregnant, is evident in his scholarly approach to his topic.

Sleamaker divides the athletic year into 13 cycles of four weeks each, with each four-week period allowing an evaluation to assess how the experiment is progressing and whether the training methods are correct or need to be altered. Thus, Sleamaker advocates that a time-trial over half the race distance (5 to 10 km is quite adequate even for marathon runners), over the same course, should be attempted every three to four weeks. The trial is run at the same intensity—for example, at the same heart rate—and the result noted. Fitness is improving if the running time improves and the heart rate during the time-trial remains the same.

Sleamaker then divides the training year into five training stages. The characteristics of the five different training stages are similar to those described in this chapter.

1. Base training (16 weeks, four cycles of four weeks) consists predominantly of slow distance running at 55% to 60% $\dot{V}O_2$max. Intervals and some form of muscle-strengthening exercises, such as weightlifting or plyometrics, are also performed during this stage.

2. Intensity training (16 weeks). The total training stress is increased by upping the total training volume and the intensity of training. This is achieved by introducing speed training in the form of intervals, race-pace training, and some races. The effort is hard but not all-out.

3. Peaking training (four weeks). The training volume falls but the intensity increases, with race-pace training and intervals being the predominant forms of speed training.

4. Racing (12 weeks). The proportion of the different training methods remains the same as in the peaking period.

5. Recovery (four weeks). Only low-intensity training is allowed.

Another training principle proposed by Sleamaker is that the training volume within each four-week training cycle should vary from week to week. In general, the percentage of the total four-week training volume rises for the first three weeks and is then reduced during the fourth week. For example, a typical pattern might be that 23% of the month's training volume is completed in the first week, 26% in the second, 29% in the third, and 22% in the fourth.

Next, Sleamaker describes six types of training—low-intensity (endurance), interval, speed, race-pace, hill, and strength training. The amount of time that each of these training methods occupies in each of the five training stages is shown in table 5.11.

The final requirement of the Sleamaker program is that the training intensity be established. A number of methods for determining training intensity have been described, and most have focused on the so-called lactate turnpoint, or anaerobic threshold. However, these techniques are erroneous for three simple reasons:

1. The anaerobic threshold does not exist (see chapter 3).

2. The physiology of the human body is not designed to recognize any "zones" of exercise intensity, as also suggested by exercise prescription according to heart rate. Rather, the body reacts in a progressive and regulated way to increases in exercise intensity.

3. This type of training advice disregards the scientific principle because it has become part of the accepted running lore without proper scientific evaluation. Instead of training subjects at different intensities, evaluating the result, and only then prescribing the training intensity that has proved the most effective, these training intensities are prescribed solely on the assumption that they will be the most effective.

Sleamaker sensibly avoids this error by prescribing five exercise intensity levels:

		% of total		Percentage per four-week cycle			
Cycle	Stage	training	Speed	Endurance	Race-pace	Interval	Hill	Strength
1	Base	6	0	80	0	0	0	20
2	Base	7	0	80	0	0	0	20
3	Base	8	0	80	0	0	0	20
4	Base	9	0	75	0	5	5	15
5	Intensity	9	5	65	5	5	8	12
6	Intensity	10	5	65	5	5	10	10
7	Intensity	11	5	65	5	5	10	10
8	Intensity	9	10	60	5	10	5	10
9	Peaking	8	15	55	10	10	5	5
10	Racing	7	10	55	15	15	0	5
11	Racing	7	10	55	15	15	0	5
12	Racing	6	10	55	15	15	0	5
13	Recovery	3	0	100	0	0	0	0

Table 5.11   Division of yearly training hours according to the training

Speed training refers to 5- to 8-second bursts repeated every 15 to 20 minutes during long, slow, distance runs.
Adapted, by permission, from Sleamaker and Browning (1996, pp. 56 and 63).

Level 1. Exercise intensities that elicit heart rates at 60% to 70% of the maximum heart rate (this level is appropriate for distance training)

Level 2. 71 to 75% (endurance training)

Level 3. 75 to 80% (endurance training)

Level 4. 81 to 90% (intervals and race-pace workouts)

Level 5. 90 to 100% (racing and peaking)

These levels are not greatly dissimilar to those proposed by Sally Edwards earlier in this chapter and are sufficiently broad to be safe and, hopefully, effective. Using these guidelines, it is possible to develop a year-round training program by following these three steps:

1. Calculate the total hours of training you will do during the year (see table 5.12).

2. Periodize the time spent training each week by dividing that amount into 23% (week 1), 26% (week 2), 29% (week 3), and 22% (week 4). The exact proportion spent training in each week can be changed from these percentages.

3. Break down the time spent each week into proportions devoted to the six training methods shown across the top of table 5.11.

   This approach allows the athlete who wishes to race more than once during the racing season the opportunity to plan appropriately (a major weakness of most of the training programs listed in this chapter and in chapter 6, which were designed with the goal of racing only one special race, usually a marathon or an ultramarathon, each year). This approach also forces the athlete to develop a structured program that lasts at least 12 months and to record what is to be done during the year. With such an excellent training record, it is relatively easy to reevaluate what was done and what might be altered next time around to ensure greater success.

   The enduring weakness that this approach shares with all training programs reviewed so far, however, is that the system is presented as a fait accompli. Yet, the scientist will always ask: What hypothesis is being tested, and how is it being evaluated?

   Thus, the final ingredient for evaluating the success of a training program is

Table 5.12   Training volumes for endurance sports

Level of competition	Hours per year		
	Running	Cycling	Triathlon
World class	500-700	700-1200	800-1400
Top citizen	400-500	500-700	500-800
Good citizen	300-400	350-500	400-500
Average citizen	200-300	200-350	300-400
Beginner	<200	<200	<300

Adapted, by permission, from Sleamaker and Browning (1996, p. 70).

that its effect on the body must be evaluated regularly. Evaluation can comprise four components—distance, speed, heart rate, and subjective feelings. These can be performed for each training session or, as Sleamaker and Browning suggest, at least once every three to four weeks. Their suggestion that the method of assessment can be a time-trial over a constant distance over a standard course, using the heart rate to control the intensity of effort, has great merit.

STEP 12: DECIDE WHETHER TO ALTERNATE TRAINING VOLUMES WEEKLY

A question not yet resolved, when training hard, is whether each training week should be of the same distance or whether there should be a varied pattern in which, for example, the normal mileage of 140 km is run the first week, reduced by 20% (to 112 km) for the second week, increased by 15% (to 160 km) for the third week, and reduced by 50% (to 70 km) for the fourth week. This possibility is argued by both Galloway (1984) and Costill (1979). Galloway feels that we all need one week's reduced training each month to allow our bodies a chance to repair themselves. This technique is described as periodization. My own feeling is that Galloway is correct and that altering weekly training distances also reduces the risk of overtraining. But the six weeks' heavy training program is probably just short enough to reduce the risk of overtraining, particularly as it leads directly into the tapering and sharpening period. The athlete who plans a longer buildup would be best advised to consider varying the training distances.

STEP 13: VIEW EACH RACE AS A SCIENTIFIC EXPERIMENT

The aim of science is to determine truth; the method we use is the scientific experiment. A scientific experiment begins with a theory or a hypothesis, simply a question that the scientist wishes to answer. The hypothesis that the runner wishes to test is whether or not a specific training program will produce a specific result, measured in terms of time and distance, in a specific person. Unfortunately, most runners never formulate this hypothesis, so they never really understand why they are training.

Instead, they project a result they wish to achieve and assume that a specific training program will secure that result, as if it is their inalienable right that this should happen exactly as they wish. This approach is the exact opposite of the scientific method because it presupposes the result even before the experiment commences.

Chapter 6 includes the story of how Mark Allen came to this realization. Having failed to win the 226-km Hawaiian Ironman Triathlon after six attempts, he suddenly realized that he had trained according to what he assumed was sufficient to win the race. Only when it dawned on him that the race might demand more than he thought was necessary (or had, until then, been prepared to give) did he win the next six Hawaiian Ironman races he entered. Consistent success will come only to those who adopt an intelligent and scientific approach to their training.

The correct way to test an overall hypothesis—in this case, developing a training program that will optimize performance—is to break the total experiment into many smaller experiments. That is how successful scientists approach their tasks. They approach their goals by progressing through many small experiments, each experiment answering a single question. These accumulated findings eventually lead to the solution to the larger question.

The reason we break up our overall experiment into many smaller pieces is so that we will avoid following any false leads for too long. Trying to answer too large a question in one big chunk increases the risk that the effort will be in vain and the time wasted.

Yet, this is exactly what most runners do. They undergo a year's training before they test the hypothesis in that one big race of the year. If their hypotheses are incorrect and they run poorly, then they have wasted their year of experimentation. They also have no idea which specific components of their training programs were at fault.

It would be far better to complete small segments of the experiment on a regular basis—at the outside, monthly. The aim of these experimental trials, which take the form of time-trials or interval sessions, is to assess how our performance is responding to the specific training undertaken in the period since the last trial.

Rereading Arthur Lydiard's book (Lydiard and Gilmour 1962), I came to the conclusion that, apart from his other innovations described earlier in this chapter, Lydiard may have been one of the first coaches to emphasize the use of frequent time-trials to assess the state of preparedness of his athletes.

In summary, the single most important point in this chapter is that athletes who wish to be consistently successful, at whatever level, must learn early in their careers to treat everything they do as part of a scientific experiment. I postulate that the athlete who best understands and can therefore control the myriad variables that influence the outcome of that experiment will be the most successful on a regular basis. In contrast, the racing performances of athletes who blindly follow training programs, assuming that the programs guarantee success, will have a random chance of success.

It is crucial to remember the essentially fraudulent nature of all training programs. They suggest that if the athlete follows the program to the letter, then a best-ever racing performance must result. Nothing could be further from the truth. The fact of the matter—and this should possibly become the 16th Law of Training—is that the key to successful training is not so much doing the training as determining how we are responding to that training. The evidence outlined in chapter 3 indicates that, as a result of genetic variance, each person adapts differently to the same training program. Therefore, every training program must be adapted to each person. And the only way to adjust successfully to a specific training program on a daily to weekly basis is to monitor how our bodies are adapting to the training stress according to the criteria described in this chapter.

STEP 14: BEWARE OF THE SELFISH RUNNER'S SYNDROME

Noel Carroll, an Irish double Olympian who has been running for more than half his life, writes about the tenuous nature of balancing running with other life commitments.

"Runners," he writes, "may make better lovers, but sometimes lousy spouses: that is the problem" (Carroll 1981, page 65).

But his message does not end at that. "Runners are an introverted lot. They like to keep their thoughts to themselves. Their behavior is at best anti-social, at worst utterly selfish. . . . It can create an atmosphere that does nobody any good, and certainly not the runner." (page 13) Carroll's analysis does not, of course, apply to all runners. But the Selfish Runner's Syndrome is an ever-present danger that needs to be avoided. It is better to be forewarned.

Running can indeed become an extremely selfish activity. I once asked one of the world's most lauded ultradistance runners what running had taught him. He answered that it had taught him how incredibly selfish he is. To compete at his level, running must come first. In this runner's case, the decision to put running first can be justified by a lack of family commitments, by the level of excellence he has achieved, and by the fact that without such selfishness he would not have reached the same heights in his running career.

The problem of the Selfish Runner's Syndrome is perhaps more acute for those runners who have family commitments and who lack the champion's talent. To put racing as the sole reason for living is inappropriate and ultimately detrimental to family life. The joy of running should be that it adds to, rather than detracts from, the runner's life. I have found that to balance everything, paying appropriate attention to work and family, requires almost as much effort as does running. Many women runners who combine a career with motherhood and still shoulder the bulk of the responsibility for cooking meals and looking after the children find themselves in a particularly difficult situation.

Conflict at home can be reduced to some extent by paying attention to the following rules:

- Limit serious running to every second year and then to only a few months of that year.
- If you work in an office, run to and from work if at all possible. Alternatively, run in the early morning or during the lunch hour or both.
- Don't allow running to affect the way you carry out your household responsibilities. Doing so provides your family with a tangible reminder that they come second.
- Be aware of "danger times"—you will know what these are in your household. At these times, be at your most attentive and, at all costs, do not open your mail to see if your running magazines have arrived, discuss running, or, worst of all, go out for a run. Weekends too must be handled carefully to ensure that running conflicts as little as possible with the family's weekend recreation.
- Don't get overtired. As a runner with a family you just have to accept that, for the sake of your family, you simply can't train hard enough to run your best. That is the price that must, quite realistically, be paid.

Other important advice offered by Carroll include the following: never complain of being tired; don't always want to go home early on evenings out; don't talk running all the time (have other topics of conversation); and always play down the importance of running in your life.

RISKS AND BENEFITS OF TRAINING AT A YOUNG AGE

Before closing this chapter, it is necessary to address the vexatious question of the training of children. There are two important questions that need to be answered:

1. At what age should children begin intensive training, including running?
2. What is the evidence that such intensive training is necessary for athletes to maximize their genetic potential?

One of the phenomena of modern sports has been the rise of child superstars, particularly in gymnastics and tennis. In running, the emergence of athletes such as Zola Budd-Pieterse has focused attention on the desirability of young children participating in very intensive training and competition. The arguments that the performances of child superstars have evoked are the following:

- The majority of children are too fragile to cope with the physical and psychological rigors of competitive sport.
- When forced to train heavily and to compete intensively, these children inevitably become athletic burnouts.
- Intensive sporting specialization at an early age robs the child of the vital experiences of a normal childhood—experiences that can never be relived.

The counterargument is that without intensive training and competitive exposure these children would never reach such heights of athletic excellence.

In researching the relative merits of these arguments, I discovered that there are no significant studies to provide us with firm guidelines. Based on this research, I concluded that most of the outstanding adult endurance runners of the past decade did not train heavily, nor were they necessarily outstandingly successful as children.

There are a number of sports, including gymnastics, ballet, swimming, and perhaps tennis, in which the most successful athletes begin specialist training at an early age. In contrast, many world-class adult runners of the past 50 years, including such achievers as Peter Snell, Sebastian Coe, and Paul Tergat, were not particularly outstanding, nor did they train excessively hard, before the ages of 16 and 18.

This was one of the most important factors determining the success of the great sportsmen and women studied by David Hemery (1986). He found that, almost without exception, none of these great athletes had specialized in their major sport before the ages of 16 to 18. In almost all cases, the push to specialization came from the athletes themselves and did not originate from their parents or coaches. Studies of elite Swedish tennis players confirm all these findings. Compared to those tennis players who failed to reach elite status, the most successful players specialized later and came from families that were less likely to be tennis-playing; the successful players were therefore less likely to have been pushed into the sport by overenthusiastic parents.

The negative effects of early specialization are probably most notable in the United States and in my own country, where early athletic success as a schoolchild seems to be an almost sure indication that an athlete will not continue to excel at a senior level. Three of the most notable American exceptions to this rule have been Jim

Ryun, Craig Virgin, and Mary Decker Slaney. On the other hand, neither Frank Shorter nor Bill Rodgers showed outstanding talent at school level. The same can be said of many world-class athletes.

Contrary to the popular misconception, most of the great Kenyan runners, including five-time World Cross-Country Champion Paul Tergat and Olympic 10,000-m silver medalist Haile Gebrselassie (figure 5.13), did not train intensively as youngsters. Indeed, according to a recent unpublished report, of a group of previously untrained Kenyan schoolboys from the Nandi area of the Rift Valley who underwent a voluntary 12-week training program under the leadership of Bengt Saltin from Copenhagen, two athletes emerged who, despite only having trained for that three-month period, were able to beat the very best Danish 10,000-m runners, who had trained since childhood. These observations suggest the predominant importance of genetic ability, not training or coaching, in determining running ability (see chapter 6).

Of course, these individual examples do not exclude the possibility that late starters might have been better runners if they had started running sooner, or vice versa. But they do show that athletes who are not outstanding as children can still make it to the top and may even be more likely to do so in some cases.

My explanation for this is that outstanding athletes seem to have a "life expectancy" of about 10 years in top competitive sport. Thus, if they specialize early and start intensive and focused training at the age of 12 years, there is a greater probability that they will not continue in the sport much beyond 22 years of age. It follows that the later athletes start intensive training, the better, as their greater physical maturity in the mid- to late 20s will allow them to train harder throughout their careers. They will then be able to make the most of their peak physical and mental years, which appear to be between the ages of 25 and 35.

It is of some interest that many great athletes and coaches have warned of the dangers of intensive, focused training before the children have matured both physically and mentally. In this chapter, I quote Alf Shrubb and Arthur Lydiard, both of whom felt that it is detrimental for children under the age of 18 to train intensively. Nelson wrote, "Never overwork a young boy. The older he grows the greater is the amount of strain he can bear; then is the time to specialize" (1924, page 14). Herb Elliott said,

> Certainly one of the messages I give kids these days is, "For God's sake, do what you enjoy doing and don't get too serious about it." You can have that attitude and approach to athletics until you are about 18 years of age and still go on to be a world-class performer. You can't in swimming, which I think is a disadvantage of that sport." (Lenton 1981, pages 25-26)

Elliott's opinion on swimming might need to be modified after the 2000 Olympic Games, at which, for the first time, older, more mature swimmers were also among the medalists. I am yet to be convinced that a genetically gifted child, taught to swim correctly at a young age, could not become an elite competitor in his or her mid- to late 20s if intensive training began only at 18 or 20.

For example, a four-year longitudinal study of Dutch speed skaters showed that there were no physiological or anthropometric variables at age 17 that could distinguish those who became successful at age 21 from those who were unsuccessful (De Koning et al. 1994). The attribute of those who succeeded was the ability to produce more power when skating. I interpret this to mean that the successful skat-

Touchline Media.

Figure 5.13   Ethiopia's Haile Gebrselassie beats Kenya's Paul Tergat by a nose to win the 10,000-m gold medal at the 2000 Olympic Games in Sydney.

ers had an inherent advantage that would become apparent whenever they started to train more intensively, irrespective of whether that was at 17 or 27 years of age.

The reason young athletes are forced to specialize at a young age is, in my view, entirely a result of environmental factors, not physiological ones. For, like 2-year-old race horses, young athletes must begin competing prematurely if they are to attract the support necessary to sustain their careers beyond their school years. Thus, they must be ranked at least nationally by the time they matriculate. Yet, in my view, it is only then that they should even begin more intensive and focused training in their chosen sports. Such is the way in which the environment conspires against the young athlete with potential.

Jumbo Elliott expressed a more or less similar opinion when asked how he would advise the father of a gifted child athlete:

> *I tell him to let the kid go out and play and have some fun. Forget about hurrying kids into competitive athletics before their bodies are more mature and able to tolerate that kind of work and abuse. It's a bad idea to start children on serious athletic programs until they are in their teens. Even at that age, too often, some eager part-time amateur coach (who probably teaches history during school hours) pushes far too hard on these young kids, with only one thought in mind—to win. My advice is this—let the kids have fun and grow up a little first. (Elliott and Berry 1982, page 140)*

Grete Waitz's advice is that before puberty young children should be encouraged to engage in a range of sports for enjoyment and to develop overall fitness. If they run, they should race the shorter distances and should only be involved in low-key training. This was the way in which both she and Joan Benoit-Samuelson, the 1984 Olympic Marathon gold medalist, started.

Waitz also writes that European coaches promote the following guidelines for children's running:

- Specialization in middle-distances (800 m to the mile [1.6 km]) should not take place before 13 to 14 years of age; in longer distances of up to 10 km, not before 15 to 16 years of age.
- Young runners should first participate in a balanced training program before they specialize.
- Aerobic, or endurance, training is important for young runners, but should be done easily.
- Young runners should be careful with anaerobic, quality training. Quality training should be avoided before puberty and, once begun, increased only in small amounts from year to year.
- Strength and sprint training are good for young runners.
- Long-term planning is crucial to prevent early peaking and burnout.

In this context, one of the sadder running experiments of which I am aware was that undertaken by a United States physician who, together with George Sheehan, was one of the first to write regularly in the popular running magazines in the early 1970s. Convinced that the children had to train hard if they were to become world champions, he "guided" them to world age-group records by the time they were 10 years old. After being "world champions" for a few years, they had had enough and retired from the sport, in which they were no longer interested. I am sure that followers of school athletics in many countries have similar stories to tell.

This, then, is the background. The cards would seem to be stacked against the child world-beater ever succeeding as an adult world-beater. At least in running, there is no evidence that early specialization is beneficial. However, there is a wealth of anecdotal evidence, not least that provided by the exceptional athletic coaches of the past 50 years, that suggests that this practice should be avoided or, preferably, outlawed.

Children who first achieve success at an older age are more likely to be the better adult runners. This may be a corollary to the first point. Possibly it is not the heavy training and early specialization in youth that is detrimental to adult performance but rather that children who show early promise in any sport, particularly running, are early maturers.

Hemery (1986) noted that the majority of the high achievers in the wide variety of sports that he studied first became successful at older ages. These possibilities deserve further study. But there are some sports in which early success, perhaps based on the good fortune of being born at the right time of the year, predicts success as an adult in that sport.

Are There Benefits of Intensive Training at a Young Age?

Those who advocate early specialization in endurance sports, such as swimming and running, usually argue that heavy training in childhood and early adulthood, at the very time when the adult body is being formed, will have its greatest effect. In fact, heavy training in childhood does not have any dramatic effect on the physiological parameters that are believed to improve running performance (Borms 1986; Naughton et al. 2000). Indeed, some suggest that the training response is blunted (C.A. Williams et al. 2000) or perhaps absent in prepubescent boys.

For example, Daniels and Oldridge (1971) and Daniels, Oldridge, et al. (1978) followed different groups of young athletes initially aged between 10 and 13 years for up to six years and measured their $\dot{V}O_2$max and running economy values every six months. They found that although absolute $\dot{V}O_2$max increased, when corrected to the increasing body mass, the $\dot{V}O_2$max relative to body mass (ml O_2 per kg per min) did not change.

The major change that did occur was a striking fall in the oxygen cost of running at submaximal speeds, owing both to growth and to training. However, the change in running economy was achieved equally by all athletes regardless of whether they started training at 10, 12, or 13 years of age. Thus, in that study the major benefit of training was an increased running economy that developed equally in all young athletes regardless of the age at which they began training.

Somewhat different results were reported in a group of Japanese runners who were studied annually for seven years between the ages of 14 and 21 and who ran two hours per day, five or six days per week (Murase et al. 1981). Relative $\dot{V}O_2$max increased from 65.4 to 75.5 ml O_2 per kg per min during this six-year period, and there was no further increase in $\dot{V}O_2$max with training after 18 years. However, this 15% increase in $\dot{V}O_2$max is no greater than would be achieved by training that began at any (older) age. For example, Jim Ryun's $\dot{V}O_2$max value of 81 ml O_2 per kg per min fell to 65 ml O_2 per kg per min when he stopped training and returned to its former value when he again trained hard (J.T. Daniels 1974). Other studies have also shown that training in childhood increases $\dot{V}O_2$max between 10 to 20% (Ekblom 1969; Andrew et al. 1972; C.H. Brown et al. 1972; Eriksson 1972; Lussier and Buskirk 1977), the same magnitude of effect that would be expected in adults undergoing equivalent training.

The extent to which the muscle mitochondrial enzymes adapt to training during childhood is no different from that reported in adults (Eriksson 1972; Eriksson et al. 1973). On the other hand, even when trained, adolescents have lower levels of muscle enzymes than do untrained adults (Fournier et al. 1982). This finding indicates that adolescents are not yet ready to adapt to training to the same degree as adults.

Other predictors of running performance, such as the lactate turnpoint, have yet to be reported in detail in children. Krahenbuhl and Pangrazi (1983) have shown that the best 10-year-old runners have higher $\dot{V}O_2$max values, run at a higher percentage of $\dot{V}O_2$max, are better sprinters, achieve higher postrace blood lactate levels, and probably have more fast-twitch muscle fibers.

My interpretation of these studies is that they simply confirm the importance of hereditary factors, rather than intensive training at an early age, as being the more important determinants of the athlete's ultimate performance. Furthermore, it seems that after age 16, those runners without the physiological characteristics necessary for athletic success stop competing (Sundberg and Elovainio 1982). This means that the adolescent athletic population comprises only those athletes who have the appropriate physiological characteristics necessary for success.

It is important to stress, however, that there is no evidence for any negative physiological effects of intensive training by itself in the prepubertal period (Baxter-Jones

1995; Damsgaard et al. 2000; Sundaresan et al. 2000). However, disordered eating, which is common in some sports, can have detrimental effects, including a delayed onset of puberty, secondary to reduced production of the hormone leptin (Weimann et al. 1999).

Is There a Risk of Physical Burnout?

The concept that children drop out of intensively competitive sport because they burn out physically is false. There is no evidence that either children or adults can train themselves to the point where they suffer lasting physical impairment. Certainly, they can overtrain acutely, but the physical burnout from overtraining lasts, at most, six weeks (chapter 7). However, we should not be blind to the relatively common practice, especially in swimming and track athletics, of exposing young children to excessively strenuous and monotonous training for which, because of their age, neither their minds nor their bodies are prepared. While one or two athletes will always survive the abuse inherent in this system and so, sadly, provide the anecdotal justification for its retention, the majority fall by the wayside and become victims not so much of physical burnout as of mental stagnation.

While we do not yet know the optimum amount of training for children, I would suggest that training for 1 to 2 hours per day is the upper safe limit. Training more than 2 hours per day crosses, in my opinion, the boundary between a healthy activity and one that may border on the abusive.

Everyone who is involved in the training of children needs to remember that the long-term outcome of such training is completely unknown. Hence, the training must be seen as a scientific experiment in which the child is usually an uninformed participant.

Were the training of children to be controlled by ethical review boards, as are all scientific experiments in humans, the children as participants would have certain rights. They would have the right to be fully informed about the nature of the experiment and its likely outcome, as well as the right to withdraw at any time should they so choose. They would also be protected from the pressure of the undue expectations of those conducting the experiment, namely their coaches and parents. Finally, all parties would sign a document in which all these points were covered in detail.

Of course, none of this ever happens, so there is no firm ethically acceptable basis for the training of children. Rather, the very children who are supposedly benefiting the most from the system remain voiceless and become its slaves.

There is an urgent need for long-term studies to establish whether intensive training of more than 2 hours per day in childhood is ultimately beneficial for those children who participate. The assumption must be that those who start young and who achieve success as adults will have benefited. But at what cost to themselves? And what of the many thousands who do not succeed in those sports as adults? Do they extract sufficient benefit to justify giving up a large part of their childhood?

Perhaps these concerns are groundless. But until we have firm data on which to base ethically sound intensive training programs for children, we do not know whether we are doing good or harm by persisting with the uncontrolled approach.

On the other hand, what we tend to forget is that many adults drop out of competitive sport when they reach the goal for which they have striven for so long and for which they have sacrificed so much. For example, Roger Bannister stopped competing shortly after he had broken the 4-minute mile barrier, at a time when he felt that his career and family had become more important (Bannister 1955). Britain's next mile world record holder after Bannister, Derek Ibbotson, captured the feeling when he wrote, "In the moment of victory I did not realize that the inner force, which had been driving me to my ultimate goal, died when I became the world's fastest miler" (Ibbotson 1960, page 13). Herb Elliott, possibly the most talented miler of all time, retired unbeaten as the Olympic champion and world record holder at the tender age of 22 so that he could study Latin at Cambridge University where, with typical obsessiveness, he chose to cram four academic years into one. I suspect that it is the same for children. I would suggest that the majority of successful child athletes retire from competitive sport for the same reasons as do adults. Either they reach the goals they set themselves, or they prefer to devote their time to developing other interests or facets of their personalities.

However, another important reason why some may stop, which is specific only to children, relates to the adult pressures to which they are exposed by parents, coaches, and the press during their competitive years. When children approach the age of about 17, they may start questioning whether they are really running for themselves or for their parents, coaches, or country.

What Are the Effects of Parental and Coaching Pressures?

Abnormal parental and coaching pressures may be the critical factors determining whether a child enjoys sport and continues to compete after adolescence. Billie-Jean King, surely one of the world's most remarkable athletes, has a brother who was also a professional athlete—a baseball pitcher. When asked whether she thought that she and her brother had been fortunate in inheriting sporting ability from their parents, she replied that they had indeed been very fortunate in the parents they had, but not for that reason. "My parents were very supportive," stated King, "but they never asked if we won. They asked how we did, whether we gave 100%, and if we were happy with ourselves. You don't have to ask children if they won; you can tell by their body language. Just look at their shoulders" (Caldwell 1983, page 23). It was this supportive, nonmanipulative attitude that she valued the most.

King's parents understood the basic psychological premise that children's self-esteem is based on what they believe their parents think of them. In sport, the parental message can be very subtle, or not, as in the case of the father who allocates pocket-money according to the number of points his child scores in a particular sport. Parents who stress the importance of winning risk raising children who, when they doubt whether they can win, may choose not to compete rather than risk losing. This is a variation of the "fear of success" syndrome discussed in chapter 8. Rather, children must be taught what King was taught—that giving 100% is all that matters. In addition, they need to learn how to lose. After all, at least 50% of people involved in competitive sport have to lose.

One of the most endearing stories about learning how to lose properly is related by Roger Kahn (1972) who recounts that Joe Black, formerly a pitcher with the (New York) Brooklyn Dodgers baseball team, took the high school team that he coached to watch the Dodgers and to meet his old coach, the legendary Casey Stengel. Black introduced his team to Stengel with the following words, "This is my team, Case. They're having troubles. They've lost 16 out of 18 games, and I wondered what the Old Master thought I ought to teach 'em.'"

"Lost 16 out of 18, you say?" Stengel scratched his chin. "Well, first you better teach 'em to lose in the right spirit." Children can cope with losing if their parents can.

In contrast to the exemplary attitude of King's parents, there are the manipulative parents who use their children's ability to serve their own ends. Often parents say that their children want to compete, but we have to ask why a young boy or girl would want to train really hard to run marathons unless he or she were given such a message by the parents?

An important point that adults overlook is that children under the age of about 14 do not think abstractly; many do not see a reward beyond the short term for the effort they put in and so, unlike adults, they do not have long-term goals. The parents who say that their young child is training to be a future world champion are, in fact, expressing a parental wish for that child and, at the same time, very forcefully conveying the parental message. That parental expectations increase the anxiety experienced by children in competition has been shown (Lewthwaite and Scanlan 1989).

And then there is the final joker in the pack—the coach or possibly the school principal who may suffer from the same problem and whose ego may be so insecure that it depends on the success of the school's athletes. (Of course, if the athlete lives in a country that also has an ego/identity crisis, then these problems will be expressed on a national scale.)

Clearly, what the child athlete needs is egoless parents, egoless coaching, and a mature nation. Where these are found, child athletes stand a greater chance of becoming an adult world-beaters. In addition, children should always be allowed to determine their own level of commitment to any particular sport.

Bruce Ogilvie (1983a; 1983b), the sports psychologist introduced in chapter 8, has stated that the most important attribute of the coach and, indeed, the parent, is "the quest to become egoless." He stresses that this must remain a lifelong goal. The goal should always be to subordinate personal needs to those of the people we are trying to help. Here are 10 helpful guidelines for parents of sporting children (adapted from Hellstedt 1988):

1. Make certain that your children know that your love and approval are not linked to whether they win or lose.

2. Be realistic about what your child is capable of achieving physically.

3. Help your child set realistic goals.

4. Encourage improved performance and skills (rather than winning) by positive reinforcement.

5. Don't use your child as a means of reliving your own athletic past.

6. Provide a safe environment, including proper training methods and equipment for sporting activities.

7. Control your own emotions at competitions and games—don't shout at other competitors, coaches, or officials.

8. Act as a cheerleader for your child and any teammates.

9. Respect your child's coaches. Discuss problems honestly and openly.

10. Be a positive role model: live healthily, enjoy your own sports, and set your own realistic goals.

Is it really so bad to be a great athlete only at school? If the child superstar retires prematurely, is it necessarily a failed outcome? In other words, why should we be so distraught if our child stars suddenly retire? Do we raise the same concerns when older athletes retire? For example, how many of our adult elite distance runners continue to compete for more than a handful of years? Yet, no one seems particularly concerned when they retire.

The problems faced by the child athlete are no different from those of the adult. Success, it would seem, depends on intense self-motivation, the acceptance of sacrifice, a supportive environment comprising egoless coaching and egoless parents, and gradual progress toward carefully delineated goals.

My personal bias is that intensive training for young runners should be delayed for as long as possible because I believe that the older the runner is when hard training begins, the better. Such intensive training should, in my view, start between 18 and 20. The value of running is that it is possible to start training at that age and still achieve your full potential. The ultimate performance level of gifted athletes may be determined by psychological factors; thus, it is best to start training so that peak physical performance occurs when the mind is strongest.

What Do Children Desire From Sport?

A study of more than 1000 young British athletes found that their behaviors during sport were determined by a relatively small set of 18 values, including sociomoral values and values of self-competence and status (see table 5.13) (Lee and Cockman 1995).

The top three values were enjoyment, achievement, and sportsmanship, whereas winning was ranked as the least important factor. Furthermore, the statement with which these young athletes concurred most strongly was keep winning in proportion.

Table 5.13 also shows that concerns about health and fitness ranked only 13th of the 18 values. The study shows that children attach moral values to their participation in sport. Teachers, parents, and coaches need to be aware that their actions influence the child's development of moral values and judgments. They also need to understand the relative unimportance that children attach to winning. Indeed, low-exercising adolescents accept that their future health will be influenced by their activity status but would prefer their physical activity to be noncompetitive (Gentle et al. 1994).

GUIDELINES FOR THE PARTICIPATION OF CHILDREN IN SPORT

Children are not miniature adults: they should be treated as children first and as athletes second. It is important to respect their limitations and to appreciate that children understand their personal limitations better than adults. Unlike adults, children who are left to their own devices will not drive themselves to the point of injury.

Table 5.13 The relative importance of selected values associated with sporting participation reported by young competitive British athletes aged 12 to 16 years

Value	Description of that value	Rank
Enjoyment	Experiencing feelings of satisfaction and pleasure	1
Achievement	Being personally or collectively successful in play	2
Sportsmanship	Being of good disposition; accepting bad luck with the good; demonstrating positive behaviors toward opponents and accepting defeats	3
Contract maintenance	Supporting the essence of agreeing to play the game; playing in the spirit of the game	4
Being fair	Not allowing an unfair advantage in the contest/judgment	5
Compassion	Showing concern for other people	6
Tolerance	Being able to get along with others despite differences	7
Obedience	Avoiding punishment	9
Health and fitness	Becoming healthy as a result of the activity, and becoming fit to enhance performance	13
Winning	Demonstrating superiority in the contest	18

Based on Lee and Cockman (1995).

Under age six. Encourage children to play and to be physically active by playing.

Six- to ten-year-olds. Awaken an interest in sports, emphasizing having fun and learning basic skills. Children at that age lack the hormones necessary to produce major physiological adaptations to training.

Parents who are runners frequently ask when their children might be able to run with them in training or even when their children may safely enter shorter distance running events. My suggestion is that anything the child initiates is acceptable. No child will voluntarily train or race at a distance or intensity that seems unpleasant. Thus, if your child asks to train with you or asks to enter a particular running event, then the child's participation can be actively encouraged as it initiates the road to a more healthy lifestyle for life.

The child will also be able to set the distance to run. For children under 10, this will seldom exceed 8 to 10 km unless the child is particularly gifted. Gifted young runners, who choose to run those distances, are at no greater risk of an unfavorable outcome or injury than are adults completing the same distances under the same environmental conditions. The key then is what the child wishes to do. If the child alone is making the decisions, then those decisions should be fully supported.

Eleven- to fifteen-year-olds. Teach sporting versatility and proper techniques so that the child can begin developing a tolerance for an increased training load.

A rough guide is that a child of this age can manage about one-third of the training load of an adult. This means that between the ages of 11 and 15 a child can train intensively for no more than 10 to 20 minutes before requiring a rest. At this age, children are motivated by the need to gain the acceptance of their peers and are unable to separate judgments about their physical ability from those about their worth as a person (Ogilvie 1983a). When judged a failure on the athletics field, the child will feel like a failure as a total being.

During these years, the child should be encouraged to participate in a wide range of sporting activities, including those that develop endurance (swimming, cycling, and running) as well as ball and other skills sports that can be played for life. The goal should be to lay the physical foundation for an active lifestyle that will be maintained for life.

Sixteen- to eighteen-years-olds. By this age range the child is ready for an increased training load (between one-half and two-thirds of that undertaken by an adult) and for specialized training, including the use of weights. From this age, children are also ready for more intensive competition. However, once again, children are not adults, and they cannot be expected to hold a competitive peak for as long as adults. A.G.K. Brown (1964) has suggested that no child be trained hard for more than six or seven weeks at a time and has proposed that a child should not be expected to maintain a competitive peak for more than a month. He suggests that the child athlete should "peak" three times per year: once each in the summer, spring, and winter or once each term in a three-term school. "If he spends the interim eating and sleeping, good luck to him!" (Brown 1964, page 65).

Most of the problems that exist in youth sports result from the inappropriate application of the win-oriented model of professional or elite sport to the child's sports setting (R.E. Smith 1984). When excessive pressures are placed on winning, children can be deprived of important opportunities for personal growth, development of skills, and enjoyment.

It is also important to recognize the wide range of maturity differences that can exist between children of the same age. Thus, at the age of six, maturity levels can vary by as much as four years; at the age of 12, by as much as six years.

Ogilvie (1983a) suggests that, when approached correctly, childhood sport should afford all children the opportunity to develop positive feelings about their bodies; it should increase their ability to interact with others more sensitively by sharing physical and emotional experiences; and it should reinforce positive attitudes toward health maintenance for life.

Coach's Role

In a sadly humorous article entitled, "How to Ruin an Athlete," Richardson (1976) describes the most effective way for the "dyed-in-the-wool, true-blue, totally conscientious coach who wants to ensure that his athletes never run again when they finish school." (page 76)

He does this by ensuring that workouts should have as little variety as possible: each day's training should be the same and should be run on the same course or track. Athletes must run sufficiently hard in training for their performances in races to show an impressive deterioration. Those whose racing performances continue to improve are not training sufficiently hard and must train even harder. All training must hurt, especially for the most fragile people. Training must also be sufficiently hard that the athletes are too tired for any social or academic life. Academic success must also be devalued.

The coach may not pay individual attention to any athlete; he should simply materialize at the track, read times off his stopwatch, bark and snarl at the runners, and disappear immediately at the end of each training session. At all times, runners must be impressed about the life-or-death nature of the sport. Impossible competitive goals must be set for the athletes so that their individual performances can be denigrated at the end of each race.

"Above all," Richardson advises, "make sure your runners know the price of success. Emphasize that the road to the Olympics is paved with blood, sweat and broken bones. To destroy an athlete, particularly a highly motivated one, requires patience, perseverance and a total lack of understanding" (page 76).

By describing the opposite, Richardson's comments clearly identify what is important. The goal should be to develop the child's self-esteem and moral judgment through sport and to give each child the interest and physical skills to remain physically active for life. If some also become professional athletes or Olympians, that is a small bonus. But this should never be the main focus of a balanced sporting program for children, which will, in the long-term, provide the greatest benefit for the largest number of children.

A coaching forum that promotes a different approach to child sport has been founded in Stanford, California (Matheson 2000). The Positive Coaching Alliance, the idea of Jim Thompson, promotes three coaching goals that are in line with those described here:

1. Help players redefine what is means to be a winner by focusing on effort and improvement, rather than on the scoreboard.
2. Fill players "emotional tanks" by using encouragement to help them play their best.
3. Honor the game by showing respect for the rules, opponents, officials, teammates, and game tradition.

Parent's Role

Ogilvie (1983a) has identified a number of negative parental attitudes. These include the parent who seems unable or unwilling to allow the activity to remain child-oriented and who has the compulsion to judge it by adult standards; the parent who is unable to maintain the appropriate emotional distance from the child's activity and makes the child's involvement in sport an extension of his own ego; the parent who is a guilt motivator and who stresses the financial and other sacrifices she is supposedly making for the child's sporting success; and the parent who fantasizes about the financial and other rewards that "my child the champion" will bring to the family.

Ogilvie has stressed that these adult pressures negate almost all of the fundamental psychological values that sport should provide for children, such as fun, emotional release, and learning to relate effectively to peers. Furthermore, the possibility is that these adult pressures will stunt the emotional and social growth of the child and lead to a restricted personality and a shaky ego. Those children who sense their worth purely in terms of a single attribute, in this case athletic ability, run a very real risk of future emotional trauma should their genetically determined capabilities fall short of their parents' expressed desires.

Ogilvie (Adler et al. 1982) suggests that the parents of children in competitive sport should answer the following three questions:

1. Is the sport regarded as directly or indirectly a measure of the child's worth as a person?
2. Have I made athletics a proving ground for the child or, vicariously, for me?
3. Do the child and I realize that no matter how remarkable the physical gift, it should not be used to prove value as a human being?

Answers to these questions will indicate whether the sport is being approached in the correct or incorrect manner.

Like coaches, parents of young children need to encourage their children to find those sports that they enjoy and will be most likely to practice for life. By being physically active themselves, parents, especially mothers, set the best examples for their children.

Only recently has it become obvious that the health choices that children make (or are taught) at a young age predict the type of lifestyle those children will follow for the rest of their lives—in particular, whether they will be physically active for life or whether they will adopt other healthy lifestyle choices. A number of studies show that those who are more physically active as adults show specific characteristics that are already identifiable in childhood and adolescence. Thus, those who are more physically active as adults

- were 2.2 times more likely to be physically active as adolescents (Janz et al 2000);
- were better than average at sport when they were at school (Kuh and Cooper 1992), including the ability to run farther during a 9-minute run test (Glenmark et al. 1994);
- engaged in more physical activities at school, including training for a longer duration and at a higher intensity (Glenmark et al. 1994);
- achieved higher marks in physical education, but not in other subjects (Glenmark et al. 1994);
- had a more positive attitude to physical activity and participated in sport outside school and in competitive activities (Glenmark et al. 1994);
- were more outgoing socially as adolescents (Kuh and Cooper 1992);
- had a higher proportion of Type I muscle fibers (this was identified in boys but not in girls; Glenmark et al. 1994);
- had fewer health problems in school (Kuh and Cooper 1992);
- were better educated (Kuh and Cooper 1992);
- had more mothers with secondary education (Kuh and Cooper 1992);
- were more likely to have attended a college or university with higher physical education activity program requirements (Adams and Brynteson 1992); and
- benefited from genetic factors that could also play a role ("the intrinsic drive to physical activity could be partly influenced by the genotype"; Perusse et al. 1989, page 1012).

In addition, it was found that physical activity in adolescence is associated with the following beneficial health outcomes:

- A slower rate of fat accretion in the subcutaneous fat layer (L.L. Moore et al. 1995; Raitakari et al. 1994; Twisk et al. 1996); higher levels of body fat in children are associated with unfavorable blood pressure and blood lipid profiles and with lower fitness levels (Harsha 1995; Twisk et al. 1996), as they are in adults
- A more favorable HDL: total cholesterol ratio, and lower serum insulin and triglyceride concentrations (Raitakari et al. 1994)
- A reduced prevalence of smoking and a lower consumption of saturated fats with a higher intake of polyunsaturated fats (Raitakari et al. 1994)
- Fewer coronary risk factors, including a lower prevalence of elevated blood pressures (Boreham et al. 1997)

It has also been established that health behaviors with respect to physical activity, smoking, and food choices are established early in life, perhaps by the sixth to ninth grade (Kelder et al. 1994; Rainey et al. 1996), so that children who will adopt high risk behaviors as adults can be identified at a much younger age. This is especially applicable to cigarette smoking, a habit that is usually established by the 12th grade. Adolescents in grades 4 to 12 who are likely to be active exhibit three characteristics: use of afternoon time for sports and physical activity, enjoyment of physical education, and family support for physical activity (Sallis et al. 1999).

In addition, the serum cholesterol concentration at age 22 predicted the subsequent incidence of coronary heart disease in midlife (Klag et al. 1993). What is more, a postmortem study of young people aged 2 to 39 who died from various causes (usually trauma) showed that the number of cardiovascular risk factors predicted the severity of the asymptomatic atherosclerosis they had developed in their coronary arteries and aorta.

Avoidance of the cigarette habit, a lower serum cholesterol concentration and percentage body fat, and a more active physical lifestyle should be the goal of health education at school.

Of some concern is the finding that participants in team sports are more likely to be obese, to smoke, to consume large quantities of alcohol (and drive without seat belts) than are runners, joggers, cyclists, and bicycle riders (Schneider and Geenberg 1992). Other studies confirm that adolescents who participate in team sports are less likely to smoke but more likely to abuse alcohol and especially to binge drink (Faulkner and Slattery 1990; Rainey et al. 1996).

FINAL WORD

In this chapter, I have presented the basic guidelines that athletes can use to develop a successful, lifelong training program. The emphasis has been on defining the 15 Laws of Training—laws learned through centuries of toil, trial, tribulation, and observation by some particularly exceptional athletes and their coaches. The wise athlete would be best advised to learn and to honor these laws rather than to transgress them.

In the next chapter, we amplify this inherited wisdom by reviewing the training successes and failures of some of the most remarkable athletes of the past century.

Learning From the Experts

In this chapter, we look at the training methods of runners who, in the past century and a half, have joined the select band of world-class athletes. The athletes presented here have been included not only because of the levels of excellence they have achieved but also because something is known about their training methods. Sadly, the majority of great athletes record only the barest details of their training methods for posterity.

The athletes described in this chapter represent middle- and long-distance running from 1500 m up to the marathon; short ultramarathon running at distances up to 100 km; and long ultramarathon running at distances from 100 to 700 km.

HISTORICAL OVERVIEW

The roots of modern distance running have been traced by Andy Milroy (1981), a sports historian who has researched the history of running, as well as the training methods of runners, particularly ultramarathon runners. Milroy relates that foot messengers were used by the Greeks and Romans to carry letters and messages over distances of up to 100 km at a time and that a 237-km race was held in the Circus Maximus in Rome at the height of the Roman Empire.

The first reference to British foot messengers was in A.D. 1040; to continental European and Turkish messengers, in the fifteenth century. Milroy writes that at the time of the Tudors (1485–1603) and the Stuarts (1603–1714), the footman was considered an essential status symbol for the English nobility. For example, a footman would carry letters between the members of the nobility and would run ahead of the nobleman's coach to clear the rough road of trees and to warn of lurking highwaymen. When the coach suffered mechanical failure, the footman would run to the nearest village to summon help. At first, footmen had little difficulty in staying ahead of the lumbering coaches as they made their way painfully over the poorly maintained dirt roads. However, in the eighteenth century, as a result of greatly improved roads, coaches were able to achieve an average speed of more than 13 km per hour, thus placing much greater demands on the footmen, who, as Milroy (1981) recounts, "seldom survived three or four years, generally dying of consumption." (p. 2) Milroy relates that the footmen of the Tudor period were usually from Ireland; later they were joined by Englishmen, Spaniards, Frenchmen, and Germans.

By the end of the eighteenth century, improvements in road conditions, particularly in Britain, made the continued use of messengers unnecessary. Messengers were retained only for racing. In Britain they were soon supplanted by professional pedestrians—trained athletes who raced against one another for financial reward in races that involved substantial betting. Race distances varied from as little as 1 mile (1.6 km) to six-day races in which some runners ran in excess of 1000 km.

Milroy (1981) states that it is difficult to explain why professional pedestrianism first developed in Britain, where races between two competitors were common from the seventeenth century onward. Three essential components—good roads, accurately measured courses, and accurate and cheap pocket watches—were also available in other parts of Europe, including France. Milroy suggests that the fascination of the British upper class with gambling was the pivotal factor and that it was betting that drove the sport in the very early days.

From the outset, there was a clear distinction between professional and amateur running. Professional running was the domain of the lower, working classes, and the earliest races were usually sponsored by public houses that built their own running tracks (Lovesey 1968). The aim was not sport, but to make money, and any working class youth who showed promise in athletics soon became a professional runner.

The more conventional (amateur) running originated in the British public schools and soon spread to Oxford and Cambridge (Krise and Squires 1982). Eton was probably the first British school to introduce formal athletics for students in 1837. Less formal cross-country running for boys in the form of games such as "hares and hounds" and "paper chases" became popular at about the same time. The 12-mile (20-km) Crick Run, held annually since 1837 at Rugby School, is the oldest long-distance run in the world.

As we shall see, road running, especially marathon and ultramarathon running, evolved from the professional sport. Professional road records antedate those of the amateurs by more than 70 years (Milroy 1987). Track running also evolved from the professionals—the amateurs wished to have similar events but "without the air of disreputability that surrounded the professional scene" (Milroy 1987). The 1896 Olympic Games formalized the marathon as an amateur event, at least until running became fully professional in the 1970s when the Olympic Games were opened to professional sportsmen and -women. Modern interest in ultramarathon running can be traced, at least in part, to the influence of Arthur Newton and the Comrades Marathon, as described later in this chapter.

DISTANCES FROM
THE MILE TO THE MARATHON

In tracing the evolution of training methods, I have summarized in chronological sequence the careers and ideas of those runners who fulfill either or both of two criteria. First, there must be something of value written about their careers, with some reasonably intelligible facts about their training methods. Second, they need to have had more than a passing influence on the history of the sport and, especially, the way in which athletes train. The athletes who, in my opinion, have made crucial contributions include the Finnish runners at the start of the twentieth century, perhaps best epitomized by Paavo Nurmi; the British ultramarathon runner, Arthur Newton; the Czech legend, Emil Zatopek; the British marathoner, Jim Peters; the host of outstanding Kenyan runners of the 1980s and 1990s; and the South African ultramarathon runner, Bruce Fordyce. Undoubtedly, the list could and should be expanded substantially, but these are the runners who have made an impact and who have been gracious enough to leave fairly comprehensive written records of their training methods and philosophies.

Deerfoot

The first great runner of whom there is some recorded history was the North American Indian, Deerfoot. He first became an international celebrity in September 1861 when, at the age of 36, he visited "a secure and insular" Britain (Lovesey 1968) to pit his running skills against the top British professionals of the day. Deerfoot's talent had first come to the attention of a British promoter and ex-runner, George Martin, who, earlier that year, had taken three leading British pedestrians to North America to compete in a series of races against American runners. It was in those races that Deerfoot's exceptional potential had become apparent.

Deerfoot's tour of Britain lasted until May 1863, during which time he visited all the major cities in the United Kingdom. In one four-month period alone, he ran 400 miles (648 km) in competition (Lovesey 1968), and in the first 14 weeks of his tour, he ran 16 races of distances from 1 to 11 miles (1.6 to 18 km) against the best British runners, losing only twice, both under unusual conditions. Only near the end of his tour was Deerfoot's invincibility challenged, in part because he had overraced and had become "rather too fond" of the British way of life and, apparently, of British beer.

Among his greatest performances were a 10-mile (16-km) race run in 53:35 and, one week later, a race in which he became the fourth man in history to cover 11 miles (18 km) in less than 1 hour. The following year, in 1862, he established the world's best performance for distance run in 1 hour, and in the first four months of 1863, he improved on that distance three times. His last race in Britain was one of his greatest. Passing the 10-mile mark in 51:26, he completed 11 miles, 970 yards (18.60 km) in 1:00:00 and 12 miles (20.2 km) in 1:02:02.05. It was not until 1953, 90 years later, that another British amateur, Jim Peters, exceeded that distance by running 16 yards farther in 1 hour. As we shall see, Peters may have been the greatest marathoner of all time.

When asked how he trained, Deerfoot replied, "I have never trained" (Lovesey 1968). Lovesey (1968) writes that Deerfoot's "invasion" of England had three major effects on distance running. First, he exposed the "cautious, strength-preserving" tactics of the British runners as unprogressive and confused them by his frequent switches of pace. Second, he brought social respectability and wide public appeal to running, and third, he inspired an exceptional group of British runners, who established running records that would last for 16 to 60 years.

Walter George

After Deerfoot, the next great distance runner was unquestionably Walter George (figure 6.1), who, in the 1880s, earned the title "Champion of Champions" for a series of remarkable running performances.

In 1882, at the age of 23, George set world records at every running distance from the three-quarter-mile to 10 miles (1.2 to 16 km; Lovesey 1968; Krise and Squires 1982) and failed by just 37 yards to beat Deerfoot's 1-hour record. He also won a string of British track and cross-country titles, and he lowered the world amateur mile record from 4:25.5 to 4:10.4. In 1885, he ran a mile in training in 4:10.2 on a course that was too long by 6 yards. Later he ran an unofficial 10 miles (16 km) in 49:29. Between 1880 and 1884, George won 12 British championship medals at four different distances and three national cross-country titles, each in record time. In the 1882 championships, George won the half-mile (800-m), mile (1.6-km) and 4-mile (7-km) races all on the same day; in the 1884 championships, he went one better by winning the 10-mile (16 km) race as well, two days after again winning the half-mile (800-m), mile (1.6-km), and 4-mile (7-km) races.

His most famous races were probably the ones he ran in 1885 against the Scotsman William Cummings, who was the professional counterpart of George, holding all the professional records at the same distances at which George competed

Figure 6.1   An elderly Walter George with Arthur Newton.

(Lovesey 1968). In the first three races they contested, George won the first, a mile, in 4:20.02; Cummings won the second and third at 4 and 6 miles (7 and 10 km) respectively. George's disappointment led to the scheduling of the Mile of the Century, run between the two great rivals on 23 August, 1886, at Stanford Bridge in London. The contestants completed the first lap in 58.25 and the half-mile in 2:01.75, and they were still locked together at the end of the third lap, and passed one another in 3:07.75. Then, Cummings suddenly sprinted to a 10-yard lead.

But he had gone too soon. George caught Cummings in the back straight, winning in the world-record time of 4:12.75. Cummings collapsed 60 yards from the finish. Remarkably, at the age of 19, and only three months after he had started running, George had announced that he would one day run the mile in 04:12 (Lovesey 1968), an improvement of 12 seconds on the then world record. Two months later, George beat Cummings over 10 miles.

By modern standards, George trained very lightly, claiming that he trained on "beer and enjoyment." For the first six years of his running career, his only training involved doing "100-up" exercises (George 1908; Lovesey 1968). This entailed little more than running on the spot, flexing his knees alternately to hip level. The idea was to build up training until he was able to repeat the exercise 100 times at maximal speed. By 1882, George ran every morning and afternoon, alternating slow runs of 1 to 2 miles with faster runs of 400 to 1200 yards and some sprinting. He finished all his long runs with a sustained burst of fast running. He did one 100-up exercise every day, including the occasional walk (Lovesey 1968). Cummings, on the other hand, seems to have trained mainly by walking up to 10 miles per day. He included a slow daily run of a mile, with faster runs once or twice per week (Lovesey 1968).

Lovesey (1968) suggests that George's contribution to running was that his intellectual approach to training brought a sense of purpose to the sport. In later life, George, who had been born in the village of Calne, Wilshire, on the Box-to-London 100-mile course, was chief timekeeper in most of Arthur Newton's record attempts in Britain (Clarke and Harris 1967).

Len Hurst

Briton Len Hurst left more complete details of his training methods (Downer 1900; Milroy 1983). Born in Kent, England, on 28 December, 1871, Hurst ran his first professional race at the age of 15, winning a 6-km race worth $10 (Milroy 1983). In the early years of his athletic career, he ran only short-distance races, but in 1893 he switched to longer distances, covering 294.6 km in a four-day event (7.5 hours of running each day).

In 1896, Hurst won the inaugural 40-km Paris-to-Conflans Marathon in 2:31:00, a time that was 27 minutes faster than Spiridon Louis' winning time in the inaugural Olympic Games Marathon, also run over 40 km that year. Hurst won this race twice more, with a best performance of 2:26:48 in the 1900 Conflans-to-Paris race. A month later, he ran 50 km in 3:36:45, a time that Milroy (1983) considers to have been a likely world record. The following year, he easily defeated American Bob Hallen in the 40-km Championship of the World.

In 1903, Hurst won the first professional London-to-Brighton race by 40 minutes in a time of 6:32:34, a 26-minute improvement on the previous record. In 1929, during the next unofficial running of this event, Arthur Newton lowered the record by a further 38 minutes. Two months later, in his last major running success at the Preston

Park Cricket Ground in Brighton, Hurst set a new world amateur and professional 40-km track record of 2:33:42.

Hurst retired in 1908 to manage a pub for the rest of his life. He was a quiet man, and he refused to write his life story. He reportedly died of cirrhosis of the liver, an occupational hazard, in 1937 at the age of 66. His achievements are commemorated each year with the award to the winning team in the London-to-Brighton race of the Len Hurst Belt, believed to have been won by Hurst in that race in 1903.

Of his training methods, Hurst wrote,

> *For a youth to attain anything like "class" honours in events from 10 miles and upwards, he . . . will have two or three years' steady work ahead of him, and must be satisfied to plod along at what, to his ambitious mind, must appear a very slow pace. . . . It is impossible for a man to possess both speed and endurance for long-distance running without a thorough training. . . . I should therefore advise . . . any amount of walking exercise, right from the time they start running. . . . Remember, never overdo yourself or pump yourself quite out. (Downer 1900, p. 117-118)*

Hurst's training included 5.75 to 6.75 hours of walking each day and between 10 and 30 km of running each day (when training for a marathon). His nutritional preference was for roast beef, roast, boiled mutton or chicken, and a limited amount of vegetables and bread, washed down with half- pint of good bitter ale. During races, he reportedly drank a mixture of egg and sherry (Milroy 1981).

Joe Binks

In 1902 Joe Binks surpassed George's amateur world mile record by running the distance in 4:16.8. His training was even more farcical than was George's. He trained one evening per week for about 30 minutes, during which he ran 5 or 6 × 110 yards at top speed, finishing with a "fast 200 or 300 yards" (Burfoot 1981a).

Later Binks became a journalist, a close friend of Arthur Newton, and organizer of the 1937 London-to-Brighton race, in which South African ultramarathoner Hardy Ballington beat Arthur Newton's course record by 1 second—a result that seems to have been engineered by Newton, who, involved in organizing the challenge to his record, apparently wished Ballington to inherit his mantle.

Alfred Shrubb

Born in Sussex on 12 December, 1878, four-and-a-half years before Arthur Newton, Alfred Shrubb set amateur and professional world records at distances from 2 to 5 miles (3 to 8 km) and from 8 to 11 miles (13 to 18 km), including the record for the greatest distance run in 1 hour.

He also won 20 British Championships between 1900 and 1904. His amateur world records, all set in 1904, included the 2 miles (3 km) in 9:09.6; 10 miles (16 km) in 50:40.6; and the 1-hour run of 11 miles, 1137 yards (18.76 km). In the last-mentioned race, he surpassed George's 22-year-old 10-mile record of 51:20. In the next 50 years, only one Englishman, Jim Peters, would run faster. Shrubb's 10-mile record was eclipsed by that of the incomparable Finn, Paavo Nurmi.

In comparison to George and Binks, Shrubb trained heavily. He was one of the first runners to record his training ideas and methods in book form (Shrubb 1910).

Table 6.1 shows the training program he followed for the 12 days before he set the 10-mile record on 5 November. Shrubb's training for the week of 24 to 30 October totaled 42 miles (68 km), of which 14 miles (22 km) were run at race pace on consecutive days. Note also that Shrubb even beat George's 10-mile record in a training run, just five days before his official race.

In his book, Shrubb (1910) expressed his views on a wide range of topics, including the American runner, who "takes his sport more seriously . . . is more highly-strung. . . and seems to set his mind more determinedly on winning than does his British rival" (p. x); child athletes ("the less serious running of any description which an athlete indulges in before 18, the better for his future prospects" (p. 17); and alcohol ("Never touch spirits of any kind. They are the worst thing an athlete can go for" (p. 71).

Prevented from competing in the 1904 Olympics because Britain failed to send a team, Shrubb traveled to and raced in Australia—a course of action which resulted in him being declared a professional in 1905. Therefore, in 1908, he joined a managed troupe of professional athletes who competed in a series of professional races in North America (H. Berry 1990). Shrubb dominated all the short-distance races up to 16 miles (26 km); the longer races were usually won by the North American Indian Tom Longboat who had won the 1907 Boston Marathon but had dropped out of the 1908 Olympic Marathon. Immediately after that race, its winner, John Hayes; the defeated Italian, Dorando Pietri; Shrubb; and Longboat were signed up to race a

Table 6.1 Training of Alf Shrubb (24 October to 4 November, 1904)		
Day	**Morning**	**Afternoon**
Monday 24	6.5 km (steady)	3.2 km in 09:17.8
Tuesday 25	–	16 km time-trial in 51:02
Wednesday 26	6.5 km (steady)	3.2 km in 09:18.6
Thursday 27	12.8 km (steady)	–
Friday 28	–	–
Saturday 29	6.5 km (steady)	12.8 km (slow)
Sunday 30	–	–
Monday 31	–	–
Tuesday 1	4.8 km (steady)	16 km in 50:55
Wednesday 2	3.2 km (fast)	8 km (steady)
Thursday 3	12.8 km (steady)	6.5 km (fairly fast)
Friday 4	Rest	Rest

From Shrubb (1910). Distances have been converted from miles to kilometers.

professional marathon. The race was run on 5 February, 1909, in Madison Square Garden (Martin and Glynn 1979). Shrubb led the race, but collapsed after 39 km when in the lead, on a track measuring 160 m per lap. The race was won by an unheralded French waiter, Henri St. Yves (H. Berry 1990). In the rematch, on 3 April, Shrubb again led for the first 40 km of a marathon derby run on an outdoor track at the New York Polo Grounds (320 m per lap), but failed to finish among the first three. His book includes training advice for the marathon race. As described in chapter 5, this training consisted mainly of walking.

Hannes Kolehmainen

Hannes Kolehmainen was the first in the dynasty of outstanding Finnish long-distance runners, which includes Paavo Nurmi and Lasse Viren and which completely dominated all the Olympic 5000- and 10,000-m races and the world records at those distances from 1896 to 1948.

In 1910, aged 20, Kolehmainen started training in earnest for the 1912 Stockholm Olympic Games. At those games, in the space of eight days, he won gold medals in the 5000 m in a world-record time of 14:36.6; in the 10,000 m, also in a world-record time of 31:20.8; and in the 8000 m cross-country race. He also set the fastest time in the 3000-m team event, in another world-record time of 8:36.6. At the next Olympic Games in Antwerp in 1920, Kolehmainen won the marathon in 2:32:35.8.

Unfortunately, no record of his training methods exists, although it is thought that he included speed play (fartlek) and did little if any training on the track (Doherty 1964). Almost certainly, his training must have been based on the Finnish methods later described by Jaakko Mikkola (1929; see tables 6.2 and 6.3). It is also certain that Kolehmainen influenced Nurmi to include speed work in his training. In letters written to Nurmi in 1918, Kolehmainen urged Nurmi to vary the speed of his training runs and to include frequent sprints, balanced by slower "shacking" (Lovesey 1968). His other great contribution was that he introduced meticulous pacing to the longer track races. His 5000-m world record set in the Olympic Games final was the first such race run with almost even splits (7:17.0; 7:19.6) and resulted in an improvement of 25 seconds on the previous record.

Clarence DeMar

Clarence DeMar (figure 6.2) is to the Boston Marathon what Arthur Newton is to the Comrades Marathon; both achieved legendary performances that helped popularize those races. DeMar won the Boston Marathon an unequalled seven times; his last victory in 1930 came when he was 41 years old. He ran in the 1912 and 1924 Olympic Games Marathons, finishing third in the 1924 race (DeMar 1937).

His achievements were the more remarkable as between the ages of 22 and 33 he ran the Boston Marathon only once (in 1917). DeMar gave three reasons for this. First, he had been told that he had a heart condition and was advised not to run. An autopsy performed after his death from bowel cancer in 1958 showed that he had no serious cardiac abnormalities and that his coronary arteries showed only mild atherosclerosis (Currens and White 1961). These findings indicate that the heart murmurs that had been heard so many years before were probably due to his high level of training and were a feature of what is now called the "athlete's heart" (see chapter 15).

© The Bettman Archive.

Figure 6.2   The legendary Clarence DeMar, "Mr. DeMarathon," in the Boston Marathon.

Second, DeMar's deep religious beliefs as a Baptist led him to question whether running for "selfish victory" was the most appropriate activity for him. He noted that some church leaders later denounced the 1928 Olympic Games as a carnival of flesh, a denouncement that, he wryly observed, ensured that those Games had the greatest attendance yet. Also, his work as a printer, with his studies in evening classes at the University of Vermont, prevented him from training properly.

DeMar was the subject of many scientific studies performed by the legendary physiologist David Dill (chapter 2) and his colleagues at the Harvard Fatigue Laboratory (Bock et al. 1928; Dill et al. 1930; Bock 1963; Dill 1965). These studies found DeMar to have good running efficiency, low lactate levels during exercise, a high lactate turnpoint, a powerful heart, and a very high $\dot{V}O_2$max (estimated to be 76 ml O_2 per kg per min at the age of 36 and measured at 60 ml O_2 per kg per min at the age of 49). Dill (1965) has also estimated that DeMar ran his best marathons at about 77% $\dot{V}O_2$max.

In his autobiography, first published in 1937 and subsequently reprinted in 1981 (DeMar 1937), DeMar left few details of his training methods. For his first Boston Marathon in 1910, he wrote:

"I trained by running leisurely [to work] with my clothes on, my only speed work being 10-mile races. Several times I had been out 15 or 20 miles instead of the usual 7 to or from work."

Before the 1911 Boston Marathon, he ran approximately 100 miles (162 km) per week for two months before the race with several 20-mile (32-km) jaunts. Most of his running was done at 8 miles per hour (5:00 per km), and his speed work was again confined to an occasional 10-mile (16-km) race. These training methods were almost identical to those of Newton, with the exception that time constraints prevented

DeMar from training as much as Newton did. Like Newton, DeMar continued to run exceptionally well, even when well into middle age.

Paavo Nurmi

Paavo Nurmi (figure 6.3), the "Flying Finn," was born in bitter poverty in Turku, Finland, on 13 June, 1897. He began running seriously at age 9 and increased his interest at age 12, the year his father died. It was said that running served as a replacement for his father. Nurmi would train with the children in his apartment block. At first, they ran around the building; then around the block. Soon they were running cross-country up to four times per week, each run being up to 10 km. These runs were always raced and were timed by the leader of the group, Jalmari Virtanen, who acted as coach (Virtanen 1989).

At age 11, Nurmi ran 1500 m against a group of leading adult runners from Turku. Despite racing in street clothes and iron-heeled shoes, he finished in 05:43, compared to the then Finnish national record of 04:20. In 1909, at age 12, Nurmi came

under the direction of Fabian Liesinen, a Finnish distance runner, who began to direct his training and his ambition. Nurmi credited Liesinen with drawing up his long-term goals.

When his father died at age 49 in January 1910, Nurmi's life changed. To assist his mother, he began work as a delivery boy for a bakery. Nurmi wrote that during this period he had no leisure time; all his spare time was spent in walking or running. Later he warned that too comfortable an existence led to laziness and poorer results in those athletic events requiring work and effort.

By the time his competitive career ended prematurely in 1932, he had competed in three Olympic Games and had won a total of nine Olympic races and placed second in three others. He did not lose any of the 80 cross-country races he ran in his life. He also set 33 world records. The Finnish runners he coached for the 1936 Berlin Olympics won 14 Olympic medals, including all three medals in the 10,000 m. In June 1996, before the Atlanta Olympic Games, *Time* magazine's

Figure 6.3   Paavo Nurmi follows another of the great Finnish distance runners of the 1920s, Ville Ritola, in the 10,000-m race in the 1928 Olympic Games. Nurmi regarded Ritola as "the gutsiest athlete" he had ever known, and he had helped train Ritola by teaching him pacing tactics.

June 24, 1996 issue selected Nurmi as the greatest Olympian of all time. At his funeral, the Finnish President, Urho Kekkonen, summarized Nurmi's status as follows: "When nature removes a great man, people explore the horizon for a successor. But none comes and none will, for his class is extinguished with him."

Nurmi began more serious training in 1912, aged 15, and at age 17—inspired by Kolehmainen's success in that year's Olympic Games—he joined the Turku Athletic Association, running his first organized competitive race in June 1914. He won the national 3000-m race for under-18s in 10:06.9, a full 10 seconds ahead of the second runner. Of this period in his running career he later wrote (Doherty 1964; Wilt 1973): "My training was very one-sided. I practised only in summer. Actual winter training was hardly known in those days. . . . I had no idea of speed work, so it was no wonder I remained a slow trudger for so many years!" It was only after his correspondence with Kolehmainen that Nurmi altered his training methods to include more speed work.

In April 1919, Nurmi, by now the regional cross-country and 5000-m champion with the fifth-fastest time in the nation (15:47.4), began an 18-month period of military conscription. By remaining politically neutral during the Finnish Civil War of 1917 to 1919, Nurmi was spared the retribution that occurred when the antisocialist, pro-German White Guard took control of Finland. In the army, Nurmi had more time to train, particularly as his regiment commander vigorously supported his career ambition to run in the 1920 Olympics at Antwerp. Nurmi also began to experiment with different training methods. In particular, he would rise 1 hour before reveille and walk at least 10 km in the fields around Turku. He continued this training, undertaken in iron-bound military boots called "Bolsheviks," into the autumn and then through the bitter Finnish winter, always in pitch dark, sometimes at temperatures of –30°C. Nurmi also included cross-country skiing in his training as he had observed that some of the best skiers were also good runners. Nurmi noticed that skaters, who used a different technique, were, in contrast, not good runners.

At 2 o'clock each afternoon, Nurmi would run repeated sprints of 80 to 800 m for a total of about 10 km, whereafter he would complete his training with a set of calisthenics. During this time, Nurmi introduced two training innovations. First, he ran behind the trains that passed on the railway line close to the barracks. By grasping the bumper of the terminal coach, Nurmi would be pulled along faster than he could normally run. Second, he carried a stopwatch when he trained. Later he used the stopwatch during racing, a habit that astonished all. Nurmi used the watch to establish his physical condition by comparing his speed with what he felt—a technique that in the 1970s became known as "listening to the body."

Of the use of his watch, Nurmi wrote:

I have never used the same speed on a track for more than 3 minutes, although a watch is always in my hand. All runners, however, do not train themselves in this manner. They must run two-thirds of any given distance before they know anything about their final record on it. On the other hand, I can say definitely after two rounds what my final time will be. . . . In a general way I should like to advise anybody who wants to train himself in running to determine on a certain record to be achieved during a summer. That determination must be made early in the spring. (Virtanen 1989, p. 91)

The result of these training innovations was that by the end of the 1919 track season Nurmi was ranked second in Finland in the 3000 m (best time 8:58.1); third in the 5000 m (15:31.5); and second in the 10,000 m (32:56.0). Given the times he was running at the time, the army was so certain of Nurmi's Olympic ambitions that he was transferred to Helsinki to serve in the Civil Guard, where he would train under Lauti Pihkala, one of the most revered Finnish athletics coaches.

During the Finnish winter of 1919, Nurmi rested before commencing training again in February 1920. Then he added a third training session, including long walks of 10 to 20 km, increasing to as much as 30 km on Sundays. Five times per week he would also walk in the mornings, covering distances of 8 to 25 km. He would always run each hill that he encountered in training.

His training during this period was influenced by the ideas of Alf Shrubb and Walter George, as interpreted by Nurmi and Pihkala. At the time, the British methods of training favored long, slow distance running on the road and over the countryside. The American methods of the day aimed to produce sprinters, not endurance athletes, and focused exclusively on developing speed. Nurmi blended both methods but emphasized endurance training.

At the 1920 Olympic Games in Antwerp, Nurmi finished second in the 5000 m to the tiny Frenchman Joseph Guillenot and first in the 10,000 m, when he reversed his defeat by Guillenot, sprinting past the Frenchman on the last lap of the race. He also won individual and team gold medals in the 8000-m cross-country race, an event no longer contested at the Olympics. The domination of the Finns in the 1920 Olympic long-distance running events was completed by Kolehmainen's victory in the marathon and other Finnish victories in the triple jump, the shot-put, and the discus, as well as a clean sweep of all the javelin medals. All told, the Finnish team of 23 athletes won 25 medals at the Games, equaling the number of gold medals won by the 167 athletes from the United States. Yet, in his personal capacity, Nurmi felt that his training during this period had been less than optimum—insufficient and with too much emphasis on long distances.

It is interesting that the non-Finnish texts conclude that from 1920 to May 1924, Nurmi trained for only six months of the year between April and September, according to the following schedule (Doherty 1964; Wilt 1973):

Morning: Walk 10 to 12 km with some sprints to supple up for the afternoon run.
   Afternoon: Run 4 to 7 km with fast speed over the last 1 to 2 km, finished off by four to five 80- to 100 m sprints.

It is clear that during this period Nurmi had begun to train during the winter, certainly in 1919 before the 1920 Olympic Games.

In addition to his Olympic achievements, and on this still quite meager training, Nurmi set a new world mile record of 4:10.4 in August 1923 in a famous race, the first "Race of the Century," against a Finnish-born Swedish resident, Edvin Wide. In the same year, he also set a world record for the 1500 m (3:53), and in a 5000-m race at the same event he passed the 3-mile mark (4.8 km) in 14:11.2, also a world record.

In his preparation for that race, Nurmi again showed his genius. Knowing that the track in Stockholm (on which the race would be held) measured only 385 m, he marked out a training track of 385 m in Helsinki so that he could calculate the lap times necessary to run the race in his prerace prediction of 4:10.0.

In 1923, Nurmi wrote an article, discovered only after this death in October 1973, listing the reasons why he thought that the Finns were the best runners in the world during the first half of the twentieth century. Nurmi listed five factors he considered important:

1. Mental approach: The Finns were used to hard work; they lived a hard life, as exemplified by his own experiences, and were courageous and determined in a single-minded, almost "stupid" way. As one journalist speculated: "Work, love of work, love of fighting against odds and obstacles has taught these men true prerequisites of athletic competition."

2. Physical strength: Nurmi believed that the Finns had strong legs, hips, and internal organs, especially hearts and lungs. These strengths were developed by their demanding way of life.

3. The Finnish landscape and climate:

   The constantly changing Finnish countryside of undulating hills, forests and marshes lessened the tedium of training. In contrast, the roads of Europe outside Scandinavia were too "level," straight, and paved with cobblestones or asphalt. These roads are not suitable for training. Walking on them at length becomes boring, especially when the surrounding area is flat. It is different here, where roads are seldom straight and where the environment varies from gentle hills to forests and meadows. These roads are not boring. At the same time, the soft sandy ground is good for the feet. (Virtanen 1989, p. 24)

   The summer weather was ideal for distance training as it was not too hot, whereas, according to Nurmi, the tough winters induced an aggression and anger that encouraged training.

4. The Finnish tradition of saunas and massage: Nurmi noted that at that time, only the Finns used saunas. In his opinion, this practice allowed harder training and more rapid recovery from competition.

5. Training methods and racing tactics: Because of their isolation from Europe and especially from North America, the Finns could develop their own ideas about training and racing. No one, according to Nurmi, told them what to do—not that the Finns, and especially Nurmi, would necessarily accept what they were told without challenge. As a result, they were free to experiment and to develop what worked best for each individual runner.

As Nurmi rested during the Finnish winter, the International Amateur Athletic Federation (IAAF), whose two senior officials were both Swedes, was faced with the uncomfortable possibility that a Finn, Nurmi, and not a Swede would win too many athletics medals at the next Olympic Games in Paris. To prejudice Nurmi's chances, the IAAF notoriously voted to schedule the finals of the 1500 and 5000 m on the same day with only 55 minutes between the events. Nurmi resolved to change his training to thwart the complicity of the IAAF officials.

Accordingly, in January 1924, he changed his training to include a late morning run, during which he ran four or five 80- to 120-m sprints, followed by a timed 400- to 1000-m run, followed by a 3000- to 4000-m run at even speed with "the last lap always very fast" (Doherty 1964; Wilt 1973). During this period, Nurmi must also have begun running longer intervals of up to 600 m.

To prepare for the 1500/5000-m combination, Nurmi organized a similar race in Helsinki in June 1924. First he ran the 1500 m in a new world record time of 3:52.6; then, 55 minutes later, he started the 5000-m race with the goal of running it in less than 15 minutes. Completing the last lap in 64.1 seconds, he finished in 14:28.2, another world record. Meanwhile, Nurmi's compatriot Ville Ritola (figure 6.3) had set the 10,000-m world record of 30:35.4 at the Finnish Olympic trials in May.

At the 1924 Paris Olympic Games on 10 July, Nurmi duly completed the double, winning the 1500 m by 50 m—slowing in the final stretch and thus missing the world record, but setting an Olympic record—and then, 55 minutes later, winning the 5000 m in 14:31.2, beating Ritola by 0.2 seconds. This time was 3 seconds outside his world record set in Helsinki but also a new Olympic Games record.

In the 1500-m race, he ran the first 500 m in a time that was faster than that of either Herb Elliott or Jim Ryun in their world 1500-m records set in 1960 and 1967 (Lovesey 1968). Nurmi also won the 3000-m team race and, on 12 July, the 10,000-m cross-country race, the latter run in severe heat that caused a number of runners to collapse from heatstroke, with only 15 of the 38 entrants completing the race. Only Nurmi appeared unaffected by the heat; even Ritola, who finished second, 1:25 behind Nurmi, entered the stadium "staggering like a drunken man" (Virtanen 1989, p. 70).

There was one other mythical aspect to those Games. The Finnish Olympic Committee, wishing to give Ritola one chance at a gold medal, forbade Nurmi from contesting the 10,000 m on the grounds that the race, to be held on 5 July, would not allow Nurmi sufficient time to recover for his attempt at the 1500/5000 m double five days later.

Nurmi was so furious that on 5 July he went to a nearby training camp and ran what was reported to be 10,000 m in less than 30:00, as timed by an independent observer, enough to have beaten Ritola's Olympic gold medal performance and world record of 30:23.2. Only many years later, in a radio interview, did Nurmi admit that the distance for his historic performance "might not have been the 10,000-m distance" (Virtanen 1989, p. 66).

Returning as heroes to Finland, Nurmi and Ritola would feature in one final famous race during the 1924 season. On 31 August, 1924, in a 10,000-m race at Kuopio, Finland, Nurmi ran 30:06.2, eclipsing Ritola's world record. En route, he also set world records for 4, 5, and 6 miles (6, 8, and 10 km) as well as for the farthest distance run in 30 minutes.

The year 1924 ended with Nurmi's first tour of North America. Arriving in New York on 9 December, he immediately launched into a period of heavy training in Van Cortland Park, refusing to race until he was ready and predicting that he would run the mile in 4:06 when properly prepared. His training during this period was the same as always—a walk of 30 to 60 minutes at a pace of 8 minutes per km at 7:00 A.M.; lunch at 11:00 A.M.; an early afternoon session of sprints and jogging in the park; and a late afternoon run on the indoor track of the 71st Regimental Armory, the site of the modern Madison Square Garden track.

Between 6 January and 26 May, Nurmi ran more than 55 races in 21 different locations in the United States and Canada. He also set 30 unofficial world records but was credited with only three, for 1 mile (1.6 km), 2 miles (3 km), and the 3000 m. But he had also established the indoor track as a viable sport in North America.

Nurmi spent the remainder of 1925 recovering from the aftereffects of his tour. He ran slower than usual and was worried by Achilles tendinopathy. It was only in July 1926 that his form returned with a world record of 8:20.4 for 2 miles (3 km), run in Stockholm, Sweden.

In 1928, then 31 years old, Nurmi started preparing for the Amsterdam Olympic Games. Despite running poorly in the Olympic trials, Nurmi was included in the Finnish Olympic team. In a thrilling 10,000 m, he beat Ritola by 0.6 seconds, finishing in 30:18.8. Ritola beat Nurmi by 3 seconds in the 5000 m, with Nurmi finishing second in the 3000-m steeplechase, from which Ritola retired, having injured his ankle in the heats. It was the last race that either would run in the Olympic Games.

Nurmi completed 1928 with a tour of Germany before focusing on another trip to North America, arriving in New York in December 1928. Between 20 January and 18 June, 1929, Nurmi again raced throughout the United States, ceasing only when his knees, legs, and feet hurt so much that he could no longer compete. Resuming light training later in the Finnish autumn, he raced little. He continued to suffer from foot pain that made it difficult for him even to walk.

Nurmi returned to form in 1930. He ran only 17 races during the year at distances from 2 miles (3 km) to 20 km, winning them all. He had set himself a new goal—that of winning the 42-km marathon at the 1932 Olympic Games.

He continued with his impressive form in 1931, setting a new world record of 8:59.6 for 2 miles, the first runner under 9 minutes, in Helsinki on 24 July. He closed the year without having lost a race in two years. During 1931, he raced a total of 103 km, compared to only 70 km in 1923. He no longer raced distances less than 3000 m and was clearly preparing for the marathon.

Accordingly, on 16 June of the following year, Nurmi ran his first 40.2-km (short) marathon in Viipuri, Finland, winning in 2:22:03.8, the fastest time ever for the distance and equivalent to 2:29:14 for the full distance. But it was a decisive race. Nurmi's legs were so sore after the race and his Achilles tendon so inflamed that he walked with a limp even as he boarded the *Mauritania*, which took the Finnish team to the United States for the 1932 Olympic Games in Los Angeles. Nurmi was entered to race both the 10,000 m and the marathon. But he would race in neither: on 28 July, the IAAF Council—again chaired by a Swede, J. Sigfrid Edström—rejected Nurmi's entry for the Games on the grounds that he had accepted "unregulated compensation" during an earlier tour to Germany. Nurmi's only known response was: "If that's the way they feel, there's nothing I can do" (Virtanen 1989, p. 172).

Nurmi continued to race in Finland as a "national amateur" in 1933, winning 12 of the 16 races he entered. His last race was on 16 September, 1934, when he won a 10,000-m race in 31:39.2.

After his retirement, Nurmi turned his attention to developing a career in construction. He also opened a haberdashery in Helsinki, which was later to be run by his only son, Matti. The construction business thrived and Nurmi became extremely wealthy. His sole business error was his failure to purchase land he was offered in Orlando, Florida, on the grounds that to care for his investment properly he would need to travel frequently to North America from his homeland. The land became the site on which Disney World was subsequently built.

Nurmi continued to run 3 miles (4.8 km) per day. He died on 2 October, 1973, after a long period of ill health. During his life, Nurmi established the Paavo Nurmi Foundation for the support of cardiovascular research as well as "general national health."

Summarizing what he had learned about his training methods, Nurmi wrote the following:

> Now as I think of my training methods at that time, I admit that it was not the correct training in every respect. . . . The greatest weakness of walking has been that it tends to make you stiff and takes too much time. Yet, I consider walking, mixed with suitable sprints, as quite a useful means of conditioning, for a runner, when it is practiced in a terrain sheltered from the wind, at suitable speed. I consider this essential for marathon runners. Just as Zatopek, who got fit from

pure running, won the marathon at the 1952 Olympic Games in Helsinki, so it could be said that I could as well have won the same distance in Paris.

The greatest mistake I made and which was formerly made in general, was the one-sided training program (too much long, slow running). It was not understood that speed training brings endurance. Instead, the one-sided training took away what even was left of speed. It was just here that the greatest danger of training hikes in winter is located. There were 300- to 600-m sprints included, but there were not enough of them. As I took my training hikes in winter on open, windy roads, my trouble was that I got thoroughly stiff. Therefore, I could make a much better effort in warm weather. On the other hand, there was too much training done during the summer. I did not dare to risk a complete resting period, though I should have needed it sometimes. (Virtanen 1989, p. 150)

The Finnish Training Methods of Kolehmainen and Nurmi

According to F.A.M. Webster (1948), the success of the Finnish long-distance runners of the 1920s was largely due to their system of winter training. Their winter-training methods were detailed in a booklet written by Jaakko Mikkola (1929) and subsequently translated into English. Arthur Newton's great South African friend, Vernon Jones, discovered an English translation in Newton's correspondence. Jones, in turn, kindly made the information available for the third edition of this book.

Mikkola records that the Finnish runners began their walking training in January or February, depending on the distances they raced; marathon runners started in January; 1500- to 10,000-m runners in February or March. The distances walked also depended on the distances the runners would race; marathon runners walked longer distances (15 to 35 km) than did the 1,500-m runners (8 to 15 km) and the 5000- to 10,000-m runners (10 to 20 km). Each group would walk these distances two to four times per week until the end of March. After about six weeks of training, they would run the last 3 to 10 km of the workout. By April, the athletes would train four or five days per week, usually twice per day; cross-country runs of 6 to 8 km would be added, as would track sessions involving sprints of 150 to 300 m and continuous runs of 1000 to 2000 m at a relatively easy pace. Walking would be gradually discontinued. By the end of March, the 5000- to 10,000-m runners were walking 60 km and running 18 km per week; the marathon runners were walking 120 km and running 24 km per week. The peak sharpening precompetition training programs that were reached in May by the 1500-m, 5000- to 10000-m, and marathon runners are listed in tables 6.2 and 6.3.

Mikkola wrote that only "an experienced and hardened man could stand the training program of the 5000- to 10,000-m runners and that, to avoid going stale, the younger runners should confine themselves to only the running workouts. Only experienced 5000- to 10,000-m runners were advised to attempt the marathon. Runners at all distances were instructed to taper for races, with the last two to three days being complete rest (Mikkola 1929).

During competition, marathon runners were advised to race to win and not to set records as it was considered useless to make schedules for such an un-

Table 6.2 Precompetition training program for a Finnish 1500-m Olympic competitor (circa 1920)

| May | 1500 m | | 5000- to 10,000 m | |
---	Morning	Afternoon	Morning	Afternoon
2	8-km walk	800 m (75%)	10-km walk	2 × 150 m (100%) 3000 m (75%)
4	2 × 150 m (100%)	2000 (easy)	Rest	5000 (85%)
6	3-km run 4 × 60 m (100%)	1000 m (100%)	15-km run	3 × 150 m (100%) 2000 m (100%)
7	8-km walk 2000 m (85%)	500 m (75%)	6-km walk 1500 m (easy)	600 m (75%)
8	Rest	2 × 150 m (100%) 800 m (75%)	1000 m (easy)	5 × 50 m (100%)
9	Rest	Rest	8-km walk	4000 m (easy)
11	Rest	1500 m (90%)	Rest	10,000 m (67–75%)
13	1000 m (easy)	600 m (90%)	8-km walk	300 m (75%)
14	Rest	3 3 150 m (100%)	Rest	8-km walk
16	1800 m (easy)	300 m (75%)	8-km walk 2000 m (easy)	300 m (75%)
17	Rest	3 3 60 m (100%) 1000 m (75%)	Rest	Rest
18	Rest	Rest	3-km run	1000 m (90%)
19	1500 m (easy)	200 m (100%)	Rest	Rest
20	1000 m (easy)	300 m (85%)	4-km run 600 m (75%)	3 × 50 m (100%)
21	Rest	800 m (jog)	Rest	Rest
24	Rest	Race	Rest	Race

Information courtesy of Arthur Newton and Vernon Jones.

predictable race. "The only schedule which a marathoner can make, and which is dependent on good fortune, is 'if nothing extraordinary happens during 2 hours and 30 minutes, then I shall succeed'" (Mikkola 1929). Although the best tactic was considered to be even-paced running, Mikkola noted that this was seldom possible in big competitions as the leaders tended to start fast. Runners were advised to run with their competitors for the first 21 to 28 km of the race and then to try the ice by sprinting to break contact, if they had the energy. Otherwise, runners were to reserve enough strength for the last kilometers,

(continued)

"in case someone should surprise." Mikkola also recognized that good marathon runners required both speed and the ability to change their pace during competition.

Arthur Newton

The first runner after Alf Shrubb to record his training ideas in great detail was the remarkable English ultramarathon runner, Arthur "Greatheart" Newton, whose competitive career spanned 13 years from May 1922 to June 1935. He was born in Weston-super-Mare in Somerset, England, on 20 May, 1883, and died in Middlesex, England, on 7 September, 1959.

During his career Newton won five of the six 90-km Comrades Marathons that he entered, setting the records for both the "up" run to Pietermaritzburg and the "down" run to Durban. He held the 86-km London-to-Brighton record; the world 30-, 35-, 40-, 45-, 50-, 60-, and 100-mile records; and the world 24-hour running record. He also covered 102,735 miles (165,403 km) in training (Newton 1935; table 6.4). In an era in which it was usual for top athletes such as Kolehmainen and Nurmi to train 30 miles (48 km) per week (see table 6.3), Newton ran as much as 30 miles per day, seven days per week.

In his day, Newton was described variously as "the most phenomenal distance runner the world has ever known" (Newton 1935) and as "one of the marvels of all time" (London Observer). It has also been said that "he may just have been, in his own way, the greatest runner ever seen" (Clarke and Harris 1967). In 1936, he received a retrospective award, the Helms Trophy for the most outstanding sportsman on the African continent.

Although Newton had belonged to an athletic club in England and had run races of up to 25 miles (40 km), it was only after he had lived in South Africa for 12 years that he became committed to long-distance running. He began running for political reasons; he believed that at the time a number of government decisions prevented him from continuing to survive economically as a farmer in Natal (now KwaZulu-Natal), South Africa. To draw national attention to his plight, Newton decided that "genuine amateur athletics were about as wholesome as anything on earth; any man who made a really notable name as such would always be given a hearing by the public" (Newton 1940, p. 20).

So it was, then, on 1 January, 1922, that the 38-year-old Arthur Newton began the second phase of his running career with a run of 2 miles (3 km), including a "long-ish" stop at halfway. For the next two days he was so "abominably stiff" that he was unable to run, but he walked instead. After five days' recovery he was able to run 4 miles (6 km). But Newton was not satisfied with this improvement. "Instead of using what commonsense I possessed, I did what the textbooks recommended: make the stopwatch your master and try to improve your times slightly every day," he reflected. Sixty years later, World Hawaiian Ironman Triathlon Champion Mark Allen would draw the same conclusions about his own training during his early career before he had become the consummate endurance athlete. Newton now decided on a more sensible approach. The result was that he started training more slowly and ran his first 10-miler (16 km) five weeks later.

On 24 May, 1922, some 20 weeks after his first run as a 38-year-old, Newton lined up at the start of the second-ever Comrades Marathon. He started the race slowly,

Table 6.3 Precompetition training program for a Finnish Olympic Marathon competitor (circa 1920)		
Date	**Morning**	**Afternoon**
April 1	18-km walk	10-km walk
2		15-km run
4	45-km walk	
6	25-km walk	
7	20-km walk	15-km run
9	15-km walk	15-km run
11		20-km run
13	15-km walk	10-km run
14	15-km run	

*Two to three 30-km runs were included in April, including one at race pace four weeks before the competition. Information courtesy of Arthur Newton and Vernon Jones.

passing into second place and continuing to win the race in 8:40.00. The following year (1923), Newton started his second Comrades Marathon properly prepared. In the 12 months since his last race, he had covered a staggering 10,642 km in training: 8205 km of running and 2454 km of walking. His training methods began to evolve: he aimed to run 100 miles (161 km) in six days of training per week.

On this second attempt, Newton won by 52 minutes, finishing in 6:56:07, bettering the old record by 2 hours and 3 minutes. It was this single performance that heralded the beginning of the modern training approach to distance running, in which all-year-round training of two or more hours per day became necessary for peak performance. Although Newton had described the essence of his training methods by the 1940s, it was really only with the arrival of athletes such as Emil Zatopek and Jim Peters in the 1950s, and the training schools of Perci Cerutty and Arthur Lydiard in the 1950s and 1960s, that the ideas that Newton had initiated in the 1920s in KwaZulu-Natal began to be propagated.

After his decisive victory in the 1923 Comrades, Newton decided to attempt the world 50-mile (80-km) running record of 6:13:58 set by the Englishman Edgar Lloyd in 1913. A 50-mile out-and-back course was measured on the Comrades route. Despite the uneven, dusty, and untarred road, Newton ran the distance in 5:53:05, thereby beating the record by 20 minutes. An incredulous report of the race in *Athletics News* questioned the possibility that this performance was a result of the hot African sun: "the first man home . . . for about 56 miles, he was doing 10 miles an hour! What stories are dished up for public consumption. . . . It was in South Africa, where the sun is hotter than here and the effect of it must be horrible" (Berry 1990, p. 16).

In 1924, Newton again won the Comrades Marathon by a large margin of 75 minutes, finishing in 6:58:22. To prove the credibility of his "impossible" 50-mile time, he traveled to England, where in October 1927 he lowered Len Hurst's record for

Table 6.4   Arthur Newton's Comrades training and racing record

Year	Age	Comrades direction	Comrades time (h:min:s)	Position	Total training distance (January–May) (km)	Monthly distances (January–May) (km)	Total distances from June–January previous year (km)
1925	42	down	06:24:54	1	3592	(752; 815; 791; 902; 322)	3988
1927	44	down	06:40:56	1	4288	(890; 811; 1043; 886; 658)	5830
1923	40	down	06:56:07	1	4760	(847; 968; 1269; 1035; 641)	3446
1924	41	up	06:58:22	1	4321	(763; 1074; 1006; 766; 712)	7283
1926	43	up	07:02:00	2	3962	(832; 678; 816; 850; 786)	2766
1922	39	up	08:40:00	1	1535	(143; 145; 306; 386; 506)	0

Newton ran his best race in 1925 on his second-lowest total training distance leading up to the race. The Comrades Marathon is run annually in opposite directions: one year, up to Pietermarizburg; the next year, down to Durban, which lies 600 m lower than Pietermaritzburg. From Newton (1935).

83.6 km from 6:34:50 to 6:11:44. Then, on 13 November, he went 18 minutes faster, lowering the record to 5:53:43 (figure 6.4). En route, he also set world records at 30, 35, 40, 45, and 50 miles (48, 57, 65, 72, and 81 km). He also passed the 42-km standard marathon mark in a time that was 9 minutes faster than that of the first English finisher in the 1924 Olympic Games. The performance ensured, when the London-to-Brighton race was revived in 1951, that the magnificent winner's trophy would bear his name. Newton's success continued with wins in the 1925 and 1927 Comrades Marathons and world records at 30, 40, 50, and 60 miles (48, 64, 80 and 96 km) (7:33:55) and 100 miles (160 km) (14:43:00) on the Gwelo-Bulawayo road in Zimbabwe (formerly Rhodesia) in July 1927. These represented improvements of 50 and 105 minutes on the respective former records. The 100-mile record was especially remarkable as the race was run at an altitude of 1500 m on a hilly course in hot conditions.

In January 1928, Newton again bettered his 100-mile (160-km) record by another 21 minutes (14:22:10)—this time in snowy, icy conditions in England. As a result of his performance, Newton became a cult figure in Britain (Berry 1990). Berry (1990) suggests that in tackling this record in the most atrocious conditions, Newton had an ulterior motive for this run. Less than two months later, Newton entered the professional Transcontinental Race that was run between Los Angeles and New York in 80 daily stages of between 30 miles (48 km) and 75 miles (120 km) each. The stakes were high as the prize for first place was $25,000. Berry (1990) believes that Newton had been offered a contract to run in that race, possibly contingent on him setting a new 100-mile world record. Newton failed to finish the Transcon-

Figure 6.4   English South African Arthur Newton finishing the London-to-Brighton run in 1924.

tinental Race; in 1928 he developed Achilles tendinopathy, and in 1929 he was struck by a car.

In 1930 and 1931, Newton teamed up with the Englishman Peter Gavuzzi for the two-man 500-mile (800-km) race in Canada, and on both occasions they won handsomely. Toward the end of 1931, Newton ran what was probably his greatest race: the 24-hour world record. This race, which cost Newton as sponsor $1000, was run on a tiny indoor track at the Arena in Hamilton, Ontario. Newton's final distance of 152 miles 540 yards (245.1 km) surpassed the previous record of Charles Rowell and remained the world's best for 22 years until it was beaten by another South African and Comrades Marathon legend, Wally Hayward, who, in 1953, ran 159 miles 562 yards (256.4 km). Milroy (1998) has suggested that Newton ran this race to discount the belief that none of the runners in Pyle's Transcontinental Races matched the ability of Rowell and the other pedestrians who competed in the six-day races in the 1880s and 1890s.

In 1933, Newton returned to the Bath Road in England where, despite Achilles tendinopathy and the fact that he did not complete the full distance, his time of 7:15:30 at 60 miles (96 km) was fast enough for another world record.

In 1934, Newton decided to make one final attempt at the 100-mile record, again on the Bath Road. On 20 July of that year, at the age of 51, Newton completed his last race and successfully lowered his time to 14:06:00. Sadly, it seems that Newton was disappointed with that run because he wrote, "There was no good fighting shy of the fact as far as the 'hundred' was concerned, I had completely failed to put up a reasonable time on the course, and I was too old to think of continuing for another year or two" (Newton 1949).

After his last 100-mile world record, Newton continued to run, although no longer competitively. He lived in Middlesex, England, and busied himself by writing the four books that were to become his legacy (Newton 1935; 1940; 1947a; 1949). As a runner, especially a self-coached one, Newton was exceptional. His four books exemplify this. They carefully chronicle his theories, providing what I believe to be the first detailed description of what would become the modern training approach to distance running. In particular, I would single out his ideas concerning year-round training; long, slow, distance training up to 160 km per week; specialization; racing infrequently; and mental preparation, all of which are covered in chapter 5 (the 15 Laws of Training).

Emil Zatopek

Czech Emil Zatopek (figure 6.5), was born on 19 September, 1922, in Moravia, Czechoslovakia, and died in November 2000. Like Nurmi, on whom he modeled himself, Zatopek completely dominated distance running in his era. In the 1948 London Olympics, Zatopek won the 10,000 m in an Olympic record time, also coming second in the 5000 m. At the 1952 Helsinki Olympic Games, he became the first and almost certainly the only man in Olympic history ever to win the three long-distance events, the 5000 m, the 10,000 m, and the marathon. What is even more remarkable is that it was the first time he had raced the full marathon distance, and he did so only three days after winning the 10,000-m final. He had won all three events within seven days. In all the races he won, he set Olympic records. By the end of that year, Zatopek held every world record from the 10,000 m to the marathon, and in 1954 he added the 5000-m world record as well. During his career, he set 18 world records. When his running career came to an end, Zatopek worked as an apprentice chemical technician in a shoe factory.

Zatopek's basic training was interval work (Doherty 1964; Wilt 1973) based on "speed and stamina" (Sandrock 1996). His rationale for this type of training was simple:

> *When I was young, I was too slow. . . . I thought, why should I practice running slow? I already know how to run slow. . . . I must learn to run fast by practicing to run fast. So I ran 100 m very fast. . . . People said, "Emil, you are crazy. You are training to be a sprinter. You have no chance." I said, "Yes, but if I run 100 m 20 times, that is 2 km and that is no longer a sprint." (Benyo 1983)*

Until 1947, Zatopek had two basic training programs that he alternated daily (Doherty 1964; Wilt 1973):

Day 1: 5 × 150 m with 150-m jogs in between; 20 × 400 m (again with 150-m jogs between each) and 5 × 100 to 150 m. The 400 m were run in times varying between 67 and 77 seconds, and the shorter sprints were run slightly faster.

Day 2: 5 × 150 m, 20 × 400 m, and 5 × 200 m.

By 1948, Zatopek had refined his daily training to 5 × 200 m, 20 × 400 m, and 5 × 200 m with a 200-m jog, lasting about 1 minute, between sessions. The 200 m were run in 34 seconds and the 400 m between 56 and 75 seconds or slower, starting at the faster speed and gradually slowing down. The total distance covered each day was about 18 km. In October 1949, Zatopek increased his training to 28 km per day.

Figure 6.5   Czechoslovakian Emil Zatopek on his way to winning the 1952 Helsinki Olympics 5000-m gold medal. At those games, he completed the unique 5000-m, 10,000-m, and marathon triple.

Zatopek later stated that he had based his training on what he had learned about Nurmi's training methods: "I never spoke with Paavo Nurmi, but running is easily understandable. You must be fast enough—you must have endurance. So, you run fast for speed and repeat it many times for endurance" (Hauman 1996, p. 50).

From the beginning of 1954, age and increasing foreign competition forced Zatopek to train twice per day. In April of that year, he increased the intervals to a total of 10 × 200 m and 50 × 400 m, thereby covering more than 30 km per day.

There is some doubt as to how fast Zatopek ran these intervals. They were certainly nowhere near the 60-second laps that have been recorded in the running folklore. It seems that "the times of the intervals were mostly slow and quite irregular. Some were practically walks, but others were sprightly—around 65 seconds. The plan was to cover the distance first, then to try to run the intervals faster" (Doherty 1964, p. 233).

Zatopek realized the importance of setting realistic goals:

> *You can't climb up to the second floor without a ladder. . . . When you set your aim too high and don't fulfill it, then your enthusiasm turns to bitterness. Try for a goal that's reasonable, and then gradually raise it. That's the only way to get to the top. (Doherty 1964, p. 6)*

Zatopek was also a great man, unaltered by fame. Of him, Australian distance runner and multi-world-record holder Ron Clarke has said: "There is not and never was a greater man than Emil Zatopek" (Sandrock 1996). On one trip to Finland, Zatopek was surprised to see a picture of himself and Nurmi in an article discussing which of the two deserved to be called the greatest athlete ever. "I can't believe they need to discuss the question," Zatopek told Finnish athletics historian, Seppo Luhtala. "Nurmi was the greatest of course. Of that there is no doubt." (Butcher 1997, p. 45)

The Origins of Interval Training

It was Franz Stampfl, the coach of the world's first sub-4-minute miler, Sir Roger Bannister, who was responsible for introducing the notion of interval training as we know it today (chapter 8).

Stampfl was born in Vienna, Austria, on 18 November, 1913. In 1930, after graduating from the Vienna Academy of Art, he moved to Ireland, where he started coaching runners. When World War II broke out, Stampfl was interned as a refugee from Hitler's "Greater Germany" and deported to an internment camp in Canada. En route to Canada, the liner on which he was traveling was torpedoed. Stampfl was one of the few people who survived the icy, oil-filled North Atlantic. From bitter experience, he learned an important lesson—that the human body is capable of far more than we believe. His ordeal led him to conclude that large "safety first" margins are built into the body, analogous to the central governor theory. From Canada, Stampfl was transferred to Australia, where he remained until 1946, when he returned to the United Kingdom. In the early 1950s, he started coaching groups of athletes at the Duke of York's barracks in London, charging one shilling for an evening's training.

Stampfl's training involved repeated intervals—for example, 10×400 m with a 2-minute jogging recovery period or, alternatively, 5×800 m, at better than race pace. This training method replaced the outdated notion of simply trying to improve your time for the total distance. Stampfl believed that interval training taught athletes to be mentally tough and to believe in their ability to extend themselves in a way they had never done before. This thinking corresponds with the theory that holds that a central governor determines exercise performance.

Stampfl's training methods contributed greatly to the so-called golden era of British middle-distance running of the 1950s. Three of the first five runners to break the four-minute mile (Bannister, Chris Chataway, and Brian Hewson) followed Stampfl's training methods.

In 1955, Stampfl became director of athletics at Melbourne University in Australia. In the same year, his classic book, *Franz Stampfl on Running* (Stampfl 1955), was published, selling more than 500,000 copies.

Norman Myers, an environmentalist and 2:37:00-marathon runner at age 46, recalls that the sum total of training advice Stampfl gave him was to "try harder." Myers, the man who coined the environmental term *hot spots* and who was trained by Stampfl while at Oxford University in the 1950s, writes: "He [Stampfl] told me that if I found that by applying his doctrine I was running faster after one month, he would offer further advice. Step two turned out to be 'Try harder still'" (N. Myers 2000).

Sadly, Stampfl was rendered a quadriplegic in a tragic car accident in 1980, and he died on 19 March, 1995. His contribution to the evolution of running training merits far greater recognition than it has received.

Jim Peters

What distinguishes Jim Peters from other athletes is that between 1952 and 1954 he became the first man to break the 2:20:00 barrier for the marathon, reducing the world marathon record from the old mark of 2:26:07 to 2:17:39. When he retired prematurely after the Vancouver Empire Games Marathon in 1954, Peters held four of the six fastest marathon times ever. No runner is ever likely to equal these performances, and it is for this reason that I consider Peters to be the greatest marathoner ever.

Regrettably, Peters is best remembered for two events over which he had little control. First, as the world record holder and clear favorite for the 1952 Olympic Marathon, Peters was badly beaten by Zatopek, who was running his first ever marathon in that race. It is documented that at about the 18-km mark, Zatopek asked Peters whether the pace they were running was "good enough." When Peters replied that the pace was too slow, Zatopek sped up and Peters was unable to respond (figure 6.6). Within a few kilometers Zatopek had gained a 10-second lead over Peters, passing the 30-km mark only 12 seconds shy of Peters' world record. Peters retired from the race shortly after 30 km (J. Peters 1955; Krise and Squires 1982; Benyo 1983).

Many assume that Peters was psyched out by Zatopek, which I feel is unfair. Two lesser known factors may explain Peters' poor performance in that race. Six

Figure 6.6 Emil Zatopek (left) passes a tiring Jim Peters (number 287, far right) in the 1952 Olympic Marathon. This apparently happened shortly after Peters suggested, in response to Zatopek's question, that they were running too slowly.

weeks before the race, Peters had won the British AAA Marathon in an astounding time of 2:20:42, an improvement of more than 4:30 on the world record. At the time, British athletic officials, including Harold Abrahams, expressed doubts that Peters would be able to recover sufficiently for the Olympic Marathon (J. Peters 1955). Their doubts were justified; we now know that it is not possible to recover fully with such a short interval between marathon races (see chapters 7 and 10).

The second factor was Peters' mode of travel to the Games. Unable to afford seats on a scheduled airline, the British athletic officials were forced to charter a four-engine York transport plane to take their team to Helsinki. The flight lasted 9 hours, during which time the plane was struck by lightning and Peters, exposed to

Table 6.5   Jim Peters' training program for October 1950

Date	Distance Km	Miles	Time (h:min:s)	Comment	Speed (min:s·km⁻¹)
2	6.4	4	25:30	Fast trot	3:59
3	6.4	4	24:00	Fast trot	3:45
4	–	–			
5	4.8	3	18:00	Fast (shorts)	3:45
6	–	–			
7	9.6	6	40:00	Cross-country run	4:10
8	–	–			
Total	27.2	17	01:47:30		3:57

Adapted from J.H. Peters et al. (1957, p. 135). © 1957 by Nicholas Kaye.

Table 6.6   Jim Peters' training program for April 1951

Date	Distance Km	Miles	Time (h:min:s)	Comment	Speed (min:s·km⁻¹)
2	14.4	9	50:30	Terribly stiff, but made it	3:31
3	9.6	6	35:00	Still stiff and tired	3:38
4	14.4	9	51:00	Still stiff	3:32
5	14.4	9	51:00	Bit better, very tired	3:32
6	–	–	–		
7	24	15	01:36:00	Nasty day	4:00
Total	76.8	48	04:43:30		3:41

Adapted from J.H. Peters et al. (1957, p. 135). © 1957 by Nicholas Kaye.

a draught, became violently ill. He arrived in Helsinki feeling sick and stiff and suffering from a headache.

Peters is also remembered for his collapse from severe heatstroke in the 1954 Vancouver Empire Games Marathon. Peters (who did not believe that extreme heat was a deterrent to a fast marathon time) failed to finish the race, while two South Africans—Jackie Mekler and Jan Barnard, who were accustomed to hot-weather running—ran conservatively, entering the stadium more than 20 minutes behind Peters but finishing second and third.

Peters is one of the few great runners to have recorded details of his training methods (J. Peters 1955; J.H. Peters et al. 1957). From what can be gleaned from his records, the key to his training seems to have been a gradual increase in his weekly training distance and intensity; a slow introduction to marathon racing; and sustained, hard effort in all his training runs. For the first four years of his running career, from 1946 to 1949, Peters ran track, cross-country, and road races of up to 16 km (J. Peters 1955) and was the British champion at 6 and 10 miles (10 and 16 km). He also ran in the 1948 Olympic Games 10,000-m final, in which he was lapped by Zatopek. Deeply embarrassed by his defeat, Peters decided to retire from running and in 1949 ran only one race. However, his coach, Johnny Johnston, persuaded him to return to running, and in November 1949 he again began regular training, with the idea of becoming a specialist marathon runner. A year later, he was following a regular training program (table 6.5; J.H. Peters et al. 1957). Although Peters' total training distance at this stage was very low, his average speed was good (3:57 per km).

By the following February, Peters had increased the regular 4-mile run to 6 miles (from 6 to 10 km) and by April to 9 miles (14.4 km). Once per week he ran a faster 4-mile time-trial in about 23:00. By the first week of April 1951, Peters was following the training program set out in table 6.6 (J.H. Peters et al. 1957). By this stage, his average speed was below 6:00 per mile (3:45 per km) and clearly not near the 5:00 per mile (3:08 per km) pace for which he strove.

In April and May that year, Peters ran two 20-mile (32-km) races, as well as his first full marathon in a course and British record time of 2:29:28, just 4 minutes off the then world record. What is noticeable about the program at this stage of his career was that, although he was running longer distances in training, his average speed had improved from 3:57 per km (table 6.5) to 3:37 per km by June, 1951 (table 6.7). His weekly training distance was only about 105 km, and this training distance had brought him within 4 minutes of the then world record for the standard marathon. In addition, he did not reduce his training during the last week before the race and did all his training in single runs.

In 1952 Peters started training twice per day. At noon he would run 9.6 km on the track in about 30 minutes (3:08 per km). In the evening, he would run either 8 or 16 km at between 3:08 and 3:17 per km. He began running cross-country and shorter road races, setting personal bests at 32 km and breaking Walter George's 69-year-old record for the 1-hour track run. He also finished eleventh in the 1953 World Cross-Country Championships. Table 6.8 records his training from June 1953 leading up to his third world marathon record (J.H. Peters et al. 1957).

For the rest of his career, Peters' training remained essentially the same. His last great race was on 26 June, 1954, when he ran the AAA Marathon in a time of 2:17:39.4. Shortly after that race, he ran his best ever 6-mile (10-km) race on the track in 28:57.8. In the 10 months leading up to that race, he had covered 7158 km. Ironically,

	Distance				
Date	**Km**	**Miles**	**Time (h:min:s)**	**Comment**	**Speed (min:s·km⁻¹)**

Table 6.7 Jim Peters' training program for June 1951

Date	Km	Miles	Time (h:min:s)	Comment	Speed (min:s·km⁻¹)
2	25.6	16	01:35:00		3:43
3	–	–	–		
4	20.6	13	01:15:00		3:38
5	–	–	–		
6	23.2	14.5	01:27:00		3:45
7	16.0	10	58:00	Fast. Legs stiff	3:38
8	19.2	12	01:10:30	Fast. OK	3:40
9	20.8+	13+	01:18:00	Tired	3:45
10	–	–	–		
11	19.2+	12+	01:11:00	Fast run. OK	3:42
12	16.0+	10+	56:00	Fast. Hot. OK	3:30
13	16.0+	10+	56:30	Fast. Hot. Terrific wind	3:32
14	16.0+	10+	10:00:00	Fast. Hot. OK	3:45
15	–	–	–		
16	42.2	26.2	02:29:28	1st. Hot, tired, but happy.	3:32
Total	**234.7+**	**146.7+**	**14:06:28**		**3:37**

Adapted from J.H. Peters et al. (1957, p. 135). © 1957 by Nicholas Kaye.

Peters' hard training and subsequent collapse in the Vancouver Marathon were contrasted with the performance of Roger Bannister, who trained lightly and did not collapse after his "Mile of the Century" race against John Landy at the Empire Games (figure 6.7). Thus, many drew the mistaken conclusion that hard training explained Peters' collapse in the Vancouver Marathon (A. Ward 1964). Six weeks after the tragedy of the Vancouver Marathon, Peters retired, largely because he was scared that he might kill himself if forced to run another marathon in the heat. He believed that the one race he still longed to win, the 1956 Olympic Marathon in Melbourne, would be run in the heat, and he was not prepared to risk his life again (Benyo 1983).

Few marathon runners before or since have matched the ferocious and unremitting intensity at which Peters (and indeed Zatopek) trained. Expressing his belief in the importance of intensive training, Peters said: "The body has got to be conditioned to stand up to the stresses and strains which it is going to meet in an actual race and therefore it is useless training at a 6-minutes-per-mile pace if you hope to race at 5+ minutes per mile" (J. Peters 1955, p. 110).

On the issue of speed and stamina, Peters said: "I rarely ran more than 16 miles a day in training. But I did good, fast, quality miles. You see, speed and stamina are yoked together" (Benyo 1983, p. 64).

Peters' training advice, inscribed on the inside of a copy of his autobiography given to ultramarathoner Jackie Mekler (who I discuss later in this chapter) some time after the Vancouver Marathon, was: "Train little, hard, and often." Peters warned against overtraining and suggested that there be a gap of at least three weeks between 32-km races and a gap of four to five weeks before a race of any kind following a marathon. "Your body and mind must be given ample time to recover from the effort." Like Zatopek, Peters did not alternate hard and easy training days, nor did he taper for his races. One wonders whether these modifications might not have made him even faster.

In his book on American Buddy Edelen, who became the next world record holder in the marathon, F. Murphy (1992) makes some profound observations on how Edelen's coach, Fred Wilt, interpreted the training lessons that these two great runners, Peters and Zatopek, gave to marathon runners.

The first interpretation was that before Peters, marathon races were won by athletes who, like Newton, simply ran longer distances in training than did anyone else. The marathon was a race for survivors, and the winners were better prepared to survive long-distance races run relatively slowly, because that was exactly what they had trained for.

The second was that Peters, who came from a tough working-class environment in London's East End, was the first to train by running fast most of the time. All his training was done at between 5:00 and 5:15 per mile (3:07 to 3:17 per km). But to achieve and maintain this high intensity, he had to run frequently—11 to 13 times per week. For example, Peter would reduce the distance of any single run and would run multiple daily workouts.

Table 6.8   Jim Peters' training program for June 1953

Date	Distance Km	Miles	Time (h:min:s)	Comment	Speed (min:s·km^{-1})
7	25.6	16	01:31:15		3:34
8	12.8	8	42:47	Fast. OK	3:20
9	9.6	6	31:40	OK	3:20
	19.2	12	01:07:06	OK	3:29
10	9.6	6	31:35	OK	3:20
	16.0	10	56:03	OK. Easing down	3:20
11	9.6	6	32:10	OK	3:21
12	10.4	6.5	33:23	OK	3:13
13	42.2	26.2	02:18:40	World record	3:17
Total	154.7	96.7	08:44:39		3:23

Adapted from J.H. Peters et al. (1957, p. 135). © 1957 by Nicholas Kaye.

Figure 6.7　Bannister chases Landy in the third lap of the famous Mile of the Century in the 1954 Empire Games. It was because of their desire to watch this race, contested at the same time as the marathon, that race officials left their positions on the marathon course prematurely. As a result, Peters was not informed of the magnitude of his lead in the last few kilometers of the Vancouver Marathon, in which he collapsed with heatstroke.

The third interpretation Wilt made, as he watched Zatopek pass Peters in the Helsinki Olympic Marathon, was that "as much as Peters had done, he had not done enough" (F. Murphy 1992, p. 21). Documenting Wilt's conclusion that Peters, like Zatopek, lacked the long continuous runs on the road, Murphy states: "Fred [Wilt] thought that if he could combine Peters' workouts at near-race pace with hard intervals like those of Zatopek, and then add long road runs at something gradually approaching the full marathon distance, he could get even better results" (F. Murphy 1992, p. 21). In Buddy Edelen, who is also discussed in this chapter, Wilt would find the tough athlete sufficiently resilient to test his new theory.

Gordon Pirie

The next great British runner after Peters was Gordon Pirie, who was born in Yorkshire in 1931. Pirie's interest in running was stimulated by his father, Alick, a former Scottish international runner who had introduced his son to competitive running through the club of which he was the secretary. After leaving school in 1948, the younger Pirie ran regularly but without competitive ambition. However, his desire for greatness was aroused when he witnessed Emil Zatopek winning the 10,000 m at the 1948 Olympic Games in Wembley. He resolved to beat Zatopek one day.

Pirie soon became disenchanted with the training methods of the other top British runners of the day, Roger Bannister (see chapter 8) and Chris Chataway. He thought these British runners too amateurish, too talented, and therefore too ready to undervalue the importance of heavy training. He wondered whether they found their training somewhat boring and decided that Zatopek's superiority over the British runners was due to his attitude and training methods. He found in Zatopek an openness, a willingness to share secrets, and an enthusiasm that he admired. Zatopek never became bored and approached life with an infectious sense of fun; he was as enthusiastic in helping his competitors as he was in running them off their feet. Also, Zatopek did not appear to feel the stress of competition; running and racing was simply a joy. Zatopek embodied the ideal for which Pirie would strive.

In 1949, Pirie started his two-year stint in the Royal Air Force (RAF). It was during this period that he adopted the training methods of Zatopek and progressed to become one of the top British track runners. In July 1951, he set the British record at 6 miles (10 km) in 29:32 and in the following year at 3 miles (5 km) in a time of 13:44.8. In July 1952, he traveled to the Helsinki Olympic Games in the same plane as Jim Peters and finished seventh in the 10,000 m in a personal best time of 30:04.2 and fourth in the 5000 m, also in a personal best time of 14:18.0. Two months later he set his third British record at 2000 m (5:21.2), and in 1953 he established new British records at 6 miles (once), 3 miles (three times), 3 km (three times), 5 km (once), 10 km (once) and 2 miles (twice). In addition, he set world records at 6 miles (28:19.4) and 4 miles (18:35.4) and was a member of the British relay team that established the 4 × 1500-m world record.

Additional highlights in his career, which lasted until 1961, were world records in the mile on grass (4:05.2 in 1954); 1.5 miles (6:26.0 in 1955); 2 miles (8:39.0 in 1958); 3000 m (twice—best time 7:52.8 in 1956); and 5000 m (best time 13:51.6 in 1958). In the 1956 Olympic Games in Melbourne, he was involved in an enthralling battle with Vladimir Kuts in the 10,000-m final before slipping, exhausted, into eighth place. In the 5000-m final, he finished second to Kuts. Even in the twilight of his career, at the 1960 Olympic Games in Rome, Pirie ran a personal best in the 10,000 m, finishing tenth in 29:15.6.

Pirie's average heavy training day is described in his book (Pirie 1961). It would seem that by 1956 he followed the routine set out in table 6.9 for four or five days per week. On the remaining two to three days of the week, he would complete only one training session.

One of the most interesting ideas to be found in Pirie's book is his discussion of two types of athletes.

They don't differ in size or muscular development. There is no apparent difference at all. But one type can run a terrific speed without training. . . . These fellows can't run slowly when they try. . . . The other type—and I fall into this category—are able only through tortuous efforts to improve our speed, but with the slightest lay-off, this hard-won ability vanishes. This first type of runner will always be the greatest. . . . Herb Elliott is the first man of the speedy type to train and race the longer distances. I believe that, if he is interested, he will be able to make a clean sweep of all the records from 1500 m to the marathon. . . .

Table 6.9 Gordon Pirie's heavy-training day	
Morning session (10 A.M.)	**Afternoon session (6 P.M.)**
30-min warm-up	30-min warm-up
800 m in 1:56	10 × 400 m in 1:01 with 300 m recovery
10-min jog	15-min cool-down
3.2 km in 8:46:6	
4 × 800 m in 2:08 with 400 m recovery	
15-min cool-down	

Reprinted from Pirie (1961). © 1961 by W.H. Allen.

The second type of runner is the fellow who flogs and flogs himself to great heights and is liable to fall quickly. But he can't possibly compete with the speed man. Trainers tell us that if you only do "so-and-so," you can run much faster. But I've tried every so-and-so method, and I can assure anyone that it is not so. (Pirie 1961, p. 72 to 73)

Pirie realized that training alone does not explain differences in running performance even in elite runners; some athletes are "more equal" than others, even before they start training. Some of the physiological characteristics that may allow a Herb Elliott to run fast over short and longer distances without undergoing the same degree of training as a Gordon Pirie were discussed in chapter 2. I would suggest that skeletal muscle recruitment patterns, skeletal muscle contractile function, and perhaps muscle elastic properties explain the greater natural speed of Elliott over the shorter distances of up to 400 m. Thereafter, the variable that becomes increasingly important is resistance to fatigue. It is this variable in his own physiology that Pirie probably tried to alter, presumably because it is the physiological characteristic that can best adapt with endurance training.

In other words, Pirie's observation that Herb Elliott would have set the marathon record would be true only if Elliott had a superior capacity for fatigue resistance that would also have adapted substantially with endurance training.

Herb Elliott

Many consider the Australian Herb Elliott (figure 6.8) to have been the greatest distance runner ever. In part, this was because of his unequalled record; during his career as a senior athlete he was never beaten in the mile or 1500 m.

Elliott was born in Perth on 25 February, 1938. Like Alick Pirie, Elliott's father was a competitive athlete who encouraged his son to run from an early age. At primary school, Elliott excelled as a sprinter. He ran his first mile at 14, finishing in 5:35. Later he ran 5:00 and concluded that any 14-year-old able to run a mile in 5 minutes could ultimately run the mile in less than 4 minutes. Two years later, he won the state 800 m (under-16) in 2:10.4. In 1954, he set the world junior mile record of

Table 6.10	Herb Elliott's training week in 1956
Monday	6-10 × 400 m or 800 m followed by 3-5 km of free running
Tuesday	8 km at peak speed
Wednesday	Training with sprinters
Thursday	30 minutes of sprint-jogging on a track; he sprinted for 30 seconds, then jogged 190 seconds before repeating the sprint
Friday	Rest
Saturday	4-10 km at peak speed on the track
Sunday	16 km hard

Data compiled from H.J. Elliott (1961, p. 148). © 1961 by Cassell and Co. Ltd.

4:25.6 and the Australian national junior 800-m record of 1:55.7. In his final year at school, besides his running achievements, he was head prefect, he rowed in the school's first eight, and he was in the school's first hockey team. In addition, he was an accomplished swimmer.

In October 1956, like Pirie eight years earlier, he attended the Olympic Games at Perth, in the company of his father. Just as Pirie had been inspired by the performances of Zatopek, Elliott was fascinated by the running of Vladimir Kuts in his races with Pirie. He then decided to commit himself to running, left home, and went to train at Portsea with the eccentric Australian coach, Percy Cerutty, thus becoming Cerutty's most famous protégé and establishing Cerutty's credentials as a coach.

The following year, Elliott set the world junior mile record twice, lowering it to 4:04.4, a time more than 2 seconds faster than Ron Clarke's previous best. He added

Figure 6.8   Australian Herb Elliott, world-record holder at 1500 m and the mile, was undefeated at those distances throughout his career.

the world junior 800-m record (1:50.8), the world senior 3000-m record (8:45.6), and the world senior 3-mile record (14:02.4). In March, he won the Australian senior mile championships in 4:00.4, the eleventh fastest time ever, and set the Australian record for 800 m (1:49.3).

On 25 January, 1958, the 19-year-old Elliott became the youngest runner to break 4 minutes for the mile, finishing in 3:59.9. At the Empire Games in Cardiff in July of that year he won the 800 m and the mile, and on 6 August he set the world mile record in Dublin (3:54.5), an improvement of 2.7 seconds on the previous record. Three weeks later in Gothenburg, Sweden, he set the world record in the 1500 m (3:36.0).

By 1959, Elliott's enthusiasm for running was waning as he was desperately hoping to win a scholarship to enter Cambridge University after the 1960 Olympic Games. He raced very little and, on Boxing Day, with no small lack of enthusiasm, began training for the 1960 Rome Olympics. Despite suboptimal training and little racing, he won the 1500 m Games, setting a new world record of 03:35.6. In the three weeks following the Games he ran four sub-4-minute miles before retiring.

During his career, Elliott was unbeaten over 1500 m and the mile, running 17 sub-4-minute miles in two years. He seldom ran more than 120 km per week in training. He also found it unnecessary to train hard during the competitive season, provided he raced twice per week and ran an occasional 16-km at peak speed. His average training week is presented in table 6.10 (H.J. Elliott 1961).

Elliott's performances in 1956 attest to his remarkable talent. He trained sporadically after a foot injury and spent most of his evenings in a coffee bar with another half-hearted athlete, inventing excuses as to why they should not train. Despite this lack of training, Elliott wrote: "Strangely, my athletic form never deserted me." (1961, p. 29)

Then, in July 1958, after "carousing about the country" for a month following the Empire Games, abusing his body by consuming too much rich food and champagne, he ran the 800 m, his weakest event, in 1:47.3, the fastest half-mile ever in Europe and only 0.5 seconds outside the world record. "To this day," he wrote, "that performance remains a mystery to me" (H.J. Elliott 1961). Perhaps Pirie's assessment of Elliott's ability was accurate after all.

Ron Clarke

Another Australian, Ron Clarke (figure 6.9), followed Herb Elliott as the preeminent distance runner of the early 1960s. However, many believe that holding the 1968 Olympics at altitude in Mexico City robbed Clarke of the Olympic gold medal that would have crowned his extraordinary athletic career.

Clarke started racing in 1953 at the age of 16 and first came to public attention during 1955 and 1956, when he set Australian junior records at distances from 800 yards to 3000 m. In 1956, he also set the Australian senior 2000-m record and was rewarded by being invited to carry the flame at the opening of the 1956 Melbourne Olympic Games. Shortly after this, Clarke married, had three children in quick succession, and began to concentrate on his career. By the time of the 1960 Rome Olympics, Clarke was a 23-year-old former athlete. The following year, he started running again. At the 1962 Commonwealth Games in Perth, he ran second to New Zealand's Murray Halberg in the 3-mile race. In July of that year, he set Australian records at 10 miles (50:02) and for the greatest distance run in 1 hour (19.36 km).

The following year, at Olympic Park in Melbourne, he set his first world records at 6 miles (27:17.8) and 10,000 m (28:15.6). In 1964, at the same venue, he added the 3-mile world record (13:07.6), and at the Olympics in Tokyo, he finished third in the 10,000 m after being passed by the first two runners in the last 60 m. He also finished ninth in both the 5000 m and the marathon, the latter in an Australian record time. In 1965, in the space of 44 days, he set 12 world records, including the 5000 m (twice, with a best time of 13:25.8); 3 miles (twice, with a best time of 12:52.4;) 6 miles (26:47.0); the 10,000 m (27:39.4, a 35 second improvement on the old world record); 16 km (47:12.0); 20,000 m (59:22.8); and distance covered in 1 hour (20.24 km). In 1966, Clarke set the Australian 30-km record (1:34:35); set world records for 3 miles (12:40.4) and 5000 m (13:16.6); and won silver medals in the 5000 m and 10,000 m at the Commonwealth Games in Jamaica. In December, he ran the second-fastest 6 miles ever (26:52.0), and in June 1967, he set a world 2-mile record of 8:19.8.

By 1968, Clarke was ready to change his image as a world-record holder who could not win major international competitions. He gave up his job, mortgaged his house, and took his family with him to the French Olympic training camp at Fontromeu. The camp was situated in the French Pyrenees at an altitude of 2200 m—the same altitude as Mexico City. For three months, the Clarke family lived rent-free in a flat that belonged to the mayor of Bolquère, a tiny village just below Fontromeu. The mayor bestowed this privilege because he liked this amateur athlete.

From R. Clarke (1966, p. 65). © 1966 by Ron Clarke.

Figure 6.9 Australian Ron Clarke set 17 world records in his career but was denied an Olympic gold medal until Emil Zatopek's famous gesture. In this picture from the 5000-m final in the 1965 World Games in Helsinki, Ron Clarke leads Frenchman Michael Jazy and Kenyan icon Kip Keino.

Twice during this period Clarke returned to sea level to race at Crystal Palace in London. During his first trip, he broke the world 2-mile record; during the second, he finished 6 seconds outside his 10,000-m world record, despite racing in gale-force conditions. During the race, he lapped Dave Bedford, who finished second, an extraordinary three times. He believed then, as did most others, that he would have beaten his world record by 20 seconds in good conditions. Had he done that, his record would have remained intact for close to 20 years.

The 10,000-m race at the Mexico City Olympics was run in the evening of the first day. With only 600 m to go, Clarke broke away from the leading group of six runners and led the race for 200 m. With 400 m to go, the Ethiopian Malmo Walde and the Kenyan Naftali Temu passed Clarke, who began to struggle. Later Clarke would write that he "went from feeling great to feeling bad in about three strides. I felt as bad with 400 m to go as I have at the finish of tough races in the past" (O'Rourke 1982, p. 1). Clarke was reduced to a jog, completing the last lap in 85 seconds. He collapsed, unconscious, at the finish; when he recovered consciousness 20 minutes later, he could not speak. The Australian team doctor, Alan Corrigan, who attended the collapsed Clarke, feared for his life. Clarke's first words, 1 hour later, were simply: "Where am I?" Remarkably, the next day Clarke competed in the final of the 500 m, finishing sixth. He was the first sea-level resident to finish in both races.

Clarke continued to run for a further two years, but he lacked the luster of his earlier career. Some 14 years after his collapse at the Mexico City Games, Clarke underwent corrective surgery for a ruptured heart (mitral) valve. Whether his collapse at Mexico City contributed to the development of his heart condition is a matter of debate to this day. Interestingly, Clarke was not the only athlete to lose consciousness during those Games; even today, the reason for these collapses remains uncertain. The end result is that the Olympic Games will never again be held at altitude.

Clarke's last great races were those he competed in during the 1968 Olympics. He retired from competitive athletics in 1970, after a career in which he had won 202 of the 313 races he had entered and set 17 world records. When Clarke visited Emil Zatopek in Prague in July 1966, Zatopek showed Clarke the measure of esteem in which others held him. As they parted at the airport, Zatopek gave Clarke a small gift, with the words: "Not out of friendship, but because you deserve it" (K. Moore 1982, p. 71). It was the gold medal Zatopek had won in the 10,000 m at the 1952 Helsinki Olympic Games.

Clarke's training methods have been described by Wilt (1972), who reports that Clarke trained almost daily all year round, with little change in pattern from one season of the year to another. Any variation was unintentional. Each day's workout was remarkably similar, and Clarke did not attempt to peak. Rather, he remained racing fit all year round, gradually increasing his training quality over his athletic lifetime. He seldom trained on the track, did not keep a training diary, and never used a stopwatch. He trained most often on grass and roads and over extremely hilly courses.

Clarke trained three times per day but regarded the evening workout as the most important part of each day's training. On weekday mornings, he ran 5 km continuously at a fast pace, usually in a full track suit, and then did some gym work. At lunchtime, he ran 10 to 12 km continuously at a fast pace, again running in a full track suit, and in the evening he would run 16 to 25 km, also at a fast pace. This workout was also usually run in a full track suit, unless the weather was extremely hot. On Tuesdays and Thursdays he included gym training; on Saturdays he trained only once, usually running 16 to 25 km, and on Sundays he trained once, covering 28 to 34 km at a continuous, fast pace over a remarkably hilly course. Occasionally, but not more than once or twice per week, Clarke would run 10 × 200-m or 10 × 400-m intervals with an equivalent recovery jog between repetitions. The remainder of his training mainly involved long, fast, continuous running at under 3:08 per km for distances up to 16 km, and close to 3:08 per km for distances up to 24 km. He ran hard and forced the pace almost without exception on most of his training runs.

Clarke seldom missed an opportunity to enter track, road, or cross-country races, and he usually raced more than once per week. He enjoyed running races of 800 to 1600 m as preparation for longer-distance races. During competition on the track, his main tactic was to share the early pace with another runner, to increase his pace in the middle third of the race so as to break away from the rest of the field, to start surging with four laps to go, and to sprint the last two laps (Lenton 1981).

Leonard Edelen

The life and training methods of America's first world marathon record holder, Leonard "Buddy" Edelen, have been documented in a biography written by Frank Murphy in 1992. Murphy records that between 1962 and 1966, Edelen ran 13 marathons, winning seven and never finishing lower than ninth (Higdon 1982). Of these, six were run in a single year between June 1962 and June 1963. Edelen set eight American track records and won the 1962 British AAA 10-mile (16-km) title. On 15 June, 1963, he ran his greatest race, winning the Polytechnic Marathon from Windsor

Castle to Chiswick in a world best time of 2:14:28, becoming the first American ever to set the world marathon record (figure 6.10). An interesting historical anecdote is that Edelen felt he had to work and run in England if he wanted to become a world-class runner.

Edelen's career started in high school in Sioux Falls, South Dakota, where in 1955 he won the South Dakota State Mile Championships in 4:28. He was undefeated in the mile as a schoolboy. While attending the University of Minnesota, he became the 1958 Big Ten cross-country champion and set a conference record for 2 miles. At this time, Edelen's training was mild and was in keeping with the type of training favored by the American collegiate athletes of the day.

In 1959, Edelen came under more direct control of American distance coach Fred Wilt, who suggested that Edelen spend the spring of 1959 in Finland to learn how the Europeans were training. By the end of that year, Edelen had increased his training to 18 miles (29 km) per day, split into two daily sessions, and was able to complete sessions of 25 × 400 m in 68 seconds each, or 4 × 3.2 km with 4 minutes' rest between sessions. As a result, during the 1960 indoor track season, Edelen won 2-mile

Photo courtesy of Buddy Edelen.

Figure 6.10   American Buddy Edelen sets a new world standard marathon record in the 1963 Polytechnic Harrier's Marathon in London. Edelen's unusual athletic career is captured in the biography by Frank Murphy (1992).

races at two major events and set an American record of 29:58.9 for the 10,000 m.

Despite his excellent early season form, he failed to qualify for the 1960 United States Olympic Games team in the 10,000 m; his poor performance in that race was later ascribed to the development of a nutritional anemia. Edelen tended to put on weight, but by restricting his food intake he had developed an iron deficiency.

In November 1960, Edelen moved to England, where he found employment teaching a range of subjects from history to home economics at the King John Modern Secondary School in Westcliffe-on-Sea, Essex. There he trained by running to and from work. His typical training week is described in table 6.11.

After a season of predominantly road and cross-country racing, Edelen won the British national 10-mile championships at Hurlington, running a time of 48:31.8, the fourth-fastest time in history. Two months later, he ran his first 42-km marathon, the Polytechnic Harriers Marathon at Windsor, finishing ninth in 2:31. It was clearly a disappointing time, given his excellent performance over 16 km.

Coach Wilt was unsparing in his diagnosis of the training errors that had led to this poor performance. Identifying three training sessions when Edelen should have rested and not trained, Wilt wrote:

> *I can't say this 40-minute jog hurt you. I can say it does not help two days before a race. This is a manifestation of uncertainty. There is a time to train and a time to rest—not halfway rest. This is a bitter lesson you have not accepted. (F. Murphy 1992, p. 57)*

Murphy (1992) also noted that Edelen ran another two hard interval sessions (45 × 100 m and 20 × 400 m) within five days of the marathon. Of his race, Edelen wrote, "I never want to run a race when I feel like that again." (p. 58) He decided that he would never again run the full marathon distance.

Yet on 21 July, 1961, he won the Welsh Marathon Championships in windy conditions in 2:22:33, just 4 seconds slower than the course record set by Jim Peters in 1953.

On 7 October, Edelen finished second by 2 seconds in the International Peace Marathon in Kosice, Czechoslovakia, in 2:28:29.8. During the race he lost 4 kg and did not drink any fluid because he had experienced stomach troubles when drinking in other races. He concluded that he must drink during races but that "it must

Table 6.11 The training of Buddy Edelen from Sunday, October 29 to Sunday, November 5, 1961		
October 29		34 km in 1:55. A moderate run. Buddy ran with a former high school and Minnesota team member, Bill Erickson. Buddy ran hard for several miles, went back for Bill, ran hard again, went back and then ran hard, continuing throughout.
October 30	A.M.	2 × 3.2 km in 10:15 and 10:25 with 3:00 jog interval; then 25 × 100 m with 30-m jog between intervals.
	P.M.	4 × 1.6 km in 4:55; 4:52; 4:41; and 4:53 with 03:00 jog between intervals
October 31	A.M.	16 km jog to sea front, followed by 2 × 3.2 km in 9:41 and 10:26.
	P.M.	Rest.
November 1	A.M.	1.6 km run to sea front; 30 × 400 m at an average time of 1:08 with 1:00 jog between intervals.
	P.M.	1.2 km warm-up; 2 x steady run; 25 × 110 km.
November 2		14 km.
November 3		1.6 km warm-up; 4 × 1.6 km in 4:52; 4:43; 5:07; and 5:06 with 3:00 jog between intervals 1.6 km warm-down.
November 4		6.4 km cross-country race in 17:25. "I ran like a bomb today."
November 5		34 km in 01:53:00.

be done in training so as to become accustomed to it" (F. Murphy 1992, p. 65). His next race was the Asahi Marathon in Fukuoka, Japan, on 2 December. In cool conditions but into a headwind on the return trip, Edelen finished fourth in 2:18:56.8.

The following winter, he trained at up to 220 km per week, racing cross-country, road, and track. Edelen then traveled to Greece to compete in the International Classic Marathon from Marathon to Athens on 19 May, 1963. His winning time of 2:23:06 bettered the course record of 1960 Olympic gold medalist, Abebe Bikila, by 38 seconds. Then, less than one month later, on 15 June, he ran what would be his greatest race, the Polytechnic Harriers Marathon. His training before the race is set out in table 6.12.

Table 6.12   Buddy Edelen's training program of the final two weeks before his marathon world record on June 15th, 1963

Date	Training log (abbreviated)	Fred Wilt's comments (abbreviated)
May 26	35-37 km 2:02. Legs sore over last 16 km. Best time ever on this course.	Excellent. You need this every week.
May 27	7 km from school. Fast pace. Legs too sore for scheduled sprints	Good judgement.
May 28	A.M. 7 km to school. Fast. P.M. 3-km warm-up, 21 × 400 m in 1:08 with 200-m brisk jog recovery. Could have run 25 repetitions.	Just fine.
May 29	A.M. 7 km to school. Fast. P.M. 24 km in 1:19. One of the fastest times on this run. Legs a bit sore over last 6 km.	Terrific training.
May 30	A.M. 7 km to school. Slower than yesterday. P.M. 1.6 km warm-up, 7 × (stride 50 m, sprint 50, jog 100, sprint 100, jog 100, sprint 100, jog 100, sprint 200 in 00:28–0:30, walk for 2:00). Legs tired at start, became heavy at the finish. 7 km home moderately fast.	Excellent but no need for the 7 km after the session.
May 31	A.M. 7 km to school. Moderately fast. P.M. 25 × 400 m in 1:13–1:17 with 0:50 jog.	Remember the big races are approaching and your volume must be cut in favor of quality plus rest.
June 1	1.6 km warm-up. 3 × (10 × 100–110 m very fast with 100 m after each); 3:00 jog between sets of 10. Still stiff from sprints on May 30. 15:00 swim in the sea.	Good judgment. Swim is fine.
June 2	16–18 km steady on road. Too tired and too windy for long run. Sea swim after the run.	Good judgment. Swim is fine.

(continued)

Table 6.12 *(continued)*

Date	Training log (abbreviated)	Fred Wilt's comments (abbreviated)
June 3	35–37 km in 2:03–2:04. Very strong wind. 15:00 swim.	Good workout that you need once a week.
June 4	6-km warm-up. 7 × (50 m jog; 50 sprint; 100 jog; 100 sprint; 140 jog; 140 sprint; 200 jog; 200 sprint; walk for 2:00). Heart recovered well but legs were shattered. Difficult to run 0:30 for the 200s. Legs very heavy. Too close to the long run. A damn tough workout. 6 km home at good clip and felt better.	Jog equal distance after each sprint. Perhaps no sprinting after a long run is best.
June 5	17–18 km in 00:54–00:55. Surprised that the run was so fast. Decided against 24-km run as legs too tired.	Just fine; good judgment.
June 6	A.M. 10 km hard all the way. P.M. 4 km warm-up. 4 × (400 m fast; 400 fast; 300 jog; 400 fast; 200 jog; 400 fast; 100 jog; 400 fast; walk for 5:00). Averages 1:04.8 for the 20 × 400. 1.6 km warm-down.	One of your best workouts ever. You are in great form.
June 7	1.6-km warm-up. 20 × 400 in 1:10–1:11 with 0:45 jog between each. 400 m home. Chose not to do 25 intervals as feeling tired from yesterday.	Good.
June 8	Club meet at Harlow. 3.2 km warm-up. 1.6 km, second in 4:23. 30:00 later, 800 m, third in 2:07. 20:00 later, 100 m leg in 4 × 100 relay.	Good effort.
June 9	35–37 km in 2:01. Fastest ever. I feel I will have a good run at Poly. 15:00 swim in the sea.	Great. You are in terrific shape.
June 10	7 km from school. 15:00 swim in the sea. Legs a bit tired from yesterday.	Excellent judgment.
June 11	A.M. 7 km to school quite fast. P.M. 3.2 km slow jogging. 5 × 100 m strides; 25 × 400 m in 1:07.4 with 200 jog in under 1:00. Total of about 27–29 km.	Good judgment in view of the upcoming Poly marathon. Otherwise I would prefer the 4 × (5 × 400 m in 1:03).
June 12	A.M. 7 km to school quite fast (bit tired in the legs). P.M. 18 km in 0:55–0:56. 15:00 swim.	OK.

June 13	Rest	
June 14	Rest	
June 15	The 50th running of the Polytechnic Harriers Marathon, Windsor to Chiswick.	Buddy Edelen, 1st in a new world record time of 2:14:28.

From F. Murphy (1992, pp. 88–89).

In that race, Edelen eclipsed Toru Terasawa's world record by 47 seconds, running 2:14:28. In the previous five years, the record had improved by only 2 seconds. Of his performance, Edelen wrote, "The days of the plodding marathon are over. It takes speed work like the 110-yard sprints I practise and the hard training on the roads to give you both the pace and the stamina you need" (F. Murphy 1992, p. 101).

Edelen felt so good and recovered so quickly after the race that he concluded,

I used to think that you needed a minimum of six weeks to recover from a marathon and that three weeks was ridiculous because although physically you could be recovered, mentally you would not be prepared to put forth another supreme effort. . . . The way it's geared and the amount of mileage I do per week seems to indicate that I can bash out a marathon and recover in a matter of a few days.

The flaw in this conclusion would only become apparent a year later when Edelen most needed to run at his best.

On 11 October, Edelen ran the Kosice Marathon, winning in 2:15:09.6, a record that was beaten only 15 years later. For the rest of 1963 and early 1964, Edelen prepared for the United States Olympic Marathon trials to be held in Yonkers in May 1964. Realizing that the race would be run in hot, humid conditions, Edelen prepared by training in four sweatshirts. The race was held in impossible conditions: 33°C with high humidity and a road temperature of 60°C. Edelen won in 2:24:22.6, winning by more than 20 minutes. Of the 128 starters, only 37 finished in less than the 4-hour limit.

Before the Olympic Marathon to be run five months later, Edelen suffered from a persistent hip pain that hampered his training. As a result, he finished the race in sixth place in a time of 2:18:12.4.

The following year saw the beginning of the end of Edelen's career. On 2 May, 1965, he won a marathon in West Germany in 2:21:00 and then, despite the persistent hip pain, finished third in the Polytechnic Marathon in 2:14:34. It was his last race in Britain. At that time, he held the sixth and seventh fastest times ever in the marathon.

He returned to the United States, settling in Alamosa, Colorado, where he studied for a master's degree in psychology. He continued to train up to 200 km weekly, desperately hoping that his pain would settle and that he would be able to run in the 1968 Olympics in Mexico City. It was never to be. Thirteen months after running 2:14:28 in the Polytechnic Marathon, Edelen finished the Denver Marathon in 2:51:00. His career was over.

Edelen was not the first, nor will he be the last, great marathoner whose resolution ultimately proved his downfall. Frank Murphy (1992) concluded that it was a combination of insecurity and self-concept that drove Edelen to train and race too much. He refused to rest before races because "he could feel his condition draining out of him." (p. 166) Coach Wilt frequently admonished Edelen, "The compulsion to run and restlessness comes from [a] mental inferiority complex. . . . I cannot kill your spirit but you are your own worst enemy. Why not be kind to Buddy Edelen? Why kill him now?" (p. 166) Murphy (1992) observed that the same motivation that made Edelen a good runner also destroyed him.

Frank Murphy (1992) uses this analysis of Edelen to support his notion that there are at least three types of successful long-distance runners. The first is the insecure person who finds reassurance in the hard grind of distance running; the second is the scientific person who "tinkers" with his body and for whom the running itself may be incidental; and the third is the person who runs simply for the joy of it. Murphy concludes that Edelen would qualify in all three categories. His insecurity stemmed from losing his mother at a young age and the presence of an abusive father. His scientific bent was shown by the meticulous preparation and subtle modifications to his training as he prepared himself. His joy of running was clear as he shared it openly with the running community in England.

The next great American distance runner, Frank Shorter, would share at least some of these traits of his compatriot.

How Abebe Bikila Won the 1960 Olympic Marathon

The first glimpse of the distance-running potential of runners from the African continent was provided at the 1960 Rome Olympics by the Ethiopian Abebe Bikila, who, running barefoot, won the marathon in a new Olympic Games record time of 2:15:16.2. In 1964, Bikila became the first runner to win the marathon in consecutive Olympics, winning in 2:12:11.2. To win that race, Bikila first had to undergo and recover from an appendix operation just five weeks before the event.

On a trip to Cape Town in 1994, Le Roy Walker, former president of the United States Olympic Committee (USOC), told me the true and previously unrecorded story of exactly how Bikila won the Olympic Marathon.

In 1960, Walker—who had also coached the U.S. Olympic track and field team and who was predominantly a coach of sprinters—was invited to coach the Ethiopian team preparing for the Rome Olympic Games in Addis Ababa. The team had assembled at an altitude of 2000 m. When introduced to the athletes at the first training session, Walker was surprised to discover that there were relatively few (East African) sprinters but a large group of distance runners. Momentarily unsure of what to do, he pointed to a distant hill and suggested the distance runners might like to jog to that hill for a warm-up while he began to work with the sprinters.

Some 90 minutes later, when the sprinters had completed their workout, Walker was surprised by the tardiness of the distance runners, who had yet to return. They returned 1 hour later, whereafter Walker commenced his first-ever training session for distance runners.

Intrigued by what had transpired, the following day Walker drove along the route on which the runners had "warmed up" the previous night. Within a few miles, he came across the first surprise as the road descended into a vast valley unseen from his vantage point on the running track the night before. By the time he reached the base of the hill to which he had directed his runners, the car's odometer indicated that he had covered 22.5 km.

Rushing back to his hotel, he immediately phoned the USOC to inquire what the current (1960) world record for the 42-km standard marathon was. When informed that it was 2:15:17, he proudly announced that from his group of Ethiopians would come the next Olympic gold medalist and the next world record holder, a boast that was fulfilled on 10 September, 1960, when Abebe Bikila achieved both in winning the Rome Olympic Marathon (figure 6.11).

If Walker's inexperience as a coach of marathon runners was not to prove an impediment to Bikila's subsequent success, he was to play one crucial role in ensuring Bikila's victory. Neither Bikila nor the other equally talented Ethiopian marathon runner, Abebe Wakgira, were prepared to run the marathon at the Olympics; both wanted to run the 10,000 m on the track in front of the Olympic

Figure 6.11   Ethiopian Abebe Bikila runs barefoot in the 1960 Rome Olympic Games Marathon. Bikila's victory in that race resulted in the first Olympic gold medal for a black African athlete and heralded the beginning of the rise to dominance of African distance runners.

(continued)

crowds. It was an interdict from the Ethiopian King, Haile Selassie, on the request of Walker, that forced Bikila and Wakgira to run the marathon, thereby sealing Bikila's position as one of the world's greatest marathon runners of all time.

Walker expresses only one regret. In his view, Wakgira was as good as Bikila, yet he performed poorly in the Rome Marathon, finishing seventh in 2:21:09, 6 minutes behind Bikila. Only later did Walker learn the reason.

In Rome, the Ethiopian team trained daily at a venue some 14 km from the athletes' residence. To save the taxi fare provided for that trip, Wakgira had chosen rather to run to and from the daily training session. The extra training proved too much. Otherwise, Walker remains certain, Ethiopia would have taken both the gold and silver medals in the 1960 Olympic Marathon.

It was at the Olympic Games in Mexico City in 1968 that the true potential of the African runners first became apparent. In those Games, African runners won every race longer than 1500 m, including the 3000-m steeplechase. Since then, African distance runners, especially Kenyans, have risen to a position of dominance unmatched in any other international sport.

Hezekiah Kipchoge (Kip) Keino

The athlete who best epitomized the African running revolution in the 1960s was unquestionably the 28-year-old Kenyan policeman, Hezekiah Kipchoge (Kip) Keino (figure 6.12).

Born in Kipsamo, in the Nandi Hills of Kenya, on 17 January, 1940, Keino began his competitive running career in 1960, inspired in part by his father, who had been a successful runner. Keino's running ability soon became apparent after he joined the police, and he was sent to the police athletic academy to pursue his running on a more full-time basis. He was soon put on a regular training program.

His first major championship, the 1962 Commonwealth Games in Perth, was less than auspicious: Keino finished last in the 3 miles and was beaten in the mile heats, but he set a national record of 4:07.0. In the 1964 Olympics, he finished fifth in the 5000 m.

In 1965, Keino beat Ron Clarke in two of three races over 5000 m and set world records at 3000 m (7:39.35) and 5000 m (13:24.2), the latter eclipsing Ron Clarke's record. He also came close to the world mile record with a time of 3:54.2 and won the 1500 m and the 5000 m at the first African Games. In 1966 he won gold medals in the 3 miles (12:57.4) and one mile (3:55.3) at the Commonwealth Games and ran the then second-fastest mile in history (3:53.4). American miler Marti Liquori wrote that Keino revolutionized mile running:

He came in at a time when even pacing was thought to be the best way to run. Keino did his kick in the second (not the last) lap. He took the focus on running evenly and shifted it, saying you can run fast in other laps. He was the first to do that and the most successful. (Sandrock 1996, p. 49)

At the 1968 Mexico City Olympic Games, Keino won the 1500 m in 3:34.9, beating the favorite, Jim Ryun, in a remarkable performance. He repeated this performance at the 1970 Commonwealth Games, winning in 3:36.6. His Olympic 1500-m record was only broken in 1984. In 1972 he earned his second Olympic gold medal by win-

Figure 6.12   The legendary Kenyan Kip Keino finishing the 1500-m final in Mexico City in the 1968 Olympic Games, run at medium altitude (2200 m). Keino ran the equivalent of a 3:52 mile at sea level, one of the most remarkable 1500-m races in history. During that race he passed the 1100-m mark 5 seconds ahead of the pace at which Jim Ryun (shown finishing second) established the 1500-m world record at sea level in 1967.

ning the steeplechase in 8:23.6. He also finished second in the 1500 m. He won bronze medals in the 5000 m at the 1968 Olympic Games and at the 1970 Common-wealth Games.

At the time of the 1968 Olympics Keino was self-coached, and, according to Wilt (1972), his training program incorporated a 10-km cross-country run in the early mornings on Mondays, Wednesdays, and Fridays. On Monday and Wednesday afternoons, he would run 4 to 8 × 400 m in 55 to 58 seconds with a 400 m recovery between sessions. On Fridays he ran 4 × 800 m in 1:53 to 1:56 with a 5-minute recovery between sessions. He did no formal training on the four other days of the week, nor did he train in the rainy season. All his training was at medium altitude (2000 m).

Wilt (1972) remarks that Keino's training was "unusually light by modern standards" and suggested that his daily work as a physical education instructor must have supplemented his formal training. Alternatively, like Herb Elliott, he may have been extraordinarily gifted, and he may have needed to train even less than Elliott.

The ability of the top black runners to achieve exceptional performances on quite modest distances but a high intensity of training is shown also by the world-class black South African runner, Matthews Temane, who we discuss later in this chapter. Keino's attitude to competition was as refreshing as his uninhibited running style, as seen from his practice, in his earlier races, of grabbing his orange cap and throwing it into the infield as he led these races into the final stretch. In his own words, "To lose or to win is all the same. If I lose, then I know somebody better than I won. If I have done my best, I have represented my nation well."

After he retired from competitive running in 1974, Keino returned to Eldoret and the Nandi Hills, where he and his wife, Phyllis, established an orphanage for displaced children, the Kip Keino Children's Home. The inspiration to set up the home had been fueled by his own childhood experiences. As a child, he had run away from the home of his abusive uncle, in whose care he had been placed. In 1987, Keino and his wife were named as Sportsman and Sportswoman of the Year by the American magazine *Sports Illustrated*. They have since opened their own Kip Keino School for 250 boys and girls. In their 30 years of service to the children of Kenya, Kip and Phyllis Keino have parented more than 100 orphaned and abandoned children. In the year 2000 alone, the Keinos were caring for 82 children.

Geographical Origins of Kenyan Runners

Most of the exceptional Kenyan runners who have achieved success since Keino have all come from a small number of tribes, notably the Kisii and Kalenjin, who comprise less than 15% of Kenya's 26 million people (SA Sports Illustrated 1991). The Nandi, who live at an altitude of 2300 m near the north-east corner of Lake Victoria, are members of the Kalenjin tribe and have won more than 50% of all Kenyan Olympic and Commonwealth Games medals.

It is thought that the Nandi arose from the admixture of the Cushites, who came to the Kenyan highlands from southern Ethiopia in about 2000 B.C.; the Nilotic people, who entered from the north in about A.D. 1000; and the region's original hunter-gatherers (SA Sports Illustrated 1991). From this union, the Kalenjin and related tribes, the Masai and the Turkana, spread down the Kenyan hills, reaching their peak distribution in about A.D. 1500. Then, as the Bantu-speaking peoples spread eastward from Central Africa, the Kalenjin retreated to their original highlands, where they split into six separate tribes, including the Nandi, who became a distinct tribe in the seventeenth century.

A more recent analysis shows the distribution of successful runners from the different geographical regions of Kenya (figure 6.13). It shows that approximately 72% of the most successful runners come from the Rift Valley, which contains only 20% of the Kenyan population. But even in the Rift Valley, it is the area populated by the Pokot, Marakwet, Tugen, Keiyo, Kipsigis, and especially the Nandi tribes that has produced most of the runners. Figure 6.13 shows that a runner from the Nandi tribe has a 23-fold higher probability of achieving success in running than does his average Kenyan counterpart. In contrast, vast tracts of the eastern half of Kenya have produced few, if any, great runners.

Some of the biological factors that might explain the dominance of the Kenyans are discussed in greater detail later in this chapter. Bale and Sang (1996) have offered some possible explanations for their extraordinary success. They suggest that the Nandi have the greatest tradition of individualism and competitiveness, which included sustained resistance to British dominance in the 1890s and extensive participation in cattle raiding, the "sport" of the Nandis. To discourage cattle raiding, the British targeted the Nandi by introducing running as a distraction. The result was that by 1937 Rift Valley athletic teams were dominated by the Nandi.

One possible explanation for the concentration of athletic talent among the Nandi is precisely the selective effects of their sport, cattle raiding. It has been proposed that the best runners would acquire the most cattle and survive for the longest by evading the spears of the recently dispossessed cattle owners. As a result, according to African custom, the best runners would procure the most wives. In this way, any genes determining running ability would tend to be conserved in the offspring of the most successful runners, whereas those without such a hereditary advantage would either die in their unsuccessful quest to acquire cattle or go unmarried. As a result, "Down through the generations, as the raiding life killed off slow runners and made fathers of the swift, the tribes must have distilled their talent. And so the Kalenjin men became not explosively muscular, but lean and tireless" (Bale and Sang 1996).

Mike Boit, the legendary Kenyan who finished third in the 800 m at the 1972

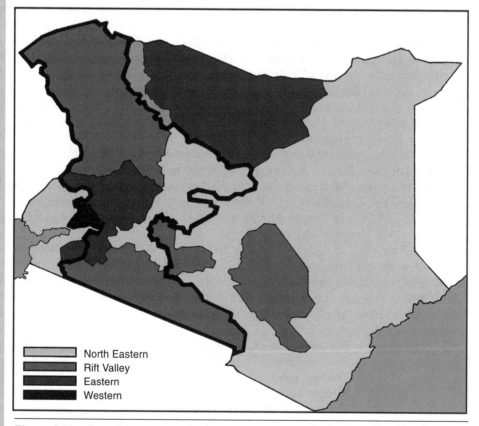

North Eastern
Rift Valley
Eastern
Western

Figure 6.13 Geographical origins of elite Kenyan distance runners. Although the Rift Valley, which comprises the Western border of Kenya, contains only 20% of the population, it accounts for 72% of elite Kenyan runners. Within the Rift Valley, the Pokot, Marakwet, Tugen, Keiyo, Kipsigis, and especially the Nandi regions, comprising a population of 2 million, produce approximately 45% of the top three finishers in all international distance races, from 1500 m to the marathon.
Adapted from J. Bale and Sang (1996, p 157).

(continued)

Munich Olympic Games (and was favored to do even better in the 1976 Games at Montreal before his country withdrew), has confirmed that this way of life was part of his heritage and could perhaps have contributed to his own success:

My tribe especially practiced a lot of cattle rustling. . . . It has been important for our society that those who could run long distances to bring back the cows survived, those who couldn't literally fell by the wayside [were killed by the Masai]. You had to pay big dowries to get married and if you were not strong enough to go out and collect two or three cows to pay the dowry, well in the end, no one would be willing to keep you. It was, literally, survival of the fittest, the strongest. (Ward 1989, p. 22)

When the British took control of East Africa, they no longer tolerated cattle raiding; they jailed the Kalenjin raiders and put them to work building running tracks. As the Nandi were the most frequent offenders, a disproportionate number of running tracks were built in their area. This laid the foundations for the Kenyan dominance of international long-distance running (SA Sports Illustrated 1992).

Manners (1998) has assessed whether factors other than this process of genetic selection may be important determinants of the success of the Kalenjin. He discounts altitude as a factor because other countries of moderate altitude, such as Nepal, Peru, and Lesotho, have not produced an equal concentration of great runners. Similarly, other tribes in Kenya live at altitude but have not produced great runners with the same frequency as the Kalenjin. Rather, Manners suggests that altitude provides the cool equatorial conditions ideal for year-round training, as well as the ideal open countryside for training long distances. Food is sufficient, and there is little malnutrition. Literacy is high, and most children attend school; therefore, they can be introduced to athletics. Yet, Kenyans are sufficiently poor in monetary terms that earning as little as $10,000 per year as a professional athlete in North America or Europe would equal 10 years' income in Kenya.

The Kalenjin's high-carbohydrate diet (D.L. Christensen et al. 1998) is not substantially different from that of subsistence farmers elsewhere in the world. Material incentives too cannot explain why the Kalenjin were already successful before runners could earn material wealth from their sport or why these incentives have failed to stimulate all the Kenyan tribes to emulate the performances of the Kalenjin.

Manners also discounts the explanation that the Kenyans become great by running to school. According to Paul Tergat, who has won the World Cross-Country Championships a record five times, this is quite simply "a myth." He continues, "In my case, home to school was just 800 m. In fact, I didn't even like running at school and I wasn't particularly good at it. It was only when I went into the armed forces and I was made to run that I discovered I had a talent for it" (Mackay 1999). Tergat's explanation for the Kenyan success is the following:

You believe Kenyan training sessions are impossible, but without trying it has no meaning. No matter how far, how hard—you must do it with your whole mind, your whole heart, and then everything is possible. Winning is ultimately in the mind. . . . No nation trains as hard as Kenya. Natural talent is not enough. To achieve something in sport, as in life, you have to work hard every day. (Mackay 1999, p. 50)

Derek Clayton

The Australian Derek Clayton was the first runner to break the 2:10:00 and the 2:09:00 time barriers for the standard marathon. His world record of 2:08:34, set in Antwerp on 30 May, 1969, lasted 12 years until it was officially broken by Robert de Castella in the 1981 Fukuoka Marathon.

Clayton is another example of a frustrated miler who found his niche in the marathon. With only a mediocre 400-m speed (52.8), Clayton realized that he would never emulate the achievements in the mile of the greatest of all Australian runners, Herb Elliott (Clayton 1980). As a result, he gradually lengthened the distances he raced on the track to 5000 m, and in his first serious marathon in October 1965, he became the Australian record holder with a time of 2:22:12. "Suddenly," he later wrote, "I was number one in something I never planned to excel in—the marathon. I had proof that I wasn't wasting my time. After years of searching, I had found my distance. I was on my way to the top" (Clayton 1980, p. 42 to 43).

Clayton's training was very hard (table 6.13). He regularly ran between 192 and 256 km per week and on two occasions ran over 320 km in a week (Wilt 1973). His total mileage for his average week was approximately 240 km. He also wrote that his interval training was 4×1 mile, and he recognized overtiredness, lethargy, and quick temper as features of overtraining (Clayton 1980).

Two features of Clayton's running career suggest that he trained too hard. He suffered a string of injuries—many of which required surgery, including four operations to his Achilles tendons, two to his knees, and one for a heel spur (Clayton 1980). Looking back, he wrote,

Unfortunately, I didn't heed my injuries, I challenged them. . . . Now I would show an injury the respect it deserves. I would rest it, exercise it, and if need be, stop

Table 6.13 Derek Clayton's training week		
Day	**Morning**	**Afternoon**
Monday	8–11 km (easy)	27 km (fast)
Tuesday	8–11 km (easy)	19 km (medium)
Wednesday	8–11 km (easy)	22 km (fast, hills)
Thursday	8–11 km (easy)	22 km (fast, hills)
Friday	8–11 km (easy)	16 km (easy)
Saturday	7 km (easy)	40 km in 2:20
Sunday	27–32 km (hills)	16 km (medium)

From Wilt (1973, p.34). © 1973 by Track and Field News. Adapted by permission.

running until it healed. Such an attitude during my competitive years might have
kept me off the operating table a few times. (Clayton 1980, p. 120)

Most of his world records came in the wake of protracted layoffs from serious
injuries (the *Zatopek phenomenon*, discussed in chapter 7), indicating that had he
rested more, he would probably have been even better (Benyo 1983).

Ron Hill

The British runner Ron Hill (figure 6.14) ran his best marathon races in 1969 and
1970, including the world's second fastest marathon ever (2:09:28), and was favored by many to win the 1972 Olympic Games Marathon. His PhD in chemistry
makes Hill one of the most academically qualified of all elite marathon runners.
Hill has also written two autobiographical books (R. Hill 1981; 1982) that describe
his running career in unmatched detail. His courage
in highlighting both his successes and his failures will
ensure that his books fulfill one of the goals he had in
writing them—namely, to teach runners where he went
wrong in the hope that they will not repeat his errors.

Figure 6.14 Ron Hill wins his
greatest race, the 1970 Commonwealth Games Marathon in
Edinburgh. His winning time of
2:09:28 was then the second fastest
marathon performance of all time
and may have been the fastest ever
on an accurately measured course.
From R. Hill (1981, p. 118). © 1981 by
Ron Hill. Reprinted with permission.

I was particularly interested in reading Hill's autobiography to find out whether there were any clues to
explain why he had not won the 1972 Olympic Marathon. It was an analysis that, not surprisingly, Hill only
made in retrospect. For that is the nature of all runners, including myself: we are so engrossed in the process of being runners that we cannot be expected to
also be objective about our own running. Yet, those
athletes who, like Bruce Fordyce, retain detached ob-
jectivity in their running are ultimately the most successful.

Hill, born in 1938, finished ninth in his first race: his
school's cross-country championships, in 1951. In 1954
he joined the local running club and for the next two
years his training was "infrequent, unplanned, and un-
scientific." He was coached by a man who trained only
in winter and who "speeded up whenever he came near
passers-by and then slowed down when there was no-
one around." (Hill 1981, p. 18) When he enrolled at
Manchester University in 1957, Hill started training and
racing cross-country and short road races regularly. He
ran his first marathon in 1961, finishing first in a time
of 2:24:22. For the seven weeks before that race, Hill
had averaged about 120 km per week. He entered a
further five marathons (with a best time of 2:14:12 on
30 June, 1964) before finishing nineteenth in 2:25:34 in
the 1964 Olympic Marathon in Tokyo. This characteristic of running extremely well prior to, but failing in,
major Olympic competition was to become a depress-
ing feature of Hill's running career.

Hill's book explains that he ran that race on "dead legs," a usual sign of overtraining (chapter 7), but he did not exhibit the other features of the overtraining syndrome—in particular, a series of poor running performances preceding the really bad race. In his last two races (at distances up to 11 km) in the two weeks before the marathon, Hill set two personal records. There is no clear explanation for his poor performance in those Olympic Games. Possibly it had something to do with traveling to and competing in a foreign country.

During the next four years leading up to the 1968 Olympic Games in Mexico City, Hill continued to specialize as a short-distance racer on the track, on the roads, and in cross-country. During this period he ran a total of six marathons, five between 2:20:55 and 2:27:21. His best and only marathon in 1968 produced the second-best time of his career at that stage, 2:17:11. Table 6.14 shows Hill's weekly training routine at this point in his career.

In training, Hill set a world record for 16 km on the track and ran an exceptional 10,000 m at medium altitude in the 1968 Olympic Games, finishing seventh in 29:53. He was the first athlete who had not trained at altitude for any meaningful period to finish, and he was only one place behind Ron Clarke, who almost certainly would have won the race had it been run at sea level. It was on the strength of this performance that Hill decided to attempt the 10,000 m and marathon double in the 1969 European Games. As a result, he began to race marathons more frequently and at a higher intensity.

Table 6.14 Ron Hill's training week for October 1968		
Day	**Morning**	**Afternoon**
Monday	11 km	16 km including fartlek
Tuesday	11 km	14.5 km including 12 × 01:10 bursts with 0:50 intervals in sets of 2, 4, and 6
Wednesday	11 km	19 km including two sets of number stride fartlek, usually up to 55 strides, then down*
Thursday	11 km	13 km
Friday	11 km	11 km
Saturday	Race	33 km with one monthly run of 45 km
Sunday	Rest	

Hill alternated two cycles of training on Monday, Tuesday, and Wednesday afternoons. On the first and third week of any month, he would perform the training described above; on the second and fourth week of the month, he would do the following:

Monday: 2 × 2:00 bursts with 1:30 rest interval; up to 20 × 0:30 bursts with 0:30 rest intervals; 2 × 2:00 bursts
Tuesday: 3 × 1.6 km fast with 0.8 km rest interval
Wednesday: Hard bursts on all the hills

* Hill defines "number stride fartlek" as running hard while counting double strides, then running the same number of double strides at an easy pace.
From R. Hill (1981, pp. 386–97). © 1981 by Ron Hill Sports Ltd. Adapted by permission.

In the next two years, Hill ran eight marathons, including the fastest (2:09:28), second fastest (2:10:30), third fastest (2:11:13), fifth fastest (2:12:39), ninth fastest (2:13:42), eleventh fastest (2:14:35), twelfth fastest (2:15:27), and fifteenth fastest (2:16:48) times in his serious marathon racing career, which lasted for seven and a half more years. Interestingly, Hill's three best marathon races were run in ascending sequence between 7 December, 1969, (the Fukuoka Marathon) and the Commonwealth Games Marathon in July 1970. Sadly, this was the premature peak of Hill's career, and he would never again be the same force in world marathon running. Hill also began to experiment with the carbohydrate-depletion/carbohydrate-loading diet and used it successfully in all his best marathons.

The first inkling of impending disaster came at the Fukuoka Marathon in December 1970, when Hill finished a disappointing ninth in 2:15:27. His comment after the race was that he never believed he would ever run so slowly again. Ironically, his time would prove to be even faster than the time he would run in the race he most wanted to win—the 1972 Olympic Games Marathon.

The explanation for Hill's poor race seems clear. He admitted that in training for that race he altered his training methods:

> I wondered what would happen if I went beyond my 120 to 130 miles per week. Would I reach another plane of fitness and capability? I had to find out. . . . But I was never really happy. A lot of the time, I felt slightly fatigued and towards the end of this increased training stint, I seemed to be doing nothing but changing in and out of running gear. (Hill 1981, p. 130-31)

The week before the race, Hill ran his highest-ever mileage, a massive 264 km, which left him with a sore throat and no competitive desire during the race.

For the next three months, Hill was troubled by a succession of six throat and chest infections. However, despite these symptoms, Hill continued to train up to 190 km per week and raced frequently, with atrocious results. Finally, in April, he reduced his average weekly training distance to 105 km and was well enough to run a 2:12:39 marathon in July and a 2:14:35 marathon in the European Marathon Championships in Helsinki in August. These races were the fifth and eleventh fastest of his career.

After the Helsinki marathon, Hill (1982) wrote,

> The successful pattern of training I have evolved over the years I feel is unique among marathon runners. This involves a series of peaks, averaging about three per year, followed by "rests." My usual rest is about four weeks, averaging 40 miles (64 km) per week and my ideal build-up to a peak occupies a period of 10 weeks. (p. 160)

Hill was also critical, justifiably in my view, of the need to prequalify for selection to the Olympic and other teams by running marathon races within three or so months of the competition. He wrote that "once the trial is over, a large measure of inspiration has gone, and the feeling is, 'I've made it,' when this is not the case at all. Usually there is not enough left for the really big race." (Hill 1982, p. 161) He also wrote something that would ultimately apply to his own career: "You may have noticed that most top marathon runners do not last long. Bikila was an exception and he raced infrequently. The others have been more or less specialist marathonmen and I am convinced that you can become marathon 'punch-drunk.' These people usually retire or deteriorate rapidly." (Hill 1982, p. 161)

In March 1972, Hill began his eight-week build-up for the British Olympic Marathon trial, in which he finished second in 2:12:51, the sixth best time of his career. After a month of reduced training, he commenced his buildup for the Olympics with two important changes in his usual routine. First, he planned to continue his peaking for 10 weeks rather than 8 because he "hoped that this extra work would lead to an extra-special performance." (Hill 1982, p. 198) He did this despite the fact that on the last occasion when he had done extra work, before the Fukuoka Marathon, the results had been disastrous.

Second, he was to train at altitude for three of the last four weeks before the marathon, despite having done a negligible amount of altitude training in his entire running career. By contrast, Frank Shorter, the athlete who would ultimately win the 1972 Olympic Marathon, had found through personal experience that after training at altitude he required at least two weeks at sea level before his speed again returned. At altitude Hill was faced with the unexpected problem of cold; he did not reduce the amount he trained, with the result that most of the time he felt "knackered," and his speed sessions were poor, which "was not surprising, considering the state of my legs." (Hill 1982, p. 204) Going to the start of the marathon, he noted that he did not "feel as bouncy or springy as he had felt before some marathons." (Hill 1982, p. 214) During the first 800 m of the race, he noted that the pace seemed much faster than what he was actually running; this almost certainly is because at altitude he had not been able to train at his peak speed, and he had not left himself sufficient time to reacclimatize once he returned to sea level.

During the race Hill was never a factor, feeling "rough" after only 5 km, at which point he fell off the pace, ultimately finishing a tired sixth in 2:16:31. For the man who had predicted on national television that the Olympic Marathon gold medal was his, this must have been a humiliating experience.

The remainder of Hill's running career is notable for two reasons. First, he continued to train twice per day and once on Sundays, just as he had since 1964—thus laying claim to the world's longest running streak. This compulsion for running tells much about Hill's personality and may explain some of the errors he made during his running career. Second, he subsequently ran some very good marathons on considerably less training than he had done before the Olympic Marathon. For example, he ran the fourth fastest (2:12:34) and eighth fastest (2:13:28) marathons of his career in April and June 1975, during a period when his average weekly training distance was only 112 km. After a similar experience in 1973 he wrote,

Winning the Enschede at the end of a rest period, on an average of only 56 miles a week, and in 2:18:06, on a hot day, and with very little effort, made me think. Yes! It made me think that 120 to 130 miles per week perhaps weren't absolutely necessary for good marathon performances. (Hill 1982, p. 253)

Hill's racing record again confirms that heavier training is as likely to produce worse racing performances as it is to produce better performances. This is clearly shown in figure 6.15, which depicts Hill's weekly training distances during his buildup periods for his 10 best marathon races. As mentioned earlier, Hill ran his fourth and eighth best marathons on his lightest training. Figure 6.16 compares Hill's training for other races in which his performances were similar but for which his training was quite different. The left panel shows races for which he trained heavily; the right panel shows races for which he trained relatively lightly, yet in which he performed no worse than when he ran almost twice as far in training.

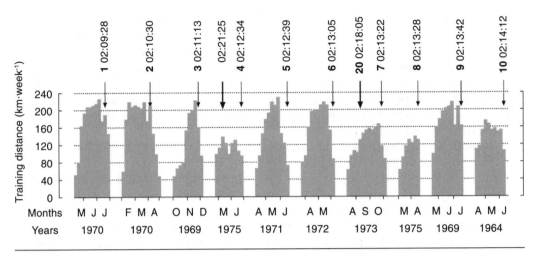

Figure 6.15 Ron Hill's weekly training distances for his 10 fastest marathons.

Significantly, if we were to apply statistical techniques to analyze the relationship between Hill's training load and his marathon performances, we would be forced to conclude that there was no statistical relationship between the amount of training he did for his various races and his subsequent performances in those races. In fact, as can be seen from figure 6.17, Hill clearly showed a training distance above which his marathon racing performance fell precipitously as he trained ever harder. According to this analysis, Hill's optimum training volume (that is, the training volume that produced his fastest marathon times) was about 160 km per week. Higher training volumes produced progressively slower performances.

This further indicates that the amount of training Hill did was not the most important factor determining his marathon performances. That he was able to run a 02:12:34 marathon on a training load of about 120 km per week reaffirms the critical importance of genetic ability, combined with appropriate but not too much training (see chapter 5, Law 6). At first, when determining your racing ability, try to achieve as much as possible on a minimum of training. Remember also that

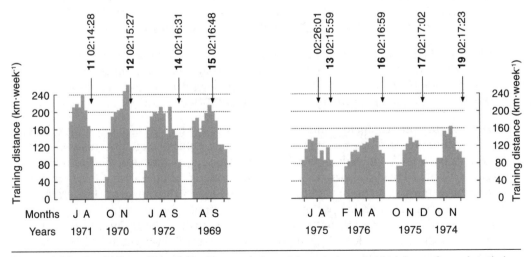

Figure 6.16 Ron Hill's weekly training distances before eight marathons in which he performed similarly

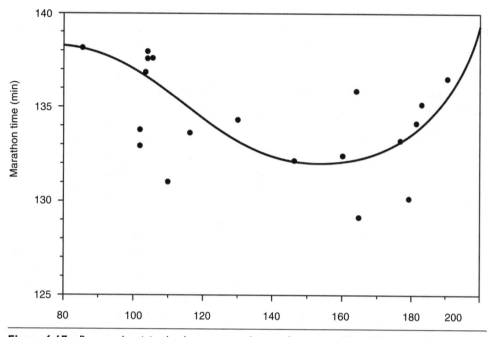

Figure 6.17 Reported training load versus marathon performance of Ron Hill: 1964-1975. Calculated from data in figures 6.15 and 6.16 by Carl Foster (1996).\

when Hill trained an average of 190 km per week for 10 weeks leading up to the 1972 Olympic Marathon, he managed a time of only 2:16:31 (figures 6.15 and 6.16).

Hill's marathon performances deteriorated when he started racing marathons regularly instead of competing in regular cross-country and short road races. Top American marathoner of the 1980s, Alberto Salazar, suffered the same fate and ascribes his failures to an overemphasis on training distance at the expense of quality training.

Hill suffered a prolonged three-month period of ill health, starting immediately after he had run six marathons, including what would be his three best ever in one 18-month period. Clearly he was, in his own words, marathon punch-drunk. It is possible that he might have done irreparable damage to his body or his mind during this period—damage that might explain why he never again reached the same heights in athletics.

Hill continued to do an excessive weekly mileage, even when he was quite ill. As he wrote: "Illness—colds, chest infections, bugs, sore throats—didn't stop me, just occasionally lowering the weekly mileage when I was really bad." As were all runners of the day, he was unaware that illness is an important sign of overtraining and indicates the absolute and urgent need for more rest, not more training.

Hill did not taper adequately for his major races, and this must surely have affected his performances adversely. Hill may have made the fundamental error of introducing change for change's sake at the most critical times in his career. This was most apparent before the 1972 Olympic Games Marathon when, despite never having trained at altitude for more than a few days, he committed himself to three weeks of altitude training just four weeks before the most important race of his life. There was no evidence then, as there is no evidence now, to suggest that a period of training at altitude inevitably improves sea-level racing performance.

The second change he made to his proven formula for success immediately before the 1972 Olympic Marathon was that he increased his peak training period by one week (see figure 6.15). A small change, you might think, but one that might have been critical if, as I suspect, he really needed to peak only for six weeks and had, in reality, already been going downhill physically when he ran his best races after the nine-week peaking period. Under those circumstances, the extra week of heavy training would have made the crucial difference. The evidence that suggests that Hill probably needed to peak for only six weeks was his statement that he usually felt a training breakthrough after about five weeks of heavy training. Thereafter, his relatively poorer racing performances (due to his heavy training) suddenly improved dramatically so that despite the continued heavy training, he was running near personal best times. If only he had begun his taper then, instead of wearing himself out by continued excessive training.

That Hill was unable to stick to the winning formula he discovered in 1969 to 1970, but chose to train harder in the hope that this would improve his performance, is a common response among runners. His experience brings to mind the wisdom in Coach Bill Bowerman's famous dictum: "If it works, don't fix it." Hill was unquestionably hindered in his career by having to hold down a full-time job. Above and beyond the personal errors that he made in his training, the fact that he had to work would have contributed to his poor performance at the 1972 Olympic Games, when he was forced to compete against athletes like Frank Shorter, who had no such commitments.

Ultimately, I suspect that it was the fanaticism that Hill shares with so many equally driven and obsessive runners that was the real cause of his few but important failures; he simply wanted to win too much. As stated by Frank Shorter, the ultimate winner of the 1972 Olympic Games Marathon, Hill was "too precise, too compulsive and too given to the scientific method" (Shorter and Bloom 1984, p. 77). Shorter preferred his own more intuitive approach (Shorter and Bloom 1984). Hill's career provides one of the best examples of why it is so important to follow the 6th Law of Training (chapter 5): "At first try to achieve as much as possible on a minimum of training." Had his "scientific method" included the experiment to identify his optimum training load (figures 5.6 and 6.17), perhaps his career would have been even more successful and might have included a gold medal in the 1972 Munich Olympic Marathon. Instead, that honor went to an American legend.

Frank Shorter

American Frank Shorter (figure 6.18) has been labeled "the man who invented the marathon," (Sandrock 1996) a title he vehemently rejects. His victory in the 1972 Munich Olympic Marathon and his second place in the 1976 Montreal Olympic Marathon, both of which were screened live on television, are believed to be the two most important events that stimulated the subsequent running explosion in the United States (Benyo 1983). I have included Shorter in this chapter to make four important points.

Shorter was not a champion athlete at school, nor even for most of his university career. This fact becomes important when discussing whether young athletes should be encouraged to strive for international success at an early age.

Shorter studied law at Yale, an Ivy League university with no athletic scholarship program and with only a volunteer track team. Conflicting interests involving skiing, studying, and singing in the choir kept Shorter from any intensive training during his first three years there. Only in his senior year, when his coach, Bob Giegengack, suggested he could become the world's best marathoner, did Shorter start to train seriously, winning the American Collegiate 6-mile title and achieving second place in the 3-mile event (Shorter and Bloom 1984).

After graduation, Shorter's performances on the track improved progressively, and his interest in the marathon was kindled. Besides his Olympic medals, Shorter's outstanding marathon achievements were his string of four consecutive victories between 1971 and 1974 in the Fukuoka Marathon, including the then third fastest marathon ever in the 1972 race.

The second important feature of Shorter's running career was that he trained initially as a track and cross-country athlete. He specialized in the 10,000 m but was also very competitive at distances as short as 2 miles. Shorter was by no means the first athlete with a track background to run the marathon. Of the runners already mentioned

Figure 6.18   American Frank Shorter winning the 1972 Olympic Games Marathon, the run that likely launched the marathon explosion of the mid- to late 1970s.

© The Bettmann Archive.

in this chapter, Kolehmainen, Nurmi, Zatopek, Peters, Edelen, Clayton, and Hill were all fast track or cross-country runners who moved up to the marathon distance.

Third, from the time Shorter ran his first serious marathon in June 1971, in which he finished second in 2:17:45, until his last competitive marathon race on 24 October, 1976, he entered 15 marathons, winning 10, finishing second three times, finishing fourth once, and failing to finish once. His career-best time of 2:10:30 came in only his sixth marathon. His second-last serious race, the 1976 Olympic Games Marathon, which was run in wet conditions that did not suit him, produced the second-best time of his career (2:10:46). In all, Shorter ran five races faster than 2:12:00 and 10 faster than 2:16:00. The average of his five fastest races was 2:11:17.

The explanation for Shorter's exceptional winning record over what, for a marathon runner, was a very long career must be found in his belief in the importance of peaking and of running only a few serious races each year. He wrote that it was "almost impossible to be in peak form twice in the same season," and for this reason, the only races for which he ever peaked were the Fukuoka and Olympic marathons. His inspiration for this approach seems to have come from other great peakers, for he wrote:

Historically, the peakers—the real peakers who pick their spots—win at the Olympics. Look at Lasse Viren or Waldemar Cierpinski or Kip Keino or Miruts Yifter, or even me. It's almost impossible for a distance runner to do both—to race frequently in top form in major competitions year in and year out and also fare well in the Olympics—Viren, at his best, was always in control. He had the peaking process down pat. (Shorter and Bloom 1984, pp. 149-50).

Shorter also recognized the psychological hold that this gave Viren over his competitors:

The mere fact that everyone is so concerned about that shows what kind of control he has over his competitors. . . . The best thing you can have is everybody thinking about you. What you might be doing, what you might be taking. It's great, let them think about you. You go train. (Hauman 1996, p. 78)

Unfortunately, little is recorded of how Shorter actually trained. Two quite different sample training weeks are found in an article by Wilt (1973) and in Shorter's autobiography (Shorter and Bloom 1984). The latter is included in table 6.15. A third sample training week, published in Sandrock (1996), is similar but not identical to table 6.16, which calls into question the general accuracy of these purported training programs. Nevertheless, Shorter summarized his training philosophy as follows:

I've always had a simple view of training for distance running; two hard interval sessions a week and one long run—20 miles or two hours, whichever comes first. Every other run is aerobic, and you do as much of that for volume as you can handle. Do this for two or three years, and you'll get good. (Sandrock 1996, p. 156)

Another point Shorter made in his autobiography is that after a period of training at altitude he required a period of 10 to 14 days at sea level before he was again at his best. It is likely that this time is required for the muscles to readapt to the faster running speed possible at sea level. As discussed, Ron Hill failed to allow for this recovery period at sea level immediately before the 1972 Olympics and paid the price.

Shorter also wrote that he did not run well in the rain. Because he did not dissipate heat very well, he got cold easily. "Rain stiffens me up, tightens my muscles, so I'm not as loose as I might be. My stride changes; therefore my form changes." All these symptoms suggest that Shorter's body, but particularly his muscle temperature, was sensitive to the cold and that even under what might normally be considered quite mild conditions, these temperatures were likely to fall, causing the muscle stiffness he described (see also chapter 4).

Shorter also noted that he could run a hard 10,000-m race a week before a marathon—as he did at the 1972 Olympics, in which he finished fifth in the 10,000-m final just five days before his marathon victory—but that he could not run a hard marathon even 10 weeks before another one. He also found that he could tell "in the first quarter-mile of a race whether or not [he would] have a good day." This feeling he described as "either being there, or [not]." He said, "I've learned I can't talk myself into this feeling." (Shorter and Bloom 1984, p. 78) I interpret this feeling, which I have also experienced, as evidence that the brain monitors sensory input from the body at a subconscious level from the moment exercise begins. Once the subconscious brain has decided how well the body can perform on that day, it resets the

Table 6.15 Frank Shorter's training week		
Day	**Morning**	**Afternoon**
Monday	11 km at 4:00–4:23 per km	16 km at 4:00 per km
Tuesday	Same as Monday	4 × 1200 m (3:06–3:12 per km)
Wednesday	Same as Monday	Same as Monday
Thursday	Same as Monday	12 × 400 m (1:00–1:01 per km)
Friday	Same as Monday	Same as Monday
Saturday	Same as Monday	Race 16 km
Sunday	32 km (first 16 km at 4:00 per km; last 16 km at close to 3:07 per km)	

From Shorter and Bloom (1984).©1984 by Frank Shorter and Marc Bloom. Reprinted by permission of George Borchardt, Inc., on behalf of the authors.

central governor and then informs your conscious mind of what you can expect—either an easy or a hard race. Since most of us believe that running performance is determined by the conscious brain, not the subconscious, we attempt to override that vital information, often with predictable results.

Shorter is also one of the few Olympic Marathon champions about whose physiology something is known. His $\dot{V}O_2$max value in 1976 was 71.3 ml O_2 per kg per minute (Pollock 1977), and his gastrocnemius muscle comprised 80% Type I fibers (Fink et al. 1977); he was 1.78 m tall and weighed 61 kg; his body fat content was 2.2% (Pollock et al. 1977). Shorter was an extremely efficient runner (Pollock 1977) whose running economy was equivalent to Derek Clayton's (see figure 2.8). Calculations showed that he sustained an exercise intensity of at least 80% when he won his Olympic gold medal (Pollock 1977), an intensity equivalent to that sustained by other world-class runners (see figure 2.13).

A fourth reason for including Shorter's biography is that he is one of the few great runners who has allowed another side of his life to be exposed: his relationship with an abusive, unsupportive father who, unlike the rest of North America, chose not to watch his son's Olympic marathon races. Thus, Shorter has stated that his father's decision to move from a lucrative medical practice in New York to become a missionary doctor to mostly Mexican-Americans and American Indians in Taos, New Mexico, was perhaps motivated by a desire for atonement for "lots of abuse, lots of philandering, lots of drunkenness. . . . Fortunately, my mother recognized the abuse and got me into boarding school by the time I was 10 years old. Although she was too passive to prevent the abuse, she was smart enough to get me out of there" (Boga 1993, p. 23).

Boga (1993) concludes that like many runners, Shorter ran against himself; he turned his aggressive feelings inward: "If not for his ability to sublimate aggression into long-distance running, to sweat the meanness out of himself, he might have become just another of life's losers. And we would have been deprived of so many transcendent moments" (Boga 1993, p. 23).

Shorter continued to run competitively in the 1980s and 1990s, competing in veteran athletics after he turned 40. Although he ran poorly in the 1980 U.S. Olympic Marathon trial, finishing in 2:23:24, the next year he finished third in the Chicago Marathon in 2:17:28. In 1987 he was still able to run the marathon in 02:36:54 and even ran a mile indoors in 4:21:95, beating both Jim Ryun and Peter Snell. In 1988, he reduced his running training and began to include cycling up to 70 km per week so that he could race the duathalon. He continues to train hard and lives in Boulder, Colorado, where a statue on the campus of the University of Colorado immortalizes his achievement, not least in overcoming a potentially crippling adversity.

Grete Waitz

Of all the athletes, male and female, who have achieved excellence in the last 50 years, Norwegian Grete Waitz (figure 6.19) has probably been one of the most charismatic. Certainly no other runner has done so much to promote women's running. Her influence on the progress of the women's world 42-km marathon record between 1978 and 1980 was similar to that of Jim Peters between 1952 and 1954.

Born in 1953, Waitz started running at 12 years of age and won her first race, a 400-m cross-country event, when she was 14. By 16 she was the Norwegian Junior Champion at 400 and 800 m. The following year (1971), aged 17, she set Norwegian records in the 800 m and 1500 m and competed in her first European Championships. In 1972 she recorded her personal best 1500 m time of 4:16 at the Munich Olympic Games. In 1974 she finished third in the same event at the European Championships in Rome and was named Norwegian Athlete of the Year for 1974.

In 1975 she was ranked number one in the world in the 1500 and 3000 m and set a world record in the 3000 m (8:46.6). In 1976 she reached the 1500-m semifinals at the Montreal Olympics and set another world record in the 3000 m (8:45.4). In 1977 and 1978 she was again ranked number one in the world in the 3000 m after winning the 3000 m at the 1977 World Cup and finishing third in the same race in the 1978 European Championships. However, it was only when she turned to road running that Waitz became an international running celebrity. Indeed, it was only at the insistence of her husband, Jack, that she took to road running rather than retiring from athletics in 1977.

Instead, in her first major road race, the 1978 New York City Marathon, she set a world best time of 2:32:30. In the 1979 race, she became the first woman to run 42 km in less than 2:30:00, finishing in 2:27:33, and in 1980 she lowered the world record further to 2:25:42. She set the world marathon record four times and won the New York City Marathon nine times. In addition, between 1978 and 1983, she won the International Amateur Athletics Federation's (IAAF) World Cross-Country Championships five times, and in 1983 she set another world marathon best of 2:25:29 in the London Marathon and won the inaugural IAAF World Championships Marathon in 2:28:09. The following year, she was second in the inaugural Los Angeles Olympic Games Marathon in 2:26:18. Five times between 1978 and 1983 she was ranked first in the world in the women's marathon by *Track and Field News*. Her consistency in marathon running is matched by her success in cross-country and road racing, in which she was unbeaten until 1982 and 1983 respectively. In Norway she was unbeaten in competition from1972 to 1984. When she retired from competitive marathon running in the 1990 New York City Marathon, her tenth, she had driven women's running to a position almost equal to that of the men.

In her book, Waitz provides a beginners' training program (table 5.9) that she proposes will allow the former armchair athlete to run 5 km continuously within 10 weeks (Waitz and Averbuch 1986).

Waitz stresses that training for competitive racing is very individual and that the elements of her personal training program are building blocks upon which aspiring runners can fashion an adequate training program. She believes that the experiences of other athletes constitute one of the greatest available resources for any runner and that we all should learn and profit from one another.

She lists five definite training guidelines:

1. Have a definite goal.
2. Set realistic goals and be flexible.
3. Do not add to or change your running program too quickly—the body needs time to adapt.
4. Do not change something that works for you.
5. Follow the hard/easy principle.

Figure 6.19 Norwegian Grete Waitz on her way to winning the 1983 World Championships Marathon in Helsinki.

She states that hard/easy is a relative principle and that its application to individual runners depends on experience and ability. For some, one hard training session per week is sufficient; others can handle three or four, while others are still able to incorporate moderately difficult training sessions between their hard and easy days.

When it comes to competitive racing, Waitz suggests reducing the expectations you and those around you have of yourself. She believes in having a winning attitude, but she suggests that this should be kept to yourself and should not be broadcast to everyone. "It's great to be confident," she says, "but let your achievements speak louder than your words. . . . Never make a bold public statement" (Waitz and Averbuch 1986, pp. 158-59).

In contrast to the advice given in chapter 5, Waitz did not practice peaking except for the two major races of her career, the 1983 World Championships Marathon and the 1984 Los Angeles Olympic Marathon. She focused on each of these races for a full year. In general, she followed the approach of Pat Clohessy and Rob de Castella, both of whom considered it too risky to sacrifice everything for a single distant goal. She also found that the mental pressure of this approach took the enjoyment out of her training.

Waitz believes quality speed training is important for all runners, even for those who just want to complete the distance regardless of time. She emphasizes that her training for the marathon was fundamentally the same as her training for 3000-,

5000-, and 10,000-m races (table 6.16), except that her total mileage was higher. But she was never a high-mileage runner in the mold of other male and female marathoners, and her peak weekly mileage never went above 160 km (Sandrock 1996). She ran quickly in training, faster than 3:45 per km (6:00 per mile) most of the time. The major difference from her training as a track runner was the addition of a weekly long run of approximately 24 to 30 km leading up to the race. As described in this chapter, this approach is the same as that of the elite male marathon and ultramarathon runners.

Waitz believes that getting to the starting line healthy and running conservatively are vitally important, and she suggests that you should always start slowly, run conservatively, and aim to run a negative split (that is, a slower first half).

Waitz states that she never started a marathon race with the intention of running a particular time and that during the race she did not pay close attention to her time as this was too stressful. She learned from the few occasions on which she ran raced specifically to break records that the pressure of this approach was just too great—she was unable to relax. The result was that she did not pay sufficient attention to her body cues. She suggests that the marathon is too unpredictable a race to allow even the top runners to estimate their finishing times with certainty. Rather, "the marathon is the kind of race you must take one mile at a time, being flexible enough to adapt to the unknown and the unexpected."

For the first two weeks after a marathon, Waitz ran as she felt and did no speed training. She believes that regardless of the competitive ability of the athlete, there should be a minimum of six months between marathon races. In her entire marathon career, spanning 13 years, she ran only 19 marathons, winning 13. Physically, she felt she could run three marathons per year, but mentally she found it difficult to run more than one per year, a practice she maintained for her entire career.

Table 6.16	Grete Waitz's training week			
	Morning (5 to 6 A.M.)		**Afternoon (4 to 5 P.M.)**	
Day	**Distance**	**Time**	**Distance**	**Time**
Monday	10–15 km	40:00–60:00	10–15 km	40:00–60:00
Tuesday	Same as Monday		6–8 × 1000 m intervals, 1–2 min rest breaks (pulse 180)	
Wednesday	Same as Monday		Rest	
Thursday	Same as Monday		Fartlek, 13 km; several 500-m sprints	
Friday	Same as Monday		Same as Monday	
Saturday	Same as Monday		15–20 × 300 m (pulse 180)	
Sunday	20–33 km fast pace distance run		Rest	

Reprinted by permission of Warner books/New York. From Waitz and Averbuch (1986, p. 106). © 1986 by Grete Waitz and Gloria Averbuch.

After the 1990 New York City Marathon, Waitz retired to live in her twin homes in Gainesville, Florida, and in Oslo, Norway. She returned to the 1992 New York City Marathon to escort Fred Lebow, the race director, who had terminal brain cancer, over the course, finishing in 5:32:34.

In her home town, Waitz is immortalized in a statue erected outside the Bislett Stadium. In addition, the Grete Waitz 5-km Run in Oslo attracts upwards of 50,000 female runners annually.

Dave Bedford

Dave Bedford, the British runner of the 1970s, set a world record of 27:30.8 for 10,000 m on the track in 1973 but achieved little other international success. I have included his training methods here (table 6.17) to warn future runners once more of the dangers of trying to do too much. Indeed, the sad conclusion that emerges from some of the biographies in this chapter is how many of the world's greatest runners of all time wore themselves out prematurely by running too much and racing, especially marathons, too frequently.

In his book, Temple (1980) states that it will take 10 or 20 years before we can say whether Bedford trained too much. I believe unquestionably that, like Clayton, Bedford tried too hard and trained too much. The proof is that he ran his best when his training had been curtailed by injury. His relatively poor competitive record in major international races might suggest that he lacked the winner's mind and thus tried to run his doubts away by training hard, but this I find difficult to believe. It is more likely that he was always overtrained and was therefore only occasionally able to run to his potential.

In answer to this criticism, Bedford stated that in reality he only ran more than 320 km in a week five times in his running career and that his average weekly training distance was between 260 and 280 km (Aitken 1984). I conclude, then, that 260 km per week of training is too much.

Table 6.17	Dave Bedford's training week		
Day	**Morning**	**Noon**	**Afternoon**
Monday	16 km	10 km	19 km
Tuesday	16 km	10 km	8 km plus 8 × 800 m in 2:12
Wednesday	16 km	10 km	6 km
Thursday	16 km	10 km	15 km plus 30 × 200 m
Friday	8 km	10 km	24 km
Saturday	8 km	24 km	16 km (fartlek)
Sunday	8 km	32 km	8 km
Total	300 km		

Data compiled from Temple (1980, p. 95). © 1980 by Stanley Paul.

Robert de Castella

Robert (Deek) de Castella began running with his father at the age of 12. When he was 14, he was coached seriously for the first time by the Australian National Distance Coach, Pat Clohessy, when he was 14. (Lenton 1982; 1983b; de Castella and Jenkinson 1984).

Clohessy started the young athlete on a training program of 60 to 80 km per week, including a long run of up to 21 km, shorter recovery runs, and hill and track work, typically 6 to 8 × 200 to 400 m. By age 18, de Castella set Australian under-19 records from 3000 to 10,000 m, and his junior time of 08:44 for 2 miles eclipsed the previous Australian record held by Herb Elliott.

De Castella's performance improved little between 1976 and 1979, but his eighth-place finish in the 1979 Cinque Mulini International Cross-Country race made him realize that he had the potential to rise to the top. Determined to succeed, he started the training program that he followed for the remainder of his competitive career (table 6.18; Lenton 1982; de Castella and Jenkinson 1984).

On this training scheme, de Castella ran the world's fastest marathon (2:08:18 at Fukuoka in 1981), the fastest time ever on an out-and-back course. He also won the marathons at the 1982 Brisbane Commonwealth Championships and 1983 Helsinki World Championships convincingly. In addition, he won the 1983 Rotterdam Marathon, which was specially staged to determine which of the three—de Castella, Salazar, or Olympic champion Carlos Lopes—was "the best." The result was that, by the end of 1983, de Castella was both the official world champion and the best marathoner in the world. His 1981 Fukuoka Marathon time was an improvement of 2:26 on his previous best, and his time of 2:09:18 in the Brisbane Commonwealth Games Marathon on a hilly course in hot, humid conditions is considered by some, including Ron Clarke, to have been the best marathon ever run up to that time. During this period, de Castella also twice finished sixth in the World Cross-Country Championships in 1981 and 1983.

Table 6.18   Robert de Castella's training week

Day	Morning	Afternoon
Monday	10 km (38:00)	16 km (60:00)
Tuesday	10 km (38:00)	10 km (38:00); 12 × 200 m
Wednesday	10 km (38:00)	29 km (hilly; 1:50:00)
Thursday	10 km (38:00)	10 km (38:00); 8 × 400 in 1:03–1:04 with a 0:45 recovery
Friday	10 km (38:00)	18 km (64:45)
Saturday	19–21 km (3:36 per km); 6 × 100 m	Race or 10 km (38:00)
Sunday	33–36 km (2:25–2:40)	8 km (31:00)
Total	208 km	

From de Castella and Jenkinson (1984, pp. 33–34). © 1984 by R. de Castella and M. Jenkinson.

Touchline Media

Figure 6.20 Robert de Castella wins the 1986 Commonwealth Games Marathon in Edinburgh.

The years 1984 and 1985 proved to be low points in de Castella's career. He ran relatively poorly in the 1984 Olympic Games Marathon, finishing fifth in 2:11:12, and was well beaten by Steve Jones in both the 1984 and 1985 Chicago Marathons. He ascribes his failures to being overmotivated and to training a little too hard, particularly when tired (Mehaffey 1986; Sandrock 1996). Interestingly, he did not race any marathons in the 12 months before the 1984 Olympic Marathon (Sandrock 1996).

However, his relocation to the medium altitude of Boulder, Colorado, and his adoption of a more relaxed approach, including doing less training, particularly when tired, seems to have rejuvenated de Castella, and his 2:07:51 in the 1986 Boston Marathon made him the world's third-fastest marathoner at the time, behind Lopes and Jones. In the same year, he repeated his victory in the 1986 Commonwealth Games Marathon, winning in 2:10:15. After four disappointing marathon races—namely the 1986 New York City Marathon, in which he finished third in 2:11:43; the 1987 IAAF World Athletics Championships in Rome; the 1988 Olympic Games Marathon, where he finished 13th; and the 1990 Commonwealth Games in Auckland, in which he finished in 2:18:50—de Castella showed that there was still life in his aging legs when he won the 1991 Rotterdam Marathon in 2:09:42. But at the 1992 Olympic Games in Barcelona, his age asserted itself, and he finished in just under 2:20. At the time of this writing, de Castella was the only man to have finished four Olympic Marathons. In addition, at the end of his competitive career, he had run faster than 2:10:00 on eight occasions.

After his last serious marathon at the 1993 London Marathon, in which he finished 33rd in 2:19:44, de Castella concluded, "My body is starting to get a little bit beat up and a little bit weary" (Hauman 1996, p. 117).

Features of de Castella's training were that he did not believe in Lydiard-type peaking but rather mixed all his training, including hill running, intervals, and long runs, each week. He stressed the importance of the long runs, which he did at between 3:54 and 4:03 per km: "Long runs are the hardest part of training to do, and the Sunday long run is the most important part of training" (Sandrock 1996, p. 391). Like Shorter, de Castella built his training around three key workouts—a hill session, a track workout of 8 × 400 m, and a weekly long run of up to 36 km (Sandrock 1996). Of the three, de Castella believed the weekly long run—starting from Poplar Avenue, Boulder, winding through the residential area and into the Rockies, and run in between 2:10 and 2:18 at an altitude of 1600 m—to be the most important. He regarded 210 to 230 km per week as adequate training, believing that further improvements in the world marathon record would come with improvements in diet, shoes, and pacing during the race. He remained unconcerned about the expectations of the general public, taking seriously only his own expectations and those of the people who were close to him.

Sandrock (1996) concluded that if ever there is a perfect running career, de Castella (figure 6.20) came as close to it as anyone.

Steve Jones

Steve Jones was born in Tredegar in the Vale of Glamorgan, South Wales, on 4 August, 1955. It was only in his late teens that he began running, almost by chance. As a cadet in the Air Training Corps stationed in his town, Jones was enticed to run an intersquadron cross-country race. His fifth-place finish qualified him for the National Championships, in which he finished twenty-ninth. He realized then that he had found something he could do well.

In 1974 Jones joined the Royal Air Force (RAF) and for the first time in his life began training regularly under the influence of his first and only coach, Bob Wallis. His break into international running came in 1977 when he won the Welsh National Cross-Country Championships, thus earning a place in the World Cross-Country Championships, in which he finished 103rd. Thereafter, he won the Welsh National Cross-Country Championships nine times and competed in the World Cross-Country Championships 11 times. But by July 1984, his only major international successes were third place in the 1984 World Cross-Country Championships and eighth place in the 1980 Olympic 10,000-m final.

It therefore came as a surprise when, on Sunday, 21 October, 1984, in his first complete 42-km marathon, Jones lowered the world record to 2:08:05, beating Olympic Marathon champion Carlos Lopes by 61 seconds. He had no idea what the world record time was or that he had broken it. He ran the race as he would a 10,000-m race, running hard from the start and putting in a race-splitting surge at 30 km. In the eight weeks leading up to that Chicago race, Jones ran the following weekly distances (in km): 160, 134, 114, 114, 160, 152, 154, and 92. Table 6.19 shows his typical training week during that period.

Like Salazar, Jones considered himself a fast 10,000-m runner who also ran marathons. He felt that a good 10,000-m runner "has at least one good marathon in him" (Sandrock 1996, p. 255).

In April 1985 Jones ran another exceptional marathon, winning the London Marathon in 2:08:15. This gave him two of the five fastest marathons ever run. He then set a world-record time of 1:01:14 in the half-marathon in Birmingham, England, in August 1985. The performance surprised many of his friends, as Jones had attended a wedding the evening before at which he had drunk "several pints of strong cider" (Sandrock 1996). His 2:07:13 performance two months later in the 1985 Chicago Marathon made him the second fastest marathoner of all time, at that point, 2 seconds behind the 2:07:11 set by Lopes at the 1985 Rotterdam Marathon.

Sandrock records that this was

> *a race that changed the way marathons were run. Never had anyone gone so fast so early and tried to keep it up so long. . . . just as Kip Keino and Filbert Bayi changed tactics with their front running in the middle-distances, so did Jones in the marathon. He showed that marathons could be raced hard the whole way. Jones, concentrating solely on winning the race, had no indication of the time as the miles flew by. (Sandrock 1996, p. 258)*

In fact, he passed 21 km in 61:42, at an average mile pace of 4:43 (2:56 per km). At 32 km, his time was 1:35:22 (2:59 per km). He ran the last 4 miles in 20:31 (3:08 per km).

Table 6.19 Steve Jones' training week		
Day	**Morning**	**Afternoon**
Sunday	24–32 km at 3:45 per km	19 km at 3:07 per km
Monday	12–16 km at 3:07 per km	10–16 km
Tuesday	11 km, including 4 × 5:00 hard	Cross-country or track race
Wednesday	11 km	10–16 km
Thursday	Hills (10 repetitions)	8–20 km
Friday	10–12 km	Race or track session (16 × 1:00 or 10 × 2:00 or 16–24 × 0:45)
Saturday		
Total	135–180 km	

After three phenomenal marathons in less than a year, it was inevitable that Jones would sooner or later experience the punch-drunk syndrome that struck Ron Hill after his momentous achievements in 1969 and 1970. First, Jones was injured. Then, at the 1986 European Championships, he ran a pedestrian 2:22:12. Still not recovered, he ran 2:12:37 in the 1987 Boston Marathon and 2:14:07 in the 1988 Boston Marathon. In June 1988 he resigned from the Air Force and moved to Boulder, Colorado. The change was clearly beneficial: Jones returned to form dramatically in the 1988 New York City Marathon run in October, winning in 2:08:20. By that time, he had lost his Reebok sponsorship and ran the race in a plain white singlet. It was to be his last very fast marathon. By winning the 1992 Toronto Marathon in 2:10:06 at age 37, he became the world's fastest marathoner, with an aggregate time of 2:08:24 for his five fastest marathons.

His last competitive race was the 1994 New York City Marathon, which he completed in 2:29. Afterwards he broke down in tears: "At 18 miles, I was a minute down on the leaders; by 26, I was 18 minutes behind. Emotionally, physically, and mentally, I was completely drained" (Sandrock 1996, p. 265).

The principal aim of Jones' training (table 6.19) was to improve his performances on the track, in particular at 10,000 m. This, he believed—as indeed he and many others have now shown—is the key to fast marathon performances. His overall weekly training distance is quite low, but it includes four sessions of speed training, in the form of either track or cross-country races, intervals on the track or road, or hill repetitions. He always trained with an intensity that no one of his era could match. His conclusion was that "it's the effort that matters on the hard days" (Sandrock 1996, p. 267).

Jones' career—like those of Ron Hill, Buddy Edelen, Alberto Salazar, and to a lesser extent, Rob de Castella—again emphasizes that the world's very best marathon runners can enjoy a purple patch during which their performances are peerless. But once the patch is past, usually in about a year or after three marathons, the athletes never again achieve the same level of performance.

Carlos Lopes

Carlos Lopes began running in Lisbon, Portugal, in his late teens and first tasted international success when he won the 1975 World Cross-Country Championships. At the 1976 Montreal Olympics, he finished second to Lasse Viren in the 10,000 m. Thereafter, his international career wavered and gave no indication of what was to follow. But in the short period from March 1983 to April 1985, the 38-year-old moved from the status of superstar to running legend and became the supreme inspiration for all those who thought they might be over the hill after the age of 35.

Lopes' comeback began in March 1983, when he completed his first standard marathon at Rotterdam in 2:08:39 and was outsprinted in the last few hundred meters by Robert de Castella. In the same year, Lopes won the World Cross-Country Championships for the second time, and in the 1984 Rotterdam Marathon he ran with the leaders before dropping out after 29 km. Later he told Frank Shorter that he had run the race for one reason only—to see how fit he was. When he found that running with the leaders required only modest effort, he knew he was in excellent shape. He dropped out so that he would not show his opponents how fit he was, nor would he risk wasting his fitness on an all-out marathon only a few months before the Olympic Games.

Three months later, on 2 July, he ran the world's second fastest 10,000 m ever (27:17.48), and five weeks later, in only his second-ever completed marathon, he won the Olympic Marathon gold medal (figure 6.21) in a time of 2:09:21. Interestingly, Lopes was hit by a car 10 days before that race and was unable to train again. He finished the race in exceptional condition—another example of the Zatopek phenomenon (see chapter 7).

Ten weeks after that, with a period of relaxed training behind him, he was still able to run 2:09:06, finishing second to Steve Jones' world record performance of 2:08:05. In 1985, Lopes won the World Cross-Country Championships for the third time, and on 29 April, at the Rotterdam Marathon, he finished in 2:07:11, bettering Steve Jones' record by 54 seconds. His comment was that with more competition, he could have run 2 minutes faster, a view that few would challenge lightly.

Published details of Lopes' training methods are scanty. According to Frank Shorter (Shorter and Bloom 1984), Lopes trained hard all the time and even when training at medium altitude seldom ran slower than 3:30 per km. He did not change his training substantially before the Olympic Games Marathon, except that he increased his long runs from 90 to 120 minutes, covering about 35 km.

Shorter believed there to be three secrets to Lopes' success. First was his innate ability to read his body signals in both training and racing so that he was always in control (as shown at the 1984 Rotterdam Marathon). Second was his ability to peak, as proven by his victories in the World Cross-Country Championships, and third was his ability to focus on his primary goals. He defeated more favored runners in the 1984 Olympic Marathon because he focused specifically on that event and was not sidetracked, as were many others, by the financial lure of other less important races in the 12 months before the Olympic Games. In addition, he again confirmed that the fastest runners at the shorter distances are the best marathon runners.

Touchline Media

Figure 6.21   Portuguese Carlos Lopes' eventual victory in the 1984 Olympic Marathon in Los Angeles was especially impressive; although a minor car accident prevented him from running for the last seven days before the mara-thon, he won the race very comfortably. He was 37 years old at the time of his victory.

Matthews Temane

One of the first runners to surpass Steven Jones' half-marathon world record was South African Matthews Selepe Temane (figure 6.22), who established a new world 21-km best of 1:00:11 in East London on 25 July, 1987.

Temane was born of Tswana parents in Hammanskraal on 14 December, 1960. His first ambition, expressed from an early age, was to become a famous soccer player. Although he won the majority of the middle-distance races that he entered at school, his sporting ambitions were focused exclusively on soccer. The only specific running that he did was jogging to school and back, covering a total distance of 15 km per day.

Figure 6.22 South African Matthews Temane running behind Zithulele Sinqe in the half-marathon championships in East London in 1986. Temane set a new world record in the event.

Eventually his mother, sensing that her son's real athletic talent lay in running, encouraged Matthews to pursue it as a career. Accordingly, he joined the Vaal Reef Goldmining Company in Johannesburg in 1981 as a sports officer and came under the care of Richard Turnbull, the coach who was to guide him in his formative years as a runner.

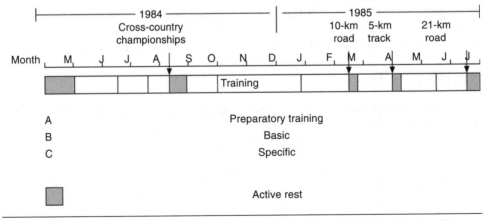

Figure 6.23 The 15-month periodization program devised by Richard Turnbull for Matthews Temane. Data from Turnbull (1985).

His first major race was the 1981 national under-21 track championships, in which he placed third in the 5000 m, despite stopping to attend to his feet during the race. Thereafter, he won national track, cross-country, and road titles at distances from 1500 m to 21 km throughout his career, and in 1987 he won every major South

Table 6.20 Matthews Temane's late basic/early specific training program for road and cross-country running

Day	Morning	Afternoon
Monday	16 km (medium)	Weight training
Tuesday	15 km (fast)	10 km (easy)
Wednesday	16 km (easy)	8 × 400-m hill runs (90% effort)
Thursday	10 km (easy)	10 km (medium)
Friday	10 km (easy)	Fartlek
Saturday	20–25 km (easy)	
Sunday	Rest	

Easy pace = 3:50 per km; medium pace = 3:20 per km; fast pace = 3:00–3:10 per km.
From R. Turnbull (1985, p. 27). © 1985 by South African Runner.

Table 6.21 Matthews Temane's late basic/early specific training program for track running

Day	Morning	Afternoon
Monday	16 km (medium)	Weight training
Tuesday	10 km (easy)	2 × 600 m each in 1:27 with 0:30 rest between intervals 2 × 400 m each in 0:50 with 0:30 rest between intervals 4 × 300 m each in 0:38 with 1:00 rest between intervals 6:00 rest between sets
Wednesday	10 km (easy)	8 × 300-m hill runs (fast)
Thursday	16 km (easy)	4 × (2 × 400 m) each in 0:56 with 0:30 rest between intervals and 4:00 rest between sets
Friday	10 km (easy)	
Saturday	18–20 km (medium)	
Sunday	Rest	

From R. Turnbull (1985, p. 27). © 1985 by South African Runner.

Day	Morning	Afternoon
Table 6.22 Matthews Temane's training program two weeks before his world 21-km record		
Monday	40:00–50:00 jog	16 km (48:00–50:00)
Tuesday	40:00–50:00 jog	Track: 2 × 800 m (2:07, 2:10); 2 × 600 m (1:34, 1:35); 2 × 400 m (0:57, 0:58)
Wednesday	40:00–50:00 jog	Cross-country 12 km
Thursday	40:00–50:00 jog	8 × 400 m hills (1:00)
Friday	40:00–50:00 jog	8 km time-trial (23:00)
Saturday	40:00–50:00 jog	Fartlek; 3 sets: 3:00 fast; 5:00 jog; 2:00 fast; 5:00 jog; 1:00 fast; 6:00 jog
Sunday	Rest	

From South African Runner (1987a, p. 33). © 1987 by South African Runner.

African road and cross-country title. His best performances during his career were 1 mile (1.6 km) in 3:55.4, the world's fastest time for the mile at medium altitude; national records at 5000 m on the track (13:25.2) and 10 km on the road (28:29 on a certified course; 28:03 on an uncertified course); and the world's fastest 21 km (1:00:11) at that time.

Turnbull believed that Temane's greatest running assets were his natural speed; his disciplined training approach, stressing rest and avoiding overtraining; and his meticulous peaking technique, in which he could reach a peak performance with only four weeks of intensive training. He drinks no alcohol, tea, or coffee and eats few sweets or chocolates.

The principles of the training program that Temane follows have been described in detail (Turnbull 1985). The program aims to produce a versatile athlete—able to compete effectively from 1500 to 5000 m during the track season and from 10 to 21 km during the winter cross-country and road season.

Turnbull divides the training program into a one- to six-week preparatory period, a 6- to 10- week basic period, and a two- to five-week specific period, always followed by a period of one to four weeks of active rest (figure 6.23). During the preparatory period, Temane does no speed training, concentrating instead on combined slow- and medium-paced runs with hill running, stretching exercises, and weight training. Intervals, fast continuous runs, and fartlek are added during the basic period, which serves as an introduction to the more intensive specific period, during which the intensity of the interval and fartlek sessions is increased, and the recovery period between intervals is lengthened. Tables 6.20, 6.21, and 6.22 provide details of Temane's training in the basic and specific training periods (Turnbull 1985).

When tested in our laboratory (Coetzer et al. 1993), Temane's $\dot{V}O_2$max was 78 ml

O_2 per kg per min; his running economy was the same as that reported for Frank Shorter and Derek Clayton (51.1 ml O_2 per kg per min at 17 km per hr); and his lactate turnpoint occurred at 21 km per hr. His body fat content was 7.4% and his mass 53 kg. Most important, he was able to run for a minute longer during the maximal treadmill test than any previous athlete tested in our laboratory, including Johan Fourie, who was ranked fourth-fastest miler in the world at that time in 1987.

It would seem that Temane's success at distances up to 21 km rested on the fact that, like the other world-class black South African distance runners, he was a very fast miler who chose also to run on the roads. He exemplified what former world mile record holder John Walker (1988) said: "If the best milers came off the track, they'd clean up on the roads."

AFRICA'S EXPERT RUNNERS

In the years since Wilson Kiprugut won Kenya's first Olympic medal with a bronze in the 800 m at the 1964 Olympic Games, the dominance of distance running, by Kenyans especially, has become a phenomenon unequaled in any other sport in the world. The following provides a measure of this dominance:

- In the 1988 World Cross-Country Championships in Auckland, New Zealand, Kenyan and Ethiopian runners filled all of the 10 top places. More remarkably, eight of the nine-man Kenyan team were among the top 10 finishers.

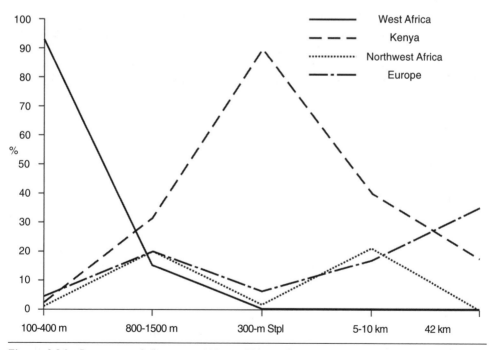

Figure 6.24 Percentage of all-time world-best 100 performances in running races from 100 m to 42 km in athletes with different geographical origins. Note that whereas athletes of West African origin dominate races of 100 to 400 m, Kenyans are dominant in the 3000-m steeplechase. Athletes of European origin tend to be more dominant at distances of 42 km or longer.
Reproduced with permission of the Royal Society of Medicine Press, London.

- At the 1988 Olympics in Seoul, Kenyan men won the 800 m, the 1500 m, the 3000-m steeplechase, and the 5000 m. Based on population percentages alone, the likelihood that this should have happened by chance is 1 in 1,600,000,000 (Burfoot 1992).

- In the 1991 World Athletics Championships in Tokyo, Kenyan men finished first and second in the 10,000 m, second in the 1500 m, and first and second in the 3000-m steeplechase.

- In the 1992 World Cross-Country Championships held in Boston, Kenyans took five of the first eight places in the senior men's race, three of the first four places in the junior men's race, and four of the top 15 places in the women's race. In this event, considered the most competitive annual distance race in the world, Kenyan men have now won the last 16 senior men's team titles and 13 of the last 14 junior men's titles. The dominance in the women's races has been equally remarkable, with seven wins in the last 11 senior women's races and nine wins in the last 13 junior women's races. On five occasions—in 1988, 1991, 1993, 1994, and 1996—the combined finishers of the top six Kenyan runners would have beaten a team of the best six finishers from the rest of the world.

- A Kenyan runner has won the 3000-m steeplechase at every Olympic Games at which the Kenyans have competed since 1968. In the 1992 Olympic Games, Kenyans won all the medals in this event. Currently, 93 of the top 100 all-time record times for the 3000-m steeplechase have been set by Kenyans (figure 6.24).

- Since first competing in the Olympic Games, Kenyan runners from the Kalenjin tribe have won 26 Olympic medals (eight gold) in track competition from 800 to 10,000 m, compared to 10 (six gold) by the United States and eight (one gold) by Great Britain (Manners 1998). And this despite the fact that Kenya did not compete in either the 1980 or the 1984 Olympic Games. As a result, Kalenjin men, comprising a population of 3 million, have won 2.6 times as many medals as have runners from the United States, which has a population nearly 100 times larger. Hence, a Kalenjin is 2600 times more likely to win an Olympic medal at 800 to 10,000 m than is a runner from the United States.

- Kalenjin runners currently hold 38% of the all-time top 10 performances at distances from 800 to 10,000 m, 37% of the all-time top 20 performances, and 29% of the all-time top 50 (Manners 1998).

- In 1996, Kalenjin runners filled 56% of the top 10 positions in distances from 800 to 10,000 m, including nine of the fastest 10 times over the 3000-m steeplechase, six of the fastest 1500-m times, and five each of the fastest 800-m and 10000-m times. Only in the 5000 m were less than half the top 10 performances for the year filled by non-Kalenjins (Manners 1998).

- Manners (1998) developed an analysis to determine how well runners "performed under pressure." He did this by comparing how well the Kalenjin runners performed under the extreme pressure of the Olympics, versus their performances in other, less pressured competitions. By evaluating every performance of Kalenjin runners in Olympic competition with their pre-Olympic credentials and by awarding performance points for running within 0.5% of their pre-Olympic best time, reaching the final, finishing in the top eight, or winning a medal, and then comparing their results with those of runners from the United States and Britain, Manners calculated the British aggregate score per runner as 1.0; for the United States, it was 1.3, and for Kalenjin runners, it was 3.0. For non-Kalenjin Kenyan runners, the value was still a respectable 2.0. Manners concluded that hereditary or acquired factors give Kenyan, and especially Kalenjin, runners a greater ability to summon a supreme effort when it matters most.

- West Africans, and African-Americans and Caribbeans of Central West African origin, specifically Liberia, Nigeria, and the Ivory Coast, have recorded 90% of the top 100 performances on the all-time list for races of 100, 200, and 400 m (figure 6.24). When the dominance of the East African runners in the long-distance events is added to this West African dominance of the sprint events, the contribution of African athletes to world athletics becomes apparent. Whereas black athletes won only 14 (42%) of the 33 medals for running events at the 1983 Helsinki World Athletics Championships, they won 29 (88%) of these medals at the 1991 Games in Tokyo. Similarly, the percentage of medals won by black women in running events increased from 7 to 34% during the same period.

- Nine of the top 11 fastest marathon times ever are currently held by African runners (table 6.23), of whom five are Kenyans. In fact, the tenth-fastest Kenyan marathon runner has run 2:07:15, making the average best marathon time for the 10 fastest Kenyans a phenomenal 2:06:48.1. This is way ahead of the averages of the next two best marathon nations, Japan (with an average of 02:08:19.7) and South Africa (with an average of 2:08:35.1).

Clearly the depth of the running talent in Kenya is remarkable. When a group of top Swedish runners traveled to Kenya in 1992, they were unable to hold their own even against schoolboy athletes. The Swedes calculated that there were probably 500 Kenyan schoolboys who were faster than the very best Swedish distance runners (O. Anderson 1992).

Table 6.23   All-time marathon list (updated to 1 August, 2001)

1	Khalid Khannouchi (Morocco)	2:05:42 (1) Chicago	24 October, 1999
2	Ronaldo Da Costa (Brazil)	2:06:05 (1) Berlin	20 September, 1998
3	Moses Tanui (Kenya)	2:06:16 (2) Chicago	24 October, 1999
4	Gert Thys (South Africa)	2:06:33 (1) Tokyo	14 February, 1999
5	Antonio Pinto (Portugal)	2:06:36 (1) London	16 April, 2000
6	Josephat Kiprono (Kenya)	2:06:44 (1) Berlin	26 September, 1999
7	Fred Kiprop (Kenya)	2:06:47 (1) Amsterdam	17 October, 1999
8	Tesfaye Jifar (Ethiopia)	2:06:49 (2) Amsterdam	17 October, 1999
9	Belayneh Densimo (Ethiopia)	2:06:50 (1) Rotterdam	17 April, 1988
9	Josephat Kiprono (Kenya)	2:06:50 (1) Rotterdam	22 April, 2001
9	Willim Kiplagat (Kenya)	2:06:50 (3) Amsterdam	17 October, 1999

In South Africa, black runners dominate all running distances between 3 and 5 km and have achieved world-class status at 21 and 42 km. A team of black South Africans won the World Half-Marathon Championships in 1999, beating the Ethiopians and Kenyans into second and third places. In addition, South African marathoners are ranked 10th and 12th on the list of all-time fastest marathoners. This suggests that the same genetic pool for distance running excellence that exists in East and North Africa must also be shared by black South Africans. Clearly, the manner in which this genetic pool distributed itself across Africa in human prehistory is of great interest. For example, how did sprinting ability concentrate in West Africa, whereas distance running ability seems more widely distributed across the rest of the continent?

Vincent Sarich, a New Zealand biologist working at the University of California in Berkeley, has made a statistical analysis of this Kenyan dominance. He notes that in the 1997 World Cross-Country Championships in Turin, the 10 Kenyan entrants finished in positions 1, 3, 4, 6, 7, 17, 19, 24, 28, and 47. The winning time was 35:11, whereas the 10 Kenyans averaged 36:04, which would have placed the entire team 12th overall in the individual event.

Sarich uses this and other information to calculate that Kenyans outperform the rest of the world in cross-country running by a factor of about 1700. This means that, whereas in the rest of the world exceptional runners appear in a ratio of about 1 elite athlete per 20 million males, in Kenya there are about 80 such elite athletes per million males (most especially, males of Kalenjin origin). As there are about 3 million Kalenjin, thus we would expect Kenya to have a maximum of about 240 elite male athletes at any time. This is not greatly different from the total of 150 invitations sent out to elite Kenyan runners encouraging them to attend the selection camp before the annual World Cross-Country Championships.

Sarich concludes that physical attributes such as height or weight and, probably, running ability are distributed normally in any population, according to an inverted U distribution (figure 6.25) around a central mean, or average, value. The nature of the distribution is defined by the standard deviation (SD) from that mean. Lines drawn to either side of the mean that include 68% of the population are known as one SD (each side of) the mean. Two SDs around the mean incorporate 96% of the population; three SDs, 99.3%; and so on. What this suggests is that elite runners in any population come from that tiny proportion of the population that exists at the extreme end of the distribution (for aerobic capacity and fatigue resistance).

Sarich calculates that if, in the average (European) population, exceptional running ability is present in about 1 per 20 million Caucasian people, this is the proportion of the population defined by a line drawn 5.3 SDs from the mean. In contrast, the distribution of elite runners in the Kenyan population suggests that the same proportion of the Kenyan population is only 3.8 SDs from the mean. Accordingly, Sarich concludes that the mean running ability of the best Kenyans is about 1.5 SDs better than that of the best runners from other population groups.

Using data from the 1997 World Cross-Country Championships, Sarich next calculates that in terms of running performance over 12 km, 1 SD is equivalent to about 3.5 minutes. Thus, his argument is that, perhaps as a result of selective processes yet to be defined, the Kalenjin tribes in the Rift Valley of Kenya have acquired superior running ability so that the average Kalenjin can run about 5 minutes (1.5 SDs) faster over 12 km than the average non-Kalenjin runner. This difference in average running ability is relatively meaningless to the average Kalenjin or average non-Kalenjin. At the center of the inverted population distribution there are so many Europeans or Kalenjins with average running ability that any 5-minute difference in running ability would be impossible to identify.

However, this relatively small difference in average running ability becomes relevant because of its effect on the number of Kalenjins who are able to run fast enough to win international running events. Whereas such performances can only be achieved by those non-Kalenjin runners who are 5.3 SDs better than the average runners in their population group, the same performances can be achieved by Kalenjins who are only 3.8 SDs better runners than the average Kalenjin.

Thus, a country like Britain, which has a population of about 60 million should produce three elite runners (1 per 20 million) who are able to compete with about 240 Kalenjin (80 per million in a population of 3 million).

Of course, the certainty is that from among those 240 Kalenjin runners, there will be some who are even faster than their average elite Kalenjin peers and, by probability, they will also be faster than the three best British runners. So, in competitions such as the World Cross-Country Championships or the Olympic Games, in which there are a restricted number of entries from each country, the fastest Kalenjin runners will outperform the very best runners from the rest of the world, in proportion to the much greater distribution of elite runners in Kenya than in the rest of the world.

The ultimate test of this hypothesis would be to hold a World Cross-Country Championship that is open to anyone able to complete a 12-km cross-country race within 1 SD of the time of the best Kenyan. The prediction would be that there would be at least 240 Kenyans in the race with the other countries represented by a maximum of 1 runner per 20 million population.

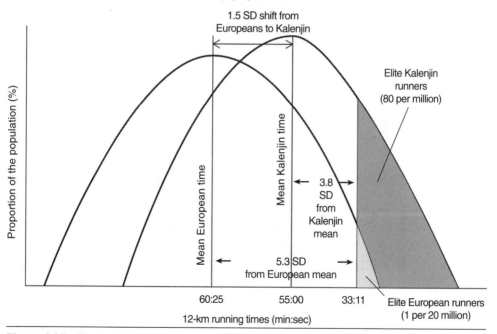

Figure 6.25 The hypothetical distribution of 12 km running times in Kalenjin males versus males from other populations. Because the "average" Kalenjin hypothetically runs 12 km 05:25 faster than the "average" European runner, proportionately many more Kalenjin (80 per million) than Europeans (1 per 20 million) can run 12 km fast enough (33.11) to be the very best in the world.

Physiological Explanations for the Superior Ability of Black Africans

There are few studies that have attempted to establish a physiological explanation for the phenomenal running abilities of black Africans—either sprinters from Central West Africa or distance runners from East, North, or South Africa. Fewer still have been published in scientific journals. The fact that none of these studies has originated in the United States is due to the peculiar sensitivities of that nation (Burfoot 1992; Entine 2000) and the malicious stereotyping of scientists who undertake such research (Entine 2000).

In one of the earliest reported studies, Andrew Bosch and his colleagues (1990) compared the physiological changes in subelite black and white South African marathon runners, all of whom had similar best standard marathon times (between 2:30:00 and 2:45:00), during a simulated marathon run on a treadmill in the laboratory. The most interesting finding in that study was that the black runners completed the treadmill marathon at a higher (89%) $\dot{V}O_2$max than did the white runners (81%). This suggested that the white runners possibly had more ability over shorter distances (measured as a higher $\dot{V}O_2$max), whereas the black runners in that study had greater endurance. Hence, they were able to match the performance of the white runners in the longer distances because they could sustain a higher percentage of their smaller $\dot{V}O_2$max during the marathon. Their outstanding characteristic appears to be a much greater "resistance to fatigue," a concept that was first discussed in chapter 2 (see figure 2.12).

The corollary to this is the prediction that if the very best white and black distance runners have the same $\dot{V}O_2$max values, then the black runners would outper-

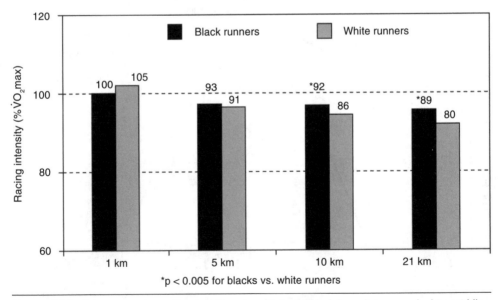

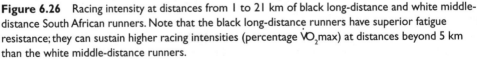

Figure 6.26 Racing intensity at distances from 1 to 21 km of black long-distance and white middle-distance South African runners. Note that the black long-distance runners have superior fatigue resistance; they can sustain higher racing intensities (percentage $\dot{V}O_2$max) at distances beyond 5 km than the white middle-distance runners.

From data from Coetzer et al. 1993.

form the white runners in endurance events such as the marathon because of their greater capacity to run for longer at a higher percentage of the same $\dot{V}O_2$max, and hence at a faster running speed. Unfortunately, this hypothesis can never be evaluated for the simple reason that there are not enough white distance runners anywhere in the world able to match the performances of the best Kenyans, Ethiopians, Moroccans, Algerians, and South Africans.

To circumvent this problem, we (Coetzer et al. 1993) compared physiological variables in the very best black South African distance (5- to 42-km) runners and the top white South African middle-distance (800-m to 3-km) runners. Generally, the white runners were 5 to 10 seconds faster in the mile (1.6 km), whereas black runners were at least 3 minutes faster at 21 km. However, at distances between 1 and 3 km, the performances of both groups of runners were quite similar.

The principal findings were that the $\dot{V}O_2$max values were slightly higher in the white milers (72 vs. 71 ml O_2 per kg per min), who were also 14 kg heavier (70 vs. 56 kg) and 12 cm taller (181 vs. 169 cm) than the black distance runners. Black distance runners also had a slightly higher proportion of Type I muscle fibers (63% vs. 53%). But the key finding was that black runners trained and raced at a higher percentage $\dot{V}O_2$max. Thus, black runners were able to race 21 km at 89% of their $\dot{V}O_2$max, whereas white runners could only sustain 80% $\dot{V}O_2$max for that distance (figure 6.26). Furthermore, tests of muscle function showed that when undergoing repeated cycles of contraction and relaxation, the muscles of the black distance runners were able to complete more contraction/relaxation cycles before they developed marked fatigue. This probably reflects the ability of the black athletes to continue recruiting a large muscle mass.

Thus, we concluded that the superior performance of black distance runners at distances from 5 to 21 km was due to their greater capacity to resist fatigue during repeated muscle contractions, perhaps due to an ability to sustain higher levels of skeletal muscle recruitment before developing fatigue. In particular, we concluded that the classical Cardiovascular/Anaerobic Model of Exercise Physiology and Athletic Performance (figure 2.4) could not explain the superior endurance capacity of the black distance runners in that study.

Hence, the important finding of that study was that the Cardiovascular/Anaerobic Model may be unable to discriminate between good and superior performance in events lasting more than a few minutes, which constitute the bulk of sporting events. It is consistent with the finding that the $\dot{V}O_2$max is a relatively less reliable predictor of endurance performance in athletes whose abilities are relatively homogenous (tables 2.1 and 2.2). The failure stems from the inability of this model to measure or predict fatigue resistance during prolonged *submaximal* exercise on the basis of physiological variables and of the performance measured during the single bout of progressive, maximal exercise to exhaustion, used to determine the $\dot{V}O_2$max.

Another surprising finding was that, unlike the usual finding in white distance runners, the black distance runners had a much higher proportion of Type II (white) fibers, making up 40% to 60% of all their muscle fibers (figure 6.27, A and B). This pattern is typically found in white middle-distance runners. Yet, the clear evidence is that the muscles of white middle-distance runners do not have the same resistance to fatigue as do those of the black distance runners we studied, despite their having the same proportion of Type II fibers. Hence, one possible conclusion is that the Type II fibers of the black runners are fundamentally different from those of the white middle-distance runners and are characterized by extreme fatigue resistance.

A   B

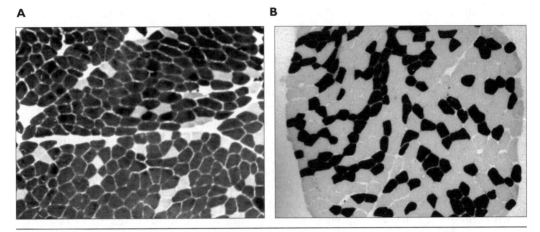

Figure 6.27   Skeletal muscle fibers of a white South African ultramarathon runner (A) and a black South African Olympian (B) at 10,000 m. The dark staining Type I fibers make up approximately 90% of the muscle fiber of the white ultramarathon runner and approximately 50% of the muscle fibers of the black 10,000-m runner.

In chapter 2, we discussed the evidence that the Type I (red) fibers are more fatigue resistant than the Type II (white) fibers. Clearly, this did not apply to the Type II fibers present in the black South African distance runners we studied.

Two other studies specifically of Kenyan runners (Saltin, Kim, et al. 1995; Saltin, Larsen, et al. 1995; Saltin 1996) failed to provide a definitive physiological answer for the manifest superiority of those runners. The overriding conclusion was that the Kenyans' $\dot{V}O_2$max values were not inordinately high. In the words of the senior author, Bengt Saltin, "A comparison of some data on some of the very best runners in Kenya during the last decades and world-class runners in Scandinavia does not reveal much that was not already known or could be anticipated" (Saltin 1996, p. 7). Hence, the Cardiovascular/Anaerobic Model was again unhelpful in explaining Kenyan dominance.

Those studies also reported a detailed analysis of the skeletal muscle characteristics of some top Kenyan schoolboy and adult runners; these data were compared with those from top Scandinavian runners. Kenyans had about 70% Type I fibers, slightly higher than the South African value but not different from the value for the Scandinavian runners. Apart from this, there were no unique findings to explain the Kenyan superiority.

More recently, Weston et al. (1999) compared physiological measures in a group of subelite black and white South African runners matched for 10-km race time and training volume. Again, it was found that black runners were able to run for longer at the same exercise intensity. Black runners also had a higher percentage of Type II fibers (51% vs. 33%) than did white runners. In addition, the activity of the skeletal muscle mitochondrial enzyme, citrate synthase, was 50% greater in black runners. Black runners also had lower blood lactate concentrations during submaximal exercise. A relationship between superior fatigue resistance, higher muscle citrate synthase activity, and lower blood lactate concentrations in black runners supported a skeletal muscle basis for the superior performance of the black athletes during laboratory testing. Weston's subsequent study (Weston et al. 2000) also found that subelite black runners were more economical than white runners.

To summarize, black African distance runners are characterized by a muscle fiber composition different from that found in white distance runners, as they seem to have more Type II fibers. This pattern found in black distance runners who perform best at distances from 5 to 42 km is more similar to that found in white middle-distance runners who race at distances up to 3 km. Yet, these Type II fibers seem to exhibit the same functional characteristics as those normally described for the Type I fibers. In particular, they have a high capillary density and high mitochondrial enzyme content, and they are extremely fatigue resistant.

The outstanding characteristic of black runners is their ability to maintain a higher exercise intensity during prolonged exercise, indicating superior fatigue resistance. There is no evidence that black runners have superior cardiovascular function and a greater capacity to transport oxygen to their exercising muscles. Hence, it is unlikely that the classic Cardiovascular/Anaerobic Model can explain their superior athletic ability (Noakes 1998b). Rather, their lower blood lactate concentrations during exercise are more likely to be the result of specific skeletal muscle characteristics.

According to the Energy Depletion Model, superior performance in races lasting longer than 2 hours would most likely result from a greater capacity to delay the onset of liver or muscle glycogen depletion during prolonged exercise, perhaps as a result of a greater capacity to store carbohydrates before exercise or a greater capacity to use fat as a fuel during exercise. However, black runners dominate those race distances that are completed in less than 1 hour, which calls into question the relevance of this model. Nevertheless, there is a need to establish the capacity of black runners to store carbohydrates in muscles and liver and to determine the rate at which they utilize that carbohydrate during exercise. The lower-than-expected blood lactate concentrations during exercise in black runners could certainly indicate alterations in glycogen or lactate metabolism during exercise. Slower rates of body carbohydrate use would, theoretically, enhance endurance performance by allowing higher exercise intensities at lower blood and muscle lactate concentrations and by delaying the onset of body carbohydrate depletion.

According to the Integrated Neuromuscular Recruitment Model, a rising body temperature caused by a progressive heat retention in the body can limit performance during prolonged exercise. The ability to accumulate heat at a slow rate when running very fast would be advantageous.

Factors that slow the rate of heat accumulation when running fast are a small size and a high running economy (efficiency). These are both well-described characteristics of black African distance runners. A slower rate of heat accumulation when running fast might contribute to the success of African distance runners. Indeed, the only study (Bosch et al. 1990) of this possibility found that black marathon runners maintained lower skin temperatures than did white runners running at the same pace. The possible relevance of this very interesting finding has lain hidden for more than a decade, even from the scientists who discovered it.

The basis of the Biomechanical Model of superior athletic ability is that skeletal muscles function as elastic energy return systems that act more like springs than torque producers during exercise. The more the muscle acts as a spring, the less energy it consumes and hence the more efficient it is. The more efficient, more elastic muscle will enhance performance by slowing the rate of accumulation of metabolites causing fatigue during exercise and the rate of rise in body temperature, as discussed above.

Empirical observation of the running stride and the anatomical structure of the lower limbs of African athletes, especially Kenyan runners, suggests, at least to me, that an evaluation of the elastic elements of the legs of elite Kenyan runners should be very rewarding. It is remarkable how thin and birdlike their legs are and how springy their strides appear to be, especially when they have raced 5 to 10 km, at which distance the difference from other non-African runners becomes more apparent. I interpret this as evidence that stretch-shortening fatigue develops more slowly in African runners, indicating a different pattern of neural recruitment during fatiguing exercise.

I am not alone in suggesting a biomechanical basis for the success of the Kenyans. Patrick Rono, a Kenyan runner of international class, has made the following observation, "A group of us were sitting watching a local competition one day. . . . A British runner was over here in Kenya running against us. We noticed first the big difference in leg structure; his legs were like oak tree trunks whereas ours were like willows. When we jumped we floated over; when he jumped it was a major upheaval" (Tanser 1997, p. 135).

Finally, the Psychological/Motivational Model predicts that a conscious choice can explain superior performance. Some importance has been attached to the practice of circumcision without anesthesia in adolescent Kenyan boys. Acceptance as an adult requires that the young boy show no emotion during the procedure. Compared to that, running makes few demands.

But clearly there must be inordinate motivation to train and race as hard as do the elite Kenyan runners. The factors explaining this capacity need to be addressed.

To summarize, there are many possible, but as yet, no clearly established, physiological explanations for the success of the Kenyans. Nor is it certain that any physiological differences will definitely be genetically based, although my bias, like that of Saltin (see sidebar, p. 447), is to believe that this is likely the case. Such a genetic advantage would have resulted from centuries of exposure to the specific environmental and other challenges posed by living at altitude and practicing cattle raiding. Perhaps it is a question that will be solved in the near future when the difficulties attending research of this nature on the African continent are surmounted.

Training Methods of the Kenyans

Each of the great runners described in this chapter changed the course of running by introducing some innovation that was subsequently adopted and, in time, became accepted as a desirable training technique.

Thus, the Finns before Nurmi were the first amateur runners to train on a regular basis, including in the harsh Finnish winters. Nurmi introduced a greater emphasis on speed training, and this was studied, modified, and taken to its extreme by Zatopek. Newton reintroduced the concept of high volume training, which he probably learned from the pedestrians of the late nineteenth century. Peters then began to combine the high volumes of training of Newton with the speed of Zatopek, to which Buddy Edelen added the single, weekly long run at fast speed. Steve Jones repeated the same approach. The athletes trained by New Zealand coach Arthur Lydiard developed the concept of peaking, which was used by Frank Shorter and Lasse Viren to great effect.

It follows then that the dominance of the Kenyans could, in part, be explained by some training innovation that will influence training theories in the future. There are three current sources of what appears to be reliable training information about the Kenyans. The monograph *Train Hard, Win Easy—The Kenyan Way* by Toby Tanser (1997) includes training histories of a wide range of elite Kenyan runners. Tanser, himself an established runner, traveled through Kenya for five months collecting the information from interviews with top Kenyan runners who ran distances from 800 m to the marathon.

The second reliable source is an article coauthored by Kenyan runner Ibraham Kinuthia (Kinuthia and Anderson 1994) and published in the Owen Anderson newsletter, *Running Research*. Another is an article by anotherAmerican runner, 2:14:00 marathoner Tom Ratcliffe (1994), who traveled to Kenya to train at the high-altitude training camp where the male and female teams that represent Kenya at the annual World Cross-Country Championships are selected. I have presented that information for which there is more than one source, which is therefore more likely to be accurate. If there is to be a reasonable analysis of the contribution that training makes to the success of the Kenyans, then it is important that there be some reliable information of exactly how they train.

Kenyans chose neither to live nor to work alone (Tanser 1997). Thus, they prefer to train in groups. As a result, small training groups congregate throughout the Rift Valley, usually around a more established international runner. In these training camps, there are no daily chores, and both male and female runners can concentrate solely on running. In addition to these unofficial training groups, there are established annual training camps that cater to different groups of athletes.

The Armed Forces Training Camp is located 30 km from Nairobi, in the N'gong Hills, which Isak Dinesen (Karen Blixen) wrote about in the opening sentence of the novel *Out of Africa* (Blixen 1985). The camp comprises three sections—one for the army, one for the navy, and one for the air force—and caters to cross-country and track athletes from November to March and to field athletes thereafter.

The Iten Training Camp is organized twice per year by Brother Colm O'Connell, with financial support from Nike. Brother Colm, a former headmaster of St. Patrick's High School, coached many great Kenyan runners while they attended his school. Acclaimed athletes from St. Patrick's include Olympic gold medalists Peter Rono (1988: 1500 m) and Matthew Birir (1992: 3000-m steeplechase).

The National Training Camp for the World Cross-Country Championships was initiated by Kenyan coach Mike Kosgei, who coached the Kenyan cross-country teams from 1985 to 1995. He established this training camp at the St. Mark's Teacher Training College, located at an altitude of 1900 m on the eastern slopes of Mount Kenya, near the town of Embu. A select group of runners are invited to this camp for final selections to the four teams that will represent Kenya in the championships.

Kenyan dominance of distance running began shortly after Kosgei was appointed coach and had initiated the training camp concept, where he taught his athletes to run as a team. The arrival of his first multiple World Cross-Country Champion, John Ngugi, at that initial camp was also crucial, as Ngugi set the training standard. He would rise before all the others and run by torchlight, returning in time for the official early morning run.

One route to international running success for the Kenyans appears to be through the St. Mark's training camp and on to the World Cross-Country Championships. Therefore, it is perhaps appropriate to begin by analyzing the training a Kenyan would go through en route to those championships. Training for the less-established runners begins at the beginning of October. This is exactly the opposite for those Kenyans who are established competitors on the professional European running circuit. Established runners usually return home in October and do not resume training until December or January. This, in the words of Paul Tergat, five-time World Cross-Country Champion and silver medalist in the 1996 Olympic Games 10,000-m race, is the time to rest the normal Kenyan way—to eat, relax, and put on weight (Tanser 1997, p. 188), advice not dissimilar to that given by Mark Allen.

Athletes in training during this period do three daily workouts—at 6 A.M., 10 A.M., and 4 P.M. The 6 A.M. and 4 P.M. sessions are moderately easy and of 7 to 10 km and 30 to 45 minutes respectively. On some days, the afternoon run is replaced with stretching and strengthening exercises. It is the mid-morning run that is done with effort. Kinuthia and Anderson (1994) list a typical week's training as shown in table 6.25.

The training load during this period therefore averages between 180 and 200 km. At the end of October, the top runners are selected to attend the special Armed Forces Training Camp, which begins in November in the N'gong Hills. During this period, the cross-country season begins, which means that the athletes' average weekly training distance falls to accommodate the races and especially the traveling entailed. During this time, the athletes train only twice per day, with one easy run between 7 and 10 km and a second daily run according to the schedule shown in table 6.24. The total distance is approximately 100 km, of which 25% to 30% is at 10-km race pace or faster.

In November and December, some of the established Kenyan runners train at Nyahururu at an altitude of more than 2400 m. This is an appropriate altitude to stimulate red blood cell production, perhaps the most important single adaptation achieved by training at altitude (chapter 13).

January is an especially important month, as it is the last month before the series of cross-country championships at district and provincial levels, at which runners are selected to attend the National Championships in February. Training during this period typically comprises one easy run of 30 minutes each day, with the daily sessions set out in table 6.24. By this time, the intensity of all training sessions has increased, and most easy runs end with the final 800 to 1600 m being run at race pace. As a result, although the training volume is 80 to 100 km, 25% of the total is run at race pace or faster.

In February, the training volume falls further to between 60 and 80 km per week, but the training speeds increase. On the last Saturday of February, the Kenyan National Cross-Country Championships are held, and the national team is selected for a month's training at St. Mark's Teachers Training College in Embu. It is there that the real Kenyan training begins (table 6.24).

At St. Mark's camp, the Kenyans revert to three training sessions per day, except on Sundays. The first run of the day is at 6 A.M. and usually entails a 40- to 50-minute run (less for the women and junior men), the last few kilometers being run at between 3:15 and 3:52 per km. The final run of the day is at 4 P.M. and is usually between 12 and 16 km. After a slow start, the tempo increases to 10-km race pace over the last few kilometers. Sunday is a relative rest day with a single run of 22 km at a moderate pace.

The main training session of the day is at 10 A.M. Owen Anderson (Kinutia and Anderson 1994) identified seven different sessions that Kosgei developed for the hard morning session:

Table 6.24 Kenyan Training

Typical October training

Day	Comment
Monday	A long run of 18–20 km at a moderate pace. By the end of October, this will be run in 56:00–62:00.
Tuesday	15 full repetitions of a steep 200–300 m climb. By the end of the month, these intervals will be done at close to race pace.
Wednesday	Either a 10-km speed play (fartlek) session or 12 km in about 35:00.
Thursday	15–18 km at a moderate, relaxed pace.
Friday	The same hill session as on Tuesday or 45:00 of easy running.
Saturday	A race of 10–12 km or else interval repetitions of either 200, 400, 800, or 1000 m.

Armed Forces Training Camp

Monday	18 km long run or no training if returning from competition.
Tuesday	18 km long run if the session on Monday was missed or else speed work consisting of 400- or 800-m repetitions.
Wednesday	8 or 10 km hill running or speed play (fartlek).
Thursday	7–10 km easy
Friday	Travel to competition or jogging for 30:00.
Saturday	10–12 km competition or the same distance as a race with teammates
Sunday	No second workout because of travel.

National Cross-Country Championships

Monday	Long run of 60:00.
Tuesday	Interval session of 12 × 400 m; 6 × 800 m or 5 × 1000 m; all at race pace or faster.
Wednesday	Easy run of 45:00.
Thursday	8 km in 24:00 or 8 km of fast fartlek.
Friday	Circuit training.
Saturday	Interval session of the same overall structure as that for Tuesday.
Sunday	Long run of 60:00.

Adapted from Kinuthia and Anderson (1994).

1. A 10-km fartlek session over hilly terrain, in which 2 minutes of hard running is followed by either 2 or 1 minute(s) of jogging. The speed of the fast running increases from about 3:45 per km to about 2:28 per km. When the 2:2 work:rest ratio is used, the 10 km is covered in about 36 minutes; when the 2:1 ratio is followed, the 10 km is covered in about 31 minutes.

2. Intervals of between 100 and 1000 m—the session continues until all runners can do no more.

3. An easy 5-km run followed by 20 × 400 m in 0:56 to 0:54, or 10 × 800 m in 1:58 to 2:08, and then by another 5 km at between 3:34 and 4:00 per km.

4. Two or three 5000-m repetitions at between 15:00 and 15:15.

5. A 15-km run at about 3:30 per km followed by 20 × 200 m in 0:27 to 0:30, followed by a 5-km jog.

6. A 22-km run at a speed of about 3.25 minutes per km, with the speed increasing over the last 6 km. The last kilometer is run in about 2:38.

7. A hill session preceded by 12 km of slow running at 5:00 per km over rolling terrain. The hill session involves 200-m repetitions up a hill reportedly inclined at 40°. The senior men complete 25 repetitions, which is the absolute limit, even for these extraordinary athletes.

The four weeks of training at St. Mark's camp involve weekly training averages of between 190 and 230 km, of which 25% to 30% is at a high intensity (table 6.24).

You might well ask if this training program is the real secret to Kenyan success. I, personally, am unconvinced, as the training does not appear to be more intense than that undertaken by non-Kenyan runners, such as Lasse Viren (Sandrock 1996), who, training by himself at altitude also three times per day, four days per week,

Table 6.25	The training program of a modern Kenyan runner	
Day	**Morning**	**Afternoon**
Feb 24	17 to 18 km in 1:20	9 km at high speed; 15 × 200 m hill work
25	10-km fartlek, high speed	15 km in 60:00
26	20-km easy regeneration; 20 min flexibility	8 km easy running
27	15 km in 60:00; 20 × 100 m at 70% effort	15 km easy fartlek
28	15 km in 1:05:00; 20:00 gym	8 km easy jogging
March 1	Competition or 13 km at competitive speed	Rest
2	10 to 12 km in 55:00; 20:00 flexibility exercise	Active rest

Adapted from Kosgei and Abmayr (1988). Permission granted by the International Amateur Athletics Federation (IAAF).

ran prodigious mileages in excess of 250 km per week but maintained a high intensity. The training volumes and intensities achieved by Peters, Edelen, and Jones seem to match those achieved by the Kenyans at St. Mark's camp.

The obvious difference seems to be that whereas few non-Kenyans have been able to achieve equally demanding training programs, a large number of Kenyans are exposed to rigorous training each year and are able to cope. It is the depth of ability that really sets the Kenyans apart. Of course, the depth then provides its own advantages, which include the opportunity to train together and to race as a team. For example, we can assume that, besides his natural reticence, the reason why Viren trained alone was simply because there were few if any other runners from Europe who could match his training intensity.

Thus, perhaps the message of the Kenyans is that the best runners will come, in future, from groups of runners who train together, probably at altitude, and who come from those populations able to produce large numbers of truly exceptional athletes in an environment conducive to running. In Kenya this includes a cool climate at altitude; dirt roads over a hilly, often beautiful and unspoiled countryside; and a level of material poverty that makes this physically demanding lifestyle desirable but is not severe enough to cause want in the basic staples of life, including adequate housing, food, and sanitation.

"So . . . If You Can Run, Then Any Kalenjin Can Run"

The debate between those who support a genetic explanation for the success of the Kenyan distance runners and those who support an environmental one will most likely be resolved in this century, as genes determining athletic ability are identified in the Human Genome Project. Until then, we will each continue to favor our own particular bias.

John Manners (1996), who has observed Kenyan runners for the past 20 years, tells the delightful story of marathoner Paul Rotich, who was one of several Kenyans at South Plains Junior College in Levelland, Texas, in 1988. At the time, however, Rotich was not on a track scholarship. "I was fat. I weighed 80 kg, and I had never run in my life." But as he had run out of money, he decided to try to win an athletics scholarship. Too embarrassed to be seen training in the day, he began by running at night. By the time he graduated four years later, he had won All-American honors 10 times in track and cross-country. When he returned to Kenya, he was met by his cousin, who remarked: "So, it is true. If you can run, then any Kalenjin can run."

A more scientific analysis of this phenomenon has been reported by Professor Bergt Saltin, whose research on the Kenyan runners is described earlier in this chapter. In this study (Arlidge 2000), Saltin trained three groups of schoolboys, none of whom had ever previously undergone any athletic training, in three different locations—in the Nandi Hills and in Eldoret (both in the heart of the Kalenjin running district in the Rift Valley; see figure 6.13) and in Copenhagen, Denmark. After three months of training, the groups raced one another over 10 km. Predictably, the Nandi schoolboys performed the best.

To determine how good the Nandi schoolboys were, Saltin invited the best two to race Thomas Nolan, one of Denmark's top-ranked distance runners, over 10,000 m. After the race, Nolan described what happened: "In the beginning,

(continued)

they ran quite fast. It was a hot day. I had confidence. I thought, 'Let them run. They don't know much about running because they have not done running before.'

But after the first 5000 m, the two young Kenyans maintained their lead. "I could not catch them up—they were getting farther and farther away. I think they were 50 or 60 m ahead when we came to the finishing line." Saltin's reported conclusion, unpopular in some quarters (B. Hamilton 2000; Entine 2000), is that "There are definitely some genes that are special here [in Kenya]. The genetic inheritance is there" (Aldridge 2000).

The HGP conclusion is not universally accepted (outside of the United States where debate on this issue is perhaps more restrained than in the rest of the world) since it is unlikely to be correct given that there are clear "racial" differences in responses of different populations to medications etc. that cannot be ignored. In June 2002, I attended a conference in which marked differences in insulin resistance were noted between Asian Indians and Europeans, such that body fat tables designed for Europeans are of a lesser value in assessing diabetes risk in Indians. This sort of argument is addressed in detail in Entine's book. But here we are not talking race but geographical/environmental influences on a specific population over centuries (i.e., it is the Kalenjins, not all Kenyans, who seem to be advantaged). Those influences can induce biological adaptations a la Darwin. Since some of these influences may benefit running, certain populations may be advantaged in running ability (or reduced risk of developing diabetes, etc.). The latter is accepted but the former apparently not. We have to interpret and report the truth as we see it just as sociologists will continue to report an opposite conclusion.

DISTANCES FROM 50 TO 100 KILOMETERS

Besides Arthur Newton, there are two modern runners whose achievements set them apart in the short ultradistance races of 50 to 100 km. The first is a Scotsman, Bruce Fordyce, who achieved greatness in the Comrades Marathon, the race that Arthur Newton popularized and that, with more than 10,000 entrants annually (25,000 in 2000) continues to be the most competitive short ultradistance marathon race in the world. The second is Mark Allen, six-time winner of the 226-km Hawaiian Ironman World Triathlon Championships.

Bruce Fordyce

According to his mother, Bruce Fordyce (figure 6.28) won his first race at the age of three and then did little serious running until after he had left school (Aitken 1983). At the age of 20, during an Old Boys' rugby match, he became aware that his fitness had fallen precipitously and he resolved to start running. In June 1976 he heard about the Comrades Marathon and started training with the idea of running the race the following year.

In his first run in 1977, Fordyce finished 43rd in 6:45:00. Only the following year, when he finished in 14th place in 6:11:00, did his potential become apparent. Thereafter, his running improved remorselessly. During the competitive phase of his running career, he won the Comrades Marathon eight consecutive times and the

London-to-Brighton Marathon three times, a feat never before achieved. He lowered the up-Comrades record three times and set the down-record, and he ran 4:50:21 for 50 miles (80 km), a world best, during the 1983 London-to-Brighton race.

What Fordyce perfected was consistency. In his competitive running career, he had very few bad races. This is arguably because he controlled all the variables that determine ultramarathon success. In doing so, he has, in my view, made the most important observations about training for short ultramarathons since Arthur Newton. Furthermore, his ideas seem to be of value for other endurance athletes, including swimmers, cyclists, and triathletes.

Table 6.26 presents in detail all the training distances Fordyce ran up until 1990, when he retired from competitive racing. As can be seen, he ran his first Comrades in 1977 on little training (1575 km between 1 January and 31 May). Then, in training for the 1978 race, he became injured and was only able to run a total of 285 km in January and February (compared to 472 km the previous year). This was the single most important event that shaped Fordyce's thinking. When the injury resolved, Fordyce increased his training and subsequently finished fourteenth in that year's Comrades Marathon. He is convinced that with a little more racing experience he might have done even better.

Fordyce subsequently told me that this performance made him suspect that runners such as Newton and Mekler had possibly trained too much for the race. He was particularly impressed by Dave Levick's Comrades performance in 1971 when, on a grand total of only 130 km of training in January and February, he ran one of the great Comrades, finishing second in 5:48:53 and going on to win the 1971 London-to-Brighton race in record time. Thus, Fordyce concluded that high training mileage starting in January and February, three months before the Comrades Marathon, was probably not necessary for a peak performance.

With the insight of the athletic genius that he is, Fordyce resolved not to follow the usual pattern of most runners, who, tasting success for the first time in a marathon or ultramarathon, conclude that they would do even better the next time by increasing their training mileage. (To underline the wisdom in Fordyce's thinking, compare the practice and beliefs of Ron Hill as well as the training Jackie Mekler did in 1958 and 1959 with what he did in 1963 and 1965.)

Fordyce decided to keep his total training distance down and, following the lead of another Comrades multiwinner, Alan Robb, he introduced more speed work and hill training. Thus, for the 1979 race, he increased his training distance for January to May by only 800 km, and for the remainder of his competitive career he kept this distance at about 2900 km for the last five months before the race. After 1979, his major training refinements were to define exactly what type of speed training he required and when. He also discovered that it was not possible to race ultramarathons too frequently, particularly leading up to the Comrades.

In 1983, Fordyce ran the Comrades and London-to-Brighton ultramarathons within 14 weeks of one another. As he took four to six weeks to recover from the Comrades and tapered for the last two weeks before the London-to-Brighton race, he had only six to eight weeks to prepare for that race. During that period he was only able to do two runs of 50 km or longer. Despite this, he ran one of the world's fastest times for 50 miles in the 1983 London-to-Brighton race. From his performance in this race, Fordyce concluded that it is not essential to do too many long runs to achieve success in distance running.

The only hiccups in his progress were injuries that occurred in March of 1979

and 1980 and in February of 1982. He believes that these were the result of starting specific Comrades training too soon, and this further convinced him of the need to be careful in January and February and to introduce intensive speed training only later. Of particular interest was that despite the low mileage he ran in February 1982 (282 km) owing to injury, he still won the Comrades that year.

Fordyce's training ideas are frighteningly simple. When asked to list the reasons for his success, he offered the following:

- He rarely did too much.
- He believed his leg strength worked in his favor. He found that in comparison to his competitors, he was particularly strong when running uphill or into the wind. Recently, Fordyce told me that he had noticed a common characteristic among the great short-distance ultramarathon runners he knew. Although they were all small, their legs were very muscular for their size—

Figure 6.28   Bruce Fordyce.

Sunday Times.

quite different to those of the Kenyans and the black South Africans against whom he had raced. He wondered if the inability of black South Africans to dominate the 90-km Comrades Marathon, as they do all other long distance races, might be because their legs are too thin.

- He also observed that he and many of the other leading South African ultramarathon runners, as well as Don Ritchie, have a common Scottish ancestry, and he wondered whether there is a Northern European gene for small bodies, big legs, and superior ultramarathon ability.

- He always exercised extreme caution and never lost focus in training or racing. In particular, he was careful not to overtrain (see chapter 7).

- He worked at improving his natural speed by racing on the track at 1500 to 10,000 m in the summer off-season. This had the effect of increasing his peak "cruising speed," particularly in the second half of ultramarathon races. This was best exemplified in the 1987 Comrades Marathon, in which he was 4.5 minutes behind the leader with 20 km to go, but which he won by 6.5 minutes, the latter all made up in the last 8 km. During that race he was timed at 03:20 per km between 60 and 70 km, equivalent to a standard marathon in 2:20:00, or only three minutes slower than his best.

- He believed in perfectionism, paying attention to all possible details, to the point of paranoia.
- He also trained at altitude.

Table 6.26   Bruce Fordyce's training and Comrades Marathon record (1977–1990)

Year	Age	Comrades direction	Comrades time (h:min:s)	Position	Total training distance (January–May) (km)	Monthly distances (January–May) (km)	Total distances from June–January previous year (km)
1990	34	up	05:40:25	1	2884	(525; 488; 520; 767; 584)	3132
1988	32	up	05:27:42	1	2901	(534; 440; 577; 734; 626)	2901
1987	31	up	05:37:01	1	2872	(513; 483; 563; 792; 521)	3389
1986	30	down	05:24:07	1	2960	(508; 518; 564; 750; 620)	2779
1985	29	up	05:37:01	1	2844	(568; 429; 500; 747; 600)	3168
1984	28	down	05:27:18	1	2713	(498; 404; 488; 760; 563)	2993
1983	27	up	05:30:12	1	2904	(498; 488; 552; 752; 614)	3055
1982	26	down	05:34:22	1	2960	(544; 282; 665; 786; 682)	3495
1981	25	up	05:37:28	1	3047	(619; 561; 561; 768; 538)	3139
1980	24	down	05:40:31	2	2925	(570; 410; 645; 610; 690)	3226
1979	23	up	05:51:15	3	2698	(503; 400; 423; 738; 634)	2472
1978	22	down	06:11:00	14	1887	(204; 81; 400; 670; 532)	1890
1977	21	up	06:45:00	43	1575	(216; 250; 359; 345; 405)	1146

Information courtesy of B. Fordyce.

During the latter phase of his career, he found that with age he had to reduce the intensity of his interval and hill sessions. I have consolidated the ideas that Fordyce expounded on training into a nine-point plan for the short ultramarathons, which in this case would be run in late May or early June.

1. Start gently in January and February regardless of fitness. Train hard over distances of 6 to 10 km, and do not run more than 110 km per week, with long weekend runs of up to 25 km. Fordyce includes one speed session per week on the track during January and February.

2. Start specific ultramarathon training only in mid-March. Fordyce began to move toward his peak by increasing his training distance to 130 km per week, and in April, which he considers to be the most important month, this rose to 176 to 192 km per week. He sustained this heavy training (beyond 130 km per week) for a maximum of eight weeks. A study showing a dramatic fall in both performance and $\dot{V}O_2$max during the sixth week of training (in athletes who underwent an intensive laboratory-based six-week peaking training program) provides further evidence for this six- to eight-week training rule (Mikesell and Dudley 1984).

3. Do specific speed training. Fordyce's speed sessions included hill training, which he hated but believed to be absolutely vital; time-trials of 8 to 10 km; cross-country races of up to 12 km; and track intervals (Fordyce 1996). For hill training, he ran a 410-m hill in 90 seconds, doing five to eight repetitions for the last four to five weeks before the race. Done any more frequently, this hill training caused fatigue the next day, which Fordyce considered to be a bad sign. For the first session, he ran six to eight hills at a slow pace; in the last two sessions, he ran fewer hills but at a faster pace (Fordyce 1996).

Interval sessions on the track were either six 800-m intervals run at 2:15 to 2:20, four 1-mile intervals run at 4:45 to 4:50 per mile, or a combination of intervals from 800 to 1200 m. In the eight-week period Fordyce averaged between 11 and 14 hard training sessions on Tuesdays and Thursdays and ran two cross-country races of 12 km. He advises,

Choose quality rather than quantity when training. Train for speed, not distance. The idea is not to be able to sprint—after all, most ultramarathons are decided long before the final meters are run—but to be able to raise cruising speed. I know that if I can race 10 km in under 30 minutes, I am going to find 3.5-minute kilometers fairly easy (Fordyce 1989, p. 32).

Fordyce did not believe his training to be any different from that of the standard marathon runners of his era, such as Rob de Castella. The only exception would be that an ultramarathoner would need to run more very long runs than those who are concentrating purely on the standard marathon (Aitken 1983).

After his fifth Comrades victory in 1985, Fordyce went through a period in which his running enthusiasm waned. His answer was to start racing on the track between November and March. This specific track training resulted in him achieving the following personal best times: 1500 m in 3:59 (at altitude); 1 mile in 4:10 (on the road); 3000 m in 8:36 (at altitude); 5000 m in 4:28; and 10,000 m in 30:28. This also helped increase his cruising speed in the latter stages of an ultramarathon.

4. Don't do too many long runs. Fordyce did surprisingly few long runs during the ultramarathon buildup (1 × 56 to 70 km, 8 × 42 to 56 km, 3 × 32 to 42 km, and 6 × 32 km) and never finished his club's 70-km pre-Comrades training run. He told me that after five-and-a-half hours on his feet, he has had enough and just "gets into the nearest car."

5. When in doubt, rest. As Fordyce explains,

> *My training advice is going to be different. . . because I place my emphasis on rest and recovery. I do believe in hard training, but there is only so much hard training that the body can take, and the timing and duration of any hard training phase is very important. During the hard training phase, never be afraid to take a day off. If your legs are feeling unduly stiff and sore, rest; if you are at all sluggish, rest; in fact, if in doubt, rest.* (Fordyce 1981, p. 4 to 5)

Fordyce also advocates running cautiously:

> *Caution is probably the most important word in the Comrades runner's dictionary. Caution should be applied both to training and to racing. It means not "flying off" at the sound of the Comrades [starting] gun; it means experimenting carefully with new ideas long before the race; and it means not falling into the trap of excessive training mileage. The concept of caution does not clash with confidence and self-belief. It is the dominant rule that should govern all your thinking about the race.* (Fordyce 1996, p. 18)

6. Don't run an all-out marathon 10 to 12 weeks before the ultramarathon. Fordyce selected his races carefully:

> *If you want to do well on the day that really matters, don't try to do well on the days that aren't as important. . . . Enter as many marathons as you like, but treat them as training runs—don't race. I enter a lot of local marathons as I find them an extremely pleasant way to run a weekend 42-km training run. I probably only race hard once (over the full marathon distance) in the five months before Comrades. (Fordyce 1981, p. 11)*

7. Taper before the race. In the years before Fordyce dominated the Comrades, it was generally held that the last month before the race was the time to train the hardest. Thus, the training mileages of previous Comrades greats, including Newton (table 6.5), show that they all trained their greatest distances in the last month (May) before the race. Only in the 1970s and 1980s has the concept of tapering become more popular.

Thus, Fordyce modified the ideas of the earlier Comrades runners by resting more in May and training hardest in April. He achieved this by following a definite taper, not dissimilar to that advocated by Newton.

8. Gauge your fitness by performance in shorter races and speed sessions. In chapter 5 we discussed the need for runners to gauge their fitness at any point in training. Two refinements that Fordyce included were the ability to gauge his fitness on the basis of performance in short-distance races and speed sessions.

Fordyce (1985) writes that when he could run 8 km in close to 25:00 (at medium altitude), he was ready for the Comrades. It is of interest that American marathoners Frank Shorter and Alberto Salazar said essentially the same for the standard marathon. Both judge their preparedness for the standard marathon on the basis of their times over 10 km. Not that this is anything new. At the turn of the century, the pedestrian Barclay wrote, *in the progress of his training, his condition may as well be ascertained . . . by the manner in which he performs one mile at the top of his speed, as to walk a hundred; . . . if he performs this short distance well, it may be concluded that his condition is perfect. (Downer 1900, p. 143)*

The short races that Fordyce ran before the Comrades included 6 or 7 8-km time-trials, one 10-km race, two 12-km cross-country races, one 21-km half-marathon, and one 32-km race. Note that he raced nothing longer before the Comrades. As I suggest in chapter 7, muscle damage seems to become progressively worse in races longer than about 28 km. Fordyce raced frequently at safe distances that were unlikely to cause muscle damage. He learned to gauge his fitness by his performance during his training sessions.

9. Do specific strength training for downhill ultramarathons. After his first down-Comrades victory in 1982, Fordyce remarked that the down-Comrades was not a race but a "survival trip." He referred to the more severe muscle damage caused by the downhill nature of the course. Before the 1984 race, he decided that he would have to do something to reduce that damage. Evidence suggests that strength training of the quadriceps (front thigh) muscle group may reduce the degree of muscle damage during downhill running. Thus, for the 1984 race, Fordyce underwent a weekly program of strength training for his quadriceps muscles and included more regular downhill running sessions. The details are included in his second book (Fordyce 1996).

Mark Allen

All of the athletes included in this chapter achieved exceptional success in their sport. For many, the duration of their success was relatively short. Their stories tell much about the factors that exhaust the body prematurely. At the other extreme are those athletes whose careers defy the normal. One such runner was Bruce Fordyce, whose repeated successes in the demanding Comrades Marathon will probably never be equaled. Californian Mark Allen is another athlete whose dominance of his sport, the 226-km Hawaiian Ironman Triathlon, arguably the toughest one-day endurance event in the world, was quite exceptional.

The experiences of Fordyce, Allen, and the third member of this trio of uniquely successful ultradistance athletes, Ann Trason, presented subsequently, provide additional information on approaches to training and racing that can ensure an especially long and productive racing career.

Allen's athletic career started in 1968, at age 10, when he began swimming competitively. For the next 12 years, he followed a regimented training program based on the simple philosophy of "Do more faster—if I could just train more yardage, and train faster, then I would most certainly race faster. Or so I thought" (Maffetone 1996, p. 9). This is reminiscent of Frank Stampfl's "Try harder still." Allen concluded that his results from this training program were mediocre at best. "Do more faster really only worked for those so talented that their genetics were going to override the lunacy of their training and take them on to greatness anyway" (Allen 1996, p. 9).

Allen's conversion from a burned-out swimmer to the world's best triathlete began in 1981 when he watched Julie Moss, the athlete who would later become his wife, crawl dramatically to the finish of that year's Hawaiian Ironman Triathlon race. Within days, he decided to try the triathlon, entering his first standard triathlon. Finishing fourth in a demanding event for which he had not trained, he learned two crucial facts. First, he discovered that he had a natural ability in this sport. The three athletes finishing ahead of him in that race were the three best in the world at that time—Dave Scott, Scott Molina, and Scott Tinley. Second, he learned that the triathlon race was not over until the finish line. In all his swimming races, he had learned that once he fell behind, he could not improve his position. Hence, he had become programmed to failure. Yet, in his very first triathlon he had discovered that perseverance would be rewarded. By being more patient, he had been able to repass close to the finish those runners who had passed him earlier.

At that time, his training continued to be based on the old "Do more faster" model. His results were again unpredictable, in part because, unlike the non-weight-bearing sport of swimming, the weight-bearing component of running introduced an additional damaging component.

Allen's career as a full-time professional triathlete began in 1983 when he entered his first Hawaiian Ironman Triathlon, having won his first triathlon, the Horny Toad Half-Ironman in San Diego, in 1982. In the same year, he won the Nice International Triathlon Championships. His record in the Nice and Hawaiian triathlons is a record unmatched and perhaps unmatchable, as Allen became the world's best triathlete at the standard (51.6 km), intermediate, and Ironman distances for more than a decade. He won 66 of the 96 races that he entered, finishing in the top three in 90% of his races. Between 1988 and April 1991, he was unbeaten in 20 races. He was also the first-ever winner of the International Triathlon Union World Olympic Distance Triathlon in Avignon, France, in 1989, and he is the only triathlete to have won the Triple Crown, with victories in Zofingen, Nice, and Hawaii in the same year (1993). His 15-year career as a professional triathlete ended with his final Hawaiian Ironman victory in 1995, at age 37. His consistent success is reminiscent of the domination that Paavo Nurmi achieved in distance running in the 1920s. Indeed, it may be appropriate to suggest that Allen is to the triathlon what Nurmi was to distance running in the 1920s.

Another turning point in Allen's career was in 1984, when he met Phil Maffetone, an applied kinesiologist who suggested that Allen was training too hard to be continually successful in the medium to long term. Accordingly, he proposed that Allen should train less hard for a period of up to three months each year. Using the Maffetone formula (chapter 5), Allen was encouraged to train at a heart rate of 150 beats per minute for the first three months of each new training year. Using this approach, Allen's performances became more consistent so that he won the 140-km World Championships in Nice, France, 10 times. Despite never being beaten in that race, he still had a weakness in his approach—he was unable to convert his international dominance at the standard 51.6-km triathlon distance or the Nice Triathlon (140 km) to success in the 226-km Hawaiian Ironman.

In six Hawaiian Ironman races between 1982 and 1988, Allen had been in contention, only to be reduced to a walk sometime in the last 90 minutes, or 21 km, of the race. Thus, in his very first race, aiming to finish in the top 100, he was in second place when his bicycle suffered a mechanical failure. In 1983, he finished in third place after leading the race by 13:00 at the start of the run; in 1984, he was leading the run by 12 minutes but was passed by Dave Scott, with 21 km to go. He finished fifth. In 1986, he finished second. In 1987, he held a 5-minute lead over Scott with 16 km to go. Again, reduced to a walk, he was passed by Scott before the finish, again finishing second. In 1988, he again led the race after the cycle leg, before being passed by Dave Scott in the run, finishing fifth.

Before the 1989 race, he decided to change his mental approach. As described in chapter 8, he realized that he feared the race and had developed a negative mindset toward the entire experience, especially the uncompromising environment in which the race was held. He had also tried to win the race by training as hard as he thought necessary to win. Realizing that this race might require more than he had been prepared to give, he decided to do "whatever it takes" to win.

That he corrected his failings was shown by his five consecutive victories between 1989 and 1993. Then in 1995, at age 37, he returned to win the race a sixth time. Like Fordyce, Allen became a ruthless perfectionist. Of his approach, Paul Huddle (another triathlete and coach of Paula Newby-Fraser) wrote,

> The amazing thing about Mark was that every year, you would think he'd back off, but he was always upping the ante. The big conception was that he was relying on his spiritual practice, but the fact is he was always trying to extract every ounce from every corner of his training. Always trying to improve on how he was doing it.

In early 1989, Allen went to Queenstown, New Zealand, for six weeks of intensive training. It raised him to a new performance level. He was, he said, finally "starting to live what it was going to take to win the race" (Allen 1998b). He had also learned patience; the patience to know that the race is won only when you cross the finish line. In that race, perhaps the classic Ironman of all time, he had raced for 8 hours alongside the other great American Ironman triathlete, David Scott. Only in the last 4 km had Allen been able to pull away, winning by less than a minute (see figure 6.29).

His next four consecutive victories through 1993 left Allen emotionally and physically exhausted. At age 35 he retired for 18 months to a more cloistered existence in an attempt to regain his physical and emotional strength, hoping that he would still achieve one final Ironman victory. After 18 months, his body responded and he returned to contest the 1995 Hawaiian Ironman at age 37, wondering whether he was too old. The mental aspects of his remarkable victory in that race are described in chapter 8.

Allen's training approach was to divide his year into three phases (Allen 1996b; table 6.27). The first phase would begin in January after two months of rest in November and December following the Hawaiian Ironman Triathlon, which is contested on the first Saturday in October closest to the appearance of the new moon. During the first phase, his Patience Phase, Allen combined aerobic training with weight training. This period would last three months. During this time, he would not train at a heart rate in excess of that allowed by the Maffetone formula, which was about 150 beats per minute during the last five years of his career. During this period of training, he was swimming 21 km per week, cycling 500 km per week, and running for 6 hours (approximately 90 km) per week. Thus, his total endurance training time was about 27 hours per week during this period. Allen would also undertake two strength training workouts each week but would always leave at least two days between sessions.

To monitor his progress, Allen would complete an 8-km run at his maximal allowed aerobic heart rate of about 150 beats per minute. During his Patience Phase, his average pace when running at that heart rate would fall progressively. When he first started training according to the Maffetone approach, his aerobic pace during this test was 4:05 per km. During this phase, Allen would expect his running speed at his aerobic heart rate to fall by about 3 to 4 seconds per km per week.

Photo courtesy of Lois Schwartz

Figure 6.29 Mark Allen and Dave Scott in the 1989 Hawaiian Ironman Triathlon, the epic race in which Allen won by less than 2:00 after the two had raced neck-and-neck for more than 8 hours. Allen broke away in the last 4 km of the marathon leg.

When Allen retired in 1995, his aerobic pace had improved to 3:19 per km, as the result of a steady progression during his entire career. For physiologists used to reporting human training studies lasting a few months, this is a remarkable finding. It shows that the human body may continue to adapt for 10 or more years to the form of prolonged, intensive training undertaken by Allen.

He would terminate his Patience Phase when either

- his speed during the 8-km aerobic run was no longer improving or was, in fact, deteriorating, indicating that he was no longer adapting to the aerobic training, or
- he was about five or six weeks before the first race of the season, usually a standard distance triathlon.

During the second phase of his training, the Speed-Work Phase, Allen reduced his training slightly but added two speed sessions, one on the bicycle and one running fartlek session. As a result, his training volume during this period included swimming 18.5 km per week, cycling 480 km per week, and running 8 hours per week.

Allen advised that when he was young, presumably under 30, he could complete 10 to 12 weeks of this type of training. As he aged, he found it more difficult to

Table 6.27 Mark Allen's three training phases

"Patience"

	Swim	Bike	Run
Monday	4 km	48 km	60:00
Tuesday	4 km	Rest	01:15:00
Wednesday	Rest	176 km	30:00
Thursday	5 km	40 km	Rest
Friday	Rest	96 km	30:00
Saturday	6 km	144 km	50:00
Sunday	2 km	Rest	02:00:00
Totals	21 km	504 km	06:05:00

"Speedwork"

	Swim	Bike	Run
Monday	3 km	64 km	40:00
Tuesday	4.5 km	64 km	01:15:00 on trails Fartlek
Wednesday	Rest	144 km anaerobic effort	60:00
Thursday	3 km	Recovery ride	30:00
Friday	3 km	Rest	A.M. 50:00 P.M. 30:00
Saturday	5 km	144 km	15:00-20:00 run follows the ride
Sunday	Rest	32 km aerobic effort	Up to 2:30:00
Totals	18.5 km	448 km	7:35:00 = 120 km

"Push"

	Swim	Bike	Run
Monday	4 km	30 km. Easy	30:00. Easy
Tuesday	Rest	90-240 km; last 30% at anaerobic effort	50:00
Wednesday	5 km	Rest	A.M. 90:00 Hills. Hard effort P.M. 30:00. Easy
Thursday	4 km	120 km. Flat—no hills	40:00
Friday	4 km	180 km. Hills	50:00. Hills
Saturday	5 km	Speed. Short and fast	Trails or track. Short and fast
Sunday	6 km	50 km. Easy	2:30:00. Aerobic effort
Totals	28 km	≈ 800 km	8:20:00 = 130 km

Compiled by Svensson pp. 88, 90, and 94.

maintain this volume of training for as long. At age 37, he could maintain this training for six weeks. He predicts this would be reduced to five for athletes over 40 and to none for athletes over 50.

At the end of the previous phase, Allen would judge whether he had reaped all the benefit from this training schedule when his running pace at his aerobic heart rate plateaued. He wrote that

> *the key is to watch for a slowing of your pace at your maximum aerobic heart rate. When this happens, it's time to go back to your base-building phase. . . . It's very subtle, but if your heart rate starts going up for a given effort in workouts, you know that you're on the edge—just resting won't help; you have to modify your training. (Allen 1996b, p. 92)*

Allen notes that many other athletes would probably try to train through this plateau in an attempt to reach an illusive higher level of fitness. But Allen stresses that this will fail, as continuing to train when the body's adaptation has plateaued will lead only to mental burnout, overtraining, injury, and a subpar performance on race day. When this happens, Allen's advice is, "If you're burned out, put a big 'R' for rest in your training diary, close it and put it away. Rather go and play" (Allen 1996b, p. 92).

As he has grown older and is therefore unable to sustain this training phase for as long as before, he spends a few weeks of recuperation training, perhaps even including a full week of rest, in July and early August. During this period he does no speed training but reverts to training that does not elevate his heart rate above 150 beats per minute.

Eight weeks before the Hawaiian Ironman, Allen begins the Push Phase of his training. This consists of four hard weeks of training and a four-week taper. During this time, Allen does not race at all. This period of training is, in my view, the most taxing training ever recorded by any modern human athlete, exceeding even that of the Kenyans (table 6.28). During his peak training week, Allen will swim 28 km (8 hours), cycle approximately 800 km (22 hours), and run for a further 8 hours, for a total training time of 38 hours, equivalent to the hours many of us spend at work during a five-day working week. To develop both speed and endurance, Allen reverts to doing long intervals of up to 20 minutes in both cycling and running during his long rides or runs.

During his four-week taper period, Allen progressively reduces his cycling distance by 160 km per week so that in the final week of his taper, which includes the distance cycled during the Ironman, he cycles only 240 km. This means that he only cycles 60 km in the final six days before the Ironman. He reduces his weekly running distance by 24 km per week and only runs 16 km in the last six days before the Ironman.

Other advice offered by Allen includes the following:

- The key workouts each week during the Speed-Work and Push Phases are the two long-distance and two speed workouts, one each cycling and running. All training is built around those workouts.
- During the Speed-Work Phase, only one or preferably two, but certainly no more, sessions should be set aside for all-out speed training.
- His longest run before the Ironman was always five weeks before the race, and his longest cycle, four weeks before. His toughest speed session was three

weeks before the race, during the tapering period.

- For his long runs he would begin at 1 hour and then increase in stepped fashion by 10 minutes every second week, dropping back to the duration of the run two weeks earlier in the intervening week. Thus, the duration of the first seven consecutive long runs would be 60, 70, 60, 80, 70, 90, 80 minutes. After 15 weeks, this would increase to the 150-minute long runs that Allen maintained during the Speed-Work and Push Phases.

- In a discussion I had with him in Pajulahti, Finland, Allen added that the key to his longevity was the three months of gentle aerobic training in the Patience Phase. His belief is that once you begin speed training, the body enters a hyped-up state that wears you down, as you are unable to sleep properly and recover adequately during this period. Thus, in his opinion, intensive training produces a cumulative fatiguing effect, which is not due solely to the actual training performed but also to a residual effect that acts during the recovery period between training sessions.

- In response to my question why more triathletes do not follow his methods, which have clearly proved effective, Allen answered that many athletes are too ego-driven. They can't wait to perform well and will not accept anyone else's ideas.

The similarities between ideas, training methods, and successes of both Bruce Fordyce and Mark Allen are so striking that one is left to assume that all are causally related (that is, that their ideas and training methods produced their successes). I would suggest that the next athletes to match their successes will do so by adopting their training ideas.

DISTANCES OF MORE THAN 100 KILOMETERS

One of the first modern references to an ultradistance performance was that of Captain Barclay, who in 1806 walked 160 km in 19 hours. Three years later he ran a mile every hour for 1000 consecutive hours (41 days and 16 hours). Barclay was clearly an unusual man. A wealthy landowner, the sixth Laird of Vry, he had at the age of 21 submitted to the training of a tenant farmer, Jackey Smith, then the most celebrated British trainer of pedestrians. This involved a major role reversal, uncommon in a society in which a gentleman never accepted orders from those who were his social inferiors.

Smith's training program lasted four to six weeks and included running, walking, and hard physical labor (Radford 1985). Smith was a hard taskmaster, once forcing Barclay to complete a 110-mile time-trial. The training that Barclay received from Smith provided the basis for Barclay's training methods, which he applied in 1807 when he himself became an athletic trainer.

Barclay believed that the novice runner who had already undergone a 12-day period of taking a course of "physic," comprising a dose of "Glauber's salts," was ready to start training. Barclay's training ideas are documented in Walker's *Manly Exercises* (quoted by Doherty 1964), in *Running Recollections and How to Train* (Downer 1900), and in *Pedestrianism* (Thom 1813).

Another component of the Barclay method was time-trials—a feature of the training of Walter George and Alfred Shrubb. Barclay also paid great attention to diet

(Thom 1813; Downer 1900). He preferred foods of animal origin, in particular lean beef, mutton (occasionally), and the legs of fowl. All veal, lamb, pork, fish, eggs, and fatty or greasy substances—in particular milk, butter, and cheese—and salts, spices, and seasonings were prohibited. Vegetables were also avoided, and biscuits and stale bread were the only foods of vegetable origin that could be consumed. The only liquor allowed was old home-brewed beer, not exceeding three pints per day, and half a pint of red wine after dinner. The drinking of other liquids, water especially, was strongly discouraged. Too much water was believed to "swell the belly," to be "bad for the wind," to "take up space" needed for solid food, and to promote "soft, unhealthy flesh."

Hereditary factors seem to have been important in Barclay's success. His father was said to have been so powerful that "finding a stray horse in one of his fields, he lifted it on to his shoulders and threw it over the hedge" (Milroy 1987). While a member of parliament, his grandfather would walk to Westminster from his home in Urie at the start of each parliamentary session and "would pick up many a prize hat for cudgel play, and wrestling on the road" (Downer 1900 p. 131). Barclay was also very strong; he once lifted a 100-kg man with one hand and placed him on a table (Milroy 1987).

Early Pedestrians

American Edward Payson Weston inspired one of the most heroic and interesting eras in the history of running. Weston, who became known as the father of pedestrianism, was born in Providence, Rhode Island, on 15 March, 1839 (Osler and Dodd 1977; 1979). He first gained fame in 1861 by walking a distance of 713 km from Boston to Washington to attend the inauguration of President Lincoln. In 1867, he walked from Portland, Maine, to Chicago, Illinois, covering a distance of 2135 km in 26 days. Thereafter, his goal became that of covering 800 km in six days, or 144 hours. He finally succeeded at his third attempt in December 1874, thereby winning a gold watch, plus the title Pedestrian Champion of the World.

The following year Daniel O'Leary, an Irish immigrant to North America, walked 800 km in Chicago and challenged Weston to a match to decide the world champion. The race, held from 15 to 20 November, 1875, was won by O'Leary, who covered 800.4 km to Weston's 720 km.

The following winter, Weston went to England, where he was unbeaten in a series of races. His best performance (801.6 km) was achieved at the Agricultural Hall in London, where he met Sir John Drysdale Astley, a baron and member of parliament, who agreed to back Weston against anyone else in the world. Meanwhile, O'Leary, learning of Weston's great successes in England, also traveled to London, where he challenged Weston to a showdown in April 1877. Again O'Leary triumphed, with a new world record of 837 km to Weston's 816 km. Despite losing £20,000 on Weston, Sir John Astley decided to sponsor the official World Pedestrian Championships. He donated the Astley Belt, valued at £100, and £2000 in prizes for the Long-Distance Challenge Championship of the World.

The first Astley Belt race was held at the Agricultural Hall in London in March 1878, and the second at Madison Square Garden in October 1878. Both were convincingly won by O'Leary, with a best distance of 837.7 km, a new world record. Weston entered neither.

Despondent at the American domination of this event, Astley began the search for a British pedestrian who could tackle the foreigners. He chose Charles Rowell, a 24-year-old boat boy from Maidenhead, Kent, with little athletic experience besides a modest best 15-km time of 60 minutes. Rowell, who was five foot six and weighed 63 kg, was given support and time to train. In the winter of 1879, he set sail for America to vindicate British pedestrianism.

The third Astley Belt contest was held in March 1879 at Madison Square Garden. O'Leary, worn out from too much racing, was no match for Rowell, who won with a distance of 800.2 km, a quite remarkable performance for a novice; O'Leary had retired on the third day.

Three months later, the fourth Astley Belt was contested in London. Rowell was unable to compete due to injury. Weston, who had watched Rowell's progress, had by this time realized that a good runner like Rowell would always beat a good walker. Before the race, he had started running training. Using his new technique, Weston took the lead on the fourth day of the race, finishing with a new world record of 880 km. Again, three months later, the fifth Astley Belt was contested at Madison Square Garden. Rowell regained the championship belt with a distance of 843.8 km and returned to Britain.

One week after the finish of the fifth Astley Belt race, the first O'Leary Belt race, sponsored by Daniel O'Leary, was held. O'Leary's stated purpose in sponsoring the race was to develop a pedestrian capable of bringing the Astley Belt back to the United States, but financial motives may also have played a role—O'Leary and his supporters reportedly made upward of $60,000 profit from the race.

The race was won by the novice Nicholas Murphy, who finished with a total of 808 km. One of the athletes initiated to the sport by the race was Patrick Fitzgerald of Long Island, who had earlier run 17.6 km in 59:50. Fitzgerald then competed in a number of six-day, 14-hour-a-day contests, and within two months he finished his first full six-day event, covering 838.5 km. Fourth place went to the African-American Fred Hirchborn from Boston, who covered 776 km, beating Weston. Hirchborn was nicknamed "Black Dan" since he received financial backing from Daniel O'Leary himself. His performances inspired two other African-Americans, William Pegram and Ed Williams, to join the professional pedestrian circuit (Entine 2000).

The second O'Leary Belt race was held in Madison Square Garden in April 1880. This was a far more competitive race and was won by Frank Hart, who covered 909.7 km, a new world record. En route, he set an American 24-hour record of 210.9 km. Three of the top American finishers in that race, William Pegram, John Dobler, and H. Howard, then challenged Rowell for the Astley Belt. Hart and O'Leary could see no reason to travel to Britain. Instead, they invited Rowell to a return race in America.

The sixth Astley Belt race began at the Agricultural Hall, London, on 1 November, 1880. However, they were overruled, and ended back in London. Included in the field were the Englishmen Blower Brown, who had previously set a world record of 890.5 km, and George Littlewood, from Sheffield, the latter competing in his second six-day event. Rowell took off quickly, going through 160 km in a record 13:57:13, en route to a world 24-hour record of 235.2 km covered in 22:27:00. By the end of three days, he had covered 547.4 km, and he eventually finished with a new world record of 911.4 km. Littlewood was second with 756.7 km. The first American was Dobler, who covered 724.5 km. The Americans ascribed their failure to the poor condition of the Agricultural Hall.

With three Astley Belt victories, Rowell needed only one more victory to obtain absolute possession of the coveted prize. He was challenged by Weston in the seventh and last Astley Belt race, held in June 1881 at the Marble Rink in London. With Weston came O'Leary, Frank Hart, Charles Harriman, and John Ennis: the latter two had also competed in the third Astley Belt race. Sadly, Weston fell ill the night before the race and withdrew on the third day after completing 323.6 km to Rowell's 450.8 km.

The world six-day record was improved three times by Americans in 1881; the last record was set by Fitzgerald, who covered 937 km at the American Institute Building in Manhattan in December. Rowell, who was in attendance, vowed to start training the next day for a race to take place the following February. In this race, which Rowell stated was to be his last, he wished to set a record that would last forever—1127.0 km in six days. The race was held from 27 February to 4 March, 1882, in Madison Square Garden. Also competing were the American current and former world record holders, Fitzgerald and John Hughes. In training for the race, Rowell ran and walked 64 km per day. During the race, Rowell passed 160 km in 13:26:30 and after 22.5 hours had completed 241.8 km, both new world records. He passed 320 km in 35:09:28, his third world record, and after 48 hours had completed 416 km for his fourth world record. On the third day, he passed 480 km in 58:17:06, finishing the day with 568.5 km—his fifth and sixth world records respectively.

Sadly, on the morning of the fourth day Rowell accidentally ingested a cupful of vinegar and retired from the race shortly thereafter. The race was won by the Englishman George Hazael, with a new world record distance of 967.8 km. Fitzgerald came second with 929.2 km. Rowell was clearly not prepared to retire after such a disappointment. He entered a further six-day race in September 1882, but retired after the third day because of an illness, which was later diagnosed as malaria. He went home to Britain and rested on his farm for one year. In October 1883, Rowell returned to New York and started training for a return match with Fitzgerald, to be held in Madison Square Garden from 28 April to 3 May, 1884.

This proved to be a remarkable event. On the afternoon of the sixth day, Rowell closed the gap on the exhausted Fitzgerald to less than 3 km, whereupon Fitzgerald's medical adviser, a Dr. Taylor, performed a treatment that was used at the time and lacerated Fitzgerald's legs with a mechanical scarifier. The treatment was apparently effective; the exhausted Fitzgerald was sufficiently revived for him to hold off Rowell's final challenge and to complete a new world record distance of 982 km to Rowell's 969.2 km.

During 1888, the last three important six-day events were held in Madison Square Garden. In the first, James Albert from Philadelphia increased the world record to 1001.0 km; in May, George Littlewood returned from Britain and completed 984.1 km, the second-best performance ever. Then, in November, he completed 1004.2 km in 4 hours less than six days. It was the final great race. Despite attempts at a renaissance in 1901, it would be another 90 years before six-day racing was revived.

Of the great pedestrians, Weston and O'Leary continued to walk for the rest of their lives. O'Leary made a custom of walking 160 km within 24 hours on every birthday and was able to keep this up until he turned 75, on which occasion he completed the 160 km in 23:54. O'Leary died at the age of 87; Weston, who at the age of 70 walked from New York City to San Francisco, a distance of 6279 km, in 105 days, died at 90. Osler and Dodd (1979) note that the other pedestrians were not as fortunate—Rowell died at 55, Fitzgerald at 53, and Blower Brown at 41. They wonder whether Weston's self-control, in particular his ability to quit instead of forcing himself when he was overextended, might not have been a factor in his greater longevity.

Andy Milroy (1983) has done a detailed analysis of the techniques used by the top pedestrians. He has found that professional pedestrians usually came from working-class families and were lured to this most grueling of activities by the remarkable financial incentives—one victory in a six-day race could provide financial security for life. Only the very best athletes became pedestrians, and many were world record holders for shorter-distance races.

Milroy concludes that the pedestrians' success was probably due to their willingness to cut their sleep to 3 hours or less a night, to running to a preplanned schedule of rest at least at the start, and to their ability to walk at 6.4 km per hour for long periods even when utterly exhausted.

U.S. Transcontinental Races of 1928 and 1929

The details of one of the most remarkable pair of races in the history of running can be found in Arthur Newton's *Running in Three Continents* (1940) and in the definitive history, based on the press reports of the race, *From LA to New York, from New York to LA* (Berry 1990). These races were the brainchild of Charles C. "Cash and Carry" Pyle, who thought up the idea while living in Champaign, Illinois.

Pyle was perhaps the first North American sports entrepreneur. He first signed to represent the legendary University of Illinois running back, Harold Grange. After negotiating a contract for Grange with the Chicago Bears, Pyle organized an 18-game tour for the Bears across the United States. The tour was a huge success, launching professional football in North America and securing substantial wealth for both Grange and Pyle, who split half of all the gate takings on the tour; the Bears received the remainder.

After introducing a professional tennis tour to the United States in 1926, Pyle began in 1927 to think of an event that would have the appeal of the annual Tour de France cycling race. He decided on a multistage foot-race across the width of the North American continent—"Man alone, unaided by machine, pitting his strength against the American topography"(H. Berry 1990, p. 5).

The 1928 race would follow in part the newly completed Highway 66, which linked Los Angeles to Chicago. The race distance for 1928 would be 4960 km in 84 stages, and the winner would receive $2,000, with another $24,000 to be shared by the next nine finishers. The following year the race would be run in the reverse direction in 78 stages. The end result was that 199 runners started the 1928 race and 55 finished. The following year, 69 runners started from New York and 19 finished in Los Angeles. Whereas the winner of the 1928 race, Andrew Payne of Oklahoma, received his winnings, the 1929 winner, John Salo, a Finnish runner residing in New Jersey, received nothing. The races had bankrupted Pyle.

The two most accomplished runners who started those races were Arthur Newton and Willi Kolehmainen, elder brother of Hannes Kolehmainen and considered by many Finns to have been a greater runner than his younger brother, whom he had coached. Kolehmainen had turned professional in 1912 at age 22, when he had immigrated to the United States, thereby excluding himself from Olympic competition.

The medical and physiological challenges that the runners had to overcome during these events are described by Berry in an absorbing summary.

Consider the topography of the United States of America, from the Atlantic to the Pacific. Relate this to the requirements of two-legged travel. In the Mojave Desert the temperature has a steady range, from 128 to 134°F (53 to 57°C). The air is dry and the radiant heat from the sun combines to limit the body's ability to shed the heat produced by the working muscles. (H. Berry 1990, p. vi)

Another novel situation for all but a few was the effects of high altitude, in particular while crossing the Rockies. It is accepted that at elevations over 1524 m the capacity to transport oxygen to the working muscles becomes progressively impaired. At 2438 m, the maximal oxygen uptake is about 90% of that at sea level. At 3657 m it is 80%, and at 4572 m, 70%. For days the runners were required to race at these elevations.

Two medical reports were compiled from studies of some participants in the 1928 race (J.T. Farrell et al. 1929; Gordon and Baker 1929). J.T. Farrell et al. (1929) performed X-ray examinations of the heart and limbs of 23 athletes three days after they had completed the 1928 race. There was no evidence for the enlargement of the heart, and the bones and joints were essentially normal. The authors concluded that "the data as a whole suggest that the immediate effects of long-distance running are inconsequential, since all of the changes noted may be found in individuals of similar ages without symptoms" (p. 398).

From their study, Gordon and Baker (1929) concluded that only 40 of the 199 competitors appeared capable of withstanding the stress of competition. Significant infections of the lungs and gastrointestinal tract were present in 21 runners before the race; 11 had moderate emphysema, a chronic condition of the lungs; and 18 had significant orthopedic problems in the lower limbs. A full 50% of competitors were considered physically underdeveloped (presumably malnourished), and only six had trained by running more than 25 miles (40 km) per day. Few had competed in long-distance races.

During the event, infections became more prevalent: the most common injury was tibial bone strain (shinsplints). The English runners were apparently least affected, possibly because they "ran in a more or less flat-footed manner, lifting the foot not more than 3 or 4 inches from the ground." The chief causes of withdrawal from the race were injuries (especially bone strain, muscular pain, and stiffness, which reduced running speed to the point where the athletes were unable to complete the daily racing distance sufficiently quickly), financial difficulties, and apparent loss of interest.

Of the 57 (or 55, according to H. Berry [1990]) athletes who completed the race, 43 were considered to be in excellent physical condition, even running the last 40 km of the race in under 2:50:00.

A significant observation was that "a high caloric intake, derived from all foods, was more important than any fixed dietetic regime. The most successful runners consumed readily available carbohydrate between meals, followed an unrestricted high-calorie diet at meal time and ingested meat at the evening meal" (H. Berry 1990, p. 5).

Newton (1947b) wrote that after one or two weeks of experimenting, all runners in the race settled down to a single method: "As big a breakfast as they
(continued)

could eat was tucked away immediately before the start" (p. 9). They would then run slowly for some 24 km, whereafter they would start ingesting "highly sweetened" drinks if the day's run was under 64 km. On longer stages, they would devour thin cheese or honey sandwiches. On even longer stages, they might eat more sandwiches and fruit and would drink every 8 to 10 km. At night they would eat a second heavy meal.

The final conclusion of Gordon and Baker (1929) was that "the data suggest that the comparatively normal human body, provided with adequate food and rest, may acquire during prolonged exercise unusual capacity for work apparently without serious untoward effect" (p. 8).

Modern Pedestrians

The demise of public interest in extreme ultradistance races occurred paradoxically at the exact time that interest in marathon running was rekindled by the inclusion of the event in the first modern Olympic Games in Greece in 1896. It coincided, too, with the popularization of bicycle travel.

Interest in ultradistance running was initially rekindled in England. In July 1803, a Captain Robertson had walked from Brighton to London and back in 45 hours. He repeated the feat in November 1804, covering the first leg to the famous Westminster Bridge in 14 hours.

On 30 January, 1837, two professional runners, John Townsend and Jack Berry, ran from the Elephant and Castle Pub in London to Brighton. This race was established formally in 1897 when some 50 professional runners took part in the first official London-to-Brighton race organized by the Polytechnic Harriers, with about 75% of the field reaching Brighton before the official 8:15:00 time limit. The first official amateur running of the London-to-Brighton race was in 1899.

The next crucial event was the first running of the Comrades Marathon in 1921. It was through his interest in the Comrades Marathon that Arthur Newton went to Britain to set a new London-to-Brighton record in 1924 and a new 160-km road record in 1928 before competing as the star attraction in the 1928 and 1929 U.S. Transcontinental Races. Thereafter, in 1931, he traveled to Canada for the first modern indoor 24-hour run, in which he eased past Rowell's one-day best with 152 miles, 540 yards (245 km). It would be another 20 years before another 24-hour race would be staged. The next amateur London-to-Brighton race was held in 1951. It then became the testing round for the best British and South African ultramarathon runners of the era, as before this there were few regular 100-km races on the European running circuit.

Only in 1973 were 24-hour track races again held on a regular basis in South Africa, Italy, and Great Britain. In the first such British race, Ron Bentley eclipsed Wally Hayward's previous 24-hour mark by running 259.7 km, a one-day record that stood until 1979. In May 1981, the Frenchman Jean-Gilles Boussiquet extended the record to 272.7 km; he had previously set world records of 260.8 and 264 km. The following year, the British runner Dave Dowdle increased this to 274.6 km, a distance that has since been surpassed by the modern Greek phenomenon, Yiannis Kouros.

Events longer than 24 hours have an even shorter modern history. In May 1979, the American Don Choi organized the first 48-hour race for well over 80 years. A year later, he organized the first six-day race, which he won with a distance of 645.6 km. For the rest, the history of the modern six-day events revolves around one man, Yiannis Kouros, who has set more than 56 world records at distances from 160 to 1000 km.

Yiannis Kouros

Yiannis Kouros began running as a child because, coming from a poor family, he could not afford the entertainment and luxuries available to other youngsters. By the age of 16, he was ranked among the top three schoolboys in Greece at 1500 m (4:09) and 3000 m (9:03).

Kouros sprang to international prominence when he won the inaugural 240-km Spartathlon from Sparta to Athens in September 1983. His winning time of 21:53:42 was greeted with some skepticism, particularly as he won the race by 2:45:00 and other competitors were known to have accepted car rides during the race.

Any doubts about his abilities and integrity were dispelled in April 1984, when he won each stage of the three-day, three-stage, 320-km Danube race in 23:16:15, a full 3 hours ahead of the second runner. Less than 10 weeks later, he competed in his first six-day race on Randall's Island, New York. After 48 hours he had completed 429.6 km, an improvement of 8.8 km on Ramon Zabalo's record set earlier that year, and after six days he surpassed George Littlewood's 96-year-old (1888) mark of 1004.2 km, with a final distance of 1022.1 km. Four months later, in November, running on a 1-mile circuit in Queens, New York, he set world road bests of 11:46:37 for 160 km and 15:11:48 for 200 km, and a new 24-hour world best of 285 km. Three weeks later, in his second six-day race in Colac, he increased his world six-day record by just over a kilometer to 1023.6 km.

In March the following year, in a two-day race in Montauben, France, Kouros improved his world 200-km best to 15:11:09 and his world 48-hour best to 452.8 km. One month later, he won the Sydney-to-Melbourne 966-km race in 125:07:00, and at the end of the year, in Queens, he again improved his world 24-hour best to 286.6 km. In February 1986, competing in a 24-hour indoor race on a track measuring 11 laps to the mile, he set world records at all distances up to 200 km, ending with 251.2 km, a new world indoor best—albeit only 6 km better than Newton's 1931 indoor performance in Hamilton. In October 1986, he returned to Greece and bettered his controversial Spartathlon record by more than 90 minutes.

In March 1987, Kouros again won the 1060-km Sydney-to-Melbourne race in 134:47:00, equivalent to 1127 km in six days, the distance for which Rowell had first aimed 105 years earlier. He reportedly slept for only 6 hours during the race. The following year, although the organizers asked Kouros to give the field a 12-hour start, he still won.

Kouros continued to dominate these races until 1991, when he fell out with the organizers of the Sydney-to-Melbourne race and chose to run the race solo for another group of organizers. He had also moved from Greece to Sydney in 1990 before settling in Melbourne in 1991.

For the next three years, he registered as a full-time bachelor of arts student at La Trobe University, completing his master's degree in Greek literature and at the same time becoming an Australian citizen. He returned to ultradistance running in 1994, finishing second in a seven-day race across Tasmania. In May 1995, he established new world track records in Surgeres, France, for 24 hours (285.36 km) and 48 hours

(470.78 km). The following year, he improved his 48-hour record to 473.797 km.

In Canberra in 1997, he aimed to run 300 km in 24 hours but on a wet track fell just short, completing 295.03 km. Then, in October 1997, in what he vowed would be his last 24-hour track race, he set the new world record of 303.51 km, a record which he predicts will last for centuries.

Between August 1990, when Kouros set his first 24-hour track world record of 280.469 km, and 1997, in which he set a record of 303.506 km, Kouros bettered the world record by 8.2%. He then set his sights on the 24-hour road, the 48-hour track, and the 1000-mile records. Indeed, in May 1998, he improved his 24-hour road record to 290.221 km in Basel, Switzerland.

Milroy (2000) has made a careful analysis of Kouros' impact on ultradistance running. He notes that between 1880 and 1980, performance in the 24-hour race had improved by 6% (16 km) compared to an 11% improvement in the mile during the same time. However, Kouros' 1997 record represents a 15% improvement on the 1880 record. By comparison, the mile record has improved by 14% in the same period. Thus, Kouros' efforts have brought the rate of improvement in the 24-hour race in line with those recorded in other distances over the last century. In effect, one man's efforts have, in some ways, been equivalent to those of all the best milers of the last century.

An important factor that helps explain Kouros' remarkable success is that, like Fordyce and Ritchie, he has a relatively fast best marathon time (2:24:01) for an ultramarathon runner. He also has a remarkable ability to go without sleep for prolonged periods of time. In the Colac race, in which he set the current six-day world record, he was off the track for only 4 hours during the entire 144 hours of the race. Like the famous pedestrians, he taught himself to race-walk at 6.4 km per hour for prolonged periods, and his approach in these races, like Rowell's, is to run hard from the start and then walk a great deal. Of his training little is known, except that he runs 20 to 25 km per day. He prefers races of 100 to 300 km. He is also virtually a vegetarian, eating very little meat.

Physiological information on Kouros has been published (Rontoyannis et al. 1989). At the time of testing, Kouros was 1.71 m tall, weighed 64 kg with 8% body fat, and had a $\dot{V}O_2$max of 63 ml O_2 per kg per min. Data for his energy balance during the 1985 960-km Sydney-Melbourne race, which he won by more than 24 hours in 125:07:00, were also provided. During the five days of the race, Kouros averaged 11.7, 8.3, 8.1, 8.9, and 6.2 km per hour, which corresponded to 57%, 41%, 40%, 44%, and 30% of his $\dot{V}O_2$max; he slept for a total of 4 hours, 40 minutes; and he rested for an additional 9 hours, 40 minutes. His daily energy expenditure ranged from 15,367 Kcal on the first day to 7736 Kcal on the fifth day, and his daily energy intake ranged from 13,770 Kcal to 7800 Kcal over the same period. Overall, his total estimated energy intake (55,970 Kcal) exceeded his energy expenditure (55,079 Kcal).

To maintain his high rate of energy consumption, Kouros ate every 15 minutes: his intake included Greek sweets; dried fruits and nuts; biscuits soaked in honey or jam; and fresh fruit, such as pears, melon, watermelon, grapes, apples, bananas, plums, pineapple, and dates. His only meat intake was a small amount of roast chicken on the morning of the fourth day. Carbohydrates provided 96% of his total energy intake. The true magnitude of Kouros' eating ability is shown by comparing his daily energy intake with that of cyclists in the Tour de France, the group of athletes with the highest recorded rates of daily energy intake. Only those cyclists whose rates of daily energy consumption equal their rates of use are able to finish the race (Brouns et al. 1989a; 1989b; Saris et al. 1989). Remarkably, the daily rates of energy expenditure of cyclists in the Tour de France (24,000 kJ; 5700 Kcal) are considerably lower than the 7736 to 15,367 Kcal achieved by Kouros during his ultradistance races. Kouros drank small amounts of water, fruit juice, or Gatorade every 10 to 15 minutes. His daily fluid intake varied from 22 L on the first day to 14.3 L on the fourth day and averaged 800 ml per hour that he ran. He finished his race 500 g lighter than he started.

His only medical complaints were severe constipation and frequency of urination, the latter possibly owing to what may have been an excessively high fluid intake for his rate of energy expenditure (chapter 4). Bladder trauma resulting from the continuous running may also have contributed.

Milroy (1998) has suggested some other reasons for Kouros' unprecedented success. These include his physical strength; during his career Kouros changed shape, becoming progressively more muscular in his upper body, trunk, back, and legs. Today, he looks more like a mesomorphic wrestler than an ectomorphic runner. Kouros has achieved this by following by a sustained program of weight training for his upper body and legs and by using a rowing machine to strengthen his back and torso.

He is also a stickler for his prerace preparation. During races he uses music to put himself into a trance-like state (a "zone"). This may explain why his greatest races have been on tracks, closed road loops, or open highways with limited traffic, where he can more easily enter this trance. He has not run as well on uneven terrain.

His pace judgment has improved progressively over the past 15 years so that his effort over a 24- or 48-hour period is apportioned more equally between the four quarters of the race. In his most recent races, the total distance he covers in the four quarters of the race are approximately 27.5%, 25.8%, 23.6%, and 23.1% of the total distance. This represents a substantial reduction in the proportion run in the first quarter, with a sizeable increase in the final quarter.

Eleanor Adams

Englishwoman Eleanor Adams is considered to be the greatest woman ultradistance runner ever. The only woman who has come close to matching Adams' performances is American Ann Trason, whom we discuss in the following section.

Adams' competitive abilities over a range of running distances have never been matched by any other male or female. She has set world track and road records at distances from 40 to 1600 km and holds the women's course records for the 240-km Sparta-to-Athens Spartathlon, the 1060-km Sydney-to-Melbourne race, and the 234-km Death Valley to Mount Witney race in California, in which she has recorded the second fastest time ever by any competitor of either gender. This race stretches from the lowest to the highest point in the United States—particularly remarkable for a native of Britain who trains in moderate environmental conditions. Another race in her long list of credits is a victory in the 1986 86-km London-to-Brighton race.

Adams first began competitive running at school and represented Yorkshire on the track and at cross-country at distances from 800 m to 4 km. She was also the county school champion at 800 m. After leaving school, she studied physical education and continued to compete in cross-country events. After graduating she taught, married, and soon had three active children, which left her with insufficient time to do much more than regular jogging. Her competitive instincts were reawakened in 1979 when she finished second in her age group in a 4-km fun run in Hyde Park, London. The next week she joined a local running club and entered an 8-km race. For the next year she raced regularly in road and cross-country races, and in 1980 she ran her first 42-km standard marathon, finishing as second woman home in a time of 3:24:00.

In 1982 Eleanor Adams won the same marathon in 2:54:00 and, in the same year, achieved her then best standard marathon time of 2:49:52. Inspired by the first modern British six-day race in Nottingham in 1981, she entered her first 12-hour ultradistance race at Barnet in 1982 and set an unratified world track record at 50 miles (6:41:02). In October, she set new world records at 20 miles (2:13:19) and at 25 miles (2:53:54) in a 100-km track race. In November, she entered her first 24-hour race in Nottingham, completing 175 km and winning the mixed race. En route she set world records at 30 miles (3:35:42), 50 km (3:44:08), and 40 miles (4:55:17). The following year at the same site, she set the then world best of 653 km in the six-day race. In the same year, she set the women's record of 32:20:00 in the 240-km Spartathlon.

During 1984, her record-breaking zeal continued. In February, at the Milton Keynes, Adams set the world 24-hour indoor record of 121.75 miles, plus seven additional indoor records at 30 miles, 50 km, 40 miles, 50 miles, 100 km, 150 km, and 100 miles, and 24 hours. In March, in the 48-hour Mountauben race, she set new world records for 300 km (42:28:48), 200 miles (47:24:51), and 48 hours (202 miles, 77 yards). In July, in a six-day race in New York, she completed 734 km, and in November, in the Colac Six-Day Race, she set a new world record with 806 km.

In the 1985 Montauben 48-hour race she set a new world record (207 miles, 988 yards), and at the Nottingham 24-hour race in August she set world records at 200 km (20:48:35.3) and at 24 hours (138 miles, 777 yards). In October, she completed the Chicago 80-km race in 06:04:28, setting the second-fastest time ever by a woman. In 1985 and 1986 she won the 1060-km Sydney-to-Melbourne race, and in February 1986 she set a new six-day race record of 808 km. In July of that year, in Honefoss, Norway, she set track records at 160 km (15:25:46) and at 200 km (20:09:28). In September, she won the London-to-Brighton race in 6:42:40.46.

In February 1987, in the Milton Keynes indoor race, Adams set an absolute world 24-hour best of 227.26 km, including world indoor records for every distance from 30 miles upward. In May, she completed a 1600-km round-Britain race in 16 days, 22 hours, and 51 minutes. In July, she completed the 234-km Death Valley to Mount Witney run in 53:03, the second-fastest time ever by a runner of either gender.

Adams (1987) ascribes her success as a woman ultradistance runner to good organization. She points out that, after her running, she (unlike many male runners) very often has to return home to cook meals and attend to her children's needs. As a single parent, Adams has the added responsibility of providing for the financial needs of her children. She therefore has to fit in her training around her family and her career.

At the peak of her career, Adams worked as a substitute teacher and aimed to work three days per week, leaving two free weekdays, on each of which she ran 32 to 36 km in a single run. On workdays, she completed two to three sessions of a total of 32 km per day, giving an average weekly total of 160 km. Before the 1600-km race around Britain, she increased her weekly average to 200 to 220 km per week.

All of her training was done alone at about 11 km per hour. On weekends, she raced any distance but always chose the longest available race. In summer, she also often raced midweek. These races served as part of her speed training for the long ultradistance races, and she did not rest for them. She also did not do any specific training for marathons. As a result, she feels that her best marathon time of 2:48:23, run six weeks after the Death Valley run, could be improved considerably. Adams preferred to compete in a long race every six weeks, completing a total of six or seven ultramarathons per year. She did not feel it necessary to do long runs in training. In fact, she told Bruce Fordyce that not only did she not train for a six-day race, but she didn't know how she could. She believed that the best way to train for such races was "to rest up as much as possible" (Fordyce 1996, pp. 29–30).

Her racing advice for long ultradistance races is to second someone else to gain an impression of what happens in these races. She warns prospective competitors to expect the worst and to take everything they are likely to need, and extras besides. This includes food, hot drinks, clothing for all weather, and several pairs of shoes. As a runner's feet tend to swell during six-day races, Adams recommends taking along a larger pair of shoes as well. Adams' best times were 36:04 (10 km); 57:36 (16 km) 1:18:21 (21 km); 2:48:23 (42 km); and 8:04:48 (100 km).

Ann Trason

Running at the elite level is extremely demanding, with the result that few athletes ever survive at the pinnacle of the sport for more than a few years. The relative brevity of the competitive careers of the world-class marathon runners such as Buddy Edelen, Ron Hill, Alberto Salazar, and Steve Jones, among others, has been emphasized repeatedly throughout this book. Although the decade-long competitive careers of Bruce Fordyce and Mark Allen stand in stark contrast to this more usual trend, it is the diminutive 47-kg Californian, Ann Trason, whose dominance of the sport defies belief. Trason (figure 6.30) has raced ultradistances for more than 15 years without any evidence of impairment.

Trason, born in San Francisco of a Czechoslovakian father and a Canadian mother, was introduced to running at age six, when she won her first local competition. Delighted with her obvious talent, her father enrolled her in a local running club. Although at that stage she was disinterested in the sport, she continued to run and soon discovered that she longed for her daily run after school. By the time she entered high school, she had increased her training distance and continued to excel in local events. At 17, Trason ran 10 km in 35:11, and in her senior year she finished sixth in the national high school championships, despite being the second youngest competitor. During that year she also completed a 32-km race in 2:03 and concluded that to be the longest distance any sane person should run at one time. Her high school talent did not go unnoticed; she was offered an athletics scholarship to the University of New Mexico, which she entered in 1978. But injury in her freshman year terminated her track career; she gave up competitive running and transferred to the University of California at Berkeley.

While at Berkeley, Trason did little competitive running. It was only at age 23, when she started working, that she again started running. Trason relates that her mentor at work, a Cape Townian, was the first to tell her about the Comrades Marathon. Her competitive edge soon reasserted itself, and she began to train for a half-Ironman triathlon by swimming in the morning, running at lunchtime, and cycling in the evenings. She recalls that this type of training always left her tired (Boga 1993).

Despite a top-100 finish in her first half-Ironman, Trason concluded that the combination of training did not suit her, and the subconscious influence of her mentor began to assert itself. An advertisement for the April 1985 American River 50-Mile (80 km) Run (the first half on a bicycle path, the second half on a single track trail from Sacramento to Auburn, California) caught her attention. Despite never having run further than 32 km, she trained for six weeks, entered the race, and ran 80 consecutive km in 5:16 per km, setting a new course record of 7:09:00, despite temperatures of 40°C. During the same year, she also set a personal best marathon time of 2:40:55. Trason had uncovered a talent but was reluctant to pursue it. She promised both herself and her mother that she would never again run an ultramarathon. But her promise was short-lived. In the very next calendar year, she aimed to complete a marathon, an ultramarathon, a 320-km cycle race, and a triathlon. But after completing the first three events in three months, Trason collapsed, dropping out of her next race. She learned then that her greatest weakness was her tendency to overdo things.

The next decisive events in Trason's progression as an ultradistance runner happened by chance in the summer of 1986, when a friend invited her to come along on a 48-km run along the Western States Trail near Lake Tahoe in northern California. The race on this course is run at elevations of between 1000 and 2000 m over rock-strewn trails. Another feature of the Western States 100-Mile Endurance Run is that it is usually raced in extreme heat alternating with bitter cold, and it includes an infamous climb of 520 m at 74 km. As Trason later recounted,

> *I just immediately fell in love with it. I fell down, of course; I fell down and this great billowing cloud of dust rose up. But instead of choking me, it felt like the cloud was lifting me up, like I was protected. I've always felt protected by trails—all trails, but Western States in particular. (Trason 2001)*

She knew then that she "wanted to become an ultrarunner, not just someone who occasionally might run an ultramarathon" (Trason 2001). And so began her quest.

Trason's next major performance came in her return to the 1987 American River 50-Mile Run, in which she won the woman's race in 6:23, a new course record, finishing sixth overall. Later that year, she finished third overall in the Firetrails 50-Mile Run in 7:30. She then decided to tackle her real love, the Western States 100-Mile Endurance Run, perhaps the world's toughest ultramarathon.

Trason's first attempt in June 1987 was unsuccessful, as she was forced to retire halfway due to a knee injury. The following year, she did substantially better. However, with 11 km to go, she began to vomit continuously. Given intravenous fluids by one group of doctors, she was then declared ineligible to continue by the chief race physician. She responded by entering and winning her first completed 160-km race in the Leadville Trail Race in Colorado, finishing seventh overall in 21:40:26 and breaking the course record by more than an hour, despite again suffering debilitating nausea and vomiting for the last 64 km of the race. Later that same year, while traveling in Europe, she entered the World 100-Km Championships at the last moment. Trason took the lead after 42 km, winning the women's race in a world best of 7:30:49, finishing 21st overall.

But it was in 1989 that Trason's extraordinary ability began to express itself. In March, she set a new world 160 km track best of 14:29:44, setting American records at 80 and 100 km en route. Then, in June at the Western States race, she finally completed the full distance, winning in 18:47:46, a new course record. She won the race for ten years in a row, from 1989 to 1998, and again in 2000 and 2001, the latter in a new master's record time. In September, she competed in the United States National 24-Hour Road Championships, which she won outright, setting the world 160-km road record (13:55:02) en route to a new American 24-hour best of 230.275 km. During that race, she also established a personal best time at 200 km (19:25:05). A month later, she established a new 80-km world road record of 5:54:17 in the Edmund Fitzgerald 100-Km Race, continuing to win the race in 7:33:13.

In 1990, Trason repeated her victory in the Western States, improving her time and the course record to 18:33:34, and in August she again won the Leadville 160-Km Trail Run, improving her course record to 20:38:51. In October, she again won the Edmund Fitzgerald 100

Figure 6.30 Ann Trason winning the Comrades Marathon.

Km, four weeks after winning the Portland 42-Km Marathon in 2:42:07.

She began racing early in January 1991, setting a new world 80-km road record of 5:45:42 while winning the Jackson 100-km race in Dallas, finishing second overall. Five weeks later, on 23 February, Trason established new world records at 40 miles (4:23:13) and 50 miles (5:40:18) in the Houston 50-Mile (80 km) Ultramarathon. Then on May 4, in the Sri Chinmoy 100-Mile (160 km) race in Queens, New York, she finished in first place overall, setting new world records at 100 miles (13:47:42) and 12 hours (146.10 km). On June 29 she won the Western States race, setting a new course record of 18:29:37 and finishing ninth overall, and on August 3 in Hayward, California, she set world track records at 50 miles (6:14:34), 100 km (7:48:14), and 12 hours (147.637 km), again winning the race overall.

In 1992, she won the Western States race, again lowering the course record, this time to 18:14:48. In December, she set her personal record of 2:39:15 in the California International Marathon. In 1993 she won the Western States race in 19:05:22, returning in 1994 to establish another new course record of 17:37:51. In August of that year, in what she considers one of her two best races, she won the Leadville 100-Mile Trail Run in 18:06:24. In that race, she led for the first 136 km before being passed by the eventual male winner. She finished second, 20:00 behind the winner, in the fourth fastest time ever on that course. In April 1995, she returned to the American River 80.5-km race after a break of eight years, winning again in 6:11:58, an improvement of 11 minutes on her previous record. In June, she won her seventh consecutive Western States race in 18:40:01.

What is perhaps even more remarkable about that performance was that, inspired by Alberto Salazar's Comrades Marathon victory in 1994, on May 31, 1995, Trason found herself at the start of the Comrades Marathon. Suffering from a viral infection, she withdrew after 45 km. Yet, 24 days later she was able to produce one of her greatest performances. Three months after her 1995 Western States victory, she won the International Athletics Union 100-Km Road World Championships in Winschoten, Netherlands, finishing in 7:00:47. This included her personal record for 50 km (3:22:28). Before the end of 1995, she also ran 17:11 for 5 km and 1:14:15 for 21 km, indicating a versatility that has perhaps been unmatched in the history of the sport.

Devastated and embarrassed by her "failure" in the 1995 Comrades Marathon, Trason returned in 1996 determined to repay her sponsors' faith but without any thought of foregoing the Western States race. The complication was that the date for the 1996 Comrades Marathon had been moved from 31 May to 17 June, leaving Trason with just 12 days to recover before the Western States race. Undeterred, Trason first won the Comrades Marathon in 6:13:23, and then, barely a week later, after traveling halfway around the world and crossing nine time zones, she again won the Western States race in 18:57:36.

The remainder of 1996 was spent searching for a medical cure for her persistent hamstring injury. As a result, she underwent surgery in November. This was followed by a two-month recuperation period, in which her leg was in plaster of Paris. Despite the difficulties of 1996, Trason returned to competition in May 1997, winning the Avenue of the Giants Marathon in 2:46:36 before repeating her victory in the Comrades Marathon, becoming the second woman to finish under 6:00:00, just 4 minutes outside Frith van der Merwe's course record. This is the second running achievement of which Trason is the most proud. Just 12 days later, she again won the Western States race, winning in 19:19:49. In September, she set a personal record for 64 km of 4:35:54 during a 100-km race in Nantes, France, from which she withdrew.

In 1998 Trason established another landmark, as she won five 100-mile trail races in 14 weeks; in June, the Western States in 18:46:16; in July, the Vermont 160-Km Endurance Run in 17:11:23: in August, the Leadville Trail 100-Mile Race in 20:58:32; and in September and October, the Wasatch and Arkansas 100-Mile Runs, thereby winning the Grand Slam of ultrarunning.

In 1999, for the first time in ten years, Trason did not race in the Western States, nor in any other major events. She returned in 2000 with repeat victories in the Western States (19:44:42) and Vermont endurance run (16:04:16). In May 2001, competing for the first time as a Masters athlete, she won the Miwok 100-km race in Sausalito, California, in 8:55:49, and in June she won the Western States in 18:33:34, setting a Masters record and her fifth fastest for the course. A month later, she won the White River 80-Km Trail Run in Washington State in 7:57:52.

At the time of writing, Trason held the course and Masters record for the Western States; she has set the eight fastest women's times for the course as well as 12 of the fastest 14 women's times. Of her passion for that race, Trason has said, "You get consumed by the Western States and forget there's life beyond the race." Of the race itself she says, "After 50 miles, your body just hurts. You have to keep telling yourself that your mind is stronger than your legs" (Licking 1998). In addition, she has set 20 world records and currently holds the world records for 100 km (road), 100 mile (road and track), 50 mile (road), and 12 hour (road and track).

Ann Trason describes her training as the following:

[I have] a very basic program with a major emphasis on consistency. I do not believe that one workout or type of workout is all that critical. What I find important is to have 10 to 12 weeks of solid training leading up to an event. An average week comprises one speed session, one up-tempo run and one long run. The rest of the week is for rest and recovery, with easy running and a social run on hilly trails. Weight lifting two to three times a week is also part of my regiment. My mileage averages around 160 km a week. I tend not to keep a running log.

***Long runs** I believe in the specificity of training, especially as it relates to my long runs. For example, if I am training for a 100-mile trail run, then my long runs are on trails, varying in distance from 35 miles to 50 miles. When training for Comrades or a 100-km road-race, then I run at least half of my long runs on roads. Distances again vary from 30 to 40 miles. I have found that I cannot run all my long runs on pavement or road or else I break down with injury. The altitude profile of the race for which I am training dictates the terrain over which I will do my training runs. If I am peaking for a hilly race, then I will run my long runs on hills. During these runs, I practice eating and drinking precisely what I will be consuming during the event for which I am preparing.*

***Up-tempo/quality runs** These comprise runs of 20:00 to 40:00. They are run on level roads or on my treadmill. The speeds at which I run these workouts are inversely proportional to the length of my long runs. That is why I call them quality, up-tempo runs and not tempo runs. My goal is to run faster than race pace, concentrating on my form.*

***Speed sessions/hill work** This is the least favorite component of my training. Speed sessions are run on a track and hill work on roads if I am training for an ultramarathon on the roads, but both are run on trails if I am training for a trail race. Hill repeats are usually 400 m long, with no more than 10 repeats in one workout. My track workouts vary in distance with repeat intervals of 400 to 1600 m. The length of my long runs determines the length of rest I take between repeats. The greater the distance of my long run, the more emphasis I put on full recovery between repeats. The cumulative distance of the repeats is never more than 8 km.*

***Rest and social runs** Recovering mentally and physically is a key element in my training. I take my easy days very easy, running 8 to 10 km twice a day on my favorite trails. In addition, I find that social, group runs are a wonderful way to rejuvenate one's spirit and enthusiasm for running. For the last 16 years, I have run with the same group every Wednesday evening. We run the same 22-km loop every week; the only thing that changes is the stories we tell.*

***Weight training** One would never know from looking at me but two to three times a week, I lift weights for both my upper and lower body. My routine takes no more than 30:00 and comprises a large number of repetitions using low weights. Sit-ups and push-ups are done on a daily basis.*

CONCLUSIONS: TRAINING METHODS OF THE ELITE

The overriding conclusion I have drawn from this survey is that available records of the training methods of elite runners are inadequate. As a result, some of what is written in this chapter may yet prove to be inaccurate. However, in the remaining section, I have attempted to consolidate what I have learned from the runners I have reviewed.

Remarkable Performances Achieved on Little Training

Walter George, for example, ran 16 km in less than 50 minutes on 2 miles of training per day, and Deerfoot ran marginally faster without ever training outside the races he ran; Alf Shrubb ran similar times on 67 km of training per week; Paavo Nurmi trained only six months of the year and then only about 16 km per day; and Jim Peters in his marathon debut came within 4 minutes of the world marathon record despite training only 77 km per week. Similarly, Ron Hill ran some phenomenal marathons on relatively little training. Attention has also been drawn to the low training mileage but high training intensities of African runners such as Kip Keino and Matthews Temane.

While a number of publications refer to the extraordinary distances run by the Kenyans in training, I suspect that this is only a part of the explanation. It fits the prevailing paradigm that running performance is determined exclusively by training. If Kenyans dominate international distance running so decisively, it must be because they train so much farther and harder than everyone else. Hence, writers from Europe and North America may search for any evidence to support their bias. In so doing, they also tend to belittle the efforts of their top distance runners. Thus, a popular explanation for the inability of top American, European, and Australian marathoners to compete with the Africans is simply because they are too lazy to train hard. Indeed, one Australian writer has suggested that

> *East Africans have developed an aura of invincibility, both in their own minds and the minds of their Caucasian opponents. . . . While there are many factors involved in the rise of East African running success, I believe that Caucasian belief and attitude systems are significant perpetuating factors. Until our athletes, coaches and support staff accept responsibility for their own performances, I believe the current level of athletic domination by East African athletes will continue. (Hamilton 2000, p. 94)*

However, the author fails to explain why three nations—the United States, the former German Democratic Republic, and Australia—are able to dominate Olympic competitions across a wide variety of disciplines, but for all their human and technical resources are unable to match the successes of East Africans in distance running. In addition, he fails to explain why there are no Kenyan sprinters to match the sprint performances of the West Africans.

Yet, there are indeed black South African runners who have run 2:07:00 and 2:08:00 marathon races, despite having trained little more, or perhaps even less, than did Jim Peters (tables 6.8 and 6.9), Buddy Edelen (table 6.12), or Steve Jones (table 6.20).

This does not mean that these athletes do not train at very high intensities or that the successes achieved by the Kenyan cross-country teams do not result from the extraordinarily demanding three-week training camp they undertake before competition (table 6.28). The point is that there seems to be something else involved as well. For example, South Africa's best marathoner, Gert Thys, reports that he trains 140 km per week. Yet, his best five marathon times of 2:06:33 (Tokyo 1999), 2:07:45 (Chicago 1998), 2:07:52 (Boston 1998), 2:08:30 (Beppu 1996), and 2:09:31 (Fukuoka 1993) made him the world's fastest marathon runner of the twentieth century with an average time of 2:08:02.2, better than the 2:08:24.0 of Steve Jones. Thys trains twice per day; with three quality sessions on track or road with his favorite of 5×1500 m in 4:10 each. He also includes one weekly long run of 30 km in about 1:55.

This observation that many of the top athletes achieved world-class performances on little training emphasizes the importance of genetic ability—not everyone can achieve such performances on what others might consider to be relatively little training. It also highlights the law of diminishing returns. To improve performances even further, these athletes have to increase their training markedly, thereby risking overtraining. For example, Jim Peters had to double his training distance and maintain the same intensity to lower his marathon time by nearly 12 minutes from 2:29:28 to 2:17:39.

Many Were Not Outstanding School Runners

While at school, neither Arthur Newton, Emil Zatopek, Jim Peters, Gordon Pirie, Peter Snell, Kip Keino, Ron Hill, Frank Shorter, Steve Jones, Carlos Lopes, Matthews Temane, Bruce Fordyce, Mark Allen, nor Charles Rowell gave any indication of their latent talents. Snell, for example, was only the third fastest miler in his school. On the other hand, Herb Elliott, Ron Clarke, Buddy Edelen, Rob de Castella, Yiannis Kouros, Grete Waitz, and Eleanor Adams all performed exceptionally during their younger days.

Many Train Similarly

Jim Peters ran 160 km per week at high intensity, averaging approximately 3:20 per km. Grete Waitz also trained about 160 km per week. Edelen, Clarke, Hill, Shorter, de Castella, and Jones all ran up to 180 to 200 km per week, probably at an intensity similar to that of Peters, but without apparent detriment to their performances. But Clayton, Pirie, and Bedford, who tried on occasion to run up to 256 km per week, proved that such weekly training distances are too great for most runners. On the other hand, Herb Elliott, Kip Keino, and Matthews Temane all trained considerably less (up to 110 km per week), yet all set world records at distances from 1500 m to 21 km.

Interestingly, the best modern short and long ultramarathon runners, including Bruce Fordyce, Yiannis Kouros, Eleanor Adams, and Ann Trason, seldom ran more than 160 to 180 km per week—considerably less than the training distances of Arthur Newton and pedestrians such as Charles Rowell, who ran up to 300 km per week. Thus, it would seem that elite runners perform best in the marathon and ultramarathon races when they train between 120 and 200 km per week, with an increasing likelihood that they will perform indifferently when they train more than

200 km per week, as vividly shown by the experiences of Ron Hill. This is confirmed by the experiences of Alberto Salazar, who set the since disallowed world marathon record in 1981.

Following his early marathon successes, which he achieved relatively soon after impressive performances (particularly at 10,000 m) on the track, Salazar increased his weekly training distance from 176 to 208 km. He reasoned that more distance would allow him to run faster marathons. The result was that his training intensity fell, he was running tired most of the time, and his performances in both the 10,000 m and the marathon fell off alarmingly, culminating in a disappointing run in the 1984 Olympic Marathon. Salazar subsequently stated that he would return to those training methods that originally worked for him (lower mileage and more speed work), that he would again train as a 10,000-m runner, and that he would run another marathon only when he was again able to run 10,000 m in a world-class time (Higdon 1985).

In fact, Salazar never again ran a world-class standard marathon, indicating that, like Edelen and Hill, his feverish period of racing in the early 1980s took something from his body that he never regained. Salazar described his illness thus: "My immune system was totally shot. I caught everything. I was always sick, always run down. . . . I was sick constantly. I had 12 colds in 12 months" (Hauman 1996, p. 91).

During this period, Salazar consulted widely and experimented with a variety of medical treatments, none of which produced any lasting effects. However, in 1993, on the advice of a running doctor, he began using the drug Prozac, which acts by increasing the brain serotonin levels. Within days, his running had improved to such an extent that he thought the watch he used to time his training runs had broken. Quite remarkably, this treatment provided Salazar with one more great race. In 1994 he confounded everyone by winning the 90-km up-Comrades Marathon in 5:38:39, having led for the last 65 km of the race. This was an astonishing performance for a novice ultramarathon racer. Sadly, the effects of the therapy were not long lasting. Salazar's illness and inability to run returned in 1995. Salazar's experience highlights the long-term, and very real, physical dangers of heavy training and frequent competition.

If marathon and short ultramarathon runners perform poorly when they substitute distance training for speed work, the experience of D. Cooper (1990) suggests that the opposite applies for the very long ultramarathon runners (24 hours to 6 days), who should be encouraged to emphasize distance training with the virtual absence of speed training.

Most Achieved Success at Shorter-Distance Races First

Kolehmainen, Nurmi, Zatopek, Peters, Edelen, Clayton, Hill, Shorter, de Castella, Salazar, Jones, Lopes, Temane, and Waitz were all excellent track or cross-country exponents before they achieved success at longer distances on the road, especially in the marathon. Some still excel at the shorter distances. The same applies to the growing dominance of international marathon races by Kenyans who first achieved success as track or cross-country athletes.

Similarly, the great ultramarathon runners, Fordyce, Trason, Rowell, and Kouros, have all run fast over distances from 10 to 42 km. Allen also dominated both short-

and long-distance triathlons. This evidence proves beyond doubt that the faster the athlete at short distances, the greater his or her potential in the marathon and ultimately in the ultramarathon. As Buddy Edelen remarked in his speech after setting the 1963 marathon world record of 2:14:28, "The days of the plodding marathon are over. It takes speed work like the 110-yard sprints I practice and the hard training on the roads to give you both the pace and the stamina you need" (F. Murphy 1992, p. 101). The experience of Fordyce confirms the importance of speed training for ultramarathon runners (Fordyce 1996), as does that of Allen for the ultradistance triathlons.

This truth was again confirmed in the 1984 Olympic Marathon, won by 1984 world cross-country champion Carlos Lopes, who, two months before the Olympics, ran the second fastest 10,000 m ever (27:17:41). Second place in the Olympic Marathon went to John Treacy, also a former world cross-country champion, running his first marathon ever. Alberto Salazar ran his best marathons when he was training for 10,000 m on the track, and Steve Jones set his 1984 world marathon record in his first marathon when training specifically for track and cross-country racing.

It comes as no surprise, then, that the Kenyans dominate track, cross-country, and marathon races; that Fordyce had amongst the fastest mile, 5000-m, and 10,000-m times of all the top finishers in the Comrades Marathon that he raced; that at the height of their careers, Van der Merwe and Adams were the fastest female marathon runners competing in the short and long ultramarathons; and that Yiannis Kouros is one of the fastest marathon runners competing in the long ultramarathons. The truth is that if you are unable to beat these runners at 1 mile or 10,000 m, you will also never beat them at any other distance, even up to 700 km. Of course, besides their speed at shorter distances, these runners also have superior fatigue resistance (chapter 2).

Most Included Regular Speed Work

Rowell, Hurst, Newton, and DeMar achieved greatness without much attention to speed training. However, they were the last of a breed, and subsequent runners have shown that regular speed training is absolutely essential for success in marathon and short (not long) ultramarathon races. Nurmi, Zatopek, Pirie, Keino, Edelen, and Shorter stressed interval training on the track; Peters, Elliott, Clarke, and Clayton ran at high intensity most of the time; and Hill, de Castella, Jones, Temane, Fordyce, and Waitz combined hill training and interval sessions on the track. Clearly, there is no single method of speed training that works for everyone.

Paradoxically, the universal importance of speed training has been proven most convincingly by the ultramarathon runners, in particular by Fordyce, who have completed the training circle that began with the pedestrians Charles Rowell and Newton. Fordyce has shown that the Newtonian approach of high mileage remains as a basic training principle but that subsequent improvements in running performance will not come simply by running more miles at the same relatively slow place. This type of training is probably only appropriate for the very long ultramarathon races of up to 700 km. But the performances of Kouros and Adams, both of whom have achieved exceptional performances in races of up to 100 km on about one-half the training of Rowell and Newton, indicate that not everyone needs so much training to excel at those distances.

These runners have shown that improvements in the short ultramarathons will come with better speed training, validating the statement by Krise and Squire that "there's nowhere to hide from speed; it will inevitably inhabit every distance" (1982, p. 102). Similarly, the lower mileage, high-intensity approach of the elite South African marathoners such as Thys and the Kenyans (when not training at St. Mark's camp) is similar to that of Peters, Edelen, Elliott, and Jones. In fact, there is very little difference in the training approach, practice, and philosophies of Peters, Edelen, Salazar, Jones, and the modern Kenyan runners.

This suggests that the great distance runners of the future will be those who are genetically endowed to cope with short periods of very high-intensity peaking training, of the intensities achieved by these great runners.

Most Ran Their Best Marathons When Inexperienced

This was clearly shown by Ron Hill, who ran his best marathon race in 1970 after he had been racing marathons seriously for one year. During the remaining 7.5 years of his serious athletic career, he never again ran as fast.

Similarly, despite his peaking approach to marathon racing, Shorter ran his best marathon ever in only his sixth attempt and did not improve further in his last eight serious marathons. At the end of his career, Shorter concluded that top runners can run only five or six top-level marathons. "A similar question is how many times can you really give 100%?"(Hauman 1996, p. 117). Shorter concluded that he personally had given 100% only four times, twice in the Olympics. Rob de Castella set the world marathon record at his sixth attempt at the distance in 1981 and failed to improve further during the next four years, despite heavy training and high expectations, especially for the 1984 Olympic Games Marathon (de Castella and Jenkinson 1984). A similar fate struck Jones and Lopes, whose average time for the first three marathons of their careers was sub-2:08:00. Both showed a significant drop in performance thereafter.

Runners seem to have a limited number of fast marathons in them. They will shorten their careers considerably if those races are run in rapid succession, as in the cases of Hill, Lopes, and Jones. Sub-2:09:00 former South African marathoner Mark Plaatjes (1986), now resident in Boulder, Colorado, has suggested that elite marathoners should race a maximum of one or two marathons per year for two years before taking a complete break from marathoning for a full two years. Plaatjes also notes that it took the two favorites for the 1984 Olympic Marathon, de Castella and Japan's Toshihiko Seiko, two years to recover from their disappointing performances in that race (Plaatjes 1986).

Another finding that adds credence to this belief is that, with only few exceptions, the winners of the Olympic Marathon have been relatively inexperienced marathoners (Beinart 1986; table 6.28). Thus, the first three post-World War II champions (Delfo Cabrera in 1948, Emil Zatopek in 1952, and Alain Mimoun in 1956) were running their first marathons. Since 1948, the average number of marathons run by the Olympic champions before their first win has been 3.1 (Hauman 1996). When Bikila and Cierpinski won their second Olympic Marathons, they had run 9 and 14 marathons respectively.

An analysis of world records supports the conclusion that runners' best marathons occur early in their careers. Clayton set his first world record in his fifth marathon; Peters set his world records in his third, fifth, eighth, and tenth marathons. Clayton set his second world record in his eighth marathon and never again ran as fast. Salazar's disallowed record of 2:08:05 (subsequently corrected to 2:08:40 on the basis of a short course) came in his second race, as did Jones' record of 2:08:05. Lopes' record of 2:07:12 came in his fourth marathon; his Olympic victory in Los Angeles came in his second. In that race the total number of previous marathons by the three medalists was three.

Exceptions to this rule were Hill, who ran 2:09:27 in his 18th marathon; Rodgers, who ran 2:09:27 in his 23rd marathon; and de Castella, whose best time of 2:07:51 came in his 13th marathon (Hauman 1996). Perhaps they might have run even faster had they run fewer marathons with greater focus.

If you had to pick future winners of the Olympic Marathon, you would be wisest to back the fast 10,000-m runners who have run either no previous marathons or only one. The same applies to the athlete most likely to break the world marathon record: that athlete is likely to be a relatively unknown African runner with world-class times at 5 to 10 km, running in his first or second marathon (on a flat course in cool, windless conditions).

Table 6.28   Prior Marathon racing experience of the Olympic Games Marathon winners (1932–2000)

Olympic year	Athlete	Number of marathons run before Olympics
1932	Juan Carlos Zabala	1
1936	Kitei Son	"A few"
1948	Delfo Cabrera	0
1952	Emil Zatopek	0
1956	Alain Mimoun	0
1960	Abebe Bikila	1
1964	Abebe Bikila	4
1968	Mamo Wolde	Unknown—converted track runner
1972	Frank Shorter	4 (in 13 months)
1976	Waldemar Cierpinski	4
1980	Waldemar Cierpinski	13
1984	Carlos Lopes	1
1988	Joan Benoit	11
	Gelindo Bordin	~ 6
1992	Valentina Yegorova	12
	Hwang Yuong-Cho	3
1996	Fatuma Roba	5
	Josiah Thugwane	19
2000	Naoko Takahashi	4
	Gezahegne Abera	4

Updated from Beinart (1986, p. 45). © 1986 by Track and Field News. Adapted by permission.

The Training Synthesis of Carl Foster

Carl Foster, the North American exercise physiologist who combines a rare ability to undertake cutting-edge exercise physiology research and to apply that knowledge to the training of elite athletes, especially speed skaters, has noted that the 15 Laws of training (chapter 5) overlap substantially with the core ideas of Arthur Lydiard, coach Jack Daniels, and Stephen Seiler, an expatriate American who currently teaches exercise physiology in Norway.

Arthur Lydiard's ideas

1. You can't train hard and race hard at the same time.
2. If you can run more than 100 miles (160 km) per week during the buildup period, don't run more, run faster.
3. 100 miles (160 km) per week is relatively easy: 20 miles (32 km) one day, 10 miles (16 km) the next day.
4. Once the base training is done, success is related to a controlled buildup of training intensity. .

Jack Daniels' core concepts

1. Don't leave your race on the training track.
2. Alternate hard and easy days, in fact only two to three hard days per week.
3. Build improvement around the judicious use of intensity (repetition training and threshold training).
4. If recovery training does not leave you recovered, try resting entirely.

Stephen Seiler's training beliefs

1. Build the program around two high-intensity interval sessions per week.
2. Most of the noninterval training should be at fairly low intensities (below the exercise intensity at which the blood lactate concentration begins to rise).
3. Avoid the middle intensities (slightly increased blood lactate concentrations); they do little more than tire you out.
4. If you are not training easily enough on the easy days, you will not be able to train hard enough on the hard days.
5. The total volume of low-intensity background training serves as a platform for progressively higher-intensity specific training. Thus, an athlete who can tolerate 15 hours per week of background training will be able to tolerate higher-intensity specific training than an athlete who can only tolerate 10 hours per week of background training. The limits of tolerability of background training are specific to the sport with cycling/swimming at the upper end and running at the lower end, developed over months and years of training, and highly variable among people.

From C. Foster and Lehmann, p. 37–38, 1997.

On the basis of these ideas, Foster has produced the four following testable hypotheses for endurance training.

1. The minimal volume of training necessary to compete effectively throughout the duration of the event may be described by a curvilinear function. (This concept was depicted in figure 5.6.)

2. Training intensity is probably the single most important factor in correct training. Foster suggests that, just as there is an hypothesized curvilinear relationship between the total volume of training and performance in a specific event, there is also likely to be a curvilinear relationship between the volume of higher intensity (that is, specific race pace) training and performance. He suggests that the exact numerical relationship between the volume of training, either total or high intensity, and the resulting performance needs to be determined experimentally.

3. More variation in the day-to-day training load is likely to result in more effective adaptation to training, as also discussed in chapter 7. Currently there are no experimental studies to determine the optimum combinations of training loads on the hard and easy days.

4. The adaptive response to the addition of specific (speed) training is quantitatively dependent on the total volume of training performed during the buildup (base-training) period. (This is essentially a summary of Tom Osler's observation that the volume of the base training determines the peak that can be attained during peaking training.)

Once again, the optimum volume of base training to produce the highest peak has yet to be studied.

FINAL WORD

Over the years, many runners have told me that this is the most enjoyable chapter in the book. Certainly, it is the one that I believe provides the best practical advice, as all runners must train. Furthermore, besides the time runners spend talking about their training, training is the single activity that will occupy the greatest proportion of their recreational time. This being so, it is best to spend that time in the most productive way possible. This chapter is invaluable, as it synthesizes the training wisdom acquired through the hard effort, substantial heartbreak, and occasional joy of the hundreds of thousands of individual runners. However, there are two crucial weaknesses to this wisdom. First, it has been generalized. Yet, we know that each athlete is a unique person who will by nature respond differently to other people. Second, all the theories, although "proven" in practice, lack a numerical certainty. For example, we do not know the exact volume of training undertaken for a precise period that will produce the greatest peak in performance. Thus, the challenge for the runner is to take this information and to perform those personal experiments that will provide the numerical answers to each runner's ultimate question: what training will produce the best results for me?

CHAPTER

7

■ ■ ■ ■ ■

Avoiding Overtraining

From the moment you send off your first race entry form, you become a racer and enter a new world. Only later will you become aware that you have crossed the threshold that divides jogging for health from training for peak racing performance. The former jogger in you will suddenly discover that singular endeavor that demands nothing less than total harmony between the spirit and the newly perfected body. With that first race, you catch the first glimpse of your true potential.

The danger is that novice racers often try to achieve too much. The mind, in striving for perfection, soon demands more than the body can deliver. Unless they exercise caution, impetuous and overzealous racers will find themselves falling prey to the most common, and least understood, of all running ailments—overtraining.

Despite all the running I did, each new training season my avaricious mind would ensure that I spent a few weeks rediscovering this illness in myself. Ironically, I now spend a great deal of time comforting runners whose training greed has reduced them to the walking wounded.

In some runners, the first signs of overtraining are generalized fatigue, recurrent headaches, diarrhea and weight loss, sexual disinterest, and a loss of appetite for food or work. Others find that they are no longer able to sleep properly and are troubled by early morning wakening, an inability to relax, listlessness, a generalized swelling of lymph glands, worsening allergies, colds or flu, or respiratory infections that resist conventional therapy. All fail to understand why, despite such hard training, their racing performances continue to deteriorate.

In fact, all these symptoms are diagnostic. These runners have stretched their bodies beyond their individual breaking points. They are told that rest—not more training—is required, and that all they can do is rest and wait for nature to heal what medicine does not yet comprehend.

INDICATORS OF OVERTRAINING

Probably the earliest scientific reference to overtraining was made by McKenzie (1923), who noted that exhaustion after exercise was of three kinds:

1. Acute exhaustion accompanied by marked breathlessness, from which recovery was rapid
2. Fatigue of the whole muscular system, which required a day or two of rest
3. Chronic fatigue, caused by "slow poisoning of the nervous system," which he called staleness, and from which recovery was prolonged and could last weeks or even months

It is interesting that McKenzie reported these symptoms at a time when athletes trained relatively little, which suggests that factors other than training alone may have been involved.

The next important observation of the condition we know today as overtraining was made by Heiss (1971), who described an increased susceptibility to infection as an important component of the overtraining syndrome. He noted that the incidence of upper respiratory tract infections among competitors at the 1928 Winter Olympics increased sharply immediately before and during the competition. At subsequent Olympics, this trend was again apparent, and Heiss considered these infections to be a sign of overtraining.

Subsequent descriptions of the overtraining syndrome (Bresnahan and Tuttle 1950; Budgett 1998; Carlile 1963; 1964; Counsilman 1968; Flynn 1998; Karpovich and Sinning 1971; Keretzty 1971; Lehmann et al. 1997; 1998; Lehmann, Gastmann, et al. 1999; Mellerowicz and Barron 1971; O'Toole 1998; Reidman 1950; Ryan 1983; Webster 1948; Wolf 1971) have not added materially to these clinical observations. However, Tom Osler synthesized these ideas into readily understandable terms. In his 30-page classic, *The Conditioning of Distance Runners*, Osler (1967) describes the symptoms he observed in himself when he had trained too much.

Table 7.1 contains a comprehensive list of indicators of overtraining taken from a large number of sources. The runner's natural response to these indicators, most particularly to the combination of a poor racing performance followed by illness, is to think that it is necessary to train even harder (Foster and Lehmann 1997). What other possible explanation can there be for a bad performance? The urgency to train hard is only exacerbated by the time lost as a result of illness. But because these assumptions are wholly incorrect, the athlete's bout of intensive training only compounds an already grave situation. The truth is that once athletes are even mildly overtrained, they are already past peak condition. And the only way to save the situation is to stop training immediately until the body is rested and the desire to run and compete again returns.

The single most important reason most runners are prone to overtraining is, I believe, that we lack the ability to make an objective assessment of our ultimate performance capabilities. We simply will not accept that we are mortal and that we have a built-in performance range beyond which training and other interventions cannot take us. We believe that the harder we train, the faster we will run, and we

Table 7.1 Indicators of overtraining/staleness syndrome

Emotional and behavioral changes	References
Loss of enthusiasm and drive; generalized apathy; an "I don't care" attitude; loss of the joy of life	(1, 3, 6–10, 18–25)
Loss of joy and thirst for competition; desire to quit during competition	(2, 4–9, 11)
Lethargy; listlessness; tiredness	(1, 2, 4–6, 10, 11)
Peevishness; complaining; easily irritated; miserable; anxious; depressed; ill-humored; unable to relax; bored	(1, 2, 4–8, 10, 11, 26)
Inability to concentrate at work; impaired academic performance	(1)
Changes in sleeping patterns—in particular, insomnia	(1, 5, 10)
Sleep does not refresh	(1, 2, 4–7, 11)
Loss of appetite	(1, 2, 4–8, 10)
Loss of libido	
Poor coordination; general clumsiness	(9)
Increased fluid intake at night; feeling thirsty	(1, 12)

Physical changes	
Impaired physical performance—in particular, inability to complete routine training sessions	(1–7, 18–25)
Gradual loss of weight	(1, 2, 4, 6–8, 11)
Athlete looks drawn, sallow, and dejected, with sunken eyeballs	(1, 2, 8)
Increase in early morning heart rate of more than five beats per minute	(1, 2, 12, 15, 17)
Abnormal rise in heart rate upon standing, and during and after a standard workout	(4, 7, 14)
Slower recovery in heart rate after exertion	(8, 11)
Postural hypotension	(2, 11)
Heavy-leggedness, sluggishness that persists for more than 24 hours after a workout	(9)
Muscle and joint pains	(4, 7)
Persistent muscle soreness increases from session to session	(9, 11)
Swelling of lymph glands	(4, 8)
Gastrointestinal disturbances—in particular, diarrhea	(4)
Increased susceptibility to infection, allergies, headache, and injury	(3, 4, 7–9, 11, 16)
Minor scratches heal slowly	(1, 2)

Loss of menstruation (amenorrhea)	
Increased blood eosinophil count; serial T-wave changes on the electrocardiogram	(4)
Mild form of hypothalamic, sympathetic, and adrenocortical insufficiency	(24)

Key to references

1 R.T. McKenzie (1923)
2 Webster (1948)
3 Heiss (1971)
4 Carlile (1963, 1964)
5 Karpovich and Sinning (1971)
6 Bresnahan and Tuttle (1950)
7 Mellerowicz and Barron (1971)
8 Counsilman (1968)
9 Osler (1967)
10 Wolf (1971)
11 Ryan (1983)
12 R.L. Brown (1983)
13 Czajkowski (1982)
14 Conconi et al. (1982)
15 Reidman (1950)
16 Peters and Bateman (1983)
17 Dressendorfer et al. (1985)
18 Lehmann et al. (1997)
19 Lehmann et al. (1998)
20 O'Toole (1998)
21 Budgett (1998)
22 Flynn (1998)
23 Lehmann, Foster, et al. (1999)
24 Lehmann, Gastmann, et al. (1999)
25 D.C. McKenzie (1999)
26 O'Connor and Smith (1999)

ignore the evidence that indicates that this is blatantly untrue. Thus, we train harder and run worse. And then, in the ultimate act of stupidity, we interpret our poor races as an indication that we have undertrained. Consequently, we go out and train even harder (Foster 1998). As stated by Foster and Lehmann, "Many [runners] would prefer to fail gloriously than to feel that they will stand on the starting line less than fully prepared" (1997, p. 187).

Personal experience, gained from my own running and from treating overtrained runners, led me to the conclusion that this syndrome typically develops in one of two ways—it is either

1. due to athletes' training very intensively for a protracted period or
2. due to athletes' running a series of races in short succession, also following a period of intensive training.

Other important factors include inadequate recovery between days of intensive training (Foster and Lehmann 1997; Foster 1998), which is contrary to the 5th Law of Training (chapter 5), and training monotony, which is a measure of the degree to which the same type and volume is done, monotonously, day after day. Doing exactly the same training each day would constitute a high degree of monotony. The combination of a high training load with a monotonous training schedule is more likely to induce overtraining (Foster 1998).

PREVENTING OVERTRAINING

The essential problem in avoiding this condition is understanding the different stages of the overtraining syndrome—especially distinguishing between the generalized fatigue that appears to be an essential ingredient of proper training (now termed *overreaching;* O'Toole 1998) and the shade more of fatigue that indicates the start of the overtraining syndrome. According to the former world-class middle-distance runner and 5000-m world-record holder, Brendan Foster, clear signs of overtraining are when you "wake up tired and go to bed even more tired." Thus, the key to diagnosing overtraining is knowing when fatigue at either end of the day has become excessive.

The person who first distinguished between these subtle grades of fatigue was James Counsilman, former swimming coach at Indiana University, author of *The Science of Swimming* (Counsilman 1968), and one of the oldest people ever to swim the English Channel.

Stages of Overtraining Syndrome

Counsilman stresses that as long as the training performance is stable or improving, feeling tired does not in itself mean that the athlete has done too much. He states of his own athletes:

> *As long as the swimmers keep swimming fast in practice, doing good repeats and good efforts, work them hard or harder. Even after they begin having the feeling of general fatigue, they will continue to swim well in practice. So keep them working hard up to the point at which their performances in practice begin to suffer. (Counsilman 1968, pp. 237-238)*

Counsilman believed that during the intensive, precompetition phase of training, his swimmers should not be allowed to recover fully before the next training session. He felt that allowing them to do so did not produce as good long-term results as did the training that kept them in the "valley of fatigue" during the training week and before the day or days of reduced training, usually at the weekend. To give visual expression to his ideas, Counsilman produced a figure on which figure 7.1 is based. The three lines (A, B, and C) indicate changes in fatigue levels in three different athletes who train hard for five consecutive days, with rest or recuperative training days on Saturday and Sunday. As the athletes become progressively more tired from Monday to Friday, their levels of fatigue increase and encroach into the fatigue zone, or the valley of fatigue. The modern term for this would be *overreaching training*.

Line A represents changes in fatigue levels in an athlete who trains only moderately hard and becomes mildly fatigued after five days' training, barely reaching the fatigue zone. During the recovery period on Saturday and Sunday, his fatigue level decreases to a level slightly lower than that at which it was the previous Monday. Line B represents the same changes in an athlete who pushes himself to the upper limit of the fatigue zone. When he recovers, his body superadapts to a fatigue level very much lower than that at which he started. Counsilman's inference is that this athlete's fitness and ability to resist training fatigue would have increased correspondingly. The athlete depicted in line C trains the hardest of the three. As a result, his fatigue level goes through the fatigue zone, deep into the failing adaptation (early overtraining) zone. When he rests on Saturday and Sunday, his fatigue level does not recover before the start of the following week. If this athlete recommences hard training before he has fully recovered, his level of fatigue will increase further during the next week of training, indicating that his training has progressed from overreaching to overtraining and that his physical condition is beginning to show the first signs of the overtraining syndrome. Without an adequate rest period, continued training at this intensity or load will cause the athlete to develop the overtraining syndrome.

A Fall in Performance

Counsilman suggests that the first and, unfortunately, the most subtle indicator that the athlete has dropped too far into the fatigue zone and is therefore over-training is that his performance in training falls off. Arthur Newton too had noted this, for he wrote: "Inability to produce your best when you are apparently in good form is the first sign of incipient staleness" (Newton 1947a, page 22. Of course, athletes who do not carefully monitor their training performances will never spot this subtle indicator. I would suggest that this is the single most important reason why every athlete should record and analyze the results of all training and racing in great detail. One of the essential factors in the success of Bruce Fordyce (and I suspect of the other great peakers, such as Frank Shorter, Lasse Viren, and Mark Allen) was his method of meticulously monitoring the results of each training ses-sion he ran. By comparing his performances in identical workouts over many years, he could tell precisely what his physical condition was on any day of any year. As a result, he always knew what training he still needed to do to produce his peak performance on the one day that really mattered.

Indeed, I believe the reason for the time-trials suggested by Lydiard (7th Law of Training, chapter 5) is to monitor the athlete's level of fatigue and resistance to

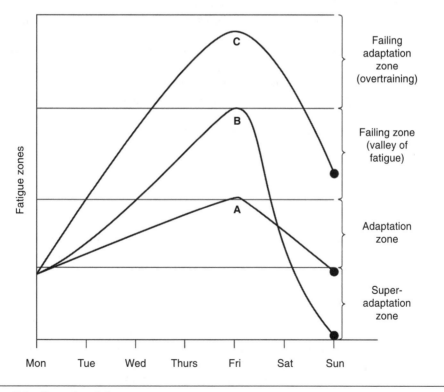

Figure 7.1 Counsilman's fatigue zones.
Adapted from Counsilman (1968, p. 236).

the stress of fast running. First, this should be done not against the stopwatch but on the basis of heart rate and the level of effort—according to the Borg Scale (table 5.2)—required to produce that performance. Second, it should be based on the athlete's rate of recovery after the time-trial. As long as the athlete's performance is improving, as shown by a faster running time for the same or lesser heart rate and effort and a more rapid recovery, then the athlete is not overtraining. An athlete who has to run harder at a higher heart rate to achieve the same time has been training too hard. The body then needs a period of rest and reduced training in order to do its best.

Heavy Leg Syndrome

If athletes fail to identify that they are doing too much and continue to train hard or, more commonly, if they believe that a fall in performance indicates the need for more intensive training, they are likely to develop the feeling of heavy legs during exercise. This condition has been graphically labeled *the plods* by South African ultramarathoner and sport physiotherapist Graeme Lindenberg. The most common symptoms of the plods are sore muscles; a heavy-legged, sluggish feeling; generalized fatigue; malaise; and, not uncommonly, diarrhea. These symptoms always disappear completely within 24 to 48 hours if the athlete is sensible enough to rest completely or to jog only a few kilometers. This rapid response to rest is what differentiates the heavy legs from the later stages of overtraining. The first run after the rest should be an absolute pleasure—there should be no trace of muscle soreness, and you should be able to run an effortless 30 seconds per kilometer or more faster than normal. Grete Waitz calls this condition a *mini burnout* (Waitz and Averbuch 1986).

Of course, the problem is that when you are training hard, it is usual for the legs to feel slightly stiff and lethargic at the start of a run. However, this feeling should pass as the run progresses. One method of deciding when the level of muscle soreness is inappropriate is to score all training runs on the basis of how your legs felt during the run. Muscle soreness that either persists or gets worse during the training run indicates that that particular run should be abandoned. There should be a period of 24 to 48 hours' rest to allow full muscle recovery before another hard or long training session is undertaken.

Super Plods

If your legs do not feel strong in the next run following the rest period, then you have developed the super plods and must rest for a further period until your legs recover fully. These more serious symptoms indicate that you have gone beyond overreaching and are now well on the road to overtraining.

Athletes who continue to race or to train hard when they have these symptoms can only crash into what we recognize as the full-blown overtraining state, with some or all of the symptoms listed in table 7.1. The most common symptoms found in a group of overtrained runners (Barron et al. 1985) were persistent muscle soreness, loss of interest in training and competition, increases in resting heart rate, and changes in sleeping patterns. Once these symptoms were present, recovery took between five and eight weeks, during which time there was absolutely no possibility that the athletes could train properly, let alone race.

Other Factors

Although training and racing too much are usually the essential ingredients for overtraining, various authors have listed other factors that predispose an athlete to overtraining or that exacerbate these overtraining symptoms. These factors include poor nutrition, drug use, lack of sleep and inadequate rest, adverse climatic conditions, "irregular living" (which I assume refers to anything not listed here that interferes with a stable lifestyle), work pressures, emotional conflicts and emotional turmoil, monotonous training, and miscellaneous stress—the everyday wear and tear of living (Carlile 1963). You should always remember that training is a holism (Law 15, chapter 5) and that certain aspects of the athlete's lifestyle will contribute to overtraining.

Monitoring the Early Signs

Obviously, very few runners develop the full-blown overtraining syndrome, yet many run races less well than they should because they fail to observe the early symptoms that differentiate overreaching from overtraining. The most practical way to prevent overtraining is to have an objective observer (a coach or friend) tune into the early symptoms of overtraining. Certainly, you are less likely to be sufficiently objective about your overtraining symptoms. My own ability to recognize overtraining in others, but not in myself, is a typical example.

The signs that provide some of the earliest clues that an athlete is overtraining have been described in detail by Richard Brown in his studies of athletes running for the Athletics West Track Club in Eugene, Oregon (R.L. Brown 1983). This Nike-sponsored club came into being at a time of great optimism in American distance running and had among its members many of the brilliant American distance runners of the early 1980s, including Alberto Salazar and Mary Decker-Slaney. The indicators to monitor include

- a progressive loss of weight,
- an increased fluid intake (particularly in the evening),
- a progressively later bedtime each evening,
- a decreased number of hours of sleep, and
- a persistent increase of 5 to 10 beats per minutes in early morning pulse rate.

Czajkowski (1982) developed another practical test of overtraining while monitoring the training status of Polish cross-country skiers. Each morning the skiers measured their heart rates, first on awakening and then again exactly 20 seconds after they stood up. He found that as the skiers became overtrained, their waking pulse rates rose, and, more important, the difference between their lying and standing heart rates increased (figure 7.2). Note the steep and sustained increase in the resting heart rate once the athletes became overtrained.

However, the fundamental weakness in this and most other techniques that aim to detect overtraining is that the signs that the athlete is overtrained—the higher waking and standing heart rates once the athlete is overtrained (July to October in figure 7.2)—occur when it is already obvious to everyone that the athlete is overtrained. What is needed is a variable that changes before the athlete is obviously suffering from the overtraining syndrome. In other words, a test is needed that will identify some alteration (in May or June in figure 7.2) that would predict by a few weeks the actual development of the overtraining syndrome. A marker that identifies what is already obvious is of no value.

Another technique that uses the heart rate to identify overtraining is the one developed by Conconi and his colleagues (1982) for determining the heart rate inflection point. In chapter 3, I outline the reasons why this test has no physiological basis. However, their relevant finding—contrary to their assertions about the lactate turnpoint and the heart rate inflection, and more likely to be correct—was that as the athlete became overtrained, the heart rate became higher at any given running speed (figure 7.3). This, of course, is exactly the opposite of the heart rate response to correct training, in which the heart rate at any running speed is reduced. Interestingly, Carlile had described essentially the same phenomenon in swimmers some 20 years earlier (1963).

The reason the resting heart rate rises with overtraining is unknown. Dressendorfer et al. (1985) studied 12 runners running 500 km in 20 days and found that the early morning heart rates fell for the first eight days of the race (as the athletes became fitter), but thereafter rose progressively (presumably as the athletes became overstressed and overtrained). They hypothesized that the rising heart rates might indicate progressive fatigue of the heart muscle. However, I doubt this. It is more likely that the elevated resting heart rate reflects heightened activity of the sympathetic nervous system, reflecting the increased stress on the body and inadequate recovery.

It is easy to measure the heart rate during training, so it is surprising that so few athletes and coaches use it as an indicator of overtraining. In particular, the sophisticated Polar heart rate monitors or the Body iQ systems, with their capacity to download previously recorded information into a computer (chapter 5), are essential pieces of equipment for all serious athletes.

However, the first detailed study of heart rate and blood pressure changes with heavy training using this more sophisticated technology has failed to identify any early markers of the overtraining syndrome (Vusitalo 1998). Thus, the early promise of this technique has still to be realized. More recently, a group of French scientists used changes in heart rate variability to predict changes in the autonomic

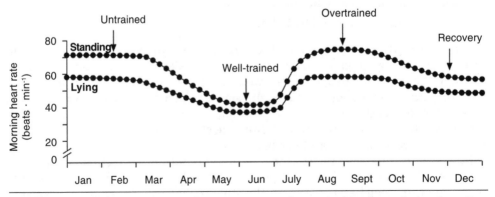

Figure 7.2 The effects of training and overtraining on early morning lying (lower line) and standing (upper line) heart rates.

Adapted, by permission, from Czajkowski (1982, p. 210).

nervous system with training (Pichot et al. 2000). *Heart rate variability* refers to minute beat-to-beat differences in the exact timing of consecutive heart beats. Thus, whereas a heart rate of 60 beats per minute suggests that there is exactly one second between all the consecutive heart beats measured in 1 minute, in fact, the gap between heart beats varies substantially and might, for example, range from 0.8 to 1.2 seconds in a person with a heart rate of 60 beats per minute. It is found that the greater the heart rate variability, the healthier the heart. More important, heart rate variability is reduced when the sympathetic nervous system is more active and is increased when parasympathetic activity is increased. Heart rate variability disappears during exercise at intensities above about 50% $\dot{V}O_2$max, when sympathetic activity is increased. Pichot et al. (2000) found that heart rate variability measured at night decreased progressively during three weeks of intensive training, indicating increased sympathetic and reduced parasympathetic activity. The authors suggest that changes in heart rate variability measured at night might provide an accurate method to optimize training and prevent overtraining.

One runner who used the exercising heart rate to indicate his physical condition during training was Lasse Viren, one of the first athletes to use an early Polar heart rate monitor in the late 1970s. In July 1972, before the Munich Olympic Games, Viren set a world record for 2 miles (8:14), raising the possibility that he had peaked too soon for the Games, which were to be held in September. To check for this, his coach had Viren run a standard workout of 20 × 200 m; his time for each repeat was measured, as was his heart rate as soon as he finished (Daws 1978). At that time it was not possible to measure the heart rate during exercise out of doors. In June, Viren averaged 30 seconds and 192 beats per minute. In July, before the 2-mile record, he averaged 29.3 seconds and 186 beats per minute, and in August, 28.2 seconds and 172 beats per minute. What is clear is that he was continuing to improve.

Another runner who has written about overtraining is Grete Waitz (Waitz and Averbuch 1986). Her remarkable consistency must be due in part to her ability to detect the early signs of overtraining. She writes,

> *I judge my fatigue more by my moods. If it's hard to sleep or I am cranky, impatient or annoyed, I am probably overtraining. In my case, family and friends often know when I am overtraining even before I do. When I begin to snap at Jack [her husband], he knows it is time to analyze my training and probably cut back."* (Waitz and Averbuch 1986, page 74)

Waitz suggests that positive answers to three or more of the following questions probably indicate that it is time to reduce training:

Does your normally comfortable pace leave you breathless?

Do your legs feel heavy for far longer than usual after a hard workout or a race?

Do you find it especially hard to climb steps?

Do you dread the thought of training?

Do you find it hard to get out of bed in the morning?

Do you have a persistent lack of appetite?

Are you more susceptible to colds, flu, headache, or infections?

Is your resting heart rate 5 to 10 beats higher than usual?

Is your heart rate during exercise higher than usual?

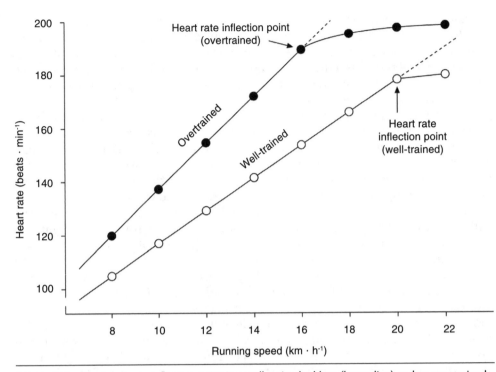

Figure 7.3   The heart rate inflection point in a well-trained athlete (lower line) and an overtrained athlete (upper line).

After Conconi et al. (1982).

Waitz wrote that the feeling in her legs and the way she breathed during exercise indicated when she could no longer push herself in training. Usually, heaviness in her legs would go away after a few minutes of running. When the feeling persisted, she knew she should rest rather than train.

Her observations on appetite are particularly interesting. Two studies (Reichelt et al. 1978; Trygstad et al. 1978) show that humans and animals produce a circulating substance that reduces appetite. They suggest that overtraining increases production of this substance, which makes a reduction in appetite another possible marker of overtraining (Greenwell 1991).

Waitz's advice for avoiding overtraining was to never try overcoming fatigue by force. Like Fordyce, she stressed that, when in doubt, runners should rest rather than train hard. She also cautioned against being overambitious and racing too much.

Blood Tests

A host of studies have been performed in an attempt to isolate changes in one or more factors in blood that can predict incipient overtraining (Urhausen et al. 1987; Lehmann et al. 1992; 1997; Hooper et al. 1993; Gastmann et al. 1998). Sadly, these studies have failed to identify a single blood parameter that can be used in a practical way to identify when an athlete is overtraining.

One possible explanation for this failure could simply be that overtraining represents the most extreme example in which the central governor is maximally activated to ensure that the athlete cannot exercise anymore and thus cause further damage. Since the central governor does not disclose its presence through anything measurable in the blood, its importance in the genesis of this condition will also not be detectable simply by measuring changes in the blood.

PREDICTIVE FACTORS

To my knowledge, the first edition of *Lore of Running* (1985) was one of the first books to include a substantive chapter on the overtraining syndrome. It was perhaps this chapter that stimulated the rash of new publications and research studies on overtraining in the late 1990s.

Many of these studies have attempted to identify early markers of overtraining, and some have evaluated the place of psychological markers for predicting overtraining. The consensus would seem to be that biological markers (in particular, blood concentrations of a variety of hormones, of chemicals relating to muscle damage and nutritional status, and of markers of immune function and hematological status) are indifferent predictors of the onset of overtraining (Flynn 1998; Fry et al. 1993; Hooper and Mackinnon 1995; Hooper et al. 1995; Budgett 1998; Rowbottom et al. 1998; Lehmann, Gastmann, et al. 1999).

As Harm Kuipers, former Olympic gold medalist in speed skating and now a leading exercise physiologist, has stated,

> *Unfortunately our present laboratory tools are much less sensitive than the athlete's body and the athlete's mind; these are the most sensitive and important instruments to detect overtraining. Athletes should learn the "feel" of the body, and the state of mind. The first signs of insufficient recovery and early overtraining are increased effort of normal training tasks, and change in the Mood State. Therefore I would suggest to have all athletes keep a training log in which, not only training data are registered, but also subjective perceptions of the training and state of mind. . . . (Kuipers 1998a)*

It is now clear that besides alterations in training and racing performances, and in other physical tests (Koutedakis et al. 1995), the most effective predictors of the development of the overtraining syndrome are measures of psychological state (Berglund and Säfström 1994; Hooper et al. 1995; Hooper and Mackinnon 1995; Foster and Lehmann 1997) and training load (Foster and Lehmann 1997; Foster 1998).

Thus, Berglund and Säfström (1994) found that the mood state, measured with the Profile of Mood State (POMS) questionnaire, of a group of 14 world-class Swedish canoeists preparing for Olympic competition deteriorated progressively as the subjects undertook increasingly more demanding training. Mood state improved during the three-week tapering phase before competition. On the basis of abnormally highs POMS scores, the training load was reduced in nine athletes, all but one of whom recovered within a week of reduced training. The athlete who did not respond to one week's rest recovered after a second week of reduced training, indicating that he was on the threshold of developing the overtraining syndrome. In contrast, the training load was increased in some subjects whose mood states were inappropriately high during training, suggesting that they were not training sufficiently hard.

Hooper et al. (1995) studied a group of 19 competitive Australian swimmers during a six-month training period. Besides regular measurement of blood samples, the swimmers completed daily training logs that included their training details and ratings of their quality of sleep, fatigue, stress, and muscle soreness on an arbitrary scale of 1 to 7. Body mass, early morning heart rate, and the incidence of illness and other medical problems were also recorded.

The four best predictors of overtraining were found to be the logbook entries for fatigue, muscle soreness, stress, and quality of sleep. In contrast, blood biochemical measures were inaccurate predictors of overtraining. As a result, the authors (Hooper and Mackinnon 1995) concluded that the four best markers for monitoring overtraining are

1. performance on standard exercise tests;
2. self-analysis of well-being by the athlete;
3. Profile of Mood State (POMS); and
4. submaximal, maximal, and postexercise recovery rates for heart rate, oxygen uptake, and blood lactate concentrations.

In contrast, they concluded that body mass, resting heart rate and blood pressure, and various blood cellular and biochemical markers (including hormone, hemoglobin, and ferritin concentrations; red cell and white cell counts; and creatine kinase activity) were poor markers of overtraining. Carl Foster was one of the first people to evaluate the relationship of training volumes to the development of both physical complaints and the risk of overtraining (Foster and Lehmann 1997; Foster 1998). He developed a seven-part complaint index (table 7.2) to evaluate the physiological and psychological symptoms experienced by the athletes during training.

Foster also developed a system to quantify the intensity of each training session. This was achieved by having the subject rate the global intensity of the training session according to a modified Borg Scale (table 7.3). When the intensity score for the individual training session was multiplied by the duration of each training session, a single number representing the training load for the session (session load) was calculated. When each day's training for a week was calculated and summed, a number of different calculations could be made.

For example, table 7.4 lists a hypothetical example of seven days' training by an athlete who indulges in a variety of activities. The daily training load is calculated as the duration of the activity multiplied by the average rating of perceived exertion, estimated from table 7.3. The daily average load is then calculated as the seven-day total divided by seven.

There is nothing particularly revolutionary in the logic behind these calculations. Their importance is that the training load calculated in this way can be related to athletic performance with increased training. When measured like this, they lead to a predictable improvement in athletic performance as a curvilinear, or exponential, function (figure 5.7).

According to that model, it is then possible to calculate your optimum training load using the guidelines in figure 5.6. However, it is the next step in logic that takes these concepts to another level. Foster reasoned that training volume alone was unlikely to be the sole cause of overtraining. For example, a study in horses (Bruin et al. 1994) found that thoroughbred race horses could not be overtrained if they were trained progressively harder with a hard day/easy day training program (Law

5, chapter 5). However, when the training load on the easy training day was increased so that the horses did not have any rest days, they soon developed symptoms of overtraining. Those authors concluded that day-to-day variability in the training load may protect against overtraining. To verify this theory, Foster and his colleagues developed a training monotony index to evaluate the extent of the daily variability in each athlete's training.

Table 7.2 Foster's psychological complaint index

To complete this index, answer the question, "How do you feel today?" in each of the seven subcategories. Place a mark through the index at the point that best represents how you feel about each of the complaints that athletes frequently have. The words or expressions are intended to serve as guides.

No complaints			Moderate complaints				Severe complaints			
0	1	2	3	4	5	6	7	8	9	10

Feel great					Feel OK				Feel horrible	
0	1	2	3	4	5	6	7	8	9	10

Fresh					Tired				Exhausted	
0	1	2	3	4	5	6	7	8	9	10

Good morning			Is it morning already?						Oh s—!	
0	1	2	3	4	5	6	7	8	9	10

Perky					OK				Lethargic	
0	1	2	3	4	5	6	7	8	9	10

Dynamic					Sluggish				Toast	
0	1	2	3	4	5	6	7	8	9	10

Muscles feel good				A little sore					Muscles ache	
0	1	2	3	4	5	6	7	8	9	10

Total score: $\dfrac{}{7}$ = average score: _____

From Guten (1997, p. 180). © 1999 by W.B. Saunders Co. Reproduced with permission.

Table 7.3   Foster's modified rating of perceived exertion scale

Approximately 30 minutes after completing a training session, describe the overall effort put into the training session according to the following rating scale.

Rating		Borg's description	Runner's description
0.0	}	No effort	Rest
0.5	} Green	Very, very easy	
1	}	Very easy	Really easy
2	}	Easy	Easy
3	}	Moderate	Moderate
4	} Yellow	Somewhat hard	Sort of hard
5	}	Hard	Hard
6	} Orange		HARD
7	}	Very hard	VERY HARD
8	}		The coach tried to kill us
9	} Red	Very, very hard	I feel like death warmed up
10	}	Maximal	Oh s—!

Permission granted by C. Foster.

To do this, they calculated the standard deviation (SD) of the daily training load (table 7.4) according to the following equation:

$$SD = \sqrt{\frac{\Sigma d^2}{N-1}}$$

where d = the difference between the value and the mean and N = the number of training sessions in the week. This gives a measure of the day-to-day variability in the training load. By dividing the average daily load by the standard deviation of the training load, Foster then calculated the monotony of training.

Figure 7.4 illustrates this concept. This figure presents the daily training loads of two runners over a 14-day period. Runner A shows large daily changes in training load whereas runner B does the same training every day. Hence, the training patterns of runner B are more monotonous than those of runner A. The weekly training load can be determined with further calculations. When this number is multiplied by the monotony factor, a rating of *strain* is also made (table 7.4).

Using these tools, Foster and his colleagues studied a group of competitive speedskaters over periods ranging from six months to three years. The weekly training load was calculated as the sum of each session load completed during the week. When this number was multiplied by the monotony score for that week, a strain score was produced.

On the basis of these tools, they were able to show that 84% of all illnesses occurred when athletes exceeded their individual training thresholds for training load, training strain, or monotony. An interesting observation was that a training load of 4000 units per week (comparable to the training load achieved by many elite athletes) could be achieved either by training hard for four days a week with two light training days and a rest day (similar to runner A in figure 7.4) or by training six days

Table 7.4	An evaluation of the load, monotony, and strain of a specific training program according to Foster			
Day	**Activity**	**Duration (min)**	**RPE (units)**	**Load (duration × RPE)**
S	Cycle 100 km	180	5	900
M	Weight training	120	7	840
T	Jog 5 km	20	2	40
W	In-line roller intervals	90	6	540
T	Cycle 50 km	75	7	525
F	Jog 5 km	20	2	40
S	Weight training	120	7	840
	Daily average load			532
	Standard deviation of the daily load			367
	Monotony (daily average load ÷ standard deviation)			1.45
	Weekly load (daily average load × 7)			3,724
	Strain (total load × monotony)			5,400

Reproduced with permission. The original was used during a lecture given by Carl Foster at the Seventh International Conference of the South African Sports Medicine Association, Johannesburg, South Africa, September 1999. Permission granted by C. Foster.

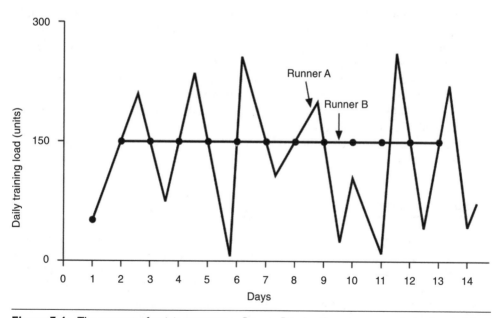

Figure 7.4 The concept of training monotony. Runner B trains the same way each day (same daily training load). Runner A varies his daily training load substantially and alternates days of heavy and light training. According to Foster, runner B is at higher risk for injury, illness, and poor racing performance because her training is more monotonous than is the training of runner A, even though the weekly training load of both athletes is quite similar.

a week with a lesser intensity but greater monotony and with only one easy training day (something similar to the pattern adopted by runner B in figure 7.4).

Foster and his colleagues found that the first training program, with fewer days of similar training, would be less likely to result in overtraining but would not produce a lesser training effect. As a result, they concluded that the risk of overtraining is increased by

- one-sided, monotonous training without alternating hard and easy training days;
- a lack of one complete rest day per week;
- a high total and increasing training load combined with significant nontraining stress factors; and
- too many competitions (Lehmann et al. 1998).

PHYSIOLOGICAL CHANGES

No one as yet knows the exact bodily changes that cause the overtraining syndrome. There are, of course, those armchair experts who will tell you that overtraining is all in the mind, that it is purely due to a mental failure—the sporting equivalent of a lack of character. I believe that such statements show that these experts have yet to learn firsthand that, when physically stretched, the body, not the mind, is always the first to quit. Overtrained runners find that while their minds are ready to run, their bodies would much rather be asleep in bed. And the more their minds force them to train, the more their bodies resist until, in the race, their bodies have the final say.

Originally I believed, in common with others (Foster and Lehmann 1997; O'Toole 1998), that the heavy leg syndrome experienced after a single long training run or after an unbroken period of heavy training was probably due to complete depletion of the body's carbohydrate stores. But that does not explain why the super plods last longer than the 24- to 48-hour period required to restock body carbohydrate stores, nor why it is not possible to run good marathons within 8 to 12 weeks of one another. It would seem that this prolonged period of recuperation after races and longer training runs must indicate that other recovery processes, either in the muscles or in other parts of the body, or both, are taking place. The prolonged recovery from overtraining supports this idea. Let us consider some of these processes.

Evidence of Muscle Damage and Recovery

A number of recent studies show that muscles are damaged by severe, prolonged exercise such as marathon running and that recovery from this damage takes substantially longer than was originally thought by some of the runners presented in chapter 6. Recall the words of former world-record holder Buddy Edelen, who believed that he could probably "bash out" a world-class marathon every month or so. Recall also that athletes who have tried to adopt that approach have all had short, albeit spectacular, marathon careers.

The first relevant study showing the impact of muscle damage on recovery rate was that of Hikida et al. (1983), who performed muscle biopsies on a group of marathon runners the day before, immediately after, and three, five, and seven days after a competitive marathon. They found strong evidence of muscle cell damage that was worst at one and three days after the race but was still present in the sample taken seven days later. Some runners' muscles even showed damage in the prerace samples. The authors concluded that both the intensive training and the marathon itself induce muscle cell damage, which explains the muscle cell soreness that accompanies heavy training and, in particular, marathon racing. Their data show that recovery from this damage is prolonged. Thus, we can conclude that at least part of the reason for the persistent muscle soreness that is so characteristic of the overtraining syndrome is due to persistent muscle damage.

In a related study, Matin et al. (1983) injected a radioactive substance (technetium 99 m pyrophosphate) into the blood of a group of ultramarathon runners after races of 80 and 160 km. By scanning the athletes with special detectors, they were able to identify where the radioactive material (which is taken up by damaged cells, including heart, muscle, and bone) was concentrated. There were abnormally high concentrations of radioactivity localized exclusively in the muscles of the lower limbs of all the athletes. After uphill running, the increased radioactivity was found in the adductor (inner thigh) muscles, whereas after downhill running, the hamstrings, quadriceps, and buttock muscles were the most affected. They also noted that the runners who complained of the worst postrace muscle soreness had the greatest abnormalities on scanning. The authors suggested that the greater the muscle pain after a race, the longer the recovery time required. Table 7.5 contains a simple classification of muscle soreness and the length of time for which hard training and racing should be avoided if the different grades of muscle soreness develop.

Next, Warhol et al. (1985) performed serial muscle biopsies on a group of 40 runners for up to 12 weeks after a 42-km marathon. Biopsies taken 48 hours after the race showed varying degrees of damage to the myofibrils, mitochondria, and sarcoplasmic reticulum. The damage was patchy, and, at worst, affected 25% of the fibers; in other runners, little damage was apparent.

Biopsies taken seven days after the marathon showed evidence of early resolution of the acute injury. The contents of the damaged myofibrils had been removed, leaving only empty (ghost) muscle tubes. There was also evidence of an ingrowth of satellite cells, which would ultimately regenerate new muscle cells to replace those damaged during the marathon. One month after competition, there was little evidence of residual damage but clear evidence of muscle cell regeneration and repair. Evidence of regeneration was more marked in biopsies taken eight to ten weeks after the race.

The researchers concluded that damage occurred to muscle fibers that were depleted of their glycogen and lipid stores; that the injury was focal and seldom exceeded more than 10% of the muscle fibers examined; that the degree of injury varied among runners; that the injury did not induce necrosis (death) of muscles, nor did it activate an inflammatory response, but that it was instead characterized by muscle fiber degeneration and drop-out; and that the injury was completely reversible within 10 to 12 weeks. However, they did notice that veteran runners did have some areas of fibrosis in their muscles, suggesting incomplete repair. A modern interpretation would be that it is the persistent and repetitive eccentric loading of the muscles, and not energy depletion, that causes this muscle damage.

These findings have been confirmed by a study by Harm Kuipers and colleagues (Kuipers, Janssen et al. 1989), who studied a group of novice runners training for a

42-km marathon and showed that, as the length of the athletes' training runs increased, so did the incidence of pathological changes in their muscles. They concluded that these findings reflected a continuous degeneration and regeneration of muscle.

Sjöström et al. (1987) performed muscle biopsies on an athlete who ran an average of 67 km per day for seven weeks. The biopsy taken before the start of the event was normal. However, marked abnormalities were present in the biopsy taken seven weeks later, after completion of the run. The muscle fiber size varied considerably, and regenerating and degenerating muscle fibers were observed. Average muscle-fiber size was reduced. It appeared that Type II (fast twitch) muscle fibers were more susceptible to injury. The researchers found evidence of increased connective tissue and an infiltration of inflammatory cells.

Similar changes were subsequently found in the muscles of a group of sub-2:40 marathon runners (Sjöström et al. 1988). Interestingly, Sjöström et al. reported that the running speed of the subject who ran 67 km per day for seven weeks "has continuously decreased since the experiment" (1987, p. 519). As described in chapter 6, the evidence is clear that athletes who race marathon and ultramarathon races frequently in any single year usually perform poorly for a considerable time afterward, suggesting that this form of muscle damage is either a cause or perhaps a marker of changes that impair running performance for quite prolonged periods.

St. Clair Gibson and colleagues (1998) from our laboratory at the Sports Science Institute of South Africa performed muscle biopsies on a 28-year-old former professional distance runner who experienced a sudden, persistent, and unexplained decline in running performance and an inability to tolerate high training loads. The subject had begun running since age 10, and, at age 17, he was the South African national junior champion with a best 10-km time of 28:35. During his professional career, he trained about 6000 km per year. Biopsy of his vastus lateralis (thigh) muscle showed normal muscle fibers but grossly abnormal mitochondria.

His arm muscles did not show these abnormalities, suggesting that it was the running training of the leg muscles that caused the abnormality rather than some other condition, which would have affected all muscles equally. It is interesting that three-time Tour de France winner, Greg Le Mond, showed similar abnormalities (Derr 1995). These findings indicate that heavy training is associated with muscle

Table 7.5	Classification of muscle soreness	
Grading	Symptoms	Indication
0	No discomfort	Continue training
1	Some discomfort on feeling muscle No racing for 2 weeks	Reduce training for 7 days
2	Discomfort on walking Unable to squat without discomfort	Reduce training for 14 days No racing for 1 month
3	Severe pain Walking with difficulty	Reduce training for at least 1 month No racing for 2 months

damage. We have also shown these abnormalities in a group of athletes from a variety of endurance sports, all of whom had trained intensively for many years and who developed persistent muscle soreness, unexplained fatigue, and a rapid, sustained fall in athletic performance (Derman et al. 1997) that could not be explained on medical or psychological grounds.

A related issue is the progressive inability of those who trained heavily at a younger age to match the performances of their peers who began training later in their lives. Does very heavy training at a young age cause a form of irreversible muscle damage to become apparent only 10 to 15 years later? Bruce Fordyce has reflected on this possibility. It is not clear whether he was writing from personal experience, but my discussions with him suggest that he was:

> We are still in a relatively early stage of understanding the effects of years on distance runners. Bill Rodgers and his contemporaries are really the first generation of elite runners who we can study to understand what happens after years of punishing training and racing. We are beginning to see signs that there is a pattern. It appears it is possible to get ring weary, even a little punch drunk. Runners who have competed at the highest levels for years are still able to race well at shorter distances but they seem to suffer badly at distances of the marathon or beyond. Their legs get tired and sore earlier and the onset of fatigue is both draining and devastating. We know that top runners have a finite number of truly world-class marathons in their systems. Thereafter, they can still run well but truly great performances are gone forever.

> The Masters [marathon] record can and will be broken, but it will be broken by a young master, a fresh master. By that we now understand to mean a 50-year-old who only started running in his [or her] forties. This would be a runner who has not grown ring weary and whose legs were still relatively fresh for the task of running 42 km in close to 2:30. The runner will break the record, but will probably rue the fact he didn't discover his talent in his twenties. (Fordyce 1999, page 23)

These examples are not typical of the overtraining syndrome in that the condition appears to be persistent and not reversible in the short term and seems to be caused by currently unknown factors, in addition to sustained heavy training and frequent competition, especially at marathon and ultramarathon distances. However, the point is that muscle is a fragile organ and can clearly be damaged in ways that we have yet to understand fully. Indeed, my colleague Malcolm Collins, in collaboration with Gillian Butler-Browne at the national center for scientific research within the department of development and cytoskeleton at the Pitie-Salpetriere medical school in France, has recently established what appears to be very good evidence that the skeletal muscles of athletes whose exercise capacity becomes impaired after many years of heavy training lose their capacity to regenerate when redamaged by training or racing. These changes have occurred at the level of the athletes' genetic material and are hence irreversible. Perhaps it is these changes that explain the observations of Fordyce, Rodgers, and Weight and indicate that accumulated training impairs racing performance far beyond what can be explained reasonably on the basis only of aging.

The question that remains is, How far can you train and race before inducing the acute, mostly reversible form of muscle damage described by these authors (Hikida et al. 1983; Matin et al. 1983; Warhol et al. 1985; Sjöström et al. 1987; 1988)? One obvious way to discover this is to monitor muscle soreness after races of different distances. Distances that do not cause muscle soreness do not, presumably, cause significant muscle damage. My experience is that, in runners trained for the distance, races of up to 21 km usually do not result in marked postrace muscle soreness.

To study this, we (Strachan et al. 1984) monitored a blood protein (C-reactive protein), the levels of which rise when there is acute (immediate) tissue damage anywhere in the body. We found the C-reactive protein levels rose markedly after marathon and ultramarathon races, reaching levels after the Comrades Marathon normally found in patients with minor heart attacks. In races shorter than 21 km, no significant rise occurred. This suggests that muscle cell damage only starts to occur in races longer than 21 km and becomes progressively worse the longer the race. (Kuipers, Janssen et al. 1989) have drawn the same conclusion. Indeed, my guess is that the damage to the skeletal muscle genetic material identified by Collins and Butler-Browne, which appears to result from many years of heavy training and racing, is probably related to the frequency with which severe muscle soreness develops and the amount of racing and training that is done with sore muscles.

We do not yet know how long it takes to recover from acute muscle damage and the resultant muscle soreness. But it would seem that it takes much longer than most runners are currently prepared to allow (chapters 10 and 11). I suspect that the rapidity with which this severe form of muscle damage develops is determined by how many kilometers you run in races when the muscles are sore or very sore. Thus, ultramarathon races in which the muscle soreness increases exponentially with distance run beyond about 65 km would most likely be particularly damaging. Similarly, starting to run too soon after races that cause muscle soreness, before the muscles have had a change to recover properly, will probably exacerbate the damage caused by racing the longer distances.

Evidence of Chronic Muscle Fatigue

As discussed in chapter 3, research in swimmers and runners has shown that even daily training can produce chronic muscle fatigue that only recovers after a prolonged period of reduced training or rest before competition.

Costill and his colleagues (Costill 1985; Costill et al. 1985) have shown that the peak muscle power of swimmers was at its lowest when they trained the most. They also found that muscle power increases progressively during a seven-day taper immediately before competition. Similar findings have now been reported in runners (chapter 3). These findings confirm the importance of a relatively long taper before competition, as first proposed by Forbes Carlile (1964) and now advocated by most elite athletes (chapter 6). The subtle biochemical or other changes that explain this phenomenon are not clear, nor has the optimum duration of the taper been established with any certainty.

Another possibility is that the poorer muscle performance during heavy training or overtraining is due not to muscle damage but to a reduced capacity to recruit the active muscles. In chapter 2, it is argued that the brain's inability to recruit sufficient muscle fibers in the active muscles may explain the fatigue that develops during high-intensity exercise, during hypoglycemia, and during prolonged exercise when the body temperature is elevated. The study of Koutedakis et al. (1995) indicates that overtrained athletes have a reduced capacity to activate their muscles during exercise as the result of reduced brain (neural) recruitment.

This indicates that overtraining also affects brain function—in particular, the ability of the motor centers in the brain to activate sufficient muscle fibers in the active muscles during exercise. Again, this would act as a protective mechanism. By preventing the athlete from continuing to train when in the overtrained state, the brain is acting to prevent any further damage. This mechanism would also explain why athletes with irreversibly damaged muscles find exercise so difficult. The sensory feedback from those damaged muscles stimulates the central governor to ensure that only a small muscle mass is recruited during exercise. In addition, the governor stimulates other brain centers so that even mild exercise is perceived as being more strenuous than it really is.

Perhaps this explains why how you feel is the best predictor of when you are beginning to develop the overtraining syndrome. The feelings of abnormal fatigue are simply the brain's way of telling you to rest because you have already done too much.

Evidence of Neurohumoral Basis

The best lead we have in attempting to understand the nature of the whole body damage that occurs with overtraining comes from the landmark studies of the legendary Canadian biochemist Hans Selye. Selye (1956) exposed laboratory animals to a variety of stressful situations and observed their behavior. His observations are summarized in figure 7.5.

Selye hypothesized that an organism exposed to a specific stress initially undergoes an alarm reaction, during which resistance to that stress is reduced. If the organism survives this alarm reaction, it passes into the so-called st*age of resistance*, with increased resistance to the specific stress to which it has now become adapted, but with reduced resistance to other *stresses. But because* all organisms have limited adaptation energy (Selye 1950), they will ultimately reach the stage of exhaustion when exposed to an unremitting stress.

Could it be that the overtrained runner is behaving like Selye's experimental anim*als, entering this ex*haustion phase with impaired resistance to the specific stress of running and to less specific stresses such as allergy and infection? This would help explain the increased susceptibility to infection of overtrained runners (table 7.1).

In studying the biochemical basis of the overtraining syndrome, we (Barron et al. 1985) used hearsay evidence that suggested that an even more severe form of the

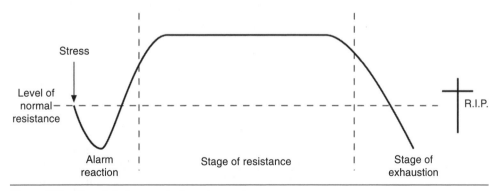

Figure 7.5   Hans Selye's general adaptation syndrome.

overtraining syndrome had been observed in athletes from Eastern European countries. These athletes allegedly continued to overtrain for months, possibly years, and finally developed an illness known as Addison's disease. In this condition, there is depression, progressive weight loss, an inability to maintain blood pressure when standing (postural hypotension), and severe physical incapacitation.

Similar but less severe symptoms have been described in overtrained runners (table 7.1). The cause of Addison's disease is a failure of the adrenal gland to secrete adequate amounts of certain hormones essential for life, in particular the hormone cortisol, which circulates in the blood and is essential for the myriad adaptations the body makes when adapting to any imposed stress, including running.

Accordingly, we set out to determine whether overtrained runners were able to normally secrete cortisol in response to an appropriate biochemical challenge (Barron et al. 1985). A strong yet safe stimulus for cortisol secretion is a fall in the blood glucose level, which can be induced experimentally by injecting an appropriate dose of insulin into an obliging subject.

We tested a group of overtrained runners to measure how they responded to the stress of having their blood glucose levels dropped precipitously by an insulin injection. As we expected, these runners exhibited an abnormal cortisol response: they were unable to increase their blood cortisol levels appropriately in response to the massive challenge of severe hypoglycemia. This abnormality was not due to a failure of the adrenal gland itself, as originally suggested by Webster (1948) and Selye (1956), but to exhaustion of the hypothalamus, the gland that orchestrates the entire hormonal response of the body. This corresponds with the other overtraining symptoms of depression, loss of appetite, and loss of libido (table 7.1), all of which are also influenced by the functioning of the hypothalamus.

After a six-week period during which the overtrained runners rested and jogged only occasionally, we found that their hormonal response to insulin-induced hypoglycemia returned to normal, but that this occurred some time before they had recovered fully. This suggests that some other recovery processes may also be required before the overtrained athlete can again run normally. Others (Luger et al. 1988; Urhausen et al. 1998) have since reported abnormalities in hypothalamic-pituitary-adrenal function in both heavily trained and overtrained athletes. These findings are similar to those reported by Barron et al. (1985). Luger et al. (1988) noted that these changes are "reminiscent of those seen in patients with anorexia nervosa and depression," whereas Urhausen et al. (1998) concluded, as we did, that hypothalamic-pituitary dysfunction is present in overtraining.

Another study (MacConnie et al. 1986) confirms that intensively training male runners running 125 to 200 km per week also show hypothalamic dysfunction, but to a lesser degree than we found in our overtrained runners. Specifically, these male runners show reduced spontaneous luteinizing hormone (LH) release from the pituitary, the same abnormality found in female runners with menstrual abnormalities. It is possible that these changes may be related to the negative changes in mood state reported by W.P. Morgan et al. (1987).

Different research groups have attempted to use this information to predict which athletes are overtraining. P.J. O'Connor et al. (1989) have shown that salivary cortisol concentrations rise in response to heavy increases in training. Heavy training also causes serum testosterone levels to fall. Thus, the ratio of serum testosterone to cortisol concentrations also drops with heavy training (Urhausen et al. 1987).

However, no one has yet been able to use information based on these biochemical tests to differentiate specifically between those athletes who are overtraining and those who are training intensively but adapting appropriately to the heavier training load.

PSYCHOLOGICAL CHANGES

W.P. Morgan and his colleagues (1987) reported the first detailed study of psychological changes with increased training. They studied groups of swimmers and showed that mood disturbances—characterized by reduced vigor and increased feelings of fatigue, depression, and anger—developed during the periods of most intensive training. These changes, similar to those found in people with marked depression, reversed spontaneously with rest or tapering of three to six weeks. The researchers suggested that monitoring mood states with the appropriate psychological questionnaires may prevent the development of staleness and overtraining. Similar findings have been reported in judo athletes (S.M. Murphy et al. 1990). These symptoms are the best predictors of overtraining, as shown by the studies of Foster and Lehmann (1997), Foster (1998), and Hooper and Mackinnon (1995) described earlier in this chapter.

However, an important limitation of some of these studies is that they have not differentiated between athletes who are undergoing a period of intensified training and those who are unable to train intensively because they are overtrained. The former are much easier to study than are athletes who are severely overtrained; hence the dearth of definitive studies of the true overtraining syndrome.

To summarize, bodily changes caused by overtraining include the following:

- Histological changes in muscle, including evidence of muscle fiber and mitochondrial abnormalities. In athletes who suffer from impaired athletic performance after years or decades of heavy training, there may also be alterations in the genetic material in the exercised skeletal muscles, suggesting that those muscles have a reduced capacity to respond to the stress of exercise, to repair damage after exercise, and to adapt to training.

- A reduced capacity of the brain to recruit the muscles used in the activity for which the athlete is trained.

- An impaired capacity of the hipothalamic-pituitary-axis to mount the normal hormonal response required to adapt to any external stress, includ:ng daily heavy training.

- Reduced sympathetic nervous system activity both at rest and during exercise (Foster and Lehmann 1997, Lehmann et al. 1997).

Thus, the overtraining syndrome appears to be caused by a major disruption in the body's ability to respond to normal stresses, such as infection or running. It is possible that this gross abnormality represents the protective response of a totally exhausted body. Rather than suffer the additional damage that would result if the body were allowed to continue training in this depleted state, the body responds by making training impossible—in particular, by preventing the brain from recruiting the muscles normally used in training. We runners must learn to respect the messages that our bodies give us, especially if the message is that we have already done too much. Perhaps it would be fitting to change George Sheehan's cautionary words "listen to your bodies" to "listen to your (subconscious) brain."

DIFFERENTIATING OVERTRAINING FROM OTHER CONDITIONS

In chapter 6, I present the evidence that suggests that elite marathon runners can expect only a limited number of fast marathons before their performances begin an inevitable decline. At present, we have been unable to find an explanation for this curious phenomenon. The following example illustrates this point. I was consulted (as a sports physician) by two elite athletes who were being treated for a supposed medical condition, hypothyroidism. The fact that prolonged and appropriate treatment for supposed hypothyroidism did not affect their subsequent running performances ruled out any causal relationship between the diagnosed medical condition and their catastrophic loss of running ability. This was despite the clear evidence that true (as opposed to a fictional) hypothyroidism does indeed impair running performance, a diagnosis that is often missed because it is such a subtle illness (Lathan 1991). Faced with a problem that they couldn't solve, the doctors of these two athletes had molded the facts to fit their medical preconceptions, which is always a dangerous exercise. However, until we fully understand the medical basis for the overtraining syndrome, this will continue to be a common error.

These two athletes were not suffering from the overtraining syndrome, as recovery from this syndrome is always accompanied by a subsequent return of athletic ability. The more likely diagnosis was that they had a syndrome that we, in our ignorance, have called the Fatigued Athletes Myopathic Syndrome (FAMS; Derman et al. 1997). Given the increasingly widespread use of performance-enhancing drugs (chapter 13), the long-term effects of which are not known, another possibility is that the early burnout of some modern professional athletes, especially cyclists, could perhaps be linked to their use of illicit ergogenic drugs.

The point is that those who do not recognize either the overtraining syndrome or FAMS often search for a medical diagnosis to explain the symptoms of these two different conditions. Instead, we should only consider the possibility of a medical condition being the cause of the runner's overstraining syndrome or FAMS if the runner's history differs in a substantial way from that described in this chapter, and if the condition does not resolve completely after a period of adequate rest (usually about six weeks). If symptoms persist beyond six weeks, a further detailed medical evaluation is essential. Should such tests fail to identify a cause, FAMS should be considered the most likely diagnosis.

A word of caution, however. There are two medical conditions that can produce a condition of impaired running performance and generalized fatigue suggestive of the overtraining syndrome, which therefore need to be excluded in all athletes who present with what appears to be the overtraining syndrome. The first is impaired functioning of the thyroid gland, causing hypothyroidism (Lathan 1991), and the second, the post-viral fatigue syndrome. Hypothyroidism can be diagnosed by the appropriate blood tests, in particular the immunometric thyroid stimulating hormone (TSH) assay. However, there are no specific tests to confirm a diagnosis of the post-viral fatigue syndrome.

As its name indicates, the post-viral fatigue syndrome develops after a viral infection. The diagnostic feature is that the sufferer is unable to exercise; even exercise of a few minutes' duration leaves the patient excessively fatigued for some days. Each attempt at exercise has the same effect. Resolution of symptoms takes at least a few months but can extend over years. The only effective treatment is complete rest until all symptoms disappear and exercise no longer produces excessive fatigue. The relationship between FAMS and the post-viral fatigue syndrome is unclear at present.

Abnormal fatigue and listlessness are also common features of depression, a diagnosis that must always be excluded in patients presenting with these symptoms. The distinction is usually quite easy: severely depressed people, like those children suffering from the overeager parent syndrome, are totally resistant even to the thought of exercise. However, athletes with either FAMS or the postviral fatigue syndrome are forever expressing their frustration at the fact that they want to exercise but are unable to because of the incapacitating fatigue that develops after each exercise bout.

TREATING OVERTRAINING

If you have developed the full-blown overtraining syndrome, it is essential to rest completely for 6 to 12 weeks. Continued training or racing when you are seriously overtrained is counterproductive, because your racing performance will be poor and the continued exertion will probably result in injury or a major infection; it may induce FAMS. My observation is that even early overtraining, which manifests itself in the form of a cold or other infection 7 to 14 days before a standard or ultramarathon, will slow a runner between 5 and 20 minutes in the marathon and between 45 and 60 minutes in the ultramarathon. In the second place, continued training when you are overtrained only prolongs the period you will ultimately have to rest. The sooner you accept the inevitable, the better.

The advice I give to overtrained runners is that they should only start running again when they have the desire, and then only slowly. But for many, including some of the experts profiled in chapter 6, overtraining is usually a chronic, relapsing condition so that, to prevent this form of condition, some intellectual insight is required on the part of the runner.

Competitive distance running is one of the most demanding physical activities to which the human body is exposed. I conclude this on the basis of the relatively short careers of most competitive distance runners, especially marathon runners (chapter 6). That some athletes run long distances, including marathons, with distinction does not prove that the human body is a marathon machine any more than the conquest of Everest indicates that humans are a high-altitude species. Both simply indicate the extreme adaptive flexibility we have inherited. While we adapt well to a variety of opposing stresses, humans are generalists, and we lack the ability to adapt specifically to any single, severe stress, such as competitive distance running, for any great length of time.

All runners need to appreciate the true nature of the human body, which is one of fragility, even though it can be trained to achieve remarkable feats. Therefore, it is essential for runners to match their mental desires to the frailty of their bodies so that their minds do not repeatedly demand more of their bodies than they can deliver.

Olympic gold medalist and exercise physiologist Harm Kuipers defines, in a nutshell, the mental approach of those athletes most likely to become overtrained: they train principally so that they can train harder, in the mistaken belief that the race always goes to the athlete who has suffered the most in training. Kuipers states,

> *Although little is known about the optimal amount of high-intensity training, athletes are usually inclined to do too much. It even appears that many athletes do high volumes of training [so as] to be able to sustain the amount of work they think they have to do. In effect, they train hard to adapt so they can train even harder. (Kuipers 1998b)*

The most successful athletes are likely to be those who consistently train less hard than their competitors believe is necessary.

Some years ago, shortly after the 1996 Atlanta Olympic Games, I was invited to participate at a joint meeting of the American College of Sports Medicine and the United States Olympic Committee on overtraining. There, the scientists discussed their concepts of overtraining and overreaching with a group of United States Olympic coaches in track and field and swimming.

During the informal discussions, I fell into conversation with a swimming coach who originated from the southern hemisphere. As if to goad the scientists, he informed us that his top swimmer, a multi-Olympic medalist, would only now begin to start training "properly." He boasted that in 1997 she would train 10% more than in 1996, and in the 12 months leading up to the 2000 Olympic Games in Sydney, she should aim to swim 50% more than she had before the Atlanta Olympics.

My comment was that I would be surprised if his swimmer ever made it to the pool at the Sydney Olympics. She did, but only barely.

Put out of the sport by an overtraining injury to her shoulder, which required arthroscopic surgery, she qualified for only one final in the Sydney Olympics. It is tragic that those athletes with the most talent, who perform the best on the least training, are also those at greatest risk of falling prey to overeager coaches, who, lacking the wisdom of the truly great coaches, restrict their athletes' great potential by ignorantly forcing them to overtrain.

FINITE PHYSICAL CAPACITY

When I was running competitively in the 1970s, the concept that runners could train too hard was anathema and was quickly dismissed by the runners with whom I ran. Indeed, an early article I wrote on the topic was passed off as evidence that I was just too lazy. Yet the signs were everywhere. Dave Bedford, the hardest trainer of the era, performed poorly in the 1972 Olympic Games. My friend Dave Levick, who won the 1971 London-to-Brighton Marathon and the 1973 Comrades Marathon in record time after finishing second in the 1971 race, performed increasingly poorly the harder he trained in later years. The performances of Alberto Salazar, who trained and raced hard in the late 1970s and early 1980s, suddenly fell off precipitously.

The early 1980s were an exciting time for American distance running. In particular, the natural successor to Frank Shorter and Bill Rodgers seemed to have arrived in the person of Alberto Salazar, a native of Cuba who had grown up in Massachusetts. He was faster than both Shorter and Rodgers, ran with a ruthless abandon, and had a youthful confidence that some interpreted as arrogance.

In fact, Salazar described himself as an "arrogant, antagonistic athlete who was never satisfied with any race, any victory. I was always so obsessed with the next race or workout that I could never relax or enjoy life" (Wischnia 1994, page 80). However, it seemed natural to assume that Salazar would bring both a world record and the Olympic gold medal back to the United States and thus sustain the glory of Frank Shorter's inspiring victory in the 1972 Olympic Marathon in Munich.

Between 1980 and 1983, Salazar set three American records; he won the Boston Marathon in 1982 in 2:08:51 and the New York City Marathon three times (1980, 2:09:41; 1981, 2:08:13; 1982, 2:09:29). In the 1981 race, he set a new world record that was subsequently disallowed as the course was 148 m short.

But the promise failed to materialize. By 1983, Salazar was no longer the world's best marathoner; he had to run too hard qualifying for the 1984 Los Angeles Olympic Marathon, in which he finished fifteenth in 2:14:17.

For the next 10 years, Salazar searched for the answer to his sudden inability to run fast without being continuously sick and injured. He concluded that three episodes of heatstroke during races run in the heat, combined with years of hard training at such a high level, had damaged his hypothalamus, leading to dysfunction of his hormonal system. Although he continued to run during this period, he "felt horrible and hated it. I couldn't let it go" (Wischnia 1994, page 82). He also felt lethargic and moody.

Then, some months after officially retiring from the sport after dropping out of the 1992 United States Olympic Marathon trials, Salazar met a physician, also a competitive masters runner, who had successfully treated himself with an antidepressant medication, Prozac. Salazar began taking the medication; within days, he began to feel better and to run faster. Suddenly, he was able to run mile repetitions 30 seconds faster per mile than before taking the medication. His blood hormone concentrations also normalized.

Most remarkably, he was again able to train competitively, and in the winter of 1993, he began training 100 km per week. His thoughts turned to the Comrades Marathon, a race at which his loss of speed would not be a hindrance. By February 1994, he was running 200 km per week—slower than in his heyday but including more longer runs that month: eight of 42 km and two of 64 km. By April, convinced that he could win the race, he officially entered the 1994 Comrades Marathon, arriving in South Africa two weeks before the event. He telephoned me shortly after arriving in this country. When I asked him how fit he was, he replied that he had run 32 km on his home treadmill in about 1:38. From this information, I predicted that he would win the Comrades Marathon, since I was unsure of any other entrant in that race who could equal that performance on a treadmill. During the race, Salazar ran just like the novice ultramarathon runner he was.

After only 20 km, Salazar took the lead. The last runner to win the race after leading from so early was Jackie Mekler, 30 years earlier, when there were only 272 entrants (compared to more than 8000 in 1994), none of whom could seriously challenge Mekler.

Salazar passed through the halfway mark in 2:44:00, a new record for the uphill run, with a lead of some 7 minutes. But by 50 km, his early pace was beginning to tell. He wished only to stop running. He began to pray and to say his Catholic rosaries. With 16 km to go, his lead had been reduced to 5 minutes—enough, he calculated, to allow him to win if he just kept running. He held on to win by 2 minutes in 5:38:39. It was, he concluded, a miracle—more satisfying than anything he had ever done in his life. But the miracle was short-lived. Salazar's goal to run the 1994 New York City Marathon and the United States National 100-Km Championships in February 1995 never materialized. He retired finally from the sport in January 1998. At his retirement, he said, "I run 30 minutes a day, and if I leave it at that, I'm fine. If I run any more than that, I feel terrible" (Salazar 1998, page 8). His concluding summary reviewed what his life as a runner had taught him:

The biggest thing I've learned isn't simply that I trained too hard all those years. Everyone says, "Alberto trained way too hard and burned out." To be a world-class runner, you have to train hard. But what I did learn is you can't do those hard workouts unceasingly. In order to be good, you have to train at a high level, but you must allow your body time to recover. You need to take time off. You need to run easy on some days, and you need to take at least a month off at the end of the season. I never did either.

I look back on the last 10 years and all the frustrations, and, in a way, I'm glad that it happened the way it did. If I had been running great all this time, I don't know what I would be like or what my priorities would be now. I might be divorced, and my kids might hate me. I'm thankful that God tested me in a way that has allowed me to understand what the priorities in life should be. More than anything, I learned there's a lot more to life than just seeing how fast you can run. (Wischnia 1994, p. 84)

During a trip to Eugene, Oregon, in 1986, I had the privilege of lunching with Salazar, who had always been a special hero of mine, and discussing his medical condition. At the time, my colleagues and I (Barron et al. 1985) had published a study showing that the hypothalamus can fail under the demands of heavy training. I told him that I was sure that his symptoms were due to hypothalamic dysfunction as a result of years of heavy training or, now in retrospect, to the three episodes of heatstroke that he had suffered. What we did not discuss was that whereas the hypothalamic dysfunction had resolved spontaneously within six to eight weeks of adequate rest in less competitive, more recreational runners, I was less certain that his condition would resolve, given that it was more severe and had already been present for more than three years.

Perhaps guided by this advice, Salazar reportedly continued to be treated medically but without real benefit. Only when he began using Prozac in 1993 did his symptoms resolve completely, albeit for a relatively short period. (This information was widely reported by Salazar after his Comrades victory; hence it is not privileged medical information.) Prozac is a selective serotonin reuptake inhibitor (SSRI) and is used for the treatment of depression and certain behavioral disorders, such as obsessive-compulsive behavior and, occasionally, bulimia and anorexia nervosa, both of which have features of the obsessive-compulsive disorders. Prozac acts to increase brain serotonin concentrations, which are believed to be low in people suffering from depression.

Salazar's primary affliction was not, in my view, depression. People who suffer from depression do not wish to exercise. Salazar was naturally depressed, but only because he could not train hard; this is the opposite response to that found in people suffering from depression.

Perhaps Salazar's assessment was correct. Heatstroke may indeed have damaged the delicate chemical balance in one or more parts of his brain, including the hypothalamus, leading to multiple hormonal abnormalities. Prozac may have worked initially by correcting that chemical imbalance in the hypothalamus in the short term. It is likely that the central governor exists either in, or in close proximity to, the hypothalamus. Hence, damage to these hypothalamic centers would impair the functioning of the central governor, causing the perception of effort to be altered and generating feelings of perpetual fatigue, even at rest.

Perhaps in the end, the Prozac became ineffective because of adaptations within the brain cells on which it originally worked so effectively. The nature of all chemical processes in the brain is that they undergo changes with time. Therefore, the risk is always present that a treatment that was initially successful may become ineffective with time.

Alternatively, Salazar's muscles, damaged by years of heavy training, may also ultimately have failed when he increased his training volume and maintained that high volume for 1993 and 1994. Perhaps Salazar's Comrades Marathon victory proved to be the proverbial final straw.

Salazar's career poignantly exemplifies the great benefits and equivalent risks of a career as a professional marathon runner. It also epitomizes what his father told him before he entered his first New York City Marathon in 1980: "Much is asked of those to whom much is given." Salazar's inspiration extends beyond his fearless running to include the capacity to accept with dignity and courage the death at a young age of that which defined him—his exceptional running ability.

Some two decades later, the evidence is absolutely clear. The body only has a finite capacity to adapt to the demands of intensive training and competition. Runners must choose, early in their careers, whether to spread that capacity over a long career, as did Bruce Fordyce and Ironman triathlete Mark Allen, or to use it up in a spectacular but short career, as did Buddy Edelen, Ron Hill, Alberto Salazar, and Steve Jones. This is the reality that both elite and nonelite athletes must confront every day that they run.

FINAL WORD

In this chapter, I reviewed the evidence pertaining to overtraining, a condition that exists in athletes who train too hard for too long and who follow monotonous training programs. Overtraining first leads to an impaired exercise capacity and is followed by a predictable range of medical and other complaints. Recovery occurs rapidly in those who wisely choose to rest as soon as any of the symptoms develop.

But those, like Alberto Salazar and other athletes presented in chapter 6, who continue to overtrain for months or years risk developing a more serious condition from which it may be impossible to recover fully.

Perhaps, as our understanding of the overtraining syndrome improves, the acute incapacitating form of the condition may occur less frequently than in the past. However, I am still concerned about the large number of young, amateur runners and swimmers, especially in the competitive collegiate circuit, who train harder than they should, performing indifferently as a result, without ever developing the full-blown overtraining syndrome. By preventing this overreaching, which affects such a large group of athletes, athletes would immeasurably improve the quality of their performances, as well as the satisfaction of their athletic experiences.

CHAPTER

8

■ ■ ■ ■ ■

Training
the Mind

Despite all I have written about preparing the body for running, I suspect that the preparation of the mind is the more important factor determining running success. In the first part of this chapter, I provide guidelines on how best to prepare and occupy the mind for competition. Next, I look at the psychological changes that occur with training, including the vexatious question of whether runners ever become addicted to running. I conclude the chapter with a section dealing with some psychological characteristics of those more likely to seek attention for the treatment of running injuries. (The complete approach to running injuries is covered in chapter 14.)

BANNISTER'S MENTAL APPROACH

When, some years ago, I performed one of the great academic rituals—the inaugural address by a newly appointed professor—I dedicated the lecture to Sir Roger Bannister. I did this by borrowing for my title one of Sir Roger's many exquisitely fashioned observations: "The human body is centuries ahead of the physiologist" (Bannister 1955). The statement's strength lies in the nature, the training, and the achievements of the man who made it.

At the time he penned these words, shortly after he became the first man to run the mile in less than 4 minutes and hence one of the all-time legends of running, Sir Roger was studying the physiology of his own body as part of his training as a medical student. Moreover, he was studying an aspect of exercise physiology that has once again become relevant and popular, almost 50 years after his original work.

As described in chapter 13, his initial research interests were the effects of inhaling oxygen-enriched air on the physiological and emotional responses to maximal exercise (Bannister and Cunningham 1954; Bannister et al. 1954). He discovered that a running speed that exhausted him after about 8 minutes when he inhaled room air (21% oxygen content) could be sustained for 16 minutes or more when he inhaled oxygen-enriched air (60% to 100% oxygen content). He also noted that switching from room air to oxygen-enriched air immediately reduced the sensation of fatigue when running at a high intensity. This proves that one of the sensory feedbacks to the central governor comes from sensors that monitor the oxygen content of one or more of the body's vital organs—perhaps the heart, brain, or respiratory muscles, including the diaphragm.

Bannister's friend Norris McWhirter has described in heroic terms what occurred in the Oxford laboratory of Bannister's tutor, British physiologist D.J.C. Cunningham:

> *Roger did some physiological research . . . attempting to determine whether pure oxygen or a mixture of air and oxygen was better for the body under stress. They had a treadmill—absolutely remorseless, this machine. It was the equal of running up Everest in 6 hours; anyone would break. You had to breathe from great gasbags and they had blood guns which sprang a blade into your finger to measure lactic acid levels as you laboured on. You poured sweat, your spine turned to rubber, and driving up the incline there was the most extraordinary effect on your chin and knees meeting in the front of you. Near the end, there was blood all over, and when you broke, you staggered and rolled off onto a mattress, trying to hit the "off" switch as you went down. Roger himself ran to breaking point on at least 11 occasions. Compared to that, the 4-minute mile was like a day off. (K. Moore 1982; p. 90)*

It would be logical to assume that it was the physiological knowledge gained from these laboratory runs "up Everest" that enabled Bannister and not other, possibly more gifted athletes (such as Arne Anderson, Gunder Haegg, Wes Santee, or John Landy) to become the first to break that mystical 4-minute barrier—particularly as Sir Roger, constrained by his medical studies, was only able to train for about 1 hour per day during his lunch hour. However, this is an incorrect assumption.

Certainly, Bannister did not believe that his scientific knowledge afforded him any advantage. He was of the opinion that his medical training taught him to observe and understand himself better: "A medical training aims at increasing the power of careful observation and logical deduction. Because understanding other people starts from understanding ourselves, the self-analysis that sport entails can be very helpful to the medical student."

What, then, was Bannister's secret? I think success came first to him because he, better than anyone, perceived that the battle for the 4-minute mile was fought in the mind, not in the body. Some weeks before Bannister's great race, Gunder Haegg, the man who in 1945 came within 1.3 seconds of breaking the 4-minute mile, wrote: "I think Bannister is the man to beat 4 minutes. He uses his brains as much as his legs. I've always thought that the 4-minute mile was more of a psychological problem than a test of physical endurance" (Doherty 1964, page 216).

Bannister's genius told him what was most important—the conditioning of the mind until it would "release in four short minutes the energy I usually spend in half an hour's training." In his preparation, Bannister reduced the race to its simplest common denominator—400 m in 1:00 or multiples thereof. He trained until running 400 m in 1:00, 24 km per hour, became automatic. As he states, "in this way the singleness of drive could be achieved, leaving my mind free for the task of directing operations so that it could fix itself on the great objective ahead" (Bannister 1955, page 184).

And when that great objective had been achieved at Oxford's Iffley Road track on 6 May 1954 (figure 8.1), Bannister's unique experience enabled him to write one of the most significant paragraphs in running literature: "Though physiology may indicate respiratory and cardiovascular limits to muscular effort, psychological and other factors beyond the ken of physiology set the razor's edge of defeat or victory

Figure 8.1 Roger Bannister completing the world's first sub-4-minute mile on the Iffley Road track in Oxford, England, on 6 May 1954.

and determine how closely the athlete approaches the absolute limits of performance" (Bannister 1956, page 224).

I conclude that the key to Bannister's success was his trained intuition, which convinced him of the importance of his mind in determining his racing performances. It is also clear that he came upon these conclusions independently and that he had little help from coaches or, more important, professional psychologists.

That Bannister was ahead of his time is shown by the dearth of material on this topic during the period in which he was racing. Only recently has the value of sports psychology become more widely accepted. Even today, the conclusion is that most athletes are "physically overeducated but emotionally undereducated" (Tutko and Tosi 1976, page 11). Readers may find it useful to compare Bannister's intuitive approach to mental preparation for racing with that suggested in other books on the topic (Tutko and Tosi 1976; Nideffer 1976;1985; Rushall 1979; 1995; Kauss 1980; Orlick 2000; Liebetrau 1982; Garfield and Bennett 1984; Porter and Foster 1986; Potgieter 1997; Jackson and Csikzentmihalyi 1999).

OTHER MENTAL APPROACHES

Brent Rushall (1979; 1995), currently a professor in the department of exercise and nutritional sciences at San Diego State University, has proposed that a majority of successful athletes use quite similar psychological strategies to prepare themselves for competitions. This suggests that, regardless of their sports, successful competitors employ similar mental approaches to competition, which are different, presumably, from those used by unsuccessful athletes. Table 8.1 provides a practical classification of these concepts. To support the explanation of these concepts, I have chosen appropriate quotes from Bannister's writings to illustrate his intuitive understanding of these ideas. His writings confirm that he had a natural insight into his own psychology, perhaps a feature of those "natural" athletes who achieve exceptional performances with a minimum of psychological support.

During Training and Precompetition

Mental approaches need to be used in practice, not just in competition. Using the following tactics in training and before a competition will help you carry over these methods into your race.

Set Training and Racing Goals

It is perhaps redundant to state that anything of value must start with a vision, or goal, and that sometimes the more unattainable the goal may appear, the more likely it will come to pass. This is probably the view held by many runners who have successfully completed more demanding athletic events, such as the Comrades Marathon or the Hawaiian Ironman Triathlon.

More than most, Bannister had to have a supreme goal to justify the sacrifices he made. In particular, because medicine was always the core of his life (K. Moore 1982), he had to justify the time spent away from his studies. Beaten into fourth place in the 1952 Olympic Games 1500-m final because he was "not nearly tough enough" to run two heats and a final in three days, Bannister found his goal. "My running has become something of a crusade. . . . I could accept being beaten in the

Table 8.1   Mental approaches of successful performers

During training

Goal setting

- Judging competitive ability accurately

Arousal control

- Not being upset by problems before competition
- Calming yourself before competition

Visualization

During competition

Goal setting

- Putting more effort into competition than into training
- Planning your racing strategy

Arousal control

- Controlling nervousness at the race start
- Not worrying about the competitors

Performing during competition

- Dominating from the beginning of the race
- Allowing for the unexpected
- Concentrating and focusing
- Giving a maximum effort, regardless of the result
- Performing to expectation

After competition

- Learning from each race
- Understanding the value of a coach

Olympics—that had happened to many stronger favourites than me. What I objected to, was that my defeat was taken by so many as proof that my way of training was wrong" (Bannister 1955, page 164).

And thus, with the significant help of his coach, Franz Stampfl (Lenton 1983a; 1983b; K. Moore 1982), and his running companions, Chris Brasher and Chris Chataway, Bannister set out to prove that it was still possible in 1954 to be a champion on as little as 1 hour of training per day. In December 1952, when the Australian John Landy ran a mile in 4:02.1, the race for the 4-minute mile had begun.

A key component to goal setting is that the athletes must judge their competitive abilities accurately. Bannister trained principally by running repeated intervals of 400 m. When, in April 1954, he was able to run 10×400-m intervals in 59 seconds with a 2:00 rest between intervals, he considered that he was ready. Then, eight days before his greatest day, he ran a 3/4 mile in a high wind. The watch recorded a time of 2:59.9. "I felt that 2:59.9 for the 3/4 mile in a solo training run meant 3:59.9 in a mile race." (Bannister 1955, page 185).

The value of goal setting may simply be that it programs the central governor to accept a greater maximum effort before it senses danger, thereby reducing the allowed pace by decreasing the mass of muscle that is activated. This theory is based on the Integrated Neuromuscular Recruitment Model. Notice specifically that Bannister trained his central governor to accept exactly what he had to do: running repeated 400-m laps at between 59 and 60 seconds—no more and no less. In part III I describe the techniques that can be used to identify your realistic racing goal for a particular race on the basis of your recent racing performances.

The importance of proper goal setting is shown by the outcomes of the different mental attitudes adopted by Bannister and Landy in May and June 1954. In June 1953, Bannister and Brasher ran a 4:02 mile during an invitation race at a schoolboys' athletic meeting. Having come so close under such artificial conditions, Bannister realized that he was capable of running a 4-minute mile. In contrast, Landy, who by April 1954 had run the mile under 4:03 on six occasions, declared: "It is a brick wall. I shall not attempt it again" (Bannister 1955, page 181).

Yet, no sooner had Bannister broken the 4-minute mile than Landy's brick wall crumbled. On 21 June 1954, on the Turku track (now the Paavo Nurmi track) in Nurmi's hometown in Finland, Landy set new world records of 3:41.8 for 1500 m and 3:58.0 for the mile, the latter an improvement of 1.4 seconds on the record Bannister had set just six weeks earlier and perhaps close to 3 seconds faster than Landy had ever before run the mile.

It would seem that Bannister's success, and conversely Landy's failure, was simply because Bannister was able to convince his central governor of what was achievable. Landy's governor could only be convinced once it had clear evidence that someone else had achieved that (impossible) performance. This perhaps explains, in part, why Landy's mile performances were constrained for more than a year, with the result that he performed well below his subsequently proven physical ability. I suspect that the really exceptional athletes do not place the same subconscious limits on their performance as do the rest of us.

Put More Effort Into Racing Than Into Training

Bannister clearly had the ability to put more effort into racing than into his training. This fact is borne out by his comment that he needed to "release in four short minutes the energy . . . usually spent in half an hour's training."

It is not clear why it is possible to put more effort into racing than into training. My interpretation is that the central governor allows a superior effort only under specific and very special circumstances—for example, during the Olympic Games or in other events once it has been convinced of the importance of the goal. Thus, the function of goal setting may simply be to convince the brain that this really is a very important race for which it must allow a performance that would not be allowed in training.

Control Arousal

I learned early in my medical career that there are two types of doctors—those who can cope in an emergency because they retain the ability to think clearly and logically, and those, like myself, who are best excluded from the scene of a disaster because we become mentally incapacitated at the merest mention of a crisis. The difference between these two opposing responses are physiologically based; in those like me, a part of the alarm response to danger (the fight-or-flight response) includes intense inhibition of the thought center in the brain. In a crisis, we have one goal—to stop thinking and to run away as fast as possible. I assume that in those of my medical colleagues who are able to think clearly in a crisis, these nerve pathways in the brain are simply not active.

The point is that perceived danger, including the thought of running a demanding race, produces different levels of arousal and different emotional responses in each of us. Yet, we perform best when that arousal is controlled and is at an optimum level. Besides the effects of arousal on our emotions and ability to think, our motor functioning is also affected by overarousal, which impairs fine and coordinated motor function. This is true in training as well as in racing

Fortunately, success in running does not depend on precise motor control; hence, excessive arousal will not impair the less precise motor functions of running. Rather, arousal affects the chosen pacing strategy in the early part of the race. The biggest danger facing an overaroused runner is starting a race too fast.

An important component of arousal control is not to be upset by events that occur before competition. Focus only on those factors that influence your performance and over which you have an influence. No human—neither Bannister nor Allen—is able to control factors such as the wind or the rain. Thus, it is not helpful to worry about them. Without divine intervention, you will not be able to change what is to be. Instead, in preparing for competition, you should focus exclusively on those variables over which you have complete control—for example, the extensive list of race preparations presented in table 8.1.

In the hours before the 4-minute mile, Bannister "forgot some apprehensions" by staying with his friends in Oxford. He wrote that "the calm efficiency of Eileen (Wenden) had helped me to still my own restless worries. Never was this factor so important as on this day" (Bannister 1955, page 189). Before his victories at the Empire and European Games, Bannister went for long walks to seek the mental calm he needed.

The essential lesson is that each runner needs to discover those behaviors that induce a calming effect before competition. For Bannister it was his friend's home; for Bruce Fordyce it was secreting himself away from the public in his hotel room or watching videos with a few select friends; for Paula Newby-Fraser it was reading a long and engrossing novel for the last two to three days before the Hawaiian Ironman Triathlon.

Visualize Your Race

Visualization is the process in which you run the race in your mind many times before you run the real race with your whole person. Bannister clearly describes how he used this technique to good effect. The interesting question is from whom did he learn this invaluable technique? Was it perhaps intuitive?

For the last five days before the Iffley Road race, Bannister rested as he began to store nervous energy. Then, he ran the race in his mind. "Each night in the week before the race there came a moment when I saw myself at the starting line. My whole body would grow nervous and tremble. I ran the race over in my mind. Then I would calm myself and sometimes go off to sleep" (Bannister 1955, page 186).

An interesting recent finding is that thinking about a specific exercise task produces the same brain activity that occurs when the actual task is performed. The brain is somehow duped into believing that the task is actually being performed.

In chapters 10 and 11, I discuss the importance of visualizing your performance over the last 25% of any course over which you are to race. The theory is that you will perform better on any course if you know the important details beforehand and have visualized yourself running there. Interestingly, the "stopping thoughts"—in effect, the attempts by the conscious brain under orders from the central governor to make you stop running—begin during the final 25% to 35% of any race. Why then, you may ask, is it so helpful to visualize your performance over the last section of any race?

I believe that the more information the central governor has about the course still to be run, the more accurately it can plan its pacing strategy. I vividly remember a pivotal moment in one early Comrades Marathon before I had learned the course and had begun to understand the importance of visualization. Having run 80 km, with about 10 km to go, I rounded a blind corner to be suddenly faced with a steep hill that I had not anticipated. My conscious brain—acting, I presume, on behalf of the central governor—in effect said, "But you did not tell me about this hill!" Together with this idea came the sudden urge to stop running, which appears to be the ultimate goal of the central governor during this section of the race.

For it to calculate the necessary pacing strategy that will enable you to finish in reasonable health, the brain has to know as much detail about the remaining 25% to 35% of the race as is possible. Without that information, it follows the course of least resistance and makes its calculations on the basis of the easiest possible course (that is, a flat one). When the course turns out to be hilly, not flat, the central governor revolts and uses the absence of information as a powerful excuse in its attempts to stop you running.

Visualization may be somewhat less important for shorter-distance races in which it is physically possible to run the distance in training and to prepare the central governor for the actual demands it will face during the real race. In chapter 11, I discuss the value of either driving over the last 25% of the course or actually filming the course to aid the practice of visualization. Do not ever underestimate the amount of information the subconscious is storing during those processes.

Plan Your Race Strategy

Bannister realized that there were four essential requirements for a sub-4-minute mile: a good track, the absence of wind, warm weather, and even-paced running. He knew that only Landy could ever race him to a 4-minute mile but that if he were to wait until the next planned event it would probably be too late. As a result, the famous Iffley Road race was conceived, and coach of the English trio, Franz Stampfl (Lenton 1983a; 1983b), set about planning the details of how Chris Brasher and Chris Chataway would pace Bannister during this epic race.

Coach Stampfl's innovation in that race was to devise a legitimate pacing strategy. When Bannister and Brasher had run 4:02 the previous year, their pacing strategy had been too blatant, and British athletic officials would not recognize the performance. Thus, the runners knew that a repeat of that specific strategy would be unacceptable. The probable change in strategy was to have Bannister run the last lap by himself, as he did in the actual race.

Bannister's other famous race was the Mile of the Century in August 1954, in which he ran against Landy in the final of the Empire Games mile in Vancouver. By that time, Landy was the world record holder. However, in this race, Bannister improved his best mile time to 3:58.8, 0.8 ahead of Landy.

Describing the tactics he used in this race, he wrote:

Tactical plans for big races have to be thought out in advance. The runner must be prepared both to meet possible moves by an opponent and to retain the flexibility to modify his scheme if something happens unexpectedly. The simpler plans can be, the better, because the mind can be free during the race. My plans were extremely simple. I had to force John Landy to set the pace of a 4-minute mile for me. . . . I must reserve my effort of willpower for the moment when I would fling myself past him at the finish. Until then, I would be entirely passive, thinking of nothing else throughout the whole race. (Bannister 1955, page 203).

Bannister had to ensure that Landy would not opt for the tactic of running from behind in the race. Therefore, in his last mile race before the Empire Games, Bannister ran easily for the first three laps and finished with a final lap in 53.8. He hoped that this would convince Landy, who lacked finishing speed, that he would have to lead from the start.

Thus, Bannister entered the Mile of the Century with a clearly defined and ultimately winning strategy. In addition, he successfully forced Landy to adopt the strategy that he believed would be most advantageous for him, not for Landy.

The importance of the correct racing strategy is that it informs the central governor before the race of what is to be expected. Bannister was successful in the race because his pacing strategy maximized his physical ability. Landy's too-fast early pace caused his central governor to become overactive. As a result, he slowed down prematurely over the last 200 m.

Focus on What You Can Control

At the start of a race, it is crucial to focus only on those variables over which you have control—that is, your emotions and how you will conduct yourself. Don't be concerned about how you feel, how your competitors appear, or the environmental conditions. This essential information will simply be incorporated by your subconscious and conscious brain to ensure that you choose an optimum racing pace.

On the day Bannister achieved the 4-minute mile, the wind only abated when he stepped onto the track. Not surprisingly, Bannister was "in a blue mood" and uncertain whether he should bother to run that special race (Lenton 1983a; 1983b). However, Stampfl was convinced that Bannister should run and that if he missed that opportunity, there would not be another. He states,

I knew a bit of rain or wind would make no bloody difference because he was capable of a 3:56 or 3:57 mile. So maybe he'll run a little slower but he would still break 4 minutes. If he doesn't do it today he'll never do it because . . . how is he going to build up again? When will there be another occasion? What about coping with this kind of mental pressure? How do you know the weather will be better at some future date? For all these reasons Bannister, in my opinion, would never have done it again. (Lenton 1983a, p. 30).

Bannister's nervousness at the start is shown by his anger at a false start in the first sub-4-minute mile race: "I felt angry that precious moments during the lull in the wind might be slipping away. The gun fired a second time" (Bannister 1955, page 185).

The point, of course, is that any emotional upsets before competition exist only in the athlete's brain and are purely the attempts by the conscious brain to prevent a maximum effort, even before competition. This is the same as the conscious brain attempting to interfere with your performance when you tire about two-thirds of the way through your race. Mark Allen's Ironman experience is an example of this.

Explaining the psychological reasons for his success, Allen argues that it is easy to be motivated at the 7:00 A.M. start of the Ironman. But as the race progresses, "it's like you're tested to the core of your intent" (Allen 1998b, page 40). Allen acknowledges that his failures before the 1989 Hawaiian Ironman were caused by his inability to understand the race sufficiently to know the core question: "Do I want to do well on my terms? Or do I want to do it on the terms of what the race is going to require?" (Allen 1998b, page 40). He concluded that he had not run to his potential during his first six Ironman races because he had not been prepared to run the race on its terms. Worse, his repeated failures and the physical beating he had taken had caused him to fear not just the race but the very island itself. While he desperately wished to win, he concluded that he "wasn't willing to do it under the terms and conditions of the race. I wanted to win in a certain way, putting in a certain amount of training, going through a certain amount of pain, but what it was going to take, was going to a new level" (Allen 1998b, page 41). The new psychological approach required that he no longer fear the island. He had also to become more patient during the race, by realizing that the winner was the first athlete over the finish line, not at any intermediate point before this.

As he explains, Allen came to realize that it was possible to see the island as paradise, not as Hell:

> I was beginning to see the aspects of the lava fields, thinking of them as paradise. What could be more of a paradise than to learn something about yourself, broaden yourself? You pick vacations that are usually in very pretty places and you recall those memories and you go, "Wow, that's such a beautiful place." It's the same with the experiences of the Ironman. It's in a harsh environment, but you can look back and think back to the power of what it felt like to complete it, to cross the finish line—and for me, to have won it. I can now look back and it's the same as the memory of something that is visually appealing. I can see . . . in those moments where I felt my strength and when I made it through tough points and made the choice to take it all the way to completion instead of backing off or dropping out. And this is a nice memory. (Allen 1998b, page 42)

With this altered mental approach, combined with a more intensive physical preparation, Allen won the next five Ironman triathlons between 1989 and 1993. However, he was aging and emotionally exhausted. He decided to take a break from his sport to recover his emotional drive. This took more than a year, but by race day in October 1995, he had recovered sufficiently and had trained hard enough to believe that he had a real chance of achieving a sixth and final victory.

But he did not swim or cycle as well as he had in his previous Ironman races. As a result, at the end of the bicycle leg, he was in fifth place, 13 minutes behind 24-year-old Thomas Hellriegel. As a result, he started experiencing severe self-doubt:

> I was far from the space between thoughts, that internal state of quiet and confidence where all the analysis and judging has ceased; I was mentally sabotaging myself. . . . I thought, "I don't need this anymore, I should just drop out. I'm 37 years old. It's too painful. I've won this thing five times. People will understand. Just drop out." (Allen 1998b, page 42)

About 5 km into the run, he was faced with the crucial decision as he approached the road leading to the apartment at which he was staying: Was he to give in or would he continue? "And then I thought, 'If I could just continue on and finish this thing . . . I would feel absolutely ecstatic." (Allen 1998b, page 43)

As fate would have it, the runner in fourth place, ten seconds ahead, decided at that precise moment to walk. Allen, his immediate crisis over, ran into fourth place.

With 14 km to go, Allen had closed to 4:00 behind Hellriegel. To continue at that pace would mean that he would only catch Hellriegel at the finish—too late. At that point, Allen remembers the internal fight between his two voices of good and evil. The evil voice was asking, "Hey, how are you going to catch him, he's so far ahead, he's 24 years old, you're 37?" To which the good voice responded, "You've got to live what you've been asking yourself. You asked for all of this help, from your friends and your family. You have to give it 100%." The evil voice retorted, "What do you mean 100%? I'm giving 100%!" Allen continues,

> But then I realized, no, I was holding back, just a little bit because . . . I essentially wanted some billboard to come out of the lava and say: "If you give 100%, you will catch Hellriegel and you will win." It was like a safety valve. If I only gave 97%, I could say, "Well, if I don't catch him, I probably could have done it." One thing was certain: If I didn't give it 100%, I definitely wasn't going to win. And I know that I had to give it 100% and that there was no guarantee. It might mean that I catch him, it might mean that he finishes five seconds in front of me, but that's what I had to do. (Allen 1998b, page 43)

With 5 km to go, Allen passed Hellriegel, finished the race in first place, and immediately retired, the Paavo Nurmi of the triathlon, the ultimate triathlete. What is particularly compelling about this story is that Allen is one of the most physically gifted athletes in any sport who trained as hard as was humanly possible. Yet, the ultimate success of his career rested on his insight that taught him the core question: Was he prepared to give whatever it took to win the Ironman or just what he was prepared to take? Only when he had answered that question could he make the physical and psychological adaptations necessary for his success.

In his final race, he could have succumbed to the will of the central governor, which, in the persona of his evil voice, was tempting him with the sanctity of stopping. Why he chose not to stop remains the greater question and the enduring fascination of sport.

During Competition

Now that you have honed several mental approaches in training and in preparing for your competition, you can focus on specific tactics during the race.

Dominate From the Start

Elite athletes prefer to stamp their authority on the event from the beginning. Clearly, this is not always appropriate in track running, particularly for an athlete like Bannister, whose major competitive attribute was his fast finish. Bannister's major racing tactic was to save himself for the finish. However, when it became apparent that this approach was inappropriate, as it threatened to be in his race with Landy in the 1954 Empire Games, Bannister was prepared to risk everything by altering his strategy, despite the knowledge that this might blunt his key competitive advantage, his fast finish.

Most of the great runners described in chapter 6 aimed to take control of the race from the start, but none more so than Paavo Nurmi and Emil Zatopek. I suspect that dominant runners intimidate the central governors of their competitors, forcing the intimidated governors to restrict the performances of their owners.

It is possible that Bruce Fordyce dominated the Comrades Marathon in the 1980s to the extent that he did because his actions convinced his competitors that they could not beat him. In other words, their central governors were preprogrammed from the outset by Fordyce to ensure their failure. Perhaps Mark Allen's dominance in the triathlon similarly rested on his ability to dominate the subconsciousness of his competitors.

The race that, more than any other, convinced me that athletes intimidate one another during competition was the 1996 Olympic Games marathon, won by South African Josiah Thugwane. Irrespective of physical ability, it was the athlete who was emotionally dominant who won. I suspected that Thugwane would win during the last 10 km, when he relentlessly set the pace and aggressively countered every move made by his two rivals, South Korean Lee Bong-Ju and Kenyan Erick Wainaina. Yet, Thugwane won by only 8 seconds, the closest finish in the history of the event. Since neither Bong-Ju nor Wainaina died at the finish, they could have run faster. However, they chose not to because, in my view, Thugwane's dominant attitude convinced their central governors that to go any harder would be futile since Thugwane would respond assertively to whatever they did. They were unwittingly coerced into accepting a slower pace that would still ensure an Olympic medal. This model gives credence to the old adage that the winning athlete is the one who craves victory the most.

Allow for the Unexpected

In his race with Landy, Bannister exhibited his ability to change plans during the race. When Landy had built up a commanding lead by the end of the second lap and showed no signs of tiring, Bannister realized that he would have to forego his prerace plan.

> To have any finish left, I must be able to follow at his shoulder throughout the early part of the last lap. How could I close the gap before the bell? If I were to stand any chance of winning I must reach his shoulder before then. I must abandon my own time schedule and run to his. This was the turning point of the race. (Bannister 1955, p. 214)

As a result of his altered plan, Bannister caught and passed Landy on the final turn of the race.

Bannister's ability to change his strategy late in the race, yet still to win in a faster time than he had ever run before, suggests that he was the superior athlete who never quite pushed his central governor to its limit. This is consistent with coach Stampfl's belief that, given ideal circumstances, Bannister had the ability to run the mile in 3:56 to 3:57.

Concentrate and Focus

Bannister had the ability to concentrate on a strategy throughout the entire contest, to concentrate on technique when tired, and to handle the pressures in the final stages of a close competition. In describing his decision to change tactics half-way through his epic Mile of the Century race with John Landy, Bannister said,

> *I won back the first yard, then each succeeding yard, until his lead was halved by the time we reached the back straight of the third lap. . . . I now connected myself to Landy again, though he was still 5 yards ahead. I was almost hypnotized by his easy shuffling stride. . . . I tried to imagine myself attached to him by some invisible cord. With each stride, I drew the cord tighter and reduced his lead. . . . As we entered the last bend, I tried to convince myself that he was tiring. With each stride now I attempted to husband a little strength for the moment at the end of the bend when I decided to pounce. . . . When the moment came, my mind would galvanize my body to the greatest effort it had ever known. I knew I was tired. There might be no response, but it was my only chance. This moment had occurred dozens of times before. This time the only difference was that the whole race was being run to my absolute limit. . . . In two strides, I was past him, with 70 yards to go, but I could not accelerate further. (Bannister 1955, p. 215-216)*

Give a Maximum Effort

Reading between the lines, it seems to me that one of Bannister's most important learning experiences was the 1952 Olympic Games. Shortly before the games, the organizers announced that semifinal heats would be held in the 1500-m race for the very first time. This immediately put Bannister at a disadvantage, which he knew was fatal, as he was not trained to run three hard races in three days. Then at the Games, Bannister saw the awesome running of Zatopek: "Zatopek isn't human in his achievement. . . . While he goes for a 20-mile run on his only free day, we lie here panting and moaning that the Gods are unkind to us" (Bannister 1955, p. 214). At the same Games, Bannister experienced the special pressures of the Olympics: "Now, with the whole athletic world concentrated in a few square miles, all sense of perspective was lost. Around me every man was giving his best—fighting to the last gasp." And in the emotional stresses that this produced, Bannister and the other British athletes, "tied in knots with anxiety, realized more about our weakness and strength as we wound up our minds for the trial" (Bannister 1955, p. 156-15) This taught Bannister that he had much to learn about his own self-control, a realization that almost certainly helped him in his later races.

Finally, after days of mental torture, Bannister went out to contest the 1500-m final: "I hardly had the strength to warm up. As I walked out in front of those 70,000 spectators, my step had no spring, my face no color. The ruthless fighting of the semi-final, the worry and lack of sleep, had exhausted me." Despite this, Bannister ran the best he could. Lying second at the last bend, he reached down for his finishing kick, but it was not there. As he states, "my legs were aching, and I had no strength left to force them faster. I had a sickening feeling of exhaustion and powerlessness as Barthel came past me, chased by McMillen" (Bannister 1955, p. 214) Nevertheless, Bannister would finish in fourth place, only 0.8 seconds behind the winner.

This ability to extend himself when exhausted is also described in his account of the closing stages of the 4-minute mile race:

> *My body had long since exhausted all its energy, but it went on running just the same. The physical overdraft came only from greater willpower. With 5 yards to go, the tape seemed almost to recede. . . . I leapt at the tape like a man taking his*

last spring to save himself from the chasm that threatens to engulf him. (Bannister 1955, p. 192)

Perform up to Expectation

Bannister's ability to handle the pressures in the final stages of a close race was evident in not only the 4-minute mile and his race with Landy, but also in the 1500-m final of the European Games:

Never did my finishing burst serve me so well. There was no longer any need to call on emotion to produce the ability to take an overdraft on my energy. There had been times in other races when I felt real fear as I tore down the finishing straight as if my life depended on it. . . . This time it was different—I was calm. . . . My mind remained quite cool and detached. It merely switched over the lever, and well-worn channels carried to my body the extra energy that my mind unleashed. (Bannister 1955, p. 24)

After Competition

Your mental training doesn't end once you cross the finish line. It is important to learn from each race and to decide how to continue improving.

Learn From Each Race

On this issue, Bannister was resolute:

Improvement in running depends on continuous self-discipline by the athlete himself, and acute observation of his reactions to races and training and above all on judgment, which he must learn for himself. The runner has to make his own decisions on the track—he has no coach there to help him. If a man coaches himself then he has only himself to blame when he is beaten. Each race is an experiment. There are too many factors that cannot be completely controlled for two races to be the same, just as two similar scientific experiments seldom give exactly the same results. By learning, often unconsciously, from mistakes, I discovered my reaction—both desirable and undesirable—to many of the situations I was likely to meet in big races. (Bannister 1955, p. 121)

Perhaps it was these words, more than any others, that inspired my conclusion that training and racing must be approached as a scientific experiment. Therefore, the athlete who best understands and adopts this approach will be the most successful.

Understand the Value of a Coach

Bannister believed in individual experience: "The things a man learns for himself he never forgets. . . . The things a man does by himself, he does best." Although originally reluctant to have a coach, in Franz Stampfl, Bannister found a man who complemented him perfectly: "Stampfl's greatness as a coach rests on his adaptability and patience. He watches and waits for the moment when the athlete needs him. . . . Franz is an artist who sees beauty in human struggle and achievement" (Bannister 1955, pp. 187, 204).

For the historical record, it should be noted that Bannister downplayed Stampfl's crucial contribution to his success in the Iffley Road race in his autobiography (Bannister 1955). For his part, Stampfl (Lenton 1983a; 1983b) claims that the major achievement in the Iffley Road mile was not having Bannister run 3:59, but training Chataway and Brasher to the point at which they would be able to pace Bannister for the first three-and-a-quarter laps. Stampfl points out that when he (Stampfl) first arrived at Oxford, Brasher was unable to run two laps in 2 minutes, yet on the day of the Iffley Road race, he had to run two and a half laps at that pace. Similarly, Chataway had a best mile time of only 4:08, yet in the race he had run three and a quarter laps at sub-4-minute-mile pace. In addition, Stampfl later trained Chataway and Brian Hewson to become the world's fourth and fifth sub-4-minute milers after Bannister, Landy, and the Hungarian Laszlo Tabori.

Brasher subsequently confirmed that Stampfl was indeed the major strategist for the race and that his omission from Bannister's book would not have been a falsehood in Bannister's eyes: "He had labored through eight years of preparation, all of it inspired by a dream of self-reliance, of doing it alone. When the time came, he wrote the dream instead of the reality" (K. Moore 1982, page 92).

What we can perhaps glean from Bannister's experience is that even one of the most intellectually astute, biologically trained athletes in the history of the sport needed the help of a coach to ensure that his ultimate performance was achieved. This would seem again to confirm the importance of the 11th Law of Training—train with a coach (chapter 5).

From this brief introduction highlighting the importance of the mind in athletic performance, we now consider how the mind works and how it can be controlled to produce optimum competitive performance. Here I aim to present the basic scaffolding on which a more detailed knowledge can be constructed.

More detailed discussions of this topic can be found in any of the psychological texts to which I refer. I believe that all athletes, regardless of their levels of prowess, would benefit by reading at least one of these books.

PSYCHOLOGICAL PREPARATION FOR SPORT

Our psychological makeup comprises our thoughts, emotions, and behaviors and how we interact with others. Each of these factors influences how we ultimately behave (perform) in sport. Thus, it is essential that we control these psychological variables if we wish to produce a particular behavior (winning).

However, the behavior of different humans to the same stimulus is not always predictable. Similarly, different stimuli can produce the same response in different people. This is because behavior is not just a simple reflex response to each stimulus. A stimulus is processed in the brain and is interpreted in terms of what psychologists call each person's belief system:

stimulus —> belief system —> response (behavior).

The belief system interprets all incoming stimuli and then activates the response that is appropriate for that person, depending on what the athlete believes about him- or herself and the prevailing situation. Another important concept is that the belief system, although strongly ingrained, is not fixed, but subject to modification. Thus, many athletes who perform less well than they should do so because they have belief systems that are programmed for failure. The only way such athletes will ever perform to their potential is if their belief systems can be successfully reprogrammed to ensure that their psychological belief systems match their physiological capacity.

To make these concepts more understandable, consider a hypothetical situation. Imagine that you are leading the next Olympic Games marathon, with 10 km to go. It has been your life's ambition to win the race. You have paced yourself well, you are running as well as you possibly can, and you are beginning to think that this might just be your year. Quite suddenly and somewhat unexpectedly, another athlete appears at your shoulder.

In this situation, you are likely to respond in one of three ways: you will surge and try to break away from your challenger there and then; you will run with your challenger and try to break away at a later stage of the race; or you will throw in the towel and immediately drop behind. Can you predict what you would do in this situation? Your response to the challenge will be determined by how you process the stimulus of being passed, how you relate it to the beliefs you have about yourself (your self-concept), and the thoughts and emotions that are aroused—in particular, those relating to the possibility of defeat.

These, in turn, are modified by your attitude to the specific event in which you are competing (that is, how important it is to you) and, most important, by your attitude to the person who is passing you. If, for example, you know that the athlete passing you has won his last five marathons and is known for his strong finish, your response is likely to be very different from the way you would respond to a runner who is known to tire greatly in the last 10 km of the race.

The thoughts and emotions that are likely to cross your mind might lead you to make a verbal comment indicating your distaste for this particular runner. Figure 8.2 illustrates what might actually go through in your mind in this type of situation. As you can see, the stimulus activates emotions and thoughts, termed self-talk, which will be either positive or negative, and will have either a beneficial or a detrimental effect on your performance. The behavior that results, whether positive or

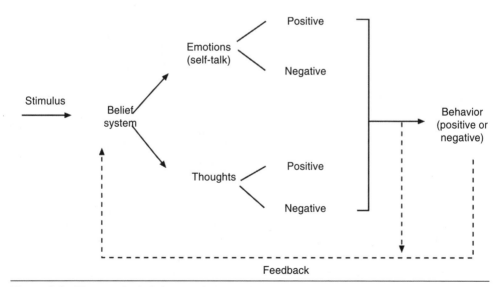

Figure 8.2 The stimulus-belief system-behavior diagram.

negative, will feed back into your belief system, with the result that the next time you are in the same situation, you are more likely to respond in the same way.

If you win the race, you will have a greater belief in yourself and will consider yourself a winner. But if you fade out of contention, chances are that your belief system will be imprinted with the loser's image and the next time around you will again act as a loser. This example should be enough to convince you that the control of emotions and thoughts is essential to produce optimum performance. As Liebetrau has said, "Emotions put the fuel in the tank and thoughts provide the steering and other skills of driving" (1982, page 7).

Although I know of some world champions who have read this book, few of us will ever be in the position to win an Olympic medal. Therefore, the relevance of this section on positive self-talk may seem a little inconsequential as few of us are ever likely to have to gird ourselves mentally for a final winning effort. What really interests me, however, is the origins of the self-talk that develops as we enter the last third of any race and its relevance to human physiology, an important aspect that seems to have been completely ignored by sport psychologists.

The point is that the most obvious feature of any all-out physical sporting effort is that it is always accompanied by self-talk, the ultimate goal of which, it seems to me, is entirely contrary to what the athlete is trying to achieve—to finish the race as quickly as possible. For if the self-talk I experienced was the same as that heard by others, its simple message was always the same: "'Stop running this race, now."

According to the central governor theory (chapter 2), subversive self-talk begins when your governor is being bombarded by a glut of sensory information from painful muscles, perhaps activating a *mechanostat;* or as a result of approaching glycogen depletion, activating the *glycostat* (see chapter 13); or from a rising skin or whole body temperature, in which case the *thermostat* is activated. The central governor's response is to exhort the conscious brain to stop, since to continue would be to risk immediate disaster or, more probably, long-term muscle damage (see chapter 11).

Nevertheless, the reality is that in each race, a point is reached at which it becomes necessary to face the mental challenges posed by self-talk and to develop mental strategies to cope, regardless of whether you are finishing first or last in the race. Although in chapters 9 to 11 I outline some of the methods I used during my running career, I am unaware of any texts that provide other solutions. Perhaps the challenges issued here will stimulate sport psychologists to study this fundamental psychological phenomenon.

Interestingly, as my colleague Alan St. Clair Gibson pointed out to me (St. Clair Gibson, Lambert et al. 2001), the existence of self-talk proves that fatigue is a centrally regulated process in the brain. For, if it were not the case and if fatigue were due purely to peripheral mechanisms as predicted by the Cardiovascular/Anaerobic Model (chapter 2) or the Energy Supply/Energy Depletion Model (chapter 3), exercise would cease the instant the muscles became exhausted and stopped working, having gone as far as they could. Why would the brain need to be informed, and of what possible value would this self-talk be? Since the muscles had reached their limits, the brain would not need to stop the exercise, nor would there be any possibility of the brain forcing the exhausted muscles to continue exercising. The analogy is the popular phrase that it is useless flogging a dead horse.

With this background, we are now in a position to consider emotions and thoughts in more detail. Such knowledge may also help us control the emotional response to the self-talk that begins in the last 25% of races.

Controlling Emotion

It is well documented in psychology texts that there are seven basic emotions: joy, sadness, anger, love, fear, shame, and surprise. Other emotions are regarded as combinations of these basic seven. The emotions you feel in any situation and how you respond to them will depend on four factors: your basic personality, how much control you have over your emotions, your emotional reactivity, and your flexibility. Control of these emotions is achieved by controlling the thoughts that cause them.

Renowned sport psychologist Thomas Tutko, formerly a professor of psychology at San Jose State University, has developed a technique to identify a person's emotional profile and to indicate how that person will react according to seven separate psychological traits—desire, assertiveness, sensitivity, tension control, confidence, personal accountability, and self-discipline (Tutko and Tosi 1976).

1. Desire is the measure of your intent to be the best or to do your best. Those with low desire express an "I don't care" attitude; those with high levels of desire are perfectionists. Both extremes are problematic, but it is the perfectionist who is more likely to persist in sport. Because perfectionists set goals that are unattainable, they live with a constant anxiety. Since they never achieve their goals, they are never content with their performances. To overcome this, perfectionists need to reassess their (unrealistic) goals and to realize that they are the cause of their anxiety. In turn, they need to focus on short-term goals, not the final results.

2. Assertiveness is the measure of the extent to which you believe you can influence the outcome of what you do. Those with low assertiveness are easily intimidated. They feel inadequate when someone else succeeds at their expense and they tend to support underdogs. Those with high assertiveness are known as killers. They frequently see sport participation as a "savage battle rather than an enjoyable challenge" (Tutko and Tosi 1976, page 68). Such activity is usually defensive since it is a front to protect a low self-esteem and the fear of being threatened or humiliated.

3. Sensitivity is the ability to enjoy sport without becoming overly disturbed at the outcome. Those with low sensitivity are known as stonewallers. Nothing can influence how they respond to any situation. In contrast, the supersensitive respond inappropriately and consider each failure, however slight, as a personal affront. The supersensitive must learn to separate the event from the emotional response that each evokes. Consequently, they are the most in need of training in emotional control.

4. Tension control is the measure of your ability to remain calm and focused under stress. Those with poor tension control are the nervous wrecks. They are unable to control their physical responses to stress. Because their motor function is impaired, they become relatively ineffective in sports that require high degrees of motor coordination. Those with excellent control are known as icebergs. Excessive tension control is detrimental if it prevents athletes from taking risks, from enjoying their participation, or from undertaking efforts to improve.

5. Confidence is the measure of your belief in your ability. Those with little confidence are insecure. Those with too much confidence are cocky. People are cocky either because they use bravado to cover an inner lack of confidence or because they truly believe that they are so talented that they need not work to achieve success.

6. Personal accountability is the measure of the extent to which you accept personal responsibility for your actions. Those with low personal accountability tend to hide behind alibis. Those with high personal accountability act as if "sports means always having to say I am sorry" (Tutko and Tosi 1976, page 84). Like the perfectionists, they feel guilty for everything except a perfect result.

7. Self-discipline is the measure of your willingness to develop and to persist with a personal game plan. Those with low self-discipline are known as the chaotics since they are unable to stick with any plan. Those with high self-discipline are known as the lemmings since their mental rigidity prevents them from changing their plans.

By grasping the extent to which each of us expresses these different traits, we gain a better understanding of our personal foibles and, in turn, learn how best to control our specific personalities in the heat of competition.

Controlling Thought

The thoughts we experience in sport are influenced by our concept of or attitude toward our opponents and ourselves. Attitudes are collections of thoughts and emotions that we have concerning others and ourselves, and these attitudes help determine the emotions we feel at any time. This can best be exemplified by returning to our previous example. The arrival of another athlete at your shoulder 10 km from the end of the Olympic marathon could stimulate two possible lines of thought that would result in quite different outcomes in the race. Clearly, the athlete who thinks, "This year I really thought I had it. I have worked so hard and now I have blown it. I really am a loser . . ." will drop off the pace and fall back. However, there is a far greater chance of success for the athlete who thinks, "Well, here she is. The woman they call the best marathon runner ever. And she has only been able to catch me after 32 km. I will just tuck in behind the about-to-become ex-number one, let her do the work for a change, and see if I can break her later. After all, my 10-km time is as good as hers, and in a close finish I have the crowds behind me as they always back the upstart."

The difference between a strong or weak belief system is determined by your self-concept (what you believe about yourself), which is, in turn, established by your record of past performances, your body image (what you honestly believe you can achieve in sport), and the attitude that the significant people in your life (such as your parents, partner, friends, and coaches) have toward you and your participation in sport. The self-concept can be further divided into what you really think about yourself (your real self) and what you would like to be (your ideal self).

How the significant others in your life influence your performance can be shown by extending the imaginary example a little further. Had you fallen off the pace in the last 10 km of the Olympic marathon, your coach or other important person in your life might have said the following to you, "You really were awful. We were sure you had it sewn up and then you let that overrated athlete beat you. How could you?"

This type of verbal abuse is likely to stimulate one of the following responses: "He is right. I really am a loser. I will never win a major marathon," or, "No, he is wrong. I ran my heart out. But he couldn't know. Now I am more determined than ever to show them what I can do." (A third response may be to rid yourself of any persons who could be stupid enough to express themselves in that way.)

Our next step must be to analyze the self-concept and to discover how it is possible to improve those areas in which there may be specific weaknesses.

Analyzing the Self-Concept

In his book, Chris Liebetrau (1982) proposes the following approach to the analysis of self-concept. To begin with, he suggests dividing a few pages in a notebook or training logbook into the following three columns: stimulus; self-talk/belief system response (thoughts); emotions and behaviors.

The idea is to complete this form by first describing your response in terms of the emotions and behaviors that you experience in a variety of sporting situations. For example, in the Olympic marathon situation described above, the aroused emotions might have included fear, anger, and frustration at being passed, or alternatively, joy that another runner was finally going to make you earn your victory.

The next step is to record the stimulus that caused your particular response—in this case, being passed at 32 km in the Olympic marathon. Finally, the thoughts that were evoked by that sporting situation are listed. In the example we gave, the thoughts could indicate the belief system of a winner ("I can stay with her. I am just as good as she is") or that of a less confident belief system ("I have blown it. I really am a loser").

Liebetrau suggests that analyzing detailed records of about 20 sporting situations like this in both racing and training will highlight the strong relationship between a positive belief system and a favorable (that is, winning) response. Conversely, negative thoughts usually result in unfavorable responses.

The second reason for writing down these responses is to show the importance of being able to analyze all sporting situations in terms of the three components listed above (stimulus, belief system, and response). With the help of the coach, the athlete must learn to dispute these negative thoughts as they occur. In addition, the athlete should practice applying positive self-statements as often as possible in all sporting situations. The more frequently these statements are made, the more likely they are to become fixed beliefs.

One important point made by all sport psychologists is that athletes should never use the word *must* unless they are 100% certain of achieving an easy goal. If a *must* statement is followed by failure, the athletes will not be able to trust their future beliefs. The catastrophic consequences of a *must* statement are best shown by completing the second half of such sentences with the clause "or else I am a failure"—for example: "I must win the Olympic marathon, or else I am a failure." Failure to win at the Olympics will then have very serious consequences for the athlete's belief system; it will undermine whatever confidence the runner might have had and will make success in the next attempt at that goal even less likely.

Improving the Self-Concept

Central to this notion of the importance of psychological factors in determining racing performance is the idea that a positive self-concept is associated with a strong belief system. But self-concept is not static: every day the self-concept faces new challenges that will either enhance or detract from it. In a sense, there is a vicious cycle: success breeds success and failure the opposite. Therefore, the only way to break this cycle is to strengthen the self-concept.

Liebetrau suggests using the following technique to strengthen the self-concept. Write down a description of the person you aspire to be (that is, your ideal self). Next, describe the person you consider yourself to be (your real person). Included in these descriptions must be lists, real versus ideal in each case, of personal attributes, sporting achievements, motivations, dedication, training habits, relationships with coach and team members (if applicable), overall and specific fitness levels, sporting skills or talents, and sporting achievements.

Next, imagine your real and ideal selves as two separate identities following each other around in your daily life. Pay special attention to the attributes in the ideal and real selves that differ the most. Imagine the two selves in various sporting situations that you experience. At first, the ideal self goes through the same motions as the real self; ultimately, the abilities of the ideal self surpass those of the real self and thus produce the performance you as an athlete desire. Begin to visualize yourself as your ideal self in everyday situations. Finally, imagine how your ideal self would have coped with previous competitive failure. In a similar way, you can rehearse forthcoming competitive events by imagining how your ideal self would successfully complete such events.

Clearly, these are difficult techniques that cannot be mastered overnight but must be practiced continuously for months, perhaps years. It is probable that they will not be developed to maximum benefit without the assistance and advice of a qualified professional, such as a sport psychologist.

Psychological Price of Success

We all know of athletes who perform exceptionally in training, only to fail miserably in competition. While some of these people might simply overtrain (chapter 7), a significantly large number of others will suffer from various psychological syndromes. One such syndrome has been termed the *fear of success-competitive inhibition syndrome* (Ogilvie 1980). Ogilvie lists the following five stresses, which success can breed and which are believed to contribute to this syndrome:

Social and emotional isolation: Success may isolate athletes from their families (in particular, spouses and friends) and may evoke jealousy among others with whom the athletes come into contact. Paradoxically, the increased acceptability with fans only intensifies the runners' loneliness because fans expect their heroes to be superhuman.

Guilt about displaying aggression: Athletes who have been taught since childhood that aggression is an unacceptable behavior may have difficulty expressing the necessary aggression during competition. Recall that the ability to dominate the subconscious of your opposition may be a key component for success.

Fear of discovering physical limits: Athletes who are brought up by perfectionist parents, who reward only winning or extreme excellence, may be unwilling to test themselves to the limit lest they fail. Therefore, they rationalize their need not to compete by falsely denying the importance of competition, success, or failure; therefore, they assiduously avoid such competition. Another way such an athlete can avoid competition is by being perpetually injured during training, by being a so-called "training-room athlete" (Ogilvie and Tutko 1971). Such athletes have strong feelings of inferiority but cannot simply opt out of the sport because of fear of isolation or rejection. Injury enables training-room athletes to avoid competition, which they fear might expose their physical limits, but to remain members of the team, thereby preserving their egos. In addition, injury allows them to live the fantasy that, but for the injury, they would have been exceptional athletes.

Fear of displacing idols: Athletes who have used idolization of former champions to motivate their own performances may become anxious when in a position to challenge the idols' records. Note, by contrast, the healthy attitude of Elana Meyer, Olympic 10,000-m silver medalist at the 1992 Barcelona Olympic Games: "I never really had a hero. If you do you can end up limiting yourself. What would happen if I had made Ingrid Kristiansen into a hero? What would happen when I had to go out and try to beat her?" (Meyer, 1991)

The responsibility of being first or the champion: Once athletes set their first records, their followers expect records at every competition. Thus, only perfection becomes acceptable to the fans, and any performance below a record may be treated with resentment.

The fear-of-success syndrome is only one of many psychological causes of competitive failure. It has simply been mentioned here to highlight the powerful role played by psychological factors in competitive failure. Similarly, it also underlines the need for any athlete whose performances are continually under par to seek help from an appropriate specialist.

PSYCHOLOGICAL PREPARATION FOR COMPETITION

In the following section, I not only highlight the range of techniques that an athlete can use to prepare for an event, but I also outline some of the significant psychological strategies that can be employed during competition.

Controlling Anxiety

As competition approaches, athletes tend to become more anxious and begin to experience precompetition arousal. Anxiety that leads to controlled arousal is necessary but anxiety that leads to inappropriate thinking can be detrimental.

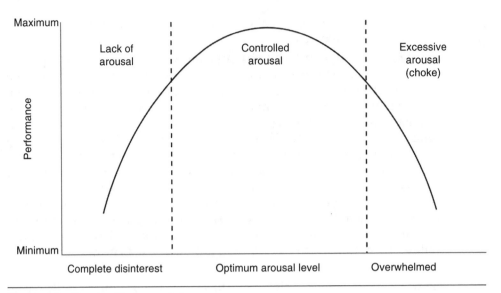

Figure 8.3   The simplified arousal diagram.
After Rushall (1979).

Rushall (1979) suggests that the nature of the thoughts that are aroused by anxiety indicate whether or not the anxiety is likely to be detrimental. He classifies these thoughts as being irrelevant, self-orientated, or task-orientated. Of these, self-orientated thoughts are the most dangerous and take the form of irrational concern about minor aches and pains and possible equipment failure. These thoughts obstruct the athlete's mental preparation. Thus, the athlete who lets such thoughts get in the way clearly needs to seek professional help.

The concept of arousal is shown in figure 8.3. It is found that athletes perform best when their level of arousal immediately before competition is in the midrange (optimum arousal level). Inadequate (left side of graph) or excessive (right side of graph) arousal levels lead to reduced performance.

Cratty (1983) believes that the optimum arousal level differs for different activities. Optimum performance in a simple, well-rehearsed activity like running can occur over a wide range of arousal levels. But as the activity becomes more complex and less well rehearsed, the range of arousal levels that will allow optimum performance becomes very narrow (figure 8.4). However, others believe that this hypothesis is unproven and too simplistic. As a result, the complex relationship between arousal, stress, and performance has yet to be adequately explained (Potgieter 1997).

An alternative theory to the relationship between arousal and performance is that proposed by Mihaly Csikszentmihalyi of the University of Chicago. Csikszentmihalyi grew up in Eastern Europe during the Second World War. Although faced with the potential for extreme unhappiness, Csikszentmihalyi dedicated his life to the study of its antithesis, happiness. He discovered that mountain climbing and playing chess transported him from his unhappy circumstances. He developed the concept of *flow* (Csikszentmihalyi 1975; Jackson and Csikszentmihalyi 1999). This theory proposes that there is a zone of optimal performance, in which athletes experiences flow; the zone can only be entered when athletes are challenged by activities that falls within their perceived abilities. Thus, optimum flow, defined

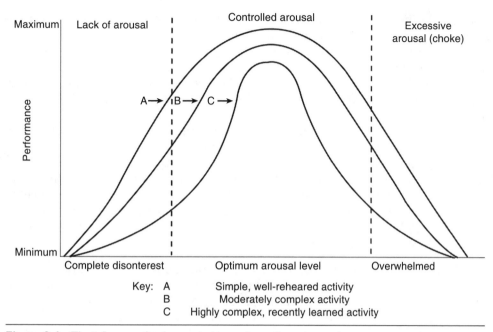

Figure 8.4   The influence of task complexity on the optimum arousal patterns.

as "an harmonious experience in which mind and body are working together effort-lessly, feeling that something special has occurred" (Jackson and Csikszentmihalyi, 1999, page 5) develops when athletes are challenged by the most demanding activi-ties that they still perceive to fall within their abilities or skill levels (figure 8.4). The characteristics of the flow state are the following (Potgieter 1997):

- The athlete is fully aware of her actions but is not self-conscious.
- She reacts automatically but does not have to analyze her actions.
- Her attention is totally focused on the task at hand, and she is not concerned with her ego.
- Although she has a feeling of control, she loses herself by becoming engrossed in what she is doing.
- She is not concerned with external rewards or outcomes.
- The task itself is the focal point and provides intrinsic motivation.

According to this theory, when the challenge exceeds the perceived skill level, anxiety develops. However, when the ability exceeds the challenge, the athlete be-comes bored. In my office, I have a poster showing a surfer turning off the bottom of a giant 6-m winter wave at the Banzai Pipeline in Oahu, Hawaii. The caption, "If surfing does not make you feel alive, then you are probably dead," captures Csikszentmihalyi's meaning explicitly: Surfing the Pipeline carries the real risk of death since the treacherous waves break on a coral reef less than 1.5 m below the surface. It would be unwise for anyone, save the most highly skilled surfers, to ride that wave—and even then not with any absolute certainty that tragedy will not occur. All the ingredients for being in the zone are provided when highly skilled surfers are challenged by a wave as demanding as the Banzai Pipeline.

Similarly, the reason why so many athletes feel so alive when they run marathon or ultramarathon races is because the challenge matches their perceived level of skill. According to Jackson and Csikszentmihalyi (1999, page 50), "Life is most exhilarating when we are deeply involved in a complex challenge. The best strategy for enjoying life is to develop whatever skills one has and to use them as fully as possible"—this is perhaps, the perfect description of what the goal of life should be.

It follows then that anxiety will arise whenever the challenge is perceived to exceed your ability level. Thus, the simple solution to avoiding stress is either to increase your level of ability (by training) or to choose only those challenges that fall within your perceived abilities. But without stress, you risk perpetual boredom.

Thus, if you choose challenges that match or threaten to exceed your level of ability, you need to know how to control the anxiety and the state of arousal that your choice will cause. Potgieter (1997) has reviewed a variety of techniques available for the control of arousal.

1. Simulation training involves training under conditions similar to those expected in competition. For runners, emphasis should be on learning the course on which the race is to be run. In all races, but especially in marathon and ultramarathon races, the important part of the course is the last quarter, when the central governor is under intense sensory barrage and has commandeered the conscious brain for its own devious ends. Athletes who have run over that part of the course in their minds will be better able to control their prerace anxieties.

2. Distraction involves taking your mind off the upcoming competition by reading, listening to music, or watching videos or television. Eight-time Hawaiian Ironman triathlon winner Paula Newby-Fraser writes that she always buys the most recent bestseller at the airport before traveling to major competitions (Newby-Fraser and Mora 1995). When immersed in her book, she is able to lure her mind away from thinking about the forthcoming race until such time as she is ready to focus on it. Classic texts on sport psychology that I would recommend reading at the time of heightened arousal are *Sports Psyching* (Tutko and Tosi 1976) and the revised editions of *The Inner Game of Tennis* (Gallwey 1997) or *The Inner Game of Golf* (Gallwey 1998). The important lesson of sport psychology that they impart will never be more easily learned than when you free up your time to analyze the mental aspects of your sport and what those mental demands teach you about yourself.

3. Positive interpretation of arousal means that the normal physiological changes that occur with arousal should be interpreted positively, as a sign that the body is readying itself for competition, rather than as a negative response indicating heightened anxiety and neurosis.

4. The thought-stopping strategy (Ziegler 1978) is an allied technique. Negative thoughts and speculations invariably increase feelings of apprehension and tension so that once you start imagining your "inevitable" failure, doubt, fear, and panic set in. These negative thoughts must be stopped and replaced by positive thoughts and self-statements, and task-orientated association. In this way, you shift the focus of attention to the positive aspects of your performance.

5. Projecting confidence, control, and calmness even though you may be harbor-

ing feelings of anxiety is an effective tactic. Useful calming techniques include smiling and talking slowly. Physical behaviors that allay anxiety include activities such as bathing, massage, stretching, or doing warm-up exercises.

6. Autogenic phrase training is another calming technique that you can use to concentrate on your muscular and autonomic functions (that is, your heart and breathing rate), as well as on your mental state. You begin by lying in a relatively relaxed body position (preferably outstretched on your back) and imagining that your limbs and abdominal area are growing warmer. Once these areas have warmed, you imagine that they have become heavier, and once this has been achieved, you begin to repeat a personal autogenic phrase that reflects your desired mental and physical arousal state, such as "I feel strong, relaxed, and confident." Frequent repetition of this procedure establishes a conscious association between the desired arousal state and the autogenic phrases so that when you repeat your personal autogenic phrases, the conditioned controlled arousal response is elicited. This technique can induce changes in muscle temperature, in heart and respiratory rates, and in the brain's electrical wave patterns (Duffy 1976).

7. Progressive relaxation, developed by Jacobson (1929), is another technique used to induce muscular relaxation. It is particularly effective for people who have trouble falling asleep (Berkovec and Fowles 1973). With this technique, you begin by contracting and relaxing your muscle groups, progressing from one muscle group to another until the major muscle groups have exercised. The reason for first contracting each muscle group is to teach you to appreciate what muscle tension feels like. Without conscious experience and recognition of what the two extreme sensations of muscle tension and muscle relaxation feel like, you will not be able to induce voluntarily the appropriate degree of muscle relaxation. Like all psychological techniques, progressive relaxation should be practiced regularly some months before the major competition so that you have acquired the appropriate proficiency with the technique by the time you need to use it.

Progressive relaxation is best practiced in a quiet, comfortable room that is free from distractions. The best place is usually your own bedroom, and this should be warm and carpeted, with the lights dimmed. Go through the following five-step sequence:

- Lie on your back on the floor with your hands resting on or next to your abdomen, with your legs extended and your feet rotated outward. Ensure that you are comfortable, then relax as much as you can.
- Clench your right fist and feel the tension in your right hand and forearm.
- Relax and feel the fingers of your right hand become loose. As you do so, contrast the feelings of contraction and relaxation.
- Repeat the above procedure first with the right hand again, then with the left hand twice, and then with both hands together.
- Repeat the same sequence for all the major muscle groups in the body, particularly the muscles of the face, neck, shoulders, upper back, chest, stomach, lower back, hips, thighs, and calves. Exercise all muscle groups, taking care not to rush the sequence. At all times carefully note the extent of the difference in the sensations of relaxation and contraction.

Practice the complete sequence of progressive relaxation exercises three times per day for 15 minutes, with the last session scheduled immediately before going to sleep. The beneficial effects of the procedure should become apparent within a few weeks.

8. Hypnosis has been used in an attempt to control precompetition arousal and to enhance athletic performance. While the subjects are under hypnosis, it is proposed that they will not become anxious or fearful before the next competition but will be confident and will successfully cope with the pain of competition. However, the consensus is that hypnosis has, as yet, no proven role in enhancing sporting performance or controlling precompetition anxiety (Potgieter 1997).

9. Meditation is a state of concentration in which you focus on a meditation object without intellectual comment or judgment. "Meditation," as Potgieter writes, "is freedom from thoughts" (1997, page 153). If the focus is on a sound, a mantra, it may be repeated aloud or silently. Transcendental meditation and Zen meditation represent specific philosophies or schools of meditation. Transcendental meditation has been shown to induce a relaxation response with reduced oxygen consumption, heart rate, and respiration rate and increased brain wave activity. It is used for the treatment of anxieties and phobias.

10. Biofeedback involves the use of equipment that measures various physiological parameters, including muscle electrical activity, brain activity, heart rate, blood pressure, and skin temperature. Reduced activity in these measures provides positive feedback that a relaxation response has been achieved. It is argued that constant use of this equipment enhances the relaxation response.

In summary, a number of techniques exist to reduce anxiety and control arousal before competition. Learning to use one or more of these techniques may be of value not only in your sport but also in the control of anxieties that inevitably arise in your day-to-day life.

Visualizing

The use of mental imagery is an important relaxation technique and literally involves running the race in the mind beforehand. Marty Liquori showed the importance of mental imagery when he stated that the race must be won in the mind a hundred times before it is finally won in reality.

There are number of important features that determine the success of using the mental imagery technique.

- Have a positive attitude—it's essential to success.
- Practice imagery in a quiet place when you are in a relaxed state.
- Include as much detail as you can using as many of the senses—vision, hearing, smell, touch, taste, and motion—as possible. Besides seeing the road, you need to hear the crowds, smell the environment, feel the road under your feet or the wind in your face, and taste your athletic drinks.
- Have a purpose for each imagery session.
- Set goals.
- Segment the event or break it up into manageable segments, each of which has a goal.

Rushall (1979) provides the following guidelines for the latter two components of imagery practice. First, an overall goal must be established, and, as discussed earlier in this chapter, this goal must be realistic.

Second, presuming a realistic overall goal has been established, the event must be segmented, and realistic intermediate goals must be set for each of these segments. For example, the athlete who wishes to run the standard 42-km marathon in 3:30:00, a pace of 5:00 per km, would have the intermediate 1, 8, 10, 16, and 32-km goals of 5, 40, 50, 80, and 160 minutes. Note that the early goals are much easier to achieve than are the latter, as the athlete tires and finds it more difficult to maintain pace. However, achieving intermediate goals stimulates the athlete to keep trying. Setting goals that are initially too high will only be demotivating. Another important reason for setting realistic initial goals is that the stopping wish can be more easily overcome. As repeatedly emphasized, usually after 80% to 85% of the activity has been completed, your conscious brain will ask you whether you should continue. This is the so-called stopping wish. But if you still have a realistic chance of achieving your overall goal when you first experience the stopping wish, the chances are that you will continue. In addition, if you have practiced mental imagery and visualized how you will respond to the stopping wish, you will be less likely to succumb to the dictates of your central governor.

Third, the more detailed and precise the preplanned goals, the more pain and discomfort you will endure to achieve the goal. Performance is likely to be better if the final evaluation allows for the attainment of a number of different goals rather than a single goal. Thus, it is important to not set the initial competitive goals too high, but to allow for a gradual improvement in performance over the years so that you do not become demotivated by repeated failures. Bruce Fordyce's running record is an excellent example of this approach (see chapters 3 and 6).

Fourth, the importance of mental imagery is that it allows you to practice the activity an unlimited number of times and to review past successes and failures. It is also possible to imagine yourself exceeding performances achieved in practice.

Finally, there are a number of additional pointers that can aid performance, which you should therefore try to remember while practicing mental imagery (Rushall 1979; Liebetrau 1982; Potgieter 1997):

- Make a public commitment to your goal.
- Play your game and not your opponents' game. The issue of whether you are a better athlete than your opponents is one you can do nothing about; you have your equipment and they have theirs. What you can do something about is how much of your physical and mental equipment you will be able to put to good use.
- Enjoy the challenge and the event; participate as if you were a child.
- Concentrate on yourself and not on your opponent or your previous success; build on your confidence with self-congratulation.
- Keep a narrow focus of attention.
- Think about the significance of the event for you personally.

Using Strategies During Competition

During competition, it is essential to segment or compartmentalize your race by breaking the overall task into smaller, more manageable segments. Substantial evidence shows that this technique improves running performance by as much as 2% to 5% (Rushall 2001).

Next, it is important to cultivate a positive and constructive mental dialogue during racing. To achieve this, we each need to discover the specific thoughts and ideas that can spur us on. The evidence is that performance is enhanced when the athlete's mental state is positive but can be impaired by a negative mindset (J.E. Dalton et al. 1977; Rushall 2001).

Examples of positive self-talk techniques include encouraging yourself, concentrating on the effort you are making, evaluating your goals for the different race segments, and carrying on general self-talk to maintain a positive attitude (Rushall 2001). This can include the use of emotive mood words that stimulate an enhanced performance, perhaps by temporarily loosening the rigid control of the central governor. It is highly likely that we all run our best when we concentrate intensely and purposefully on what we are doing, thereby excluding all extraneous thoughts, including those relating to pain. Thus, we are *in flow* or *in the zone* (Jackson and Csikszentmihalyi 1999). This thinking strategy has also been called *task-relevant thought content* (Rushall 2001).

Experimental evidence to suggest that the best athletes use this technique has been provided by William Morgan, an exercise psychologist from the University of Wisconsin (W.P. Morgan and Pollock 1977; W.P. Morgan 1978; Sachs 1984a). Morgan reported a study that contrasted the mental strategies used during competition by a group of elite, world-class American marathon runners, including Frank Shorter, Kenny Moore, Don Kardong, and Jeff Galloway, with those of a group of nonelite, average runners.

He found that during competition the elite runners exhibited *associative characteristics,* which means that their thoughts were totally absorbed in the race itself. They concentrated on strategy, on staying loose, and on running as efficiently as possible by closely monitoring subtle physiological cues from their feet, calves, thighs, and respiration. Their marathon pace was governed not by the clock but by their bodies. According to the governor theory, these athletes were allowing their pace to be set by the central governor on the basis of its integration of all the different sensory information coming from those organs that determine performance.

Since the central governor really does know what each athlete's physiological capacity is—in fact, it sets that capacity—it is perhaps not surprising that these elite runners did not believe in the existence of the so-called marathon wall. Rather, because they made their conscious brains subservient to the subconscious governor, they were able to choose the exact racing speed that avoided a sudden and precipitous fall off in performance at the wall. One said, "The wall is a myth. The key is to read your body, adjust your pace, and avoid getting into trouble" (W.P. Morgan 1978, page 43). In reality, these athletes had learned that optimum performances can only be achieved when the pacing strategy is dictated by the subconscious and not by some predetermined plan, invented by a hopelessly overoptimistic conscious brain and shaped by a host of imaginary variables, including expectations, hopes, and presumptions, none of which has anything to do with the athlete's true physiological state before or during the race. Since it is only the central governor that can monitor the athlete's true physiological state, it is only the pace chosen by the subconscious governor that will ever be the best possible under the prevailing circumstances.

Intense concentration on task-relevant information is also thought to reduce the discomfort that is felt when racing. Thus, it is perhaps understandable why these athletes believe that the wall befalls only those who ignore the subtle physiological cues that differentiate between the correct racing pace and one that is too ambitious—the classic error made by those who allow their conscious brains to override the finely tuned pacing strategies provided by the central governor.

As would be expected, these elite runners also segmented the race by concentrating on holding the correct pace for the kilometer they were actually running, instead of worrying about the fact that they had many more kilometers to run. This technique is also known as *staying in the present* (Potgieter 1997). It is also found that the more intense the activity, the shorter each segment must be (Rushall 2001). As described in chapter 10, when extreme fatigue develops, for example in the last 10-km of the standard marathon, the segments must also become shorter (usually 1 km), whereas 5- to 10-km segments are appropriate at the start of that race.

In contrast to the mental techniques used by elite athletes, Morgan found that the average marathon runners tended to dissociate during competition—to fix their minds on subjects totally unrelated to running. Morgan also reported that the need for the average runners to dissociate became overwhelming as the race progressed and they were overcome by discomfort. My conclusion from this explanation and my own observations is that as athletes mature with years of training and racing experience, they gradually learn how to pace themselves optimally. Perhaps this indicates that they eventually learn to transfer the responsibility for pacing from the conscious brain to the subconscious governor. Those who never effect this transfer of responsibility will remain frustrated, as they will always underperform compared to what they, but not their subconscious governors, believe to be their true abilities. Perhaps the sooner you learn this lesson, the more fulfilling your running career will be.

Helgo Schomer (1984; 1986; 1987), a sport psychologist from the University of Cape Town, studied the relationship between the marathon runner's perception of effort and the mental strategies employed during exercise of different intensities. Using lightweight microcassette recorders, he recorded the thought patterns during training of three distinct groups of marathon runners: a group of male and female novice runners training for their first marathon, a group of average male marathon runners, and a group of elite runners with best marathon times in the region of 2:20. These runners were encouraged to speak into the tapes to record the thoughts that went through their minds.

The surprising finding, which contrasts with that of Morgan (1978), was that runners in each group, regardless of their proficiency, spent progressively more time in associative thought as the intensity of their perceived effort, measured on the Borg scale described in table 5.2, increased. Thus, irrespective of whether they were elite or novice runners, as they perceived their exercise becoming harder, they altered their thinking from being mainly dissociative to being mostly associative, in line with the findings of Sachs (1984a). Schomer (1987) also found that the associative thoughts could be classified as body monitoring, personal commands or instructions, reflection on the athlete's emotional state, or pace monitoring.

He concluded that athletes who wish to use associative thoughts optimally must discipline their minds to focus on the task at hand, with careful monitoring of their energy reserves and emotional states. They should also give themselves positive encouragement and praise for their efforts and calmly consider the correctness of their pace in relation to that of their opponents.

Similarly, Schomer found that dissociative thoughts during running typically comprised reflections on the runner's life, personal problem solving, work and career planning, considerations of the environment and the course, and conversational chatter. These thought patterns are probably beneficial for novice runners in that they maintain motivation by distracting their thoughts from the discomfort they may be feeling. However, for more serious runners, dissociative thinking patterns, particularly during races, probably indicate that they are not running optimally since they are not in flow, nor are they likely to be running according to the dictates of the central governor. It is my contention that the central governor directs associative thinking patterns and positive self-talk when it, and not the conscious brain, is solely responsible for the pacing strategy. When the conscious brain is in charge, the probability is that negative self-talk will try to dominate.

Indeed, there is good evidence to suggest that the intensity of associative, content-relevant thinking must increase during the final quarter of competition if performance is to be optimized (Rushall 2001).

PSYCHOLOGICAL BENEFITS OF RUNNING

When I began running, I perceived the benefits as being purely physical. I have since discovered that many of the benefits of exercise are in the mind. The most persuasive evidence for this is provided in the classic running books of Sheehan (1975; 1978b; 1980; 1983) and Fixx (1977).

A criticism that can be leveled at some of these writings is that we runners are all too neurotically involved in the activity to be totally objective. For this reason, it is important to review some of the more scientific studies that highlight the psychological benefits that can be gained from exercise. However, it is perhaps equally important to consider the following: if running has so much psychological benefit to offer, can it be too much of a good thing for some people? Sachs and Buffone (1984) have written the most detailed scientific review of this topic.

Positive State of Mind

One random survey (R. Carter 1977) found that 72% of those who exercised sufficiently to maintain a moderate level of fitness—equivalent to running 10 km per week—claimed that they were very happy. In groups who answered that they were either pretty happy or not so happy, only slightly more than one-third were physically fit. Therefore, a significant association was found between happiness and optimum physical fitness. This does not necessarily prove that exercise increases happiness. Happiness could be a factor that determines whether or not people will choose to exercise.

Reduced Tension and Anxiety

Anxiety levels were reduced after vigorous exercise, either in the laboratory or out of doors (Bahrke and Morgan 1981; Yeung 1996; W.P. Morgan 2000). Chronic exercise (training) also decreases anxiety levels (Topp 1989), and trained people have lower levels of anxiety than nonexercisers (Stephens 1988; Nuori and Beer 1989; Scully et al. 1998). In addition, the anxiety-reducing effect of exercise may last longer than that produced by other methods (Raglin and Morgan 1987). Running has been used in the management of those with severe anxiety (Berger 1984), including panic disorder (Broocks et al. 1998; O'Connor, Raglin, et al. 2000), without inducing panic attacks (O'Connor, Smith, et al. 2000).

Other diversional activities, such as biofeedback, meditation, and quiet rest, are apparently equally effective (Bahrke and Morgan 1981; Petruzzello et al. 1991), but in my own experience, exercise has a specific effect on reducing my anxiety that I cannot achieve any other way. Perhaps exercise training has a specific effect on the brain. One study (Broocks et al. 1998) suggests that regular training reduces the activity of the serotonin receptors in the brain. Reduced sensitivity of these receptors to stimulation might explain the antidepressant and anxiolytic effects of exercise.

When compared with a single dose of tranquillizer, a single exercise bout (15 minutes of walking at a heart rate of 100 beats per minute) has a significantly greater effect on resting muscle tension. De Vries (1981) concludes that exercise has a substantial acute and long-term tranquillizing effect. Runners also exhibit less anxiety about death than do nonrunners (Guyot et al. 1984; North et al. 1990).

Decreased Depression

Jogging has proved an effective adjunct in the treatment of depression and may be at least as effective as, and is certainly cheaper than, conventional drug therapy in mild cases (Griest et al. 1981; Berger 1984; Buffone 1984; Kostrabula 1984; McCann and Holmes 1984; Martinsen et al. 1985; North et al. 1990; Scully et al. 1998; Weyerer and Kupfer 1994). Cross-sectional studies show that depressive symptoms decrease with increasing levels of physical activity (Farmer et al. 1988; Ross and Hayes 1988; Stephens 1988; Weyerer 1992; W.P. Morgan 2000) so that the physically inactive are three times more likely to suffer from depression than those who are physically active (Weyerer 1992). Furthermore, Farmer et al. (1988) suggest that physical inactivity may be a risk factor of depressive symptoms. Also, in prospective studies, it was found that those who either did not exercise or reduced their levels of physical activity were at increased risk of developing depression during the subsequent decade (Camacho et al. 1991), whereas increased levels of physical activity reduced levels of depression in adolescents (R. Norris et al. 1992).

Although physically active subjects in a Harvard alumni study (described in chapter 15) were at slightly lower risk of developing depression or committing suicide in later life, personality traits reflecting feelings of isolation, rejection, and low self-esteem were the better predictors of these outcomes. This might explain why another study of North American physicians did not show any difference in the risk of developing depression between exercisers and nonexercisers (Cooper-Patrick et al. 1997).

Increased Quality of Life

University students who participated in a 15-week jogging program showed a significant increase in their reported quality of life measured on the Pflaum scale, whereas a control group showed no such change (A.F. Morris and Husman 1978). Female long-distance runners also scored higher on this scale than did college students and nonrunners (A.F. Morris et al. 1982).

Positive Personality Traits

There have been a number of studies of the effects of exercise training on personality (Dienstbier 1984). Canadian researcher McPherson and his colleagues (1967) reported that healthy adults who have exercised regularly for four or more years exhibited greater energy, patience, humor, ambition, and optimism and were more amiable, graceful, good-tempered, elated, and easygoing than were a group of people just commencing an exercise-training program. Similarly, Ismail and Trachtman (1973) from Purdue University in Indiana reported that high-fitness adults had greater emotional stability, imaginativeness, and self-sufficiency than did adults with low levels of fitness. Membership of the high-fitness group was associated with self-assurance, imagination, emotional stability, and self-sufficiency.

Subsequent studies have shown that exercise training increases self-confidence, emotional stability, self-sufficiency, conscientiousness, and persistence (Buccola and Stone 1975; Sharp and Reilley 1975; Young and Ismail 1976a; 1976b; 1977; Scully et al. 1998) and reduces anxiety, tension, depression, and fatigue but increases vigor (Blumenthal et al. 1982a). Runners in particular were found to be more introverted, stable, self-sufficient, and imaginative than inactive controls, and they were also lower on anxiety and higher on self-esteem (Hartung and Farge 1977). These benefits also appear to rise with increasing amounts of exercise. Thus, marathon runners score higher on these variables than do joggers who, in turn, score higher than do inactive men (Wilson et al. 1980). Body image and self-esteem are also increased in people who exercise regularly (Eide 1982). Exercise training also increased self-concept and mood in incarcerated delinquent adolescents (McMahon and Gross 1988).

These studies have led the eminent sport psychologist Bruce Ogilvie, coauthor of *Problem Athletes and How to Handle Them* (Ogilvie and Tutko 1971), to state:

> *Distance running has character-strengthening effects as well as physical effects. Running can generate certain qualities that have tremendous payoffs in our society: qualities such as dependability, organization, the willingness to take risks and push to the limit, and tenacity; qualities we need to survive in our world today. The nature of distance running demands and nurtures these qualities. (Ogilvie 1981, page 52)*

Stress Resistance

My personal experience has been that exercise greatly increases the ability to cope with the minor irritations and stresses experienced each day, especially at work. It is as if running allows me to see the triviality of some of the problems I confront daily. Alternatively, it may be that prior exercise alters the concentrations of certain chemical transmitters in the brain, including the endorphins, and that these then dampen our responses to stress.

Suzanne Kobasa and her colleagues (1982) postulated that there might be a special type of personality, alias *hardy*, that is better able to cope with stress than others. Kobasa and her colleagues found that hardiness protected against illness, particularly under severely stressful conditions, and that hardiness was increased by regular exercise. Thus, stress-resistance was greatest in those hardy personalities who also exercised. Dienstbier et al. (1981) studied a group of runners when they had not run and after they had run either 10 km or a standard 42-km marathon. The physiological responses to various stimuli, including noise and cold exposure, were reduced after they had run in comparison with their responses when they had not run. Furthermore, the runners perceived that when they were tested after running, these factors were less stressful.

An important observation was that in these experiments the subjects were tested up to 5 hours after they had run; thus, the stress-reducing effect of running lasted for at least that long, something I have also observed with my own running.

Howard and his colleagues (1984) found that people who exercise regularly are more resistant to the detrimental physiological and psychological effects of the so-called stressful life events. The stressful life events include such tragedies as divorce, financial hardship, or loss of a spouse.

Thus, for example, physically active people were better able to cope with the loss of a spouse than were their inactive peers. The same conclusions were drawn from a study of adolescents who had experienced stressful life events (Brown and Lawton 1986; Brown and Siegel 1988). Those who were physically active were less debilitated by these events. In addition, Roth and Holmes (1987) showed that exercise training was the most effective method of reducing the depression that resulted from a stressful life event. In their review of all the published studies relevant to this topic, Crews and Landers (1987) and Scully et al. (1998) all concluded that endurance-trained subjects show a reduced physiological response to psychosocial stress, as confirmed by more recent studies (Holmes and Roth 1988; Blumenthal et al. 1990; Claytor 1991).

Another view is that exercise may also acutely increase pain tolerance (Gurevich et al. 1994).

Fewer Minor Medical Complaints

Although this is not strictly a psychological benefit of exercise, it has been shown that physically fit women complain less of minor medical conditions such as colds, allergies, fatigue, menstrual discomfort, backache, and digestive disorders than do less fit women (Gendel 1978). The author concluded that many complaints may be due simply to a lack of physical fitness. The symptoms of the premenstrual syndrome (PMS) are also reduced by a relatively gentle exercise program involving 30 minutes of exercise three times per week (Scully et al. 1998).

Improved Mental Functioning

Two preliminary studies (Ismail and El-Naggar 1981; Lichtman and Poser 1983) suggest that exercise training increases mental functioning, as shown by increased scores after exercise in a variety of tests of mathematical and other reasoning abilities. Rats that exercise for life also show improved memory retention as they age (Samorajski et al. 1985). Creative thinking may also increase after a bout of exercise (Steinberg et al. 1997).

More Awareness of Health

I have found that of all athletes, runners and other endurance athletes are by far the most conscious of their physical and mental health. This results, I suspect, from the process whereby endurance athletes learn to listen to their bodies. They learn, early in their athletic careers, that the physical demands of running and other endurance activities are such that they can be performed with pleasure and satisfaction only if they care well for their bodies.

The result is that endurance athletes become health-aware and follow good health practices (Heinzelman and Bagley 1970), not because they are primarily health-conscious, but because they are performance-conscious. The potential long-term health benefits of this attitude should not be dismissed lightly. For example, Breslow (1979) has shown that longevity and physical health are strongly influenced by seven health practices: the avoidance of smoking; taking regular exercise; eating moderately and controlling body weight; eating regularly; eating breakfast; drinking alcohol moderately or not at all; and sleeping 7 to 8 hours per night. It was found that at 45, a person who had observed all seven health practices had a greater life expectancy of some 11 years over a person of the same age who had followed three or fewer of these rules (Belloc 1973). By comparison, the greatest medical advances known to us, which have taken place since the early 1900s, have increased the longevity of men aged 45 by a mere four years (Breslow 1979). Thus, Breslow has concluded that "the patterns of daily living, including eating, physical activity, use of alcohol and cigarettes, largely determine both health and how long one lives" (page 2093). Because running influences all these behaviors positively, it is one of the most powerful health tools known to humankind.

How Runners Perceive These Benefits

Kenneth Callen (1983) used a questionnaire to survey 424 runners of both sexes in the small college town of Columbia, Missouri. His results, detailed in table 8.2, show that the surveyed runners believe they derive important mental and emotional benefits from exercise (in particular, relief from tension and enhanced self-image, mood, and self-confidence). As many as 69% of the runners experienced a "high" during running. This occurred more commonly in those who ran more than 35 km per week and had been running for more than 15 months. The high—which was described as a feeling of euphoria with a lifting of spirits, increased creativity and insight, and a sense of well-being—usually occurred in the second half of the run; it occurred roughly every second run and became more likely to occur the longer the run. Callen suggests that the high may be a form of autohypnosis, with the first half of the run being used to induce the hypnotic state.

PSYCHOLOGICAL ADDICTION OF RUNNING

As the running revolution of the 1970s took hold and the literature describing its benefits grew, it was only natural that a counterliterature should develop. The major contention of this countermovement was that running is detrimental because it is "addictive" (Sachs and Pargman 1984).

Arguments for Addiction

One definition states that addiction occurs when involvement in an activity eliminates choice in all areas of life. On this basis, an addiction must be distinguished

Table 8.2 A summary of a psychological survey of 424 runners	
Responses	**% of total***
1 Reasons for starting running	
To improve health	70
For fun	55
Weight control	54
Competition	32
2 Mental and emotional benefits of running	
Relieves tension	86
Better self-image	75
More relaxed	75
Better mood	66
More self-confident	64
Other (happier, more alert, relieves depression, more content, thinking more clearly)	53-58
3 Experienced the "runner's high"	69
4 Experienced a trance or altered state of consciousness during running	56

* Respondents could list as many benefits as they wished.
From Callen (1983, p. 145). © 1983 by American Psychiatric Publishing.

from a habit, commitment, or compulsion, none of which excludes all other activities. My experience is that the great majority of runners are not addicted to such an extent that running completely dominates all other aspects of their lives. Rather, I believe that running fits the description of a compulsion and that the term *addiction* is inappropriate.

A feature of an addictive state is that withdrawal symptoms develop when the addict cannot indulge in the addiction. Two authors have described the withdrawal symptoms that they consider indicative of running's addictive nature. Psychologist William Morgan (1979) lists the following array of withdrawal symptoms: depression and anxiety usually accompanied by restlessness, insomnia, generalized fatigue, tics, muscle tension and soreness, decreased appetite, and constipation or irregularity. In general, the benefits of vigorous exercise are reversed. Exercise addicts give their daily run(s) higher priority than their jobs, families, or friends. They run first and then, if time permits, they work, love, and socialize. And they often exercise to the point where overuse injuries have near-crippling effects, pain becomes intolerable, and they search for the perfect shoe, orthotic, injection, or psychological strategy that will enable them to run again.

Sacks (1981) has emphasized the psychological component of these withdrawal symptoms:

> *The running addict is characterized by a compulsive need to run at least once and sometimes twice per day. . . . if prevented from running, such runners become irritable, restless, sleepless, and preoccupied with guilty thoughts that the body will decondition or deteriorate in some way. The running addict recognizes the irrationality of those feelings and thoughts, but they are inescapable and can be relieved only by running.*

Biochemical

This argument contends that running is addictive because it stimulates the release of certain hormones inside the brain, the endorphins or encephalins, which give the runner a pleasurable feeling during jogging—the so-called runner's high (Callen 1983). The brain then becomes dependent on these pleasure-producing substances, just as it does with other potentially addictive substances, such as heroin, cocaine, or morphine. But, as with all addictions, the euphoric feelings can be maintained only if the dosage (that is, the running distance) is continually increased (see also chapter 14).

Psychological

Other writers have noted that the withdrawal symptoms described by runners who are forced to stop running for a period of time are mainly of a psychological, rather than a physical, nature. The psychological withdrawal symptoms that they describe include guilt, irritability, anxiety, tension, restlessness, and depression. These writers also note that runners, possibly like myself, tend to lay too much emphasis on the mental benefits of running, and they suggest that this may indicate that such addicted runners use their running to cope with major underlying psychological problems. Victor Altshul (1981b) suggests that if jogging is indeed able to mask anxiety and depression, as these runners testify, albeit for relatively short periods, then it follows that many people with these psychological abnormalities will use running as an effective and cheap home remedy. Like Sacks, Altshul also notes that compulsive running frequently starts in response to a major emotional upheaval.

In a paper that went unnoticed before the current interest in running addiction, Crawford Little (1969) offered another suggestion as to why some may be compelled to run. He noted that among patients referred to him for the treatment of neurosis, 42% did not show the slightest interest in any form of physical activity. However, an equal percentage were the exact opposite. These "athletic neurotics" seemed to overvalue the importance of health and fitness and revealed an inordinate pride in their previous sickness-free progress through life and their excess physical stamina, strength, or skill.

Subsequently, Little (1981) concluded that athletic neurosis is not a trivial, short-lived illness. He suggests that while excessive athleticism is not in itself neurotic because it does not cause any suffering in either the subject or the subject's family, it can place the athlete in a vulnerable preneurotic state, leading to a manifest neurosis in the event of an appropriate threat. However, despite this, Little contends that the overall benefits of the exercise movement of the 1980s far outweigh the negligible risk that a relatively small number of athletic neurotics will be produced. My experience is that although this syndrome is real, I have detected this diagnosis in relatively few of the runners that have consulted me over the years.

Another psychological condition that is said to predispose addictive running is obsessive-compulsive behavior. In its extreme form, obsessive-compulsive behavior is characterized by a rigid, intensely focused attitude; preoccupation with technical detail; over-reliance on intellectuality with a loss of emotional responsiveness; worry and marked self-criticism; overconcern for moral and professional responsibility, with emphasis on what should be done; and a constant routine activity performed with the use of a schedule and checklists.

Running is attractive to the person with obsessive-compulsive behavior because it provides a rigidly defined goal (such as running an ultramarathon) that justifies a constant, routine activity (training) and preoccupation with detail (training methods, diet, shoes, reading this book, etc.). Signs that suggest an obsessive-compulsive attitude to running include a need to run every day (the training freak) and to run every race on the calendar.

Another academic, Arnold Cooper (1981), professor of psychiatry at Cornell University in New York, observed that you "scratch marathoners once and they tell you how wonderful they feel. Scratch them twice and they tell you about their latest injuries" (page 267). This made Cooper wonder whether "addicted" runners suffer from masochistic needs.

The inescapable feature of running, according to Cooper, is the masochistic need to inflict pain by running great distances. This, he concludes, "seems to be a repetition of the infant's desperate need to create everything—even their own pain." (page 271). By completing a marathon, runners demonstrate their omnipotence by triumphing over their frailty while secretly enjoying their self-inflicted pain, which would normally be forbidden by their own conscience and society's. Together, these victories provide illusions of immortality. The result is a hypomanic state experienced as the runner's high.

Cooper concludes that we all share pathological narcissistic and masochistic tendencies but that most of us find ways of diverting these tendencies toward useful activities. The marathon runner is likely to be quite far along the narcissistic-masochistic spectrum and, "almost uniquely, carries on a useless activity that symbolizes society's need for a special hero who will enact the infantile triumphs requisite for healthy functioning and who also enables the audience to share vicariously in some of his or her forbidden pleasures" (Cooper 1981, page 272). This, of course, provides a quite different interpretation of the reasons why we run marathons (see chapter 10).

Along the same lines, Blumenthal et al. (1985) propose that habitual or obsessive running is best understood as a coping strategy for the regulation of a person's emotional state. They point out that our emotional state comprises positive affects (such as excitement and enjoyment) and negative affects (such as distress, tension, anger, fear, and shame), and suggest that running enhances positive affects and reduces negative affects. Thus, they postulate that running represents one method by which people learn to regulate their emotional states.

In addition, they suggest that different runners may learn to use running either as a stimulant to improve feelings of self-esteem and self-worth or as a reward for some actions of which they are proud. They may actually run only when they are happy (positive affect runners), or they may use running only as an antidote, to control their distress (negative affect runners). In this scheme, the negative affect runners are the ones at risk if they begin to believe that running is the sole method of reducing distress. As running replaces other effective methods of stress management and controlling one's emotions, the runner begins to believe that the only way to reduce distress is to engage in running behavior. This belief heightens the runner's dependence on running: hence, the development of an addiction.

Arguments Against Addiction

The published evidence of the withdrawal symptoms experienced by runners forced to stop running are somewhat less dramatic than Morgan (1979) and Sacks (1981) would have us believe. For example, Morgan (1979) based his conclusion on eight brief case reports involving two runners who developed withdrawal symptoms when they were forced to stop running because of injury; three joggers who continued to exercise with chronic injuries, one who missed a staff meeting and went running instead; a counseling psychologist who expressed guilt as his midday run cut into 30 minutes of his counseling time, for which he was being paid; and finally, an Olympic wrestler who, in addition to his wrestling training, would wake up in the middle of the night and run 8 to 10 km.

In one of the few scientific studies of these symptoms, Baekeland (1970) found that daily exercisers refused to participate in a study for which they would be paid to stop exercising for a month. Many asserted that no amount of money would stop them exercising. Therefore, Baekeland was forced to study less addicted people who only exercised three times per week. He found that a month-long period without exercise impaired sleep, increased sexual tension, and increased the need to be with others. Thaxton (1982) found that runners who trained five days per week were more depressed if they did not run on a scheduled running day.

Thus, it would seem that the documented evidence for the withdrawal symptoms in runners is distinctly sparse. Clearly, we require more than eight brief case reports from one scientist to confirm the existence of this condition.

Biochemical

There is now good evidence to suggest that endorphin levels in the blood rise during exercise (Francis 1983; Harber and Sutton 1984); that the degree to which they rise correlates with the increase in the feelings of pleasantness engendered by the exercise (Wildmann et al. 1986); and that blocking the action of these endorphins prevents some of the euphoric feelings experienced after running (Janal et al. 1984; Allen and Coen 1987; Daniel et al. 1992) and may impair performance during submaximal exercise (Surbey et al. 1984). These findings therefore support, at least superficially, the premise that elevated endorphin levels caused by exercise could explain the addictive nature of running. However, there are two weaknesses in this argument.

First, it is now known that endorphins play an integral part in the normal stress response of the body. Any stress to which the body is exposed will cause endorphin levels to rise. We also know that not all stresses (for example, being chased by a lion) are likely to be addictive. Second, because the proposed mechanism for the running addiction is neurochemical (that is, addiction to endorphins), the implication is that anyone who ever runs will become addicted in the same way as someone who takes an addictive drug. Thus, a runner who makes a rational decision to start running would ultimately become dependent on a neurochemically based addiction that would override the rational thinking process, making it impossible to stop.

But the evidence is that not all joggers experience the runner's high (Callen 1983; Sacks 1981), nor are they addicted to the extent of developing the symptoms described by Morgan (1979) and Sacks (1981). The fact that the runner's withdrawal symptoms are mainly psychological rather than physical further suggests that the addiction is not neurochemically based. This suggests that either the condition does not exist or an entirely different explanation must be sought.

Psychophysiological

It is difficult to dispute that most runners are attracted to running because it provides a powerful psychological support system that enables them to cope better with their own unique life stresses.

The relative sanity of runners as a group is shown by the finding that runners exhibit increased emotional stability and score low on neuroticism and anxiety (Morgan and Costill 1972). Indeed, even obligatory runners enjoy excellent psychological health (Blumenthal et al. 1984). Runners are also of above-average intelligence and are more imaginative and self-sufficient than average, although they tend to be more introverted. In addition, runners have been shown to score higher on psychological scales that measure needs for thrill and adventure, and one study has suggested that running may be an important method for thrill and adventure seekers to acquire sufficient sensory input to keep their needs satisfied (Pargman 1980).

It would seem that an explanation for attraction or addiction to running must take into account all these psychological attributes of runners. One suggestion (Pargman 1980; Sachs and Pargman 1984) is to consider that adherence to running is either a commitment—dedication on an intellectual basis—or an addiction—dependence on a psychochemical basis, for which, as I have indicated, there is still no credible basis (Scully et al. 1998). The committed runner may run regularly for health or social reasons (such as the desire to forestall a heart attack), or for financial reasons, or for prestige, power, or narcissism. According to this view, a professional runner is not addicted to running but committed to earning a living. Sachs and Pargman (1984) suggest the involvement of the committed runners in their sport should be termed a *healthy habit,* not an addiction.

Two psychologists from the University of Illinois, Mary Ann Carmack and Rainer Martens (1979), were the first to attempt a more complete explanation of the way in which social, psychological, and physiological factors interact to determine the extent of a person's involvement in running. They quantified the extent of this involvement on the basis of assessing the following aspects of the runner's lifestyle: the time spent thinking and reading about running; the distances involved in traveling to races and the frequency of competition; the number of marathons run; the number of friends who were runners; the percentage of new friends met since starting running who were also runners; the amount of money spent on books and magazines about running, and on running equipment and accessories; the extent to which changes in eating, drinking, and other lifestyle patterns had been made to accommodate the daily run; and the duration and intensity of running itself.

Using this Carmack-Martens Commitment to Running Scale, two North American sociologists, Paul Joseph and James Robbins (1981), studied four different groups of runners whose commitment to running was classified according to the criteria listed below and related their level of commitment to various indices of work satisfaction and commitment:

Group 1: Running as the most important commitment. This group ran at least 64 km per week and raced often; most of their friends were runners and they read about running at least weekly.

Group 2: Running as a crucial commitment. This group ran between 18 and 64 km per week and raced frequently. They were less involved in the running subculture than were group 1 runners.

Group 3: Running as a hobby. This group also ran between 18 and 64 km per week but had no interest in the running subculture.

Group 4: Running as an occasional activity. Runners in this group ran only when they felt the urge. They usually stopped running in winter or during bad weather.

The authors made three important findings. First, they found that all runners, regardless of their level of commitment, valued self-involvement at work, but this self-involvement had to be an active involvement in which the employees were able to focus on themselves and the contribution they could make.

Second, the authors found that the more committed these runners were to their running, the greater the tendency to rank running as a more important source of self-identity than their work. Thus, the more committed runners are to running, the more they feel they can best be understood through running.

Finally, the greater the dissatisfaction with certain aspects of work (in particular, the potential it gave for self-development, self-involvement, or competition) the greater the tendency to rank running over work as the more important source of self-identity. This was particularly marked in those who were dissatisfied with the capacity for self-development offered by their work and hence shifted their identity from that of worker to that of runner.

Joseph and Robbins conclude that those associating with their leisure roles rather than their work roles—in this case, runners—are either attracted to a particular set of work needs, comprising a philosophy of work that stresses the cultivation of self (a chance to relax, to be alone with one's problems, to counter the seriousness of life, to forget about personal problems) or they are frustrated by their job experience because of its failure to provide opportunities for their self-development in terms of, for example, control over the outcome of their efforts; the ability to see the unambiguous results of those efforts; the chance to be totally involved and to make a contribution to society; and the chance to provide challenge, adventure, and friendship.

These authors suggest that, in sociological terms, their findings indicate that there is the gradual rejection of the previous social norm that people should identify themselves exclusively through their work. "Running," they suggest, "represents a quite legitimate rebellion against the unwarranted hegemony of work as the primary focus of self-identity" (Joseph and Robbins 1981, page 142).

They also point out that this shift in identity would not have been possible if there had not also been an expansion of leisure time. However, they note that this is selective and does not involve all social classes. Thus, runners come from a social class that enjoys the privilege of an expanded leisure time and therefore the possibility for this shift in self-identity.

Finally, they conclude that the fact that there exists this need to search for alternative or supplemented areas of self-understanding indicates that ambiguity exists. If running takes on compulsive and irresponsible features of its own, they maintain that running itself contains elements of pathos, uncertainty, and insecurity. The unsettling elements of the search for self-identity through running imply that all is not as it should be in other aspects of the runner's life. By pouring ourselves into running, Joseph and Robbins suggest, we unconsciously adopt a form of social amnesia and therefore escape from activities that continue to be important.

But perhaps the reason many of us run may simply be because it provides us with a simple way to play. Another pair of American psychiatrists, Samuel Perry and Michael Sacks (1981), point out that the word *sports* comes from the word *disport,* which means to carry away (that is, from work). They confirm there are three features of sport that also make it play: it produces nothing in the real world (once sport has purpose, it is no longer play but becomes work); play is separate from the real world (the opposite of play is not work, but reality); and although it is a purposeless activity in a make-believe world, the feelings expressed in play can be very real and very intense.

For many of us, running permits a return to the make-believe world of our childhood in which we can do anything, including win the Olympic marathon, in our dreams: "Like children, we pretend because we can never completely accept reality for what it is. Pretending is make-believe, an illusion" (Perry and Sacks 1981, page 74).

So running is the personal private playground in which we develop our private personal creations. By running, runners are able to control how, when, where, how far, and how fast they run; they can call "time out" when they have had enough and they can set their own goals—all the ingredients essential to a play activity. And the success of this make-believe is shown by the answer to the question, Who else but the runner could be proud of finishing ten-thousandth in a marathon?

Naturally, I have wondered how all this applies to myself and my compulsion to run, which now extends over more than 30 years and which has included many different primary focuses.

I am struck by the apparently purely physiological basis for my initial attraction to running, which occurred during that first decisive 1-hour run described in the preface. It was as if my brain had been hit by a surge of chemicals that transported me into a different world, full of harmony, emotional tranquility, and insight. Later, I learned that it was only runs of an hour or more that would induce this state and that longer training runs of 2 to 4 hours produced an even more intense state, the classic runner's high. Other activities, such as cycling, failed to induce a high of the same intensity regardless of their duration. The sole exception is vigorous mountain hiking lasting 4 or more hours.

Discussions with my immediate family indicate that whatever genes determine this response, they are not shared by either my wife or my children, none of whom experience the same feelings during prolonged exercise, but only during high-intensity exercise of short duration. My son, Travis, who has earned a black belt in an explosive sport, karate, indicates that he shares the emotional profile of Sir Roger Bannister, who wrote to the effect that running the mile suited his personality since it required that he expend all his emotional and physical energy in an explosive burst of activity lasting just 4 minutes.

My conclusion then is that marathon runners come from that segment of the human population whose brains have evolved to reward prolonged, sustained activity of moderate to low intensity. Perhaps we are the direct descendants of that group of humans—the ancestral hunters—who outran their prey during many hours of pursuit. Our reward was not the slain animals but the gorgeous feelings of tranquility and universal insight that the prolonged chase produced. Far from feeling tired, I suspect that this physiological response spurred the ancestral hunters with the desire to hunt each day, clearly an important survival strategy.

Others, like my son and Sir Roger, were designed to protect the tribe from predation by wild animals and other marauding humans. Their joy was to be involved in high-risk, physically explosive activities, of the precise kind that I find completely distasteful and from which I would escape at the earliest opportunity. Since fighting, and not hunting, was probably the more important activity of ancestral humans, so it may be that the fighting, and not the running, brain is in the majority in modern human populations.

I believe that the attraction to running is, in the first place, physiologically based, probably on the basis of specific, genetically determined receptor-mediated metabolic pathways in the brain. Those who lack those specific metabolic pathways are unlikely ever to become committed lifelong runners. They will run only for as long as there is a desired goal. Once that goal is achieved, running will be replaced by another interest better suited to the specific brain physiology.

Since the psychological models of this running attraction or addiction ignore this essential physiological basis, they provide numerous explanations, each of which seems entirely plausible and any number of which we can selectively apply to our own experiences. But without the essential physiological basis, I believe that we would not be runners, irrespective of the seemingly plausible psychological explanations for our compulsion. I believe we run because the brain demands it and rewards us with desirable feelings and emotions when we follow its commands.

PSYCHOLOGY OF INJURY

The final way in which psychology has an impact on the runner is through injury. In chapter 14, I present all I know about the causes and cures of running injuries. Although we now have the knowledge (at least in theory) and the tools, the shoes, and the orthotics to cure all runners, we are discovering that there are other factors that limit the effectiveness of treating some runners' injuries. We find that some conventional remedies are useless because, like a good percentage of ordinary medical patients, some runners can never get better. Their problem may be more a mental than a physical one, perhaps a condition that could be more aptly termed *excessive pronation of the brain.*

Over the years, I have had my fair share of treatment failures with runners like these. There are certain factors in each athlete that influence how that athlete will interact with the injury and with the practitioner consulted about the injury (Nideffer 1983).

There are essentially two groups of injured runners: those who wish to be in control of their treatment and those who wish to be controlled. Obviously, their needs are quite different. The former require little more than simple advice of the type provided in this book. The latter require very precise and detailed instructions and are only likely to recover if an adviser can be found who will give advice in that manner.

I like to be in control of myself, and I expect the athlete to do the same. For this reason, I am relatively ineffective with injured runners who need to be controlled. Those runners may need to choose a more pedantic physician, more devoted to detail than am I.

Those athletes whose self-confidence is low more often than not require the doctor to take charge of their treatment. If left to do things by themselves, they become excessively stressed and anxious. The opposite extreme is the athlete whose level of self-confidence is too high, frequently unjustifiably so. Such athletes find it difficult to trust and listen to the opinions of others. They have unshakable confidence in their own way of doing things and know better than their doctors how to do things. Under pressure, this tendency often increases. All doctors will have difficulty with this type of athlete.

People also differ in the speed at which they make decisions. I tend to make quick decisions and therefore become frustrated with people who take a long time to consider all the possible consequences of their decisions. These athletes should consult more patient physicians who better understand their needs.

Quiet, introverted athletes become even more so when injured, and it is often extremely difficult to extract all the necessary information about their injury from them. In contrast, the extroverted athlete may use denial and joking to avoid facing the reality of the injury. This approach will pose a problem should it prevent the athlete from acknowledging the gravity of the situation. Athletes who better understand how their levels of introversion or extroversion affect their actions will be better able to help themselves when injured.

When we express ourselves, we are acting on both an intellectual level and an emotional one, and the amount of importance we attach to either component will differ. The expressiveness of some of us academics, in particular, is dominated by the intellectual function. There is a tendency to be logical and rational, to exhibit so-called left-brain dominant behavior, and usually not to express much emotion. When people of this type are injured, a structured treatment protocol, rather than understanding and commiseration, is what is required.

Others, who are right-brain dominant, may express themselves more through emotions, which might be positive and supportive, negative and critical, or confrontational. Patients who become negative and critical when injured are unlikely to elicit sympathy from those they consult. Again, the point is that all runners need to understand how their personalities influence interactions with those health care professionals they consult. You will receive the best care when your personality matches that of the person who provides that care or when your care provider understands these issues and will treat you according to your specific, psychological needs.

Typical Response to Injury

All athletes, regardless of personality, will go through a similar pattern of response to injury.

1. Denial: At first, the athlete refuses to accept that the injury has occurred and simply denies its possibility. Examples of runners who ran to their deaths, denying that they could possibly have heart disease, are detailed in chapter 5.

2. Anger (rage): When the injury can no longer be denied, the athlete becomes enraged and blames either the doctor, a spouse, or some third party for the injury. Occasionally, athletes will blame their bodies for this betrayal and may even subject it to further abuse, for example, by continuing to run.

3. Depression: When denial and rage no longer work, the athlete moves on to the (penultimate) stage of depression.

4. Acceptance: Finally, the athlete learns to accept the injury and to modify ambition to accommodate the inadequacies of the mortal body. When this occurs, the athlete is likely to be over the injury.

Sooner or later, ambition will again rise, the desire to do more will again increase, and the athlete will enter what Victor Altshul (1981a) has labeled the stage of renewed neurotic disequilibrium. In this stage, the neurosis is caused by the tension between the athlete's rational realization that it is necessary to stay within the limits of his talents (and injury risk) and the neurotic need to train more to achieve ever-greater running ambitions. "In running, as in all human endeavors," Altshul concludes, "the battle for mature self-acceptance must be perpetually fought."

I am uncertain whether it is possible to increase the speed at which the athlete progresses from denial to acceptance. But understanding that the process is quite normal is usually helpful.

Other Injury Patterns

I conclude this chapter by considering the unusual characteristics of some patients who seek medical care, sometimes for running injuries. This information may be of value if you can identify yourself among these descriptions. Alternative caregivers may benefit from this knowledge if it enables them to identify and treat those with the different psychological traits.

The importance of understanding the psychology of injury is that it helps us understand why we respond to injuries in our own peculiar way. By understanding why we respond as we do, we gain a better insight into our psychological makeup and the type of medical approach that will most likely help us get over the injury.

It has been found that the illness attitudes and beliefs of runners differ from those of the general population (Currie et al. 1999) since runners are more likely to reject a psychological explanation for their symptoms, to deny the importance of life stresses, to express their concerns in terms of somatic (bodily) complaints (including, perhaps, injury), and to be somewhat more hypochondriacal.

Munchausen Syndrome

Baron von Munchausen lived in Hanover in the mid-eighteenth century and achieved notoriety as a teller of extraordinary tales about his life as a soldier in the Russian army and as a hunter and sportsman. The connection of Munchausen's name to a medical condition was made in 1951 by British physician Dr. Richard Asher, who nearly became father-in-law to Beatle Paul McCartney, and who described a group of patients who were so addicted to surgery that they learned to tell detailed, very appropriate, but totally untrue stories about their imagined illnesses, fooling the surgeons into believing they desperately needed whichever surgical operation they desired.

Asher recognized three types of Munchausen syndrome: the neurological type, who presented with paroxysmal headache, fits, or loss of consciousness; the hemorrhagic type, who specialized in bleeding from the lungs, stomach, or other sites; and the acute abdominal type (laparotomophilia migrans), who presented with severe abdominal pain, mimicking that of a surgical emergency.

A variant of this condition is the Munchausen by Proxy syndrome, named also the Polle syndrome in memory of Baron von Munchausen's son, who died mysteriously at one year of age (Meadow 1987). In his variant, a parent actively induces a medical condition or injury in the child—for example, by introducing foreign substances into the body—with the result that the child is hospitalized. In this way, the parent can attend hospital and be ministered to by doctors without being ill (Meadow 1977; Meadow 1987; V. Frederick et al. 1990).

The Munchausens are probably rare among runners. Yet, I have met one or two runners whose love of running was, I suspect, exceeded only by their love of surgery. Perhaps in some small way, the overeager or pushy parent syndrome is a benign form of the Polle syndrome, since it is the parent, not the child, who benefits most from the precocious performances of the pushed prepubescent.

A variant of the Munchausen syndrome is the runner who has to have a (simulated) injury that is, and always will be, incurable, with or without surgery. We recognize that in conventional medical practice such patients have dependent personalities and use their simulated illnesses to avoid work or family responsibilities. To be successful, they require a sympathetic, long-suffering audience either in the form of the overly attentive, too good, soft-hearted spouse, or the equally caring hospital doctors and nurses.

I view runners with simulated injury as being totally harmless. They benefit from the attention and care they are given, receiving rewards that might not be forthcoming in other areas of their lives. I have learned to view all running injuries as potential attention-seeking behaviors. Some runners need to be treated as if they are special, even for only a few minutes. The doctor's duty is to identify these patients and to respond appropriately.

Overly Eager Parent Syndrome

This injury syndrome is forever linked in my mind with the case of the student athlete whose father phoned me to say that I had to help his son, who was going to captain the national schoolboy rugby team three months later. Apparently, the young man had been unable to play for some months because of a back injury that had resisted the attention of the best physicians, orthopedic surgeons, chiropractors, physiotherapists, acupuncturists, homeopaths, and naturopaths in the country.

Needless to say, the boy did not have a serious back injury, nor did he ever play for his country. Rather, he was an example of an extremely talented but reluctant athlete who was forced to play by an athletically frustrated father. As Ogilvie and Tutko (1971) point out, by being "injured," the reluctant athlete achieves several objectives: he can make his father feel guilty for pressurizing him, he can frustrate his father's misplaced aspirations, and he can avoid the undesired competition.

Two pointers that make the diagnosis very likely are the presence of an overbearing parent whose desire for the child's success is clearly abnormal and the extreme reluctance of the "injured" athlete even to try participating in the activity. Thus, all encouragement for the athlete to return to the sport is vigorously rejected. This contrasts absolutely with the usual situation of the athlete with a real injury, who must be restrained from returning too quickly to the sport.

More recently, I was consulted by another talented young rugby player, also with an overeager father, who would faint for up to 40 minutes during exercise. When an exhaustive examination failed to disclose any life-threatening brain or heart condition, the diagnosis of a psychological sport-avoidance condition was made, and the boy and his father were counseled appropriately.

Iatrogenic Injury Syndrome

Iatrogenic is Greek for *doctor-induced*. And there are a number of ways in which doctors, either alone or in combination, can ensure that certain running injuries never heal. First, there is the situation in which the runner with a real injury suffers the misfortune of being shunted from one disinterested doctor to another without ever getting better. The runner soon concludes, or is told openly, that the injury is incurable, that it will be impossible ever to run again, or that (this is a particular favorite) he or she will inevitably develop arthritis (see the 10th Law of Running Injuries in chapter 15). After such provocation, it is understandable that any subsequent twinge or ache confirms the runner's sorry plight and produces the "arthritic cripple."

Psyche-Out Injury Syndrome

This is one of the most common psychological running injuries. In these cases, the runner uses injury either to explain a poor performance or to prevent a good performance in a forthcoming race. This idea was discussed earlier in this chapter in the section on the training-room athlete. Another variant is the runner who becomes psychologically injured shortly before an extreme event, such as an ultramarathon. These runners lack the psychological mechanisms to cope with these longer races and are best encouraged to stick to the shorter distances. There is no disgrace in being scared of overextending yourself.

My-Injury-Is-Unique Syndrome

This category is a wastebasket for a group of conditions that I, as yet, cannot accurately subdivide. Runners with this syndrome are usually outwardly intelligent and successful people. They usually argue that their injury is unique, that I will most certainly know nothing about it, and that I definitely will not be able to help them. These runners usually exude a certain amount of hostility. They may even ask me if I am sufficiently qualified to be practicing medicine. Indeed, one such runner even introduced himself by asking whether I had good medical protection in case he had to sue me. Another variant of this syndrome is the runner who vehemently accuses me of causing the injury, either because of something I wrote, or alternatively failed to write, or because of something someone said I had written or said.

I suspect that these runners are simply transferring their own psychological insecurities onto me. Fortunately, understanding the psychological game that is being played allows me to avoid a subjective response to the injured runner's challenge.

FINAL WORD

Understanding how your mind works—and how your unique personality influences how you will respond to different events during training and racing—is discussed to aid you in the preparation of your mind. A mental approach to training and racing is presented, as is the evidence that regular physical activity provides substantial benefits for mental health.

Since injury is a common feature of running, especially if you are running more than 50 km per week, it is essential for injured runners to understand that we all go through the normal process of denial, anger, depression, and finally acceptance when we are injured. We need also to understand how our personalities and those of our caregivers will either hinder or enhance recovery.

Despite the great deal I have written about physiology and medicine in this book with relatively scant attention to psychology, perforce reflecting the focus of my academic training, I believe that the mind remains the most important frontier for exercise science and medicine in this new millennium. An understanding of the way in which the central governor works and the nature of the psychological tricks it plays promises to be a good place to start.

■ ■ ■ ■ ■

TRANSFERRING TRAINING TO RACING

■ ■ ■ ■ ■

I n part II, I evaluated the variables that determine how the body and mind can best be prepared for racing, and I provided a number of general training guide lines. In part III, I build on these guidelines by looking more closely at the specific training methods that are likely to produce the best results at three different racing distances—10 km and half-marathons (chapter 9), the 42-km standard marathon (chapter 10), and ultramarathons of more than 42 km and up to 160 km (chapter 11).

The advice in these chapters needs to be considered in sequence. Thus, the novice runner whose ultimate goal is to run a 90- to 100-km ultramarathon in 18 months' time would first need to train and race according to the guidelines provided in chapter 9 for distances of 10 to 21 km. After that, the runner should start concentrating on the marathon (chapter 10). Only then would it be advisable to move into the final phase of preparing for and racing the ultramarathon (chapter 11).

Copy the following prerace checklist and place in a prominent place. By checking the list regularly, you will ensure that you do not overlook anything obvious in your racing preparation no matter the distance.

36 to 13 weeks before race day

✔ Run a series of progressively longer races to get used to the atmosphere of races, to practice pacing, and to learn how to drink while running.

✔ Make sure that you have a digital watch with a stopwatch function to time yourself. This is especially important for learning how to pace yourself.

✔ Send in your race entry form in good time (i.e., 3 months before the race).

12 to 5 weeks before race day

✔ During the last 12 weeks before the race, do not run races longer than 28 km.

✔ The period from the ninth to the fourth last week must be reserved for heavy (peaking) training.

✔ Ensure that the shoes you plan to race in are broken in.

✔ If racing out of town, check that you have comfortable and quiet accommodation (away from road noises) at the site of the race and that the food choices and other amenities are satisfactory. If traveling by air, check that you have organized transportation from the airport to your hotel.

4 to 1 weeks before race day

✔ Start your taper by reducing training to 70%, 50%, and 40% of maximum for the fourth-, third-, and second-last training weeks.

✔ Save the shoes you are planning to race in by running in them once or twice a week.

✔ Consider the need for heat acclimatization.

✔ Decide on the pace you plan to run.

✔ Study the course, especially the last 10 km of the standard marathon and the last 25 km of an ultramarathon.

✔ Begin mental preparation by visualizing yourself running on the course and passing the 1-, 10-, 16-, 21-, and 32-km marks at the times appropriate for your pacing schedule.

✔ Memorize the exact details of the last 10 km—in particular, the number and length of all the uphills and downhills, when they come, and for how long they last.

✔ Imagine yourself running that section, and think about how you will cope with the inevitable fatigue you will feel.

✔ Check that all your racing gear fits and is in perfect condition.

✔ Attach your race number to your racing shirt and pack your racing gear in a bag.

7, 6, and 5 days before the race

✔ If on the carbohydrate-depletion diet, run a longish run (up to 21 km) on day 7, and thereafter begin the low-carbohydrate diet for 2-1/2 to 3 days.

✔ Run up to 12 km on days 6 and 5.

✔ Sleep as much as possible at night, and try to nap in the afternoons.

✔ Be less fastidious than usual at work.

4 and 3 days before the race

✔ Run very little (up to 5 km) or not at all.

✔ Eat a high-carbohydrate diet as outlined in chapters 3 and 15.

✔ Rest and sleep as much as possible.

✔ Don't think too much about the race.

2 days before the race

✔ Do not run.

✔ Continue eating a high-carbohydrate diet, and rest as much as possible.

✔ Travel to the site of the competition if the race is out of town.

✔ Remember to take your own bed linen and pillows and other personal possessions from your room.

✔ Drive over the course, particularly the final section.

✔ Go to bed early.

The day before the race

✔ Do not run.

✔ Continue eating a high-carbohydrate diet but switch to low-residue carbohydrates.

✔ Avoid all dairy produce and other food to which you may be allergic.

✔ Spend the day relaxing and keep your mind occupied with things other than the race.

✔ Lay out all the clothing you will need for the next day.

✔ Get into bed well before 10 P.M. Before going to sleep, set at least two alarm clocks to wake you.

Race day

✔ Wake up slowly.

✔ Drink your favorite early morning beverage.

✔ Repeat positive statements.

✔ Dress for the race, applying petroleum jelly where necessary and taping your nipples (if you are a man) to avoid chafing.

✔ Check that you have toilet paper for the race.

✔ Check the weather to see whether you will need to wear or take additional clothing with you to the start.

✔ Eat a light breakfast 2 to 2-1/2 hours before the start of the race.

✔ Make sure that you use the toilet.

✔ Arrive at the race start no later than 30 minutes before the scheduled start.

✔ Take the starting-line test (see pp. 587-588), and if it is clearly going to be a hot day, adjust your race schedule accordingly.

✔ Line up in the appropriate position and think about the race; visualize your race one more time. Start the race slowly. Remember that the best pacing strategy is to allow your subconscious governor to be in charge for at least the first half of the race.

✔ Relax and enjoy the journey!

10K to Half-Marathon

I have little experience in training for distances between 10 and 21 km. Accordingly, I have had to defer, once again, to the published training methods of those runners and coaches who are recognized internationally for their successes—Jeff Galloway, Jack Daniels, Pete Pfitzinger, and Grete Waitz. However, those runners who are aspiring to join the ranks of the world-class should refer to chapter 6, where the training methods of the Kenyan cross-country runners, who dominate these distances internationally, are outlined. In chapter 5, I introduced a number of training programs for beginners. In the following section, I look specifically at beginners' programs for distances up to 21 km.

JEFF GALLOWAY'S TRAINING PROGRAM

Table 9.1 outlines Jeff Galloway's training programs for runners who wish to run 10 km in less than 40 minutes. (Slower runners should refer to the training advice provided in chapter 5, table 5.10.) With minor modifications, this program can also be used by those who wish to run 10 km in less than 38, 35, or 32 minutes. The major difference is that the number of hill repetitions during the hill training period increases up to a maximum of 12 for those wishing to run this distance in less than 35 minutes. Also, the speed of the 400-m repetitions is increased so that runners should run the repetitions in 1:25 to 1:23 if they wish to run a 38-minute 10 km; in 1:18 to 1:16 for a 35-minute 10 km; and in 1:12 to 1:09 for a sub-32-minute 10 km.

Week #	Mon	Tue	Wed	Thur	Fri	Sat	Sun (longer runs)
Table 9.1 Galloway's 32-week training program for a 40-minute 10 km							
			Base training				
1–14	0–3	9–13	0–3	9–13	3–6	0	Starting with longest run in last 2 weeks, increase 1.6 km per week up to 19 km
			Hill training				
15	0–3	8–10 (Hills)	0–3	9–11	3–6	0	19
16	0–3	10–13 (Hills)	0–3	6–9	3–6	0	9
17	0–3	13–16 (Hills)	0–3	9–11	3–6	0	23
18	0–3	16–19 (Hills)	0–3	9–11	3–6	0	11
19	0–3	10–13 (Hills)	0–3	11–13	3–6	0	26
20	0–3	10–13 (Hills)	0–3	6–9	3–6	0	13
21	0–3	10–13 (Hills)	0–6	11–13	3–6	0	27
22	0–3	10–13 (Hills)	0–6	11–13	3–6	0	13
			Speed work				
23	0–3	8 × 400 in 01:30	0–6	11–13	3–6	0	27
24	0–3	10 × 400 in 01:30	0–3	6–9	0	5 (race)	13
25	0–3	12 × 400 in 01:30	0–6	11–13	3–6	0	27
26	0–3	14 × 400 in 01:30	0–6	11–13	0	10 (race)	13
27	0–3	16 × 400 in 01:30	0–6	8–9	3–6	0	27
28	0–3	18 × 400 in 01:30	0–3	6–9	0	0	13
29	0–3	20 × 400 in 01:30	0–6	6–9	0	5 (race)	27
30	0–3	6–8 × 400 in 01:30	0–6	11–13	3–6	0	27
31	0–3	7 × 400 in 01:30	0–6	8–9	0	5 (race)	27
32	0–3	7 × 400 in 01:30	0–3	8–9	0	10 (goal race)	13

All distances are in kilometers or meters.
From J. Galloway (1984, p. 114). Reproduced by permission.

Neither of Galloway's books (1984; 1996) include training programs for 21-km races. However, some additional training advice has been included in table 9.1, as well as in his marathon training programs (tables 10.4 to 10.6). Note the emphasis he gives to cross-training and to regular walking in training and racing.

JACK DANIELS' TRAINING PROGRAM

This program involves a 24-week, four-phase program (table 9.2). The first three weeks of phase 1 are for steady, easy running. Runners may train twice per day if they are in good condition. However, if they have been resting for a prolonged period, they should only train once per day. In phase 2 (weeks 7 to 12), some quality running is added. The training distance may also be increased. Phase 3 training (weeks 13 to 18) is the toughest phase of the program. During this period, runners may enter some races as this will help them identify their current VDOT

Table 9.2 Daniels' advanced 24-week training program for races of 5 to 15 km

Week	Day 1	Day 2	Day 3	Day 4	Day 5	Day 6	Day 7
1–3	Easy	Easy	Easy	Easy	Easy	Easy	Easy
4–6	Long 25% 5–6 × 00:20–	Easy 5–6 × 00:20–00:30 strides	Easy 00:30 strides	Easy	Easy	Easy 5–6 x 00:20–00:30 strides	Easy 5–6 × 00:20–00:30 strides
7	Long 25% (24) 5–6 × 00:20–00:30 strides	Easy	2 × 200 m plus 1 × 400 m at R pace 5%	Tempo 1.6-km repetitions at T pace with 01:00 recovery 8% (10)	Easy	Easy	Intervals of 02:00 hard; 01:00 easy; 01:00 hard; 03:00 easy; 00:30 hard; 00:30 easy 8% (10)
8	Long 25% (24) 5–6 × 00:20–00:30 strides	Easy	Easy 5–6 × 00:20–00:30 strides	Repeat 400 m at R pace 5%	Easy	Easy	Intervals of 02:00 hard; 01:00 easy; 01:00 hard; 00:30 easy; 00:30 hard; 00:30 easy 8% (10)
9	Long 25% (24) 5–6 × 00:20–00:30 strides	Easy	2 × 200 m plus 1 × 400 m at R pace 5%	Tempo 1.6-km repetitions at T pace with 01:00 recovery 8% (10)	Easy	Easy	Interval sets of 04:00 hard; 03:00 easy. 8% (10) 5–6 × 00:20–00:30 strides
10	Long 25% (24) 5–6 × 00:20–00:30 strides	Easy	Easy 5–6 × 00:20–00:30 strides	Repeat 400 m at R pace 5%	Easy	Easy	Intervals of 02:00 hard; 01:00 easy; 01:00 hard; 00:30 easy; 00:30 hard; 00:30 easy 8% (10)
11	Long 25% (24) 5–6 × 00:20–00:30 strides	Easy	2 × 200 m plus 1 × 400 m at R pace 5%	Tempo 1.6-km repetitions at T pace with 01:00 recovery 8% (10)	Easy	Easy	Interval sets of 04:00 hard; 03:00 easy. 8% (10) 5–6 × 00:20–00:30 strides
12	Long 25% (24) 5–6 × 00:20–00:30 strides	Easy	Easy 5–6 × 00:20–00:30 strides	Repeat 400 m at R pace 5%	Easy	Easy	Intervals of 02:00 hard; 01:00 easy; 01:00 hard; 00:30 easy; 00:30 hard; 00:30 easy 8% (10)
13	Long 25% (02:00) 5–6 × 00:20–00:30 at 1.6 km race pace with 01:00 rest intervals	Easy	Intervals of 1.0, 1.2, or 1.6 km with 03:00 recovery, 8% (10)	Tempo 00:20 at T pace with 4 × 200 at R pace	Easy	Easy	Race or intervals of 1.0, 1.2, or 1.6 km to suit ability; intervals last 04:00–05:00 with a 03:00–04:00 jog recovery. Up to 8% of week's mileage or 10 km (whichever is less)

Week	Day 1	Day 2	Day 3	Day 4	Day 5	Day 6	Day 7
14	Long 25% 5–6 × 00:20–00:30 at 1.6 km race pace with 01:00 rest intervals	(02:00) Easy	Intervals of 1.0, 1.2, or 1.6 km with 03:00 recovery, 8% (10)	Tempo 1.6-km repetitions (or up to 00:15) at T pace with 01:00 recovery 10% (13)	Easy	Easy	Race or intervals of 1.0, 1.2, or 1.6 km to suit a ability; intervals last 04:00–05:00 with a 03:00–04:00 jog recovery. Up to 8% of week's mileage or 10 km (whichever is less)
15	Long 25% 5–6 × 00:20–00:30 at 1.6 km	(02:00) Easy	Intervals of 1.0, 1.2, or 1.6 km with 03:00 recovery, 8% (10)	Tempo 00:20 at T pace with 4 × 200 at R pace race pace with 01:00 rest intervals	Easy	Easy	Race or intervals of 1.0, 1.2, or 1.6 km to suit a ability; intervals last 04:00–05:00 with a 03:00–04:00 jog recovery. Up to 8% of week's mileage or 10 km (whichever is less)
16	Long 25% 5–6 × 00:20–00:30 at 1.6 km race pace with 01:00 rest intervals	(02:00) Easy	Intervals of 1.0, 1.2, or 1.6 km with 03:00 recovery, 8% (10)	Tempo 1.6-km repetitions (or up to 00:15) at T pace with 01:00 recovery 10% (13)	Easy	Easy	Race or intervals of 1.0, 1.2, or 1.6 km to suit a ability; intervals last 04:00–05:00 with a 03:00–04:00 jog recovery. Up to 8% of week's mileage or 10 km (whichever is less)
17	Long 25% 5–6 × 00:20–00:30 at 1.6 km race pace with 01:00 rest intervals	(02:00) Easy	Intervals of 1.0, 1.2, or 1.6 km with 03:00 recovery, 8% (10)	Tempo 00:20 at T pace with 4 × 200 at R pace	Easy	Easy	Race or intervals of 1.0, 1.2, or 1.6 km to suit a ability; intervals last 04:00–05:00 with a 03:00–04:00 jog recovery. Up to 8% of week's mileage or 10 km (whichever is less)
18	Long 25% 5–6 × 00:20–00:30 at 1.6 km race pace with 01:00 rest intervals	(02:00) Easy	Intervals of 1.0, 1.2, or 1.6 km with 03:00 recovery, 8% (10)	Tempo 1.6-km repetitions (or up to 00:15) at T pace with 01:00 recovery 10% (13)	Easy	Easy	Race or intervals of 1.0, 1.2, or 1.6 km to suit a ability; intervals last 04:00–05:00 with a 03:00–04:00 jog recovery. Up to 8% of week's mileage or 10 km (whichever is less)
19	Long 20% Strides	Easy	Tempo 00:20 at T pace with 4 3 200 at R pace	2–4 3 1.0–1.6-km at T pace; 2 3 1.0–1.2-km at I pace; 4 3 200 m at R pace	Easy	Easy	Race or intervals of 2:00 hard; 1:00 easy; 1:00 hard; 00:30 easy; 00:30 hard; 03:00 easy (6% of week's mileage or 5 km whichever is less). Plus 4 × 200 m R pace

(continued)

Table 9.2 (continued)

Week	Day 1	Day 2	Day 3	Day 4	Day 5	Day 6	Day 7
20	Long 20% Strides	Easy	Tempo 1, 1.2, or 1.6-km repetitions at T pace with 02:00 recovery 8% (10)	2–4 × 1.0–1.6-km at T pace, 2 × 1.0–1.2-km at 1 pace; 4 × 200 m at R pace	Easy	Easy	Race or intervals of 3:00 hard; 02:00 easy; 6% of week's mileage. Plus 4 × 200 m R pace
21	Long 20% Strides	Easy	Tempo 00:20 at T pace with 4 × 200 at R pace	Easy	Easy	Easy	Race or intervals of 2:00 hard; 1:00 easy; 1:00 hard; 00:30 easy; 00:30 hard; 03:00 easy (6% of week's mileage or 5 km whichever is less). Plus 4 × 200 m R pace
22	Long 20% Strides	Easy	Tempo 1, 1.2, or 1.6-km repetitions at T pace with 02:00 recovery 8% (10)	2–4 × 1.0–1.6-km at T pace; 2 × 1.0–1.2-km at 1 pace; 4 × 200 m at R pace or easy	Easy	Easy	Race or 2–4 × 1.0–1.6-km 2 × 1.0–1.2 km at 1 pace; 4 × 200 m at R pace
23	Long 20% Strides	Easy	Tempo 00:20 at T pace with 4 × 200 at R pace	2–4 × 1.0–1.6-km at T pace; 2 × 1.0–1.2-km at 1 pace; 4 × 200 m at R pace or easy	Easy	Easy	Race or 2–4 × 1.0–1.6-km 2 × 1.0–1.2 km at 1 pace; 4 × 200 m at R pace
24	Long 20% Strides	Easy	Tempo 1, 1.2, or 1.6-km repetitions at T pace with 02:00 recovery 8% (10)	Easy	Easy	Easy	Race

Easy = Easy running or rest (to fill out the weekly training quota)
Long = Long runs. Distance specified as percentage of total weekly distance (in km) or time (in hr:min).
T = Threshold pace.
R = Race pace.
From J. Daniels (1998, p. 266–69). Reprinted by permission.

(see chapter 5). Phase 4 training (weeks 19 to 24) is the final, quality phase of the intense distance program and allows both quality training and the capacity to recover for the race. (The different training intensities advocated by Daniels have been covered in chapter 5.)

PETE PFITZINGER'S TRAINING PROGRAM

Table 9.3 presents the training program advocated by Pete Pfitzinger for athletes who wish to train more than 80 km per week for races of 15 to 21 km. The different training intensities he proposes can also be found in chapter 5.

Table 9.3 Pfitzinger's advanced training program for races of 15 to 21 km

Weeks to goal	LR1	LR2	Lactate threshold workouts	VO₂max workouts	Basic speed	Week's distance (km)	Percentage of peak
14	12	9	2 × 3.2 km LT	—	—	80	70
13	13	9	—	5 × 3:00 on grass, golf course, or trails	—	86	75
12	13	9	2 × 3.2 km LT intervals	—	8 × 100 m	93	81
11	14	10	—	—	5 × 3:30 moderately steep hill	93	81
10	14	10	16-km run with long hills or 6.4-km tempo run	—	10 × 100 m	99	86
9	15	10	—	5 × 3:30 moderately steep hill	—	106	92
8	16	11	8-km tempo run	—	12 × 100 m	99	86
7	15	11	—	5 × 4:00 moderately steep hill	—	109	94
6	17	12	6.4-km time-trial	—	12 × 100 m	115	100
5	15	12	—	5 × 1200 m at 2 s/lap slower than 8–10 km goal pace	—	112	97
4	13	10	8-km or 10-km tune-up race	—	12 × 100 m	99	86
3	16	11	—	4 × 1600 m at 1 s/lap slower than 8–10 km goal pace	12 × 100 m	102	89
2	14	10	8-km or 10-km tune-up race	—	12 × 100 m	96	83
1	12	9	—	3 × 2 km at 8–10 km goal pace	—	86	75
Race week	9	7	Goal race	—	8 × 100 m	70	61

All distances are in kilometers. Only the key workouts are listed. Other training days should be used either for recovery or for easier running to fulfill the week's listed training distance. The training speeds corresponding to the different intensities of training (LR1, LR2, lactate threshold, VO₂max, basic speed) are described in chapter 5. From Pfitzinger and Douglas (1999, pp. 144–45). Reprinted by permission.

GRETE WAITZ'S TRAINING ADVICE

I introduced the great Norwegian distance runner Grete Waitz in chapter 6, including table 6.17 which lists a sample of her weekly training schedule for racing distances of 10 to 21 km. The crux of her program was the inclusion of at least two, or often three, quality sessions (one of long intervals, one of short intervals, and one of fartlek) and one longer run per week. All speed sessions were performed in the afternoon, wearing racing shoes.

On the day of a quality workout session, she would begin her preparation by mentally rehearsing the workout. She took these hard workouts very seriously and avoided a busy schedule on the days she ran these sessions. She would usually nap beforehand to ensure that she felt rested and prepared to run hard.

A typical interval workout on the track would be 6×800 m run at faster than 10-km race pace with a 400-m recovery between repetitions. If she did not have access to a track or other measured distance, she substituted this workout with 6×2.5 minutes of hard running with a 2-minute recovery between repetitions. During these sessions, she concentrated on doing more repetitions at a fast pace, rather than fewer repetitions at maximal effort. To progress, she did not try to run each interval faster; rather, she shortened the recovery period. The purpose of these sessions was to run faster than race pace.

Waitz's short-interval session would be 12×200 m run at close to 800-m race pace. In contrast to her approach to the longer intervals, as she progressed, she did not shorten the recovery period, but ran each interval faster. The purpose of these short intervals was to maintain her leg speed and efficiency. The final speed-work session that Waitz used was a time-trial in which she raced up to two-thirds of the distance of a forthcoming race at 5 to 10 seconds per kilometer slower than her race pace. She used this session to assess her likely race pace. If she was able to run at or near her goal 10-km pace for 5 or 6 km in training, feeling in control, then she knew she would be able to repeat that in a race. As she raced frequently, she only did time-trials occasionally, particularly when there were gaps in her racing schedule or when her confidence was at a low ebb.

RACE PREPARATION

One of the attractions of running is that it is possible to prepare properly for a race and be fairly certain of the outcome. Chance plays only a small role in running; what happens is predictable on the basis of the athlete's physical endowment, recent racing history, and training history.

Therefore, to be successful—which in my terms means running to the limit of your particular physical ability within the constraints imposed by your environment, including work, study, family responsibilities, or all three—you must follow certain rules in both training and racing. These rules ensure that the time you spend in training is not wasted and that it produces your best possible result.

Step 1: Run Progressively Longer Races

Before attempting races of 10 km or longer, start running some longer races three to nine months before your planned race. Doing so helps you become accustomed to the distractions that accompany long races. In addition, you will be able to practice any race strategies that you may have evolved. For example, one of the distractions that can pose a potential problem during a race is the large number of excited runners, all eager to run a personal best time. As a result, they often start the race too fast. If you are new to running, it is easy to be swept along with the crowd and to be distracted from your personal goals.

The best way to run a race of any distance is to run the second half at least as fast as the first half—preferably faster—because fatigue during racing does not develop as a linear function of the distance already raced. In other words, the fatigue felt at the end of a 10-km race is not simply twice the fatigue you felt after the first 5 km of that race. Rather, it follows a nonlinear function so that you may feel three to four times as tired near the finish as you felt at the halfway mark.

For this reason, always run the first half of the race well within your limits so that you do not feel excessively fatigued by the halfway mark. Rather, it is advisable to reach the halfway mark knowing that you will easily maintain, and perhaps increase, your pace during the second half of the race. Hence, do not be distracted by the horde of less inhibited runners who wish to start the race too fast. Start the race a little slower than you think ideal and speed up later.

The second distraction in the race is the presence of frequent aid stations. To ensure that you do not drink too much or too little, plan an appropriate drinking strategy. In a race of 10 km or less, it is unnecessary to drink more than once. But as you race longer distances, you will need to learn how to drink between 300 and 500 ml per hour, depending on your gender, mass, and running speed, without letting the process of drinking affect your pacing strategy or induce gastrointestinal discomfort (see chapter 4).

Step 2: Acclimatize to Heat

Another problem faced by many runners is that most of our training is done in the cooler times of the day, either in the early mornings or late evenings. The result is that most of us are not adequately acclimatized for exercise in the heat because we have not trained sufficiently in warm conditions. Thus, when forced to run in the heat, we might run less well. Fortunately, most races of distances longer than 15 km are held in the early mornings, when environmental conditions are usually mild. However, in races that either start at midday, as do some 10- to 21-km races, or that last most of the day, the chances are that, on occasion, the environmental conditions will be unfavorable. Therefore, the wise athlete will undergo a period of heat-acclimatization (chapter 4).

The initial phase of heat-acclimatization can be achieved quite rapidly. Five to eight exercise sessions, each of up to 2 hours, on consecutive days in the heat, produce optimum acclimatization, which lasts for some weeks. Thus, in the one to four weeks leading up to a hot-weather race, acclimatize to the heat, either by running in the midday heat or by training in a track-suit if you must train in a cold environment. In effect, a track-suit, particularly if worn over other layers of clothing, produces the same hot, humid conditions next to the skin as would a hot, humid environment. Thus, the body responds as if it were training in a hot, humid environment and begins to adapt exactly as it would if you were training in that environment.

In chapter 10, I describe the technique used by American distance runners Buddy Edelen and Ron Daws to train in cold environments for hot-weather marathons, in which they beat other athletes who trained in warmer environments.

Until you have gained experience, choose races that are run in cool conditions, as you will run faster, with less effort, and will recover more quickly. Once you have some experience, you can try running in hotter races, provided you acclimatize properly. But if you wish only to run in races that will be more comfortable and enjoyable, avoid racing in the heat.

Step 3: Acclimatize to Altitude

Just as you should acclimatize to heat, athletes who live at sea level and are forced to compete at altitude should undergo some short-term altitude acclimatization. However, there are certain absolutes about competing at altitude. All sea-level athletes who, by choice or necessity, compete at altitude should understand these absolutes.

The 1968 Olympic Games, held in Mexico City at an altitude of 2500 m, provided an opportunity for scientists to study the effects of altitude on human performance. By comparing the winning times at various running distances with the world records for those distances, it was found that performances at distances below 800 m were improved, whereas performances at greater distances were impaired progressively more with increasing distance.

Figure 9.1 provides a composite picture of these results and shows that performance in races of 100 to 400 m was enhanced by 1% to 2%, while performance in races from the 3000-m steeplechase to the standard marathon was impaired by 5% to 7%.

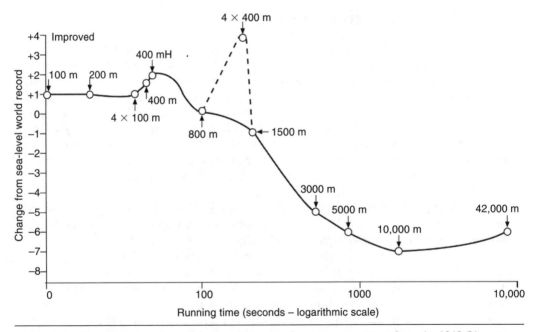

Figure 9.1 The effect of medium altitude on athletic performance: experience from the 1968 Olympic Games.

In addition, as shown in table 9.4 (Péronnet et al. 1991), performance in races of 60 to 200 m is always superior at altitude, with the benefit improving with increasing altitude. Performance in races of 400 m improves progressively up to altitudes of between 2000 and 2500 m but then begins to return to sea-level values. However, even at altitudes of 4000 m, performance is still slightly better than at sea level. Performance in races of 800 m or longer is always inferior at altitude; this deterioration in performance falls most steeply at altitudes above 2500 m.

Table 9.4 lists the equivalent world-record performances at the different racing distances at different altitudes. It shows that compared to world-record performance in a 10-km race run at sea-level, races in Calgary (altitude 1000 m), Colorado Springs, Johannesburg, or Nairobi (altitude 1800 m), Mexico City (altitude 2240 m), or La Paz (altitude 3658 m) would be slowed by 46 seconds (2.8%), 1:26 (5.3%), 1:55 (7.1%), and 6:17 (23.2%) respectively. The effect on 21-km race pace would probably be slightly greater. The world's fastest standard marathon at medium altitude was set in Johannesburg by Mark Plaatjes (2:14:45) and, in line with the prediction in table 9.4, is 6 minutes (4.7%) slower than his best time at sea level.

According to the original theory as to why performance in races longer than 800 m is impaired at altitude, the major portion of energy utilized during such races comes from oxygen-dependent metabolism. As the oxygen content of the air decreases with increasing altitude, the maximum oxygen transport capacity ($\dot{V}O_2$max) falls, resulting in a reduced ability for energy production by oxygen-dependent pathways in the mitochondria in the active muscles. If true, this theory predicts that blood lactate concentrations should be increased in acclimatized athletes during exercise at altitude. In contrast, the maximal blood lactate concentrations are reduced, giving rise to the lactate paradox described in detail in chapters 2 and 13.

The alternative theory, which I prefer, predicts that the reduced oxygen content of the air with increasing altitude will reduce the oxygen supply to the heart. This activates the brain reflex described in chapter 2, the effect of which is to limit the amount of muscle that can be activated during maximal exercise. As a result, maximum exercise capacity is reduced by this governor in proportion to the reduction in the amount of oxygen reaching the heart (see chapter 13).

If this is correct, it follows that an important physiological adaptation to altitude training would be an increase in the maximum oxygen delivery to the heart. This might be achieved by an increase in either the capacity or size of the (coronary) blood vessels supplying the heart, or in the concentration of circulating red blood cells. The latter adaptation is achieved only by living at altitudes of 2500 m or higher.

But what this theory and all others do not explain is why performance at altitude is worse for longer races (figure 9.2) that are run at lower exercise intensities. If a reduced capacity to transport oxygen explains the detrimental effects of altitude on running performance, then this effect should be greatest in shorter-distance races run at the highest exercise intensities (approximately 100% $\dot{V}O_2$max in the 1500 m) and least in the marathon, which is run at a lower exercise intensity (85% to 89% $\dot{V}O_2$max). This is a paradox that has still to be explained.

My explanation is that the rate of development of (central) fatigue is accelerated during prolonged exercise at altitude, perhaps because of increased feedback to the brain from the higher respiratory effort required when running at altitude.

In contrast to the effect of altitude on performance in endurance events, performance in the sprint events from 100 to 400 m is improved (figure 9.2) because the air resistance is reduced at altitude. These events are not affected by the body's

Table 9.4 Performance equivalent to actual sea-level world records for men and women at different altitudes

Location	Sea-level	Munich	Calgary/ Bloemfontein	Albuquerque
Altitude (m)	0	500	1000	1500
Men				
60 m	6.41	6.39	6.37	6.35
100 m	9.92	9.88	9.83	9.79
200 m	19.75	19.64	19.52	19.43
400 m	43.29	43.14	42.97	42.84
800 m	1:41.73	1:42.11	1:42.40	1:42.73
1500 m	3:29.46	3:31.24	3:32.76	3:34.33
1600 m	3:46.32	3:50.05	3:50.50	3:51.82
5000 m	12:58.39	13:09.07	13:18.61	13:28.14
10,000 m	27:08.23	27:32.52	27:54.36	28:15.97
Marathon	2:06:50.00	2:08:50.00	2:10:52.93	2:12:46.21
Women				
60 m	7:00	6.97	6.94	6.92
100 m	10.49	10.44	10.38	10.33
200 m	21.34	21.20	21.06	20.95
400 m	47.60	47.43	47.24	47.08
800 m	1:53.28	1:53.75	1:54.11	1:54.53
1500 m	3:52.47	3:54.50	3:56.26	3:58.06
1600 m	4:15.80	4:18.17	4:20.22	4:22.33
5000 m	14:37.33	14:49.65	15:00.67	15:11.67
10,000 m	30:13.74	30:40.99	31:05.49	31:29.74
Marathon	2:21:06.00	2:23:28.42	2:25:37.22	2:27:43.72

Colorado Springs/ Johannesburg	Mexico City	La Paz	
1800	2240	3658	4000
6.34	6.32	6.28	6.27
9.77	9.74	9.66	9.64
19.37	19.30	19.12	19.10
42.76	42.70	42.96	43.16
1:43.07	1:43.71	1:48.67	1:50.78
3:35.71	3:38.10	3:54.10	4:00.64
3:53.71	3:56.04	4:13.82	4:12.06
13:36.16	13:49.58	15:14.93	15:48.28
28:34.00	29:03.89	32:10.83	33:25.38
2:14:19.67	2:16:53.15	2:32:37.87	2:38:52.13
6.90	6.88	6.82	6.81
10.30	10.27	10.16	10.14
20.87	20.78	20.56	20.53
47.00	46.94	47.29	47.53
1:54.94	1:55.72	2:01.64	2:04.17
3:59.64	4:02.37	4:20.67	4:28.15
4:24.16	4:27.33	4:48.43	4:57.05
15:20.92	15:36.40	17:14.89	17:54.58
31:49.95	32:23.46	35:53.04	37:16.63
2:29:28.12	2:32:19.58	2:49:55.60	2:56:54.31

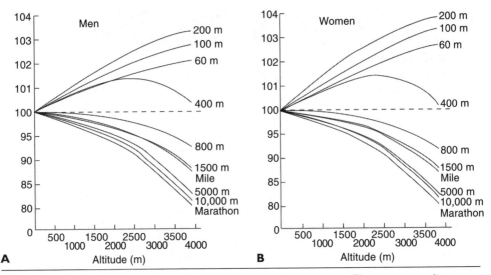

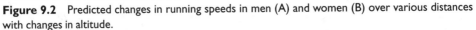

Figure 9.2 Predicted changes in running speeds in men (A) and women (B) over various distances with changes in altitude.

Reproduced from Milledge, J.S. Altitude In: *Oxford Textbook of Sports Medicine*. Second Edition. Eds: Harries, M.; Williams, C.; Stanish W.D.; Micheli L.J Oxford Medical Publications, Oxford, 1998, page 262. Reproduced by permission.

reduced capacity for oxygen transport, either because they rely on energy produced by oxygen-independent pathways or because they do not last sufficiently long for the heart to be maximally stressed, requiring a maximum coronary blood flow. As a result, they are completed before there is any risk of heart damage so that the governor described in chapter 2 is not activated.

The fourth absolute of altitude competition is that in events lasting longer than 2 minutes, athletes who live at sea level are always at a disadvantage when competing at altitude against athletes who live at altitude. The sea-level athlete suffers a dramatic fall in work performance and in $\dot{V}O_2$max immediately after arriving at altitude, and this reduction corrects only slowly and never reaches the sea-level value. Thus, the $\dot{V}O_2$max of these athletes may fall as much as 15% on the second day after arriving at an altitude of 2200 m above sea level. Over the next few weeks, their $\dot{V}O_2$max will improve gradually and will return to a value, at altitude, of 10% below the sea-level $\dot{V}O_2$max (Dill 1968), depending, of course, on the altitude. Continued training at moderate altitude (below 2500 m) does not increase the $\dot{V}O_2$max when measured at altitude or at sea level (see chapter 13). My interpretation is that such training is unable to increase maximum blood supply to the heart, perhaps because irrespective of how hard or at what altitude they train, adults have a limited capacity to increase the size of their coronary blood vessels and therefore to increase their maximum coronary blood flow further.

The effects of transferring to altitude on actual racing performance was first quantified by a study of British middle-distance runners supervised by a British physiologist, Griffiths Pugh (1967). Pugh showed that the 3-mile running times of these athletes fell by 8.5% in the first week of living at altitude, improving somewhat thereafter but remaining at 5.7% slower than sea-level performance after four weeks at altitude. Thus, even after four weeks' acclimatization at altitude, performance in a 3-mile race was slowed by about 43 seconds in world-class athletes from sea level who were unaccustomed to running at altitude (figure 9.3). Pugh concluded that it would take a "matter of months rather than weeks" for full acclimatization to altitude to take place. In fact, even this view was optimistic; full acclimatization, in which the performance of sea-level athletes matches that of altitude residents, does not occur.

Indeed, the winning time for the 5000 m at the Mexico City Olympics was 5% less than the sea-level world record (see figure 9.1) and was set by the Tunisian Mohammed Gammoudi, who lived and trained at altitude, as did Kip Keino and Nabiba Temu, who finished second and third respectively. Temu would go on to win the 10,000 m from the Ethiopian Mamo Wolde, who also won the marathon at those Games, with Gammoudi in third place. The point that I am making is that the disadvantage of training and living at sea level cannot ever be overcome in competition at altitude.

The practical implications of this are that the sea-level athlete who must compete at altitude should compete either immediately upon arrival at altitude or only after living at the altitude for three or more weeks. The worst time to compete at altitude is within three to six days of arriving.

There are two options in preparing for competition at altitude. You should either train exclusively at altitude or else live at altitude 22 hours per day and travel to a lower altitude, preferably sea level, for training sessions. The potential benefits are

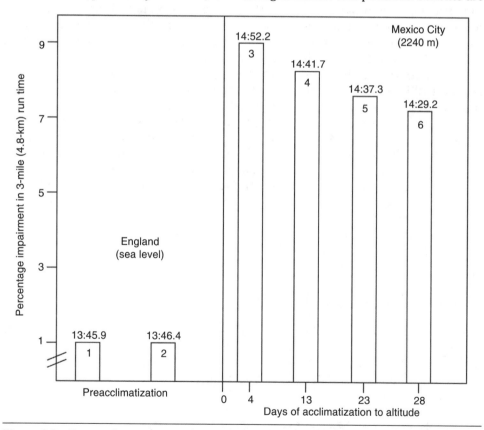

Figure 9.3 Percent changes in running performance with acclimatization to altitude: experience of British middle-distance runners at the 1968 Mexico City Olympic Games.

*Compared to all-time personal best performance.

Graph drawn from data in Pugh (1967a). © by the Physiological Society.

that the body acclimatizes to altitude by living there, not by exercising there. Indeed, the problem with training at altitude is that because of the reduced oxygen content in the air, you are never able to train quite as fast as you would at sea level. Thus, when you are training at altitude, your racing fitness for sea-level competition falls slightly, despite your enhanced ability to perform at altitude. By training at sea level and living at altitude, you adapt to altitude without losing your sea-level racing edge. Theoretically, you enjoy the best of both worlds. This is discussed in more detail in chapter 13.

Besides the pioneering study of Pugh (1967), discussed earlier, there do not appear to be any studies that indicate that training at altitude optimizes performance at altitude. This reflects, in part, the fact that since the 1968 Olympics at Mexico City, very few international athletic competitions have been held at altitude. Interestingly, living and training at medium altitude does not reduce the detrimental effect of increasing altitude on $\dot{V}O_2max$ nor does it increase $\dot{V}O_2max$ at sea level (Tucker et al. 1984). Thus, the focus of research interest has shifted to the use of high-altitude training to enhance performance at sea level.

The evidence reviewed in chapter 13 suggests that there is negligible support for the idea that living and training at an altitude below 2000 m will aid performance in races of 10 to 21 km run at sea level. A popular explanation for this failure of altitude training to improve sea-level performance, at least in the shorter track and distance races in which speed is essential, is that it is not possible to train sufficiently fast at altitude. On the other hand, there is some evidence suggesting that living at altitude and training daily at a lower level, the "live hi, train lo" regime, may enhance performance in races of 5 to 10 km (and perhaps longer) that are run at sea-level. Although these studies seem to show a beneficial effect of living high and training low, they fail to show any beneficial effect of high-altitude training alone on running performance at sea level. This is the expected response. But this finding does not exclude the possibility that marathon and ultramarathon runners might benefit from altitude training, as they do not need to train as fast as middle-distance runners do. The alternative argument—that training while inhaling oxygen in higher than normal concentrations (hyperoxia) is likely to be more beneficial than training at altitude where the oxygen content of the air is reduced (hypoxia)—is also presented in chapter 13.

Whereas the elite athlete may benefit by living high and training low, novice runners should not be tempted to do the same. Far greater benefits can be achieved by following the standard training advice given in chapter 5.

Step 4: Taper Your Training

The importance of undergoing a decent taper is discussed in chapter 5, where scientific studies on tapering are also presented. Surprisingly, few authors have discussed the importance of tapering for 10- to 21-km races. None of the programs of Galloway, Daniels, or Pfitzinger advocate any taper before races of these distances.

Step 5: Decide Your Race Pace or Effort

During the week before the race, you need to think about your race tactics. There are essentially three ways to run a race: according to your body, according to your heart rate monitor, or according to your stopwatch. When running according to your body, you monitor effort; when running according to your heart rate monitor or stopwatch, you monitor either heart rate or pace, or perhaps both.

For the first few races, it is best to run according to your body and to allow the governor to take charge. Start every race very slowly at an effort that the governor will allow you to maintain for the entire distance. It is disastrous to start too fast in any race, but especially in your first longer race. Bitter experience has shown that any time you gain in the first half of any race is paid for in double in the second half.

There is certainly no better advice for the first-time racer than the motto of a popular North American running club: *Start slowly, then taper off.* The golden rule is that the effort for both halves of the race must be as close to as equal as possible. You should never listen to those who advocate that you must run the first half of any race faster so that you will have spare time to cushion your reduced pace in the second half. In fact, the too-fast early pace is the very reason for the excessive fade in the second half. The great runners have an exquisite ability to judge not only pace but also effort. My personal advice, gained from many unhappy experiences, is that you should always aim to run the second half of any race, regardless of the distance, slightly faster than the first. I found that it was always preferable to speed up in the second half when others were slowing down. This gives the impression that you are running much faster than you really are, and the mental lift of passing others is great. In addition, in running conservatively, you are sparing not only physical, but also mental, energy—the latter being crucial in the longer-distance races.

Even when you are running a race according to effort rather than pace, it is necessary to have some idea of how fast you are likely to run. This is another important reason it is essential to have run previous races of shorter distances before attempting longer races. The times you ran in those races can be used to predict the time you can expect to run in your chosen race. This is done by checking one or more of the tables devised by Davies and Thompson (table 2.3), Daniels and Gilbert (table 2.4), Tom Osler (table 2.6), or Gardener and Purdy (table 2.7) or the nomogram of Mercier, Leger, and Desjardin (figure 2.14), which allow you to predict realistic race times on the basis of performances in shorter races. You would then run your race according to a pacing schedule that will give you two halves run in equal times.

The third possibility is to run according to a predetermined heart rate. It is likely that in due course this will become one of the most effective methods. However, at present there is insufficient information on how to do this properly.

For example, it is known that heart rates are artificially elevated, perhaps by anxiety or excitement, when racing (Mbambo and Lambert 2000) so that any relationship between heart rate and running speed established under training conditions no longer applies. The difference too can be quite large. Thus, the pace you wish to race at may elicit a heart rate of 10 to 15 beats per minute higher during competition than during training. As a result, if you run at a heart rate that you measured in training while running at your desired race pace, then, because the excitement of the race will have raised your heart rate by 10 to 15 beats per minute, at that heart rate, you will be running at a slower-than-desired pace during the race. Accordingly, it would seem that you will only gain experience about what is the ideal heart rate for you during races of different distances by using a heart rate monitor during competition.

Remember that the central governor theory predicts that all pacing strategies are ultimately regulated in the subconscious so that any conscious override, be it according to a consciously determined pacing strategy or according to a specific heart rate, will produce an optimum result only if it concurs with the subconsciously determined strategy.

Reviewing my racing memories, I think that the subconscious governor plays the dominant role in that it always has the last say. Thus, when you run a disappointing race, it is because your conscious estimation of what you are capable of is blinded by hope and exceeds that which the subconscious governor will allow you to do. If you run too fast early in the race, for example, the governor steps in and slows you down, even though your conscious drive wills you to run faster. My governor, at least, was also somewhat conservative, indeed lazy, and usually preferred me to race slightly less hard than I was perhaps physically capable of. The key is that you may need just a little, but not too much, conscious override to achieve the optimum pacing strategy that will allow you to run your best in any race of any distance.

Using a heart rate monitor or a predetermined pacing strategy can be a conscious assistance to the governor but may also be a hindrance if it causes you to ignore those bodily sensations that warn you that you are running too fast. You need to remember that the governor is the source of that information and is trying to warn you to slow down. If you continue to ignore the governor, it will eventually act, forcing you to slow down.

If you are an ambitious and driven racer, the best pacing advice is to slow down, if in doubt. If you are to take a more conservative approach to racing, in the mould of Bruce Fordyce, you will probably already be allowing the governor to guide your pacing strategy, which, in my view, is the much better option.

Generally, women appear to be better pacers than men, especially during very long distance races (see chapter 11).

Step 6: Eat Healthy Foods

There is no evidence to suggest that carbohydrate depletion in either the liver or the muscles limits performance in races of 10 to 21 km (Sherman et al. 1981) or that carbohydrate loading will necessarily enhance performance in races of this duration (Hawley, Schabort et al. 1997). There is no reason you should undertake a specific carbohydrate-loading program before races of this distance.

Instead, ensure that you eat a healthy diet with moderate to high carbohydrate content for the last 48 hours before the race. Eating breakfast before the race and ingesting carbohydrate during it will ensure that your blood glucose concentration does not fall during the race, impairing performance (chapter 3).

A disconcerting experience for any runner is to have the race interrupted by an unscheduled pit stop. The emotion of the moment, combined with half an hour or more of hard running, will shake loose even the most resolute bowels. One way of avoiding a pit stop is to ensure that the intestine is empty before the race. To do this, eat only highly refined, low-bulk carbohydrate foods that leave little residue (white bread, cookies, sweets, rice, potatoes) 16 to 24 hours before the race.

I suspect that another reason many runners may have to go to the toilet during races is that they may have very mild forms of milk or food intolerances. George Sheehan (1975) was the first to observe that the stress of competitive running caused gastrointestinal disturbances in some athletes and that these were prevented if they avoided milk or other dairy products either completely or for 24 hours before competition. It is also possible that intolerance to other foods, such as gluten, may be a problem. If you find that your stomach wants to work during races, try altering your prerace diet to establish whether you have a form of food intolerance.

Step 7: Prepare Mentally

The psychological aspects of running are discussed in chapter 8. These include understanding yourself, your mental weaknesses and strengths, and your self-concept. With regard to competition, the important features are to control your anxiety and arousal levels before the race and to run the race in your mind as often as possible before you attempt it in reality. It is also advisable to store creative energy by avoiding all demanding creative activities in the last few days before the race.

Store Creative Energy

In the week before the race, runners wanting to run a good race should devote some time to mental preparation. For the novice runner about to face the taxing ordeal of a first race, I suggest that this be done in solitude. The first priority is to store creative energy; running requires mental energy, and if this energy has been exhausted in other pursuits, there will be insufficient remaining to complete the race successfully.

There are at least three ways in which runners can harness their creative energy before the race. The first is by reducing their training loads. This not only allows the body time to recover but also stores the mental energy normally used during training. The second way is by sleeping more, relaxing, and avoiding any extraneous stresses, particularly at work. Acute sleep deprivation impairs performance during prolonged exercise (B.J. Martin 1981) and should therefore be avoided. Interestingly, resistance to this effect differs markedly from person to person (B. J. Martin 1981). The third way to harness creative energy is by avoiding any new creative activities at work or school.

Mentally Rehearse

The next important mental strategy is to run the race in your mind. Set realistic goals and then divide the distance into manageable segments. Clearly, these skills are not acquired overnight but take years of practice.

If we assume that you have established realistic goals along the lines prescribed earlier in the chapter, your task is to break up the race into small segments and to imagine yourself running each of these segments in turn, in the times that you have set yourself. It is easy to segment 10-km races into single kilometers: these races are really too short to require additional tactics. Races of 21 km can also be segmented into individual kilometers or into a race comprising an 11-km segment followed by two 5-km segments.

However, even though these races are not as long as the marathon, in which proper segmenting is crucial for success (see chapter 10), they still seem long when you are in the last one-third of these races. Knowing what the course is like—the last 3 km of the 10-km race and the last 6 km of the half-marathon—substantially reduces your anxiety during that part of the race, not to mention the difficulty you may have in finishing the race. Survey the course beforehand to be certain that you know enough about it so that you can adapt your strategy and prepare your mind appropriately.

You may be tempted to avoid seeing the course lest that vision induce an unnecessary panic attack. But you will always run better and with less anxiety over a course that you have studied or, ideally, that you have driven or run over.

A special priority is to know where the hills are on the course, especially those in the last third of the race. The reason for this is simply that near the end of any race, you are so tired that an unexpected hill can be discouraging. If you know where the hills are on the course, you can run with the goal of conserving some mental and physical energy specifically for those final hills.

However, even if you know the course very well and have visualized yourself running it, you should still drive the course one last time the day before the event, paying special attention to the last section. As you drive the course, imagine how you will feel on race day as you run the various sections, and remind yourself of the positive self-statements that you will use as you become progressively more tired.

Step 8: Give Yourself Enough Travel Time

It is probable that your first 10- or 21-km race will be run close to your home, so any advice on travel would be inappropriate. However, if you have to travel out of town for the race, refer to the advice given in chapters 10 and 11.

Step 9: Assemble Your Gear

Assemble your running gear the night before the race to ensure that you have everything. Pin your race number onto your vest and drape the vest on a chair near your bed. Seeing your racing number on awakening will help motivate you. Pack a kitbag with petroleum jelly, hair clips (if your hair is long) toilet paper, extra safety pins, your race watch, preferably a heart rate monitor, any food supplements you require before or during the race, and a snack for after the race. Also pack your favorite training hat and alternative clothing (such as old T-shirts, gloves, and rain gear), a change of shoes, and clothing for after the race. If you are unsure whether water will be provided at the start of the race, also pack a bottle of your favorite sport drink.

As far as racing clothing is concerned, heat is a major problem in many summer races, and an essential way to remain cool during running is to dress as lightly as possible. Remember that excessive heat accumulation when running fast in hot environmental conditions is an important cause of fatigue or even collapse. Running pants and vests should be lightweight and porous. The most suitable racing vests are of the nylon fishnet variety or the newer materials such as CoolMax.

On the other hand, when conditions are likely to be cold, especially if the day is also wet and windy, the risk of developing hypothermia increases—especially in thin runners with little muscle bulk. Under these conditions, wear more than one layer of clothing, cover the arms, and make every attempt to stay as dry as possible. However, wind combined with wet conditions is the greatest enemy, and the only sure protection is to wear rainproof clothing, such as Gore Tex running jackets, at least over the upper body.

The shoes you choose to race in should be sufficiently worn-in to be comfortable but not too old to be worn out. To prevent having a pair of shoes wear out a few days before a major race, leaving no time for breaking in a new pair, I would keep aside a pair of just worn-in shoes and use them only for racing. One absolute rule is never to run a long race in a pair of shoes you have not previously used in one or more long training runs. In longer races, it may be advisable to apply petroleum jelly to your feet before putting on your socks. This helps prevent blisters.

A question that always arises is whether the weight of your racing shoes influences the time taken to complete the course. There is, in fact, some evidence that very light racing shoes can reduce the energy cost of running by up to 3%, a substantial saving over 42 km (Cavanagh 1980).

But the reason racing shoes or flats are able to save this energy is that they sacrifice on certain other important characteristics. For example, Cavanagh (1980) found that when comparing the best training shoe with the worst racing flat, there were differences of 100% and 400% in rear and forefoot cushioning in favor of the training shoe. He concluded that it is unwise for all but the best runners to race in racing shoes as the risks are likely to outweigh the benefits. The risks are sore feet, added stress on the musculoskeletal system, and a greater chance of injury. (Runners with specific problems, such as pronation, may be particularly at risk and may find that because racing shoes provide insufficient support, they increase fatigue.) It is safest to run in a comfortable, more sturdy training shoe. Avoid fancy racing shoes until you are an expert or have been running and racing for two or more years without injury.

The final prerace preparations on the day of the race will be to apply petroleum jelly to those areas of the body that are liable to chafe (in particular, the groin). Also, cut your toenails; and for men, who lack the protection afforded by a bra, apply sticking plaster to your nipples to prevent so-called jogger's nipples or jogger's breasts. However, this is more likely to occur during marathon and ultramarathon races.

Step 10: Get Enough Rest

It is important to get enough rest before the race and to go to bed at the normal time. We become conditioned to awakening at a certain time each morning, and this time is not influenced by how late we go to bed. Athletes who go to bed late at night thinking that they will simply awake later the next morning are wrong. They will wake at the same time and will therefore sleep fewer hours. It is especially important to go to bed very early the second-last night before the race and to sleep as many hours as possible that night.

But despite having gone to bed at the correct time, you may find that you are unable to go to sleep, or you may be unable to stay asleep (frequent awakening), or you may awaken early and be unable to go back to sleep.

To fall asleep quickly, Liebetrau (1982) suggests using *calm scene visual imagery*. With this technique, you imagine that you are at a tranquil spot. You then imagine every possible feature of the place in the greatest possible detail, including all the sensations that could be seen, heard, smelled, or felt. With practice, the scene becomes more vivid and more detailed. After many trials, the scene that works most effectively can be identified.

Even when using these techniques, it is often difficult to sleep very deeply the night before a major race. This may make novices feel uneasy, as they may worry that their performance will be impaired. In fact, the opposite is true. The night before the race, the mind is restless because it is preparing for what lies ahead. A good night's sleep before the race probably indicates that the runner is not properly psyched up.

There may also be some benefit in using a short-acting pill of the benzodiazepine group. Triazolam has been shown to improve sleep without interfering with athletic performance measured in the laboratory (Zinzen et al. 1991). However, if you are to race in the morning, be aware that some medications have residual effects immediately on waking.

What about sex the night before the race? Old ideas, it seems, die hard. Tom Osler (1978) writes that in ancient Greece, sexual intercourse was strictly prohibited for athletes, as it was believed to sap the athlete's strength. The earliest reference to this topic was by Andrews, who wrote, "I have come to the conclusion, based on long experience, that the married state is not the best for an athlete, and that in all cases continence is essential to success" (1903, page 57).

Current feeling is that sexual activity, in moderation, has no effect whatsoever on physical performance. In the words of the famous American baseball coach, Casey Stengel, "It's not the sex, but the staying up all night looking for it, that fatigues the athlete" (Mirkin and Hoffman 1978, page 169). Surprisingly, despite the fact that this is one of the most frequently asked questions at prerace talks, the topic has not attracted much scientific interest. However, a report released at the time of the 2000 London Marathon claimed that those London marathoners who reported having sex the night before the race ran about 5 minutes faster than those who reported no such activity. The scientific question would be whether the two groups were identical in all aspects except for the presence or absence of sexual activity on the eve of the marathon or whether the difference in their marathon times was due to some other confounding variable. No doubt runners will interpret these data according to their preference in this matter.

Step 11: Wake Up Right

Both Liebetrau (1982) and Rushall (1979) stress the importance of correct waking procedures for determining how the athlete will feel and perform during the rest of the day. They give the following guidelines:

- Avoid using an alarm clock with a loud and jarring ring. The ideal is to be nudged awake by a gentle alarm or by a quiet knock on the door.

- Make your drink of choice so that you can wake up gradually while enjoying the sensory pleasure of drinking.

- Repeat some positive statements about how well you feel, what a beautiful day it is, and how excited you are about the race.

- Smile and generally get yourself into a happy, humorous frame of mind. Then do some stretching and deep-breathing exercises. As soon as you are in a positive mood, get dressed and continue to repeat positive self-statements.

- Avoid thinking about the competition, as this will produce anxiety and high levels of arousal too early before competition. Should you begin to be aroused, practice the mental-relaxation techniques described in chapter 8.

Step 12: Eat a Prerace Breakfast

Provided you eat dinner the night before a 10- or 21-km race, you do not have to eat breakfast before the race. But if you are accustomed to eating before running in the morning, you should not feel compelled to change. The reason eating breakfast is not essential before races of up to 21 km is that such races do not cause muscle or liver glycogen depletion, making hypoglycemia an unlikely cause of fatigue at these distances (see chapter 3). The main effect of the prerace breakfast is to restock the liver glycogen stores that have been partially depleted by the overnight fast and to prevent hypoglycemia from developing.

There may be a role for ingesting a caffeine-containing drink before races of any distance. Although early studies suggested that caffeine may be the most effective ergogenic agent known to exercise physiology, these studies were performed in the laboratory in subjects who were asked to exercise for as long as they could at a fixed exercise intensity. We now know that because this method of testing does not allow the athlete to follow a pacing strategy of the kind used during races, in which a known distance must be completed in the shortest possible time, it produces variable results. When subjects were allowed to choose their own pacing strategies in an effort to complete a long-distance (100-km) cycling time-trial in the laboratory, caffeine had no effect (Hunter et al. 2002).

Caffeine may be of value if you are competing in an event in which you are trying to go as far as possible. But if you are racing to finish a known distance in the shortest possible time, caffeine may be less helpful than is generally believed (chapter 13).

Step 13: Warm Up

Having prepared both mentally and physically, it is finally time to take to the road. Check in early at the race start and leave yourself at least 30 minutes for adequate stretching, a gentle warm-up, and a final mental tuning.

Stretching is essential to overcome the overnight tightness and inflexibility that will have developed in your most-trained muscles—the calves, hamstrings, and back muscles. Set aside about 15 minutes for this. Some runners have told me that a hot bath is also helpful in overcoming this early-morning stiffness.

A thorough warm-up is only necessary if the race is short, the field is relatively small, and you wish to run hard from the start of the race. This time also allows the solitude necessary for the final mental planning. I warm up by jogging for 15 to 20 minutes with a few bursts at race pace. When less fit and noncompetitive, I considered this warm-up an unnecessary drain on my limited energy reserves. Under those conditions, I would warm up during the first 3 km of the race by running even slower than I expected to run for the remainder of the race.

Once you have stretched and warmed up, with 5 minutes to go before the race start, drink between 300 and 500 ml of cold fluid, preferably the carbohydrate-containing solution of your choice. This fluid helps reduce the extent of dehydration during the race by ensuring that, even as the race starts, fluid (and energy) is being absorbed from the intestine.

Then, as you amble nervously over to the horde of gathered runners, take the "starting-line test." This test, first described by Tom Osler (1978), states that if, while standing at the start in your skimpy running clothes, you do not feel cold,

Table 9.5   Heat stress warnings for runners based on the Wet Bulb Globe Temperature (WBGT) index*

WBGT Color warning code	Risk	Warnings
Below 15°C White	Risk of hypothermia	Hypothermia may develop in slow runners in long races and in wet, windy conditions.
Below 18°C Green	Low	Heat injury can occur, so caution is still needed.
18–22°C Yellow	Moderate	Runners should watch closely for signs of impending heat injury and slow pace as necessary. Environmental conditions may deteriorate as race progresses.
23–28°C	High	Runners must slow their running pace and be very aware of warning signs of heat injury. Do not run if unfit or ill or if sensitive to heat or humidity.
Above 28°C	Extremely high	Even with considerable slowing of pace, great discomfort will be experienced. Races should not start under these conditions.

* Runners who are not accustomed to running in the heat must exercise greater care at any temperature.
Adapted from Hughson et al. (1983, p. 102).© 1983 by McGraw-Hill. Reproduced by permission.

then the weather for that day is too hot for you to run your best race. That being the case, you should remember the running axiom "In the cold you run for time, in the heat you run for a place," and act accordingly.

Novice runners should be warned that they might beat the distance, but they will never beat the heat. The novice who is too ambitious in the heat will suffer the ultimate indignity of turning to pulp and being passed by patriarchs like myself who have learned from bitter experience that heat is indeed the great equalizer.

Since Osler's description of the starting line test, the Wet Bulb Globe Temperature (WBGT) index (a more scientifically accurate measure of the environmental heat load) has been devised (see chapter 4). Guidelines on how athletes should conduct themselves in races run at different WBGT indexes have been proposed by Richard Hughson and his colleagues (1983; table 9.5) and adopted by the American College of Sports Medicine (1985).

In races in which the WBGT index is not routinely measured, it is advisable to follow the guidelines set out in table 9.6. Note that these guidelines are based on what is termed *the dry bulb temperature* (that is, the temperature measured with an ordinary thermometer). The dry bulb temperature is also the temperature that is reported in the news media.

Unlike the WBGT index, the dry bulb temperature does not take the relative humidity of the air or the amount of solar radiation into account. On humid days when there is no cloud cover (and therefore no protection from solar radiation), the dry bulb temperature seriously underreads the heat load to which the runner is exposed. Table 9.6 makes provision for this.

Table 9.6 Heat stress warnings for runners based on dry bulb temperature

Season[a]	Color warning code		
	Green[b]	Yellow[c]	Red[d]
Spring	Less than 12°C	12–23°C or less than 12°C but humidity greater than 50% and a cloudless sky	Greater than 23°C or temperature between 12 and 23°C but humidity greater than 50% and a cloudless sky
Summer	Less than 18°C	18–27°C or less than 18°C but humidity greater than 50% and a cloudless sky	Greater than 27°C or temperature between 18 and 27°C but humidity greater than 50% and a cloudless sky
Winter	Less than 10°C	10–20°C or less than 10°C but humidity greater than 50% and a cloudless sky	Greater than 20°C or temperature between 10 and 20°C but humidity greater than 50% and a cloudless sky

a. The season influences the runner's resistance to heat by altering the level of heat-acclimatization, which is best in summer, less in spring, and least in winter.
b. Green indicates go.
c. Yellow indicates run with caution and be aware of the risk of heat injury. Runners should monitor themselves carefully for the early warning symptoms of heat injury and must be prepared to slow their paces should these occur.
d. Red indicates extreme caution. Athletes uncertain of their abilities to complete the distance should not run. The only way to finish is by running much more slowly than normal.
From Hughson (1980, p. 119). © 1980 by Canadian Medical Association.

Rowland Richards and colleagues (1984) have suggested that the WBGT index is in fact not the best predictor of heat injury risk during distance running and have proposed an alternative index, the corrected effective temperature (CET). Their views are based on their decade-long experience in treating large numbers of heat-related casualties in one of the world's largest fun runs, Sydney's annual 14-km City-to-Surf race, which attracts in excess of 25,000 runners. Richards and colleagues point out that the WBGT taken at the start of the race may not reflect conditions later on during the day as the race progresses, nor does this value necessarily apply to all sections of the course. In addition, they suggest that the WBGT does not adequately reflect the two factors that affect the runner's ability to stay in thermal balance during distance races—the amount of radiation from the sun (global radiation) and the wind velocity. The CET, on the other hand, gives adequate weighting for both these factors.

Figure 9.4A shows how the CET is derived from the dry bulb temperature and humidity, and figure 9.4B, from the global radiation and the wind velocity. Figure 9.4A shows that at any given dry bulb temperature, the effective temperature falls with decreasing humidity. Thus, for example, when the humidity is only 20%, a dry bulb temperature of 30°C corresponds to a CET 6.5°C lower (that is, of 23.5°C). Similarly, increasing wind velocity decreases the rise in CET for any given amount of global radiation. Whereas full sun conditions in late winter in Sydney (latitude 34° south) cause an elevation of CET by 5°C, at a wind velocity of 20 m per second, conditions of full sun increase the CET by only 0.75°C.

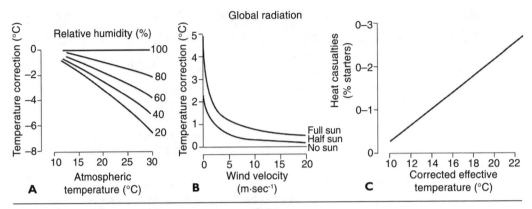

Figure 9.4   The corrected effective temperature (CET).

From Richards et al. (1984, p. 805–8). © 1984 by the Medical Journal of Australia. Reproduced with permission.

Figure 9.4C shows the value of the CET in predicting the likely number of heat-related casualties in the Sydney City-to-Surf race. The number of casualties increases from less than 0.02% of starters at CET values of 10°C or less to more than 0.25% (a 15-fold rise) at CET values of 22°C or greater. Richards et al. (1984) found that the CET was better able to predict the number of heat casualties occurring in their race than was the WBGT. However, they warn that in order to provide an adequate margin of safety, race officials should be prepared to cater to 50% more heat casualties than predicted by their data.

Browne (1986) has provided a simple diagram from which runners can assess heat stress associated with running in different environmental conditions of humidity and air temperature (figure 9.5). This figure shows that running at air temperatures of up to 25°C is relatively safe even at relative humidities of up to 100%. However, once the air temperature exceeds about 27°C, rising humidity is associated with progressively greater stress and the increasing likelihood that the danger limit will be approached. In fact, as discussed in chapter 4, these recommendations need to be considered in light of the runner's body mass. Whereas light runners (approximately 50 kg) are relatively less affected by increasing humidity at any environmental temperature, it poses a real problem for heavier runners (more than 70 kg), even at quite low dry bulb temperatures (approximately 25°C). Thus, heavier runners need to be aware that the environmental humidity poses a greater threat to their health and ability to run fast than does the dry bulb temperature. Accordingly, if your body mass is more than 70 to 80 kg, you need to be careful when competing in races run in humid conditions, even if the dry bulb temperature is not particularly high.

Finally, the ACSM has produced its own guidelines for determining the relative safety of distance races held under different environmental conditions (see figure 4.15). Those data show that races held in temperatures below 25°C and humidities below about 40% are considered to be of low risk. But once the humidity exceeds 80%, an environmental temperature of 25°C constitutes a high to a very high risk.

Although we do not yet know the precise extent to which racing performance is affected at higher environmental temperatures, Foster and Daniels (1975) have calculated that for each degree Celsius that the dry bulb temperature is above 7°C, the final running time will be increased by 40 seconds. Maughan (1990) has reported

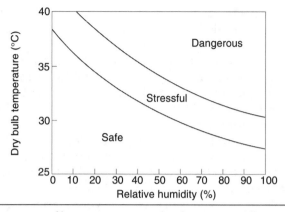

Figure 9.5   Assessment of heat stress associated with running in different environmental conditions of humidity and air temperature.

From Browne (1986, p. 23). © 1986 by S. Browne.

that the average marathon winning time is least in races run at dry bulb temperatures of 12 to 13°C (figure 9.6). This is in line with the world male and female marathon records, both of which were set at dry bulb temperatures of between 10 and 12°C, and with ultramarathoner Arthur Newton's observation: "I know that a distinctly moist day, cloudy, the thermometer about 55 degrees F [13°C] and with little or no wind, is what suited me for racing purposes" (Newton, 1935, page 81).

On the basis of questionnaire data, Browne (1986) has concluded that at temperatures greater than 25°C, marathon finishing times will be 7% to 10% slower than in races run in cooler conditions. Thus, a 2:16 marathon in the heat is equivalent to a 2:10 marathon in cold conditions. Similarly, Jack Daniels (1998) has published a table suggesting that an athlete wishing to run a marathon in 2:10:00 will slow by 2:00 if the temperature is 21°C, by 4:00 at 27°C, and by 6:00 at 32°C. For a

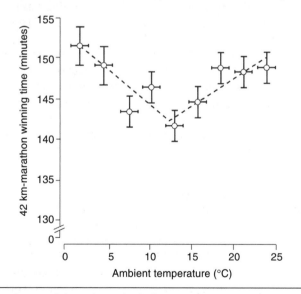

Figure 9.6   The influence of the ambient dry bulb temperature on the average winning times in the standard marathon.

From E.C. Frederick (1983a, p. 52). © 1983 by E.C. Frederick.

3:00:00 marathon, the respective impairments would be 3:00, 5:30, and 8:30; and for a 4:00:00 marathoner, these would be 4:00, 7:00, and 11:30. Compared to the data in figure 9.6, these calculations would appear to be conservative.

Thus, runners who take the starting-line test and who know the dry bulb temperature that is likely to be reached during the race should adjust their racing times accordingly. A runner who is heavier than 70 kg needs to be even more cautious if the humidity is greater than 70%. With experience, you will learn how much the heat impairs your racing performance.

The final problem that you will have to overcome before you start the race is to decide where you to stand in this now heaving, jovial horde. My advice to the novice runner is to start as close to the back as possible. In all races, there is such a wealth of racing talent that the front runners will always start very fast. And a fast start always has a ripple effect: it tends to make everyone start too fast. The further back you are in the pack, the less is this effect. If your aim is just to finish a race, you should be in the back row from the start.

Step 14: Run a Good Race

If you are running in a race with a small field (less than 500 competitors), the first thing you should do when the gun goes off is to start the stopwatch function on your digital wristwatch or heart rate monitor. You will soon learn that, next to your running shoes, a heart rate monitor with a digital stopwatch is your most critical companion in any race, and the more so the longer the race.

However, in the very populous 10- and 21-km races, the slower runners who start further back can lose several minutes at the beginning of the race owing to the vast number of competitors who need to get moving. Under these circumstances, the best idea is to start your watch when the race starts and record your first "lap" when you actually cross the starting line. Thus, you will eventually know your actual running time, in addition to your slower official finishing time. More important, you will also know your actual time over the first kilometer of the race.

Having recorded the time that you actually crossed the starting line, your immediate priority should be to achieve the correct running pace as quickly as possible. For novice runners, this is often difficult to get right. The only way to correct this is to calculate the running pace over each of the first two kilometers by calculating your actual running times at the first and second kilometer marks, not your total elapsed time from the official start of the race. If you fail to make this correction, you will calculate that you are running slower than you actually are and may therefore be tempted to speed up and run too fast, too soon.

Pacing

If you choose to pace yourself with your watch instead of according to the dictates of your central governor, at the first kilometer mark, it is essential to check your actual running time since crossing the starting line. By subtracting the time when you cross the start from that at the first kilometer, you will be able to calculate your running pace for the first kilometer. If it is far too fast, as it usually is, the only way to get into the correct pace may be to walk for a short distance. This will break your running rhythm and will enable you to make a fresh start at a slower pace. Without this walking break, it is absolutely impossible to slow down adequately. This process should be repeated at each kilometer mark until you finally slow to the correct pace. This approach will prevent runners, and particularly novices, from running too fast early in the race.

The goal of pacing is to run the race at an even pace (that is, so that the times for the first and second half of the race are equal). Although there are no studies of the optimum pacing strategy for running races longer than 1500 m (Foster et al. 1994), the current consensus is that even-paced running is the optimum tactic for all racing distances and that this becomes increasingly more important, the longer the race (chapters 10 and 11).

Running in a Group

In chapter 2, we discussed the importance of drafting during cycling and racing on the track. It was also suggested that drafting may be of value during marathon racing for those running faster than 18 km per hour, or for everyone when running into a facing wind.

Yamaji and Shephard (1987) found that competitors in the two leading Japanese distance races, the Fukuoka and Tokyo marathons, form clusters, the density of which increases linearly with faster running speeds. Therefore, clustering was most apparent among the best runners. Runners probably cluster because this reduces wind resistance, increases the competitive sprint, allows each runner to survey the other runners, and reduces uncertainty about the correct racing pace (Yamaji and Shephard 1987).

Drinking and Sponging

Drinking and sponging is relatively unimportant in a 10-km race completed in less than 60 minutes. Certainly, the fastest runners will not improve their performance by trying to drink during races of this distance. Furthermore, fluid ingestion might impair performance if it interferes with breathing and concentration in those running at very high intensity during these races.

In contrast, in longer races, including the 21-km half-marathon, it is important to start drinking by about the 3-km mark. If it is a warm day, it is also advisable to sponge for the first time at this point. It is important to start drinking early, as the rate of fluid absorption from the intestine continues at a constant rate and cannot make up for time lost if the stomach stays empty for some time after the start of the race.

Thereafter, you should drink at rates of between 400 and 750 ml per hour according to the guidelines presented in chapter 4. Provided you are drinking as you feel thirst (ad libitum), you will most likely fall within the range of fluid intakes that are safe. Overdrinking will also not be dangerous since the duration of the race is too short for serious overhydration to occur (see chapter 4).

Mental Imaging

Once you have settled into the race (usually after a few kilometers) and are running at the appropriate pace, start associating if you wish to race at your best possible pace. The key to associating is to concentrate on precisely what you are doing each step of the way and to exclude the distractions of all the runners surrounding you.

If your goal is to complete the race and to enjoy the experience, then you should continue to dissociate. Interacting with other runners and spectators and concentrating on everything but what you are doing will bring you the result you seek.

Late-Race Problem Solving

Near the end of any race, regardless of its distance, fatigue becomes a real issue because humans tend to choose pursuits that challenge their limits. After completing the first 5-km race, novices want to run 10 km, a distance for which their bodies are not yet properly prepared. The same applies for the 21-km distance.

The result is that the last third of these races will probably cause a feeling of progressive fatigue and growing despair. Fortunately, neither are particularly severe in races of these distances, nor do they last particularly long, in contrast to the situation in marathon and ultramarathon races, in which these twin evils must be subdued for some hours.

The solution is to adopt the associating form of mental imagery and to segment the remaining race distance into manageable segments, usually of 1 km. You then focus all your efforts on getting through the next race segment without any concern about the total distance still remaining. At first, almost imperceptibly, the remaining distance starts to shorten until quite suddenly, it becomes manageable.

Your first race has been completed successfully. Congratulations.

AFTER YOUR RACE

After races of 10 to 21 km, all runners will be mildly dehydrated and should drink sufficient liquid to correct any dehydration and sodium chloride loss incurred. The best drinks to correct this dehydration are those that you usually favor and that you will therefore drink in the required volumes.

The body can only correct its water losses after exercise if the sodium chloride losses are replaced at the same time (Nose et al. 1988a; 1988b). The body, as it were, concerns itself with correcting the sodium chloride losses and allows the water deficit to be restored only when the sodium deficit has been corrected. Thus, it is important to ingest some salt, probably in the form of salty food, such as pretzels or potato chips, after prolonged exercise.

When the joy or alternatively the disappointment with the race result have dimmed, it is necessary to start analyzing what went right or wrong with the race. In short-distance races of 10 to 21 km, the errors are usually in training and in the pace chosen early in the race.

Although insufficient training is the most likely cause of a poor run by a novice, as you become more experienced and hence more greedy, so that your conscious mind tries to wrestle control from your more conservative subconscious governor, poor performances will far more likely be the result of training too much, racing too frequently, and using an over-optimistic pacing strategy. These errors can be avoided by following Laws 6 and 10 in chapter 5.

If you suspect that you have indeed overtrained, then it has been a valuable experiment, provided you interpret it correctly. For you have now established an amount of training that exceeds the amount you personally require to run your best. By reducing the volume of training you do before your next race and perhaps by adding more speed training, your next performance should be closer to your ideal.

RACE RECOVERY—WHEN TO RACE AGAIN

Aim to race no more than three 10- or 21-km races per year if you wish to race your very best in each. This means that there should be a three- to four-month interval between races of these distances. These guidelines are much more conservative than those followed in the 1970s. In his classic text, the late George Sheehan (1972), an inveterate racer, suggested that 8-km races could be run weekly, 16-km races every two weeks, 21-km races once a month (but no more than five per year), and marathons every three months (but no more than two all-out marathons per year).

Interestingly, his advice for ultramarathons was far more conservative and, in my view, correct. He suggested that recovery from an 80-km race took one year and that such races should only be run once every two years.

Perhaps the point is that recovery from racing always takes longer than the conscious mind will admit. The more conservative your racing schedule, the better you will race and the longer your racing career will be. But if you run for fitness, health, and pleasure and do not run yourself to complete exhaustion, either in training or in racing these distances, you could run a 10-km race every week for perhaps 10 to 12 races before taking a break of one to two months.

On the other hand, 21-km races should be run less frequently, perhaps once every two to four weeks, also over a period of three months, before a recuperative break would be appropriate. The temptation to experiment with something new increases as the race approaches. Remember: never try anything new for the first time in any important race. The time to experiment with alterations to the guidelines is in minor races, in which the results are not crucial to your running career.

FINAL WORD

In this chapter, I have introduced some essential training methods and racing techniques that will help novice runners complete 10-km races successfully. For most runners, 10-km races are, and should be, enough. You should not be coerced into thinking that simply because you have now completed a 10-km race, progression to a marathon is mandatory. However, chapter 10 has been written for those who, despite this gentle warning, wish to go further.

Marathon

The marathon is less a physical event than a spiritual encounter. In infinite wisdom, God built into us a 32-km racing limit, a limit imposed by inadequate sources of the marathoner's prime racing fuel—carbohydrates. But we, in our human wisdom, decreed that the standard marathon be raced over 42 km.

So it is in that physical no-man's-land, which begins after the 32-km mark, that the irresistible appeal of the marathon lies. It is at that stage, as the limits to human running endurance are approached, that the marathon ceases to be a physical event. It is there that you, the runner, discover the basis for the ancient proverb: "When you have gone so far that you cannot manage one more step, then you have gone just half the distance that you are capable of." It is there that you learn something about yourself and your view of life. Marathon runners have termed it *the wall.*

Before the 1970s, the marathon was regarded as such a demanding event that only the most physically gifted dared to tackle it. As British coach Harry Andrews remarked:

> *It requires strength and a dogged determination to become a successful long-distance runner. Every man will improve with training, but only those possessed of the above qualifications, and also blessed with a strong stomach and sound digestive organs, should go in for long-distance work, as it is particularly trying to those parts of the constitution. (1903, page 71)*

Arthur Newton (chapter 6) wrote similarly: "Before the 1914 to 1918 War, the marathon was considered an event for only the favoured few who had unusual toughness and stamina."

THE MARATHON BOOM

After 1976, following the introduction of the big city marathons—first in New York, then in London, Berlin, Rome and, in time, many other great cities around the world—the notion of marathon running being reserved for a select few was turned on its head. Televised live, these races provided the visible evidence to dispel the myth that only the physically elite could complete such grueling events.

Perhaps aided by the massive success of the classic running books, Jim Fixx's *Complete Book of Running* (1977) and George Sheehan's *Running and Being* (1978), the popularity of marathon running rose exponentially between 1976 and 1980 (figure 10.1). For example, the number of runners in the New York City Marathon rose from 126 in 1970 to 2002 in 1976 and to 16,315 in 1984. By 2000, there were 29,327 finishers. Similarly, the London Marathon attracted 6,255 in its first race in 1981, a figure that swelled to 30,066 in 2001. Even the popularity of the two premier ultramarathons in the southern hemisphere, the 56-km Two Oceans Marathon in Cape Town and the 90-km Comrades Marathon in KwaZulu-Natal, showed a similar but more modest growth over the same time period. We may never know what explains this remarkable social phenomenon that stretched simultaneously across North America, Europe, and even into the southern hemisphere.

Equally surprising has been the second marathon revolution that began in the mid- to late 1990s. It differed from the 1976 revolution in the respect that the new growth in marathon running occurred in older runners merely wishing to complete the marathon distance, irrespective of the time in which they took to do it. The new revolution reflects a maturing approach to the value of running. The sole focus is no longer on each runner's finishing time. Now it seems that there is equal merit in just finishing—a welcome change.

In this chapter, we begin by considering a range of different marathon training programs for those runners who have already progressed from beginner status to being capable of completing a 21-km half-marathon.

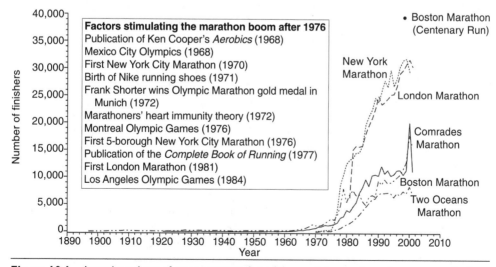

Figure 10.1 Annual numbers of competitors in five of the most famous long-distance races in the world—the Boston, London, and New York City Marathons and the 56-km Two Oceans and 90-km Comrades Marathon. Note that there was a sudden upsurge in interest in 1977 following the first running of the New York City Marathon through the city's five boroughs.

TIM NOAKES' BEGINNERS' PROGRAM

If you are a novice and have completed all the training necessary to run a half-marathon—for example, you have followed an introductory program from chapter 5 or 9—you should be ready to start training for a marathon, should you so wish. Again, it is necessary to emphasize that if you started as a complete novice with no recent running experience, you should have undergone at least 25 weeks of training. If you start on the next phase of this program without an adequate base of 25 weeks of training, you will be at greater risk of injury once you start running more intensively with less rest between long runs.

Table 10.1 presents the program that I suggest as the natural extension of Grete Waitz's program for beginners (table 5.9). The program in table 10.1 ensures that the runner who is training for 160 minutes per week and who has successfully completed a 10-km race will be able to complete a standard marathon in a further 26 weeks. It is a slight modification of the one used successfully in 1983 to train 26 novices to complete a marathon within 36 weeks of their first 20-minute walk.

The key to the program is the gentle extension in daily training volumes, with special emphasis on long runs that, in line with the method used by Mark Allen (see chapter 6), increase in a gradual stepwise progression by 10 minutes every second week. Note that this program includes both times and distances. The times are calculated for those running 6 minutes per km or slower, the distances for those who run faster. Neither the listed distances nor the times should be exceeded.

This program is clearly for those runners wishing to complete a marathon comfortably with a low risk of injury and with the highest possible probability of success. It does not include speed or hill training that, if done properly, will undoubtedly improve race time substantially. Other programs, like those of Jeff Galloway included later in this chapter, incorporate this type of training.

Many programs advise on the exact mileage that runners should cover when training for a marathon. This begs the question of what science tells us about the optimum training distances for marathon runners. In fact, there are few studies of the actual distances people run in training for a marathon. Thus, we do not really know what the optimum training distance is for the majority of novice marathon runners. The distances advocated in this program have been arrived at empirically, but they are compatible with the findings of a study by Grant et al. (1984). When evaluating the training patterns of 88 runners in the 1982 Glasgow Marathon, Grant and colleagues found that the average distance run in training was 60 km per week for the 12 weeks before the race and ranged from 24 to 103 km. This study also debunked two important myths. First, there is no relationship between weekly training distance and marathon time (as shown by Franklin et al. 1978). Second, despite their apparent inadequate training, the runners did not slow down dramatically after hitting their predicted collapse point at about 27 km.

Thus, they could find no evidence to support the collapse-point theory proposed by Ken Young (1978). This theory holds that runners who do not train more than 101 km per week collapse and are reduced to a shuffle when they race more than three times their average daily training distance for the last eight weeks before the marathon. Finally, as in the study of Franklin et al. (1978), these novice marathoners were unable to predict their marathon times accurately. However, the accuracy of their predictions did improve the closer they were made to race day.

Table 10.1   Noakes' 26-week marathon training program

Week	Monday	Tuesday	Wednesday	Thursday	Friday	Saturday	Sunday
1	30	–	30	–	35	25	40
2	–	25	40	–	30	25	30
3	–	35	30	–	30	25	50
4	–	20	–	35	–	20	40
5	–	40	20	–	45	20	60
6	–	40	20	–	50	20	50
7	–	30	50	–	50	20	70
8	–	40	50	–	50	20	30
9	–	50	40	–	60	20	80
10	–	30	55	30	55	–	70
11	–	60	35	60	40	–	90
12	–	65	40	30	40	–	80
13	–	60	30	50	35	–	100
14	–	70	40	60	40	–	90
15	–	70	30	60	35	–	110
16	–	70	40	70	30	–	100
17	–	70	35	70	35	–	120
18	–	85	40	75	40	–	110
19	–	80	45	70	40	–	130
20	–	80	40	75	25	20	120
21	–	85	35	75	20	20	140
22	40	80	40	40	35	–	130
23	40	90	40	90	40	–	150
24	–	90	40	90	40	–	60
25	40	–	40	30	–	60	20
26	40	20	10	–	–	–	Race

All entries are for running time in minutes.

TIM NOAKES' ADVANCED PROGRAM

During my marathon running career, I achieved personal best times of 2:50:20 (42 km), 3:59:49 (56 km), and 6:49:00 (90 km). I achieved these times on the training programs described here. I present them as an option for those with a similar physiology and training capacity. A measure of my physiological capacity were my best times for certified courses of 1:00:59 for 16 km (3:48 per km) and 1:21:39 for 21 km (3:52 per km).

My personal training approach was similar to Newton's. It included plenty of long, slow distance to the exclusion of speed work. This was because I originally switched to running (from rowing) with the express intention of completing the Comrades Marathon, regardless of finishing time. For the first six to eight years of my running career, I trained exclusively by running long, slow distances. However, I now firmly believe that this training approach, which emphasizes distance training to the virtual exclusion of speed work, although very safe, is not the best way to train for any distance, including ultramarathons. I endorse Roger Bannister's view that high-mileage distance training increases the athlete's speed of recovery from effort but does not increase racing speed. The athlete must achieve a balance by doing just the right amount of speed training, according to the guidelines described in chapter 6.

Thus, the evidence is that the fastest middle-distance and cross-country runners are the best runners at all distances, even up to the very long ultramarathons (see chapter 6). However, there is one important proviso—they need to have superior fatigue resistance. But superior fatigue resistance alone will not make a world-class marathon or ultramarathon runner. For that, both speed and fatigue resistance are required, as shown by the comparison of the running performances of Sebastian Coe, Daniel Komen, and Haile Gebrselassie.

With this background, I include details of the training practices I followed when running marathon races on a regular basis between the ages of 22 and 36. After that, I found that I could no longer train as hard as the program required. However, with the aim of addressing more mature runners, I have included some ideas on how to modify training with advancing age.

Modifying Training for Age

George Sheehan once said that you should never write a book on training and racing for runners. As soon as you did, it would signal that you were a *has-been*. In my case, he was quite correct. After completing the first edition of this book in 1985, I never again ran a decent race.

Of course, I would suggest that the two events were not causally linked. My desire to write the book coincided with my growing perception that I had learned as much as I possibly could from the physical acts of training and racing. I perceived that from then on, my focus should rather become an intellectual one that distilled that practical experience with the growing body of scientific knowledge on running and the physiology of the body. But I also suspect that these intellectual justifications occurred at a time when I first began to notice that running was becoming less easy, partly because of age and partly because of the effects of 15 years of heavy training and frequent racing.

The point is that both increasing age and years of heavy training reduce the amount of training that you can do. This is shown somewhat dramatically in the lifetime running experience of Basil Davis (see figure 2.19). After age 45, Davis' ability to train fell precipitously, despite his continuing conscious desire to train and race at a high level.

The training programs presented in this book were all designed for men and women in the prime of their athletic careers. The problem is that we do not know how they should be modified for older athletes, since few have written on this topic. Runners, you see, are never meant to age or to become so frail that they are unable to train as hard as did the world-class athletes in their prime.

The best advice I can give is that if you are over 45 or if you have been competing for more than 15 to 20 years, you should not try to train according to the guidelines given in the training tables in this and other chapters. Rather, you should aim to achieve a certain percentage of what is written, say 60% to 75%. As you learn more about your body's abilities, you can modify that percentage accordingly. Remember always to follow the 6th Law of Training (At first, try to achieve as much as possible on a minimum of training).

A general rule is that older runners perform better on less training since the margin between optimum training and overtraining (see chapter 7) is much less, which makes it easier to overstress the older body and to perform poorly as a result. The runners at greatest risk are those who have always run and who were once competitive. It takes great insight and wisdom to realize that the glory days are past and that a new perspective must be reached.

The initial goal of my hard training program (table 10.2) was to condition myself to be able to run 110 km per week, a distance that I have also found to be optimal for the majority of recreational runners who have major time constraints.

Table 10.2 Noakes' typical base training week

Day	Morning	Evening
Monday	5 km	7 km
Tuesday	7 km	7 km
Wednesday	7 km	7 km
Thursday	7 km	7 km
Friday	5 km	5 km
Saturday	24–32 km	—
Sunday	—	8–14 km
Total	96–110 km	

Increasing Volume

For the first 10 weeks or so of my more intensive training program, I would gradually increase my training from 90 to 110 km per week. At first, my average training speed would be slower than 5:00 per km, I would struggle up each and every hill, and the longer runs would be particularly tiring. I judged the stress of these runs not only by how I felt during each run, but also by how quickly I recovered after the run. A run that had been too long or too hard would make me want to sleep for an hour or two; I would be unable to do any mental work that day, and the following day I would run tired. A run that had been just the right length would leave me a little tired, and I would need to sleep for only a short time, after which I would be able to do an hour or two of mental work, should I so choose. By the following day's run, my body would have recovered sufficiently to ensure that my gentle recovery run of between 6 and 14 km would be effortless. During this phase, I would run three to five short races of up to 16 km. Any longer races that I might enter would constitute long training runs.

This break-in phase lasted for 10 to 12 weeks, during which time my long weekend runs would not be less than 24 km and not longer than 32 km. The major indications that this phase had had its desired effect were that I started to finish the long runs so fresh that I wanted to run farther on the following long run. At the same time, my average training speed increased, and the hills that I ran became much easier. When this happened, I was ready to move on to the second phase of my program, the so-called peaking phase.

Most of this training was done to and from work over a hilly terrain. During my Tuesday and Thursday afternoon runs, I would sometimes include slightly faster runs, either track or hill repetitions.

Interestingly, studies have been unable to show that training more than 120 km per week produces any additional physiological benefits for competitive racers (Sjodin and Svedenhag 1985). This weekly distance is used by the middle-distance athletes trained by Bill Bowerman and is also advocated by Herb Elliott (Lenton 1981). This is about half the distance I would normally run when not training hard. An important reason I did not run farther in training is that if I started increasing my mileage, say up to 160 km per week, I began to feel that I was doing nothing but running. I imagine that I felt much the same as Ron Daws did while training for the 1968 Olympic Marathon in the dark mornings and evenings of a Minnesota winter (Daws 1977). He wrote that there were times when he returned from his runs not knowing whether he should be going to bed or getting ready for a day's work. Once I reached that state, I was no longer able to maintain my interest in running. I had approached the point Mark Allen wrote about in the early years of his training for the Hawaiian Ironman Triathlon (see chapter 6). He was prepared to do only as much as he considered necessary to win the race, whereas he later learned that the race required more. Only when he trained as much as he now thought the race required did he start to win. I never crossed that divide between being average and achieving something better. Perhaps I had come to accept that on account of my physiology, it was not worth the effort.

In addition, I discovered that heavy training not only affected my creativity, but it also interfered with other commitments, inducing other adverse stresses such as inadequate sleep, excessive fatigue, family displeasure, and missed deadlines. While gentle running enhances a person's productivity and creativity, too much training has the opposite effect. Arthur Newton recognized this, for he states:

Aggressively serious physical effort left me with a positive disinclination to study anything that needed real brain work. So much of my available energy was used for training that only a mere trickle was left over for recreational purposes, not nearly enough to permit me to delve into metaphysics or similar intricate matters which always beckoned me. I regretted it all the time, for I felt I was losing a great deal in the way of education, yet to neglect even a small part of my training might make all the difference between reasonable certainty and chance, and I dislike the latter. (Newton 1947a, page 66).

I suspect that the biochemical explanation for this is that heavy training causes depletion of certain brain chemicals, the reduction of which also explains the relaxing and tranquilizing effect of running and, in the long term, the overtraining syndrome. This effect also explains why serious runners cannot hold down jobs that demand excessive mental effort, particularly in the afternoons and especially during periods of intensive training. Training burns up creative energy, leaving little space for other intellectual matters.

The converse also applies. While engrossed in writing this book—a task many times more demanding than preparing for the Comrades Marathon—I sometimes found it difficult to run regularly and for any reasonable duration. The creative energy needed to coax me outdoors had been expended in the compilation of these pages.

Indeed, if there is one contentious issue in training for distance running, it is the exact value of running many miles at these low exercise intensities. That the majority of runners spend most of their time training at quite low exercise intensities has been shown by a number of studies. For example, a study of 13 elite New Zealand distance runners (D.M. Robinson et al. 1991) found that their average training intensity was characterized by the following: their average heart rate was 145 beats per minute; their average percentage $\dot{V}O_2$max was 64%; and their average running speed was 15.6 km per hour, which corresponds to 77% of the speed at which the lactate turnpoint occurred. Remarkably, only 4% of their training involved running at speeds greater than that at which the lactate turnpoint occurred.

Another study found that the average training pace of a group of top German female marathoners corresponded to only 60% $\dot{V}O_2$max, or less than 77% of the running speed at which their blood lactate concentrations reached 4 mmol per liter.

Similarly, Gilman and Wells (1993) found that most of the training of a group of women of average ability training for an 8-km race was at an easy or moderate intensity, with very little training (less than 9%) at a hard intensity. In contrast, 70% of the 8-km race was run at heart rates equivalent to 96% of maximum. The authors also concluded that the runners had overestimated the volume of high-intensity training they performed and that they would have benefited from the use of heart rate monitors.

Our own more recent studies (Mbambo 1999) showed that, whereas heart rates were in excess of 170 beats per minute for 62% of their racing time, a group of 10 long-distance runners training under a coach ran at those heart rates for only 10% of their training time when doing long, slow distance and for only 25% of that time when doing high-intensity training (figure 10.2). In that study, the average duration of the races and the long, slow distance (LSD) and high-intensity training (HIT) sessions were similar (about 40 to 60 minutes). Hence, to accumulate the same total number of heart beats at rates faster than 170 beats per minute, athletes would need to run about three high-intensity training sessions for each 10- to 15-km race that they ran. Mbambo (1999) also showed that during races heart rates were always higher than predicted from measurements made at the same running speed during training, and that running in the heat predictably elevated the heart rate.

In chapter 2, I discuss recent studies that suggest that cutting out much of this slow training, but retaining the speed training, does not impair performance, at least over shorter distances of 5 to 10 km. However, I am not yet ready to conclude that all low-intensity training is unnecessary. Certainly, provided the total training volume is less than 110 km per week, this low-intensity training would not seem detrimental. But its value for running performances, certainly over the shorter distances, has not yet been proven. Recall also the evidence in chapter 6 showing how well many elite runners have performed on relatively little training. The major benefits of heavy training volumes in excess of 120 km per week are to increase the strength of the connective tissue in the muscles and the resistance to the eccentric muscle damage that produces fatigue after running 30 or more kilometers, which then increases your ability to keep running beyond the marathon wall.

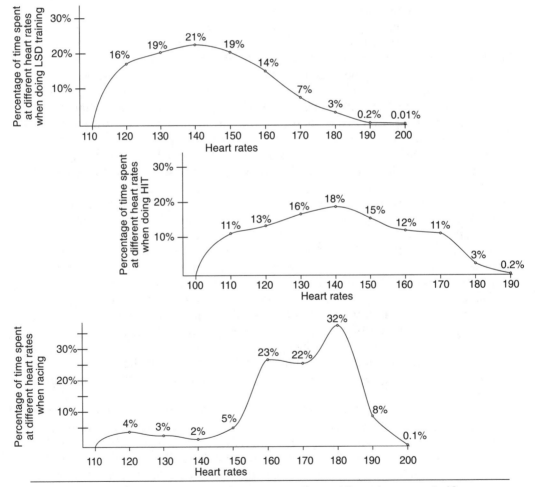

Figure 10.2   The percentage training and racing times spent at different heart rates in 10 runners.
LSD = long slow distance training , HIT = high-intensity training.
From data of Z. Mbambo (1999).

Peaking

The aim of peaking is to increase the training load further by adding speed training sessions, in the form of either intervals, speed play (fartlek), time-trials, or short-distance races (5 to 16 km) for a period of four to six weeks before competitions. As described in chapter 5, this form of training produces dramatic changes in racing speed. But if maintained for too long, it can induce early symptoms of overtraining (chapter 7). Thus, it is a high-risk/high-reward period of your training.

The next phase of my 20-week hard training cycle differed, depending on the length of the race for which I was preparing. For shorter distances, I emphasized mostly speed training and maintained the weekly training distance at about 120 km per week. For ultramarathon, I emphasized distance training and long weekend runs, only adding speed training when I had completed the heavy distance training.

During the peaking phase (table 10.3), I would emphasize speed training sessions, either on a Tuesday or a Thursday, and would run two or three races of 10 to 16 km (but no farther). I found that these are the optimum racing distances for preparing for both the 10-km race and the marathon. Longer races tend to cause more severe muscle damage from which recovery is slow. Also, from a psychological viewpoint, the marathon breaks up neatly into two 16-km races and one 10-km race. Thus, during the marathon race, I would concentrate on running as close to my best times for each of these distances as was possible. When properly prepared, it is remarkable how close you can come to this goal. More general ideas on speed training are included in chapter 5.

During the second-last week before the marathon, I would reduce my training to between 50 and 80 km of easy running and would rest and carbohydrate load for the last three days before the race. During the intervening four days, I would incorporate three days of mild carbohydrate restriction and runs of 12 to 18 km, depending on how I felt.

The value of either procedure is not really known. Recall that carbohydrate restriction is not necessary to optimize carbohydrate storage during carbohydrate

Table 10.3 Noakes' six-week marathon peaking program			
Day	**Morning**	**Evening**	**Effort**
Monday	5	7	Jog
Tuesday	7	16	Moderate/hard
Wednesday	7	7	Jog
Thursday	5	16–21	Moderate/hard
Friday	5	5	Jog
Saturday	10–16-km race	—	Race
Sunday	20–32 km	—	Moderate
Total	≈120 km		

loading (chapter 3). Also, the ideal taper for marathon and ultramarathon runners has not yet been established in a scientific trial. The optimum taper for a short-distance race (800 m to 5 km) might well be that described by Shepley et al. (1992) in which high-intensity interval training of decreasing volume is performed for the last five days before race day. For the long ultramarathon races (over 100 km), it may be better to continue heavy training right up to race day, as suggested by Cooper (1990) (see chapter 11).

My bias is to believe that there should be more rest and less running during the tapering phase and certainly more days in which you do no training at all. In chapter 5, I refer to the Zatopek phenomenon, in which elite athletes have achieved remarkable performances after a period of reduced training—in the case of Zatopek, even after being hospitalized for two days before his record-breaking performances. Some 30 years since this phenomenon was first recognized, I realize that I ran one of my best 56-km ultramarathon races after a period of enforced rest. I ran the race a mere three weeks after undergoing surgery to my foot, which prevented me from running for two weeks. In the last week before the race, I had only been able to fit in a few jogs. Without trying, I ran a time that was less than 40 seconds slower than my best over the distance, achieved three years later after a much more intensive training program but during a race for which I did not taper properly. The last word on the ideal taper has yet to be written.

JEFF GALLOWAY'S PROGRAMS

Galloway's classic books (Galloway 1984; 1996) also include training programs for athletes wishing to run their first marathon (table 10.4) or marathons in under 4:00:00 (table 10.5) and in less than 2:39:00 (table 10.6) as well as other intermediate times (Galloway 1996). The training programs are very similar, with quite small differences in the total volume of training, the number of intervals run, and the speed of those intervals. The result is that runners wishing to develop their own programs for a sub-3:30:00 marathon, for example, would choose a program that falls between that for a 4:00:00 and a 3:00:00 marathon.

Galloway's key training principles are to run slow enough so that you can hold a normal conversation when training and so that you can finish each run tired but strong. On run/walk days, walk for 2:00 to 3:00 and then jog for 1:00 to 2:00. Progress to walking 3:00 and jogging 2:00. Advanced beginners can walk 2:00 followed by a 2:00 jog. Always alternate walking and running to speed recovery without losing training benefits. Best results in the chosen marathon race are achieved if you have covered the full distance in training. If you have been unable to complete the full distance in training, run slowly and take more walking breaks during your chosen marathon race. Gradually introduce your body to eating and drinking during your long runs.

Galloway's beginners' marathon program (table 10.4) is a 26-week training program for those whose goal is merely to finish the marathon. The program requires that the athlete run only three to six times per week. During the week (Monday to Friday), the distances never exceed 7 km. The key to the training program is the long weekend training runs, which start at 5 km and increase quite rapidly to 16 km after seven weeks. Thereafter, a long weekend run usually alternates with a shorter run; the longer runs increase (every second week) by 3 km so that by the end of week 26 the athlete is ready to run the marathon.

Week	Monday	Tuesday	Wednesday	Thursday	Friday	Saturday	Sunday
1	W 30	RW 30	W 30	RW 30	W 30	Off	5–7 km RW
2	W 30	RW 30	W 30	RW 30	W 30	Off	6–8 km RW
3	W 30	RW 30	W 30	RW 30	W 30	Off	8–10 km RW
4	W 30	RW 30	W 30	RW 30	W 30	Off	10–12 km RW
5	W 30	RW 30	W 30	RW 30	W 30	Off	12–14 km RW
6	W 30	RW 30	W 30	RW 30	W 30	Off	14–15 km R
7	W 30	RW 30	W 30	RW 30	W 30	Off	15–16 km R
8	W 30	RW 30	W 30	RW 30	W 30	Off	16–18 km R
9	W 30	RW 30	W 30	RW 30	W 30	Off	18–19 km RW
10	W 30	RW 30	W 30	RW 30	W 30	Off	10 km R
11	W 30	RW 30	W 30	RW 30	W 30	Off	20–22 km R
12	W 30	RW 30	W 30	RW 30	W 30	Off	12 km R
13	W 30	RW 30	W 30	RW 30	W 30	Off	24–25 km R
14	W 30	RW 30	W 30	RW 30	W 30	Off	12 km R
15	W 30	RW 30	W 30	RW 30	W 30	Off	27–29 km R
16	W 30	RW 30	W 30	RW 30	W 30	Off	13 km R
17	W 30	RW 30	W 30	RW 30	W 30	Off	30–32 km R
18	W 30	RW 30	W 30	RW 30	W 30	Off	14–15 km R
19	W 30	RW 30	W 30	RW 30	W 30	Off	14–15 km R
20	W 30	RW 30	W 30	RW 30	W 30	Off	35–37 km R
21	W 30	RW 30	W 30	RW 30	W 30	Off	14–16 km R
22	W 30	RW 30	W 30	RW 30	W 30	Off	14–16 km R
23	W 30	RW 30	W 30	RW 30	W 30	Off	40–42 km R
24	W 30	RW 30	W 30	RW 30	W 30	Off	14–16 km R
25	W 30	RW 30	W 30	RW 30	W 30	Off	14–16 km R
26	W 30	Off	W 30	Off	W 30	Off	Marathon
27	W 45	RW 45	W 30–60	RW 40	W 30–60	Off	12–16 km RW
28	W 45	RW 45	W 30–60	RW 45	W 30–60	Off	14–24 km RW
29	W 45	RW 45	W 30–60	RW 45	W 30–60	Off	19–32 km RW

All entries are running or walking times in minutes or distances in kilometers.
From J. Galloway (1996, p. A6). Refer also to Galloway's Web site: **www.runinjuryfree.com.**

Table 10.5 Galloway's 4-hour marathon training program

Week	Monday	Tuesday	Wednesday	Thursday	Friday	Saturday	Sunday
1	XT	R 40–50	R 20–30	XT	R 40–50	Off	4–6 hills (8–11 km)
2	XT	R 40–50	R 20–30	XT	R 40–50	Off	5-km race (9–11 km)
3	XT	R 40–50	R 20–30	XT	R 40–50	Off	7–8 hills (11–13 km)
4	XT	R 40–50	R 20–30	XT	R 40–50	Off	9–10 hills (13–14 km)
5	XT	R 45–50	R 25–35	XT	R 45–50	Off	5-km race (14–16 km)
6	XT	R 45–50	R 25–35	XT	R 45–50	Off	3–5 × 1600 m (18 km)
7	XT	R 45–50	R 25–35	XT	R 45–50	Off	5-km race (13 km)
8	XT	R 45–50	R 25–35	XT	R 45–50	Off	5–7 × 1600 (22 km)
9	XT	R 45–50	R 25–35	XT	R 45–50	Off	5-km race (11 km)
10	XT	R 45–55	R 25–40	XT	R 45–55	Off	24–26 km easy
11	XT	R 45–55	R 25–40	XT	R 45–55	Off	5-km race (14 km)
12	XT	R 45–55	R 25–40	XT	R 45–55	Off	27–29 km easy
13	XT	R 45–55	R 25–40	XT	R 45–55	Off	6–8 × 1600 m
14	XT	R 45–55	R 25–40	XT	R 45–55	Off	30–32 km easy
15	XT	R 45–55	R 25–40	XT	R 45–55	Off	5-km race (16 km)
16	XT	R 45–55	R 25–40	XT	R 45–55	Off	6–8 × 1600 m
17	XT	R 45–50	R 25–40	XT	R 45–55	Off	35–37 km easy
18	XT	R 45–55	R 25–40	XT	R 45–55	Off	5-km race
19	XT	R 45–55	R 25–40	XT	R 45–55	Off	4–6 × 1600 m
20	XT	R 45–55	R 25–40	XT	R 45–55	Off	40–42 km easy
21	XT	R 45–55	R 25–40	XT	R 45–55	Off	5-km race
22	XT	R 45–55	R 25–40	XT	R 45–55	Off	3–5 × 1600 m
23	XT	R 45–55	R 25–40	XT	R 45–55	Off	43–45 km easy
24	XT	R 45–55	R 25–40	XT	R 45–55	Off	5 km or 4 × 1600 m
25	XT	R 45–55	R 20–25	XT	R 45–55	Off	4 × 1600 m
26	R 40	Off	R 30	Off	R 30	Off	Marathon
27	W 45	RW 30	W 30–60	RW 40	W 30–60	Off	RW 11–16 km
28	W 45	RW 45	W 30–60	RW 45	W 30–60	Off	RW 14–24 km
29	W 45	RW 45	W 30–60	RW 45	W 30–60	Off	RW 19–32 km

XT refers to cross-training. Numbers in parentheses for Sundays refer to total distance to be covered in the session including warm-up, warm-down, and recovery between intervals. Long runs should be run at 1:15 per km slower than you can run at that distance. Walk for 1:00 every 4:00 to 6:00; every 6:00 for distances up to 28 km, every 4:00 m for longer distances. Hills should be run at 10-km pace. Mile repetitions (1600 m) should be at marathon goal pace (5:41 per km). Use time in 5-km races to predict marathon performance. Run at projected marathon pace for 2 to 5 km on Wednesdays and Fridays. Running pace on Tuesdays should be 38 seconds per km slower than projected marathon pace. When in doubt, run slower, run less, or rest.

From J. Galloway (1996, p.A14). Refer also to Galloway's Web site: **www.runinjuryfree.com.**

Table 10.6	Galloway's 2:39:00 marathon training program						
Week	Monday	Tuesday	Wednesday	Thursday	Friday	Saturday	Sunday
1	XT	R 40–50	R 20–30	XT	R 40–50	Off	4–6 hills (8–10 km)
2	XT	R 40–50	R 20–30	XT	R 40–50	Off	5-km race (9–10 km)
3	XT	R 40–50	R 20–30	XT	R 40–50	Off	7–8 hills (11–13 km)
4	XT	R 40–50	R 20–30	XT	R 40–50	Off	9–10 hills (13–15 km)
5	XT	R 45–50	R 25–35	XT	R 45–50	Off	5-km race (14–16 km)
6	XT	R 45–50	R 25–35	XT	R 45–50	Off	5–7 × 1600 m (18 km)
7	XT	R 45–50	R 25–35	XT	R 45–50	Off	5-km race (13 km)
8	XT	R 45–50	R 25–35	XT	R 45–50	Off	6–8 × 1600 m (20 km)
9	XT	R 45–50	R 25–35	XT	R 45–50	Off	8–10 × 1600 m (20 km)
10	XT	R 45–55	R 25–40	XT	R 45–55	Off	24–26 km easy
11	XT	R 45–55	R 25–40	XT	R 45–55	Off	5-km race (14 km)
12	XT	R 45–55	R 25–40	XT	R 45–55	Off	27–29 km easy
13	XT	R 45–55	R 25–40	XT	R 45–55	Off	10–11 × 1600 m
14	XT	R 45–55	R 25–40	XT	R 45–55	Off	30–32 km easy
15	XT	R 45–55	R 25–40	XT	R 45–55	Off	5-km race (16 km)
16	XT	R 45–55	R 25–40	XT	R 45–55	Off	11–13 × 1600 m
17	XT	R 45–50	R 25–40	XT	R 45–55	Off	35–37 km easy
18	XT	R 45–55	R 25–40	XT	R 45–55	Off	5-km race
19	XT	R 45–55	R 25–40	XT	R 45–55	Off	5–8 × 1600 m
20	XT	R 45–55	R 25–40	XT	R 45–55	Off	42–44 km easy
21	XT	R 45–55	R 25–40	XT	R 45–55	Off	5-km race
22	XT	R 45–55	R 25–40	XT	R 45–55	Off	5–8 × 1600 m
23	XT	R 45–55	R 25–40	XT	R 45–55	Off	45–48 km easy
24	XT	R 45–55	R 25–40	XT	R 45–55	Off	5 km or 4 × 1600 m
25	XT	R 45–55	R 20–25	XT	R 45–55	Off	4 × 1600 m
26	R 40	Off	R 30	Off	R 30	Off	Marathon
27	W 45	RW 30	W 30–60	RW 40	W 30–60	Off	R/W 11–16 km
28	W 45	RW 45	W 30–60	RW 45	W 30–60	Off	R/W 15–24 km
29	W 45	RW 45	W 30–60	RW 45	W 30–60	Off	R/W 19–32 km

Guidelines as for table 10.5. Run the long runs 1:15 per km slower than you could. Alternate walking and running during the long runs by walking 1:00 minute every 8:00 to 10:00 from the beginning of every long run. Walk for 1:00 every 1600 m in runs over 28 km. Hills are run at 10-km race pace and 1600 m repeats should be in 5:40. The number in parentheses after hill and speed sessions and races refers to the total distance for that session, including warm-up and cool-down.

From J. Galloway (1996, p. A24). Refer also to Galloway's Web site: **www.runinjuryfree.com.**

Galloway places great emphasis on walking in training and especially in racing. Thus, the program in table 10.4 enables you to finish the marathon without spending an inordinate amount of time training. The key is to emphasize the walking component if you are to benefit optimally. Galloway's training programs for faster runners include some high-intensity training sessions.

JOE HENDERSON'S PROGRAMS

Joe Henderson is one of the most prolific writers on running, having written more than a dozen books, many of them classics. Henderson is perhaps best known for coining the phrase *LSD (long slow distance)*. He also penned the loving biography of running's greatest writer, George Sheehan (Henderson 1995).

His marathon programs (Henderson 1997) include 100-day marathon training schedules for "cruisers, pacers and racers." These programs are built around different combinations of five common ingredients—long runs, half-long runs, fast runs or races, easy runs, and rest days. The programs are flexible and enable athletes to tailor their training to their personal needs and choices. The three programs differ in the frequency and amount of training, the length of the long runs, and the inten-

Table 10.7 Henderson's cruiser training program			
Week	Big days	Other runs	Rest days
1	19–22 km	R 30–45 × 3–4	2–3
2	19–22 km	R 30–45 × 3–4	2–3
3	19–22 km	R 30–45 × 3–4	2–3
4	19–22 km	R 30–45 × 3–4	2–3
5	19–22 km	R 30–45 × 3–4	2–3
6	19–22 km	R 30–45 × 3–4	2–3
7	19–22 km	R 30–45 × 3–4	2–3
8	19–22 km	R 30–45 × 3–4	2–3
9	19–22 km	R 30–45 × 3–4	2–3
10	19–22 km	R 30–45 × 3–4	2–3
11	19–22 km	R 30–45 × 3–4	2–3
12	19–22 km	R 30–45 × 3–4	2–3
13	19–22 km	R 30–45 × 3–4	2–3
14	Marathon	R 30–45 × 3–4	2–3
15	19–22 km	R short and easy × 3–4	3–4

Abbreviations as for the other tables in this chapter. This program is built on short runs during the week with progressively longer weekend runs; the latter are the focus of the training program.
Adapted, by permission, from Henderson (1997, p. 13).

sity of the hard training sessions. The cruisers' program introduces the concept of walking frequently in training. Thus, at the start, the cruiser is encouraged to walk for at least a minute after 1.6 km of a long run; the first long run of between 20 and 23 km takes place in week 1 (table 10.7).

Clearly, this program is meant for those who have already been running for some time, as it is inappropriate for the complete beginner, who must first start with a few weeks of walking. Nevertheless, Henderson makes the important point that those runners who wish to finish a marathon, regardless of time, should include walking in both their racing and training, according to the Galloway approach.

The pacers' program is essentially the same as the cruisers' program except that there are fewer rest days per week and the "other runs" are between 30 and 60 minutes. The racers' program incorporates only one rest day per week and includes one day of fast training, between 2 and 5 km or a 5- to 10-km race on the third, sixth, ninth, and eleventh weeks.

ART LIBERMAN'S BEGINNERS' PROGRAM

Art Liberman coaches via the Internet (**www.geocities.com/Yosemite/6004/index.html**). His training program includes four days of training each week with three days of complete rest (table 10.8). The emphasis is on the long training runs at the weekend. To succeed on this program, you must be prepared to walk frequently in both training and racing. Liberman suggests that you walk for 60 seconds for every 10 minutes that you run.

This is an ambitious program. I would only advise those with a previous history of athleticism (that is, people who always showed competence in other physical

Table 10.8 Liberman's beginner's training program for a 5:00:00 or slower marathon

Week	Mon	Tue	Wed	Thu	Fri	Sat	Sun	Week's total
1	Rest	6	Rest	8	Rest	6	16	36
2	Rest	6	Rest	8	Rest	6	16	36
3	Rest	6	Rest	8	Rest	6	16	36
4	Rest	6	Rest	8	Rest	6	16	36
5	Rest	6	Rest	8	Rest	6	16	36
6	Rest	6	Rest	8	Rest	6	16	36
7	Rest	6	Rest	8	Rest	6	16	36
8	Rest	6	Rest	8	Rest	6	16	36
9	Rest	6	Rest	8	Rest	6	16	36
10	Rest	6	Rest	8	Rest	6	16	36
11	Rest	6	Rest	8	Rest	6	16	36
12	Rest	6	Rest	8	Rest	6	16	36

Distances are in kilometers. Liberman proposes that the longer training runs be run/walked or run at a comfortable training pace. Shorter runs can be run faster than marathon goal pace, but the longer runs must be at slower than goal pace. From Liberman (1999, p. 67). Permission granted by Art Liberman, State of the Art Marathon. For more on beginning marathon running, access Liberman's Web site: **www.runinjuryfree.com.**

sports but who have only recently started running) to attempt it. The advantage of the beginners' program that we developed (table 10.2) is that it is suitable for all beginners, regardless of athletic ability.

BOB WILLIAMS' ADVANCED PROGRAM

Bob Williams is a veteran coach from Portland, Oregon. His program (table 10.9) is designed for athletes who have run consistently for three years or more, who have completed at least three marathons, and who want to run faster. The keys to his 12-week program are twice-weekly speed sessions incorporating

- tempo runs done at about 12 seconds per km slower than 10-km race pace (they should also cover no more than half of the total distance listed for each tempo session on table 10.9);
- pace runs at marathon race pace;
- short intervals of 200 to 400 m at 5-km race pace; and
- long intervals of 800 to 1600 m at 10-km race pace.

Table 10.9   Williams' advanced marathon training program for a 3-hour marathon on 65 to 95 km training each week

Week	Mon	Tue	Wed	Thu	Fri	Sat	Sun	Total
1	8	5 × 800 m	8	5 (tempo)	Rest	24	6	69
2	8	3 × 1600 m	8	16	Rest	20	6	69
3	8	4 (tempo)	8	8 × 200 m	Rest	28	5	78
4	8	4 × 1600 m	8	9 (pace)	6	0	Race	64
5	8	6 × 200 m	8	5 × 1000 m	8	34	5	83
6	8	8 × 400 m	8	7 (tempo)	8	20	Rest	69
7	8	5 × 1600 m	8	16	Rest	37	6	90
8	8	8 (pace)	8	8 × 200 m	5	0	Race	64
9	8	6 × 200 m	8	5 × 1600 m	8	5	40	96
10	8	8	8	6 × 800 m	Rest	10 (pace)	5	64
11	8	5 × 1600 m	8	16	Rest	20	Rest	64
12	8	5 × 1600 m	8	6	5	Rest	Marathon	80

Distances are in kilometers unless indicated. Williams advises that the key workouts are on Tuesdays, Thursdays, and Saturdays. Training on the other days should be at an easy pace. Tempo runs are at 12 seconds per km slower than 10-km race pace. Gradually develop that pace after a 3 to 5 km warm-up and hold that pace for the distance indicated. Then cool down for another 3 to 5 km. Pace runs are at race pace and follow the usual 3 to 5 km warm-up to that pace, followed by a 3 to 5 km cool-down. Short intervals (<800 m) are run at 5-km race pace with a 400-m jog between intervals, following the same 3 to 5 km warm-up and cool-down procedure for other faster sessions. Long intervals (800 to 1600 m) are run at 10-km race pace.
From R. Williams (1999, p. 70). Reproduced by permission of Robert Williams.

He also proposes that long runs be at 35 to 55 seconds per km slower than your marathon goal pace.

PETE PFITZINGER'S ADVANCED PROGRAM

I reviewed Pete Pfitzinger's training ideas in chapter 5. The features of his serious marathon training program, for those who are able to run more than 96 km per week, are listed in table 10.10. His program includes training sessions at the four different intensities.

Table 10.10 Pfitzinger's advanced marathon training program

Weeks to goal	Long run 1	Long run 2	Lactate threshold workouts	V̇O$_2$max workouts	Basic speed	Weekly distance	% of peak
17	24	16	—	—	—	96	70
16	26	18	—	—	10 × 100 m	100	74
15	27	18	2 × 2.4 LT intervals	—	—	100	78
14	24	18	2 × 2.8 LT intervals	—	—	109	80
13	29	19	—	6 × 1 km at 8—10-km race pace	—	112	82
12	24	19	2 × 3.2 LT intervals	—	—	112	82
11	30	19	—	6 × 1.4 at 8—100km race pace	—	118	87
10	26	21	6.4 tempo run	—	—	106	78
9	32	21	8 tempo run	—	—	125	92
8	27	21	—	—	12 × 100 m	125	92
7	34	22	10 tempo run	—	—	131	96
6	27	22	Last 3.2 of LR2	—	12 × 100 m	125	92
5	35	22	—	—	12 × 100 m	136	100
4	24	19	8—15 tune-up race	5 × 600 m at 6-km race pace	—	121	89
3	32	22	—	—	12 × 100 m	121	89

Three-week taper

Week	Mon	Tue	Wed	Thu	Fri	Sat	Sun	Mileage
2	10	12	18 with 12 × 100 m	13	8	8—15 tune up race	27	106
1	Off	10	3 × 1.6 at 10-km race pace	15	10	10	21	78
Race week	8	8	13 with 5 depletion run	8	Off	7	Goal race	43 (up to race day)

All distances are in kilometers. Only the key workouts are listed. Other training days should be used either for recovery or for easier running to fulfill the week's listed training distance.

Adapted, by permission, from Pfitzinger and Douglas (1999, pp. 66–67).

JACK DANIELS' ADVANCED PROGRAM

Jack Daniels' 24-week advanced marathon training program is presented in table 10.11. The different training intensities that he advocates were also described in chapter 5.

Table 10.11			Daniels' advanced marathon training program				
Week	Day 1	Day 2	Day 3	Day 4	Day 5	Day 6	Day 7
1–3	Easy	Easy	Easy	Easy	Easy	Easy	Easy
4–6	Long (25%)	Easy 5–6 × 00:20–00:30 strides	Easy 5–6 × 00:20–00:30 strides	Easy	Easy 5–6 × 00:20–00:30 strides	Easy 5–6 × 00:20–00:30 strides	Easy
7 80%	Long (25%) or a maximum of 02:30:00	Easy 5–6 × 00:20–00:30strides	Easy	Easy plus 03:00 easy; 8% (10)	Sets of 4:00 hard	Easy 5–6 × 00:20–00:30 strides	Easy
8 80%	20:00 at T pace; 5–6 strides	Easy 5–6 × 00:20–00:30 strides	Easy easy, 8%	Sets of 04:00 hardplus 03:00 (10)	Easy 5–6 × 00:20–00:30 strides	Easy	Easy
9	5 × 05:00–06:00 at T pace with 01:00 rest; 60:00 easy	Easy	Easy	Easy 5–6 × 00:20–00:30 strides	Sets of 1000, 1200, or 1600 m at I pace; 03:00–05:00 recovery 8% (10)	Easy 5–6 × 00:20–00:30 strides	Easy
10 90%	Long 25% (2:30:00)	Easy 5–6 × 00:20–00:30 strides	Easy	Sets of 1000, 1200, or 1600 m at I pace; 03:00–05:00 recovery 8% (10)	Easy	Easy 5–6 × 00:20–00:30 strides	Easy
11 90%	2 × 10:00–12:00 at T pace with 02:00 recovery; 80:00 (16 km) easy; 15:00–20:00 at T pace	Easy	Easy 5–6 × 00:20–00:30 strides	Sets of 04:00 hard (5-km pace) with 03:00–05:00 recovery 8% (10)	Easy	Easy	Long 25% (2:30:00)
12 70%	Easy	6 sets of 05:00–06:00 at T pace with 01:00 recovery 5–6 × 00:20–00:30 strides	Easy	Easy 5–6 × 00:20–00:30 strides	Sets of 1000, 1200, or1600 m at I pace; 03:00–05:00 recovery 8% (10)	Easy	Easy
13 100%	Long 25% (2:30:00)	Easy 5–6 × 00:20–00:30 strides	Easy	4 × 10:00–12:00 at T pace with 02:00 recovery	Easy 5–6 × 00:20–00:30 strides	Easy	Easy

The percentage below the week number indicates the percentage of the peak training distance that should be covered during the week. Other abbreviations are the same as in table 9.2. Adapted, by permission, from J. Daniels (1998, pp. 250–53).

Week	Day 1	Day 2	Day 3	Day 4	Day 5	Day 6	Day 7
14 90%	4–55 × 05:00–06:00 at T pace with 01:00 recovery; 60:00 easy; 15:00–20:00 at T pace	Easy 5–6 × 00:20–00:30 strides	Easy	Easy	4 × 05:00–06:00 at T pace with 01:00 recovery; rest for 05:00; 3–5 × 06:00 at T pace with 01:00 recovery	Easy	Easy
15 80%	19 km (1:40:00) at projected marathon pace	Easy 5–6 × 00:20–00:30 strides	Easy	Easy	15:00–20:00 at T pace with 03:00 recovery; repeat above; 10:00–20:00 at T pace	Easy	Easy
16 100%	Long (02:30:00)	Easy 5–6 × 00:20–00:30 strides	Easy	20:00 at T pace; 10:00 jog; 20:00 at T pace	Easy 5–6 × 00:20–00:30 strides	Easy	Easy
17 90%	2 × 10:00–12:00 at T pace with 02:00 recovery; 80:00 (16 km) easy; 15:00–20:00 at T pace	Easy 5–6 × 00:20–00:30 strides	Easy	Easy	8 × 05:00–06:00 at T pace with 00:30 recovery	Easy	Easy
18 70%	24 km (2:00:00) at projected marathon pace	Easy 5–6 × 00:20–00:30 strides	Easy	Easy	4 × 10:00–12:00 at T pace with 02:00 recovery 5–6 × 00:20–00:30 strides	Easy	Easy
19 100%	35 km (2:30:00)	Easy	Easy	Easy	20:00 easy; 15:00–20:00 at T pace; repeat	Easy	Easy
20 80%	4 × 05:00–06:00 at T pace with 01:00 recovery; 16 km (80:00) easy; 4 × 05:00–06:00 at T pace with 01:00 recovery	Easy	Easy	Easy	60:00 easy; 6 × 05:00–06:00 at T pace; 15:00 easy	Easy	Easy
21 70%	35 km (2:30:00)	Easy	Easy	35:00–40:00 Easy; 15:00–20:00 at T pace; repeat	Easy	Easy	Easy
22 70%	24 km (2:00:00) at projected marathon pace	Easy	Easy	Easy	4 × 10:00–12:00 at T pace with 02:00 recovery	Easy	Easy
23 80%	2 × 10:00–15:00 at T pace; 811 km easy	Easy (14%)	Easy	Easy (10–12%)	3 × 10:00–12:00 at T pace with 02:00 recovery	Easy (10–15%)	Easy (10–12%)
24	24 km (2:00:00)	Easy (16%)	4 × 04:00 with full recovery	Easy (16%)	Easy (10–15%)	20:00–30:00 easy	20:00–30:00 easy or race

INDIVIDUAL RESULTS MAY VARY

Bear in mind that all training programs are essentially fraudulent because they presume the outcome of an experiment (the time for running a certain distance), the result of which is necessarily unpredictable, unless of course, the athlete's inherent athletic ability is known and appropriate reckoning has been made.

It is misleading to think (and this is certainly not what Jeff Galloway, for example, is suggesting) that an athlete who runs 4 hours on the program listed in table 10.5 will progressively improve to sub-3:00 and then to sub-2:39 by following the programs for those times. The extent of your progress will be determined by your inborn, hereditary abilities. However, the faster your time in that first marathon, the greater your potential, particularly if you trained relatively lightly.

As a novice, understand that your performance will improve as you progress from the less demanding to the more advanced training programs, but the extent of that improvement will be different for everyone. We truly are, as the late George Sheehan emphasized, unique, never-to-be-repeated experiments of one. And never more so than when we train for the marathon. Thus, only the more genetically gifted will be able to achieve the listed goal times when they train according to the more advanced programs detailed here.

But if you wish to train progressively harder in successive years, with the goal of continuing to increase your best marathon times, it makes sense to gradually increase your training over the years, according to the programs provided in tables 10.9 to 10.11. Remember also that your fourth to sixth marathon is likely to be your fastest and that you will have little hope of making marked improvements thereafter (see chapter 6).

PREPARING TO RACE

The three most important physical variables, encompassed in Laws 9 and 13 of chapter 5, are whether or not you peak for the race, whether you undergo a decent taper, and how recently you ran a major race. The important mental variables are whether you have analyzed your self-concept and trained yourself to improve that concept; whether you have practiced mental imagery and visualized the race beforehand; and whether you have controlled your arousal levels immediately before the race (chapter 8). In this chapter, we refine these concepts and consider other important variables that need equally careful control.

Step 1: Run Shorter Races First

Run races of 10, 16, 21, and 32 km before attempting a marathon These races allow you to calculate the pace that you are likely to run in a marathon (see tables 10.12 and 10.13). In addition, they enable you to practice the pacing and drinking techniques you will need during your marathon. It is essential that your drinking technique be well practiced before your important race. These races allow you to practice under appropriately competitive conditions in the presence of many other equally eager runners, conditions that are impossible to recreate when training on your own or even in a small group.

Table 10.12   Predicting likely standard marathon times on the basis of performance in shorter-distance races

Distance (km)	Your time	Predicted $\dot{V}O_2$max (ml·kg^{-1}·min^{-1})	Predicted 42-km time
10	00:37:21	56.3	02:52:34
16	01:01:54	56.3	02:52:34
21	01:22:38	56.3	02:52:34
32	02:08:54	56.3	02:52:34

Table 10.13   Predicting likely standard marathon times on the basis of performance in shorter-distance races

Distance (km)	Your time	Predicted $\dot{V}O_2$max (ml·kg^{-1}·min^{-1})	Predicted 42-km time
10	00:37:21	56.3	02:52:34
16	01:05:23	52.8	03:02:06
21	01:31:59	49.7	03:11:35
32	02:37:37	44.5	03:30:23

Step 2: Cut Back on Long Races

Don't compete in a race longer than 28 km 12 to 16 weeks before a marathon. Part of the tapering process involves running the right number of races in the weeks and months leading up to the race (Law 7, chapter 5). Experienced runners who offer interesting insights on the issue of tapering are Tom Osler (1978), Jeff Galloway (1984), Bill Squires (1982), and Bob Glover and Pete Schuder (1983).

All these writers concur that, at the very least, there should be an eight-week recovery period after an all-out standard marathon race. My own feeling is that this is not sufficient and that full recovery of the muscles and the mind takes a minimum of 12 to 14 weeks after a standard marathon. This conclusion is based on the physiological evidence, my personal experiences, and an analysis of the racing records of the great marathoners described in chapter 6. We need only compare the careers of Edelen, Hill, Salazar, and Jones with those of the more cautious racers Bruce Fordyce and Mark Allen to conclude that the more marathons you race in quick succession, the shorter your racing career will be. I also suspect that the more marathon races you run in rapid succession, the less likely is it that you will ever achieve your true potential.

My advice is therefore not to race marathons competitively more than every four to six months. In fact, for the elite runners, it is best to race only one marathon every year. Recovery from races shorter than 25 km is believed to be much quicker as they do not cause significant muscle damage. For these races, Osler's rule of thumb of one day of recovery per mile (or kilometer) raced, is probably adequate for the experienced runner. However, for the novice, two days of recovery may be more appropriate for each kilometer raced.

In my opinion, it is much better to race short distances more regularly during the buildup to a marathon or ultramarathon and to conserve the pain and temporary muscle damage for one all-out effort. As an athlete, you have only so many really good races in you, which makes it all the more essential to choose your races wisely. Furthermore, I have learned that performance in your one chosen race cannot be predicted from how you performed in any marathon you might have run during the last 12 weeks before that race. Rather, I suspect that the best measure of condition for both marathon and ultramarathon distances is your most recent time over a short-distance event of 8 to 16 km (see Fordyce in chapter 6), provided, of course, that you have been training for a distance event.

Step 3: Acclimatize to Heat

Marathons can extend into the heat of the day, especially for runners who take 4 or more hours to complete the distance. Hence, heat acclimatization is important if the race is to be run in the warm part of the season or if, like the Boston Marathon, it starts at midday.

In his book (1977), Ron Daws, a former United States marathon runner, explains how to use the track suit technique as part of a heat-acclimatization program—a method he mastered in 1968 and, in so doing, earned himself a place in the Olympic Marathon. Daws collapsed with heat exhaustion at the 40-km mark of the 1964 United States Olympic Marathon trials, run at midday in New York City with dry bulb temperatures of 35.5°C. The race was won by Buddy Edelen, who had been training in England in temperatures of approximately 10°C. Edelen's secret was that he trained each day wearing five layers of clothing. Daws subsequently used the same method for heat acclimatization. His technique was to train with five layers of clothing four days per week for three weeks, or a total of 12 training days. He found that it was not possible to train each day with full clothing and trained in normal running attire on alternate days. As a result of his attention to detail, Daws comfortably won positions on United States marathon teams, the selection races for which were again run in extreme heat.

If a race is to be run at a time of day at which you do not normally train, it is probably helpful also to at least do some training at that time of day. There is evidence to suggest that, at least in exercise of relatively short duration, performance is enhanced when training is done at the same time of day at which the event takes place.

Step 4: Acclimatize to Altitude

In chapter 9, I discuss the importance of incorporating altitude training when attempting to perform optimally in a competition held at altitude. However, as the majority of marathons around the world are run at sea level, this is largely an academic question. But you would certainly be ill-advised to run a marathon at altitude if you wish to run your best time.

Table 9.5 lists the equivalent world-record performances at the popular racing distances at different altitudes. Notice the significant effect that altitude has on a world-record performance. In the marathon, there is a difference of between 6 and 8 minutes between a marathon run at sea level and one run in Denver, Johannesburg, or Nairobi, all of which are at altitudes of between 1600 and 1800 m. Attempting a marathon race in La Paz, Bolivia, at an altitude 3658 m is not recommended, as even the world-record holder would be slowed by more than 26 minutes.

The highest marathon in the world is "run" at the base camp of Everest at an altitude of 5400 m. In 1994 and 1995, five elite marathon runners (with best times of between 2:18 and 2:30) ran two experimental high-altitude marathons in the region of Everest at average altitudes of 4300 and 5200 m respectively (Roi et al. 1999). Their average race pace at sea level was 17.3 km per hour; at 4300 m it was 12.3 km per hour, and at 5200 m, 11.5 km per hour. The 35% reduction in running speed during the marathon was due to a 37% decline in $\dot{V}O_2$max; at altitude, the athletes still raced at the same percentage $\dot{V}O_2$max as at sea level. According to the models of exercise physiology developed in chapter 2, this is because of the reduced skeletal muscle mass that can be recruited during exercise at altitude. The reduced muscle activation protects the heart and brain from having to function with a reduced oxygen supply.

Conversely, what is the evidence that training at altitude will enhance sea-level performance in the marathon? In chapter 13, I review in detail the evidence for and against altitude training or, conversely, the "live hi, train lo" variant on performance in middle-distance races. These data show that only the "live hi, train lo" variant may enhance middle-distance running performance at sea level. In as much as training that improves middle-distance running performance is also likely to improve marathon performance, a tentative conclusion might be that this variant may also be beneficial for marathon performance.

But to conclude that living and training at altitude is unlikely to improve marathon performance, we have to ignore the evidence that the best marathon runners in Kenya and South Africa, two of the three countries with the fastest average times for their 10-fastest marathon runners, live and train exclusively at altitude, as did some of the best marathoners reviewed in chapter 6. In addition, during the 1980s and 1990s, many of the best international ultradistance triathletes chose to train at altitude in Boulder, Colorado. The important question we have to ask is whether living and training at altitude enhances the performances of marathon and ultramarathon runners even though such training has no beneficial effect on middle-distance runners.

The essential difference between middle- and long-distance running is that marathon and ultramarathon races are run at much slower speeds (at about 16 to 21 km per hour). When required, the good athlete who trains at altitude will be able to run faster than in training and will therefore have no difficulty in retaining sufficient leg speed for the marathon and ultramarathon races. Yet, this athlete will always be running at a higher percentage of $\dot{V}O_2$max and at higher blood lactate levels and will therefore be running harder than if the same training had been done at the same speed at sea level.

Indeed, if athletes do the same amount of training, they will benefit more by performing that training at altitude. The important reason is that their performance at both sea level and altitude increases more than if they did the same volume of training at sea level (Terrados et al. 1988).

Logic suggests that the optimum altitude for marathon training is the highest

Table 10.14 Pacing schedules for the standard marathon

Distance (km)	1	8	10	16	21	32	42.2
Time	00:03:00	00:24:00	00:30:00	00:48:00	01:03:18	01:36:00	02:06:36
	00:03:10	00:25:22	00:31:42	00:50:43	01:06:53	01:41:26	02:13:46
	00:03:20	00:26:38	00:33:18	00:53:17	01:10:16	01:46:34	02:20:32
	00:03:30	00:28:00	00:35:00	00:56:00	01:13:51	01:52:00	02:27:42
	00:03:40	00:29:22	00:36:42	00:58:43	01:17:26	01:57:26	02:34:52
	00:03:50	00:30:38	00:38:18	01:01:17	01:20:49	02:02:34	02:41:38
	00:04:00	00:32:00	00:40:00	01:04:00	01:24:24	02:08:00	02:48:48
	00:04:10	00:33:22	00:41:42	01:06:43	01:27:59	02:13:26	02:55:58
	00:04:20	00:34:38	00:43:18	01:09:17	01:31:22	02:18:34	03:02:44
	00:04:30	00:36:00	00:45:00	01:12:00	01:34:27	02:24:00	03:09:54
	00:04:40	00:37:32	00:46:42	01:14:43	01:38:32	02:29:26	03:17:04
	00:04:50	00:38:38	00:48:18	01:17:17	01:41:25	02:34:34	03:23:50
	00:05:00	00:40:00	00:50:00	01:20:00	01:45:30	02:40:00	03:31:00
	00:05:10	00:41:22	00:51:42	01:22:43	01:49:05	02:45:26	03:38:10
	00:05:20	00:42:38	00:53:18	01:25:17	01:52:28	02:50:34	03:44:56
	00:05:30	00:44:00	00:55:00	01:28:00	01:56:03	02:56:00	03:52:06
	00:05:40	00:45:22	00:56:42	01:30:43	01:59:08	03:01:26	03:59:16
	00:05:50	00:46:38	00:58:18	01:33:17	02:03:01	03:06:34	04:06:02
	00:06:00	00:48:00	01:00:00	01:36:00	02:06:36	03:12:00	04:13:12
	00:06:10	00:49:22	01:01:42	01:38:43	02:10:11	03:17:26	04:20:22
	00:06:20	00:50:38	01:03:18	01:41:17	02:13:34	03:22:34	04:27:08
	00:06:30	00:52:00	01:05:00	01:44:00	02:17:09	03:28:00	04:34:18
	00:06:40	00:53:22	01:06:42	01:46:43	02:20:44	03:33:26	04:41:28
	00:06:50	00:54:38	01:08:18	01:49:17	02:24:07	03:38:34	04:48:14
	00:07:00	00:56:00	01:10:00	01:52:00	02:27:42	03:44:00	04:55:24
	00:07:10	00:57:22	01:11:42	01:54:43	02:31:17	03:47:26	05:02:34
	00:07:20	00:58:38	01:13:18	01:57:17	02:34:10	03:54:34	05:09:20
	00:07:30	01:00:00	01:15:00	02:00:00	02:38:15	04:00:00	05:16:30
	00:07:40	01:01:22	01:16:42	02:02:43	02:41:20	04:05:26	05:23:40
	00:07:50	01:02:38	01:18:18	02:05:17	02:45:13	04:10:34	05:30:26
	00:08:00	01:04:00	01:20:00	02:08:00	02:38:48	04:15:00	05:37:36
	00:08:10	01:05:22	01:21:42	02:10:43	02:52:23	04:21:26	05:44:46
	00:08:20	01:06:38	01:23:18	02:13:17	02:55:16	04:26:34	05:51:32
	00:08:30	01:08:00	01:25:00	02:16:00	02:59:21	04:32:00	05:58:42
	00:08:40	01:09:22	01:26:42	02:18:43	03:02:56	04:37:26	06:05:52
	00:08:50	01:10:38	01:28:18	02:21:17	03:06:19	04:42:34	06:12:38
	00:09:00	01:12:00	01:30:00	02:24:00	03:09:54	04:48:00	06:19:48
	00:09:10	01:13:22	01:31:42	02:26:43	03:13:59	04:53:26	06:26:58
	00:09:20	01:14:38	01:33:18	02:29:17	03:16:22	04:58:34	06:33:44
	00:09:30	01:16:00	01:35:00	02:32:00	03:20:27	05:04:00	06:40:54
	00:09:40	01:17:22	01:36:42	02:34:43	03:24:02	05:09:26	06:48:04
	00:09:50	01:18:38	01:38:18	02:37:17	03:27:25	05:14:34	06:54:50
	00:10:00	01:20:00	01:40:00	02:40:00	03:31:00	05:20:00	07:02:00

altitude that allows the normal training load to be undertaken, including speed training at faster than race pace. If that altitude exceeds 2500 m, the added benefit will be an increased production of red blood cells with an increase in the blood hemoglobin concentration. This may be the most important adaptation achieved by altitude training (see chapter 13) and, perhaps, the one that really determines its effectiveness.

It is notable that some of the best Kenyan runners are those who can still run fast at quite staggering altitudes, almost reproducing sea-level performances. For example, Willem Sigei, world cross-country champion in 1993 and 1994 and former world-record holder at 10,000 m (26:52), reportedly ran eight 1-mile intervals in 4:30 with a 400-m recovery jog at the Nyahururu training camp in Kenya (Kinuthia and Anderson 1994) at an altitude of more than 2450 m. At that altitude, he was training as fast as he needed to run in the World Cross-Country Championships held at sea level. In addition, he was training at an altitude sufficiently high to induce an increase in his blood hemoglobin concentration. Logically, this type of training at that altitude would also be appropriate for a 42-km marathon.

Due to logistical problems, in particular the cost of the experiment and the number of athletes that would need to be tested, it is unlikely that we will ever have a definitive scientific answer to whether training at altitude is beneficial for marathon and ultramarathon runners. In the absence of such evidence, each athlete will need to determine on an individual basis whether training at altitude improves performance in marathon and ultramarathon races.

Conversely, the athlete might consider the opposite—that training at sea level while inhaling oxygen enriched air during speed-training sessions might be even more beneficial (chapter 13).

Step 5: Taper Your Training

The principles of tapering were discussed in chapter 9 and the scientific evidence for this practice in chapter 5. In general, my belief is that the longer the race for which you have trained and the harder you have trained, the more tapering you should do and the less you should exercise during the last week. This is necessary to allow full recovery of the shock-absorbing capacity of the trained muscles. Recovery of this function becomes important beyond the marathon wall. In contrast, too much rest before a shorter distance race may cause you to lose the leg speed necessary for optimum performance in races of up to 21 km. But in the marathon, inadequate recovery of the shock-absorbing function of the muscles will have a more marked effect on your performance. Perhaps the brain must also be adequately rested to ensure that it can continue to recruit the muscles appropriately once the pain of the marathon becomes increasingly severe.

Of those who have written on the topic, Galloway (1984) advises that training should be reduced by 30% the second-last week before a marathon race, and that you should run only 30% of the usual weekly total distance in the first four days of the last week before the race. For the last three days, he suggests running only 2 to 5 km daily.

The tapering approach that I advise is presented in table 10.1.

Step 6: Choose Your Race Pace

Having run a series of shorter-distance races (step 1), you will find that it becomes easier to predict a likely time in the marathon.

Let us assume that your times in races of 10, 16, 21, and 32 km were 37:21, 1:01:54, 1:22:38, and 2:08:54. According to the data of Daniels and Gilbert, each of these performances equates to a $\dot{V}O_2$max of 56.3 ml O_2 per kg per min and a final marathon time of 2:52:34. Clearly, this athlete is well trained, as her performances do not deteriorate with distance. This indicates a high degree of fatigue resistance (see chapter 2).

In contrast, table 10.13 shows the case of a runner whose performance deteriorates with increasing distance. This runner is inadequately trained for the longer distances and cannot expect to run the standard marathon even in the time predicted from his 32-km time. He should probably aim to run his marathon as if his predicted $\dot{V}O_2$max were only 40.1 ml O_2 per kg per min, giving him a predicted marathon time of 3:48:57. Thus by comparing your relative performances at different distances, you can estimate the degree of slowing that you will experience in races longer than 32 km and hence your probable time in the 42 km marathon. By starting that race at a pace based on these calculations, you can enhance your performance and enjoyment.

The importance of attempting to predict your standard marathon time on the basis of the times at shorter distances is that very few novices have any idea of the time they are likely to run in their first marathon. One North American study (Franklin et al. 1978) revealed that 65% of first- and second-time marathoners predicted they would run faster than they actually did. Worse still, some 15% of the first-time and 8% of the second-time marathoners predicted they would run 1 hour faster than they subsequently did. In contrast, it was found that experienced marathoners could predict their marathon times accurately to within a few minutes.

If you are running the marathon without ever having raced any of these distances, and you do not have the faintest idea what time you are likely to do, only one tactic remains—let your subconscious governor take control. As it knows what is best for you, you will be under the most excellent control. I suggest then that you line up 5 m behind the last row of runners at the marathon start and start the race at the slowest pace at which your governor feels comfortable that will get you to the finish in less than 4:30:00 (i.e., 6:23 km per hour) or less than 6:00:00 (i.e., 8:32 km per hour), whichever is the marathon cut-off time. If, after the 34-km mark, it is clear that this pace is too slow for you, then, and only then, it is advisable for you to risk speeding up.

Having decided on the pace at which you are to run the marathon, you then calculate the split times you will run at 1, 8, 10, 16, 21, and 32 km (table 10.14). I describe later how to incorporate this information into the prerace mental strategy.

Step 7: Carbohydrate Load (and Deplete)

Whereas carbohydrate loading is of unproven value for 10-km racing, for marathon races it is clear that you must carbohydrate load before the race, eat a prerace breakfast, or ingest carbohydrate during the race. It is advisable to do at least a little of all three to ensure that premature carbohydrate depletion, especially a low blood glucose concentration (chapters 3 and 4), does not cause you to run slower, with more discomfort than is necessary.

The original scientific rationale for the carbohydrate-depletion, carbohydrate-loading regime was presented in detail in chapter 3. The basic theory is that the body's carbohydrate stores are filled more completely when you eat a very high-carbohydrate diet three to seven days before competition. In this carbohydrate-loaded state, you can expect to perform better, especially in events lasting longer than 90 minutes, but probably also in events as short as 4 minutes. However, the issues that remain unresolved are

- whether the three-day carbohydrate-depletion phase that precedes the carbo-hydrate-loading phase is necessary,
- whether there are any dangers associated with the depletion phase of the diet,
- the length of time for which you should load carbohydrates,
- which type of carbohydrate (simple or complex) you should eat,
- the exact amount of carbohydrate (in grams) you should eat each day during the loading phase, and
- whether you need to supplement the carbohydrate intake by drinking com-mercially available carbohydrate-loading drinks during the loading phase.

For now, suffice it to say that it is probably unnecessary, and perhaps unwise, to follow an absolutely rigid three-day depletion phase. A modified depletion phase in which carbohydrate is restricted and during which you only run short distances in training is probably better for those who believe that this technique improves their performance. However, the depletion phase may not be necessarily as dangerous as some have suggested.

The loading phase need last only three days, during which you should eat mainly complex carbohydrates. Eat 500 to 600 g of carbohydrate each day during the load-ing phase. In practice, take in some form of carbohydrate-loading drink as it is diffi-cult to eat 500 g of carbohydrate on a normal diet.

But you need also to remember that eating breakfast before the race and ingest-ing carbohydrate during the race may be as valuable for your performance as is carbohydrate loading (chapter 3). Indeed, if you only carbohydrate load and do not ingest adequate amounts of carbohydrate during the race, you risk developing hypoglycemia, which will cause you to slow dramatically and thus negate all the hard work you expended in your training. Carbohydrate loading does not protect you absolutely from this risk during a marathon race. Thus, the optimum approach is to carbohydrate load before and to ingest carbohydrate appropriately during the race (chapter 13).

Step 8: Prepare Mentally

The longer the race, the more important it is to prepare the mind for the challenge that lies ahead. Most committed runners would agree that if told unexpectedly that there was a 21-km race in their area the following day, they would plan to run the race without hesitation. If informed that the race was a marathon, they would very likely pass up the opportunity. The reason is that it probably takes four to eight weeks to prepare mentally for the rigors of such an arduous race.

I suspect that this is because the degree of discomfort experienced after 30 km in the marathon is the worst that most men, and most women outside of child-birth, ever experience. In order to cope with this, the mind needs to understand fully why it should drive the body through that pain barrier. Thus, before attempt-ing the marathon, it is especially important to follow the guidelines on mental preparation described in detail in chapter 9.

The reason to run progressively longer distances in both training and racing before attempting the marathon is so that you can convince your mind that your body can indeed go the distance. Recall the evidence in chapter 3 that suggests that a large component of the fatigue experienced during prolonged exercise may result from a reduced central drive from the brain to keep recruiting enough muscle during exercise, so-called central fatigue. How does the body learn by how much it must progressively reduce muscle recruitment during prolonged exercise? To what extent is this learning process acquired during the long races or training runs that you complete in preparation for the marathon? Does this explain why it is unusual for a novice runner to race his best marathon or ultramarathon on a first attempt? Perhaps the inexperienced brain has yet to be programmed to exhaust the body as completely as is possible. It is probable that this central fatigue acts to prevent unnecessary harm to the body. Hence, to run your best, you must fool your brain to allow you to run closest to that chasm of harm.

Although I currently believe that this central (brain) component of fatigue is not under conscious control, it cannot be reversed by simply willing it away as there may well be some component of conscious programming that occurs during racing and training. Perhaps the confidence acquired through training slows the rate at which this central fatigue develops during marathon racing.

Thus, in training for the marathon, it is important to build up confidence to help ensure that you are able to go the distance. This may preprogram the subconscious governor that comes into play late in the marathon, allowing you to encroach more closely on that safety margin that the brain has developed to protect you from harming yourself unnecessarily.

Store Creative Energy

During the last 10 to 15 km of the marathon, it is necessary for your mind to take control and to drive your ailing, complaining, and increasingly unwilling body toward the finishing line. In fact, these complaints must have their origins in the brain itself, for it is in the brain, not in the muscles, that pain is registered and interpreted. These complaints evoke the responses of the first voice of which World Champion Ironman triathlete Mark Allen writes (see chapter 8).

In fact, this self-talk is simply the result of attempts by the subconscious governor to usurp control of the conscious brain to ensure that you stop running. The nature of this self-talk and how it has evolved remain one of the great mysteries in the exercise sciences. Complete mastery of this self-talk is what each athlete strives for during training and racing. The world's greatest athletes, like Mark Allen, are those who are best able to overcome this internal mental battle.

To overcome the malevolence of this first voice, the mind must be properly rested and focused on what it will be expected to do. During the week before the race, it is therefore essential that you prepare mentally for the big day.

It is during this period of mental preparation that marathon runners are frequently at their most eccentric. A surgical colleague who missed one ultramarathon because of influenza now refuses to work for the last seven days before the race. When not running during this period, he dons a surgical mask, takes leave of his family, cloisters himself in a sterile environment, and finds solace in reading books from his large library of Eastern philosophers. At such times, only those who are known to be free of "marathon-destroying germs" have access to him.

This particularly eccentric reaction should not be regarded as especially odd. As a correctly trained runner, you are on the knife's edge. You are mildly irritable and at an increased risk for infection. You have worked hard for what will be a once-only chance. Your body is ready. Now you must seek out the correct environment so that the final arbiter of marathon performance—the mind—can be equally well prepared.

Mentally Rehearse

The standard marathon can be segmented into two 16-km races with a final 10-km stretch tacked onto the end. Thus, when preparing to race the standard marathon, I set time goals for the 16- and 32-km markers. In this way, I was never concentrating on a goal more than 16 km away. To ensure that everything was going according to plan during the race, I would check my pace over various individual kilometers along the route. The positive reinforcement engendered by knowing that you have run another kilometer in the correct time has a calming and reinforcing effect.

In mental practice for the marathon, I visualized the times I had set myself. Then, for the last 10-km of the race itself, I would run from each kilometer board to the next, timing myself at each marker. If I was on time at 32 km, the motivation to maintain my pace through each of those last 10 individual markers was very high. On the other hand, if these intermediate goals were not achieved, it meant that I was having a bad day and that my subsequent goals in the race had to be modified accordingly.

Present-day runners have it somewhat easier than in the past. When I first began running marathons in 1972, the only marker boards we were likely to see were those at 32 km, where our times were recorded for the first time. Thus, it was impossible to segment to the same degree as you can now, with marker boards placed every kilometer, even in the ultramarathons. You need to ensure that you take full advantage of this courtesy currently provided by modern race organizers.

The final essential mental rehearsal is to visualize the last section of the race and to plan how to deal with the real fatigue that develops during races, as well as with what runners call "bad patches," which Rushall (1979) refers to as "dead spots." Dead spots occur when athletes lose their mental control, either because they have grown tired of concentrating on the same mental track or because a powerful distracter has suddenly appeared.

When a dead spot occurs, do not panic. Try to regain your mental control as rapidly as possible. The best way to do this is to introduce positive self-statements. My approach was to concentrate on the goals that I had already achieved in the race. I would remind myself how well I was doing and how proud I would be of my performance. If this failed, I would think about some aspect of my work that was going well and was giving me pleasure. The mental battle the 37-year-old Mark Allen had to win before he could finish first in his last Hawaiian Ironman Triathlon is presented in detail in chapter 8.

The second problem is how to cope with the real fatigue that occurs after 32 km in the standard marathon and, to a far worse degree, after 70 km in a short ultramarathon or after 120 km in a long ultramarathon.

The key is to prepare mentally for when the pain will begin. In the marathon, the pain starts becoming a problem after about 28 km, and in the ultramarathons, after either 65 or 100 km. Thus, in your mental preparations you must imagine the feelings of increasing fatigue that you will experience and how these will affect you generally.

Another important mental tactic is to know that when the discomfort comes, it is, at first, worst on the uphills. I used to comfort myself by saying that the next downhill would allow me to recover. As I had already committed every detail of this part of the course to memory (step 10) and had "run" that part of the course frequently in my mind, I knew precisely when the next downhill section was due and so could motivate myself more easily to persist for just a little bit longer until the next downhill.

An essential technique is to know the exact geographical details of the final 10 km of the marathon. To do this, drive over the last 10 km of the race and record the details in a notebook (in particular, the exact situation, length, and severity of all uphill and downhill sections). Use this information when doing your mental preparation before a race.

It is essential that you know exactly how many hills there are. This allows you to run each hill with the confidence that there is now one less hill before the finish. In contrast, if you do not know the course, the tendency is to become progressively more upset and therefore distracted with each successive hill. When this happens, the mind tends to play its own special tricks. Sensing a weakness, it is likely to offer some particularly unhelpful suggestions, such as, "If you feel this bad on this hill, imagine how bad it will be if the rest of the course is uphill!"

My advice to an elite runner competing on an unfamiliar course is to film the course beforehand on video and to use that film, not only to learn the course, but also to help with mental preparation for the race. If you want to run your best possible race, this advice certainly applies to you.

However, when the fatigue becomes all-embracing and running downhill is just as tiresome as running uphill, you must confront the pain, accept it, and concentrate your efforts on not allowing the discomfort to slow you down or, worse, to stop you completely. You can do this by focusing on your time through each successive kilometer. A technique I found useful was to think only of getting to the next marker in a particular time. However tired I was, I could usually imagine getting to the next marker. With time, the individual kilometers add up and finally you arrive within striking distance of the finish. Usually, I knew I was home when I reached the final few kilometers of a marathon or ultramarathon.

Surprisingly, in retrospect, this distance was the inverse of the distance already run. Thus, whereas the certainty of finishing an ultramarathon is relatively secure when you are still 4 km from the finish, I only ever thought the marathon was over when running the last kilometer.

Once you approach this distance from the finish, you can begin to convert it into a time, knowing that the distance to the finish requires less than 15 to 20 minutes to complete. This gives a finite limit to the amount of discomfort that you still have to endure. Positive self-statements during this phase of the race are very helpful.

In sum, once you have decided on a concise running strategy, you need only convince yourself that it is possible.

Step 9: Arrive at the Competition in Good Time

Unlike your first 10- or 21-km race, it is very likely that you will need to travel out of town for your first 42-km race. If the competition is to be held at altitude and you live at sea level, the best time to arrive is either immediately before, or three or more weeks before, the competition. Generally, if the marathon is to be run at altitude and you are a sea-level runner, the best advice is rather to choose an alternative marathon that is run at sea level.

If the race is to be held out of town but at low altitude, it is advisable that you do the following:

- Arrive at least two days before the race and allow one day of recovery for each day spent driving there.

- Allow one day of recovery for each three hours spent flying to your race destination.

- If getting to the competition involves traveling across one or more time zones, allow one day of recovery for each time zone crossed. When crossing more than six time zones, allow 14 days to resynchronize your biological clock (Loat and Rhodes 1989). If your flights cross 10 or more time zones, always take a westward flight, as the body adapts better to the lengthening of the day of travel (traveling west) than to the shortening of the day (traveling east; Loat and Rhodes 1989).

Where possible, check the points listed in the following paragraph to ensure that your travel and accommodation arrangements run smoothly. By doing this, all unfamiliar events and sights will be reduced to a minimum, and as many minor frustrations as possible avoided (Liebetrau 1982).

If you are flying to the site of competition, ensure that you arrange transport to the hotel. Check that the hotel rooms are comfortable, free from noise, and close to those of your friends. The noisiest rooms are likely to be those nearest the street, the kitchen, the lounge, the dining room, and the bar. Ask the hotel manager for details about your allocated room to ensure it is far away from these areas. At the same time, inquire about the availability of any special foods that you may need, as well as about facilities, such as indoor training facilities, saunas, and a swimming pool.

Once in the hotel, familiarize yourself with the room. Liebetrau (1982) suggests taking along some personal possessions, such as photographs, your pillow from home, and the bedclothes and pajamas in which you have recently slept. This ensures that unfamiliar smells and skin sensations do not interfere with your ability to fall asleep and to stay asleep. Bruce Fordyce may not have learned much from reading this book, but he did indicate that after reading an earlier edition, he started taking his bedclothes with him. This alone must surely explain his long and distinguished career?

Not everyone will have the luxury of sleeping alone in a hotel room the night before the chosen marathon. If you plan to share a room with someone, it is advisable to discuss beforehand what time you plan to go to bed and what time you plan to wake up. Make sure that you are emotionally compatible with your roommate, as you will both need emotional space to compose yourselves mentally before the race.

Step 10: Drive Over the Course

If you have not had the opportunity to drive the course previously (and hence have not had the chance to practice visualizing yourself running this section of the course), it is essential that you now do so (see also chapter 9).

If you know the location, severity, and distance of the hills in the first 30 km of the course, you do not need to drive over that section of the course. Rather, drive the last 12 km of the course and record the exact location, severity, and distance of each uphill and downhill section. Then, commit these to memory so that you are able to concentrate appropriately when you run the race a few days later. As suggested earlier, you should consider filming that part of the course to aid your mental preparation.

Step 11: Eat Right

In chapter 9, I emphasize the importance of ensuring that your intestine is empty before the race and that you do not develop diarrhea as the result of a food intolerance. In addition, before the marathon it is important to ensure that you eat enough on the last day to fill both your muscle and liver glycogen stores (chapter 3). Failing to fill these stores may cause premature fatigue due to hypoglycemia, especially if you do not ingest sufficient carbohydrate during the race. Guidelines on how much you need to drink and the optimum solutions for the marathon are described in chapter 4.

Step 12: Assemble Your Gear

In addition to the gear guidelines provided in chapter 9, one essential item for the marathon, which is usually unnecessary for a 10- or 21-km race, is sufficient sheets of toilet paper for one pit stop in a marathon, two in an ultramarathon. Put these into a plastic bag with a watertight seal. Pin the bag inside your shorts or in a pocket. Ideally, the pocket should also be big enough for you to take along any food you may need, especially if you are running an ultramarathon. If your shorts do not have such a pocket, consider sewing one into them.

Nowadays, it is possible to buy lightweight energy belts in which you store any foods or energy bars that you may wish to eat during the race. However, it is advisable to first use one in training before wearing one during a marathon or ultramarathon.

As mentioned in chapter 4, you may find it easier to eat foodstuffs—fruits (such as bananas), sandwiches, and potatoes—during marathon and ultramarathon races. Many people find that they become nauseated after eating a large number of energy bars during a race. If this has been your experience, consider experimenting with other forms of energy replacement.

Note also that it is crucial to pack accessory clothing if you think it may be cold at the start of the race or during either part or the whole of the race. There is nothing worse than trying to run your best when you are cold. The difference between feeling cold and being comfortable during a marathon run in cool conditions may simply be a long-sleeved T-shirt. A good safety procedure is to always wear extra clothing to the race start if you are in any doubt about the weather on race day. If the day turns out warmer than expected, the extra clothes can be easily discarded. I have yet to meet the runner who has too few T-shirts. An occasionally discarded T-shirt helps address this imbalance.

If there is any risk of rain, it is important to wear a rainproof outer garment, especially if you are running more slowly than about 5:00 km per hour. As described in chapter 4, wet clothing is an excellent conductor of heat, increasing the risk of hypothermia, especially when running slowly in windy conditions (Noakes 2000b). Lean runners with little muscle bulk, especially women, are at greater risk, particularly if they run slowly when wet and poorly clothed. In general, small, lean athletes need to be careful, even if they plan to run quite fast and to maintain high rates of heat production. They lose heat so effectively that small changes in environmental conditions can put them at risk of hypothermia.

Step 13: Get Enough Rest

In chapter 9, I stress the importance of getting enough rest. Before a marathon, you also need to ensure that you do not spend too much time on your feet during the final 24 hours before the race. It is far better to spend the day relaxing and reading or watching videos or doing whatever physically undemanding activities you prefer.

Also be sure you get enough sleep the night before and wake up properly on race day. Both of these are discussed in more detail in chapter 9.

Step 14: Eat a Prerace Breakfast

The food you eat for breakfast before an early morning marathon (or ultramarathon) has an important influence on running performance (see chapters 3 and 4), particularly in runners who do not ingest sufficient carbohydrate during these races. The ingested breakfast carbohydrate restocks the glycogen stores in the liver and provides a store of carbohydrate in the intestine ready for use as soon as exercise commences. This can be sufficient to delay or prevent the onset of hypoglycemia, especially if you drink too little carbohydrate during the race itself.

Thus, after an overnight fast, the liver carbohydrate stores will have been depleted by about 50 g. But optimum liver carbohydrate stores are essential if blood glucose levels are to be maintained near the end of marathons or longer races. Even after an all-night fast, liver glycogen stores will be adequate to prevent hypoglycemia developing during races of 10 to 21 km. Thus, as explained in chapter 9, there is no need to eat breakfast before those races. However, the liver glycogen stores depleted by an overnight fast are not sufficient to sustain the blood glucose concentration during a marathon race, and certainly not during an ultramarathon.

The prerace breakfast should contain easily digestible carbohydrates (bread, cornflakes, sugar, honey) and must be eaten at least 2 or 3 hours before the race starts. Food eaten within 1 hour of the race stimulates the release of the hormone insulin, which increases the amount of carbohydrate you will use during the race. All studies show that carbohydrate ingested before exercise either improves subsequent performance or has no measurable effect (see chapter 3). In my view, this is because any carbohydrate ingested before exercise will increase the liver glycogen stores, thereby delaying the onset of hypoglycemia. It is this hypoglycemia, rather than muscle glycogen depletion, that is more likely to cause a dramatic reduction in running speed near the end of marathon or ultramarathon races.

The final breakfast supplement that the runner might choose is two cups of coffee. Originally, it was thought that the 200 mg of caffeine contained in the cup of coffee primed the body for prolonged exercise by stimulating the release of those body hormones that mobilize free fatty acids from fat tissue. More recent evidence suggests that caffeine offers no such metabolic advantage, at least in runners who have carbohydrate loaded and eaten breakfast (Weir et al. 1987), and that any potentially beneficial effects of caffeine on performance during open-ended exercise probably result from caffeine's action as a mental stimulant.

Because caffeine is a drug that also acts as a mental stimulant, its use to excess constitutes doping and is in contravention of the rules governing competition under the International Amateur Athletics Federation (IAAF). There is no evidence that taking more than about 300 mg of caffeine, equivalent to about two-and-a-half to three cups of coffee, has any additional benefits for the runner, so that there is, in fact, no added benefit in taking caffeine in large amounts. One possible complication of caffeine is that it promotes urine formation (diuresis). Thus, any benefit that caffeine-loaded runners might have gained from the stimulatory effects of caffeine may be lost as they have to stop to relieve themselves during the race. However, it is not known whether this diuretic effect persists during exercise, when the body is becoming dehydrated.

A fatty meal (steak, eggs, bacon, dairy produce, etc.) with some carbohydrate (breakfast cereal, bread, and honey) eaten 4 to 5 hours before the race should be of benefit if it causes free fatty acid levels in the blood to rise, inducing a carbohydrate-sparing effect according to the Glucose-Fatty Acid Cycle (chapter 3). Indeed, many legendary ultramarathon runners, including Arthur Newton and Wally Hayward, ate fatty meals before their ultramarathon races.

With this said, there is no convincing evidence that this cycle works in humans (chapter 3). Thus, there is no reason to believe that a fatty meal will improve performance as the result of this specific metabolic effect. But this does not exclude the possibility that such foods could have a performance-enhancing (ergogenic effect) in some runners for reasons that we do not yet understand. If you choose to eat a fatty meal before competition, you should do so secure in the knowledge that the value of this practice is unknown but that it is unlikely to be detrimental. Again, the challenge is for you to find out what works best for you, irrespective of what current science teaches.

Step 15: Warm Up

As marathon races have become increasingly popular, it has become necessary to arrive at the start sufficiently early to secure a favorable position in the assembling crowd of runners. If you are racing for a good time, you will want to be reasonably close to the front of the field. As a result, unless you are an elite athlete, you may not be able to warm up before the start of the race. What is more likely is that you will be forced to stand fairly still in the crowd of marathoners for at least 30 minutes.

Use the first 2 to 3 km of the race as your warm-up, gradually increasing your pace up to a point that you aim to maintain for the rest of the race. But before you start, it is crucial to take the starting-line test described in chapter 9 so that you make an initial decision on how you should alter your pace according to the weather conditions you are likely to experience during the race. Remember that the longer the race, the more you will be affected, especially by the adverse effects of high humidity.

Step 16: Run a Good Race

If you are competing in a popular marathon and are not near the front of the race, you should start your stopwatch the moment the race starts and then record your first lap as you cross the start line. This will allow you to calculate the exact time you ran for the first kilometer of the race, as well as all subsequent splits, as described in chapter 9. To do this, your stopwatch will need to store 43 laps, not 42.

Drinking and Sponging

It is essential to drink the correct solution in the appropriate volumes during the marathon race. In chapter 4, I discuss the composition of the drinks that are most appropriate for marathon races. To recap, it seems that some of the mental fatigue experienced by less trained (but nevertheless competitive) runners during the last 10 km of a marathon, and in highly competitive runners during the last 30 km of the short ultramarathon, results from insufficient carbohydrate ingestion. Runners who ingest insufficient carbohydrate will be unable to maintain normal (greater than 4.5 mmol per liter) blood glucose concentrations during the latter half of these races. A fall in the blood glucose concentration can be prevented by ingesting a reasonable volume of a 6% to 10% carbohydrate solution throughout the race.

In this regard, I continue to be surprised that there are some big international marathons at which only water is provided. It is as if the organizers still adhere to the discredited notion that you drink during races to prevent dehydration and hyperthermia, not to prevent hypoglycemia. It is simply not possible to run your best without taking in some carbohydrate.

Thus, to ensure that you take in enough carbohydrate, you should drink about 400 to 800 ml of a carbohydrate-electrolyte sports drink each hour during the marathon. The lesser amount would be appropriate for smaller athletes, including most women, whereas the higher amount would be correct for faster runners competing in hot, humid conditions in which sweat rates in excess of 1 liter per hour are more likely. It is not possible to drink more than 800 ml per hour when running at a high intensity, regardless of how rapidly you are sweating. The reason for this is that humans appear to have a design flaw in that the desire to drink and the capacity of the intestine to absorb fluid decrease as the exercise intensity (and hence the metabolic and sweat rates) increases. Despite this, there is no evidence to suggest that runners unable to drink enough to match their sweat rates suffer physical harm as a result, nor that they will run more slowly than if they simply drink *ad libitum* as their thirst dictates. This again confirms the value of being a small (less than 50 kg) marathon runner whose sweat rate will always be lower than those of heavier runners racing at the same pace. Smaller runners are therefore more likely to be able to match their sweat rates with the smaller fluid volumes that their intestines can absorb when running at race pace.

Thus, even if conditions are such that the sweat rate is more than 800 ml per hour, it is not possible to drink sufficiently to match that sweat rate if you are running at your peak effort. Attempts to do so will only produce a feeling of stomach and intestinal fullness that is likely to hinder, rather than enhance, performance (T.A. Robinson et al. 1995).

Paradoxically, it is only those runners who run slowly and walk frequently and who therefore have no such need (because their sweat rates will be correspondingly much lower) who are able to ingest fluid at rates in excess of 1 liter per hour. But because their exercise intensity is low, their fluid requirements are much less, probably as little as 100 to 200 ml per hour. By drinking so much, they risk developing water intoxication, a medical condition called hyponatremia, which is now being reported with increasing frequency, precisely in this type of runner.

If you are a slow runner, or if you start walking in the marathon, your fluid requirements will be low so that you must drink much less during those races, perhaps 200 to 400 ml per hour. If, as will inevitably happen before the race, you are told to drink as much as you possibly can regardless of how fast you run, lest you suffer the mythical risks of dehydration, refer your ill-informed and dangerous tormentor to chapter 4 of this book, which outlines the dangers of this practice.

Mental Imaging

Whereas it is relatively easy to concentrate fully on your bodily sensations—to maintain full association—when running a 10-km race, this becomes progressively more demanding the longer the race.

For the average runner, it is probably best to run the first 10 to 16 km of the marathon without fully associating, thereby sparing the mental effort of associating for when it is really necessary (that is, during the last 16 km of the race).

I only ever achieved a state of complete association in one marathon race. Not surprisingly, this was my best. I felt my involvement with the present was so intense that time stood still. It was, in retrospect, a trancelike state, much like a mantra. I experienced in that race what I later heard 2:11:00 marathoner Johnny Halberstadt describe as "an intense concentration on only what I was doing—on breathing, on efficiency of movement, on running as fast as possible" (Halberstadt 1982). There was no room for extraneous thoughts or for considering how well I was running. As Halberstadt stated, "Once you think you are running well, you have already lost it."

When I finished the race, I remembered little of the last 10 km—only the incredible rapidity with which, in contrast to all other races, they had seemed to pass. I am not sure how you learn to associate, but I do not think it just happens. I suspect that it needs considerable practice. In modern parlance, this trancelike state is now known as *the zone*. It seems that performance in many sports in which conscious override can interfere with performance—for example, in high-skill sports such as cricket, tennis, golf, archery, and target shooting, among others—can be enhanced by entering the zone. This allows the subconscious to take charge without interference from the conscious brain. Techniques for entering the zone are discussed in chapter 8.

Midrace Problem Solving

Kilometers 10 to 28 usually pass quite uneventfully and involve the best running. I found that, without any increased effort, I ran at a slightly faster pace during this section of the race. As a result, I learned to save my effort for the second 16 km, during which I would aim to run slightly faster than the first 16 km. I have since wondered whether we are able to achieve this faster pace because we become lighter the further we run as a result of fluid (sweat) losses and fuel that has been used. Nevertheless, there are a number of problems that may occur during these kilometers.

Refusing to Quit

In every good race I ever ran, I had the desire to quit. I am not sure whether this is a personal idiosyncrasy, but I suspect that it is common to all runners and results from the attempts of the central governor to usurp control of the conscious brain.

However, I only quit in one race, for which there were extraneous factors. In retrospect, I realized that I was also profoundly hypoglycemic in that race, so this desire to quit is not irresistible and is usually quite easily overcome.

In earlier editions of this book, I advised runners not to bail from any longer race unless they were elite athletes or had medical conditions. However, I have since started to question this advice. Perhaps it matters not whether you are an elite or an ordinary runner—if you are running badly on the day, why continue to struggle to the finish?

The reason elite runners should quit when they are running poorly is simply that they are probably underperforming as a result of muscle damage. This usually indicates that these runners have been overtraining or have raced too frequently before that race, or have not recovered fully from a previous race (chapter 6). It makes no sense to continue aggravating that muscle damage by continuing the race. Thus, their best option would be to stop running and to commence a period of rest. Continuing to run simply compounds the problem by prolonging recovery, seriously affecting future chances of racing well again.

I now firmly believe that the type of muscle damage caused by racing the longer distances, which is characterized by pain during exercise and by prolonged postexercise muscle soreness, is cumulative and may have long-term consequences. If this is indeed true, it makes no sense to incur that muscle damage for no good reason, other than finishing a marathon or longer race in a disappointingly slow time.

I therefore modify my previous advice by suggesting that recreational runners should also only quit marathon races if the same conditions apply. Remember that the reason you are running slowly is that your brain is trying to tell you to stop running (the Integrated Muscle Recruitment/Central Governor Theory). It is responding to negative messages from the muscles, which are trying desperately to impress on your subconscious that they are distressed and in need of rest. Therefore, the pain you feel is in direct proportion to the degree of conscious effort you need to summon in your ridiculous obsession to finish what your muscles have long since decided is a futile endeavor.

On the other hand, if you quit the race for reasons other than abnormal fatigue, the sense of failure will stay with you for a very long time and will increase the likelihood that the same thing will happen in the next race. Extreme fatigue is, by itself, not a reason to quit any race. Much of the marathon battle is mental anyway, and often fatigue becomes more bearable the nearer you get to the finish.

Therefore, however fatigued you might feel when the desire to quit arises, the question you need to ask is whether this fatigue is normal or whether it is unusual and is due to overtraining and overracing in the buildup for the race. If your racing time is what you expected, then the fatigue is normal. You then have no excuse to quit.

Should you quit, remember there is no second chance. I strongly dissuade you from getting into the nearest car. Instead, start walking and keep walking until the race is officially over. Don't be concerned if your progress is slow. As ultramarathoner Jackie Mekler advised, "At all costs, keep moving *forward*" [my emphasis] (Mekler 1984). You have to be extremely well disciplined to restart any race once you have sat or lain down. Worse, particularly in a long race, once you stop, you have trouble restarting because the exhausted muscles or perhaps the fatigued brain, refuse to restart.

However, runners would be advised to quit immediately when the following occur:

- Severe diarrhea or persistent vomiting. These symptoms indicate that something is seriously wrong. Furthermore, they compound the normal fluid losses incurred by sweating. They may also cause marked sodium chloride losses that must be replaced by drinking salt-containing drinks, which are usually not available at drinking tables. Replacing fluid losses from diarrhea without also replacing the salt losses could possibly lead to water intoxication if excessively large volumes of fluid are ingested.

- Light-headedness, drowsiness, or aggressiveness. These signs could indicate that the runner is hypoglycemic, hyponatremic, or suffering from hyperthermia or hypothermia, the latter if the race is run in cold, wet conditions. Such athletes should be removed from the race (which they may strongly resist) and placed under medical supervision. If these symptoms do not respond within 15 minutes to adequate carbohydrate ingestion, then the athlete is probably either hyper- or hypothermic or possibly even hyponatremic and should receive the treatment described in chapter 4.

- Chest or stomach pain. Symptoms like these that are obviously not due to a stitch but continue, causing the runner to walk, are important warning signals. They may indicate something rather ominous and must therefore be taken very seriously. On occasion, they may indicate an impending heart attack, which, although very uncommon, has been reported in marathon runners (Noakes 1987b).

Under these circumstances, it is essential not to be a hero. Seek medical advice. Strange things do happen in marathons, just as they happen in every other sport, and these are best treated immediately. The medical literature is littered with examples of athletes who continued to run when they would have been better advised to stop (see chapter 14).

Including Walking Breaks

Provided all is going well and you are not forced to stop for any of the reasons previously discussed, you may find you have a desire to walk. During the 1970s and 1980s, walking during a marathon was considered taboo. But thanks to the activism of Jeff Galloway and others, walking during marathon running is being advocated increasingly as a virtue. Thus, in the more accepting marathon culture, the real crime is to start walking when you are already exhausted. Start walking sooner than later. Do not wait until you are too exhausted to continue running.

If you are unsure of whether you are able to run the entire marathon or ultramarathon distance, alternate regular running and walking. For example, do 20 to 25 minutes of running, followed by 5 to 10 minutes of walking. By spreading the distance walked over the entire course, instead of only resorting to walking at the end, you have a chance to recover every 20 minutes or so. You will probably find that you will cover the same distance with less discomfort and in a shorter time. Alternatively, you may consider walking 1 minute for every 5 that you run. Another approach is to walk only on the uphills, which is good advice for hilly ultramarathons but does not allow much walking time on a flat marathon course.

Tom Osler (1978), one of the first modern proponents of walking in racing and training, concluded that anyone capable of running 42 km can easily run 80 km if they alternate regular walking and running in the ratio described previously.

Alleviating Stitches

Stitches are a common problem that appear to be caused by

- breathing with the chest, rather than with the diaphragm;
- taking small breaths (panting) without exhaling fully, thereby stretching the diaphragm;
- stretching certain ligaments in the abdomen that attach the intestine to the diaphragm (Plunkett and Hopkins 1999); or
- an inflammatory response in the peritoneal lining of the intestine (Morton and Callister 2000).

The most effective treatment is prevention. You can learn to prevent stitches by breathing with the diaphragm and by strengthening the abdominal muscles with regular sit-ups. Should a stitch develop during a race, two measures that frequently help are to exhale very deeply to stretch the diaphragm, thereby breaking its spasm, or to breath out when you land on the foot opposite to the side on which the pain is felt. This helps reduce *cecal slap,* a descriptive term first used by a British physician who noted that he developed diarrhea and pain in the right side of his abdomen after running his first marathon (Porter 1982). He suggested that this was due to contact of the first part of the large bowel—the cecum (which sits immediately above and to the right of the pelvis)—with the anterior abdominal wall, and that this caused bruising of the cecum.

I further suggest that the stitch may also be exacerbated by contact of part of the large bowel with the diaphragm. Thus, if the cecum slaps against the anterior abdominal wall, there is no reason other parts of the bowel cannot also strike the diaphragm. If you get a stitch on your right side, it may be that landing on the right foot drives the right side of the large bowel into the diaphragm. By breathing out when you land on the left foot, you may reduce the amount of contact between the bowel and the right side of the diaphragm, thereby reducing the likelihood of the cecum striking the diaphragm.

Runners tend to get stitches when running downhill, particularly following a tough uphill section. This may be due to sudden contact of the cecum with the anterior abdominal wall and the large bowel with the diaphragm. The bowel is then more likely to strike the diaphragm, initiating the stitch. Running fast uphill may also be more likely to induce panting with inadequate stretching of the diaphragm when exhaling.

Plunkett and Hopkins (1999) found that tightening the abdominal muscles or even wearing a wide belt around the abdomen and tightening it at the onset of the stitch may also be helpful in some cases.

Alternatively, if the stitch is due to inflammation of the peritoneal linings of the abdomen, as proposed by Morton and Callister (2000), it is not immediately clear how it might be prevented.

Coping With Camber

Poor camber on road surfaces is a source of discomfort. Many downhill sections of races, especially ultramarathons, are characterized by severely cambered roads that result in additional stress being placed on one side of the body.

My solution to this problem, which can be very tiresome, particularly when the runner is fatigued, is to run in the gutter, which is usually relatively flat. A slippery road surface is another potential hazard. While the gutter is usually less slippery, you may have to contend with running over stones, bottles and litter. Hopefully, as marathons become more popular, more attention will be paid to keeping the gutters clean.

Taking Pit Stops

Another potential nightmare for runners is having to go to the toilet during the race. The key here is forward thinking. Try to find an appropriate spot as soon as is possible. Well-prepared runners will have brought their own toilet paper with them and will thus be spared the agony of also having to look for some. In urban marathons, garage restrooms are convenient pit stops.

In a race where time is of the essence, runners will have to urinate on the run. For those who, like me, are a bit bashful, this is best done when you have just passed a seconding station so that the water or sponge can be used to disguise your actions. At this stage during the race, the attention of the other runners is usually diverted, and they are less likely to notice. If your finishing time is not important, it is perhaps more hygienic for all concerned to use the most convenient restroom.

Late-Race Problem Solving

In a marathon, the race really begins from 32 km onward, during the last 10 km. From here to the finish, the marathoner's brain speaks of logic and therefore appeals to the first voice, which will argue that there is no justifiable reason to continue. The marathoner's only recourse is to call on the spirit, which fortunately functions independently of logic. It accepts that marathon running goes beyond logic—that humans were not designed to race marathons any more than they were designed to scale Everest. And the human spirit soon learns that the marathon is one way for ordinary people to define irrevocably their own physical, mental, and spiritual limits. By the 32-km marker, the marathoner must be ready to define these personal limits.

My advice is to ignore all logic and to take solace in the realization that every other runner feels just as bad as you do. You should view your own efforts as being every bit as important as anything else you have done previously up to now.

Everyone Slows Down

There are very few studies of the actual pacing strategies adopted by marathon runners. Certainly, my impression has always been that the best runners are able to maintain the same pace for the entire race, whereas the less skilled runners slow substantially more during the race. Both observations are probably wrong.

A study (Buoncristiani and Martin 1993) of runners in two Japanese marathons, the Tokyo and Osaka marathons (both of which are run on essentially flat, out-and-back courses), found that the running pace over successive 5-km segments of both races fell progressively as a nonlinear function of race distance in both the best 10% and the worst 10% of the runners (figure 10.3A) so that there was relatively little difference in the degree to which the fastest and the slowest runners fatigued in that race. The data were then collated for a total of six marathons, three each at the two venues, and graphs for mean split times versus distance were calculated for the Osaka (figure 10.3B) and Tokyo (figure 10.3C) marathons. These graphs show that runners in the Osaka race slowed by about 3:30 between 0 to 5 km and 40 km and by a somewhat lesser margin (approximately 2:30) in the Tokyo Marathon. Interestingly, women slowed less than did the men, a point discussed again in chapter 11.

Predictably, the authors try to explain this phenomenon on the basis of metabolic and other changes in muscle that produce a peripherally based metabolic fatigue, as predicted by the Energy Depletion Model (chapter 3). However, this is an implausible argument since there is a progressive slowing even after the first 5 km, long before significant metabolic changes will have occurred in the muscles. What is much more likely is an explanation based on a central neural mechanism in which there is a progressive reduction in the mass of skeletal muscle that can be activated, according to the Integrated Neuromuscular Recruitment Model. But the rapid increase in slowing after 30 km might be due to additional biomechanical factors (see the Biomechanical Model in chap. 2).

When we did our own analysis of 10-km split times measured at the 1995 and 1997 100-km IAU World Challenge race run over a flat 10-km loop course in Winschoten, the Netherlands (Lambert, Dugas et al. 2001), we came up with a somewhat different response between the faster and slower runners in those races. Thus, as shown in figure 10.4, the fastest group of runners in those races maintained higher speeds for longer than did the slowest group of runners (figure 10.4A). But both groups slowed progressively. A marked fall-off in running speed occurred after 40 to 50 km in the slowest group of runners and after 50 to 70 km in the fastest runners (figure 10.4A). Furthermore, the rate of the decline in running speed was much steeper in the slower runners than in the faster runners (figure 10.4B). Hence, the fastest runners had superior fatigue resistance.

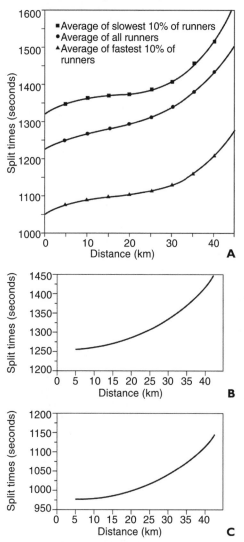

Figure 10.3 Mean 5-km split times for the top and bottom 10%, as well as the mean (average) of competitors in the 1990 Osaka Marathon, Japan (A) and for the average of three races each in the Osaka (B) and Tokyo (C) Marathons. Note that runners slow progressively during these races, essentially as an exponential function (B and C) but that the better runners (the top 10% in A) slow marginally less during the last 12 km than do the slowest runners (bottom 10% in A).

From Buoncristiani and Martin (1993, pp. 28-29). © 1993 by Springer-Verlag, Heidelberg. Adapted by permission.

(continued)

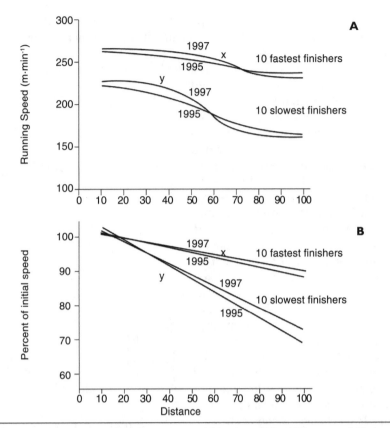

Figure 10.4 Running speeds for successive 10-km laps of the 10 fastest and 10 slowest runners (A) and normalized running speed vs. distance for those runners (B) in the 1995 and 1997 100-km World Challenge races at Winschoten, the Netherlands. Note that the fastest runners (line x in A) begin to slow down later in the race than the slower runners (line y in A) and do not slow as rapidly during the race as the slower runners (compare gradients of the respective lines in B). Faster runners complete the race when still running at about 90% of their initial pace. Slower runners finish at about 70% of their initial pace.

From M.I. Lambert, Dugas, et al. (2002). By permission of M.I. Lambert.

The authors concluded that the faster runners ran at a more constant speed and were able to maintain their initial speed for longer before slowing. It is not possible to explain this gradual and progressive slowing on the basis of a peripherally based energy depletion model since that model does not allow for a gradual but progressive fatigue that already develops after 40 km.

AFTER YOUR RACE

After a marathon, the immediate priority is to drink sufficient liquid to correct any dehydration and sodium chloride losses that may have occurred. This ensures that the kidneys increase their urine production as soon after the race as possible, and it is especially important for faster runners. Slower runners who have drunk adequately during the race and who may be slightly overhydrated need to be careful about not drinking too much after the race, thereby becoming water-intoxicated (hyponatremic). Unconfirmed reports suggest that there have been at least two deaths in marathon runners who drank too much both during and after races because they believed they were dehydrated. The increasing frequency of this condition, especially in recreational women runners who take more than 5 hours to complete marathons, has been emphasized repeatedly.

You should be able to pass urine within six hours of completing a marathon. If you are not able to, it is possible that you may have developed acute kidney failure, an extremely rare condition in marathon and ultramarathon races. However, if you have not passed urine within 12 hours of completing a race, contact a doctor, preferably a kidney specialist. If you are developing acute kidney failure, the earlier you seek a medical opinion, the more likely it is that the severity of the failure can be lessened and the need for blood dialysis prevented.

A runner's appetite is usually suppressed for a few hours after a marathon. When it returns, there is usually a mild craving for high-fat or high-protein foods, such as steak. According to Bruce Fordyce, the only time he eats steak is during the first three days after ultramarathons. It is probable that the protein in the steak is needed to repair the racing-induced muscle damage.

The day after the race is usually characterized by varying degrees of mental and physical fatigue and, in some, mild depression. Typically, your legs will be stiff on account of the muscle damage, and anything except sleeping will seem to sap all your available energy. This usually lasts for 48 hours after a standard marathon and for 7 to 10 days after a short ultramarathon.

Little can be done about these feelings, except to accept them as normal, to sleep more, and to avoid excessive physical and mental activity. I suspect that the depression is due to depletion of brain neurotransmitters—an exaggerated response of the same type that in a milder form explains the ability of running to reduce anxiety.

From the second day after the race, there is an increased likelihood of developing symptoms of infection or inflammation. In a study of the incidence of symptoms of upper respiratory tract inflammation or infection (sore throats, nasal symptoms, cough, or fever) after the 56-km Two Oceans Marathon, Edith Peters and Eric Bateman (1983) found that 47% of runners who ran the race in less than 4 hours developed such symptoms in the first 14 days after the race, whereas only 19% of those finishing the race in between 5:30 and 6:00 developed these symptoms. The frequency of these symptoms in the slower runners was the same as that of members of their households during the same period, whereas that of the faster runners was much higher. These symptoms were not trivial, and in 47% of runners they lasted for more than seven days. Taking vitamin C, both before and after these races, may reduce the probability of developing these symptoms (E.M. Peters et al. 1996). Other studies have confirmed that there is a greater risk of contracting these symptoms after ultramarathons (E.M. Peters et al. 1992; 1997) and marathons (D.C. Nieman et al. 1990) than after shorter-distance races of 5 to 21 km (Nieman, Johannsen, et al. 1989). Similarly, runners that train heavily are also at increased risk of developing these symptoms.

At present, we do not know whether these symptoms are due to a bacterial or viral infection or whether they represent an inflammatory or allergic response to the high rates of ventilation sustained for many hours during the races. Thus, there is uncertainty about whether to treat the symptoms with antibiotics or with anti-inflammatory or antiallergenic medications.

However, the best form of treatment is rest. My bias, first suggested to me by my colleague Wayne Derman, is to believe that these symptoms are probably of an allergic or inflammatory origin and are not due to infections. This seems especially likely given the increased probability that athletes will suffer from allergies.

After about one week, when your enthusiasm for running starts to return, it is a good idea to analyze the race in detail to find out what errors you made both in the race and in training. If you ran well, it is probable that your training was appropriate and that you paced yourself well during the race. If you ran badly, it may be that your training was not appropriate, that you raced too much in the previous 12 months, or that you ran too fast too early in the race. The most common errors made by runners are overtraining, training too hard too close to the race without a decent taper, or racing too frequently and too recently. You should also pay attention to the balance between speed and distance training. Was the balance correct in your training? Did you carbohydrate load effectively, or did you become hypoglycemic during the race because you failed to carbohydrate load properly, to eat the correct prerace meal, or to ingest sufficient carbohydrate during the race? If you quit mentally during the race, analyze your responses. Did you start having negative thoughts at some point in the race? There is also the possibility that you did in fact run to your genetic potential (chapter 2) but that you are not yet willing to accept the reality.

FINAL WORD

In the early 1970s, when I started running, little was known about the appropriate rest period between marathon races. My coach, Dave Levick, the winner of the 1973 Comrades Marathon, raced a marathon and an ultramarathon within six days of one another, only weeks before his record victory in that Comrades. I now wonder how much more he might have achieved had he known what we now know. By the 1975 race, his career was on a downward slide.

Nowadays, people tend to be far more cautious. Bruce Fordyce (1985) has, more than anyone, forced us to realize the damaging effects of marathon races and the slow recovery from them. The studies of muscle damage due to marathon running would seem to confirm his ideas, as there is indeed evidence to show that a specific form of muscle damage may explain the fatigue that develops during marathon racing or the impaired running performance in those who have raced for more than 20 years.

Even the best runners in the world have only a certain number of good marathons in their legs before they develop the so-called punch-drunk syndrome.

To reiterate the point made earlier in this chapter, I suggest that you race an absolute maximum of two marathons per year, or one marathon and one ultramarathon. But it is better to race only one marathon or ultramarathon each year if you still wish to be running competitively in 20 to 30 years. Ideally, there should be at least four, but preferably six, months between these races. The better the athlete, the fewer marathons that should be run each year. Elite runners should start their careers knowing that they have only two or three really great marathons in their legs and another two or three marathons that will not be quite as good. Perhaps then they would be more careful in choosing which marathons to run.

If you develop an infection after any race, regardless of its length, you should not race again for another four to six weeks, as you need to give your immune system a chance to recover fully.

I come from the one place on earth where the ultramarathon is the ultimate running test. In South Africa, your running achievements count for little unless you have run the Comrades Marathon, the race first immortalized by Arthur Newton and later by Wally Hayward and Bruce Fordyce, among others.

The ultramarathon poses a number of interesting challenges. It is the one race in which any small errors in training or racing strategy will be severely punished. Whereas training or racing errors in races of 10 to 42 km cause discomfort that lasts perhaps 15 to 45 minutes, ultramarathoners who bring training or racing errors to their races will regret them bitterly during the many hours ahead.

TRAINING PROGRAMS FOR BEGINNERS

There are some runners for whom the marathon is not enough and whose ultimate aim is to progress to distances longer than 42 km. In this chapter, I present a number of training programs that will help prepare aspirant ultradistance runners for these events. These programs target novice, intermediate, and elite runners.

Basic Beginners' Program

Those runners who have completed a marathon, perhaps according to the programs given in tables 10.2 and 10.3, and who wish to tackle an ultramarathon of up to 90 km can do so by graduating to the 22-week training schedule shown in table

11.1. This training program has been designed for novice runners who wish to complete an ultramarathon of 80 to 100 km in relative comfort.

Table 11.1	A 22-week ultramarathon training schedule					
Week	Monday	Tuesday	Wednesday	Thursday	Friday	Saturday	Sunday
1	48(8)	60(10)	60(10)	78(13)	–	96(16)	–
2	–	48(8)	60(10)	96(16)	78(13)	–	114(19)
3	–	96(16)	96(16)	78(13)	96(16)	–	114(19)
4	–	96(16)	96(16)	78(13)	96(16)	–	144(24)
5	–	96(16)	66(11)	96(16)	96(16)	–	156(26)
6	–	96(16)	66(11)	96(16)	114(19)	–	192(32)
7	–	114(19)	72(12)	96(16)	132(22)	–	240(40)
8	–	114(19)	72(12)	96(16)	132(22)	–	120(20)
9	–	114(19)	96(16)	96(16)	114(19)	–	240(40)
10	–	114(19)	96(16)	96(16)	96(16)	–	120(20)
11	–	96(16)	132(22)	96(16)	114(19)	–	288(48)
12	–	96(16)	132(22)	96(16)	114(19)	–	120(20)
13	–	96(16)	132(22)	96(16)	114(19)	–	288(48)
14	–	96(16)	132(22)	96(16)	114(19)	–	240(40)
15	–	96(16)	132(22)	96(16)	114(19)	–	120(20)
16	–	96(16)	132(22)	96(16)	132(22)	–	288(48)
17	–	114(19)	114(19)	96(16)	96(16)	–	360(60)
18	–	78(13)	96(16)	114(19)	132(22)	–	120(20)
19	–	96(16)	132(22)	96(16)	132(22)	–	240(40)
20	–	96(16)	114(19)	96(16)	96(16)	–	120(20)
21	48(8)	96(16)	96(16)	114(19)	96(16)	–	60(10)
22	48(8)	48(8)	30(5)	–	–	–	Ultra

The coding used in this table—for example, 48 (8) on day 1 of week 1—means that you run for either 48 minutes or for 8 km, whichever is shorter. As in tables 10.2 and 10.3, the distances and times are calculated for an athlete whose normal speed is about 6:00 per km, the training speed of most recreational male and female ultramarathon runners. If your training speed is faster than 6:00 per km, pay attention to the *distances* given on the training schedule. If your training speed is slower than 6:00 per km, refer to the *times* given in the training schedule. If slow runners try to run the distances listed, they will be doing too much.

However, before advancing directly to the ultramarathon program in table 11.1, you should either have run your first marathon in less than 3:45:00 or should have been running for one to two years. Athletes who ultimately wish to be good marathon or ultramarathon runners should not follow beginners' programs. Instead, first race at shorter distances of up to 15 km on the track, cross-country, and road. Only after you are running your fastest possible times over 10 km should you consider entering marathon and ultramarathon races. This echoes the advice given in chapters 6 and 10. As Grete Waitz has written, "The roots of every great runner, and all great running, are on the track" (Waitz and Averbuch 1986, page 102). Thus, the best way to destroy running talent is to become a marathon or ultramarathon runner at an early age and to burn out by doing too much intensive speed work or long-distance training before the age of 18 to 20.

The major difference between training for shorter-distance races, including the marathon, and training for ultramarathons is the length of the long weekend runs. These runs are the most important features of the ultramarathon training program and should increase gradually from 16 to 60 km. As a guideline, anyone able to complete two 32-km training runs in the final six weeks before the marathon can be confident of finishing that race, regardless of how well the rest of training has gone. If you were to drop all other training, the only component you should not drop would be the long weekend training run.

Oliver-Tabakin Novice Program

In 1979, two veteran Comrades runners, Don Oliver (19 Comrades medals) and Dennis Tabakin (18 Comrades medals), initiated a six-month program in which they trained novice runners to complete the Comrades Marathon within the obligatory cutoff time of 11 hours.

Although it is not possible to do full justice to their program, the key principles that Oliver and Tabakin developed during two decades of coaching include several short-term objectives. Each month the training objective is for the runner to run only slightly farther than the successful target achieved the month before. Runners build up confidence as they prove to themselves that they can reach their targets easily. This philosophy emphasizes the importance of training the central governor (see chapter 2) to accept what might otherwise be concerned impossible. Table 11.2 presents their monthly training program from December to June.

The program has been extremely successful—in its 22-year history, 95% of the estimated 6500 novices who followed it won their first medal. More recently, Tabakin established the Jardine Joggers Running Club, which assists disabled runners. To date, 195 disabled athletes have participated in this program.

Table 11.2 The Oliver-Tabakin monthly training program for Comrades Marathon novices

December
Objective: To get used to running six days per week so that you can accumulate the necessary kilometers in five month's time.

Week	Mon.	Tues.	Wed.	Thurs.	Fri.	Sat.	Sun.	Total
1	Rest	8	6	10	8	5	15	52
2	Rest	8	6	10	8	5	15	52
3	Rest	8	6	10	8	5	15	52
4	Rest	8	6	10	8	5	15	52

January
Objective: To only do one 21-km race in less than 02:15:00. Too much too soon will spoil it all.

Week	Mon.	Tues.	Wed.	Thurs.	Fri.	Sat.	Sun.	Total
5	Rest	8	8	10	5	5	15(race)	51
6	Rest	8	8	10	6	5	21(race)	58
7	Rest	6	8	10	8	5	15(club run)	52
8	Rest	6	8	12	8	5	21(club run)	60

February
Objective: To finish a 32-km road race in less than 03:15:00. A 32-km is a nice, chewable chunk. After that, runners can consider a marathon.

Week	Mon.	Tues.	Wed.	Thurs.	Fri.	Sat.	Sun.	Total
9	Rest	10	8	12	10	5	25(club run)	70
10	Rest	5	10	5	10	5	32(race)	67
11	Rest	8	8	10	10	6	21(race)	63
12	Rest	8	8	12	5	8	21(club run)	62

March
Objective: To qualify for Comrades by running a 42-km marathon in less than 04:15:00. Run your first ultramarathon in this month. Do not run more than 15 km on the day after a long weekend run.

Week	Mon.	Tues.	Wed.	Thurs.	Fri.	Sat.	Sun.	Total
13	Rest	8	8	12	5	5	42(marathon)	80
14	Rest	Rest	8	10	8	8	15	49
15	Rest	8	8	10	5	50(race)	Rest	81
16	Rest	6	8	12	8	8	15	57
17	Rest	8	8	12	8	8	30(club run)	74

April

Objective: To finish a 50-km ultramarathon in less than 05:30:00. Run the second of two pre-Comrades 42-km marathons in this month.

Week	Mon.	Tues.	Wed.	Thurs.	Fri.	Sat.	Sun.	Total
18	Rest	8	8	10	6	6	42(race)	80
19	Rest	8	8	12	8	8	15	59
20	Rest	8	8	12	5	50(race)	Rest	83
21	Rest	8	8	12	8	10	15(club run)	61

May

Objective: To run the 62-km long club run (week 23) in less than 08:30:00. This run, five weeks before race day, is compulsory and is the last stepping stone.

Week	Mon.	Tues.	Wed.	Thurs.	Fri.	Sat.	Sun.	Total
22	Rest	8	6	12	8	5	25	64
23	Rest	8	8	10	8	5	62(long club run)	101
24	Rest	Rest	6	10	8	6	32(race)	62
25	Rest	6	6	8	6	8	21(race)	55

June

Objective: To finish the Comrades Marathon in less than 10:45:00. Wind down with a few days rest and you are ready for your medal. Take a pacing chart along with you.

Week	Mon.	Tues.	Wed.	Thurs.	Fri.	Sat.	Sun.	Total
26	Rest	6	6	10	6	6	10(race)	44
27	Rest	8	6	6	5	5	8	38
28	6	6	Rest	Rest	Rest	90	Rest	02

All distances are in kilometers. Total training distance for 28 weeks = 1781 km.
Reproduced with the permission of Don Oliver and Dennis Tabakin.

INTERMEDIATE TRAINING PROGRAMS

In the previous chapter, I described my own training program for racing a marathon. In effect, this program was part of a longer program designed to prepare me for a 90-km ultramarathon after about five months of concentrated training. In the following section, I outline this program, as well as the ultradistance training programs of Norrie Williamson and Bob de la Motte.

Tim Noakes' Peaking Program

In training for the ultramarathon, I began with a 10-week break-in period similar to the one described for the marathon (table 10.2). Thereafter, I would start increasing the weekly distance I ran in training with the aim of peaking with two weeks of 160 km (table 11.3).

Note that the difference between the training program described in table 10.2 and the one in table 11.3 is that the total running distance on Tuesdays and Thursdays is greatly increased, as is the distance of the long weekend training runs. The relative rest days of Monday, Wednesday, Friday, and Sunday are much the same.

During this phase, the key was to gradually increase the total distance run each week by upping the distance run on the three long training days. However, I was careful not to succumb to overreaching (see chapter 7). If I developed any of the overreaching symptoms, I would not run on the relative rest day and approached the next hard training day with caution. If these symptoms remained even after a full day's rest, the next hard training day became a light training day, and this continued until all symptoms had disappeared. What is remarkable is how quickly the body recovers when given a chance. With just 24 hours' rest, I had usually recovered fully, and the next training session was inevitably a delight.

Two other important indicators of whether the training load is optimal are the times run over a regular training course and performance in interval sessions or time-trials. I frequently ran the same course to and from my place of work. By regularly checking my running times over that course, I could immediately spot when I was doing too much, as the run would take longer and would require more effort. Conversely, fast, effortless runs indicated that I was approaching my peak. At the time, I did not have a heart rate monitor, as they were not readily available. Use of a monitor would have helped me determine when I was overreaching or, conversely, approaching a peak (see chapter 5).

During the four weeks before the ultramarathon, I reduced my training volume from 100% in the fifth-last week before the race to 26% during the last week before the race. This was done in accordance with the formula that Bruce Fordyce devised. Although the scientific basis for different tapering regimes is described in chapter 5, what I did and what Bruce Fordyce advised were determined more by

Table 11.3 Noakes' six-week peaking training program for the short ultramarathon

Day	Morning	Evening	Effort rating
Monday	5 km	7 km	Jog
Tuesday	16–21 km	8–15 km	Moderate
Wednesday	7 km	7 km	Jog
Thursday	16–21 km	8–15 km	Hard
Friday	5 km	5 km	Jog
Saturday	42–60 km	—	Moderate
Sunday	—	12–16 km	Jog
Total	138–184 km		

what we learned from other runners and from personal experience than from a detached analysis of the scientific evidence. I suspect that we still do not advocate sufficient rest during the last 7 to 10 days before an ultramarathon.

During this period, I also emphasized speed-work sessions. I tried to run four or five such sessions during the four-week period. If the ultramarathon was to be run on a hilly course, I would concentrate on hill running. Again, the provisos regarding the proven value of different tapering methods, discussed in chapter 10, apply.

Norrie Williamson's Program

Williamson has competed in a range of ultradistance events from 56 to 1000 km, including a record setting (131:27:00) run from Johannesburg to Durban. He has competed in more than 100 ultradistance events, including the 262-km Spartathlon in Greece and the 226-km Hawaiian Ironman Triathlon. He captained the South African team that won the inaugural three-day London-to-Paris Triathlon, which included a four-man relay swim across the English Channel. He has also represented Scotland and Great Britain in 100-km and 24-hour championship races.

In 1989, Williamson published a definitive book, *Everyman's Guide to Distance Running*, which includes a detailed training program for aspirant Comrades runners. The book was the first of its kind and was also translated into Zulu. A revised 14-week version of the program is presented in table 11.4. Further information on Williamson's complete 20-week Comrades training program can be found on his Web site, **www.sa-active.co.za/coachnorrie.**

Schedule 1 in table 11.4 (first column) is for novice runners who have not trained heavily for distance running before, who have not run an ultramarathon before, and who aim to finish a run similar in length to the Comrades (90 km) in 9:30:00 to 11:00:00. The requirement is that the athletes will need to train five days per week and that they should be able to run 50 to 85 km per week when in peak training. Personal best times when starting the training program should be 10 km in more than 51:00, 21 km in more than 2:00:00; and the marathon in more than 4:00:00.

Schedule 2 (second column) is for runners able to run six days per week, covering a distance of between 60 and 100 km per week, during the heavy training period. The aim for these runners is to finish the race between 8:00:00 and 9:30:00. Runners wishing to enter this program should have run 10 km in between 45:00 and 51:00; 21 km between 1:40:00 and 2:00:00; and marathons between 3:30:00 and 4:00:00.

Schedule 3 (third column) is for athletes who are able to train six days per week, with occasional days of double training. Runners should have at least a full year's running experience behind them and should be able to handle a maximum of 120 km per week in training. They should also have included speed training in the last six months. Their personal best times for 10 km should be between 40:00 and 45:00 minutes; for 21 km, between 1:25:00 and 1:40:00; and for marathon, between 3:10 and 3:30. Their target will be to finish the Comrades between 7:30:00 and 8:15:00. Williamson advises that runners who are able to run a marathon between 2:55:00 and 3:10:00 have a borderline option of finishing the Comrades Marathon in less than 7 hours. However, they might need to adjust the training program slightly—in particular, by increasing the volume of training done, especially two months before the race.

This program includes speed work training and hill sessions. The hill sessions are similar to those described by Galloway. However, Williamson also stresses the use of speed play, or fartlek training, especially repetitions of hard training intervals with adequate recovery periods.

Table 11.4 Williamson's 14-week Comrades training program		
Schedule 1 (novice) 9:30–11:00	**Schedule 2 (intermediate) 8:00–9:30**	**Schedule 3 (competitive) 7:30–8:30**
Week 1		
1 0	0	0
2 6 × 100 (H)	12 km including 5-km time-trial	12 km including 5-km time-trial
3 10–12 (W)	8–10 (W)	18–20 (W)
4 4 × 01:00 (03:00) recovery (S)	17–20 km	10 (W)
5 0	8	A.M.: 8 km; P.M.: 6 × 400 (H)
6 25	7 × 400 (H)	10–15 (W)
7 18–21	35	38–40
Week 2		
1 0 (W)	0 (W)	0 (W)
2 10	2–5 × 00:35 (H)	A.M.: 8
		P.M.: 10 × 400 m at 10-km pace (T)
3 15–18	16	20–25
4 8 (W)	8 (W)	8 (W)
5 4 × 01:00 (03:00) (S)	3 × 02:00 (05:00) (S)	A.M.: 8; P.M.: 2–6 × 00:35 (H)
6 0	8–10 or 0	10–15
7 10-km race	15 at 21-km pace	20 with 2 × 4 at 10-km pace
Week 3		
1 0	0	0 (W)
2 6–7 (H)	6–10	3 ×800 m (01:30) at 10-km pace (T)
3 15–18	18	20
4 8 (W)	12 (W)	12 (W)
5 0	3 × 02:00 (05:00) (S)	2–6 × 00:35 (H)
6 30–35 at 90-km pace	35–40 at 90-km pace	40 at 90-km pace
7 10–12 at 42-km pace	12 at 42-km pace	15–18 at 42-km pace
Week 4		
1 0	0	0 (W)
2 6–7 (H)	6–10	3 × 800 m (01:30) at 10-km pace (T)
3 15–18	18	20
4 8 (W)	12 (W)	12 (W)
5 0	3 × 02:00 (05:00) (S)	2 × 6 (00:35) (H)
6 20–25 at 90-km pace	25–28 at 90-km pace	25–28 at 90-km pace
7 10–12 at 42-km race	12 at 42-km pace	15–18 at 42-km pace
Week 5		
1 0	0	0 (W)
2 8	4 × 01:00 (02:00) (S)	4 × 400 m (03:00) at 3-km pace (T)
3 0	10	15
4 3–5	6 × 03:30 (02:00) (S)	6 × 400 m (02:00) at 10-km pace (T)
5 0	0 or 3	0 or 8
6 8	8	10
7 50–60 at 90-km pace	50–60 at 90-km pace	50–60 at 90-km pace

	Schedule 1 (novice) 9:30–11:00	Schedule 2 (intermediate) 8:00–9:30	Schedule 3 (competitive) 7:30–8:30
Week 6			
1	0	0	0 or 5
2	8 or 0	8	8–10
3	10	12–15	15–18
4	0 (W)	4 × 200 m (H)	5 × 200 m (H)
5	10 including 3 × 200 m (H)	10 (W)	10–12 (W)
6	20–22	20–22	20–25
7	0 (W)	0 (W)	0 (W)
Week 7			
1	8–10	5 ×400 m (H)	A.M.: 8 P.M.: 5–6 ×1000 at 15-km pace (T)
2	4 × 01:00 (02:30) (S)	18–22	21–25
3	16 (W)	8 (W)	10 (W)
4	0	8 × 00:30 (02:00) (S)	A.M.: 8; P.M.: 8 ×400 m (H)
5	2–4 × 01:00 m (02:00)	8–10	12–15 (W)
6	0 (W)	0 (W)	0
7	42-km race	42-km race	42-km race
Week 8			
1	0	0	0
2	10	15–18	A.M.: 8; P.M.: 4–5 × 1000 at 15-km pace (T)
3	4–5 × 200 m (H)	2–5 × 00:35 (H)	18–21
4	15–17 (W)	5–8 (W)	10–12
5	0	4 × 02:00 (05:00) (S)	A.M.: 8; P.M.: 7 × 400 (H)
6	22–25	8	10–15 (W)
7	18	30–33	30–35
Week 9			
1	0 (W)	0 (W)	0 (W)
2	2 × 5 × 00:35 (H)	6 × 400 m (H)	A.M.: 8; P.M.: 2 × 2000 m at (03:00) at 10-km race pace (T)
3	15–18	8 (W)	16
4	8 (W)	15 (W)	A.M.: 8; P.M.: 2–6 × 00:35 (H)
5	4 × 01:00 (03:00) (S)	8 (W)	(W) or 0
6	0	25–30	32–35
7	10-km race	20–25	25–28
Week 10			
1	0 (W)	0 (W)	0 (W)
2	8–10	12 including 5-km time-trial	A.M.: 8; P.M.: 5–6 × 1000 m at 15-km pace (T)
3	3 × 02:00 (04:00) (S)	8	23–25
4	15 (W)	15–17 (W)	A.M.: 8; P.M.: 6 × 400 m (H)
5	0	8–10	10 or 0 (W)
6	30 at 90-km pace	8–10	50 at 90-km pace
7	20–25 at 42-km pace	50–60 at 90-km pace	A.M.: 0; P.M.: 15–18

(continued)

Table 11.4 *(continued)*

	Schedule 1 (novice) 9:30–11:00	Schedule 2 (inter-(mediate) 8:00–9:30	Schedule 3 (competitive) 7:30–8:30
Week 11			
1	0 (W)	0 (W)	0 (W)
2	2 × 6 × 00:35 (H)	8	12 including 5-km time-trial
3	18–20	18	10–12
4	8–10 (W)	8 (W)	25 (W)
5	0	8 × 00:30 (02:00) (S)	A.M.: 8; P.M.: 2–6 × 00:35 (H)
6	3–4 × 02:00 (04:00) (S)	8–12	20
7	35–35 at 90-km pace or 21 km at 42-km pace	34–38 at 90-km pace 21 km at 42-km pace	30 at 90-km pace or 21 at 42-km pace
Week 12			
1	0 (W)	0 (W)	0 (W)
2	0 or 8	8–10	8–10
3	2–6 × 00:35 (H)	4 × 01:00 (03:00) (S)	8 × 400 m (01:30) at 10-km pace (T)
4	8–10 (W)	10 (W)	15–18 (W)
5	8–10	10	12 with 8 km time-trial
6	4 × 02:00 (04:00) (S)	8 × 00:30 (01:00) (S)	10–15
7	10 at 90-km pace	0	0
Week 13			
1	8	2–4 × 00:35 (H)	10
2	0	0	0
3	12–15	16	2 × 2000 m (03:00) at 10-km pace (T)
4	2–4 × 00:35 (H)	23 at 90-km pace	17 at 42-km pace
5	0	8	8–10
6	18 at 90-km pace	15 at 90-km pace	23 at 90-km pace
7	0	4 × 01:00 (02:00) (S)	15 at 90-km pace
Week 14			
1	0	0	0
2	4 × 01:00 (03:00) (S)	4 × 01:30 (04:00) (S)	4 × 400 m (03:00) at 3-km pace (T)
3	0	0	0
4	3 × 01:00 (03:00) (S)	8	3 × 400 m (03:00) at 3-km pace (T)
5	0	0	0
6	3 × 00:30 (02:00) (S) or 0	4 × 00:30 (02:00) (S)	4 × 01:00 (03:00) (S) or 0
7	90-km race	90-km race	90-km race

All distances are in kilometers.
Key: (W) = Weight training   (S) = Speed work (Fartlek)
       (T) = Track workout   (H) = Hills
       5 × 01:00 (02:30) means 5 intervals of 1 minute fast running with 02:30 recovery between intervals

TRAINING PROGRAMS FOR ELITE RUNNERS

Elite runners (best marathon time under 2:20:00 for men and under 2:35:00 for women) wishing to step up to the short ultramarathon need look no further than Fordyce's training advice in chapter 6. However, it always surprises me that so few of the best ultramarathon runners ever incorporate Fordyce's wisdom into their training schedules. Why reinvent the wheel? It is far better to begin with that which has already proven successful and to improve it further by careful evaluation of the type that Fordyce has always applied. By failing to take the lead from those who know, we may simply repeat the errors of those who have gone before us.

There are only three modern ultradistance athletes whom I know to have been as successful in their careers as was Bruce Fordyce—Hawaiian Ironman triathletes Paula Newby-Fraser and Mark Allen and Californian ultradistance runner Ann Trason. Newby-Fraser openly acknowledges that Fordyce's ideas were the key to her success.

The worst way to train for ultramarathons is to overtrain. As stated in chapter 7, it is not necessary to train as hard as you possibly can to run your best. You will simply overtrain and will race poorly as a result.

Recall Harm Kuiper's injunction that the main goal of many athletes is to train so that they can train even harder. Whatever they may pretend, these runners do not really train so that they can race faster, but simply so that they can train some more.

PREPARING TO RACE

The main difference between marathons and ultramarathons is the amount of time you spend on your feet. In addition, the degree of discomfort and fatigue that is experienced is substantially worse and must be countered for a far longer period.

Step 1: Complete One Race of More Than 42 km

Alberto Salazar's experience in his first and only ultramarathon, the 1994 Comrades Marathon (figure 11.1), recounted in chapter 7, should give first-time ultradistance runners an inkling of what is at stake. When describing his experiences in the race, Salazar, renowned as one of the hardest trainers and toughest competitors in the history of running, concluded that winning Comrades was more satisfying than anything he had ever done.

Before attempting to race in an ultramarathon, however, it is advisable to complete at least one ultradistance race. This will enable you to appreciate the different challenges you will face. Compared to an ultramarathon of 90 km or more, the 42-km marathon is little more than a sprint. The most important mental adaptation is the realization that racing ultramarathons is all about patience—about conserving your efforts, both mental and physical, until you are absolutely certain that any increase in speed will not cause you to slow precipitously in the last 20 km of the race. These 20 km alone will require more effort and mental fortitude than you have ever expended in any other previous race, including your toughest marathon. Your aim in running your first ultramarathon should simply be to cover the distance and to give you a glimpse, however fleeting, of what will be required to race effectively over these much longer distances.

Step 2: Race 30 Km or Less 12 Weeks Before the Ultra

In chapter 10, I suggest that recovery from a competitive marathon may take at least 12 to 14 weeks. Therefore, it is not advisable to race the marathon distance in the last 12 weeks, but preferably longer, leading up to the race. In fact, the ideal is that you should not race anything longer than about 30 km in preparation for an all-out ultramarathon effort. However, provided you do not race, it is acceptable to complete a marathon 12 or more weeks before the ultramarathon.

Similarly, recovery from a short ultramarathon may take up to six months and between 9 and 12 months for runners who compete in 160 km/24-hour events. Although you may be able to race two marathons per year, runners who wish to race ultramarathons regularly for more than a few years should limit these to one per year, with the possibility of running one other long race three to four months before, or four to five months after, that ultramarathon.

Fordyce used this knowledge to his advantage. He never ran a marathon or longer race at 100% effort in the three months before the Comrades. There is a long list of athletes who have tried to prove otherwise and who have paid the inevitable price for their injudicious actions, which result from greed and ignorance.

Paradoxically, barely three months after the Comrades Marathon, Fordyce was able to win the 86-km London-to-Brighton race three years in succession (1981 to 1983); this included establishing one of the world's fastest 80-km times in 1983. In the same period, he also won the 1984 AMJA 50-miler (80 km) in Chicago and the 1987 80-km Nanisivik Midnight Sun Marathon. This I ascribe to the fact that he always started the Comrades Marathon slightly undertrained and, with the exception of 1982 and 1985, did not run himself into an exhausted state at the end of those races. To win those northern hemisphere races he did not have to run to his limits. If you wish to run your best for more than a few years, you should only race one marathon or ultramarathon each year.

The possibility remains that had Fordyce followed his own advice more closely in his early years, he might not have denied himself the elusive 10th Comrades Marathon victory that he so richly deserved.

Figure 11.1   Alberto Salazar wins the 1994 Comrades Marathon in 5:38:39 after leading for 75 km.

Step 3: Acclimatize to Heat

Unless they start at night, ultramarathon races usually extend past midday, increasing the possibility that they will be run in the heat. If this is the case, it is important that you enter the race properly heat acclimatized according to the principles described in chapter 10.

The easiest way to acclimatize to heat is to run your longer runs in the heat. If you train in cool conditions but expect to race in the heat, then you need to train with additional layers of clothing.

Step 4: Acclimatize to Altitude

In chapter 10, I review the possibility that training at altitude might aid marathon performance in the standard marathon. According to the logic developed there, training at altitude might be even more likely to benefit ultramarathon runners. The reason is that the pace in ultramarathons is sufficiently slow that training faster than race pace will be achieved more easily at altitude than is the case when training for shorter-distance races of 10 to 42 km. The dominant ultramarathon runners in South Africa have usually lived and trained at altitude (1800 m), not in the sea-level cities of Cape Town and Durban. Furthermore, it has become increasingly popular in recent years for ultramarathon runners in South Africa to train at altitudes of up to 2000 m for some period before the Comrades Marathon. Recall, however, that this altitude is not ideal if you wish to increase the number of circulating red blood cells and the blood hemoglobin concentration (chapter 13), for which living at altitudes greater than 2500 m may be necessary.

Training for those ultras that are held at altitude, such as the Leadville (Colorado) 100 miler (160 km) or the Western States (California) 100-mile/24-hour race, must obviously include a prolonged period of residence and training at altitude. Athletes who live at sea level will always be at a significant disadvantage when racing at those altitudes.

Step 5: Taper Your Training

I believe that the longer the race distance, the more important the taper becomes and the longer it should be. Thus, before an ultramarathon, it is necessary to taper for longer and to rest more than before shorter-distance races.

Fordyce tapers for the last three weeks before his ultramarathons and runs very little in the last 10 days before the race (see chapter 6). This basic tapering procedure has worked for him, and I suggest that it could be used successfully by all ultradistance runners.

The tapering program for the Hawaiian Ironman Triathlon developed by Mark Allen, perhaps one of the hardest training athletes in the history of endurance sports, also stresses a large reduction in training volume in the last four weeks before the race (chapter 6).

While observing the 1998 Hawaiian Ironman Triathlon, I was struck by what I consider the needless training, especially running, that many triathletes were performing during the last week before the race. I strongly believe that the compulsion for training, so necessary to complete the arduous preparation for ultramarathon foot-races and triathlons, must be replaced with an equal compulsion for near total rest the week before an important race.

Fordyce's tapering approach before an ultramarathon is much more radical than was usual for ultramarathoners of earlier eras. For example, Arthur Newton's rule was that you should reduce training by 15% during the third-last week before the race, and by a further 10% in the second-last week. He continued to train quite hard until the fourth-last day before competition. The same approach was followed by other world-record holders of that era, including Wally Hayward and Jackie Mekler. To my knowledge, we have no record of the tapering approach of the six-day racers of the late nineteenth century. As many of Arthur Newton's training ideas probably originated from the pedestrians, it is likely that he advocated the approach that the pedestrians also used.

Step 6: Decide on Your Race Pace

Correct pacing is essential for any race. But the consequences of poor pacing in an ultramarathon are always devastating. The general rule—that each minute that you run too fast in the first half of a 10- to 42-km race will cost you twice that time in the second half—probably does not apply to the ultramarathon. Here the cost of each minute run too fast in the first half of the race may be more like 3 or more minutes in the second half. There are numerous examples of ultramarathoners whose time for the second half of an ultra was 50% to 75% longer than for the first half.

It is essential to predict your likely finishing time in an ultramarathon as accurately as possible so that you can establish a realistic pace from an early stage of the race. The method for predicting your likely 42-km marathon time on the basis of your best performances at shorter distances was described in chapter 10 (tables 10.12 and 10.13). The same method can be used for predicting ultramarathon times. However, it is difficult to predict your degree of fatigue resistance at distances beyond 42 km and up to say 160 km, unless you have run a reasonable number of races at intermediate distances (for example, 56, 80, and 100 km). Any prediction is likely to be quite incorrect if you have no previous racing experience at those distances.

Provided you have trained appropriately for your ultra, you will probably be able to complete the race in a time predicted for that distance for an athlete with the $\dot{V}O_2$max value corresponding to your marathon time on one of the tables in chapter 2 (tables 2.3, 2.4, 2.6, or 2.7).

Remember, however, that this will be the very best possible time that you can achieve at that distance. For example, if your fatigue resistance in races longer than 42 km is less than that predicted for shorter-distance races of 5 to 42 km, you will run substantially slower than that time.

With this method, the time predicted is the best you can hope for. A safer approach would be to aim to run the first half of your ultramarathon about 10 to 30 minutes slower than the halfway time predicted by this method. The value of this is that if you are able to achieve that predicted time, you can gradually speed up during the second half so that your finishing time will be close to your predicted optimum. When you race your second ultramarathon, you will then be able to run slightly faster over the first half of the race and come closer to your best ideal time. Never downplay the dangers of running the first half of any race, but particularly an ultramarathon, too fast.

If your actual 42-km time shows that your fatigue resistance is not optimum— that is, your times follow the pattern shown in table 10.13—it is not possible to predict what your optimum ultramarathon time will be. Again, remember that the ultramarathon finishing time predicted by the $\dot{V}O_2$max value that corresponds with your 42-km marathon time on the tables in chapter 2 will be much faster than you can expect in your current state of training. Thus, you will need to add a substantial amount of time to that prediction to ensure that you do not start the race with a goal that is hopelessly optimistic. Even then you should follow the advice given in the previous example, which is to run the first half of the ultramarathon 10 to 30 minutes slower than your predictions suggest you should. This will enable you to speed up, rather than slow precipitously, in the second half of the race.

This advice is easy to give because it has been won the hard way—through bitter experience. I once asked friends with whom I had started running marathons and ultramarathons to identify the single most important piece of advice that they would pass on to new runners. Almost without exception it was always to run the second half of any race faster than the first. Ironically, almost no runners willingly follow that advice until they discover it the hard way. But if you are clever, you will listen to the voices from the past. This priceless wisdom is, in my view, the most useful piece of advice in this chapter.

Women's Success in Ultras

Women have started showing their dominance in races lasting 24 to 144 hours. Milroy (1992a; 1992b) ascribes this success to the following factors:

■ Women tend to be less aggressive and competitive and are less likely to force the pace. They are more likely to run conservatively in the first half of the race. The same may apply to older men.

■ Women have a greater capacity for using fat, the principal fuel used during prolonged exercise. In addition, women have more fat to burn and may therefore lose less muscle during long-distance races. For example, a 43-year-old female Canadian who ran across the width of Canada (7250 km) in 112 days, covering an average daily distance of 65 km while maintaining an average speed of 7.9 km per hour, developed a daily energy deficit of 4300 kJ (Mertens et al. 1996). During the race, she shed 17 kg, 14 of which was fat and only 3 kg of which was muscle, reducing her percentage body fat from 36% to 23%. A male runner with an equivalent starting weight (76 kg) with 15% body fat (11 kg) would not have been able to sustain such an extreme fat loss and would have needed to eat more, or he would have lost more muscle, ultimately compromising his performance.

Trekking unsupported in the Arctic or Antarctic is the activity that is most taxing on the body fuel reserves since starvation is the ultimate cause of death (Huntford 1985; 2000) or the termination of the attempt. Logically, women would do better in these events than men, but they have seldom been given the opportunity to prove their potential superiority in this sport. .

■ Their greater subcutaneous fat stores give women an advantage during exercise in the cold. Thus, it is not surprising that the current records for swimming both the Irish Channel, which is substantially colder than the English Channel, and Loch Ness are held by women.

(continued)

■ Milroy also describes the outcome of a 48-hour race, held in Blackpool, England, in November 1988, in which the consecutive night temperatures were –2 and 0°C. Despite the participation of the top British male runners, women finished first, third, sixth, and seventh. The race was won by Hilary Walker, who established what was then the best 48-hour performance. The thinnest male runner dropped out within the first 10 hours.

■ Women are better adapted to withstanding physical stress than are men. Their greater survival capacity under extreme conditions (for example, starvation during war) is legendary. This is in line with my theory that women would be superior performers in Arctic and Antarctic explorations.

■ Women are better adapted to withstanding psychological stress than are men. Indeed, women perceive equivalent levels of exercise as less stressful than do men (Koltyn et al. 1991). Milroy writes: "In my experience in long ultras of 100 km upwards, men are more likely to quit if things go wrong or conditions get difficult, whereas women keep going" (1992a).

Milroy concludes, "Men depressed by finishing second to the fair sex should be philosophical. In the greatest ultra of them all—life—women consistently achieve greater performances, outliving their male peers. Basically, they are just tougher."

Step 7: Carbohydrate Load Correctly

The advice to carbohydrate load before exercise of any duration is part of the Holy Grail of sports nutrition. However, it is advice that is not beyond suspicion, especially when applied to ultramarathons.

In chapter 3, we discussed the paradox that the Hawaiian Ironman Triathlon poses for exercise physiologists. It is, quite simply, that if we believe that muscle glycogen is essential for endurance performance because its depletion causes exhaustion, then we are quite unable to explain the running performance in that race of athletes such as Mark Allen and Dave Scott, both of whom have completed the final 42-km running leg in approximately 2:40:00. Yet, every prediction is that after cycling 180 km in hot and windy conditions at 40 km per hour, their muscles must be almost completely depleted of muscle glycogen. Hence, their unique performances in the running leg must be due to the superior capacity for fat oxidation by their muscles; it is unlikely that this capacity is influenced at all by prerace carbohydrate loading.

In my view, the main value of carbohydrate loading is that it reduces the probability that hypoglycemia will develop, especially if you do not eat a proper meal before the race or if you do not ingest sufficient carbohydrate during the race to offset the development of liver glycogen depletion and hypoglycemia.

While it is still advisable for ultramarathon runners to carbohydrate load before the race, they need also to be aware that carbohydrate loading alone is not enough and will not, by itself, prevent the development of hypoglycemia after 5 or more hours of an ultramarathon race.

To ensure that hypoglycemia does not cause you to slow unnecessarily during the last few hours of a short ultramarathon, not only must you carbohydrate load, but you must also eat a prerace meal and ingest carbohydrate during the race.

In the long ultramarathons of 160 km or further, less carbohydrate is needed to prevent hypoglycemia because the running speeds are so much slower. In addition, the slower running pace of the long ultramarathons makes it somewhat easier to eat during those races.

Make sure you keep eating correctly all the way up to the race. It is important to ensure that you ingest adequate carbohydrate in the 12 hours before the race (that is, at dinner the night before and at breakfast on race day).

Step 8: Mentally Prepare

If you are preparing for an ultramarathon according to the guidelines proposed in this book, you will already know what it takes to prepare mentally for the rigors of the marathon. Bear in mind that in a 90- to 100-km ultramarathon, the real discomfort starts at about 65 km. As a result, your mind will need to control the complaining first voice for the final 25 to 35 km, almost as much as the full marathon distance. This fact alone should encourage prospective ultramarathon runners to put extra emphasis on mental preparation before the race.

For this very reason, you must undergo a prolonged physical tapering period before any ultramarathon. You should also use this period to focus on the upcoming race and on resting the mind to store creative energy. In the final week before an ultramarathon, Bruce Fordyce would go into virtual seclusion, cut off from the outside world. Although few recreational runners have the time to do this, the important point is that the more time you can spend in solitude and in personal reflection during this period, the better you will cope with the mental demands of the last 25 to 35 km of the ultramarathon.

Step 9: Mentally Rehearse

The concept of segmenting the marathon into manageable sections is described in chapter 10. This involves dividing the marathon distance into two 16-km sections with a final 10 km in which each kilometer is run as a separate segment.

My experience of ultramarathon running was largely in the 56-km Two Oceans Marathon, which I ran 15 times (best time 3:59:00), and the Comrades Marathon, which I ran 7 times (best time 6:49:00). However, I only *raced* the Comrades four times, and for those races I developed the following strategy:

- I always aimed to run the second half of the race faster than the first, and in my best races I achieved this. Fordyce incorporated this strategy into his race tactics, showing that it was also the best technique for the elite ultramarathon runners. To perfect this, you must run slower than you might think necessary during the first half of the race. In other words, during the first half, you allow the subconscious governor to determine your race pace. To achieve a finishing time of about 5:30:00, Fordyce used to run 10 minutes slower during the first half (2:50:00) than in the second half (2:40:00). Interestingly, Fordyce used the same strategy in the "up" run to Pietermaritzburg, as well as in the "down" run to Durban, despite the very real differences in the level of difficulty of the first half of these two runs. Using this technique he, perhaps not surprisingly, became the most effective up runner in the history of the race.
- I set a goal time for the last 42 km of the race. This was particularly effective

as the last 42 km comes in the "dead" part of the race when you have just passed the halfway mark (and have therefore achieved your first major time goal) and are at risk of losing focus. By setting a new goal, you immediately refocus, and—based on your prior planning and recent racing times, as well as on how you feel at that point in the race—you can begin estimating a likely finishing time on the basis of how fast you think you can run the final 42 km.

- I knew the exact course details of the last 25 km. During the month before the race, I would run the last 25 km in my mind at least once per day, usually just before falling asleep each night. In this way, I would know the exact position, length, and severity of each uphill and downhill section.

The benefit of this technique is that you are able to focus your mind on the exact task at hand. For example, when faced with an uphill section, you can control your mind by telling yourself that this is the fourth-last hill in the race. Then, you can recover on the downhill sections and start planning how you will run up the third-last hill and so on. Without this technique to occupy your mind, you will encounter the inevitable negative thoughts that become your constant companion during this arduous section of the race.

By following this technique, you will not be faced with the daunting situation of coming around a blind corner only to discover another long uphill section. That is enough to break anyone's spirit. But if you know the exact location of each hill, as you round the corner, it is almost as if you are being greeted by an old friend, waiting to challenge you. And you, eager to accept that challenge, will not buckle under the weight of it.

Drive over the course to know exactly where all the hills are on the course, particularly those that occur in the last 25 km. Besides running the course in your mind, it is also ideal to practice on the relevant sections of the course, most especially the last 25 km, at least a few more times. This perhaps explains in part why runners tend to improve their performances on the same ultramarathon course once they become more familiar with the exact details of the route. In other words, the more time you can spend learning the geography of the course, the easier it will be to perform your best.

Step 10: Allow Enough Time to Acclimate

If you have to travel out of town for the race, especially if you have to go to a foreign country to compete, follow the principles described in chapter 10.

Step 11: Assemble Your Gear

The necessary principles are described in chapters 9 and 10. It is especially important to take additional clothing to the start of the ultramarathon. The athlete, who may be on the road for anything up to 24 hours, must be prepared for every eventuality in an ultramarathon and should take four sets of clothing—one each for hot, cold, and intermediate temperatures and a separate kit for a race run in the rain. In rainy conditions, it is important to stay as dry as possible, particularly if it is also cold and windy. A waterproof garment, such as a rain jacket, will provide protection from the rain and prevent hypothermia (see chapter 4).

Fordyce has an extra bit of advice that he applies to both marathons and ultramarathons, and that is to do one long training run, a dress rehearsal, in the exact running gear in which you plan to race. Fordyce advocates paying exact attention to detail, including pinning your race number to your vest. On one point he is absolutely adamant:

> The golden rule is—nothing new. Nothing you wear or use on race day should be untried. Everything from running shoes to race drinks should be well worn in and tested. During the months and weeks preceding the race, try everything—all the new ideas and equipment that you feel might improve your race time. By the time race day arrives, you need to be absolutely sure about every detail of your race equipment. (Fordyce 1996, p. 21)

If you are a male, apply tape to your nipples. The pain from chaffed nipples is severe. In fact, in one race, it was so painful that I was forced to stop running until I found some sticking plasters at an aid station. Women should wear racing bras to prevent chaffing. As obvious as it may seem, avoid wearing lacy bras or bras with metal clasps or metal underwiring. Continual rubbing against the skin can be extremely painful. If you feel that you need extra support, opt for a supportive racing bra made out of cotton. Make sure that your bra, your underwear, and your socks have been washed several times to soften them before you wear them to race in.

On race morning pay particular attention to the range of weather conditions you are likely to experience during the race. While there is little you can do about an increasingly hot day—except shedding unnecessary clothing—you cannot add clothing you do not have if the weather at the start is colder than you expected, or if conditions deteriorate and become colder, wetter, and windier. Dress more warmly than expected if you are in any doubt about the likely weather conditions (see chapter 10) and ensure that you have access to additional clothing, if needed, during the race.

Step 12: Get Enough Rest

The main principles are covered in chapters 9 and 10. However, during the final 24 hours before an ultramarathon, it is especially important to be on your feet as little as possible. You should rather indulge yourself by doing absolutely nothing physical besides that which is necessary to read or to watch television or videos. See chapters 9 and 10 for more guidelines on getting proper rest and for the best way to wake up ready for race day.

Step 13: Eat a Prerace Breakfast

A prerace breakfast is, in my view, essential before any ultramarathon (see chapter 10). Some runners are reluctant to eat before competition because they do not eat before their long morning training runs. I think this is a mistake. All the evidence shows that a prerace breakfast is only likely to help, rather than hinder, subsequent performance in both training and racing. By avoiding breakfast, runners increase the risk of developing hypoglycemia, unless of course they ingest adequate carbohydrate during those runs.

Learn to eat breakfast before your long early morning training runs. Once you have adapted to this, it will become second nature to eat before your ultramarathon races. Over the years, I learned to eat breakfast cereal with fruit and then to begin running within 10 to 20 minutes. This appeared to make the long training runs easier. Recall that in the early years of my running career, runners drank little and ate even less during training runs. Perhaps if you eat and drink appropriately during training runs, breakfast will not play such an important role. However, I would still advise you to eat breakfast on race day.

Step 14: Prepare for the Start

The major ultramarathon races that I ran in the mid-1980s were popular events with large numbers of competitors. In these large fields, the aim should be to find a starting position that will allow you to start running within the first few hundred meters of the starting line. This will enable you to start the race at a slow pace, an ideal warm-up procedure after standing around on the start line for up to an hour.

In contrast, many of the world's ultramarathon races have relatively small fields with fewer entrants, making it impossible to carry out your usual warm-up procedure. But because the average pace maintained during the ultramarathon is usually much slower than during races of 10 to 42 km, there is often little reason to perform a very extensive warm-up, and the first few kilometers can be run gently as a warm-up.

As the race can last at least 4 to 7 hours, it is crucial to know what weather conditions you are likely to encounter later in the day. Therefore, not only must you take the starting line test (see chapter 9) to decide whether you need to adjust your projected race pace on the basis of the likely weather conditions during the first part of the race, but you should also update this assessment every 2 to 3 hours, especially when the sun comes up (if the race starts before sunrise). At that time, it will be possible to decide whether the rest of the race will be run in cool or warm conditions. If the latter, the sooner you start running conservatively, the better.

Step 15: Run a Good Race

In chapters 9 and 10, I emphasize the importance of timing your first kilometer and of having accurate early split times so that you can determine your running pace. It is essential to settle into the correct pace early in the ultramarathon. Bad pacing in a standard marathon may leave the athlete with, at worst, 12 to 14 km of discomfort. By making the same mistake in the short ultramarathon, you could end up having to struggle through 30 km or more until the end.

The solution then, is to start all races conservatively, aiming to run the first half easily according to the body and using what is left in the second half. As I have already suggested, it is usually best to run through that section of the race that is the most difficult—the last quarter—as quickly as possible, but to delay the time of reaching that point for as long as possible. This is best done by starting very conservatively and saving your effort for when it is most needed.

Drinking, Eating, and Sponging

The importance of drinking sufficiently to prevent excessive dehydration and hypoglycemia during marathon running is explained in chapters 4 and 10. As the race pace during ultramarathons is usually slower than during marathon races, it follows that fluid requirements will be slightly less in ultramarathons than in marathons, provided the environmental conditions, especially the humidity, are similar. Thus, hourly fluid requirements are somewhat less during ultramarathons than during marathons. However, the requirement for ingested carbohydrate, especially near the end of the short ultramarathons, is probably greater than during marathons, provided you are still running at a reasonable intensity and have not started walking or jogging more slowly. Once you slow down, your fluid and carbohydrate needs fall precipitously. Continuing to drink and eat too much under those conditions will most likely make you feel ill and could cause you to vomit and even develop water intoxication, the hyponatremia of exercise.

The opposite problem is that many competitive runners, who are able to sustain high running speeds for virtually the entire race, probably begin to drink less near the end of ultramarathons because they lose their thirst. Thus, just when they need to ingest more carbohydrate near the end of these races, because their liver glycogen stores are approaching depletion, their thirst dictates that they drink less. As a result, they place themselves at risk of developing hypoglycemia, as occurred to me and the other short ultramarathon runners described in chapter 4.

To prevent this, it is essential that you ingest some form of high-carbohydrate drink or food regularly after 50 km of ultramarathons, particularly if symptoms of hypoglycemia (depression, faint-headedness, and difficulty in concentrating) develop. If you experience the same symptoms in a marathon, follow the same advice but take in the high-carbohydrate drink or food after 28 km.

The evidence is incontestable that any athlete running hard in any race lasting more than 4 hours must take in an additional source of carbohydrate during the race. Many of the conventional drinks provided during races do not contain sufficient carbohydrate; thus additional carbohydrate may need to be added.

Although there has been an increasing emphasis on the use of energy bars as an energy source during ultramarathon races, they are only one of many options. You need to establish for yourself whether you find a particular bar more palatable and digestible than others; whether you can continue to eat those bars for some hours while running without developing side effects, including nausea or vomiting; or whether more conventional foodstuffs, such as bananas, cooked potatoes, other fruits, sandwiches, or even cooked foods, are not more acceptable to you. I suspect that we have overemphasized the importance of carbohydrate, which may create the impression that the intake of other foods is not important. The fact is that during ultramarathons in which you run sufficiently slowly, you could choose to eat any of a number of different foodstuffs. The key is not to be afraid to experiment and to follow your instincts. Usually your body will tell you what it wants and what will be best. Provided you take in some carbohydrate (20 to 60 g per hour), it doesn't matter if the food you eat also has a high-fat or high-protein content.

On a cold day you should worry less about the total volume that you drink and more about the amount of carbohydrate you are ingesting; on a hot day, run more slowly and take more care about the volume of fluid you ingest. As you are running more slowly, your glucose requirements will be less, but near the end of the race, when you are still reasonably hydrated, you should switch to drinks with a higher carbohydrate content (10% to 15%) if you are still running hard and according to your planned racing schedule.

Mental Imaging

It is quite impossible to remain focused and to continue associating for the full duration of any ultramarathon. The lower running intensity will enable you to dissociate your mind from what you are doing, at least for a substantial portion of the race.

Thus, the goal, at least for the first half of the ultramarathon, should be to enjoy yourself by talking to other runners and enjoying the scenery and the occasion. You need, all the time, to remind yourself that you have done a considerable amount of training and that you have suffered a great deal for this race, and that you will not run many similar events in your life. Thus, you need to enjoy the race as much as possible and try to make the moment last as long as possible. Your first ultramarathon may be the most exciting race you will ever run and will probably be the one you remember most fondly. You may run other ultramarathons in your life, but none is likely ever to recapture the joy of that first race. Thus, your overriding aim should be to enjoy this memorable race as much as you possibly can.

But reality will unfortunately intrude sometime after halfway, as the pain and discomfort envelope you. At this stage of the race, you will need to develop the skill of focusing on the moment—on each running stride—and to be unperturbed by considerations of how far you still have to run. To do this, follow the advice given in chapter 10.

Midrace Problem Solving

The principles of problem solving are covered in detail in chapter 10. The same principles apply for ultramarathon races. However, pay special attention to the question of walking during the ultramarathon. The principles of successful walking are as follows:

- Continuous running during marathon and ultramarathon races produces a specific form of fatigue due to eccentric-induced muscle damage with associated changes in neuromuscular function (see chapter 2).
- Once this fatigue develops, it is irreversible, causing the runner to slow precipitously or even to be reduced to walking. Complete recovery may take weeks to months.
- First Tom Osler and then Jeff Galloway discovered (each independently) that bouts of walking repeated frequently before the onset of this terminal fatigue allow you to cover a much greater distance with less discomfort. Hence, other than training, frequent walking is the best known technique to enable you to run farther before developing this terminal fatigue.
- As discussed in chapter 5, it is best to start walking early in the race and to repeat your walking breaks regularly and frequently.
- For those able to race the entire distance, it is important to ingest adequate carbohydrate during the last half of an ultramarathon (chapter 4) if you continue to race at your best possible pace.
- If you slow substantially and begin to walk, do not fall into the false trap of thinking that you are dehydrated and that by drinking sufficiently you will recover dramatically and speed off to the finish.

In chapters 2 and 3, we discuss the many types of fatigue that may develop during marathon and ultramarathon running, and none can be reversed acutely by drinking copious amounts of fluid. This fluid will simply cause water intoxication, a condition that can have fatal consequences (see chapter 4).

AFTER YOUR RACE

Postrace tactics are discussed in detail in chapter 10. However, in this section, I elaborate on the reasons 5% to 10% of finishers in ultramarathons seek medical attention after they finish these races. Although I have dealt with the medical aspects of these conditions in chapter 4, in this chapter I discuss the practical relevance of this information.

The most common serious cause of collapse in ultramarathon runners is the hyponatremia of exercise (water intoxication). This condition occurs in those who drink excessive volumes of fluid during exercise and who, as a result, retain excessive amounts of fluid in their bodies.

The most immediate problem associated with this condition is that excess fluid stored in the brain causes a progressive loss of consciousness, leading to epileptic seizures and ultimately death when either breathing or the heart beat ceases. This can be further compounded if the athlete is incorrectly treated with intravenous fluids for incorrectly diagnosed dehydration.

The prevention of the condition is simple—do not drink more fluid than you lose in the form of sweat during running. The treatment is equally simple—allow the kidneys to excrete the fluid excess by not giving the athlete fluid either by mouth or, more important, by intravenous infusion. It appears that there have been deaths worldwide in marathoners, especially females, who were incorrectly and inappropriately treated with intravenous fluids for a dehydration that was in fact, the precise opposite: serious overhydration.

If you or a friend or relative, especially a woman, should ever collapse during or after a marathon or ultramarathon race, you need to ensure that anyone treating you knows about this condition and does not simply tell you that you are dehydrated and in need of urgent intravenous fluids. In my view, intravenous fluids have no role in the treatment of collapsed runners (Noakes 1995; 1999a; 1999b) and are more likely to be dangerous than beneficial. Although it may be necessary to replace salt in runners with symptomatic hyponatremia, this can be achieved by ingesting salt tablets during recovery. Athletes who are unconscious may need to receive sodium intravenously, but only concentrated (3%) sodium solutions can be given at slow rates (about 50 ml per hour).

Indeed, I try to instill in my students that should they ever be present at an endurance event and notice the obvious presence of hundreds of liters of intravenous fluids, they will be correct in assuming that the medical staff at that event are ignorant of what they are really treating. Intravenous fluids can only be given, without risk, if the athlete's blood sodium concentration is known and is greater than 135 mmol per liter, indicating that serious hyponatremia with fluid overload of the major organs is not present.

The most common and most inconsequential cause of collapse in ultramarathon runners is a postural hypotension (drop in blood pressure) that develops immediately after the athlete finishes the race and stops walking or running. In those who are susceptible, the blood pressure begins to fall within seconds of stopping running, and, within 30 to 90 seconds, it can have dropped sufficiently low that the athlete begins to feel dizzy and wants to lie down.

The condition can be prevented if the athlete continues to walk for 5 or 10 minutes at the race finish. Or alternatively, the moment the athlete finishes the race, he should lie down and elevate his pelvis and legs above the level of his heart—the head-down, or Trendelenberg, position. In this position, the runner will recover rapidly without becoming dizzy, as the blood pooled in the legs returns normally to the heart, instantly stabilizing the circulation and causing the blood pressure to rise appropriately. This method is our treatment of choice for this condition.

Treating a collapsed athlete with the feet and pelvis elevated above the level of the heart increases recovery time and also reduces the risk of unnecessary, expensive, and dangerous treatment such as intravenous fluids (Holtzhausen and Noakes 1997; Myers and Noakes 2000; Noakes 2000b). Indeed, perhaps the best way to treat all ultramarathoners is to have them lie down with their legs elevated as soon as they finish the race. I suspect most would recover more quickly immediately after the race if this technique was used more widely.

RACE RECOVERY

Once you have completed the ultramarathon race to your satisfaction, it is time for a good rest. I suggest that for three months you should do little or no running but concentrate on other non-weight-bearing activities, such as swimming, cycling, or working out in the gym. This allows the weight-bearing function of your leg muscles to recover. Once that has happened and your legs again feel light and springy, you can consider returning to running training.

We (Chambers et al. 1998) found that leg muscle strength measured grossly as vertical jump height was reduced by 20 cm immediately after the Comrades Marathon and recovered only 18 days later. In addition, exercising heart rate was elevated for up to a month after the race. These findings explain why you should not expect to run comfortably for a long time after the ultramarathon. In fact, a minimum of one month's near total rest is desirable.

As a result of the damage caused by the ultramarathon, I would suggest that if you wish to specialize as an ultramarathon runner, you should race only once each year or perhaps, even better, only every second year at the ultramarathon distance. If you race more frequently, you will never achieve the fastest time of which your body is capable.

If, on the other hand, you are an occasional ultramarathon runner, I would suggest that you only run one such race every second or third year. Finally, the advice I would have liked to receive when I was running ultramarathons is to alternate one year of running with one year of triathlon training. By doing more cycling and swimming and less running, you will spare your legs and thus be able to continue doing ultradistance running in the long term.

The ultramarathon may be the most exciting challenge you ever undertake in your running career. But it is a demanding event that can leave deep scars, equal to the great moments it bestows. Treat this race with respect and it will reward you in ways perhaps unequalled by any other race. But if you abuse it, it may bite back—if not immediately, perhaps some time in the future.

RUNNING ULTRAS AS YOU AGE

When I started running regularly in 1969, I assumed, like many, that running would continue to be my sole sporting preference forever and that my competitive desires would never pale. Now I see that no sporting choice is, or should be, immutable; there certainly is a time for every sporting purpose. I made my first change in my competitive running career in 1986 at the age of 36, shortly after the publication of the first edition of this book.

In 1984 and 1985 I was fortunate to join Bruce Fordyce and Norrie Williamson as manager of South African teams that competed in the London-to-Paris Triathlons of those years. These fascinating races comprised a 160-km relay run from London to Dover on the first day; a 32-km relay swim across the English Channel on the second day; and a 360-km cycle ride from Calais to Paris on the third day. This exposure stimulated my interest first in cycling and then in swimming. Once I had learned to swim in the open sea, I was ready for the triathlon, an event that added another five years to my competitive interests.

My brief foray into the triathlon taught me a number of valuable lessons. First, it taught me that cycling and even swimming are wonderful and enjoyable activities. The value of both is that they are non-weight-bearing activities, an attribute that, I believe, becomes increasingly important the older you become. In addition, swimming taxes and develops the upper body, a region that is poorly developed in runners.

Whereas many believe that it is the joints that must be protected as you age, the evidence clearly is that moderate running for life does not increase the risk of developing osteoarthritis. Rather, my experience is that it is the shock-absorbing characteristic of the muscles themselves that is most impaired as you age. In chapter 5, I recount Bill Rodgers' observation that muscle soreness has become a constant training and racing companion now that he has entered his sixth decade. This is the most obvious characteristic I have noted in myself. Any more demanding run, be it as little as a 10 km run at a faster pace, usually causes increased muscle stiffness that lasts for 24 to 36 hours. It is as if the muscles have developed a reduced capacity not only to absorb shock during running but also to recover after training. Because this effect is not likely to improve suddenly, it perhaps makes sense to spend an increasing amount of your training time in non-weight-bearing activities as you age. If muscles do indeed have a finite number of repair cycles, a topic that our research unit at the University of Cape Town is actively researching, it is important to ensure that those repair cycles last a lifetime, rather than for a limited period of, say, 20 years of heavy training and racing in your midlife.

Some runners are reluctant to participate in activities other than their primary specialization, running. They often consider swimming too difficult to learn. As the world's worst swimmer, who once swam 3.2 km in the open sea, I conclude that it is possible for anyone to learn to swim at any age, provided you are prepared to devote sufficient time to the task and that you have a goal, such as a triathlon.

Some argue that cycling is dangerous. This is certainly true, yet adaptations can be made to reduce the risks. Another complaint about cycling, which unfortunately cannot be overcome, is that it is simply not possible to cycle subconsciously and so to dream as you can when you run. For those, like me, who run to dream, this is a very special attribute that can also be achieved in swimming in open water, but never to the same extent in cycling. But recall Arthur Newton's observation: when you first start running, all your mental effort is required just to keep running, but with time this responsibility is taken over by the subconscious so that the mind is free to pursue other thoughts. I have also experienced this in cycling, but it may take years, rather than months, and it must never occur to the same extent as in running, or your life will be in danger.

A substantial advantage of cycling is that it is possible to cover large distances in a short time even when relatively unfit. One of my greatest pleasures, when training for the Comrades Marathon, was a 60-km training run around the Cape Peninsula, arguably one of the most scenic runs imaginable. While it would take months of training before I could attempt the run, that distance is no more than a comfortable cycling excursion, even when you are untrained.

Since my introduction to cycling, I have been able to convince other hardened yet aging runners of the value of combining cycling with a running training program. This has been particularly valuable for those with serious orthopedic problems, most especially severe lower back pain or osteoarthritis of the knee (usually resulting from injuries sustained in contact sports such as rugby), and for those who were simply no longer able to run. Cycling has allowed them to continue enjoying the benefits of exercise, albeit in a different way.

Some of you will, of course, be wondering how the author of *Lore of Running* could possibly be advocating cycling or even swimming and the triathlon as an alternative pursuit to running. However, other aging runners have also committed this treason. Tom Osler, author of one of the first classic running books (Osler 1967), told me that since turning 50, he has realized that the aging body needs diversity to maintain its functioning. As a result, Osler now trains in five sports—running, cycling, swimming, canoeing, and weight training. The late George Sheehan also became a cyclist and a swimmer in his 70s. Even Frank Shorter and Bruce Fordyce currently compete in the duathlon (running and cycling) and in cycle races. I can only conclude that this must be the correct approach for the aging runner. Indeed, these ideas, somewhat revolutionary in the 1990s, are now well accepted, and cross-training has become more widely practiced by those who train and race at the shorter running distances.

There comes a time in each of our running careers when we must reevaluate the importance we attach to running and, especially, the price we are paying for that behavior. As soon as we realize that our remaining lives can be measured in hours, days, or months, we are forced to answer for the decisions we have taken in our lives and how they have affected our families, our colleagues, and our friends.

Shakespeare believed that there were seven Ages of Man, three of which—schoolboy, lover, and soldier—emphasized the physical. My personal experience as a marathon and ultramarathon runner suggests that there are also three Sporting Ages. In the first age, up to about 16 years, sport is played in such a way that the activity itself is the reward while the outcome is of little consequence. That was my experience of surfing at the age of 15. The freedom of surfing contrasted with the structured, goal-orientated, sport-as-work ethic that I experienced in the traditional sports I played at school. I am not certain that we do our children any favors by introducing the work ethic into sport when so young.

The age for sport-as-work should, in my opinion, not begin before the age of 18 to 20. It is only then that we should be directing our competitive urges toward an end. We need that competitive period as we measure ourselves in early adulthood when our physical powers are blooming. The passion of that period of our lives, and the wonderful rewards and valuable lessons that hard training and competitive sport can bring, must be enjoyed to the full. Goal-orientation is important; to waste that energy on play would be futile.

However, I now know that this period of goal-orientation must also come to an end; there is a time when the primary element of play must return to our sport, when the goal-orientation must be subjugated. Perhaps each runner can compete for 15 to 20 years, after which it may be time to return to a second sporting childhood. Indeed, there may be both physiological and philosophical reasons for this.

The philosophical reason may simply be that, after 20 years of competition, you should have resolved those competitive physical urges that drove you before. The continual need to assert and assuage your ego should hopefully have diminished. After 20 years, it is time to relax more, and to enjoy it. That, surely, is the just reward earned by so much hard training and exhaustive racing.

The physical reasons are even more compelling: the body at 40, or 50, or 60, is not the same body it was at 20, even though the brain may think so. Whereas continued physical activity will delay the processes of decay that accompany aging, it cannot reverse the process. Your body is not 20 forever, even though I suspect your mind can be. That some athletes, such as Wally Hayward (who completed the 1988 Comrades Marathon in 9:44:15 at age 79, beating more than half the field) or John Campbell (who ran the standard marathon in 2:11:15 at age 42) or Carlos Lopes (who won the Olympic Marathon gold medal at age 37), are apparently able to overcome this process is the classic red herring. They are genetically exceptional. We must not base our expectations of what will happen to the rest of us on the basis of one or two individual case histories. Instead, we should be basing our expectations on the results of scientific studies of the bodily changes that occur with aging in the vast majority of us. Sadly, these studies do not make for great reading (chapter 2), as they show that the body undergoes substantial physiological changes after the age of 50, changes that accelerate somewhat after 60.

Aging athletes who have completed many races, including many ultramarathons, and who have run many miles in training but wish to continue their sport for as long as possible should pay heed to the following guidelines:

- Accept that your best is past. Aging is a real phenomenon, regardless of what the media would have us believe. Even aging actors and actresses must resort to unphysiological measures, particularly cosmetic surgery, to perpetuate the myth of eternal youth. But sooner or later, the truth will express itself. I suspect that the battle against age must be fought with stealth and wisdom. Pretending that it does not exist, or that it can be fought with the same methods that brought athletic success in our twenties, is inappropriate.

- Assess the cost of remaining competitive. When the cost of trying to remain competitive outweighs the benefits, it is perhaps time to discard the competitive urges and to turn to recreational running for health and fitness only. The decision should be one of wisdom, not of weakness and capitulation.

- Accept that training becomes more difficult. With age, training is harder both physically and mentally. The physical changes described in this chapter reduce our ability to train as much, as intensely, or as frequently as in our youth. Hence, most of the more intensive programs described in chapters 5 and 6 are inappropriate for those over 40. Yet, at present, no one has offered any real alternatives. Perhaps they are too scared to admit that aging could ever occur in the physically active marathon runners, who were once erroneously promised immunity from heart attacks (Bassler 1977). My intuition tells me that it is important to cut down on the total amount of running you do after 40, especially if you ran many miles in your youth. My unproven suggestion is that most "normal" runners (and this excludes the obvious exceptions such as Wally Hayward and Basil Davis) have a limit of possibly 20 years' involvement in competitive distance running. Thus, those who start at the age of 20 become increasingly injury-prone and show a more marked fall in performance after the age of 40. Those who start at 40 can expect the same result at the age of 60. It is not chronological age that determines the runner's age; rather it is the years of heavy training. This is a distinction that many have difficulty accepting. It is indeed possible to be an old runner at 40.

The age- and training-related changes in muscle and tendon reduce the ability to sustain heavy training loads and increase susceptibility to injury. Hence, the aged athlete, regardless of chronological age, will need to train less frequently, less intensively, and with a lesser total training load. Jeff Galloway suggests that the aged runner should only run every second day and should limit total training distance to less than 50 km per week.

As this training volume is probably inadequate for maintaining a favorable physique, it is advisable to introduce other non-weight-bearing activities, such as cycling, swimming, canoeing, and weight training of the upper body.

The intensity and volume of intensive training, such as speed work, especially intervals, need to be reduced, possibly drastically. The distinction between high-intensity training that is beneficial and that which is harmful narrows with age. A good starting point would be never to exceed half the number of intervals you ran in your twenties. This would need to be reduced even further with each subsequent decade. One 70-year-old runner told me that a single 400-m interval was now quite adequate for him. He had found that when he tried to do more his racing performances fell off substantially. To maintain muscle strength, people who do not swim or canoe may wish to include weight-training activities, especially for the upper body.

- Accept that continued heavy training may be detrimental. I have alluded to the possibility that the rate of aging of connective tissue could possibly be increased by years of continued heavy training. Also, the rate of deterioration of previously injured joints in the lower limbs and back could be accelerated by continued weight-bearing activities.

For those committed runners who develop more serious injuries, including osteoarthritis, a simple conversion to cycling may allow them to continue exercising for as long each day as they wish and to compete in ultradistance competitive cycling events without discomfort. Most will soon discover that, unlike running, cycling does not cause symptoms either during the activity or on the days that follow.

The problem in giving this advice is to overcome committed runners' prejudice against any activity other than running. Besides their preconception that cycling is dangerous, they consider cycling to be less demanding physically and therefore less beneficial than running. However, after they have climbed a few long, steep hills on a bicycle, this view will soon change.

Some recent studies have also suggested that heavy training in those over 50 may cause a reduction in bone mass (Michel et al. 1989; 1991)—the very opposite of the effect at a younger age. Heavy training was described as more than 6 hours per week after the age of 50 and more than 3 hours per week after the age of 70. There is also the finding that people with high blood pressure may be at increased risk of suffering a stroke if they train more than about 2 to 4 hours per week.

Similarly, it has been found that many years of endurance training appears to be a risk factor for the heart rhythm abnormality, atrial fibrillation (see chapter 15). This too is not a benign condition since a person with atrial fibrillation has a reduced life expectancy, in part because of an increased risk that blood clots will develop in the atrial cavity of the abnormally beating heart with possible dispersion to the brain, causing a stroke. Clearly, these studies need to be confirmed before any absolute conclusions can be drawn. But they do suggest caution. We really cannot assume that what was good for us at 20 will be equally good at 70.

FINAL WORD

Some important messages derived from the final section of this chapter are as follows:

- Age is a factor that needs to be considered when drawing up a training program. The need to be more careful in training becomes more important with age. The more intensive training programs listed in chapters 5 and 6 may be unrealistic for most runners aged over 40. In particular, the volume and intensity of training need to be reduced. Until such time as specific programs are developed for older athletes, it may be most appropriate to follow the scientific approach proposed in chapter 5, in which the effects of training on performance are evaluated frequently.

- Be wary of previous injuries and, most especially, chronic joint injuries.

- Do not specialize in one activity only. It may be more appropriate to include a range of activities that train both the upper and lower body in both weight-bearing and non-weight-bearing activities.

- Accept that body weight is a significant factor in the ease with which we adapt to running. In general, the lighter you are, the easier it is to run and probably the less likely it is that injuries will develop. In contrast, men heavier than about 90 kg and women heavier than 75 kg will find running more difficult. Non-weight-bearing activities are particularly beneficial for heavier people.

CHAPTER 12

Pushing the Limits of Performance

J ust how fast can men and women run? Most theories on this topic are unsatisfactory because they are based on instinctive answers that are firmly grounded on personal beliefs rather than on any scientific information. The important question to ask is whether we in fact have any scientific basis for projecting how running records will improve in our lifetimes and beyond.

PHYSIOLOGICAL BASIS OF RECORDS

The first scientist to analyze human athletic records was A.V. Hill (1925). To answer the question "For how long can a given effort be maintained?" Hill plotted the average speeds for all male and female world running records against the time for which those speeds had been maintained (figure 12.1).

From the graphs that he generated, he made the following conclusions:

- Very high running speeds could be maintained for only relatively short times, the fastest running speeds being recorded in the 200 m race (point A). This is because humans only reach their peak running speed after about 50 m and slow down relatively little over the next 150 m of the 200-m race. Hence, the average speed over 200 m is faster than that over 100 m.

- Running speeds fell rapidly in events lasting more than 20 seconds and leveled off in events lasting more than 10 to 15 minutes (point B).

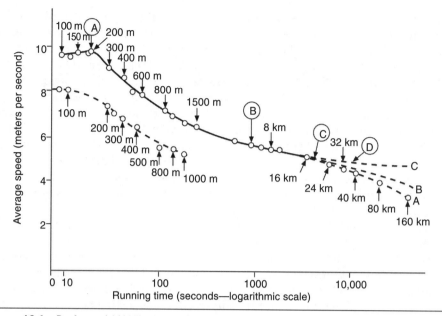

Figure 12.1 Professor A. V. Hill's plot of average running speeds for male (top line) and female (bottom line) world-record holders up to 1925.

From A. V. Hill (1925, p. 484). Reprinted with permission from Elsevier Science.

- In running events lasting more than 60 minutes (point C), a further reduction in performance occurred, and this became exaggerated the longer the performance. This reduction was particularly marked in running races longer than 40 km (point D).

- The women's world running records were only 79% of the corresponding male records. The way in which this has changed in the recent past provides a measure of the extent to which this male/female difference can be ascribed to either hereditary or environmental factors and, indeed as we shall see, the extent to which this difference can be reduced by the illegal use of anabolic steroids.

Hill then considered the physiological basis of these observations. He estimated that the oxygen debt mechanism, probably an incorrect concept (chapter 2) but one that he was among the first to popularize, would support exercise for at least 50 seconds. Hill concluded that the fall-off in performance after 20 seconds of exercise must happen because the body is unable to release all its available energy stores in such a short time. The modern version of this model, the Energy Supply/Energy Depletion Model of Athletic Performance described in chapter 3, is based, in part, on Hill's analysis of these athletic records. As argued in chapter 3, the reason this model cannot be correct is that any failure to generate energy fast enough will lead to irreversible muscle contraction and muscle rigor, not fatigue.

Perhaps because he recognized the weakness of this theory, Hill proposed that mechanical and nervous factors, rather than the depletion of energy reserves, must be the critical factors limiting performance in explosive short-term activities. This fits in with the notion of there being a central (brain) governor that limits exercise to prevent damage to the heart and other organs.

To explain why there was only a gradual decline in the speed that could be maintained in events lasting between 10 and 60 minutes, Hill concluded that these activities were limited only by the athlete's maximum ability to consume oxygen, the $\dot{V}O_2$max value. As that value was preset before the athlete began the race, performance during races within that range of distances would not differ substantially.

Of course, this is an interesting speculation. Hill first had to assume that the $\dot{V}O_2$max determines performance in races lasting 10 minutes. Then, because he knew that performances fell little in races up to 60 minutes, he had to conclude that the $\dot{V}O_2$max also determines performance in these longer races. He did not consider the possibility that performances in races at these distances might be determined by another physiological factor or set of factors (chapter 2) independent of $\dot{V}O_2$max values and oxygen transport. However, this did not prevent scientists from propagating this exclusive model for the past 75 years.

Despite its flaws, Hill's conclusion is especially interesting because it is the understanding of the very factors limiting performance in this range of running distances that is the most troublesome for the traditional Cardiovascular/Anaerobic Model of Athletic Performance. Like Hill, proponents of this model believe that the accumulation of lactate explains the progressive fatigue that develops during these races. But this explanation cannot be correct. In races lasting between 30 and 60 minutes, blood lactate concentrations rise early in the race but fall progressively thereafter and are lower when fatigue is increasing sharply near the end of the race than they are earlier in the race when the athlete is not as tired (Schabort et al. 2000). Hill might have been wiser to extend his original central (brain) governor theory to explain the progressively slower times that can be sustained in races lasting 10 to 60 minutes. This governor would be responding to information about the runner's rising body core temperature and other information still to be determined, including, for example, the rising rate of ventilation and the increasing discomfort from shortness of breath (dyspnea) that it causes. The evidence for the action of such a governor is presented in chapters 2 and 4.

Next, Hill offered two suggestions to explain the further, more rapid deterioration in the speed that can be maintained in races between 16 and 160 km (line A in figure 12.1). He postulated that fatigue in these events might be due to exhaustion of the material of the muscle or to incidental disturbances that force runners to stop before their muscular systems have reached their limits. He suggested that to sustain the effort required to maintain speed, a runner's glycogen supply would need to be bolstered by carbohydrate feeds. Here Hill was anticipating the Energy Depletion Model of Athletic Performance described in chapter 3. The weakness of this particular model is that muscle glycogen depletion leads to muscle rigor, not fatigue.

Second, Hill felt that the greatest athletes of his time had confined themselves to distances of up to 16 km. If athletes of the caliber of Alf Shrubb and Paavo Nurmi had run marathons and longer races regularly, they would have broken the records by producing performances that corresponded with line B or, better still, line C. In chapter 6, I argue that the best marathon runners are those athletes who, like Nurmi, are also the fastest at the distances of 1.6 to 21 km. Indeed, had Nurmi not been declared a professional and banned from the 1932 Los Angeles Olympic Games Marathon, he might well have proved Hill's prediction correct.

Hill ascribed the inferior performances of the women to a lower capacity for power production. It was an opinion he came to regret. In truth, few women participated in competitive athletics in the 1920s, which goes some way to explaining the poorer performance of women in those years compared to men. The homocentric bias of that period, still apparent when I began running in 1969, blinded Hill's judgment. This trend continued until relatively recently.

Women in the Marathon

Looking back from the start of the third millennium, it is difficult to comprehend the restrictions that women athletes have had to overcome in their quest for athletic equality. New Yorker Nina Kuscsik, one of the first women to complete a sanctioned marathon legitimately, reviewed the history of women's participation in long-distance running at the 1976 New York Academy of Sciences Conference on the marathon (Kuscsik 1977).

Kuscsik suggests that the first female marathoner may have been Melpomene, who, "accompanied by a bicycle escort," allegedly completed the first Olympic Games Marathon in 1896 in about 4:30:00 (p. 863). Not surprisingly, the Olympic Committee refused to grant permission for her to enter the race, an action that would have been in accord with the beliefs of Baron Pierre de Coubertin, founder of the modern Olympic Games. In 1928 de Coubertin stated, "As to the admission of women to the Games, I remain strongly against it. It was against my will that they were admitted to a growing number of competitions" (Kuscsik 1977, p. 864). Melpomene was clearly way ahead of her time. In Britain, women runners were ridiculed and labeled as "brazen doxies" (p. 863).

Rumor has it that a second woman, Stamata Revithi, may also have competed in the inaugural Olympic Marathon. Revithi, a mother of a 17-month-old boy, had apparently arrived in Athens to be told that she could become rich if she were to run the marathon and win (Martin and Gynn 2000). However, signed documents proving that she began the marathon at 8:00 A.M. and arrived at the finish at 1:30 P.M. have never been found, which, as Martin and Gynn (2000) suggest, might indicate that Melpomene and Revithi were indeed the same woman.

In 1921, an international governing body for women's athletics, the Feminine Sportive Federation International (FSFI), was formed. The FSFI successfully lobbied for the introduction of five athletic events for women at the 1928 Olympic Games, including the 800 m as the longest race. Unfortunately, some competitors in the 800-m final collapsed, providing the Olympic Committee with sufficient ammunition to have the event removed from future Games—a move that Kuscsik believes derailed women's distance running by 50 years. The decision to bar women from running in the 800-m event had been taken even though, in 1926, Gertrude Ederle became the first woman to swim the 32-km English Channel, breaking the men's record by 2 hours (Lutter 1994). At the time, the idea that women should not tax themselves in competition was supported by physical educators in the United States.

The prevailing belief was that women were

not physically fit for the excitement and strain that this competition affords [and should] play for enjoyment, not to specialize and win. . . . The aim of athletics among women has been the establishment and maintenance of a high standard of health and vigor, rather than some brilliant achievement. (Kuscsik 1977, p. 865)

(continued)

This bias was clearly inspired by the social norms of the pre-World War II years, as well as by prevailing attitudes toward women, which were that a woman's primary function was to reproduce. As exercise, sport, and education, especially, were seen to be detrimental to uterine function, all were to be avoided. Vigorous sport, especially competition, were thought to divert blood away from the uterus and therefore cause it to atrophy; moreover, it was thought that exercise increased the risk that injury would damage the "inner mechanism of the female frame."

As a result, during the first two decades of the twentieth century, young women were only encouraged to participate in aesthetic sports. In 1923, the Women's Division of the National Amateur Athletic Federation in the United States replaced competitive sport with "play days" during which young women from a number of neighboring schools congregated for a day of sporting activities that included basketball, volleyball, field hockey, and swimming, but also hopscotch, dodge ball, relays, and folk dancing. "Frequent breaks for juice and cookies prevented the players from overexercising themselves and gave them time to socialize. . . . The idea was to have fun rather than to excel as an individual" (Lutter 1994). Although young American women were allowed to play cricket, lawn tennis, golf, and a less vigorous form of basketball, the national pastime, baseball, was considered "too strenuous for womankind, except as she may take part in the grandstand" (Howell 1982).

Despite these constraints, the Roaring Twenties saw the beginning of the emancipation of women and the growth of a strong movement that began to campaign for the right to vote. More important, women constituted in excess of 25% of the labor force in the United States and, as a result, became more independent and began to acquire the money to participate in sport both as a part of work teams and in leisure time. But during the Great Depression, women lost valuable ground as it was considered unpatriotic for a woman to take a man's work. As a result, women gave up some of the autonomy they had gained in the 1920s (Lutter 1994). World War II reversed that bias, as women who did not work were now considered unpatriotic. However, when male soldiers returned from the war, the situation was reversed for a third time as a woman was again expected to

> stand behind her man and be available for her family. Working with her body or pursuing physical activities somehow did not fit into the updated version of what a family woman should be. And, predictably, the emphasis was on protecting her most valued assets: her reproductive organs and her femininity. (Lutter 1994, p. 271)

Since it was still believed that vigorous exercise could interfere with reproductive function, young women continued to be discouraged from participating in physical activity.

The reintroduction of the 800-m event at the 1960 Olympic Games rekindled interest in long-distance running; the following decade was characterized by the increasingly assertive actions of people wishing to participate in long-distance competitions, including marathon races. At that time, the body governing athletics in the United States, the Amateur Athletics Union (AAU), did not allow women to race farther than 800 m. In response to growing pressure, this limit was increased tenfold to 8 km by 1968. But for some, this concession was too little. The desire to compete with men in the 42-km marathon footrace had become an obsession for some women.

Hauman (1996) recounts that the first recorded time by a woman marathon runner was that of Englishwoman Violet Piercy, who, in October 1926, ran the Polytechnic Marathon course between Windsor and London in 3:40:22. The next recorded time for a woman is that of Californian Merry Lepper, who completed the 1963 Western Hemisphere Marathon in Culver City, California, in 3:37:05, despite having to punch an irate official who tried to remove her from the race. To enter the race, she had hidden on the sidelines before jumping in to join the men. In 1966, Roberta Gibb Bingay completed the Boston Marathon unofficially in 3:21:40. However, Will Cloney, the race organizer, insisted that Bingay had not run the race. "She merely covered the same route as the official race while it was in progress" (Kuscsik 1977, p. 867).

The following year, Bingay again completed the race (in 3:27:00), but the attention that year was focused on Kathrine Switzer. Switzer entered the race officially by not disclosing her first name; she started the race in disguise, with a hood covering her head. When it became apparent that a woman was running with the men, race organizers Will Cloney and Jock Semple tried to intercede physically. But a body block administered on Semple by Switzer's football-playing boyfriend dissuaded his further efforts (figure 12.2). Switzer finished in 4:30:00. Within days, her membership of the AAU was terminated on the grounds that she had exceeded the allowable distance for women, had run with men, had fraudulently entered an AAU race, and had run without a chaperone.

But the male bastion was crumbling, and women were finding it easier to run marathons. What is more, their times were improving dramatically. In 1971, during the New York City Marathon, Beth Bonner and Nina Kuscsik became the first women to officially break the 3-hour barrier. As a result, the AAU increased the legal limit for women to 16 km and agreed that selected women be allowed to enter the Boston Marathon officially.

Figure 12.2   Kathrine Switzer's boyfriend blocks the attempt of the race organizer, Jock Semple, to oust her from the 1967 Boston Marathon.

© The Bettman Archive

(continued)

During the next running of the marathon, the organizers agreed to allow women to enter, provided they raced in a separate race, which was to start 10 minutes before the men. But the women competitors had something else in mind: when the starting gun went off, they sat down and waited the 10 minutes for the men's race to begin.

In the face of this open rebellion and a pending human rights lawsuit for practicing discrimination in a public place (Kuscsik 1977), the AAU finally capitulated. In 1972 the legal running limit for women was raised to 42 km, and the AAU declared that men and women could compete in the same races and begin from the same starting line at the same time. The same year the United States Congress passed Title IX, which prohibited discrimination on the basis of gender in educational institutions receiving government funding. As a result, women could no longer be denied equal access to sport in any educational institution in the United States.

Admission of women to ultradistance races followed shortly afterward. In 1975, women were allowed to compete officially in the Comrades Marathon for the first time. A handful of women had run the race unofficially before 1975, but the numbers were small and their performances were unremarkable when compared to the subsequent achievements of other women who have run the race since then.

Since 1972, progress in women's distance running has been relentless. During the late 1970s and early 1980s, attention was focused on Norwegian Grete Waitz, who, on the global stage provided by the New York City and London Marathons, personally lowered the world women's marathon record by more than 7 minutes between 1979 and 1983 and proved that the best women distance runners could outrun all but the very best men.

In 1984, another milestone was passed when the women's marathon was finally included in the Olympic Games. American Joan Benoit-Samuelson overcame potentially crippling injury, knee surgery, and illness to win a dramatic race after leading for more than three-quarters of the way. Like others who have been forced to rest before a major race, Benoit-Samuelson later ascribed her victory to the period of rest following surgery:

> I believe I was in the best shape of my life before the knee injury. I think I would have had the race of my life at the [U.S.] Olympic trials and I think I would have had nothing left for this [Olympic Marathon] race. I feel the injury and the timing were perfect. (Martin and Gynn 2000, pp. 341–42)

It was largely due to the efforts of the original campaigner, Kathrine Switzer, that the women's marathon was included in the Los Angeles Olympic Games. Switzer had raised corporate sponsorship for, and from 1978 onward directed, a series of annual women-only marathon championship races. In 1982, faced with the reality that women's marathon racing was becoming firmly entrenched worldwide, the International Olympic Committee (IOC) announced that a women's marathon would indeed be included in the 1984 Olympic Games in Los Angeles.

In the year after the Olympics, Norwegian Ingrid Kristiansen, fourth in the inaugural Olympic Marathon, lowered the women's world marathon record to 2:21:06—a record that was not broken until 1999; Kristiansen set world records at 5000 m, 10,000 m, and 15 km and, along with Grete Waitz and Portugal's Rosa

Mota, became the dominant women's marathon runner during the mid-to-late 1980s. Fittingly, it was these three athletes, together with Joan Benoit-Samuelson, who filled the first four positions in the inaugural Los Angeles Olympic Marathon.

But when historians of the future choose those remarkable achievements that finally proved women's rightful place with men in the toughest endurance events, they may well include the performances of Paula Newby-Fraser in the 1988 and 1989 Hawaiian Ironman Triathlon, of Frith van der Merwe in the 1989 Comrades Marathon, and of Ann Trason in the Western States 160-km race.

The Hawaiian Ironman Triathlon, comprising a 3.8-km sea swim, a 180-km cycle ride, and a 42-km run, is considered by many to be the toughest single-day sporting event in the world. Before 1988, the margin between the winning male and female competitors had been 1:01:12. But in 1988, Paula Newby-Fraser, a Zimbabwean now resident in San Diego, California, completed the course in 11th position overall, in a time of 9:01:01, just 30:01 or 6% slower than that of the male winner. Her time in the final 42-km run (3:07:09) was only 4:27 (2.4%) slower than that of the male winner. In 1989, Newby-Fraser improved her course record to 9:00:56. Newby-Fraser's performance in the 1988 Hawaiian Ironman event is widely regarded as the greatest endurance performance in history. In 1990, she was selected as the professional sportswoman of the year by the Women's Sports Foundation, ahead of other notable female professional athletes, including Steffi Graf. By 1998, Newby-Fraser had won the Hawaiian Ironman Triathlon a record eight times and had been labeled the greatest triathlete of all time.

South Africa's Frith van der Merwe also features prominently in the record books. Despite having raced excessively in the preceding months, Van der Merwe finished the 1989 Comrades Marathon in fifteenth position overall in a field of 11,000 runners. Her time of 5:54:43 was better than the winning times in all the Comrades races run before 1963 and was only 2 minutes slower than the fastest time of the legendary Wally Hayward. When corrected for the expected 10% difference in performance between men and women, her time was the fastest ever run in the race.

PREDICTING PERFORMANCE LIMITS

Another approach to the analysis of world records is to plot the measured variable (time, height, or distance) against the year in which the world record in that event was established. The rationale behind this approach is that in each event there must be a speed, height, weight, or distance that will prove to be the ultimate limit for human performance. This limit can be predicted mathematically because, as any particular record approaches this limit, each improvement on the previous record will be even smaller and the time period between each new record will grow ever longer. Thus, the curve of any graph plotting these records would start to flatten out. In mathematical terms, it would become asymptotic. (Records that are not approaching their limits will continue to improve linearly; where rapid improvement is occurring, the graph might even ascend.)

The first scientist to adopt this approach was German-born Ernest Jokl, an emeritus professor of physical education at the University of Kentucky. Jokl made the German 1928 Olympic Games team as an alternate in the 400-m hurdles but did not compete. Between 1928 and 1932, he was director of the Institute of Sports Medicine in Breslau, Germany, perhaps the first of its kind in the world. Expelled from Germany in 1932 on religious grounds, he settled in South Africa, where he established a course for teaching physical education at the University of Stellenbosch. His influence was such that a new word, *jokkel* (meaning "to exercise"), was incorporated into the Afrikaans language. He left South Africa in 1948, settling in the United States.

Jokl and his colleagues (1976) concentrated on nonrunning events and noted that, with two exceptions, all world records in these events showed a linear improvement, indicating that the ultimate performance limit was not yet in sight and could not be predicted at the time.

The first exception to the rule of linear improvement in world records occurred in the long jump, in which the record curve started to become asymptotic in 1935, when American Jesse Owens jumped a distance of 8.13 m. In the following 33 years, the record improved a mere 0.22 m. Then, the impossible occurred. At the 1968 Mexico Olympics, Bob Beamon added 0.55 m to the record, an estimated record progression of 84 years—roughly equivalent to a 6-second improvement in the 400-m world record or a 24-second improvement in the mile running record. It was, according to Jokl, the greatest single feat in the recorded history of athletics and a record that, as shown in figure 12.3, should be safe for another 84 years. The factors contributing to Beamon's remarkable performance were the altitude and the following wind speed, which at 2.0 m per second was the maximum allowable (Brearly 1977). Both factors helped him attain a faster sprinting speed than had previously been achieved by a long jumper (Ward-Smith 1986).

But as we now know, the American Mike Powell eclipsed Beamon's record within

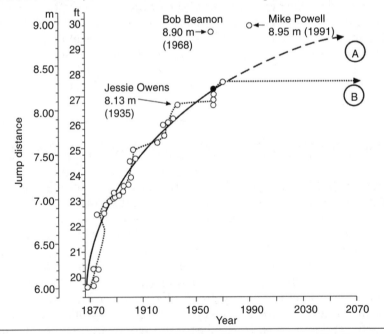

Figure 12.3   Record progression in the men's long jump. The performances of Bob Beamon and Jesse Owens could not have been predicted on the basis of earlier world records set between 1870 and 1968. **A** (dashed line) is the projection of the world long jump record based on the record performances between 1870 and 1975. **B** (dotted line) shows the apparent plateau in performance between 1968 and 1991 without the performances of Bob Beamon and Mike Powell.

From Jokl et al. (1976, p. 7). © 1976 by S. Karger AG, Basel. Reprinted by permission.

23 years (figure 12.3), even though he was competing at sea level in the 1991 World Championships in Tokyo. This suggests that the previous long-jump record was, in reality, not limited by human physiology. It could be that the long-jump training techniques were inadequate and had stagnated, or that the athletes best suited to long jump were simply not attracted to that event.

The second unusual pattern occurred in the women's 400-m freestyle swimming event. The women's swimming record had manifested a dramatic upward curve. Furthermore, when Jokl wrote the article, the gap between the men's and women's record was closing, and this raised the statistical possibility that in the late 1980s or early 1990s women would swim the 400 m as fast as men.

A similar pattern of accelerated improvement in women's world running records between 1960 and 1995 was noted by Brian Whipp and Susan Ward, two physiologists from the University of California in Los Angeles. Whipp and Ward plotted the relative rates of improvement in male and female world running records for distances from 200 m to 42 km, from 1895 to 1995 for male athletes and from 1915 to 1995 for female athletes (figure 12.4; Whipp and Ward 1992).

They noticed that the rate of improvement for women was faster at all running distances than for men (figure 12.4B). Then, despite the potential pitfalls they foresaw, they could not resist extrapolating these record progressions into the future. Naturally, if the records were progressing faster in the women's events and if that rate of progression was to be maintained, then the point must be reached at which women's performances would equal those of the men (figure 12.4C). While this crossover point was predicted to occur after 2030 for the 400 and 1500 m and even later for the 200 and 800 m, the projected intersection for the marathon was predicted to occur in 1998.

However, this did not happen. Between 1985 and 1999, the women's marathon world record did not change. In September 1999, the Kenyan Tegla Loroupe set a new world record of 2:20:43 in the Berlin Marathon. Two years later at Berlin, Naoka Takahashi from Japan further lowered the record to 2:19:46. She held that record for

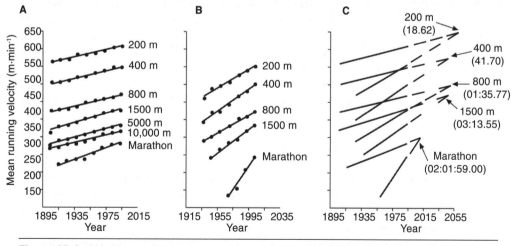

Figure 12.4   World record progressions with time for men (A) and women (B) at running distances from 200 m to the 42-km marathon. The linear regression lines for the running events that are common to men and women are plotted in C and extrapolated to their points of intersection. The values in parenthesis are the predicted world records (h:min:sec.hundredths) at the points of intersection (that is, at the points when the women's records are predicted to pass those of the men). That this has not occurred indicates that the predictions were based on an erroneous supposition. Reprinted with permission from Whipp and Ward (1992, p. 25). © 1992 by Macmillan Magazines Limited.

a week, until Kenyan Catherine Ndereba ran 2:18:47 at Chicago. At the end of 2002, the difference between the men's and women's world marathon records was 13:05.

In fairness to the authors, who have been unjustly criticized in some quarters, they did not predict that women would outrun men at some future date. In fact, they specifically wrote that "the suggestion that women could, so soon, be running those [marathon] races as fast as men seems improbable at first appearance" and "whether the world record progression rate will begin to slow, either relatively abruptly or more progressively, will only become apparent in the future" (Whipp and Ward 1992, p. 25) Rather, they posed four relevant questions:

1. Why is the world record progression in the various events so linear over an interval of approximately a century?
2. Why is the slope of the record progression so similar from the sprints to the 10,000 m?
3. Why is the record progression in the marathon appreciably greater?
4. Why is the record progression for women increasing at such a rapid rate relative to that for men?

Their fourth question is the easiest to answer. The rapid improvement in the women's marathon world records noted by Whipp and Ward (1992) reflected a sociological, not a physiological, phenomenon. The surge in the women's marathon during the 1980s led to an increase in the number of faster, competitive female athletes, with the result that the marathon record improved precipitously. Moreover, Grete Waitz, one of the best female track runners of the era, was enticed by the potential financial rewards into running the New York City Marathon in 1978. Her world-record performances, in which she personally lowered the world record by 7 minutes, launched the golden era of women's marathon running.

Initially, the marathon was dominated by European, especially Scandinavian, and North American women. But, in the last few years, as is the case with the men, an increasing number of East African runners, including former world-record holder diminutive Tegla Loroupe from Kenya, the 1996 Olympic gold medalist and three-time winner of the Boston Marathon, Fatuma Roba from Ethiopia, and current world-record holder, Kenyan Catherine Ndereba, have begun to make their mark on women's marathon running. This too represents a significant sociological shift, as African women have begun to assert themselves in a traditionally male-dominated domain.

But, in the past 10 years, the women's marathon curve has flattened predictably (see line D in figure 12.9) as the record has become more representative of women's current physiological limits. Thus, for the reasons I will outline later in this chapter, there is no probability that, even if all the current social constraints that limit the opportunities for African women to become world-class distance runners were removed overnight, women's marathon performances or indeed their performances at any other distances would suddenly eclipse those of men.

But besides these sociological factors, another theory has been developed to explain the dramatic improvement in women's running performances identified by Whipp and Ward after 1960 (figure 12.4). It is a theory that Jokl and colleagues, and perhaps not even Whipp and Ward, could have anticipated.

Steven Sailer, a United States businessman and avid writer on a host of topics of current interest (**http://members.aol.com/stevesir**), and Steven Seiler, an American exercise physiologist currently working at Agder College in Norway, collected data for the top six finishers in World Track and Field and Olympic final competitions between 1952 and 1996. All in all, they collected data from a total of 182 championship finals (Sailer and Seiler 1997). Like Whipp and Ward, they wished to determine changes in the gender gap in performance during that time. But crucially, their analysis included performances after 1989, the year that saw the collapse of communism in Eastern Europe.

Those researchers showed that the intergender gap in running performances reached its minimum for the 800 m in the 1970s and for all other events except the marathon in the 1980s. The difference ranged between 9% and 13% for all events, with the lowest average difference of 11% occurring in the mid-1980s (see figure 12.3.) Between 1970 and 1989, 70% of the top female finishers came from East Germany and Russia. Interestingly, whereas East German women set 49 world records in the sprints and relays during that 19-year period, only 7 of 48 world records set at 5, 10, and 42 km were set by East European runners, and none by East Germans. The most enduring of these records is Czechoslovakian Jarmila Kratochivilova's 800-m record of 1:53.28 set at the 1983 World Championships, a record that some consider to be unsurpassable.

However, by the mid-1990s, the average difference between men's and women's world athletic records had increased dramatically to 12%, indicating that something unusual had happened. Other evidence confirming that women's running performances fell off in the 1990s comes from a comparative analysis of the progress of men's and women's world records between 1989 and 2000. Thus, the men's world records in track running events have improved by 1% since 1989, including 38 new world records. In contrast, there has been no average improvement in the women's world track records during that time, and only seven women's world track records were broken between 1989 and 1999. What is more, none of these new records was set by an East German.

Sailer and Seiler conclude that increased female participation in sport and running, allied to an increasingly professional approach to sport and better coaching, should have led to progressively better performances in the 1990s, continuing the trend established in the 1970s and 1980s. However, given that drug use was rife among elite female athletes who dominated running during the earlier period and that these drugs significantly improved athletic performance (chapter 13), it is likely then that more stringent doping control techniques, including the deterrent effect of out-of-season testing first introduced in 1989, was the single factor that reversed the progress in women's world running achieved up to 1989. Thus, Sailer and Seiler conclude that the increasing gender gap in running performances since the mid-1980s is the strongest indirect evidence that the widespread illegal use of anabolic steroids by female athletes could have accounted for the markedly superior female performances achieved during those years, compared to the less-good performances during the last decade of the twentieth century.

Interestingly, women's performances in the ultramarathons also improved substantially, relative to those of men, during the period surveyed by Sailer and Seiler. For example, a comparison of the original curve of A.V. Hill (figure 12.1) and the most recent curve (figure 12.5) shows that neither the men's nor the women's performance curve shows the same dramatic fall in performance in races longer than 80 km that the men's curve did in 1925 (figure 12.1, line A). This can be explained quite simply. As Hill suggested, the best runners of the early 1900s, such as Alf

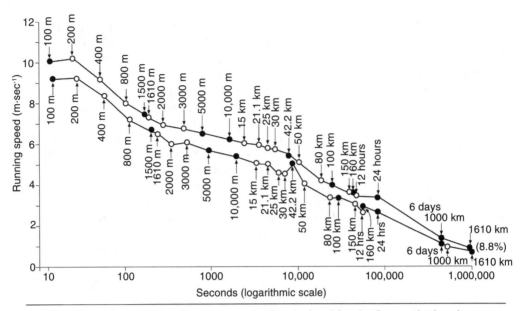

Figure 12.5 World record performance in males (top line) and females (bottom line) at distances from 100 m to 1610 km, current to 2001.

Shrubb and Paavo Nurmi, did not compete in, nor did they train specifically for, races longer than 16 to 42 km, with the result that these races did not necessarily attract the top middle-distance competitors. But since Arthur Newton's day, progressively faster and more talented runners, such as Wally Hayward, Don Ritchie, Bruce Fordyce, and Yiannis Kouros, have become interested in the marathon and ultramarathon and have improved human performance in those races dramatically.

The same argument can be used to explain the unremarkable performances of women in races longer than 42 km, even up to 1983, when the difference between men and women was 44% at 80 km and 27% at 24 hours. Thus, the performance difference between men and women was three times greater for the 24-hour race than it was for the 100 m, the opposite of that predicted by the theory discussed subsequently, which holds that women have superior endurance compared to men. In accordance with this theory, the intergender gap in running performance should shrink progressively as the racing distance increases to the ultramarathons and other multiday events.

But by 2001, these female-male differences had shrunk considerably to 17% at 50 miles; 13.6% at 100 km; 9.6% at 100 miles; 24.5% at 24 hours; 15.9% at 1000 km; and only 8.8% at 1610 km (1000 miles).

It would seem that before the 1990s the glamour event for women was the standard marathon and that this distance attracted the best athletes. As was the case with the men before 1929, the ultramarathons have only recently started attracting elite female marathon runners. Indeed, the remarkable ultramarathon performances of Frith van der Merwe, whose best standard marathon time was only 6 minutes slower than the then women's world record, shows what will happen when the world's best female marathoners start running the ultramarathon. In fact, the performance of van der Merwe in the 1989 Comrades Marathon was exactly 9.9% slower than the then best-ever performance of a male in that race. This could be the smallest intergender difference in running performance yet measured.

The result of this is that the gap between female-male performances in ultramarathon races has narrowed to the same 11% to 12% difference that is also present in the short track events from 100 to 10,000 m, as well as in the marathon.

This essentially means that the inherent quality of the athletes competing in the longer-distance races is now similar in men and women. In other words, the historically much larger female-male performance difference in the longer-distance races was due simply to the relatively poorer athletic ability of the women who chose to run those longer races. But now that the relative quality of athletes attracted to male and female ultradistance races is similar, the gender gap in ultradistance performance has narrowed to equal that of races from 100 m to 42 km.

What these records do not explain are the biological factors responsible for these gender-related differences. The interesting scientific question that they raise is why the magnitude of the performance difference between men and women is so similar in both the sprints and in the endurance events (11%). It is possible that the same biological factors that cause women to run more slowly in the sprints also explain why they are slower by a similar margin in the endurance events, such as the standard marathon. Clearly, this is at variance with the classical teaching, which holds that speed and endurance are determined by different factors. Or does it confirm Arthur Lydiard's belief (Lydiard and Gilmour 1978) and Gordon Pirie's observation (1961) that athletes' potentials are determined by their speeds over 100 m?

Will Women Ever Outrun Men?

Despite the exceptional distance-running performances of female athletes such as Grete Waitz, Paula Newby-Fraser, Frith van der Merwe, and Ann Trason and the rapid improvements in female track world records up to 1990, and in the ultramarathons between 1990 and 2000, the reality is that women's performances are inferior to those of the elite men at all distances, including the ultramarathon.

However, an interesting paradox we noticed among South African ultramarathon runners was that recreational male and female runners who were matched for performance at a short distance, say 10 or 21 km, usually did not perform equally at longer distances of 42, 56, or 90 km. The longer the distance, the greater the time by which the female runner would beat the male, suggesting that women have superior fatigue resistance (see chapter 2). If this difference also exists in groups of elite athletes, then there should be some (very long) running distance at which the best women will ultimately beat the best men. To test this hypothesis that average women runners perform progressively better than average male runners as the running distance increases, we evaluated the racing performances of 28 male and 28 female runners whose performances in the Two Oceans Marathon were matched (Bam et al. 1997; figure 12.6).

By comparing their best racing performances at all distances from 10 to 90 km, we found that the men were significantly faster at distances from 10 to 42 km. However, women became increasingly faster than the men at distances beyond 66 km. Accordingly, we concluded that the women ultramarathon runners in this study had greater fatigue resistance than did equally trained men whose performances were superior up to the marathon distance.

The same findings were reported by Speechly et al. (1996), who compared another group of equally trained average South African male and female marathon

(continued)

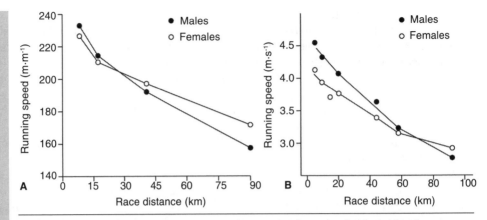

Figure 12.6   Comparative performances at other running distances of male and female ultramarathon runners matched for performance at either 42 km (A) or 56 km (B). When the performances of men and women matched for running ability at 42 or 56 km are compared at shorter (10- or 21-km) distances and at the 90-km Comrades Marathon, it is found that the men outperform the women at the shorter distances, whereas women start to dominate at the longer distances. This suggests that subelite women runners have superior fatigue resistance compared to men of equal running ability at shorter distances. Surprisingly, this effect is not noted in the performances of the world's best runners (figure 12.5), in whom the performance gap between men and women is relatively similar from 100 m to 1610 km.

Adapted by permission from Speechly et al. (1996) and from Bam et al. (1997). © 1997 by Lippincott, Williams, and Wilkins.

runners who were also matched for performance at 42 km, rather than at 56 km. They found that female runners were, on average, shorter (by 11 cm), lighter (by 15 kg), and fatter (by 6%), with a marginally lower $\dot{V}O_2$max (48 vs. 51 ml O_2 per kg per min). But females ran significantly faster at 90 km because they sustained a higher percentage $\dot{V}O_2$max at that distance (60% vs. 50% $\dot{V}O_2$max), as they did at 42 km (73% vs. 65% $\dot{V}O_2$max). The decline in the percentage $\dot{V}O_2$max with increasing running distance was also significantly less in females, confirming that a superior fatigue resistance explained the superior 90-km performance of the females whose $\dot{V}O_2$max, running economy, and training volume were not greater than those of the males with whom they had been matched.

In contrast, the study of Sparling et al. (1998) found that the intergender difference in the world's best times for races from 1500 m to 42 km was essentially the same (11.1% vs. 11.2%). Furthermore, these differences have now been stable for more than a decade.

Thus, the authors found no evidence for the theory that the rapid improvement in women's marathon performances in the 1970s and 80s indicated they would one day outrun men. Nor did their findings correspond with our hypothesis that at distances beyond 42 km, women show superior fatigue resistance. The gender gap in running performance did not reduce, as our hypothesis suggests it should, as the racing distance increased.

Why, then, does analysis of the performance of average runners suggest convincingly that women have the superior fatigue resistance whereas an analysis of world records set by the world's best runners fails to reveal any such difference? The most likely explanation is that a gender-related but not a gender-specific (that is, a genetically determined) difference explains these discrepant findings.

My guess is that average runners show average differences between the genders, whereas those differences become much less at the extremes of the populations from which the very best performers come. For example, while the average male marathon runners are likely to be taller and heavier with less body fat than the average female marathon runners, these differences are likely to be much less when the world's best male and female runners are compared. It is probable that the world's best male and female marathon and ultramarathon runners are all equally small and light (less than 45 kg) with a low percentage body fat, albeit marginally greater in the women.

One possibility is that the clear differences in fatigue resistance between the genders that we and Speechly et al. (1996) found could be due to differences in the body sizes of the average male and female runners in our respective studies. As a result, the generally smaller women are at an advantage that becomes increasingly apparent as the race distance increases. But since these size differences are much smaller in the world's best marathon and ultramarathon runners of both genders, we would expect the real relative advantage of the average female runner over the average male runner to disappear when the performances of the elite athletes of both genders, whose body sizes are much more similar—both being equally tiny—are compared.

My conclusion is that the fatigue resistance of the very best male and female ultramarathon runners is not different, which indicates that any gender-related differences in fatigue resistance is not gender specific but is more likely the result of the smaller body mass of the average female runner compared to the average male runner. The point has been made repeatedly that smallness is a key advantage in marathon and ultramarathon running (Dennis and Noakes 1999; Kay et al. 2001).

On the basis of all this information, we can now safely predict that until women can run short distances as fast as men, the curve showing future improvements in marathon times will remain lower than that of the men, essentially in proportion to how much slower women are than men at the shorter running distances. We can make this prediction with certainty, given the clear relationship between running performance at short and longer distances. We can predict marathon performance from 5- or 10-km race time (tables 2.3, 2.4, 2.6, and 2.7) and the recent analysis of world records by Sparling et al. (1998). In addition, it appears that women are not inherently more fatigue resistant than men. However, being, on average, smaller than men, the average woman will be at an advantage over the average male at the longer distances, at which her smaller size is beneficial.

Perhaps the reason that East, North, and South Africans, as well as Asians, are so successful in distance races is that they are generally smaller than Europeans and North Americans.

PREDICTING FUTURE WORLD RECORDS

Whipp and Ward (1992) observed that, during the past century, world running records have improved linearly but at different rates for the different distances, with the fastest rate of improvement being in the marathon. However, these observations were also made some years earlier by three Chicago physicians, Ryder,

Carr, and Herget (1976). This team of researchers plotted the speed (in meters per minute) of every male world record ever set at both metric and nonmetric running distances against the year in which the record was established. They found that there was a linear improvement in the speed of every record in each event equivalent to about 0.6 m per minute per year for the 100 m and 0.9 m per minute per year for the standard marathon (figure 12.7).

On the assumption that the future improvement in running world records would continue to follow a linear projection, the authors used their analysis to predict future world records. The prediction for 2000 was that the 10,000 m for men should have been run in less than 26:00 (compared to the actual 2000 world record of 26:22); the men's marathon world record should be less than 2:00:00 in 2004; the 5000 m for men less than 12:00 by 2020; and the mile for men below 3:30 by 2028 (table 12.1).

Unfortunately, the authors did not analyze women's records, and, as a result, equivalent predictions for women are currently not available. Furthermore, because women have only competed at some running distances since the 1960s, there are few data available. Additionally, since the rate of progression of women's records may have been artificially accelerated in the 1980s by the illicit use of anabolic steroids, with little progress since 1989, any predictions based on the data currently available are likely to be incorrect.

However, there is an alternative theory that contrasts with the belief that male world running records are continuing to improve in a linear manner (Ryder et al. 1976; Whipp and Ward 1992). This theory holds that the rate of progression of world running records may already show evidence of flattening. This view is championed

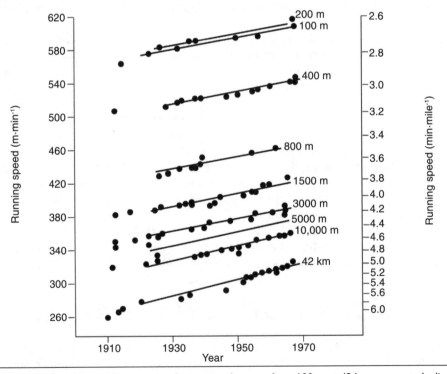

Figure 12.7 World record progression for running distances from 100 m to 42 km appears to be linear.
Adapted from Ryder et al. (1976, p. 112). © 1976 by Scientific American. All rights reserved.

Time	Year	
Distance (m)	2004	2028
100	9.56	9.34
200	18.97	18.52
400	42.49	41.32
800	1:38.30	1:35.10
1000	2:08.80	2:04.30
1500	3:22.20	3:14.70
1609 (mile)	3:38.30	3:30.00
2000	4:40.00	4:28.90
3000	7:12.10	6:54.10
5000	12:24.80	11:51.90
10,000	25:44.00	24:31.00
16,000	42:48.00	40:39.00
20,000	53:57.00	51:09.00
30,000	1:24:42.00	1:20:01.00
42,000	2:00:00.00	1:53:13.00

Table 12.1 World-record predictions (h:min:s.hundredth) for male running races from 100 m to 42 km for 2004 and 2028

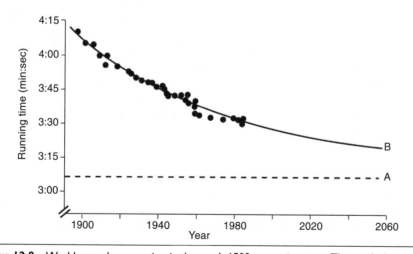

Figure 12.8 World record progression in the men's 1500-m running event. The graph shows a nonlinear (asymptotic) slowing in the velocity of successive new world records, first becoming apparent after about 1940. The broken line A indicates the projected ultimate world record, calculated as the time at which the asymptotic line B ultimately flattens out, sometime after 2100 (see also table 12.2).

Distance (m)	1980	1984	1990	2000	2010	2020	2030
Table 12.2 **Hugh Morton's predicted male world running records (min:s.hundredths) from 1980 to 2100**							
100	9.87	9.95	9.80	9.74	9.68	9.63	9.58
200	19.98	19.92	19.81	19.66	19.52	19.40	19.29
400	44.08	43.86	43.70	43.34	43.01	42.71	42.44
800	1:42.60	1:41.70	1:41.70	1:40.90	1:40.10	1:39.40	1:38.70
1500	3:32.50	3:30.80	3:29.90	3:27.50	3:25.40	3:23.50	3:21.80
1609*	3:50.70	3:49.30	3:48.60	3:46.70	3:44.90	3:43.30	3:41.90
3000	7:31.50	7:32.10	7:24.60	7:18.00	7:12.00	7:06.90	7:02.10
5000	13:10.50	13:00.40	13:00.30	12:51.00	12:42.60	12:35.00	12:28.50
10000	27:42.50	27:22.40	27:21.80	27:03.00	26:46.00	26:30.10	26:16.80

*1609 m = 1 mile.

by Hugh Morton, a statistician at Massey University in Palmerston North, New Zealand (Morton 1983; 1984). Morton has paid particular attention to the progress of the men's 1500-m world record since the record was first recorded in the late nineteenth century. Using sophisticated mathematical techniques, he has provided strong evidence, both mathematically and visually (figure 12.8), that the record progression in the 1500-m race is best described by a curving (asymptotic) line, not by the straight line of Ryder et al. Certainly, a straight line can be fit to these data, but the curving line fits better, suggesting very strongly that a true asymptote is being approached in this event. When he applied the same mathematical techniques to other races, Morton obtained the same results.

All track records were best considered to be asymptotic, which means that the rate of future progression of these records will slow progressively until a point is reached at which progress will be barely observable, indicating that the human performance limits have been reached. Using his equations, Morton has predicted the ultimate records for certain distances and expected times for each decade for the next 120 years (table 12.2). The striking feature of Morton's predictions, when compared to those of Ryder and his colleagues (table 12.1), is how very much more conservative they are. Ryder et al. predict that by 2028 the mile will be run in 3:30, while Morton can only offer us a 3:41.9-mile by 2030. Similarly, the prediction of Ryder et al. for the 10,000 m is some 95 seconds faster than that predicted by Morton by the year 2028.

I am inclined to believe that Morton's ideas are closer to the truth. For example, a close look at the men's world standard marathon record (figure 12.9) shows that the straight line of Ryder et al. (line A) hides a more complex reality. Thus, a line drawn by freehand (line B) seems to be made up of two asymptotic lines. The first asymptote ends in 1952 with the appearance of Jim Peters and his dramatic 7-minute improvement in the world record in just two years. The second asymptote has only just ended with the recent spate of improvements in the world marathon record. Whether these improvements will continue or whether the record will fall progressively further behind the prediction line of Ryder and his colleagues remains to be seen.

2040	2050	2060	2070	2080	2090	2100	Ultimate
9.54	9.50	9.47	9.44	9.41	9.39	9.37	9.15
19.19	19.09	19.00	18.92	18.85	18.79	198.73	18.15
42.18	41.95	41.74	41.54	41.36	41.20	41.04	39.33
1:38.10	1:37.60	1:37.10	1:36.70	1:36.30	1:36.00	1:35.70	1:33.00
3:20.20	3:18.80	3:17.60	3:16.40	3:15.30	3:14.40	3:13.60	3:05.70
3:40.60	3:39.50	3:38.40	3:37.50	3:36.60	3:35.80	3:35.10	3:28.40
6:57.80	6:53.90	6:50.40	6:47.20	6:44.30	6:41.70	6:39.40	6:16.90
12:23.00	12:16.30	12:11.20	12:06.60	12:02.50	11:58.70	11:55.30	11:22.90
26:04.20	25:52.80	25:42.50	25:33.20	25:24.80	25:17.10	25:10.20	24:04.60

From H. Morton (1984).

Figure 12.9 also shows the rapid improvement in the women's marathon record from 1965 to 1981, with a very marked asymptote thereafter (line D). This indicates that the women's marathon world record has been improved four times since 1980 for a total improvement of 04:58 during those 20 years. Had the early improvement by women been sustained, they would already have outrun men in the marathon (line C) as originally observed by Whipp and Ward (1992; figure 12.4).

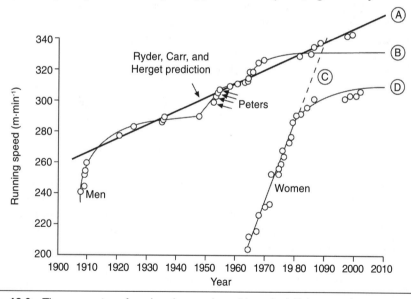

Figure 12.9 The progression of men's and women's world standard 42-km marathon records. Note that whereas the extrapolation of the women's record progression between 1965 and 1982 suggested that their performances would surpass those of men in about 1990 (line C crossing line A), as originally concluded by Whipp and Ward (1992; see figure 12.4), women's marathon records after 1982 in fact followed the asymptotic projection along line D. This indicates that sociological, rather than biological, factors explained the rapid improvements in women's performances from 1965 to 1982, with biological realities becoming increasingly important thereafter.

British Olympian Ron Hill, who in 1970 ran the marathon in 2:09:28, then the world's fastest marathon time, agrees with Morton. Hill has since stated: "Unless doctors find a method, or evolution results in bigger people with longer legs, we'll never get down to 2 hours. I think it's impossible simply because I don't believe the human body is capable of carrying that much energy store in available glycogen or fat" (Temple 1981, page 68).

In fact, the likelihood that a Kenyan or Ethiopian will run a marathon in less than 2:00:00 in the next decade does not seem as improbable to me now as it did to Hill in 1981. Such an athlete will not only have long legs (relative to size), but he will also be small (weighing less than 50 kg), with elastic legs able to resist the eccentric damage caused by running so fast. He will also have a large maximum capacity for blood (coronary) flow to his heart, thereby enabling him to achieve a high maximum cardiac output. Since the size of his muscle glycogen stores are not as crucial to his performance as Hill originally thought, these will not need to be abnormally large. Most important, the future world record holder will need to have a central governor in his subconscious brain that is preprogrammed to believe that his body is capable of a sub-2:00:00 marathon.

Physiological Determinants

In chapters 1 through 4, I discuss the different physiological models that can be used to assist in our understanding of human athletic performance. Until recently, the Cardiovascular/Anaerobic Model has enjoyed uncontested dominance.

Two Canadian researchers, Francois Péronnet and Guy Thibault (1989), have used the Cardiovascular/Anaerobic Model to analyze past world record performances and to develop a model that predicts what the world records should be at different running distances in the future. Their ability to predict all records from 60 m to the marathon with an absolute accuracy of 0.7% suggests that their predictive equations have merit, even though they may be based on a physiological model that does not make biological sense.

In essence, their model is based on three physiological principles. Each body has the capacity to produce a large and measurable amount of energy for a short period of time. This capacity, incorrectly called *anaerobic power* (A), essentially provides all the energy in explosive-type events, such as sprinting (chapter 2). Thus, world records in races of 60 to 400 m are a measure of the levels of anaerobic power found in the best physical specimens of the human race. *Maximal aerobic power* (MAP), characterized by the $\dot{V}O_2$max measurement, is one of the two major determinants of performance in longer races. The maximum power generated by an athlete during 7 minutes of exercise equals the MAP. The proportion of the MAP that can be sustained in events lasting longer than 7 minutes—termed the *endurance capability* (E)—is the second critical determinant of performance capacity in longer-distance events. This corresponds to the concept of fatigue resistance developed in chapter 2.

Péronnet and Thibault then generated an equation incorporating these three variables. The equation predicts the power that the world's best athletes can sustain for any running duration. By converting that power output to a running speed, it is possible to predict the world record times for all running distances.

The authors then used this equation to study running records since 1912 to determine what had occurred in terms of A, MAP, and E during the subsequent years.

In so doing, they hoped to explain for the first time the physiological basis for the changes in these world records in the past 80 years. Their findings may address two of the questions posed by Whipp and Ward (1992): why has there been a linear progression in world records for more than a century, and why is this rate of improvement faster in the marathon than in races of shorter distances?

They found that there had been progressive and essentially linear increases in A and MAP since 1912, but that E in males had remained unchanged during this period. In contrast, E had also increased linearly in females since 1957, the first year of their analysis of women's records. Assuming that these linear increases in A and MAP would continue for the foreseeable future, these authors produced their own table of projected world records for the years 2000, 2028, and 2040 for men (table 12.3) and for 2000, 2028, and 2040 for women (table 12.4). A comparison of their data with that of Ryder et al. (table 12.1), shows that Péronnet and Thibault's predictions for 2040 approximate those of Ryder et al. for 12 years earlier, again suggesting that Ryder et al. were overly optimistic. Now that it is 12 years since the publication of their predictions, it is possible to compare these predictions to the actual world records in 2000 to determine how accurate they were.

This comparison (table 12.5) shows that the predictions of Ryder et al. (1976) were too optimistic for all the distances—by 2.3% at 100 m and by 4.6% at 42 km. Morton's predictions were substantially more accurate with an overprediction of 0.5% at 100 m and an underprediction of 0.5% at 10,000 m. The predictions of Péronnet and Thibault, on the other hand, are conservative yet accurate for all the distances, with the exception of the 30,000 m. Since this race is run infrequently, it suggests that the scientists are correct and that the athletes are about 1:30:00 slower at the distance than they should be.

Table 12.3 Projected men's world records in running events

Distance (m)	World record (h:min:sec.hundreths)			
	2000	2028	2040	Ultimate
100	9.74	9.57	9.49	9.37
200	19.53	19.10	18.92	18.32
400	43.44	42.12	41.59	39.60
800	1:39.88	1:36.18	1:34.71	1:30.86
1000	2:09.72	2:04.81	2:02.86	1:57.53
1500	3:25.45	3:17.45	3:14.27	3:04.27
1609	3:41.96	3:33.29	3:29.84	3:18.87
2000	4:45.15	4:33.89	4:29.41	4:11.06
3000	7:22.54	7:03.91	6:56.87	6:24.81
5000	12:42.72	12:09.39	11:56.19	11:11.61
10,000	26:43.63	25:52.27	25:04.01	23:36.89
20,000	56:29.26	53:55.74	52:54.94	49:26.16
21,100	59:55.03	57:11.96	56:07.38	52:20.03
30,000	1:27:56.69	1:23:55.10	1:22:19.46	1:16:16.08
42,195	2:05:23.72	1:59:36.08	1:57:18.47	1:48:25.25

From Péronnet and Thibault (1989, page 463). Reprinted with permission of the American Physiological Society.

Table 12.4	Projected women's world records in running events			
	World record (h:min:sec.hundreths)			
Distance (m)	**2000**	**2028**	**2040**	**Ultimate**
100	10.66	10.46	10.44	10.15
200	21.46	20.95	20.90	20.25
400	46.85	45.34	45.18	44.71
800	1:51.16	1:46.95	1:46.53	1:42.71
1000	2:27.74	2:22.03	2:21.45	2:12.50
1500	3:47.93	3:38.91	3:38.00	3:26.95
1609	4:10.79	4:00.83	3:59.82	3:43.24
2000	5:22.19	5:09.27	5:07.96	4:41.48
3000	8:11.98	7:50.61	7:48.46	7:11.42
5000	14:19:33	13:41.56	13:37.75	12:33.36
10,000	29:38.41	28:19.04	28:11.04	26:19.48
20,000	1:02:50.97	1:00:00.06	59:42.85	54:48.13
21,100	1:05:27.19	1:02:28.97	1:02:11.03	57:59.39
30,000	1:36:34.12	1:32:09.07	1:31:42.38	1:24:05.12
42,195	2:18:43.34	2:12:19.55	2:11:40.91	2:00:33.22

From Péronnet and Thibault (1989, page 463). Reprinted with permission of the American Physiological Society.

The predictions to 2040 suggest that there are some barriers that will never be surpassed—a sub-9.00 100 m, a sub-1:29 800 m, or a sub-3:00-mile. Although the 5000-m record will go below 12 minutes, it will not drop below 11 minutes. The 10,000 m still has a long way to go before it reaches the predicted limiting time of 23:36.89. Compared to the 2000 record, the world marathon record is predicted to improve by more than 17 minutes in the next 40 years, a projection which currently seems improbable.

Interestingly, the male athlete who runs the mile in less than 3:30 in 2040 will, according to these predictions, have a $\dot{V}O_2max$ of between 90 and 91 ml O_2 per kg per min, and the first athlete to break the 3-minute mile barrier in the year 2172 will have a $\dot{V}O_2max$ of 112 ml O_2 per kg per min. This makes you wonder who will be the first athlete with a $\dot{V}O_2max$ greater than 100 ml O_2 per kg per min. Currently, the highest value reported in a male runners is 85 ml O_2 per kg per min in John Ngugi and Dave Bedford (see table 2.1). This is not greatly different from values of 81.5 ml O_2 per kg per min measured in Don Lash—who set the mile world record at 2 miles, becoming the first man to break 9:00 for 2 miles at the time he was studied in 1939— or of 82 ml O_2 per kg per min in Kipchoege Keino, 1968 Olympic gold medalist at 1500 m and world 5000-m record holder in 1965 with a time of 13:24.2.

These findings seem to suggest that increases in $\dot{V}O_2max$ do not adequately explain the progressive improvements in running world records in the past century. I suggest that these improvements have largely resulted from changes in fatigue resistance brought about by the progressive adoption of superior training methods since Zatopek and the entrance of the more fatigue-resistant African runners into world athletics since the 1964 Olympic Games. But once the limits of fatigue resistance have been approached, as may now be the case, further improvements in running performance will certainly require further increases in $\dot{V}O_2max$ or the discovery of populations that are even more fatigue resistant than the Kenyans, Ethiopians, Algerians, and Moroccans.

But Péronnet and Thibault (1989) do not believe that an athlete with a $\dot{V}O_2max$ greater than 100 ml O_2 per kg per min will ever be born. Their prediction of the ultimate running records closely approximates those of Morton (see table 12.2); their ultimate mile time of 3:18:87 for men will require a $\dot{V}O_2max$ of 98.4 ml O_2 per kg per min, which they feel is a reasonable expectation. Only time will tell. According to my model, the limits will ultimately be determined by the maximum capacity for (coronary) blood flow to the heart. There must be a physiological limit to which the size of the coronary blood vessels can grow.

A different physiological model has been proposed by researchers from the Space Telescope Science Institute in Baltimore, Maryland (Savaglio and Carbone 2000), who used a different mathematical equation to compare running and swimming world records in males and females. They found that both running and swimming world records can be described by two distinct critical phenomena. In essence, a single equation describes both phenomena, but the value of a particular constant in that equation has quite different values for racing distances lasting less than 2:12 to 2:48, equivalent to running distances of less than 1000 m or more than 1500 m

Table 12.5 Comparison of male world records (h:min:sec.hundreths) in running events in year 2000 with the predictions of various scientists				
		Scientists' predictions		
Distance (m)	2000 world record	Ryder et al. (1976)	Morton (1984)	Péronnet & Thibault (1989)
100	9.79	9.56	9.74	9.74
200	19.32	18.97	19.66	19.53
400	43.18	42.49	43.34	43.44
800	1:41.11	1:38.30	1:40.90	1:39.88
1000	—	2:08.80	—	2:09.72
1500	3:26.00	3:22.20	3:27.50	3:25.45
1609	3:43.13	3:38.30	3:46.70	3:41.96
2000	4:44.79	4:40.00	—	4:45.15
3000	7:20.67	7:12.10	7:18.00	7:22.54
5000	12:39.36	12:24.80	12:35.00	12:42.72
10,000	26:22.75	25:44.00	26:30.10	26:43.63
20,000	—	53:57.00	—	56:29.26
21,100	59:17.00	—	—	59:55.03
30,000	1:29:18.80	1:24:42.00	—	1:27:56.69
42,195	2:05:42.00	2:00:00.00	—	2:05:23.72

From Péronnet and Thibault (1989, page 463). Reprinted with permission of the American Physiological Society.

and swimming distances of less than 200 m or more than 400 m. They suggest that this reflects the switch from events requiring anaerobic energy production to those requiring aerobic metabolism.

But this does not really reflect any further advancements in our understanding. For example, according to the Central Governor Model of Exercise Physiology, that division at 2:12 to 2:48 could just as easily represent activities that are completed before a maximum cardiac output (and coronary blood flow) is achieved, and hence before the governor is activated (chapter 2) and begins to regulate performance to prevent bodily damage, especially to the heart.

None of these researchers analyzed world records for races longer than the standard 42-km distance. To see whether the same rules applied to longer races, I applied the same mathematical techniques used by Ryder and his colleagues to the records in races from 48 km to 24 hours. Unfortunately, in most of these races, there are too few results to permit any reasonable inferences to be made. However, in two ultramarathon races, the 83- to 87-km London-to-Brighton race and the 90-km Comrades Marathon, there are sufficient records to allow reasonable graphs to be drawn.

The records of both these races show the same pattern as that found by Ryder and his colleagues in the shorter distances and show that there is a linear improvement in running speeds ranging from 0.88 to 1.11 m per minute per year.

Limiting Factors

Ryder and his colleagues explained this phenomenon of the linear progression in records in the following way. The champions stop, not at a given speed, but when they set a record. Succeeding champions do the same. They telescope in their relatively short racing lives all the achievements of the great runners of the past and then stop with a gold medal, just as their predecessors did. Since it is the medal and not the speed that stops them, the speeds they reach cannot be considered in any way the ultimate physiological limit. This explanation seems reasonable. Almost certainly, throughout their careers, elite athletes program themselves to run just fast enough to win gold medals or to set world records. It makes no sense to run 30 seconds faster than the opposition if one thousandth of a second will do. This was the approach adopted by pole vault world-record holder, Sergei Bubkei. Bubkei set a new world pole vault record on 14 occasions, usually by only 1 cm. Using this approach, he improved the world record by 19 cm over a period of 10 years between 1984 and 1994. Might he have achieved the same overall improvement the first time he broke the world record, had he attempted it?

This explanation is also compatible with the idea that human athletic performance is somehow preprogrammed into the subconscious brain even before the activity begins. Thus, the brain will pace the body according to certain learned parameters, one of which is the speed at which previous world records have been set. It follows that a knowledge of previous world records will probably be the single greatest influence on the subconscious control of the speed at which athletes' brains will allow them to run during world-record attempts.

Furthermore, this explanation is compatible with the belief of many elite athletes, including former world-record holders Roger Bannister, Herb Elliott, and Derek Clayton, that psychological, rather than physiological, factors ultimately separate the world-record holders from the rest.

But a possibility not mentioned by these authors, to which we must not be blind, is that the linear improvement in these athletic records may be an artifact of the relatively short period during which these records have been recorded, especially for women. Although we have been running for millions of years, accurate running records have only been kept for men during the past hundred years or so, and the data used by Ryder and his colleagues cover only the past 60 years. As women have been racing distances longer than 800 m for less than 40 years, the period of observation is even shorter for them.

What seems more likely is that the current world records are already on the asymptotic part of the record curve and that the linear part of the curve is hidden in our prehistory before the advent of the stopwatch, the measuring rod, and the human desire to measure oneself in athletic competition.

That this explanation is probably valid becomes more apparent if we consider the world records for the extreme ultradistance races. In these races, few records have been set, but, more important, some of the best records for men were set 100 years ago and have been improved little, if at all, since then. Since women were not allowed to run marathons or longer distances before 1972, the same phenomenon does not apply to women's running records.

For example, the world records set by Charles Rowell in 1882 for 160 km and 24 hours stood for 71 and 49 years respectively before they were ultimately broken by Wally Hayward and Arthur Newton, both of whom were competing in single-day events. Yet, when Rowell established these records, he still faced five days of competition. During the next two days, he set records that were only broken in 1984 by Yiannis Kouros. But in the past 15 years, Kouros has single handedly improved the long ultradistance world records to the levels at which they should be, based on the projection from the performances of Charles Rowell and the other pedestrians, more than 100 years ago.

FINAL WORD

In this chapter, I have reviewed the evolution of running records set over the past century. What is particularly striking is the marked improvement in women's records during the past 30 years. These improvements can largely be attributed to sociological factors, as before 1972 women were barred from running marathons and other long-distance races. However, in recent years, following the official sanctioning of female competitors in these previously male-dominated events, women's world-best marathon and ultramarathon times improved dramatically, since these races now attract women who are best suited to these distances. As a result, the performance gap between men and women has stabilized between 8% and 12% for most running distances. However, short of genetic engineering exclusively of women, this gap will remain forever.

While both men and women will continue to run progressively faster for the foreseeable future, there are limits to human performance, with each new record pushing the human inexorably closer to those limits.

PART IV

RUNNING HEALTH

C hapter 12 covered the evolution of and the limits to record-setting running performances for men and women. As we come closer to reaching our human genetic potential, more athletes search for substances that might give them an edge over their competition. Part IV moves beyond the topic of record-seeking by offering in chapter 13 a review of those ergogenic aids—both legal and illegal substances or methods that may enhance performance—that have sufficient scientific evidence to support or refute the claims made about their efficacy. The information presented illustrates that no ergogenic aid can compete on a percentage improvement basis with good training. Furthermore, the costs to overall health inherent with taking several of the ergogenic aids covered within the chapter may pose the risk of a higher cost than benefit.

But does training or running itself pose a health risk for runners? Some antirunning scientists would have us believe that running is a threat to our overall health. Certainly the risk of injury is ever present for runners, but, as explained in chapter 14 in the 10 laws of running injuries, if the cause of the injury can be found, it can often be alleviated or cured and prevented from happening again. In chapter 15, I present evidence that few medical conditions are caused or worsened by regular exercise. In fact, a substantial number may be completely prevented or at least substantially alleviated by such exercise.

CHAPTER
13

■ ■ ■ ■ ■

Ergogenic Aids

Sooner or later the desire to run faster becomes a dominating passion. And so begins the search for those aids that, in addition to training, have an *ergogenic* (or performance-enhancing) effect. Judging from the exponential growth in the sales of ergogenic aids in Europe, the United States, and South Africa over the past decade, I'd say this compulsion is widespread.

There are at least two reasons the number and variety of ergogenic aids marketed to runners will continue to expand. First, the natural human desire to acquire a performance edge will not suddenly be assuaged. As the financial rewards for professional sport continue to skyrocket, so too will the market for potential ergogenic aids continue to grow. Second, unlike prescription drugs, which are only marketed after an exhaustive process of development and testing (costing in the order of $250 million for each successful product), nutritional products that claim to have an ergogenic effect do not currently require any substantial development or evaluation before they are released on a willing, trusting, and usually remarkably gullible public. Furthermore, provided advertisers do not claim to cure specific medical conditions, there are few legal restrictions on the sometimes outlandish claims attached to products. This wholly unacceptable state of affairs results from the actions of a United States senator who initiated legislation in Congress in the early 1990s specifically to remove nutritional supplements from the scrutiny of the U.S. Federal Drug Agency, the organization that licenses all other pharmaceutical agents for use in the United States, and hence, indirectly, in the rest of the world. Not surprisingly, the senator's home state is one of the world's major exporters of nutritional ergogenic aids.

In this chapter, I review those products that are promoted for their alleged ergogenic effects. These are the aids to which most runners will have been exposed, either in the advertising media or in discussions with their running friends. I have only included those aids about which there is some credible scientific evidence and from which a dispassionate judgment of their efficacy can be made, independent of the advertising hype. I have included not only nutritional supplements but also pharmaceutical agents (many of which are banned), such as anabolic steroids and erythropoietin (EPO), as well as other interventions, such as altitude training.

My aim here is to present the hard scientific evidence, such as there is, that either supports or refutes the value of each of these aids. In addition, I have tried to quantify the magnitude of benefit that the athlete might expect from a particular intervention. By analyzing the cost or the inconvenience of any particular intervention, or both, we can calculate a simple cost/benefit ratio for the different products or aids.

For example, if you can estimate with reasonable accuracy the magnitude of the benefit you are likely to achieve by traveling to, training, and living at altitude, compared to the benefit of taking creatine or another nutritional substance, you will be better able to make an informed decision about what interventions or aids are best for you. Obviously, it will be to your advantage to use the many relatively cheap aids that have clearly established benefits and to avoid those costly interventions that have dubious benefits. Unfortunately, we live in a culture that teaches that the more expensive the intervention or aid, the greater the benefit you can expect. With ergogenic aids, this is not necessarily the case.

HOW MUCH BENEFIT CAN YOU EXPECT?

Athletes and scientists differ substantially in their assessment of the magnitude of any benefit they would consider to be important. Scientists refer to a change as being either significant or nonsignificant. Their main aim is to prove that the effect they measure—for example, a change in fitness following a training program—occurs with high probability as a direct result of the actual physical training undertaken by their subjects. At the end of the experiment, they wish only to conclude that the effect they measured (in this case, a change in fitness) resulted, beyond a reasonable doubt (that is, with a greater than 95% probability), from the experimental intervention (the exercise program) and not from some other extraneous factor, such as a different diet or a lifestyle change that took place concurrently with the training program.

Thus, when scientists report a significant finding, they simply mean that there is more than a 95% probability that the effect they measured (an increase in fitness) was a direct result of the intervention they evaluated (physical training) and was not caused by any other extraneous factor that their experiment was designed specifically to exclude.

In contrast, athletes interpret a significant effect only in terms of their own experience and expectations. They wish to know whether a specific intervention or ergogenic aid will help them run faster or farther, or preferably both. Also, the degree of improvement they would accept as significant varies substantially, depending on their performance level. Thus, an athlete like Maurice Green, wishing to break the 100-m world record, is looking for an improvement of less than 10 milliseconds

(0.01 second), representing an improvement to his best previous performance of less than 0.1%. In contrast, a 3:30:00 marathon runner may think that anything less than a 30:00 improvement (14%) in his best marathon time is too small and therefore not appealing.

INTERVENTIONS WITH PROVEN ERGOGENIC EFFECTS

Sport scientists are currently unable, and indeed may never be able, to establish beyond a reasonable doubt that a particular aid produces the minuscule effect that would be attractive to Maurice Green and other world-class competitors. Rather, because of financial and other constraints, the smallest significant effect we are currently able to detect with reasonable certainty is probably about 1.5% to 2%. Larger effects become increasingly easier to detect. But a 1.5% effect represents a 0.147 second improvement in the world 100-m record or an improvement of 1:53, close to 2 minutes, in the 42-km marathon. Clearly, many of the world's elite athletes would be content to use aids that are able to enhance performance by much less than the limiting 1% to 1.5% effect detectable by current scientific methods.

Therefore, I have attempted to rank the different performance-enhancing practices, including ergogenic aids and the use of illicit doping agents, in sequence, according to the magnitude of the effect that the average runner might expect to achieve from using them. In this way, I hope to distinguish those aids or interventions that are really important from those that can safely be ignored. However, the actual percentage advantages I have calculated should be interpreted as a best-guess approximation. They are presented only to provide some sort of numerical ranking for the different interventions—for example, by comparing the magnitude of benefit that you can except from a specific aid to the magnitude of benefit you might expect from physical training.

Exercise Training

Before I began training as a runner, I could only run 1 km at 16 km per hour. With training, I eventually sustained that speed for 15 km, a 1500% increase. Similarly, whereas I was initially able to run 2 to 3 km at 13.4 km per hour, I eventually ran 90 km at that pace, an improvement of 3000%. During this period, my best 1600-m speed increased from about 6:00 to 5:00, an improvement of 16%. I suspect that this is the range of performance changes that most ordinary athletes can achieve with dedicated training over many years.

The point is simply to establish a rough idea of the magnitude of improvement that you can achieve by proper training alone—perhaps a 10% to 25% improvement in speed over a short distance and a 1500% to 3000% increase in the duration for which a specific running speed can be sustained. The latter measures the change in fatigue resistance (chapter 2). Thus, if you wish to improve your fatigue resistance, your best investment is training. Nothing else will ever be able to increase your performance and fatigue resistance by 1500% to 3000%.

Training-induced improvements in speed over a short distance are more moderate. Yet, there is no ergogenic aid that will produce a 10% to 25% improvement in running speed over a short distance—not even the illicit use of anabolic steroids.

It is important to stress that correct training of the type described in earlier chapters will produce benefits that are at least one to three orders of magnitude superior to those that can be achieved by even the most expensive ergogenic aids. Sadly, this knowledge is unlikely to deter many from the ultimately futile quest for the supreme ergogenic elixir that can be used instead of training.

Thus, the most potent ergogenic elixir is training. With training alone, a runner can expect a 10% to 3000% improvement in performance. Unfortunately, because training cannot be packaged for oral consumption, it will never compete with the immodest hype surrounding the newest ergogenic practices, all of which inevitably originate from some exotic location.

Anabolic Steroids and Other Banned Hormones

The use of anabolic steroids is banned in all competitions that fall under the auspices of the International Olympic Committee (IOC). The ban applies to all sporting codes, including running, swimming, and the triathlon. The magnitude of the effect of steroids is substantial. Steroids are believed to enhance power by up to 20% and speed, endurance, racing performance, and rate of recovery from competition by as much as 10%. Hence, the use of anabolic steroids by competitive athletes constitutes cheating since their use falls specifically outside the rules that determine fair play in international sport.

As a sports physician, I will not prescribe anabolic steroids to athletes, as this conflicts with the ethics of the medical profession. However, as the author of this book, I have the responsibility to provide accurate information on these drugs, irrespective of how distasteful that information may be for those who believe in ethics and fair play and whose desire is to ensure that sport should, for once, be untainted.

Anabolic steroids were first used by power athletes, including weightlifters and shot putters in the Olympic Games, perhaps as early as 1954. The dominance of female athletes from the German Democratic Republic (GDR), formerly East Germany, in the late 1970s and 1980s suggests that these drugs were first used by sprint and middle-distance runners during that period. These athletes established records that still stand two decades later. Speculation about the authenticity of these "remarkable" performances has been confirmed by the publication of official doping records on former GDR athletes (Franke and Berendonk 1997), as well as by a series of court cases against sport officials who provided anabolic steroids, which had unfavorable, long-term medical consequences, to young female athletes.

The efficacy of these agents has been confirmed by the fact that the records set in those years have yet to be equaled (see chapter 12) and that drug use was an essential part of the GDR sporting machine. It is also notable that Ben Johnson ran substantially faster when he used steroids before the 1988 Olympic Games, where he set the since disallowed world record, and when he again tested positive four years later than he did in the intervening years, when he presumably was not using the drugs. He effectively proved that without anabolic steroids, he was not a world-class sprinter.

Table 13.1 reflects information contained in an official publication of the Stasi, the GDR secret police. It lists the expected improvements that could be achieved by athletes following programs of anabolic steroid use for four years. Graphs that show performance improvements in selected GDR track and field athletes when using anabolic steroids are provided by Franke and Berendonk (1997).

Table 13.1 Expected performance enhancement for male and female track and field athletes using cycles of anabolic steroids		
	Improved performance of:	
Event	Males	Females
Shot put	2.5–4 m	4.5–5 m
Discus throw	10–12 m	11–20 m
Hammer throw	6–10 m	?
Javelin throw	?	8–15 m
400 m	?	4–5 s
800 m	?	5–10 s
1500 m	?	7–10 s

The report notes that "Remarkable rates of increased in performance were also noted in the swimming events of women...."
? = unreported data
From Franke and Berendonk (1997).

There is also mounting evidence to suggest that endurance athletes, including runners, use low doses of anabolic steroids to improve recovery from heavy training and to allow a heavier training load. Two leading East European female distance runners—Leipzig-born Uta Pippig, three-time winner of the New York City Marathon, as well as the Berlin and Boston marathons, and Maria Bak, winner of the Comrades Marathon in 1998 and 2000—were served banning sentences after testing positive for the illicit use of anabolic steroids. It is of interest that Pippig reportedly trained in excess of 200 km per week. Some weeks, she did up to 290 km per week (Sandrock 1996, p. 535), a very high mileage for any athlete, male or female.

In chapters 5 and 6, I discuss the optimal frequency with which runners should race in marathons or ultramarathon races. In accordance with Law 7 in chapter 5, I advise runners not to race more than two marathons per year. This conclusion was drawn on the basis of all the accumulated evidence available in the early 1990s, perhaps before distance runners fully appreciated the perceived benefits that could be gained from anabolic steroid use. Although some athletes in the 1960s, 1970s, and early 1980s—most notably Buddy Edelen, Ron Hill, Alberto Salazar, and Frith van der Merwe—were able to break this rule for some years before their performances fell away as a direct consequence, there is absolutely no suggestion that their performances were in any way artificial.

Needless to say, suspicion is now being cast over those marathoners who seem to be able to race frequently and for longer periods, and who recover more rapidly than did their counterparts from the 1980s and 1990s, as well as those athletes, particularly marathoners, who run very fast in their first or second marathons, only to disappear just as suddenly thereafter. Is this because modern runners are somewhat different from runners from all previous generations? Or are evil forces at work?

While there are no scientific studies to show that low doses of anabolic steroids improve endurance performance by allowing a heavier training load and more frequent racing, there is, however, strong evidence to suggest that anabolic steroids, as used by strength-trained athletes, increase muscle strength and muscle size substantially. Concomitant with their use, there is also a marked change in body composition, especially in women.

Anabolic steroids decrease the amount of fat in the buttocks, thighs, and upper arms of women (Lovejoy et al. 1996). As a result, women using steroids appear more masculine (androgenization) and have a lower than expected percentage body fat. For example, one study compared professional Australian female bodybuilders with elite Australian male and female athletes (K. Norton, quoted by Myhal and Lamb 2000). The female bodybuilders had a higher ratio of fat-free (muscle and bone) mass to body height than did the other two groups; the difference in the two female groups was 38%. In addition, the female bodybuilders had less than half the percentage body fat measured in the male runners (4.5% vs. 10%).

Similarly, in the only controlled clinical trial of which I am aware, 600 mg per week of testosterone enanthate was administered to healthy men for 10 weeks (Bhasin et al. 1996). Testosterone increased cross-sectional areas of the arm and thigh muscles and increased bench-press and squatting strength by 9 and 13 kg respectively in the group that did not train while taking steroids. However, the effects of weight training and testosterone administration were synergistic. This combination increased bench-press and squatting strength by 12 and 38 kg compared to changes of 10 and 25 kg with training alone. Fat-free mass also increased by 2 kg with training alone, by 4 kg with testosterone administration alone, and by 6 kg with the combination of exercise and testosterone administration.

As a result of the IOC ban on anabolic steroids, the sale of anabolic steroid prohormones (such as dehydroepiandrosterone [DHEA], androstenedione, and noradrostenedione) has soared, largely because manufacturers of commercially available supplements wish to capitalize on athletes' desire to improve performance by taking products that might mirror the effects of steroids. The theory is that these prohormones are converted into anabolic steroids in the body, thereby producing identical effects to those of the established and widely used anabolic steroids. Of course, the intent behind the use of prohormones is no different from that which spurs the use of the parent anabolic steroids. Thus, the intent behind the use of prohormones also constitutes cheating.

At present, the efficacy of these prohormones is unknown (Burke, Desdrow, et al. 2000; Myhal and Lamb 2000). It is also alleged that the illegal use of the other hormones that may have anabolic effects—growth hormone (GH), insulin-like growth factor (IGF-1), and human chorionic gonadotrophin (HCG)—is common among some athletes wishing to increase their strength, speed, or power.

Because there are no clinical trials measuring their effects in athletes, the magnitude of benefit, if any, is not yet known. However, there is no reason to believe that they do not have a significant effect, as athletes would not risk using them if they did not.

Increasing Oxygen Delivery

The Cardiovascular/Anaerobic Model (chapter 2) predicts that superior athletic performance will be achieved by altering those factors that enhance oxygen delivery to the muscles. This can be achieved by increasing the following

- forward blood flow from the heart (cardiac output);
- the capacity of the blood to bind oxygen because of an increased red blood cell (RBC) mass or concentration; or
- the capacity of the muscles to process that oxygen as the result of an increased density of capillaries or an increased mitochondrial volume and enzyme content, or both.

Thus, according to this model, one of the most effective interventions would be to enhance the oxygen-carrying capacity of the blood by increasing the number of red blood cells in the bloodstream. This can be achieved by living and training at medium altitude; living at altitude but training at sea level (the "live hi, train lo" protocol); sleeping in a high-altitude (alpine) or nitrogen house; reinfusing your own red blood cells, so-called blood doping; or by using the banned hormone erythropoietin (EPO).

Live and Train at Medium Altitude

Living at altitude, where there is less oxygen in each liter of air that is inhaled, reduces the amount of oxygen carried in the blood in proportion to the altitude above sea level. According to the Cardiovascular/Anaerobic Model, training under these conditions should increase the anaerobic stress on the body.

Thus, proponents of this model argue that, during maximal exercise, the athlete's muscles are working under more anaerobic conditions than at sea level. Hence, the body will be forced to adapt by improving its ability to process oxygen, thereby reducing the rate at which lactate and hydrogen are produced by the exercising muscles. This will delay fatigue and enhance performance, especially at altitude. In addition, when the athlete returns to sea level, these adaptations will increase the ability to use what is now the usual amount of oxygen in the inspired air. As a result, performance will be enhanced, at least in those sporting activities in which performance is determined by a limiting oxygen delivery to, or use by, the exercising muscles.

Two events helped crystallize the notion that training at altitude would be of special value to distance runners. The first was the scheduling of the 1968 Olympic Games at altitude (2200 m) in Mexico City. The distance events in those Games were dominated by athletes from East and North Africa, who were used to living at altitude. When East African runners subsequently also began to dominate middle- and long-distance running races, even at sea level, the natural conclusion was that athletes who trained at altitude had an unfair advantage during competitions regardless of whether they were contested at altitude or sea level.

Second, a series of scientific studies was conducted on elite U.S. runners, including mile world-record holder Jim Ryun (Daniels and Oldridge 1970), who trained at altitude before returning to sea level for competition. Ryun (figure 13.1) trained at altitude in Alamosa, Colorado (2450 m), a total of three times. In his book (Ryun and Phillips 1995), Ryun recalls that on his first run in Alamosa, he stopped after 600 m. He finished his first timed mile (1.6 km) at that altitude in 4:32, a full 37 seconds (16%) slower than his most recent best performance at sea level. Later, in the 1968 Olympic Games, Ryun ran 1500 m in an astonishing 3:37.8, equivalent to a 3:56 mile at altitude or a 3:46 mile at sea level (table 9.4). But in that race he was beaten by Kip Keino, who ran 3:34.9, the equivalent of a 3:42 sea-level mile, passing

Wichita Eagle, Kansas.

Figure 13.1 The 18-year-old Jim Ryun wins the mile in 3:58.3 at the Kansas State Championships on 15 May, 1965. A year earlier, Ryun had become the first high school athlete in the United States to break the 4-minute barrier in the mile. A month later, on 27 June, 1965, Ryan ran 3:55.3 to beat Olympic champion Peter Snell in the mile. This U.S. high school record held for 36 years until bettered by Alan Webb, who ran 3:53.43 on 27 May, 2001, in the Prefontaine Classic in Eugene, Oregon.

1100 m 5 seconds faster than Ryun's then sea-level world record. Keino's performance has to be considered the greatest 1500 m of all time. Clearly, although altitude training had helped Ryun improve his running performance at altitude by an astonishing 16%, it was insufficient to match the performance of the Kenyan, who was born and had lived at altitude all his life. A group of British middle-distance runners who trained in Mexico City at the same time also improved their 3-mile running performances by 3% (Pugh 1967a). But even after training at altitude for four weeks, their 3-mile performances were still 6% slower than they were at sea level (see figure 9.3). Sir Roger Bannister was again correct. When asked what would it take to become thoroughly acclimatized to altitude, Sir Roger had answered simply: "There are two ways. Be born at altitude . . . or train there for 25 years" (Ryun and Phillips 1995, pp. 73–74).

But in 1967, when Ryun returned to sea level to compete in the buildup to the Olympics, he ran extremely fast, establishing a new world 1500-m record of 3:33.10, beating Keino by 4.01, and bettering Herb Elliott's previous record of 3:35.6. For the proponents of the Cardiovascular/Anaerobic Model, who believe in the benefits of altitude training on sea-level performance, this proved irrevocably the value of training at altitude to enhance performances at sea level.

However, when I spoke to Ryun at a scientific meeting at Stanford University in California 21 years later, he expressed doubts as to whether altitude training had been the sole, or even the most important, reason for his excellent performances in the summer of 1968. He later ascribed his success to the rest he obtained when traveling to and from altitude. In fact, he stated to me: "I had never rested so much before races in my life." Ryun was, in my opinion, an athletic genius who trained harder than he needed. He almost certainly did not taper sufficiently before races, a common failing in U.S. distance runners of that era and a problem that I believe still prevails today.

In the 30 years since those Olympic Games, a large number of studies have evaluated, in a more objective way, the effects of altitude training in runners. First, there are studies investigating the physiological and performance effects of acute and chronic exposure to training at medium altitude. These studies show that whereas running performance at altitude improves with continued exposure to living and training at altitude, neither the maximum oxygen consumption ($\dot{V}O_2$max; Fulco and Cymerman 1998) nor the maximum heart rate alters with continuing residence and training at altitude (Saltin 1996). Physiological changes that do occur are a reduction in heart rate and blood lactate concentrations during submaximal exercise (Saltin 1996). Hence, the changes in running performance that occur with residence and training at altitude, as clearly established by Ryun's example, are accompanied by clear physiological changes that are measurable during submaximal, but not during maximal, exercise.

But there is no evidence to suggest that these adaptations translate to measurable physiological changes measured during either maximal or submaximal exercise at sea level before and after altitude exposure (Pugh 1967a; Mizuno et al. 1990; Svedenhag et al. 1991; Jensen et al. 1993; Saltin 1996; D.M. Bailey et al. 1998).

The second group of studies looks at the results of training at altitude on athletic performance at sea level. It is extremely difficult to conduct these studies because they require that a control group of runners of matched ability remain at sea level and train simultaneously and at the same intensity as the group of athletes training at altitude. Furthermore, it is difficult to control for the natural expectation of both athletes and scientists that athletes training at altitude will benefit more than will those who train only at sea level. If the scientists were not inclined to believe this, would they undertake the research in the first place?

In other words, the studies cannot be adequately controlled, or *blinded*, to ensure that neither the athletes nor the scientists are aware of who trained at altitude and who trained at sea level. This is an important consideration, as part of any effect might simply be the belief that training at altitude is beneficial, the so-called placebo effect. Athletes who believe their altitude training was beneficial will force themselves to run harder during the final testing that measures the effects of altitude training. This altered self-belief will influence the outcome of the experiment, regardless of the real effects of training at altitude.

Since the 1950s, there have been at least 92 studies of this topic (Bailey and Davies 1997). Of these studies, 76 are scientifically unintelligible because they were conducted without an adequate control group of athletes who performed the equivalent training program at sea level at the same time that the intervention group was training at altitude. Of the remaining 16 studies, only 4 found that the performance of the altitude-trained group improved more than that of the group who trained similarly at sea level (Bailey and Davies 1997). An important finding is that the more carefully the study is controlled, the greater the probability that a negative or negligible effect of altitude training will be found (Böning 1997; Bailey et al. 1998). This is a common finding in any study of an intervention (in this case, training at altitude) that has either a small effect or none.

In fact, one of the most carefully conducted studies (Bailey et al. 1998) found that the racing performance of middle-distance athletes was impaired immediately when they returned to sea level after a period of training at altitude. The authors concluded that the higher rate of infection at altitude and an inability to train at the same speed as at sea level explained why the athletes in that study did not benefit from training at altitude.

There is other indirect evidence suggesting that high-altitude training may be of little value in improving the performances of runners competing at distances ranging from 1500 to 10,000 m. Péronnet (1994) found that the rate of progression of world running records at those distances did not increase after 1968 when world-class athletes first began to train at altitude. In fact, no world records were set at those distances between 1968 and 1971. This is most unusual and had not occurred in the 36-year period between 1930 and 1968. It seemed that the very reason no world distance running records were set in these four years was because all the world's best athletes suddenly began to train at altitude.

Furthermore, the rate of progression of the men's world records for those distances was slower between 1968 and 1994 than between 1950 and 1968, the opposite of what would be expected if altitude training enhanced running performance at sea level.

The author concluded that

> these observations fail to show any overall beneficial effect of the introduction of altitude training on sea-level performance for elite male runners. . . . Accordingly, the beneficial effects of altitude training for sea-level performance remain to be convincingly demonstrated and should not be taken for granted. (Péronnet 1994)

In summarizing this research, Saltin concluded that "it is clear that the available scientific data do not support the 'myth' that training at medium altitude adds something significant to an athlete's maximal aerobic power" (1996, p. 10).

However, Saltin's unambiguous conclusion needs to be interpreted correctly. The fact that altitude training does not improve sea-level running performance in certain events or increase the maximal aerobic power ($\dot{V}O_2max$) is damaging for the Cardiovascular/Anaerobic Model of Exercise Physiology and Athletic Performance. But it does not exclude the possibility that the benefits of altitude training are real but too small for modern scientists to measure, or that athletic performance in some events at other running distances could still be enhanced by a period of altitude training. This would occur, for example, if oxygen deficiency in either the muscles (Cardiovascular/Anaerobic Model) or heart (Integrated Neuromuscular Recruitment Model) does not limit performance in those events.

In other words, altitude training could still be invaluable if it alters, more effectively than an equivalent amount of sea-level training, those physiological factors that determine running performance at running distances that are not limited by an oxygen deficiency somewhere in the body. Such events could be marathon and ultramarathon footraces and long-distance cycling and triathlon events, for example. The effects of altitude training on performance in those events have not been studied. Thus, the potential of any altitude-related training benefit for cyclists and triathletes or ultramarathon runners cannot be discounted on the basis of the current (incomplete) evidence.

Nor can the placebo effect of altitude training be discounted. Athletes who believe that altitude training is beneficial are likely to perform better when they return to sea level, even if the altitude training had no physiological benefit.

Furthermore, for many athletes, training in a more rural, less cluttered environment, at altitude, offers the chance of a "time out" from their more stressful lives in their home environment. The quality of their training would understandably be enhanced under those more favorable training conditions. By focusing exclusively on the physiological benefits of training at altitude, scientists may have missed an important reality.

It is also important to understand why it is so difficult for scientists to prove that training at altitude definitely improves running performance at sea level. It may be that the effect is quite small and that the cost of proving such a negligible effect conclusively may be prohibitive. For example, the smaller the effect, the more athletes needed to prove such an effect. Most altitude training studies typically include about 20 runners in the two study groups, the control and intervention. But statistical analysis shows that a study using this number of subjects can only detect an improvement in performance of greater than 3%. Yet, the difference between first and fourth places in Olympic competition is usually only a fraction of 1%. But for the study to detect an effect even as large as 1%, 100 athletes would need to be included in the trial. At present, logistical and financial considerations make such a trial impossible.

Thus, most of the studies that have been undertaken were not designed to identify an effect the size of which (less than a fraction of 1%) would still be perfectly acceptable to an elite Olympic athlete who only requires a tiny improvement to ensure an Olympic medal, not the scientifically detectable 3% improvement that would take the athlete to another, quite unattainable and unrealistic level of performance.

Conversely, we might conclude that even if altitude training does indeed improve running performance, any effect must be quite small, perhaps less than about 1%, compared to the effect of the same training undertaken at sea level. The size of this effect is perhaps so small that it can easily be negated by other detrimental effects of training away from home for prolonged periods. On the other hand, this small effect might be all that the elite Olympic athlete requires to become the gold medalist. Hence, we can perhaps never fully exclude the possibility that altitude training is a crucial training option for the very best athletes looking for a tiny training edge. Indeed, the fact that so many world-class athletes from a wide variety of sports choose to train at altitude suggests that either there must be some real benefit from this form of training or else there are many foolish coaches and athletes in the world.

Alternatively, it can be argued that altitude training may be of little value because the physiological model that gives it legitimacy may be incorrect. As discussed in chapter 2, the alternative explanation is that the heart, not skeletal muscle, may be at greatest risk of developing an oxygen deficiency during maximal exercise both at sea level and at altitude (figure 2.5). That model requires the existence of a governor to terminate exercise before the heart is damaged, especially during maximal exercise at altitude.

The governor model predicts that altitude training will only be of value if it induces adaptations that increase the amount of blood reaching the heart during maximal exercise—perhaps requiring an increase in the capacity of the coronary blood vessels supplying the heart muscle—or improve the heart's power and efficiency so that it can produce a higher (cardiac) output at the same oxygen demand.

The adaptation most likely to achieve these benefits would be any increase in the amount or concentration of the circulating red blood cells, the exact adaptation identified by Chapman et al. (1998) as crucial for any beneficial performance effect of training at altitude.

However, training at altitude will not definitely ensure that the number of red blood cells are increased (Bailey et al. 1998). Recent studies show that residence and training at an altitude of 1800 m for 18 days failed to increase red blood cell mass (Friedmann et al. 1999). Similarly, elite Australian athletes who slept for 8 to 11 hours per night in a high-altitude or nitrogen house for either 23 nights at 3000 m (Ashenden et al. 1999a) or for 5 (Ashenden et al. 2000) or 12 (Ashenden et al. 1999b) nights at 2650 m failed to show any increase in red blood cell production. This suggests that the optimum altitude to achieve this effect has yet to be established and might be as high as 4000 m. As there are relatively few hospitable locations at such high altitudes, this finding presents some very real logistical problems for those athletes who wish to base their high-altitude training on a firm scientific foundation.

This failure of altitude exposure to increase the red blood cell mass would then explain why the $\dot{V}O_2$max does not increase during continuing residence at altitudes less than perhaps 2500 m. Without an increase in oxygen supply to the heart, either at altitude or at sea level, the governor model predicts that an increase in the maximum cardiac output necessary to raise the $\dot{V}O_2$max cannot occur. Hence, it is clear that exposure must be to altitudes equal to or greater than 2500 m if there is any chance that running performance will improve consequent to an increased red blood cell mass (Levine and Stray-Gundersen 1997).

In contrast, the presence of the postulated governor, reducing the intensity of exercise that can be sustained at altitude, must also cause the skeletal muscles to lose some of their sea-level capacity. At extreme altitude, this process of de-adaptation causes a 20% to 25% reduction in muscle cell size and a reduced concentration of mitochondrial enzymes, as found in climbers exposed to a simulated 40-day climb to an altitude equivalent to the summit of Mount Everest (Green et al. 1989a). It is difficult to believe that these de-adaptations would enhance running performance at sea level. Indeed, other studies show that any training-induced changes in mitochondrial enzyme concentrations at altitude will only equal those produced by training at the same relative intensity at sea level (Saltin 1996). As far as muscles are concerned, training at altitude has no magical effect; muscles respond to the relative intensity of effort and are unable to detect whether that same training is being performed at sea level or at altitude.

Interestingly, this governor model can also explain why, despite their markedly superior performance at extreme altitudes, the leg muscles of Sherpas have lower mitochondrial enzyme concentrations than do sedentary Caucasians living at sea level (Kayser et al. 1991). The reason is that the Sherpas' superior performance at altitude is not explained by the capacity of their leg muscles to use oxygen. Rather, the governor model predicts that it is either their bodies' ability to provide their hearts with a greater oxygen supply during exercise at extreme altitude or their superior heart function that would ultimately determine the Sherpa's superior performance at altitude. This superiority would result from

- a higher red blood cell concentration;
- an increased ventilatory function, which allows more oxygen to be transferred from the lungs to the blood during exercise at altitude;
- a more extensive network of blood vessels in the heart, which is able to accommodate a larger coronary blood flow;
- an increased volume of mitochondria in the heart; and
- perhaps, as a result, superior myocardial efficiency so that an even larger cardiac output can be achieved at these higher levels of blood and oxygen supply to the heart.

There are fundamental differences between people living at high altitude and those living at sea level. This is shown by the smaller difference in $\dot{V}O_2$max measured at sea level and at medium altitude in people who were born and who live at altitude. Hence, altitude natives whose $\dot{V}O_2$max is the same as that of matched sea-level residents when both are tested at sea level have substantially higher $\dot{V}O_2$max values at altitude (Favier et al. 1995b), perhaps because they are better able to supply their hearts with oxygen during maximal exercise at altitude.

Finally, because of the increased risk of infections of either the upper respiratory or gastrointestinal tracts at altitude (Bailey and Davies 1997), altitude training may prove less effective than expected. Thus, any potential but small benefit of altitude training may be lost by the debilitating and sometimes prolonged effects of an intercurrent illness acquired while living at altitude.

Train at Sea Level, Live at Altitude

An alternative method that can be used to improve exercise performance by increasing the red blood cell mass, without the disadvantage of training at high altitude, has become known as the "live hi, train lo" technique. Using this method, athletes live at altitude but train at a lower altitude or at sea level, especially when doing high-intensity training (Levine and Stray-Gundersen 1992). The proposed benefits of training at sea level are as follows: the athlete can train at the necessary competitive speeds; the established negative effects of living continuously at altitude, including the increased risk of infections at altitude (Bailey et al. 1998), are reduced; and the beneficial adaptation of the increased red blood cell mass is maintained.

Thus, two carefully controlled and meticulously conducted studies (Chapman et al. 1998; Levine and Stray-Gundersen 1997) have found that subelite middle-distance runners who lived at 2500 m but who trained daily for four weeks at 1300 m showed a 1.4% (14-second) improvement in 5000-m time-trial performance for up to three weeks after returning to sea level.

In contrast, athletes who either trained at sea level for the same period or, equally important, lived and trained at medium altitude (2500 m) did not show any improvement in racing performance at sea level. That finding is again consistent with the conclusion that, even if high-altitude training does improve racing performance at sea level, the effect is too small (perhaps less than 1%) to be established by current research methods.

The authors concluded that two adaptations are necessary to achieve a beneficial effect from living at high altitude and training at sea level. First is the increase in red blood cell mass that enhances potential oxygen delivery to the skeletal muscles (and heart according to the Central Governor Model). Although this occurred equally in both groups living at altitude, it was only the group that trained at a lower altitude that improved its sea-level running performance. This adaptation alone is insufficient to improve running performance at sea level. Second, the authors concluded that it was the inability of the group training at high altitude to train sufficiently fast that explains why they did not benefit from the increase in red blood cell mass. Thus, they argue that if the benefits of training and living at high altitude are to be realized, the athlete's muscles must still be trained at the speeds achieved in competition.

The major physiological adaptation measured in the group that lived high and trained low was an increased $\dot{V}O_2$max, accompanied by a reduced cardiac output during submaximal exercise at sea level. Despite the fact that the "live hi, train lo" group improved their racing performance at sea level, neither skeletal muscle capillarization nor enzyme content was altered with any form of training (Stray-Gundersen and Levine 1999). This was a surprising finding for these authors, but not for those who argue that increased oxygen delivery to the heart and not to skeletal muscle is the crucial factor explaining why an increased red blood cell mass enhances athletic performance.

The authors also noted substantial individual variation in the response to altitude training. They concluded that those athletes who benefited from altitude exposure experienced heightened erythropoietin (EPO) production by their kidneys and, as a result, demonstrated an increase in red blood cell mass and subsequently in $\dot{V}O_2$max (Chapman et al. 1998).

In summary, these authors suggest that athletes will only benefit from training or living at altitude if they fulfill three criteria. First, they must live at an altitude sufficiently high to stimulate their production of EPO so that their red blood cell mass increases. This altitude should not be less than 2500 m. Second, they must either have adequate whole body iron stores or must receive adequate amounts of iron so that they can increase their red blood cell mass appropriately in response to the increased EPO production by their kidneys. Third, they must be able to train at the same running velocities that they normally achieve at sea level. This requires that they perform their high-intensity training at altitudes as close to sea level as possible.

As a result of the negative results derived from studies of training at altitude, alternative options have also been evaluated. These include the use of red blood cell infusions or of repeated injections of the hormone erythropoietin (EPO; ACSM 1996c), or sleeping in a high-altitude (alpine) or nitrogen house through which air with a reduced oxygen and increased nitrogen content is circulated. All of these techniques aim to increase oxygen delivery to the exercising muscles (and heart) by increasing the mass of circulating red blood cells. There is clear scientific evidence to suggest that EPO use and blood doping has a substantial ergogenic effect. Both techniques are currently banned by the IOC, and the race is on to develop appropriate detection techniques for use in Olympic and other competitions.

Blood Doping

When the great modern Finnish athlete Lasse Viren came back from four years in the athletic wilderness to win his third and fourth gold medals at the 1976 Montreal

Olympic Games, some people viewed his success with indignant skepticism. The charges against Viren were that he had blood doped—a technique that involves artificially increasing an athlete's circulating red blood cell count by reinfusing red blood cells previously drawn from that athlete and stored under special conditions for a minimum of four to six weeks.

Blood doping, or blood boosting, as it has also been called, violates the Olympic ruling that makes it illegal for any physiological substance to be taken by an abnormal route or in an abnormal quantity for the "sole object of increasing, artificially and in an unfair manner, the performance of that individual while participating in a competition" (Raynes 1969, p. 145).

In 1976 the central doping issue at the Olympic Games was anabolic steroids. There was no firm evidence that blood boosting worked, so that apart from the irresponsible and unsubstantiated charges against Viren, this never became a major issue.

But by the 1980 Olympic Games, all that had changed. After these games, the Finnish runner Kaarlo Maaininka, who won silver and bronze medals in the 10,000- and 5000-m events, freely admitted to receiving two units of blood shortly before these races. Some members of the 1984 United States Olympic cycling team also blood doped before the games (Klein 1985), and Italian Francesco Moser apparently traveled to Mexico City, where he twice lowered the outdoor 1-hour cycling record, allegedly accompanied by "an entourage of two cardiologists and eight men 18 to 20 years of age who were chosen several months before because of their blood type compatibility with Moser" (Brien and Simon 1987, p. 2762).

Scientific studies suggest that blood boosting does indeed work, as it should according to either the Cardiovascular/Anaerobic or the Central Governor Model (chapter 2). According to the Cardiovascular/Anaerobic Model, the extra oxygen-carrying capacity of the blood will increase oxygen delivery to the active skeletal muscles, thereby reducing muscle anaerobiosis and skeletal muscle lactate production, allowing a higher peak work rate to be achieved. According to the Central Governor Model, the extra oxygen delivery to the heart will allow a larger muscle mass to be recruited during maximal exercise, enabling a higher maximal work rate to be achieved.

Thus, in 1980, Fred Buick and his colleagues (Buick et al. 1980) performed a study in which each of an elite group of long-distance runners was subjected to a maximal treadmill test, during which the runners' $\dot{V}O_2$max and maximal treadmill running times (a measure of their endurance performance) were measured. After the test, 900 ml of blood was withdrawn from each athlete and stored. After five weeks, blood tests showed that the athletes had recovered from the inevitable anemia caused by this blood loss. The treadmill tests were repeated to ensure that the period of anemia had not affected either the athletes' $\dot{V}O_2$max values or their maximum treadmill running times.

After the second treadmill test, blood reinfusion took place. Half the athletes were then reinfused with their own stored blood, while the other half received a (sham) infusion of a small amount of an intravenous salt solution not expected to have any effect on performance. Then, 24 hours later, all athletes were again retested on the treadmill by technicians who had no idea who had received the blood and who had received the sham infusions. By doing this, Buick and his colleagues ensured that neither the athletes nor the technicians were motivated to extract greater efforts in the knowledge of which athletes had been blood boosted.

After the test, and under the same rigorous experimental conditions, the athletes received a second infusion: those who had previously received the sham infusion now received their blood quota; those who had already received their blood quota were given a sham infusion. The treadmill tests were repeated 24 hours, one week, and four months later.

Blood reinfusion had a dramatic effect. There was a 6% increase in the $\dot{V}O_2$max and a massive 39% increase in the treadmill endurance running time. Furthermore, these increases were maintained for seven days. Since that original study, at least three others have shown essentially similar results (Gledhill 1982 and Gledhill et al. 1999). For example, Brien and Simon (1987) found that 10-km running time was reduced by 1:09 (4%) after infusion of 400 ml of red blood cells. This benefit was still present 13 days after reinfusion, as it was in a study of cross-country skiers (Berglund and Hemmingson 1987). Conversely, blood reinfusion does not seem to reduce the impaired exercise performance that occurs at altitude (A.J. Young et al. 1996; Pandolf et al. 1998). The reasons for this finding are not immediately clear. One possibility is that at altitude, but not at sea level, the brain must first "learn" that the red blood cell mass and oxygen delivery to the heart has increased. It is only once the brain has been reprogrammed that it will allow an increased maximum exercise performance at altitude.

These studies confirm the original finding, first made in 1972 (Ekblom et al. 1972), that established that blood boosting improves both endurance performance and $\dot{V}O_2$max. Although exercise physiologists continue to interpret these studies as confirmatory evidence for the Cardiovascular/Anaerobic Model of Exercise Physiology, they are equally compatible with the Central Governor theory, which holds that maximum exercise performance will be improved by any intervention that increases blood flow to and oxygenation of the heart, which then allows the central governor to recruit a larger muscle mass, which demands an increased maximum cardiac output with an increased blood flow to the exercising muscles.

Perhaps the most important conclusion from these studies is that muscles have reserve capacity during maximal exercise so that either the same muscle mass is able to take up more oxygen after blood doping or, more probable in my view and according to the Central Governor Model, a larger muscle mass can be recruited during maximal exercise after blood doping, as a result of an increased oxygen delivery to the heart.

Blood doping may also enhance heat tolerance during exercise (Sawka et al. 1987; Patterson et al. 1995). Other effects of blood doping are to reduce blood lactate concentrations during exercise (Spriet et al. 1987) and to alter the lactate turnpoint to a higher running speed (Celsing et al. 1987). Both these effects will reduce the perception of effort during running.

If the intensity of effort that can be sustained during prolonged exercise is determined by feedback from sensory receptors throughout the body to the central governor, and if the circulating lactate concentration is one of the chemicals that is sensed, then this effect on lactate metabolism would explain why blood doping also enhances performance during prolonged exercise when no ergogenic effect is due to a greater maximum capacity for oxygen transport (to heart or muscles).

Techniques to detect blood doping depend on the origin of the blood used for the infusion. A reinfusion of blood that originally came from the athlete is called an *autologous transfusion*. Alternatively, the blood may come from another (compatible) donor, in which case the transfusion is termed a *nonautologous blood transfu-*

sion. Transfusion from an incompatible donor causes death, induced by massive red blood cell destruction. Other risks of blood transfusion include the transmission of the HIV/AIDS or the hepatitis B or C viruses.

Nonautologous blood transfusion can be detected relatively easily from a blood sample, which, depending on the size of the transfusion, will indicate that a proportion of the red blood cells, usually up to 10%, is allogenic (that is, they have a different genetic code than the 90% of red blood cells produced naturally by the athlete's own genes).

Methods to detect autologous blood transfusion are based on the work of Berglund and colleagues (Berglund and Hemmingson 1987; Berglund et al. 1987; Berglund 1988). These authors showed that the measurement of serum levels of erythropoietin (EPO), iron, and bilirubin can identify 50% of boosted athletes within the first seven days of blood doping. The principle is that blood reinfusion causes an increase in the blood hemoglobin concentration that suppresses the production of the kidney hormone, EPO, responsible for regulating red blood cell production. In addition, the reinfused red blood cells are older and more fragile, having been stored outside the body for a substantial time. They are therefore more likely to rupture (hemolyze) during exercise, causing an increase in blood iron and bilirubin concentrations.

An alternative technique may be to measure the distribution of red blood cell size, as the reinfused cells are likely to be larger than the athlete's remaining red blood cells. Thus, the size distribution of the athlete's red blood cells will probably show an abnormal distribution of large cells (Berglund 1988).

However, since the mid-1980s, the detection of blood doping is no longer necessary, since it seems that athletes no longer have any need to use this laborious doping technique, as a more practical and far more effective technique can be used to achieve the same result. This involves the illegal use of the hormone, EPO, itself.

Using Erythropoietin

Erythropoietin (EPO) is a hormone, produced naturally by the kidney, which stimulates the production of red blood cells by the bone marrow. It was previously only available in small quantities worldwide, but advances in biotechnology in the mid-to-late 1980s made it possible to produce EPO, effective in humans, in essentially limitless quantities. Originally, the EPO was developed to treat the anemia that develops in people who have chronic diseases, especially kidney failure, and who are therefore unable to produce their own EPO. However, it was only a matter of time before the greater availability of EPO, together with the knowledge that blood doping works, encouraged athletes to begin experimenting with this drug and, in so doing, cause a sustained increase in their red blood cell numbers. Erythropoietin was first used by professional cyclists in Europe in the mid-1980s.

A tragic early result may have been the death of 18 professional European cyclists in the late 1980s. The causes of their deaths have yet to be explained, and any link to the use of EPO is purely speculative (ACSM 1996c). The assumption that EPO was involved is made largely on a temporal basis; these deaths occurred shortly after EPO first became commercially available. The suspicion—now confirmed by exposés made at the 1998 Tour de France (Whittle 1999), including those by Willy Voet, who has admitted to providing EPO to the Festina cycling team since 1994 (Voet 1999)—is that the use of EPO had become widespread in professional cycling in the early 1990s.

Yet, it is not immediately apparent how EPO use can cause death. When used in controlled conditions, the hormone has an excellent safety record, as might be expected for the use of a naturally occurring hormone (ACSM 1996c). It is possible that the early deaths may have been caused by uncontrolled use of the drug. Athletes may have increased their red blood cell masses to levels that ultimately proved fatal. The drug is now believed to be widely abused by many other elite endurance athletes, including cross-country skiers, swimmers, distance runners, and triathletes. According to the Central Governor Model, EPO should improve performance in any event requiring maximum effort for more than about 90 seconds, since blood flow to the heart should begin to reach maximum values after that time, so that the central governor would begin to be activated to limit performance in events that last longer than that duration.

There are three different techniques that can be used to control the use of EPO. The first is to set an upper limit to the percentage of the total blood volume that can be occupied by the red blood cells. This value, known as the hematocrit, is usually between 43% and 45%, which means that the red blood cells usually occupy between 43% and 45% of the volume of blood circulating in the body. As a result, the International Cycling Union (Union Cycliste Internationale) instituted a rule prohibiting male professional cyclists from competing in sanctioned events if their prerace hematocrits are greater than 50%; the corresponding value for females is 47% (O'Toole et al. 1999). In effect, this has established a goal for EPO therapy, which is to increase the hematocrit to 50% in males and to 47% in females (Voet 1999). It is extremely likely that a male cyclist with a hematocrit of 50% would have a significant advantage over another equally trained cyclist with the same genetic ability but whose (untreated) hematocrit was an honest 45%. Interestingly, various studies of Tour de France cyclists between 1980 and 1986, before the introduction of EPO, found that the hematocrits of those athletes ranged from 43% to 48%, so that none were over 50%, and hemoglobin concentrations were also substantially below 17 g per dl (Saris et al. 1998).

Allegedly, the highest hematocrit yet recorded (73%) in a live human being was in a Tour de France cyclist noted for his climbing ability, whose blood was examined after he was admitted to a hospital following a serious cycling accident. The highest value recorded in one study of Hawaiian Ironman triathletes was 52% in a male and 48% in a female (O'Toole et al. 1999). Whether or not those high values were drug-induced is not clear since they might also be at the upper limit of the normal range in athletes not using EPO, although I have doubts about this.

Similarly, in 1997 the Fédération Internationale de Ski (FIS) introduced a limiting hemoglobin concentration of 18.5 g per dl. However, despite nearly 30 years as an exercise scientist, I do not recall ever measuring a hemoglobin concentration greater than 17 g per dl in any South African athlete, let alone a value of 18.5 g per dl. If such high values occur naturally, then, in my experience, they do not occur often in South African athletes. Hence, the rulings are not ideal, as they still discriminate against the honest athlete while rewarding the dishonest athlete for being only a "little" dishonest. It is interesting that average blood hemoglobin concentrations and hematocrits in European cross-country skiers have increased in the past 15 years since EPO first became more freely available and these rulings were applied for the first time

In 1989, during the first Skiing World Championships, the FIS introduced mandatory blood testing at international skiing competitions, especially cross-country skiing. Results showed that the mean hemoglobin concentrations for both men and women were about 9% below the general population reference values of 15.6 g per dl for men and 14.4 g per dl for women (Rusko et al. 1998; Videman and Forsythe 2000). These values have jumped dramatically, so much so that by 1996 the highest value measured in a male skier was 18.0 g per dl; in a female skier, the highest value measured was 15.5 g per dl.

Now that upper normal limits have been established, the natural inclination for some athletes will be to titrate their EPO doses to ensure that they stay within this abnormal range of blood hemoglobin concentrations, as professional cyclists do (Voet 1999).

A twist to the story occurred in the 2001 World Skiing Championships in Lahti, Finland, at which six Finnish skiers tested positive for the use of the banned blood volume expander, Haemophes. This blood volume expander works by artificially reducing the blood hemoglobin concentration and the hematocrit of athletes using EPO, enabling them to attain a greater circulating mass of red blood cells but without transgressing the liberal FIS regulations. These positive tests, devastating to the pride of the nation that produced the world's greatest athlete, Paavo Nurmi (chapter 6), indicate the extent to which illicit drug use has pervaded international sport. The Finns do not believe that their skiers were alone in the use of illicit agents in that competition but that, like Paavo Nurmi in 1932, they were the ones targeted for exposure.

The second technique used to control the use of EPO is to detect the subtle differences in the molecular structure of the EPO produced commercially from that produced by human kidney cells (Wide and Bengtsson 1990). The molecules are differently charged. This difference in charge can be detected in blood or urine samples for up to seven days after injection (Wide et al. 1995).

The third detection technique, developed at the Australian Institute for Sport in Canberra, measures changes in those red blood cells, the reticulocytes, that increase immediately when EPO is administered and that subsequently mature into adult red blood cells (Parisotto et al. 2000). This research showed that by measuring four different reticulocyte parameters it would be possible to identify 52% of current or recent users of EPO with fewer than seven false positives per 100,000 tests. However, these tests would probably need to be performed within 7 to 14 days of the last EPO injection.

The latter two detection methods were used at the 2000 Olympic Games in Sydney. One effect was that a number of endurance athletes who had been selected to compete in those Games chose rather to stay at home, perhaps out of fear that their illegal use of EPO might be detected.

Of course, athletes who knew the outcome of that research before the Games were at an advantage, since they would have been able to continue using EPO closer to the Games, safe in the knowledge that, provided they stopped 7 to 14 days before competition, they would escape detection.

The benefits of illegal EPO use are equivalent to those achieved by blood doping (Ekblom and Berglund 1991; Ekblom 1996). However, the clear advantage of EPO is that it improves performance both in training and in competition, an advantage not provided by blood doping used only intermittently, the benefits of which are lost after about three to six weeks. Furthermore, the effects of EPO are rapid.

For example, one recent study from Norway showed that hematocrits increased from 43% to 51% within four weeks of EPO use on alternate days (Birkeland et al.

2000). During the same period, the $\dot{V}O_2$max rose by 7% from 64 to 68 ml O_2 per kg per min, an increase that exceeds any that could be achieved by even the most intensive training in already well-trained athletes with quite high $\dot{V}O_2$max values.

But what this last study shows is the relative dearth of quality studies of the effects of EPO use on athletic performance. The analogy with anabolic steroids is striking. The two most abused drugs in international sporting competition have evoked the least scientific interest among the research community. We are surely forced to question why this should be.

The Next Alternatives

As detection techniques for blood doping and EPO use continue to improve, it is likely that some athletes will continue searching for other alternatives. The first alternative will be mimetic proteins that produce the same effects as EPO but that are structurally different (Wrighton et al. 1997) and are hence undetectable by methods that identify injected, exogenous EPO.

The second alternative will be an artificial hemoglobin produced by recombinant gene therapy. It is only a matter of time before this technology is used to develop an artificial blood substitute that will ensure that blood stores can be sustained independent of the rate of blood donations and without the risk of transmitting the HIV/AIDS or other viruses.

If the past is anything to go by, endurance athletes will be among the first in the queue to test these products when they become available.

Using a High-Altitude or Nitrogen House

Erythropoietin production is stimulated whenever the oxygen supply to the kidney is reduced. This occurs whenever the oxygen content of the blood is reduced (for example, during exposure to altitude). Since the early 1990s, a number of researchers have been experimenting with techniques to stimulate altitude exposure in those living at sea level. Two techniques have become popular.

The first is the high-altitude (alpine) or nitrogen house, in which a low oxygen, high nitrogen gas mixture is fed into the room in which athletes rest and sleep for 12 to 16 hours a day. The second is a simple tent that fits over the athlete's bed, for use when during sleep. The value of both is that the athlete sleeps at altitude but is able to train at sea level; thus the disadvantage of a reduced training intensity at high altitude is avoided. In addition, the athletes remain in their usual living and training environments.

These techniques only induce an increase in red blood cell production if the simulated altitude is greater than 2500 m. Although no studies have yet reported the effects of living in a high-altitude house on subsequent running performance, there is no reason to doubt that the technique will be effective, provided it increases the red blood cell mass sufficiently to increase blood and oxygen supply to the heart.

According to the governor theory, any increase in oxygen flow to the heart, whether achieved by blood doping, EPO use, or living at a real or simulated altitude, will delay the activation of the governor during high-intensity exercise. Thus, these techniques could improve performance in events lasting as little as 1 minute, with perhaps a peak effect in events lasting 4 to 10 minutes, when oxygen supply to the heart is likely to be the main sensory feedback to the central governor and hence the major determinant of performance.

However, the magnitude of any benefit is likely to be proportional to the extent to which the red blood cell mass increases. In as much as living at a real or simulated altitude is less effective in increasing the red blood cell mass than is the use of EPO, it is likely that these techniques will prove to be substantially less effective ergogenic aids than the illegal use of EPO.

Training With Oxygen-Enriched Air

The Central Governor Model predicts that it is the oxygen delivery to the heart that determines performance during high-intensity exercise. Hence, exercising with an increased, not reduced, oxygen concentration in the inspired air should enhance performance. One method that can be used to achieve this is to inhale air that contains an increased percentage of oxygen. For example, at sea level room air contains 21% oxygen, whereas at an altitude of 2000 m it is as if the inhaled air contains only 17% oxygen. (In fact, the oxygen content of air at all altitudes is always 21%. But because the barometric pressure falls at increasing altitude, the physiological effects on the body are as if the percentage oxygen concentration in the air has been reduced. Hence, at sea level, many but not all physiological effects of altitude can be simulated by exposing subjects to air that has been modified by reducing the percentage of oxygen that it contains.) At the summit of Mount Everest, the equivalent percentage oxygen in the inspired air is 4%, which explains why climbing at altitude is so taxing, with a rate of ascent of about 50 m per hour.

The first scientists to report the effect of oxygen inhalation before exercise on subsequent performance were Leonard Hill and colleagues (1908). The subjects in this study were Just himself and a man named Holding, two Cambridge University students who had competed in the Olympic Games. The pair was studied on the Stanford Bridge track in London on 27 July, 1908. Just inhaled 100% oxygen for 2 minutes, after which he ran 880 yards in 1:55.5, a 3-second improvement on his Olympic qualifying time of 1:58.5 and equal to his previous best performance ever. He reported "an absence of distressful dyspnea [the sensation of uncomfortable and distressing breathlessness], of grogginess about the legs, and of stiffness of the muscles after his great effort" (L. Hill et al. 1908, p. 500). Twenty minutes later he again inhaled oxygen and ran 440 yards in 53:6. Of his record-breaking run, Just reported: "I travelled so easily that the pace seemed much slower than it really was; and even sprinting, which usually tires me very much, seemed quite easy" (p. 500). This performance further surprised Just because he had been smoking heavily and had run three 800-m races in seven days. Holding also inhaled oxygen for 2 minutes and then ran 440 yards in 50.5, and "to the astonishment of the officials, he was no more blown than after a 100-yard race. The best time in which he had ever done the quarter before was 51 seconds. At the trials for the Olympic Games, he did not do it in less than 52 seconds" (p. 500). Some 30 minutes later, Holding lowered his best 100-yard time by 0.5 sec to 11.00, again after inhaling oxygen for 2 minutes.

The authors concluded that the results showed convincingly that "athletes, by inhaling oxygen, can both break the world's records and relieve themselves of the great distress which follows their greatest efforts" (p. 500). They go so far as to say that the

> occasional breathing of oxygen could prove of benefit in long-continued efforts such as the marathon race and the Channel swim. In horse-racing, too, the use of oxygen would, we think, have a notable influence. By breathing oxygen before

and after each severe trial is run or rowed during training, it seems likely that the development of the muscles would be improved and "staleness" from overtraining prevented. (L. Hill et al. 1908, p. 500)

Not surprisingly, A.V. Hill and his colleagues were the next to test the effects of an increased oxygen content of the inspired air on athletic performance (Hill et al. 1925). Their logic followed directly from their theory that there must be a governor in the heart to prevent heart damage during maximum exercise when, in their model, the heart must develop an inadequate blood supply.

They reported that

the use of gas mixtures containing a high pressure of oxygen enables a considerably higher oxygen intake to be attained. The increase is often so large that it cannot be due simply to more complete saturation of blood in its passage through the lungs. It is suggested that a governor mechanism exists, either in the heart muscle itself, or elsewhere, that tends to coordinate the output of the heart with the degree of saturation of the blood leaving it. The high values of oxygen intake attained, especially while breathing oxygen mixtures, allow an approximate calculation of the maximum output of the heart. Apparently, under some circumstances of severe exercise, the output in many may reach 170 to 220 c.c. per beat, or 30 to 40 liters per minute. Assuming these high values, a further approximate calculation of the work done by the heart emphasizes the great importance, in muscular exercise, of an adequate coronary blood supply to the heart muscle itself. (Hill et al. 1925, p. 166).

They subsequently concluded that "the limit to which the muscles can be driven, while breathing air, is set, not so much by the exhaustion of the muscles themselves as by the distress (cardiac and cerebral) resulting from either the rise of hydrogen-ion concentration of blood, or its imperfect saturation with oxygen while passing rapidly through the lungs" (Hill et al. 1925, p. 135).

Since those early reports of L. Hill et al. (1908) and of A.V. Hill et al. (1925), a number of other studies have established that the inhalation of air with an increased oxygen percentage improves exercise capacity (Bannister and Cunningham 1954; Ekblom et al. 1975; Adams and Welch 1980; Peltonen et al. 1995; 1997; 2001).

Interestingly, Sir Roger Bannister, the world's first sub-4-minute miler, was among the first to study the effects of this technique. Sir Roger was an experimental subject in those trials. These studies were published in 1954, the same year that Sir Roger established his historic feat, suggesting that he may have completed those laboratory studies sometime before his famous run on the Iffley track. Inhaling air enriched with oxygen at either 66% or 100%, Sir Roger ran about 100% longer to exhaustion on a treadmill set at 10 km per hour and at a 1 in 7 gradient. Of his experience, Sir Roger wrote the following:

R.G.B. noticed with surprise that he felt mentally elated when breathing 66%, but not when breathing pure oxygen. The exercise was incomparably easier than in any of the previous runs at this intensity; breathing was effortless and he stopped running more from boredom than from exhaustion. (Bannister and Cunningham 1954, p. 130)

Another subject, D.J.C. Cunningham, "felt that he could continue to run indefinitely" while inhaling 66% oxygen. A third subject, identified as N.D. McW., "thought that there was a definite elation which he distinguished from the mere absence of discomfort. He would have been prepared to run indefinitely had he not had to catch a train" (Bannister and Cunningham 1954, p. 130).

The other observation of Bannister and Cunningham (1954) was that subjective improvements occurred within a few breaths of inhaling the oxygen-enriched air, indicating that these effects cannot be due to alterations in the skeletal muscle metabolism, in particular the rate of production of lactate and hydrogen ions, but must result from immediate changes in oxygen tensions somewhere in the body. The authors suggested that receptors sensitive to oxygen, the carotid or aortic chemoreceptors, might be responsible. Alternatively, according to Hill's governor theory, they postulated that oxygen "might act by improving cardiac function."

The modern studies of Peltonen et al. (1995; 1997; 2001) from the unit for sports and exercise medicine at the University of Helsinki, Finland, have added substantially to our understanding of how hyperoxia improves exercise performance. By studying rowers performing a simulated 2500-m race on a rowing ergometer, they showed that the rower's ability to produce a maximum rowing stroke at the end of each 500 m of the race fell progressively due to reduced electromyographic (EMG) activity (Peltonen et al. 1997), indicating the development of a central, neural fatigue. But the reduction was less in hyperoxia, when the rowers inhaled air with an increased oxygen concentration, indicating that the inhalation of oxygen-enriched air allows a greater maximum skeletal muscle recruitment. Subsequently, they have shown that the maximum cardiac output is increased when oxygen-enriched air is inhaled and reduced in hypoxia, when oxygen-depleted air is inhaled (Peltonen et al. 2001).

Hence, these findings are compatible with the Central Governor theory and completely at odds with the Cardiovascular/Anaerobic Model. The Cardiovascular/Anaerobic Model logically predicts that the maximum output of the heart is always the same, since it is limited by an inherent and immutable (in the short term) inability to alter its maximum pumping characteristics. The pumping characteristics always reach the same limiting maximum capacity during maximum exercise at sea level, thereby inducing skeletal muscle anaerobiosis, as described in chapter 2. If the oxygen demands of the skeletal muscles must always be protected, then the same maximum cardiac output must be achieved during hypoxia and hyperoxia. This is especially so during hypoxia, when the amount of oxygen carried in the blood is reduced, and the sole way to sustain oxygen delivery to the tissues is to maintain or increase the maximum cardiac output, and not to decrease the cardiac output, as found by Peltonen et al. (2001).

But the Central Governor Model predicts that reduced oxygen delivery to the heart during maximum exercise when air with a reduced oxygen percentage is inhaled will prematurely activate the central governor, reducing the maximum amount of muscle that can be recruited and hence lowering the peak work rate that can be achieved. As a result, cardiac output and peak EMG activity will be reduced, in line with the findings of Peltonen et al. (1995; 1997; 2001).

What are the practical implications of this work? First, if the Central Governor theory is correct, then performing high-intensity training while inhaling oxygen-enriched air may be more beneficial than performing the same exercise when inhaling either normal air or air with a reduced oxygen pressure, as occurs at altitude.

The reason for this is that a higher exercise intensity will be achievable during that training when oxygen is inhaled. If this is sufficient to reset the governor to allow a higher exercise intensity in the next few exercise bouts when normal air is inhaled, then there will be a short window of opportunity during which the athlete will be able to run faster even when inhaling normal air. Of course, if the governor has no memory but reverts to its former levels of function immediately when the next exercise bout in normal air begins, then this potential benefit will not be realized.

Since we currently have no data on this possibility, we can only speculate. It is perhaps possible that Sir Roger broke the 4-minute mile because of the experimental runs he performed in the research laboratory at Oxford while inhaling oxygen-enriched air.

Second, if this theory is indeed correct, then training at either medium or high altitude or living high and training low may be the wrong options. It might then be better either to stay at sea level and perform high-intensity training while inhaling oxygen-enriched air or else to live at the very high altitudes (above 2500 m) known to stimulate an increase in the red blood cell mass and to do all training while inhaling oxygen-enriched air. Of course, some may choose the third option, which is to exercise in hyperoxia and to stimulate red blood cell production using the banned hormone erythropoietin.

An important consequence of all this is that the fate of the high-altitude training theory and all the high-altitude training camps situated around the world hangs in the balance, pending the outcome of this scientific debate.

Ingesting Carbohydrate to Prevent Hypoglycemia

In chapter 3, I discuss the history of how hypoglycemia came to be recognized as a significant cause of fatigue during prolonged exercise and how its prevention improves performance.

In a recent laboratory study (Claassens et al. 2002), we showed that the prevention of hypoglycemia by infusing glucose in subjects who began exercising in a carbohydrate-depleted state and who were therefore at high risk of developing hypoglycemia increased the duration they could continue exercising at about 70% $\dot{V}O_2max$ by a minimum of 26%.

This does not simply mean that if you ingest carbohydrate to prevent hypoglycemia you will necessarily improve your performance by as much as 26%. What it does mean is that if you are involved in an event that will definitely cause you to develop hypoglycemia—for instance, if you are able to sustain a relatively high exercise intensity (65% $\dot{V}O_2max$ or higher) for more than 3 to 4 hours—your performance will improve substantially if you ingest sufficient carbohydrate to prevent hypoglycemia. This point was discussed in detail in chapter 3, and the conceptual basis for it is shown in figure 3.6. But if you do not develop hypoglycemia during such events, perhaps because you fatigue prematurely for any of the other reasons described in the different fatigue models (chapters 1 to 4) or because you naturally burn more fat during exercise and are therefore less reliant on carbohydrate, then all the carbohydrate in the world will not improve your performance. Instead, you should aim to improve your performance by addressing those other weaknesses, perhaps by training more appropriately.

The different methods that can be used to prevent hypoglycemia by appropriate carbohydrate ingestion during exercise are covered in chapter 4.

Interestingly, there are believed to be two mechanisms by which hypoglycemia can impair exercise performance. First, there is suggestive evidence of a glucose sensor in the brain that responds to falling blood glucose concentrations by activating a counterregulatory response. The goal of this regulatory response is to raise the blood glucose concentration (Boyle et al. 1994) and thereby protect the brain from damage caused by an inadequate energy supply. This sensor becomes less sensitive to a falling blood glucose concentration in people who have previously experienced bouts of hypoglycemia (Boyle et al. 1994).

Second, Hevener et al. (1997; 2000) have shown that receptors in the walls of the (portal) veins draining from the liver, into which the liver secretes the glucose necessary to maintain the blood glucose concentration, must sense either the glucose concentration or its rate of change from some normal value. By extrapolating these findings from rats to humans, it is possible that if, during exercise, those receptors sense that the liver is not producing glucose sufficiently rapidly, they would inform the central governor, which, in turn, would then reduce the mass of muscle that is active according to the Integrated Neuromuscular Recruitment Model that we have developed in this book. At the same time, the governor informs the athlete's conscious brain that he is tired, inducing the symptoms of hypoglycemia described in chapter 3. The blood glucose concentration at that time could be normal (Claassens et al. 2001), indicating that, in that instance, the central governor may not be responding to the blood glucose concentration in the brain but to the glucose concentration at another site closer to the liver.

These two findings might also explain why the blood glucose concentrations at exhaustion can differ substantially among people. For example, some subjects will terminate exercise at a blood glucose concentration of 4.5 mmol per liter while others can continue exercising even though their blood glucose concentrations are below 2.5 mmol per liter (Claassens et al. 2002). The brain sensors for glucose may respond to different blood glucose concentrations, perhaps as a result of prior episodes of hypoglycemia (Boyle et al. 1994), which train the brain to tolerate lower blood glucose concentrations in subsequent bouts of exercise. This would be more likely in those people whose diets contain lower carbohydrate contents and who ingest insufficient carbohydrate during prolonged exercise. Alternatively, the glucose concentration in the portal vein, where it is being sensed, or the rate at which the liver is producing the glucose may possibly be the same in those whose blood glucose concentrations are quite different at exhaustion. For example, athletes whose muscles use more carbohydrate during exercise ("carbohydrate burners") would be more likely to stop exercising at higher blood glucose concentrations since any small discrepancy between high rates of glucose production by the liver and high rates of glucose use by the muscles would cause a sharp fall in blood glucose concentrations. In contrast, if rates of glucose production and use are lower, as found in habitual "fat burners," then any discrepancy in their respective rates will cause blood glucose concentrations to fall more slowly. Hence, the governor can be more lenient, allowing the blood glucose concentration to fall further before it calls an end to exercise by reducing the mass of muscle that is activated. Of course, all this is speculative, and substantial research will be required before it is shown to be either correct or fanciful.

Preexercise Carbohydrate Loading

Since carbohydrate loading increases the preexercise liver (and muscle) glycogen stores (chapter 3), it will delay the onset of hypoglycemia during prolonged exercise (Bosch et al. 1996b). This effect alone should be expected to enhance endurance performance by about 20%. In addition, the higher preexercise muscle glycogen concentrations should further enhance performance by allowing more exercise to be performed before the central governor is activated and in turn terminates exercise before complete muscle energy depletion can develop.

Analysis of all studies of the effects of carbohydrate loading on endurance performance suggests that this intervention increases the duration of exercise that can be sustained at a given exercise intensity by about 20% and shortens the time required to complete a given amount of exercise by about 3% (Hawley, Schabort, et al. 1997). The extent to which this effect delays the onset of hypoglycemia or increases the muscle glycogen content, or a combination of both, is not yet known (Burke, Hawley, et al. 2000; Claassens et al. 2002). It is interesting that the magnitude of this effect is similar to that achieved by ingesting carbohydrate to delay the onset of hypoglycemia during exercise.

My bias, as argued fully in chapter 3, is to believe that the dominant effect is the prevention of hypoglycemia, with a somewhat smaller effect due to the higher starting muscle glycogen concentrations. This would explain why carbohydrate loading had little effect when subjects also ingested carbohydrate during exercise to prevent hypoglycemia (Burke, Hawley, et al. 2000) and conversely, as argued in chapter 3, why the effect of carbohydrate loading is exaggerated in those studies in which liver glycogen concentrations are reduced artificially before exercise, thereby expediting the onset of hypoglycemia in those subjects who have eaten less carbohydrate before exercise.

But this interpretation is based on a fairly simple understanding of how the body works (that is, it responds only to a crisis that has already developed—either the blood glucose concentration has fallen too low, or the muscle glycogen stores have already become depleted). But if the brain is much cleverer than exercise physiologists currently believe, then a more intriguing possibility exists.

Ingesting Fluid During Exercise

Moderate amounts of fluid ingested during prolonged exercise enhance performance, as described in chapter 4. The magnitude of the effect will vary depending on the manner in which it is measured. Below et al. (1995) showed that performance time during a bout of high-intensity exercise, lasting about 10 minutes, that followed 50 minutes of cycling exercise, improved by 6% with water ingestion and by another 6% when the fluid included carbohydrate. Using a similar testing protocol, Walsh et al. (1994) showed the same effect. However, bear in mind that these studies compared drinking during exercise to not drinking at all during exercise of relatively short duration and high intensity. They did not address the question of whether drinking more than a certain amount was more or less beneficial or whether these findings also apply to more prolonged exercise at a lower intensity, especially in cool conditions. In chapter 4, I review the evidence that drinking ad libitum is as effective as forced (but not over-) drinking in maintaining performance and physiological function during prolonged exercise, whereas overdrinking, perhaps to quite a moderate extent, impairs performance.

One possible explanation for this unexpected finding is that the act of drinking itself may be an important determinant of the performance-enhancing effects of fluid ingestion. Perhaps sensory receptors from the mouth and throat feed information to the central governor about the rate of fluid replacement during exercise. Provided they have evidence that some fluid is being replaced, their input to the central governor may be limited or absent. In contrast, if no fluid is ingested, they may inform the central governor that performance must be reduced by decreasing the mass of muscle that can be recruited.

Time to fatigue during very prolonged exercise increases substantially when water is ingested. Again, the magnitude of the effect will depend on the nature of the exercise that is undertaken (see chapter 4).

If fluid ingestion improves performance by a central (brain) mechanism, then that effect will only ever be identified if that specific brain mechanism is investigated. Since, to my knowledge, no researcher has yet evaluated any possible role of the brain in this effect, then the possibility that fluid ingestion could improve performance through a central mechanism has been neither shown nor excluded. Nevertheless, the conclusion is that if the exercise bout is sufficiently long, those who do not drink are likely to stop exercising approximately 25% sooner than are those who drink. But this does not mean that those who drink more will continue for even longer than those who only drink ad libitum. This possibility has not been studied.

In summary, there is clear evidence to suggest that people who do not drink anything during exercise of whatever intensity or duration will perform less well than they would if they drank ad libitum. However, whereas drinking more than ad libitum has not been shown to improve performance further, drinking to excess can be fatal (see chapter 4).

It is important not to confuse the clearly established ergogenic effect of water ingestion on performance with the complete absence of any evidence that high rates of fluid ingestion during exercise reduce the risk of developing medical complications during prolonged exercise in the heat (Noakes 2001).

Caffeine

There is a formidable body of evidence showing that caffeine, even at dosages allowable in Olympic competition, has a substantial ergogenic effect, especially on the duration for which a specific exercise intensity can be sustained (time to fatigue).

A series of Canadian experiments (Graham and Spriet 1991; Spriet et al. 1992) has shown that the ingestion of between 3 and 6 mg of caffeine per kg of body weight approximately 1 hour before endurance exercise improved time to fatigue when cycling at a fixed exercise intensity by between 20% and 50%. A Dutch study (Pasman et al. 1995) of more highly trained cyclists also found that time to fatigue at approximately 85% $\dot{V}O_2$max increased by 23%.

Caffeine also improves performance during all-out efforts lasting from 4 to 5 minutes. For example, exercise time at $\dot{V}O_2$max increases by approximately 20% (Jackman et al. 1996), performance during 1500-m running by approximately 1.5% to 1.7% (Wiles et al. 1992; MacIntosh and Wright 1995), and performance in 2000-m rowing in both men (Bruce et al. 2000) and women (Anderson et al. 2000) by approximately 1%. Performance during repeated bouts of exercise—for example, during swimming intervals—is also improved (Collomp et al. 1992).

Caffeine also increases the maximum force that can be developed during a maximum voluntary contraction (MVC; Kalmar and Cafarelli 1999) by about 3%. This effect is due to increased skeletal muscle recruitment by the motor cortex in the brain. Indeed, caffeine ingestion allows more work to be performed at the same perception of effort (Cole et al. 1996). Or, stated differently, the same exercise intensity produces a lower perception of effort after caffeine ingestion. Similarly, the maximum instantaneous power produced during brief bouts of cycling increases by about 6% following caffeine ingestion (Anselme et al. 1992). In addition, caffeine increases the duration that an isometric contraction can be sustained at 50% MVC by 28% (Kalmar and Cafarelli 1999).

Given the overwhelming evidence supporting caffeine's ergogenic effects, we were extremely surprised by the results of our own studies, which failed to show that caffeine ingested even at quite high doses improved performance during a 100-km simulated cycling time-trial that included repetitive sprints of 1 or 4 km at specified distances during the trial (Hunter et al. 2002). A key difference in those trials is that the cyclist chooses his own pacing strategy, which is remarkably consistent from trial to trial (Schabort, Hawley, et al. 1998) and is not influenced by caffeine ingestion.

In as much as most athletes are more interested in their time-trial performance than in maintaining a constant running speed for longer before they become exhausted, we believe our study to be a more relevant measure of the true ergogenic value of caffeine for endurance athletes competing in events lasting 1 to 4 hours. Hence, my personal conclusion is that caffeine ingestion will be of little value in endurance events lasting more than 1 hour. In longer events, when the ability to stay awake becomes an important variable determining performance, then the ability of caffeine to increase alertness in the fatigued state may indeed prove ergogenic.

In chapter 3, we analyzed the evidence that caffeine may enhance time to fatigue by way of a postulated metabolic effect of slowing the rate of muscle glycogen use. No convincing evidence for a metabolic mechanism has ever been established (Graham et al. 1994). While fatigue during prolonged exercise probably results from a central neural (brain) effect, it is more likely that caffeine improves time to fatigue, speed, and strength by a stimulatory effect on the central nervous system.

Indeed, caffeine stimulates the release of a variety of central nervous system neurotransmitters, including the catecholamines, dopamine, noradrenaline, adrenaline, and serotonin (Arnaud 1998). These transmitters increase vigilance, alertness, motivation, clarity of thinking, mental concentration, feelings of well-being, and a sense of energy. They also improve mental performance when you are fatigued or bored.

It is not immediately obvious why these same effects do not improve performance during a simulated 100-km cycling time-trial. However, our interpretation is that performance in that event is predetermined by a pacing strategy established by the subconscious brain even before the exercise begins. During exercise, the brain interprets information from many different organs in the body and modifies its original pacing strategy accordingly. The brain's goal is to deliver the athlete to the finish in the most efficient way, without causing bodily damage. Since the determinants of this pacing strategy were apparently not influenced by caffeine ingestion (Hunter et al. 2002), it can be concluded that caffeine did not alter performance.

In contrast, because there is no pacing strategy involved in exercise time to fatigue—the same constant work intensity must be sustained for as long as possible—the brain must function differently and the conscious/subconscious decision to terminate exercise can be delayed by the caffeine circulating in the bloodstream. This is consistent with caffeine's known effects to increase vigilance, motivation, and mental performance when fatigued. Similarly, in short-duration exercise lasting minutes rather than hours, a stimulatory effect on the brain, perhaps acting directly on the governor itself to allow an increased skeletal muscle recruitment, would explain the ergogenic effect of caffeine.

In summary, the practical advice to the runner is that caffeine is a valuable, essentially harmless, and legal agent that can enhance certain types of performance, but perhaps not the most important for the endurance runner. Provided it is used within the legal limits set by the IOC, there is no reason why runners should not ingest it. I predict that its greatest potential in running races would be to alleviate boredom and increase alertness during prolonged events lasting 12 or more hours. But in races of shorter distances (1 to 5 km), it is likely to be of little or no value.

Caffeine doses greater than 9 mg per kg are likely to exceed the legal doping limit imposed by the IOC. For example, when cyclists rode for 1 hour at about 85% $\dot{V}O_2$max, only subjects who ingested less than 5 mg per kg body weight were below the legal limit. When subjects ingested caffeine at the highest dose of 13 mg per kg body weight, their average urinary caffeine concentration was 15μg per ml, well in excess of the legal limit. Furthermore, such high doses did not improve time to fatigue more than did doses of 3 to 6 mg per kg (Graham and Spriet 1995; Pasman et al. 1995). But these high doses are increasingly likely to cause side effects, including insomnia, anxiety, nervousness, headaches, heart palpitations, and tremor.

Popular sources of caffeine include coffee (50 to 100 mg per cup), brewed tea (30 to 60 mg per cup), cola drinks (50 mg per 375-ml can) and over-the-counter medications (100 to 200 mg per tablet). However, there is doubt as to whether coffee is as good an ergogenic agent as is pure caffeine taken in tablet form. This is probably because coffee contains a range of other chemicals that negate any potential ergogenic effects of pure caffeine.

Interestingly, caffeine is metabolized in the body to paraxanthine, theophylline, and theobromine, and the effects attributed to caffeine represent the sum of the effects of all four compounds. Paraxanthine is the most active ingredient. Current IOC doping control only measures the concentrations of caffeine in the urine. A more effective method would be to measure the urinary paraxanthine concentration, as it is only a matter of time before paraxanthine is used instead of caffeine.

Caffeine excretion is not affected by exercise (Van der Merwe et al. 1992), unlike the excretion of some of the currently banned stimulants, including pseudoephedrine (Gillies et al. 1996). Furthermore, caffeine does not increase urine production during exercise (Wemple, Lamb, et al. 1997) although it does so at rest.

Sodium Bicarbonate or Sodium Citrate

As described in chapter 2, the Cardiovascular/Anaerobic Model, first popularized by A.V. Hill and colleagues in the early 1920s, predicts that fatigue during high-intensity exercise lasting from 2 to 10 minutes and perhaps longer results from an inadequate oxygen supply to the maximally exercising muscles. As a result, the muscles are forced to work anaerobically, producing lactate and hydrogen ions (H+). According to this model, the accumulation of these chemicals is believed to inhibit a variety of contractile and metabolic processes in the active muscles, thereby causing fatigue and preventing the continuation of exercise at that particular intensity (Fitts 1994).

Hence, it is theoretically possible that the ingestion of chemicals such as sodium bicarbonate or sodium citrate, which maintain higher blood and muscle pH during exercise by buffering the acids released during high-intensity exercise, might enhance exercise performance.

To achieve this effect, athletes usually ingest about 0.3 g sodium bicarbonate or 0.5 g sodium citrate per kg of body weight about 2 hours before exercise. These buffers elevate blood pH concentrations for about 3 hours after ingestion, with a peak effect occurring between 1 and 2 hours after ingestion.

A large number of studies (Matson and Tran 1993) have established that bicarbonate ingestion may improve performance in high-intensity exercise of short duration, such as running events of 800 to 1500 m and swimming events of 400 to 800 m. Of the studies that have been completed, 54% showed a beneficial effect (Matson and Tran 1993). The beneficial effects varied in magnitude from 2% to 62%. The greatest effects were measured in the earliest studies, which suggests that these studies were the least well designed. Studies with poor experimental design are more likely to find either very large effects (a false positive result) or to miss a real effect that is small (false negative result). Also, studies in which the ingested dose of sodium bicarbonate induced the greatest degree of alkalosis of the blood were more likely to measure an effect. The most marked effects were also measured in studies that evaluated time to fatigue, in which the ergogenic effect was as large as 35%. In general, the more intense the exercise and the greater the rise in blood lactate concentrations, the larger the effect of induced alkalosis.

As changes in muscle pH do not cause fatigue during exercise lasting more than 30 minutes, it would seem unlikely that ingestion of bicarbonate or citrate would enhance performance in endurance events of that duration. Although we (Schabort et al. 2000) were unable to measure any such benefit in a 40-km laboratory cycling time-trial, two other studies did indeed report a beneficial effect (Potteiger et al. 1996; McNaughton et al. 1999) during 30-km cycle trials in the laboratory.

In summary, bicarbonate ingestion before high-intensity exercise of short duration produces an ergogenic effect of variable degree in about 50% of the studies that have been reported. This suggests that the response is likely to be highly individual, with some subjects, say 20%, showing a marked effect; a larger number, perhaps 40%, showing a much smaller effect; and the remaining 40% showing no effect at all. Paradoxically, of the three studies of more prolonged exercise (30 to 60 minutes) at a lower intensity, two have shown an ergogenic effect of between 3% and 5%, whereas the third showed no discernable effect (Schabort et al. 2000).

There are no foods that produce this effect. Thus, the athlete who wishes to "soda load" with carbonate must ingest a concentrated solution of either sodium bicarbonate or sodium citrate. However, a decided disadvantage of this is that the high dose of alkali causes quite marked diarrhea within about 1 hour of ingestion in about 50% of subjects.

Soda loading clearly contravenes the doping regulations controlling athletics, and bicarbonate and citrate are likely to be listed as banned agents in the near future. In addition, excess bicarbonate can be relatively easily detected in the urine within a short time of bicarbonate loading.

The product is mentioned here not to be condoned but merely because it allows further practical insights into the factors that may limit running performance (Linderman and Fahey 1991).

One untested possibility is that bicarbonate loading might enhance performance during interval training, allowing the athlete to train at a faster pace, especially in the final few repetitions of an intensive interval session. However, there is still no guarantee that this technique would definitely translate into superior racing performance. As might be expected, the ingestion of acidic substances before exercise impairs performance (Hultman et al. 1985).

In summary, soda loading is of no proven value for distance runners but may enhance performance in very short distance sprints. However, the gastrointestinal discomfort that it produces may well offset any potential physiological advantage and certainly puts practical restrictions on its use.

Thus, the advice would seem to be that if you wish to use either bicarbonate or citrate as an ergogenic aid, you will first need to determine whether you are a *responder* or *nonresponder* to these chemicals. You also need to be aware that both these agents, most especially bicarbonate, act as laxatives, the effects of which usually strike 2 to 3 hours after ingestion.

Preexercise Cooling

There is clear evidence (chapter 4) to suggest that the central governor will only allow prolonged exercise to continue if the whole body temperature is lower than some limiting maximum value, which is unique for each person. It may well be that in hot environmental conditions the athlete's subconscious chooses a race pace that will minimize the rate at which the body accumulates heat and at which its temperature rises (Marino et al. 2000), specifically to ensure that the limiting maximum temperature is not reached before the race finish line.

According to this theory, lowering the body temperature before exercise should allow the athlete to run faster for longer before that limiting temperature is reached.

A number of studies have shown that precooling can improve subsequent athletic performance (Hessemer et al. 1984; Schmidt and Brück 1981; Olschewski and Brück 1988; Lee and Haymes 1995; Booth et al. 1997; Kay et al. 1999; Marsh and Sleivert 1999). The benefit is most likely to occur in activities lasting less than 30 minutes. After this, skin and body temperatures equalize in subjects who have undergone precooling, as well as in those who have not (Booth et al. 1997; Kay et al. 1999).

The effect of precooling is large. In the study of Kay et al. (1999), subjects cycled 6% farther during 30 minutes of exercise at their peak sustainable pace. The same group found that subjects ran 304 m (about 4%) farther during a 30-minute treadmill run in hot (32°C), humid (60%) conditions (Booth et al. 1997). A related technique is to cool the skin during exercise. Cooling the head improved cycling time to fatigue at 75 % $\dot{V}O_2$max by 50%. Head cooling prevented the normal rise in the temperature of the inner ear (tympanic) membrane but had no effect on the rectal temperature.

Creatine Supplementation

Creatine is a normal constituent of mammalian muscle, where it functions as an essential component of the phosphocreatine (PCr) molecule. PCr in turn serves as an energy source for the resynthesis of adenosine triphosphate (ATP), the ultimate energy source for muscle contraction. The average daily dietary creatine intake is about 1 g. As daily creatine turnover is about 2 g, the body must manufacture 1 g per day to cover the shortfall. Creatine is produced in the liver from a precursor produced in the kidneys. To increase muscle PCr concentrations, you need to ingest either high doses (20 to 25 g per day) of creatine for five days or lower doses (3 to 5 g per day) for up to 28 days. A maintenance dose of 2 to 3 g per day is then recommended. When creatine is ingested in these high doses, the body terminates its usual creatine production.

In the 1980s Eric Hultman, one of the originators of the muscle biopsy technique and the carbohydrate-loading diet, noted that muscle PCr concentrations fall steeply during high-intensity exercise. As a result, he wondered whether fatigue during high-intensity exercise lasting 2 to 60 seconds might be caused by PCr depletion. Using the same logic that launched the carbohydrate-loading diet, he proposed that increasing the preexercise muscle PCr concentrations might enhance performance during high-intensity exercise of short duration. He then began the search for techniques to increase muscle PCr concentrations and came up with the idea of creatine supplementation.

The end result of his speculation was that by 1999 approximately 4 million kg of creatine were sold across the globe, mainly in North America, but with large and expanding markets in Europe, Australasia, and Southern Africa. The value of these markets has been estimated at $200 million annually.

Analysis of research only undertaken after creatine was launched commercially comes to six principal conclusions (Mujika and Padilla 1997; M.H. Williams and Branch 1998; Kraemer and Volek 1999; Demant and Rhodes 1999; Graham and Hatton 1999; Jacobs 1999; ACSM 2000; Rawson and Clarkson 2000):

1. There is no evidence that creatine supplementation increases performance during a single burst of maximal exercise lasting less than 90 seconds. This includes sprint cycling, sprint running, and sprint swimming. This is a particularly surprising finding, given the original hypothesis that increased muscle PCr concentrations should increase performance during a single bout of maximal exercise that causes muscle PCr concentrations to fall sharply. It shows that scientific hypotheses must never be taken too seriously. However, one recent study (McNaughton et al. 1998) reported that kayak performance was significantly enhanced by 16% during a 90-second bout of maximal exercise and by 7% in a 5-minute maximal exercise bout.

2. The majority of, but not all, studies show that creatine supplementation improves performance during repeated bouts of high-intensity exercise—for example, during interval sessions of running, cycling, or swimming. The effect seems to be that creatine supplementation allows a more rapid recovery between exercise bouts. As a result, more work can be performed in the last few intervals of the session. Hence, creatine supplementation improves fatigue resistance and enhances performance during interval training. If athletes are able to train harder during their interval sessions, this benefit might enhance subsequent competitive performance. However, this hypothesis has yet to be tested.

3. Almost all studies show that creatine supplementation enhances adaptation to a weight-training program. Thus, for example, the amount of training performed and the gain in muscle mass, strength, and the size of muscle fibers are all significantly greater in those who ingest creatine during training (Volek et al. 1999). These authors concluded that the ingestion of creatine allows more work to be done in each training session. However, a direct effect of creatine on muscle development during weight training cannot be excluded.

4. Performance during endurance cycling, swimming, or running events lasting 10 or more minutes is not improved and may in fact be impaired, perhaps as a result of an increased body mass that usually accompanies the use of creatine.

5. The response to creatine supplementation is highly individual. Studies suggest that the populations that have been studied fall more or less equally (that is, 25%) into one of four groups: nonresponders, low responders, average responders, and high responders (Myburgh 2000).

6. There is currently no evidence to suggest that creatine use carries any short- or long-term health risk when used by healthy athletes (Poortmans and Francaux 2000).

One theoretical risk at present would be from impure creatine that is contaminated with other chemicals, especially toxic metals. When large doses (20 g) of creatine are ingested daily, even trace impurities could have harmful effects. Thus, if you choose to ingest creatine, be certain that the product is pure and that it is produced by a reputable manufacturer.

Another risk is that the creatine may have been spiked with an anabolic steroid that is not declared on the product label. The advantage to the athlete is that the spiked creatine will act more like an anabolic steroid; the disadvantage is that the athlete may test positive for the illicit use of anabolic steroids. Indeed, the recent spate of positive tests for nandrolone in world-class athletes from a variety of disciplines—including soccer, a sport that is not usually considered a hotbed of anabolic steroid abuse—suggests that the probable cause of their positive doping tests are nutritional ergogenic aids willfully spiked by the manufacturers with anabolic steroids or prohormones. While the actions of these manufacturers may be premeditated, they may not be illegal since the United States law only requires that substances comprising 10% or more of the product need be declared on the label.

In summary, there does not appear to be any good reason why distance runners should use creatine, particularly as it can cause weight gain. Cyclists and triathletes are the only endurance athletes who might benefit because competitive cycling involves bouts of high-intensity exercise followed by prolonged periods at a lower exercise intensity. If creatine supplementation also hastens recovery from the high-intensity bouts that occur during competitive cycling races, then it may offer a small advantage to elite cyclists. Athletes need to be wary that their creatine supplement has not been spiked with anabolic steroids.

Environmental Aids

In addition to the ergogenic effects of training and supplements that can be ingested, there are several environmental factors, such as running surface and lane choice, that can aid performance.

In 1976 two Harvard University engineers, Thomas McMahon and Peter Greene (McMahon and Greene 1978; 1979), were approached by the university's athletics department to design an indoor running track that would reduce the risk of injury, as well as optimize the athletes' running speeds during competition.

Their intuition told them that the softer or more compliant the track surface, the lower the risk of injury. But a soft surface would also be slower because, when running on an absorbing surface, the athlete would spend so much time sinking into and rebounding from that surface, that speed would be considerably reduced.

To establish which surface compliance would both optimize running speed and lower injury risk, McMahon and Greene performed a series of experiments to determine the effects of surfaces differing in their hardness on the two important components of running speed—ground contact time and stride length. Contrary to expectation, which was that an unyielding, hard surface would be the fastest, they discovered that, because of an inbuilt shock-absorbing or dampening component in muscle, ground contact time was least and stride length greatest when the running surface was of intermediate hardness—specifically when the track compliance was in the range of two to four times the compliance of human muscle. The stiffness of the track and that of the athletes had to be "tuned" for one another. When this was achieved, the authors predicted that the runners' track times would be reduced by between 2% and 3%, a predicted improvement on the world mile record of up to 7 seconds.

Their prediction has yet to be validated as few, if any, outdoor tracks have been built to the specifications determined by these innovative workers.

P.C. Jain (1980) of the department of physics at the University of Zambia has made the observation that the world running record for the 200m run in a straight line is about 0.4 seconds faster than that run on a conventional, curved running track. The slower time when running on a track results from overcoming the centripetal force as you run the curves. As the centripetal force is an inverse function of the radius of the curve, it follows that the runner in the outside lane will be less affected than the runner in the inside lane.

Jain calculates that the difference between adjacent lanes will constitute about 0.012 and 0.024 seconds in 200- and 400-m races respectively, accounting for a difference of up to 0.8 and 1.6 seconds between the inside and outside lanes in 200- and 400-m races. He concludes that these differences are sufficiently important that they should be corrected for. He suggests either that the distance of the inside lanes be shortened or that these races should start before the curve, rather than on it, as dictated by current practice. Thus, the start for the outer lane should be moved from on the curve to the point where the straight part of the track meets the curved section. In this way, the athlete in the outside lane would have to run the entire curve and would therefore run a longer distance on the curve (because of the greater radius of the curve). Runners in the inside lane would run a shorter distance on the curve. The advantage gained by running in the outside lane would be neutralized, as runners in that lane would be exposed to the same centripetal force as before, but for a longer time.

Pacing

The scientific literature has not convincingly answered the question of which pacing technique produces the optimum result. In chapter 5, I suggest that it is better to run long-distance races with a negative split (that is, running the second half of the race faster than the first). In contrast, the work of Foster et al. (1994) suggests that a fast start produces a better overall result in short-distance races.

Sometimes it is best to look at the very best runners to establish what they do. Figure 13.2 shows the 1-km split times for three world-record 10,000-m runs of Haile Gebrselassie. His pacing consistency is quite remarkable and seems to be

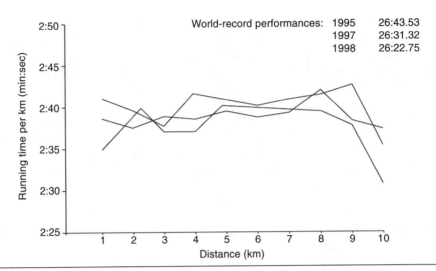

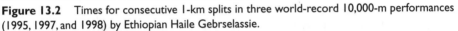

Figure 13.2   Times for consecutive 1-km splits in three world-record 10,000-m performances (1995, 1997, and 1998) by Ethiopian Haile Gebrselassie.

Data on running times provided in a personal communication (Sears 1998).

similar to that adopted by Paavo Nurmi. One is reminded of Paavo Nurmi's statement to the effect that he already knew what time he would run in any track race after he had completed the first two laps. Clearly, the same applies for Gebrselassie.

Note in figure 13.2 that the fastest 1-km times were always recorded in the last 1 km of each race, indicating an impeccable pacing strategy and showing that Gebrselassie runs his fastest when he is theoretically the most tired. This phenomenon is impossible to explain according to any of the current models of exercise physiology presented in chapters 1 to 4, with the exception of the Integrated Neuromuscular Recruitment Model. The Cardiovascular Anaerobic Model is particularly unhelpful since it predicts that a rise in muscle metabolites constrains exercise performance. According to that model, such metabolites must reach peak concentrations at the time the race pacing strategy is first adopted, usually within the first 200 to 400 m of the race. Because the world 10,000-m record is set at intensities that exceed the lactate threshold, rising blood lactate concentrations from 1 to 9 km should cause a progressive slowing of pace, which would be slowest in the final kilometer, the opposite of what is found.

The most likely explanation is that pacing strategies are determined centrally in the brain before the race, with continuous modifications based on sensory input from the environment (including the state of competitors, the environmental conditions, etc.) and from different sensory organs in the body. The goal of pacing is to maintain the fastest pace at which body homeostasis is still maintained.

INTERVENTIONS WITHOUT PROVEN BENEFIT

Several supplements and vitamins are thought by athletes and their coaches to provide ergonomic benefits, however, many of these substances have not shown any proven benefit to performance. I highlight some of the most popular of these substances below.

Glycerol

The ingestion of glycerol causes an acute increase in the plasma volume, the volume of fluid circulating in the bloodstream. Although some studies suggest that this improves performance during high-intensity exercise lasting about 30 minutes (Hitchins et al. 1999), other studies do not show any such effect either on performance (Latzka et al. 1998) or on metabolism during exercise (Watt et al. 1999).

Hence, the conclusion we can draw is that glycerol ingestion before exercise has no ergogenic effect. According to the Central Governor Model, there is no logical reason to expect glycerol ingestion to enhance performance since it does not increase oxygenation of the heart. However, it might mask EPO use by reducing the hematocrit or hemoglobin concentrations to legal values.

Medium-Chain Triglycerides

Increased blood fatty acid concentrations should stimulate fat and reduce carbohydrate metabolism according to the hypothetical glucose-fatty acid cycle (chapter 3), thereby potentially enhancing endurance performance. Accordingly, of a large number of studies that have evaluated whether the ingestion of medium-chain fatty acids will improve endurance performance, only our study (Van Zyl et al. 1996) found such an effect. The overwhelming majority of studies (Hawley 2000), including another from our laboratory (Goedecke, Elmer-English et al. 1999), failed to show any benefit.

Thus, the balance of modern evidence is that fat ingestion during prolonged exercise does not enhance performance. This is compatible with the theory that factors other than carbohydrate depletion may determine performance during prolonged exercise (chapter 3).

Branched-Chain Amino Acids

In terms of the central governor theory, fatigue is nothing more than a sensory manifestation of a central control mechanism, the goal of which is to prevent bodily harm during exercise. This form of central control contrasts with a peripheral fatigue that results from metabolic changes in the exercising muscles. An alternative form of centrally determined fatigue that is also metabolically based, so-called central fatigue, has also been proposed (Newsholme et al. 1987; Davis 1995).

According to this model, fatigue is caused by the accumulation of fatiguing metabolites in the brain—in particular, increasing concentrations of serotonin (5-hydroxy tryptamine). In line with this theory, the nutritional interventions that reduce serotonin accumulation in the brain should also improve endurance performance. In particular, this theory holds that the ingestion of carbohydrates or branched-chain amino acids, or both, can influence the accumulation of serotonin in the brain and therefore influence the rate at which central fatigue develops.

The brain serotonin concentrations are believed to be altered by changes in the blood concentration of the unbound amino acid, free tryptophan, from which brain serotonin is derived. Exercise increases the amount of free tryptophan present in the blood because the rising free fatty acid concentrations displace tryptophan from circulating albumin, the blood carrier for both tryptophan and free fatty acids.

Hence, a rising concentration of free fatty acids, secondary to progressive muscle glycogen depletion (Weltan et al. 1998a; 1998b), and falling blood insulin concentrations will cause the circulating levels of free tryptophan and, at least theoretically, brain serotonin concentrations to increase. In this way, exercising muscle that is becoming progressively glycogen depleted might be able to inform the brain of its predicament, inducing central fatigue.

The entry of tryptophan into the brain, across the blood-brain barrier, is controlled by a specific transport mechanism that tryptophan shares with the branched-chain amino acids, valine, leucine, and isoleucine.

If these theories are correct, the onset of central fatigue could be delayed by reducing the circulating free fatty acid concentrations by ingesting carbohydrate before and during exercise (chapter 3) and by increasing blood concentrations of those branched-chain amino acids that share the specific brain transporter with tryptophan (J.M. Davis et al. 1992).

In support of this hypothesis are the following findings:

- Blood tryptophan levels increase as a linear function of increasing blood free fatty acid concentrations (J.M. Davis et al. 1992).

- As a result, the ratio of the concentration of blood free tryptophan to branched-chain amino acids also rises (J.M. Davis et al. 1992).

- Carbohydrate ingestion improves endurance performance (chapter 3) and also attenuates the rise in plasma free fatty acid concentrations and hence circulating tryptophan concentrations. These changes should reduce brain serotonin concentrations but, for obvious reasons, this has not been studied, at least in humans.

- Drugs that block the action of serotonin in the brain, the so-called serotonin antagonists, improve exercise performance in rats (Bailey et al. 1993), as do drugs that decrease the activity of the brain serotonin receptors (Abdelmalki et al. 1997). Conversely, drugs that inhibit the breakdown of serotonin in the brain and that increase brain serotonin concentrations reduce the endurance performance of humans (Wilson and Maughan 1992).

The practical question raised by this hypothesis is whether the ingestion of branched-chain amino acids during prolonged exercise enhances performance. Blomstrand et al. (1991) initially reported that the running performance of "slower" (but not "faster") marathon runners improved when they ingested branched-chain amino acids. In addition, mental performance after a 30-km cross-country race was also improved in those runners who ingested branched-chain amino acids.

However, other studies, including our own (Velloza 1996), have failed to confirm this effect (Burke, Desbrow, et al. 2000). One potentially detrimental effect of the ingestion of branched-chain amino acids during exercise is that it also increases plasma ammonium concentrations (MacLean and Graham 1993). Plasma ammonium concentrations also rise during prolonged exercise as muscle glycogen concentrations fall (MacLean et al. 1991). The belief is that elevated plasma ammonium concentrations would be detrimental to endurance performance since they may provide sensory feedback to the governor, thereby inducing a heightened sensation of fatigue.

L-Tryptophan

According to the serotoninogenic central fatigue hypothesis described in the previous section, the ingestion of L-tryptophan should impair endurance performance by increasing brain serotonin concentrations.

Surprisingly, an early study (Segura and Ventura 1988) reported than L-tryptophan ingestion did the exact opposite, increasing total exercise time by 50% in male athletes running at about 80% $\dot{V}O_2$max. The performance of one subject improved by 260% and another by 160%. Such large changes have to be due to something other than L-tryptophan ingestion; otherwise, we can all stop training and simply ingest L-tryptophan before any race. A subsequent study failed to find any beneficial effect of L-tryptophan ingestion on running time to exhaustion at 100% $\dot{V}O_2$max (Stensrud et al. 1992).

Other Amino Acids

There is no evidence to suggest that other amino acids—including arginine, ornithine, lysine, glutamine, and B-hydroxy B-methyl butyrate (HMB, a metabolite of the amino acid leucine)—have special ergogenic properties, irrespective of the quantities in which they are ingested.

Chromium Picolinate

Chromium is an essential trace element for which no studies have shown an ergogenic effect when ingested in higher than trace concentrations (Burke, Desbrow, et al. 2000).

Most IOC-Banned Stimulants

A popular belief is that any drug or intervention that is banned by the IOC must have a proven ergogenic effect. But this is not correct. To appear on the banned list, a drug must have the potential for that effect, usually because it is related in some distant way to another stimulant, like the amphetamines, which were originally thought to be ergogenic (Karpovich 1959; Smith and Beecher 1959). However, more recent studies have produced less certainty about the true ergogenic effects of even the amphetamines (M.H. Williams and Thompson 1963; Swain et al. 1997).

Many of the stimulants banned by the IOC are found in over-the-counter medications that can be bought without a prescription and that are used to treat minor intercurrent illnesses, such as colds and influenza.

There are few studies of the true ergogenic effects of these banned stimulants. Two separate studies failed to show that two banned stimulants, pseudoephedrine (Gillies et al. 1996; Swain et al. 1997) or phenylpropanolamine (Swain et al. 1997) enhanced performance during either a 40-km cycling time-trial or a $\dot{V}O_2$max test.

Recently, because both these agents have been linked to an increased risk of hemorrhagic stroke, the United States Federal Drug Agency requested their removal from all over-the-counter preparations but has fallen short of demanding their banning (Fleming 2000). Similarly, South Africa has followed these recommendations. The first study showed that phenylpropanolamine used in appetite-suppressant medications profoundly increases the risk of stroke in women; the use of phenylpropanolamine in cough or cold remedies also increases risk but to a much lesser extent (Kernan et al. 2000). Hence, the use of phenylpropanolamine is considered an independent risk factor for hemorrhagic stroke in women. Whether males are also at risk when they use phenylpropanolamine could not be established (Fleming 2000) since very few males use appetite suppressants.

The second study (Haller and Benowitz 2000) found a relationship between certain adverse effects, including hypertension (high blood pressure), heart palpitations, and stroke, in those who ingested dietary supplements that contain ephedra alkaloids, also referred to as *ma huang*. Ephedra alkaloids, including ephedrine, are used as energy boosters and for weight loss. Adverse effects include death and disability. To date, no deaths have been recorded, but 13 cases of permanent disability have been documented.

Fleming (2000) makes the crucial point that a loophole in the Dietary Supplement and Education Act of the United States Congress enables inadequately tested drugs to be marketed as dietary supplements without restrictions. In practice, since most of the dietary supplements sold in South Africa originate in the United States, this ruling also applies in South Africa. Yet any product containing the ephedra alkaloids is a drug, and its sale should, at least, be regulated. If it is as dangerous as this study suggests, the product should be banned. Fleming suggests that the Dietary Supplement and Education Act needs to be amended to close this loophole.

Vitamins

Many years ago a medical friend and I ran a marathon on N,N-dimethyl glycine—purely in the interests of science. Reports in the medical literature had claimed that dimethyl glycine (an impostor vitamin, also called vitamin B15) worked better than training (Pipes 1980). A group of 12 male college athletes who had used the substance for just one week had reportedly increased their $\dot{V}O_2$max values by 28% and their times to exhaustion while running on the treadmill by 24%—increases that you or I would be lucky to achieve in a lifetime of training.

In the end, I am glad to report, vitamin B15 was a total, unmitigated failure. This experimental race proved that vitamin B15, like many of the ergogenic agents reviewed in this chapter, was no replacement for training. There is no evidence to suggest that any vitamin taken in excess of the daily requirement can enhance athletic performance.

Antioxidants

Supplementation with an antioxidant cocktail containing ascorbic acid (vitamin C), alpha-tocopherol (vitamin E), and coenzyme Q10 failed to improve maximum exercise performance, $\dot{V}O_2$max, or the performance or metabolism of muscles stimulated to contract to exhaustion with an externally applied stimulator (Nielsen et al. 1999).

L-Carnitine

L-carnitine is a constitute of the (palmityl carnitine transferase) enzyme complex that transfers fatty acids across the inner mitochondrial membrane for their subsequent oxidation in the Krebs cycle.

In chapter 3, I discuss the theory that fatigue during prolonged exercise may result from the tardy rate at which fatty acids can cross the inner mitochondrial membrane. As a result, according to the Energy Depletion Model, once the muscle runs out of glycogen during prolonged exercise, the sustainable exercise intensity must fall to one that is still sustainable by the (lower) peak rate of fatty acid oxidation.

Increasing the amount of L-carnitine in the diet should increase the amount of palmityl carnitine transferase in the inner mitochondrial membrane, thereby increasing the muscle's capacity to oxidize fat when muscle glycogen concentrations are low. This, in turn, enhances endurance.

Unfortunately, a series of studies has established that L-carnitine supplementation failed to increase muscle L-carnitine concentrations (Vukovich et al. 1994; Barnett et al. 1994), to increase the amount of fat oxidized during exercise (Vukovich et al. 1994; Brass and Hiatt 1998), or to alter performance during five bouts of all-out swimming over 91 m (Trappe et al. 1994) or during more prolonged exercise, including marathon running (Colombani et al. 1996).

Hence, the available evidence does not support the use of carnitine supplementation as an ergogenic aid in healthy athletes (Brass and Hiatt 1998), although the exercise capacity of people with vascular disease of their legs or with end-stage kidney failure (Brass and Hiatt 1998) may improve with supplementation.

Other Studied Practices

There is no published scientific evidence to support any claims that taking bee pollen, ingesting spirulina, or phosphate loading can improve athletic performance.

Ginseng is a generic term encompassing a wide variety of compounds derived from the oriental plant family Araliaceae (Dowling et al. 1996). The active ingredients (specific glycosides also referred to as ginseng saponins or ginsenosides) have been used for several thousand years as adaptogenic and restorative agents (Bahrke and Morgan 2000). These products are used to treat a wide variety of medical conditions, from nervous disorders to anemia and impaired libido. The most recent review concludes that there is "an absence of compelling evidence" to suggest that ginseng either improves athletic performance or reduces fatigue "in conditions associated with that complaint" (Bahrke and Morgan 2000).

ERGOLYTIC SUBSTANCES

One of the possible consequences that few people have considered is whether the expensive ergogenic aids might indeed prove to be ergolytic (performance impairing). In the absence of carefully controlled clinical trails, as is required by all pharmaceutical agents, there is no reason to believe that this might not be the case and that some ergogenic aids may indeed be ergolytic, at least in some people. Currently, the two popular drugs with known ergolytic effects are alcohol and cigarettes.

Ethanol

Ethanol ingested 10 minutes before and at 30 minutes during a 60-minute treadmill run at 80% to 85% of $\dot{V}O_2$max caused 75% of subjects to terminate exercise prematurely, largely because they became progressively hypoglycemic (Kendrick et al. 1994). When they ingested either caffeine or a placebo, all the same subjects in the trial completed the exercise bout. Ethanol also increased heart rate and blunted the expected rise in blood free fatty acid concentrations during exercise.

Tobacco

A number of cross-sectional studies show that chronic smokers have a reduced maximum exercise capacity (Leon et al. 1981; Sidney et al. 1993; Sandvik et al. 1995) and are slower by 2% to 10% over 2.4 km (Conway and Cronon 1988; 1992; Song et al. 1998), by 15% over 3.2 km (Jensen 1986), and by 2% to 16% in a 12-minute running trial (Marti, Abelin, et al. 1988), with the least effect in light smokers and the greatest effect in heavy smokers.

FINAL WORD

Correct training improves athletic performance more than any other single intervention. The two next most effective interventions—the use of the illegal doping agents, the anabolic steroids or erythropoietin (EPO)—transgress the ethics of sport by providing an unfair advantage to those who use them.

The major threat confronting our particular code of sport is that all world-class runners, whether in sprinting or in distance running, have to decide if they are going to compete honestly but at a probable disadvantage or if they intend using one or more banned substances in the hope that the protection offered by the farcical doping controls currently in place in international sport (Franke and Berendonk 1997) will mask their deceit. Compared to the effects of training and illicit drug use, the benefits of using other ergogenic aids are relatively modest.

Perhaps the main point of this chapter is to highlight the substantial discrepancy between the magnitude of the benefits that are claimed for the different ergogenic substances and the real extent of those benefits when quantified experimentally. The reality is that very few ergogenic aids are of any value.

Finally, you need to be aware of the dearth of appropriate legislation controlling the production, marketing, and sale of these products—legal loopholes make it easier for doping agents or even harmful drugs to be included in nutritional supplements. We also need to be cautious about the unrestricted and often false advertising claims attributing the alleged ergogenic benefits to any nutritional supplement for which there are no medicinal qualities.

CHAPTER

14

■ ■ ■ ■ ■

Staying Injury Free

R unners are often given dire warnings about the dangers that running poses to their physical well-being, if not to their lives. For example, American cardiologists Friedman and Burch describe jogging as a form of mass suicide and see runners as deserving prey for motor vehicles or coronary arteries (Friedman et al. 1973; Burch 1979). Some orthopedic surgeons dismiss running as an outrageous threat to the integrity of the human knee. Such activity, they predict, will leave runners with "knees so badly deteriorated as to be crippling" (Sonstegard et al. 1978).

Because health is not the sole aim in running, most runners dismiss the dire threats of imminent cardiological demise or chronic orthopedic disability. Not only do these threats miss the point, but they are also simply not true. When studies are performed by disinterested scientists, not antijogging activists, it is found that "daily physical activities or sports cannot be incriminated as an important contributory factor in sudden death in the general population" (Vuori et al. 1978, p. 287; see also chapter 15) and that jogging cannot be considered a factor in the development of osteoarthritis, at least of the hip (Puranen et al. 1975), although more vigorous training by elite athletes may increase slightly the risk of this condition (see the 10th Law of Running Injuries later in this chapter).

The reason these somber medical warnings fail to impress is that they come from those who have learned everything from the outside, without ever bothering to engage in that most fundamental learning process—personal experience.

The only danger that stems from running and that is a cause for concern is the epidemic of running injuries—the modern-day athletic pandemic. What makes running injuries so dangerous is that doctors often do not think about the root cause and, as a result, treatment also fails. Running injuries have a unique feature: an identifiable and treatable cause. And until that cause is rectified, the conventional approach—the rest, the drugs, the injections, and the surgery—is an expensive waste of time.

George Sheehan was the first to conclude this (Sheehan 1972; 1975; 1978a). Suffering perpetually from injuries, Sheehan was the first to admit that his colleagues could not help him. The medical elite were powerless to cure, much less to prevent, his myriad of running injuries. At the same time, Sheehan was writing the world's only medical column in *Runner's World* magazine. In his writings, Sheehan espoused the traditional orthopedic advice: the runner's injury must initially be treated with rest, physiotherapy, and drugs. When these measures failed, the natural route to follow was cortisone injections and, ultimately, surgery. Even then, the outlook was grave. In the early 1970s, most injured runners soon became ex-runners.

But through his special connections with the running world, Sheehan was soon to learn of runners' experiences that suggested that this traditional approach was off target. A high school runner told Sheehan that his knees only hurt when he trained in a particular pair of shoes. Another suffered pain only when he ran continuously in one direction on a banked track. Someone else found that running on the outside of his foot helped alleviate a painful knee. Sheehan himself observed that the slant of the road seemed to be a factor, because he experienced discomfort only when running continually on one side of the road, but was pain free when running on the opposite side.

The ultimate revelation came from the experience of the exmarine who refused to stop running despite severe knee pain, which was resistant to every possible therapeutic intervention that Sheehan or anyone else had prescribed. He was finally saved when he developed foot pain in addition to his knee injury and was referred to a foot specialist (podiatrist). The in-shoe foot support (orthotic) that was prescribed to relieve the foot pain not only cured his foot injury but also his knee pain. From this fortuitous event, Sheehan drew the empirical conclusion that the runner's foot might have something to do with other running injuries distant from it. The date given for the first prescription of orthotics to a runner is 11 December 1970 (Boga 1993, p. 195); the podiatrist was Richard Schuster of Queens, New York.

And then there is the famous story about Dave Merrick (Sheehan 1975). Merrick, a champion high school runner, was sidelined at college with severe knee pain for which he received the textbook treatment: 14 months of rest, corrective exercises, drugs and cortisone injections, and, finally, surgery. When surgery proved unsuccessful, the whole process was started again and continued for a further 18 months, until surgery was again suggested. But that time Merrick demurred. Instead, he sought out Sheehan, to find out whether runners might know something not yet chronicled in the medical textbooks.

As Merrick later told the press, the meeting nearly started badly: "I thought Dr. Sheehan was nuts at first. I thought he was some kind of quack. Here my knees are all swollen and he looks at my feet" (Sheehan 1978a, p. 117). By that time Sheehan had sufficient experience to believe that when Merrick's feet were corrected, the injured knee would take care of itself. And so it did. Within a week of fitting a pair of custom-made in-shoe supports, Merrick was back on the road. Within six weeks he had won his college's 2-mile indoor championship, and within a further three months he was the university cross-country champion. An inexpensive in-shoe support had succeeded where any amount of expensive conventional therapy had failed.

In the years since these first therapeutic miracles, Sheehan and others have taught us that the key to the successful treatment of running injuries is to be on the lookout for that mysterious X-factor, that hidden cause responsible for the runner's injury. We have learned that the very factors that make an athlete great—genetic endowment, training methods, and training environment—are the same factors that are responsible for the athlete's injuries. A myriad of inbuilt biomechanical afflictions exist, each a potential destroyer—the internal twist of the femur or tibia, the squinting patellae, the bow legs or knock knees, the short leg, and the flat or high-arched feet (Krivickas 1997; Neely 1998a; 1998b).

When these genetic factors are exposed to the hostile environment of shoes and surfaces and expected to withstand impossible training loads, injury becomes not only possible but inevitable. Thus, treatment of the injury must take into account every possible contributory factor—the genetics and the unique physiology and biomechanics of the individual athlete; the environment (more specifically, the surface on which the athlete runs); the type of shoe that is worn; and the training. As Sheehan wrote in 1977,

> *Athletes, whether they are motor geniuses or not, simply multiply their training until disability occurs. . . . The distance runner achieves excellence by making the most of his genetic endowment through training in his environment. This formula for greatness is also the cause of his [sic] diseases of excellence. The physician must take a holistic view of his illness and act accordingly. (p. 880)*

Experience with my own running injuries is not dissimilar from that of Sheehan. During a 42-km marathon, a few months after my first Comrades Marathon in 1973, I developed a persistent injury that resisted all the conventional medical advice and put me out of running for a year. Only when I attended the 1976 New York Academy of Science Conference on the Marathon (Milvy 1977) and heard the presentations by George Sheehan (1977), Richard Schuster (1977), and Steven Subotnick (1977) did I begin to appreciate that attention to my running shoes and the use of an orthotic might cure my injury. These measures worked. After 18 months of intense frustration in which I was able to run only once or twice a week, I was again able to run without pain. The injury was desperately uncommon—an inflammation of the (pes anserinus) bursa on the inner side of the knee. However, it was only some years after the injury had been cured that I finally made the correct diagnosis.

TEN LAWS OF RUNNING INJURIES

This experience, together with knowledge gained from treating those injured runners kind enough to risk my advice, has led me to formulate what I call the 10 Laws of Running Injuries.

Law 1: Injuries Are Not an Act of God

Injuries that occur in sport fall into one of two groups: they are caused by either extrinsic or intrinsic forces. Extrinsic injuries result when an external force acts on the body (for example, in contact sports, such as rugby, ice hockey, and boxing). The first sports medicine specialists were probably the doctors who looked after the Roman gladiators. In modern times, the orthopedic surgeons who first cared for athletes in major contact sports were the first exponents of sports medicine. The result of all this is that textbooks of orthopedics and sports medicine have until very recently restricted their focus to extrinsic injuries and have ignored injuries occurring in noncontact sports. Fortunately, this has now changed, and the first medical textbook specific to the medical problems of runners was published in 2001 (O'Connor et al. 2001).

Intrinsic injuries, on the other hand, result from factors inherent in the body itself and have nothing to do with external trauma. They result from the interaction of at least three identifiable factors—the athlete's genetic build; the environment in which training is performed, including the shoes that are worn; and the athlete's training methods. Only the genetic factor remains constant; environmental factors, especially the type of shoes worn, and training methods change constantly.

Hereditary influences that may predispose to running injuries relate to lower limb structure, which largely determines how our hips, knees, and ankles and their supporting structures—muscles, tendons, and ligaments—function during running. Because of differences in genetic structure, virtually no two runners function identically. More important, perfect mechanical function is exceedingly rare and is restricted to the handful of runners who run as far as they like in whatever shoes they might choose without ever being injured. The rest of us run despite varying grades of biomechanical disaster. Take any ten of us and you will probably find every possible biomechanical running abnormality ever described (and a few that defy description).

The fundamental teaching in the biomechanics of running injuries is that the ankle joint functions most effectively when the talar bone is correctly aligned in the ankle joint, in the so-called neutral position. Figure 14.1A shows the typical foot of a runner with a flat foot, in which the talar bone has descended as the subtalar joint has pronated so that the foot can comfortably reach the ground. When the subtalar joint is returned to its neutral position (figure 14.1B), the arch of the foot is reformed, showing that flat feet are caused by a misalignment of the ankle joint.

One theory is that this apparent abnormality occurs because the foot position shown in figure 14.1A is better adapted to gripping a vertical structure, like a tree,

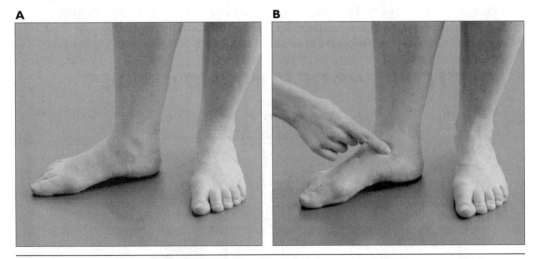

A   **B**

Figure 14.1   An athlete with flat feet (A) and with feet in the corrected position (B).

than to either walking or running on a flat surface. Hence, it is concluded that this abnormality is a throwback to the human's origins from a tree-dwelling ancestor. It is currently believed that this biomechanical abnormality contributes substantially to many different running injuries and that shoes or orthotics that compensate for this abnormality by holding the foot in the more neutral position (figure 14.1B) are important for effective treatment that will produce a long-term cure.

There are several common anatomical afflictions that may potentially predispose athletes to running injuries, including

- reduced ankle range of motion;
- leg-length asymmetry (short leg syndrome);
- anteversion of the femoral neck;
- increased quadriceps (Q) angle;
- genu varum (bow legs);
- genu valgum (knock knees);
- forefoot or rearfoot malalignment (figure 14.2)—or, in its worst form, the malicious or miserable malalignment syndrome, comprising twisting (internal rotation) of the femur, squinting (kissing) patellae, knock knees, externally rotated tibia, and flat feet (excessive foot pronation; see figure 14.3); and
- high-arched (pes cavus) or flat (pes planus) feet (Cowan et al. 1996; Krivickas 1997; Neely 1998a; 1998b).

These biomechanical abnormalities are likely to predispose the athlete to lower limb injuries.

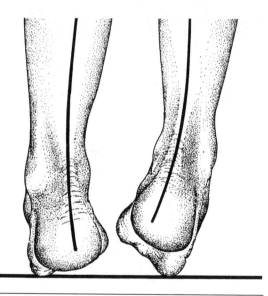

Figure 14.2 Feet assume the neutral position when not bearing weight. The deviation from the vertical at the heel in this picture is known as *rearfoot varus;* the deviation from the horizontal on the forefoot is known as *forefoot varus.* Note that this foot appears particularly well adapted for tree climbing.

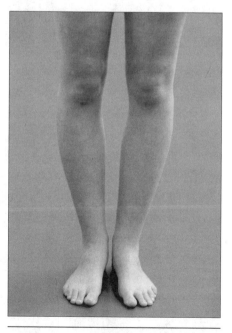

Figure 14.3 An athlete with the malicious malalignment syndrome, comprising internal rotation of the femur, squinting (kissing) patellae, external tibial rotation, and flat feet.

To this daunting list must be added another set of predisposing factors: female gender, age greater than 24 years, a high body mass index or high percentage body fat (documented in military populations), low levels of physical fitness at the commencement of the training program, and a previous history of injury (Neely 1998a; 1998b).

The development in the early 1970s of a hypothesis proposing how these structural abnormalities interfere with the normal functioning of the foot and lower limb during running and how they interact with running surfaces, shoes, and training methods to cause injury led to the single most important practical advance in sports medicine in the 1980s. That the theory now appears to be an oversimplification

Figure 14.4, A-F   Lungelo Ndaba demonstrates the running stride on the treadmill. During the first part of the support (or stance) phase (figure 14.4A, left leg), an inward rotation of the leg, begun during the previous swing phase, continues. By midsupport (B), the direction of rotation reverses to one of outward (external) rotation and this continues at toe-off (D through F).

(Ilahi and Kohl 1998; Razeghi and Batt 2000; Nigg 2001) is less important than is the fact that it produced methods of treatment that have proved relatively effective. Of course, when we better understand the real biomechanical cause of these injuries, our treatments will improve. But in the meantime, and until we know better, we must stick with the explanation that has proved to be practically helpful for the past 25 years. This explanation proposes a common pathway by which these common biomechanical abnormalities cause running injuries by altering the biomechanics of the running stride.

The running stride (figure 14.4) is divided into two major phases, the short support

Figure 14.4, G-L   Immediately after toe-off during the longer swing (or recovery) phase of the cycle, the leg begins to rotate inward (G through L). This rotation continues during the latter part of the swing phase. The big toe moves toward the midline of the body during this rotation.

The labels in this caption refer to the action of the left leg only.

(stance) phase and the longer swing (recovery) phase. One running cycle is from heel strike to the next heel strike of the same foot. During each running stride, the leg rotates in the following sequence: during the longer swing phase of the cycle (figure 14.4, A through F, right leg), the leg rotates inward (internal rotation), and this continues during the first part of the support phase (figure 14.4B, left leg). By midsupport (figure 14.4C, left leg), the direction of rotation reverses to one of outward (external) rotation, which continues at toe-off (figure 14.4, E and F, left leg).

As soon as the foot is planted on the ground (figure 14.4B, left leg), the frictional forces between the sole and the surface prevent the foot from passively following the internal/external rotation sequence occurring in the lower limb. Therefore, a mechanism has to be present to allow the rotation sequence of the upper limb to continue without involving actual movement of the foot in relation to the ground. To achieve this, the subtalar component of the ankle joint acts as a universal joint, transmitting the internal rotation of the lower limb (in the transverse plane) into an inward rolling or pronatory movement at the ankle (in the frontal or horizontal plane; see figure 14.5). As the ankle joint pronates, it unlocks the joints of the midfoot, allowing these also to roll inward. The importance of this movement is that it absorbs and distributes the shock of landing and allows the foot to adapt to an uneven running surface.

In the athlete with normal running mechanics, after 55% to 60% of the stance phase has been completed, the upper limb begins to rotate externally, and the ankle rotation reverses itself and rotates outward (supination) until, just before toe-off, the ankle and midfoot joints lock in a fully supinated position. This results in the lower limb becoming a rigid lever, allowing for a powerful toe-off. Thus, in the ideal running gait there is an early, limited degree of pronation, followed sometime near the middle of the stance phase of the running stride by supination of the subtalar joint.

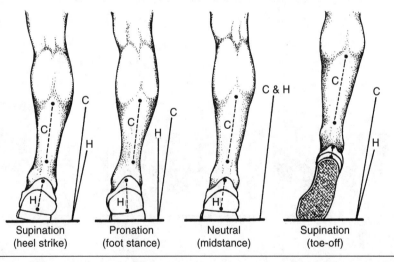

| Supination | Pronation | Neutral | Supination |
| (heel strike) | (foot stance) | (midstance) | (toe-off) |

Figure 14.5 Ankle joint pronation during the foot contact phase. At heel strike, the calf alignment lies nearer to the midline than the line of heel alignment. At foot stance, this relationship is reversed as the ankle joint pronates rapidly so that line H lies medial to line C. At midstance, lines C and H overlap, indicating the neutral foot position has been reached as a result of resupination of the ankle joint, which starts before midstance. At toe-off, the position of full supination is recreated.

C = calf alignment   H = heel alignment

The original theory, proposed in the mid-1970s, holds that very few runners have a sufficiently normal biomechanical structure to allow this normal sequence of events. Despite the lack of any firm scientific grounds for this theory, the design of running shoes and the treatment of injured runners are still to a large extent based on it (Ilahi and Kohl 1998; Nigg 2001). We are taught that most of us are saddled with feet that either do too much rolling—the hypermobile foot—or else roll too little—the so-called rigid, or clunk, foot. And when these feet are attached to minor malalignments in the lower limbs, the theory holds that it is remarkable that any runner can escape injury.

It is theorized that athletes with hypermobile feet pronate excessively during the stance phase of the running cycle so that, instead of reversing ankle pronation in midsupport (figure 14.4D, left leg), pronation continues. As a result, the foot leaves the ground in a pronated and not in the normally supinated position shown in figure 14.5. It is then argued that this excessive ankle pronation during the latter stages of the stance phase of running is the specific biomechanical abnormality that causes certain running injuries, not only in the foot and ankle but also higher in the lower limb. The latter effect results from abnormal internal rotation of the tibia (shin) bone, a consequence of excessive ankle pronation (Hintermann and Nigg 1998).

In contrast, it is argued that the rigid foot fails to pronate sufficiently, and this causes another set of injuries, as the lower limb is unable to pronate enough to absorb the shock of landing.

It is on the basis of this theory that shoes are designed and marketed according to their ability either to resist overpronation (antipronation shoes) or to absorb shock (neutral or cushioned shoes). Perhaps surprisingly, the facts we now have do not convincingly support the theory, even though shoes designed according to that theory seem to be relatively effective in preventing injury.

Therefore, the major weakness of the theory is that despite more than 20 years of intensive and highly sophisticated research, no one has yet been able to show that running shoes either reduce the risk of new injuries or cure established injuries specifically by preventing excessive pronation in those with hypermobile feet or by increasing shock absorption in those with rigid feet (Razeghi and Batt 2000; Nigg 2001).

Benno Nigg, a biomechanist from the University of Calgary in Canada, who has studied and helped in the design of running shoes for more than 20 years, has identified the following paradoxes (Hintermann and Nigg 1998; Nigg 2001):

- Overpronation probably causes a maximum of about 10% of all running injuries (Walther et al. 1989; Nigg 2001).

- Approximately 70% of runners with lower limb injuries improve when they use orthotic devices (James et al. 1978; Bates et al. 1979; McKenzie et al. 1985; Gross et al. 1991), which should act by controlling their excessive pronation.

- Neither specifically designed running shoes (Reinschmidt et al. 1997; Stacoff et al. 2001) nor orthotics (Nigg et al. 1998; Nigg 2001) measurably alter the degree to which the ankle pronates during the stance phase of running. Indeed, those studies found that differences in lower limb biomechanics when running barefoot, with shoes, or with shoes and orthotics were negligible, at least in the parameters that those researchers measured. Thus, Nigg (2001) has concluded that "These experimental results do not provide any evidence for the claim that shoes, inserts or orthotics align the skeleton. . . . One may even challenge the idea that a major function of shoes, shoe inserts or orthotics consists in aligning the skeleton." Of course, the possibility remains that these researchers were not measuring the really important biomechanical changes that are produced by these shoes. But the point is that they were unable to show that running shoes produce those biomechanical changes to the running stride that we have always believed in.

■ Specific anatomical abnormalities are not predictably related to specific running injuries (Wen et al. 1997; Razeghi and Batt 2000; Nigg 2001).

To this list of paradoxes must be added the findings of a study of two groups of New Zealand runners. One group included runners who had never suffered running injuries, and the other, runners who had suffered injuries at or below the knee.

The study found that uninjured runners had greater hamstring flexibility and a running gait that produced lower levels of impact loading but higher rates of ankle pronation. This is paradoxical since, according to the conventional theory, high rates of ankle pronation should increase injury risk. No other anatomical or biomechanical factors differed between the groups. Hence, the authors concluded that reduced impact loading seems to be important in reducing injury risk in runners—a finding that mirrors my personal experience treating my own running injuries but that conflicts with the finding of another study, which found that subjects with higher impact loadings had fewer running injuries (Nigg 2001).

Attempts to alter impact loading by changes in the hardness of the midsole material in the running shoes are largely ineffective (Nigg 2001). Furthermore, running on hard surfaces does not increase the risk of running injuries compared to running on soft surfaces (Van Mechelen 1992). Nigg (2001) acknowledged that as we are unable to conclude that impact forces are an important factor in the development of chronic or acute running-related injuries, or both, the paradigm of cushioning to reduce the frequency or type of running injuries needs to be reconsidered.

To explain these anomalies, Nigg (2001) has proposed a novel model of how the shoes, shoe inserts, and orthotics alter muscle function both before (muscle preactivation) and during the stance phase of the running cycle to produce preferred joint movement patterns in the lower limb.

Nigg (2001) proposes that the impact forces when the foot strikes the ground serve as an input signal to the body. This signal produces a response—muscle tuning—in the body in time for the next foot strike. The function of muscle tuning is to minimize vibrations in the tendons and muscles and to support a preferred movement pattern.

The input signal to the body is filtered first by the shoe sole and second by the shoe insert or orthotic, before being sensed by the plantar surface (sole) of the foot. This sensory information passes to the brain, which then produces the necessary muscle preactivation and related movement patterns to optimize performance and comfort with that specific combination of shoes, orthotics, running surfaces, and degree of muscle fatigue. As a result, the ideal combination of shoe and shoe insert or orthotic reduces muscle activation, improves running comfort and economy, and (presumably) reduces the risk of injury.

In this way, shoes, shoe inserts, or orthotics do not act by altering the preferred joint movement patterns. Rather, they alter lower limb muscle function during the stance phase of running, thereby influencing comfort, the development of fatigue, and hence running performance.

As I survey the proliferation of running shoes and the complexity of their design compared to what was popular and seemingly very effective during the 1980s, I begin to wonder whether Nigg might not be on the right track. Indeed, Nigg's proposal is that the "needs of a large segment of the population can be served with four or five specific groups (of running shoe/orthotic combinations)" (2001, p. 8). Perhaps it is time that we began to design and prescribe shoes not solely on whether they are antipronation or cushioning shoes. The finding that shoes do not alter pronation indicates that a thorough testing of the new ideas proposed by Nigg is long overdue.

Law 2: Each Injury Progresses Through Four Grades

Unlike extrinsic injuries, in which the onset is almost always sudden and dramatic—for example, in the case of a rugby player caught in a ferocious tackle—the onset of intrinsic running-related injury is almost always gradual. Running injuries become gradually and progressively more debilitating, typically passing through four stages or grades.

> **Grade 1:** An injury that causes pain after exercise and is often only felt some hours after exercise has ceased.
>
> **Grade 2:** An injury that causes discomfort, not yet pain, during exercise, but that is insufficiently severe to reduce the athlete's training or racing performance.
>
> **Grade 3:** An injury that causes more severe discomfort, now recognized as pain that limits the athlete's training and interferes with racing performance.
>
> **Grade 4:** An injury so severe that it prevents any attempts at running.

Appreciating the distinction in the severity of running injuries allows a more rational approach to treatment. An athlete with a grade 1 injury requires less active treatment than does the athlete with a grade 4 injury. Similarly, the athlete with a grade 1 injury does not have to be excessively concerned about the injury as long as it does not progress to being a grade 2 injury. Should the injury progress, the athlete needs to pay more attention to it.

Runners need not fear that a grade 1 injury that has existed for some time will suddenly deteriorate into a grade 4 injury. (The only exceptions are stress fractures and the iliotibial band [IT band] friction syndrome, both of which can become severe and incapacitating very rapidly.)

The grade of the injury helps the doctor define each athlete's pain or anxiety threshold. The athlete who seeks attention for an injury only when it reaches grade 4 clearly has a different anxiety threshold from that of the athlete who seeks urgent attention for a grade 1 injury. Obviously, the advice given for each type will also differ greatly: a runner with a grade 1 injury requires substantial psychological support; a runner with a grade 4 injury requires a psychological analysis of why running is so important that the athlete will only stop when forced to do so.

Law 3: Each Injury Indicates a Breakdown

This law can be viewed as a corollary to the first law, which holds that there is a reason running injuries occur. This law simply emphasizes that once an injury has occurred, it is time to analyze why the injury happened. Often the injury is due to the fact that the athlete has reached the breakdown point, usually because a higher level of training has been sustained for longer than one to which the body can adapt. Occasionally, it is the result of a more sudden change in training routine. The athlete may be training harder, farther, or on a different terrain or in different or worn-out running shoes, all of which can precipitate a physical breakdown.

Every athlete has a potential breakdown point—a training intensity and a racing frequency at which breakdown becomes inevitable—whether this point is a weekly total of 30 km or 300 km in training or a racing frequency of 1 or 50 races a year. Indeed, the more races you run, the longer your longest training run; and the faster you run, the greater your risk of injury (Van Mechelen 1992, p. 61). The key to preventing and treating injuries is to understand that just as most of us will never win a big race because of certain genetic limitations, so our genes limit our choice of shoes, influence the surfaces that we can safely train on, and ultimately determine what training methods our bodies can handle. Only when we learn this perspective will we have sufficient wisdom to be injury-resistant. The corollary, of course, is that athletes who are frequently injured do not yet appreciate their bodies' thresholds. When a running injury occurs, the factors that the wise runner needs to consider are training surfaces, training shoes, and training methods.

Training Surfaces

Running surfaces are often too hard or too cambered and accordingly, in terms of the Nigg model (2001), require increased muscle activity to produce the preferred lower limb movement patterns. The ideal running surface is a soft, level surface, such as a gravel road, which is more forgiving and requires less muscle preactivation to ensure optimum shock absorption. Unfortunately, we are usually forced to run on tarred roads or concrete pavements. Furthermore, roads are usually cambered, and this forces the foot on the higher part of the slope to rotate inward (pronate) excessively, while the range of movement of the foot on the lower part of the slope is reduced. In addition, the leg on the lower side of the camber is artificially shortened and therefore acts as a short leg. Running on a concrete surface increased the risk of injury in women but not in men (Macera et al. 1989).

Grass surfaces, although soft, can be uneven, while the sand on beaches is either too soft (above the high-water mark) or too cambered (below the high-water mark). Athletic tracks are of varying hardnesses and introduce the problem of running continuously in one direction around a curve. This causes specific stresses on the outer leg, which must overstride to bring the athlete around each corner.

Similarly, uphill running puts the Achilles tendon and calf muscles on the stretch and tilts the pelvis forward, while downhill running accentuates the impact shock of landing and pulls the pelvis backward, thereby extending the back. Downhill running also causes the muscles to contract eccentrically, thereby increasing muscle damage (Schwane et al. 1983). Overstriding, more common when running downhill, also increases the loading on the anterior calf muscles.

A running injury may first occur shortly after the runner has changed to uphill or downhill running, or to running on the beach or on a Tartan or cinder track, or to running continuously on an unfavorable road camber. The best plan of action is to vary the terrain on which you run, to run in both directions around a track, and to avoid running on the beach, except for an occasional session.

Front of running shoe

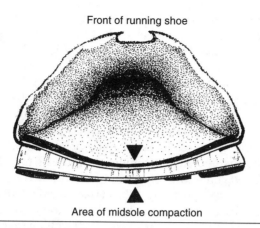

Area of midsole compaction

Figure 14.6 The dissected midsole of a well-used running shoe, showing compaction of the midsole material under the forefoot in the front of the shoe. This compaction will be missed if the shoe is examined only from the outside. Feeling the midsole simultaneously from the inside and outside is the only way to detect this compaction.

Training Shoes

Injury may follow a recent change in shoes, either simply from one pair of shoes to another, or from a training shoe to racing flats or spikes or, more commonly, from one model to another. Other significant potential factors in injury include running in worn-out shoes, either with worn-off heels, with heel cup and midsole having molded to your genetic foot faults (usually collapsing inward), or with midsoles that have flattened out or become hard (figure 14.6).

Surprisingly, one study found that runners who used the more expensive shoes (Marti, Vader, et al. 1988) or who owned two pairs of shoes (Walther et al. 1989) had more injuries. This probably reflects selection bias: only runners who run greater distances in training or who have been injured previously are likely to buy expensive running shoes or to own more than one pair of shoes.

Training Methods

High training volumes and previous injury are two of the most important predictors of injury (Powell et al. 1986; Marti, Vader, et al. 1988; Brill and Macera 1995; Van Mechelen 1992). But injury may also follow a sudden increase in training distance or speed (training too much, too fast, too soon, too frequently; Van Mechelen 1992; Brill and Macera 1995; Almeida et al. 1999) or may occur when undertaking too many races or long runs.

Novice runners, women in particular, are especially prone to injury if they run too frequently and too far and are too ambitious during their first three months of running (Brill and Macera 1995). Risk of injury is also greatest in those who have not been particularly active or physically fit before beginning more intensive training (Jones et al. 1993; 1994). Beginning runners who increase their training according to the rapid improvement in the fitness of their heart, lungs, and leg muscles may exceed the capacity of their bones (which adapt more slowly) to cope with the extra load caused by running and may develop tibial or fibular bone strain (shinsplints) or a stress fracture. It is for this reason that it is advisable to follow the structured training programs for beginners proposed in chapters 5 and 9.

Different training methods can also promote muscle strength and flexibility imbalances. Every kilometer that we run increases the strength and inflexibility of the muscles most active in endurance running—the posterior calf, hamstring, and back muscles—with a corresponding reduction of strength in their opposing muscles—the front calf, front thigh, and stomach muscles. This strength/flexibility imbalance has traditionally been regarded as such an important risk factor in injury that many authorities (Anderson 1975; Uram 1980; Beaulieu 1981), but not all (Osler 1978), believe that it is important to maintain muscle flexibility as you train. For this reason, flexibility (stretching) exercises are usually prescribed to both prevent and cure injuries. However, insufficient stretching has not been found to be a risk factor for injury. In fact, injured runners were those who stretched for longer before running (Jacobs and Berson 1986; Ijzerman and van Galen 1987). Indeed, a careful analysis of all the published literature (Shrier 1999; 2000) and a controlled clinical trial (Pope et al. 2000) all conclude that preexercise stretching, even when combined with adequate cool-down and warm-up sessions (Van Mechelen 1992; 1993; Brill and Macera 1995; Pope et al. 2000) does not influence the incidence of lower limb injuries. However, a full description of the commonly prescribed stretching exer-

Table 14.1   A summary of the factors that may be related to running injuries

Factors significantly related to the risk of developing running injuries	Factors unrelated to the risk of running injuries	Factors with an unclear or contradictory relationship to the risk of running injuries
Previous injury	Age	Body height
Lack of running experience	Gender	Malalignment of the lower limb
Competitive running	Warm-up	Restricted range of joint motions
Excessive weekly running distance	Stretching exercises	Frequency of training
Low body mass	Running hills Running on hard surfaces	Level of performance
	Participation in other sports	Consistency of training patterns
	Time of the year	Shoes
	Time of the day at which training is undertaken	In-shoe orthotics
	Increased walking distance	Running on one side of the road

Based on Van Mechelen (1992) and including conclusion of Colbert et al. (2000).

cises is included in this chapter for those who wish to follow a regular stretching program.

Table 14.1 provides an analysis of all the factors that have been evaluated and their postulated relationship to the risk of developing a running injury (Van Mechelen 1992).

Law 4: Most Injuries Are Curable

Only a small fraction of true running injuries are not entirely curable by simple techniques, and surgery is only required in very exceptional cases. For example, in a study of 200 consecutive running injuries seen at our sports injury clinic, we (Pinshaw et al. 1983) found that within eight weeks of following the simple advice described in this book, nearly three-quarters of the injured runners were pain free and running almost the same training distance as before injury. In addition, most of the runners who were not helped had not adhered to our treatment protocol.

Armed with this knowledge, the first priority of any caregiver is to reassure injured runners that they can almost certainly be completely cured. The only possible exceptions to this rule are the following types of injuries:

- Those that occur in runners with very severe biomechanical abnormalities for which conventional measures are unable to compensate adequately. Such runners are always likely to become injured whenever they train sufficiently hard. However, in my experience, only a small number of runners have such severe mechanical abnormalities that they are unable to run without injury.

- Those that result in severe degeneration of the internal structure of important tissues, in particular the Achilles tendon. There is now a growing appreciation that most injuries to the Achilles tendon are due to degeneration of the tendon (tendinosis), not inflammation (tendinitis) (Khan et al. 1999). Degenerative conditions tend to heal poorly, requiring more prolonged periods of rest than do inflammatory conditions. In addition, the prospects of a complete cure without recurrence are rather small.

- Those that occur in persons who start running on abnormal joints (in particular, hips, knees, and ankles). The typical patient with this problem is the former rugby or football player who has damaged one of these major joints and undergone major surgery. The joint is never again quite the same after major surgery, and by the time such players start to run, usually in their late 30s, their joints have often degenerated to the point at which they cause pain during running.

An important corollary to this fourth law is that if you are not completely cured of your running injury by the experts with whom you consult, it is time to look elsewhere. But treat even the advice of runners with some caution, and do not accept it unconditionally without seeking a professional assessment from someone knowledgeable about running and sympathetic to runners.

Law 5: Sophisticated Methods Are Seldom Needed

Most running injuries affect the soft tissue structures (tendons, ligaments, and muscles), particularly those near the major joints. These structures do not show up on X rays. You should therefore be wary of the practitioner whose first reaction to your injury is to order an X ray. Unless that X ray can be justified, you are probably better off putting the money that would have been spent on the radiological examination into a good pair of running shoes.

The diagnosis of most running injuries is made with the hands, so the advice of any caregiver who does not carefully feel the injured site before making a diagnosis must be treated with caution. As with any injury, a correct diagnosis requires a careful, unhurried approach in which the injured athlete is given sufficient time to explain the situation and describe the training methods used. The doctor must have the time and the patience to listen carefully and sympathetically. Seldom is it necessary to use expensive tests to establish the diagnosis, and the treatment prescribed is usually very simple. Indeed, I believe that 60% of the doctor's success is due to an ability to understand what the injury means to the patient, the fears that the injury engenders, and how best to allay those fears. For this, the doctor needs to understand the patient's psyche and understand why the patient came at that particular time to have the injury examined (see also chapter 8).

However, if the injury persists, it may be necessary to undergo a more sophisticated evaluation with a magnetic resonance imaging (MRI) scan. These scans specifically show the soft tissues in previously unimaginable detail and will detect those rare and unexpected injuries that defy the more simple and conventional diagnostic methods described here.

Law 6: Treat the Cause, Not the Effect

Because all running injuries have a cause, it follows that the injury can never be cured until the causative factors are eliminated. Therefore, surgery, physiotherapy, cortisone injections, drug therapy, chiropractic manipulations, and homeopathic remedies are likely to fail if they do not correct all the genetic, environmental, and training factors causing the runner's injury. Remember the following axiom: the runner is an innocent victim of a biomechanical abnormality arising in the lower limb. First treat the biomechanical abnormality and then, and only then, attend to the injury. Even though we may not yet fully understand the exact biomechanical abnormalities that cause specific running injuries (Razeghi and Batt 2000; Nigg 2001), the overriding belief that biomechanics determines injuries remains intact.

Unfortunately, there are some runners whose injuries exist more in their heads than in their legs. Runners in this group are characterized by their failure to respond to those forms of treatment that would normally be expected to succeed. An approach to the management of these injuries is described in chapter 8.

Law 7: Complete Rest Is Seldom the Best Treatment

If an injury is caused solely by running, then the logical answer for those who know no better is to advise avoidance of running (rest) as the obvious cure. Rest does indeed cure the acute symptoms, but like any therapy that does not aim to correct the cause of the injury, it must ultimately fail in the long term, because as soon as the athlete stops resting and again starts running the lower limbs are exposed to the same stresses as before, and the injury must inevitably recur. Furthermore, there is no doubt that rest is "the most unacceptable form of treatment for the serious runner" (James et al. 1978).

Complete rest is unacceptable to most serious runners, because running involves a type of physical and emotional dependence. An athlete who is forced to stop running for any length of time will usually develop overt withdrawal symptoms (Mondin et al. 1996), and either the runner or, not uncommonly, the runner's spouse will immediately commence the search for anything that will allow the distraught runner to return to the former running tranquility.

The only injuries that require complete rest are those that make running impossible. For example, the athlete with a stress fracture simply cannot run, no matter how strong the desire to do so. Thus, my approach is to advise runners to continue running, but only to the point at which they experience discomfort. In other words, they are only allowed to run to the point at which their injury becomes painful. In addition, supplementary or alternative activities can be prescribed. Fortunately, most current runners are not the complete specialists typical of former years, and many also swim, cycle, or exercise in the gym. These alternative activities, including running in water using a flotation device, can provide the daily physical stimulus to which most athletes are accustomed without adversely affecting the healing of the injury. Indeed, there is a possibility that mild exercise, including water activities, may stimulate healing.

If these treatments are effective, then the runner's discomfort should become progressively less during running, making it possible to run progressively further. On the other hand, if the pain does not improve on treatment, then either the treatment is ineffective (occasionally because the runner has a psychological basis for the injury) and an alternative method of treatment must be tried, or else the diagnosis is wrong.

Furthermore, if the injury does not respond to what should be adequate treatment within three to five weeks, then the alarm bells should ring very loudly. The failure of an injury to respond indicates that you may be dealing with an obscure injury, such as effort thrombosis of the deep veins in the calf, or an injury unrelated to running (for example, a bone cancer) for which another form of treatment may be urgently required.

Law 8: Never Accept As Final the Advice of a Nonrunner (MD or Other)

Over the years I have come to the conclusion that all people consider themselves experts on sport. People who are otherwise extremely wary about expressing opinions on subjects about which they may actually know something feel no such restraint when the topic of sport arises. This applies equally to sport injuries and their management.

How, then, do you know whose advice you can trust? I suggest four simple criteria:

1. Your adviser must be a runner. Without the first-hand experience of running, this person will not have sufficient insight to help you. Of course, this does not mean that all the advice you get from runners will be sound—only that there is a greater probability that it will be correct.

2. Your adviser must be able to discuss in detail the genetic, environmental, and training factors likely to have caused your injury. If the practitioner is unable to do this, together you will go nowhere.

3. If unable to cure your injury, your adviser should feel as distressed about this failure as you do. The person from whom you seek help must understand the importance of your running to you. It is patently ridiculous to accept advice from someone who is antagonistic to your running in the first place.

4. Your adviser shouldn't be expensive, as most running injuries can be cured without recourse to expensive treatments.

Other advice given by Tom Osler (1978) is that you should tell the practitioner that you will only consider the possibility of treatment after all the choices are clear and you have had time to reflect on them. After hearing the treatment that has been suggested, go home and discuss it with other runners. At all times, be conservative in the advice you accept. Finally, Osler reminds the runner to remember that "God heals and the doctor sends the bills." Osler's comments are particularly apt as they were written at a time when so little was known about these injuries and how they should be treated.

Law 9: Avoid Surgery

The only true running injuries for which surgery is the first line of treatment are muscle compartment syndromes and interdigital neuromas. Surgery may also have a role in the treatment of chronic Achilles tendinosis of six or more months' duration (Smart et al. 1980; Leppilahti et al. 1994; Testa et al. 1999), low back pain from a prolapsed disc (Guten 1981), and the iliotibial band friction syndrome (Noble 1979; 1980; Firer 1992), but only when all other forms of nonoperative treatment have been allowed a thorough trial.

The obvious danger of surgery is that it is irreversible: what is removed at surgery cannot be returned. It is a tragedy, as I have seen on more than one occasion, for a runner to have undergone major knee, ankle, or back surgery for the wrong diagnosis. Not only will that surgery fail to cure the injury, but it may seriously affect the unfortunate athlete's future running career.

Surgery should only be considered for a small group of injuries, and only when such injuries are grade 3 or 4. These concerns do not apply as rigidly to athroscopic surgery, in which a small flexible fiberoptic cable is placed inside the joint through a small skin incision. This procedure allows visualization of the joint surfaces and all the relevant structures within the knee, enabling a more accurate diagnosis to be made or, alternatively, showing that the joint is normal. Corrective surgery can also be performed with miniature instruments, also introduced through small skin incisions. Since the entire knee is not opened in this procedure, recovery is usually rapid.

Law 10: Recreational Running Does Not Appear to Cause Osteoarthritis

Osteoarthritis is a degenerative disease in which the articular cartilage that lines the bony surfaces inside a joint becomes progressively thinner until the bone beneath the cartilage on both sides of the joint ultimately becomes exposed. In the advanced stages of osteoarthritis, the exposed bones rub against one another, causing pain and severely limited joint movement. The view of some orthopedic surgeons is that this degenerative process can be initiated and exacerbated by long-distance running (Sonstegard et al. 1978).

However, the more modern evidence shows that if running does indeed increase the risk of osteoarthritis, this occurs only in those elite athletes who run many miles in their careers. Recreational joggers are not at any increased risk of developing osteoarthritis (Panush and Inzinna 1994; Buckwater and Lane 1997).

Nevertheless, it is important that the literature on this topic should be presented, most especially those studies that show a (moderately) increased risk for osteoarthritis in elite athletes, including runners.

Puranen and his colleagues (1975) obtained the hip X rays of 74 former champion Finnish athletes, who had run for a mean duration of 21 years. Advanced degenerative osteoarthritic changes were found in three runners (4%) but were present in more than twice as many (9%) of the control subjects treated at that hospital for conditions other than hip diseases. In two runners with advanced radiological changes, their symptoms were insufficiently severe to restrict their running, even at the ages of 75 and 81. It was reported that despite what his radiograph showed, the 75-year-old runner would not even consider interrupting his lifelong obsession with marathon running.

Similarly, in other studies of highly active sportspeople, including professional soccer players (Adams 1976), physical education teachers (Bird et al. 1980; Eastmond et al. 1980) and even sport parachutists (Murray-Leslie et al. 1977), the incidence of osteoarthritis was no higher than that found in the nonathletic population. Neither Wally Hayward, when studied in 1981 (Maud et al. 1981), nor Jackie Mekler had any evidence of osteoarthritis, despite the prodigious distances they ran. In no large series of people with osteoarthritis is there a preponderance of athletes (Jorring 1980), as would be expected if sport were a significant cause of osteoarthritis.

Sohn and Micheli (1984) found that the incidence of osteoarthritis in a group of runners who competed between 1930 and 1960 at seven universities in the eastern United States was lower than that of a matched group of swimmers who competed at the same universities at the same time, whose joints had not been exposed to the same loading stresses as had those of the runners. A Danish study (Konradsen et al. 1990) found that the incidence of osteoarthritis in 30 Danish orienteers during the 1950s, most of whom continued running 20 to 40 km per week for 30 years, was no different from that in controls. Similarly, runners with a mean age of 60 who had run an average of 3 hours per week for 12 years did not have a greater prevalence of osteoarthritis but did have a 40% greater density in their vertebral bones (Panush et al. 1986).

Lane et al. (1986) reported that the incidence of osteoarthritis was not higher in a group of 41 runners aged 70 to 72 than it was in a matched control group. A similar finding was reported by Panush et al. (1986). The study of Lane and her colleagues (1986) also found that the bone mineral content of the runners, both male and female, was approximately 40% greater than that of the controls. A subsequent prospective, five-year follow-up study of 35 runners aged 63 at the start of the trial found that at age 68, although X ray evidence of osteoarthritis had increased in both runners and controls, there was no difference in the radiographic scores for osteoarthritis in runners who were still running, in those who had stopped running, or in control subjects who had never run (Lane et al. 1993). Runners in that group ran an average of 163 minutes a week.

In a related study, Lane et al. (1987) showed that runners develop fewer musculoskeletal disabilities as they age, and develop them at a slower rate, than do nonrunners. Thus, far from making them more infirm and disabled, their running preserves the functional integrity of their joints and muscles. Similarly, female former college athletes were not found to be at increased risk of developing osteoporotic fractures in later life than were nonathletes (Wyshak et al. 1987).

Other evidence to support this belief is that experimental osteoarthritis in rabbits is not made worse by running (Videman 1982); that the absence rather than the presence of normal weight bearing across a joint leads to degenerative changes similar to those found in early osteoarthritis (Palmoski et al. 1980); and that even in patients with the more serious form of arthritis (rheumatoid arthritis), regular exercise seems to delay rather than to expedite the progression of the disease (Nordemar et al. 1981).

Many sportspeople who develop osteoarthritis have had previous joint surgery. In the study of Murray-Leslie et al. (1977), 75% of sport parachutists who developed osteoarthritis had undergone previous surgery for removal of a torn cartilage (meniscectomy). It was those athletes who exercised on abnormal joints who ultimately developed osteoarthritis. Another study (Kohatsu and Schurman 1990) found that obesity, significant knee injury, and heavy daily physical labor, but not leisure-time physical activity, increased the risk of osteoarthritis.

The type of sport injuries requiring surgery are typical of those that result from an external blow to the joint, as occurs in contact sports, such as football or rugby, or from rapid changes in direction that occur in both contact and noncontact sports that are contested at speed. Thus, those who blame running as a significant cause of osteoarthritis are blaming the wrong sport. They should rather focus on contact sports or other sports in which there are frequent, rapid changes in direction. Nevertheless, we cannot ignore a growing body of evidence showing that running at a very high level of competition, sustained for many years, is associated with a measurable, but small, increased risk of osteoarthritis.

A famous study of a large group of residents of Framingham, Massachusetts—the Framingham study was the first to show that there are certain personal risk factors for heart disease, including cigarette smoking, high blood pressure, and high blood cholesterol concentrations (see chapter 15)—reported that the most physically active residents were at increased risk of osteoarthritis, as were those residents who were the most obese (Felson et al. 1988; McAlindon et al. 1999).

But residents who participated in light to moderate physical activity were not at any increased risk of osteoarthritis. Essentially, the same conclusions were drawn from a study of elderly women (Lane et al. 1999). As might be expected, weight loss of 5 kg reduced the risk of osteoarthritis in women in the Framingham study (Felson et al. 1992).

A 15-year study of 27 long-distance runners revealed that those who were running the fastest in 1973, when the study began, had the most marked radiological changes of degenerative hip disease at follow-up. The authors concluded that past long-term, high-intensity, and high-mileage running cannot be dismissed as a potential risk factor for premature osteoarthritis of the hip (Marti et al. 1989).

A Swedish study of 233 men who underwent hip replacement surgery for advanced osteoarthritis found that men who were exposed to high levels of sporting activities for more than 29 years had a 3.5- to 4.5-fold increased risk of developing osteoarthritis (Vingård et al. 1993). For men who were also involved in high levels of physical work in their occupations, the risk was increased 8.5-fold. The most hazardous sports were racket sports and track and field, in which risk was increased 3.3- to 3.7-fold respectively for those with high exposure for the longest time. Risk was increased 2.1-fold for long-distance runners in the same category. Sports in which there was less impact loading on the joints, including golf, swimming, hiking, bowling, and ice hockey, were not associated with any increased risk.

Two Finnish studies (Kujala et al. 1994a; 1995) have evaluated the prevalence of osteoarthritis in former elite male Finnish athletes. The first study (Kujala et al. 1994a) evaluated 2049 male athletes who had represented Finland in international competition between 1920 and 1965. The study found that athletes from all types of competitive sports were at slightly increased risk of seeking medical care for osteoarthritis—1.9-fold increased risk for endurance athletes and 2.2-fold increased risk for power athletes. Interestingly, endurance athletes first sought medical care for osteoarthritis at a much older average mean age (71 years) than did athletes in other sports (58 to 62 years).

The second Finnish study (Kujala et al. 1995) compared the prevalence of osteoarthritis of the knees in former top-level Finnish athletes participating in long-distance running, soccer, weightlifting, or shooting. The study found that previous knee injuries (4.7-fold increased risk), a high body mass index (1.8-fold increased risk), and playing soccer (5.2-fold increased risk)—because of the likelihood that soccer would cause a previous knee injury—were the principal risk factors for knee osteoarthritis. In contrast to its effects on the hip (Kujala et al. 1994a; Räty et al. 1997), long-distance running did not increase the risk for premature osteoarthritis of the knee.

A study of former elite British female long-distance runners and tennis players also found a 2- to 3-fold increased risk for the development of X ray changes suggestive of osteoarthritis (Spector et al. 1996). But athletes did not report pain any more frequently than did nonathletes, who generally had fewer radiological signs of osteoarthritis. Interestingly, it appears that women are more likely than men to develop osteoarthritis when exposed to high levels of habitual physical loading of their joints (Imeokparia et al. 1994).

In summary, people who participate in regular, vigorous, competitive athletics for most of their lives are at increased risk of developing osteoarthritis. The risk is increased if they also develop a joint injury during their sporting careers or if they also load their joints during their work. Sports that involve both impact and torsional loading, such as soccer, racket sports, and track and field, are associated with greater risk than long-distance running. Competitive long-distance running at an elite level appears to increase the risk only of hip osteoarthritis. But for those more sedentary patients who develop osteoarthritis, a supervised walking program reduces symptoms and improves functional capacity (Kovar et al. 1992; Ettinger et al. 1997).

INJURY SELF-TREATMENTS

Boston podiatrist Rob McGregor tells his injured running patients that they must not contact him until they have tried everything they can think of to cure their own injuries. Only when they have run out of ideas are they allowed to consult him.

Given the understanding that running injuries have identifiable causes, not all of which we comprehend fully, it follows that the runner, the person closest to these causes, should be in the best position to analyze and correct them. Furthermore, with the possible exception of stress fractures, the development of virtually all running injuries is a gradual process. Thus, with very few exceptions, the runner will have a fairly long warning period. It is during this time that the clever runner should begin to analyze, according to the following guidelines, why the particular injury developed in the first place.

Step 1: Decide Whether Your Injury Is Due to Running

Although virtually all running injuries are intrinsic injuries, we occasionally see a runner whose injury, although causing discomfort only during running, was actually caused by a non-running-related incident that was so mild that it was disregarded. Thus, a trivial knee or ankle injury suffered in a long-forgotten contact-type team sport may cause symptoms only when the person takes up running many years later. It is important for a runner to identify any of these preexisting injuries; otherwise they will not respond to the treatment approach prescribed in these pages and may ultimately require surgical correction.

The first priority is to ensure that the injury is truly running-related and that it is not due to external trauma. If there is doubt, then the pointers to remember are the following:

- Intrinsic injuries come on gradually and never involve the joints. One of the most common injuries—runner's knee—causes pain around the joint but is not a joint injury.

- With the possible exception of chronic muscle injuries, some types of stress fracture, and occasionally the iliotibial band friction syndrome, all running injuries will be cured (albeit temporarily) after four to twelve weeks of complete rest. They then recur only when the athlete again reaches that weekly training distance equivalent to the breakdown point. In contrast, extrinsic injuries do not improve no matter how long they are rested, and they cause discomfort immediately when running recommences.

If you are certain that your injury is a true running injury, proceed to step 2. You can, of course, consult a doctor at this stage, but the cure may be as simple as changing to a better pair of running shoes, in which case the visit to the doctor will have wasted both the runner's and the doctor's time.

Step 2: Diagnose and Determine the Cause

Assuming that you are satisfied that yours is an intrinsic injury, the next step is to make a specific diagnosis of the injury and to establish whether the injury has occurred simultaneously with a change in one or more factors in your training milieu (see table 14.1).

Shoes

The first question to ask yourself is, *Have I recently changed to a different type of running shoe?* Any athlete who continues to train in the normal way, but who becomes injured within two to four weeks after changing to a different running shoe, must consider that the new shoe is the cause of the injury. In this case, the treatment is obvious. Either go back to the old pair of running shoes or, if these are in bad repair, start running in a new pair of the same model as your last successful pair. An unfortunate feature of modern running shoes is that the exact design and construction of a particular model seldom stays the same for more than a few years. Thus, the unwary runner may fail to appreciate that the features of a popular running shoe, in particular the materials used in its construction, may alter with time, making that particular model less compatible with the runner's specific needs.

The second question to ask is, *If the shoes are not new, are they worn out?* The major areas of failure in the running shoe are the heel-counter, the midsole, and the outersole. The heel-counter may have lost its rigidity and may have been dragged inward. This is the typical pattern in athletes whose feet rotate inward (pronate) excessively. The athlete who runs in shoes similar to these is said to be running *next to* the shoes.

The midsole material in the heel is particularly prone to compaction, especially in running shoes in which the midsole material is very soft. Look at your shoes from behind. Is the height of the midsole at the heel significantly higher (1 cm or more) on the outsides than it is in the middle of the shoe? If so, this means that the midsole underneath the inside heel has compacted down. The degree of imbalance (1 cm) in the heel would be more than sufficient to produce a running injury. These considerations indicate the importance of checking your shoes regularly from behind.

The midsole material in the forefoot can also compact, particularly in runners who mainly land on the balls of their feet, so-called forefoot strikers. Figure 14.6 shows this marked midsole compaction. The midsole material under the small and big toes measures 0.8 cm and that under the second and third toes, 0.6 cm, showing 25% compaction. Note that this compaction may not be apparent when the shoe is examined from behind, as the midsole material at the heel may not have compacted.

The only way to detect this midsole compaction under the forefoot is to put one hand inside the shoe and the other outside, as demonstrated in figure 14.7. The index and middle fingers of the inside hand are placed into the indentation where the second and third toes fit, and the same fingers of the other hand are placed on the outersole overlying this area. The thickness of the midsole is then assessed by squeezing it between the fingers and comparing the midsole thickness at that site with what is felt under the rest of the forefoot. Frequently, the midsole under the

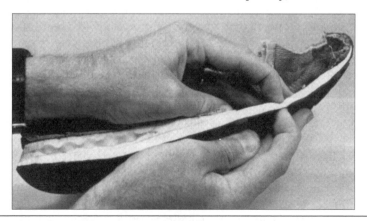

Figure 14.7 Testing for midsole compaction under the forefoot in a shoe that has been bisected in its long axis. By applying pressure between the ends of the fingers inside and outside the shoe, the full extent of midsole compaction can be identified since the compacted areas will be thinned and less resilient than the areas of midsole in which less compaction has occurred.

forefoot is completely compacted so that the fingers of the inner and outer hands are separated only by the thickness of the outersole. Most runners whose shoes reach this state will usually know about it; when they land on a stone underneath the big toe, they will feel immediate pain.

Last, the midsole may have hardened, or "bottomed out." Figure 5.2 shows the thumb compression test used to compare the relative hardnesses of the midsoles of different running shoes and the degree to which a particular shoe has bottomed out. With experience, you learn how much indentation is appropriate for your own shoe. The test is also essential to check loss of shock-absorbing capacity with time. For example, figure 14.7 shows the indentation test being performed on a five-year-old running shoe. This shoe allows no indentation; the midsole has essentially fossilized, and the owner of these shoes might just as well have run barefoot on the tarmac. The tarmac would probably have been softer.

Shoes differ in the rapidity with which the midsole compacts and hardens. Some studies in the 1980s on EVA midsoles (Cavanagh 1980; Cook et al. 1985a; 1985b) noted the loss of shock absorption over time. Cook et al (1985a ;1985b) noted that the greater the original cushioning of the shoe, the more rapid the deterioration in cushioning. Thus, a shoe that was initially selected for its ability to absorb shock might prove to be inappropriate in the long term. They also noted that wetness reduced the cushioning properties of the shoes. However, once the shoes had re-dried, they returned to the level of cushioning consistent with the mileage they had "run." Thus, the injured athlete must remember to check that the midsole of the running shoe has not compacted completely.

It seems unlikely that midsoles made from encapsulated air would ever alter their shock-absorbing capacity, except when they puncture, but this has not yet been studied. Perhaps the point is that these historical studies describe what happens to the midsoles of shoes that are constructed from materials other than air.

The last important area of shoe wear is the outersole. Figure 14.8 shows the different wear patterns found in three different running styles. In the normal wear pattern (figure 14.8A), the outersole wears at the outer edge of the heel, under the ball of the foot between the first and second toes, and then at the front of the sole, underneath the second and third toes. In contrast, the extreme pronator (figure 14.8B) strikes on the inside of the heel and wears all along the inside border of the sole of the shoe and, in particular, underneath the big toe. The third type of sole wear is found in the runner whose foot supinates excessively (rotates outward) during running (figure 14.8C). The supinator's sole wear pattern is the exact opposite of that found in the pronator, as the main wear is concentrated on the outer border of the sole, from heel to toe.

I am not sure to what extent excessive outersole wear, particularly at the heel, influences injury risk. There is some merit in the argument that wear, particularly at the heel, is an adaptation to the individual athlete's particular mechanical makeup. Thus, the athlete who wears rapidly at the heel has a reason for doing so. Indeed, one shoe company produced shoes with heels that were rounded in the direction of the heel wear. Heels of this type reduce the extent and rate of pronation (Nigg 1985) and may therefore be of value in the treatment of pronation-related injuries, such as runner's knee. These heels do, however, increase peak landing forces at heel strike.

This argument suggests that applying excessive repair patching on the heel is probably wrong and may be a factor in injury. However, the wisest course of action is probably to experiment to find out what is most helpful for you.

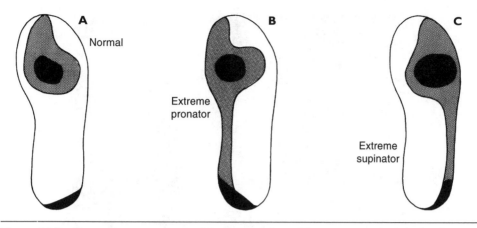

Figure 14.8 Outersole wear patterns of the shoes of three different runners. In the normal wear pattern (A), the heel wears on its lateral side and in the forefoot underneath the first and second toes. The extreme pronator (B) strikes on the medial side of the heel with the wear along the inner shoe border. The extreme supinator wears exclusively along the outer border of the outersole (C).

Biomechanical Structure

As described earlier in this chapter, the conventional belief is that the lower limb mechanics of injured runners may exhibit one of two characteristic patterns: either the ankle joint rotates inwardly (pronates) too much, or it does not pronate enough. The foot with an ankle joint that rotates too little is frequently called a high-arched clunk foot, whereas the foot with an ankle joint that pronates too much is referred to as a hypermobile, flexible, low-arched (or flat) foot (Schuster 1977). However, there is some evidence that this distinction may be less absolute than previously believed (Razeghi and Batt 2000). That is, some people with high-arched clunk feet may pronate more than others with flat feet (Kvist et al. 1989). Furthermore, there is little evidence that the height of the arch, a measure of the rigidity or clunkiness of the foot, actually predicts the forces transferred to the lower limb when running (Nachbauer and Nigg 1992). Yet the distinction may have some value, as injury patterns may follow foot types (Kaufmann et al. 1999), and those with either high-arched or flat feet may have the highest incidence of injuries and discomfort when running (Kvist et al. 1989; Cowan et al. 1993; Kaufmann et al. 1999).

According to the explanation of Benno Nigg described earlier, excessive or abnormal pronation may cause injury because of the need for increased muscle activity to control what is, in fact, the preferred joint movement pattern for the person with that specific lower limb configuration. Hence, according to Nigg's theory, treatment must aim to alter the muscle function of the lower limb when running since the degree of subtalar joint pronation cannot be reduced by use of shoes or orthotics, or both.

A popular method for differentiating between a flexible or rigid foot is the so-called bathroom test. In this test, you place your still-wet foot on the bath mat first when you are sitting, and then when you are standing. Alternatively, the same test can be performed by standing on wet sand. The imprint of most runners will look like imprint B in figure 14.9 when they are sitting. If the standing foot imprint is like imprint C, the runner has a rigid foot, whereas imprint A is that of a flat foot. The importance of identifying the foot type is that the two abnormal foot types are

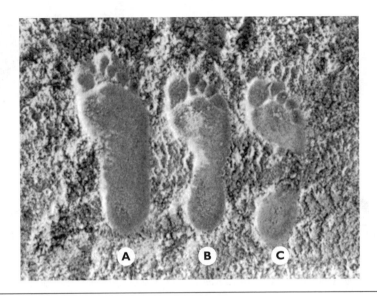

Figure 14.9 Footprints in the sand. Imprint A is that of the flat foot, imprint B corresponds to a normal foot, and imprint C is that of a high-arched, rigid foot.

probably associated with a higher risk of injury and more discomfort when running. Thus, some sort of intervention will be more likely to ensure that runners with either of these foot types are better able to run with less discomfort and a lower risk of injury.

Clunk Foot

According to the conventional theory, the clunk foot is generally a rigid, stable, immobile, high-arched structure that is unable to perform the most basic function of the running foot—adequate shock absorption through controlled, appropriate pronation (Schuster 1977). Because of its stability, the clunk foot provides a powerful lever at push-off and thus is the ideal foot for the sprinter. But in long-distance running, in which adequate shock absorption is essential, particularly during days of heavy training or in a long race when fatigued muscles lose their ability to absorb shock, the clunker may become a source of disaster—so much so that possibly 30% to 40% of injured runners have this type of foot. As the high-arched foot is unable to absorb sufficient shock, it places additional stresses on other shock-absorbing structures, particularly around the knee, which may break down.

Whether or not these ideas are still absolutely correct will probably become apparent in the next decade. But until we have better information, treatment advice based on these ideas does seem to be valid. Perhaps the only issue that requires a more detailed analysis is whether the clunk foot can also pronate excessively and, if so, what treatment is required. I am sensitive to this possibility because my clunk feet pronate excessively and the shoes that I find most comfortable to run in must be the softest available, currently the new (2000) Nike Pegasus, into which I place a very soft orthotic. Hence, in my case, increased shock absorption, achieved in part by the use of a soft orthotic that some might consider contraindicated for the clunk foot, is an essential requirement for more comfortable running.

Hypermobile Foot

Also according to the conventional theory, the hypermobile foot is usually an excellent shock-absorber because of its ability to pronate but is very unstable during the push-off phase of running (Schuster 1977). Instead of having a firm lever from which to push off, the runner with the hypermobile foot is all but attached to the ground by a bag of delinquent bones, each going its own way and causing the lower limb to rotate too far inward during the stance phase of running. It is this excessive inward rotation that appears to put runners with this type of foot at an increased risk of injury. But exactly how this abnormal movement pattern contributes to injury or causes specific injuries is still unclear (Razeghi and Batt 2000; Nigg 2001).

Normal Foot

A normal foot is neither high-arched nor flat and neither supinates nor pronates excessively during running. People with this type of foot appear to be at a reduced risk of developing a running injury.

Biomechanical Structure and Shoe Design

Until the mid-1970s, running shoes were developed without attention to the possibility that they could cause or cure running injuries. But when it was discovered, quite by chance, that in-shoe orthotics were an effective treatment for many lower limb injuries in runners, the pronation theory of running injuries (my terminology) was established (Subotnick 1977). As a result, shoe manufacturers began to develop antipronation shoes that would cure all existing running injuries and prevent any new injuries. That this laudable ideal has yet to be realized suggests that the theory is not entirely correct (Nigg 2001).

In general, then, running shoes are designed and marketed on the basis that they provide either adequate shock absorption or motion control. These are two quite different characteristics that can only be built into the same shoe with great difficulty. In general, the more a shoe is built for motion control, the more rigid it must be and consequently the less shock it can absorb. Conversely, the better the shock-absorbing capacity of the shoe, theoretically the less well it will control the motion of the ankle. Yet, the paradox is that running shoes may not really achieve either of these goals (Nigg 2001). Although some original studies suggested that altering the hardness of the shoe reduced the degree of ankle pronation it allows (Clarke et al. 1983b; Stacoff et al. 1988), more recent studies have not been able to confirm these findings.

This discrepancy can be explained by the different techniques used to study ankle movements during running. The early studies used markers placed on the outside of the running shoe to estimate what was happening to the ankle bones, which were hidden by the heel-counters of the running shoes from the direct view of the posteriorly located recording cameras. More recent studies using removable markers surgically embedded into the ankle bones have shown that whereas markers applied to the heel-counters of the running shoes do indeed suggest that the ankle pronates less when antipronation running shoes are used, the actual movement of the ankle bones inside the running shoe is not influenced by the type of shoe that is worn. In other words, the ankle joint continues to pronate as before within the heel-counter of the running shoe, but the firmer heel-counters of modern shoes do not distort as much. Thus, it is as if the ankle joint is pronating less when antipronation running shoes are worn. But the reality is somewhat different.

Early studies also suggested that the design of the heel influences the extent of pronation—in particular, that the more extensive the lateral heel flare, the greater the pronation (Nigg et al. 1987; Nigg and Bahlsen 1988; Nigg and Morlock 1987; Stacoff et al. 1988), whereas a medial flare (Clarke et al. 1983b) or a rounded heel (negative flare) reduces pronation (Nigg and Morlock 1987). These early studies also suggested that a straight-lasted shoe controls pronation more effectively than does a curve-lasted shoe even if the midsole is of the same hardness (Stripe 1983). But in view of current uncertainties of the exact role of the shoe in controlling pronation, it seems that these studies need to be repeated with the more sophisticated methods currently available. The point is that if these specific shoe designs do indeed reduce injury risk, then they probably act in ways other than simply controlling pronation (which they do not achieve).

In addition, shoes of different hardness or softness do not alter the overall loading of the lower limb (Clarke et al. 1983a; Frederick 1986; Nigg et al. 1987; Nigg 2001). Nor do viscoelastic shoe insoles reduce landing forces during running (Nigg et al. 1988; Nigg 2001). But risk of injury has been reduced in army recruits who used either neoprene insoles (Schwellnus et al. 1990) or a modified basketball shoe (Milgrom et al. 1992) during training, suggesting that the protective action of these interventions may result from factors other than increased shock absorption.

It seems that runners alter their gait and muscle activation patterns (Komi et al. 1987) when running in a harder shoe or when running barefoot. Thus, the degree of pronation is reduced when running barefoot (Frederick 1986; Smith et al. 1986; Stacoff et al. 1991) because of changes in running patterns. In particular, the maximum rate at which the knee bends at landing increases with barefoot running and with the hardness of the shoe (Frederick 1986; Lafortune et al. 1996). It is thought that this is an energy-inefficient mechanism (McMahon et al. 1987) that could make barefoot running or running in harder shoes less efficient than running in softer shoes (Frederick 1986).

Hence, there is increased muscle activation to absorb any extra loading caused by the harder running shoes. Thus, it seems probable that the real effect of shoes in causing or preventing injury may result either from the different patterns of lower limb muscle activation that they cause or from biomechanical alterations in gait that have yet to be identified.

In summary, the current hypothesis is that shoes should still be prescribed according to the original method, but the logic is now different. Whereas before the rationale was that shoes would either reduce or increase the extent of pronation, depending on the degree to which they incorporate the traditional antipronation characteristics, now it is theorized that shoes do not actually alter the extent of pronation. Rather, they optimize the muscle activation patterns that will produce the lower limb gait pattern that is predetermined by each person's unique biomechanical structure. This theory predicts that, by altering those muscle activation patterns, the appropriately prescribed shoe will reduce injury risk or will cure the injury that is already present. Accordingly, see chapter 5 for more on the principal characteristic that makes a shoe soft enough to optimize muscle activation patterns in runners with different foot types.

Are Running Shoes an Expensive Gimmick?

Steven Robbins, a biomechanist from Montreal, suggests (somewhat controversially) that modern athletic footwear is unsafe. This assertion is based on the finding that impact loading is not reduced, especially by expensive running shoes that are promoted as having additional features that protect against injury—such as more cushioning and "pronation correction" (Robbins and Gouw 1991). Additionally, Robbins and colleagues claim the incidence of running injuries is reportedly 123% higher (Robbins and Waked 1997) in wearers of expensive running shoes and in those who show brand loyalty than in those who run barefoot, who wear less expensive shoes, or who have no such brand loyalty.

The gist of their argument is that the plantar (under-) surface of the foot contains sensors that detect the loading forces under the foot. If the foot is encased in a soft shoe with a smooth inner sole, the plantar surface of the foot misinterprets the actual loading being transmitted to the skeleton and the soft tissues when running. In other words, an illusion is created in which the runner thinks that because the plantar surfaces of the foot are comfortable, the loading of the skeleton must also be appropriate and not excessive. As a result, the running stride alters in such a way that the runner will tend to bounce more. The end result is that the loading of the skeleton will, according to this theory, actually be greater than if the runner ran barefoot. Robbins and Gouw (1990; 1991) suggest that by running in expensive shoes, athletes therefore expose their skeletons to more loading than if they ran barefoot. Thus, the risk of injury is increased, not reduced, by wearing expensive shoes. In contrast, running barefoot is beneficial because the plantar surface of the foot is exposed to the real loading conditions of the body and is not misled. Hence, these authors propose that barefoot running should be promoted. But as this is impractical, they suggest that footwear be modified so that the sensory illusion produced by the cushioned midsole is removed.

More recently, the authors have changed or perhaps amplified their original hypothesis to include a supposed effect of deceptive advertising by the manufacturers of expensive athletic footwear (Robbins and Waked 1997). Thus, in their newer proposal they suggest that "Products deceptively advertised as performing well, that are actually ineffective, might attenuate caution sufficiently to heighten injury frequency above levels existing before their introduction" (p. 299). They further propose that as no athletic footwear "regardless of manufacturer and price range" has ever been shown to protect against injury, "advertising good protection is deceptive." As the more expensive running shoes are advertised as having superior protective characteristics than cheaper products, the advertising of the more expensive (branded) running shoes is even more deceptive.

Therefore, they postulate that deceptive advertising about the protective nature of expensive running shoes causes those runners using expensive (branded) shoes "to eschew cautious behavior, resulting in higher impact" and therefore—according to their model, which postulates that more impact equals more injuries—to suffer more running injuries.

To test their hypothesis, these workers recruited 15 young men and had them

(continued)

step onto a force platform that was either bare or covered with a layer of EVA 2.5 cm thick. Subjects were asked to step repeatedly onto the force platform when it was either bare or covered with one of three differently colored EVA mats. However, the hardness of the EVA in all three mats was identical.

Before the subjects stepped onto the force platform covered with EVA, they received one of three messages:

1. a neutral message in which the EVA was described as never before having been used in a shoe sole, so that its effect was unknown;

2. a deceptive message in which the material was praised for its superior impact absorption, its "advanced technology," and its being "state of the art"; or

3. a warning message that stated that this EVA was associated with frequent injuries from excessive impact and instability and was found only in cheap running shoes.

Their results showed that subjects landed harder on the force platform after they had been given the deceptive message, supporting their hypothesis that footwear advertising changes running behavior so that greater impact may be produced, leading to more injuries (at least according to their theory of injury causation).

Accordingly, they proposed that expensive running shoes should carry a public health warning stating that "protection against injury with this product is only realizable if they remain as cautious with the new product as they were with the one it replaced" (Robbins and Waked 1997, p. 302). Such labeling, they conclude, would reduce injury frequency by an impressive 55%.

That study, however innovative it may be, can be criticized on the ground that it has little relevance to the real world. The conclusion is drawn from an experiment that lasted a few minutes, whereas runners use their "deceptively advertised" running shoes for many hours. It is likely that, after some hours of running, feedback from sensory receptors in the lower limb would inform the subconscious brain that the pair of deceptively advertised, expensive running shoes was not doing what it claimed. Hence, the subconscious mind would override that part of the conscious brain to which the deceptive advertisers appeal and alter the running gait, thereby normalizing the forces on the lower limb. Indeed, a study stimulated by the Robbins hypothesis confirmed that when young women were misinformed about the true cushioning characteristics of the shoes in which they were tested while walking, such information did not influence their ground reaction forces during the gait cycle (McCaw et al. 2000). The authors proposed that "The outcome of this study lends support to the quote attributed to Abraham Lincoln, sixteenth president of the United States, 'You can fool some of the people all of the time, and all of the people some of the time, but you cannot fool all of the people all of the time'" (Hertz 1939 p. 136).

Furthermore, Robbins' overall thesis can be criticized on the grounds that there is no conclusive evidence suggesting that increased loading of the lower limb is an important cause of running injuries (Nigg 2001). Indeed, injury rates were no different in groups of runners with high, medium, or low peak impact forces when running (Nigg et al. 1998). In fact, runners with the highest rate of loading had significantly fewer injuries than those with low loading rates. Also, there is no conclusive evidence that runners who habitually run in "deceptively advertised, technologically advanced, state of the art" running shoes actually expose their skeletons to greater levels of loading than do runners running either barefoot or in "cheap shoes with old technology," or that they do actually suffer more injuries as a result.

The weakness of this argument is that even if you find that runners wearing technologically advanced running shoes have a much higher incidence of injury than those runners who either run barefoot or who run in cheap shoes with old technology, this does not prove that cheap shoes prevent, and expensive shoes cause, running injuries. As discussed in chapter 15, only prospective studies can prove this causal relationship. Cross-sectional studies investigating injury patterns among runners who choose what shoe they run in—in this case technologically advanced or primitive—are open to the effects of confounding variables. For example, runners who have been injured previously and who are therefore at increased risk of another injury would be much more likely to buy technologically advanced running shoes. The real meaning of the finding that injured runners are more likely to run in technologically advanced, expensive, and branded shoes cannot be determined from a cross-sectional study.

The only way to prove that the cost of the shoe influences injury risk would be to undertake a prospective longitudinal study in which a very large number of runners are randomly assigned to groups that run for at least 12 months, either barefoot or in cheap or expensive running shoes (see the Harvard Graduate Study [chapter 15] for an understanding of how these trials are conducted). After 12 months, the incidence of injury in the three groups would be compared. Provided that the runners in the three groups were reasonably well matched for their likelihood of developing a running injury, and provided they had exposed themselves to equivalent amounts of running during those 12 months, any differences in the incidence of running injuries between the groups would provide a measure of the injury-preventing or injury-promoting effects of different classes of running shoes. Until such time as a study like this is performed, no one—not Robbins, nor anyone else—can make the dogmatic claim that running barefoot or in cheap shoes prevents injury or that the use of expensive shoes causes running injuries.

The Robbins hypothesis is a classic example of a theory that has been developed on the basis of a few selective facts and that avoids those unpleasant facts that do not support the theory. This technique is known as fitting the facts to the theory, rather than developing a theory that takes account of all the known facts.

However, Robbins does make one very telling point—there is no definitive evidence to prove that the use of expensive running shoes reduces the risk of injury. That data he quotes to prove that expensive running shoes cause an increased incidence of injury are invalid as they are cross-sectional (Marti et al. 1989). This apparent relationship could be caused by any number of other confounding variables already discussed. Conversely, to prove that expensive running shoes prevent injuries would require the longitudinal studies just described. Until these studies are completed, the theory that expensive running shoes prevent running injuries is as conjectural as is Robbins' contrarian hypothesis.

(continued)

The challenges posed by Robbins are the following:

- Just as we do not know if expensive running shoes increase the risk of running injury, we do not know if they prevent injuries. Without this information, are we really able to determine the real value of these expensive shoes?

- Robbins makes the point that there are unlikely to be substantial differences in the design or construction of specific types of shoes between different brands of running shoes. Hence, it is unlikely that there would be any real differences in injury frequency among runners using different brands of shoes. Recall Nigg's (2001) conclusion that five or six different shoes/orthotic combinations would probably cater for the needs of almost all runners.

- The most significant point of Robbins' challenge is that there is a pressing need for large-scale epidemiological studies, funded by the major shoe manufacturers, to determine which characteristics of specific running shoes prevent or alternatively cause injuries in different runners with defined lower limb mechanical characteristics.

Perhaps, just as the pharmaceutical companies must expose their drugs to extensive testing before they may be released for use by the general public, the time has now dawned for running shoes too to be subjected to similar considerations. The same argument should apply equally to substances that are claimed to have an ergogenic effect (chapter 13). Were that to come about, Robbins' campaign, based on heretical and unsubstantiated claims, would have been particularly worthwhile.

Any understanding of the interaction between the shoe and the lower limb biomechanics is made even more complex by the finding that the tendons and ligaments of the foot are designed to absorb shock when running barefoot (Alexander 1987; Ker et al. 1987). Furthermore, these structures in the foot act as highly efficient springs, converting as much as 93% of the energy they absorb on landing into elastic recoil at toe-off. Compared to these structures, the midsoles and outersoles of running shoes are relatively inefficient, as they convert only 40% to 50% of this energy back into elastic recoil (Alexander 1987; Alexander and Bennett 1989); the remainder of the energy heats up the midsole. Running shoe manufacturers, who have only considered the shock-absorbing function of the midsole, have only recently focused on the importance of elastic recoil (Alexander and Bennett 1989; Turnbull 1989). Those companies that have made claims about the value of their "energy return systems" would seem to have overstated their cases; few differences in energy return capacity were initially found between different running shoes (Alexander and Bennett 1989). More recently, Nike introduced the Nike Shox range of running, basketball, and cross-training shoes, which feature energy-returning springs in the heel (see figure 2.11). These shoes have been designed to increase energy return to the lower limb. But even a shoe that was 100% effective in energy return would only save the runner about 10% of the energy lost from the body with each step (Alexander and Bennett 1989).

Matching the Shoe to the Athlete

When it became apparent that running shoes should be designed for either shock absorption or motion control (Subotnick 1977), the need arose to grade the different models of running shoes according to their relative capacities for achieving these two aims.

Most running magazines now provide up-to-date information on the popular brands of running shoes, essential reading for any runner preparing to buy new running shoes, but especially important for runners who, because of their injuries, require a particular type of shoe. Other important resources are *The Running Shoe Book* (Cavanagh 1980) and *Biomechanics of Running Shoes* (Nigg 1986).

More recently, my colleagues at the University of Cape Town, Martin Schwellnus and Wayne Derman, developed the so-called Sports Shoe Injury Prevention System (SSIPS). This system attempts to match the biomechanical characteristics of the athlete with the specific functional characteristics of the shoe.

Using this method, the athlete is evaluated for the type of foot (figure 14.9), for the alignment of the forefoot and rearfoot, and for flexibility of the calf and hamstring muscles. The running gait is then inspected to determine the extent of any obvious excessive pronation or supination. Next, the athlete's shoes are examined for wear patterns and for specific characteristics. This is done to determine the suitability of that shoe for that particular athlete. On the basis of this examination, a specific score is calculated, with a low score indicating the need for a neutral shoe and a high score indicating the need for a motion control/antipronation shoe.

Each new running season, the available stock of running shoes is evaluated by a group of clinicians involved in the care of running injuries. Each running shoe model is then categorized into the neutral, stability, or motion-control categories on the basis of a specific numerical score—that is, the sum of five values that the shoe scores in five specific categories: heel counter rigidity; lasting (whether curve lasted, semicurved, or straight lasted, and whether board or combination lasted); the presence of a medial wedge; midsole hardness and stability in the vertical plane according to the Running Shoe Pronation Testing Technique (figure 5.3); and heel flare. Thus, each model of running shoe is given a specific numerical value that covers a continuum, and it is the specific score more than the category that will determine the correct shoe for each runner.

Once runners undergo this evaluation, they receive a score and a list of three to four suggested shoes, the numerical scores of which match the runners' scores. The runner then chooses from the list the shoe that is most comfortable. A popular feature of this system is that the assessment need only be done once, provided the athlete's running or injury profile does not change. Furthermore, the listing of shoes is updated annually.

Using In-Shoe Orthotics

The revolution in the understanding and treatment of running injuries began with the chance finding that in-shoe orthotics could cure a number of running injuries that had been resistant to all other forms of conventional treatment popular in the early 1970s (Sheehan 1977). The effectiveness of orthotics has since been confirmed. In two separate studies, 76% to 96% of runners with orthotics reported complete resolution or great improvement of their symptoms (Gross et al. 1991; Donatelli et al. 1988).

Although it was originally argued that orthotics worked by reducing both the total amount of rearfoot pronation and the maximum rate of pronation (Bates et al. 1979; Taunton et al. 1985; Frederick 1986; Smith et al. 1986), compatible with the belief that orthotics cure running injuries that are caused by excessive subtalar joint pronation (Kvist et al. 1989), there is now less certainty that this is the real reason for this effect. Kilmartin and Wallace (1994) argue that there is insufficient evidence to suggest that placing the foot in a more supinated position when running, as was supposed to occur with the use of an orthotic but which we now know does not happen (Nigg 2001), is more advantageous than leaving the foot in a more pronated position.

Similarly, Nigg et al. (1999) contest that in the original study, which concluded that orthotics alter ankle pronation during running, shoe- and skin-mounted markers were used. However, these markers fail to track the real ankle movements. Thus, when bone pins are used to measure the real ankle movements during running, neither running barefoot, running with shoes, nor running with shoes and orthotics altered the degree of ankle pronation (Stacoff 1998). Hence, orthotics must influence injury risk and running comfort by mechanisms other than controlling the amount of ankle pronation.

Accordingly, Nigg et al. (1999) proposed that the function of the orthotic, like that of the shoe, is to minimize the (stabilizing) work of the lower limb muscles during running. This is achieved by stabilizing the joints and by reducing tissue vibrations (Nigg 1997). This information is relayed to the brain from sensory organs on the surface of the foot, in the muscles, and in the joints. Together, this information produces the optimum muscle activation patterns for each athlete's specific biomechanical characteristics (Nigg 2001).

Training

After looking at your shoes, the next important factor to consider is whether your training methods or racing patterns have changed and whether these changes might explain the injury.

The common changes that occur in training methods are an increase in the amount of speed work done, either in the form of harder or more frequent interval sessions or in speed-play sessions or time-trials; an increase in the total distance run in training (in particular, the introduction of single long training runs); or an increase in the amount of uphill or downhill running. Running too many races too close together is another important precipitating factor (Jacobs and Berson 1986). It would seem that injury risk increases linearly with increasing running speed, daily and weekly running distance, and number of days run per week (Samet et al. 1982; Koplan et al. 1982; Powell et al. 1986; Jacobs and Berson 1986; Blair, Kohl, et al. 1987; Marti 1988; Macera et al. 1989; Walter et al. 1989; Brill and Macera 1995; Jones et al. 1993; Jones et al. 1994; Almeida et al. 1999).

If injury occurs after a change in any of these, then it is logical to go back to the training you were doing before the injury occurred and to reintroduce the suspected causative factor gradually.

Also ask yourself, have your training surfaces changed recently? The most important features of training surfaces are their hardness and degree of camber. Hard running surfaces include roads, pavements, and some running tracks; softer surfaces include dirt roads, trails, grass, and beach sand.

All road surfaces are cambered to ensure adequate drainage of rainwater into the gutters at the roadside. When running on a cambered road, the foot nearest the center of the road is often forced to pronate excessively, whereas the foot nearest the verge has restricted pronation. This apparently trivial difference can be sufficient, over many kilometers, to cause injury on one side of the body. For example, the athlete with flexible feet that have an increased tendency to pronate may develop an injury such as runner's knee on the leg that is positioned closest to the center of the road. This is because the foot on that side will be forced to pronate even more to compensate for the road camber, and this may be just enough to cause the injury.

While grass surfaces are soft and not usually cambered, they are uneven. This unevenness detracts from their overall attractiveness as a running surface, as they will tend to favor excessive ankle pronation. Similarly, beaches are highly cambered below the high water mark and very soft above it.

Finally, recall if you have previously been injured. A previous injury is a strong indicator of future injury risk (Macera et al. 1989; Walter et al. 1989; Jones et al. 1993; Jones et al. 1994; Brill and Macera 1995; Neely 1998a; 1998b). Thus, it is especially important that once you have been injured, that you reduce the risk of future injuries by following the advice contained in this chapter, especially that which is specific to the type of injury you initially suffered.

Once you have changed shoes and corrected any possible errors in training or in the choice of running surfaces, it is entirely possible that the injury will have been cured. Our experience (Pinshaw et al. 1983; Lindenberg et al. 1984; Pretorius et al. 1986) is that these simple procedures are effective enough to produce a cure in more than 60% of runners within three to six weeks. The point is that some running injuries can be cured without an accurate diagnosis ever being made. However, if injury persists despite these simple measures, then an accurate diagnosis must be made (see step 6).

Step 3: Warm Up Before Exercise

As the name implies, warm-up suggests a process in which the temperature of the body, and especially of the muscles, is increased before exercise. Warm-up may be either passive, such as taking a warm shower, or active, where the athlete generates internal heat by exercising. Furthermore, warm-up can be defined as either general or sport-specific (Safran et al. 1989). A general warm-up could include activities such as jogging, stretching, doing calisthenics, and using light weights. The sport-specific warm-up includes the specific movements that would normally be used in the sport. Runners should generally warm up by jogging.

The particular physiological effects of warming up are to increase respiration and circulation, especially to the active muscles; to increase the temperature of the muscles; and to reduce their viscosity, thereby increasing their flexibility (Shrier and Gossal 2000).

More important, there is now firm experimental evidence that muscles that have warmed up are more resistant to tearing (Safran et al. 1989). In other words, they require greater forces to induce tearing than they would when not warmed up. These experimental findings are in line with the observation that acute muscle tears occur more frequently when sprinting in cold environmental conditions when, presumably, the muscles are colder.

The effect is substantial. In fact, some researchers conclude that "the evidence suggests that athletes should drop the stretching before exercise and increase warm-up" (Shrier and Gossal 2000). In other words, it is the warm-up, not the stretching, that prevents injury.

Step 4: Stretch

Stretching is not something that most runners do willingly. Runners who somehow manage to squeeze in 1 or 2 hours of running a day never seem quite able to find the additional 5 to 10 minutes needed for adequate stretching. There are a variety of reasons for this. First, most inflexible runners are unconvinced that stretching is beneficial. Secondly, we are ignorant of what is involved. Third, experience has taught us that stretching hurts; and finally, we are haunted by the suspicion that we may be doing it wrong anyway. There are now some excellent references that review all aspects of stretching (Anderson 1975; Uram 1980; Beaulieu 1981; Shellock and Prentice 1985; Alter 1996; 1998; Shrier and Gossal 2000). The information presented here is a synthesis of the ideas in these books.

Muscles have a complicated mechanism that prevents them from ever being damaged by overstretching. Muscles contain tiny stretch receptors that are attached to the working parts of the muscle—the muscle fibers. When a muscle is stretched suddenly, the degree of stretch is sensed by the stretch receptors. They then send messages back, via the spinal cord, to the nerves that control the contraction of the muscles in which the receptors lie (that is, the stretched muscles). As the intensity of the stretch increases, the stretch receptors begin to fire more rapidly and more strongly. Ultimately, these impulses exceed a certain threshold, and the stretched muscle contracts and shortens, preventing the muscles from being overstretched.

A general rule is that the intensity of the muscle contraction induced by a stretch reflex varies with the rapidity with which the stretch is applied. The faster the stretch is applied, the more powerful the contraction it evokes. Another important stretch reflex, the inverse stretch reflex, performs an exactly opposite function to that of the conventional stretch reflex. The receptors for this reflex are not embedded in the muscle fibers but are situated in the muscle tendons. These receptors are sensitive to the tension present in the muscle tendons.

As the muscle contracts, the tension in the tendon rises, and the tension receptors are activated. As in the conventional stretch reflex, these receptors send messages to the nerves controlling the contraction of the muscles in which these receptors lie. But in contrast to the conventional reflex, when these tension receptors in the inverse stretch reflex are activated, they inhibit the contraction of the relevant muscle. Therefore, the inverse stretch reflex provides a protective mechanism that prevents a muscle from contracting so strongly that it ruptures its own tendons. If the tendons sense that the muscle is contracting too powerfully, the tendon receptors cause the contraction to be "switched off." One theory holds that it is the inhibition of this reflex during prolonged exercise that contributes to cramping during exercise (see chapter 15).

How does stretching increase flexibility? When muscles are stretched, they exhibit two characteristics of a viscoelastic substance—creep and stress relaxation. Thus, unlike an elastic band that stretches immediately to a final length when a constant force is applied, the length of stretched muscles increases gradually with time (creeps). This is similar to any viscous substance, such as molasses. Stress relaxation occurs when the tone of the muscle suddenly falls after a period of constant stretching at the same length.

Stretching acutely reduces muscle stiffness by decreasing viscoelasticity and by reducing muscle tone during the stretch. If muscles are stretched for 30 seconds per day, these acute changes are retained and enhanced so that ranges of motion allowed by the stretched muscles are increased.

Benefits

The three main arguments in favor of stretching (Beaulieu 1981; Shrier and Gossal 2000) are that it reduces the risk of injury, promotes less muscle soreness after exercise, and improves athletic performance. However, the cold light of scientific investigation has not been kind to these traditional dogmas. As already discussed, there is insufficient evidence to suggest that intermittent daily stretching reduces the risk of injury (Shrier and Gossal 2000) and that stretching reduces postexercise muscle soreness. Rather, a regular stretching program induces a state of tolerance so that the stretched muscle only feels less stiff after exercise (Shrier and Gossal 2000), with the result that the factors causing the stiffness remain unchanged.

In addition, there is no published evidence to suggest that regular stretching improves running performance. However, the one condition that may well be prevented by regular stretching is muscle cramping during prolonged exercise (Schwellnus 1999). Thus, those who choose to stretch need to know that the benefits of this most popular practice have still to be established.

Dangers

Shrier and Gossal (2000) make the perhaps obvious point that irrespective of the technique of stretching that is used, stretching will always be more controlled than most athletic activities. Thus, stretching is likely to be less dangerous than the sport itself if performed properly and unaggressively.

Beaulieu (1981) suggests that if runners become sore and even injured after stretching, it is because they are not stretching properly. He suggests that if runners better understood the physiology of stretching, they would be less likely to injure themselves during the process.

How does this information help us determine the most effective stretching techniques? First, it indicates that the stretch must always be applied gradually. A slow buildup of stretch has the least stimulatory effect on the stretch receptors. Thus, these receptors remain at rest, and the tension in the stretched muscle is kept to a minimum. This is important because the best stretches are achieved when the tension inside the stretched muscles is low. Second, the inverse stretch reflex explains why a muscle that has been gradually stretched for 60 to 90 seconds will suddenly "give" as the inverse stretch reflex relaxes any remaining tension in the stretched muscle.

Techniques

There are four basic stretching techniques: ballistic, passive, contract-relax, and static stretching.

Ballistic stretching. This is the technique favored by school coaches and football players, and it involves bobbing up and down while touching your toes. Ballistic stretching is usually considered to be an ineffective method as it simply activates the stretch reflex, causing the stretched muscle to contract rapidly and the athlete to bob up with remarkable speed. The tension inside the muscle during ballistic stretching is about twice that in a static stretch. However, although it is possible that this form of stretching increases the risk of injury, there is no published evidence suggesting that this is in fact so.

Passive stretching. In this method, a partner applies additional external pressure to increase the extent of the stretch. This method is particularly popular among gymnasts. Beaulieu's considered opinion is that this method of stretching is invaluable for expert stretchers who participate in sports such as gymnastics or ballet dancing in which extreme flexibility is important, but that it is potentially risky for inexperienced stretchers. If you choose this method, ensure that both you and your partner are experts in this type of stretching.

Contract-relax stretching. In a contract-relax stretch (also called proprioceptive neuromuscular facilitation [PNF]), the muscle to be stretched is first actively contracted and then stretched as soon as it relaxes. The theory behind this technique is that the active muscle contraction activates the inverse stretch reflex, and, as originally believed, the muscle tension during the subsequent contraction is reduced. In fact, this does not occur. Instead, the contracted muscle remains slightly active during the subsequent stretch. Thus, the tension in the stretched muscle is actually higher, not lower, than during a static stretch. However, there is no evidence to suggest that this technique increases the risk of injury during stretching. A variant of this stretching technique is the contract-relax-antagonist-contract method, in which the muscle that is the antagonist of the muscle being stretched is contracted immediately following relaxation of the muscle being stretched. With this technique, if the quadriceps muscle, for example, is first contracted, the hamstring muscle will then be stretched. PNF stretching appears to be the most effective technique for increasing the range of motion of different muscles. However, this effect is achieved by increasing the muscles' tolerance to stretch without altering the muscles' viscoelastic properties, defined subsequently.

Static stretching. During static stretching, the stretch position is assumed slowly and held for at least 30 to 60 seconds. There is a slow buildup of tension in the muscle. Thus, the stretch reflex is not activated. As the tendons are stretched gradually, the inverse stretch reflex is activated and muscle tension falls (stress relaxation), enabling the muscle to be stretched a little further. As static stretching causes the smallest increase in muscle tension, it is believed to be the most effective stretching technique.

Current scientific evidence indicates that the contract-relax-antagonist-contract technique is superior to the contract-relax technique for increasing flexibility (Etnyre and Abraham 1986). The ballistic stretch technique is the least effective of the four methods of stretching (Wallin et al. 1985).

Following detailed studies, Gracie Hughes (1996) concluded that the optimum static stretching program consists of static stretches, each lasting 30 to 90 seconds, repeated three to nine times. If this program is performed three times a day, a consistent increase in muscle and joint stretchability will occur within seven to nine days. Hughes also found that stretching in the supine position (lying on your back) produced greater benefits than did stretching in the erect position.

Once the desired degree of flexibility has been achieved, a single stretching session per week will maintain that flexibility. Continuing to stretch three to five times a week will produce further improvements in flexibility (Wallin et al. 1985).

Stretching Program

I've modified Beaulieu's following guidelines for a successful stretching program:

- Expect results only after weeks or months of regular stretching.
- Follow a stretching program all year round, or, in a seasonal sport, begin at least six weeks before the beginning of a season.
- It is not necessary to exercise first before starting to stretch. Beaulieu's contention that stretching should follow a gentle warm-up (for example, a 5-minute jog) because warm muscles stretch better and are less likely to get injured is true for the calf muscles but not for other muscles (Williford et al. 1986; Shrier and Gossal 2000). Furthermore, this effect lasts for 30 minutes only. The same applies to cycling (Shrier and Gossal 2000).
- It is best to stretch both before and after exercise. If this is not possible, stretch before exercise. The increased muscle flexibility that results after a period of stretching lasts for up to 3 hours.
- Select stretching exercises carefully. Start with the easiest and build up to the more advanced.
- Alternate the muscles that are stretched—for example, the calf, then the quadriceps, and then the hamstrings.
- Assume the stretching position slowly and hold it for the duration of the stretch—ideally 30 seconds. Stretch the muscle to the point at which tightness is felt in it. At no time should the stretch cause discomfort or pain.
- Beaulieu recommends the 20 stretches that follow (figure 14.10, A through T). Perform exercises A, B, C, E, H, J, O, and P if insufficient time is available for the total program. Some of the exercises commonly used by runners (exercises R, S, T) are too risky for inexperienced stretchers. Exercises Q through T are specifically designed to prevent and treat lower back pain. Each can be repeated up to 10 times, as frequently as required.

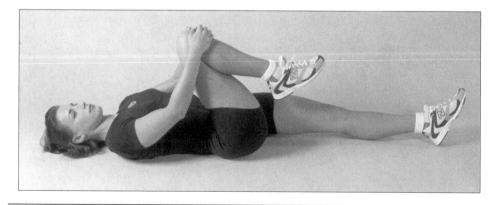

Figure 14.10   Exercise A: Hamstrings. Pull the knee to the chest; repeat with the other leg.

Exercise B: Quadriceps. Grasp the foot with one or both hands and pull it toward the buttock. Repeat with the other foot.

Exercise C: Back. Rock gently back and forth 8 to 10 times.

Exercise D: Abdomen and chest. With elbows on the floor or with arms extended, push the upper torso back with your arms. Keep the pelvis on the floor, and push the head as far back as it will go.

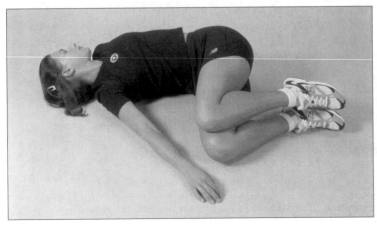

Exercise E: Hip and sartorius. Lie on your back with one leg bent over an extended leg or with both legs bent. Repeat, bringing legs to the other side.

Exercise F: Shoulders. Put one elbow behind your head. Gently pull the elbow toward the center of your back. Repeat, placing other elbow behind your head.

Exercise G: Lower leg. Leaning on a wall, keep your back foot flat and your head up. Slowly bend your arms and lower your body toward the wall. Repeat with the other leg.

Exercise H: Groin. With your feet together and your hands on your ankles, push down on your knees.

Exercise I: Sitting hamstrings. Sitting with one foot pressed against the inner thigh of the opposite leg, grasp the ankle of your extended leg and pull your body forward. Repeat, extending the other leg.

Exercise J: Lying hamstrings. While lying on your back, grasp one leg and pull it toward your head, keeping it as straight as possible. Repeat with the other leg.

Exercise K: Quadriceps. Lie on your side and pull the upper leg back to your buttocks. Repeat on the other side.

Exercise L: Hip and sartorius. Sitting, cross your right leg over the left, and bring your left arm to the right side of your right knee as shown. Push on your right leg with your left arm, and twist your body. Turn your head to the side (toward your right shoulder). Repeat with the other hip.

Exercise M: Hamstring. Standing, place one leg on a wall or ledge that is about hip height. Bend forward toward the raised leg, and reach toward the foot. Attempt to extend the raised leg as straight as possible, so that the legs form a 90° angle.

Exercise O: Pelvic area, abdominals, and back. Lie on your back with your knees bent, your feet flat on the floor, and your arms at your sides. Tighten your stomach muscles, and flatten the small of your back against the floor, without pushing down with the legs. Hold for 5 seconds, then slowly relax and repeat.

Exercise N: Hamstring. Standing with your feet shoulder-width apart, bend at the waist to touch your toes. (Avoid this exercise if you have back problems.)

Exercise P: Abdominals and quadriceps. Start in the same position as in exercise O. Grasp your right knee, and gently pull it toward your right shoulder. Return to the starting position, and repeat with the left leg.

Exercise Q: Quadriceps and hamstrings. Start in the same position as in exercise O. Use your hands to pull both legs to the chest. Grasp both knees and pull them toward your shoulders. Let the knees return to arm's length, and repeat.

Exercise R: Abdominals. Start in the same position as in exercise O. While holding this position, curl your head and shoulders up and forward. Hold for 5 seconds, then slowly return to the starting position. Be careful not to strain your neck.

Exercise S: Abdominals and back. On your hands and knees, relax your abdomen, and let your back sag downward. Then tighten your stomach muscles and arch your back.

Exercise T: Trunk. Starting on your hands and knees, tuck in your chin, and arch your back upward. Then slowly sit back on your heels while letting your shoulders drop to the floor. Relax. Return to the starting position, keeping your stomach tight and back arched.

Dominque Donner, a top South African triathlete, demonstrates these exercises.
Exercises A through O from Beaulieu (1981). © McGraw-Hill. Adapted with permission of McGraw-Hill.
Exercises P through T from Rovere (1987). © by McGraw-Hill. Adapted with permission of McGraw-Hill.

Step 5: Strengthen Muscles

Recent studies have shown that specific running injuries are associated either with imbalances in the relative strengths of the different muscles acting at those sites or with weakness in a specific muscle. In such instances, muscle strengthening will probably reduce the risk of injury, preventing its recurrence. There is clear evidence to suggest that acute muscle injuries can be prevented by strengthening muscles and eliminating muscle imbalances between opposing muscles (Garrett et al. 1987; Safran et al. 1989). For example, the introduction of specific muscle testing and strengthening programs reduced the incidence of acute hamstring tears in the University of Nebraska football team from 8% to 1%. Similarly, the recurrence rate dropped from 32% to 0% (Heiser et al. 1984).

Specific muscle strengthening exercises that are of special value to runners are shown in figure 14.11, A through J. These exercises are prescribed to elite runners by Justin Durandt, senior consultant in the Discovery Health High Performance Center at the Sports Science Institute of South Africa in Cape Town. The value of these exercises is that the muscles of runners, who only run gradually, lose strength with time, giving rise to the classic observation that the more runners train, the less their ability to jump (Costill 1979). This probably occurs because of a progressive change in myosin ATPase activity (see chapter 1) as all the trained muscle fibers take on the characteristics of slower contracting, more fatigue-resistant Type I fibers. Commence with a warm-up and stretching. A warm-up should be a minimum of 10 minutes and may consist of one of the following activities: running on the road or treadmill; skipping; working out on the Stairmaster; cycling, or jogging on the spot. Stretching should only take place once the warm-up has been completed.

From the perspective of injury prevention and performance enhancement, it is important that initial strength levels be maintained, especially in those muscles that are not trained by running, such as the hip abductors and adductors.

The recent trends in injury prevention and rehabilitation emphasize strengthening and conditioning of the gluteus medius and other muscles acting through the iliotibial band, which act to stabilize the pelvis. Similarly, the muscles that stabilize the knee, including the vastus medialis, and the invertors and evertors of the ankle, also need to be trained.

Figure 14.11 Exercise A: Lunges (2 × 10 repetitions). Alternate between right and left legs. Do not allow the front knee to bend further forward than across the vertical line extending from the toes of the front foot. Stop this exercise if you experience knee pain.

Exercise B: Hip flexion (2 × 10 repetitions). Do not use a heavy weight with this exercise (2.5 kg max). Rather, use an elastic band. Attach the elastic band to the ankle, with the other side tied to a support. Lift your thigh upward until it is parallel to the ground. Keep the supporting leg slightly bent at all times.

Exercise C: Chair squat (3 × 12 repetitions). From the standing position, lower your body. Pretend you are sitting on a chair, but do not go further down than 90°. Stop if back or knee pain develops.

Exercise D: Leg press (2 × 20 repetitions). Push the weights away from your body by extending your knees. During the movement, point your toes slightly outward. Release the weights slowly—2 seconds for pushing the weights away, 4 seconds for returning to the weights to their original position. Do not bend your knees more than 90°, and stop if knee or back pain develops.

Exercise E: Standing calf raises (3 × 20 repetitions). In this exercise, the ankle plantar flexes (extends) as a result of calf muscle contraction. Note that when stepping into and out of the calf raise machine, you should bend your knees and not your back. In the first set, point your feet slightly outward so that the weight is carried on the outer part of your foot. In the second set, point your feet slightly inward so that you are bearing weight on the inner part of foot. In the third set, point your feet slightly outward so that you are bearing weight on the outer part of the foot.

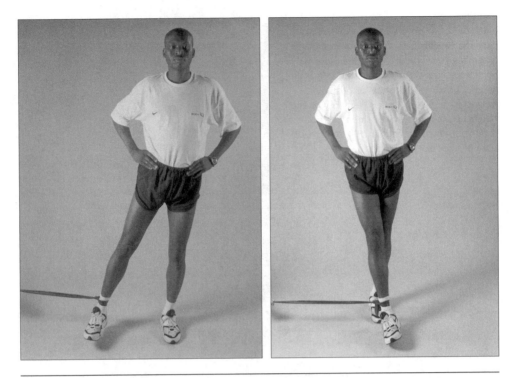

Exercise F: Inner and outer thigh (2 × 10 repetitions). In this exercise, you use a band or pulley. Pull the band across your body to exercise the inner thigh muscles and away from the body to train the outer thigh muscles. Bend the knee of the foot that is on the ground. Always tense the lower abdominal muscles prior to lifting the thigh. Do not use your hands for support. Stabilization should come from the gluteus and lower abdominal muscles. Keep the pelvis stable throughout the movement.

Exercise G: Push-ups (3 × 10 repetitions with 30 sec rest between each set). Push your upper body away from the ground by extending your elbows. Place your hands shoulder width apart, and keep your buttocks in the air. For a less strenuous exercise, cross the legs.

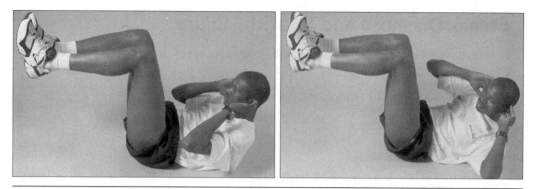

Exercise H: Stomach crunches (2 × 15 repetitions of each). For straight crunches, lift your torso off the ground toward your flexed knees. For side-to-side crunches, lift and rotate your torso to bring each elbow toward the opposite knee.

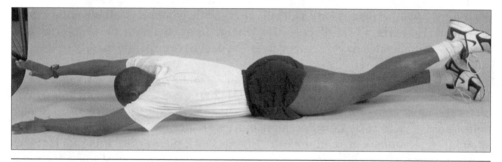

Exercise I: Alternate arm/leg raise (2 × 5 repetitions). Lie on your stomach and lift one arm and the opposite leg 5 cm off the ground. Hold for three seconds. Keep your chin on the ground throughout the exercise. Repeat using the other arm and leg.

Exercise J: Bridging with leg extension (2 × 10 repetitions). Lie on your back. Tense your lower abdominal muscles, and then lift your buttocks about 10 cm off the ground. Slowly lift and bend one knee in toward your chest while keeping the other foot on the ground. Then slowly push the leg outward as you straighten it, keeping your stomach muscles tight. Return the foot to the ground, and repeat the same procedure with the other leg.

Step 6: Diagnose and Treat the Injury

Running injuries typically affect the following structures, in roughly the order of frequency listed:

- ligament-to-bone or tendon-to-bone attachments,
- bones,
- muscles,
- tendons,
- bursae (fluid-filled sacs that lie between tendons and bones and allow free movement of the tendons over the bones),
- blood vessels (arteries and veins), and
- nerves.

Each injury has particular characteristics that help in its diagnosis. As a result, each injury will be discussed in detail, along with comments about appropriate treatment. However, I first discuss the relative frequencies of these injuries and how these frequencies have changed over the past decade as the quality of running shoes has altered.

Following six different surveys (James et al. 1978; Cavanagh 1980; Clement et al. 1981; Pinshaw et al. 1983; MacIntyre et al. 1991; 2001), the knee was concluded to be by far the most common site of injury (19% to 44%), followed by tibial and fibular bone strain (15% to 18%). Less common injuries are Achilles tendonitis, now known as Achilles tendinosis or tendinopathy (5% to 11%); plantar fasciitis (5% to 14%); stress fractures (5% to 6%); and muscle injuries (5% to 6%). In all studies, the most common knee injury is *runner's knee,* now known as *patellofemoral pain syndrome (PFPS),* with the iliotibial band friction syndrome originally accounting for only about one-fifth to one-third of the total running injuries to the knee. However, the incidence of this injury has risen in the most recent survey (MacIntyre et al. 2001), and it now accounts for up to 9% of all running injuries.

The major changes that have occurred in the patterns of running injuries since 1970 have been that the incidence of Achilles tendinosis has fallen markedly from about 20% to 5% of all injuries, whereas the incidence of bone strain (from 10% to 18%) and especially patellofemoral pain syndrome (from 23% to 44%) has risen sharply. The incidence of the iliotibial band syndrome has also increased (MacIntyre et al. 1991; 2001), especially in military recruits, where it now accounts for up to 10% of all injuries (Kaufman et al. 1999) and is more common than the patellofemoral pain syndrome. My guess is that this reflects the more recent trend toward firmer running shoes with less cushioning.

In my view, the decline in the incidence of Achilles tendinosis is probably not the result of the increased heel height in modern running shoes and increased time spent stretching by modern runners as is the view of one expert (McKenzie et al. 1985) but has occurred because the nature of runners has changed. Achilles tendinosis is more common in older athletes who have trained at high intensity, including frequent sessions of interval training, for many years. Before the mid-1970s, such athletes made up the majority of all runners. Today, their numbers have been diluted by the much larger number of recreational runners, who are likely to be at a much lower risk of contracting this particular injury. The reason the incidence of the other injuries has risen may be, as Cavanagh (1980) suggests, the introduction of softer running shoes that control pronation rather poorly. My impression is that in the 1990s, shoes became firmer. Thus, according to Cavanagh, a reversal of this injury trend in the 1990s would be predicted.

Another recent change is an increase in the incidence of meniscal (cartilage) injuries (MacIntyre et al. 2001) that are more usually associated with contact sports, such as rugby, or twisting sports, such as soccer and skiing. The reason for this change in runners is unknown.

TYPES OF INJURIES

I now describe the common injuries—where in the body they occur, what seems to cause them, and how best they should be treated.

Ligament-to-Bone or Bone-to-Tendon Injuries

The five common injuries that I include in this group are the patellofemoral pain syndrome (PFPS, also known as runner's knee), the iliotibial band friction syndrome, plantar fasciitis, the Osgood-Schlatter syndrome, and tarsal tunnel syndrome.

Patellofemoral Pain Syndrome

The term *runner's knee* was first coined by George Sheehan in the early 1970s to describe a running injury that produces a set of very specific and characteristic symptoms: The pain is localized around the kneecap. The pain first occurs during running and does not result from external trauma. The pain usually comes on after a predictable distance. It becomes gradually worse but is exacerbated by very long races. Walking up or down steps causes discomfort, as does squatting on the haunches. Sitting with the knee bent for any length of time causes discomfort. This is called the "movie sign" (Insall et al. 1976) because patients with this injury soon learn to choose aisle seats at the movies so that they can periodically stretch their knees into the aisle, thereby relieving the pain. The conventional medical approach to sporting injuries—cortisone injections into the painful area—never provides a permanent cure in this, as in most running injuries. In the original description of this condition, the damaged tissues in this injury were thought to lie behind the kneecap in the cartilaginous lining of the knee joint between the kneecap and the two other bones (the tibia and femur) that constitute the knee joint. Thus, runner's knee was considered to be chondromalacia patella—a condition well-recognized by orthopedic surgeons and in which there is degeneration of the joint cartilage on the undersurface of the kneecap.

If this were indeed the case, it would mean that running had caused degeneration of the joint cartilage, which, in time, would almost certainly lead to arthritis. If we follow this logic, we could conclude that runners who have a high incidence of the prearthritic condition, chondromalacia patella, must ultimately develop arthritis. The 10th Law of Running Injuries counters this untruth. Runners are not at increased risk of knee osteoarthritis, although the risk of hip arthritis is increased in elite athletes who continue to train intensively for many years.

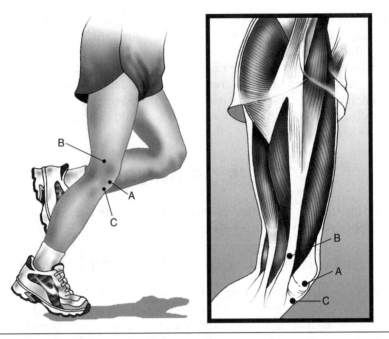

Figure 14.12 Sites of pain in the common running injuries affecting the knee, including the patellofemoral pain syndrome (runner's knee) (A), the iliotibial band (ITB) friction syndrome (B), and Osgood-Schlatter's syndrome at the growth plate in the tibial tubercle (C).

Fortunately, we now know that runner's knee is not chondromalacia patella and has nothing to do with the cartilage that lines the undersurface of the kneecap (Pretorius et al. 1986). Stan James, an orthopedic surgeon and runner and the man whose medical expertise helped Joan Benoit win the first women's Olympic marathon, together with his colleagues (1978), was the first to notice that the area of most severe knee pain in runners with this condition was actually on the inner or outer border of the kneecap at the site where the patella tendon and the medial and lateral retinacula attach (figure 14.12). Clearly, they are not the sites affected by chondromalacia patella. James and his colleagues (1978) therefore coined the term *peripatellar pain syndrome* to describe this condition. Others use the terms *medial retinaculitis* (Clancy 1980) or *patellofemoral pain syndrome* (Clement et al. 1981).

James' hunch has since been confirmed by sophisticated studies showing that the ligaments and indeed the bone in this condition are abnormal (Devereaux et al. 1986), as they show degenerative changes that almost certainly explain the marked pain caused by this injury (Merkel et al. 1982). Not all runners with this condition develop osteoarthritis; rather, they tend to get better without the need for heroic measures such as surgery (Karlsson et al. 1996; Natri et al. 1998). As a result, the term *patellofemoral pain syndrome* (PFPS) is now preferred, and *chondromalacia patella* has been abandoned (Krivickas 1997).

If the history of injury is suggestive, the diagnosis of PFPS can be confirmed by a simple test, shown in figure 14.13. In this test, the runner relaxes the quadriceps (upper thigh) muscle. The left hand pushes the top end of the patella so that the bottom tip comes away from the knee joint. Firm pressure with the thumb and forefinger along the lower border of the patella reproduces the pain the athlete feels when running.

PFPS is the injury that is cured, par excellence, by the prescription of antipronation shoes and corrective orthotics and would thus appear to be due to excessive muscular activity associated with higher degrees of ankle pronation. While it has been assumed that runners with this condition must have hypermobile feet that pronate excessively—either because the foot itself is at fault or because it is compensating for other abnormalities in the lower limb (Pretorius et al. 1986), including an increased Q angle or femoral neck anteversion—there is as yet little concrete evidence to support this theory (Karlsson et al. 1996; Krivickas 1997). In fact, the most recent study (Duffey et al. 2000) found that the ankle joints of runners with PFPS pronated less than did those of controls. In that study, runners at greater risk of injury "had higher arched feet, replaced their shoes more frequently, pronated less through the first 10% of stance, and had weak knee extensors" (p. 1825). Another long-term follow-up study also found that strengthening the quadriceps muscle on the af-

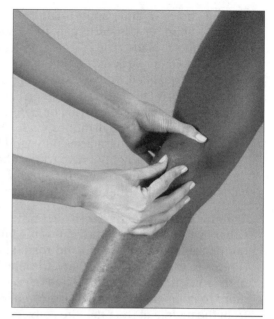

Figure 14.13 Palpating the kneecap to make a diagnosis of PFPS. The top hand pushes down, lifting the lower pole of the patella. Pressure from the thumb and forefinger of the lower hand onto the lower borders of the inferior pole of the patella reproduces the discomfort of this condition. The most likely cause of this pain is bone bruising at the site at which the patella ligament inserts into the lower pole of the patella.

fected side was an important predictor of recovery (Natri et al. 1998), suggesting that muscular factors may be more important in this injury than was generally appreciated. Other factors associated with this injury are presented in the following sections.

Shoes and Orthotics

In my clinical experience, the most important additional factor associated with this injury is inappropriately soft running shoes that fail to control pronation and that may have collapsed on the inside, as has the shoe shown in figure 14.6. However, this conflicts with the findings of Duffey et al. (2000), which suggest that excessive pronation may not be a factor in this condition.

Since the mid-1980s, all the major running shoe manufacturers have developed shoes that are advertised specifically to limit ankle pronation during running—the so-called antipronation shoes. While it is unlikely that these shoes actually limit ankle pronation, these shoes are the most effective in treating this injury (see chapter 5 for more on selecting these shoes). Additional shoe advice for the runner who needs an antipronation shoe can be found in the most recent shoe surveys published in the more popular running magazines, such as *Runner's World*. To determine which of these shoes have proven to be successful on the road, it is advisable for the runner to discuss these shoes with other runners and particularly the salesperson at a specialist running shop.

If the choice of more appropriate running shoes does not cure the injury, then the only hope for long-term pain-free running is to have a custom-built orthotic (arch support) made. The current problem experienced all over the world, except perhaps in some parts of the United States, is that specialist podiatrists who are sufficiently qualified to make such supports are difficult to find. And unless the orthotic is correctly made, the injury will not improve. The best advice I can offer is to find runners who are wearing orthotics with which they are pleased and to find out where they had the orthotics made. At present, orthotics that can be bought over the counter at pharmacies only tend to help those with mild forms of PFPS.

If this injury does not improve within about a month, runners should realize that the shoes and orthotics they are using have failed to correct whatever biomechanical abnormality it is that causes the injury.

Training Errors and Surfaces

Other likely factors include training too far, too hard, and too soon; always running on the same side of a cambered road; and interval training and racing too often (Pretorius et al. 1986). Note that if the injury occurs on the leg nearest to the middle of the road, it is most likely related to excessive pronation, as that foot will pronate more to compensate for the road camber. If the injury occurs on the leg farthest from the middle of the road, the converse applies.

Biomechanics

These are likely to include flat feet (pes planus) or alternatively high-arched feet (Duffey et al. 2000), reduced ankle flexibility (Kaufman et al. 1999), femoral neck anteversion (Krivickas 1997), and an increased Q (quadriceps) angle at the knee (figure 14.14; Messier et al. 1991). Runners with a Q angle greater than 168° are at significantly greater risk of developing this condition.

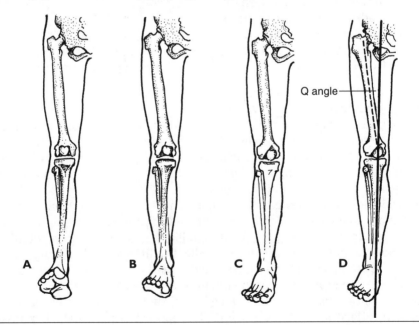

Figure 14.14 The Q angle affects the running stride: heel contact (A), ankle pronation begins (B), lower leg twists inward (C), and increased Q angle during the running stride (D). The technique for measuring the Q angle is shown in figure 14.15.

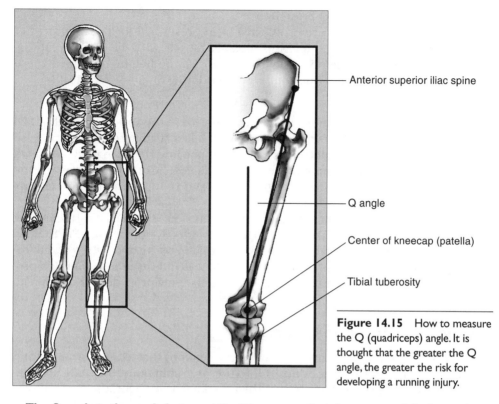

Anterior superior iliac spine

Q angle

Center of kneecap (patella)

Tibial tuberosity

Figure 14.15   How to measure the Q (quadriceps) angle. It is thought that the greater the Q angle, the greater the risk for developing a running injury.

The Q angle is the angle between the line connecting the center of the kneecap to the anterior superior iliac spine on the pelvis and the line connecting the tibial tuberosity and the center of the kneecap (figure 14.15).

The successful treatment of PFPS should aim to correct the biomechanical factors that are believed to cause it. I have found it useful to support the subtalar ankle joint during running. In the past, we assumed that this form of treatment cured the problem by reducing excessive ankle pronation during running, but this now seems to be an unlikely explanation. Nevertheless, the advice to the runner is to run in those shoes that are advertised to limit ankle pronation. If this fails, a custom-built orthotic (arch support) is prescribed.

Using this simple approach, we (Pretorius et al. 1986) were able to cure 68% of runners with this injury within four weeks after only one consultation lasting about 20 minutes. Others have also reported that orthotics cured more than 80% of runners with this condition (Gross et al. 1991). The remaining paradox is how orthotics work given that they do not limit ankle pronation, especially if excessive ankle pronation may not be associated with this injury (Duffey et al. 2000). As someone unable to run without orthotics in the softest running shoes available, I suspect that orthotics act by improving cushioning while allowing ankle pronation to continue without causing excessive or abnormal muscle functioning.

Other less essential methods of treatment include calf muscle stretching and correcting any possible muscle strength/flexibility imbalances between the quadriceps and hamstring muscles. The role of muscle imbalance in this injury has not yet been established, but runners with this injury show reduced endurance of the quadriceps muscles (Messier et al. 1991), and those who improve their quadriceps strength the most show the best recovery (Natri et al. 1998).

Stretching and Strengthening Exercises

While no specific stretching exercises have been prescribed for the treatment of this condition, strengthening the vastus medialis muscle with the chair squat (figure 14.11C) or leg press exercise (figure 14.11D) can be helpful, provided these exercises do not cause pain or discomfort either during or after exercise.

Specific Treatment

The first-aid treatment of runner's knee is to apply ice to the sore area for about 20 minutes twice daily. Two aspirins (or equivalent) taken 30 minutes before exercise are also said to be quite helpful. Cortisone injections into the knee joint, although suggested by some writers, must be avoided at all costs as they do not reach the site of the injury, which, as shown in figures 14.12 and 14.13, is around the kneecap, not in the knee joint itself.

Quite recently, an Australian physiotherapist proposed a special taping technique, the McConnell technique, which was particularly effective in treating PFPS. However, a prospective, randomized trial found that patients treated with a standardized physiotherapy program recovered as quickly as did those in whom this program was combined with the use of the McConnell taping procedure (Kowall et al. 1996).

Iliotibial Band Friction Syndrome

The iliotibial band is a thickened strip of fascia (tendon) that extends from the hip across the outside of the knee to insert into the large shin bone, the tibia, immediately below the line of the knee joint. When the knee is straight, the fascia lies in front of a bony prominence at the outside of the knee, the femoral epicondyle, but as the knee bends, the fascia begins to move toward that bony point. When the knee has bent through about 30°, the fascia may make contact with the femoral epicondyle, and it is this contact that is believed to cause pain in this condition.

The classic feature of iliotibial band friction syndrome injury is severe pain, well localized over the outside of the knee, directly over the lateral femoral epicondyle. The pain is absent at rest and only comes on during exercise. Even though possibly quite unable to run, the athlete is usually able to walk long distances or play other sports (for example, squash, rugby, or tennis) without discomfort, although walking down stairs may be painful.

During running, the pain usually becomes so severe that it limits the runner to a specific running distance, which may be as little as 100 m in some, and as much as 16 km in others. The pain usually comes on rapidly and, once present, stops further running. Downhill running, in particular, aggravates the symptoms in all runners. Sometimes, but rarely, symptoms are present only during downhill running. In such cases, the runner may be able to continue running on the flat or uphill as long as the downhills are avoided.

Another important feature of this injury is that the pain subsides almost immediately when the athlete stops running. For this reason, athletes are frequently reluctant to see their doctors lest they be considered hypochondriacal. However, should the athlete again try to run, the pain returns rapidly. (We use this feature to help in the diagnosis. Should an athlete present with an injury that sounds like the iliotibial band syndrome but in whom no sign of injury can be found, we simply ask the patient to go for a run and to return when the pain develops. After a short run, the site of the pain, and therefore the diagnosis of the injury, usually becomes obvious.)

Figure 14.16 The anatomy of the iliotibial band, showing the area of localized pain experienced in the IT band friction syndrome. One theory is that the condition is caused by repeated friction on the undersurface of the posterior fibers of the IT band as it crosses the lateral femoral epicondyle during repeated bouts of flexion and extension of the knee.

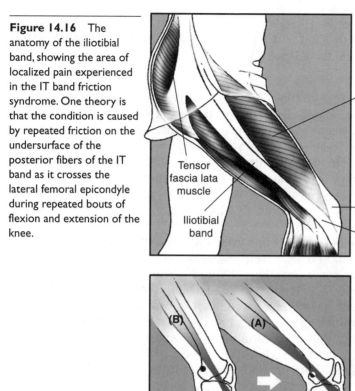

The most important finding on examination of the knee is an area that is exquisitely tender to pressure. This area is well localized to the outside of the knee joint, immediately overlying the femoral epicondyle (figure 14.16). Downhill running aggravates the pain. The diagnosis is confirmed by a test first described by a South African orthopedic surgeon (Noble 1979; 1980). In the Noble test, pressure is applied to the lateral side of the knee directly over the femoral epicondyle. The knee is slowly straightened from about 90° of flexion. At about 30° of flexion, as the band slips over the femoral epicondyle directly underneath the examiner's finger, the pain that the athlete feels during activity is reproduced.

This injury is believed to occur because of repeated rubbing of the posterior edge of the iliotibial band against the lateral femoral epicondyle, just after foot strike in the gait cycle (Orchard et al. 1996). In addition, runners with this injury may show an enlarged bursa between the iliotibial band and the femoral epicondyle with thickening of the iliotibial band (Ekman et al. 1994) or even an extension of the knee joint capsule between the epicondyle and the iliotibial band (Nemeth and Sanders 1996). In some, injury may develop at the site of the insertion of the iliotibial band into the lateral epicondyle of the tibia (Rockett et al. 1991).

Some of the factors that we (Lindenberg et al. 1984; Messier et al. 1995) and others have found to be associated with the injury (but which we cannot be certain caused the injury) include the following.

Shoes and Orthotics

Of our sample (Lindenberg et al. 1984), 66% of injured runners were running in hard running shoes with poor shock-absorbing properties at the time of injury. Hard shoes would be those designed to limit ankle pronation, which are therefore normally prescribed for the treatment of PFPS and tibial bone strain. Indeed, it is not uncommon for an athlete treated too enthusiastically for either of those conditions to return some weeks or months later with the initial injury cured but with an iliotibial band friction syndrome that has been caused by shoes and orthotics that have altered muscle recruitment patterns by increasing the perceived hardness of the shoe and orthotic.

Initially, all injured runners should be advised to buy soft running shoes that do not resist pronation. Chapter 5 discusses how to choose such a shoe.

Finally, in runners with severe bow legs or very high-arched, rigid feet, it may be necessary for an orthopedic technician to build a lateral (outside) wedge into the midsole of the shoe. Such a wedge forces the foot to pronate inward, thereby improving its shock-absorbing capacity by up to 25% (Kvist et al. 1989). In addition, if the athlete has a short leg, the sole of the shoe on the short-leg side should be built up to compensate for the shortness. However, runners with this injury are no more likely to have a short leg than are uninjured runners (Messier et al. 1995).

Training Errors and Surfaces

It would seem that heavy training mileages, sudden increases in training, and too much racing are important training errors that explain why this injury occurs most commonly in the peak racing season. Thus, Messier et al. (1995) found that runners with this injury ran higher weekly mileages but at a slower pace for fewer months than did control runners who did not develop the injury. In addition, injured runners ran more on composition tracks, and they also swam more. Hence, the picture we have is of an injury that is more likely to occur in the less experienced runner who has been training at the current level for less time than uninjured runners.

Indeed, the reason that a South African orthopedic surgeon was among the first to describe this condition (Noble 1979) was that he began to see the condition so frequently among ultramarathon runners training for the Comrades Marathon. Typically, the condition would occur two to three months before the race at the very time when the less experienced runners were beginning to increase their weekly training distances, especially by including weekly long (30 to 60 km) weekend training runs. Certainly, my clinical experience has been that this condition is most likely to occur in the novice marathon and ultramarathon runner in the last few months before the chosen race, particularly when runners have altered their training to include many longer runs on weekends. In those who train less and race shorter distances, the injury seems also more likely if the longer weekend runs are much longer, perhaps two to three times as long, as the longest single training run during the rest of the week.

Athletes with this injury should be encouraged to reduce their training. They are allowed to run with discomfort, but once the injury becomes painful, they must stop.

A novel alternative form of treatment was developed by the United States Marine Corps in San Diego, California. Aronen et al. (1993) found that immobilization of the knee for three days, during which time injured marines wore immobilization braces on their injured knees and walked only with crutches, effectively cured almost all acute injuries. During their immobilization, marines also took antiinflammatory medication, iced their knees three times per day, and performed stretching exercises of the iliotibial band six times per day.

Once the initial symptoms had disappeared after three days, marines could return to running but could run only until they felt tightness on the outside of their knees, whereafter they were told to stop running immediately. Until they were again running pain-free at the previous training mileages, they were encouraged to continue with their stretching exercises and to use ice and antiinflammatory medications. Following this regime, the authors reported that 99% of more than 2000 injured marines have recovered completely. This is a far better result than I have ever achieved using a treatment regime that did not include complete immobilization for the first three days of the injury.

Excessive downhill running and running on hard surfaces seem to be factors in this injury. Another important factor identified in our study (Lindenberg et al. 1984) was that injury occurred on the side of the body corresponding to the side of the road on which the runner most often ran. Runners who ran on the right-hand side of the road normally developed the injury on their right-hand side.

Thus, training should be done on flat, soft surfaces and all downhill running must be avoided until the injury has resolved. Runners also may want to change their normal habits and to switch to running on the opposite side of the road. This advice must be followed only with the greatest caution. Note also that not all studies find that running on crowned, or cambered, roads is a factor that favors this injury (Messier et al. 1995).

Biomechanics

My clinical impression, supported by findings from an early study, is that the important hereditary structural factors associated with this injury are bow legs and high-arched, rigid feet (Sutker et al. 1981), although not all studies support this conclusion (Kaufman et al. 1999) as runners with flat feet can also develop this injury. But the theory is that rigid feet are unable to absorb adequately the shock of landing, which is then transferred in some way to the iliotibial band, and this ultimately leads to the injury. Runners with this injury were also found to be shorter and less strong than uninjured runners (Messier et al. 1995).

Thus, in my experience, about 70% of cases of the ITBS occur in runners whose lower limbs do not appear to pronate sufficiently during running. The study of Messier et al. (1995) found that the feet of runners with this injury landed in a more neutral, less supinated position and were thus likely to pronate less during the stance phase of the running cycle. If this is the case, the reduced amount of pronation must cause other musculoskeletal adaptations to compensate for a reduced capacity for shock absorption in the foot itself.

Messier et al. (1995) also found that the maximum braking force was less in runners with this condition, so that the higher the weekly running mileage and the lower the braking force, the greater the probability of injury. Indeed, an equation using only these two variables could correctly classify 68% of their subjects as either injured or uninjured.

Lower braking forces could result from muscular weakness. Fredericson, Cookingham, et al. (2000) found that runners with this injury were significantly weaker in the muscles producing hip abduction—the gluteus medius and the tensor fascia lata—than were uninjured runners. They postulated that weak hip abductor muscles will increase the stretch of the iliotibial band, promoting injury especially in the fatigued state. Furthermore, a six-week rehabilitation program to strengthen the gluteus medius muscle cured 92% of their injured runners (Fredericson, Guillet, et al. 2000).

The evidence would seem to confirm that treatment should aim to increase the ability of the limb to absorb shock, achievable in a number of ways, and to increase the strength of the muscles that stabilize the hip during running.

Stretching and Strengthening Exercises

I prescribe three special lateral stretches. In the first, all the weight is carried on the injured side, and the upper body is bent away from the injured side, with the chest facing forward. This stretches the iliotibial band and is performed for 10 minutes daily. Do the second two stretches while sitting. The beginning stretch requires that you place the foot on the injured side on the lateral side of the extended knee of the uninjured side. By rotating the upper body toward the injured side, use the elbow opposite the injured knee to push the injured knee toward the opposite side (figure 14.17A). Once the iliotibial band and associated muscles become more flexible, adopt the more advanced stretch, in which the arm corresponding to the injured side is placed around the injured knee, and the opposite hand grasps the foot and pulls the knee across the body toward the opposite armpit (figure 14.17B).

Also perform strengthening exercises for the gluteus muscles. Figure 14.11F (an exercise for the outer thigh) is one appropriate form of exercise. The same exer-

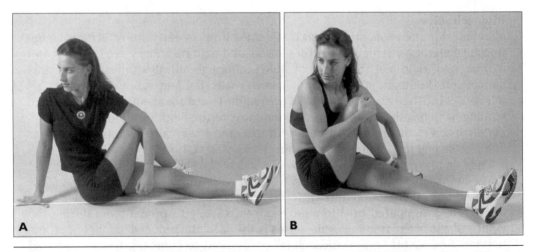

Figure 14.17   To perform the IT band stretch for the right knee, sit with both legs extended and then place the right foot on the lateral side of the extended left knee and use the left elbow to push the right knee to the left, away from the body (A). As the IT band flexibility improves, a more effective stretching technique is to flex the affected knee and grasp it with the arm of the same side, while the hand of the opposite arm holds the foot (B). Contracting the arm holding the injured knee pulls that knee toward the opposing shoulder, stretching the IT band and the gluteus muscles in the buttocks.
Aronen et al. (1993. p 65).

cise can be performed by lying on the uninjured side and by lifting, in the vertical plane, a weight attached to the foot on the injured side.

Specific Treatment
Other treatment options include icing the tender area of the knee, using anti-inflammatory medications (Aronen et al. 1993), injecting hydrocortisone into the affected area, and performing strengthening exercises for the gluteus medius muscle (Fredericson, Guillet, et al. 2000). The ideal exercise is side-lying leg lifts, which isolate the gluteus medius muscle. Patients build up to 3 sets of 20 repetitions each, performed daily.

Occasionally, in very resistant cases, a small surgical procedure may be performed, in which the section of the tendon that comes to ride over the femoral epicondyle is excised (Noble 1979; 1980). Although the results of the surgery are most encouraging (Firer 1989; 1992; Martens et al. 1989), most would advocate that the hydrocortisone injections and surgery only be tried after all the other treatment options described (Aronen et al. 1993; Fredericson, Guillet, et al. 2000) have been tried, or if the athlete simply cannot afford the time necessary for conservative treatment to succeed. Indeed, Fredericson, Guillet, et al. (2000) have never referred a patient for surgery and believe that this is because they advocate an aggressive rehabilitation program.

Even using our more simple methods of treatment, which at the time included neither immediate knee immobilization nor strengthening of the gluteus medius muscle, 83% of the injured runners in our sample were cured completely of the injury (Lindenberg et al. 1984); 58% of all runners were cured within three weeks; and the remaining runners, who were completely cured, became symptom-free within six weeks to six months. Had we added early immobilization of the injury, the use of anti-inflammatory medications, and strengthening of the gluteus medius muscle, the results would have been achieved more quickly.

Thus, in the past decade, the management of this condition has improved dramatically. The pessimistic opinion expressed in previous editions of this book—which suggested that we could not expect to cure everyone with this condition—can now be replaced with a message of significant optimism. Early aggressive management of this injury should produce a rapid cure in most runners.

Plantar Fasciitis

This is one of the less common injuries, accounting for only about 5% to 14% of injuries in all the large cases reported in the literature. The symptom of this injury is pain directly in front of the heel, usually first noticed during running; it later becomes noticeable when these patients get up in the morning. For the first few steps, they hobble by putting all their weight on the heel; they will not extend the ankle or push off with the big toe. (The same features are present in Achilles tendonitis.) Someone suffering from a heel bruise, on the other hand, will hobble on the toes to prevent the bruised heel from coming into contact with the ground. On examination, the diagnostic feature is extreme point tenderness at the origin of the plantar fascia from the calcaneus (figure 14.18, A through C).

The mechanism of injury in this condition is believed to be excessive subtalar joint pronation, which causes a bowstring stretching of the plantar fascia, especially if toe-off occurs with the ankle fully pronated. However, confirmation of this concept is still lacking (Warren 1984). Other factors associated with the injury

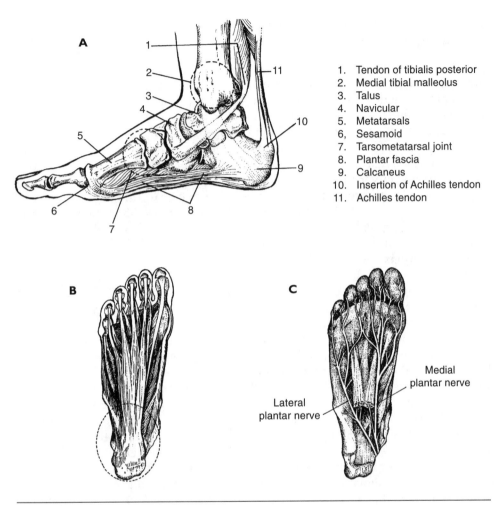

1. Tendon of tibialis posterior
2. Medial tibial malleolus
3. Talus
4. Navicular
5. Metatarsals
6. Sesamoid
7. Tarsometatarsal joint
8. Plantar fascia
9. Calcaneus
10. Insertion of Achilles tendon
11. Achilles tendon

Medial plantar nerve

Lateral plantar nerve

Figure 14.18 The relevant anatomical features of the ankle (A); the origin of the plantar fascia from the calcaneus, or heel bone, (B); and the nerves to the forefoot that run beneath the plantar fascia and may be entrapped or inflamed, causing the tarsal tunnel syndrome (C).

include high-arched, rigid feet and leg-length inequality (McKenzie et al. 1985; Messier and Pittala 1988; DeMaio et al. 1993). In addition, runners with this injury show reduced ankle motion on the affected side; muscle strength on the injured side is also below normal (Kibler et al. 1991).

Stretching and Strengthening Exercises
None have been described or tested. Logic suggests that exercises that increase the eccentric strength of the foot muscles should be beneficial. Indeed, calf-muscle stretching (figure 14.10G) and strengthening would seem to be especially important (Warren 1984) in view of findings of deficits in these measures in runners with this injury.

Specific Treatment
Until the exact mechanism of this injury has been determined, efforts to treat this injury should initially include measures to increase shock absorption and limit the

muscular activity associated with increased ankle pronation. Thus, all the measures described for the treatment of PFPS and Achilles tendinosis must be tried. It may be necessary to adjust the orthotic slightly to ensure that it does not contact the painful area under the heel bone. Uphill running and speed work should be avoided until the injury has resolved.

Quite recently, a novel technique that involves wearing a foot splint at night was tested (Batt et al. 1996). The aim of the splint is to maintain the tension in the plantar fascia by holding the ankle in a position of dorsiflexion with the toes extended. The splint is worn for up to 14 weeks.

The remarkable finding was that 30 of 33 (91%) cases of plantar fasciitis treated in this way healed completely within an average of 12.5 weeks, whereas only 6 of 17 (35%) patients treated with a standard treatment of anti-inflammatory medication, a viscoelastic heel cushion, and stretching were healed within the same time period.

If these methods fail and symptoms persist for longer than 12 months despite all these measures, surgery may prove effective (Snider et al. 1983). In these runners, there is evidence of major histological (tissue) changes in the fascia at the site of pain.

Tarsal Tunnel Syndrome

A condition that may cause symptoms indistinguishable from those of plantar fasciitis is the tarsal tunnel syndrome (Jackson and Haglund 1991; figure 14.18, A through C). The tarsal tunnel is an anatomical structure on the inside of the heel bone, through which runs the posterior tibial nerve and a group of tendons stretching from the calf to the toes. High degrees of ankle pronation cause nerve irritation along the medial side of the heel and into the arch of the foot, perhaps a consequence of excessive activity of the posterior tibial muscle in people with high degrees of subtalar joint pronation.

The condition can be distinguished from plantar fasciitis because, in the tarsal tunnel syndrome, tapping over the tarsal tunnel causes a tingling sensation in the area of distribution of the posterior tibial nerve—a sensation that is not produced in plantar fasciitis. Treatment aims to reduce the excessive muscular activity present in people with high degrees of ankle pronation. Hence, the prescription of antipronation shoes and orthotics is the first line of treatment. Other predisposing causes of the condition, including pregnancy, gout, and rheumatoid arthritis, among others, should be excluded.

Osgood-Schlatter Syndrome

This is a condition specific to growing children who develop discomfort well localized over the tibial tubercle (see figure 14.12), into which the patella tendon inserts.

In growing children, the tibial tubercle is an epiphysis (area of bone growth), or epiphyseal growth plate, and repeated contractions by the powerful quadriceps muscle, which inserts via the patella tendon into the tibial tubercle, can cause minor separation of the epiphyseal cartilage from the underlying bone. The condition resolves when the cartilage in the epiphysis is replaced by bone, usually at the age of about 15 years.

During childhood, the growth of the bones occurs in a cartilaginous growth plate that separates the bone shaft (metaphysis) from its end (the epiphysis; figure 14.19).

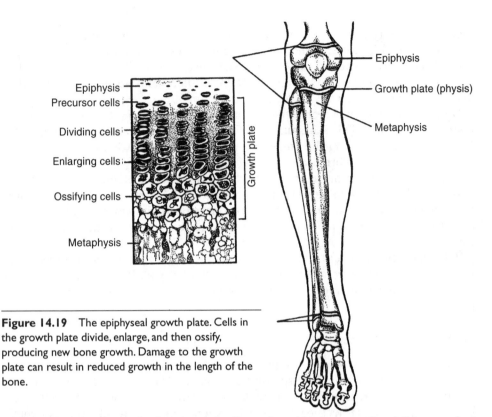

Epiphysis
Precursor cells

Dividing cells

Enlarging cells

Ossifying cells

Metaphysis

Growth plate

Epiphysis

Growth plate (physis)

Metaphysis

Figure 14.19   The epiphyseal growth plate. Cells in the growth plate divide, enlarge, and then ossify, producing new bone growth. Damage to the growth plate can result in reduced growth in the length of the bone.

The cartilaginous growth plate is gradually replaced by bone as the child grows but only solidifies into true bone when the child has matured, usually between the ages of 15 and 19 years.

The main risk posed by the growth plate is that because it comprises cartilage, which is much weaker than bone, it is more likely to be damaged if an external force is applied to the bone—for example, during a rugby tackle. There is considerable concern that vigorous exercise increases the risk of displacement or even death of the growth plate, with potentially catastrophic effects. For example, were the growth plate to be displaced in such a way that the epiphysis and the metaphysis were no longer in the appropriate alignment, subsequent growth in that bone would occur at a slant. Alternatively, if the growth plate were severely damaged, this could result in the death of the growth plate and failure to grow further in length. Thus, the child who suffered a growth plate injury in one long bone, such as the tibia or femur, would be left with unequal growth on the two sides of his or her body. In 1956 the Committee on School Health of the American Academy of Pediatrics came out strongly against contact sport for preadolescents in particular, on the basis that such sport would lead to a high incidence of growth plate injuries (Committee on School Health 1956). However, subsequent research has clearly established that the risks had been greatly overstated.

In a study of 12,338 sporting injuries in children under 15 years of age, Larson and McMahan (1966) found an incidence of growth plate injuries of only 6%. It would appear that the risk of growth plate injuries, even in children involved in body contact sports, is relatively low and certainly not a cause for undue concern.

More recently, it has been suggested that children who participate in long-distance running risk damaging their growth plates (Caine and Lindner 1984). Again, it appears that the risks have been overstated, and no one has yet reported a high incidence of these injuries in child runners. As I have yet to see such an injury in a young runner, I am currently unimpressed with the argument that long-distance running will increase the risk of growth plate injury in children.

In the past, immobilization of the knee was a popular method of treating this condition. But today, we know that this is unnecessary and that time alone will cure the injury. Until such time as the tibial epiphysis fuses, the athlete with this condition is allowed to continue exercising with discomfort, but not with pain. Activities that cause pain sufficiently severe to limit exercise must be avoided. There is certainly no need for the young athlete with mild symptoms to rest completely, an option that is still prescribed too frequently. Rest is an unfortunate prescription because there is no evidence that it alters the natural course of the condition, which is to resolve completely as the child ages. In addition, it introduces the negative consequences of a child unable to exercise at a crucial time of life.

Bone Injuries

The two common bone injuries in runners are (tibial and fibular) bone strain and stress fractures.

Tibial Bone Strain

In the 1900s, before the running revolution, there was really only one running injury. As long as you were a runner, and you hurt somewhere between the big toes and the hip, you had shinsplints. This lack of diagnostic precision was probably not really much of a handicap because our understanding of running injuries was so rudimentary anyway that whatever therapy was suggested invariably failed (Sheehan 1975).

Today, however, shinsplints (now more accurately referred to as tibial or fibular bone strain) is a diagnosis reserved for one specific and curable injury—a bone injury localized to one or both of the calf bones (the tibia and the fibula) in one or more of three positions (figure 14.20). Other terms more anatomically correct than shinsplints include *posterior tibial syndrome* (James et al. 1978), *tibial stress syndrome* (Clement 1974; Clement et al. 1981), and *medial tibial stress syndrome* (Mubarak et al. 1982). I prefer the term *bone strain,* as this locates the tissue that is more likely to be the site of pain (Batt et al. 1998).

Bone strain typically develops through four stages of injury (2nd Law of Running Injuries). In the first stage, vague discomfort, poorly localized somewhere in the calf, is noted after exercise. As training continues, the discomfort comes on during

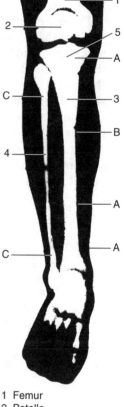

1 Femur
2 Patella
3 Tibia
4 Fibula
5 Tibial plateau (medial)

Figure 14.20 Anatomical sites at which tibial bone strain (shinsplints) can occur: (A) posterior shinsplints, (B) anterior shinsplints, and (C) lateral shinsplints. Novice runners are more likely to develop bone bruising at either end of the tibia, but especially at the medial tibial plateau.

exercise. At first it is possible to "run through" this pain, but if training is continued without treatment, the pain soon becomes so severe that proper training is neither enjoyable nor possible. This is a grade 3 injury. Ultimately, the injury may be so bad that anything more strenuous than walking is quite impossible. A grade 4 bone strain injury has become a stress fracture.

In making a diagnosis of bone strain, it is important to differentiate the injury from a chronic tear in the tibialis anterior or tibialis posterior muscles. This is done by feeling for the site at which maximal tenderness is felt. In bone strain, this is always along either the front (anterior or medial tibial bone strain) or back (posterior tibial bone strain) borders of the tibia or along the outside (lateral) edge of the fibula (fibular bone strain; figure 14.20). Usually the bone in the affected area has a rough, corrugated feeling owing to the buildup of a new bony (periosteal) layer at the site of the irritation. Applying firm finger pressure to these areas produces exquisite, well-localized, nauseating tenderness. The discomfort thus produced is usually severe enough to cause the injured runner to screech involuntarily and to pull the leg away. Quite frequently, there is also mild swelling over the injured bone so that, when the finger-pressure is released, a small indentation is left in the tissues overlying the injured bone.

There are several elaborate explanations for the cause of bone strain, but I am not sure that all are entirely satisfactory. In the mid-1970s, the most popular explanation was that bone strain was due to the buildup of pressure in one or more of the tight muscular compartments of the leg during exercise (figure 14.21). Thus, the logical treatment was to prevent the effects of this pressure buildup through a surgical procedure in which the tight lining of the muscular compartment was cut. Certainly, this type of treatment is very effective in the compartment syndromes discussed subsequently, in which there is an increase in pressure, but it is without effect in true bone strain (Allen and Barnes 1986).

We now know that in true bone strain there is no such pressure buildup (Mubarak et al. 1982; Wallensten and Eriksson 1984; Detmer 1986). Rather, this is an injury of

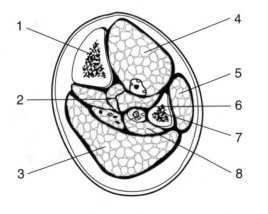

1 Tibia
2 Blood vessels
3 Superficial posterior compartment
4 Anterior compartment
5 Lateral compartment
6 Tibialis posterior
7 Fibula
8 Deep posterior compartment

Figure 14.21 The muscle compartments of the right calf viewed from above. Note that the deep posterior compartment is frequently involved (60%). However, diagnosis of involvement of the deep posterior compartment is most difficult. As a result, this condition is frequently missed.

Based on data of Martens et al. 1984.

bone (Batt et al. 1998) or, less commonly, periosteum (Bhatt et al. 2000) and is probably related to excessive ankle pronation (Viitasalo and Kvist 1983; Sommer and Vallentyne 1995), perhaps related to an increased Q angle (Cowan et al. 1996) or to exposure to excessive shock to which the bone is initially unable to adapt, or as a result of excessive activity of the medial soleus muscle (Michael and Holder 1985). Interestingly, as early as 1938, Webster (1948) suggested that shin soreness was often, but not always, caused by the "lowering of the arches of the foot."

It has been suggested that the area of abnormality in some cases of bone strain is restricted to a narrow band of bone along the inner border of the tibia (Michael and Holder 1985) to which the thick covering (fascia) of the soleus muscle inserts. These authors postulate that excessive muscular activity resulting from high levels of ankle pronation causes increased tension in this fascia, the so-called soleus syndrome, ultimately leading to the bone injury of bone strain. They therefore suggest that if control of excessive ankle pronation does not cure the injury, then surgical dissection of the fascia is likely to be successful. Detmer (1986) calls this injury the Type II medial tibial stress syndrome and suggests that surgical resection of the fascia of the posterior compartment and attention to the damaged periosteal lining are usually required. The most likely explanation for the majority of cases of bone strain, however, is that the injury occurs in bones that are undergoing remodeling in response to an increased loading stress.

It is now established that the initial response in bones subjected to increased loading is the activation of specialized cells, osteoclasts, whose function it is to cause bone resorption (that is, the removal and absorption of bone tissue; Johnson et al. 1963; Li et al. 1985). The resorbing bone also becomes highly vascular (that is, it has a high concentration of blood vessels) and, possibly because of this increased vascularity, may be identified by bone scanning (Matheson et al. 1987) or magnetic resonance imaging (Lodwick et al. 1987). This phase has been termed *osteoclonal excavation* (Lodwick et al. 1987). During this phase, the bone strength is probably reduced, placing the bone at increased risk of fracture (Scully and Besterman 1982). Movement at the site of bone weakness induced by exercise could explain the deep-seated pain of bone strain. The phase of osteoclonal excavation passes gradually into one in which new bone is laid down at the site of bone resorption by other specialized bone cells, the osteoblasts.

My interpretation is that bone strain and stress fractures develop in those whose bones either undergo excessive osteoclonal excavation or whose osteoblastic response is either delayed or initially ineffectual. Indeed, Marguiles et al. (1986) showed that the bone mineral content of Israeli army recruits who failed to complete their basic training, most commonly because they suffered stress fractures, increased significantly less than did the bone mineral content of those recruits who did not suffer stress fractures. Significantly, 85% of the fractures occurred within the first eight weeks of training. It is believed that it takes at least 90 days for the resorbed bone to be completely replaced by mature, strong bone; the rate of this response slows with increasing age (Johnson 1964). I suggest that bone strain indicates excessive osteoclonal excavation with the development of focal or diffuse areas of bone weakness. These weaker areas are sensitive to touch and to the increased loading stress of exercise. Myburgh et al. (1990) have indeed shown that athletes with stress fractures have reduced bone density owing to a low-calcium diet, menstrual abnormalities, or both.

Additional support for this theory comes from the finding that army recruits who participate in ball sports, principally basketball, have a substantially lower risk of developing a stress fracture than do recruits who participate in other sports (Milgrom et al. 2000). Other sports, including jogging, martial arts, and weightlifting, are not protective, whereas swimmers are actually at increased risk. Milgrom et al. (2000) have shown that basketball loads the bone substantially more than does running, especially during rebounding. They theorized that basketball elicits maximal bone adaptation and hence greatest protection from stress fractures, once the bone has adapted fully. They speculate that this would occur over a period of two years and suggest that playing basketball is an excellent method for reducing the risk of bone injuries caused by running or military training.

Furthermore, Crossley et al. (1999) have reported that athletes who developed tibial stress fractures have smaller bones than do uninjured runners but that the mineral content of their bones is not reduced, nor do they have higher ground reaction forces and hence higher levels of bone loading when they run.

These studies show that athletes who suffer bone injuries have weaker bones, either because they are smaller in cross-sectional areas, or because they have a lower bone mineral density. Furthermore, a prolonged period of heavy loading, produced especially by jumping and landing in sports such as basketball, increases bone strength or stiffness and reduces the risk of contracting a future bone injury.

It has also been suggested that overstriding is a factor in the development of anterior tibial bone strain. Overstriding is especially common during fast downhill running. In overstriding, the athlete's stride is too long and causes the shoe to strike the ground forcibly at the extreme back of the heel, making the forefoot slap onto the ground. In trying to prevent this slapping movement, the muscles in the front of the calf are forced to overwork, and ultimately pain develops at the point where they attach to the tibia.

Posterior tibial bone strain, by far the most common form of bone strain, is associated with high levels of ankle pronation (Viitasalo and Kvist 1983; Messier and Pittala 1988), and it probably results from either the inadequate shock-absorbing ability of bones unused to the stresses of running or from excessive muscular activity in those with high degrees of ankle pronation. In my clinical experience, most novice runners who develop bone strain within their first three months of running usually recover without any specific treatment, besides possibly changing to a more appropriate running shoe. This suggests that their bones become stronger and are therefore better able to absorb the shock of running after six months or so, just as the lower limb bones of basketball players probably develop their superior stiffness over two or more years. On the other hand, my impression is also that when the high degrees of ankle pronation are treated in experienced runners with bone strain, they are usually cured within a short time.

Exactly how these two mechanisms of increased muscle activity secondary to excessive ankle pronation and reduced bone stiffness or strength cause the bone pain of bone strain is not known. My guess is that the excessive muscle actions found in people with high levels of ankle pronation causes localized bone traction injuries. Alternatively, runners with high levels of pronation may be more likely to develop a torque, or twisting force, in the tibia and the fibula, and this could eventually lead to minute bone cracks (grade 1 to 3 injuries) at the sites of greatest bone resorption. Ultimately, these may progress into full-blown stress fractures (grade 4 injury). How inadequate shock absorption causes the identical injury is not known at present.

Bone strain is most common among three groups of athletes: middle-distance high school track athletes; novice joggers and army recruits, particularly during their first few months of training; and more experienced runners, particularly when they start training intensively for competition. The factors associated with the injury are discussed in detail below.

Shoes

Novice runners may develop tibial bone strain from training in unprotective running shoes, perhaps even canvas tackies. For trained distance runners who have recently developed tibial bone strain, the choice of training shoes may be inappropriate, or the shoes may be worn out in one or more of the ways described earlier in this chapter. Most often, the shoe will have collapsed to the inside, or else the midsole may have hardened to stone.

Training Errors and Surfaces

Although there is no published evidence to support this, I suspect that high school track athletes are particularly likely to develop tibial bone strain. They train very little in the off-season, so that when the new school year begins, there is usually about a month in which to prepare for the first track meeting. Each day, the athlete is exposed to an impossible training load (too much speed work, too often, too soon; no hard-day/easy-day routine) under the worst possible environmental conditions (running continually in one direction on a hard, unforgiving running surface in hard, uncompromising shoes). Unless the athlete has perfect lower limbs, the result is predictable. By the time the first major track event arrives, these athletes either have such advanced bone strain that they are unable to do their best, or else they are watching from the sidelines, nursing stress fractures.

Joggers and long-distance runners who develop tibial bone strain may exhibit some of these behavior patterns, but there are frequently additional factors as well. Typically, joggers with bone strain have been running for between 5 and 12 weeks, frequently to lose weight, so that they are a shade heavy; and they have progressed too rapidly (Devas 1958; Richie et al. 1985; Myburgh et al. 1988). For whatever reason, female joggers seem to be at greater risk than male joggers. This high risk of bone strain in novice joggers is the reason I advocate a period of walking in the first weeks of the beginner's training program (chapter 5).

On the other hand, trained distance runners who have recently developed tibial bone strain have usually altered their training methods in one or more of the ways described previously. They may have suddenly increased training distances or introduced speed work or hill-running sessions. Alternatively, they may have recently resumed training and pushed it too hard, too soon.

Biomechanics

Foot type (either flat [Devas 1958; Michael and Holder 1985; Viitassalo and Kvist 1983; Myburgh et al. 1988; Sommer and Vallentyne 1995] or high-arched [Bennell et al. 1995] feet), leg-length discrepancy (Friberg 1982), and external rotation of the hip (Giladi et al. 1991) have all been associated with tibial bone strain. In addition, there may be inadequate flexibility of the ankle caused by tight calf muscles. A squatting test has been designed to identify those who have the greatest degree of lower limb malalignment and who are at greatest risk of injury (Allen et al. 1986).

While tight calf muscles may be inborn, they may also develop in athletes who train hard without stretching adequately. Hard training also develops muscle imbalances, and it is believed that the strength of the posterior calf muscles is increased more by running than is the strength of the anterior (front) calf muscles. This strength imbalance may then play a role in injury.

Menstrual Abnormalities or a Low-Calcium Diet

There is growing evidence (chapter 15) that the majority of sportswomen who have abnormal menstrual patterns also restrict their dietary energy intakes (Cann et al. 1984; Drinkwater et al. 1984; Lindberg et al. 1984; Marcus et al. 1985; Nelson et al. 1986; E.C. Fisher et al. 1986; Cook et al. 1987; Zanker and Swaine 1998). The important result is that their trabecular bones especially (that is, those mainly of the spine—in particular the vertebrae) but often also the cortical (limb) bones (Gonzalez 1982; Lutter 1983; Linnell et al. 1984; K.P. Jones et al. 1985; Prior et al. 1990; Drinkwater et al. 1990; Snead et al. 1992; Myburgh et al. 1993; Micklesfield et al. 1995; Rencken et al. 1996; Rutherford 1993; Tomten et al. 1998; Pettersson et al. 1999) are likely to become weaker—first, because the blood levels of the female hormone estrogen, which is required for normal bone mineralization, are depressed, and second, because their dietary calcium intakes may be too low to maintain normal bone mineral content (Grimston, Engsberg, et al. 1990; Grimston, Sanborn, et al. 1990). Their weaker bones are more prone to the development of bone strain, stress fractures, and curvature of the spine (scoliosis) in early adult life (Lindberg et al. 1984; Marcus et al. 1985; Lloyd et al. 1986; Warren et al. 1986; Barrow and Saha 1988) and almost certainly to more serious problems, such as pathological hip fractures complicating severe osteoporosis, in older age. This combination of anorexia nervosa, amenorrhea, and osteoporosis in athletic women is known as the Female Athlete Triad and is discussed in detail in chapter 15.

Men are not immune to the detrimental effects of eating disorders on bone mineral density. Thus, men with anorexia or bulimia nervosa also develop osteoporosis (A.E. Andersen et al. 2000). In addition, the extent of the osteoporosis is worse in men than in women with equivalent eating disorders.

The effect of a low calcium intake is shown by the finding that the dietary calcium intake of sportsmen and sportswomen with shin soreness (bone strain and stress fractures) is abnormally low and is a predisposing factor for the injury (Myburgh 1989; Myburgh et al. 1988; 1990).

Stretching and Strengthening Exercises

Specific calf muscle stretching exercises for this injury are shown in figure 14.10. The most effective strengthening exercise for the calf muscles is shown in figure 14.11, E, standing calf muscle raises.

Specific Treatment

The treatment of bone strain depends on the severity of the injury and its location. Grade 1 injuries, which cause pain only after exercise, do not require heroic measures. The first priority, as in all injuries, is to determine whether anything has changed recently in the runner's training methods. A return to previous training methods (if possible) may be all that is required to cure the injury. For example, track athletes who develop the injury shortly after the introduction of regular speed sessions on the track should simply run fewer intervals, less often, less fast, until the injury clears up. Alternatively, they should run their intervals on a softer surface in running shoes that absorb shock better than do spikes.

The novice runner who has been running for less than three months can be reassured that it is likely that the injury will disappear in 4 to 10 weeks without any specific treatment, and without even a reduction in training. In this group of runners, special attention must also be paid to the running gait—in particular, these runners should be taught how to run with a shuffle and to avoid overstriding. Another trick is to avoid pushing off with the toes: the toes should be allowed to float inside the shoe. Some American podiatrists suggest that padding should be placed under the toes to help achieve this.

The next option is to consider a change in running shoes. If examination of an old pair of shoes shows that the runner pronates to a high degree, then a firmer shoe that is more likely to control the muscular activity associated with excessive pronation is necessary.

If, on the other hand, the old shoes do not reveal patterns of excessive pronation, the problem becomes one of deciding whether the shoe is too hard or not quite hard enough. Under these circumstances, I usually advise runners to buy slightly softer running shoes than the ones in which they have been running. Should that prove ineffective, there is still the option of prescribing an arch support to control the muscle function associated with high levels of pronation.

A specific form of treatment is to apply ice massages to the sore areas for 20 to 30 minutes per session, two to three times per day. The ice should be placed in a plastic container and then massaged gently up and down the leg over the sore areas. Whether physiotherapy, drugs, or injections really make any difference at this stage of the injury is not clear. Certainly, they do not substitute for a thorough evaluation and correction of the factors causing the injury.

A woman who is not menstruating regularly should consider the possibility that a lack of circulating estrogen may be contributing to her injury. If she will admit to knowingly restricting her food intake, she must be advised to increase her food intake until normal menstrual patterns return. Alternatively, she should consult a gynecologist for an opinion about the advisability of taking replacement estrogen and progesterone therapy (Prince et al. 1991). Although there is some evidence that the use of oral contraceptives is associated with a lower incidence of stress fractures (Bennell et al. 1999), it remains uncertain as to whether estrogen therapy is of any value in this condition (Bass and Myburgh 1999).

The reason is that women runners with amenorrhea have a form of osteoporosis that is due to a low rate of bone turnover (Zanker and Swaine 1998), whereas estrogen lack alone causes a high rate of bone turnover, preventable by estrogen replacement. Hence, estrogen therapy for the osteoporosis caused by the Female Athlete Triad would probably not be beneficial.

Those women who are menstruating normally but who are restricting their dietary calcium intakes, usually by avoiding dairy produce, which provides most of the calcium in the diet, should consider taking supplementary calcium in the form of calcium tablets (500 to 1000 mg per day).

Other risk factors for the development of osteoporosis in women include alcohol or tobacco use, a sedentary lifestyle, and the use of certain drugs (in particular, anticonvulsant drugs and thyroid hormone). White and oriental women who are of slender build, who undergo an early menopause, and who have a family history of osteoporosis are particularly at risk of developing this condition (Johnston and Slemenda 1987).

It is important to stress that exercise increases bone mineral content and reduces the risk of osteoporosis in all people at all ages (chapter 15) with the sole exception of young, amenorrheic women whose blood estrogen levels are low (Smith and Raab 1986; Johnson and Slemenda 1987; Chow et al. 1987; Dalsky et al. 1988). However, the effect is greatest when exercise is undertaken at a young age, probably before puberty, and when the activity involves leaping and landing (Bass and Myburgh 1999).

When, despite trying everything listed, pain is always present during running (grade 2 and 3 injuries), the only real hope of a cure is to acquire an adequate custom-built arch support (orthotic) to wear when running. When the injury advances to this stage, it indicates that the runner's genetic structure will never cope by itself with the amount of training the mind desires. And the only way to compensate for these genetic limitations is to wear an orthotic. But remember that only when the orthotic is correctly adjusted will it cure the injury. If the orthotic fails to cure the injury, it is likely that it has not been made sufficiently well to provide the precise degree of motor control required to cure the injury. Usually, all that is required is for further minor corrections to be made to the orthotic. However, if the injury fails to respond to conventional treatment, the possibility that it is the soleus syndrome of Michael and Holder (1985) should be considered, and a surgical opinion should be sought.

If the level of a grade 4 injury is reached, the stage of stress fracture, the treatment is physical rest and mental exercise in the form of deciding what caused the injury. Whether a first stress fracture is an indication to buy an orthotic depends largely on the major factor causing the injury. If the major error has been in the training methods, then these should be corrected first. If, in spite of careful attention to all the factors listed, the injury returns, then an orthotic is likely to be the only long-term solution to the injury. The most frustrating aspect of a stress fracture is the enforced layoff from exercise that it entails. Exercise that the athlete is allowed to do while recovering from a stress fracture is described subsequently.

Stress Fractures

Unlike the common bone fractures occurring in contact sports, such as rugby, in which a single external blow causes the bone to fracture, the runner's bone may fracture as a result of repeated minor trauma accumulating over weeks or months. It is a concept that runners usually find difficult to accept. They want to know, how can something as strong as bone fracture so easily? We do not know, but it happens quite frequently.

Probably the first doctor to recognize this injury was Breithaupt (1855), a German military doctor. As these fractures occurred most commonly in new army recruits recently introduced to marching, they became known as march fractures, a name that persists to this day. It is of great interest that only three animals, all athletes, develop these injuries—humans, racehorses, and greyhounds.

The symptoms produced by a stress fracture are simple and unmistakable—there is rapid onset of pain, well localized to any of a number of the bones, usually of the lower limb. (Stress fractures of the vertebrae, ribs, and upper arms have been described, but these are uncommon in runners and occur mainly in sports in which the upper body is stressed.) In a Finnish study of 142 stress fractures in athletes (Orava et al. 1978), 55% occurred in the tibia, 23% in the metatarsals (toe bones), 14% in the fibula (small calf bone), 6% in the femur (thigh bone), 1% in the ankle bones (navicular), and 1% in the groin (pubic arch) bone (figure 14.22). The pain is

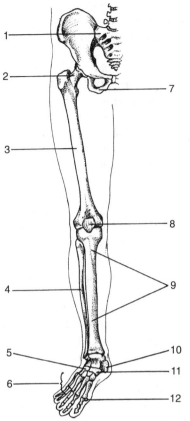

1	Sacrum 0.1%	7	Pubic arch 2%
2	Femoral neck 4%	8	Patella
3	Femoral shaft 2%	9	Tibia 55%
4	Fibula 14%	10	Calcaneum
5	Cuboid bone	11	Navicular
6	Metatarsals 23%	12	Sesamoid bone

Figure 14.22 Anatomical distribution of stress fractures in runners.

Adapted from Orava et al. (1978, p 22). © Elsevier Science.

usually bearable when the athlete is at rest or when walking, but as soon as any running is attempted, it becomes unbearable, making running impossible.

The diagnosis of stress fracture is simple. First, the injury is usually of quite sudden onset, and there is no history of external trauma. Warning symptoms are usually mild—runners get little notice of the tragedy about to befall them. Then, they are suddenly no longer able to run. Second, they will find that hopping on the injured leg (the hop test) is painful (Matheson et al. 1987). In those with fractures of the pelvis, standing on one leg (the standing test) is very painful and may be impossible (Noakes, Smith, et al. 1985). Third, the diagnosis may be confirmed if tenderness is felt, localized to the bone. Even gentle pressure on the injured bone will illicit exquisite, nauseating pain. For absolute diagnostic certainty, however, a fourth feature is required: the injury heals itself completely within two to three months of complete rest, depending on its site. Fractures of the foot bones usually heal within six weeks, with an increased healing time as one moves up the bones of the leg. Thus, the tibia and femur may require 8 to 12 weeks to heal and the pelvis up to three to four months, if not longer (Noakes, Smith, et al. 1985).

Unfortunately, few runners will accept a two-month rest period without some visible evidence that the diagnosis is correct. We usually have to resort to X rays and bone scans, both of which are not without their own drawbacks. In quite a high percentage of cases (up to 57%; Matheson et al. 1987), X rays will

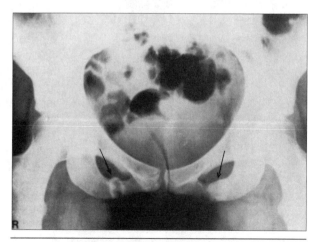

Figure 14.23 A pelvic X-ray showing a healing stress fracture on the left (arrowed) and a bone traction injury on the right (arrowed).

fail to reveal the presence of a stress fracture if they are taken earlier than three weeks after the initial injury. In effect, the fracture is so small that it cannot be seen. Only when new bone is being formed, which is more dense than the old bone it replaces, does the fracture show as a line on the X ray (figure 14.23).

Convention is that the runner with a stress fracture that fails to show up on the first X ray is asked to come back three weeks later for a second X ray. In fact, this is not necessary, because that X ray has already revealed all that we need to know— that the pain is not due to something like a bone infection or another bone abnormality (such as a bone cancer) that is unrelated to running and that requires more energetic medical attention than stress fractures. If the X ray shows nothing, but the pain is localized to the bone and the runner is unable to run, the injury is almost certainly a stress fracture.

A newer technique to detect stress fractures is bone scanning. This involves the injection of a radioactive material into the bloodstream. At least in theory, this radioactive material is taken up by bone cells that are extremely active. These active cells then show as an area of increased radioactivity, a hotspot, when photographed through a special camera (figure 14.24), and they indicate areas of active bone resorption and bone remodeling. It is found that virtually all runners who have the clinical features of a stress fracture but who have normal X rays usually have these hotspots, indicating that they do indeed have stress fractures that for some or other reason, probably because they are too small, could not be identified on X ray. However, even this technique may not reveal every stress fracture. Furthermore, for each symptomatic fracture that the bone scan identifies in any person, another two sites of increased uptake of radioactivity are present somewhere else in the athlete's skeleton (Matheson et al. 1987). These sites are asymptomatic: they do not cause the athlete noticeable discomfort. Matheson et al. (1987) have coined the term *bone strain* to identify areas of active bone remodeling that can be identified by bone scanning. When the area of remodeling is small, the athlete may complain only of bone strain; when the area is large, a stress fracture may develop.

My view is that bone scanning for these injuries is really only necessary if the injury fails to heal within 6 to 12 weeks (longer for the larger bones, such as the femur, tibia, and pelvis; shorter for the smaller bones, such as the fibula, metatarsals, and small ankle bones) or if it recurs within a few weeks of the runner starting to run again.

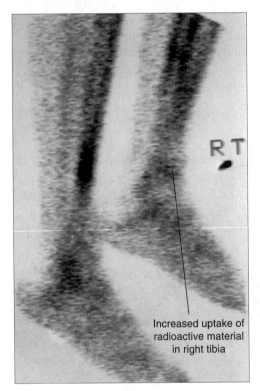

Increased uptake of radioactive material in right tibia

Figure 14.24 A bone scan showing a stress fracture with a well-localized increase in radioactive material in the right tibia.

Image provided courtesy of A. Fatar, MD, in the department of radionuclear medicine at Groote Schuur Hospital in Cape Town, South Africa.

Figure 14.25
A CT scan showing a fracture in the cortex of the left navicular bone.

Image provided courtesy of Dr. Richard de Villiers.

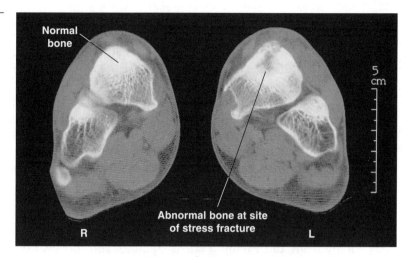

Failure of the injury to heal completely with the appropriate period of rest is not a usual feature of a conventional stress fracture. Rather, it suggests that something else, unrelated to running, is going on in that bone that would indicate the need for a thorough evaluation by an orthopedic surgeon.

Two other specialized investigations can be used to identify stress fractures. Computerized tomography (CT) produces a far more detailed picture of the fine architecture of bone (figure 14.25) and is able to identify the smallest disruptions in that architecture, identifying stress fractures that may be invisible to most other diagnostic techniques. But this technique is seldom necessary except in the diagnosis of the fractures of the small bones of the feet—for example, of the navicular bones (Khan et al. 1992; Kiss et al. 1993).

Magnetic resonance imaging (MRI) is extremely useful in detecting injuries of the soft tissues (muscle ligaments and tendons) and shows specific changes in the bone lining, the periosteum, diagnostic of stress fractures (Batt et al. 1998). As this technique does not expose the patient to radioisotopes, it may be valuable in certain patients. However, it is more expensive than bone scanning.

Causes

The exact reason why stress fractures occur is not known. However, the reason must be that the bone fracture is at the site at which there is an abnormal concentration of forces. Thus, two factors are involved. First, there must be an abnormal concentration of stress at one particular site in the bone and, second, the bone must be insufficiently strong to resist those forces, probably because of the osteoclonal excavation described in the previous section.

At present we do not know the exact biomechanical reasons for the accumulation of these forces at specific sites in the different fractures, nor why the bones of some, but not all, runners are insufficiently strong to resist those forces. However, we do know that there are a number of risk factors for this injury, which will ultimately give us the clues to understanding these injuries. Following are the seven most important factors associated with stress fractures (Bennell et al. 1999):

1. **Female sex.** Women are more prone to stress fractures than are men (Hulkko and Orava 1987; Kannus et al. 1987). This has become especially apparent now that women have been accepted to the American Military Academies and have

followed the same training programs as the men (Protzman 1979; Scully and Besterman 1982; Brudvig et al. 1983). The frequency of stress fractures in these women is up to 12 times higher than that in the men in the same programs. Recently, it has been suggested that it is the amenorrheic women who are especially at risk of developing stress fractures (Marcus et al. 1985).

2. **Menstrual abnormalities or a low-calcium diet.** The very strong relationship between menstrual abnormalities and stress fractures (Bennell et al. 1999) was explained in the previous section. Our studies (Myburgh 1989; Myburgh et al. 1990) found that stress fractures were 12 times more frequent in people with low dietary calcium intakes. In these studies, a low calcium intake was by far the best predictor of risk of stress fracture. Similarly, Bennell et al. (1995) found that female athletes with a stress fracture were more likely to diet and to restrict their food intakes. Furthermore, women with a past history of oligomenorrhea—irregular periods, fewer than six per year (chapter 15)—were six times more likely to develop a stress fracture, and those who were careful about their weight were at eight times greater risk. They concluded that the prevention and treatment of stress fractures in female athletes should include a thorough assessment of menstrual characteristics and dietary patterns.

3. **Shoes.** Excessively hard running shoes (in particular, training spikes) may be a factor explaining this injury, especially in track athletes. However, my clinical impression is that shoes play less of a role in this injury than do major errors in training methods and other factors listed here. There is no convincing evidence that shoes or even orthotics alter the risk of stress fractures (Bennell et al. 1999). However, neoprene (Schwellnus et al. 1990) but not viscoelastic (Gardner et al. 1988) insoles reduced the incidence of stress fractures in military recruits. Neoprene insoles also reduced the overall incidence of all overuse injuries.

4. **Training errors.** The traditional explanation based largely on clinical observation is that stress fractures typically occur in novice runners or in competitive runners who suddenly increase their training load, run one or more very long races, or return too quickly to heavy training. It is perhaps easy to understand why novice runners should be at risk since hard training during the early period of bone weakening from osteoclonal excavation is more likely to cause a fracture. In the beginner's training program that we developed (see chapter 5), most of the stress fractures that occurred happened in the period between 8 to 12 weeks after the commencement of training, just as the runners were getting sufficiently fit to run more than 10 km regularly. Their increased levels of muscle and heart fitness therefore occurred at just the wrong time, and their bones were not yet sufficiently strong to cope with the added stress of suddenly running much longer distances. Another adverse feature of suddenly increasing your training distance is that it causes accumulated muscular fatigue that may then reduce the muscles' ability to absorb shock. When the muscles are tired and unable to absorb shock, that function is passed over to the bones, which must therefore become more likely to fracture.

With regard to more conditioned athletes, two studies suggest a link between increased risk of stress fractures in women, but not in men, who ran higher mileages in training (Brunet et al. 1990), and in female ballet dancers who trained for more than five hours per day (Kadel et al. 1992). Hence, training volume may indeed be an independent risk factor for stress fractures (Bennell et al. 1995), as suggested by the clinical experience.

5. **Genetic factors.** Three principal genetic factors are associated with stress fractures (Bennell et al. 1999): the high-arched foot (Giladi et al. 1985; Simkin et al. 1989), which fails to absorb shock adequately and is associated with fractures of the femur and metatarsals (Matheson et al. 1987); the pronating low-arched foot, which causes abnormal biomechanical function in the lower limb, part of which may actually be a shearing motion in the tarsal bones, the tibia, and the fibula, predisposing those bones to fracture (Matheson et al. 1987); and leg-length inequalities (Friberg 1982). Friberg (1982) found that 87% of army recruits with stress fractures had leg-length inequalities. A total of 73% of fractures of the femur, tibia, and metatarsals occurred on the side of the long leg, whereas 60% of fibular stress fractures occurred on the side of the short leg. Conversely, there is no convincing evidence that the Q angle is related to stress fracture risk.

   Thus, if you have a stress fracture, you should check your old shoes to determine whether they are too hard or whether they indicate that you pronate to a high degree (figures 14.6 and 14.9). To determine whether there is a leg-length inequality, it is normally necessary to be examined by a health care professional, but the side and site of the stress fracture may suggest which leg is short. The leg-length discrepancy should be corrected with an appropriate in-shoe orthotic.

6. **Low bone density.** Myburgh et al. (1990) found that stress fractures occur in athletes who have reduced bone density, most likely as a result of an inadequate calcium intake (in men) or of menstrual dysfunction (in women), both of which are probably related to a significant eating disorder. However, not all studies report this relationship (Bennell et al. 1995; Bennell et al. 1999), suggesting that low bone density is not as important a risk factor as perhaps abnormal eating and menstrual patterns.

7. **Race.** People of African descent are apparently less prone to stress fractures than are Caucasians (Blickenstaff and Morris 1966; Brudvig et al. 1983).

Specific Treatment

The usual treatment for most stress fractures is 6 to 18 weeks of rest, depending on the site of the fracture. Because these fractures seldom become unstable and are therefore not liable to go out of alignment, they do not need to be placed in plaster. In fact, complete immobilization of stress fractures in plaster of Paris may reduce the speed with which they heal. Immobilized muscles weaken considerably, and the bone may become demineralized. The latter two effects will, of course, be corrected once the athlete starts exercising again, but the point is that they are unnecessary complications.

Instead of plaster of Paris, interest has been focused on using a removable pneumatic leg brace (Aircast) that can be worn during the day and removed at night or for bathing. Athletes with tibial stress fractures treated with a pneumatic leg brace returned to full, unrestricted activity within three weeks, whereas athletes treated in the conventional manner, without bracing, only returned to full sporting activity after 13 weeks (Swenson et al. 1997).

For runners who simply will not rest, it is possible to continue exercising in water in a specially designed pool using a flotation device. Alternatively, you can run in shallow water without the use of a flotation device (Town and Bradley 1991). I first saw such a pool in Eugene, Oregon, in the practice of Dick Brown, former coach of Alberto Salazar and Mary Decker-Slaney. Brown was enthusiastic about his observation that this activity appeared to increase the rate of healing of fractures of the lower limb. Alternatively, runners with fractures of the tibia or fibula may achieve complete relief from their symptoms and may be able to continue their activities simply by wearing the same pneumatic leg brace (Dickson and Kichline 1987) that has been shown to increase the rate of healing of tibial stress fractures substantially.

Another United States Olympian, marathoner Ed Eyestone, and his colleagues (Eyestone et al. 1993) found that six weeks of running in water while using a flotation device maintained the $\dot{V}O_2$max and 2-mile (3.2-km) racing performance of trained athletes (who were not being treated for stress fractures) just as effectively as did an equivalent training program of the same intensity and frequency with cycling or running on dry land.

There are two exceptions to the general rule that stress fractures do not need to be immobilized if rapid healing is not a priority. First, a stress fracture of the neck of the femur is an extremely serious injury and requires the urgent attention of an orthopedic surgeon, as the injury can have very serious consequences. Second, there is clear evidence that navicular stress fractures heal more rapidly if immobilized and may fail to unite properly if not treated in a plaster cast as soon as the diagnosis is made (Khan et al. 1992).

The real challenge, however, for the runner recovering from this injury is, first, to keep physically active to avoid the runner's withdrawal symptoms and, second, to find out why the injury happened in the first place, and in so doing, to prevent being thwarted again.

Muscle Injuries

Muscle injuries in runners fall into four categories: delayed onset muscle soreness (DOMS), acute (sudden) muscle tears, chronic (insidious) muscle tears, and muscle cramps (including side cramps).

Delayed Onset Muscle Soreness

DOMS (Armstrong 1984; Friden 1984) is that feeling of muscle discomfort that comes on 24 to 48 hours after unaccustomed or particularly severe exercise, especially if it involves eccentric muscle contractions (Clarkson et al. 1992). It is not due, as many believe, to an accumulation in the stiff muscles of lactate (lactic acid) because the lactate concentration in muscles exhibiting delayed muscle soreness is not elevated. The misconceptions surrounding lactate are discussed in chapter 3. The likely cause of this DOMS is damage of the muscle cells, in particular the connective (supporting) tissue and the contractile proteins (Clarkson and Sayers 1999; Morgan and Allen 1999).

Recent evidence suggests that there are at least three phases to the muscle damage that occurs with exercise (MacIntyre et al. 1995). The first phase begins within hours of unaccustomed exercise in trained athletes and is associated with the leakage of moderate amounts of muscle enzymes into the bloodstream; peak enzyme leakage occurs at the time of peak muscle soreness (that is, 24 to 48 hours after exercise; Noakes 1987a; Noakes, Kotzenberg, et al. 1983a; Strachan et al. 1984).

The characteristic feature of DOMS is that pain develops when the muscle is forcefully stretched and becomes worse after bouts of eccentric exercise. This led to the early belief that "the pains are located in the intramuscular connective tissues, as they are most apt to develop after exercises that have extended the muscles" (Asmussen 1956, p. 113).

William Abraham (1979) was the next to advance this concept. He showed that the excretion in the urine of connective tissue breakdown products is increased in people with delayed muscle soreness and that peak urinary excretion coincides with the time when the subjects report the greatest muscle soreness. Indeed, it is now generally accepted that this soreness, better termed stiffness, is due to damage to the connective tissue in the muscle (D.A. Jones et al. 1987).

The second phase of muscle damage occurs approximately four to six days after unaccustomed eccentric exercise in untrained athletes (D.A. Jones et al. 1986; Newham et al. 1986). It is associated with much higher rates of enzyme leakage into the blood, infiltration of muscle by inflammatory cells (Round et al. 1987), and degeneration of muscle cells, with the latter peaking 10 to 12 days after exercise (D.A. Jones et al. 1986; O'Reilly et al. 1987). Muscle glycogen content is also reduced in the damaged muscle (O'Reilly et al. 1987). Replacement of damaged muscle cells is already well advanced 20 days after exercise. This represents the final, or regenerative, phase in muscle injury.

Armstrong (1984) has postulated that repeated powerful muscle contractions, especially those occurring during eccentric contractions, cause muscle cell damage, allowing calcium to flood into the cells, leading to cell death that peaks 48 hours after exercise. Initiation of an inflammatory response stimulates nerve endings in the damaged tissue, causing the typical pain of delayed muscle soreness. The site of maximal damage appears to be the Z-band of the sarcomere, the point at which the thick filaments are anchored (see chapter 1). These Z-bands are therefore the intrasarcomeric structures that are subjected to the greatest strain during eccentric muscle contractions, particularly during downhill running (Friden, Seger, et al. 1983; Friden 1984; Friden et al. 1984). This suggests that the initial damage results from mechanical trauma. In addition, damage may be more pronounced in ST, Type II fiber (Snyder et al. 1984).

Z-band disruption with release of protein breakdown products may then lead to fluid accumulation and swelling of the muscles (Bobbert et al. 1986), which may, in turn, cause the delayed muscle soreness. Protein degradation may also be due to the activation of special intracellular enzymes, the lysozymes (Friden 1984; Salminen et al. 1985). Friden et al. (1986) have shown that intramuscular pressure is greater during and after eccentric exercise than after concentric exercise, whereas Bobbert et al. (1986) found that the volume of legs with muscle soreness was increased. These studies suggest that an elevated intramuscular pressure resulting from muscle swelling may be an important factor in DOMS (Friden, Sfakianos, et al. 1988b).

An alternative postulate is that oxygen-centered free radicals, which are released into tissues that are actively utilizing oxygen, as do muscles during exercise, may explain this damage (Davies, Quintanilha, et al. 1982; Maughan et al. 1989). These free radicals are believed to attack lipids, particularly in cell membranes, damaging them in a peroxidation reaction. It is postulated that vitamin E deficiency exacerbates this process, but there is no evidence that this damage can be prevented by an excessive vitamin E intake (Jackson 1987). That the blood levels of serum lipid peroxides rise after eccentric exercise and follow the same time course as do changes in serum enzyme activities has recently been shown (Donnelly et al. 1987).

Finally, another study found an increase in the concentration of inorganic phosphate in muscles with delayed soreness (Aldridge et al. 1986), owing possibly to accumulation of phosphate at the sites of damage.

The important practical points to remember about delayed muscle soreness are that this soreness indicates that the muscle has been overstressed; that persistent muscle soreness is a very strong indicator of overtraining; and that it takes considerable time for the muscle to recover fully from this injury. Refer also to the "Race Recovery" and "After Your Race" sections in chapters 9, 10, and 11. In another study, Crenshaw et al. (1993) found that frank disruption and death of some muscle cells occurred in athletes who complain of pronounced muscle soreness after marathon and ultramarathon races.

The only known ways to reduce the degree of muscle soreness and therefore muscle damage during prolonged exercise are the following:

- Distance training.
- Downhill training or training with eccentric exercise (Schwane and Armstrong 1983; Friden, Sjostrom, et al. 1983; Byrnes et al. 1985; Schwane et al. 1987). It is the eccentric contractions that occur during downhill running that cause the most muscle damage. The study of Byrnes et al. (1985) showed that a single bout of downhill running offered protection from muscle damage during a similar bout of exercise for up to six weeks. This effect may be due either to an increase in the number of sarcomeres or, more likely, to an increase in Z-band strength (Friden 1984; see chapter 9) or reduced lysozomal activation (Salminen et al. 1985).
- Weight training to increase the strength of the quadriceps muscle (see Fordyce's ninth point of ultramarathon training in chapter 6).
- Using anti-inflammatory medications. Anti-inflammatory agents used acutely (during or within hours of exercise) appear to have little effect on delayed muscle soreness (Editorial 1987; Donnelley et al. 1988; 1990). However, when used daily for 15 days before muscle-damaging exercise, preadministration of a popular anti-inflammatory drug significantly reduced muscle damage, measured both histologically and by changes in blood creatine kinase concentrations and symptoms of DOMS (O'Grady et al. 2000). However, this study raises the disturbing possibility that the use of these agents for up to two weeks before prolonged exercise, such as marathon or ultramarathon races, might speed up recovery. This finding is disturbing because many marathon and ultramarathon runners, especially in South Africa, already consume potentially dangerous amounts of these drugs during competition. This finding might encourage even greater use. The long-term consequences of such use are not yet known. Acute complications that can occur during these races include acute kidney failure (see chapter 15), the risk of which may be increased by the unrestrained use of these anti-inflammatory drugs.
- Massage and ultrasound. There is no evidence that these therapies speed up recovery from DOMS (Tiidus 1999).

Acute Muscle Tears

This is the classic muscle injury of the explosive sports, such as sprinting, squash, soccer, and tennis. The athlete is suddenly overcome by agonizingly severe pain in the affected muscle; there is immediate loss of function. The muscle is in spasm, is extremely tender, and swells over the next few hours. The skin overlying the injury may show bruising.

Acute muscle tears are believed to result from a combination of muscle strength imbalance between opposing muscle groups (Burkett 1970), especially reduced eccentric hamstring muscle strength (Jönhagen et al. 1994); inflexibility of the affected muscles; inadequate warm-up (Sutton 1984); and muscle fatigue (Worrell 1994). The initial thinking was that the sprinter's hamstring tear is caused by an activity (very fast running) that overdevelops the front thigh muscles (quadriceps) at the expense of the hamstrings, which become correspondingly weaker. When this strength imbalance reaches a critical value, the quadriceps overpowers the hamstring, causing a severe muscle tear (Burkett 1970).

The newer theory is that the hamstring tears during the eccentric phase of its contraction (that is, as it contracts powerfully but lengthens during the swing phase of the running cycle, as the hamstring contracts to slow the forward movement of the foot and lower limb, peaking immediately before foot strike; positions A through I for the right leg in figure 14.4).

The reason the tear is more likely to occur during the eccentric phase of the muscle contraction is that the intramuscular forces are greatest during eccentric contractions, and fewer muscle fibers are active. Hence, individual muscle fibers are subjected to greater forces during eccentric than during concentric contractions.

Thus, immediately before heel strike, the forward movement of the limb is under the joint control of the quadriceps muscle contracting concentrically and the hamstring muscle contracting eccentrically. The modified theory is that a hamstring tear can result if the concentric strength of the quadriceps muscles is too great or the eccentric strength of the hamstring muscles is too weak, or a combination of both. It is further postulated that other muscles prone to acute tearing show the same relationship; that is, they are too weak in their eccentric contractions to cope with the overstrong concentric contractions of their antagonist muscles.

Imaging and Initial Treatment

The site of the muscle tear can now be identified with computed tomography (Garrett et al. 1989; Speer et al. 1993) or magnetic resonance imaging, both of which show that inflammation and edema, rather than bleeding, are the major components of the injury. Follow-up investigations show evidence of muscle atrophy, fibrosis, and calcium deposition (Speer et al. 1993).

The immediate treatment of the acute muscle tear is to apply ice to the tender area without delay, to rest and elevate the injured limb, and to apply a firm compression bandage over the site of the tear as soon as the initial ice application is completed. Athletes below 18 years of age should be seen by an orthopedic surgeon to check that they have not pulled off the pelvic epiphysis, to which the hamstring muscles are attached. Next, and most important, comes specific treatment and early rehabilitation.

Specific Treatment and Rehabilitation

Until relatively recently, a serious acute muscle tear was considered to be such a severe injury that rest for six to eight weeks was the only treatment prescribed. In the early 1970s, a group of Sydney doctors under the leadership of Anthony Millar, head of the Institute of Sports Medicine, developed a treatment regime that clearly showed that such a conservative approach was not necessary. They found that an intensive regime involving vigorous treatment of the injured muscle, together with muscle stretching and strengthening for as many as six half-hour sessions a day, beginning 48 hours after injury, could return most athletes with serious acute muscle injuries to competitive sport within 10 to 14 days (Millar 1975; 1976). Since then, this accelerated rehabilitation program has become the international standard.

The critical issue in acute muscle injuries, particularly those of the hamstring, is to prevent their recurrence. This can only be achieved if the muscle imbalance is corrected by increasing the eccentric strength of the hamstrings without overdeveloping the concentric strength of the quadriceps. Preferably, specific eccentric muscle strengthening exercise should be performed on an isokinetic exercise machine, under expert supervision. Alternatively, to increase eccentric hamstring muscle strength, the athlete should do the following exercise, either standing or lying prone on a couch. The exercise involves kicking the leg into rapid knee extension and stopping the movement suddenly 20 to 30° before full knee extension, allowing the hamstring to contract concentrically thereafter. The patient performs three sets of 15 repetitions every second day, starting without weights and gradually increasing in increments of 0.5 kg. Powerful sprinters may reach a maximum weight of 5 kg after about eight weeks of training. The strengthening effects of this training method can be measured only with isokinetic dynamometers, which analyze both eccentric and concentric muscle function.

Hamstring stretching (figure 14.11, A, I, and J, but not M and N) should be performed religiously, also under supervision. There must be a gradual return to running, and no fast sprinting may be undertaken before the eccentric strength of the injured hamstring equals that of the uninjured leg; when activity does not cause pain; after an adequate warm-up; and following a period of pain-free running at a slightly slower speed. When these procedures are followed, the incidence of hamstring injuries in people participating in explosive sports is reduced substantially (Heiser et al. 1984).

More recently, hyperbaric oxygen therapy has been developed for use in the management of acute muscle injuries. An early study of muscle stretch injury in rabbits found evidence of earlier tissue healing and a more rapid recovery of muscle strength in rabbits exposed to five 60-minute sessions of hyperbaric oxygen therapy beginning 24 hours after injury (Best et al. 1998). This finding should encourage similar studies in human athletes.

Chronic Muscle Tears

Chronic muscle tears (or muscle knots) are probably the most common injuries seen in elite long-distance runners. The importance of chronic muscle tears is that they are probably the third most common injury among all groups of runners (Pinshaw et al. 1983) and are especially common among the elite runners; they are usually misdiagnosed; they can be very debilitating; and they will respond only to one specific form of treatment. Remarkably, this group of injuries is seldom adequately described in English-language textbooks of sports medicine. One early

German textbook (Krejci and Koch 1979) included an adequate description of this injury.

The injury is usually reasonably easy to recognize. The characteristic features are that the pain starts gradually, in contrast to the acute muscle tear, in which the onset of pain is sudden. At first, the pain comes on after exercise. When the pain starts to occur during exercise, it is possible at first to run through it. But the pain grows progressively worse until it becomes sufficiently severe to interfere with training, so that speed work, in particular, becomes impossible. The pain is almost always localized to a large muscle group—either the buttock, groin, hamstring, or calf muscles. The pain is deep-seated and can be very severe but passes off rapidly with rest. Typically, there are other features suggesting that the damaged muscle has gone into protective spasm (for example, the inability to push off properly with the toes).

In contrast to bone or tendon injuries, both of which improve if sufficient rest is allowed, chronic muscle tears never improve unless the correct treatment is prescribed. As a result, the patient can rest for months or even years without any improvement. Indeed, I have seen one runner who struggled for five years with a chronic muscle injury, having given up all hope that he could ever be cured.

To confirm that the injury is indeed a chronic muscle tear, all the runner or, preferably, a physiotherapist need do is to press firmly with two fingers into the affected muscle in the area in which the pain is felt. If it is possible to find a tender hard "knot" in the muscle, the injury is definitely a chronic muscle tear. I cannot emphasize sufficiently just how sore these knots are—they are excruciating. Finally, because the injury occurs in muscle, it will not show on X ray.

Thus, attempting to diagnose this injury with X rays is futile. But magnetic resonance imaging may well show the abnormality. Nevertheless, such sophisticated diagnostic techniques are unnecessary as the diagnosis can be made with certainty on the basis of the history and the typical finding of one or more painful muscle knots in the affected muscle.

The mechanism of injury in chronic muscle tears is currently unknown but is probably related to the same mechanism causing acute muscle injuries: namely, weakness of the affected muscles during eccentric contraction. I am impressed by the fact that the person who has recurrent chronic muscle tears will tend to tear the same muscles at the same site every time, usually when starting to do either more speed work or more distance training. I developed five such sites during my running career. Similarly, Bruce Fordyce suffered from chronic tears of his calf muscles virtually every March, as he began his intensive Comrades Marathon preparation. In fact, he credits his victory in the 1982 Comrades Marathon to the treatment he received for a chronic calf muscle tear (in particular, cross-frictions that made him scream; Cameron Dow 2001).

I conclude that chronic muscle tears occur in the various muscles at specific sites that, for reasons unknown, develop eccentric muscle weakness. This weakness is exposed during faster running. When the eccentric loading exceeds the muscle's eccentric strength, a small section of the muscle is strained and develops an inflammatory response, as also seen in acute muscle injuries. This initial tear is too small to cause discomfort. However, once the initial tear has occurred, a cycle of repair and reinjury and reinflammation develops that leads ultimately to the large tender knot, probably comprising muscle fibers surrounded by inflammatory scar tissue as found in experimental muscle injuries (Nikolaou et al. 1987).

Stretching and Strengthening Exercises

While neither stretching nor strengthening exercises will cure a chronic muscle tear, appropriate stretching (figure 14.10) and strengthening (figure 14.11) exercises for the specific injured muscle may prevent recurrences of the injury. In particular, eccentric strengthening exercises are especially important in muscle injuries.

Specific Treatment

Conventional treatment, including drugs and cortisone injections, is a waste of time in this injury. The only treatment that works is a physiotherapeutic maneuver known as cross-frictions, as first popularized by Cyriax (1978). A better term would be *crucifixions,* because nothing, not even the runner's toughest race ever, is as painful as cross-frictions applied, however gently, to a chronic muscle tear.

And therein lies the key to the treatment of these injuries. A chronic muscle tear will only resolve if the cross-frictions are applied to the injury site (in this case, the tender knot in the muscle) and applied with the correct pressure. In earlier editions of this book, I advocated that these cross-frictions could only be effective if they reduced you to tears and were applied by a physiotherapist or masseur who had big hands, the forearms of a gorilla, and unbridled sadism. However, my physiotherapy colleagues now inform me that this advice is incorrect. Apparently, there is no longer a need for strong arms and vicious intent. Rather, it now seems that such sadism is neither necessary nor ideal. Often gentler cross-frictions may be more effective, especially in older athletes or in injuries that have been present for more than a few months.

Most chronic muscle tears respond rapidly to a few sessions of cross-frictions. The treatment is correct if the pain while running becomes gradually less so that progressively greater distances can be covered. Most injuries will require between 5 and 10 sessions of therapy, each lasting 5 to 10 minutes, after which most runners should be able to run entirely free of pain. Injuries that have lasted for six months or more may require a longer period of treatment. I have mentioned that these injuries tend to recur. To prevent recurrence, runners should be especially fastidious about stretching the muscles that tend to be injured, especially before any fast running, in particular before early morning races. Furthermore, it is essential that at the first sign of reinjury, you go immediately for more massage. A little treatment early on in these injuries saves a great deal of agony later.

Muscle Cramps

Muscle cramps are defined as spasmodic, painful, involuntary contractions of muscles. Although muscle cramping is an important feature of some serious muscle disorders, the cramps experienced by runners are, despite the inconvenience and discomfort they cause, usually of little medical consequence and tend to occur either at night (nocturnal cramps) or during unusually prolonged exercise (exertional cramps).

It is clear that the propensity for cramping differs: some are almost never affected; others will always develop muscle cramps if they run far enough. One runner informed me that in 10 attempts, he had never been able to run more than the first 50 km of a 90-km race because of severe cramping that always developed as soon as he went further than 50 km. His cramping was so severe that he would fall to the ground, writhing in agony as all the muscles in his body went into seizure.

His propensity for cramping was not influenced by how much he trained or what he ate or drank before or during the race. I conclude that he has a minor muscle or nerve abnormality that only becomes apparent during prolonged exercise.

Exertional cramps tend to occur in people who run farther or faster than the distance or speed to which they are accustomed. Other identified risk factors for muscle cramping include older age, a longer history of running, higher body mass index, shorter daily stretching time, irregular stretching habits, and a family history of cramping (Schwellnus 1999).

Thus, the athlete whose longest regular training run is 30 km is likely to develop muscle cramps during the last few kilometers of a 42-km standard marathon, particularly if he is an irregular stretcher and has a family history of cramping. There is no evidence of a gross disturbance in blood electrolyte levels in runners with cramps (Maughan 1986; Schwellnus 1999) nor of the theory that ingesting electrolytes (such as sodium chloride, magnesium, or zinc) will prevent cramps from developing. Dehydration also seems an unlikely candidate; runners who develop cramps during exercise are no more likely to be dehydrated than are runners who do not develop cramps during the same race. Thus, an excessive fluid intake is not likely to be of value. Indeed, hyponatremia induced by an excessive fluid intake can lead to cramping (see chapter 4).

The first factor that appears to reduce the risk of cramping is simply more training, especially long-distance runs in those who run marathon and longer races. Attention to adequate fluid and carbohydrate replacement before and during exercise, and not running too fast too early in the race, may also be of value.

Another factor that may be important is adequate stretching before and during prolonged exercise. The director of the University of Cape Town Sports Medicine Program, Martin Schwellnus (1999), has produced convincing evidence that muscle cramps result from alterations in the sensitivity of the reflexes that originate from the muscle and tendon tension receptors. It is postulated that during prolonged exercise the inverse stretch reflex, the one that inhibits excessive muscle contraction, becomes inactive due to reduced sensory input coming from the type Ib Golgi tendon organs, whereas stimulatory impulses from the alpha motor neurons in the spinal cord to the type Ia and II muscle spindles is increased (figure 14.26). Stimulation of the muscle spindles increases the likelihood that the muscles will contract. It is argued that these changes occur especially in muscles that contract in a shortened position for prolonged periods of time. Typical examples are the diaphragm muscle in all activities (see description of the stitch below), the hamstrings and the quadriceps muscles in running and cycling and also the calf muscles in swimming or when sleeping at night. Only muscles that undergo lengthening (stretching) frequently during prolonged exercise may be prevented from cramping. For it is the lengthening (stretching) of the muscle that activates the protective stretch reflex, originating from the Golgi tendons.

Without regular activation of this protective reflex, the muscle can go into spasm. The Schwellnus theory predicts that cramps should be prevented if the activity of the inverse stretch reflex is maintained during prolonged exercise. This is done by regularly stretching the tendons of the affected muscles. This stretching reactivates the dormant stretch reflex.

However, it is clear that those athletes who suffer severe muscle cramping during prolonged exercise are not likely to be helped by any advice that we currently have. Presumably, those athletes have an uncontrollable increase in muscle spindle

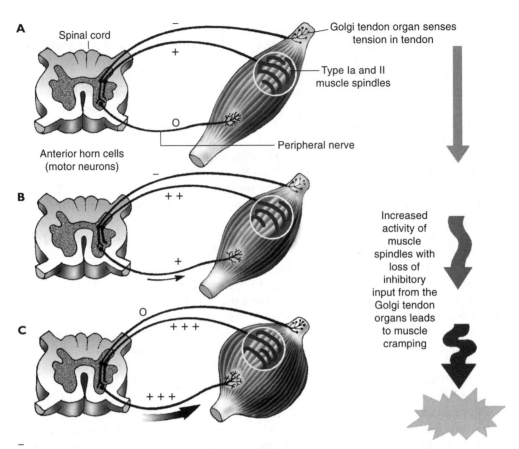

Figure 14.26   The Schwellnus theory of how muscle cramps occur. According to this theory, muscle cramps occur when fatigue leads to abnormalities in the mechanisms that control muscle contraction. Muscle spindles react to stretch by producing afferent signals that trigger motor neurons (anterior horn cells) that cause the muscle to contract; Golgi tendon organs inhibit contraction in response to increased muscle tension. A simplified view of the anatomy is seen in A. During a normal contraction (B), excitatory and inhibitory signals are in balance. In a fatigued muscle (C), spindle activity increases and Golgi tendon organ activity decreases, resulting in increased muscle membrane excitability that can lead to a cramp. Contraction of the muscle in its shortest position (inner range) also inhibits Golgi afferent activity.

Schwellnus (1999, p. 113). © McGraw-Hill Inc. Adapted with permission of McGraw-Hill Inc.

activity, leading to uncontrollable cramping. Besides the Comrades Marathon runner mentioned earlier, I have since seen another Comrades runner, who, despite following all our best advice, was never able to run more than 70 km in that race before he too collapsed on the side of the road with intensive and sustained whole-body muscle cramping that prevented him from standing, let alone walking or running.

Clearly, he has an inbuilt defect, perhaps in the design of his muscle spindles, that is too minor to cause any problems during everyday activities, including running, but that prevents the muscles from contracting normally in a sustained burst for more than a few hours. Because the condition is so rare and is not life-threatening, it may be many years before it attracts sufficient research attention and before the causative abnormality is identified.

The cause of nocturnal cramps is unknown but is probably no different from that producing exertional cramps. Stretching the affected muscles before going to bed each night has been found to prevent this form of cramp completely, further suggesting the accuracy of the Schwellnus theory. Additional support for this theory comes from the condition known as the stitch (see also chapter 5).

In contrast, quinine, which is widely prescribed for the treatment of nocturnal cramps, seems to have no significant effect on this condition (Sidorov 1993) and should therefore not be prescribed, particularly as this drug does cause some mild side effects.

Side Stitch

A number of different conditions cause the form of exercise-induced abdominal pain known as *the stitch*. My contention is that one specific form of the stitch is due to a cramp of the diaphragm muscle. It occurs most often when the athlete is running fast and when breathing is uncomfortable. Under these circumstances, the athlete tends to pant so that the diaphragm muscle contracts in a shortened position and is never fully lengthened; full lengthening only occurs when the athlete exhales fully. The stitch can be broken, as can any muscle cramp, by lengthening the muscle. To do this, the athlete must exhale fully and forcefully, attempting to empty the lungs completely of all their contained air. Thus, breathing out fully at regular intervals, rather than panting, should prevent this form of the stitch from developing or should cure it when it happens

Tendon Injuries

Unlike muscle injuries, which are usually poorly recognized by runners and their advisers, tendon injuries do not usually present a diagnostic problem to anyone, particularly when they occur, as they invariably do, in the Achilles tendon.

Achilles Tendinosis

The first inkling of Achilles tendinosis (formally called *Achilles tendonitis*) usually comes with that first step out of bed in the morning. As soon as the afflicted foot touches the ground, there is a feeling of discomfort or stiffness behind the ankle. This is usually enough to cause some initial limping, which tends to wear off after a few minutes of walking. These symptoms constitute a grade 1 injury. If the condition is allowed to progress unchecked, discomfort may also be noted after exercise, particularly after long runs or fast intervals (grade 2), and this may deteriorate gradually through grades 3 and 4 of injury (see the 2nd Law of Running Injuries).

Most runners realize that the injury is an Achilles tendinosis because the pain is well-localized to the tendon, which is tender to touch at one or more sites. However, two serious conditions involving the Achilles tendon, which need to be differentiated from Achilles tendinosis but which are nevertheless related, are partial or complete tendon ruptures. In these conditions, either a large portion of the tendon or the complete tendon ruptures, causing sudden pain and weakness in the affected ankle. Although complete Achilles tendon rupture is an uncommon injury in distance runners, it tends to occur in middle-aged undertrained athletes involved in sports in which the Achilles tendon is exposed to sudden violent eccentric stretching, as occurs in squash, tennis, or sprinting. However, the incomplete tear is frequently seen in distance runners.

The importance of recognizing complete or partial Achilles tendon ruptures is that they are conditions for which either early surgery (Ljungqvist 1967) or complete immobilization is essential if a good result is to be achieved.

Thus, if the onset of Achilles tendon pain is sudden and debilitating, unlike the gradual onset described for typical Achilles tendinosis, then it is essential that the runner consult a surgeon experienced in the care of running injuries without delay so that the appropriate surgery can be performed immediately. The area of torn tendon begins to degenerate shortly after injury, making surgery extremely difficult after any delay.

The diagnosis of Achilles tendinosis is usually very easy. The discomfort is localized to the tendon, and, on pinching the tendon between the thumb and index finger, one or more exquisitely tender areas are located. A partial tendon rupture will feel exactly the same, while in a completely ruptured tendon, it should be possible to feel a complete gap in the tendon. An important feature of a complete tendon rupture is that it prevents normal walking on the affected side; the runner with a completely ruptured Achilles tendon is unable to push off with that ankle because the calf muscles that provide the power for push-off are no longer attached to the ankle by the Achilles tendon.

Our understanding of the pathological changes that cause pain in the Achilles tendon has been revolutionized in the past five years (Khan et al. 1999). This has followed the finding that tendon inflammation (tendonitis) is not present in the vast majority of athletes who complain of chronic, well-localized Achilles tendon pain. Rather, the affected areas of the tendon have lost their normal glistening appearance to the naked eye. Microscopic examination reveals that the principal constituent of the tendon, the collagen fibers, are disorganized and degenerate. The substance bathing the fibers, the ground substance, is also altered, and there is a proliferation of fibrous (scar) cells within these areas of damage. Nowhere is there any evidence that the affected tendon has been invaded by inflammatory cells—the essential microscopic feature to support a diagnosis of inflammation. These same abnormalities are also present in Achilles tendons that rupture (Maffulli et al. 2000) but are not found in the Achilles tendons of elderly patients undergoing lower limb amputations and who had never complained of symptoms in their Achilles tendons.

The authors (Khan et al. 1999) conclude that these findings indicate the presence of tendinosis, a noninflammatory, degenerative condition of unknown etiology, and not a tendonitis, as was formerly believed. They further conclude that, to be effective, treatment must address the degenerative nature of the condition.

The reasons the Achilles tendon should be especially prone to localized areas of degeneration is unknown. Clement et al. (1984) hypothesize that excessive ankle pronation causes a whipping action, or bowstring effect, in the Achilles tendon. This produces a twisting force in the tendon. They also propose that the Achilles tendon has a relatively poor blood supply in the area in which it typically develops the injury—that is, 2 to 6 cm above the site of insertion of the tendon into the heel bone. They suggest that this whipping action interferes with the already tenuous blood supply to the area, leading ultimately to degeneration of small areas of the tendon in that region. More recent studies have not shown that the blood supply is particularly tenuous at the commonest sites of injury.

A second hypothesis is that the calf muscles undergo rapid eccentric shortening at heel strike, followed by rapid concentric contraction at toe-off, and that these rapid alterations in muscle action may cause degeneration in the Achilles tendon (Smart et al. 1980), perhaps as a result of tiny but repetitive microtears (Gibbon et al. 1999).

There may be a number of factors associated with this injury, although few, if any, have been studied rigorously in controlled scientific trails (Almekinders and Temple 1998). Hence, many of our ideas are based on clinical impressions that may require significant modification in the future.

Shoes and Orthotics

Factors involving shoes include running in heelless spikes or low-heeled shoes (racing flats) and running in shoes that are either worn out or inappropriate for the runner's specific biomechanical needs—in particular, shoes that do not limit the excessive muscular activity caused by high degrees of pronation or that have a heel height lower than 12 to 15 mm and a very stiff sole that fails to bend easily at the forefoot. If the Achilles tendon acts as a spring, then softer running shoes with an appropriate orthotic may also be indicated.

Wearing high heels at work during the day promotes calf-muscle shortening and, perhaps, eccentric weakness of the calf muscles. The only time that it may be a good idea to wear high-heeled shoes is during the early treatment phase of this injury.

My general rule is that an injury is an absolute indication to buy a new pair of shoes, probably of a different make. When choosing a shoe to treat Achilles tendinosis, you should look for antipronation models with rigid heel-counters and firmer midsole material that best control the excessive muscular activity associated with high degrees of ankle pronation. In addition, the rigid heel-counter may also increase the capacity of the heel pad to absorb shock (Jorgensen and Ekstrand 1988).

Most authorities agree that a 7 to 15 mm heel-raise should be added to the running shoes, either as an addition to the heel or as firm felt material inside the running shoe (Clement et al. 1984). This is especially important in runners who have tight calf muscles, high-arched feet, or leg-length inequalities.

If the Achilles tendinosis resists all such treatment, then an in-shoe support (orthotic) is indicated. Ideally, these should be made professionally, as they usually require expert readjustment before they are completely effective. The orthotic should preferably be made from a soft material. My bias is still to believe that a lack of cushioning is also a factor in this injury. Another factor that will help the runner decide whether an orthotic should be prescribed is the degree to which the foot is overpronating during running. Athletes who pronate badly will almost certainly require an orthotic.

Training Errors and Surfaces

Training factors may include any sudden increase in training distances (in particular, single, very long runs); too many speed sessions, including track or fast hill running (particularly if these are carried out running mainly on the toes, as opposed to the heel-toe pattern of long-distance running); a sudden return to heavy training after a layoff; and increased inflexibility of the calf muscles caused by too much training and too little stretching (Smart et al. 1980; Clement et al. 1984). In addition, runners with Achilles tendinosis were found to stretch less frequently than uninjured runners (McCrory et al. 1999).

Age and Years of Heavy Training

Some now believe that the main propulsive forces for running come not so much from the muscles but from the tendons. The suggestion is that we terrestrial animals bounce along on our tendons. However, it is clear that with age the tendons lose their bounce, a factor possibly explaining why we run more slowly with age. I suspect that this loss of bounce also increases the susceptibility to injury of the aging Achilles tendon. My strong clinical impression is that chronic degeneration of the Achilles tendon is one of the major causes of retirement from running of those older athletes who have run many miles, especially fast miles, in their training and racing careers. Indeed, one study (Haglund-Åkerlind and Eriksson 1993) has shown that runners with Achilles tendon injuries had trained for significantly more years and covered significantly longer distances per week than had runners without the injury. Another study (McCrory et al. 1999) also found that runners with this injury had run for more years and at a faster pace than uninjured runners. Age is indeed a significant risk factor for Achilles tendon injuries (Almekinders and Temple 1998) with the peak incidence between 30 and 50 years.

Biomechanics

Biomechanical factors include tight, inflexible calf muscles; hypermobile, flat feet (Kaufman et al. 1999); or, alternatively, the high-arched, cavus or "clunk" foot (Clement et al. 1984; McCrory et al. 1999; Kaufman et al. 1999). Loss of the shock-absorbing capacity of the heel pad has also been implicated (Jorgensen 1985).

In support of the hypothesis that high degrees of ankle pronation cause this injury, McCrory et al. (1999) found that runners with Achilles tendinosis pronate more than do uninjured runners. Hence, runners with this injury touched down in a more (inverted) supinated position, pronated more and at a faster rate, and achieved the maximum pronation velocity in a shorter time. These data provide strong evidence that high levels of ankle pronation are associated with, and likely cause, Achilles tendinosis.

There is some evidence that people with the ABO blood group are at increased risk of developing Achilles tendinosis.

Stretching and Strengthening Exercises

Appropriate calf-muscle stretching exercises must be done for 10 to 20 minutes each day. The most effective stretching exercises for this injury are the calf muscle stretches shown in figure 14.10.

Eccentric loading of the Achilles tendon should begin as soon as pain allows. Credit for this major innovation belongs to Stanish et al. (1985; 1986) who first noted that Achilles tendon ruptures occur most frequently when the Achilles tendon is stretched eccentrically. They also noted that those with Achilles tendinosis complained of the greatest pain when the tendon was stretched eccentrically during downhill running or when stretched experimentally in the laboratory. Accordingly, they developed an eccentric stretching program to increase the strength of the Achilles tendon during eccentric loading. A recent study (Haglund-Åkerlind and Eriksson 1993) has also shown that the eccentric strength of the calf muscles of runners with Achilles tendon injuries is significantly less than that of uninjured runners, whereas eccentric strengthening of those muscles speeds up recovery, as already discussed (Khan et al. 1999). Hence, eccentric calf-muscle strengthening is a logical treatment for this condition.

Eccentric exercise can be performed by standing with the ball of the foot on the edge of a step with the heel extended over the edge. Under the influence of the body's weight, the heel is gradually lowered until the Achilles tendon is fully stretched. Contraction of the calf muscle returns the heel to its horizontal position, whereafter the sequence is repeated. Three sets of 10 repetitions each should be performed daily. For the first two days, the sets should be performed slowly; for the next three days the exercise should be done at a moderate pace; and thereafter the repetitions should be done at the fastest speed that does not induce pain. After seven sessions, weights should be added in the form of sandbags over the shoulders.

Alternatively, all exercises can be done in the gym using the machine designed for "calf-raising" (Alfredson et al. 1998; figure 14.11E), except that the focus of strengthening must be on the eccentric (calf-lowering), not the concentric (calf-raising), component of the exercise. The strength-training activity is continued until the condition resolves. Thereafter, this training should be continued once or twice a week.

Specific Treatment

As we now know that this injury is due to degeneration, not inflammation, whatever treatment is prescribed must incorporate this new reality. For example, an inflammatory condition will usually settle, with complete healing, within three to six weeks. Furthermore, medications that reduce inflammation, such as hydrocortisone injections or other anti-inflammatory medications, would be expected to enhance healing. In contrast, a degenerative condition will not be improved by anti-inflammatory medication. It is less likely to recover fully without long-term sequelae and may take substantially longer (months to years) to settle.

Thus, Khan et al. (1999) propose the following guidelines for the management of Achilles tendinosis and other degenerative conditions of tendons:

- Relative rest should start earlier, as soon as the first symptoms develop, by which time there is already likely to be significant tendon degeneration, and should last for much longer (months rather than weeks).
- Eccentric muscle strengthening should start early, as such loading accelerates the repair of the tendon cells. A number of studies confirm the value of eccentric strengthening in the treatment of tendon injuries (Niesen-Vertommen et al. 1992; Alfredson et al. 1998; Holmich et al. 1999; Khan et al. 1999).
- The value of anti-inflammatory medications and corticosteroid injections is unproven (Almekinders and Temple 1998; Khan et al. 1999) and would not seem to have a logical basis in the treatment of a degenerative condition.
- Physical therapies, including ultrasounds, laser photostimulation, and electrical stimulation, stimulate tendon repair when studied in animal models (Khan et al. 1999).
- Ice therapy may reduce the extent of tendon degeneration.

The first step is to stop running; early, complete rest is more likely to limit the extent of further degeneration in the tendon, thereby speeding up recovery. I would advocate a period of 7 to 21 days of complete rest from running, as soon as the first symptoms develop. Instead, activities that do not load the Achilles tendon—such as swimming, gentle cycling, running in water with a flotation device, and upper body weight training—can be substituted for running.

During this time, initial treatment for the injured Achilles tendon is to apply an ice pack to the sore area for as long as possible each day. An orthopedic colleague maintains that his Achilles tendinosis was cured by keeping the injured foot in an ice bath for up to 8 hours a day, which is fine if you don't trade your Achilles tendinosis for severe frostbite. A less demanding schedule would involve applying an ice pack for at least 30 minutes three times a day, especially immediately before and after running.

Anti-inflammatory drugs or cortisone injections can be used, or both, but my personal approach is to avoid both drugs and injections on the ground that there is no good evidence to suggest that they add benefit to the normal treatment described here (Shrier et al. 1996; Almekinders and Temple 1998). Also, the condition is not due to an inflammation that these drugs can reverse. In addition, the use of drugs poses some potential risks.

First, this type of treatment can suggest that a cure can be bought or swallowed, whereas what is really essential is that you learn why the injury developed. Only then will you learn how to avoid injuring yourself repeatedly. This is especially important with a degenerative condition. Second, there is the cost involved and the question of whether that money could not be better spent elsewhere (for example, in buying a new pair of more appropriate running shoes).

Third, specifically with regard to cortisone injections, there is a general feeling that cortisone should never be allowed near an Achilles tendon unless the injector knows exactly what he or she is doing. The risk is that cortisone injected into the tendon may make it more liable to rupture completely (Ryan 1978), although no human studies have yet confirmed this possibility (Shrier et al. 1996).

I suggest that the best approach in this condition is to treat any factors that might cause or exacerbate the injury and to assist the healing process in the degenerative area with relative rest and appropriate physical therapy.

I advocate absolute rest from running for at least the first one to three weeks after the onset of symptoms. Thereafter, the amount of running you do will depend on the grade of injury at the time you seek medical care.

In general, as long as the injury remains in the first injury grade, it is probably not necessary to alter your training program dramatically after the initial week's rest. But for a grade 2 injury (pain coming on during exercise), a reduction in all speed running, in racing, in long runs, in weekly training distance, and particularly in hill running is advisable. When the injury reaches grade 3 (pain coming on during exercise and impairing performance), only short-distance jogging, running in water, cycling, swimming, and upper body strengthening exercises in the gym are allowed. With a grade 4 injury (pain prevents running), there should be no running whatsoever, but alternative activities can be done. During this time, eccentric strengthening of the calf muscles must continue.

One way of tailoring training to the injury is to use the pinch test after each run. If the pinch test indicates that the tendon is becoming progressively more tender after each run, or after a particular training session, then this suggests either that total training should be reduced or that that particular training session should be avoided. Alternatively, if the tendon becomes progressively less tender, then the treat-ment is succeeding and training distance and intensity may be increased gradually.

Physiotherapy or physical therapy is advised for all injuries like this and should be mandatory for all injuries worse than grade 1. All the appropriate physiotherapeutic modalities should be used, especially in the early phases of the injury when they may aid the initial healing process. Thereafter, gentle cross-frictions may be applied to the tender areas of the tendon.

The following list summarizes one approach to the treatment of Achilles tendinosis.

Grade 1: Morning discomfort in tendon

- Rest one week before resuming training as before.
- Stretch calf muscles for total of 20 minutes each day.
- Try new running shoes that prevent excessive pronation.
- Add 7- to 15-mm heel rise to running and street shoes.
- Monitor injury progress with the pinch test.
- Use physical therapy and drug therapy if costs permit.

Grade 2: Pain during running, but not affecting performance

- Continue approach for grade 1.
- Modify training to reduce speed work, hill running, long runs, and weekly distance.
- Try an orthotic.
- Try physical therapy (in particular, cross-frictions).

Grade 3: Pain during running that is affecting performance

- Continue approaches for grades 1 and 2.
- Rest for three weeks.
- Try regular cross-frictions.
- After 3-week rest, resume jogging, cycling, or swimming (no serious running) until injury reverts to grade 2, then try serious running only when injury reverts to grade 1.

Grade 4: Running impossible.

- Try approaches for grades 1, 2, and 3.
- If these fail, visit an experienced orthopedic surgeon.
- Consider surgery only when all other techniques, included repeated sessions of cross-frictions, have not worked.

The critical points to remember are that the injury must be differentiated from partial or complete Achilles tendon ruptures, both of which require either urgent surgery or immobilization, and that during the acute injury episodes, anything that will provoke further damage should be avoided because the more damage there is, the more likely it becomes that surgery will become necessary.

The immediate results of this type of treatment approach are usually very encouraging. Of a total of 86 runners treated in this way, 73 (85%) reported an excellent result, and only one (1.16%) graded the result as fair (Clement et al. 1984). A second study has reported equally good results (D.L. Anderson et al. 1992).

Similarly, the long-term outcome in this condition is also encouraging. In a study of 83 patients with this condition who were followed up eight years after their initial injury, even though 30% had undergone surgery, 84% had recovered fully to their previous activity levels and 94% were either without symptoms or had only mild pain with strenuous exercise (Paavola et al. 2000). Some 41% had begun to suffer symptoms in the initially uninvolved Achilles, indicating that even though many runners will eventually develop Achilles tendinosis bilaterally, it does not necessarily have to interfere with their running.

Surgery

The ultimate danger in recurrent Achilles tendinosis is that the degenerative process, which initially starts inside the tendon, will progress to involve the sheath surrounding the tendon. When this happens, adhesions (connections) are formed between the tendon and its sheath. As this happens, the free movement of the tendon inside its sheath becomes progressively impaired, and the tendon becomes susceptible to repeated attacks of tendinosis, each of which leaves the runner progressively more debilitated, until ultimately it is almost impossible to run at all.

Fortunately, this injury can now be effectively treated by a delicate surgical procedure, which removes the tendon sheath, along with any areas of tendon scarring. When performed by an experienced surgeon, this procedure has a very high success rate (Smart et al. 1980; Leppilahti et al. 1994).

Surgery should be considered for the treatment of Achilles tendinosis only when all other interventions have failed and the injury has been present for some substantial time (at least six months or more) and its effects are debilitating.

In the usual form of surgery, the tendon lining is first removed, and then areas of definite degeneration are excised. More recently, a form of outpatient surgery has been developed in which a scalpel blade is inserted into the area of maximal tendon thickness or degeneration and held in place as the subject extends and flexes the ankle (Maffulli et al. 1997). This procedure is performed under local anesthetic. The incision is then repeated at four other sites: 2 cm above and below and 2 cm on the inside and outside of the original incision. This form of treatment cured 70% of a group of long-distance runners for whom conservative therapy had failed. The authors suggest that, not least because it is simple and effective, this technique should be the operation of choice for the management of Achilles tendinosis when conservative treatment has failed.

Other Tendon Injuries

Achilles and patellar tendinosis, described in the foregoing pages, are by far the most common forms of tendinosis. Another tendon that is sometimes involved is the popliteus tendon, which runs around the outside of the knee. In this injury, there is pain on the outside of the knee just below the site at which the iliotibial band syndrome causes pain (see figure 14.17). The injury is said to occur with downhill running, although no one has yet studied a large enough number of runners with this injury to confirm this observation.

The treatment that I prescribe for this injury is the same as that used in the treatment of Achilles tendinosis—in particular, the use of the appropriate shoes and orthotics to control the excessive muscular activity associated with high degrees of ankle pronation. The injury is uncommon and usually responds rapidly to this treatment. Other forms of tendinosis should also be treated according to the regime described for Achilles tendinosis.

Injuries Due to Interference With Blood Circulation

Obstruction to either the arterial blood flowing into the muscles or the venous blood returning to the heart can produce incapacitating symptoms that make running impossible and even dangerous.

Acute and Chronic Compartment Syndromes

This group of injuries occurs infrequently and in the past was often confused in the literature with bone strain. In the compartment syndromes, exercise causes an abnormal rise in pressure in one or more of the muscular compartments of the lower leg (Wallensten 1983; Davey et al. 1984; Martens et al. 1984; Detmer et al. 1985; Rorabeck 1986; Wiley et al. 1987; Rorabeck et al. 1988; Schepsis et al. 1993; Biedert and Marti 1997; see figure 14.21). It is likely that the pressure rise occurs because fluid accumulates in the muscles during exercise. Normally there is sufficient space in these compartments for the muscles to swell without there being any increase in pressure. However, in people who develop this injury, the muscle compartments are tight and do not allow sufficient room for such swelling. Thus, the pressure rises abnormally in those compartments during exercise, and the resulting pressure increase may be so great that it interferes with the blood flow to the muscles, causing them to become painful (Styf et al. 1987), especially when stretched eccentrically against resistance. This is a helpful diagnostic technique. As the intracompartmental pressure rises, nerve function may also be affected, leading to a tingling sensation or a feeling of pins and needles in the foot.

At present, the only factors known to be associated with this injury are hereditary—muscle compartments that are too small to accommodate the normal swelling of their contained muscles during exercise or muscles that are simply too big for their compartments.

The most common symptom in the chronic form of this injury is the onset of pain during or after exercise. At first, the pain is mild and disappears rapidly as soon as the runner stops running. However, with time, the pain becomes increasingly severe and begins to interfere with running. Ultimately, the pain is so severe that it forces the patient to stop running. The pain usually subsides within minutes of stopping exercise but recurs with exercise, as soon as the same running speed is reached.

The runner usually has no difficulty localizing the site of pain, which is one or more of the large muscle groups—usually the anterior calf muscles, less commonly the deep posterior and lateral calf muscles. An observant athlete may also notice that as they become painful, the affected muscles lose their normal suppleness and become very hard to the touch. But as the pain disappears, the hardness gradually dissipates. This too is a key diagnostic finding. In addition, the affected muscles are most painful when stretched eccentrically. If the anterior calf muscles are affected, the athlete will adopt a typical gait in which the forefoot begins to slap on the ground, thereby avoiding repeated powerful eccentric contractions of the anterior calf muscles.

While most cases of compartment syndrome present with the gradual (chronic) development of symptoms, there is another extremely dangerous presentation. In this acute form, the athlete has no previous warning. The muscles suddenly become increasingly painful after a single exercise session. Instead of abating with rest, the pain intensifies and soon becomes so overwhelming that the runner is unable to do anything but think about the painful leg. The runner may also notice loss of sensation in the skin overlying the muscles, and ultimately there may be paralysis of those muscles, which have become board-hard. If the runner were to feel for the arterial pulses in the foot, it would become apparent that they had disappeared.

This injury constitutes an emergency. In effect, what has happened is that the pressure inside the muscles has built up to such an extent that it has caused complete obstruction of blood flow to the affected muscles. As these muscles now have an inadequate blood supply, they begin to die. The treatment is therefore to relieve the pressure without delay. This is achieved by the same surgical procedure used in the management of the more insidious (chronic) form of compartment syndrome (Rorabeck et al. 1983). The only difference is that in this acute form, the surgery must be performed as an absolute emergency as soon as it becomes clear that the pain will not subside.

Differentiating Compartment Syndromes From Bone Strain

I estimate that the ratio of runners suffering from true bone strain to those with the compartment syndrome is of the order of 100:1 to 200:1. This indicates just how uncommon this injury is.

A true compartment syndrome can be differentiated from bone strain with relative ease for the following reasons:

- A compartment syndrome causes pain localized to the muscles, not the bones, of the lower limb.
- The pain usually gets worse after running (acute compartment syndrome).
- The injury never gets better, even after months of rest, whereas in bone strain, after a few months of rest, the runner will usually be pain-free until the breakdown training level is again reached (the 3rd Law of Running Injuries).
- After running, the affected muscles become absolutely rock hard, and the foot may be pulled into a strange position (because of transient muscle paralysis).
- There may also be changes in skin sensation and, occasionally, severe muscle cramping.

Specific Treatment

There is only one form of effective treatment for this injury, and that is a surgical procedure in which the lining of the tight compartment is split, allowing the muscle to expand freely inside its compartment (Rorabeck et al. 1983; Detmer et al. 1985; Detmer 1986; Biedert and Marti 1997). Rest and other forms of conservative treatment are almost always unsuccessful (Wiley et al. 1987; Rorabeck et al. 1988). It is important that all the involved compartments are identified and surgically treated (Martens et al. 1984; Rorabeck 1986; Rorabeck et al. 1988). Often the superficial posterior compartment and not the deep posterior compartment is released during surgery. If the symptoms arise from the deep compartment, the treatment will be ineffectual.

If the initial diagnosis is correct, response to treatment is excellent. The athlete is again able to run without pain as soon as the surgical wound has healed. If, on the other hand, the initial diagnosis was incorrect and the athlete was suffering from true bone strain, surgery will obviously not bring about any improvement (Allen and Barnes 1986). Therapy will also fail if the cause of the problem is popliteal artery entrapment syndrome. There are no stretching and strengthening exercises that are of any proven value for this condition.

Popliteal Artery Entrapment Syndrome

This is an extremely uncommon injury that causes pain in the leg during exercise. It is caused by the contraction of an anomalous portion of the gastrocnemius muscle that surrounds the main artery in the calf, the popliteal artery. Contraction of that muscle during exercise causes obstruction of the artery, preventing blood flow to the calf. It is this absence of blood flow that causes the pain during exercise. This is a diagnosis only for the experts, and the only effective treatment is surgery. Usually, the diagnosis is only considered when all other possibilities have been considered and treatment has failed.

Effort Thrombosis of the Deep Calf Veins

Clotting of blood (thrombosis) in the deep veins of the calf is an extremely dangerous condition that can be precipitated by exercise. Ultramarathoner Len Keating has described his own experiences with this injury (Keating 1982).

Keating relates that he continued training and racing through the pain, which began in his calf and spread to the back of his knee. He ascribed his problems to Achilles tendonitis, initially, then to hamstring troubles. The day after racing a half-marathon, he says,

> I couldn't walk or even sit without pain. About six days later, the pain subsided and I continued running. I decided to run a 50-km race and for the first time in my entire running career, I pulled out of a road race at the 40-km mark, limping badly and in some distress. (Keating 1982, p. 18).

After continuing to train lightly, Keating found that he could not walk the day after "a hard 16 km" and that his leg, in particular his calf, had begun to swell. A visit to his doctor confirmed a deep vein thrombosis, with clotting stretching from Keating's ankle through to his abdomen.

Effort thrombosis of the deep calf veins is another very uncommon injury: I probably see and hear of less than 10 such cases each year. The factors precipitating the clotting are unknown, although the use of oral contraceptive medication by women and periods of prolonged inactivity (for example, bed rest or sitting in an airplane on intercontinental flights) are likely explanations in some cases. Once the clot has formed, it blocks the main route for blood to return from the legs to the heart. The blood then accumulates in the legs, at first causing the pain that Keating described but later, as the extent of the clot increases, making the legs swell.

The main danger of this condition is that a part of the blood clot can dislodge and travel up the leg veins through the heart to lodge in the small arteries of the lungs. If sufficiently large, the dislodged clot can cause death within minutes; if smaller, it can cause death of small areas of the lung. When this occurs, the patient will experience marked chest pain and may cough up blood.

The only treatment is immediate hospitalization to allow for the safe administration of drugs that reduce blood clotting, supportive bandaging of the leg, and a complete avoidance of all exercise for a period of up to 6 to 12 months. During this period, blood clotting is controlled with appropriate medication. Fortunately, recovery is usually complete but may take 6 to 12 months. In 1984, Keating returned to racing, winning a 161-km road race in 13:32:00.

Nerve Injuries

Recently it has become apparent that a group of nerve entrapment syndromes can cause pain, especially in the foot. These injuries are resistant to all forms of conventional therapy (Henricson and Westlin 1984; Murphy and Baxter 1985). The nerves involved in these conditions are the following:

- The nerve to the abductor digiti quinti. This nerve runs deep to the plantar fascia in the foot and, when entrapped, causes pain that is indistinguishable from that of plantar fasciitis.

- The deep peroneal nerve as it crosses either the talus or the tarso-metatarsal joint. Entrapment of this nerve can cause pain at the site of the entrapment on the top of the foot, often with radiation of the pain to the toes.

- The posterior tibial nerve entrapped by an accessory navicular bone (os naviculare). Entrapment of this nerve causes pain to be felt on the bottom (plantar) surface of the foot, as well as on the inside of the heel. This nerve is also involved in the tarsal tunnel syndrome, described earlier.

- The medial plantar nerve below the calcaneonavicular joint. This entrapment causes pain to be felt on the inside of the foot, just above and in front of the site at which the plantar fascia is tender in people with plantar fasciitis. Surgical decompression of these nerves at the site of entrapment is the only effective form of treatment.

- The peroneal nerve as it crosses the head of the fibula. Entrapment of this nerve causes pain and tingling to be felt on the lateral aspect of the lower leg (Leach et al. 1989).

- The sural nerve lateral to the musculo-tendinous junction of the Achilles tendon (Fabre et al. 2000). Entrapment causes chronic calf pain.

Surgical decompression of these nerves at the site of entrapment is the only effective form of treatment.

Heel Bruise

An injury that is less understood is the heel bruise. In this condition, pain is felt in the heel pad directly under the calcaneus. On examination, a small, exquisitely tender area can be palpated. The site of maximum tenderness is usually in the middle of the heel; this distinguishes the injury from plantar fasciitis, in which the pain is located nearer to the arch of the foot (figure 14.18, A through C), or from a calcaneus stress fracture, in which the pain is best reproduced by compressing the calcaneus on both sides between the thumb and forefinger.

The heel pad comprises specialized tissue designed both for shock absorption and for energy return (Jorgensen 1985). With age, the thickness and therefore presumably the functional capacity of the heel pad decreases, and this may predispose the runner to injury.

The most effective treatment for this condition is the use of a special (Tuli) heel cup designed to maintain the mobile tissues of the heel pad underneath the heel at heel strike. This prevents the heel pad from compressing and dispersing on both sides of the heel. When this is achieved, the shock-absorbing capacity of the heel pad is enhanced (Jorgensen and Ekstrand 1988).

FINAL WORD

Anyone who has ever run for some time soon learns that injury is an ever-present risk. Fortunately, there is now sufficient information available to suggest practical ways in which the incidence of running injuries can be reduced. This chapter provides much of that information.

CHAPTER

15

■ ■ ■ ■ ■

Running and Your Health

Georgel Sheehan was one of the first people to dare suggest that most runners do not actually run to be healthy. Accordingly, he proposed that runners be classified into one of three groups—joggers, racers, and runners—on the basis of their motivations for running (Sheehan 1978b).

Joggers, Sheehan contended, are the physically reborn who preach the gospel of jogging for health and longevity. They will bore anyone incautious enough to ask with evangelical details of how jogging saved their lives. And as they begin to discuss the evidence that exercise increases longevity and protects against coronary heart disease (with names like Morris and Paffenbarger tripping off their tongues as if they were the jogger's nearest and dearest friends), they will be inspecting you carefully, looking for those telltale signs indicating your need for physical reform.

Fortunately for all of us, most joggers grow up. As joggers mature, they begin to realize that the passions that motivate people to become healthy are the same as those that transform the jogger first into a racer and then finally into a runner. Sooner or later, the jogging bore may find that jogging has become boring. The exercise prescription that has made the body healthy has failed to do anything for the mind. The mental challenge to start exercising and become healthy has gone. It is time to move on—to enter a race.

As soon as joggers mail their first race entry forms, they become racers and enter a new world. The racer, you see, no longer has any concern for health. The sole concern is performance, with the desire to run faster. Every training session, every waking moment, is concerned with what will make the legs run farther in less time. As the racer's expectations can never be satisfied, it is not possible to train sufficiently, or race enough. The result is that if there indeed are any medical dangers associated with jogging, they occur almost exclusively among the racers.

Sheehan suggests that running competitively (racing) does for the mind what jogging does for the body. The race provides the fear, the excitement, the physical challenge from which our modern, repetitive, unchallenging nine-to-five lives have sheltered us.

Ultimately, the jogger/racer may evolve into a runner who is unconcerned about the health aspects of running and whose psyche no longer needs the challenge of the race. The runner runs to meditate, to create, and to become whole. Sheehan writes: "Running is finally seeing everything in perspective. . . . Running is the fusion of body, mind and soul in that beautiful relaxation that joggers and racers find so difficult to achieve" (1978b, p. 287).

With this introduction, let us discuss the real and perceived medical problems associated with running in general and racing in particular.

EXERCISE AND THE RESPIRATORY SYSTEM

Most people who develop constriction of the bronchial airways during exercise are aware that they suffer from asthma and are under medical treatment for this condition. For this reason, I will not discuss this topic in detail but will cover it briefly along with exercise and lung cancer risks, and respiratory infections, including rhinorrhea (athlete's nose), pulmonary edema, and the phenomenon of the "second wind."

Exercise-Induced Asthma

In essence, the bronchial airways of asthmatics are especially sensitive to a number of stimuli, including, for example, cold air, infections, cigarette smoke and other pollutants, and various allergic stimuli (such as house dust, animal dander, and certain foods). When exposed to these stimuli, the muscles lining the respiratory airways go into spasm, causing severe narrowing of the small air passages. This narrowing acts like a ball valve, allowing air to enter the lung but preventing its escape during normal exhalation. Thus, during an attack, the asthmatic has great trouble exhaling and the lungs become progressively more distended by trapped air, causing progressive respiratory distress.

The important practical points about asthma and its management are as follows.

- The condition must be treated by a medical practitioner.

- The vast majority of asthmatic symptoms can be adequately controlled, if not completely eliminated, by the use of appropriate medication (Hansen-Flasschen 1998). However, some of these medications contain substances that are banned by the International Olympic Committee (IOC). Thus, if you are an elite athlete who is likely to undergo doping control during competition, you must ensure that you use only those drugs that are cleared by the IOC for use during competition.

- Far from avoiding sport, asthmatics, especially children, should be encouraged to be as active as possible in sport, not only because the exercise will frequently reduce the amount of medication they need to control symptoms

(King et al. 1989) but also because of the psychological benefits of participating in an activity. Running, however, is not the exercise of choice for asthmatics. For reasons that are not entirely clear, running is more likely to produce asthmatic attack than is, for example, swimming. If the asthma is well controlled, however, running can be encouraged.

- Despite the value that regular physical activity has for children with asthma (King et al. 1989), it is also clear that asthma is more common in elite athletes, especially endurance athletes, such as long-distance runners (Helenius et al. 1997) and cross-country skiers (Wilber et al. 2000), as well as power athletes (Nystad et al. 2000), than it is in the general population. Women are particularly at risk (Nystad et al. 2000). Risk rises with increased hours of training per week and is greatest in the group that trains the most (about 20 hours per week; Nystad et al. 2000). These findings invite the hypothesis that strenuous physical training is a risk factor for the development of asthma.

Nystad et al. (2000) speculate that three factors may contribute to the higher incidence of asthma in athletes:

1. Repeated damage from overstimulation of the mechanisms that protect against dry air-induced damage to the linings of the respiratory airways (repeated injury may lead to chronic inflammation)
2. Recurrent infections that may be more common in athletes who train intensively
3. Increased exposure to environmental factors, including air pollutants, that may increase the risk of developing asthma

Lung Cancer

The risk of developing lung cancer, a condition usually associated with cigarette smoking, is substantially reduced in physically active men (Wannamethee et al. 1993; Lee and Paffenbarger 1994; Thune and Lund 1997), although no effect was found in women (Thune and Lund 1997).

Respiratory Infections

The high incidence of the symptoms of respiratory infections in competitive runners in the week following major competitions (Nieman 1994) was discussed in chapter 10. The reason for the high incidence of these symptoms is unknown but may be related to two factors. The first is trauma to the membranes of the respiratory passages caused by sustained high levels of ventilation. Such damage will be exacerbated if the environmental temperatures are low. The second is exercise- and diet-induced (Kono et al. 1988) impairment of the body's resistance to infection owing to alterations in the function of the immune system (Lewicki et al. 1987; Nieman, Berk, et al 1989; Nieman, Johanssen, et al. 1989; Berk et al. 1990; Mackinnon and Jenkins 1993; Nieman 1995; Pedersen and Hoffman-Goetz 2000) or of the cilia in the respiratory tree that clear the airways of mucous and bacteria (Müns et al. 1995). However, there is growing evidence that these symptoms cannot be due to infections since they occur too soon (28 to 48 hours) after exercise, whereas the normal incubation period for viral infections is three to five days longer. Thus, trauma-induced inflammation is the more likely mechanism causing symptoms of respiratory infection.

Regardless of the mechanism, you need to remember that you are at high risk of respiratory tract inflammation, allergy, or infection when you race competitively, especially in cold conditions. After such races, be extremely wary of starting training too soon. Remember that these symptoms always mean that you have done too much and are in need of rest, not more training. I continue to be amazed at the number of athletes who are ignorant of this basic fact and who continue to train through illness either before or after competition, and who are unable to understand why they perform so poorly for as long as they continue to train. Only when they stop training and rest will they have any chance of again performing to their potential.

When should an athlete with a respiratory or other infection compete again? The most comprehensive advice I could find is that followed by the Swedish cross-country skiers, who are particularly prone to respiratory infections because they train and compete in very cold temperatures. Because they train in the cold, they are also more likely to suffer bronchoconstriction (asthma) if they exercise with respiratory infections, and they are at increased risk of developing asthma in the long term, particularly if they suffer frequent respiratory infections.

Swedish cross-country skiers receive the following advice, equally applicable to runners (Bergh 1982):

- Never train hard and never race when you have an infection or are otherwise in poor health. If possible, seek the advice of a physician.

- Do not train or compete if you have a fever, a sore throat, or a bad cold or if you have just been vaccinated (within 3 to 7 days).

- You can continue training but should not train hard or compete if you have recently been ill, have a light (head) cold, or have a slightly blocked or runny nose with no fever or sore throat. Do not resume training until you are completely well and consult your physician. If you have a cold or other contagious condition, do not train, race, or go to training camps with other athletes.

- To race when you are not completely well is misguided loyalty to your teammates, club, or organization and leaders. Racing when you are ill can have serious consequences, as you may risk your health or your life.

Runners are frequently unwilling to take antibiotics to treat their infections because of their fear that antibiotics will jeopardize their performances. In fact, it is the infection that jeopardizes running and indicates that runners have overtrained. Antibiotics have not been shown to affect performance adversely (Kuipers et al. 1980).

Nasal secretions are increased during exercise (Stanford and Stanford 1988), possibly due to the increased humidification of the inhaled air. The effect is reversed relatively quickly after the cessation of exercise. This condition could possibly also be part of an allergic response.

Pulmonary Edema

Fluid may accumulate in the lungs (a condition known as pulmonary edema) of healthy athletes if the heart fails temporarily, as reported in two Comrades ultramarathon runners (McKechnie et al. 1979); if there is marked fluid overload caused by excessive fluid consumption before (Weiler-Ravell et al. 1995) or during exercise (Noakes 1993); or if the athlete is treated inappropriately with excessive volumes of intravenous fluids after exercise for the wrong reasons (for example, the treatment of cramps; Noakes 1998a) or, even more inappropriately, for an unrecognized heart attack after ultramarathon running (Noakes et al. 1977), the symptoms of which were ascribed to the "dehydration myth."

The fluid content of the lungs increases transiently after prolonged exercise (Caillaud et al. 1995), and this reduces the capacity of the lungs to transfer gasses. The cause and significance of this finding is unknown.

Second Wind

The second wind is one of the more interesting and least understood phenomena in exercise physiology. It is defined as the subjective sensation of reduced breathlessness (dyspnea) that comes on after a few minutes of hard exercise.

Perhaps one of the first references to this phenomenon comes from Webster. He suggested without any experimental justification that

> When the second wind, that feeling of renewed energy that the runner experiences, comes on, a certain alkaline substance, created or multiplied in the blood by the process of training, begins to neutralize the acidity that has been produced by exercise activity running on into the beginning of fatigue. (Webster 1948, p. 119)

The only scientific studies of the second wind are those of Scharf, Bark, et al. (1984) and Scharf, Bye, et al. (1984), who showed that, at the onset of the second wind, there was a change in the function of the muscles of inspiration. Specifically, there was a reduction in the number of muscle fibers recruited, indicating that the contractility of the inspiratory muscles, particularly the diaphragm, had increased. They suggest that a redistribution of blood flow to the diaphragm and stimulation of the contractility of the inspiratory muscles by adrenaline and other hormones could explain this change.

They also suggest that the progressive breathlessness that develops during prolonged exercise may represent a reversal of the second wind—that is, a progressive failure of the contractility of the inspiratory muscles, requiring the recruitment of more muscle fiber, causing the subjective sensation of increasing breathlessness.

EXERCISE AND THE CARDIOVASCULAR SYSTEM

Although the exact cause of coronary heart disease is unknown, certain known risk factors are associated with the disease. Therefore, the risk of developing the disease increases with the number of risk factors present. The most important risk factors include the following.

- **Cigarette smoking.** Smoking is one of the most powerful coronary risk factors and acts to increase the rate of development of coronary atherosclerosis (see chapter 5) by mechanisms as yet unknown. The most likely effect is a direct action of one or more constituents of cigarette smoke on endothelial and media cells in the arteries. The increased risk associated with cigarette smoking only abates about 15 years after stopping smoking (Robinson et al. 1989). It has been suggested that "smoking may be the gateway to an unhealthy lifestyle in general" (Prättälä et al. 1994) and that "about half of all regular cigarette smokers will eventually be killed by their habit" (Doll et al. 1994). On the other hand, smokers who are physically active have a 40% lower risk of heart attack than do smokers who are not active (Paffenbarger et al. 1978; Hedblad et al. 1997). Physically active smokers live longer than inactive smokers (Hedblad et al. 1997; Ferrucci et al. 1999) so that their further life expectancy at 65 or 75 is as good as, or perhaps marginally better than, that of sedentary nonsmokers (Ferrucci et al. 1999). Exercise also improves the maintenance of smoking cessation in women (Marcus et al. 1995).

- **Elevated blood pressure** (hypertension). Hypertension increases the risk of heart attack (and stroke). The accepted cutoff blood pressure, above which risk begins to rise more substantially, is 140/90 mmHg.

- **Elevated blood cholesterol levels** (hypercholesterolemia)—in particular, a reduced ratio of high-density lipoprotein (HDL) to total cholesterol (Stampfer et al. 1991). Confirmation of these levels as direct cause of heart attack comes from studies showing that a new group of medications, the statins, lower blood cholesterol concentrations and reduce the risk of heart attack, even in those with "average" blood cholesterol concentrations, whether or not they already have diagnosed heart disease (Sacks et al. 1996).

As is the case with all these risk factors, people who are physically active are at lower risk of developing coronary heart disease at any level of risk factor, including any blood cholesterol concentration (T.B. Harris et al. 1991). This means that exercise provides a measure of protection against coronary heart disease even in the presence of one or more coronary risk factors.

The contention that low blood cholesterol levels may be undesirable because of an increased risk of cancer (Schatzkin, Hoover, et al. 1987) is not supported by other studies (Sherwin et al. 1987; K.M. Anderson et al. 1987). Hence, as is the case with systolic blood pressure, statistically speaking, the lower the blood cholesterol concentration (or the systolic blood pressure), the lower the risk of developing heart disease. But the risk for heart disease increases exponentially with rising blood cholesterol concentrations (or blood pressure). Thus, whereas small changes in those with high blood cholesterol concentrations (or markedly elevated blood pressures) substantially reduce the risk for heart disease, even quite large changes in the blood cholesterol concentrations or blood pressures of those who are already at low risk because their blood cholesterol concentrations (or blood pressures) are already low may produce a disappointingly small effect. Those who benefit from any intervention, be it increased physical activity or a lowering of blood cholesterol concentrations or blood pressure, are those who are at the greatest risk to begin with. Those who are most unhealthy stand to benefit the most; the very healthy benefit the least, because they are already at such low risk.

Interestingly, the presence of the common coronary risk factors—hypertension, hypercholesterolemia, and obesity—is associated with poor endurance capacity in healthy, asymptomatic younger people (Abbott et al. 1989).

- **Elevated blood concentrations of fibrinogen** (Kannel et al. 1987; Ridker 1999), **high-sensitivity C-reactive protein, and homocysteine** (Ridker 1999). Blood fibrinogen levels are lowest in those who are the most physically active (Connelly et al. 1992; Ernst 1993) and are reduced by physical training (Meade 1995). Furthermore, the concentration of tissue plasminogen activator, whose function is the opposite of fibrinogen, rises with increasing levels of physical activity (Eliasson et al. 1996).

  Whereas elevated blood fibrinogen concentrations increase the risk of heart disease, it is the combination of an elevated high-sensitivity C-reactive protein concentration with a low ratio of total cholesterol to HDL cholesterol that is really important. Hence, this combination is associated with a fivefold increased risk of heart attack, compared to a threefold increased risk if the blood cholesterol ratio is considered alone (Ridker 1999).

  Blood C-reactive protein concentrations are an indirect marker of inflammatory processes in the body (Strachan et al. 1984); the finding that their elevated concentrations in blood can predict risk of future heart attack invites the hypothesis that inflammation is involved in, or may indeed cause, coronary artery atherosclerosis (Ridker et al. 1998). If this is correct, it may explain why the long-term use of the anti-inflammatory drug aspirin is so effective in reducing the risk of further heart attacks in those with coronary heart disease (ISIS-2 Collaborative Group 1988).

- **Lower social class.** Risk rises appreciably with decreasing social class (Lapidus and Bengtsson 1986; Wing et al. 1987). This is due, at least in part, to an increasing prevalence of the classic coronary risk factors—cigarette smoking, elevated blood cholesterol concentrations, increasing body mass index, and elevated blood pressure—in the lower socioeconomic classes (Shewry et al. 1992).

- **European ancestry.** There are also ethnic differences in the incidence of the disease, which is highest in North Americans and Europeans and lowest in Africans and those living in less developed countries. Part of the effect may be due to differences in diet and physical activity patterns. Life expectancy is also less in people living in less developed countries, most especially in African, South American, and Asian countries that have been engulfed by the HIV/AIDS epidemic. Coronary heart disease is a disease of aging and will therefore be less common in populations dying at younger ages from other causes.

- **Male gender.** Males are more prone to heart disease than are females. This effect is probably related to the presence of testosterone and other androgenic hormones that are present in low concentrations in women. Some also believe that body iron stores may be related to the risk of heart attack (Salonen et al. 1992; J.L. Sullivan 1992; Roest et al. 1999; Salonen et al. 1999). In line with this theory, the monthly loss of iron through menstruation may offer women increased protection against coronary heart disease. Furthermore, physical activity also reduces body iron stores (Lakka et al. 1994) and serum ferritin concentrations (Pate et al. 1993), the latter being a measure of body iron reserves.

  Women lose their relative protection from heart disease following menopause, after which they have low or absent blood estrogen concentrations. If estrogen protects women from heart disease before menopause, then estrogen therapy after menopause should reduce their subsequent risk of developing this condition. At present, there is uncertainty whether estrogen replacement therapy initiated after menopause can prevent or delay the development of coronary heart disease (Nabel 2000) but definitive studies—the Women's Health Initiative and the Raloxifene Use for the Heart (RUTH) trial—are currently in progress.

- **Family history of heart disease.** People who have a close family history of heart disease, either in grandparents, parents, uncles, aunts, or siblings, are at increased risk. When such relatives have died from heart disease before the age of 45, it suggests that the family may carry the genes for very high blood cholesterol levels, displaying the so-called familial hypercholesterolemia. Members of families with a history of early deaths from heart attack should consult their doctors and have their blood cholesterol levels and blood pressures monitored.

- **Certain disease states, such as diabetes.** Diabetes is one of the most malignant chronic diseases, with a long-term prognosis little better than that of many of the cancers. Arterial damage is a cardinal feature of diabetes that substantially increases the incidence of heart attack, stroke, peripheral vascular disease, and kidney failure, all due to arterial disease.

- **Short stature and early aging.** The reason people of short stature (under 1.7 m) should be at increased risk of heart disease is unknown (Herbert et al. 1993). Men, but not women, who show early signs of aging, including graying hair, frontal baldness, and facial wrinkling, are at increased risk of heart attack (Schnohr et al. 1995).

- **Male- ("apple-," or abdominal-) type obesity.** In the male form of obesity, there is excess accumulation of body fat in the abdominal organs, giving the typical beer belly. This type of obesity is associated with multiple metabolic abnormalities, including hypercholesterolemia, glucose intolerance, high blood insulin concentrations, and hypertension, so-called Syndrome X. As a result of this clustering of risk factors, people with this form of obesity are at increased risk of developing heart disease (Després et al. 1990; Avery 1991).

- **Increased body mass index with high waist-to-hip-circumference ratios.** Nonsmoking white American men with a body mass index, calculated as weight in kilograms divided by height in square meters, between 23.5 and 24.9 kg per meter have the lowest mortality from death from all causes (Calle et al. 1999). The effect is less apparent in African-Americans. In women, the optimum body mass index is between 22.0 and 23.4 kg per meter. Similar findings have been reported in the Dutch.

The waist-to-hip-circumference ratio may be a better predictor of death from all causes (Folsom et al. 1993), perhaps because it provides a more accurate measure of the amount of fat stored in the abdominal organs. It is believed that fat stored at that site is more closely linked to the risk of disease than is fat stored at other sites (Peiris et al. 1989).

Interestingly, patterns of body fatness are established already at age 25 (Voorrips et al. 1992). Furthermore, even quite high levels of physical fitness (running more than 64 km per week) cannot prevent a remorseless increase in body mass index (approximately 0.5 kg per meter per decade) and waist-to-hip-circumference ratio (1.9 cm per decade) with advancing age (P.T. Williams 1997). Nevertheless, those who run the most have the most favorable body mass indexes and waist-to-hip ratios, in part because they have the most favorable ratios at all younger ages.

P.T. Williams (1997) suggests that this progressive accumulation of body fat may be caused by an age-related decline in blood testosterone concentrations since the administration of testosterone to middle-aged men reduces their waist-to-hip circumference ratios (Rebuffe-Scrive et al. 1991). He calculates that, to maintain the same body mass index with increasing age, runners would need to increase their training distance by 23 km per week each decade. This would mean that an athlete running 64 km per week at age 30 would need to more than double his weekly training distance to 133 km per week at age 60 and to 156 km per week at age 70, a physical impossibility at that age (chapter 11).

- **Inappropriate alcohol intake.** The intake of moderate amounts of alcohol, especially wine (Grønbæk et al. 1995), is associated with a reduced mortality from all causes, including heart attack and strokes in middle-aged to elderly men and women (Rimm et al. 1991; Thun et al. 1997; Berger et al. 1999; Sacco et al. 1999). The protective mechanisms remain uncertain, as does the exact amount of alcohol that is protective. In general, optimum benefits are achieved with no more than one to two drinks per day (Thun et al. 1997; Berger et al. 1999; Sacco et al. 1999). Whereas wine appears to be especially effective (Grønbæk et al. 1995), the protective value of beer and other spirits is less well established. The protective effect of alcohol is greatest in those who metabolize alcohol the most slowly because they have a particular allele of the enzyme alcohol dehydrogenase 3 (ADH3; Hines et al. 2001). People with that genotype also had the highest blood HDL-cholesterol concentrations.

However, the beneficial effect of appropriate alcohol consumption on mortality is quite small and does not compensate for the very much (twofold) increased risk associated with cigarette smoking. Hence, combining moderate alcohol consumption with smoking, a common practice, will not nullify the detrimental effects of smoking on the arteries and heart. Furthermore, alcohol consumption at younger ages is associated with increased mortality from trauma and other conditions, including poisoning (Rehm et al. 1993), and it presumably increases the probability that alcoholism will develop in those with the brain disorder that predisposes to the condition (Nestler and Aghajanian 1997; Leshner 1997).

The evolutionary origins of human alcohol consumption and alcoholism have been traced by Dudley (2000). He proposes that fruit-eating (frugivorous) birds and mammals, including the human ancestors, may have learned to identify the smell and taste of ethanol in decaying fruit as a marker of energy-dense foods. As a result, alcohol-seeking behavior may have evolved in mammals, including humans, as a spur for nutritional reward. Since ethanol is infrequently available in the wild, alcoholism in those animals with any genetic predisposition is unlikely to occur. But the widespread availability of alcohol in modern society will inevitably convert an evolutionary, beneficial alcohol-seeking behavior in animals to alcoholism in some humans with a genetic predisposition once they are exposed to alcohol.

- **Hostile personality type.** Persons with the so-called type-A personality originally defined by Meyer Friedman and Ray Rosenman (1959) possess three characteristics: they are highly competitive and ambitious; they speak rapidly and interrupt others frequently; and they are seized by anger and hostility with uncommon frequency. In short, they are unable to sit back and relax but are consumed by hostility, haste, impatience, and competitiveness. The traditional belief has been that such people have a greater risk of developing coronary heart disease than do people without these characteristics, the so-called type-B personalities. It is suggested that, of the three personality characteristics, it is the tendency of the type-A personality to hostility that explains the increased risk of heart disease (R.B. Williams 1987).

  But even hostility is not the best description of the dangerous personality characteristic. Rather, it appears that a mistrust of others, cynicism, is the toxic element in the type-A personality that explains this apparent increased susceptibility to coronary artery disease. The type-A person at risk of heart disease exhibits an absence of trust in the basic goodness of others, believing them to be mean, selfish, and undependable. Tutko (Cimons 1988) has suggested that there are two subsets of the type-A person: the type-A-hostile and the type-A-controlled. He argues that the type-A-hostile is the classic type-A-person whose actions are motivated by hostility and anger. In contrast, the type-A-controlled is motivated "by excitement and reward, by the challenge of what he is doing. He's like a kid in a candy store. When he wants more, it's because he loves what he is doing" (Cimons 1988, p. 46). Furthermore, it has been found that middle-aged men who are without symptoms of heart disease but who express hostility are more likely to have silent coronary atherosclerosis than those without such hostility (Barefoot et al. 1994).

  Another study (Ragland and Brand 1988) suggests that, at least after an initial heart attack, the risk of sudden death or heart attack is lower in type-A than in type-B people. Thus, the degree to which the type-A personality characteristics contribute to an increased risk of coronary heart disease remains controversial. Interestingly, owners of pets have an enhanced survival after heart attack (Friedman et al. 1982) and lower blood pressures and blood cholesterol and triglyceride concentrations (W.P. Anderson et al. 1992). Perhaps pet owners are likely to have less-hostile personalities, or else pets may moderate the hostility of their owners.

- **Depression.** Men who are depressed are at an increased risk of developing heart disease (Hippisley-Cox et al. 1998).

- **Chronic infection with chlamydia pneumoniae.** In contrast to the more accepted theory—that coronary heart disease occurs as the result of arterial damage caused by the interaction of cholesterol, elevated blood pressure, and inflammation—is the "germ theory," which holds that the arterial damage results from chronic infection with as yet unidentified viruses or bacteria. An early study found that patients with acute heart attack were more likely to have evidence of recent or longstanding infection with the bacterium chlamydia pneumoniae (Saikku et al. 1988). This organism was subsequently isolated from the atheromatous coronary artery plaques of patients dying from coronary heart disease (Kuo et al. 1993; Ramirez 1996). More recently, Strachan et al. (1999) found that people with elevated 1gA antibodies to chlamydia pneumoniae had increased mortality, mainly from fatal heart attack, over a 13-year period. They suggest that treatment for this infection may improve survival in people with coronary heart disease.

Lack of Physical Activity

Six researchers have contributed significantly to our understanding of the relationship between activity level and coronary heart disease. Jeremy Morris, Ralph Paffenbarger, David Siscovick, Ken Cooper, Steven Blair, and Urho Kujaala and their colleagues concluded separately that those who actively exercise are less likely to suffer from coronary heart disease.

Morris' Studies

One of the first studies to suggest that physical inactivity may be an important risk factor for coronary artery disease was reported in 1953 by Jeremy Morris and his associates at the London School of Tropical Medicine (J.N. Morris et al. 1953). They found that conductors on the London Transport system had a 30% lower incidence of heart disease than did the sedentary bus drivers. A similarly favorable result was found for mail carriers when compared to less active postal clerks, who performed sedentary work.

However, subsequent analysis suggested that fat, heavy-smoking, high-blood-cholesterol people likely to develop heart disease chose sedentary occupations, while thin nonsmokers with low blood cholesterol levels chose active occupations (J.N. Morris et al. 1956; Oliver 1967). This finding suggests that physical activity at work was not the sole determinant of heart attack among higher or lower risk groups.

In an attempt to exclude the possibility that people at increased risk of heart attack choose sedentary occupations, Morris' group next studied 16,882 British civil servants, all of whom were involved in sedentary occupations and who were quite similar in respect of their coronary risk factors. This group was then subdivided on the basis of whether they performed vigorous exercise in their leisure time. Vigorous exercise was classified as swimming, tennis, hill climbing, running, jogging, mountain walking, or fast cycling, but these authors did not quantify how often or for how long the required activity had to be.

The heart attack rate in the vigorously active group was one-third of that in the less active group (J.N. Morris et al. 1973). Furthermore, vigorous exercise in leisure time even offered a measure of protection for smokers and for those with high blood pressure, but, for obvious reasons, these subgroups had a higher heart attack rate than did nonsmoking, vigorously active civil servants whose blood pressures were normal (Chave et al. 1978). A subsequent study (J.N. Morris et al. 1980) confirmed that physical activity provided a degree of protection even for fat civil servants of small stature who smoked or who had high blood pressure, diabetes, or even chest pain. Furthermore, whereas the heart attack rate in the active group stayed the same between the ages of 40 and 60 years, the rate in the inactive group more than doubled during those years.

J.N. Morris and colleagues (1980) concluded that "vigorous exercise is a natural defense of the body with a protective effect on the ageing heart against ischemia [a reduced blood flow usually caused by progressive atherosclerotic narrowing of the coronary arteries] and its consequences" (J.N. Morris et al. 1980, p. 1207). Vigorous activities included participation in sports and games such as running and jogging, cycling, rugby, squash, badminton, tennis, football, boxing, swimming, hockey, and rowing as well as recreational activities such as aerobics, calisthenics, hill climbing, and gardening (digging, tree-felling) at least twice a week.

In contrast, participation in nonvigorous activities, including walking, golf, dancing, and table tennis, provided no beneficial effect, even in those who walked up to 7 hours per week.

Paffenbarger's Studies

The next outstanding studies in this field are those by Ralph Paffenbarger and his colleagues (Paffenbarger and Hale 1975; Paffenbarger et al. 1977; 1978; 1983; 1984a and b; 1986; 1993; 1994; Lee and Paffenbarger 1992; 1994; 1998; Sasco et al. 1992; Helmrich et al. 1991). Paffenbarger is an experienced ultramarathon runner, having completed the grueling Western States Hundred-Miler (a mountain race through the Sierra Nevada mountains of northern California) on five occasions, as well as the Comrades and the Two Oceans Marathons in South Africa. He is currently emeritus professor of epidemiology at the Stanford University School of Medicine and has written his own book incorporating his research findings and advice on exercise for optimum health and a longer life (Paffenbarger and Olsen 1996). American sports journalist James Fixx wrote an excellent review of Ralph Paffenbarger and his work in his *Second Book of Running* (Fixx 1980) in a chapter entitled, "Is Running Really Good for Us?"

Indeed, it is a sad paradox that Fixx was one of the few journalists to grasp the complexities encountered by scientific studies attempting to measure the cardiovascular benefits of running. His subsequent sudden death during exercise was sadly seen by many as proof that exercise could not be good for anyone, and Fixx's own meticulous reporting of Paffenbarger's research (Fixx 1980) was forgotten in the rush to incriminate jogging as the cause of his death. But Fixx was never under any illusion that running could prevent heart disease absolutely, for he wrote to the effect that, although strange to believe, runners also die.

In the early 1950s, Paffenbarger chose to study two populations: people who were vigorously active in their occupations (the San Francisco Longshoremen Study: Paffenbarger and Hale 1975; Paffenbarger et al. 1977; 1984a) or in their leisure time (the Harvard Graduate Study: Paffenbarger et al. 1978; 1983; 1984a; 1986; 1991; 1993; 1994; Lee and Paffenbarger 1992; 1994; 1998; Sesso et al. 2000; Paffenbarger and Lee 1997). As the finding from both studies are complementary, only the Harvard Graduate Study will be considered in detail. The special value offered by the Harvard alumni study was that excellent medical data had been collected years earlier, when the alumni were students at Harvard. This made it possible for Paffenbarger to begin a study on subjects whose medical histories were known for up to 40 years previously, staring in 1916. He was therefore able to start a project that covered the life span of his experimental subjects and that would provide significant information in his own lifetime.

In the Harvard study, Paffenbarger et al. (1978) graded leisure-time activity according to the following classification: 10 stairs climbed every working day each week = 118 kJ per week; one city block walked every working day each week = 235 kJ per week; participation in light sports = 21 kJ per minute; participation in vigorous exercise = 42 kJ per minute.

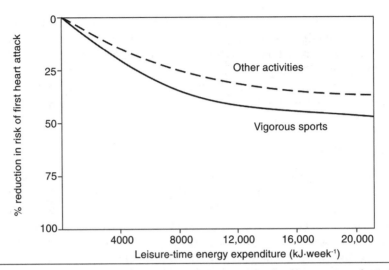

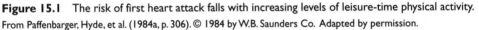

Figure 15.1   The risk of first heart attack falls with increasing levels of leisure-time physical activity. From Paffenbarger, Hyde, et al. (1984a, p. 306). © 1984 by W.B. Saunders Co. Adapted by permission.

Using this classification, they found (Paffenbarger et al. 1984a) that men who reported climbing 50 or more steps each working day had a 20% lower risk of suffering a heart attack than men who climbed less; those who walked five or more blocks daily were at 21% lower risk than those who walked less; and those who reported vigorous sporting activity in leisure time had a 27% lower risk than those who did not exercise vigorously. Participation in light sporting activity did not influence cardiac risk.

When total leisure-time physical activity was calculated, it was found that risk of a first heart attack fell with increasing leisure-time physical activity and was 39% lower in those expending more than 8400 kJ of energy in leisure-time exercise each week (figure 15.1).

Calculating Weekly Kilojoule Expenditure

Runners wanting to calculate their weekly kilojoule energy expenditure to estimate their likely health benefits according to the Paffenbarger studies can do so by referring to figure 15.2. This figure shows that the kilojoule energy expenditure per kilogram of body weight (y-axis on the right) increases linearly with increasing running speed.

To calculate your total energy expenditure during a particular exercise session, you need to know your body weight, the duration of exercise, and your average running speed. An 80-kg runner whose average running speed is 10 km per hour (6:00 per km) expends approximately 0.83 kJ per kg per minute, or 66 kJ per minute, during exercise. To expend more than 8400 kJ of energy per week, the value shown by Paffenbarger et al. (1984a) to be associated with a 39% reduction in heart attack risk, this runner would need to run at that speed for 8400 ÷ 66 minutes (that is, 127 minutes) per week. Similarly, a 50-kg runner whose average training speed is 16 km per hour (3:45 per km) expends approximately 1.14 kJ per kg per minute (57 kJ per minute) and would need to run 147 minutes per week at that speed to achieve the same total energy expenditure.

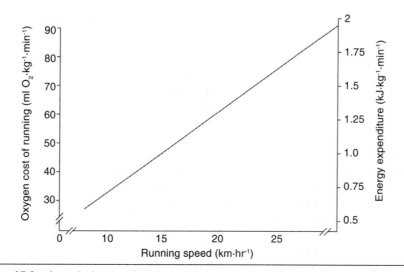

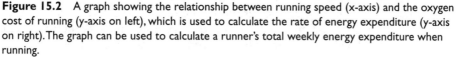

Figure 15.2 A graph showing the relationship between running speed (x-axis) and the oxygen cost of running (y-axis on left), which is used to calculate the rate of energy expenditure (y-axis on right). The graph can be used to calculate a runner's total weekly energy expenditure when running.

Certain heart rate monitors, including the Polar OwnCal watch, calculate energy expenditure during exercise on the basis of the athlete's mass and heart rate. This calculation is possible because, when a large number of people are studied, there is a linear relationship between energy expenditure and heart rate. Hence, the measured heart rates during exercise can be converted to an estimated energy expenditure in kilojoules or calories.

However, there is a large interindividual variability in this relationship, so that the actual kilojoule value calculated by the watch may be either too high or too low. Therefore, the real value of these calculations is not in the precise accuracy of the numbers that they provide but rather in the trends that they identify. Thus, measuring energy expenditure on a weekly basis during training enables us to estimate how we compare to the Paffenbarger data (figure 15.1) and can provide an added (health) incentive to maintaining higher levels of physical activity on a weekly, annual, and lifetime basis.

The Harvard Graduate Study has also produced a number of other important findings, including the following.

- A leisure-time energy expenditure of less than 8400 kJ per week was as strong a risk factor for a first heart attack as were those other well-established heart attack-risk factors (smoking, high blood pressure, and high blood cholesterol levels). Thus, on the basis of this study, physical inactivity must now be considered to be as important a risk factor for heart disease as the other three risk factors, an opinion that has since received universal support (Powell et al. 1987; Fletcher et al. 1992; Bijnen et al. 1994). It has been subsequently shown that alumni expending more than 8400 kJ per week have a 20% lower risk of developing all forms of coronary heart disease (Sesso et al. 2000), regardless of the duration of their exercise bouts. Hence, equal benefit could be achieved by longer bouts of lower-intensity effort or shorter bouts of more intensive exercise, provided the weekly energy expenditure exceeded 8400 kJ (Lee et al. 2000).

- Only Harvard graduates who remained active after graduation were protected from heart attack. The genetic athletes who won fame and glory on the Harvard sports fields in their college days had a reduced heart attack rate only if they continued to exercise vigorously in the years following their graduation. This suggests strongly that it is continued exercise for life, not genetic ability, that is associated with a subsequent reduction in heart attack risk. More recent findings suggest that, if anything, the health of the former university athletes tends to deteriorate more rapidly with age than that of those who were not athletic at university. This is possibly because the body type of the university athlete proficient in power sports, such as football and baseball, is more likely to be mesomorphic (muscular). Mesomorphy is not associated with longevity or good health in later life (Sheehan 1973), perhaps because mesomorphs may have a higher proportion of Type II fast-twitch muscle fibers. Power athletes with a higher proportion of Type II muscle fibers are at greater risk of developing coronary heart disease than are endurance athletes (Lean and Han 1998; Kujala et al. 2000), perhaps because they have more coronary risk factors, including lower blood levels of the protective HDL cholesterol (Tikkanen et al. 1991; 1996).

- Exercise offered protection even in the face of other coronary risk factors (Paffenbarger et al. 1978; Sesso et al. 2000). Thus, Harvard graduates who were short in stature, had a parental history of heart attack or hypertension, smoked, were overweight, had high blood pressure, or had a history of diabetes or stroke were still at a 50% lower risk of heart attack if they expended more than 8400 kJ energy per week in leisure-time activities than were alumni with the same risk factors who did not exercise. Figure 15.3 compares the risk of developing a heart attack in smokers and nonsmokers who differ in their amounts of habitual physical activity. The highest risk (relative risk of 1.00) is found in those who smoke more than 10 cigarettes per day and who are not sufficiently physically active, expending less than 500 kJ per week in physical activity (column D). In contrast, those nonsmokers who are the most active (column C) have the lowest risk (relative risk of 0.25), indicating a 75% lower risk of heart attack than inactive nonsmokers. However, it is worth noting that physically active smokers (column I) have a relative risk of heart attack of about 0.5, which is even slightly lower than that of inactive nonsmokers (column A). Therefore, the risk of heart attack is no higher in physically active smokers than in physically inactive nonsmokers. This occurs because cigarette smoking and physical inactivity are equivalent risk factors for heart disease. The avoidance of both risk factors produces the most favorable result (column C).

- Alumni who reported vigorous leisure-time exercise had a lower risk of fatal heart attack at all levels of total weekly energy expenditure (figure 15.1). Thus, additional benefit seemed to be gained by including vigorous exercise in the exercise sessions. Lee and Paffenbarger's more recent study (1994) found that vigorous but not nonvigorous exercise was inversely related to mortality.

- Those graduates who had suffered a heart attack but who reported 8400 or more kJ per week of leisure-time energy expenditure had a 29% lower heart attack fatality rate than did those graduates who had also suffered heart attacks but who did not exercise as vigorously.

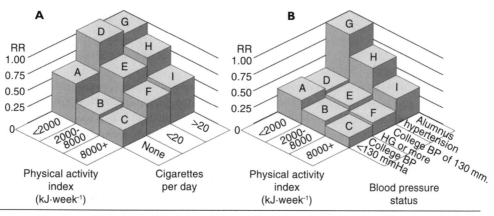

Figure 15.3 The risk of heart attack is reduced in cigarette smokers who are physically active (A). Thus, the relative risk (RR) of first heart attack is greatest in inactive subjects who smoke (columns D and G) and least in those nonsmokers who are the most physically active (column C). Physically inactive nonsmokers (column A) reduce their risk of heart attack as they become increasingly more physically active (columns B and C). Similarly, inactive smokers (column G) reduce their risk of heart attack as they become more physically active (columns H and I). Thus, exercise acts to reduce heart attack risk, even in the face of other risk factors. The same applies for blood cholesterol concentrations (not shown) and for blood pressure (B). Adapted from Paffenbarger, Hyde, et al. (1984b). © 1984 by the American Medical Association.

- Vigorously active graduates had a 27% lower risk of developing high blood pressure than did less active alumni (Paffenbarger et al. 1983). The heavier the graduate, the greater the degree to which exercise reduced the risk of developing hypertension (figure 15.4). Even high rates of total energy expenditure in activities of low intensity were not protective. Rather, protection was present only in those who included moderately vigorous activities, such as tennis, cycling, swimming, or running (Paffenbarger and Lee 1997).

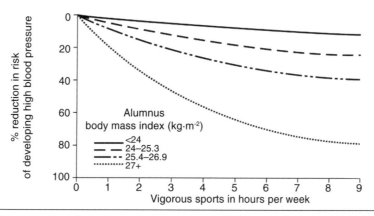

Figure 15.4 The risk of developing hypertension increases with increasing body mass index. However, this risk is reduced in proportion to the number of hours spent exercising each week. Note that the reduction in risk is greatest in those who are the heaviest (highest BMI line) and least in those who are the leanest (lowest BMI line). This is, in part, because those who are lean are at low risk of developing hypertension, whether or not they exercise, whereas those who are heavy are at substantially increased risk. From Paffenbarger, Wing, et al. (1983, p. 253).

- Paffenbarger et al. (1984a) calculated that if five risk factors for heart attack (physical inactivity, cigarette smoking, obesity, high blood pressure, and a family history of heart attack) were removed from all the Harvard alumni, the risk of heart attack would be reduced by 67%.

- Paffenbarger and his colleagues (1986) have shown that the longevity of alumni who exercised vigorously for life is increased. Thus, graduates who continued to expend more than 8400 kJ per week in leisure-time physical activity from the age of 35 years onward enjoyed a two-and-a-half year gain in life expectancy (figure 15.5). Those who began vigorous exercise only after 50 years had a one-to-two-year extension in longevity. A number of other studies support this conclusion that lifelong physical activity probably increases longevity by one to two years (Pekkanen et al. 1987; Heyden and Fodor 1988).

- Paffenbarger's study group has now lived sufficiently long for the effect of recent changes in physical activity patterns to be evaluated. Indeed, this information provides one of the strongest tests of the general hypothesis that physical activity reduces the risk of heart disease. If recent changes in physical activity do not produce changes in line with the findings described, there might be a serious flaw in these findings.

- Fortunately, Harvard alumni who increased their levels of habitual physical exercise to more than 8400 kJ (2000 kcal) per week sometime between 1977 and 1985 reduced their heart attack risk by 26% (Paffenbarger et al. 1993), identical to the reduction enjoyed by those who had always exercised at that level. They also increased their longevity by up to one year. These effects were equivalent to those achieved by stopping smoking. In contrast, the heart attack risk of alumni who stopped regular vigorous exercise increased by 20%. This detrimental effect was greater than the effect of taking up smoking. Hence, an important conclusion from that study was that it is never too late to start exercising. Equally, it is never a good time to stop.

Figure 15.5 Life expectancy increases in proportion to the amount of exercise performed for life. This graph shows that those who expend more than 8000 kJ per week from age 35 increase their left expectancy by 2.5 years. Even beginning exercise late in life is beneficial. Thus, even at 70 years old, an increase in physical activity might prolong life by eight months.

From Paffenbarger, Hyde, et al. (1986).

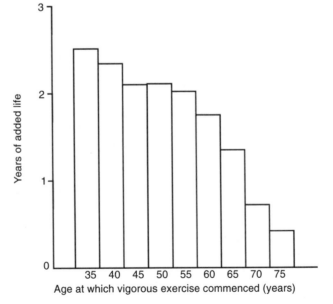

- The effects of changes in body weight on mortality from all causes and from coronary heart disease and cancer were evaluated (Lee and Paffenbarger 1992). Those alumni who remained weight-stable for life were at the lowest risk of mortality from all causes and from heart disease, whereas those who either lost or gained more than 5 kg were at the greatest risk. Lesser amounts of weight loss or weight gain were associated with intermediate risks. Changes in weight did not alter the risk of developing cancer.

- A sister study performed on alumni from the University of Pennsylvania showed that for each additional 2100 kJ per week of energy expenditure, the risk of developing non-insulin-dependent diabetes fell by 6% (Helmrich et al. 1991). Female alumni in that study were also at lower risk of developing breast cancer if they were physically active (Sesso et al. 1998).

- Alumni who had a body mass index greater than 26 kg per m but who expended more than 10,460 kJ per week had a significantly lower risk of colon cancer. In addition, physical activity did not influence the risk of colon cancer in alumni with lower body mass indexes (Paffenbarger et al. 1994). Highly active alumni also had a significantly lower risk of lung cancer. Risks of rectal, prostatic, or pancreatic cancers were not influenced by physical activity.

- Risk of stroke was reduced in alumni who expended more than 4200 kJ per week and fell further in those expending 8400 to 12,596 kJ per week (Lee and Paffenbarger 1998). However, no further reduction occurred with greater weekly energy expenditure. As in the previous studies, activities of light intensity did not reduce risk further.

- Physically active alumni were at a reduced risk of depression but not of suicide (Paffenbarger et al. 1994). The earliest publications of the Harvard Graduate Study focused on factors predicting risk of suicide (Paffenbarger and Asnes 1966), a condition for which this population were at greater risk than most Americans.

- The risk of Parkinson's disease was also slightly reduced in physically active alumni (Sasco et al. 1992).

Siscovick's Studies

The third researcher who has made a significant contribution in this field is David Siscovick, a research cardiologist currently working at the University of North Carolina.

Siscovick and colleagues (1982; 1984a; 1984b) collected detailed information on all people who died suddenly in Seattle, Washington, during a one-year period. Analysis of 145 sudden deaths in a group of people who were, to all intents and purposes, absolutely healthy right up to the moment they died showed that those who exercised vigorously on a regular basis had an overall risk of sudden death approximately two-thirds lower than that of the nonexercisers (figure 15.6; compare lines A and C). However, the risk of sudden death in the habitually exercising group increased acutely during exercise (vertical column D in figure 15.6). Thus, although habitual exercisers had a reduced risk of sudden death, that subset of exercisers with advanced heart disease who would ultimately die suddenly were more likely to die while they were exercising than when they were at rest.

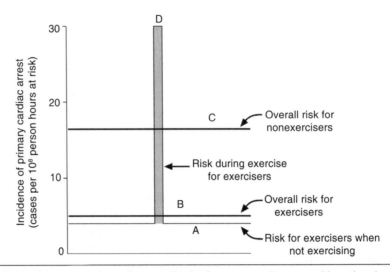

Figure 15.6   Habitual exercise reduces the overall risk of primary cardiac arrest. Note that the risk of cardiac arrest is steeply elevated (column D) during exercise in those regular exercisers who are at risk of sudden death. But as the risk of cardiac arrest for exercisers when they are not exercising (line A) is about 60% lower than the overall risk for nonexercisers (line C), the total (overall) risk for exercisers (line B)—which is the sum of the risk during exercise (column D) and the risk when not exercising (line A)—is still very much lower than the risk for nonexercisers. Hence, the apparent paradox: although exercise may kill you acutely during a single exercise bout (if you are so predisposed by an underlying heart condition), if you survive sufficient bouts of exercise, you will live longer than if you had not exercised.
Data from Siskovitch et al. (1984a; 1984b).

   This finding explains why the sudden death of athletes usually occurs during exercise and also why such events do not prove that exercise is dangerous and should therefore be avoided. In fact, if the habitual exercisers were to stop exercising, their risk of sudden death would increase threefold, as shown in figure 15.6, since their incidence of cardiac arrest would rise from line A to line C, a 66% increase. This group (Lemaitre et al. 1999) has also shown that moderate physical activity, including walking for exercise or gardening, performed for more than 60 minutes per week was as effective as more vigorous or prolonged exercise in reducing the risk of sudden cardiac arrest.

   Therefore, the studies of Siscovick and colleagues confirm the finding that the risk of sudden death is reduced in people who exercise regularly. But they also show that there is an increased likelihood that those people who have heart disease in spite of their regular exercise will die during their exercise bouts. Interestingly, the degree of benefit is directly related to the higher the level of coronary risk; people who are at low risk of dying suddenly from coronary heart disease benefit less from vigorous physical exercise than do those who are at high risk either because of a family history of heart disease or because they are smokers who have other risk factors already described.

   As Siscovick et al. have stated, "Efforts to discourage clinically healthy people at risk of primary cardiac arrest from continuing to engage in vigorous exercise may be inappropriate" (1984b, p. 625). More recently, Siscovick et al. (1997) found that coronary risk factors and markers of subclinical (asymptomatic) heart disease fell with increasing intensities of leisure-time physical activity in men and women older than 65. They therefore concluded that the intensity of exercise undertaken in later life was an important determinant of benefit.

Exercise Versus Sudden Death

If exercise has a protective role in heart disease, why is it that some athletes die suddenly during exercise? This is a question that the media, in particular, seem unable to resist. In an attempt to find an answer, I have looked at this phenomenon from a historical perspective.

The marathon race itself commemorates the immortal run of an unknown soldier, fully armored and "hot from battle," to Athens. His mission was to inform the Greek capital that the invading Persians had been defeated on the plains of Marathon. Within seconds of delivering the joyous words, "Rejoice, rejoice, victory is ours," the messenger reportedly died. While this event was probably mythical (D.E. Martin et al. 1977), genuine tragedies have since been documented in actual marathon races.

The Greek physician Galen was one of the first to express an opinion on the risk of exercise on the heart. He wrote,

> *Athletes live a life quite contrary to the precepts of hygiene, and I regard their mode of living as a regime far more favorable to illness than to health. . . . While athletes are exercising their professions, their body remains in a dangerous condition but, when they give up their professions, they fall into a condition more parlous still; as a fact, some die shortly afterward; others live for some little time but do not arrive at old age (Hartley and Llewellyn 1939, p. 657).*

The first modern sport to attract a similar concern was rowing. In 1845, the seventh Oxford and Cambridge Boat Race was the first to be rowed on the current course on the Thames between Putney and Mortlake. No sooner had it moved to its longer course through the British capital than an irate letter written by one Frederick C. Skey, past president and Fellow of the Royal College of Surgeons, appeared in *The Times of London,* charging that "The University Boat Race as at present established is a national folly" (Hartley and Llewellyn 1939, p. 657). Skey claimed that rowing was bringing young men to an early grave. A scientific study published shortly afterward by John Morgan (1873), a Birmingham physician, proved that Skey was in error. Morgan showed that the life expectancy of university oarsmen was not reduced. If anything, it was slightly longer than that of the average Englishman of the period.

The introduction of professional marathon running to the United States after the 1908 Olympic Games marathon (Martin and Glynn 1979) induced the following judgment:

> *It is only the exceptional man who can safely undertake the running of 26 miles, and even for them the safety is comparative rather than absolute. The chances are that every one of them weakens his heart and shortens his life, not only by the terrible strain of the race itself, but by the preliminary training, which produces muscular and vascular developments that become perilous instead of advantageous the moment a return to ordinary pursuits and habits puts an end to the need for them. (New York Times 1909)*

In 1968, this issue was revived in a letter that appeared in the *Journal of the American Medical Association* (Moorstein 1968), stating that all members of the

(continued)

1948 Harvard rowing crew had since died "of various cardiac disease"—an assertion that was enthusiastically denied by these oarsmen, who reported that they were all alive and well (Quigley 1968).

In the 1890s, North Americans suddenly discovered the bicycle, and medicine had another sport about which to express its alarm (M.M. Sherman 1983). Prospective cyclists were warned that prolonged bending over the handlebars could cause *kyphosis bicyclistarum,* or, in lay terms, *cyclist's stoop* or *cyclist's spine.* Then, too, there was cyclist's throat, caused by the inhalation of cold, dusty air, and *cyclist's face,* the determined grimace that indicated the excessive tension caused by riding a bicycle. The incidence of hernias and appendicitis were also said to be more common in cyclists, and these too were related to the cycling position. Manufacturers were urged to develop a cycle that could be pedaled in the upright position. Women who cycled, it was said, were especially prone to uterine prolapse and to distortion of the pelvic bones and hardening of the muscles of the pelvic floor, both of which would cause difficult labor, should they ever stop cycling long enough to become pregnant.

Finally, of course, there was *cyclist's heart.* The working life of the heart was limited to only a certain number of heartbeats, these physicians asserted, and the faster heart rate during cycling would only waste these precious beats and, in so doing, lead to premature heart failure.

One of the next references to the dangers of exercising on the heart was made in 1909 by five eminent British physicians who initiated a chain of correspondence in *The Times of London* by stating that "school and cross-country races exceeding one mile in distance were wholly unsuitable for boys under the age of 19, as the continued strain involved is apt to cause permanent injury to the heart and other organs" (Friend 1935; editorial 1938).

Again, this view was easily refuted. From an analysis of 16,000 schoolboys covering a period of 20 years, Lempriere (1930) could find only two cases of sudden death during exercise that were not due to accidents. He concluded that "heart strain through exercise is practically unknown," a conclusion echoed by Sir Adolphe Abrahams (1930; 1951), who denounced the concept of the strained athletic heart. Instead Lempriere (1930) made this very significant observation: "The real risk lies in boys playing games or running after some minor illness, generally slight influenza, and in times of epidemics it is impossible to be sure that no unfit boy takes part."

Running again became a medical cause célèbre in the 1970s, as the popularity of the sport mushroomed. One of the first articles to question the safety of such activity reported that half of 59 sudden deaths occurred during or immediately after severe or moderate physical activity, especially jogging. The authors questioned "whether it is worth risking an instantaneous coronary death by indulging in an activity, the possible benefit of which . . . has yet to be proved" (Friedman et al. 1973, p 1327). They also considered "the possible lethal peril of violent exercise to [heart] disease patients" (Friedman et al. 1973, p. 1327).

Blair and Cooper's Studies

Many regard the publication of Ken Cooper's classic book *Aerobics* (1968) as one of the greatest influences on the physical fitness boom that began in the 1970s.

The influence of Cooper's book can possibly be ascribed to two factors. Cooper was the first to suggest that endurance-type (aerobic) activities were especially beneficial to health—until that time, most people believed that strength, not endurance, was the key to health. More important, Cooper devised a method (Cooper's aerobic points) of grading the amount of exercise performed and thereby assessing the relative health benefits you could expect from participating in different activities for different durations and at different intensities. In accordance with this method, the optimum amount of exercise needed to ensure good health were 30 points in one week. To achieve this you would, for example, need to walk 4.8 km five days per week; run 3.2 km five days per week; cycle 9.6 km five days per week; swim 900 m five days per week; or play handball, basketball, or squash for 40 minutes five days per week. Remarkably, these guidelines are not greatly different from the current activity guidelines of the American College of Sports Medicine (ACSM).

Cooper's next significant contribution was to establish the Cooper Clinic in Dallas, Texas, for health screening and exercise prescription. By 1981, more than 13,000 medical evaluations and exercise prescriptions had been performed. Realizing that this information would be of great value if the health of the participants were to be followed into later life, Cooper initiated the Institute for Aerobics Research, housed in the grounds of the Cooper Clinic. He contracted epidemiologist Steven Blair to follow the future health of the Cooper Clinic patients, in much the same way that Morris and Paffenbarger followed their respective study populations.

In 1989, Blair and his team reported that participants who were judged to be physically fit on the basis of their treadmill running performance at the initial screening test had lower mortality from all causes of death, from heart disease, and from cancer at specific sites, than did those who were judged unfit on their initial assessment. As in the studies of Morris and Paffenbarger, risk reduction occurred even in the presence of risk factors, so that those at high risk benefited the most from increased levels of physical fitness. Furthermore, sporting activity at high school or college was not associated with any alteration in risk (Brill et al. 1989).

Subsequent studies from Blair's group have shown that fitness levels, measured as the number of minutes that subjects can continue to exercise during a progressive maximal exercise test to exhaustion, is inversely related to mortality from all causes and from coronary heart disease in men (Blair et al. 1996) and women (Blair et al. 1993; Blair et al. 1996). People who increased their fitness over a five-year period reduced their mortality risk by 44% (Blair et al. 1995). Members of the moderate-to-high fitness groups usually walked between 2 and 3 hours per week (Stofan et al. 1998), compatible with the current recommendation that 30 minutes of exercise on most days of the week is an optimum exercise dose for most people.

Using the same population group, Wei et al. (1999) have also shown that sedentary, obese men are at a 2.6 times higher risk of developing coronary heart disease than are men of normal weight. But regular physical activity reduced risk independent of their levels of obesity, indicating that part of the increased risk for obese men results from an associated physical inactivity.

Although it was not stated in their article (Wei et al. 1999), in other presentations by Blair and colleagues I have heard it suggested that physical activity normalizes coronary risk in the obese, in much the same way as it does in those who are smokers or who have high blood pressure (see figure 15.3).

Finnish Studies

An unusual characteristic of the Finnish health care system is that all hospital discharges from both public and private hospitals are recorded on a central register. This makes it possible to determine diagnoses and associated medical costs in different Finnish groups, including former athletes.

Using this technique, a series of studies have shown that Finnish former elite athletes have increased life expectancy (Sarna et al. 1993), which is greatest in endurance athletes (76 years), less in power athletes (72 years), and least in the matched reference group of healthy but nonelite athletic Finns (70 years). Former elite athletes also maintained healthier lifestyles for life. They remained physically active, were more likely to eat fruits and vegetables and to avoid vitamin supplements, and were less prone to taking up smoking or to consuming butter, high-fat milk, and alcohol (Fogelholm et al. 1994). Greater habitual physical activity and a lower smoking incidence could partly explain the greater life expectancy of those athletes.

This group of former elite Finnish athletes also had a substantially lower risk of developing or dying from coronary heart disease or cancer, or of developing diabetes or hypertension (Kujala et al. 1994b; Sarna et al. 1997; Kujala et al. 1999; Kujala et al. 2000; Pukkala et al. 2000). However, endurance athletes had a greater reduction in the risk of developing coronary heart disease than did power athletes (Kujala et al. 2000), perhaps because endurance athletes participated more often in vigorous exercise after retiring from world-class competitive sport. In another study, mortality among the best Finnish weightlifters between 1977 and 1982 was 4.6 times higher than the expected rate for elite Finnish athletes, whereas elite Finnish weightlifters between 1920 and 1965 had a normal life expectancy (Sarna et al. 1993). The authors suggest that the increased use of anabolic steroids by power athletes after the 1970s might explain that phenomenon.

Former athletes also had lower total blood cholesterol and higher HDL-cholesterol concentrations with a reduced oxidation of LDL-cholesterol (Kujala, Ahotupa, et al. 1996). Although their risk of developing knee but not hip (Kujala et al. 1999) osteoarthritis was marginally increased, they were less likely to develop occupational disabilities. As a result, those athletes made less use of hospital care, with the greatest reduction (29%) being achieved by the endurance athletes and the least (5%) by the power athletes.

Kujala et al. (1998) have tried to establish the extent to which genetic factors alone might explain the superior health of former elite Finnish athletes. By studying pairs of Finnish twins in which one twin was more active than the other, they found that the more active twins had lower mortality rates despite having identical or very similar genetic material. Hence, in people with shared genetic material, physical activity reduces mortality rate from all causes of death.

Lack of Physical Fitness

One of the complexities that bedevils studies of the role of physical activity in the prevention of heart disease is the definition and measurement of an elusive "physical fitness" in the general population. For example, chapter 2 shows that elite athletes inherently have superior athletic ability, whether or not they are highly trained at the time when their physical fitness is evaluated. Hence, athletes with superior genetic endowment may perform better on certain fitness tests, such as a maximal treadmill test to exhaustion, even when they are untrained, than will many with lesser genetic ability but who may train very hard, even to the point of exceeding the weekly energy expenditures that are associated with a reduced risk of heart disease. Is it really physical *fitness* that is a measure of the capacity to undertake physical activity, or is it the physical *activity* itself that protects against heart disease?

The studies of Paffenbarger and Morris showed that physical activity itself was associated with protection against heart disease, whereas the studies of Blair and colleagues showed that higher levels of physical fitness, measured as treadmill running time during a maximal exercise test, were associated with reduced risk of coronary mortality. Hence, these studies measured beneficial effects of either physical activity or physical fitness. But the question remains: do some people who are physically inactive enjoy a measure of protection from heart disease simply because they are physically fit on a genetic basis (that is, they are genetic athletes)? Blair et al. (1995) showed that such people would improve their health even further by being physically active and by improving their fitness.

Whatever the outcome of this debate, it is clear that physical fitness, measured as the exercise duration that can be sustained before reaching exhaustion during a progressive maximal exercise test, is an independent predictor of death from all causes and from heart disease in a variety of populations (Ekelund et al. 1988; Sandvik et al. 1993; Vanhees et al. 1994; Snader et al. 1997; Roger et al. 1998; Wei et al. 1999; Tauqir et al. 2000).

Indeed, in one study, low fitness increased the risk of death at least as much as did diabetes, an elevated blood total cholesterol concentration, hypertension, or current cigarette smoking (Wei et al. 1999). Another study has found that coronary risk factors are more closely related to levels of physical fitness than to habitual physical activity levels (Løchen and Rasmussen 1992). Even in marathon runners, those who finish in the fastest times have fewer coronary risk factors than do the slowest marathon runners (Ketelhut et al. 1996). Furthermore, not only did the fastest runners have 16% higher blood concentrations of the protective HDL-cholesterol fraction and 13% lower concentrations of the damaging LDL-cholesterol fraction before they raced, but they also showed a much greater (40%) increase in blood HDL-cholesterol concentrations during the race than did the slowest runners (9%). That runners have higher than expected HDL-cholesterol concentrations was first noted in 1977 (Wood et al. 1977) and subsequently confirmed in a number of other studies (Hartung et al. 1980; P.T. Williams 1990a; 1990b; 1996). What is particularly interesting is the finding that subjects who adapted most effectively to training and who showed the greatest increases in their HDL-cholesterol concentrations with training were those who had the highest HDL-cholesterol concentrations at the start of the training program (P.T. Williams et al. 1982). This suggests that HDL-cholesterol concentrations are related to some other factors that also determine athletic ability, perhaps skeletal muscle fiber composition including a higher proportion of Type I muscle fibers.

As a result of all these findings, Ketelhut et al. (1996) have questioned whether the factors that determine the level of these coronary risk factors might also determine the ability to develop physical fitness.

My interpretation, according to the Integrated Neuromuscular Recruitment Model (see chapter 2), is that the governor determines the physical fitness level during progressive maximum exercise to exhaustion in response to the adequacy of coronary blood flow to the heart. As a result, those who are able to exercise for longer before the governor terminates exercise would be expected to have a better, less diseased coronary circulation and hence to be at lower risk of developing symptomatic heart disease in the immediate future. However, this theory cannot explain why a superior coronary circulation also protects against death from all causes or why, in healthy athletes who do not have any evidence for coronary artery disease, higher levels of physical fitness (and hence, according to this model, greater coronary blood flow) are associated with fewer coronary risk factors and a superior adaptation of those risk factors to physical activity—for example, greater increases in HDL-cholesterol concentrations in response to physical activity (Ketelhut et al. 1996; P.T. Williams et al. 1982; P.T. Williams 1996).

To determine the extent that inherent athletic ability (physical fitness) protects against heart disease, we need to compare heart disease mortality or heart attack rates, or both, in those who differ in both their inherent athletic ability and their levels of habitual physical activity.

It is of interest that moderate-to-high levels of physical fitness in the participants in the Dallas Aerobics Study are achieved by expending between 2100 to 5300 kJ per week in leisure-time physical activity (Stofan et al. 1998). This 2.5-fold difference in the amount of weekly exercise required to produce the same level of fitness in different people provides an indirect measure of the hereditary contribution to physical fitness.

What is therefore needed is a test that can identify those with high levels of physical fitness who do not participate in regular physical activity. One possibility is the rate at which the heart rate recovers after exercise, since this is known to be influenced by physical activity. Indeed, a delayed decrease in the heart rate during the first minute after maximal exercise is a powerful predictor of subsequent mortality (Cole et al. 1999), independent of the level of physical fitness measured as the peak work rate achieved during such testing. We can expect future work to disentangle the effects of physical activity from those of physical fitness.

Heart Disease

Can deaths that occur during running be attributed solely to the activity of running? The general public seems to have difficulty understanding this concept, as people tend to assume that there is always a cause -and-effect relationship between any two apparently related phenomena.

To illustrate the point, let us imagine the example of a rugby or ice hockey player whose neck is broken, causing paralysis, as the result of an illegal maneuver during a match. Clearly in this case, there is a direct relationship between the illegal maneuver and the subsequent paralysis. Had the player not been playing the match at that moment and had he not been the target of a maneuver, he would not have been paralyzed.

Now, let us consider the runner who dies suddenly while running. Can we be certain that if the runner had not been running at that particular moment, he would still be alive? The answer is a decided no; whereas in the normal course of events, people do not suddenly break their necks developing paralysis, we all know that a large number of people with heart disease die daily from heart attacks, without ever running. Thus, unlike the rugby or ice hockey player's broken neck, the condition of sudden death is not necessarily specific to sport. The question that then arises is whether running triggered the fatal event.

Virtually all people who die suddenly during exercise have a serious disease, usually of the heart, that adequately explains the cause of death (Noakes et al. 1984b). This was true of James Fixx.

Fixx, a running guru in the United States, was at high risk of heart disease because his father had died from a heart attack at a very early age (43 years). In addition, Fixx had not always lived an exemplary life and had been a heavy smoker in his younger days. He also had a markedly elevated blood cholesterol concentration (Noakes 1987b).

Fixx unquestionably had warning symptoms that he chose to ignore. His fiancée relates that he had complained of chest tightness during exercise and said he was going to Vermont to see whether the fresh Vermont air would not alleviate the symptoms, which he considered to be due to allergy (Medical World News 1984; Higdon 1984). He promised that if the Vermont air failed to offer him respite he would see a physician. The air did not help, and he died while running on his first day in Vermont. Interestingly, some months before his death, he had visited Ken Cooper's Aerobics Center in Dallas and had politely refused to undergo an exercise stress test to check the state of his heart. Possibly even then he had had an inkling of what was in store.

An autopsy showed that Fixx had severe disease of the (coronary) blood vessels supplying the heart, with near-total narrowing by arterial disease (atherosclerosis) of one and 80% narrowing of another coronary artery. There was also evidence of a recent heart attack. In addition, his heart was somewhat large, suggesting the possibility of concurrent hypertrophic cardiomyopathy.

On the day Fixx died, 1000 other Americans would also have died from heart attacks (Zipes et al. 1981). Had the press reviewed the features of those heart-attack victims, they would have concluded that, at least with regard to his regular exercise, his death was the exception, and that heart attacks occur most commonly in males who have high blood pressure, smoke heavily, have high blood cholesterol levels, and take no exercise—a conclusion that is the opposite of that drawn from reports that highlight the exception to the rule.

Thus, Fixx's death followed a familiar pattern that helps to emphasize the points already made. One interesting possibility not considered by many is that regular exercise actually enabled him to outlive his father by nine years. The term *the athlete's heart* was coined in the late nineteenth century by those who mistakenly believed that exercise caused damage that led to an enlarged, weakened heart with death at an early age from heart failure.

The types of heart disease associated with sudden death during exercise differ depending on the athlete's age. Athletes older than 40 are more likely to die from coronary atherosclerosis causing an acute heart attack, whereas athletes under the age of 40 who die suddenly during exercise are more likely to have a condition known as hypertrophic cardiomyopathy, in which the heart is abnormally enlarged. However, some young athletes who die suddenly during exercise have genetically elevated blood cholesterol levels (familial hypercholesterolemia), which cause them to develop severe atherosclerosis at an early age, leading to sudden death in their teens or early twenties.

Neither coronary atherosclerosis nor hypertrophic cardiomyopathy is caused by exercise, however vigorous. The exact cause of coronary atherosclerosis is currently unknown but is related to all the factors discussed earlier in this chapter. Regular physical activity acts to delay or prevent coronary atherosclerosis. There is also no evidence that hypertrophic cardiomyopathy is either improved or aggravated by exercise. Because these athletes have severe or advanced disease, they are at high risk of dying suddenly, irrespective of whether they exercise.

A number of studies have tried to determine whether exercise increases the risk that people with advanced heart disease will die suddenly during exercise. Some have found that moderate exercise does not increase the risk of sudden death (Vuori et al. 1978; P. Lynch 1980), whereas others have found that more vigorous forms of exercise, such as cross-country skiing or running, are associated with a five- to sevenfold greater risk of sudden death (Vuori et al. 1978; P.D. Thompson et al. 1982; P.D. Thompson 1982). This means that if the same population had not participated in the activity but had stayed at home, the number of deaths during the same period would have been only one-fifth or one-seventh. The magnitude of this risk increase is perhaps difficult to imagine since the risk of sudden death in that group of relatively healthy athletes is, in any case, negligible.

Three more recent studies have also established that heavy physical exertion (Mittleman et al. 1993; Willich et al. 1993), including sexual activity (Muller et al. 1996), can trigger the onset of heart attack, including sudden death. But in all those studies, the risk of heart attack was substantially lower in those who were habitually physically active. The period of increased risk was roughly the first hour after physical exertion (Mittleman et al. 1993).

Paul Thompson and his colleagues (P.D. Thompson et al. 1982) conducted a study that provides a more meaningful grasp of the real magnitude of this increased risk. They found that between 1975 and 1980, 12 men died while jogging in Rhode Island, 11 from heart attacks. Five of these men were known to have heart disease before their deaths. The incidence of death during jogging was one death per 396,000 hours of jogging, which is about seven times the estimated heart attack rate during more sedentary activities. Thus, in that study, the unequivocal evidence was that jogging increased the risk that the jogger with severe heart disease would die while exercising. The same conclusion can be drawn from the data of Siscovick et al. (1982; 1984a; 1984b).

This finding should not be used, however, to overestimate the risk of exercise. For example, in the Rhode Island study, there was one death per 7620 joggers per year, clearly an infinitesimal risk for each individual jogger. Furthermore, it would be totally impractical to screen all 7620 joggers in Rhode Island in an attempt to identify the one jogger at risk of sudden death each year. Dr. Peter Wood from Stanford University has calculated, on the basis of these data, that a middle-aged jogger with no known cardiac disease who decides to continue running for one more year is at considerably lower risk of dying suddenly than is a middle-aged nonrunner who continues to drive his car during that year (Wood 1987).

More recently, Maron, Poliac, et al. (1996) calculated, on the basis of cumulative 30-year data from two United States marathons, that the overall prevalence of sudden cardiac death during marathon running was 0.002%, or 1 death per 50,000 race finishers. The risk was about 100-fold less than the overall risk of living for one year. But when expressed relative to person-hours of exercise, marathon running (1 death per 215,000 hours) was more "dangerous" than noncompetitive forms of exercise (1/375,000 hours), jogging (1/396,000 hours), or cross-country skiing (1/607,000 hours). For the individual person, it means that you need to accumulate 215,000 hours of marathon running, equivalent to 53,750 four-hour marathons, before you are likely to die suddenly while racing a marathon. Most would accept this as a perfectly reasonable risk and one that should not deter us from continuing to run marathons, provided that symptoms of heart disease discussed subsequently are not present when we run.

If exercise did increase the risk of sudden death or heart attack, by how much did exercise actually shorten the life expectancy of the runner who was in any case at high risk of dying suddenly and unexpectedly? Indirect evidence that the exercise probably does not greatly decrease life expectancy under such circumstances comes from a study of the 1978 Rhode Island blizzard (Faich and Rose 1979), which caused the daily death rate from heart attack to increase from the usual February average of 27 deaths per day to 48 deaths per day. This rate remained high for three of the first five days after the storm but subsequently decreased below the normal daily average, so that the total number of heart-attack deaths for February that year was the same as for previous years. Thompson concluded that "These results suggest that the added physical and emotional stress arising from the storm eliminated those who would have succumbed to ischemic heart disease [heart attack] in the near future" (1982, p. 227). In the same way, jogging deaths may occur in those whose time is up and who would be due to die within the next few days or weeks even if they avoided all forms of exercise, including walking.

It is important to understand that silent heart disease may be present even in people who are extremely physically fit (Noakes et al. 1984a; Rowe 1991; Katzel et al. 1998; Damon et al. 1999). For example, we have reported cases of marathon runners who completed the 90-km Comrades ultramarathon only weeks before their subsequent deaths from severe advanced heart disease (Noakes et al. 1984b). One 42-year-old runner completed a 42-km standard marathon in 3:06:00 just three weeks before (as shown in the autopsy) he had complete occlusion of one major coronary artery and 75% narrowing, with atherosclerosis, of the other two. In addition, there was evidence of hypertrophic cardiomyopathy (Noakes and Rose 1984). An even more disturbing example was the sudden death of a 57-year-old within one minute of his winning a 3,000-m race in a meet record time of 10:30.2 (Sadaniantz et al. 1989). Autopsy revealed severe coronary artery disease in the three major coronary arteries and an enlarged heart, also suggestive of hypertrophic cardiomyopathy. Hence, it is quite wrong to assume that because someone is fit enough to complete competitive races (including marathons and even ultramarathons) in quite respectable times, that person cannot have very serious heart disease (Noakes 1987b). On the other hand, in some cases of sudden death or heart attack during exercise, no structural heart abnormality may be found (Noakes 1987b; Tse and Lau 1995; Chillag et al. 1990; Bouvier et al. 1997) and the mechanism of death remains uncertain although the heart is clearly the cause.

The majority of people who die suddenly during exercise frequently also have symptoms of heart disease that they ignored, choosing to continue exercising rather than to seek medical advice (Drory et al. 1991). Thus, in our study of heart attacks and sudden deaths in marathon runners, we found that fully 81% of these cases had had warning symptoms (Noakes et al. 1984b; Noakes 1987b). Six athletes completed marathon races, and three the Comrades ultramarathon, despite symptoms of chest or abdominal pain sufficiently severe to force them to stop running and to walk and run intermittently. Despite severe chest pain, one athlete continued to run a 16-km race and collapsed at the finish. Another runner continued training for three weeks, including a 64-km training run, with chest pain severe enough to force him to walk on numerous occasions. Loss of consciousness, in particular, is a grave sign that must be thoroughly investigated. Other warning signs include gastrointestinal symptoms and a recent febrile illness.

A large number of people die each day from heart attacks, a point that is sometimes ignored. The vast majority of these people are sedentary, heavy smokers with uncontrolled high blood pressure and elevated blood cholesterol levels. If only those sudden deaths occurring in athletes are reported in the press, the public may develop a distorted impression of the relative dangers of exercise, as was the case in the past. Fortunately, the overwhelming evidence for the cardiovascular benefits of exercise ensure that the distortion is no longer possible.

The data of Siscovick et al. (1982; 1984a; 1984b) clearly show that people who have undetected heart disease (and who are therefore at risk of sudden death) reduce their overall risk of sudden death if they exercise regularly. However, during exercise, their risk is increased acutely (see figure 15.6, column D).

In contrast, we now know that people involved in dynamic, endurance-type activities live longer and have less coronary artery disease than their more sedentary counterparts. We also know that a normal heart cannot be damaged acutely by severe exercise, even at medium altitude, because performance in such activities appears to be limited by a governor in the brain that restricts the amount of exercise that can be performed, specifically to prevent heart damage.

Today we use the term *athlete's heart* to describe cardiac characteristics found in trained athletes (table 15.1). The heart of the trained athlete has a slow resting heart rate that may be as low as 28 beats per minute in some world-class marathon runners as the result of increased activity of the parasympathetic nervous system. Increased parasympathetic activity increases the variability in the beat-to-beat heart period (the RR interval) both at night and during the day (Goldsmith et al. 1992). Increased RR variability is the sign of a more healthy heart.

Table 15.1 Cardiovascular values in untrained, trained, and world-class athletes			
Cardiovascular quality	**Untrained**	**Trained**	**World-class**
Resting heart rate (beats·min^{-1})	75	60	28–36
Maximum heart rate (beats·min^{-1})	185	183	174
Heart volume (ml)	750	820	1200
Resting stroke volume (ml)	61	80	125
Maximum stroke volume (ml)	120	140	200
Resting cardiac output (L·min^{-1})	4.6	4.7	4.5
Maximum cardiac output (L·min^{-1})	22.2	25.6	34.8
$\dot{V}O_2$max (ml·kg^{-1}·min^{-1})	41	50	80

The maximum heart rate is also slightly reduced in these athletes, probably as a result of an increased maximum stroke volume. As a result, the trained heart can achieve higher maximal cardiac output, but at a lower heart rate. Indeed, the volume of the heart is up to 60% greater in world-class athletes than in untrained subjects, and this enlarged heart pumps more blood with each stroke, both at rest (resting stroke volume) and at maximum exercise (maximum stroke volume), because of enhanced contractility and a superior filling capacity (Fagard et al. 1989; Gledhill et al. 1994; Jensen-Urstad et al. 1998). The result is that the maximum cardiac output, the amount of blood pumped each minute by the heart during maximum exercise, and the $\dot{V}O_2$max are much greater in world-class athletes than in untrained subjects.

In the words of the cardiologist Joseph Wolffe, "The heart of the athlete is a better developed, physically more adequate organ that functions more economically than the heart of the physically untrained" (1962, p. 23).

A problem faced by cardiologists is the clinical differentiation of the healthy athlete's heart from the condition hypertrophic cardiomyopathy that may occur on a genetic basis as a result of at least four different genetic mutations on chromosomes 1, 11, 14, and 15 (Maron et al. 1995) and that may therefore be coincidentally present in athletes. This condition is characterized by the presence of an enlarged heart and an increased risk of sudden death. Hypertrophic cardiomyopathy is the leading cause of sudden unexpected death in athletes younger than about 30 years (Liberthon 1996). Furthermore, up to 40% of patients with this condition may die suddenly during or after exercise (Maron et al. 1982). Fortunately, measurement of the thickness of the left ventricular wall and the size of the left ventricular cavity with echocardiography can usually distinguish the two conditions (Pelliccia et al. 1991; Maron et al. 1995).

The usual left ventricular wall thickness is up to 12 mm in highly trained athletes but may range from 20 to 50 mm in people with hypertrophic cardiomyopathy (Maron et al. 1995). Difficulties arise in those with left ventricular wall thicknesses of 13 to 16 mm, into which range some athletes (less than 2%) with normally enlarged hearts and some patients with hypertrophic cardiomyopathy fit. The distinction between health and disease is helped by the finding that more than 30% of athletes have an enlarged left ventricular cavity greater than 55 mm, whereas values below 45 mm are more common in people with hypertrophic cardiomyopathy. The diagnosis of hypertrophic cardiomyopathy becomes increasingly more probable and that of the athletic heart increasingly less likely as the thickness of the left ventricular wall increases and the size of the left ventricular cavity decreases.

Heart Damage

Although the clear evidence is that appropriate exercise is beneficial for the heart, some recent studies suggest that there may be some detrimental consequences of acute prolonged exercise, such as ultramarathon running or completing the Ironman Triathlon, or of very high levels of activity sustained for many decades.

In 1979, we reported the development of acute heart failure in two athletes during the 90-km Comrades Marathon (McKechnie et al. 1979). Their condition resolved rapidly during recovery after the race, and there was no evidence of any structural form of heart disease. Since then, other studies have shown acute, rapidly reversible abnormalities in left ventricular function in runners in a 24-hour race (Niemelä et al. 1984), in Ironman triathletes (Douglas et al. 1987; 1990), and in participants in 100-mile (160-km) race in Silverton, Colorado, run at altitudes ranging from 2350 to 4300 m (Seals et al. 1988). Five of fourteen study subjects in that race developed pulmonary hypertension, right ventricular dysfunction, and wheezing that resolved within 24 hours.

The abnormal heart rhythm, atrial fibrillation, which carries long-term health risks, was found to occur in 5% of top Finnish orienteers and in only 0.2% of age-matched controls (Karjalainen et al. 1998). The higher prevalence of atrial fibrillation occurred even though these orienteers had a lower reported incidence of coronary heart disease, lower mortality from heart disease, and fewer risk factors for atrial fibrillation. Another study also found a higher than expected incidence of arrhythmias in veteran athletes (Jensen-Urstad et al. 1998). A follow-up study of 20 veteran British runners, some of whom were record holders or national champions, found that two required the insertion of pacemakers for the treatment of abnormally slow resting heart rates (Hood and Northcote 1999).

Orienteering has also been associated with two other types of heart disease. A dramatic increase in risks of sudden death occurred in Swedish orienteers between 1979 and 1992, most often due to inflammation of the heart muscle (myocarditis; Wesslén et al. 1996; Friman et al. 1997). The cause of the outbreak remains uncertain. A subsequent study showed that 62% of a group of Swedish orienteers had abnormal heart movement during strenuous exercise, indicating concealed left ventricular damage. The cause of that abnormality is also unknown but could perhaps result from unrecognized but nonfatal bouts of myocarditis. Preventive measures introduced in 1992 prevented further deaths and should, according to this theory, also have prevented further bouts of subclinical heart damage.

Heart Murmurs

There was a time when heart murmurs automatically disqualified anyone from doing any exercise, as it did Clarence de Mar in the 1910s and Wally Hayward in the 1930s. However, as a result of the great advancements that have been made in the field of medicine, it has become apparent that a vast majority of heart murmurs, particularly in athletes, do not indicate the presence of disease. The interpretation of the cause of a murmur will depend on the presence or absence of other findings, which together will then suggest whether the murmur is likely to be a normal finding or whether it signifies likely heart disease (Pflieger and Strong 1992). We now know that up to 80% of runners have heart murmurs and added (third and fourth) heart sounds when evaluated by experienced cardiologists (Singh et al. 1975; Parker et al. 1978).

Thus, many runners will have heart murmurs that are a feature of their fitness and do not indicate disease. The athlete who is concerned that a heart murmur may indeed be due to disease should consult a heart specialist who, with the aid of sophisticated equipment, will be able to establish beyond doubt whether the murmur is due to significant heart disease.

Myocarditis

Myocarditis is caused by inflammation of the heart muscle, often as the result of a viral infection. In most of the more severe viral infections (in particular, influenza), the virus attacks muscle cells throughout the body, causing marked changes in the ultrastructure of these cells and reducing the activity of the important oxidative and glycolytic enzymes essential for cellular energy production (Astrom et al. 1976; Astrom 1977). This explains why muscle pains and stiffness, much like those felt after a marathon, are a common feature of many of these infections and why strength and endurance are reduced especially during, but also for some period after, a viral infection (Daniels et al. 1985; Friman et al. 1997). For example, exercise performance was impaired in one elite athlete for more than 15 months after a viral infection (Jakeman 1993) that also caused a myocarditis.

Indeed, the heart cells are also frequently involved in such infections, and if strenuous exercise is performed when the heart cells are infected by virus, serious consequences, including sudden death, can result (Neuspiel 1986; Drory et al. 1991).

This possibility was most clearly demonstrated by 16 cases of sudden death among 3000 elite Swedish orienteers between 1979 and 1992. During this period, the average annual death rate among these otherwise extremely healthy people was about 1 per 2500 athletes, compared to an expected death rate of 1 per 200,000 healthy Swedes of the same age. The approximately 90-fold greater risk of sudden death in these orienteers was "considered to represent an increased death rate" (Friman et al. 1997). Histological evidence showed that myocarditis was present in at least 75% of the decreased orienteers, raising the probability that a common viral or bacterial agent, perhaps chlamydia pneumoniae, had infected these orienteers, perhaps because their immunity was impaired as a result of their heavy training. There was a notable absence of other likely causes of sudden death (in particular, coronary atherosclerosis or hypertrophic cardiomyopathy) in the hearts of these athletes.

Strict preventive measures were introduced to Swedish orienteering following the 16th death in November 1992. All ranked orienteers were forced to stop training for the first six months of 1993, and all elite competitions were canceled for that year. Orienteers were also advised to avoid all training when suffering from an infection. The results appeared to be impressive; no further deaths were reported to the end of 1995, and the problem appears to have been resolved.

This tragedy provides strong support for the advice that no one should exercise at all during the febrile stage of any viral or bacterial infection, and that athletes should exercise only very lightly for at least 7 to 10 days after the body temperature has returned to normal. This means that if you have influenza within 7 to 10 days of a race, you must not enter that race; if the infection occurs 10 to 21 days before the race, you may run that event, but only at a gentle pace, provided that you feel completely well before the race and that your resting heart rate has returned to normal. A persistently elevated heart rate at rest or during exercise raises the probability that the heart has been infected and that there is a persisting myocarditis. Only if the infection occurs more than three weeks before a race can you run hard in the race, but the chances are that the results will be less than spectacular. If doing well in the race is very important, it is best to avoid the race and to save your efforts for another race, when full recovery from the long-term effects of the infection is more likely.

Abnormal Heart Rhythms

When studied during exercise, well-trained runners have a high incidence of abnormal heart rhythms, one or two of which would normally be considered to indicate serious heart disease if present in sedentary people (Pantano and Oriel 1982). Pantano and Oriel conclude that, by themselves, these variations in heart rhythms may be normal and do not necessarily indicate heart disease, provided the athlete is without symptoms, especially during more vigorous exercise.

But, as described earlier, the pathologically abnormal heart rhythm, atrial fibrillation, may be a direct consequence of many years of heavy endurance training (Karjalainen et al. 1998), as may be the development of an abnormally slow heart rate.

High Blood Pressure

Vigorous lifelong exercise reduces the likelihood that high blood pressure (hypertension) will develop (Paffenbarger et al. 1983; Hernelahti et al. 1998); acute exercise lowers postexercise blood pressure, especially in those with elevated pressures (Brownley et al. 1996); and exercise training reduces blood pressure in approximately 75% of hypertensive subjects (Hagberg and Brown 1995) and in those with normal blood pressures (Halbert et al. 1997). Nonetheless, some athletes have or develop this condition and require treatment.

High blood pressure is considered to be present when the blood pressure readings exceed 140/90 mmHg. The convention 140/90 means that the average systolic blood pressure (the pressure present in the large arm arteries when the heart is actively contracting) is 140 mmHg, and the average diastolic pressure (the pressure present when the heart is relaxing) is 90 mmHg. Blood pressure readings in excess of 140/90 mmHg are associated with an increased risk of developing stroke or heart attack, underlining the need to treat people whose blood pressures exceed these values. Hypertension is usually caused by increased constriction of the arteriolar blood vessels, in part from increased sympathetic nervous activity or increased responsiveness to that stimulation. Sympathetic activity increases blood pressure by stimulating the heart, increasing the heart rate and constricting the blood vessels. Exercise training reduces the resting blood pressure by reducing the activity of the sympathetic nervous system (Grassi et al. 1992; Kingwell et al. 1992).

Currently, there is complete consensus that people whose blood pressures exceed 140/90 mmHg should be treated with varying combinations of exercise, weight loss through diet and exercise, and drug therapy, but there is a lack of agreement about the exact blood pressure reading above which drug therapy becomes essential. Blood pressures that are consistently raised above 165/95 mmHg are a definite indication for drug therapy. Athletes whose blood pressures are raised to those levels should not exercise vigorously until their elevated blood pressures are controlled.

Conventional treatment of people with hypertension should begin with nonpharmacological approaches before medications are used. The nonpharmacological approach includes regular aerobic exercise (Hagberg and Brown 1995); mild sodium restriction (Thelle 1996); mild kilojoule restriction for weight reduction when indicated; restriction of alcohol intake; and behavior modification (in particular, relaxation techniques).

Unfortunately, most of the drugs used for the pharmacological management of high blood pressure produce a number of trying side effects for the athlete—in particular, they interfere with exercise performance, probably through combined effects on the brain, heart, and skeletal muscle and on metabolism. They must therefore be prescribed with discretion, especially to competitive athletes.

Interestingly, people who have normal blood pressures at rest but who develop abnormally elevated blood pressures during exercise testing are at increased risk of developing hypertension (Tanji 1992) and need to be monitored carefully so that their hypertension can be identified early.

Postexercise Collapse

Chapter 4 includes a detailed description of exercise-associated collapse, a condition that occurs in athletes, especially ultramarathoners and Ironman triathletes, shortly after they cross the race finishing line. Postexercise collapse is also known as orthostatic intolerance. Within about two minutes of stopping exercise (especially if it has been in the heat and if the athletes stop running suddenly and have to join the finish line queue for any length of time), affected athletes begin to feel dizzy and nauseous and may feel that they are about to faint. The natural response is to fall to the ground. Lying down rapidly reverses these unpleasant symptoms. Facial pallor, especially pallor of the lips, is a characteristic feature—it is as if the blood drains from the athlete's face.

The most probable physiological abnormality is a sudden hypotension caused when the muscle pump in the leg ceases as the athlete stops running (see chapter 4). This causes blood to pool in the legs with reduced return to, and therefore filling of, the heart. Originally, the reduced return of blood to the heart was believed to cause the output of the heart to fall, resulting in hypotension. But a unique series of forgotten experiments performed in the 1940s (Barcroft et al. 1944) showed that a reduced pressure inside the heart induces a reflex vascular dilatation, and it is this unexpected response, rather than any reduction in the output of the heart, that causes the blood pressure to fall precipitously. The condition also occurs in athletes who train in the upright position and not in swimmers, who train in the supine position (Savard and Stonehouse 1995).

In contrast, the normal corrective response that the body should make is to immediately constrict (not to dilate) all the blood vessels in the body, especially in the intestine, arms, and legs. This response, which occurs normally in other circumstances, is impaired after exercise (Halliwill et al. 1996), most especially after prolonged exercise in the heat (Franklin et al. 1993). This response is also impaired in those who faint frequently (vasovagal syncopy), including the rare condition of vasovagal syncopy that occurs during (as opposed to after) exercise (Piepoli et al. 1993; Sneddon et al. 1994; Thomson et al. 1995; Thomson et al. 1996). Patients with this condition may faint during exercise, even though their hearts are normal. Their condition is caused by inappropriate vasodilation, secondary to an abnormal stimulation of mechanical receptors in the heart (Sneddon et al. 1994).

There are other changes that make this condition either more or less likely in endurance athletes (Raven and Pawelczyk 1993). For example, the leg veins of endurance-trained but not strength-trained athletes are more distensible than those of the untrained (Louisy et al. 1997). As a result, these trained veins could store more blood immediately on the cessation of exercise, increasing the probability that exercise-associated collapse will develop. In addition, the filtration of fluid by the leg capillaries is substantially higher in endurance-trained athletes (Hildebrandt et al. 1993). As a result, more fluid is transferred from the blood into the tissues in trained athletes on the cessation of exercise. Continual leakage of fluid in that way could explain why the development of postexercise hypotension and collapse may be delayed in some athletes (Hildebrandt et al. 1993).

At the onset of exercise, the body allows the blood pressure to reach values well above those that it will allow when the body is at rest. The physiological term for this phenomenon is *baroreceptor resetting*—the baroreceptors that control the blood pressure are reset to accept higher blood pressure during exercise than at rest. The value accepted by the reset baroreceptors is a function of the exercise intensity and may reach values of 220/90 mmHg during maximal exercise. However, as exercise continues, the acceptable blood pressure range falls progressively (Norton et al. 1999), suggesting a continuous resetting of the baroreceptors to lower values during exercise.

This raises the possibility that, immediately on the cessation of exercise, the baroreceptors are again reset but to an even lower blood pressure than that which prevailed before the start of the exercise bout. This would explain why the resting blood pressure remains below the preexercise value for some time after the cessation of exercise. But this reset blood pressure range, immediately after very prolonged exercise, may be too low in some athletes to allow them to stand without collapsing (Holtzhausen et al. 1994) after exercise, hence causing exercise-associated collapse.

Alternatively, the inability of some to maintain an adequate blood pressure on the cessation of exercise may result from partial failure of the autonomic nervous system (G.D. Smith et al. 1993), perhaps on the basis of one or more genetic defects in the action or metabolism of the sympathetic messenger, noradrenaline (Shannon et al. 2000). This condition is important is for the following reasons.

- It explains why postexercise collapse does not have to be solely and exclusively due to dehydration, as proponents of the dehydration myth have vehemently argued since the 1980s (see chapter 4). If postexercise collapse is not due to dehydration, then treatment with intravenous fluids is not indicated and should be avoided because of the risk that those athletes who are also fluid-overloaded will be adversely affected by such treatment (Noakes 2000b).

- Sudden death frequently occurs on the cessation of exercise, particularly in those with hypertrophic cardiomyopathy (Maron 1992). It has been proposed that the precipitous fall in the return of blood to the heart on the cessation of exercise is especially dangerous in this condition because it can induce the abnormal type of ventricular contraction that leads to sudden death in people with that heart condition.

- Fainting can also occur during exercise; this provides the single exception to the rule that fainting with or without loss of consciousness during exercise in an otherwise healthy person is always caused by a significant and potentially serious cardiac condition.

The practical point is that it is never a good idea to stop suddenly after exercise. Instead it is advisable either to keep walking around quiet briskly for the first 3 to 5 minutes after exercise, so that the muscle pump ensures an adequate return of blood to the heart, or else to lie down immediately, preferably with the legs and pelvis elevated above the level of the heart.

Stroke

If regular exercise reduces the probability that high blood pressure will develop, and if high pressure is an important risk factor for stroke (in which there is bleeding from or clotting within one or more blood vessels of the brain, causing neurological consequences), then it follows that regular exercise should reduce the risk of stroke.

Indeed, a number of studies show that physical activity reduces the risk of stroke in men and women (Wannamethee and Shaper 1992; Shinton and Sager 1993; Kiely et al. 1994; Gillum et al. 1996; Lee and Paffenbarger 1998; Sacco et al. 1998; Lee et al. 1999), young and old, black and white (Sacco et al. 1998).

However, the relationship between stroke and increasing physical activity is U-shaped, which means that moderate amounts of exercise (up to 12,600 kJ per week in Harvard alumni) are the most protective, with increasing risk at lower rates of energy expenditure and no additional benefit at higher levels of energy expenditure or intensity (Kiely et al. 1994; Lee and Paffenbarger 1998).

A possible explanation for this finding comes from the study of Shaper et al. (1994). They also showed a U-shaped relationship between habitual levels of physical activity and risk of heart attack, so that risk was least in people doing moderate or moderately vigorous exercise. This conflicts with the finding that mortality from heart disease falls with increasing physical activity in the Harvard alumni.

As Shaper et al. (1994) knew the blood pressures of their subjects, they were able to show that the increased risk of heart attack with increasingly vigorous exercise occurred only in those subjects with established hypertension. People with normal blood pressures continued to benefit even from vigorous exercise. Hence, they suggested "some caution" when encouraging vigorous exercise in hypertensive subjects, particularly if additional risk factors for coronary heart disease (such as an elevated blood cholesterol concentration, current smoking, or a parental history of heart disease) were present.

While their advice relates to the risk of heart attack, it probably applies equally well to the risk of stroke. Since people with high blood pressure are at increased risk of either condition, this advice should apply equally to the prevention of both heart attack and stroke in people with established hypertension.

Peripheral Arterial Disease

Arterial disease (atherosclerosis) does not confine itself solely to the arteries of the heart and brain, leading to heart attacks and strokes, respectively. Atherosclerosis may also extend into the blood vessels of the legs. When present, such atherosclerosis may limit blood flow to the legs during exercise, causing pain (claudication) that is essentially the same as the pain (angina pectoris) that is felt when the blood supply to the heart muscle is limited by atherosclerosis in the coronary arteries.

Not unexpectedly, physical activity reduces the risk of developing atherosclerotic peripheral vascular disease (Housley et al. 1993). The effect is most marked in habitual smokers.

In contrast, there is one form of peripheral arterial disease that occurs only in athletes, cyclists in particular. This condition was first recognized in 1979 in a highly trained 23-year-old cyclist (Mosimann et al. 1985) who had no apparent risk factors for atherosclerosis. Since then, about 20 cases per year have been described (Abraham et al. 1997; Schep et al. 1999).

The condition is caused by fibrosis thickening (endofibrosis) of the wall of, most commonly, the external iliac artery in the groin and upper thigh. As the wall thickens, blood flow is progressively reduced until symptoms of one-sided leg pain, first during all-out effort, later during less intensive exercise—for example, hill climbing and cycling—begin to develop consistently. The consistent pattern of the pain—which always comes on at the same muscular effort, the oxygen requirement of which exceeds the supply capacity of the obstructed blood vessel, with rapid resolution at rest (as the blood flow again becomes adequate)—strongly suggests the diagnosis. Self-diagnosis can be aided by looking at the foot on the affected side. Usually the foot becomes increasingly pale as the blood flow to the limb becomes inadequate. The normal color of the foot usually returns within 2 to 5 minutes, depending on the severity of the obstruction.

Treatment of the condition requires that the obstruction be removed, either by surgical reconstruction of the artery (endarterectomy) or by replacement with a vein graft. Stretching with a balloon catheter inserted through the skin into the leg arteries (angioplasty) is not recommended (Schep et al. 1999) and should be actively avoided (Schep and Bender 2000).

The long-term results of these different forms of treatment are not known. It seems highly probable that all will provide only temporary relief if the causative factors persist—most likely the high rates of blood flow during exercise that produce large shear forces at the sites of endofibrosis and the frequent hip flexions that occur in cyclists, estimated to be 8 million per year in professional cyclists (Schep and Bender 2000).

Unfortunately, it seems that some athletes are peculiarly prone to this condition, and I would expect that recurrences of the condition are probable if they continue to exercise vigorously, especially to cycle. Thus, a change of sport may be the sole long-term solution (Schep and Bender 2000).

RUNNING AND THE GASTROINTESTINAL SYSTEM

The most common gastrointestinal problems that affect runners, especially during competition, are increased bowel activity causing mild but irritating diarrhea (the so-called runner's trots), progressive nausea, and a disinclination to eat or drink, especially during the last third of marathon and ultramarathon races. This section will help you to understand these and other gastrointestinal disorders associated with running.

Runner's Trots

Up to 60% of runners are troubled by abdominal cramps, diarrhea, or the urge to defecate during or after competitive running (S.N. Sullivan 1981; Keeffe et al. 1984; Larson and Fisher 1987; Riddoch and Trinick 1988; Rehrer, Beckers, et al. 1989; Rehrer et al. 1992; Peters et al. 1993; Gil et al. 1998). Some studies, but not all (Gil et al. 1998), found that men were more frequently affected than women (Keeffe et al. 1984; Riddoch and Trinick 1988).

The physiological mechanisms that explain why the gastrointestinal symptoms develop during running are not known, and some popularly accepted theories, including a reduced intestinal blood flow (mesenteric ischemia), seem increasingly improbable (Gil et al. 1998). My feeling is that exercise per se is not the cause; these symptoms are much more common in running than in cycling, swimming, or walking (Peters et al. 1999). Thus, it is likely that the increased mechanical mixing and bouncing caused by running (Larson and Fisher 1987), aided possibly by increased blood levels of hormones that increase bowel motility (Sullivan et al. 1984)—including Vasoactive Intestinal Polypeptide, Motilin, and Peptide YY (Gil et al. 1998)—may be the principal cause of these symptoms. Symptoms are also more common in runners who become dehydrated by more than 4% during competition (Rehrer, Janssen et al. 1989). However, not everyone develops these symptoms when running. Thus, other predisposing factors, perhaps even psychological (Gil et al. 1998), may need to be present.

In chapter 9, I introduced the theory that some runners with runner's trots may suffer from mild milk or other food intolerance. One runner told me (Noakes 1982a) that he had been suffering from intense intestinal cramping for years. These cramps came on a few hours after he had completed a hard training session or a race of more than 5 km. Once the discomfort began, he would have to retire to bed. The spasms of colicky abdominal pain eventually abated about 5 hours later. After much unsuccessful trial and error, that runner finally decided to remove all dairy produce from his normal diet, with dramatic results: he was again able to train and race hard without developing intense abdominal cramping after exercise. He has subsequently had minor recurrences, but only when he has inadvertently eaten dairy produce that has been disguised in various foodstuffs, such as sauces.

Although that runner did not strictly suffer from runner's trots, his story was important to me because, after hearing it, I decided to reduce the amount of dairy produce in my own diet. The first result was that I cured myself of an irritable bowel syndrome—a condition of episodic left-sided bowel cramping that is said to be due to psychological factors—and was suddenly able to run any distance race without stopping. On reflection, I remembered that those races in which I had had the most problems were also those in which I had ingested the most milk in the days before the race.

When I subsequently discussed this with a gastroenterologist, Mervyn Danilewitz, I was told that my complaint was not unusual. His own studies (Danilewitz et al. 1984) have shown that milk (lactose) intolerance is present in a high percentage (66%) of people with irritable bowel syndrome, and he has cured a number of runners with the trots by advising them to avoid dairy produce for at least 24 hours before competition.

People who are milk-intolerant have reduced amounts of the enzyme lactase in the walls of their small intestine and are said to have lactase deficiency or to be lactose-intolerant. The enzyme lactase is required for the normal breakdown of the milk sugar, lactose, into its two component simple sugars, glucose and galactose.

The bowel content of lactase is low in all humans at birth but then rises steeply within a few days as the infant starts to drink milk. However, after two or three years, the bowel lactase content falls and can reach very low levels, especially in certain race groups (such as African-Americans, black Africans, Chinese, and Ashkenazi Jews). Only in northern Europeans and their descendants and in certain nomadic African cattle-herding communities is the incidence of lactose intolerance low (Kretchmer 1972).

The result is that in many communities there is a wide range in the amount of bowel lactase present in different people. Those who have a high content of lactase will be able to ingest large amounts of dairy produce without developing the symptoms of milk intolerance; those with no lactase at all will be unable to metabolize any dairy produce and will have severe milk intolerance. In between are people like me, who have some bowel lactase and are therefore able to cope with a certain, critical amount of dairy produce (in my case, milk in hot beverages only).

The reasons that lactase deficiency causes these symptoms are as follows. The lactose, which escapes small bowel digestion, is greedily attacked by the bacteria present in the large bowel. The bacteria, in turn, ferment the lactose into organic acids and carbon dioxide. The gases cause the bowel wall to become distended and therefore painful, and the organic acids probably stimulate contraction of the muscles in the bowel wall. In addition, water is drawn into the bowel by the osmotic action of the organic acids. The result is that people with lactase deficiency develop bloating, flatulence, belching, cramps, and a watery, explosive diarrhea when they ingest dairy produce.

Why lactase deficiency also seems to cause loose stools during competitive running is not as easy to explain. Possibly, it is the fermented byproducts of lactose that stimulate the bowel to become more active during running.

Very recent research suggests that people who develop bowel symptoms, the so-called spastic colon, may suffer from nothing more than an overgrowth of bacteria in the colon. Thus, the runner's trots may also be caused by a bacterial overgrowth that does not cause symptoms either when certain provocative foods are avoided or when exercise is not undertaken.

The practical point is that if you regularly develop the trots during running, you should initially stop taking dairy products for 24 to 48 hours before competition. If this prevents the trots, you have discovered the cure. If not, consider the possibility that you may be sensitive to another common foodstuff in your diet—even fructose (Anderson and Nygren 1978). Another tip is to eat a low-residue diet for 24 to 48 hours before competition (Keeffe et al. 1984; Larson and Fisher 1987; Moses 1990) so that the colon is relatively empty when you start exercise. During exercise, hypertonic carbohydrate solutions may cause symptoms in some susceptible people (Rehrer et al. 1992).

Prevention of this condition requires that the athlete identify any provocative foodstuffs and remove them from the diet for 24 to 48 hours before competition. Eating a low-residue diet during this time is also helpful, and every effort should be made to have a bowel movement before arriving at the race start. A light meal and a warm beverage followed by gentle exercise may be needed to stimulate a prerace bowel movement.

The drugs codeine, diphenoxylate hydrochloride, and loperamide, all of which reduce bowel activity, may be used occasionally if these other measures are ineffective and factors other than exercise or diet are involved (S.N. Sullivan 1992). The possible use of antibiotic therapy to reduce a potential bacterial overgrowth has still to be evaluated.

Bloody Diarrhea

Between 8% and 80% of runners may have bloody stools after competitive running (Porter 1983; McMahon et al. 1984; Stewart et al. 1984; McCabe et al. 1986; Eichner 1989; R.L. Fisher et al. 1986; Gil et al. 1998), and, in some, the condition may mimic serious disease (Cantwell 1981). The frequency of the condition rises with increasing race distance (Gil et al. 1998) and is common in those who run long distances: 85% of ultramarathon runners develop blood in their stools after exercise (Moses et al. 1989; Baska et al. 1990). The condition occurred in less than 2% of cyclists competing in a seven-day race (Wilhite et al. 1990) and in no walkers participating in a four-day event (J.D. Robertson et al. 1987).

At present, the cause of the bleeding is unknown, as even detailed investigations in some runners have failed to find anything that would explain the bleeding (Cantwell 1981; R.L. Fisher et al. 1986; Gil et al. 1998). Other studies found evidence of bleeding from the stomach (Eichner 1989) or hemorrhagic colitis (Moses, Brewer, et al. 1988). The condition, which is more common in younger, faster runners (McMahon et al. 1984), particularly when they have suddenly increased their training or competitive running (Stewart et al. 1984), resolves within three days. The condition is more frequent in runners who ingest analgesic drugs before or after competition (J.D. Robertson et al. 1987). However, the volume of blood lost is inconsequential, amounting to less than 0.5 ml of whole blood per day. Thus, it is unlikely to be an important source of blood loss and cannot explain the development of anemia in runners.

If the condition persists beyond three days, medical advice should be sought. Causes of bloody diarrhea that will require medical or possibly surgical intervention include bowel infections and bowel tumors. If no cause is found, the athlete should be encouraged to avoid anti-inflammatory drugs for 12 to 24 hours and aspirin for two to three days before heavy training or competition (Eichner 1989).

Nausea

Heavy or prolonged exercise frequently causes mild nausea and a decreased appetite during and for a few hours after exercise. In some runners, vomiting may occur, particularly during or after hard exercise (Keeffe et al. 1984).

Sullivan (1981) found that 6% of runners complained of nausea or retching after competitive running and 50% had a reduced appetite for 30 to 150 minutes after hard competition. After an easy run, the percentage of runners who reported an increase, decrease, or no change in appetite was about equal. The effects could be due to increased episodes of gastro-esophageal reflux induced by exercise (N. Clark et al. 1988; Soffer et al. 1993).

Two other important causes of nausea and retching or vomiting during exercise may simply be ingesting too much fluid during exercise, especially during ultramarathons or ultratriathlons, or motion sickness resulting from the incessant up-and-down movement of the head for hours on end.

Drinking too much fluid during exercise causes the retention of a progressively increasing volume of unabsorbed fluid in the intestine. This occurs because the maximum rate of intestinal fluid absorption may be quite low in some humans, perhaps as little as 500 to 800 ml per hour, especially during exercise. Eventually, the accumulated fluid will induce nausea and vomiting.

The point is that vomiting should alert runners to the probability that they have drunk too much—not too little as is sometimes mistakenly believed—and are therefore at risk of developing water intoxication (hyponatremia; see chapter 4). Drinking less in future races may be all that is required to prevent the condition. Dehydration does not cause vomiting. Hence, drinking more when you start vomiting because you believe you are dehydrated is precisely the wrong treatment.

If the condition is due to motion sickness, antinausea medication (for example, 5 mg of Stemetil) taken about 1 hour before you expect to become ill and again every 2 hours until exercise stops will cure the problem. Higher doses may be needed by some. Interestingly, susceptibility to motion sickness increases with increasing levels of fitness (Cheung et al. 1990). However, if the medication is without effect, then the condition is not due to motion sickness and other causes must be sought.

The only clinical investigation comparing gastrointestinal function in runners who develop nausea during exercise with those who do not found that symptomatic runners were more likely to suffer gastro-esophageal reflux and to have slower bowel transit times and higher intestinal permeability during exercise, especially running, than asymptomatic runners (Van Nieuwenhoven 1999).

Colon Cancer

A host of studies have shown that high levels of physical activity at work or in leisure time are associated with a reduced risk of colon cancer in both men and women (Lee and Paffenbarger 1992; 1994; Wannamethee et al. 1993; Sternfeld 1992; Macfarlane and Lowenfels 1994; Longnecker et al. 1995; Giovannucci et al. 1995; Thune and Lund 1996; Neugut et al. 1996; Martinez et al. 1997; Slattery et al. 1997). Physical activity during early adulthood, however, offers no protection (P.M. Marcus et al. 1994).

Exercise may protect against colon cancer by increasing gastrointestinal motility (Kohl et al. 1988). One theory is that cancer of the colon occurs when toxic cancer-forming (carcinogenic) dietary substances remain in contact with the linings of the colon for prolonged periods because of poor bowel motility. A general effect may also be present: rats that exercise are more resistant to the development of chemically induced cancers of both the colon (Andrianopoulos et al. 1987) and breast (Cohen et al. 1988).

Exercise is thought to increase bowel motility, thereby shortening the time it takes for food (and the carcinogenic substances contained in that food) to pass through the bowel—the bowel transit time (Cordain et al. 1986; Keeling and Martin 1987; Oettlé 1991; A. Harris et al. 1991; Koffler et al. 1992). Thus, the carcinogenic agents have less time to damage the colon linings, thereby inducing cancer. This, it is speculated, reduces the overall risk of colon cancer. However, not all studies find that exercise reduces the bowel transit time (Bingham and Cummings 1989; Meshkinpour et al. 1989; Lampe et al. 1991; Coenen et al. 1992; G. Robertson et al. 1993).

Alternatively, colon cancer may be caused by a combination of low levels of habitual physical activity and high levels of both energy intake and body mass, so that those at greatest risk are those in the most unfavorable energy balance, as they have all these three characteristics (Slattery et al. 1997).

In support of this theory is the finding that physical activity reduces the risk of colon cancer even in those with high energy intakes and body masses (Lee and Paffenbarger 1992; Slattery et al. 1997). This invites the hypothesis that colon cancer may result from factors that are distant to the colon but that are related to individual metabolic profiles—in particular, the tendency to obesity, especially of the central or abdominal type that is more prevalent in men.

Diverticular Disease

Diverticular disease of the colon occurs when the lining of the bowel herniates between the muscular layers. These herniations, or diverticula, can become infected, causing abdominal discomfort and low-grade ill health. Physical activity (jogging and running in particular) is associated with a reduced incidence of this disease (Aldoori et al. 1995).

Gall Bladder Disease

Gallstones, which are also associated with obesity, are more prevalent in women, especially those who have had multiple pregnancies. But recreational physical activity reduces the risk that gallstones requiring surgical removal will develop in both women (Leitzmann et al. 1999) and men (Leitzmann et al. 1998). Leitzman et al. (1998) calculate that 34% of symptomatic gallstones in men could be avoided if those at risk performed 30 minutes of endurance activities five days a week.

Gastrointestinal Absorption

The transit time of food in the small bowel, where the absorption of most foodstuffs occurs, may (Keeling et al. 1990) or may not be influenced by exercise (Ollerenshaw et al. 1987). It is possible that reduced transit time through the small bowel may interfere with food absorption during exercise. Other studies have found that this transit time is in fact prolonged by exercise (Meshkinpour et al. 1989; Moses, Ryan et al. 1988).

Blood in the Urine (Hematuria)

Like most marathoners, I am an obsessional urine-watcher, an avid follower of the effect of running, climate, and a host of other minutiae on the production of this critical human end-product. And in common with most runners, my concern is never greater than when this process has been most threatened by those three or more hours of renal insult imposed by the marathon race.

Only after that first, ceremonial postrace voiding can we marathoners again feel secure. Imagine then what should happen if, at this critical first voiding, you should see what appears to be your very life blood disappearing before your eyes. The emotional impact is catastrophic. It is enough to suggest complete internal dissolution. A case, one runner said with feeling, of total body failure.

The athlete's sense of destruction is only compounded by the visit to the doctor. For 10 days later, having survived a series of exhaustive tests, the athlete is confronted with the assurance that nothing is wrong. The runner is, as it were, being asked to forget the unforgettable, to dismiss the incident as a figment of postrace dementia.

Fortunately, there is no longer a need for this limited understanding of bloody urine (runner's hematuria). Thanks to the Royal Navy, we have at least one valid explanation for this diagnostic failure. However, runners who detect blood in their urine should consult a physician to narrow down the possible causes and to ensure that it is nothing serious.

Bladder Trauma

With orders to get to the root of the problem, Surgeon Captain Blacklock (1977) of the Royal Navy Hospital in Gosport in Hampshire, England, investigated a group of naval athletes who developed bloody urine after exercise. He used an operative procedure in which a small fiber-optic tube, a cystoscope, is passed into the bladder, allowing its inner walls to be visualized. Through his cystoscope, Blacklock saw what he had suspected: angry, bleeding bruises in the membrane lining the bladder walls. Blacklock repeated the procedure seven days later and found that the bruises had cleared.

Blacklock has proposed that these bruises are caused by the impact of the two walls of the empty bladder against each other during running. While each impact may by itself be very minor, when the action is repeated with each running stride over a longer period, the trauma can become quite marked. This postulated mechanism would also explain the inconsistency with which any single athlete develops hematuria after exercise. When running with a urine-filled bladder, the athlete would be protected from injury. This proposed mechanism also allows a simple technique to prevent bladder bruising. Always run with a half-filled bladder and never urinate immediately before running.

That bladder bruising is the likely cause of most cases of hematuria after exercise is shown by a study of 45 runners in the 90-km Comrades Marathon. An estimated 25% had hematuria after the race (Kallmeyer and Miller 1993), and bleeding from the bladder was the likely cause in all but one of the affected athletes.

Red Cell Leakage

The glomeruli of the kidney are a network of blood vessels enclosed in a special membrane, through which the blood is filtered as the first stage in the production of urine. Under normal circumstances, the glomeruli do not allow red blood cells to be filtered into the urine, as these cells are too large to pass through the filtering membrane. However, there is now quite good evidence that a high percentage, if not most, of the red blood cells found in urine after exercise have escaped through the glomeruli (Fassett et al. 1982; Kincaid-Smith 1982). Red cells that have passed through the glomeruli can be identified because they are of smaller volume than normal red cells (Naicker et al. 1992). They show the effects of having been squeezed through the glomeruli.

This suggests that glomerular permeability is transiently increased during exercise, allowing the passage of some large substances that are normally unable to pass through the glomeruli. Once the exercise stops, these changes reverse themselves within 24 to 48 hours, and the glomerular membrane again becomes impermeable to red blood cells.

Hemoglobinuria

Hemoglobinuria is the passage of the red blood cell pigment, hemoglobin—the pigment that gives blood its color—in the urine. It occurs when the red blood cells traversing the blood vessels in the feet become damaged by the constant impact of the feet against the hard road surface during running, so-called foot-strike hemolysis. Some cells are destroyed, releasing their contained hemoglobin into the bloodstream, passing into the kidneys, from where it is excreted in the urine (Buckle 1965).

The precipitating factors for hemoglobinuria are hard running surfaces and poorly designed running shoes (in particular, shoes that do not absorb sufficient impact shock). Prevention of the condition is usually quite simple and involves the prescription of running shoes with a soft midsole, especially under the forefoot (Dressendorfer et al. 1992). The condition is probably less common since the advent of running shoes with superior cushioning. Indeed our study (Steenkamp et al. 1986) failed to show any evidence of foot-strike hemolysis in six woman runners during a 42-km marathon race.

Some athletes are especially prone to hemoglobinuria. Godal and Refsum (1979) and Banga and his colleagues (1979) have investigated athletes whose performances dropped inexplicably whenever they commenced hard training. All were found to have genetically fragile red blood cells that presumably started to break down in large numbers when the athletes exposed their more fragile red blood cells to the trauma of foot-road contact.

This caused the runners to become anemic, and their performances fell precipitously. It is entirely possible that because other similar types of as yet undescribed idiosyncrasies predispose some athletes to sufficiently high rates of red blood cell destruction during exercise, they eventually develop an iron-deficiency anemia.

Even in apparently healthy runners, there is a more rapid turnover of red blood cells, and the average red blood cell lifespan is reduced from the normal value of about 110 days to about 70 days (Weight, Darge, et al. 1991).

Myoglobinuria

Myoglobinuria occurs when, for reasons not well understood (Knochel 1972), myoglobin escapes from the exercising skeletal muscles and appears in the urine. Unlike hemoglobin, myoglobin is highly toxic to the kidneys and in high concentrations may be an important factor explaining the acute kidney failure that occurs not uncommonly in events such as the Comrades Marathon (MacSearraigh et al. 1979). A group of researchers from Addington Hospital in Durban (Schiff et al. 1978) found that 57% of a group of Comrades runners had elevated blood myoglobin levels (myoglobinemia) after the race and 14% had myoglobin in the urine (myoglobinuria).

It would seem that runners prone to severe myoglobinuria may have subtle, as yet undefined, muscle cell abnormalities that make them prone to acute renal failure and possibly also to heatstroke (Noakes 1987a).

The first decision that the athlete who passes bloody urine has to make is whether to consult a doctor. In general, I would advise that the first time you pass the bloody urine you should consult your doctor and, depending on the findings on initial testing, you either will be able to ignore subsequent episodes or will require additional medical evaluation.

If there is any associated low back (loin) pain or fever; if the bloody urine also occurs at rest when no exercise has been performed; if it fails to clear up within 24 to 48 hours after exercise; or if the condition fails to respond to appropriate treatment (soft shoes or running with a half-filled bladder), seek medical attention without delay.

Loin pain indicates that the site of bleeding is likely to be the kidney, and this would be a strong indication that an abnormality such as kidney stones is probably the cause. In contrast, if there is associated lower-abdominal (suprapubic) or groin pain or discomfort, or discomfort in the urethra, the bleeding is probably of bladder origin. Similarly, the passage of blood clots suggests that the bleeding comes from the bladder (editorial 1982a).

Exercise-related hematuria always resolves within 72 hours (Blacklock 1977; Fletcher 1977; Siegel et al. 1979; editorial 1982ab) so that its persistence beyond three days is abnormal and must initially be considered to be due to a disease process, like that of bladder cancer (Mueller and Thompson 1988), unrelated to running. Hence, symptoms that persist for more than three days must be investigated.

Factors Unrelated to Exercise

Hematuria may also be caused by something that has nothing to do with running. Runners are not immune to the conventional, run-of-the-mill medical conditions such as kidney stones, growths, or infections, all of which may first expose themselves by the passage of bloody urine after exercise. These conditions, which can include kidney stones or cancers or infections of the kidney or bladder, require some form of medical treatment. Hence, there is always a need to investigate runners with persistent hematuria to ensure that a treatable condition unrelated to exercise is not overlooked.

Athletic Pseudonephritis

That the urine may contain protein and white and red blood cells after exercise has been known for more than 70 years. This led Gardner (1971) to coin the term *athletic pseudonephritis* because these changes are identical to those found in a very serious kidney disease, glomerulonephritis. As most forms of glomerulonephritis are ultimately lethal, it is understandable that the finding of these substances in the athlete's urine would cause considerable concern to those unaware that, in athletes, such changes are almost always due to exercise, not disease.

There is no reason to believe that these findings are anything but a transient response to exercise that clears completely within three days of rest (Fletcher 1977). It seems likely that the same changes that cause the kidneys to leak red blood cells during exercise also cause the kidneys to leak large protein molecules and other cells.

Acute Kidney Failure

Exercise-induced acute kidney failure has been described most commonly in 90-km Comrades Marathon runners (MacSearraigh et al. 1979), although sporadic cases among 42-km standard marathoners have also been described (Lonka and Pedersen 1987). Although acute kidney failure is not an uncommon complication of heatstroke, in these marathon runners the kidney failure developed even though they did not develop heatstroke. The mechanism is unknown; the failure is not simply a result of severe dehydration or prolonged exercise. In contrast to the widely held belief, kidney function remains essentially unchanged even during prolonged exercise (Irving et al. 1986a; 1989; 1990b) except in those athletes at risk of developing acute kidney failure (Irving et al. 1990a).

I suspect that there may be an individual susceptibility to this condition on the basis of a specific musculoskeletal defect that predisposes the muscle to break down during severe exercise and leak myoglobin (Noakes 1987a). When the myoglobin is filtered through the kidney, it acts as a toxin, causing kidney failure. There is also a feeling that the intake of certain analgesic drugs (such as aspirin [acetyl salicylic acid]) or the nonsteroidal anti-inflammatory drugs (such as indocid [indomethacin], brufen [ibuprofen], and naproxen) may increase the risk of kidney failure during exercise (Goldszer and Siegel 1984; Vitting et al. 1986), perhaps by reducing kidney blood flow (Walker et al. 1994).

Alternatively, the excessive use of nonsteroidal anti-inflammatory drugs for the treatment of sporting injuries, for example, has been associated with irreversible kidney failure in susceptible athletes (Griffiths 1992).

The first indication that you might have kidney failure is that you pass little or no urine for the first 24 hours after a long race. The wise athlete will recognize the seriousness of this sign and will immediately go to the nearest hospital that has a specialized unit for the treatment of kidney failure—in particular, a unit able to perform renal dialysis, which may well be necessary. Failure to recognize this early symptom of kidney failure means that you are likely to start feeling rather ill 36 to 48 hours after the race and will probably visit the doctor with a severe headache due both to the sudden steep rise in blood pressure and the retained metabolic end-products caused by the kidney failure. By this stage, the kidney failure will be well established and you will probably have to undergo repeated renal dialysis until the kidneys recover, usually within 10 to 21 days.

Although the condition is seldom acutely fatal, the long-term prognosis of people who develop acute renal failure during exercise is unknown, nor is it known how the condition might be prevented in those susceptible to it. The most important factor is for runners not to ingest nonsteroidal anti-inflammatory drugs during prolonged exercise. These agents are, in any case, ineffective during exercise and, by reducing kidney blood flow during exercise (Walker et al. 1994), only increase the likelihood that kidney failure will develop.

Kidney Stones

A survey of entrants in the 1977 New York City Marathon showed that there was an abnormally high incidence, about five times normal, of kidney stones among male runners (Milvy et al. 1981). Runners most likely to develop kidney stones were those who had been running for the longest time, who ran the greatest mileages in training, and who were the fastest runners. They were also more likely to develop discolored urine after training or racing.

There seems to be a similar high incidence of kidney stones in our population of local runners, and this stimulated our research into the effects of marathon running on the composition of calcium and other crystals normally present in the urine (Irving et al. 1986b; Rodgers et al. 1988; 1991; 1992). We found that the urine of marathon runners had the same distribution of calcium crystals as that found in people at risk of developing kidney stones. Black African runners did not show this pattern (Rodgers et al. 1992). Sakhaee et al. (1987) also found that exercise increases the urinary concentration of stone-forming constituents.

These findings are compatible with the well-established observations that kidney stones are more common in people living in hot environments. Thus, it has been presumed that the repeated bouts of dehydration caused by running predispose to the formation of kidney stones, but other factors may also be operative. For runners the message is clear. Avoid dehydration by drinking appropriately during but also immediately after exercise—especially in hot weather. But do not drink so much that you develop hyponatremia (chapter 4).

Urinary Incontinence

One study (I. Nygaard et al. 1990) found that 30% of women noted incontinence during exercise and that bouncing exercises, such as running or aerobics, caused the highest incidence of symptoms. A total of 20% of those with incontinence were forced to avoid certain activities altogether, and 55% wore a pad during exercise. Clearly, there is a need to pay greater attention to this problem and to establish more effective methods to treat the condition.

EXERCISE AND MENSTRUATION

There are four specific questions concerning menstruation and exercise that scientists have been researching:

1. Can strenuous exercise at an early age affect the age of onset of menstruation (menarche), which normally occurs at about 13 years of age?
2. Can strenuous exercise training undertaken after menarche cause a subsequent cessation of menstruation (secondary amenorrhea), and if so, are there any long-term dangers associated with prolonged secondary amenorrhea?
3. Does menstruation influence competitive performance, and if so, can menstruation be controlled before competition?
4. Can vigorous exercise influence female fertility independent of any changes it might cause in menstrual patterns?

Menarche

The outstanding observation is that menarche (the onset of menstruation) occurs at an older age in athletes than in nonathletes and that menarche is latest in those who compete at the highest levels in certain sports in which a small size provides a competitive advantage. Thus, swimmers, in general, tend to be the least affected, whereas gymnasts, figure skaters, divers, and ballet dancers have the latest menarche (Malina 1983; Moisan et al. 1991). Note that sports that require girls to be the thinnest and smallest are associated with the greatest delay in menarche (Moisan et al. 1991). But the process of sexual maturation, which occurs before the onset of menarche, may not be delayed in those who train consistently and compete regularly between ages 7 and 15 (Plowman et al. 1991).

Doctors Rose Frisch and Janet McArthur (1974) have postulated that there must be a certain percentage of body fat present before menstruation can begin. Hence, poor nutrition may delay menarche. A reduced percentage body fat may not delay sexual maturation—only the onset of menarche. However, there is no evidence to suggest that body fat alone determines the age at which menarche occurs or explains its delay in some athletes (Malina 1983; Baxter-Jones et al. 1994).

There is no evidence to suggest that athletic girls come from a different (lower) social class than do nonathletes or that they come from larger families. Both these variables (lower social class and being born into a large immediate family) are associated with a delayed menarche (Malina 1983).

The most popular theory, for which there is an accumulating evidence (Baxter-Jones et al. 1995; Sundaresan et al. 2000), is that late-maturing girls with a late menarche are more likely to succeed in sport. The chief proponent of this hypothesis is Texan Bob Malina (1983; 1994a; 1994b). The first part of this thesis holds that the physique of the late-maturing girl is different from that of early maturers and is better suited to athletic success. Late maturers characteristically have long legs for their stature, narrow hips, and a generally linear physique; they have less weight for height and less body fat, and they tend to perform well in motor tasks such as dashes, jumps, and throws. The android body shape of female distance runners is typical of the late maturers.

Early maturers, on the other hand, have relatively broad hips and short legs and higher levels of body fat, all of which are detrimental to performance, particularly in events in which the body must be projected or carried. Early maturers may also be at greater risk of developing obesity (Van Lenthe et al. 1996).

Malina quotes evidence to show that, at least in boys, heavy training does not influence the rate of physical maturation. In other words, training in boys cannot override or indeed influence the normal maturation processes that are under hormonal control. If the same occurs in girls, it suggests that Malina is indeed correct and that exercise selects rather than produces late maturers.

The second part of the Malina hypothesis is that early maturers move away from sport, whereas late maturers are selected toward sport. He points out that early maturers are at a social disadvantage because they are out of phase with the emotional and physiological development of girls their age and particularly boys their age, who in any case mature two years later than do girls. The result is that these girls will tend to be socialized away from sport and into activities that, until recently, society has viewed as being more closely associated with femininity. If the social standing of girls is determined by their ability to attract the attention of older boys, rather than by their athletic achievements, then they will be encouraged to go with their strengths. Incidentally, the only sport for which this argument probably does not apply is swimming, in which early maturers may be at an advantage owing to their greater size and absolute strength. But, in time, the greater height of the late maturers becomes more advantageous.

In contrast, the late maturer is likely to be socialized into sport, as that is where her advantage lies, and her late maturation will keep her less interested in her traditional feminine role. Furthermore, her greater success in competitive sport is likely to motivate her to maintain an active interest in sport. As a result, it is the late maturers who comprise the athletic populations of the teens and early 20s.

A third possibility explaining the superior athletic ability of late maturers may be some factor other than body build. For example, late maturers may enjoy one or more physiological advantage in their hearts, brains, or muscles (see chapters 1 through 3). To date, we have no scientific information on this possibility.

Intensive, focused training of many hours per day before menarche could delay its onset, possibly by slowing accumulation of body fat, either by a direct effect of exercise on body mass or through attempts by the athlete to maintain a low body weight by dieting, including a low-fat diet, since a higher dietary fat intake accelerates the onset of menarche (Merzenich et al. 1993). This could explain why the age at menarche of swimmers is the least affected. Swimmers can afford to be less concerned about their weights than are runners, as a swimmer's body weight is supported by the water rather than by her legs. Conversely, ballet dancers in particular (Druss and Silverman 1979) but also gymnasts, who diet rigorously to maintain their prepubescent-like appearances, would be especially prone to delayed menarche.

Maternal age at menarche also predicts menarcheal age in the daughter. Together with the type of sport in which the young girl participates, maternal menarcheal age is the best predictor of age at menarche of the daughter. This leads to the hypothesis that the arrow of causality is indeed reversed, so that intrinsic genetic factors passed on by the mother that delay the onset of menarche encourage adolescent girls to continue participating in those sports in which smallness is essential for success. Because they are genetically equipped to be the better performers, they train more intensively. Cross-sectional studies of successful competitors in these different sports will then conclude that the intensive training caused the delayed menarche, not the reverse.

There is now growing evidence (Stager, Robertshaw, et al. 1984; Stager et al. 1990; Baxter-Jones et al. 1994) to suggest that competitive sports select out the late maturers whose potential in most sports is superior to that of early maturers and that menarche is relatively unaffected by vigorous exercise in adolescence. Rigorous dieting, perhaps as part of an eating disorder, with a consequent slowing of the rate of body fat accumulation, could further delay the menarche in late maturers participating in activities that traditionally demand slimness for aesthetic appeal.

Menstrual Irregularity

Just as menarche is later, so is the incidence of menstrual irregularity higher in most groups of athletes (in particular, among long-distance runners and ballet dancers) than in nonathletes (Noakes and Van Gend 1988). The question that arises is whether exercise causes this higher incidence of menstrual irregularity or whether girls who are prone to menstrual irregularity are more likely to be attracted to vigorous exercise or ballet dancing. Before we consider these two possibilities, it is necessary to define what is meant by menstrual irregularity. Long-term menstrual irregularity can take one of the following forms:

Amenorrhea: the absence of any previous menstrual cycles, or menstrual cycles lasting longer than 90 days in a female who has previously menstruated

Oligomenorrhea: menstrual cycles lasting between 35 and 90 days

Short luteal phase: menstrual cycles lasting fewer than 23 days

Short-term menstrual irregularity is any short-term departure from the normal menstrual pattern experienced by the person. This might take the form of an early or delayed onset of menstruation or an increased or reduced number of flow days, for example.

Low Percentage Body Fat

Frisch and McArthur (1974) proposed that a critical percentage of body fat (17%) is required before a young girl will start menstruating and that a slightly greater percentage (22%) is required for the maintenance of menstruation. With improved nutrition and increased body fat at an early age in North America, there has been a parallel decrease in the age at which menstruation begins, providing indirect support for this hypothesis. In subsequent studies on ballet dancers, Frisch and her colleagues (1980) reported a high incidence of amenorrhea among those dancers with percentage body fat lower than 22%, thereby adding further support to this theory.

Studies of female distance runners have found essentially the same relationship. Young women who weigh less than 53 kg and who lost more than 4.5 kg after they began running are more likely to develop menstrual irregularity (Speroff and Redwine 1980). Another study of 168 women divided into inactive controls, "joggers" who ran between 8 to 48 km per week, and "runners" who ran more than 48 km per week found that although each group had almost identical average heights, they differed greatly with respect to percentage body fat and body weight (Dale et al. 1979). The runners were approximately 6 kg below average body weight for height, and their higher incidence of menstrual irregularity correlated with their lower percentage body fat. Numerous other studies have shown that amenorrheic runners are lighter than normally menstruating runners or controls (Schwartz et al. 1981; Shangold and Levine 1982; Carlberg et al. 1983; Webb and Proctor 1983). Amenorrheic runners also tend to be the better performers (Shangold 1980; Van Gend and Noakes 1987; Webb and Proctor 1983), at least in the short term. However, persistent malnutrition must impair performance in the long term. My clinical impression is that elite athletes with more serious eating disorders perform well for 3 to 5 years before their bodies finally rebel and their performances fall off.

However, the percentage body fat theory is not the complete answer (Reeves 1979; Caldwell 1982; Malina 1983; Noakes and Van Gend 1988). For example, some ballet dancers and swimmers who develop irregular menstrual cycles during training become more regular in the off-season even without significant changes in body weight (Abrahams et al. 1982; Cohen et al. 1982; Russell et al. 1984). Furthermore, some amenorrheic runners are of normal body weight, and other studies have found no difference in height, weight, or percentage body fat between amenorrheic and menstrually regular runners or controls (Malina et al. 1978; Dale et al. 1979; Fishman 1980; Wakat et al. 1982; Sanborn et al. 1987).

In summary, there is no conclusive evidence that percentage body fat plays an exclusive role in determining menstrual patterns in athletes. Rather, it is likely to be a contributing factor acting with other variables. One possibility is that loss of fat from specific depots may induce the amenorrhea. Brownell et al. (1987) suggest that depletion of the fat stores distributed below the waist in the hips, thighs, and buttocks—the lactation fat stores—may be associated with menstrual dysfunction. Indeed, female athletes with menstrual dysfunction have lower body fat stores in all regions of the body (Frisch et al. 1993) and an increased capacity for hydroxylation of the female hormone, estrogen, to an inactive metabolite.

Alternatively, a low percentage body fat may be associated with superior athletic potential and the desire to train sufficiently hard to become a top competitor. The stresses of heavy training and intense competition might then induce the menstrual irregularity. One study has reported that amenorrheic runners associated more stress with their running than did normally menstruating runners (Schwartz et al. 1981), while another found that amenorrheic runners tend to be more emotionally distressed than normally menstruating runners (Galle et al. 1983). The links between amenorrhea and eating disorders, including anorexia nervosa, are discussed in detail later in this chapter.

Another possibility is that the rapidity of weight loss may play a more important role than the amount lost per se, as evidence suggests that a rapid loss of 15% of body weight influences menstruation (McArthur 1982; Wentz 1980). Alternatively, the low percentage body fat may be indicative of an eating disorder.

Age at Menarche

Generally, it has been found that the later the menarche, the higher the incidence of subsequent menstrual irregularity. For example, one study (Feicht et al. 1978) found that amenorrheic middle-distance runners had a later age of menarche than did menstrually-regular middle-distance runners (14.1 vs. 13.3 years).

However, the likely explanation for the relationship between a late menarche and subsequent menstrual irregularity is probably that late-maturing girls (who, as we have discussed, are of a different body build than are early maturers) may be more prone to menstrual irregularity than are early maturers. This notion will be explained in greater detail later in this chapter.

Training Volume

A number of studies have shown a direct relationship between the degree and frequency of menstrual irregularity and training load, measured in runners as the distance run per week. Thus, one study (Feicht et al. 1978) found that 43% of athletes running more than 128 km per week had menstrual irregularity and that there was a linear relationship between the incidence of amenorrhea and distance run per week (figure 15.7). In comparison, the incidence of amenorrhea among university-age girls was found to be only 6%. Hence, the idea arose that exercise alone would cause menstrual irregularity, provided some threshold of training volume, perhaps different for each athlete, was crossed.

It is important, however, to remember that two variables can be related in a cross-sectional study without the one directly causing the other. Rather, this apparently causal relationship might be explained by a common dependence on a third factor

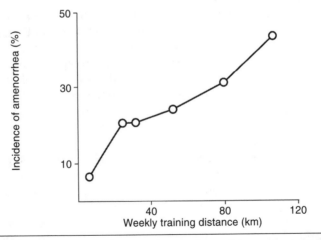

Figure 15.7 An apparent relationship between the prevalence of absent menstrual periods (amenorrhea) and the weekly training distance. The implication of this figure is that more than 30% of women running 80 km or more per week can expect to lose their periods. In fact, the relationship is spurious. Athletic women who lose their periods do so because they are eating too little, not because they are running too much.

From Feicht (1978, p. 1145). © Elsevier Science.

that is the real cause of the condition. Alternatively, the arrow of causality may be reversed. For example, the menstrual irregularity might cause the exercise, not the reverse. Interestingly, the incidence of menstrual dysfunction did not rise with increasing training volume in female swimmers (compare to figure 15.7).

It is now clear that exercise alone does not cause menstrual irregularity. Rather, the arrow of causality is indeed reversed so that young women with menstrual irregularity caused by other factors, most especially malnutrition resulting from covert or overt eating disorders, are more likely also to train excessively.

Evidence for this finding is that in other cross-sectional studies training load is unrelated to menstrual status in runners (McArthur 1982; Schwartz et al. 1981; Shangold 1980; Shangold and Levine 1982; Speroff and Redwine 1980; Wakat et al. 1982; Van Gend and Noakes 1987; Cokkinades et al. 1990; Myburgh et al. 1992; Tomten et al. 1996) and that swimmers and cyclists show no increase in the prevalence of amenorrhea with increasing training load, even when they train at loads never achieved by runners (Sanborn et al. 1982). This may be because they maintain body weight and therefore presumably an adequate nutritional status, however hard they train.

More significantly, prospective, longitudinal studies, in which the same group of athletes is studied for months or years as all undergo the same intervention, have now established that exercise alone seldom causes significant menstrual dysfunction in postmenarcheal women who start exercise with normal menstrual periods (Rogol et al. 1992; Bonen 1992; Warren 1992; N.I. Williams et al. 1995). If changes occur, they are usually subtle and transient, causing only some minor alterations in cycle lengths. Furthermore, exercise alone does not cause amenorrhea (Henley and Vaitukaitis 1988; Warren 1992; Beitins et al. 1991). Rather, it appears that menstrual dysfunction occurs when exercise is combined with an energy-deficient diet (Myerson et al. 1991; Loucks and Heath 1994; N.I. Williams et al. 1995; Loucks and Verdun 1998; Loucks et al. 1998; Thong and Graham 1999; Harber 2000) as originally proposed by us in 1987 (Van Gend and Noakes 1987).

This has led to the theory that leptin, the production of which by the fat cells is reduced when an energy deficit reduces the size of the body fat stores, may be the peripheral signal that links an energy deficit with menstrual dysfunction, thereby providing "a critical link between fat and fertility" (Thong and Graham 1999, p. 317).

Age

Younger athletes appear to be more prone to menstrual irregularity. In two large surveys of 900 runners (Speroff and Redwine 1980) and 550 runners (Lutter and Cushman 1982), proportionally more young women developed menstrual irregularity. However, most of these young women also had histories of menstrual irregularity before they even started running, which implies that the running was not the primary cause of the menstrual irregularity. Rather, it may be that young girls with menstrual irregularity are particularly attracted to vigorous exercise such as long-distance running.

Previous Menstrual Irregularity

In a survey of women completing the 1979 New York City Marathon, it was found that the incidence of menstrual irregularity in the respondents was 19% even before they began training (Shangold and Levine 1982). This is much higher than the rate in the "normal" population, which is about 6%. The same higher-than-expected incidence of menstrual irregularity before they started exercise has been found in ballet dancers (Abrahams et al. 1982) and in participants in the 1983 Two Oceans Marathon (Van Gend and Noakes 1987).

There can really only be one interpretation of these findings, and it is that some factor that promotes menstrual irregularity may inspire women to take up running, just as women who have late menarche may also be selected toward running or other sports that favor leanness. This propensity for menstrual irregularity then continues unchanged while the athlete trains. For this reason, it is found that the best predictor of a girl's menstrual status after she begins to run is her menstrual status before she began running (Van Gend and Noakes 1987; Cokkinades et al. 1990; Myburgh et al. 1992). If she had regular menstrual periods before she started running, the likelihood is that she will remain regular once she begins running, provided she continues to eat enough to remain in energy balance.

Parity

Parity indicates the number of children conceived. The evidence suggests that women who have not borne children are more likely to develop running-related menstrual irregularity than are those who have conceived (Dale et al. 1979; Baker et al. 1981).

Hypothalamic Dysfunction

The hypothalamus is a very specialized area at the base of the brain that is responsible for control of, among many other things, menstruation. Current thinking is that the hypothalamus becomes dormant in runners with amenorrhea; thus, it fails to produce those hormones that are necessary to induce the cyclical ovarian and uterine changes that lead to menstruation (figure 15.8). In particular, it is the loss of the cyclical, low-frequency, high-amplitude spikes in luteinizing hormone (LH) secretion by the pituitary in the midcycle that causes the menstrual dysfunction. These cyclical LH spikes are dependent on cyclical stimulation arising from the GnRH cells in the hypothalamus. This is analogous to the situation we found in overtrained male runners, who also show disturbed hypothalamic function (Barron et al. 1985). The question that remains is, what causes this hypothalamic dysfunction?

Two theories are currently popular (De Crée 1998). The first is the "energy deficiency hypothesis," which holds that calorie restriction induces changes in the circulating concentrations of thyroid hormones, insulin, leptin, and insulin-like growth factor (IGF), which then suppress the function of the GnRH-secreting cells in the hypothalamus. The second theory holds that the high blood cathecoloestrogen concentrations found in amenorrheic athletes interfere with hypothalamic GnRH function, perhaps in combination with simultaneously elevated brain endorphin concentrations. Exercise increases the production of cathecoloestrogens, especially in those with reduced body fat content.

In summary, the view first expressed in the second edition of *Lore of Running* has been confirmed. By itself, exercise training, however vigorous, is an inadequate stimulus to cause significant hypothalamic dysfunction in female athletes. Rather, the hypothalamus fails only when several key ingredients are present: dietary restriction combined with strenuous exercise and intensive competition in female

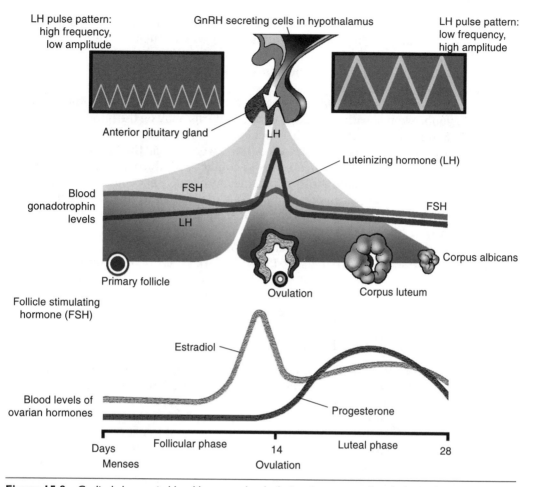

Figure 15.8   Cyclical changes in blood hormone levels during the menstrual cycle. In the follicular phase (first 14 days) of the menstrual cycle, the primary follicle secretes increasing amounts of estrogen. Ovulation is stimulated by the release of gonadotrophin-releasing hormone from the hypothalamus. This stimulates a surge in the amplitude but a reduction in the frequency of LH release from the anterior pituitary gland, initiating ovulation. The primary follicle, without its expelled egg, becomes the corpus luteum, which excretes progesterone to maintain the lining of the uterus. Menstruation occurs when the corpus luteum ages and stops secreting progesterone so that the lining of the uterus sloughs off.

athletes whose hypothalamus is sensitive (possibly as a result of hereditary predisposition). There is growing consensus for this multifunctional explanation (Loucks 1990; Henley and Vaitukaitis 1988; Myburgh et al. 1992; Thong and Graham 1999; De Crée 1998).

Nutrition

There is no published evidence showing that a single nutritional deficiency is uniquely related to menstrual dysfunction in exercising women (Watkin et al. 1991). One interesting observation has come from a study showing that amenorrheic runners ate one-fifth the amount of meat eaten by normally menstruating runners (S.M. Brooks et al. 1984). While 82% of amenorrheic runners ate less than 200 g per week of meat (poultry or red meat) and were classified as vegetarians, only 13% of normally menstruating runners ate as little meat. However, the total animal protein intake was not different between the groups, as the amenorrheic runners took more dairy produce. Fat intake was lower in the amenorrheic runners, as also reported by Deuster et al. (1986). Thus, a low intake of either red meat or fat may be one factor in menstrual irregularity in athletes.

Only more recently has it been recognized that an energy-deficient diet, especially in young women with restrictive eating patterns, may be the important nutritional link to menstrual dysfunction, especially amenorrhea.

In retrospect, we (Van Gend and Noakes 1987) were among the first to make this connection, but because the concept was in conflict with the existing paradigm, it took close to a decade before the idea became more widely accepted. The basis for our conclusion was simple: among a large group of ultramarathon runners, most of whom had normal menstrual periods, almost all those with amenorrhea had a present or past history of anorexia nervosa (Van Gend and Noakes 1987). Sometimes the evidence is so clear that it cannot be ignored.

A number of other reports (Henry 1982; N. Clark et al. 1988) confirmed a high incidence of restrictive (anorexic-type) eating patterns in elite North American female runners, and it is this group of elite runners that is particularly prone to menstrual irregularity, as discussed above.

Anorexia Nervosa and Bulimia Nervosa

Anorexia nervosa is a condition in which a person quite simply stops eating and starts starving to death. However, the term is misleading, because it literally means "loss of hunger on a psychological basis." In fact, there is no loss of hunger in this condition; people with anorexia nervosa suffer from intense hunger and food preoccupation but deny the hunger and will themselves not to eat (Blumenthal et al. 1985). They choose to avoid fats and sugar, in particular. A better definition for this condition might be "self-induced starvation syndrome." Anorectics have a morbid fear of being fat. They also suffer from a severe distortion of body image and see themselves as being morbidly obese even when they are so thin that they are at death's door.

Bulimia nervosa is characterized by binge eating followed by purging that can include self-induced vomiting, diuretic and laxative abuse, and rigorous exercise. Patients with bulimia do not try to lose weight; rather they purge to prevent weight gain induced by binge-eating. Bulimics binge as an outlet for feelings of frustration, disappointment, anger, loneliness, and boredom. Unlike anorectics, bulimics acknowledge the abnormality of their uncontrolled and uncontrollable behaviors. In addition, they do not suffer from a distorted body image. As their weight is normal, bulimics remain hidden in the normal population, whereas the thinness of anorectics makes their condition more obvious. However, there is often no rigid distinction between the two conditions, and many patients may show the characteristics of both.

Weight and Noakes (1987) confirmed that abnormal eating attitudes are most prevalent among the most competitive runners. Rosen et al. (1986) found that 47% of a group of female American collegiate runners practiced one or more pathogenic weight-control behaviors, such as self-induced vomiting or binge eating more than twice weekly or the use of laxatives, diet pills, or diuretics. The prevalence of these abnormal behaviors was even higher among gymnasts (74%). Swimmers, too, were found to use these practices to reduce or control their weight (Dummer et al. 1987). Some 27% of elite Norwegian runners and cross-country skiers met the criteria for anorexia nervosa or bulimia (Sundgot-Borgen 1994; 1999).

A nationwide survey of 2459 male and 1786 female runners in the United States found that 8% of males and 24% of females had increased scores on the questionnaire designed to detect abnormal eating attitudes (Kiernan et al. 1992). Interestingly, men but not women with elevated scores were more likely to be running the highest mileages in training. A relationship between abnormal eating attitudes and menstrual dysfunction has been established (Brooks-Gunn et al. 1987a; 1987b; Rippon et al. 1988; Walberg and Johnston 1991; Perry et al. 1996).

Gadpaille et al. (1987) have also reported that 11 of 13 amenorrheic runners reported major psychiatric disorders, especially depression, in themselves or in first- or second-degree relatives; 62% also had eating disorders. All these findings were significantly different from normally menstruating runners.

Together these findings suggest either one or a combination of two possibilities (Rippon et al. 1988). Women who are prone to menstrual dysfunction may be attracted to long-distance running. Socially induced pressures for thinness then induce abnormal eating attitudes and the adoption of the psychological characteristics found in women with anorexia nervosa. Alternatively, women who have the psychological characteristics of anorexia nervosa may eat calorie-restricted diets from an early age and develop menstrual dysfunction as a result. They then choose professions for which leanness is a positive attribute, such as modeling, gymnastics, or ballet, or physically demanding activities that will assist in maintaining their leanness, such as long-distance running. Their menstrual patterns will remain disturbed for as long as they continue to eat too little.

The evidence to date suggests that the menstrual dysfunction and the restrictive eating patterns displayed by these athletes stem from a disturbed psyche that underlies both abnormalities.

Anorexia Nervosa and Compulsive Exercise

An article (Yates et al. 1983) written by three running doctors from the department of psychiatry at the University of Arizona (Alayne Yates, Kevin Leehey, and Catherine Shisslak) and entitled "Running—An Analogue of Anorexia?" appeared in the prestigious *New England Journal of Medicine* in February 1983. It caused an immediate outcry because it suggested that those who exercise the most, the compulsive exercisers, may have similar personality characteristics to those described for young women with anorexia or bulimia. The study raised the interesting possibility that a condition of "compulsive exercising" may indeed exist and could be quite common among those male and female runners who train the most.

The article began by noting that the 1970s were characterized by two major social events: the rise among adolescent females of the incidence of anorexia nervosa to the point at which it is now regarded as a major public health problem in developed countries, and an almost simultaneous increase in the number of joggers and runners in the same countries. The possibility that the two conditions may be related first occurred to the authors during a research project in which they interviewed 60 runners who regularly ran more than 80 km per

(continued)

week. During these interviews, they noted similarities between the character, style, and backgrounds of some runners, whom they labeled *obligatory runners,* and the anorectic women they were accustomed to treating in their psychiatric practices. The similarities they noted were the following.

Singular dedication: Although the anorectics' goal is physical attractiveness and that of the obligatory runners is physical performance, the authors contend that both pursue their different goals with a degree of dedication that is alarming and potentially dangerous.

Personality characteristics: Anorectic females are usually described as having been model children reared in middle- to upper-class homes, often in families that are overtly concerned with achievement, diet, and exercise. They tend to be introverted, intensely active, and liable to depression. Some 24% of anorectic women are said to be "very athletic." Typically, anorectic women have a hazy sense of self as children and are dependent on others for opinions of their own self-worth. Successful dieting reduces the anorectic's anxiety and introversion and may produce a similar high to that experienced by runners.

In their survey, the authors found that their obligatory runners had similar characteristics to these anorectic women. They were self-effacing, hardworking high achievers from affluent families who were uncomfortable with anger, who were reluctant to express emotions, and who tended toward introversion. Their heightened commitment to running usually occurred at a time of identity crisis, heightened anxiety, or depression. Running improved their sense of self-worth, and the ritualization of shoes, clothing, books, food, training, and racing helped strengthen this self-image. These obligatory runners were totally obsessed with weight and felt unwell, anxious, depressed, and bloated when unable to run.

To explain this, the authors suggested that running may be an effective way for people who do not like to express anger openly to channel and release that anger. If unexpressed, the accumulated anger would then contribute to the runner's depression or "withdrawal symptoms." Thus, if running is indeed an effective and acceptable release of this pent-up anger for people who dislike expressing their anger, this would explain runners' withdrawal symptoms when they stop running.

Finally, the authors noted that both groups are characterized by asceticism, a tendency to social isolationism, and an aversion to passive receptive pleasures (such as eating, socializing, and visual entertainment).

Cultural reinforcement: The authors noted that society commends runners for their performance, while dieters are praised for their slimness. However, they also observed that when taken to extremes, a cultural bias becomes apparent, because although we praise overcommitted, elite runners for their dedication and courage (if they compete well despite injuries), anorectic women, the elite of the dieters, are classified as ill and are stigmatized by society.

Typical but different ages of anorectic women and obligatory runners: Women become anorectic in late adolescence, while obligatory runners become obsessed only in their thirties and forties. The authors suggest that this is because a girl's attractiveness really becomes an issue of self-worth only when she enters the dating arena in early or mid-adolescence. In contrast, the test of male physical powers first occurs in adulthood when the male has achieved a stable career, and, for the first time, he notices that his physical and sexual prowess are beginning to decline. So, the adult male with an identity crisis runs to overcome the crisis; the heightened physical and sexual prowess that result from running give him the feeling of heightened security and self-worth that he desires.

Yates et al. (1983) conclude that, in modern society, most people experience some anxiety about their appearance or strength and may decide to go on a diet or exercise program. In most cases, these lifestyle changes are beneficial. However, a small number of runners and dieters will go overboard in either their diet or their exercise programs. These people then become analogous to religious fanatics or workaholics and are identifiable by their extreme inflexibility, their adherence to rituals, their repetitive thoughts, and their intense need to control themselves and their environments. Something else must be present to push the normal exerciser or dieter into the obligatory, or anorectic, phase. This factor, the authors suggest, probably relates to the instability of the self-concept and must therefore place obligatory runners at high risk of developing depression, anorexia, and other disorders should they have to stop running and thereby lose their psychological crutch.

Since publication of that paper, many have sought to identify groups of compulsive exercisers for detailed study. In particular, the hypothesis under evaluation is whether compulsive exercise forms a psychological variant of the anorexia/bulimia syndrome.

For example, James Blumenthal and his colleagues (1984) from Duke University compared the psychological profiles of 43 obligatory runners with those of 24 patients who had been diagnosed with anorexia nervosa. They found that the psychological profile of the obligatory runners was quite normal, whereas that of the anorectic patients was clearly abnormal. They concluded that "obligatory runners do not suffer from the same degree of psychopathology as do patients with anorexia nervosa" (p. 520).

Similarly, we (Weight and Noakes 1987) found that the incidence of abnormal eating attitudes of the type present in people with anorexia nervosa was no greater in groups of female marathon and track runners than it was in the nonrunning population. However, abnormal eating attitudes were more prevalent in the more competitive women runners, suggesting that some women runners who are at risk for developing anorexia nervosa may use competitive running to control their anorectic tendencies. But this interpretation cannot explain the attraction running has for the vast majority of women runners.

Le Grange and Eisler (1993) propose that an excessive or compulsive exerciser is someone who is driven by a "relentless pursuit of fitness" and gives increasing priority to an exercise routine, thereby developing increased exercise tolerance. Compulsive exercising develops when the exerciser is no longer able to regulate the exercise routine because withdrawal symptoms develop if the exercise schedule is interrupted. They reviewed the literature to establish whether there was any evidence that the same factors causing anorexia in

(continued)

some people would cause excessive exercising in others, hence confirming the hypothesis that excessive exercising is a variant of anorexia nervosa.

Le Grange and Eisler conclude that whereas patients with anorexia nervosa suffer from a "morbid fear of fatness," excessive exercisers will diet specifically to lose weight so that they can perform better—"the pursuit of fitness (and performance)." But when the exerciser's "pursuit of thinness" exceeds the "pursuit of performance" so that the excessive weight loss impairs performance, the divide between the conditions may have been crossed. They also note that whereas patients with anorexia nervosa frequently suffer from depression either as the cause or a result of the condition, excessive exercise is not associated with depression. In contrast, exercise is sometimes used to control a tendency toward depression, as clearly described by Beck Weathers, the Mount Everest climber (Weathers and Michaud 2000).

Le Grange and Eisler also believe that there is no evidence to suggest that excessive running provides the same boost to self-esteem and identity as does dieting for the anorectic. Nor do they believe that all excessive exercisers are characterized by obsessive-compulsive or perfectionist tendencies, or that they are ineffective or self-effacing persons with low self-esteem who avoid direct expressions of anger.

Le Grange and Eisler propose that the defining characteristic of excessive exercisers is their single-minded commitment to physical fitness, which becomes the driving focus of their lives just as dieting is the sole focus of the patient with anorexia. But such commitment does not prove that the conditions are linked or related. Nor is there any evidence that excessive exercisers are biochemically addicted to exercise as a result of altered brain function in the same way that patients with anorexia nervosa may become euphoric as the result of starvation. The authors conclude that it is misleading to suggest any link between the two conditions and that the differences are greater than any superficial similarities.

Support from this conclusion comes from the study of Krejci et al. (1992), which found that, compared to females with bulimia, compulsive female exercisers were not dissatisfied with their bodies, did not have the same drive to be thin, did not have a distorted body image, were not depressed, and were not overly intent on restricting dietary fat and sugar intakes. However, obligatory exercisers did have a higher than normal drive to be thin. They were all perfectionists, but this was not to the pathological extent found in patients with anorexia nervosa.

Two other studies (Bamber et al. 2000a; 2000b) have drawn exactly the same conclusion. The psychological characteristics of two groups of exercise-dependent runners were compared to exercisers who had only an eating disorder and to sedentary controls who neither exercised nor suffered from an eating disorder. The first group of exercise-dependent runners included exercisers who were preoccupied with exercise, who developed significant withdrawal symptoms when they could not exercise, and whose preoccupation significantly impaired other aspects of their lives, but who were without evidence of a mental disorder to explain these behavior patterns. The second group exhibited exercise dependence and eating disorders and therefore included female athletes who had the first three of these four characteristics but who also had evidence of an eating disorder and associated mental characteristics.

The results showed that the psychological profile of the first exercise-dependent group were indistinguishable from those of sedentary controls. In contrast, the psychological profile of the exercise-dependent/eating-disorder group was indistinguishable from that of the eating-disorder group who exercised without evidence of exercise dependency. Furthermore, the female athletes in that group displayed all the characteristics that typify people with anorexia nervosa. The authors concluded that exercise dependency does not exist as a single pathological entity separate from anorexia/bulimia. Hence,

Where exercise dependence was manifest, it was always in the context of an eating disorder, and it was this co-morbidity, in addition to eating disorders per se, that was associated with psychological distress. As such, these qualitative data support the concept of secondary [in association with an eating disorder], but not primary, exercise dependence. (Bamber et al. 2000b, p. 423)

They also emphasize that people with other behavioral abnormalities (for example, pathological gamblers) have a very high prevalence of other psychological morbidities (such as lifetime mood or anxiety disorders) or personality disorders (present in as many as 87% of pathological gamblers; Black and Moyer 1998). In contrast, female athletes with exercise dependence showed no such bias and, in contrast, were characterized by high levels of self-esteem.

More recently, the focus has shifted to the links between obsessive/compulsive tendencies, anorexia nervosa, and compulsive exercising (C. Davis et al. 1994; 1995). This model theorizes that it is the combination of weight preoccupation and obsessive-compulsive behavior that drive the excessive dieting or the exercise dependency, or both. Clearly, it is only in some men and women in whom the confluence of both factors produce anorexia nervosa. This model predicts that, compared to patients with anorexia nervosa who exercised only moderately, athletes with the excessive exercising/eating disorder score the highest on measures of obsessive/compulsive behavior tendencies (C. Davis et al. 1997). The authors even suggest that the greater obsessive compulsiveness of those with the excessive exercising/eating disorder could result from the exercise alone, since a majority of patients with anorexia nervosa report high levels of physical activity, including participation in competitive sport or a marked increase in training load (Sundgot-Borgen 1994), even before the onset of anorexia nervosa (Davis et al. 1994). In addition, a majority reported that their physical activity patterns increased when they ate the least (Davis et al. 1994; Davis et al. 1997), a characteristic also found in food-deprived, exercising laboratory rats (Davis et al. 1997). The authors suggest that starvation may increase brain serotonin concentrations that then drive the increased physical activity of these patients (and rats). Thus, they invoke a brain neurochemical link to explain how starvation can lead to higher levels of physical activity in young women who have the psychological predisposition to develop anorexia nervosa.

In summary, there is no evidence to suggest that those who exercise excessively are psychologically disturbed so that a novel psychiatric condition—obligatory exercising—has to be invoked. Rather, obligatory exercising occurs in some young women with anorexia nervosa and is simply another symptom or variant of that basic disorder. Thus, as McCutcheon and Ayres (1983) have

(continued)

> written: "We have reached a sad state of affairs where perfectionism is a dirty word. . . . It is indeed sad that those who try to reach beyond their limits to pursue excellence are subjected to ridicule. . . . Accusing the dedicated athlete of neuroticism is to libel the pursuit of excellence" (p. 17).
>
> Perhaps the truth is that any human activity that provides a solid measure of ego satisfaction—be it academic, professional, political, religious, business, or sport-related—is particularly attractive for those with hazy self-esteem. Thus, just as there are obligatory runners and dieters, there are obligatory academics, obligatory professionals, obligatory politicians, obligatory priests, and obligatory executives, all of whom probably have similar personalities but none of whom have an identifiable psychiatric condition, although there must be a psychological predisposition yet to be identified.
>
> Therefore running is no more or no less an analogue of anorexia than is any human activity that improves self-esteem and satisfies the ego. The danger, then, is the psychological predisposition, not the activity. So running, like all these human activities, is beneficial when it improves feelings of self-esteem and self-worth, all of which may improve the way obligatory-type people cope with their lives. In addition, the effect is more likely to be beneficial.
>
> What Yates et al. (1983) should have told us is that obligatory runners and dieters, like obligatory people active in any of these activities, need to be aware of the limits to which any single activity can satisfy uncomfortable personality traits without introducing those additional behaviors that can ultimately be devastating.

Female Athlete Triad

Prior to 1984, it was assumed that the menstrual dysfunction found not uncommonly among elite female distance runners was without medical consequences (Zaharieva 1972) and, at very worst, was a welcome relief from an annoying physiological function. But the study of Drinkwater et al. (1984) exploded that belief by showing that female athletes with amenorrhea had reduced bone density. At first, there was a reluctance to accept this finding because it was so unexpected; everyone "knew" that running increased bone density. Furthermore, all aspired to be elite runners, whose thinness and unimaginable performances contributed toward the picture of health that epitomized the 1980s.

Unfortunately, a host of studies have now established beyond doubt that women who have persistent menstrual disturbances—and who therefore fail to produce adequate amounts of estrogen or progesterone so that they develop amenorrhea, oligomenorrhea, or the short luteal phase (Prior et al. 1990; Prior and Vigna 1991; Snead et al. 1992)—will develop weak osteopenic bones at increased risk of injury. Once the bones have lost more than about 10% of their mineral (especially calcium) content, they become increasingly liable to fracture. It follows that women with prolonged and persistent amenorrhea will develop decalcified bones, which are at risk of fractures not only in later life but also during their athletic careers. In addition, athletes with menstrual dysfunction, either oligo- or amenorrhea, may be more prone to musculoskeletal injuries (To et al. 1995).

This syndrome of three distinct medical conditions—disordered eating, amenorrhea, and osteoporosis/osteopenia—has since been termed the Female Athlete

Triad (Yeager et al. 1993; ACSM 1997). I note that, perhaps not surprisingly, the acronym FAT has yet to be applied to this syndrome, which is always described by its full title.

The overriding concern in this condition is that the degree of osteopenia develops in proportion to the duration of the menstrual dysfunction; it affects all the bones in the body; and it is largely irreversible (ACSM 1997). This osteopenia places the Female Athlete Triad athlete at increased risk of stress fractures while she continues to compete and at increased risk of hip fractures after the menopause.

Therefore, persistent menstrual dysfunction is not beneficial in the long term, so that runners need to do whatever is required to prevent its development. As soon as the condition develops, corrective measures must be initiated. If an increased calorie intake is all that is needed, then the psychological support will need to be provided to ensure that this can be achieved.

Hence, the current suggestions are that athletes with menstrual dysfunction should

- decrease training activity by 10% to 20%;
- increase energy intake gradually, perhaps by including a high-energy sport drink in the usual diet;
- increase weight by 2% to 3% of current body weight; and
- increase calcium intake to 1.5 g per day (Steen 1997).

Regaining weight to about 90% of a standard body weight is usually enough to ensure the resumption of menstruation (Golden et al. 1997). An increase calcium intake can be achieved by increasing the consumption of low-calorie, high-calcium foods such as skimmed milk, low-fat yogurt, and cottage cheese in addition to calcium supplements. Vitamin D aids in the absorption of calcium; thus, supplementation with this vitamin is of value.

Finally, the runner should discuss the need for estrogen therapy with a specialist gynecologist, as estrogen therapy may reduce the rate of bone loss and therefore the long-term risk of shinsplints, stress fractures, and ultimately osteoporotic fractures (Naessén et al. 1990; Cauley et al. 1995). However, it remains uncertain whether estrogen replacement therapy will reverse bone loss in amenorrheic runners (Bennell et al. 1999), and early studies suggest that any effect is likely to be quite small (Gibson et al. 1999). Hence, at present, the best long-term option is prevention of abnormal eating behaviors and amenorrhea in the first place.

Osteoporosis

Physically active women whose menstrual periods are normal (or were normal during their reproductive years) have increased bone mass in the femoral neck (Greendale et al. 1995) or the lumbar spine, or both (Pocock et al. 1986; Howat et al. 1989; Wolman et al. 1990; Heinrich et al. 1990; Cheng et al. 1991; Shimegi et al. 1994; Gardner and Poehlman 1993)—the two sites most commonly involved in osteoporotic fractures in elderly women. Physically active women with normal menstrual periods also have a lower risk of femoral neck fracture (Boyce and Vessey 1988; Wickham et al. 1989; Paganini-Hill et al. 1991; Nieves et al. 1992; Coupland et al. 1993; Jaglal et al. 1993; 1995). Bone density is also increased in physically active men (Snow-Harter et al. 1992; Välimäki et al. 1994; Need et al. 1995).

The sites at which bone density is increased in men and women depend on the type of physical activity that is undertaken and the bones that are loaded by that activity (Bennell et al. 1997). Thus, activities such as basketball, volleyball, jogging, aerobics that include jump training (Heinonen et al. 1996), boxing, figure skating (Slemenda et al. 1993), ballet dancing (N. Young et al. 1994), and especially weightlifting (Suominen 1993; Sabo et al. 1996; Hamdy et al. 1994; Bennell et al. 1997)—all of which load both the spine and lower limbs—are usually associated with increased bone density at those sites. Weight training is associated with increased bone mineral density of the upper limbs as well (Hamdy et al. 1994; Bennell et al. 1997). Importantly, it seems that exercise undertaken in the prepubertal years is especially important because it increases bone density and the size of the bone cortex more than does equivalent exercise undertaken at any other age (Bass 2000).

In contrast, neither cycling (Beshgetoor et al. 2000) nor swimming (Stewart and Hannan 2000) and sometimes not even running (Brahm et al. 1997) is associated with an increased lumbar bone density; nor does running or cycling alone increase bone mineral density of the upper limbs (Hamdy et al. 1994; Stewart and Hannan 2000). Indeed, cyclists in the Tour de France have decreased bone density in the lumbar spine, hip, and femoral neck (Sabo et al. 1996), although other studies do not find a reduced femoral bone density in cyclists (Beshgetoor et al. 2000; Stewart and Hannan 2000). It appears that endurance exercise, such as running, may either reduce (Brahm et al. 1997) or increase (Hetland et al. 1993) the rate of bone turnover, depending on the weekly mileage that is run. Higher weekly training volumes are associated with higher rates of bone turnover and a reduced likelihood that bone density will be increased (Bilanin et al. 1989; MacDougall et al. 1992; Hetland et al. 1993; MacKelvie et al. 2000).

Other factors that influence bone density are a high intake of soluble calcium salts or dairy produce (Reid et al. 1993; Metz et al. 1993) combined with high levels of physical activity, especially during adolescence (Slemenda et al. 1991; Welten et al. 1994; Ruiz et al. 1995; Van den Bergh et al. 1995), and the use of the contraceptive pill or estrogen replacement therapy after menopause (Ulrich et al. 1996; Kohrt et al. 1998). The combination of exercise and estrogen replacement therapy has a greater effect on bone mineral density than does either intervention alone (Kohrt et al. 1998). Furthermore, the gains in bone mineral density achieved with the combined intervention are not lost if the amount of physical activity is subsequently reduced while the estrogen replacement therapy is continued (Kohrt et al. 1998). Vitamin K supplementation may also play a role in preventing bone loss with aging (Craciun et al. 1998).

Other significant factors besides menstrual dysfunction that reduce bone density or increase the risk of osteoporotic fractures, or both, include cigarette smoking (Välimäki et al. 1994; Law and Hackshaw 1997); high dietary intakes of protein and phosphorus (Metz et al. 1993), both of which increase urinary calcium losses; frequent consumption of carbonated drinks by adolescents (Wyshak 2000); caffeine use; and moderate alcohol consumption (Hernandez-Avila et al. 1991).

Athletic Performance and the Menstrual Cycle

The stage of the menstrual cycle affects certain physiological functions during exercise (Quadagno 2000). Thus, rectal temperature (but not heart rate nor the level of perceived exertion) is higher during the luteal phase of the menstrual cycle. The

$\dot{V}O_2$max also does not appear to be different when measured at different times during the menstrual cycle. Muscle strength, but not endurance, is increased during that part of the cycle when blood estrogen concentrations are increased (the late follicular and early luteal phases). This suggests that estrogen increases muscle strength, a finding that is supported by research showing that hormone replacement therapy increases muscle strength in postmenopausal women (Phillips, Rook, et al. 1993; Greeves et al. 1999).

There is a pervasive belief that these physiological changes must have some influence on the exercise capacity of the female athlete at different times during the menstrual cycle (Quadragno 2000). The evidence suggests that physical and mental performance does alter during the menstrual cycle, but there is some uncertainty regarding exactly when in the menstrual cycle performance is most affected.

In a study in which athletic performance was carefully measured during the entire menstrual cycle, Brooks-Gunn et al. (1986) found that performance in high-intensity, short-duration exercise was best during the menstrual phase of the cycle and worst immediately before menstruation, in the premenstrual phase. Another study also showed that women performed better during maximal exercise testing in the laboratory in the first eight days of the cycle than in the last eight days. Body temperatures were also higher during exercise performed in the premenstrual period (Stephenson et al. 1982a). In contrast, Bale and Nelson (1985) found that 50-m swimming performance was best from the 8th to the 15th day of the menstrual cycle but was worst on the first day of menstruation. However, as 16 of the 20 swimmers believed that their performances were affected by menstruation, a psychological effect cannot be excluded. For example, impaired performance may result from inattention due to premenstrual discomfort (Pierson and Lockhart 1963). Another study (Quadagno et al. 1991) did not find any effect of the menstrual cycle phase on 100-m freestyle swimming performance. Studies of more prolonged exercise have shown either no effect (De Souza et al. 1990; Lebrun et al. 1995) or impaired performance during the menses (Fomin et al. 1989; Quadagno et al. 1991).

In summary, it remains uncertain whether exercise performance alters substantially during the different phases of the menstrual cycle. This probably means that the response is very individual, with about equal numbers of women showing either no effect or a detrimental one.

How, then, do some women compete effectively at all phases of the menstrual cycle (Erdelyi 1962)? Either the menstrual cycle does not affect their athletic performance (or the most successful athletes are those who are the least affected by any premenstrual or menstrual drop in athletic performance) or else successful athletes use oral contraceptives to control their menstrual cycles since exercise performance does not alter during the artificial menstrual cycle produced by the use of oral contraceptives (Quadagno 2000). Alternatively, it may even be that some successful athletes are amenorrheic. Amenorrhea, because it avoids the premenses, may reduce the variability in athletic performance. But the long-term damage caused by amenorrhea exceeds any small benefit that this might offer.

Interestingly, women who participate in contact sports are at increased risk of traumatic injury during the premenstrual and menstrual periods, and pill users have a lower incidence of traumatic injuries than nonpill users (Moller-Nielsen and Hammar 1989). The explanation for either finding is unclear but could relate to the nature of the women who use or do not use the pill.

Premenstrual Symptoms and Endometriosis

Moderate exercise training significantly decreases the severity of premenstrual symptoms (Prior et al. 1986) and reduces the risk of developing endometriosis—a rare condition in which the lining of the uterus, the endometrium, may also be found at scattered sites outside the uterus. Since this errant endometrial tissue is functionally intact, it bleeds in response to the normal menstrual cycle. If the errant endometrium bleeds into a confined space, pain develops (Cramer et al. 1986). Exercise likely has little direct effect in reducing the symptoms of this condition.

EXERCISE AND OTHER CANCERS

If exercise alters the production of the female hormones—particularly if it delays menarche, thereby postponing the time at which the female reproductive organs are first exposed to estrogen—then it may influence the development of those female cancers that are believed to be estrogen-dependent (Kramer and Wells 1996) and that may be more likely in those whose organs are exposed to estrogen at the youngest ages.

Thus, some early studies found that the risks of benign and malignant cancers of the breast, ovary, uterus, cervix, and vagina; malignant cancers of the digestive system, thyroid, bladder, lung, and other sites; and cancers of the blood-forming tissues (lymphoma, leukemia, myeloma, and Hodgkin's disease) were lower in former college athletes than in nonathletes (Frisch et al. 1985; 1989; Wyshak et al. 1986). The incidence of cancers of the skin, including melanomas, was found to be no different between the former athletes and nonathletes.

The authors concluded that the regular physical activity of the former college athletes reduced their risk of developing these cancers. The risk of osteoporotic fractures developing in later life was not different between former athletes and nonathletes (Wyshak et al. 1987).

These conclusions must be treated with caution. The lifelong physical activity patterns of these women were not determined. Thus, there is no proof that the former athletes were more physically active during their working lives than their peers, although it is likely that they were. The possibility that hereditary factors explained this difference is unlikely, as the family history of cancer in the athletic and nonathletic groups was the same. The incidence of diabetes was also lower in the group of former college athletes (Frisch et al. 1986).

More recent studies have indeed established that physical activity, maintained for life, reduces the risk of developing breast cancer, especially in those women who do not gain excessive amounts of weight during their adult lives (Bernstein et al. 1994; Friedenreich and Rohan 1995; Mittendorf et al. 1995; McTierman 1997; Zheng et al. 1993; Thune et al. 1997; Sesso et al. 1998; Carpenter et al. 1999; Rockhill et al. 1999).

One avoidable risk factor for breast cancer is alcohol. Two recent studies show that even very moderate amounts of alcohol (two drinks per week) are associated with an increased risk of breast cancer in women (Schatzkin, Jones, et al. 1987; Willett et al. 1987). The risk of endometrial (uterine) cancer is also lower in those who are physically active (Shu et al. 1993; Sturgeon et al. 1993), perhaps because they are less likely to be overweight.

Prostatic cancer is one of the most common forms of cancer in men. One study found a weak relationship between increased levels of physical activity in men and increased risk of prostatic cancer (Le Marchand et al. 1991), whereas others have found the opposite: that the risk of this cancer is reduced in those who exercise the most (Brownson et al. 1991; Thune and Lund 1994; Oliveria et al. 1996). The current conclusion is that "the bulk of evidence at this time does not support an overwhelmingly beneficial effect of exercise on prostate cancer risk" (Oliveria and Lee 1997, p. 97). But physical activity reduces the risk of developing benign prostatic hyperplasia and associated lower urinary tract symptoms (Platz et al. 1998).

Two studies found an unaltered risk of testicular cancer in those who exercised the most (Thune and Lund 1994; Paffenbarger, Hyde et al. 1987) whereas a third found that a sedentary lifestyle reduced the risk of developing testicular cancer (United Kingdom Testicular Cancer Study Group 1994).

EXERCISE AND MALE FERTILITY

There is clear evidence, then, that exercise training in combination with other factors (in particular, inadequate nutrition and high levels of competitive and other stresses) can induce cessation of menstruation in female athletes by inhibiting the normal cyclical release of hormones from the hypothalamus and pituitary glands. In females, any failure of the hypothalamus or pituitary glands is immediately apparent because menstruation ceases.

In men, however, the condition might go unrecognized, as the only likely signs would be a loss of libido and infertility, symptoms to which most male runners are likely to admit only with reluctance. Thus, the question has been posed whether males who train intensively also show changes in the functioning of these glands.

Early evidence of this possibility was our finding, discussed in chapter 7, of hypothalamic-pituitary failure in overtrained male athletes (Barron et al. 1985). It should be noted that this abnormality was not present in runners who were training in excess of 160 km per week and were racing frequently but who were not overtrained.

More recently, a number of studies (Wheeler et al. 1984; 1991; Ayers et al. 1985; Hackney et al. 1988; 1990; De Souza et al. 1994) have found reduced blood levels of the male hormone testosterone in trained male distance runners, possibly on the basis of hypothalamic dysfunction (MacConnie et al. 1986; Hackney 1996). However, the study of Ayers and his colleagues (1985) showed that these changes were mild and were not associated with changes in libido, sexual performance, or fertility, as judged by the quality of the semen produced by these runners. Thus, the conclusion is that these low serum testosterone concentrations are not associated with reproductive dysfunction (Cumming et al. 1989; Hackney 1989; Lucía et al. 1996) and are due to decreased production of hypothalamic and pituitary hormones necessary for testosterone production by the testes, as well as a decreased capacity of the testes to produce testosterone after exercise (Kujala et al. 1990).

Interestingly, Ayers et al. (1985) noted that 2 of the 20 runners whom they studied were clearly abnormal and were infertile. However, these two runners were thinner, had lost more weight, and had experienced more stress in their lives than the other runners. They felt that these two runners were more typical of the anorectic-type runners of the Yates hypothesis (discussed earlier), which equates obligatory running in males with anorexia in females. They concluded that heavy training alone was not associated with a detrimental effect on libido or sperm production in male runners. But changes in both libido and sperm production have indeed been reported in trained athletes who increased their training from 1 to 2 hours per day for two weeks (Griffith et al. 1990). In contrast to these negative effects of heavy training on libido, people who begin a moderate training program (60 minutes per day, three to four times per week, at 75% $\dot{V}O_2$max) report enhanced sexual behavior (White et al. 1990). The degree of sexual enhancement is directly related to the improvement in physical fitness.

However, another study (Baker et al. 1988) found that pregnancy rates achieved with semen donated from athletic males was reduced and that sperm from these athletes was of decreased volume with impaired motility. This finding has been confirmed. De Souza et al. (1994) reported that athletes running more than 100 km per week or more than 8 hours per week showed a significant reduction in the number of normal and motile sperm, with an increased number of immature sperms. None of these abnormalities were present in athletes who ran less than 40 to 60 km per week or 2 to 5 hours per week. In addition, sperm from high-mileage runners had reduced penetration or cervical mucus when tested in vitro (De Souza and Miller 1997).

They concluded that although the sperm function of heavily training runners was not grossly abnormal, the changes they measured might be sufficient to cause subclinical fertility problems in some male runners. Probably the important practical point from these findings is that male runners should consider stopping running if their wives are having difficulty becoming pregnant.

Another possible complication of reduced blood testosterone concentrations in male runners training more than 100 km per week may be a reduced femoral or vertebral bone density, or both; the densities of these bones may be no higher than those of nonrunners and lower than those of runners running less than 60 km per week (Bilanin et al. 1989; MacDougall et al. 1992; Hetland et al. 1993; Goodpaster et al. 1996b; MacKelvie et al. 2000).

This has led De Souza and Miller (1997) to suggest that there may be a training

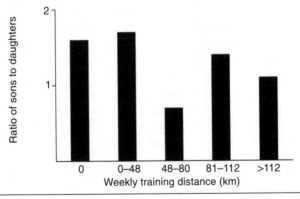

Figure 15.9   The ratio of sons to daughters born to fathers who were running different weekly mileages at the time of conception. Fathers who ran either fewer than 48 km per week or more than 80 km per week were more likely to have sons. Only fathers who ran between 48 and 80 km per week were more likely to have daughters.

Adapted with permission from Crawford et al. (1992, p. 272).

volume threshold of about 100 km per week, above which the beneficial effects of exercise on bone density may be reversed and subclinical fertility changes may begin to develop.

Inspired by these findings, James (2000) has suggested that changes in male hormone concentrations induced by heavier training may explain why the gender of the offspring of runners seems to be influenced by the training volume of their fathers (Crawford et al. 1992; figure 15.9). Thus, the ratio is U-shaped, with the ratio of boy-to-girl offspring being 1.6 to 1.7 (indicating that 62% of children born were boys) for nonrunners or those who run less than 48 km per week and 1.1 to 1.4 for fathers who run more than 80 km per week. In contrast, the ratio was least (0.7— indicating that 60% of offspring were girls) in fathers who ran between 48 and 80 km per week.

According to this theory, runners who wish to conceive boys should therefore either stop running or run more than 112 km per week. Those desiring girls should run between 48 and 80 km per week.

EXERCISE AND FEMALE FERTILITY

Exercise can influence a woman's fertility in two other ways. First, exercise can reduce the duration of the luteal phase (see figure 15.8) of the menstrual cycle (Shangold et al. 1979; Prior et al. 1982; Prior and Vigna 1991). This will effectively prevent pregnancy because it will cause sloughing of the uterine lining before any fertilized egg has the chance of becoming established in the womb lining.

Second, exercise may prevent ovulation. O'Herlichy (1982) has reported two amenorrheic Irish runners who failed to ovulate in response to the fertility pill, clomiphene citrate, even in high doses. However, when both stopped running, ovulation was soon induced by normal or low doses of the drug.

That exercise may indeed be a factor in infertility is suggested by the study of B.B. Green et al. (1986), who interviewed 346 infertile women attending an infertility clinic and found that infertile women were more likely to participate in vigorous exercise for more than 1 hour per day than were fertile women. Vigorous exercise for less than 1 hour per day was not associated with infertility.

The message is that any woman runner who is having difficulty becoming pregnant should be open to the possibility that her running may be a factor. Stopping running may be all that she need do to ensure conception. Occasionally, however, the opposite can occur. A colleague's wife, who had struggled for more than a decade to conceive, started running and gave birth to her first child nine months to the day after finishing her first 56-km ultramarathon.

An early study found that sexually active runners are less likely to use oral contraceptives than are nonrunners. Thus, two independent studies (Shangold and Levine 1982; Jarrett and Spellacy 1983a) reported that runners make far greater use of diaphragms for birth control than do nonrunners (37% and 44% vs. the U.S. national average of about 3%) and far less use of oral contraceptives (6% and 13% vs. the national average of 44%). It would seem that runners who are concerned about their health are particularly concerned about the potential risks of oral contraceptive use. Whether these patterns still apply in the newest generation of female runners is not known.

I shall not discuss the relative risks of the use of oral contraceptive pills (Prior and Vigna 1985). Clearly, this is a matter for each woman and her gynecologist. In addition, ideas change. Those experts whom I have consulted are generally in agreement that the risks of oral contraceptive use are small. It is possible that those women runners who, for perceived health reasons, choose not to use oral contraceptives, may be oversensitive to the potential dangers of those drugs. Alternatively, it may be that oral contraceptives impair running performance (Prior and Vigna 1985) and that this effect makes them less acceptable for runners.

One effect of some oral contraceptives is that they decrease blood HDL-cholesterol levels. As elevated HDL-cholesterol concentrations are associated with a reduced incidence of coronary heart disease, anything that reduces blood HDL-cholesterol concentrations is clearly undesirable. However, regular exercise raises HDL-cholesterol concentrations in women who use oral contraceptives (Gray et al. 1983; Merians et al. 1985). All users of oral contraceptives should, in fact, run.

As yet there is no consensus on whether all women should take hormone replacement therapy after menopause. Although such use will prevent the development of osteoporosis, any effect in preventing the subsequent development of coronary heart disease has yet to be shown (Nabel 2000). Although women using hormone replacement therapy have a lower mortality, especially from heart disease and stroke, for the first five years after beginning hormone replacement therapy, the benefit becomes less with time, in part because the risk of developing breast cancer begins to increase after 5 to 10 years of hormone replacement therapy (Grodstein et al. 1997). Women with risk factors for heart disease benefited more than did women with no coronary risk factors.

A new group of drugs, the selective estrogen-receptor modulators (SERMs), are currently under evaluation. These drugs act on one or more of the sites at which naturally occurring estrogen acts, including bone, breast, uterus, and heart. The goal is to develop a SERM that protects against heart disease and osteoporosis without promoting the development of estrogen-dependent cancers of the breast and uterus. Raloxifene is a SERM that decreases postmenopausal bone loss without affecting the uterus but may protect against breast cancer. Its effectiveness in preventing coronary heart disease is currently under investigation in the Raloxifene Use for the Heart (RUTH) trial.

Another potential benefit of hormone replacement therapy is the prevention of muscle strength losses in the first few years of menopause (Greeves et al. 1999). Some athletes take oral contraceptives as a means of controlling their menstrual cycles. The athlete may deem that control of her menstruation is necessary if she knows that her performance is affected during the menstrual cycle and if a major race is likely to occur while she is menstruating. To determine this, she must establish her menstrual cycle length and monitor her training and racing performance during the different phases of the menstrual cycle by the careful use of a running logbook. Remember that the evidence is far from conclusive that the stage of the menstrual cycle affects athletic performance.

To ensure that she competes at the most favorable period in her menstrual cycle, the athlete may take either estrogen or progesterone in high doses for varying periods of time. When she stops taking the medication, a "withdrawal bleed" is induced, as occurs at the end of the menstrual cycle when estrogen and progesterone levels suddenly fall. Oral contraceptives have the effect of shortening one or more of the cycles previous to competition: it is done three to six months before competition so that there is a resetting of the menstrual cycle and so that when the athlete is no longer on medication, the competition will fall in her midcycle. If the menstrual cycle needs to be shortened by only a few days, either of these drugs needs to be given for only two to three days near the end of the luteal phase. If the cycle needs to be reduced by up to 12 days, these drugs must be given from day 5 until day 14 of the menstrual cycle. Withdrawal bleeding then occurs on day 16 (Dalton and Williams 1976).

The athlete who fails to take these precautions but who, at the last moment, realizes that her competition will occur during menstruation can delay menstruation by taking high doses of progesterone in the form of a suppository.

There is no evidence to suggest that running influences the timing of the onset of menopause. However, hot flashes are only half as common in active postmenopausal women as they are in inactive women (Hammar et al. 1990).

EXERCISE AND PREGNANCY

Scientific studies of the physiological effects of exercising during pregnancy have focused on blood flow to the fetus, hyperthermia during exercise, and the risk of premature labor. These three topics need to be understood if the safety of exercise during pregnancy is to be established (Dale et al. 1982; Gorski 1985). In the following section we discuss these three topics as well as the benefits of exercising during pregnancy and guidelines for exercising safely during pregnancy.

Blood Flow to the Fetus

Blood flow to the fetus decreases during maternal exercise in pregnant ewes (Lotgering et al. 1983), but compensation occurs so that overall oxygen supply to the fetus remains unchanged. The same reduction in blood flow could apply in humans (N. Morris et al. 1956), but more recent studies do not show this (D.H. Moore et al. 1988; Rauramo and Forss 1988; Shangold 1988).

If the fetus receives an inadequate oxygen supply, then the fetal heart rate should either rise or fall as a result. Different studies have measured decreased (Dale et al. 1982; Jovanovic et al. 1985), unchanged (Carpenter et al. 1988; Sorensen and Borlum 1986; Spinnewijn et al. 1996) or increased fetal heart rate (Dressendorfer and Goodlin 1980; Collings et al. 1983; Collings and Curet 1985) and increased fetal breathing movements (Marsal et al. 1979) during maternal exercise. But studies showing a reduction in fetal heart rate during exercise may have been erroneous, as modern techniques that avoid an artifact induced by the motion of the mother's body show that fetal heart rate does not change during maternal exercise (Paolone et al. 1987).

Indeed Sady et al. (1989) have found that cardiac output is higher both at rest and during exercise in pregnant women. They suggest that there may be a luxurious blood flow to the uterus during exercise, thereby ensuring an adequate blood flow to the fetus during exercise.

Perhaps the more important question is this: are babies born to women who have exercised during pregnancy of lower birth weight and at increased risk of suffering abnormalities? That would be the expected outcome if maternal exercise impairs the oxygen supply to the developing fetus. Here the evidence is clear: the children born to women who have exercised during pregnancy are of normal weight and do not show any increased risk of birth abnormalities.

Thus, a number of studies confirm that exercise during pregnancy does not increase the risk of an adverse outcome of pregnancy (Beckman and Beckman 1990; Clapp 1991b; Lokey et al. 1991; Schramm et al. 1996). Furthermore, the vast majority of studies (Zaharieva 1972; Pomerance et al. 1974; Dale et al. 1982; Collings et al. 1983; Jarrett and Spellacy 1983b; Collings and Curet 1985; Hall and Kaufmann 1987; Kulpa et al. 1987; Sternfeld et al. 1995; Kardel and Kase 1998) found that the birth weights of the offspring of those who exercise during pregnancy are normal. Two studies (Clapp and Dickstein 1984; Bell et al. 1995) have shown that women who continue to exercise for at least 30 minutes three times per week for the duration of pregnancy deliver earlier and have lighter offspring. However, the difference was due solely to a lower fat mass in the offspring of the exercisers (Clapp and Capeless 1990; Clapp 1991b). Exercise was not associated with an increased incidence of fetal abnormalities in those studies (Clapp 1989; 1991b). At five years of age, offspring of mothers who exercise during pregnancy continue to have a lower body fat content (Clapp 1996).

In contrast, Hatch et al. (1993) found that the babies of mothers who were fit before their pregnancies and who continued to exercise either lightly or more vigorously during their pregnancies weighed more at birth than did those of nonexercisers. Babies born to heavier exercisers were 300 g heavier than babies born to unfit, nonexercising women. The authors suggested that popular guidelines for exercising during pregnancy may be too stringent for well-conditioned women whose pregnancies carry low risk.

Reviewing all this information, the scientist who has contributed perhaps the most research on this topic—Professor J.F. Clapp III (Clapp 1994) of the Cape Western Reserve University School of Medicine in Cleveland, Ohio—proposes that the physiological adaptations to exercise and pregnancy are complementary and are designed to protect the fetus. Although he acknowledges that the safe upper limit for exercise during pregnancy has yet to be defined, he suggests that the pregnant mother can continue to benefit from exercise without undue risk to the fetus. He proposes that the training program should be flexible and individualized and that the health of the mother and the progress of the pregnancy should be monitored regularly so that exercise continues to be at an appropriate level.

Indeed, anecdotal evidence suggests that highly trained women can continue to exercise vigorously without adverse effects to their babies. Thus, Kardel and Kase (1998) studied 42 competitive endurance athletes who continued to train six days per week, including either 1 or 2 hours of endurance training (stationary cycling, cross-country skiing, running, or fast walking) per day on two of those days; 25 or 35 minutes of interval training at peak maternal heart rates between 170 to 180 beats per minute on two days per week; and strength training two days per week. Most of these athletes continued to exercise to within four days of the onset of labor. Birth weights were no different between groups and were within or were higher than birth weight ranges for other pregnancies of healthy women.

Another case study (Bailey et al. 1998) of a competitive marathoner (best time 2:34:00), who continued to train an average of 107 km per week up to three days before delivery, showed that her twins, delivered by elective Caesarian section, were normal, healthy, and of an appropriate weight.

Hyperthermia and the Fetus

An elevated maternal temperature (hyperthermia), from whatever cause, may be detrimental as it may cause fetal damage (D.W. Smith et al. 1978), especially if the maternal temperature exceeds 39.2°C during the first three months of the pregnancy (Artal and Sherman 1999). From the information reviewed in chapter 4, it would seem likely that a woman exercising moderately in a cool environment for up to 30 minutes would not show a marked rise in body temperature, so that moderate exercise of this duration is probably quite safe (R.L. Jones et al. 1985). Indeed, Clapp (1991a) has shown that the body temperature at any workload falls with gestation, owing to an enhanced capacity of the pregnant female to lose body heat during exercise. Thus, moderate exercise would not seem to pose any thermal dangers to the fetus.

Were the pregnant mother to exercise vigorously in hot environmental conditions (Wet Bulb Globe Temperature index more than 22°C) for more than 30 minutes, however, then her body temperature might reach levels that could cause fetal damage. But these concerns are largely theoretical since no mother is ever likely to exercise for a prolonged period in environmental conditions that are uncomfortably hot.

Premature Labor

This, fortunately, is one topic on which we have a consensus. Gertrud Berkowitz and her colleagues (Berkowitz et al. 1983) from the department of obstetrics and gynecology at the Mount Sinai Medical Center in New York compared social and health-related data in women who had either delivered their babies prematurely (before 37 weeks of gestation) or after a normal gestational period (after 37 weeks). They found that significantly fewer women who participated in leisure-time physical activity delivered prematurely and suggested that exercise might protect against premature labor.

My own interpretation is that some other feature of women who choose to exercise during pregnancy makes them less likely to deliver their babies prematurely. For example, the women least likely to deliver prematurely typically have those social features that are common in the running population—they are generally from the upper socioeconomic class, consume little alcohol, and have good nutrition and a positive attitude to their pregnancies.

Although the authors were able to control for many of these factors in their study and still showed that exercise during pregnancy was associated with a reduced incidence of premature labor, the possibility remains that something other than the exercise, perhaps inherent in those mothers who choose to exercise, may explain their lower risk of premature labor. Nevertheless, it is clear that regular, moderate exercise during pregnancy certainly does not increase the risk of premature labor (Hatch et al. 1998), nor does it increase uterine activity (Veille et al. 1985; Klebanoff et al. 1990; Clapp 1991b). In striking contrast, high physical exertion at work increases the risk of premature labor and low birth weight (Homer et al. 1990), stressing the need to limit work-related physical activity of pregnancy women.

Benefits of Exercise During Pregnancy

The benefits of exercise for the pregnant woman are presented in detail in the sections that follow. However, firm scientific evidence on some of these points is lacking (P. Edwards et al. 1983). What evidence there is indicates that exercise during pregnancy increases or maintains physical fitness without detrimental effects (Erkkola 1976; Clapp and Capeless 1991). These benefits can be grouped as either short- or long-term.

Short-Term

The mother feels better, has more energy, and suffers less from the common complaints that are associated with pregnancy (Sternfeld et al. 1995; Horns et al. 1996)—in particular, constipation, back pain, and reduced energy. Her weight gain is better controlled. Most important, the risk that the mother will develop hypertension during pregnancy is reduced in physically active mothers (Marcoux et al. 1989).

The rate of weight gain during pregnancy remains within the normal range but falls slightly in late pregnancy in those who exercise (Clapp and Little 1995).

During Labor

The fit mother is better able to cope with whatever happens during delivery (in particular, the possibility of complications). Strong abdominal muscles aid the expulsion of the baby, and well-toned pelvic floor muscles stretch better during delivery and recover more quickly afterward.

However, these differences may be more psychological than physical. In the studies reported to date, contrasting results were found regarding the effects of training during pregnancy on the outcome of labor. In four studies, the labor and delivery of women who had exercised during pregnancy were no different from those of women who had not (Pomerance et al. 1974; Dale et al. 1982; Collings et al. 1983; Kulpa et al. 1987).

In contrast, Erdelyi (1962), who studied the pregnancy outcomes of 172 Hungarian athletes (66% of whom continued their sporting competition during the first three to four months of pregnancy), found that these athletes had fewer complications than normal during pregnancy and that there was no increased risk of spontaneous abortion. Labor and delivery were normal, except that the rate of Caesarian sections was half that of the control group, as was the duration of the second stage of labor. Hall and Kaufmann (1987) also found a lower incidence of Caesarian section in mothers who had trained during pregnancy; trained mothers also returned home more quickly from the hospital and bore children whose condition stabilized more rapidly at birth (Hall and Kaufman 1987). Zaharieva (1972) also reported that the second stage of labor was only half as long in Olympic athletes as in nonathletes. A similar finding was reported by Clapp (1990; 1991b). Wong and McKenzie (1987) found that the third stage of labor was shorter in trained mothers, whereas Beckman and Beckman (1990) reported shorter first and second stages of labor in active mothers. Another study (Varrassi et al. 1989) found that trained mothers experienced less pain during labor and had higher serum endorphin concentrations. The blood concentrations of the stress hormones, including cortisol, were lower in trained mothers, suggesting that these women experienced less stress during labor than did the untrained. Possibly as a result of the shorter labor, there is less evidence of fetal distress at birth in infants born to active women (Clapp 1990; 1991b).

Long-Term

The mother who has been active during pregnancy will find it easier to lose weight and to recover from the effects of the delivery and pregnancy. Lactation is not influenced by exercise during the postpartum period, so that neither the volume nor composition of breast milk is altered (Lovelady et al. 1990; Dewey et al. 1994). However, women should not feed their infants shortly after maximal exercise since the higher lactate concentration of postexercise milk reduces the infant's acceptance of that milk (Wallace et al. 1992).

Exercise Guidelines

Based on this rather inadequate scientific information, the following recommendations concerning exercise during pregnancy have been proposed (Jopke 1983; Lotgering et al. 1985; Snyder and Carruth 1984; Sady and Carpenter 1989; Wolfe et al. 1994; Artal and Sherman 1999).

- The main determinant of the optimum exercise level for the mother during pregnancy is her prepregnancy fitness and activity levels. Thus, as one writer has said, "Pregnancy is not the time to train for a marathon or a competitive event" (P. Edwards et al. 1983, p. 89). It follows then that the time to start training is before rather than after conception. However, those who do wish to start a moderate program during pregnancy, as advocated by some experts (Artal and Sherman 1999), should aim to exercise between 20 and 30 minutes daily at a comfortable pace. The correct intensity is one at which you can hold a conversation (chapter 5).

- Recommendations regarding the optimum amount of exercise during both the menstrual period and pregnancy have changed substantially in the past century (Artal and Sherman 1999). At the end of the nineteenth century, menstruation was regarded as a period of "ill health" in which ordinary occupations were to be suspended or modified. In addition, women were advised to avoid long walks, dancing, shopping, riding, and parties "at this time of the month invariably and under all circumstances" (Ehrenreich and English 1979). A woman was considered "indisposed" for the entire nine months of her pregnancy and was advised to recuperate for many months after her delivery by lying in bed (Lutter 1994). This advice did not apply to working women, who risked losing their jobs if they missed even a single day of work either due to menstruation or following childbirth. In the 1950s, pregnant women were advised to walk 1 mile (1.6 km) per day, preferably divided into several sessions. In 1985, the American College of Obstetrics and Gynecology (ACOG) suggested that exercise be limited to 15 minutes daily at a maximum heart rate of 140 beats per minute. By 1994, the College had revised that recommendation substantially and now advises that women with uncomplicated pregnancies can exercise safely according to the guidelines provided to nonpregnant women (ACOG 1994).

- Aerobic exercises and weight training using lighter weights are advised. Sports in which there is a risk of injury due to collision are unacceptable. Waterskiing and scuba diving are to be avoided: the first because of the danger of forceful entry of water into the uterus, causing miscarriage; the latter because of the risk of decompression sickness and the risks associated with exposing the fetus to elevated blood-oxygen content. Sports requiring good balance and coordination need to be modified during pregnancy because of changes in the center of gravity that make a fall more likely.

- Caloric intake must be increased in proportion to the amount of exercise undertaken.

- Experts are reluctant to advise competitive athletes to continue their more demanding training and competitive programs during pregnancy since there are insufficient data on which to make firm recommendations. Those competitive athletes who wish to continue their intensive training can take heart in the knowledge that the new guidelines of the ACOG do not specifically forbid such activity and even suggest that pregnancy should not influence the mother's choice of physical activity, which could therefore include competitive endurance sports. In addition are those studies showing that the health of the newborns of competitive athletes who remain vigorously active to within days of the onset of labor is not compromised (Kardel and Kase 1998; Bailey et al. 1998). However, women who participate in vigorous competitive exercise must ensure that they maintain their body temperatures below about 39°C, especially during the first three months of pregnancy (particularly soon after conception). Exercising at a lower intensity and avoiding exercise in the heat are the most practical ways to ensure that the body temperature does not increase excessively during exercise.

- Women who should probably be discouraged from exercising during pregnancy are those who have preexisting chronic medical conditions, such as diabetes, heart disease, or high blood pressure (hypertension), or who have a history of previous medical problems during pregnancy (Snyder and Carruth 1984; ACOG 1994; Artal and Sherman 1999). Small or underweight women, who statistically have an increased risk of delivering premature and underweight babies, should also be discouraged, as should overweight adolescents, who frequently begin a crash exercise-diet program once they become pregnant. Weight loss during pregnancy is associated with certain brain abnormalities in the infant. Thus, any form of maternal weight loss, from rigorous dieting alone or in combination with exercise, must be condemned (Snyder and Carruth 1984). I suspect that athletic women with eating disorders are another potentially high-risk group that would need careful monitoring to ensure that they gain weight appropriately during pregnancy.

- Much of the added physiological stress on the mother during exercise is caused by the added weight of the fetus. Thus, exercises in which the body weight must be carried (such as walking, jogging, tennis, and aerobic dance) are more stressful than are those in which the body weight is supported (such as cycling and swimming). For this reason, stationary cycling, low-impact aerobics, swimming, and other water exercises are the preferred forms of exercise during pregnancy.

- Exercise performance becomes gradually impaired during pregnancy, especially during the last three months. Therefore, exercise should be more gentle during the last trimester.

- It is important to listen to the body at all times. Any abnormal symptoms—but especially pain, bleeding, fainting, the onset of contractions, or the cessation of fetal movements—are an indication for urgent medical consultation and an absolute contraindication to continued exercise (Sady and Carpenter 1989).

There are two gold standards against which the effects of exercise during pregnancy must be measured. The first is the well-being of the baby: does exercise jeopardize or enhance the health of the baby at birth and during its developmental years? Second, does exercise increase the risk of complications either before or during labor?

What scientific evidence there is has not shown that any exercise, however vigorous, when maintained during pregnancy has any detrimental effects on either of these factors. Rather, such exercise seems to have certain beneficial effects.

RUNNING AND IRON DEFICIENCY

A popular belief is that long-distance runners, and women in particular, are especially prone to the development of iron deficiency that may present as an iron-deficiency anemia. Iron is needed for three major body processes: for the formation of hemoglobin, which binds with oxygen, thereby carrying the oxygen from the lungs to the mitochondria in the heart and skeletal muscles; for the formation of myoglobin, which stores and transports oxygen in the muscle cells; and for a group of enzymes known as the ferrochromes, which exist in the mitochondria and whose function is essential for the production of ATP.

Total body iron stores are about 4.0 g, of which 2.7 g is present in hemoglobin, 1 g is present as ferritin or hemosiderin in the liver and bone marrow, and 0.3 g is found in myoglobin and the mitochondrial enzymes (Jacobs 1984).

The evidence that we have at present is that when anyone, an athlete or otherwise, becomes iron deficient, the first stores to be depleted are the liver and bone-marrow iron stores. Only when those two stores are depleted does the iron content of the mitochondrial ferrochromes start to fall, and then only do blood hemoglobin levels fall. Anemia, diagnosed as a fall in the blood hemoglobin content, is the final, not the first, indication of body iron deficiency.

Studies Showing Iron Deficiency in Runners

Body iron stores can either be assessed directly by sampling the bone and measuring its iron content, or, more easily, can be estimated by measuring the levels of ferritin in the bloodstream. At least in untrained people, the ferritin levels in the blood bear a direct relationship to the size of the body iron stores; they are high when body iron stores are replete and low when body iron stores are depleted. As we shall see, however, this relationship may be altered in runners. Low blood ferritin concentrations—under 30 to 50 ng per ml (Dufaux et al. 1981; Clement and Asmundson 1982; Dickson et al. 1982; Clement and Sawchuk 1984) have been reported in as many as 20% of male, competitive, long-distance runners. The incidence of low blood ferritin levels among competitive female runners may be even higher. Two studies (Clement and Asmundson 1982; Nickerson and Tripp 1983) have found that 60% to 80% of female runners had subnormal blood ferritin levels.

Recent studies have confirmed these findings by directly measuring the bone marrow iron stores. Using a thick needle to take bone from the exposed area of the hip bone, Scandinavian (Ehn et al. 1980) and Israeli (Wishnitzer et al. 1983) researchers reported the virtually total absence of bone marrow iron stores in different groups of long-distance runners, all of whom had normal blood hemoglobin levels.

Originally, low blood ferritin levels and the absence of bone marrow iron in these runners were seen as an indication of a severe iron deficiency, even though the runners were not anemic. However, Hallberg and Magnusson (1984) have offered an alternative and quite plausible explanation. They compared a group of runners with very low blood ferritin levels and absent bone marrow iron stores with runners with high levels for both these parameters. They found that the rate of production of red blood cells and their quality was no different between the two groups, suggesting that the low serum ferritin levels and absent bone marrow iron stores did not indicate a true iron deficiency. They suggested that as a result of red cell destruction in their feet while they ran (foot-strike hemolysis), the runners stored their iron in the liver rather than in the bone marrow. Thus, the conventional methods used to diagnose iron deficiency in nonrunners are not applicable to runners.

Our findings and those of Celsing et al. (1986) are compatible with this interpretation. We (Matter et al. 1987) found that iron therapy did not improve the exercise performance, the $\dot{V}O_2$max values, or the running speed at the blood lactate turnpoint of a group of female runners who had low serum ferritin levels but whose blood hemoglobin levels were normal. Celsing et al. (1986) showed that four weeks of severely depleted or absent tissue iron stores, induced by blood withdrawal, did not affect the activities of a variety of iron-dependent mitochondrial enzymes. Maximum exercise tolerance after blood reinfusion was not different from that measured before blood withdrawal. Thus, the four weeks of anemia did not have any long-term effects on performance, once blood hemoglobin levels were restored. A related study, in which acute anemia was produced by diet, blood donation, and menstruation over 80 days and reversed by iron supplementation for a further 100 days, failed to show any effect of either iron depletion or repletion on maximum exercise performance (Lukaski et al. 1991). The rate of increase in $\dot{V}O_2$max during exercise was lower and the rate of CO_2 and lactate production higher with iron deficiency, suggesting to the authors that iron deficiency affects muscle metabolism during exercise. Peak lactate concentrations were noticeably higher with iron deficiency (16.2 vs. 12.6 mmol per liter) even though maximum exercise capacity was unaltered.

Other studies have also failed to show that iron supplementation aids performance in subjects with low serum ferritin concentrations but without anemia (Powell and Tucker 1991; Fogelholm, Jaakkola, et al. 1992; Telford et al. 1992) or that supplementation with iron improves training adaptations in athletes with low blood ferritin concentration (Klingshirn et al. 1992; Zhu and Haas 1998). Similarly, iron injections did not alter either blood hemoglobin concentrations or the mass of red blood cells in female athletes with low serum ferritin concentrations (Ashenden et al. 1998). Hence, these subjects were not iron deficient before iron therapy, as those parameters would have increased with iron therapy if a true iron deficiency had been present initially.

All these studies concluded that iron therapy should be reserved only for runners whose blood hemoglobin levels are subnormal. In the absence of established anemia, shown by low blood hemoglobin levels, low serum ferritin levels can probably be ignored, as they do not affect athletic performance (Garza et al. 1997).

Iron Deficiency With Anemia

Once true iron deficiency develops, the hemoglobin content of the red blood cells falls and the cells become smaller, are less able to carry oxygen, and are more fragile, with a reduced life expectancy. People with iron-deficiency anemia suffer from a reduced blood oxygen-carrying capacity that causes a reduced $\dot{V}O_2$max. With appropriate iron therapy, $\dot{V}O_2$max and running performance improve (LaManca and Haymes 1993).

The possible causes of iron-deficiency anemia in runners have not been established. It may be due to excessive iron losses in sweat (Vellar 1968; Paulev et al. 1983) or excessive blood losses in the gastrointestinal tract or in urine from hematuria and hemoglobinuria, or both. Hemoglobinuria may result from accelerated intravascular hemolysis (Selby and Eichner 1986; Weight, Byrne, et al. 1991). In some female runners, excessive menstrual blood losses may contribute to iron deficiency. Another cause may be impaired gastrointestinal absorption of ingested iron, which has been reported in some iron-deficient runners (Ehn et al. 1980). A deficient dietary intake must also be considered, because intensively training runners tend to eat high-carbohydrate, vegetarian-type diets that usually have low iron contents. In addition, some elite runners, women in particular, may severely restrict their caloric intakes. At present, however, the consensus is that anemia in athletes is caused by the same mechanisms that cause anemia in the sedentary population and that there is no specific entity, the anemia of exercise (Weight and Noakes 1993).

As a result, true iron-deficiency anemia is extremely rare in runners (Pate et al. 1993).

Sport Anemia

So-called sport anemia (dilutional anemia) has been found in endurance athletes that have subnormal blood hemoglobin levels without necessarily being iron deficient. In competitors at the 1948 Olympic Games, it was noted that the athletes competing in sports requiring great endurance had the lowest hemoglobin levels (Berry et al. 1949). The endurance athletes in the 1968 Dutch (De Wijn et al. 1971) and Australian (G.A. Stewart et al. 1972) Olympic teams in particular were found to have blood hemoglobin levels that were lower than those of their team coaches and managers. Interestingly, the Australian athletes with the lowest hemoglobin levels subsequently performed the worst in the Games. Clement and colleagues (1977) reported essentially the same findings in the 1976 Canadian Olympic team.

Currently, the cause of these low hemoglobin levels is unknown. As none of these earlier studies measured blood ferritin levels or performed bone marrow biopsies to measure body iron stores, we do not know whether this sport anemia is due to iron deficiency or simply to dilution as a result of an increased circulating blood volume (Weight, Darge, et al. 1991). Interestingly, Selby and Eichner (1986) found that male and female competitive swimmers showed a fall in hemoglobin levels over a five-month competitive season. Yet, their hemoglobin levels did not fall into the anemic range, and the serum ferritin levels were low in 57% of the women and only 10% of the men.

The current belief is that a low hemoglobin level in an endurance athlete is abnormal and requires investigation and treatment. As already explained, the causes of this anemia are likely to be the same as those for anemia in the sedentary population. An increase in blood hemoglobin levels in response to iron therapy would indicate that iron deficiency was the cause of the low hemoglobin level.

Early Season-Training Anemia

Since 1966 (Yoshimura 1966), it has been known that people who start exercising for the first time, or who undergo a period of very intensive training, develop an anemia that can be quite severe, causing blood hemoglobin levels to fall by up to 18% (Londemann 1978), possibly due to an increased rate of red blood cell destruction. This anemia has been described in rugby players (Yoshimura 1966), in tennis players, and in people exercising on a bicycle ergometer (Shiraki et al. 1977), in Norwegian army recruits participating in a period of intensive training (Londemann 1978), and in young women participating in an exercise/fitness class (Hegenauer et al. 1983).

This anemia usually corrects itself within about three to eight weeks (Shiraki et al. 1977; Hegenauer et al. 1983) and can be prevented by eating a high-protein diet (2 g protein per kg body weight per day; Shiraki et al. 1977). The anemia appears to be caused by the release into the bloodstream of a chemical substance, possibly lysolethicin from the spleen, which in turn precipitates the rapid destruction of a large number of circulating red blood cells. Iron ingestion does not prevent the development of this anemia (Hegenauer et al. 1983). To prevent the condition, novice runners should increase their dietary protein intakes for the first month or so of their training.

Changes in the Blood

Immediately after very prolonged exercise (marathon or ultramarathon racing), there is a marked increase in the number of white blood cells in the bloodstream—a change that reverts to normal within 48 hours (Dickson et al. 1982). Between 24 and 48 hours after prolonged races, blood hemoglobin levels tend to fall (Dickson et al. 1982), probably from excess water retention by the kidneys for the first three days after prolonged exercise (Irving et al. 1990b).

There are no major changes in the levels of any other blood components (in particular, blood urea, uric acid, creatinine, and bilirubin) after any exercise, regardless of its duration (Noakes and Carter 1976; 1982). Marked changes do occur in the activities of certain enzymes in the bloodstream—in particular, in the enzyme creatine kinase, which normally exists inside the cells and whose function is to transfer phosphate from phosphocreatine to form ATP. This enzyme is released into the bloodstream during exercise, probably as a result of muscle cell damage (Noakes 1987a).

In general, postexercise blood creatine kinase activity varies with the duration of the activity and is higher the longer the race, presumably because the longer the race, the greater the muscle damage that occurs (Noakes 1987a). Training reduces the extent to which the blood creatine kinase activity rises during and after exercise (Noakes and Carter 1982), also presumably because training reduces the amount of muscle damage that occurs with exercise (Schwane and Armstrong 1983).

Finally, it is important to be aware that an elevated creatine kinase activity in the blood is used in the diagnosis of heart attack. Thus, the runner who is admitted to hospital within 24 hours of a long run may be unjustly diagnosed as having had a heart attack if the doctors are unaware that running causes blood creatine kinase activity to be increased to levels normally found in heart attack patients (Noakes, Kotzenberg, et al. 1983a; Noakes 1987b). C-reactive protein concentrations are also used as an indicator of a recent heart attack and are also increased after exercise. Indeed, blood C-reactive protein concentrations after a 90-km ultramarathon can reach levels found in people with moderately sized heart attacks (Strachan et al. 1984).

The troponin molecule, which constitutes an important part of the skeletal muscle thin (or actin) filament, is also released into the bloodstream after both heart attacks and exercise. Fortunately, physicians are now aware that prolonged exercise, especially marathon or ultramarathon running, can cause changes in the blood that are normally only present in patients suffering from heart attacks.

RUNNING AND THE IMMUNE SYSTEM

I have already discussed those studies that show that the symptoms of inflammation and infection are increased immediately after competitive racing (chapter 10) and that infection is an important feature of the overtraining syndrome (chapter 7). The reasons for this are unknown but probably indicate that the body's immune system (and with it the athlete's resistance to infection) is impaired by heavy training and intense competition (Lewicki et al. 1987; Nieman, Berk, et al. 1989; Nieman, Johanssen, et al. 1989) and by weight loss (Kono et al. 1988).

Paradoxically, mild exercise releases a protein, endogenous pyrogen (Cannon and Kluger 1983), that causes the body temperature to rise. This elevation of body temperature, corresponding to the fever stage of infection, is beneficial because it creates an internal environment that is less favorable for the growth and multiplication of invading bacteria and viruses. In addition, blood levels of the antiviral protein interferon increase, as does the activity of "killer" white cells (Hanson and Flaherty 1981; Viti et al. 1985). Mild exercise should reduce acutely the risk of an athlete developing an infection. This gives rise to the concept that mild to moderate levels of physical activity enhance immunity, whereas high levels of training and competitive stress increase the risk of infection.

Chronic training does not influence immune function even in groups of runners who claim to have had fewer infections since they started running (R.L. Green et al. 1981). However, much is still to be learned about the influence of exercise and overtraining on the immune system (Keast et al. 1988). My impression is that during the past decade a considerable amount of research has been done in this field but without any great practical advances being made.

HEADACHES AND OTHER NEUROLOGICAL CONDITIONS

A number of different types of effort headaches exist (Dimeff 1992; McCrory 2000). Acute effort migraine has been described in weightlifters, runners, and cyclists involved in short-duration exercise of high intensity. These headaches usually disappear within a short time.

More common are the headaches that come on gradually after prolonged exercise of a lower intensity. These headaches become progressively worse over the next 3 to 6 hours (Massey 1982). The condition occurs more frequently in those who are poorly conditioned or older than 40, and it is found to be worse at altitude (Diamond 1991). It may be related to benign vascular sexual headache, in which headache occurs during sexual activity as a result of spasm of blood vessels in the brain (Silbert et al. 1989; 1991).

As one who suffers from effort headaches, I have discovered that they occur only when I run longer distances in the morning and are most likely to occur when I am less well conditioned. When well trained, I seldom, if ever, suffered from headaches.

What is important about effort headaches is to know that such a condition exists. If the headaches follow the patterns described here, it is probably safe to assume that they are not due to a serious disease. If, on the other hand, the headaches do not follow this pattern, or if they become progressively more severe and frequent or are not always related to exercise, then it is important that they be investigated fully by your doctor. Cases in which effort headaches were due to serious disease have been reported (Rooke 1968).

It is also worth noting that the effort headache may indicate the presence of a food allergy, and an attempt should be made to identify the responsible foodstuff. The nonsteroidal anti-inflammatory agents, including the drug indomethacin (indocid), may be useful in this condition (Diamond 1982).

The study of Denio et al. (1989) suggests that epileptics who exercise have fewer epileptic seizures than those who do not exercise. The incidence of Parkinson's disease is also slightly lower in the physically active (Sasco et al. 1992), and the symptoms of the condition may be lessened by physical activity.

ENDORPHINS AND THE RUNNER'S HIGH

The drug morphine has been known to have potent pain-relieving (analgesic) actions for more than 150 years, but it was only in the mid-1950s that morphine's mechanism of action in the body became clear. The critical finding was that morphine acts on specific morphine receptors lining the outer membranes of many cells throughout the body.

The fact that human cells have receptors for a drug prepared from the poppy plant suggests that the body produces its own morphine-like substances and therefore requires such receptors for their action. This realization prompted an international search to isolate and identify these endogenous (internally-produced) morphine derivatives, which became known as the encephalins and endorphins. In the decade since their initial isolation, the encephalins and endorphins have been found to play a role in drug and alcohol dependence; in the pain relief produced by acupuncture; in disorders involving menstruation; in gastrointestinal disorders, including stomach ulcers; and in other physiological control mechanisms, including the control of blood pressure, respiration, food intake, and drinking behavior (Copolov and Helme 1983).

When it was found that endorphin levels increase during exercise (Harber and Sutton 1984), special interest arose in the possibility that elevated endorphin levels might explain the mood changes that occur during running—in particular, the euphoria of the "runner's high" and the increased resistance to pain that occurs during exercise (Black et al. 1979) and with training (Scott and Gijsbers 1981).

Currently, the view seems to be that endorphins form part of the natural stress response of the body. When the body is under stress, be it when jogging gently or running away from a lion, brain endorphin levels will rise. And because not all stressful events are associated with a high, it follows that elevated endorphin levels will not always produce positive mood changes.

However, another study (Allen and Coen 1987) does show that high doses of naloxone, a drug that blocks the actions of endorphins in the brain, prevents the normal positive mood changes that develop during and after running. They suggest that the increased endorphin activity induced by exercise contributes to the postexercise calmness experienced by runners. But naloxone does not reduce the increased resistance to pain experienced during exercise (Droste et al. 1991).

Thus, the current feeling is that endorphins may play a role in the runner's high, but probably do not alter pain perception during exercise. Interestingly, Dr. William Morgan (1985), the psychologist who originally described compulsive running behavior in terms of a chemically based addiction (chapter 8), seems now less sure about the chemical nature of this addiction. This is in line with the suggestion that it is the personality, not the activity, that determines susceptibility to running addiction.

RUNNING AND DIABETES

The major disease of the endocrine system that has relevance to running is insulin-dependent diabetes. This is caused by an absolute lack of the hormone insulin that is secreted by the pancreas and is essential for the normal regulation of metabolism, both at rest and during exercise. Insulin-dependent diabetes usually has its onset in childhood, for reasons that are unclear. One possibility is that a viral infection causes selective destruction of those pancreatic cells that produce the hormone.

Insulin is required for the normal entry of glucose into the muscle cells and therefore for its storage as glycogen in both muscle and liver. Thus, in the absence of insulin, the untreated diabetic has difficulty metabolizing ingested carbohydrate. The insulin lack prevents the increased amounts of glucose released from the liver during exercise from entering the muscle cells to act as an important fuel (chapter 3). Thus, blood glucose levels rise, leading ultimately to coma. On the other hand, exercising too soon after an insulin injection is particularly hazardous if it induces hypoglycemia. This occurs because insulin favors glucose storage in the liver and increases glucose uptake by the muscle. As a result, less glucose enters the bloodstream from glycogen breakdown in the liver, but more glucose is extracted by the muscle. This imbalance in the rate of glucose release into the bloodstream by the liver and its removal from blood by the muscles can cause the rapid onset of hypoglycemia.

People with diabetes who are receiving insulin and who wish to take up exercise should be encouraged to do so because the training will reduce their insulin requirements, improve the quality of their diabetic control, and probably reduce their risk of developing the long-term complications of diabetes (Moy et al. 1993), many of which are serious. Regular exercise also encourages people with diabetes to take charge of their disease, and it provides the same (if not greater) psychological benefits that are enjoyed by all athletes. With care, selected people with diabetes can do virtually any exercise, including running ultramarathons or completing the Ironman triathlon.

The following are the main points that exercising diabetics need to know (Draznin 2000):

- Start an exercise program only if you can find the necessary medical support.
- Buy an automated blood glucose analyzer so that you can monitor your blood glucose levels regularly (every 20 minutes) during exercise. In well-controlled diabetics, the risk of hypoglycemia developing during exercise even of quite short duration (10 to 30 minutes) is high. Only by monitoring your blood glucose concentrations regularly during exercise can you ensure that this does not happen.
- Always exercise at exactly the same time of day so that the amount of (injected) insulin in your bloodstream and in your body storage sites is always the same. This is essential because the amount of insulin in these sites will determine the body's metabolic response to that exercise.
- Reduce your daily insulin requirements as you exercise more.
- Always carry a supply of rapidly absorbable carbohydrate, preferably a 20% glucose polymer solution, with you during exercise. Ensure that you drink a sufficient amount of this solution to maintain your blood glucose level above 3.5 mmol per liter during exercise
- Increase your carbohydrate intake after exercise (to restock reduced muscle glycogen stores) to prevent a steep fall in blood glucose levels (hypoglycemia) some hours after exercise. Beware of developing hypoglycemia at night while you are asleep. This is more probable if exercise is taken in the afternoon or evening, if insulin is injected during that time, and if you do not eat sufficient carbohydrate in the evening after your exercise bout.

These guidelines are not meant to be comprehensive. They are offered here simply to remind diabetics that they can and should exercise as much as they wish but that they must approach their exercise with diligence and intelligence, with a thorough knowledge of exercise physiology (chapter 2) and metabolism (chapter 3) and with the backup of suitably qualified and interested medical personnel. More information can be obtained from two excellent books on the topic (Cantu 1982; Betteridge 1987).

The second form in which diabetes can occur is non-insulin-dependent diabetes mellitus (NIDDM). This form occurs in later life and is usually associated with abdominal-type obesity. Regular exercise reduces the risk of developing NIDDM (Helmrich et al. 1991; Manson et al. 1991; Burchfiel et al. 1995; Manson et al. 1992); this effect is greatest in those at highest risk (Helmrich et al. 1994; J. Lynch et al. 1996) because of a history of obesity, a history of hypertension, or a parental history of diabetes. Regular exercise also decreases the likelihood of developing complications, especially kidney disease and nerve dysfunction (peripheral neuropathy) in those with insulin-dependent diabetes (Kriska et al. 1991).

FINAL WORD

When I began my clinical medical training in the early 1970s, I was reliably informed by my teachers that exercise was dangerous for human health. Since I seemed to feel far better the more I exercised, I concluded that my teachers could not be trusted.

Fortunately, the past 30 years have confirmed that intuition. The evidence presented here shows that few medical conditions are either caused or worsened by regular exercise, whereas a substantial number may be completely prevented or at least substantially alleviated by such exercise. Indeed, it now seems that regular physical activity might be the cheapest and most effective preventive medicine yet discovered.

References: For the complete reference list, visit www.humankinetics.com/references/Noakes.pdf. For a printed copy of the list, within the US, please send a self-addressed, postage paid, 8-1/2 x 11 envelope to *Lore of Running* Editor, Human Kinetics, P.O. Box 5076, Champaign, IL 61825-5076.

Index

Note: The italicized *f* and *t* following page numbers refer to figures and tables, respectively. Italicized page numbers indicate runner photos.

About the Author

Dr. Timothy Noakes is Discovery health professor of exercise and sports science at the University of Cape Town and director of the medical research council/UCT research unit for exercise science and sports medicine at the Sports Science Institute of South Africa in Newlands. Noakes received his MD from the University of Cape Town. In 2002 Dr. Noakes received the DSc degree from the University of Cape Town for seminal research findings in the exercise sciences. He is a veteran of more than 70 marathons and ultramarathons. He is an editorial board member for many international sport science journals and a former president of the South African Sports Medicine Association. In 1999, he was elected as one of 22 founding members of the International Olympic Committee's Olympic Science Academy. Noakes is also a fellow of the American College of Sports Medicine. He and his wife, Marilyn Anne, reside in Cape Town, South Africa. *Lore of Running* received the 2003 Book Award of the Universtiy of Cape Town.